A Dream
Of Greatness

Books by Geoffrey Perrett

History
DAYS OF SADNESS, YEARS OF TRIUMPH:
The American People 1939–1945

A DREAM OF GREATNESS:
The American People 1945–1963

Fiction
EXECUTIVE PRIVILEGE

A DREAM
OF GREATNESS

The American People
1945–1963

Geoffrey Perrett

Coward, McCann & Geoghegan
New York

Excerpt from *Collected Poems* by Vachel Lindsay reprinted with permission of Macmillan
Publishing Co.,Inc., copyright 1914 by Macmillan Publishing Co., Inc., renewed 1942 by
Elizabeth C. Lindsay.
Excerpt from *Manchild in the Promised Land* by Claude Brown reprinted with permission
of Macmillan Publishing Co., Inc., copyright ©1965 by Claude Brown.
Excerpt from *Nobody Knows My Name* by James Baldwin reprinted by permission of
The Dial Press, copyright ©1954, 1956, 1958, 1959, 1960, 1961 by James Baldwin.

Library of Congress Cataloging in Publication Data

Perrett, Geoffrey.
    A dream of greatness.

    Bibliography
    Includes index
    1. United States—Social conditions—1945–1963
1. Title.
HN58.P38   309.1′73′092   78-10343
ISBN 0-698-10949-X

PRINTED IN THE UNITED STATES OF AMERICA

TO THE MEMORY OF MY WIFE

ANN PERRETT

1940–1976

CONTENTS

Part III: *Rocking!*

Part IV: *Falling Short*

Part V: *Lightning Always Strikes the Highest Peaks*

Is not the pastness of the past the profounder,
the more complete, the more legendary, the more
immediately before the present it falls?
   —THOMAS MANN, *The Magic Mountain*

Introduction

This book aims to provide a reliable chronicle of events between August 1945 and November 1963, to interpret those events, and to explore new approaches to social history.

Most attitudes toward the past are still colored to some degree by nineteenth century ideas, first that "history is past politics" and second that real history has to be set far back. These attitudes have led writers of large-scale social histories to become defensive, to describe their work as being somehow "informal" or as providing a mere "narrative." The social history of recent times has been reduced to a kind of backward-looking journalism. Insofar as it has been within my ability to do so, I have tried to correct these imbalances and to show that *real* history can be written about the recent past and can be written on a large scale.

The political historian has had another advantage besides the winds of intellectual fashion in his favor. He knows exactly what he is dealing with (official papers, great events) and with whom (great men). The social historian by contrast has to make what he can of humble men and women and even humbler materials.

He also faces myriad points at which he can begin. This can be nearly as frustrating as having almost nowhere to begin. A living, dynamic society does not lock up its important papers for twenty years, fifty years, or until all of those affected are safely dead and unable to invoke the libel laws. A modern society churns out its "documents" daily. They are so commonplace as a rule that they are more likely to excite derision than respect—there are the best-selling books, hit records, pamphlets on child-rearing, surveys of sexual and other practices, changing fashions in speech, dress and manners, figures on church attendance, advertisements, inane fads, terrible crimes, examples of madness, perversion, per-

11

versity, the grotesque and the mundane, the inspiring and the vulgar, the bombastic and the banal. These matters are often not even derided; they are ignored. Nothing is so invisible as the familiar.

Yet even the humblest materials are expressions of the life within. And the social historian is fascinated by life, in contrast with the political historian, who is fascinated by power. To make use of the mixture of trash and riches at his disposal, the social historian above everything else needs perspective; otherwise, he is certain to be overwhelmed.

Perspective is frequently confused with distance. It is a commonplace notion that one needs to be well removed in time from complex events in order to make sense of them. But distance is only—distance. Perspective refers to an angle of vision, a way of seeing things in relation to one another and in relation to the world at large. It comes from looking at things from a specific point of view. Distance is neither a substitute for perspective nor an assurance of it. Some of the most valuable works we possess have no distance to speak of, such as Boswell's life of Johnson. Yet Boswell's perspective—which held that Dr. Johnson was a great man of enduring interest to posterity—was surely right, and helped make sure that all who came after Boswell viewed Johnson from much the same perspective.

This book is the result of thousands of hours spent raking through minutiae, exotica, and the obvious. And in the end it claims to say something that makes sense of this material. That is perspective. I have had to try to see things whole in order to see anything at all. The alternative would have been to produce an indigestible lump of a book, another of that genre Charles Lamb termed biblia abiblia—items which have the outward appearance of books but which are actually unreadable.

Because there is no general agreement on the proper methods and materials to be employed in large-scale social history, I have devised my own forms and rules as needed. This is an effort begun in my first book, *Days of Sadness, Years of Triumph: The American People 1939–1945*, and more fully realized here.

The problem of what to do with politics in a social history has troubled a number of eminent modern social historians. G. M. Trevelyan offered "history with the politics left out." But this made sense only up to 1919. Until then one-third of the adult population had 100 percent of the vote, nearly two-thirds of the population had not been to high school, communications were unreliable, and travel was the prerogative of a very small minority. Politics did not exist in a meaningful sense to the majority of people, even in a country which considered itself democratic.

But now almost all adults have the vote, have been exposed to "civics" or something of the kind at high school, and have been brought up in an age of radio, television, and inexpensive travel.

There is a more subtle consideration. Each of us has a personal life to live. But consciously or subconsciously, directly or indirectly, we also live the life of our times. The life of society mingles with our individual existence. Since World War I every Western democracy has lived an intensely politicized life, and not only because of the challenges posed first by Fascism and then by Communism. To describe American life in the twentieth century "with the politics left out" could be done. It would also be completely unreal.

The answer to what should be done with politics in a social history is not to exclude it but to keep it in its place. The emphasis from first to last must be upon everyday life and ordinary people. In this work that is where the emphasis is to be found. The people it mentions are usually quite ordinary, but at times they are caught up in extraordinary events, such as Elizabeth Eckford of Little Rock and Robert "Tut" Patterson of Sunflower County, Mississippi, a convict named Chessman and a war bride named Knauff, a legless veteran and a black janitor, a confessed perjurer and a little girl with the prosaic name of Brown who became famous; there are the people who built backyard bomb shelters and the Jesuit who said that it was moral to shoot a man intruding on another man's shelter; there are the victims of the heroin "plague" and there are the Beats; there is the first tranquilizer generation and the last polio generation; Mrs. Robert Finkbine, who shook the nation's conscience by trying to secure an abortion, and a Louisville couple who sold a house to a young black family; there are the returning veterans and the new suburbanites—plain people, for the most part.

This is also a book with a case to make. What makes a book interesting is what makes a man interesting—ideas. The principal idea of this book— that is, the perspective it offers—is that from V-J Day 1945 until November 22, 1963, the people of the United States were engaged in a conscious attempt to become the greatest nation in history. And that self-conscious, self-willed effort so inflamed the nation's temper that it led inevitably to turbulence.

Yet it was a breathtaking ambition—to outshine Greece in its glory, Rome in its grandeur, France in its various phases of greatness, and Britain at the height of its power. There was no hesitation, no doubt. It seemed entirely natural to the Americans of these years to be the richest, the most powerful, and, were it possible, the most accomplished people in history. There was hardly an important human endeavor in which they did not attempt to take the lead.

The dates 1945 and 1963 have therefore not been chosen arbitrarily or for the sake of convenience. They serve as brackets to historical awareness. They are dates around which the entire nation has organized its memory of the recent past. If there are only three days which people remember clearly, they are December 7, 1941, V-J Day, and the day John Kennedy was assassinated. This consciousness of where one was and what one was doing on those three days is an incision into the raw material of history made not by the historian but by the people he is studying.

In pursuing the realization of the American Dream, Americans have never lost sight of three very down-to-earth objectives: abundance in a world of scarcity; liberty in a world of tyrannies; peace in a world torn by wars. Yet these three objectives have always implied something more inspiring than becoming a transcontinental Switzerland. There was always within them a dream of matchless glory.

Although the United States became the world's principal industrial power shortly before the turn of the century, and despite the involvement in World War I, the nation was hesitant about turning this dream into a reality. It nibbled at the edges, picking up a handful of islands and acting in robust imperialistic style, yet was constrained by both geography and its own ideas of proper behavior. But chiefly the opportunity was lacking. Not until the second European civil war, signaling the final and irreversible political bankruptcy of Western Europe, and not until the development of rapid and reliable global communications, overcoming America's physical isolation from Europe and Asia, was that ardent nationalist Henry Luce able to declare that this was "the American Century." The century was nearly half gone, but no matter. Most of a century is better than none.

Luce made his pronouncement shortly before the attack on Pearl Harbor. When the war ended four years later, America dominated the world. And everyone was aware that something important was about to begin. The American people came out of the war as self-consciously in pursuit of their national destiny as any people have ever been.

Not that the challenges of the postwar were taken up with a carefree smile and a light heart. It probably appeared that way to the inhabitants of a dreary camp for DPs outside Hamburg when watching American movies. But to the returned veteran who was moving with his wife and baby into a cold-water flat or, humiliatingly, moving in with his parents, the immediate postwar was ruled by the gospel of Elbert Hubbard: "Life is just one damned thing after another." The worker who saw his income drop sharply when overtime ended and the rapid postwar inflation began was no cockeyed optimist. Nor was the family that was despondently scouring the black market for a car it needed badly but could not really afford. And what of the black soldier who went back to his home in the South, his head held a little higher than before?

Letters, diaries, newspapers, and periodicals from 1945 to 1948 convey a febrile sense of dread. There are frequent warnings of an impending fiery end. There are confident predictions of political, social, and economic collapse. If the A-bomb did not get you, then the new Depression would.

Despite the petty frustrations and the cataclysmic fears, Americans also enjoyed a spiritual revival. As I showed in *Days of Sadness, Years of Triumph*, the principal social consequence of the war was that it had restored the nation's morale—bound up the deep wounds the Thirties had inflicted on people's belief in themselves, in one another, and in their country. They had met the first test of any society which aims at greatness—success in war. There were numerous failures which might be pointed out, such as widespread juvenile delinquency, appalling slums, serious maldistribution of medical resources. But compared with the social and economic difficulties confronting all the other major combatants, whose cities were shattered, whose economies lay in ruins, whose self-confidence was destroyed, these were comparatively minor. It is not hard to imagine a future generation looking back on America at the end of the war and reflecting, "To have been an American then—the world must have seemed at one's feet!"

With the passage of time what will be forgotten is that undercurrent of fear which provided the emotional setting for Auden's long poem of 1947, *The Age of Anxiety*. But the feeling that it was a wonderful time to have been an American will, in the main, be right. Not after this war was there an intellectual emigration to Europe in search of "genuine culture." There would be no new Lost Generation; only Americans abroad on the GI Bill or Fulbright scholarships. America was where life was at its most vibrant and purposeful. It would remain so for the next two decades.

The American people possessed in these years the characteristic of any nation that is coming to grips with its destiny: a moral certainty that they mattered. Mattered, that is, not only to themselves but to History. Mattered because on what they did or failed to do there hung much of the fate of the human race. And "Greatness," said Shakespeare, "knows itself."

Greatness sought or greatness won, the self-conscious pursuit of national destiny is a social phenomenon taken for granted and rarely examined. The mere word is intoned for oratorical effect. It papers over the cracks in politicians' speech. "Greatness" is so thoughtlessly bandied about that it is in danger of becoming merely a blessed word, like Mesopotamia. But I have sought to see it as an accepted part of everyday life and to see it as the mainspring behind collective efforts and aspirations.

As the narrative unfolds, it will be worth remembering that greatness is at times something like a fit. Much that occurred in these years was unedifying. But a nation in the throes of greatness lives a life that is turbulent, not placid. It produces drama, and melodrama, with a profligacy no playwright could ever match. It is such periods in the lives of nations that have produced the material of epic poetry since the time of Homer. Such history was traditionally written in epic terms. Its dominant motif has been tragedy.

Finally, I should like to declare an interest. To write about America from 1945 through 1963 is to write about the society in which I grew up. My personal introduction to the atomic age came in a school playground in Los Angeles. We children were lined up and stood, hushed and curious, looking in the direction of southern Nevada. A brief white flash on the far horizon signaled an atomic explosion at Frenchman's Flat. Several years later Elvis Presley appeared on the far horizon of adolescence, to the horror of my parents. Later still, as a soldier guarding the President, I saw Eisenhower's incredibly pink and cheerful face flash by while, with outstretched arms, he greeted a foreign people who cheered themselves hoarse. I also remember exactly how and from whom I first heard that John F. Kennedy had been shot. Only a few minutes earlier I had left a Young Democrats' meeting where we had been shown a miniature California license plate which was inscribed "JFK 1964."

In writing this book, I have bumped into my own past many times. That might have tempted me to write in a hazy glow of nostalgia. It might have had the opposite effect and caused me to write with a gloomy sense of what-might-have been. I have consciously tried to avoid both these dangers.

PART I

THE ROAD TO 1948

1

Homecoming

The war ended not with a bang but with two. In between them came ten days of false alarms and premature celebration. But there were many millions of people, and a majority of important officials, who still believed that the fanatical Japanese would contest every square inch of Japanese soil, that they would fight on—without food, ammunition, gasoline, or hope, armed only with bamboo spears and worship of their emperor—until all of Japan had been occupied. Yet this was not to be. Late at night on August 15 came the news of Japan's unconditional surrender.

Within the hour snake-dancing crowds wound through the streets of Salt Lake City in teeming rain; in San Francisco a pair of voluptuous platinum blondes cavorted naked in the fountain outside city hall to excited cheers of encouragement; in Times Square more than 500,000 celebrants bellowed joyously until, with the dawn, they had grown so hoarse they could hardly raise another cheer. For that night every man in uniform was free to make a pass at any woman who caught his eye. Strangers in the street kissed like long-parted lovers. Lovers kissed more deliriously than ever. In millions of homes there were tears of joy and relief, and prayers of thanks were given. Everyone was glad that the killing had stopped.

In the nations which win wars there is a natural cycle of emotions: determination in the beginning, spiced with excitement; as the early victories are scored, there is mounting exultation; but in time this gives way to impatience, because the end of the war comes in sight long before the fighting stops. The killing goes on and on to less and less purpose. By the time the war ends the victors are as sick of it as the vanquished.

There was thus an uneasy undercurrent to the V-J revelry; it seemed somehow self-willed and self-conscious. And the false alarms had taken the edge off the excitement. But there was another, subtler reason why

19

the rejoicing had a faintly hollow ring. As glad as people were to see the killing stop, war had one powerful attraction which peace lacked— familiarity.

War was what the American people had lived with for six years. It had dominated their lives since it broke out in Europe in September 1939. America had participated by proxy, first through aid to Britain, then through lend-lease, and then by helping the Royal Navy hunt German U-boats in the North Atlantic. The two years prior to Pearl Harbor had been years in which an army had been drafted and trained; years in which those "defense" industries were built which became, following Pearl Harbor, the war industries which secured victory over Germany and Japan. For six years war had shaped everyday life and in some important respects had improved it, as most people knew but few liked openly to acknowledge.

War had touched every family. Nor was there an American institution, from the one-room school in an agricultural hamlet to the somber offices high above Wall Street, which had not been affected. War had ended the Depression. War had put men and women back to work. War had put food on tables, clothes on backs, roofs over heads, money in pockets. For six years the war had been the big *if* in every plan, the question mark over every hope, a unifying force, a great simplifier, a source of purpose, and a concrete, attainable aim in which all might share. Suddenly it was gone. And what was there to put in its place?

Peace was an unknown quantity and on examination it lacked the glamor and excitement of war. In fact, decided one disappointed observer, it "looked a little nondescript." And nearly all the experts said that the country's economic prospects were bleak. Little wonder that a depression psychology rapidly revived. That could be dangerous because it could become a self-fulfilling prophecy if people held onto their wartime savings and failed to spend, failed to invest.

So far as the immediate economic effects of peace went, they seemed to do little more than add to the prevailing confusion. The war did not end neatly and cleanly; it only appeared to in retrospect. For millions it had effectively ended long before the shooting stopped. For other millions it did not end, to all practical purposes, until some time in 1946 when they came home and took off their uniforms.

Three million war workers had reconverted themselves before V-J Day by changing their jobs. Up to 1 million women who had taken up war work had gone back to being full-time housewives. More than 4 million men who had been in uniform had gone back to civilian life.

Labor's "no strike" pledge had ended in some plants and industries weeks before the German surrender, and afterward became a mockery as scores of strikes broke out almost daily. With Japan's surrender the strikes became official, which meant they became more effective.

Along assembly lines and slipways planes and ships were left unfinished because there was no longer a demand for them. The battleship *Illi-*

nois would never sail, nor would the powerful new aircraft carrier *Repris-al*. War plants declared a two-day holiday with pay to celebrate victory over Japan. The plant managers then spent those two days telephoning Washington to ask what they were supposed to do now. At the Boeing plant in Renton, Washington, three-fourths of a work force of 29,000 were laid off in a single day. Several major plants shut down completely. But others went on blithely turning out arms and ammunition with the evident intention of doing so until someone in authority noticed this deliberate act of lunacy and ordered them to stop.

Most of the irritating restrictions and controls of wartime were lifted in short order. Transportation was freed from its shackles. Starved for travel and vacations, and with 7 million fewer cars on the road in late 1945 than there had been in late 1941, American families hurried out and booked every hotel room, plane seat, and railroad berth available. For more than a year after V-J Day travel in the United States was a Kafkaesque ordeal: wildly overbooked hotels, waiting rooms which resembled emergency shelters in areas devastated by natural disaster, restaurant food that appeared to have been filched from pigsties, reservations which apparently reserved nothing, and baggage checks which were like lottery tickets. Never in so large a country had people been so horribly crowded. "It seemed to me," wrote a weary war correspondent returning home, "that I came homeward with an American nation which had all gone West and was in a body fighting its way East again for Christmas. The soldiers from the Pacific stood in the stations. Civilians from everywhere made queues with them at the ticket windows. They were crowded and sleepy, dirty and harassed, but rich. And astonishingly cheerful."

Night life flourished. Fads and crazes reappeared, such as making soap bubbles from loops of wire and a supply of soapy water. Radio "hams" were told they could reassemble the sets dismantled on December 8, 1941. "They were once more free to stay up all night hoarsely calling 'CQ, CQ, CQ,' into a microphone."

When Christmas drew near, there was a spending spree which made the past appear niggardly. It was a classic illustration of the definition of inflation which begins with too much money chasing too few goods. A black market developed in children's toys, and rickety second-hand bicycles sold for more than new ones would have cost, had they been available. A black market at Christmas seemed especially odious.

After Christmas was soon enough to turn to the serious business peace brought in its train. Despite the nagging doubts and fears, there was a strong undercurrent of excitement, side by side with the sense of apprehension. These days, everything seemed heightened, the good and the bad. There was a feeling of renewal, of things beginning rather than ending. While there might be problems ahead, such as unemployment, most people felt they would be all right; it was the other fellow who would have a hard time of it.

In the past six years the Americans had recovered their self-confidence.

They had drunk deeply at the well-spring of their national character—optimism, America's secular faith. Spiritually, they had been born again. An era was about to begin.

Some 16.7 million men and women saw wartime military service, and on V-J Day more than twelve million were still in uniform. The vast majority had but a single thought: they wanted out.

Getting out came down to the number of points you had. Combat, as evidenced by a campaign star, a decoration for bravery, a Purple Heart, was worth five points for each instance. Having a child under the age of eight was worth twelve points. Overseas service was worth a point a month. Military service itself was worth an additional point a month. Points became an obsession not only with the millions in uniform but with their tens of millions of relatives. On V-J Day 85 points would get you out.

The magic number dropped rapidly. By Christmas the "critical score" had dropped to fifty. But the score dropped faster than shipping became available, and the pressure on shipping space was aggravated when 70,000 war brides began to present themselves for travel to the U.S. The belief spread that the government had broken an unspoken agreement to ship men home as soon as they reached the critical score, and when a troopship failed to sail on schedule from the Philippines with 5,000 homeward-bound servicemen, their mood turned ugly. Thousands of irate American servicemen rampaged through the streets of Manila.* For several days they pointedly reported for duty staggering drunk and out of uniform.

The Army also discovered that if it continued to discharge men at the rate of 1 million a month, it would go out of existence by July 1946. It decided to cut the rate of separations to 300,000 a month. This was also considered a betrayal. When Secretary of War Robert Patterson journeyed to Japan, he was met by crowds of booing soldiers. They were shamed into silence, however, by a provost marshal who briefly described the gallantry under fire which had won Lieutenant Patterson the Distinguished Service Cross in France in 1918.

In Frankfurt, several thousand soldiers mobbed the European Theater of Operations headquarters. In Paris protesting servicemen held a candlelight procession down the Champs-Elysees, chanting obscenities. More than 100 marines stationed in Hawaii sent an insolent, whining telegram to President Truman.

---

*The conduct of American servicemen overseas created disgust at home and abroad. It is not the whole story, however. American soldiers vacationing in Switzerland made a solemn journey to Schaffhausen, which had been accidentally bombed in 1945, when 35 people were killed, more than 100 injured. The U.S. government had apologized profusely and paid compensation to the victims and their families. There was still bitterness over the incident. These soldiers made the journey to offer their personal regrets, to visit the children who had been maimed, and to lay a memorial wreath. And this was typical of many spontaneous acts of kindness shown by American servicemen.

At home, "Bring Back Daddy" clubs were formed. Legislators began to receive baby shoes in their mail, accompanied with childish scrawls supposedly from infants, reading, "Bring my daddy home."

Demobilization was proceeding with extraordinary dispatch. Only impatience made it seem slow. Soldiers and sailors, marines and airmen possessed some powerful allies in Washington. Congressmen were, almost without exception, on the side of servicemen—and their mothers', and their fathers', and their wives'—in fact, on the side of every one of a serviceman's relatives who had reached voting age.

The impatient man in uniform possessed another, less benign ally: the atomic bomb. For who, it was asked, could raise a serious threat to America now? *Life* paraphrased the lines Hilaire Belloc had written in praise of the Maxim gun some forty years earlier:

> Whatever happens, we have got
> The atom bomb, which they have not.

Separation was one of those terminal experiences in life, like getting married or losing one's virginity. No one ever forgot how it went. Louis Falstein recalled his own separation in detail: "Eleven of us boarded the train in Chicago with orders to report to Fort Dix for separation from the Army. We were a jubilant bunch of high point men . . . we presented our government meal tickets and received the inevitable stew, but this time we did not resent it. We were lavish in our tips. We called each other 'Mister.'" At Fort Dix, Falstein and his companions were marched from building to building, signed forms, killed time, chafed incessantly, and patiently sat through a lecture from the chaplain on how to readjust. "Take it easy," he advised. "Have confidence in God. Help build a better America." But God was a less pressing issue than how to convert their government insurance.

There was a last, carefully considered trip to the PX to stock up on tax-free razor blades, cigarettes, silk stockings, rouge, lipstick, and socks. But what they really wanted was "that White Piece of Paper." The future did not begin until they held that in their hands.

Sitting around, waiting for the coveted White Piece of Paper to emerge from the bureaucratic machinery, they sang:

> When this war is over we will all enlist again;
> When this war is over we will all enlist again;
> Like hell we will, like hell we will . . .

There was one final hurdle—the physical. It was enough to make a man with a chestful of combat decorations nervous. If you failed the physical, you stayed in until you were fit enough to pass it.

Having passed the physical examination, they moved on to be fingerprinted. They signed three copies of their service records. There was a short, brisk march over to the clothing depot, to exchange old army clothing for new army clothing and collect a pair of shoes in exchange for their combat boots. The right breast of their new khaki shirts bore a ruptured duck, executed in gold thread.*

Afterward came a trip to Finance, where each man received $50 in cash and a check for whatever else was owing him. Finally, there came the trip to the chapel. A WAC played "America" on the organ, Falstein remembered, a prayer was said, that White Piece of Paper was handed out in a ceremony resembling high school graduation, and after that they were free—civilians once more.

The challenge now was to get home. Incoming veterans from the Pacific discovered that the only way they could get home by Christmas was to hop a freight train. The unlucky and stoical waited in tents and barracks for a break in the transportation bottleneck. Some waited for weeks.

After separation came the homecoming, and that, many found, was another battlefield. The most famous enlisted man to return from the war was 23-year-old Army Sergeant Bill Mauldin, the cartoonist who had created Willie and Joe. Like many another returned veteran, Mauldin came back to a wife he would soon divorce.

On the West Coast, an Army veteran returned only to accuse his wife of infidelity during his absence. To prove her devotion, she poisoned his coffee, so that she might nurse him back to health. She miscalculated, and was indicted for manslaughter.

Corporal Thomas Eugene Atkins returned as one of the great heroes of the war. Badly wounded in the hip, with the other members of his platoon lying dead around him, Atkins had fought a one-man action in the jungles of Luzon, persevering under indescribable hardship. He killed forty-four Japanese soldiers single-handedly. At the White House Truman decorated him with the Congressional Medal of Honor. (Truman would say to men such as Atkins, "I'd rather have this medal than be President.") Atkins returned to Spartanburg, South Carolina, to a hero's welcome—and a dirty, drafty shack.

His family was desperately poor. His father was an itinerant sharecropper. There was no evident future for the son except to follow in his father's mired footsteps. A sense of shame, however, moved the people of Spartanburg. A hero deserved a farm of his own and a promising future. Thomas Eugene Atkins began to receive money in the mail from strangers. There were several checks for $100. But most of the money came in nickels, dimes, and quarters. Spartanburg and the surrounding area were poor. Yet in less than a month he received nearly $7000. With this he bought Thank You Farm. Then the other gifts began to arrive: a mule, pecan trees, fertilizer, an electric pump, furniture, dishes, a Bible.

James Kutcher had graduated from high school straight into the

---

*This was the popular name for what was known politely as the Golden Eagle. It showed a bird posed in a heroic attitude, its wings outstretched, within a circle decorated with a stars and stripes motif. There was a version to be worn in the lapel, but as one typical veteran complaint ran, "It's made of plastic, gets upside down in the lapel, and nobody recognizes it anyway."

Depression. For eight years he had tried, and failed to find a steady job. He had been among the first men to be drafted in 1940. The Army knew, but did not care, that Kutcher had spent much of the Depression as a member of the radical Socialist Workers Party. He went on to fight in North Africa, Sicily, and Italy, until his legs were shredded by an exploding mortar shell. One was amputated above, the other below, the knee.

After a long, painful rehabilitation he learned to walk with artifical limbs. In 1946 he finally found permanent employment, as a loans clerk with the VA. Kutcher was typical of thousands of severely wounded veterans, the man whose strength of character literally put him on his feet again. He was typical, too, of hundreds of thousands of men who did not have a permanent job until after the war. We shall meet Kutcher again, in a sadly different context.

More broadly representative in outlook and experience was John Keats. Born in 1920, he had gone into the Army in 1941. "Perhaps the most impressive lesson the Army taught us was that the America we had hitherto known as a land of breadlines and uncertain economics was, in fact, overwhelmingly wealthy, productive and powerful—once its resources were employed. . . . For the first time (in the lives of many) they were presented with all the food they could stuff into themselves." Coming home, he recalled, "The factories bordering the Philadelphia railroad yards were clattering by, with signs on them reading WELL DONE and WELCOME HOME and THE NATION IS PROUD OF YOU. I could hardly believe they were meant for me." And then: "I felt a sudden fear of leaving the Army. I had not enjoyed it; I had often detested it . . . Yet the Army had been my father, mother, big brother and reason for existence for more than four years. It was something familiar, something I understood. Outside yawned a vast uncertainty."

Some men had found in the military a home of sorts. That was what had happened to Major Claude Eatherly of the Army Air Corps. He was also one of those thousands of men who failed to make the transition from military to civilian life. Eatherly had flown over Hiroshima in advance of the *Enola Gay,* to report on the weather over the first city marked for destruction by an atomic bomb. He had nothing to do with selecting the target or ordering that it be dropped. He was far away at zero hour and saw nothing of the explosion.

He attempted to remain permanently in the Air Corps at the end of the war. He had a weak character, however, and was caught cheating on an examination at Meteorology School. A reluctant civilian, he became involved in an attempt to invade Cuba by means of a ragtag army of ex-servicemen manning war-surplus landing craft and P-38 fighters. A light bomber was reserved for Eatherly. He proposed to paralyze Havana by bombing the central business district. The object of the attack on Cuba was to force the island into the Union as the forty-ninth state. At the last moment Federal officials seized the aircraft, the landing craft, and the principal conspirators, three of whom went to prison. But Eatherly was set free. He is another veteran we shall meet again.

Ira Hayes, the Pima Indian who had helped the raise the flag on Iwo Jima, typified the plight of many of the 30,000 Indian veterans. He came home to the Pima Reservation in Arizona a hero. He also came back to unemployment, poverty, and despair. He turned, as countless Indians had turned, to cheap whiskey. Drunk much of the time, he stumbled around the reservation for several years in a stupor, pitied and scorned, until one night he stumbled into a drainage ditch and drowned in three inches of muddy water.

Once separated and at home, most veterans found it took time to become psychological civilians once more. Anyone who spends several years in uniform absorbs some of the military's values. To a soldier, sailor, or airmen most civilian pursuits appear soft and pointless. And once absorbed, values are not quickly changed. Military service itself had not completely eradicated the civilian's scorn for the military which these veterans had possessed before putting on a uniform. To the civilian, a military career appealed only to the slow-witted and submissive. But even when he scoffed, the fledgling amateur soldier, sailor, or airman was absorbing much of the military's ways and judgments. So when, years later, he was set free, he did not think highly of military life; at the same time he confronted his old job with a sinking feeling that it was a pursuit fit only for a tame and hollow man. The same dismay set in when he thought about his old friends, his neighborhood, his family. There was only one answer to this emotional confusion—time. It would take time for military values to become enfeebled for want of reinforcement.

Many veterans were further confused because they wanted the impossible—security without dullness. Most had saved some money. Those with $1,000 or so were tempted to set up a small business, usually a tavern or gas station.

The veteran was for a couple of years the object of obsessive concern. He was smothered with official, if haphazard, advice. A dozen Federal agencies offered their services, but never in a coordinated way. Most states established veterans' bodies. Some towns, notably Bridgeport, Connecticut, and Peoria, Illinois, created imaginative and responsive programs to help veterans find jobs and housing and to take full advantage of the benefits provided by law.

But the hardest problems to be faced were often matters of the heart, where outside help can do the least. For many a veteran homecoming was a return not to freedom but to responsibility (a wife, a child or two) and disillusionment. Some men wasted little time in taking to their heels. Other thousands made an effort, but failed. A wife could be as disappointed as the man. Out of uniform her husband was only too likely to seem dull and indecisive, a sorry imitation of the glamorous fighting man she so clearly remembered marrying. Yet most husbands and wives sooner or later accepted the challenge, and the disappointments, of married life and became responsible, hardworking couples.

To secure their interests in the postwar, the veterans looked to the VA, which was transformed under the brief tenure of General Omar Bradley, and to themselves. They turned mainly to the American Legion and the Veterans of Foreign Wars. The Legion's attraction was not its uniform or the antics of some Legionnaires at the annual convention. Nor were the new veterans attracted by the recreational (mainly drinking) opportunities provided by the local Legion post. The Legion's appeal was its political clout. More than a third of all Senators and Representatives were Legionnaires.

The VFW for its part attracted a large number of World War II veterans simply because it was as devoted to veterans' interests as the Legion without bearing the stigma of reaction. A year after V-J Day three-fourths of all members of the American Legion and the VFW were veterans of World War II. They were notably more liberal than the elderly men who continued to run the organizations. Among the tens of thousands of Legion posts there were some which were decidedly leftist, while others might have been happily directed by Calvin Coolidge. It is conceivable that there were more Communists within the American Legion than within the ultraliberal American Veterans Committee (whose motto, "Citizens First, Veterans Second," was viewed with the deepest suspicion by the Legion and the VFW). Communists openly bedeviled the AVC, but they were advised by the *Daily Worker* to concentrate on the Legion and to bore from within.

In the end each man or woman made his or her readjustment to civilian life. Most veterans were successfully reintegrated into American life with help from the GI Bill, their families, their friends, their employers. But the most important element was their own determination.

Although they liked to be considered straightforward and realistic, most of them were idealistic. They were shocked to find black markets flourishing in the United States. What had seemed acceptable in Naples or Manila seemed disgusting at home. Nevertheless, before long they too were buying black-market tires or meat. Their zeal was remarkable. They were accustomed to accepting responsibility and asserting themselves. They thought nothing of holding down two or three jobs. "More young men came home from World War II with a sense of purpose," Congressman Frank Smith later recalled, "than from any other American venture. I was one of them." Their confidence and determination were a by-product of the war. What most men did not achieve until they reached their forties and fifties these had acquired in their twenties and thirties.

They were young without youth.

The most pressing shortage, the veteran soon discovered, was housing, which in 1945 presented a classic example of a social problem which had gone from bad to worse for more than fifteen years because at any given time something else seemed more important, until by 1946 nothing seemed more important than housing.

Private construction had slumped badly during the 1930s. Comparatively few houses had been built in wartime. In constant prices the nation's housing stock was worth less in 1945 than in 1929. Yet the demand for housing had never been so urgent. Millions of people from rural areas had migrated during the war to urban areas. Nearly 2 million veterans had married by V-J Day and were seeking homes of their own. Wartime prosperity had lifted savings and income to unparalleled heights. The banks, awash with money, dropped mortage rates below 5 percent. With so much cheap money to be borrowed and so few houses to be had, the price of old houses, which was uncontrolled by the Office of Price Administration virtually doubled in some areas between Pearl Harbor and V-J Day. The price of new houses was controlled, and the upper limit set at $8,000. But the chance of finding a new house at the controlled price was almost as remote as the chance of being struck by lightning.

Housing was almost a handicraft. In 1946 anyone capable of erecting ten houses on a single site was considered a big-time operator. Most builders put up one house at a time.

The housing shortage put terrible strains on marriage and family life. Hundreds of thousands of families were broken up by it, if only for a few months. In Englewood, Colorado, Jay Ramsey, a Navy veteran evicted from his tiny apartment and unable to find another, dragged a divan into city hall. Mrs. Ramsey promptly occupied the divan and began to nurse the seven-month-old Ramsey infant. When the city proved unable to find other accommodation for them, the mayor allowed the Ramseys to squat in city hall indefinitely.

Then there was Leo Zale, recently of Company I, 105th Regiment, 29th Infantry Division. On his return from Okinawa a large sign greeted him at the Los Angeles docks: WELCOME HOME, BOYS — JOB WELL DONE! That was the beginning and end of a hero's welcome. Zale spent several weeks tramping around Los Angeles in search of a room. Until he found one, he slept on the beach. Elsewhere in Los Angeles a resourceful Marine veteran put his wartime experience to practical use. He pitched a tent in Pershing Square.

In Tuckahoe, New York, the new superintendent of schools arrived in town and found nowhere to stay. He tried sleeping on a friend's couch while house hunting. But that put a strain on friendship. He then moved into one of his schools at dead of night. That worked nicely, until the school board found out and told him to move.

Even United States Senators were caught short. When Glen Taylor, the new Senator from Idaho, arrived in Washington in January, 1944, he was found sitting on the Capitol steps, strumming his guitar, plaintively singing, "Oh, give me a home, near the Capitol dome, with a yard where the children can play. Just one room or two, any old thing will do, we can't find a pla-a-ace to stay."*

As late as a year after V-J Day an advertisement for an apartment in At-

---

*This provided the United States Senate with the largest number of singing cowboys ever to grace a national legislature, two, the other being Pappy "Pass the Biscuits" Daniel of Texas. The singing cowboy was a form of entertainment now mercifully extinct. It was also the only thing Taylor and Daniel had in common, apart from being United States Senators.

lanta drew 2,000 replies. Ironically, it had never been easier to buy a house, if you could find one. People would secure permission to build, take out a mortgage, find a builder, give him the money, and wait. And wait. The builder, if he were an honest man, would be waiting too—for lumber, for pipes, for wiring, for tiles. On the other hand, he might collect all the deposits the traffic would bear (usually a lot) and brazenly go out of business without ever building a single house.

A number of radical solutions were broached, nearly all impractical or unrealistically expensive. The exception was Buckminster Fuller's Dymaxion house which was logical and inexpensive. Fuller was a bald, moonfaced figure with the zeal of an Old Testament prophet combined with an engagingly eccentric nature and a passion for modern technology. His Dymaxion house was made of aluminum and was round. He and Beech Aircraft Corporation proposed to turn them out in the tens of thousands and to sell them for $6,500 each. This price included shipping, erection, kitchen appliances, and bathroom fittings. The entire structure weighed four tons, yet could withstand the worst extremes of weather. It could hardly be faulted—it met a strongly felt need; it was practical; the price was right. The only trouble was, hardly anyone could be found even during the worst housing shortage in American history who wanted to live in a tin can thirty-six feet in diameter.

The housing crisis remained the most volatile social question politicians had to deal with. To Truman, housing was a fundamental of social justice in a democratic state: everyone had a right to a decent place to live in. His friend John Snyder, a conservative Missouri banker installed as director of the Office of War Mobilization and Reconversion, lifted the restrictions on the use of building supplies. A construction boom followed. But it was a boom in the construction of bowling alleys, cocktail bars, summer resorts, racetracks, and department stores. Some houses were built, but they were houses for the rich.

Truman acknowledged the urgency of the situation by appointing a national Housing Expediter, Woodrow Wilson Wyatt, until recently the liberal mayor of Louisville, Kentucky. Wyatt banked heavily on prefabrication to provide up to 600,000 new houses each year. Prefabrication building companies appeared to spring up overnight like Shasta daisies, all of them clamoring for a share of the very limited stock of building materials available.

The Reconstruction Finance Corporation was urged by Wyatt to lend hundreds of millions of dolllars to the infant prefab industry. In most instances the RFC refused to follow Wyatt's urgings, and perhaps that was as well. For it did make large loans to one new prefab company, Lustron, which had never built a house and whose usual business was producing metal fittings for gas stations. Lustron had some important friends in Congress. It proposed to build 120,000 prefabricated, metal-skinned houses each year. But when, tens of millions of dollars and seven years later, Lustron went out of the housing business, it had contributed 2,096 houses, at an average Federal subsidy of $17,000 each.

Wyatt's hopes for prefabrication came to nothing. But that was largely because he knew nothing about prefabrication. It was not the inexpensive alternative it appeared to be. The sections could be stamped out cheaply and quickly at the factory. But then came on-site assembly, which required highly paid plumbers and electricians. Landscaping did not come in a box from the factory, nor did the driveway, nor, for that matter, did the site. Mortgage interest had to be paid, as on an ordinary house, and so did insurance. The shell amounted to less than half the cost of a house, and that was all that prefabrication produced—shells, not houses. The savings involved amounted to 20 percent of the total cost, for a house which was likely to be 20 percent less sturdy and resistant to wear.

Wyatt's housing plans never came to grips, moreover, with the challenge of dealing with 30,000 prime contractors and 200,000 subcontractors. A national housing program could succeed on a large scale only if it spawned large-scale projects, each involving hundreds or thousands of units.

The housing crisis was aggravated by strikes in crucial industries—lumber, railroads, steel. After a year of frustration and abuse Wyatt resigned as Housing Expediter, only one-tenth of his projected housing starts behind him.

Congress was meanwhile considering the Wagner-Ellender-Taft housing bill, and Truman, perhaps sensing that Wyatt would fail, increasingly pinned his own hopes on a bill which was largely the idea of Senator Robert A. Taft. It held out several enticements to real estate and banking interests. It also contained a provision for 500,000 units of public housing. The W-E-T bill was destined never to get out of the Senate Banking and Currency Committee.

Despite the shortage, there was a large and vocal body of public opinion opposed to any attempt by the Federal government to build homes for rent or sale. And although veterans were among those most in favor of the government as developer, the American Legion was one of those groups most opposed to it. The Legion sided not with the homeless veteran but with the real estate lobby, in the belief that it was fighting "Socialism."

The Federal government nevertheless played a vital role in the postwar housing crisis. It did so through existing agencies, such as the Federal Housing Administration, created in 1934. The FHA was designed to help builders provide homes for middle-income families. After 1945 it became principally an agency which helped builders, period. The FHA became a money machine for anyone with the wit to turn the handle. By applying for and receiving a loan markedly in excess of the real cost of a housing development, an enterprising builder could secure 100 percent plus financing and a no-risk profit of 25 to 35 percent on the finished project. The FHA was also generous enough to pay the architect's fees and paid the builder 2½ percent of the mortgage as his commission for going to all the trouble of arranging an FHA-financed mortgage on his houses.

The government was like a Dutch uncle in everything involving mortgages, especially where veterans were concerned. By 1947 all that a veteran needed to raise for a house was a few hundred dollars to cover closing costs. The government provided a 100 percent loan at 4 percent interest with thirty years to pay.

But well into 1947 there were tens of thousands of families living in chicken coops, attics, sheds, tents, and condemned buildings for no better reason than the general housing shortage. Tens of thousands more were still forced to begin married life by living with relatives and friends. Simply being able to get a mortgage did not get you a house.

When Richard L. Neuberger returned to his hometown in Oregon in 1946, he discovered that the biggest construction project underway was a $1 million racetrack. "While hammers fall and planks are sawed at the racetrack, veterans with HH priorities tramp from lumber yard to lumber yard vainly trying to buy construction materials for homes . . . loan companies and automobile sales agencies are putting up elaborate new buildings . . . but veterans encounter difficulty getting the tiniest screw or simplest window frame for bungalow or cottage." The veterans found that an HH priority was worth far less than a well-placed friend. Lacking that, it helped to have plenty of money. Anyone with $15,000 to spend could buy a house carried on the tax rolls as being worth $5,000.

The veterans were understandably angry. They were also puzzled. They had recently traversed arctic wastes, deserts, and rocky atolls and bomb-pocked moonscapes and despite all obstacles had within a few weeks or months built small towns with airfields, roads, and docks. But now, facing nothing more daunting than a level 100-foot lot, they were told it would take at least a year to erect upon it a modest two-or three-bedroom house.

On June 1, 1946, the chairman of the TVA, David Lilienthal, made an entry in his diary:

> Saw a new kind of "line" yesterday in Knoxville. Unemployed men, veterans. The line began at the Veterans Service Center next door to the New Sprankle Building, stretched past the entrance of the TVA office, past the telephone office, turned the corner and stretched down the hill half a block. It was that long when I went to lunch; it was even longer when I returned. Men getting their $20 a week unemployment benefits.

What he had witnessed was the local chapter of the "52-20 Club" in session. Discharged veterans were entitled to $20 a week for up to one year. Despite popular impressions of widespread, prolonged loafing fewer than 1 veteran in 100 ever retained membership in the club for an entire year.

Nearly every veteran had some savings, insurance, a bonus, and his 52-20 Club benefits to carry him until he found a job. For those who were still in need there was a veterans' welfare scheme called the readjustment allowance. Of those who applied for it, most drew it for fewer than three weeks. Almost without exception what the discharged veteran wanted was a job.

For the man who had learned a trade, such as radio repair, it was comparatively easy to find work. It was more difficult if all that you had learned was how to set up a mortar and how to use a machine gun. Every employer was required by law to give the veteran his old job if he asked for it. But since his departure a replacement had been hired and trained. Many an employer appealed to the returned veteran's conscience: naturally, he had a right to the job, no doubt about it, but the other fellow happened to be a middle-aged man, had a sick wife, or an elderly mother, several children, mortgage payments, a bad leg, had seen a lot of hardship. . . . Of course, if the veteran *insisted* on taking the job away from this poor fellow, cast him onto the trash heap, he had that right. Of course he had.

In 1944 the Selective Service System had created "superseniority" to protect the rights of veterans to their old jobs. It was an idea which labor unions resisted. It threatened to overthrow the principle of seniority which they had striven for years to establish as one of the sacred rights of labor. And some employers used the superseniority ruling to get rid of wartime union labor, replacing it with veterans who were antiunion. But most of the fury was taken out of this issue by a force neither business nor union controlled—a very high level of demand for labor.

The problem, the veteran found, was less likely to be finding a job than finding a job that appealed. The old hometown and the old job had lost the attraction they had held when viewed from a hedgerow in Normandy or a swamp on Saipan. "You guys have been turned ass-over-appetite by combat and don't want to go back to dull, tasteless jobs," was how one of the characters in the 1946 best-seller *The Hucksters* expressed it.

But it was not only the veterans whose heads had been turned by wartime thrills. There had been a massive internal migration between the outbreak of the war in Europe and the end of the war in the Pacific. Tens of millions of people had moved back and forth. Money had poured into people's pockets. Sexual liaisons had been more casual than ever. People who worked hard felt unusually free to indulge themselves in whatever pleasures were left over from controls. Nightclubs had done a better business in wartime than they had in the fabled 1920s. The consumption of stimulants, from cigarettes to alcohol, had soared. And in the exciting new era about to unfold, no one wanted to be left out. "People were probably never choosier," wrote *Time*. "They're looking for 'glamor' jobs in the so-called 'glamor plants.' No more ordinary factory surroundings for them. They're used to music and news broadcasts and de luxe cafeterias. . . . Across the land workers objected to lower pay, less interesting peacetime jobs." After years of being told how important they were, how critical was their individual contribution to victory, ordinary people felt entitled to all the good things in life, including a satisfying job.

Victory won, it had to be savored. The national celebrations continued for months after V-J Day. In late October 1945 a mightly fleet of aircraft carriers, battleships, cruisers, and lesser vessels steamed up the Hudson in a display of naval power. The President journeyed to New York on Navy Day to review the armada. Along the riverbanks more than two million New Yorkers cheered the passage of these huge gray ships, which filled the river for mile after mile.

The President addressed a vast throng in Central Park before going to visit the battleship *Missouri* and gaze at the bronze plaque fixed to the deck to memorialize the Japanese surrender. Having transferred to the destroyer *Reuben*, he reviewed the warships moored in the river. Each ship fired a twenty-one-gun salute, while overhead 1,200 Navy planes flew past in the most imposing show of air power ever presented over an American city. For once even the blasé citizens of New York were awed. For the President, whose prosaic appearance concealed a deep romantic streak, it was "the happiest day of my life."*

The Army's victory celebration came on a frosty day in early January 1946. The entire 82nd Airborne Division marched down Fifth Avenue and through the Washington Square Arch. They appeared with bayonets fixed and bared, 13,000 strong, marching on behalf of all the men who had worn the Army uniform in wartime.

It was a performance conducted with classical restraint, almost Greek in its austerity. There was no music except the rhythmic pounding of marching feet, few flags, no weapons except for those the soldiers carried, no elaborate equipment. It was the men themselves, the heart of any army, who were the spectacle. "Airborne" sounded glamorous, but they were simply airborne foot soldiers, what the British call "the PBI—poor bloody infantry." For mile after rhythmically marched mile they were cheered and applauded. The simplicity of the scene gave people the chance to reflect on what it stood for—the 300,000 soldiers who had died, the million who had been wounded. New Yorkers crowded the sidewalks and the side streets. In the daunting cold, tears glistened on cheeks.

Some of the war's unfinished business was less edifying. In Japan, Tokyo Rose was tracked down, not by the Occupation authorities, busy with other matters, but by a reporter. The famous siren who had attempted to lure American servicemen from their duty, with no apparent success, proved to be no beauty but a homely twenty-nine-year-old Nisei named Iva Toguri. There had been not one but a dozen Tokyo Roses, and she was only one of the bunch.

It was her misfortune that she alone fell within American jurisdiction. Returned to the United States, she was tried, in the press as well as in the courts, found guilty of treason, and sentenced to ten years' imprisonment.†

---

*The *Missouri* was left at her mooring after Navy Day to welcome visitors. As many as 60,000 children boarded her in a single day. The visitors inflicted more damage in two weeks than the Japanese had managed to inflict on the battleship in several years of combat. After two weeks of vandalism the *Missouri* had to be moved from her mooring and taken to Brooklyn Navy Yard for repairs.

†In 1977 she received a Presidential pardon from Gerald Ford in one of his last actions before leaving the White House.

Three men were accused of treason on account of broadcasts they had made on behalf of the enemy in wartime. One was Douglas Chandler, the "American Lord Haw-Haw," who had served the Nazis for four years. He received a sentence of life imprisonment. Another was Robert H. Best, once a respected foreign correspondent, whose anti-Semitism led him to imitate Chandler. Like Chandler, he received a life sentence. The third was Ezra Pound.

The Army took him into custody in northern Italy and proceeded to treat him as if he were a dangerous beast. He was kept in a cage like a zoo animal, except that zoo animals were treated better. His cage, fashioned from the metal strips used to lay down temporary runways in combat zones, was exposed to the fierce Italian sun by day and the riveting cold by night. As it was not far removed from a busy highway, he was kept awake by the roar of traffic and at busy times on dry days was showered with dust. Throughout the night powerful searchlights played on his cage. When it rained, he was drenched to the skin. When the wind blew, he felt its blast. But all of this was in Pound's best interests, the Army claimed, because it discouraged him from committing suicide.

The other prisoners held at the same air base were deemed less suicidal. They were thus allowed to sleep in tents and take exercise. Only after Pound collapsed mentally and physically from this ordeal was he taken from his cage and permitted the comparative luxury of an army cot under canvas. Whether calculated or not, Pound's suffering amounted to seven months of torture. "As a result of this ordeal," said his lawyer, "he went out of his mind and suffered a complete loss of memory, a state from which he did not fully recover."

Pound's standing as an avant-garde poet had doubtless encouraged the Italian government to believe he would be a useful propagandist for the Fascist cause. But his wartime broadcasts had consisted of nothing more potent than cranky anti-Semitism and some incoherent ramblings on the virtues of Social Credit economics.

Had he been Hitler, Pound's confinement in a cage would have been indefensible. Jailers are in the position of superiors to inferiors; they are responsible for them and have a moral obligation to protect them from needless cruelty and suffering. When prisoners and poets are treated as Pound was treated, there is evidently some confusion over how prisoners, poets, and crazy old men are to be regarded. The Army chose to believe that Pound was in fact more dangerous than its ordinary run of petty cut-throats for no better reason than that he wrote poetry, was bearded, and gave long-winded answers to short, simple questions.

Out of Pound's encagement came a body of poems which are often un-readable. But among them there is one poem, Canto LXXXI, which con-tains some of the best poetry written by an American in the postwar years. Art has a furtive, almost subversive character. It will find a way de-spite jailers and cages.

Once the unfinished business of celebration and incarceration was over, there remained the more important unfinished business of making something out of victory. What should be done about the Bomb? Almost everyone believed it had been right to use it to end the war. But that was the beginning of the matter, not the conclusion. What ought to be done regarding the Soviet Union? Should the Russians be helped to rebuild their economy? On this there was little disagreement. American overwhelmingly opposed a Russian loan. To nearly half the American people the Russians were already seen as both the principal danger to peace in the postwar and a deadly threat to the security of the United States. Nor were Americans convinced that Germany was no longer a threat. Most people were convinced that Hitler was still alive.

So Americans favored rapid demobilization. But they did not favor national disarmament. They wanted a military establishment in peacetime that was five times the size it had been in 1939—that is, a million-man Army and a half-million-man Navy, plus retention of the atomic bomb.

These, then, were the Americans in the first aftermath of victory. To see more closely what they looked and felt like, however, John Bartlow Martin visited Muncie, Indiana (famous as the "Middletown" studied a generation earlier by Robert and Helen Lynd), in early 1946. People there, he found, were far more concerned with domestic affairs than with international issues. They had abandoned their former isolationism, but reluctantly. They disliked the idea of loans to the British almost as much as they disliked making loans to the Russians. They were skeptical over sending food to Europe. "Europe wouldn't feed us if we were hungry," they said.

People still grew vegetables in their own Victory plots. Beer was in short supply, forcing taverns to open at 4 P.M. and to refuse to sell before 7. The Buick dealer had two cars in his showroom and 170 orders on his desk. New clothes were hard to find. Martin encountered a young veteran wearing khaki army pants who complained passionately, "Christ, I been trying all over to buy a pair of overalls."

At a Ball State Teachers College dance in the Hotel Roberts few of the girls' escorts, he noticed, "resembled the skinny awkward small-town boys, ill at ease in tuxes, whom you used to see at Indiana college dances. Instead they were older men, and serious-faced, and some had been wounded—how strange it was to see a burly man in tweeds with a ruptured duck in one lapel and a white rose in the other, and the fragile blue card of a dance program dangling from his pocket!"

No one talked about the atomic bomb or the international situation unless Martin raised the subject. Yet they knew that for every door the war had closed for the United States another had been opened. They knew only too well that they and their country stood on the threshold of a new age, filled with unusual dangers and novel responsibilities.

They had learned, or were about to find out, that each nation which fights and wins a war discovers only afterward what it has actually been fighting for. It all depends on what it does with its victory. In the aftermath of victory a nation learns the truth about itself. It is presented with countless opportunities to misuse its strength. The question was: what would the Americans do with the enormous power now in their hands?

2

Had Enough?

Throughout 1946 there were three subjects on which you could get an argument started in any bar—price controls, strikes, and Harry S Truman. All three were closely related.

The Office of Price Administration had greeted the Japanese surrender by ending the rationing of gasoline and canned goods. Its master plan called for the gradual lifting of controls and the reappearance of consumer goods at the same prices, in real terms, charged for them in 1941. This meant that manufacturers would have to absorb the inflationary increases of wartime; the OPA reasoned that business had made so much money since 1941 that it could afford to contribute heavily to price stability during reconversion.

An Executive Order issued three days after the war ended gave White House approval to the OPA plan. If all went as the OPA intended, the country would be returned to a more or less free economy in eighteen to twenty-four months. On the face of it, the government had the economy well under control.

In fact, much of it had already escaped. More broke free each week. Open markets were becoming gray; gray markets were turning black. The OPA fulminated, denounced, and protested, but with fewer than one investigator per county, it was in no position to enforce its regulations. Shortages plus prosperity made black markets inevitable. The OPA's impotence made them widespread. The economic order of 1946 was aptly described as "Over the ceiling, under the counter, and through the nose!" Up to half the population probably made a black-market purchase at some time, knowing just what it was doing.

Existing shortages were at times aggravated the better to exploit them. Fresh lumber was deliberately held back at the sawmill. In 1946 an estimated 400 to 500 million board feet were being cached against the day when OPA price ceilings were lifted. Most of the sawmills were in the South. The farther away from the South you were, the harder it was to buy lumber. Above Maryland the lumber black market was almost completely in control. And if you managed to buy the lumber you needed, chances were you then needed nails. Black-market nails cost nine times the OPA price.

Millions of shirts and hundreds of thousands of suits were cached at manufacturers' warehouses, waiting for the OPA Maximum Average Price system to be scrapped. Veterans complained that they had won the war only to lose their shirts. A delegation marched on the OPA office in Manhattan stripped to the waist.

There was a black market in meat. In a sense, there was a black market in housing, as we have seen, and at times it could be brazen. The *Portland*, Oregon, *Daily Journal* ran an advertisement which offered: "$6000 Family Home! Only $8350."

But the most pervasive black market was in used cars. The price of secondhand vehicles was less closely controlled than that of new ones. So it was not unusual to buy a Cadillac with a speedometer reading of 000010. The new price was $3,379; the "used" price was likely to be close to $6,000. But for that you admittedly received a used car which bore the factory stickers on the windshield, had mothballs in the back, and exuded that distinctive new car smell.

The black market involved an estimated one-fourth of all automobile sales. Where vulgar cash did not change hands the OPA regulations might still be circumvented by diamond rings or the deed to a plot of land. In a down-at-the-heels South Carolina small town, Leesville, the casual visitor in 1946 was regaled with an extraordinary sight: every street, every vacant lot, every alley was crammed with cars. Leesville, with a population of 2,000, on any given day had far more cars than people. For a short while it was famous as the center of a $100 million black market in used cars.

All along the Mason-Dixon line that year, where small-town sheriffs could be induced to turn a blind eye and where Northerners with cash could expect a warm welcome from Southerners who lacked it, a passing motorist might draw up to a light to find himself confronted by a stranger who had leaped onto his running board to make an offer the unwary driver was not supposed to be able to refuse.

The dealers were blamed for the used-car black market. But the dealers had to find the cars before they could sell them. Anyone with a good used car to sell in 1946 knew what it was worth, OPA ceilings notwithstanding. The bedrock of the automobile black market was the unshakable greed of ordinary, law-abiding citizens.

Many black markets involved "tie-in" sales: if you wanted a bottle of whiskey you might have to buy a bottle of wine, too; if you wanted a nice thick steak, you might also have to take a pound of tripe. Barter revived. Some people seemed to enjoy haggling for a change. Nylon stockings became a form of currency—demand was universal; they were easy to carry and impossible to forge. A pair of contestants on a Los Angeles radio show were set loose without a cent between them, but amply supplied with nylons, and given a week to reach New York. They made the journey in four days without missing a meal or going without a place to stay.

It might fairly be said that black markets put American ingenuity to the test. Americans were not found wanting. Attempting to make a purchase, the would-be consumer might encounter a would-be seller who would throw down a challenge. "Betcha I can spit further than you can." The consumer, if he or she had the wit and the determination required, would accept the challenge and would go on to lose the contest. One ingenious Oklahoma car salesman was reported to own a dog that he sold with every car. "The hound dog always shuffled back to the lot," *Time* reported.

To evade the price ceilings, many businessmen simply went out of business. They would then go into business once again, producing goods anyone might swear were identical with those formerly produced; but no, this was an entirely new line. The OPA was asked to set a new price for them. Almost without exception this would be higher than the old price. The clothing business was famous for the ease with which it eluded the OPA's grasp.

"New" businesses also hit on the discovery that it was possible to make a handsome profit without making anything else. Once a business was in possession of an office, some stationery, and a telephone it could demand its share of the raw materials essential to its existence—cloth, leather, steel, wood pulp, or whatever. It could then sell its share at a black-market price to some other manufacturer who actually intended to turn out tables or dresses or suitcases or paper.

There was still another way to defeat the OPA. Its regulations were tied to price, not quality. A dress could be bought for $10 in 1940; six years later a dress could still be bought for $10. To the OPA the two dresses were the same. But the woman who bought the two dresses could see the difference. She could feel it as well.

The National Association of Manufacturers took full-page advertisements blaming the black markets and the shortages and the drop in quality on the OPA. Fulton Lewis, Jr., a splenetic radio commentator whose hates far exceeded his loves, regularly inveighed against the OPA and suggested that it was in some way connected with the Kremlin. Wholesalers, retailers, and consumers were encouraged by the U.S. Chamber of Commerce to complain to Congress. Yet although Congress did receive a huge outpouring of anti-OPA mail, public opinion still supported price controls, by a margin of 4–1.

Congress lacked the nerve to stand up to the NAM et al., nor would it risk public wrath by destroying the OPA outright. It inflicted on it the death of a thousand cuts, forcing it to raise price ceilings over an ever-wider range of goods while steadily slashing the OPA appropriations.

The OPA was also forfeiting public goodwill by becoming a refuge for defeated Democratic politicians. And it suffered for the heavy-handed antics of some of its investigators. A widely reproduced photograph in 1946 showed an OPA agent in Los Angeles with his left hand grasping a startled, bespectacled used-car salesman by the neck, while in his right hand the OPA agent brandished a lead-filled leather sap.

Truman began to consider the OPA a political liability, as did Snyder. With support from the White House fading rapidly its days were soon numbered. Under Congressional pressure price ceilings were lifted on meat, and there was a stampede to the slaughterhouse. In the Midwest trucks lined up for miles, waiting to unload. In the summer heat many a cow and pig did not live to be slaughtered.

The lifting of price controls on meat appeared to be the end of controls. But within a month the cost-of-living index jumped 5.5 percent. Many goods rose by 20 to 30 percent the moment controls were lifted. People were stunned and frightened. For a brief, terrifying moment the entire country stared in the face of hyperinflation. Senator Taft, who had led the often fatuous and shrill attacks in Congress on price controls, received 10,000 abusive letters and telegrams. The White House and Congress hastily attempted to revive the OPA. But it was an exercise comparable in nature and difficulty to putting the bones back into a filleted fish. They created a Price Decontrol Board to use what remained of the OPA machinery to set and enforce controls over some of the most widely consumed goods and services. Rent controls, which had not been lifted, were extended. It had been one of the OPA's proudest boasts, and most popular achievements, that it had kept wartime rent increases below 1 percent.

The PDB took one bold action and thereby wrote its own suicide note. It reimposed controls on meat prices. Under Chester Bowles the OPA had tried to prepare the country to feed tens of millions of starving Europeans by controlling the grain markets. But Congress had undone Bowles's initiative. Suddenly, in the summer of 1946, the White House realized that the millions of tons of wheat currently being shoveled into feeding troughs for American farm animals would be needed in Europe before the winter was out. Curbs were hastily placed on brewers and bakers. But the most effective rationing device (namely, rationing) had been gutted. In a desperate effort to get control over the grain supply, the Administration reimposed controls on meat, and Herbert Hoover was enlisted to stump the country and call for sacrifices.

The stampede to the slaughterhouse stopped overnight. It was followed by a meat shortage, grandiloquently termed a "meat famine." In a few weeks it was hard to find even such humble simulacra of meat as hot dogs and bologna. Tens of thousands of butcher shops closed down. There was a rise in poaching. Coal miners struck, rather than work on a vegetable diet. Thousands of people stood in the rain all night at the Fourteenth Street meat market in New York in hopes of buying meat in the morning.

The meat famine destroyed public support for price controls. And with the 1946 elections looming, rather than requisition cows, hogs, and chickens Truman decontrolled meat prices. Soon everything was decontrolled except rents. The OPA boards, begun five years earlier with a single and comparatively simple task, rationing, went out of existence. In those five years 250,000 people had served without pay on 5,000 boards.

The ending of controls did not put an end to shortages, as the NAM and Senator Taft had repeatedly insisted it would. There were shortages of everything from toilet paper to New England baked beans. There was a steel shortage, and it lasted into the 1950s. What the lifting of price controls increased most impressively was not production but inflation.

That was exactly what the lately departed OPA had predicted. As an experiment it had removed price controls in the fall of 1945 on coconuts, not normally in great demand, simply to see what would happen. Within a month the price of coconuts rose by 400 percent.

Although not scrapped, rent controls were eased. One Miami landlord attempted to relieve four years of frustration by raising his tenant's rent from $25 a month to $1,000 a month. But Congress allowed only an increase of 15 percent, and said it had to be voluntary. Nearly every tenant in the country, perhaps trying to avoid having an unhappy landlord to deal with, volunteered to pay an extra 15 percent.

It was almost an accident that the country was not plunged into hyper (50 percent plus) inflation, given the ineptitude of government policy in the fifteen months following V-J Day. The Secretary of the Treasury, Fred M. Vinson, was an economic innocent, almost an economic illiterate, installed in his post because Truman liked him and he had a reputation for getting on well with people.

Not only were price controls rapidly lifted, but the amount of gold backing the currency was reduced from 40 percent to 25 percent; this made a large and rapid increase in the currency supply inevitable.

The Federal Reserve represented the wisdom of an earlier age which decreed that someone other than elected officials should have their hands on the currency printing press. "But during the war the Treasury obtained a dominant position. [And] it is more than half the truth that in monetary management the Treasury wielded power without responsibility while the Federal Reserve had responsibility without power." The Federal Reserve became little more than the place to buy Treasury bonds.

The Reserve itself had bought vast amounts of government securities during the war. This made credit curbs almost impossible to effect. Each time the government tried to impose curbs the banks in the Federal Reserve System merely dusted off their government securities, sold them back to the Federal Reserve, and in one working day had $1 or $2 billion which could then be used to underwrite new loans. And the government attempt to curb credit had in the meantime increased interest rates, so the banks made more on the new loans than on the securities they had just cashed in. Every attempt to curb credit led to a turn-in of Treasury bonds and increased the money supply.

Congress added to inflation by rapidly abandoning the wartime excess profits tax, by reducing corporation income tax, and by allowing businesses to claim back some of the excess profits tax already paid. It needs to be added, however, that insofar as this stimulated business activity, it helped preclude the widely forecast postwar economic slump.

Postwar tax cuts took effect gradually, while money continued to flow into government at levels close to those of wartime just when government spending was dropping sharply. Huge cash surpluses built up. They were used to reduce the national debt by more than $15 billion and served as a brake on inflation.

More important, perhaps, was the behavior of the nation at large. People believed the forecasts of deflation and acted accordingly. They remembered how, during the Depression, deflation had brought falling prices. They lacked the inflationary cast of mind, which impels people to hurry out to buy today before the price goes up tomorrow. They bought what they needed, often at inflated, black-market prices. Otherwise, they waited—for the price to come down. Much of their wartime savings was spent in the first year after the war. Yet compared with the national income, consumer spending was remarkable for its restraint.

By accident the United States hit upon the happy medium between consumption at sufficiently high levels to avoid a slump and a mad scramble which would have turned inflation into hyperinflation. The American people, and the Western nations whose war-racked economies now relied so heavily on American stability, were astonishingly lucky.

When the last tank rolled off the assembly line at one plant, it bore a handmade placard reading "End of the Gravy Train." And it was, for millions.

While prices rose, so did unemployment. Such is the stuff that strikes are made of, especially when, as now, earnings were falling, thanks to cuts in overtime.

Including those in uniform, the wartime labor force numbered 66.2 million at its peak in April 1945. But this included 2 million people who would normally be considered unemployable—midgets; the handicapped; children; the retired. It also included 5.5 million women who would have remained at home had there been no war. The Department of Labor estimated the "normal" labor force at 58 million. That meant that before long 8 million people were going to be out of work. One expert prediction was that up to 20 million would be out of work.

Through the winter of 1945–1946 the unemployment figure rose steadily. By April 1946 it reached 2.7 million—and stayed there, to the forecasters' bemusement. Unions had meanwhile been struggling, and failing, to maintain workers' earnings. In manufacturing they had dropped from a weekly average of $47.12 to $41.04. Among the higher paid workers, such as those in steel, the fall in earnings was far more drastic, as much as 20 percent. And this was at a time of rising prices.

Collective bargaining had been suspended during the war, and the no strike pledge had been almost universally adhered to until the spring of 1945. The unions had gained membership and closed and union shops. In the strikes which broke out in the first year after V-J Day there was, on both union and management sides, a willing engagement in a trial of strength. Clerical workers, lumbermen, textile workers, machinists, longshoremen, oil refinery workers, carpenters, meat-packers, automobile workers, steelworkers—all came out on strike before the spring of 1946.

The steel strike lasted for three months. The people of Pittsburgh had their best look at the sky in many years. In Omaha, when the meat-packers struck, the city smelled different, or rather, did not smell of anything much.

Besides the major national strikes, there were thousands of local walkouts. In Boston the fishermen refused to fish, creating a shortage of cod. In Cincinnati the bakeries were closed, setting off a revival of home baking. In Albany, New York, there were no meat deliveries. In Alabama there were no Greyhound buses.

Strikes could still be deadly. On the Toledo, Peoria and Western Railroad a clash between pickets and company guards left two men dead and several others seriously wounded. The railroad was run by George McNear, who had taken it over when it was, in his phrase, no more than "two streaks of rust." McNear hated unions; unions hated McNear. His railroad had been run during the war by the government because he refused to employ union labor. When the TP&W was returned to him, he hired strikebreakers and goons to terrorize the union workers the government had hired. One night McNear was shot to death on a Peoria street.

In Stamford, Connecticut, Yale and Towne, a manufacturer of locks and hardware, tried to abrogate its wartime maintenance of membership agreement, on the grounds that the war was over. Yale and Towne's 2,500 machinists struck. And for one day much of the city of Stamford went out on strike with them. It was a bitter dispute which dragged on for four months.

Two hundred thousand electrical workers struck. In Los Angeles, their pickets were charged by the police and clubbed down. In Philadelphia, they marched on General Electric's plant 800 strong and were charged by mounted police. The strikers were back the next day, 3,500 strong. They were once more charged by police mounted on horses and motorcycles. In all, five strikers were hospitalized, and scores arrested.

Before the wave of strikes ran its course, there was hardly a city or town which had not been affected, an industry which had not been involved. Where the national interest was directly threatened, Truman intervened, as he did in the steel strike and the strike of oil refinery workers. But he was always loath to interfere with labor. He was by temperament and upbringing a border Populist, a man to whom such phrases as "the fat cats" and "the interests" came easily.

Throughout his political career he had enjoyed union support. His difficult fight for reelection to the Senate in 1940 had left him with a heavy moral obligation to the railroad unions particularly. But when the Brotherhood of Railroad Trainmen and the Brotherhood of Locomotive Engineers moved toward a strike in 1946, he bluntly told their leaders, "If you think I'm going to let you tie up this country, you're crazy as hell."

The warning did no good. On May 23 the trains stopped running. Hundreds of thousands of travelers were stranded in the big cities. Hotels set up cots in their corridors. Panic-stricken mobs descended on bus stations and airports. Food stores and gas stations were besieged. In rural areas a feeling of despair gripped farmers who contemplated ripening crops that threatened to rot before ever getting to market.

Truman asked Congress for emergency legislation, and the mood was such that he was certain to get what he asked for. The railroad unions hurriedly accepted what they had recently said was unacceptable, an extra 18.5 cents an hour.

Truman never lacked for public support in a confrontation with labor. And however strong his personal sympathies with working people, Truman almost welcomed the showdown with John L. Lewis and the United Mine Workers. It was the turning point in the Truman Presidency, to defeat the one imposing national figure whom even Roosevelt, for all his cunning and showmanship, had never bettered. It partook, moreover, of sweet revenge; Lewis was the only person who had succeeded in making a mockery of the wartime Truman Committee. The committee had held a hearing on productivity in the mines, and Truman asked Lewis what he had to say about absenteeism. Lewis gazed balefully at the empty chairs at the committee table, then remarked that Congress was itself not exempt from the problem: "Absenteeism prevails among this committee this morning. I do not know why some of the Senators are not here, but I am sure they are away for perfectly competent reasons." Raucous, sarcastic laughter rocked the hearing room. Following his opening shot, Lewis continued in the same sarcastic vein, crushing Senatorial egos. Truman called the hearing to a premature halt.

To threaten a coal strike in 1946 was to threaten catastrophe. Since the turn of the century coal had been the lifeblood of the industrial sector. Most goods moved by train, and coal fired nearly every locomotive. It provided two-thirds of all electrical power. It provided industry with more than half its energy. But on April 1, 1946, the miners struck.

The President disliked Lewis intensely. Yet he proceeded circumspectly. Brownouts and dimouts disrupted cities in the East; New Jersey declared a state of emergency; railroads laid off 50,000 men; automobile plants cut production; passenger trains were halted; steel mills banked their fires; freight loadings dropped by 75 percent, shipping on the Great Lakes was cut by half. Still Truman stayed his hand. Congress on its own account prepared to pass emergency legislation. Lewis, the master of the war of nerves, unilaterally declared a truce and sent his miners back to work.

This was the Lewis style. He would issue warnings, make demand after demand, set deadlines, hint at calamity to follow, and then, as the showdown neared, would change his demands, dream up a new set of conditions, and set a new deadline. His was the style of guerrilla warfare, the natural tactics of the weaker party—to strike when the enemy was scattered, to scatter when the enemy prepared to strike. He never stood still, yet he never lost sight of the principal objective. In its way, his strategy was brilliant. But there was one major weakness: if he were ever brought to battle and had nowhere to run, he would be ground to pieces.

Lewis's overriding objective in 1946 was a health and welfare fund for the miners, to be financed by "royalties" on every ton of coal mined. The mineowners considered the idea outrageous. After twelve days of truce, Lewis ordered the miners out again. They followed his lead without hesitation.

On May 21 the President seized control of the mines. Lewis and the Secretary of the Interior, Julius Krug, came to an agreement which created a health and welfare fund, and set the royalty at five cents a ton. After six months the mines were handed back to their owners.

The owners repudiated the Krug-Lewis agreement. Winter was on its way. If a coal strike was a catastrophe, a coal strike in winter was a catastrophe in spades. Lewis ordered the miners out. This was the ninth major coal strike in six years, and it threatened the entire reconversion of the economy. This time, Truman knew, he would have to break the coal strike whatever the risks.

The President wanted to use the force of law without sending Lewis to prison, for he was likely to prove the most gifted martyr since St. Paul. He could well be a bigger obstacle to a settlement from within prison than within the UMW headquarters. With considerable trepidation, the government lawyers took Lewis and the UMW to court.

The phrase "Injunction granted" could still be relied on to stir the passions of every union man. And now, although Lewis's flamboyance and conceit had antagonized much of organized labor in the past, labor rallied to his support.

Lewis and the miners ignored the Federal court's injunction; the miners stayed out. Lewis appeared remarkably like a man who relished the prospect of a spell behind bars.

The government lawyers returned to Federal court. The judge, T. Alan Goldsborough, who had granted the injunction, had no desire to send Lewis to prison. The U.S. Attorney hit on an alternative: why not fine the union a quarter of a million dollars a day? The miners had been in defiance for fourteen days. That would cost them $3.5 million if Goldsborough accepted the suggestion, which he did. For good measure, the U.S. Attorney and the judge agreed to fine Lewis $10,000.

Levying fines on a recalctrant union had been done before. But never on so heroic a scale. At a single blow the UMW, one of the richest unions in the country, stood to lose one-fourth of its carefully accumulated treasury.

For once Lewis's characteristic ebullience deserted him. He was visibly staggered and now instead of striking theatrical poses brandished his stick querulously at reporters and photographers. He had been outflanked, then routed. Three days later the coal miners were back at work. The fines were later reduced by 80 percent, but there was no hiding the magnitude of Lewis's defeat.

Then, in early 1947, with the mines once more under Federal control and the UMW still arguing with the owners over a health and welfare fund, the Number Five shaft at the Centralia Coal Company mine in Centralia, Illinois, blew up. Far below ground 111 miners were burned to death. Lewis flew into a tirade which defied the courts, the President, public opinion, and Congress. He brought the miners out for six days of mourning. The President bided his time.

Lewis derided Krug as "a Hercules wearing size 12 shoes and a size five hat." Krug had not actually killed the miners, Lewis conceded. "He just permitted them to die by negligence in action."

A subsequent inquiry into mine safety* by a committee headed by Ad-

In 1946 nearly 1,000 miners were killed. In some states the casualty rate in the mines was as high as 25 percent a year. The number of cases of emphysema and silicosis was unknown but was assumed to run into the tens of thousands annually.

miral Joel T. Boone showed beyond any doubt that mine operators, almost without exception, took no serious interest in the health and safety of miners. Their bluster and evasion were thrown into relief by the austere, military-style prose of the Boone report. The only positive safety measure the mine operators freely undertook was to offer a bonus of $100 a man at any mine where a year passed without a single fatality. This device had been known in the coalfields for decades. On bonus day the mine shut down and the miners got roaring drunk. As a safety measure it had a certain poetic charm but little else to commend it.

The Boone report made the case for a miners' health and welfare fund irresistible. Lewis got his fund, and he got complete control over it. The fund provided retired miners with pensions of $100 a month, it provided disability pensions to crippled miners, but most of all, it provided a string of ten modern hospitals in Appalachia to cater to miners and their families. The UMW health and welfare fund brought modern medicine into an area where scarlet fever patients were being coated with axle grease, where the blood of a black cat was used as a cure for shingles, where copper wire was used for treating arthritis.

The UMW health and welfare fund proved a landmark in postwar labor negotiations. Collective bargaining had been traditionally about wages. After Lewis it centered increasingly on "income supplements"—employer contributions to social insurance, health and pension funds, and so on. More than any other individual Lewis issued in the age of corporate welfarism in the United States.

Not that Lewis neglected hard cash. In six years, from 1940 through 1946, he had raised the take-home pay of miners from $35 for a thirty-five-hour week to $85 for a forty-eight-hour week, raised vacation pay from nothing to $100, secured a paid lunch break, secured extra pay for night shifts, and got the companies to pay for a miner's tools.

Although the public was sympathetic to union demands for better pay and conditions, people were usually impatient with strikes. Antilabor feeling was also fanned by the press. Typical was the 1946 headline which declared, CIO FORCES SHOWDOWN WITH INDUSTRY.

The Wagner Act was widely attacked on the grounds that it had conferred on the unions extensive powers and too little responsibility. But to the unions the Wagner Act might as well have been engraved on stone and handed down on Mount Sinai. Labor could not agree to any attempt to modify it.

Yet Congress, with public support, was determined to do exactly that. The number of man-days lost to strikes had totaled 199,000 in January 1945; in February 1946 they totaled 22 million. Congress passed a bill introduced by New Jersey Congressman Francis Case which effectively nullified much of the Wagner Act. The Case bill presented Truman with a splendid opportunity to mend his fences with labor. He seized the opportunity. He vetoed the bill.

By the end of 1946 nearly every major strike had been settled. Five million people had walked picket lines that year, and for a while it had seemed little had changed since the labor turmoil following World War I.

But a great deal had changed. There was far less violence. Thanks to strike pay and wartime savings, striking workers did not now plunge their families into abysmal poverty. The unions were better led these days, and most businessmen were reasonable and decent men. The police were better trained, more disciplined, and far less brutal than the police of 1919. Finally, government at all levels this time actively promoted compromise which was fair to all parties in dispute.

Organized labor was not what it had been a generation earlier. It had not only grown during the war; it had matured. It was not without some notorious shortcomings: the AFL was too tolerant of crooks; the CIO harbored several thousand Communists. These two labor bodies, split into the craft unions on the one side and the mass of industrial workers on the other, continued to spite one another. But organized labor had grown so that it now spoke for a third of all wage and salary workers. Today's unions were big unions. Membership of 100,000 or more was not unusual.

The union offered a promising career to able, ambitious young men. Once the legendary example of working-class success had been the youth who began in the stock room and rose to become chairman of the board. That breed had virtually vanished. Now, however, there was the reality— and it involved scores, if not hundreds, of men—of the union leader who had made his way to the top of a rich, powerful organization after beginning at the shop floor, the sweatshop, the mine, or the waterfront. The successful businessman had nearly always been to college; many a successful union leader had not even finished high school.

Career unionism meant middle-class life-styles, middle-class salaries, the avoidance of risk, the avoidance of scandal. There was a new type of union leader, and its paradigm was Walter Reuther, who headed the United Automobile Workers.

In 1939, when the UAW had a membership of 150,000, it was considered a very big union. In 1945 its membership stood at 1.2 million. But as with Lewis, what made Reuther important was not so much the size of his union as the style and objectives he cultivated.

Reuther sought to equate the national interest with union interests, and vice versa. Under Reuther's guidance the UAW concerned itself with issues which transcended ordinary collective bargaining. There was a UAW policy on race, on domestic Communism, on fiscal and monetary strategies, and on most major international questions. The UAW rejected Socialism, disliked class warfare, and never called for the destruction of capitalism. Because it played an instrumental role in educating the rest of the labor movement on union objectives and methods, the consequences of the UAW's moderation were profound, even if they were indirect.

Reuther's prestige was very high even among people who had no interest in unions. His intelligence won respect even from his opponents. He was nearly always photographed wreathed in a boyish grin. But to those who knew him Reuther was a man singularly lacking in human warmth. He was an ascetic, dedicated figure who conveyed a sense that he was emotionally far removed from the petty concerns of ordinary humanity.

He neither drank nor smoked. He had few pleasures, few close friends. He was "proud to be the lowest paid head of any major union," say his biographers, and he refused to allow the UAW conventions to raise his salary beyond comparatively modest limits.

But his principal hold over the loyalty of UAW members was not his noble plainness or his principles. Reuther delivered the goods. He led the union into one of the most important of the end of the war strikes, against GM, and won. The GM settlement was widely copied throughout industry.

It came only after some dramatic confrontations. Reuther insisted that GM could raise wages without increasing the price of cars. The company disagreed; it was not as rich as Reuther claimed, said GM. Reuther demanded, "Open the books." He argued that openness was in the national interest. GM was put into the position of arguing that on the contrary, secrecy was good for the country. When a Presidential fact-finding body was created, GM refused to let even its august members look at the books. The ensuing strike was a public relations disaster for GM, and in the end the UAW secured most of what it had asked for.

At the time of the strike Reuther was only one of several UAW vice-presidents. The president, R. J. Thomas, was an old-style union leader, "a roly-poly extrovert who loved chewing tobacco and late night poker games." It was said of him that he opposed the GM strike because he did not understand it. At a tumultuous convention in Atlantic City in March 1946 Reuther narrowly (by 4,444 votes to 4,320) ousted Thomas from the presidency. It was a contest which gained added interest for being split, crudely, into right and left camps. Thomas, the traditional type of union leader, was a man of the left. Reuther, younger and more businesslike, was a man of the center (which in labor circles means right). However narrow, Reuther's victory happened to mark an important shift within the labor movement.

For several months after the Japanese surrender photographs appeared which showed bombs or propellers rolling off one assembly line while at the adjoining line the first postwar refrigerators or washing machines were rolling off. The symbolism was heavy-handed, yet it also said something important: business could hardly wait to get down to satisfying consumer demand.

To negotiate its way from war to peace, the economy had to remain active at a very high level. Had it been treated like an invalid and been nursed along step by step it would probably have slumped.

When the war ended, nearly half the gross national product was tied up in war contracts. "Cancellation of any large number of these [if] accompanied by delay or uncertainty about payment could easily tie up sufficient resources to start a depression," said one scholar. The policy laid down by the OWMR was to terminate contracts swiftly and conclusively. If haste made for error, if it encouraged fraud and deception, that was regrettable, but ultimately it would prove less costly than caution. If outright swindles were perpetrated, the law provided remedies and punishments to deal with them in due course.

No one pretended that a policy of haste was the ideal answer to contract termination. But it involved fewer risks than any policy which moved cautiously and was overly solicitous of the fate of every taxpayer's dollar would have been. And despite the appearance of having been tacked together at the last moment, the policy of swift termination, rapid settlement, had been in the making for two years before V-J Day.

By mid-1946 nearly every war contract had been terminated and settled, at a cost of $63 billion. It was a policy which succeeded in large part because it was suited to the American temper—expansive, optimistic, positive, and quickly done. If it was open to serious criticism, it was that it showed undue generosity in disposing of surplus property.

The Army and Navy had ended the war with $90 billion worth of surplus material, including 40,000 surplus homing pigeons (with dozens of little pigeons hatching every minute, increasing the surplus), huge quantities of Elizabeth Arden black face cream (for night fighting), 500 tons of contraceptives, half a million wooden rifles. Washington swarmed with bargain hunters, but where was there a buyer for an air-conditioned, glass-brick, one-of-its-kind "Mouse House," which gave off a powerful odor and bred up to 15,000 mice each week?

To dispose of its surpluses, the government hired hundreds of agents. The agent's fee often exceeded the value of the sale. One company made a sale worth $14 and charged the War Assets Administration a fee of $4,571 for doing so.

Billions of dollars' worth of surplus jeeps, trucks, bulldozers, cranes, and aircraft were rusting away at military bases around the world. The problem such surpluses posed was that bringing the equipment back to the United States would add to its cost, yet it could be sold for only a fraction of its original price.

The Surplus Property Act specifically charged the government with handling the sale of surplus goods to encourage the revival of a free enterprise economy. It was supposedly a commitment to help small businesses. In practice, it became a boost to big business. U.S. Steel was allowed to buy the world's most expensive, most modern steel plant, built at Geneva, Utah, at a cost of $202 million, at the bargain basement price of $47 million. Alcoa had run a string of government plants built during the war at a cost of $700 million. The cost to Alcoa—$230 million.

But there was still a chance for the small man to make a big buy, as Martin Wunderlick of Jefferson City, Missouri, showed. He bought 5,540 Flying Fortresses, at a cost of $2.8 million, and proceeded to cut them up for scrap. Paul Mantz, a stunt flier later famous for his work in movies, bought a sizable air force of 475 fighters and bombers. He reserved a few for his own use and cut the rest up for scrap.

Douglas Leigh bought three Navy surplus blimps for $10,000 each, which was less than 3 percent of their original cost. He fitted each blimp with thousands of light bulbs to spell out advertisers' messages in the night sky. Before long, Leigh's blimps were a sight regarded with affection up and down the East Coast.

The stimuli provided by Congress, buoyant consumer demand, and swift contract settlements all helped to keep business at a high pitch, and throughout 1946 the stock market went from strength to strength. In vain did the Treasury plead with people not to cash their government savings bonds in order to buy stocks and shares. No one wanted to be left out of the rich harvest being gathered on Wall Street.

The few businesses which were cautious were to pay a heavy price. That was what happened to Montgomery Ward. During the 1930s Sewell Avery had guided the company with a magician's touch. During the war he had carried on a seriocomic war of his own, against the Federal government. And now he decided that a slump was in the offing. Montgomery Ward was quoted at 40 to 50 percent above the price of Sears, Roebuck stock. Avery made his company sit tight on its huge cash reserves. Sears, Roebuck expanded vigorously. In a few years Montgomery Ward lost its preeminence in the mail-order field, never to regain it.

Among small business these days there was a sudden upsurge in activity, thanks to the influx of 100,000 veterans who went into business for themselves with the aid of $300 million in government-backed loans. Whatever the business it was likely to be called the "Veterans" this or that. Veterans' cab companies fought the monopolies held by Yellow or Checker. In Philadelphia they drove maroon and gold cabs with a ruptured duck painted on the doors and, because they were not allowed to levy fares, accepted "donations."

A group of former Flying Tiger pilots pooled their skills and their money to start National Skyways Freight Corporation. They were willing to fly anything anywhere—baby chicks, household goods, racehorses, flowers, or football teams. Another group of Flying Tigers under Robert Slick set up the Flying Tiger Airline. No matter how exotic or bizarre the cargo, they would carry it.

Most people had never heard of most of these small airlines. But by the end of December 1946 the United States had nearly 2,400 airlines, and all but 17 were nonscheduled carriers. Nine out of ten nonscheduled airlines were run by veterans, flying planes bought with veterans' priority certificates and money borrowed from the RFC.

The crying demand for automobiles led some hardy souls to try competing with the Big Three. Every such venture led only to grief for all concerned. The most spectacular failure was the Tucker Torpedo, few of which were ever built even though the government let Preston Tucker rent the $200 million Chicago Dodge plant for a comparative trifle—$1 million a year—at a time when Tucker had only $3,000 in the bank and when the Securities and Exchange Commission (SEC) was placing advertisements to warn people against lending Tucker the $20 million he was trying to raise. It helped Tucker pay the rent when the War Assets Administration began paying him $900,000 a year to look after the tens of millions of dollars' worth of machine tools in the Dodge plant. And Americans always rally to a plunger. Tucker raised most of the loan.

The attempts to challenge Detroit stirred interest and sympathy. There was a sentimental longing to see David beat Goliath and a residual, Depression-inspired dislike of big business generally.

But business had changed as much as the unions had, and mainly for the better. It still harbored more than a few rogues and scoundrels; it was in no position to criticize labor on that score. Of the hundreds of wartime scandals involving business during the war, none had been more odious than the conspiracy "to fix prices and block improvements on artificial limbs for war veterans," as the Federal indictment expressed it. Tens of thousands of limbless men had been burdened with prosthetic devices the design of which had not altered in thirty years, and the limb manufacturers' friends in Congress prevented the VA from undertaking prosthetic research or manufacturing artificial limbs. So crippled, weakened men were burdened with wood and steel in an age of plastics and aluminum. Not content with their monopoly, the limb manufacturers used the sudden increase in demand occasioned by the war to raise their prices dramatically. Thirty individuals and thirty-three companies were convicted on the conspiracy indictment in 1946.

Postwar Congressional investigations into "influence peddling" involving war contracts for a while focused on Howard Hughes, a probe which led nowhere until Major General Bennett "Call me Benny" Meyers was unearthed. Balding, short, mustachioed, and rotund, Benny boasted a busty, blond ex-movie starlet wife and a higher standard of living than his fellow major generals enjoyed. Benny had a lot to answer for, which he did over several years inside a Federal penitentiary.

Scandals apart, however, business had changed remarkably in recent years. Many of the old enemies of organized labor were dead or dying or had lost the stomach for the fight. The modern business corporation no longer resorted to the hired goon but to the printing press. It waged wars of publicity. The style, moreover, was subtler. It was passé to claim that an extra five cents an hour would force the plant to close. The thing to say was that of course, the workers deserved an extra five cents an hour—if productivity increased by enough to cover it.*

At General Electric a new post, Vice-President for Employees and Community Relations, was created. Its first occupant was Lemuel R. Boulware, whose approach to negotiations created envy, but almost no one else had the nerve to follow his lead. "Boulwareism" required extensive research into productivity, wages, and profits. The company would then make what it genuinely believed was the maximum offer it could

---

*It is worth noting that the wartime "miracle of production" probably involved a drop in productivity measured as total physical output per man-hour, thanks to the presence of millions of women, children, old people, and the physically handicapped. So the postwar attempts to tie wage increases to productivity increases was almost as good as a promise of more money. As the marginal workers left the labor force, productivity was bound to rise.

afford in the interests of workers, management, and stockholders. Only on the basis of "new information" could the offer be increased. To the unions it looked suspiciously like "Take it or leave it" paraded in fancy dress. But the business executives involved were almost certainly being sincere. The new generation of businessmen found haggling distasteful.

Attitudes toward business changed, thanks to prosperity, but thanks also to the rapid spreading of civilized behavior in the business community. "Between 1930 and 1946 Wall Street was a bad word and the financial market had no appeal for youth," Martin Mayer noticed during the 1950s. "All that changed after the war and today there are training programs all over the Street."

Wartime tax laws had encouraged companies to take better care of their employees, a trend further stimulated by the general shortage of able-bodied labor. A few enlightened companies began to offer pension plans to blue-collar workers as well as white. By 1946 some of the major corporations were willing to begin bargaining over novel fringe benefits. Business had found during the war that one way to avoid paying the excess profits tax was to pay the money in bonuses to employees. Business discovered, too, that the postwar wage settlements were not going to lead to the bankruptcy court. On the contrary, they allowed business to raise prices to such levels that the break-even point of manufacturing industry was dramatically lowered. Here was one more buffer against any future slump in demand; investment became safer, encouraging further investment; and failure became ever less likely. At the same time the extensive publicity campaigns which business conducted directed public wrath over higher prices against organized labor.

The reforming passions of the New Deal appeared to be as dead as high-button shoes. Liberals and conservatives alike persisted in considering it a program of radical experiments. But much closer to the truth was Alvin Hansen's conclusion: "The New Deal was not ahead of its time; it was long overdue."

During the 1930s young men with liberal ideas had flocked to Washington. In the 1940s bright young men still sought government jobs, but if they had left-wing political views, they were well advised to keep them to themselves. That old panacea known vaguely as "planning" was looked on with such disfavor that no one any longer admitted to "planning." Government agencies made plans but refused to admit that this was what they were doing.

Some of what had been done was undone. Under pressure from business, which wanted to see a pool of cheap labor maintained and to see the size of employers' contributions to unemployment insurance funds reduced, the United States Employment Service was dismantled. During the war many millions of workers had crossed state lines. When unemployed, they had turned to USES for help. The states resisted taking responsibility for them when USES was destroyed.

Nearly half of those who originally qualified for retirement pensions under the original 1935 Social Security Act were disqualified by Congress in the immediate postwar.

There was endless and passionate talk in praise of balanced budgets, much of it little more than veiled hostility to programs of social welfare.

It was against this background that Congress passed the Employment Act of 1946, one of the most important of all general welfare enactments. It had made its original appearance in the Senate in 1945 as S. 380, otherwise known as the Full Employment Act. In that form it committed Congress and the Administration to keeping the entire labor force at work by whatever means necessary.

Democrats and Republicans alike said that the government was responsible for maintaining full employment, which may seem unusual. But everyone thought that the forecasts of 8 to 20 million unemployed were going to be realized. The Republicans, bearing the cross of one Depression, did not intend to be blamed for a second.

Beyond the halls of Congress, however, there was deep opposition to the Full Employment Act, led by the NAM, General Motors, the U.S. Chamber of Commerce, and the Farm Bureau Federation.

As it turned out, no one knew how to define "full" employment in terms acceptable to both liberals and conservatives in Congress. By 1946 "Full" had been dropped from the title of the act. Gone with it were several of the more important original proposals; such as a commitment to secure a fairer distribution of income.

Liberals were not very happy with the 1946 act, considering it too weak to achieve very much. But it was a crucial piece of legislation. It settled the issue of direct government intervention in the economy once and for all. It marked the advent of Keynesian economic theory as the predominant influence on economic policy, most especially the Keynesian emphasis on maintaining aggregate demand. Finally, it created the Council of Economic Advisers. The logic of the CEA was that it should be a planning body, a quasi-independent agency with a staff of career bureaucrats. The illogic of the moment made it a tiny adjunct to the Office of the President.

When from their various vantage points Americans surveyed the economic life around them at the end of 1946, they were critical of almost everything they saw. They stared success in the face and pronounced it failure.

Expectations had risen faster than consumer goods production. Of the first 500,000 refrigerators produced after the war, half went on sale, the other half went into the showrooms. Detroit was filled with heady talk of 6 million new cars a year, but in 1946 produced only 3 million. Instead of 1.2 million new houses built as promised, there were 700,000. Even so, by the end of 1946 most of the shortages—and most of the black markets— had vanished. The farmers had brought in a record-making harvest. In the stores, after a five-year absence, sales and discounts reappeared.

Reconversion was proving to be as dramatic and as successful as the building of defense industries had been from 1940 to 1942. Had American industry been less adaptable and energetic the war would have lasted longer. For the same reason the transition to peacetime would have been far less successful. In each case, the economy was turned around in approximately two and a half years.

Had reconversion not been so rapid the postwar inflation would almost surely have been much worse and would have raged for much longer. It might well have gone to 25 to 30 percent a year and stayed there into the 1950s. In doing so, it would have wiped out the huge backlog of wartime savings. Instead, that backlog, amounting to $250 billion, was being used to finance the successful transition to an essentially peacetime economy.

Hardly anyone believed that reconversion was going well. It was, and remains, one of the most remarkable and ignored success stories in recent American history.

When Truman became President he was determined to get along well with Congress, to succeed where Roosevelt had failed. When Congress reconvened in the fall of 1945, Truman sent it one of the longest messages it had ever received from a President, 16,000 words of unsolicited advice. He asked for the swift enactment of twenty-one major programs, from a national Fair Employment Practices Commission to 1.5 million units of public housing. Several months later, in January 1946, he delivered his first State of the Union message, a record-breaking 25,000 words. Whether Congress liked it or not, Truman always let it know what was on his mind.

But his relations with Congress went from bad to worse. And when he took to the radio, to deliver a "fireside chat" urging people to put pressure on their representatives to follow the President's lead, he got nowhere.

There was bad blood between the White House and the Hill over the Congressional inquiry into the attack on Pearl Harbor. The majority report, written by the Democrats, said the Japanese were responsible. The minority report, written by the Republicans, said Roosevelt was responsible, because he had provoked the Japanese beyond endurance.

Truman found himself being crossed not only by his overt adversaries but by his ostensible friends. His new Secretary of State, James F. Byrnes, was embittered by the belief that had he not been double-crossed over the Vice Presidential nomination in 1944 he, not Truman, would now be President. The first chairman of the CEA, Edwin G. Nourse, regularly gave the President advice which a man of Truman's Populist, easy-money outlook was bound to reject. Before long there was deep mutual contempt between them.

Liberal Democrats, mourning the glamorous Roosevelt, suffered Truman with ill grace. When he forced the departure of Harold Ickes as Secretary of the Interior, they became clamorous and abusive. And when he proposed to install Edwin W. Pauley in Ickes's place, they were enraged. Pauley was a California oilman in the mold of a Gilded Age Robber Baron. Had Truman gone mad? The President, far from being mad, was grooming Pauley for a bigger job. He intended to try to unify the military services. And when the time came, "I wanted the hardest, meanest son-of-a-bitch I could get as Secretary of Defense." The liberals' clamor, however, denied him Pauley.

A Conference of Progressives spent a week in Chicago racking its brains over the problem of remaining within the Democratic Party while repudiating Truman's leadership of it. Liberals rallied at first to Henry Wallace, whom Truman retained as Secretary of Commerce, but with a notable lack of enthusiasm. Wallace, like Byrnes, believed in his heart that Truman had unfairly gained the prize which by rights had been his.

Wallace was one of the most unusual and tragic figures in recent American politics. His business acumen had made him a millionaire. He was an accomplished statistician, a man who had done agricultural research which was of lasting importance, and a man who had shown himself to be a first-rate administrator. He was a man of great gifts, but none of them was political, and few of them were endearing.

He was a health faddist: vegetarian, teetotaler, avid student of novel diets, such as living on milk and popcorn or on rice and water. When the mood struck him, he fasted. He exercised daily. In middle age he took up wrestling. He never smoked, and he never allowed anyone else to carry his suitcase. He was fascinated with Oriental mysticism and the religious beliefs of American Indians and at times dabbled in the occult. Yet throughout his life he remained a devout, practicing Episcopalian.

In 1932 he had been a registered Republican. He gave money to the Socialist candidate, Norman Thomas. He voted for Franklin D. Roosevelt. Wallace liked to talk of "new frontiers." Republicans spelled it "New Deal." His reputation as a visionary attracted liberals; the same reputation repelled conservatives. At the end of the war his short book *60 Million Jobs* was alternately hailed as the formula for success and the recipe for disaster.

Reading it now, it is difficult to understand why it created any stir at all. Wallace praised free enterprise and all its works, except unemployment. His idea of government intervention in the economy was that business should keep government informed of its payrolls, its investment plans, and its inventories so that Washington could set fiscal and monetary policies in the light of full, rather than partial, knowledge.

As Secretary of Commerce, Wallace was under the impression that he was Secretary of State. He continually thought out loud about this international problem or that, freely criticizing whatever he disliked; there was much he disliked. Because Wallace retained the support of millions of Democrats, Truman chose to turn a deaf ear and a blind eye.

Wallace was a man whose nature was ruled by an obsession with important moral questions. Such men are always difficult to deal with. He was among the first to catch within the first atomic explosions a glimpse of the death of all humanity. Either the weapons would be controlled from the outset or there would be an arms race. If there was an arms race, there would one day be a nuclear war. The stakes were so high, Wallace believed, that they justified taking risks, including the risk of trusting the Russians not to build atomic weapons if the United States voluntarily renounced its current atomic bomb monopoly. There was, within this complex man, something of a gambler's temperament.

In September 1946 he addressed a Madison Square rally at the beginning of the Democratic campaign for the upcoming November elections. His speech was a combination of pietism and realpolitik. The world was so dangerous, he averred, that the great powers had no serious choice but to learn to live with one another; this would later be known as "peaceful coexistence." The audience at the Garden was strongly to the left. Wallace attempted an even-handed critique of U.S. and Soviet policies. But every criticism of the United States was loudly applauded, and every criticism of the Soviet Union was drowned with boos. The booing forced him to cut his speech so that the rally could continue. The next day the *Daily Worker* condemned the speech.

Wallace's words created a political furor. Wallace claimed that Truman had read and approved the speech in advance. Truman said that he had not, or not exactly. Byrnes cabled from Vienna to inform the President that the United States could operate with only one Secretary of State at a time. Whom was it to be—Byrnes or Wallace? It appears that Wallace had read only parts of the speech to Truman and that Truman only half listened to or half understood the parts Wallace read. But the President's post-speech explanations were so convoluted and self-contradictory that he was called a liar in the national press.

Wallace in the meantime released the text of a letter he had sent to the President criticizing American foreign policy and the continued production of atomic bombs. Until now Truman had ignored the Byrnes ultimatum. But this time Truman demanded Wallace's resignation.

Within days the *Daily Worker* backtracked and hotly embraced the fallen Wallace. And he in turn had become convinced that the "war makers" in the Cabinet were responsible for his ouster.

To many liberal Democrats the Wallace resignation was the last straw. But had they not known all along that Truman was "a man of mediocre mind, ordinary personality, little comprehension and second-rate talents"? Of course they had.

They could hardly have been more mistaken. Truman was a man remarkable for his acute intelligence and his personal integrity. But his intelligence was often slighted because of his obviously patchy education and a cornball manner which went over well at a Midwestern Masonic hall but grated on the sensibilities of educated Easterners. And his integrity was almost an eccentricity when set alongside the behavior of some of his friends. Yet Truman was the last President who had to live on his salary. His preparation for high office had been a life of struggle and repeated disappointment. To put courage and compassion and humility into a man it was ideal.

He had been a sickly, bespectacled child whose ambition to go to West Point had come to nothing. He and his father were farmers; their chief aim in life was to stop being farmers. His father had wasted time and money on various "get rich quick" ventures. Following in his father's footsteps, he saw his own money sink into a worthless zinc mine and a dry hole. But these setbacks never dulled his liking for what he termed "hazard."

He went into the haberdashery business and went broke but not bankrupt. It took ten years, but Truman paid off all his debts. His moral courage was matched with physical bravery. The Klan was a powerful and dangerous presence in the Border states of the 1920s. When he spoke out for the equal treatment of blacks, Truman's life was threatened. Unintimidated, he went to a Klan meeting and dared them to carry out their threat.

While a county judge with heavy debts to pay, he possessed both the means and the motive to enrich himself, because county judges in Missouri let the contracts for road construction. He was scrupulous to the last cent. In 1940, while a United States Senator, he was too poor to prevent his eighty-eight-year-old mother, on whom he doted, from being evicted from her home.

He was as inspiring as mud. To listen to a Truman radio address was an experience devoutly to be missed. Reading a speech, he droned along in a whining monotone. But in private his speech was lively and direct. His favorite relaxation was not, as he sometimes liked to suggest, reading every book in the Library of Congress. It was cruising up and down the Potomac on the Presidential yacht, playing poker, drinking whiskey, talking politics.

Elevation to the White House did little to moderate the crass streak in his nature. In his first year as President he traveled to Caruthersville, Missouri, for the state convention of the American Legion, an event he had rarely missed in twenty years. There he "held open court in the little hotel lobby, out on the street, and in the corner drugstore; signed hundreds of autographs on everything from paper napkins to blank checks; walked down to the banks of the Missouri river and performed the traditional rite of spitting into it."

Truman was openly deferential to his wife and daughter. When Margaret Truman, to the outrage of thousands of ambitious and no worse sopranos, made her singing debut, it was broadcast live from coast to coast. Truman was enormously proud. But when Paul Hume, the music critic of the *Washington Post*, openly wrote what many fervently believed—that Margaret's voice was weak and wayward—the proud father was so incensed that he immediately sat down and wrote a sulfurous letter. Hume was told that if he ever had the misfortune to meet the President of the United States, then he, Hume, could expect a punch in the nose and a swift kick to the testicles. Truman put his own three-cent stamp on the letter, considering it personal rather than Presidential business, and strode briskly out of the White House to post it.

Behind this impulsive, plain-spoken man with his two-tone shoes and close-fitting suits there was a nature deeply sensitive to the tragedies and the nobility of human existence. His passion for serious music was genuine. He was not frightened by novel ideas or bold actions. His concern for small businessmen and struggling farmers, for the old, the poor, the black, the despised sprang not from liberal ideology or middle-class sentimentality. Counted a failure until nearly fifty, a life of struggle was flesh of his flesh, bone of his bone.

Truman was a joiner without peer. He belonged to almost everything available, reflecting a sly liking for the grandiose as well as a politician's calculation. He was a member of 218 organizations, from the Shriners to the Baker Street Irregulars. He would don a silly hat or join in some juvenile ritual without having to be asked twice.

His love of ceremonial led him to redesign the Presidential seal and the Presidential flag. He had the White House remodeled and, over howls of protest, put a porch on the south front. He put his profile on the ubiquitous dime. In some ways, he left more of a mark than Roosevelt.

He reached the ultimate in the world of the joiner by rising to the dignity of Supreme Grand Master, a 33rd Degree Mason. Throughout the Mississippi basin states Masonry was in those days a badge of respectability. As a farmer in southern Missouri explained matters to a visiting sociologist, "A man that knew the Masonic handshake could cash a check anywheres."

There was an idea cherished among liberals and conservatives alike that a timorous, indecisive little man had been suddenly thrust into the White House. Doubtless there were moments when Truman was unsure of himself. But as a rule he carried himself with self-assurance, and he proved willing to make the hard choice, to take the unpopular stand.

He was such a complex man that during his first year in the White House almost everyone got him wrong. And as the 1946 elections neared, Truman was blamed for every shortage, all the inflation, intractable foreign problems, and the mediocrity of the people around him. He compounded the difficulties Democratic candidates faced by putting his foot in his mouth each time he spoke. In the closing stages of the campaign he good-naturedly imposed a vow of silence on himself.

It was an election the Republicans were longing to contest. They entered the campaign under the less-than-stirring slogan "Controls, Confusion, Corruption, and Communism." All of which were said to have flourished under the Truman Administration. A Boston advertising executive, Karl Frost, suggested another slogan: "Had Enough?"

It was extremely effective. It meant have you had enough of strikes? Of shortages? Of inflation? Of Truman? It was potentially limitless in scope. Whatever you were fed up with, "Had Enough?" covered it. By the fall of 1946 almost everyone was fed up with something.

The 1946 election would be the first to see veterans both run and vote in large numbers. Candidates just out of uniform were nearly always younger and more energetic than the incumbents they challenged. They were invested, moreover, with an aura of heroism, especially when, like young John F. Kennedy, who was running for Congress in Boston, they could boast combat decorations.

Like most of the other veteran-candidates, Kennedy plied his uniform for all that it was worth. He joined the American Legion and was also president of the Joseph P. Kennedy, Jr., post of the VFW. He campaigned as "a fighting conservative" (evidently he had had enough, too) and spent money so freely that local politicians thought it witty to wear $20 bills on their lapels which, they claimed, were "Kennedy campaign buttons."

In Alabama another returned veteran was running for office for the first time. During the war the people of Barbour County had been puzzled when each Christmas they received cards mailed to them from the South Pacific bearing greetings from one George C. Wallace, a B-29 flight engineer. In 1946 Wallace filed for probate judge of Barbour County and began visiting all the people he had been sending Christmas cards to. Wallace had also stayed an enlisted man, on the sound principle that that was what most veteran-voters would turn out to have been. With so much foresight behind him, when Sergeant Wallace ran for probate judge, he was almost unbeatable.

In California, meanwhile, a strange item had appeared on the front page of twenty-six Orange County newspapers. It had arrived in the mail as a publicity handout. Unsure of what to make of it, the editors ran it on page one because it was novel:

> WANTED: Congressman candidate with no previous political experience to defeat a man who has represented the District for 10 years. Any young man, resident of district, preferably a veteran, fair education, no political strings or obligations and possessed of a few ideas for betterment of country at large, may apply for the job. Applicants will be interviewed by 100 interested citizens who will guarantee support but will not obligate the candidate in any way.

The applicants who presented themselves proved without exception to be useless. But one of the Committee of 100, a banker, remembered a young lawyer, presently a lieutenant commander in the Navy but due for release shortly from military service, by the name of Richard M. Nixon. The Committee of 100, at its wit's end, sent Nixon a telegram which posed two questions: Are you a Republican? Would you like to run for Congress?

The incumbent whom Nixon was to face was no time-serving political hack but one of the most effective members of Congress, Jerry Voorhis. The National School Lunch Act passed in 1946 was a typical piece of Voorhis's legislation—generous in spirit and the result of years of patient effort, not the kind of act to win headlines or public acclaim, but just the kind of act to do some good to those who stood in need of its provisions. Most Congressional districts would have been delighted to be represented by someone like Voorhis. But, as often happens, the price of effectiveness in Washington was the neglect of the grass roots.

Nixon adopted the simplest campaign strategy available. He cast himself as "the Fighting Quaker" and his opponent as the candidate of the Kremlin. A scurrilous smear campaign was conducted on the telephone to besmirch Voorhis's loyalty. Nixon claimed that Voorhis had the endorsement of two "Communist-dominated" organizations. He attempted, in a tortuous fashion, to show that Voorhis's voting record followed the Communist Party "line."

In later years Nixon and others would choose to play down the Republican attempt to make Communism one of the principal issues in the 1946 election. They had forgotten their Four Cs. Every effort was made to fan anti-Communist hysteria, but it failed to take hold nationally. The national concern was with domestic issues, mainly economic ones. But locally, Communism paid handsomely for some candidates, as Nixon, and at least one other candidate, discovered.

Throughout that summer of 1946 a Marine veteran was making the most of his thirty months of safe and undistinguished service. Nearly one million copies of a twelve-page pamphlet retailing the fictitious exploits of the candidate were put into the mail. And there were the equally fanciful newspaper advertisements:

Joe McCarthy was a tail gunner in WWII. When the war began Joe had a soft job as a Judge at EIGHT GRAND a year. He was EXEMPT from military duty. He resigned his job to enlist as a PRIVATE in the Marines. He fought on LAND and in the AIR all through the Pacific. He and millions of other guys kept YOU from talking Japanese. TODAY JOE MCCARTHY IS HOME. He wants to SERVE America in the SENATE. Yes, folks, CONGRESS NEEDS A TAIL GUNNER. Now, when Washington is in confusion, when BUREAU-CRATS are seeking to perpetuate themselves FOREVER upon the American way of life, AMERICA NEEDS FIGHTING MEN. These men who fought upon foreign soil to SAVE AMERICA have earned the right to SERVE AMERICA in time of peace.

McCarthy concentrated on one issue in the Republican primary against Senator Robert La Follette, who was another incumbent who had neglected his home base. After winning in the primary, McCarthy faced Professor Howard Murray, whom "Tail Gunner Joe" described as a "pinko."

Although in the case of some veterans there was a revival of the worst political instincts, the general picture was far more positive. The veterans, whether candidates or voters, represented a strong urge to improve American political life—to take it out of the hands of political bosses and local machines, to make it more representative, more honest and effective. In some localities the challenge to entrenched political interests led to violent clashes. In Athens, Tennessee, it resulted in a spectacular all-night gunfight over the ballot boxes and left 14 people with gunshot wounds.

Nationwide, the election was overshadowed by Truman's capitulation to the cattlemen. "In a world charged with atomic energy," *The Nation* grumbled, "the election has been fought in the shadow of a meatball." When the Republicans swept to victory, they did so on a tide of discontent, not a wave of Republicanism.

For Truman, it was an incalculable setback. Only after the election did he force Lewis's bluff. His popularity soared; his reputation as a ditherer was shattered at a blow. The President seemed for the first time to be big enough for the job, and his self-esteem rose visibly. To Clark Clifford, one of the few imposing figures in the Truman White House, the Truman Presidency did not really begin until the hour in December 1946 when Lewis capitulated. In breaking Lewis, Clifford said of Truman, "He was his own boss at last." He broke free from the shade of Franklin D. Roosevelt.

At the presumably welcome news of a Republican victory the stock market dropped sharply. Looking over the new crop of politicians—including sixty-nine veterans elected to Congress—the nation's press tried to spot the rising stars. And contrary to later stories of his rapid emergence from near-total obscurity, they fastened on none other than Senator Joseph McCarthy of Wisconsin.

Time had touted him from the moment he defeated "Young Bob" La Follette. In an admiring story he was portrayed as a near legend among his fellow marines, a man of astonishing physical courage and uncanny political shrewdness: "Bluff, genial . . . energetic . . . shrewd . . . optimistic . . . conservative . . . good-natured." This was Joe McCarthy, whose primary triumph had "turned one more page in a storybook career."

On his arrival in Washington, the Women's Press Club made a fuss over him. But the most fulsome story on McCarthy to appear in the national press was written by Jack Anderson and appeared in the *Saturday Evening Post:* "He is warmhearted, ingratiating and charming, and a handshaker and votegetter of heroic proportions. Still a bachelor, he is handsome in a dark, square-jawed way that has kept the Washington society columnists chirping excitedly ever since he alighted on the Capitol roost. . . . He is a muscular six-footer and his physical movements are the quick purposeful ones of the good athlete." How did McCarthy spend his time when not on the Senate floor or in his office? "Most of his evenings are spent in reading voluminous reports on pending legislation and skimming the Congressional Record. On the side, he is learning Russian."

Here, plainly, was a man to watch.

3

The New Look

The weather seemed to be turning extreme. People blamed the change on the atomic bomb. In the winter of 1947 frost destroyed the citrus crops of Florida and snow fell on San Francisco. In New York the streets rang to the sound of "White Christmas" being played interminably under a warm blue sky. On Christmas Day the snow fell. In fifteen hours some 200 million tons of snow blanketed the city. Traffic was brought to a standstill. An army of 16,000 workers spent three days hauling the snow away to sewers and the rivers. Travelers were stranded in their hotels. Food shortages appeared. Stores and factories stayed shut. On the West Coast temperatures stayed in the seventies for day after day, and much of California suffered from drought.

In April, Texas City, Texas, had seemed a thriving little town with a prosperous future. The war had poured money and people into it. Road signs hailed it as "The Port of Opportunity." Radiating inland from the docks were expensived new refineries, smelters, and chemical plants.

Early in April a French freighter, the *Grandchamps*, arrived to unload several thousand tons of ammonia nitrate fertilizer. A fire broke out. Hundreds of people, idle and curious, came down to the docks to enjoy the thrill of watching the firemen tackle the blaze. By now the ship was a floating bomb. The flames reached the ammonia nitrate fumes. The *Grandchamps* and the crowd at dockside and buildings up and down the docks vanished in a massive explosion. The blast brought down two aircraft passing over Galveston Bay.

A tide of fire—oil blazing on the surface of a wave of water—swept over the docks and wharves. Chunks of metal of up to 300 pounds in weight rained down; metal torn from the exploded freighter. In seconds the waterfront was turned into a devastated area, looking as if it had been shattered by artillery fire or bombing. Oil and gasoline gushing from shattered pipes fed scores of torrid fires.

A mile away, downtown, thousands of windows and doors had been smashed. Gas, water, and electricity supplies were cut off. The dead and dying littered the streets. Hundreds of people, thinking that the town was under attack, scrambled to their cars to flee. But still others, heedless of danger, were hurrying in the opposite direction, to tend the injured.

Another ship loaded with a cargo of ammonia nitrate, the *High Flyer*, had caught fire. The weary survivors of the Texas City fire department struggled far into the night, trying to bring the blaze under control. Shortly before dawn the *High Flyer* blew up, killing a rescue squad led by a Catholic priest, Father William Roach. The sun rose on a charnel house. Most of the people of Texas City had left. Behind them were 576 dead and more than 4,000 injured.

Like bad weather and accidents, crime flourished in the immediate postwar. New Yorkers were briefly rapt with envy for a cashier named Nickel who embezzled $800,000 from a bank. He spent it properly—on motorboats, expensive whiskey, still more expensive women, and lavish tips to bellboys and headwaiters.

Less fortunate was Willie Francis. He survived an attempt to execute him on behalf of the citizens of Louisiana when the electric chair failed. In the movies that would have meant a second chance. In Louisiana, however, it merely meant a second chance to be electrocuted. Over nationwide protests that such conduct was unsporting, Willie Francis was taken back to the electric chair. This time it worked.

In Chicago a seventeen-year-old University of Chicago sophomore, William Heirens, confessed to more than twenty serious crimes, from burglary to murder. His murder victims were a six-year-old girl and two women. He invented an imaginary partner in crime, one George Murman. And it had been George, he maintained, who had scribbled in lipstick on a bathroom wall, "For heaven's sake, catch me before I kill more." George, evil genius that he was, had imitated the handwriting of Bill Heirens. *

Other hazards awaiting unwary citizens included the VFW and the American Legion. When the VFW convened in Boston in 1946, they teamed up with local riffraff to set fires, smash windows, assault passers-by, and turn on fire hoses in movie theaters. Scuffles with the police sent ten policemen to hospital. The next year 250,000 American Legionnaires descended on Manhattan for the biggest convention in their history. They made water bombs from brown paper bags and tap water, then pelted women in the street with them. With electric cattle prods they made other assaults on female passersby. Day and night, up and down Broadway, drunk, foulmouthed Legionnaires molested strangers. Their idea of innocent ammusement was to inflict humiliation on someone else. They paraded endlessly. One Legion parade was pure Dada, a parody on cryptomilitarism: they paraded in their pajamas. The antics of the Legionnaires and others like them betrayed an uneasy, sad, defeated sexuality, which expressed itself as hostility to women. For decades Americans had tolerated their behavior. But increasingly after the war city after city refused to host such conventions; people began to react against this boorish behavior; conventions became no less noisy but far less offensive.

Americans came out of the war with their love of sports stronger than ever. After years of one-armed pitchers and one-eyed shortstops, spavined horses, and short-winded football teams they were ready for some first-class entertainment. Never had athletes been so doted on, so highly paid, or so thoroughly coached. And when, in 1948, Babe Ruth died, the entire country went into mourning.

The American love of novelty remained undiminished. Shortly after the war ended, Gimbels advertised the sale of "The fantastic, atomic era, miraculous pen." In one week Gimbels sold 30,000 at $12.50 each. Instead of having a nib at the business end, these pens carried a tiny, ink-soaked ball bearing.

The pen was the invention of a Hungarian, but it was manufactured by Milton Reynolds, a graduate of the go-for-broke school of business administration. After numerous entrepreneurial misadventures Reynolds saw a $26,000 investment in ball-point pens turn in one year into sales

---

*It is said that the first defendant to plead dual personality as a defense in a criminal trial was found guilty and the judge, passing sentence, said, "It is now my duty to send both of you away.

worth $6 million and a net profit of $1.5 million. The boast of the new pen was: "It writes under water." And that, said some disgruntled buyers, was probably the only place where it would write. The first generation of ball-point pens was by turns balky and leaky. In some, the ink fermented and blew the ball out of the tip. Nothing, however, seemed to check demand. Less than two years after its first sale, Gimbels was selling ballpoint pens for 84 cents each.

Peace ushered in a new wave of interest in the irrational. An upsurge of interest in astrology provided the nation's 25,000 practicing astrologers with better business than anyone had forecast. The backlog of clients meant a four- to six-week wait for personal readings, horoscopes by mail, and other services. *The Moon Sign Book*, an astrology annual, sold 1 million copies in a single year. The circulation of astrology periodicals rose rapidly. But the most exciting news in zodiacal circles was that the Age of Pisces was ending and the next 2,156-year cycle, the Age of Aquarius, would be an era of harmony and cooperation.

There were 10 million ostensibly rational people walking around with the feet of rabbits in their pockets or handbags. Each year millions of dollars were spent on charms, magic potions, and amulets. There was "Graveyard Dust" for those who needed it and "Evil Eye" candles. One thriving company sold tens of millions of four-leaf clovers.

The most flourishing new venture in publishing was science fiction. Five new houses, devoted entirely to publishing science fiction, came into existence. Conservative publications, such as the *Saturday Evening Post*, began to publish SF. A collection of stories by H. P. Lovecraft, *The Outsider*, little noticed on its original appearance in 1939, was selling for $60 a copy in 1948. More than a score of SF magazines appeared each month, and all made money. Trade publishing houses began to turn out dozens of SF novels and anthologies every year. Almost overnight a corpus of textual criticism appeared. All the earnest, comma-counting, brow-knitting effort taken for granted in Shakespearian scholarship was trained on SF themes and symbols.

After half a century there was a revival of the unidentified flying object. In the winter of 1896–1897 there had been a rash of UFO sightings in California, and the sightings had spread rapidly to other parts of the country. The reported objects had been remarkably suggestive of the most advanced aerial technology of their day. The most often reported object had resembled a sausage-shaped airship.

The 1947 sightings began when an Idaho businessman, Kenneth Arnold, was flying over southern Washington state. His path was crossed without warning by nine disk-shaped objects traveling, he estimated, at more than 1,000 miles an hour. Arnold was a man respected in his community, an experienced pilot and a deputy sheriff. His report was followed by scores of others.

The press coined a new term, "Flying Saucers, "whether the objects were described as saucer-shaped or not. UFOs had kept up with modern technology. Western air forces, especially those in the United States and

Britain, happened to be experimenting with circular and V-shaped designs for the next generation of jet aircraft. Speeds had also kept pace. The earlier UFOs had traveled at the (for 1897) dazzling speed of 400 to 500 miles an hour. These days they traveled at 1,000 to 2,000 mph. And in 1947 as in 1897 there came reports of flashing lights, strange noises, and falling objects.

All of which was very encouraging: it meant that life had gone back to normality.

In 1946 the divorce rate was 4.3 persons per 1,000 population, twice the prewar figure, and people wondered where it would all end. But the United States, with its twin emphases on individual freedom and personal happiness, had long been one of the world's most divorcing societies. The divorce rate had been rising steadily since the Civil War. No two states adopted the same approach. Washington allowed eleven grounds for divorce, South Carolina, none. Residence requirements ranged from six weeks to five years; the grounds, from "Indignities" to "Premarital Prostitution Unknown to Husband." In states such as New York, where adultery was the sole permitted reason for divorce, couples who were sick of one another were reduced to perjury and faked sexual liaisons with strangers.

In the immediate postwar years traditional divorce centers, such as Reno, Hot Springs, Miami, and Juárez, did land-office business. Most bigcity divorce courts were crowded. Hearings became perfunctory, the indignities recounted often provoked laughter rather than pity, and in the end the divorce was granted. The current housing shortage led to some novel property settlements whereby divorced couples continued to live in the same house or apartment.

By 1948 the boom in divorce, and the boom in marriage, leveled off. But both divorce and marriage rates remained considerably higher than they had been before the war. The baby boom reached its peak in 1947, and although it remained high, the birthrate ceased to rise. Part of the continued high birthrate comprised children who might have been born earlier, had there been no Depression. They were to this extent an expression of faith in the future, once the future seemed bright. As a measure of social morale the current level of births was the most graphic single indication of the revival of American optimism.

One intriguing feature of current births was the rise in the number of illegitimate births. Between the late 1930s and the late 1950s the rate of illegitimacy trebled.

The baby boom was important to the successful reconversion of the economy. It created extra demand for homes, schools, roads, clothing, food, and energy. It made daddy work harder. And as soon as she was able, it sent mother back to work.

Bringing up baby became so solemn it was almost a cult, and Dr. Benjamin Spock was its prophet. Ironically, Dr. Spock was the most genial and modest of men, not at all like his most earnest devotees.

There had been a similar baby obsession immediately after World War I. In both instances the aim was to make the path of parenthood run smooth. The "child-centered" family of the late 1940s was the democratization of an ideal commonly encountered among upper-middle-class families of the 1920s.

But the kind of advice being given the hoi polloi these days showed a marked improvement over that handed out circa 1914, when infants had been portrayed as autoerotic little anarchists. It had been mother's unpleasant duty to maintain eternal vigilance against thumb-sucking and masturbation: otherwise, she would unleash on an unprotected world a child filled with depraved desires and dangerous impulses. Extreme measures were condoned, such as tying baby's feet together and pinning the sleeves of baby's clothes to the sides of the crib.

Thirty years later all that had changed. Now masturbation and thumb-sucking were normal. The child who cried in 1914 was a petty tyrant seeking slavish attention. The child who cried in 1947 was a lovely little creature that was worth all the attention you could give it. Parenthood had been a duty. Now it was a pleasure. Play ("having fun") was an important part of life for parent and child alike, not a waste of time for all concerned.

Following its publication in 1946, Dr. Spock's *The Pocket Book of Baby and Child Care*, a work full of sensible advice, written in a direct and engaging style, went on to become the best-selling book to the postwar. It sold more than 20 million copies.

Dr. Arnold Gesell's *The Child from Five to Ten* also appeared in 1946 and was also a best-seller, more or less taking over where Spock left off. It portrayed a riot of confusion which few parents could match. It is dismaying to contemplate the number who took its pronouncements for gospel. Those who might display a high respect for intellectual ability in their children were sternly informed that they should "place a premium on non-verbal as well as verbal abilities." To place a premium on both is to place a premium on neither and to consider the inability to read as estimable as literacy.*

Gesell reflected a spreading hostility toward the intellect which was very strong throughout the postwar, afflicting, oddly, people who worked with children more than any other group in society. As we shall see, it was commonly found in the schools. Typical was Gesell's pronouncement: "In fact, there are many potential leaders among the non-verbal lower third." Such statements became fashionable among people who were themselves educated.

But no examples were ever cited to support such claims. It was left to the imagination to conjure up painters unable to put their names on their canvases, brilliant musicians unable to read anything but music, psychologists who had graduated from college unable to express their advice

---

*Cf. Samuel Johnson's noted remark that the difference between the lettered and the unlettered was like the difference between the living and the dead.

to their patients except through winks and nudges, lawyers who could not write briefs, legislators who could not write laws. Strong, silent leader types appear, if at all, only in Westerns. Inarticulate, illiterate people may be kindly, decent, and hardworking. Potential leaders they are not.

Parents, however, were so eager to do what was best for their children that they tended to be credulous when a healthy dose of skepticism would have done them, and their children, more good. But that is often the way with cults.

Paradoxically, the obsessive concern with children did little to improve the schools. The shortage of classrooms and teachers was astonishing for a country so rich. Long after the war ended the number of teachers pressed into service with emergency credentials rose from semester to semester. The war had emptied the schools of the better and more experienced teachers; postwar prosperity kept them from coming back. In 1947 the educational attainments of the average teacher were below those of the average teacher ten years earlier. And the dearth of teachers forced thousands of schools to close.

Incredibly, local communities, many of them virtually debt free for the first time in their history, thanks to the war boom, were reluctant to spend money on the schools. And for many a poor state, there was no realistic hope of spending more on education without help from the Federal government. Senator Taft and other important Republicans regularly supported the Administration's attempts to provide aid to education. But opposition from Roman Catholics kept the legislation from ever reaching House or Senate floor. It was legislation the nation at large supported by a three-to-one margin, to no avail.

Parents commonly found almost nothing about the local school to encourage them. The physical plant was in disrepair. The classes were overcrowded. The teachers were inexperienced and undereducated. While strict academic requirements were in decline, educational jargon was on the rise.* A Dover, Delaware, high school principal wrote in mocking vein describing the compromise between vocational and nonvocational education: "The book obstacle is allowed to remain, but the effort to overcome it is eliminated."

Ever since the turn of the century, when secondary education had for the first time embraced the majority of children, strict educational standards had been lowered in the majority of schools. The proportion of students enrolled in algebra, foreign language, or physical science classes dropped steadily. In schools offering a commercial curriculum there was a similar experience: classes in bookkeeping and shorthand shrank; those in typing grew rapidly. By the late 1940s almost every student had been exposed to courses in hygiene and physical education, if to nothing else. Half of all students had learned to play an instrument, to sing, or simply

---

*E.g., spelling drills were currently called "repetitive experience" or "sustained habituation." Such examples could be cited at tedious length.

to enjoy music passively. Americans in the postwar appeared to be rearing a new generation of clean, healthy music lovers in their schools.

The war years had seen the near death of Progressive education and the advent of "Education for Life Adjustment." It derived in part from the 1930s idea of the community-centered school, an idea whose time had evidently come, because it attached more value to a scrap drive than to a class in physics or algebra. In 1945 a group of teachers meeting in Chicago passed a resolution noting that only one youth in five went on to college, that one in five was given vocational training, and the three remaining were stranded between an academic and a vocational curriculum. What those three in five stood in need of, said the resolution, was "Education for Life Adjustment."

Life adjustment became a crusade. Columbia University Press in 1947 published *Developing a Curriculum for Modern Living* with such chapter headings as "Life Situations Are the Curriculum." Vocational training (formally known as "work experience") was hailed, as in Harl Douglass's *Secondary Education for Life Adjustment of Every American Youth*, in which English was considered useful only when it was directly useful, as in printing. "Health education," by contrast, was considered more useful than (i.e., superior to) history, chemistry, or literature.

In Illinois, where this writer went to grade school and high school and was required at a tender age to describe the kind of woman he wanted to marry (slender legs, large breasts, and half a million dollars) and sketch the house he intended to live in (it had a private runway and an Olympic-size swimming pool) the life adjusters attempted to break all learning into "real-life problems." They produced a list of fifty-five items (repeatedly referred to in the accompanying literature as fifty-six; but then, arithmetic was not among the real-life problems listed). These included: "The problem of selecting a family dentist," "The problem of developing and maintaining wholesome boy-girl relationships," and "The problem of improving one's personal appearance." The problems of learning to read, write, add, and subtract, of developing the powers of reason and the refinement of artistic sensitivity were noteworthy for their absence from the list of real-life problems.

There were doubtless sizable numbers of grade school and high school students who would not profit overmuch from a rigorous, unflinchingly intellectual curriculum. But the life adjustment movement was so hostile to the development of mental powers that in effect it assumed that students would not gain much by acquiring the rudiments of clear thought and expression. The education it offered was fit for serfs. Although it did not entirely remake the high school curriculum, it gave the downturn in academic education a shove it could have done without.

The better colleges had for some time been worried about the preparation of the high school seniors who applied for admission. In 1944 Harvard had published *General Education in a Free Society*. It had an appearance of unimpeachable sobriety. But it was at bottom a deeply romantic work, filled with such observations as: "It is through the poetry, the imaginative understanding of things in common, that minds most deeply and essentially meet." It was a work with an anonymous hero, "the complete man." His were the traits of "the whole man"—"initiative, zest, and interest, strength of resolution, driving power."* Instead of using his gifts to enrich himself, the complete man turned them to noble ends.

The Harvard report was an attempt to help rear a generation of young Americans whose character was almost Roman (of the "*gravitas, pietas, fidelitas*" school) or after the fashion of young English Victorians at their gem-like flame, muscular Christian best. New people for a new age. What those behind the report sought was more than a mere reform of the curriculum in high school and college. The principal idea advanced, that of a core curriculum, was adopted by many colleges for no better reason than that Harvard College had done so. But whether the core curriculum did much good for a school or college in the end depended on whether the school or college was any good to begin with.

In 1947 a Presidential Commission on Higher Education issued its report, *Higher Education for American Democracy*. Its aim was to help remedy the educational deficiencies either occasioned by the war or convenient to blame on the wartime emergency. The commission set a number of ambitious goals for the years ahead, including Federal scholarships and fellowships which would have provided assistance to one-fifth of nonveteran undergraduates and the most promising 30,000 graduate students each year. It also proposed that college enrollments ought to double between 1949 and 1959, with a target of 4.6 million students in 1960.

Direct Federal aid on the lavish scale the commission proposed was to prove impossible for some years. But the commission had nonetheless given colleges and universities strong moral encouragement for rapid expansion. And the Federal government was already providing $1 billion a year to higher education, via the GI Bill, in 1947 when half the 2 million students enrolled were veterans.

Education was one of the major deferred demands of the war years, along with four new tires or a new refrigerator. Millions were hungry for it. In all, nearly 8 million veterans went high school or college or took vocational training with the aid of the GI Bill. But to the horror of VA officials tens of millions of dollars was being spent on courses that included cake decorating, magic, and training horses. In Los Angeles alone millions of dollars were spent each year on flying lessons. Another favorite was radio announcing. Few of the intending pilots ever obtained a full license; hardly any of the trainee announcers was ever heard except by their fellow students at announcing school. The "schools" offering glamorous careers nearly always set their fees to within $10 of the $500 the VA allowed for vocational training courses.

The veterans who went to college found themselves living in makeshift

---

*The irreverent might be excused for considering this an excellent short description of the ideal lover, male or female.

quarters—Quonset huts, gymnasiums, trailer parks, attics, cellars. Nearly half of the veterans were married, forcing colleges to abandon their traditional barriers to married students and their wives.

The colleges that were crowded were very crowded. But nine colleges out of ten were, to their disappointment, shunned by all but a handful of veterans. The top 100 colleges and universities—the best and the best-known—took the bulk of the veterans, and their GI Bill money.

A legend sprang up that the veterans were eager, enthusiastic students. But Jacques Barzun had a slightly different recollection: "My experience was that this impression was vivid but not uniform. I found many excellent students, and as many who sat on their federal haunches, resisting what they had come to get."

The current crop of college students was older than its predecessors. They were older. They were less interested in the social side of college life. More drank, but fewer got drunk. Before the war college men had "played the field" or had "several on a string." These days they were monogamous even when unmarried. They dressed more neatly and carried themselves with a purposeful air. "Collegiate" had once been an honorific; now it was term of scorn, because the traditional antics of collegians suddenly seemed childish when compared with the decorum of the veterans.

These industrious, serious young men were a puzzle to their elders, who wanted to like them but found it hard to do so. "It is what they don't want rather than what they do that [they] know best," reported *Fortune*. "And what they don't want is risk . . . they seem, to a stranger from another generation, somehow curiously old before their time . . . security has become the great goal. . . . [They] want to work for somebody else—preferably somebody big."

The ruling passions of the postwar were security and identity. While the externals of life became ever more standardized and bureaucratic, the internal workings of individual personality were, by all accounts, becoming fragmented and confused. These outer and inner aspects of American life will appear again and again in the following pages in their various manifestations.

Traditional sex roles had been under strain for decades. But in the immediate postwar they began to crack visibly. A War Department psychiatrist discovered during the war that there were more than a few combat pilots who wanted to go to bed with women not for intercourse but in order to be held and caressed, as mom had held and caressed them. When Bing Crosby toured the South Pacific the most frequently requested song was the Brahms "Lullaby."

Out of nearly 20 million men examined for military service one in five either failed to meet the (not very high) standards of mental and emotional fitness or else actively attempted to evade military service. So of the young men aged eighteen to thirty-five there was a sizable proportion which simply could not fulfill the traditional masculine role, with its emphasis on stability, courage, and responsibility.

Ironically, military service had a feminizing influence on those who reached the required standard, at least to the extent that they learned to wash and iron their own clothes, make beds, work in kitchens, darn their socks, sew on buttons, and perform rudimentary housework such as washing floors and dusting. Within an ostensibly aggressive and masculine order they performed chores their fathers and grandfathers had stoutly considered fit only for women and children.

They also smelled different. Cosmetics manufacturers stumbled upon a new market when, during the war, they persuaded women to send cosmetics—euphemistically called toiletries—to their husbands and boyfriends. The offerings ranged from bubble baths with a flowery scent to after-shave in imitation whiskey bottles. Men loved heavily scented colognes. A salesgirl in a New York department store was quoted in reflective mood: "From all the stuff we mailed to servicemen overseas, I'll bet that jungle smelled awful nice."

While the line on the men's side was being blurred, so was the line on the women's. It was claimed that they were becoming assertive and, in a word, masculine. Much of the postwar writing on that hardy perennial the Woman Question (or Problem) was hostile and strident.

Bound up with the blurring of traditional sex roles was the fraying of family life. Until the turn of the century American society, like all Western societies, had been based on a farming economy. Family life was integral with community life. Individual life was firmly planted in family life. And such was the order which prevailed for four-fifths of the population, living outside the big cities.

By the end of World War II the order had been reversed. Now only one person in five was tied directly to the land. The community was either a town of 10,000 or more people or a city—that is, it was a place full of strangers. Family life was becoming perfunctory. Work, religion, recreation, and education, for centuries involving the home or occurring close to it, all were conducted far away, in either physical or emotional distance. Most people felt they had little control over their lives, yet the ideal of national life was individualism. The result was endless tension, which went deep and spread wide. And when that tension led people to take it out on someone or something, they did so on the people nearest them and the institution nearest them, the family.

Ordinary life was becoming so impersonalized that the individual man or woman appeared to count for nothing. Yet at the same time people were caught up in a round of pressing activities. "We spoke of life as being a rat race. Apparently no one thought it odd to equate Americans with rats," said John Keals.

Nowhere were the forces of standardization and impersonalization more clearly evident than in the suburbs. They, too, became a target for the resentment people felt at their powerlessness and obscurity.

Yet the suburbs were not really new. They had been in existence since the Civil War, at least, when tramcar lines and the railways had radiated out from the increasingly congested and dirty cities to the pastoral, unspoiled countryside. Between World Wars I and II three-fourths of all new housing had been built in the suburbs. And this was how a typical pre-1945 suburb was described: "The well-to-do residential community where most of the financially successful people of this country now reside . . . Most of the houses are in the higher income brackets, many of them are spacious and surrounded by ample grounds. . . . Building restrictions insure the uniform excellence of the dwellings." Not the way anyone would describe the typical postwar suburb, because what was happening now was the democratization of suburbia.

Millions of people had long desired to get away from the city, but until now had no way of doing so. The postwar housing shortage, and the efforts to overcome it, required the construction of large numbers of houses, at comparatively low cost and in very short order. Only the suburbs possessed land that could be bought in large parcels at realistic prices. And the Federal government was ready, through several avenues, to provide the necessary financing for building what amounted to small towns. There was only one piece missing from the equation—mass production techniques in construction. Enter Levitt and Sons of Long Island.

Abraham Levitt had begun his construction business during the Depression. In wartime, he and his sons, William and Alfred, had built more than 2,000 low-cost housing units for the Navy. In the process, they learned how to standardize the construction of housing—what Ford was to cars, they were to homes.

William Levitt had the temperament of the born salesman. Five feet eight inches tall, he would put his height as "nearly six feet." He also had vision. He bought 1,200 flat, grassy acres on Long Island's Hempstead Plain where Westerns had been filmed before the movie business went West. Potato fields had since taken over much of the plain, while to Long Island's upper middle class these open spaces were splendid for riding. It was here, where the land was level and treeless, that William Levitt decided to try mass production of houses.

Every phase of construction was broken up to be performed by teams trained solely to execute one task. The materials were prefabricated, or cut precisely to the required shape and size before they left the factory. Once the foundations had been poured, trucks rolled by to drop off standardized packages of windows, doors, pipes, shingles, plasterboard, and so on.

Levitt bought entire lumber mills to provide himself with lumber when other builders were resorting to the black market. He bought a nail factory. He hired a nonunion work force and thereby circumvented the obstacles to innovation posed by many of the construction unions.

Throughout 1947, to the mounting indignation of the Long Island horseriding set, hundreds of two-bedroom houses were finished each week amid the potato fields. *This*, they told one another, was not suburban housing. *This* was "the slum of the future."

Yet Levitt did try to give his Levittown a modicum of charm and variety. He offered four facades, although all houses had the same floor plan and arrangement of interior walls. And it was a success before it opened. Levitt took no chances; he advertised heavily. But it was mainly word of mouth that brought thousands of people out to Levittown each week, to tramp in and out of the handful of model homes. A Levitt house offered a mere 721 square feet of floor space, but the price was right ($7,990), and it included a fully equipped modern kitchen with appliances.

Levitt's influence on postwar housing was enormous. He showed that it was possible to build a town, albeit one without any civic life to speak of. He also showed how much money there was to be made selling cheap houses. He originally estimated the cost of Levittown at $30 million. He got a loan for that amount from the Federal Housing Administration and built Levittown for $25 million. And thanks to the way the FHA regulations were written, Levitt was allowed to keep the $5 million difference and call it a capital gain. By the early 1950s, when Congress finally put a stop to such windfalls, Levitt and other builders had collected $500 million in this way.

Even with mass production it took some time before the housing shortage eased noticeably. In 1948 there were still 3 million families living doubled up with some other family for want of a home of their own. In April that year one homeless family of six was found living in Pennsylvania Station. On money begged from passersby they subsisted on a diet of hot dogs. The housing shortage made a best-seller of a mordantly witty book by Eric Hodgins, *Mr. Blandings Builds His Dream House*. Blandings was by turns bilked, penalized for his innocence, undone by his ambitions, and simply unlucky. One reviewer decided, "It's too true to be funny."

The shortage led to the "Rookeries Racket," the kind of venture unmasked decades before by journalists such as Jacob Riis and presumed extinct. It battened on the hundreds of thousands of people who moved to New York each year in search of work. Often they were desperate for a place to live. Landlords obliged by taking over decaying warehouses, vermin-ridden hotels, run-down brownstones, and dilapidated office buildings, and these were carved into warrens of tiny rooms, each room holding as many beds as could be crammed into it. When one tenant moved out, another moved in within hours, so desperate was the need.

The postwar saw the advent of the "consumer society." It was launched on the $100 billion people had saved during the war. Most people did not have thousands of dollars with which to buy a sailboat or a new car. They were more likely to buy a new vacuum cleaner or their first television set. In 1946 the demand for household appliances was double the 1940 level. Some of the appliances in greatest demand, such as food freezers, had been available for years but had been considered luxuries or frivolities. The consumer society would see a change in the average home, from being labor-intensive to being capital-intensive.

It was a change partly due to the almost total disappearance of full-time domestic servants. In the late 1930s some 20 to 25 percent of American homes had a full- to part-time servant (euphemistically called help, as a concession to democratic sensibilities). War industry had robbed the middle-class home of its help, and except here and there the help did not come back after the war ended. In shopping, too, nearly everyone now had to look after himself. The wartime labor-shortage had turned the self-service supermarket from a novelty into a commonplace. Department stores similarly learned to let the customers do much of the business of looking for what they wanted for themselves, instead of paying sales assistants to do it for them. No one any longer expected to be waited on as if by right. And many shoppers appeared to prefer to look after themselves. Even the rich who still had full-time servants and could buy large amounts of deference turned discreet in the more democratic atmosphere of the postwar. "In the year 1948," wrote James B. Conant, president of Harvard and therefore well placed to view the behavior of millionaires, "the leisure class is distinctly out of fashion."

Ordinary people had become accustomed during the war to being flattered as if they were individually important, although they knew they were not. But once accustomed to such treatment, they expected it and looked mainly to business and government. Their expectations were not very high, but they were higher than they had ever been during the Depression. The Republican-controlled 80th Congress made a move which heretofore would have been considered fit only for Democrats: it removed 7 million people in the lower-income brackets from the tax net. Congress and White House alike were eager to hand the mounting government surpluses back to the consumers, instead of paying off the national debt.

Consumer spending was further buoyed by the lifting of Regulation W, a wartime measure which had curbed consumer credit. In September 1947, when veterans were allowed for the first time to cash their terminal leave pay bonds, they ignored the Treasury's pleas for caution and hurried to turn them in. In San Francisco the bank tellers had not worked so hard since the bank panics of 1932-1933. At a Bank of America branch the line stretched out of the door and down the street for two blocks.

Consumer demand had to remain high for a slump to be averted. The government's share of spending dropped from 41 percent of the GNP in 1945 to barely 9 percent in 1948. It was for consumers to take up the slack. So they continued to be wooed by politicians and business. They did not look in vain.

Prices never dropped as widely or as deeply as some forecasts anticipated. But they did stabilize throughout 1947, and the price of some items, such as meat and men's clothing, actually fell. Even the price of sex came down. In Seattle whorehouses, for example, the price of the standard service went from $10 to $3. In Newburyport, Massachussets, a hardware merchant, John Swanson, decided to take a stand against inflation by cutting his prices. Other Newburyport merchants followed suit. Other towns emulated Newburyport. In 1948 the cost of living index turned down for three straight months, marking the end of the inflation attendant on reconversion. In three years prices had risen by nearly 50 percent before they leveled off.

If was against this backdrop of sustained prosperity and growing stability that the consumer society began to mature rapidly. Tastes, like incomes, were not what they had been only a few years earlier. The most striking aspect of the change in tastes was the tendency to embrace the best and the worst and to ignore the middle ground. It is a development we shall encounter at various points in this narrative.

The consumer society placed a high value on comfort. New homes had radiant heating, a method of heating via walls and floors that was not only more efficient than radiators or hot-air vents but reflected the preference for clear lines of sight and large open spaces in the modern home.

While the technology of domestic architecture grew rapidly, the quality of the natural materials used declined. Hardwood floors, for long one of the most pleasing aspects of a middle class house, had become too expensive for the new middle class. People paid $12,000 and more for a house the drab softwood flooring of which needed to be decently hidden beneath honest linoleum. Stone was used less lavishly than before and was often faked with concrete simulacra. There were even false bricks, false wooden beams, and fake marble in expensive houses whose prewar counterparts had enjoyed the charm of authenticity.

To this extent, homes were becoming less gracious. Yet they were at the same time becoming brighter. There was a change to home furnishings in lighter colors and smaller sizes than had been fashionable before the war. Furniture was more likely to come equipped with casters or wheels; not only were people more mobile, but so were their sofas. Wall-to-wall carpeting became an essential, quintupling the demand for carpeting fifteen feet or more in width between 1939 and 1948.

Gardening equipment and furniture also became lighter and brighter. Rotary-blade lawn mowers, electric hedge clippers, and plastic hoses all appeared at the end of the war. Thanks to the introduction of tools based on magnesium, aluminum, and plastic, gardening became easier than ever and provided further encouragement to the postwar love of the outdoor life.

At night, beds were no longer piled high with blankets in winter and fires left burning in bedrooms, thanks to the rapid adoption of the electric blanket, another prewar novelty become a postwar essential. Mattresses and sofas were no longer filled with horse hair or rags but with foam rubber. Towels had traditionally been a nice, clean, utilitarian white, like the sheets. Now there was a good chance that neither would be white but would be brightly patterned.

Its expectations raised to a new pitch, the consumer society's principal collective endeavor was nagging. Instead of being satisfied that a wide range of new goods was better than the old, consumers complained that they were not different enough. Or, when they really were different, were not good enough. They had been promised so much in the atomic age, the air age, the television age. Everything was supposed to be lighter, brighter, more efficient, more streamlined.

The only wholly new product which came near to fulfilling such promises was the ball-point pen, and that tended to leak. Studebaker managed to make an impact on Detroit only once, in 1946, when it brought out a car which offered an unprecedented amount of window space for a family car and a front that looked as if it had been copied from a science fiction comic-book spacecraft. Similarly, in 1948, Buick's Riviera was a popular success thanks to a styling innovation which would be widely copied. The new Buick boasted two doors and a hard top that looked like a soft top. The Riviera offered the dashing convertible appearance, without the rattles and drafts. This was what the new consumer was looking for—an appearance of flair and innovation, combined with safety, reliability, and comfort.

It was not a life which appealed to everyone. When John Keats moved into his new house in a brand-new mass-produced suburb on the outskirts of Washington, he hated it from the moment he moved into it. As "a machine for living," he conceded, it was beyond reproach. It was also repellently antiseptic and impersonal. The development had houses and roads and people but no community life. There was a dead-levelness which was both boring and infuriating. All the men had the same kind of job. All the women were of the same outlook and interests. Children were nearly all in the same age range. There was a lot of togetherness and hardly any friendship. There was goodwill, but little emotion. There were many interests, hardly any passions. Complaints such as Keats's were comparatively few at first. In the years ahead they would grow to become a howl of impotent anguish. Yet the plain fact is, most young families who managed to earn a decent living and buy their first home were secretly—or not so secretly—pleased with themselves because they were plainly getting ahead.

We have seen that men were becoming feminized. So were women. In the first few years following the war they spent record amounts on perfume, hats, furs, handbags, and frilly underwear, accusations that they were becoming viragos notwithstanding.

The summer of 1946 had brought scanty bathing suits which consisted entirely of perfunctory bits of cloth carefully positioned. It was an innovation blamed on the French, who were, as everyone acknowledged, shamelessly immodest.

Mounting pressure from American women forced the government to lift the wartime clothing regulation, L-85, before the OPA had intended. Fashion overnight came back into fashion. Dresses and skirts became much longer. Elegance mattered; cost did not. Shoulders were bared, necklines dropped precipitously; dresses became more formal, more colorful, more flouncy.

After wearing their hair long for five years or more, women felt it was time for a change. They began to have their hair cut short, in styles reminiscent of the early 1920s, after the previous World War.

Such was the turmoil already in train when the New Look arrived in 1947. It was less a fashion than a sensation. At a stroke it regained for Paris the preeminence it long enjoyed in setting styles, which had been held in abeyance since 1939. The New Look was coined by the press. The look itself was designed by Christian Dior.

It lowered hemlines five inches below the knee. Shoulders were rounded, and waists narrowed. Manufacturers of corsets and padding prospered. The jackets of women's suits were lowered to hip length, as were blouses. Gloves with big cuffs, as worn by the Three Musketeers, were *de rigueur*.

The New Look proved protean. Sometimes the hips, not the shoulders, were padded. There were bustles on some dresses instead of wasp waists. Skirts could be either straight and narrow or voluminous and freely swaying. Whatever the variations, the change in women's fashions was for once new from top to bottom.

Some women held out against the New Look; those with beautiful legs appeared particularly resistant. Nor were men enthusiastic over the new skirt lengths. Glenn Ford, the film star, expressed the sentiments of many. A woman's legs were the one part of her body impossible to disguise "in these days of falsies, padded hips and fake shoulders," he protested. And now you could not even see them.

In the end nearly all fashion-conscious women came to terms with the New Look. This was, after all, a new age; everyone agreed with that. Would any woman want to start life anew dressed in her old clothes?

America is the most difficult country in the world to generalize about, and the easiest. It is so diversified that you can find fifty examples of anything; can prove any proposition; can disprove any other.

It remained throughout the postwar a land of paradox. Stark lunacy was likely to appear in the company of cold logic. In the midst of persecution you came up against the unexpected kindness. No nation has ever appeared less able to discharge great international responsibilities. Few have ever occupied a defeated enemy with the enlightenment, the generosity, and the good sense which the United States brought to the postwar occupation of Germany and Japan. No other Western country was so prone to hysterical overreaction to events. No other Western society aired its faults so openly.

To the outside world in these first few years after the war the Americans it saw appeared to swagger and preen. But at home, in the prosaic business of everyday life, there was less swaggering than lurching from one dilemma to the next.

A young journalist who set off to cross the country and talk to the people he encountered along the way to gauge the national mood found that the chief fear remained inflation. People talked about a possible war with the Russians. Hardly anyone liked the idea; hardly anyone thought it could be indefinitely avoided. As for domestic Communism, on the other hand, he found little overt concern. There was almost no interest in the fall election. "Only the possible candidacy of General Eisenhower seemed to raise any spontaneous interest." There was, he noted with wonder, nostalgia for the Depression years, when everyone had felt they were in the same boat, whether they were or not. The end of the war had certainly not brought the halcyon existence they had expected.

He was not alone in remarking the growing feeling of disillusionment. To help counteract it, the Administration sent a red, white, and blue Freedom Train rolling across the country, carrying to the nation's citizens the original Bill of Rights, Washington's personal copy of the Constitution, and more than 100 priceless historical documents. The Freedom Train visited every state, stopping in hundreds of towns and cities, being visited by millions. The antidote to disappointment was nationalism.

Even inspirational books were becoming muted. "It is not that the notes of the literature have become those of gloomy pessimism," concluded one study. "It is rather that optimism has become more cautious."

But visiting Europeans were struck by what they saw, even when they decided that it was not for them. The English poet and critic Cyril Connolly reported: "The American way of life is the most effective the world has ever known, but about the ends of life Americans are more in the dark than any people since the Gauls of Tacitus."

For the majority of people, life was certainly more pleasant and civilized than that enjoyed by ordinary people almost anywhere else in the world. Luigi Barzini wrote of his first postwar visit: "I rediscovered the principal pleasure of life in America, which is the absence of fear, diffidence, suspicion and envy."

Simone de Beauvoir was similarly impressed. The family she stayed with in Los Angeles in 1947 did not bother to lock their doors when they went out. How different from France! she marveled. "I liked this carefree trust. The delivery men enter quietly and leave milk, eggs and bread, and the bill on the kitchen table. The idea of burglary is not an obsession in America."

It is through such things that life as it was lived by most people is glimpsed—that is, through the things they took for granted.

4

Black and White Checks

The most antipathetic parts of the country were the highly urbanized centers of the North and the hardly urbanized sections of the South. By the quirks and ironies of history the strongest link between them in the immediate postwar was black people, migrating from the one to the other.

It was the tragic fate of the South to rear tens of millions of people who were in most respects kindhearted, courteous, and brave, but their fear of blacks so twisted and perverted their feelings on race that the logical outcome was murder. The years immediately following World War I, a time when all emotions were heightened, as they were heightened now, had brought a revival of the Ku Klux Klan. A wave of race murders had stained the South. In small towns and along country roads, crowds had gathered to stand by in fascination while some poor black man was tortured to death. Ominously, when World War II ended there was another Klan revival.

The old Klan had disappeared under a torrent of Federal liens for unpaid taxes from the 1920s, when various Klans had enrolled a membership totaling millions and some Klan leaders had become suspiciously rich. As Stetson Kennedy found when he tried to join the Klan in 1946, he had to look around before he found it. But in a bar in Atlanta a hard-drinking cabdriver named Slim announced apropos of nothing in particular, "What this country needs is a good kluxing." When Kennedy suggested that the Klan no longer existed, Slim handed him a card.

Here Yesterday, Today and Forever!
The Ku Klux Klan is Riding!
God Give Us the Men!

Nathan Bedford Forrest
Klavern No. 1
P.O. Box 1188
Atlanta, Georgia

In October 1946 a fiery cross burned at night atop Stone Mountain in Georgia to announce the rebirth of the Klan. Its presiding genius was a short, chubby, bespectacled Atlanta obstetrician, Dr. Samuel Green. The 300-foot cross burning on the mountainside could be seen for many miles. It was formed from drums of fuel oil. In the clouds of thick oily smoke stood Stetson Kennedy and 200 other new recruits. Baffled by the swirling smoke nervous Klansmen opened fire on the Imperial Wizard puffing heavily up the mountainside in purple robes. Dr. Green spent the remainder of the evening in a state of near collapse.

Thirty-seven of his fellow recruits, Kennedy noted, were policemen. Several dozen more were evidently veterans; they were dressed in the remnants of military uniform. All learned the secret left-handed handshake and the secret password, consisting of challenges and responses: "White . . ." " . . . man" and "Native . . ." ". . . born."

At a later, secret initiation ceremony Kennedy swore a blood oath, signing his name with his own blood. "I knelt in front of the altar on my right knee, placed my right hand over my heart, and raised my left hand in outstretched salute. . . . With great solemnity Carter administered the blood oath of the Klavaliers: 'Klansman, do you solemnly swear by God and the Devil never to betray the secrets entrusted to you as a Klavalier of the Klan?' '' He swore to that. '' 'Do you swear to provide yourself with a good gun and plenty of ammunition, so as to be ready when the nigger starts trouble to give him plenty?' '' He swore to that, too. '' 'Do you further swear to do all in your power to increase the white birth rate?' '' At which, Kennedy recalled, "I blurted out 'I do' with gusto."

Revived, he found, it was not the Klan as of old. Outright lynching was not encouraged. The local police, a major source of Klan members, could arrange a sudden death instead or, if time were short, could take someone into custody, then shoot him "while attempting to escape."

Kennedy and his companions one evening kidnapped a black man, beat him up, then forced him to run along a quiet country road while a carload of drunken, jubilant Klansmen roared close by him. When they tired of this sport, the driver suddenly accelerated and knocked the man down. An understanding local police department listed the death as a hit-and-run accident.

Behind the revival of the Klan was a revived fear that black people were about to challenge the mastery of Southern whites. Tens of thousands of black veterans returned to every Southern state between 1945 and 1948, and among them were many men of proud, unbending spirit. When they could not force such men to yield, white Southerners turned, in many instances, to the gun, the whip, the club, and the burning brand.

Countless minor acts of terror were perpetrated and were hardly noticed. But some outrages reached the national press. The worst was the case of Isaac Woodward. On his way home to Batesburg, South Carolina, after four years in the Army, Woodward asked the bus driver to stop at one of the scheduled halts long enough for him, Woodward, to use the toilet. Heated words were exchanged. When the bus reached Batesburg, the driver called the police. When the police chief attempted to take him into custody, Woodward's eyes were ground out with a billy club. When the police chief was subsequently tried in Federal court for violating Woodward's civil rights, he was acquitted. When he was acquitted, the packed courtroom burst into cheers.

The politics of the South seemed as firmly racist as ever. The 1946 election in Georgia brought the return to power of "Ol' Gene"—Eugene Talmadge, he of the scrawny red-neck, the galluses, and the dirty vest.

During the primary election, notices had appeared on the doors of black churches: THE FIRST NIGGER WHO VOTES IN GEORGIA WILL BE A DEAD NIGGER. In the small town of Fitzgerald two days after the primary election Marcus Snipes, a veteran who had voted in the election, answered a knock at his door and was shot to death in his doorway. On a nearby church another sign had been tacked up: THE FIRST NIGGER TO VOTE WILL NEVER VOTE AGAIN.

All across the South racial hatred worked up to a bloody pitch. Another black veteran, Roger Malcolm, was jailed in Monroe, Georgia, for stabbing a white man. A car took Malcolm from the jail, along with his wife, his brother, and his sister-in-law. On a deserted stretch of road a mob suddenly appeared. The deputy sheriff who had been driving the car stood by while Malcolm and the others were brutally murdered. That same week, in Holmes County, Mississippi, thirty five-year-old Leon McAtee was flogged to death by a dozen white men before a large and appreciative audience.

In 1947 a cabdriver was fatally stabbed in Liberty, South Carolina, and a black man named Willie Earle was charged with the crime. A mob took Willie Earle from jail and tortured him until he confessed. He was thereupon carved up like a roast of meat. His agonies were finally put to an end by a shotgun blast. The FBI identified twenty-eight members of the lynch mob. Twenty-six of them confessed. At their trial, all the defendants stood mute. All the defendants were acquitted.

At Anguilla State Prison near Brunswick, Georgia, seventeen black prisoners were shot, eight of them fatally. They all were attempting to escape, said the guards. They were making their bid for freedom under a considerable handicap: they were inside a compound which was patrolled by armed guards, it was daytime, and the compound was ringed with a twelve-foot-high cyclone fence. They had made no attempt to run away earlier in the day when they were outside the compound, working on a nearby highway, and the guards were fewer.

The truth appears to be that they had refused to work in a snake-infested swamp. The warden, whose demeanor suggested that he had been resorting to a traditional snakebite remedy, was incensed by this insubordination. To set an example for the others, he told one Willie Bell to step forward and be shot. Willie Bell stayed where he was. The warden then shot him in the legs and, having set the pattern, bellowed to the guards, "Mow 'em down!" The terrified prisoners scattered like startled birds and were shot down at the base of the cyclone fence.

In Columbia, Tennessee, a fracas between a young black man and a white repair shop owner set the entire town on edge. When the local police force descended on Mink Slide, the town's black ghetto, to arrest the young man and his mother, frightened blacks nervously opened fire and wounded four policemen. The police gathered their forces, then rampaged through Mink Slide's shanties, arresting more than 100 people and killing two men "while attempting to escape."

In Lyons, Georgia, Robert "Big Duck" Mallard, a thirty-seven-year-old black man reared in the North was known as "a biggety nigger," thanks to his enterprise and prosperity. He was guilty of such intolerable conduct as buying a new car and wearing well-tailored suits. One night a gang of white men murdered him in the presence of his wife and son. Under prodding from Northern newspapers and the *Atlanta Constitution*, Georgia officials eventually arrested a suspect—Mrs. Mallard. She was charged, briefly, with murdering her husband. Released, the distraught and terrified woman ran into the woods in a heavy rainstorm and cowered there, her mind deranged, until found by friends. Two of the men she identified as the murderers of her husband were finally tried. One was acquitted, whereupon the trial of the second was stopped.

The spate of tortures, murders, floggings suggested that not much had changed over twenty-five years. But something important had changed, on both sides. The assertion of black pride which provoked white people to commit murder was essential to winning the respect of whites. What inspired atrocities in the short term was, paradoxically, crucial to white acceptance in the long term.

Beneath its cultivation of rationality, Puritanism, and pragmatism, Anglo-Saxon culture retains a strong warrior ethic. The Anglo-Saxon people enter history like the Mongols—as marauders. In the modern age they have proved to be the most gifted practitioners of war the world has known. America, in effect, won both world wars, carrying its allies to victory. It is not too much to say that Anglo-Saxon nations have a gift for making war. With brilliance in arms has gone a warrior's view of beaten people and their reaction to defeat. The Indians were a conquered people. But even in defeat their own warrior spirit remained uncrushed; every attempt to enslave Indians failed. They died first. And in this they retained a measure of their conquerors' respect. Blacks, by comparison, were crushed even down to the spirit.

And then came the war, breaking the mold of subservience. "Many of my friends fled into the service," James Baldwin remarked, "all to be changed there, rarely for the better, many to be ruined, and many to die." Deadly race riots flared at Army bases and in naval ports. Overseas, there were race riots on Guam and in England. In Florida and California black ammunition handlers refused to load ammunition ships, not because the work was dangerous but because they were assigned to dirty, risky work solely on account of their color.

Put into uniform, the black soldier, sailor, or airman was expected to show the warrior ethic, yet many military officers refused to believe that black men could fight at all. After centuries of degradation they were presumed to have no aptitude for combat. The violence of black ghettos is the violence of the criminal, not the warrior; of the twisted soul, not the proud spirit. Blacks demanded the opportunity to fight, and while the results were not particularly impressive, they were sufficient to refute the glib assertions that blacks were by nature cowardly. As their spirit revived, James Baldwin discovered, "it destroyed their fear of white authority."

For many young blacks the war was a school in which they learned about the world at large, the condition of black people in other parts of the country, and the mental habits of citizens in a democracy. Matters which white people took for granted were likely to strike them as a revelation. Spencer Logan, a young black soldier in basic training, recalled being marched to the post movie theater to hear a lecture on what the war was being fought over. The white soldiers sat on one side of the theater, the blacks on the other, and the lecturer talked to them about democracy. The film was concerned mainly with the inherent evil of Fascism and made its point by dwelling on the subjugation of the Dutch, the Jews, the Poles, and so on. All of which was contrasted with the American way of life, with its emphasis on equality, free speech, and mutual tolerance.

Logan and his fellow trainees from the Northern cities were disgusted. But to his amazement, the trainees from the South had hardly noticed the segregation inside the theater and "had, instead, been very much surprised that the ideal of democracy expounded in the lecture even existed in America."

While blacks were becoming more assertive, the attitude of the young white men they came into contact with gradually began to change. No doubt some white servicemen became more, not less, prejudiced by firsthand acquaintance with blacks. But the effect on most appears to have been liberalizing.

In a broader perspective, it may fairly be said that only when blacks began to demand what was theirs by right did the white majority begin to take their grievances seriously. But it was generally true that the only part of white society that remained unfailingly sympathetic was among the educated young. At the universities of Oklahoma and Missouri, for example, the authorities were hotly engaged in trying to keep black students out in 1948 when the majority of students wanted to see them admitted.

The Truman Administration, moreover, committed itself to the struggle for racial equality. During every year of Truman's Presidency, a bill to create a Fair Employment Practices Committee was introduced into Congress. It was passed by the House each time and defeated with equal predictability in the Senate. Various states, notably New York, created FEPCs of their own, to no evident effect.

But the President was determined, nevertheless, to improve the lot of blacks. The blinding of Isaac Woodward horrified him, and the cold-blooded murders in Monroe, Georgia, provoked his indignation. He ordered the Justice Department to try to bring the murderers to book. The department reported back that it was powerless to do anything in the matter. In December 1946 the President did one of the few things he could do on his own; he created a Presidential committee to investigate civil rights.

The committee's report, *To Secure These Rights*, appeared in the fall of 1947.* It made no attempt to gloss over the appalling crimes against blacks in recent years. It did not evade the fact that local and state officials were often implicated in them. It accepted without demur the claims that police brutality was commonly visited on blacks, Mexicans, and Jehovah's Witnesses. The committee did not ferret out new atrocities. It simply, and utterly, rejected racism in all its forms.

Its sternest criticism was directed at the nation's capital and drew its strength from Washington's symbolic importance. Washington was where black travelers going South were forced to change to all-black rail-

---

*It is from about this time that the current distinction between civil rights and civil liberties emerges. They may be likened to a shield and a sword. Civil liberties are the shield the Federal government provides so that the individual may enjoy the rights the law provides. Civil rights by comparison are the sword wielded by the Federal government in making an active onslaught against discrimination.

road cars. Almost every aspect of life in the capital, in fact, was touched by Jim Crow. *"This is the situation that exists in the District of Columbia. The Committee feels most deeply that this is intolerable."* (Original italics.)

Its most important single conclusion was that the doctrine of "separate but equal conditions" was, in polite language, a myth. No one could honestly maintain that it had been achieved, was being achieved, or could ever be achieved. "Separate but equal" was a contradiction in terms and would remain so in any democratic state.

Truman attempted to use the committee's report as a foundation for legislation. The measures he asked for anticipated all the civil rights legislation of the next twenty years. But all that came of it in 1948 was to arouse the South to a pitch of anger that took him by surprise. His civil rights proposals got nowhere in the 80th Congress.

Yet they marked a change in the climate, a change marked by a shy, unknown, introspective young student at Crozer Theological Seminary in Pennsylvania. Martin Luther King, Jr., at a crossroads in his life set his course by this "stirring in the womb of time," which he liked to call the zeitgeist. He took hope from Truman and from A. Philip Randolph, the leader of the Brotherhood of Sleeping Car Porters, who was threatening to lead a civil disobedience movement in protest against the continued segregation within the armed forces.

Military officers continued to compare the performance during the war of the all-black (except for white officers) 92nd Infantry Division with that of the average white infantry division. But the latter, unlike the former, was not composed mainly of men possessing less than an eighth-grade education and intelligence scores barely within the range considered normal. It was impossible to train such a division adequately for warfare in the middle of the twentieth century and foolish to try to fight a battle with such a force. Even so, two of its number won the DSC. It was only when, in the closing stages of the war, black and white platoons fought side by side (each, inevitably, doing their best) that black soldiers fought as well as whites. Some high-ranking officers, however, persisted in referring to the 92nd and ignored the mixed platoons.

In 1948 Truman acted. He issued Executive Order 9981, ordering the desegregation of all military units. Doubtless he had one eye on the upcoming election. But the order was also entirely in keeping with his personal convictions. The worst that can be said was that like most human beings he acted from mixed motives.

The military complied, but grudgingly. The pressure was maintained, however, by Randolph and others. Black protest was more effective these days than it had ever been. But it was still characterized by too many leaders, too few followers. No civil rights organization had yet developed a mass following.

The National Association for the Advancement of Colored People (NAACP) continued to rely on white people for money and ideas, not from choice but from necessity. Its membership had grown rapidly during the war, and in 1948 it reached 500,000. It said volumes that when the association then decided to raise annual dues from $1 to $2 it promptly lost half its membership.

More militant but less well known was the Congress of Racial Equality. In 1947 it organized an integrated bus ride to test a recent Supreme Court ruling which outlawed segregation on interstate transportation. A Freedom Ride into the Deep South was considered too dangerous to attempt. The riders reached Durham, North Carolina, before they were arrested. Three were sentenced to serve thirty days on the local chain gang.

CORE also organized lunch counter sit-ins in 1947 in a number of Northern cities and forced them to desegregate. In 1948 CORE organized a swim-in at Palisades Park in New Jersey. A score of demonstrators were clubbed and jailed. Yet the outcome was a completely desegregated amusement park.

Such tactics were inspired largely by the recent civil disobedience campaign conducted in India by Mahatma Gandhi against British rule.

Organizations and the zeitgeist can only open doors. It is for individuals to walk through them. Each black man or woman who won the acceptance of whites really did so one at a time. And when in 1947 Jack Roosevelt Robinson, better known as Jackie Robinson, became the first black player to reach the major leagues, he possessed such personal graciousness and athletic brilliance that he became the first black man to be admired on both sides of the racial divide.

His overnight appearance came after four years of careful preparation by Branch Rickey and the Brooklyn Dodgers and by Robinson himself. For a moment it threatened to throw baseball into turmoil. When the Philadelphia Phillies arrived to play at Ebbets Field and discovered that the Dodgers proposed to play Robinson, the Phillies' manager threw a tantrum. The St. Louis Cardinals threatened to strike if Robinson was in the Dodger team when it came to St. Louis. Ford Frick, the baseball commissioner, called the Cardinals' manager to New York to inform him bluntly, "If you do this, you will be suspended from the League . . . I do not care if half the League strike. Those who do will encounter quick retribution. The National League will go down the line with Robinson, whatever the consequences." Brave words, noble sentiments, yet absolutely inconceivable only ten years earlier.

There was no more visible symbol of the zeitgeist than the sight of a solitary black player coming onto the diamond to an ecstatic ovation when all the other players were white.

The revival of the Klan obscured the changing character of Southern resistance to racial equality. The South by and large had lost none of its fear of blacks. But it was less and less willing to rely on the crudest, most violent means. It was perhaps less a change of heart than a change of circumstances. At all events, the South was changing. The South that was emerging seemed likely to be less charming than the old South, but less murderous, too.

Recent years had transformed its prospects. Malaria, which Southerners had for generations considered inevitable and uncontrollable, had been all but eliminated in only ten years. "Control of the mosquito in the South is one of the nation's greatest health success stories. What seemed hopeless in 1930 was a fact in 1950." Hookworm, which had drained the strength of as much as half the population in some rural Southern counties, was checked, thanks largely to the Rockefeller Foundation. Pellagra and other diet-deficiency diseases which had tormented black and white alike were brought under control.

Not only were the people of the South healthier than ever but so was their economy. For decades it had been held back by outside economic interests as well as by its own inherent defects. Its underindustrialization owed more than a little to the railroads. Freight rates were 37 percent higher in the South than in the Northeast. The railroads charged cheap rates to bring manufactured goods into the South but charged much higher rates for anything being shipped out. The South's economic resources, moreover, were in many instances owned by Northern corporations. Throughout the South men complained feelingly about "Colonialism." In 1947 a measure of relief was secured: the Supreme Court upheld an Interstate Commerce Commission ruling which equalized freight rates.*

The prosperity of wartime had also eased the Northern grip on the Southern windpipe. The South possessed the warm (if often wet) climate and large empty spaces conducive to training millions of servicemen. The most Anglo-Saxon region in the country was also a wonderful source of military recruits. They arrived from all over the South with little prompting. Their Army or Navy pay each month was for many the first regular cash income they had ever enjoyed.

As revenues rose, Southern towns and states and industries paid off their bonds, their mortgages, their notes and loans with unwonted zeal. Interest rates on Southern debts were halved, then halved again. The South came out of the war still the poorest region in the country but free at last from the crushing burden of debts it had borne since before the Civil War.

The news in 1946 that a mechanical cotton picker had been developed after decades of effort sent a chill through the South, and the region braced itself for disaster to follow. The machine picked only the ripe bolls, by stripping the stalk in a single raking action. Thus, it would work only in semiarid areas such as Arizona and Texas, where all the bolls ripened together, and it would pick a bale of cotton faster and for less than

---

*The reason for the disparity in freight rates, which dates from 1887, was that passenger trains made losses while freight trains made profits. In the "Official Territory"—east of the Mississippi, north of the Ohio and Potomac rivers—freight volume was so high that it could carry the passenger side's losses. But in other regions, where freight volume was not so heavy, rates were accordingly raised to provide the necessary cushion of profitability. The South was not singled out for this treatment. But given other constraints on its economic development, this was one more burden it could well do without if it were ever to become industrialized and urbanized.

human labor could ever manage. Cotton was also under threat from the development of synthetics such as rayon.

In terms of the number of people dependent on it for a living, cotton was the country's most important crop. It was the only commodity which had been exempt from wartime price ceilings. Its price rose steadily from 9 cents in 1940 to 39 cents a pound in 1946; then the price collapsed. Cotton exchanges in New York, Chicago, and New Orleans went out of existence. Lamentation swept the South. Jubilation would have been more appropriate.

Cotton has been a curse to every nation which has made it a principal crop. It was the chief justification for slavery. After Emancipation it never did, and never could, provide a decent living for the millions who picked it. The boll weevil was endemic in the Black Belt from 1910 onward, and blacks sang mournfully, "The merchant got half the cotton, the weevil got the rest."

Cotton strangled Southern agriculture, exhausting the soil, impeding the development of a diversified farm economy, impoverishing blacks and whites alike. By 1947 cotton subsidies were tying more than 1 million people to a crop and a system which offered them nothing but drudgery and pitifully small incomes.

Cotton, with tobacco, was the crop of nearly all Southern sharecroppers and tenant farmers. Sharecropping was a time-honored method for stealing from the poor. The cropper would turn over to 'the Man" all or nearly all his crop. In return, the Man gave him a payment, ostensibly the fair value of half the crop. But if the value of the entire crop was, say, $4,000, the chance of the cropper's receiving $2,000 was nil. The use of certain tools was worth so much, said the Man; the use of draft animals was worth so much more. If he happened to be lucky, the cropper might get $700 to $800. Most sharecroppers were not lucky. Had they been, they probably would have been doing something else for a living anyway. The Man handled the accounts. The cropper in all likelihood could not read, write, or do simple arithmetic. He did not challenge the accounts because even had he the nerve, he did not have the knowledge. He took what was offered and hoped that next year would be better. Too poor to own even the few simple tools and the draft animals that would have made him a tenant farmer, the sharecropper was too poor even to move. He was little better than a serf.

It was, all in all, a brutal system of exploitation, but one which kept the landowner in the same brutish condition as the cropper, if in greater comfort. It had to be destroyed if the South were ever to rise. It collapsed when the price of cotton collapsed. And when it happened, Southerners who had been terrified to live under any rule but that of King Cotton found they were perfectly capable of managing without that tyrant.

Industry was moving South to take advantage of lower wages. The CIO was moving in, too. In 1946 it launched Operation Dixie to recruit 1 million workers in the burgeoning textile industry, the sawmills, and the chemical plants. The CIO raised $1 million for its drive, but it was dogged by the AFL's decision to launch a counterdrive of its own.

Almost to a man, Southern industrialists hated unions. There were a few who took a comparatively enlightened approach like the North Carolina manufacturer who kept the unions out of his mills by a simple but effective expedient: "I always make sure that I'm five cents an hour ahead of the sons-of-bitches." But more typical was the experience of Ernie Starnes, a CIO organizer working in Georgia in 1947.

He needed to sign up more than half the workers in a mill in secret before he dared openly let it be known what he was doing and demanded recognition. Yet the mills were rife with informers. Southern plants and mills were gripped with suspicion and fear because any man or woman fired for union activities had trouble finding work anywhere else in town. In places such as Macon and Milledgeville, Georgia, the workers fired because they had dared to join a union could be seen sitting around town all day, dejected and penniless, serving as public examples.

Operation Dixie also aroused the attention of the Klan. Union organizers were not lynched and were spared the ineffable tortures inflicted on blacks. But they were beaten by sheeted men and had crosses burned on their lawns.

It took unusual courage to be a union organizer, anyway. When an Alabama-born organizer went to Alexander City, a town of 16,000 people, he entered a community where the mill, the only hotel, the town water supply, the gristmill, the creamery, and the woodworking plant all were owned by one family, the Russells. The mayor was named Russell. Life in Alexander City was controlled by the Russell Manufacturing Company.

When the organizer arrived in town he was asked to stop by city hall, where the chief of police had a message for him. It was: "Get the hell out of town" or risk being "mobbed." The draft board asked to know about his draft status and seemed eager to put him into the service of his country if it could. Wherever he went in Alexander City he had company—two policemen. Several mill employees were given half a day off with full pay to make a trip downtown, where they beat up the organizer.

The police arrested the victim. His assailants went back to the mill. The company looked to its labor relations. It organized a company union. The National Labor Relations Board had some harsh things to say about management's approach to labor at the Russell Manufacturing Company, but years later the mill remained as unorganized as on the day the organizer had arrived in town.

Against this background you would expect the CIO's chief troubleshooter in the South (Southern Public Relations Representative, to use the formal title) would have to be a burly, hard-as-nails figure, somewhat like Jimmy Hoffa perhaps. Instead, it was a white-haired little old lady who smiled sweetly, spoke softly, drove a battered Plymouth, and never carried anything more deadly than an umbrella. Throughout the 1940s, when union organizers were being thrashed, it was Miss Lucy Randolph Mason who arrived to chastise recalcitrant millowners and sheriffs. Little known in the North, she was a figure of awe in the South.

It was said that when this smiling tiny woman walked into local sheriff's offices and announced for whom she worked, several sheriffs had gaped so hard in astonishment that they swallowed their chewing tobacco. In her home state of Virginia she had once been confronted by an irate small-town politician who demanded to know, "By what right do you come into Virginia to make trouble?"

Miss Lucy modestly proffered her credentials. She was too well bred to wish to impress anyone, but in the South ancestor worship is almost as widely practiced as in the Orient, so she established who she was by citing her lineage. Three of the signatures on the Declaration of Independence, she said, belonged to relatives of hers. Before that, however, there had been George Mason, her great-great-grandfather. He wrote the Virginia Declaration of Human Rights on which the later Declaration was modeled. The blood of the famous "First Families of Virginia" flowed through her veins—the Randolphs, the Carters, the Bollings, the Beverleys, the Chichesters. And she was also related to Chief Justice John Marshall. Among her father's cousins had been an eminent soldier, General Robert E. Lee. Her father had, naturally, held high rank in the Confederate Army. One of her brothers had been killed in France in World War I. "Young man," she concluded, "I do believe that I have a right to come into Virginia and to talk civil rights to her people."

"Madam," said the retreating politician, "whatever the CIO pays you, it is worth it."

She called tirelessly on her numerous important cousins in every Southern state. She was almost certainly the only member of the DAR who was at the same time a paid-up member of the CIO. And on behalf of the latter she used her special status as an old lady of high breeding to its full advantage.

But even Miss Lucy could not save Operation Dixie. The CIO spent $6 million, saw scores of its organizers beaten or harassed, and by 1950 had fewer members in the South than it had had in 1946, when the drive began.

To Northerners, the South was little more than a primitive society, where the chief aim of communal life is to resist change. Thoughtful Southerners themselves despaired at the politics of the South, which had become part of the problem rather than part of the solution to the problem. One of the most popular radio characters in the late 1940s was "Senator Claghorn" on the *Fred Allen Show*. Claghorn made a profession out of being a Southerner and offering knee-jerk resistance to change. He drank only from Dixie cups, wore a Kentucky derby, and refused to go through the Lincoln Tunnel.

Yet there were politicans far removed from the Claghorn mold. Ellis Arnall, whom Ol' Gene had succeeded in Georgia, had been a man of liberal views on everything, including race. The 1946 gubernatorial election in Alabama was won by "Big Jim" Folsom, six feet eight inches tall, who boasted that during his campaign he had kissed 50,000 women. He also campaigned with a broom and a suds bucket, to symbolize his intention of cleaning up the handful of large corporations which dominated the state's economy. Folsom was a Populist. His victory was the triumph of veterans and small farmers over the Black Belt plantation owners. Folsom tried to repeal the poll tax and to reform the corporations. But he was generally as full of bourbon as he was sincere and genial and in the end the plantation owners and the "Big Mules"—the corporations—proved more than a match for him when it came to controlling the state legislature.

Death was overtaking some of the worst Southern politicians. Ol' Gene died shortly before being sworn in as governor of Georgia in 1947. That same year Senator Theodore "The Man" Bilbo died of cancer, just as the Senate was about to debate whether or not to seat him. Bilbo, to the surprise of no one, was found to be a crook. He had in his time praised the KKK on the Senate floor and modestly admitted to being a member. He wrote letters to his critics with the salutation "Dear Kike" or "Dear Nigger." Back in Mississippi that kind of thing won votes.

The singular politics of the South baffled the rest of the country. But that was because it was twisted at its roots, being based not on a realistic assessment of what was in the best interests of the people of the South as a whole but on the defense of segregation.

Large numbers of blacks, unable to vote in any other way, voted with their feet. Each year hundreds of thousands of them moved north and west. It was, albeit inadvertently, a positive step, because much of the fear in the South was based on simple arithmetic: white Southerners were frozen in attitudes of terror because they were afraid of being outnumbered by blacks. But since the First World War the migration of blacks out of the South was so heavy that the black proportion of the total population in most Southern states dropped steadily. By wandering steps and slow, despite its resistance to change, the South was changing.

The cities of the North and West to which blacks were moving in such large numbers had, almost without exception, contained only a marginal black presence up to World War II. Rare was the city that was as much as 10 percent black. But throughout the 1940s the percentage of black people in the central cities rose dramatically.

In the middle ages people fled their cities to escape the plague. Nowadays they fled to escape dirt, noise, congestion—and blacks. But well-meaning white people liked to believe that in moving to the cities which they themselves found noisome, the blacks for their part had moved into a better life than they had before enjoyed. It was problematical whether this was so for most. "They do not move to Chicago," James Baldwin noted, "they move to the South Side; they do not move to New York, they move to Harlem."

It was not only blacks who migrated in large numbers from the South; so did poor whites. In Chicago's Kenmore district a large "hillbilly" ghetto grew up in the 1940s. Similar ghettoes appeared elsewhere, in Detroit, Indianapolis, Cleveland, and Pittsburgh.

The slums of the immediate postwar were not the products of poverty so much as of prosperity. The poor, whatever their color, flocked to the cities in search of work—dirty, hard, menial, unskilled, offering long hours and low wages, but enough to live on. As the postwar economy waxed, so did the slums. Spreading from block to block, they were as much a manifestation of a vibrant national economy as the shiny Cadillacs rolling into the theater district each night. Prosperity enlarged the slums, made them denser and more dangerous.

They took a grip on the central city because this was where the older houses were, near the railroad tracks, because the cities had grown up around the railroad termini. Or if the city was a port, the slums were down near the docks.

Overcrowding became desperate because although the slums spread, they did so less rapidly than their population increased. During the war conditions among black war workers on the Chicago South Side were such that most enjoyed fewer than five hours' sleep each night. There was not enough space for beds. Children and adults commonly slept three or more to a bed. To sleep lengthwise was a luxury. Children were often given a quarter and instructed to go to the all-night movie house to sleep.

In Los Angeles there were twenty-two major hospitals, but only one would accept black patients. Similar conditions prevailed in other cities. As a result, the health conditions in black slums were not noticeably better than in rural black communities in the South.

The housing shortage was bad for whites; it was doubly so for blacks. The barrier which most effectively hemmed them into a small part of the metropolis was the racial covenant. It was a common practice for someone who purchased property to make a contract to sell or rent it only to someone who was white. Occasionally a real estate broker would buy a property for a black client by means of a "straw party"—a white person who would make the purchase, sign the covenant, and then defy it by selling it to the black client. For the few black people who acquired property in this fashion, it was very expensive.

Nor were racial covenants easily flouted. A black man, Henry Laws, for example, bought a small plot of land in Los Angeles during the war. He built a house on it, at 1235 East 92nd Street. When the house was finished, he moved in, with his wife, his two daughters, his son, his son-in-law, and a grandchild. The deed to the land stated that any structure built at this location location could not "be used or occupied by any person not of the Caucasian race."

Laws was sued for breaking the covenant. He attempted to buy or rent another house. But the black population of Los Angeles had doubled during the war. No house or apartment could be found for a black family of seven. Laws and the rest of the family, except the grandchild, were convicted of violating the covenant and imprisoned. Other people who did as they had done suffered similar fates.

These agreements had the character of apartheid legislation: a Gentile woman in Bethesda, Maryland, was forced to oust her Jewish husband from their home; a West Coast man was ordered to oust his half-Indian wife and their three children; a black man in Michigan was ordered not to visit his white wife at their house.

The racial covenants did not keep blacks out of the cities. They simply served to make living conditions intolerable. The wartime race riots in New York, Detroit, Philadelphia, and Newark were probably in part due to the pressures of desperate overcrowding. Among the forty recommendations set out in *To Secure These Rights* were three aimed at racial covenants. One asked Congress to act against them; another asked the states to act against them; the third asked the Department of Justice to act against them, and it did so.

In 1948 it intervened on behalf of three plaintiffs in two suits, arising in Missouri and Michigan, which challenged racial covenants. The plaintiffs had lost in the lower courts because every such case on record had upheld the constitutionality of such agreements. And when the Supreme Court* made its ruling, it too found them to be legal. But, said the Court, they had no force in law—that is, they were private agreements freely entered into, but private parties had no power to place an obligation on the courts to enforce their agreements. These agreements were unenforceable.

The racial covenant cases were the first major postwar victory of the NAACP. It won another later that year when it persuaded the Federal Housing Administration to revise its *Underwriting Manual.* Since 1935 the manual had encouraged builders to avoid what it termed "unharmonious social groups." Builders had discovered that to obtain FHA insurance, it was a good idea to build segregated housing. "The evil that the FHA did was of a peculiarly enduring character. Thousands of racially segregated neighborhoods were built, millions of people re-assorted on the basis of race, color or class, the differences built in, in neighborhoods from coast to coast."

The Home Owners' Loan Corporation followed FHA practice. When a house in a white neighborhood came up for sale a black family was automatically proscribed from taking out an HOLC loan to buy it.

Black people were also hemmed in by informal but effective credit blacklisting practices operated by banks and savings and loan associations. "Credit-blacklist maps (were) identical, both in conception and in most results, with municipal slum-clearance maps . . . the two devices, blacklist maps and slum-clearance maps, came into common use at about the same time, in the early 1940s."

Despite this welter of barriers, black neighborhoods expanded, albeit slowly, and when black families moved into some decaying white neighborhood, they were likely to be greeted at first with rifle shots, bombs, and arson. Chicago, Dallas, Miami, Detroit, Los Angeles, Cleveland, Indianapolis, and Kansas City all were racked with racial violence in the 1940s over the first black families to move into a white neighborhood.

In New York, the city that attracted the largest share of the migration from the South, the search for housing was made still worse by the arrival

* Two Justices, Robert H. Jackson and Wiley B. Rutledge, stepped down from these cases. Both men had bought property involving racial covenants. In the District of Columbia not only were such agreements the rule in the white sections of the District, but they were strictly enforced.

of competition—large numbers of Puerto Ricans. The great exodus from their sunny island began in 1946, when nonscheduled airlines began to offer a ticket to New York for only $35, less than half the price asked by the scheduled carriers.

The Puerto Ricans competed with the blacks for the lowest rungs on the ladder. Although nominally not black, they were almost as despised. Reputable New York newspapers printed columns such as: "mostly crude farmers, subject to congenital tropical diseases . . . almost impossible to assimilate and condition . . . a majority of these people are lured here deliberately, because as American citizens they can vote . . . few can obtain employment . . . they were left far behind in their own unhappy land . . . they turn to guile and wile and the steel blade, the traditional weapon of the sugar cane cutter, mark of their blood and heritage."

Most of the Puerto Rican migrants were unassailably white. But up to 35% were obviously black or brown. Discrimination by color was the usual practice among them. The darkest child in a family would be less esteemed by his parents than his lighter-colored brothers and sisters. Pregnant women rubbed their swelling bellies with talcum powder and prayed urgently for a white baby.

New York was thus the terminus of two streams of immigration. As its principal city became increasingly black, the nation would finally have to accept the fact that the problem of race was not a problem for the South. It was a problem with which the entire country would have to deal.

5

The Poisoned Cup of Power

Power may be likened to arsenic—a stimulant in small doses, deadly poison in large. Not since the early Roman Empire had one nation so dominated the Western world. But the melancholy truth was that every democracy in history had succumbed eventually to excess. Although Americans reveled in their present wealth and power they had reason to look carefully to themselves. That vigilance which they were tirelessly, and tiresomely, told was the price of liberty needed to be directed to their own country as much as to any other. They needed to stand guard against some of their own sentiments and beliefs as if against an armed enemy.

Yet there was something positive in the enormous challenges which faced them, at home and abroad, which found an echo in two aspects of American life—the passion for self-improvement and the belief in learning-by-doing. Education is the principle of a democracy. No nation was ever more willing to learn.

But while they were learning, there was one point on which they had not the least doubt—their country had become the center of the world. When the newly created United Nations began to look for a permanent home, Americans were surprised to learn that it was seriously thinking of locating itself outside the United States. It seemed unnatural.

The UN Commission held hearings, nevertheless, in London while it made up its mind on a permanent site. The governor of Massachusetts led a delegation to England to plead Boston's case. The mayor of Boston was unable to appear in person; he was in a Federal prison, serving a sentence for mail fraud. Atlantic City sent a delegation, reasoning that any city which could make a success of the Miss America Contest could make a success of world peace. Chicago made a bid which complacently maintained that it was far more cultured than Boston or Atlantic City. Philadelphia sent a judge to offer its case. The mayor of San Francisco ridiculed both Boston's and Philadelphia's pretensions of suitability: did not their harbors freeze over each winter—unlike San Francisco Bay?

When the selection committee eventually chose a site, it found one in the United States. It wanted to take over a large piece of territory on the southwest Connecticut, Westchester County borders, 20 miles north of Manhattan. The upper-class suburbanites already residing there in bucolic tanquillity were outraged. They were all in favor of international amity, but a United Nationsville of 50,000 souls, given to God knew what outlandish dress and habits, set among their spacious mansions and exclusive country clubs was unthinkable. And did the UN really need to take over 42 square miles of land for its exclusive use?

The UN began to waver, and its attention turned once again to Philadelphia. But New York suddenly made the most tempting offer of all: a free site along the East River between Forty-second and Forty-eighth streets, on what had once been known as Turtle Bay. Under the urging of Mayor William O'Dwyer and Robert Moses the Rockefeller family offered to buy the site from William Zeckendorf, who had spent years piecing together small parcels of land, covered with tenements, garages, abattoirs, and warehouses along the East River to build a vast concourse of skyscraper hotels and office towers. The Rockefellers made a gift of the site to the UN.

To Dean Acheson, it was a dreadful mistake; "Misplaced generosity placed [the UN] in a crowded center of conflicting races and nationalities." But that was itself as good a reason as any for locating it there. "New York," ran a more apt comment, "*is* the world's capital."

Most people viewed the promise of the UN with mixed emotions. They did not believe it would preserve peace, but they hoped it might. Inevitably, when the intractability of postwar international problems sank in, much of the disappointment people felt was turned into scorn for the UN. In July 1948 Steven J. Supina, a decorated veteran of thirty-three combat missions, expressed his own sense of disgust by flying over the newly finished UN Secretariat and dropping a homemade bomb. It exploded harmlessly above the UN Plaza.

Most Americans preferred to express their sense of obligation for the fate of the world in less eccentric ways. They brought to their new and daunting international obligations the charitable impulses they were accustomed to express at home. "Philanthropy," one observer found, "has been expanding toward the planetary economy." In the summer and fall of 1947 a "Friendship Train" rolled across the United States, collecting food for hungry Europeans. When it reached the East Coast it was pulling 300 boxcars of freely given food.

Countless individuals acted on their own. Gerard and Kathleen Hale of Southern California adopted the French village of Maillé as their particular concern. During the war the people of Maillé had hidden a downed RAF pilot. The Germans retaliated by burning a third of Maillé's houses and murdering one-fourth of its population. The Hales asked the people of the ravaged town what they needed to restore Maillé. They bought and shipped to France everything that was asked for—clothing, china, furniture, altar scarves, bedding, funeral cloths—and hundreds of other items the town had lost during the war.

Farmer Claude Canaday of Bloomfield, Nebraska, had got out of debt during the war. Feeling that he personally owed the hungry people of the world a share of the bounty from his 740-acre farm, he offered 1,000 bushels of corn free to the government for famine relief. That posed problems, so he sold it and gave the government a check for $1030 for relief work. "We enjoy seeing our own two boys eat so well, we hate to think of any other boys going hungry," he said.

The Hales and the Canadays were doing on a large scale what millions of Americans were doing on a smaller scale. The largest private relief program was CARE— the Committee for Remittances to Europe (later, to "Everywhere."). CARE organized a lot of chaotic enthusiasm and made it effective. People learned to stop stuffing anything they could think of into a box and sending it away in the not unreasonable belief that people in war-devastated areas would find almost anything useful. CARE offered standardized packages, which came at different prices but reflected a well-thought-out set of priorities. The donor was encouraged to choose the kind of recipient he most wanted to reach—"a Greek orphan," "a French widow," and so on.

Each month American relief agencies were remitting up to $10 million to their European counterparts for such essential needs as shoes for poor children, shelter for displaced persons. In the six years following the war, Americans gave $2 billion to relieve the sufferings of people overseas. The government, of course, gave billions more.

The government provided both food and credit. The shortsightedness of official policy toward the war's end, however, was almost beyond belief. The War Food Administrtion feared that the 30 percent increase in food production between 1939 and 1945 would bring a postwar collapse in farm prices unless something drastic was done. Farm policy was therefore set "to come as close as possible to seeing that the last GI potato, the last GI pat of butter and the last GI slice of bread were eaten just as the last shot was fired." As a result, when the war ended, the government possessed very little surplus food.

By the spring of 1946 it seemed probable that the food aid the Administration had promised during the winter would not be available. As the consequences of famine in Europe began to sink in, American photographers turned their talents to recording the sight of starving youngsters, and the press competed in publishing what amounted to starvation-atrocity pictures. It was a cheap ploy, but effective. It stirred American emotions to see children who looked very much like their own children, except for the stick-like arms and legs, shivering in the cold, clutching pots and pans while they searched for food. A sense of shame spurred government and people alike to action. And Fiorello La Guardia, who succeeded Herbert Lehman as head of the UN Relief and Rehabilitation Agency, (UNRRA) put his mind to the problem. La Guardia was probably the most overrated politican of the age. Typically, he called on the hard-pressed British, who were already sharing what they had with others and would have food rationing until 1954, to sacrifice still more. As he saw it, they were more accustomed to hardship than Americans, so would not notice its effects as much.

The country rose to the challenge not by making a policy but by resorting to expedients. Loaves of bread became smaller and darker because more flour was extracted from wheat kernels and more of the husk went into the bread. It was a tastier, more nutritious loaf than the beloved soggy white object. It was eaten with sour faces and eyes rolled heavenward in supplication.

Flour had for decades been shipped in plain muslin; now it began to arrive in the stores in ugly gray sacks stamped EMERGENCY FLOUR. In rural areas, this caused consternation. Flour sacks had helped clothe millions of the rural poor. And flour companies, cultivating customer goodwill had obligingly for years sent out brightly patterned or striped sacks, with fast colors. Pillsbury executives liked to boast that every time the wind blew hard across the South you could see "Pillsbury" on all the girls' panties.

In this moment of famine relief crisis the egregious Colonel Robert R. McCormick of the Chicago *Tribune* and other misadventures suggested that all stray dogs be rounded up, butchered, and the results shipped to feed hungry Europeans. His dislike of foreigners was well known; evidently he did not like dogs either.

By various last-ditch measures, which did not include the Colonel's suggestion, and thanks to the best harvest in history, the 1946 target of shipping 10.7 million tons of wheat to famine-threatenened areas was met in the nick of time. In all, nearly 16 million tons of emergency food aid were shipped abroad.

In 1947 the harvest was markedly below the 1946 level. To meet the government's targets, Truman asked people to observe a meatless day

each week and to go without poultry and eggs on Thursdays. It was a policy based on concern and confusion. If people did not eat chickens, for instance, the farmers held chickens back from market and meanwhile fed
them grain.

Price supports also produced surpluses which could prove embarrassing, In 1947 a widely reproduced photographed showed a potato mountain
in Foley, Alabama, deliberately set on fire after being first doused with
kerosene. It caused anger and revulsion at home and in the hungry world
outside.

When winter approached, once more Europe braced itself for a lean
time. Even with American help which provided 400 to 500 calories a day,
manual workers in much of Europe would have to live on 2,000 clalories,
which was 1,000 calories below the minimum required for them to maintain their strength.

The President created an emergency Citizens Food Committee to find
the extra food needed for the U.S. to meet its export goals. It was another
voluntary measure. Distillers, bakers, and brewers all pledged to use less
grain. Nearly all found a way to renege on their promises. The voluntary
effort came to nothing.

The winter in Europe proved one of the harshest on record. Thanks to
bumper crops in Argentina and Australia and a surprisingly good winter
wheat crop in the American southwest, there was no famine in Europe.
And by the spring of 1948 European agriculture was on the road to recovery.

The need to provide credit was less obvious than the need to provide
food, and Truman had acted precipitately and ineptly when he ended
lend-lease only days after the war ended. He failed to understand how
much other nations had come to rely on lend-lease and to integrate it with
their own economies. This was not from weakness of character or a deplorable desire to have a free lunch, but from sheer economic necessity.
Ending lend-lease was popular with Congress. It may also have been done
with an eye to making the British more amenable to pressures from the
U.S. to agree to changes in the patterns of world trade.

The British protested that they were happy to stand on their own feet.
But first they had to reconvert their economy and begin to export goods
and services again. The withdrawal of lend-lease so abruptly came as a
blow. Lord Keynes came to ask for $5 billion, as a gift. He was persuaded
to ask for a loan.

The cry of "Uncle Sucker!" was once more heard in the land. There
were unhappy memories of the defaulted debts from the First World War.
Half the nation was opposed to a British loan. The British, moreover, had
in 1945 overwhelmingly chosen a Socialist government. Why should the
world's most successful capitalists finance Socialism for the British? If the
British wanted it, let them pay for it.

The British were eventually offered a loan of $3.75 billion, at 2 percent
interest. In Britain there were angry calls for rejection. The loan was accepted with ill grace. The British, having discovered that for them history
was over, slid into debilitating attitudes of self-pity.

The Russians also wanted a loan. At the end of the war, when support for such a measure was at its peak, only one person in four was in favor, and a large majority was firmly against it. In 1946 only one person in ten continued to favor the idea of a Russian loan.

There is absolutely no evidence for the currently fashionable belief that the United States as a whole enjoyed an amicable relationship with the Russians from 1944 through 1946. Far too much is made of Roosevelt's gestures of goodwill toward Stalin. To a considerable extent they were less matters of policy than of the President's vanity. Far more important was the weight of opinion within the Administration, within Congress, and within the nation. And the truth is, Americans detested the Soviet government. Congress repeatedly gave expression to that hostility. The Russian people were admired for their fighting spirit; the Soviet Union as such was held in contempt and distrust. Roosevelt, had he lived, could not have carried a let's-be-nice-to-the-Russians policy against the sentiments of Congress and the public, supported only by a small band of New York liberals and leftists.

Stalin's priorities consisted of increasing Soviet power, first, last, and always. A Russian loan would have been used to finance the modernization of Soviet military technology before it would have provided food, housing, or consumer goods. A loan would not have altered Soviet priorities; it would have made them easier to achieve.

Congress disliked lending money to anyone. The British loan was the exception to the rule, It did as little as it decently could to help other countries. Appropriations for UNRRA were hedged about with restrictions to keep UNRRA assistance from reaching Eastern Europe or anywhere else under Soviet or Communist domination. no UNRRA money could be used, said Congress, for "rehabilitation" either. One Congressman was baffled by such attitudes: "We were willing to send Europe some bread and dried eggs but not to help them rebuild bridges, refertilize their land, or reconstruct their homes."

A new economic order was nevertheless being forged, and it relied mainly on the United States. The World Bank and the International Monetary Fund both began operations in 1946. The United States provided more than half the working capital of both bodies. They both were chaired by the U.S. Secretary of the Treasury, Fred M. Vinson.

Most people had no doubts that it had been a good idea to use the atomic bomb against the Japanese. They believed that it had brought the war to a speedy end and thus saved many more lives than it had taken.

The most disturbing aspect of the use of the bomb was that there had been no decision to use it as such. The momentum of modern weapons technology had taken effect and brought the use of the bomb against a nation already defeated and looking for a way to surrender.

Shortly after becoming President, Truman had been briefed on the bomb's construction by Secretary of War Henry Stimson. An interim committee was established to advise the President on the use to be made of this weapon. The committee made various recommendations, the first of which was: "The bomb should be used against Japan as soon as possible." Truman accepted the committee's advice. But no separate and distinguishable decision was ever arrived at. The use of the bomb was implicit in the decision to build it, undertaken years before. Years later Truman would recall, "There at Postsdam the decision to use the bomb was made." But no record exists of any such meeting occurring or any such decision being made. The assumption in all the discussions concerning the bomb was that it would be used. The sole issue at stake was how. The closest thing there is to written Presidential authority for the weapon to be used is Truman's assent to an order written for transmission to the 509th Composite Group, 20th Air Force, outlining the mission against Hiroshima.

Less than a month after the destriction of Hiroshima an editorial by Norman Cousins appeared in the *Saturday Review* under the title "Modern Man Is Obsolete." The basis of loyalty to the nation-state was that it offered security to its citizens. Was anyone secure any longer? Technology had overtaken established systems of political allegiance, and humanity would either adjust to the change by moving toward world government or slide eventually into a war between obsolete political entities armed with atomic bombs. If people could not make the adjustment to world government, Cousins thought, it might be as well to raze the great cities, burn down the universities and libraries, and revert to a simple, pastoral existence. That would at least assure the continuation of the human species.

Put between covers, *Modern Man Is Obsolete* sold 100,000 copies , but most people continued to believe that the United States could be made secure against a future atomic attack. Although some people admitted to being worried about the bomb, twice as many refused to worry, because there was nothing they could do about it.

To improve the bomb's public relations, the first postwar atomic explosion, conducted at Bikini Atoll, was treated like the premiere of a Hollywood epic. The test was broadcast over the radio on July 1, 1946, as something new in the world of entertainment. The bomb was dropped from a B-29 named *Dave's Dream*. The bomb casing bore a likeness of Rita Hayworth looking seductive; the bomb itself was known as Gilda. General Carl "Tooey" Spaatz provided the radio commentary, referring to the explosion as "the main event." The networks brought scientists into the studio to explain in cozy, down-to-Earth terms what atomic fission was all about. There were numerous references to "national defense." But no one spoiled the fun by talking about death.

The Bikini test, said rumor, would rip open the ocean floor; all of the ships involved, said rumor, would be sunk without trace; and California, said rumor, would vanish under an enormous tidal wave. It seemed tame when, in the event, five ships were sunk, fifty others were damaged, and California escaped unscathed. When rumor was confounded, the bomb became much easier to live with.

But only two months later doubt revived. The issue of *The New Yorker* for August 31, 1946, looks utterly untoward. It shows a picnic scene on the front cover. But inside there is, for once, no satire, no cartoons, no fiction, no smart quips or shopping notes, nothing but the usual torrent of advertising, and snaking in and out, weaving through the ads, is a 30,000-word article by John Hersey called, simply, "Hiroshima." No other magazine article published in the first twenty years after the war had the impact of "Hiroshima."

Hersey's text covered the bomb's effect on six survivors, each of whom escaped death by chance in all its freakishness. Within hours of publication the entire issue of *The New Yorker* sold out. It worked a profound change in American feelings. For the first time in years, if not for the first time ever, Americans felt for the Japanese the sympathy which binds all humanity. And Hersey enabled people to think of the bomb not as a vast impersonal force but as something made by men and used to destroy other people. It was the first essential step in getting people to think seriously about the bomb as a national and an international responsibility.

The demand for Hersey's account, which was spare and unemotional, led to a four-part version being broadcast over the radio to an audience of millions. Scores of newspapers carried it in serial form. Albert Einstein bought 1,000 copies of the August 31 issue of *The New Yorker* to give to his friends.

A feeling of guilt encroached on the pride Americans had until now felt toward the bomb. Serious minds were also troubled by the prospect of what lay ahead. By 1948 there were references being made to "The deuterium (or heavy hydrogen) bomb, which does not now exist but probably will be perfected some day in the not-too-distant future."

When the war ended, the Administration had barely begun to think about the control of atomic energy. The War Department, with the aid of Lieutenant General Leslie R. Groves, who had supervised the Manhattan Project, wrote its own Atomic Energy Act. This was introduced in Congress by Senator Edwin C. Johnson of Colorado and Representative Andrew May of Kentucky, both of whom were enamored of the military (May was also enamored of money to such a degree that he finished his career in a Federal penitentiary, convicted of bribery). The May-Johnson bill enjoyed the blessing of the White House. The hearings set for it scheduled only four witnesses, all friendly to the bill. If passed, it would have allowed military officers to be appointed to the proposed Atomic Energy Commission. The structure it envisaged was remarkably similar to the wartime Manhattan Engineer District. Release of research data would be severely limited. There were huge penalties for infractions, such as fines of $300,000. (One scientist, asked by a Congressional committee if this was enough, said perhaps not. He smiled. "Why not make it a million?") To scientists who had chafed for years under military control the May-Johnson bill was not really a laughing matter. They began to arrive in Washington by the hundreds to lobby against it.

Natural and physical scientists not involved in atomic energy research joined forces with the atomic scientists to oppose the May-Johnson bill, but it proved an uneasy alliance from first to last. With a $10,000 gift arranged by Robert Hutchins from the University of Chicago's "Special Education" fund, the atomic scientists rented a few rooms in an unprepossessing office building near the Capitol. They began publication of the *Bulletin of the Atomic Scientists*. The Federation of the Atomic Scientists (Fats) was formed. It directed its lobbying activities at the Senate's recently created Special Committee on Atomic Energy, chaired by Senator Brien McMahon of Connecticut. It was one of the most singular lobbies in history. World-famous scientists waited patiently in the outer offices of mediocre politicians in the hope of being able to say a few words about atomic energy. Fats was so innocent of the rudiments of public relations that it typed its press releases single-spaced and used both sides of the paper.

Congressional mail began to run heavily in the scientists' favor as their intense outburst of activity generated publicity. The White House dropped its support of the May-Johnson bill.

A new bill was introduced by Senator McMahon and Representative Helen Gahagan Douglas of California. It assured civilian control over the AEC. Research data were still restricted, but less so than under the May-Johnson bill. The McMahon-Douglas bill became the Atomic Energy Act of 1946, and with its passage the question of domestic control over atomic energy was settled.

A five-man committee appointed by Byrnes was meanwhile trying to devise a system of international control. The six were Dean Acheson, Under Secretary of State; David Lilienthal; General Groves; James B. Conant of Harvard; Vannevar Bush, the head of the Office of Scientific Research and Development; and a noted Wall Street figure, John McCloy.

"No fairy story that I read in utter rapture and enchantment as a child, no spy story, no 'horror' story, can remotely compare with the scientific recital I listened to for six or seven hours today," Lilienthal confided to his diary one evening after the committee had been in all-day session. "Seated in a prosaic office high above Lexington Avenue, I heard more of the complex story of the atomic bomb, past, present and immediate future, than any but a few men have yet heard. . . . We are going to know the facts about this whole business as no one else, having similar purpose, has ever known those facts. . . . This is a soul-stirring experience. One must be far more insensitive than I—the same thing is written on the utterly solemn and grim faces of my associates—not to feel deeply moved by having the terrible facts of nature's ultimate forces coolly laid before him as on an operating table, almost feeling them warm and stirring under one's probing fingers. Mixed with that the constant element of international rivalry and intrigue, and I feel that I have been admitted, through the strangest turn of fate, behind the scenes in the most awful and inspiring drama since primitive man looked for the first time upon fire."

The report which followed, popularly termed the Lilienthal Report, argued strongly for international control even if that involved taking risks. But it contained at least one fatal flaw: it proposed a step-by-step transfer of control over atomic energy to an international agency, and should the agreement break down before the transfer was completed the United States would still possess atomic weapons while other countries would have probably ceased their manufacture. Lilienthal, Acheson, and the rest were sincere in what they proposed. But to others it was bound to appear merely an American move to retain the American atomic monopoly.

Truman expressed his confidence in Lilienthal by appointing him the first chairman of the AEC, an appointment strenuously resisted by Senate conservatives to whom the TVA remained the most potent symbol of the New Deal. The President, however, saw the appointment confirmed and turned elsewhere for someone to make out the American case for international control over atomic energy. To the amazement and alarm of his more astute advisers, he chose Bernard Baruch.

The Baruch Plan, which Baruch modestly preferred to call "the American Plan," was formally presented to other members of the UN, who gathered at Hunter College for the occasion, the UN not yet possessing a home of its own. Baruch opened with a flourish: "My fellow citizens of the world, we are here to make a choice between the quick and the dead." The chief difference between the Lilienthal and the Baruch proposals was that the former was prepared to take the risks inherent in systematic inspection while to the latter control meant *control*, over all stocks of fissionable material, over all manufacturing processes. Baruch proposed, moreover, "immediate, swift and sure punishment" for any violation of the proposed agreement. The only possible source of the swift and certain punishment he had in mind was the United States. He seriously expected the Soviet Union to agree to this. For good measure, he called on the Soviets to relinquish their Security Council veto.

While the United Nations Atomic Energy Commission discussed these matters in a desultory way, the first of the Bikini tests was heard offstage. The Russians called for the immediate destruction of all existing atomic weapons and the publication of all available information on the construction of atomic weapons.

Only days after the war ended Churchill had told the House of Commons that the American atomic bomb monopoly would last for only three or four years. Bush and Conant offered the same opinion to Stimson. Bush also told the McMahon Committee that "if she threw her weight into it,"the Soviet Union would possess a deliverable atomic bomb by 1950. Two leading atomic scientists gave a similar warning in a best-selling book on the dangers posed by the bomb, *One World or None*. Several countries were capable of building an atomic bomb by 1951. Irving Langmuir, a Nobel laureate in physics, expected the Soviets to explode their first atomic bomb some time in 1949.

Most of the public was of much the same view—sometime around 1950 the Soviets would break the American atomic bomb monopoly. But unlike the scientists, most of whom supported the efforts to arrange international control over atomic energy, they wanted the United States to maintain its monopoly for as long as possible.

The atomic bomb marked a watershed in the place of science in the modern world. Henceforth science became too important to be left to scientists. When the war ended, the wish of most scientists was the wish of most servicemen—they wanted out. But the government and especially the armed forces had found during the war that to fight a modern war, scientists were as essential as troops, ships, planes, and ammunition.

Wisely, the government essayed nothing remotely resembling compulsion in its attempts to continue in peacetime its close wartime relationship with American scientists. It bought them, lock, stock, and laboratory. But there was a sharp clash over principle. The scientists continued to assert their right to publish their research results and to decide for themselves what research they wished to do. The difference of opinion over these points led to a five-year delay in the creation of the National Science Foundation. But in the end the scientists for the most part got their way.

Truman had meanwhile created another Presidential committee, this time to advise him on the future course of science in the United States. The President's Scientific Research Board pointed, on the one hand, to the reliance of the economy and the military on an expanding scientific effort, and on the other, it was concerned that until the war the United States had depended for basic scientific research mainly on discoveries made in Western Europe. America's contribution to basic research was remarkably small for a country of its size and wealth. And now Western Europe was in ruins. "For the first time in our history we are on our own so far as the extension of knowledge is concerned."

The board set a number of ambitious goals for American science to meet by 1957: a quadrupling of the money going into basic research, for generous Federal assistance to education, for tripling the amount of money spent on medical research, and so on. It also called for help to be given to finance the work of European scientists and the rebuilding of European research facilities, not to pick their brains, but because it was the right thing to do.

Despite being wooed so keenly, many scientists felt uneasy at being ardently pursued after decades of being considered oddballs. Nor did they care for the impact of national security policy on their traditionally free and open community. Even the head of the Weapons Evaluation Group in the newly created Department of Defense, Philip McC. Morse, protested, "No adequate course in nuclear engineering can be taught at a university; the material is too secret." As a result, the United States found itself with far fewer nuclear scientists than it was capable of training.

There were also some extraordinary attacks on scientists by Congressmen whose mathematical ability was confined to counting votes. J. Parnell Thomas, the chairman of the House Un-American Activities Committee, in March 1948 described Edward U. Condon, the head of the National Bureau of Standards, as "one of the weakest links in our security." Condon had been one of the senior administrators on the Manhattan Project and had made fun of some of Groves's security measures. Thomas admired Groves. Condon had also been an important figure in the lobby which defeated the May-Johnson bill, a measure Thomas had supported, and he and Condon had clashed over it during the hearings. Thomas came off second best. Also, the House was considering the largest appropriation request HUAC had ever submitted at the time Thomas smeared Condon. Finally, Condon had been appointed to his present post by Henry Wallace.

Condon replied to the claim Thomas had made, "If it is true that I am one of the weakest links in atomic security, that is very gratifying. The country can feel absolutely safe, for I am completely reliable, loyal and conscientious."

While Condon was attempting to shrug off Thomas's inexcusable slur on his name, another scientist who had held a very high post in the Manhattan Project found he was under intense surveillance by government investigators. When discussing sensitive matters with a visitor to his office, J. Robert Oppenheimer asked the visitor to step outside, murmuring, "Even the walls have ears." While at home, Oppenheimer digging in his garden inadvertently dug up the wiring of a listening device placed by Federal agents.

Such episodes only added to the climate of suspicion and discouragement which pervaded the scientific community in the immediate postwar.

Returning home to South Carolina after his foredoomed efforts at the Hunter College gymnasium, Bernard Baruch addressed the state legislature. He took note of the spreading dismal climate at home and abroad and said glumly, "Today, we are in the midst of a cold war." The phrase stuck in the imagination and quickly passed into everyday speech.

Americans did not need to be made suspicious of the Soviet Union; they already were. Most Americans were convinced that the Soviet leaders were brutal, expansionist, and ruthless. The ordinary Russian was probably all right. But his leaders were men steeped in mass murder, men who lied as naturally as other men drew breath, men who had only one foreign policy ambition—world domination. More than one-third of those polled favored the execution or life imprisonment of American Communists. By five to one, Americans in 1946 opposed the sale of oil, machinery, and industrial products to the Soviet Union. By the same margin they favored the creation of a Central Intelligence Agency, a body whose principal task would clearly be the thwarting of Russian designs. Only among a dwindling band of liberals did any Americans (except outright Stalinists) continue to believe that the Soviets could be trusted to behave decently. "In many Eastern European countries, whose peoples today are moving directly from feudalism to socialism, majority rule exists," wrote the editor of *The New Republic* in September 1947. Such wishful thinking was becoming more difficult to sustain almost day by day, however.

The Soviets took pains to prevent the truth about the nature of their rule from reaching the world at large. It seems perverse that those who persisted the longest in believing Russian lies were often the more, as compared with the less, educated. But in 1947 the Soviets made fools of themselves over *l'affaire* Lysenko.

T. D. Lysenko was a plant breeder who claimed to have succeeded in transmitting acquired characteristics from one generation of plants to its offspring. Soviet agriculture could do with a miracle. That was what Lysenko was offering. He was elevated at once to the Soviet Academy of Sciences. His fellow academicians, not as a rule given to believing in miracles, accepted the new doctrine rather than attempt to explain to Stalin why it was impossible. Proletarian biology swept bourgeois biology to one side, at least in the Soviet Union. Or at least in the Academy of Sciences. Unfortunately, Soviet plants proved to be unregenerately bourgeois and went on growing in the same old way.

Even a journal long sympathetic to the Soviets, *The Nation*, found the attempt to impose ideology on seeds and semen a joke: "From now on, plants and animals in the Soviet Union will transmit acquired characteristics, or the Central Committee of the Communist Pary—and the MVD—will know the reason why."

The year 1946 saw the republication of Aldous Huxley's *Brave New World*, first published in 1932. Its portrayal of a totalitarian state was considered timely, and the book was reviewed, favorably, as if it were a new work. The same year saw the appearance of George Orwell's successful anti-totalitarian fable *Animal Farm*.

The behavior of Soviet diplomats on American soil was itself something to wonder at. They were frequently involved in seriocomical misadventures of espionage (nearly always taken far too seriously by the press). They were also shown at their worst in the matters of Mrs. Oksana Kasenkina.

She was a Russian schoolteacher brought to the United States in 1946 to teach the children of Soviet diplomats working in New York. One day in 1948 Mrs. Kasenkina arrived at Reed Farm, an asylum for Russian refugees maintained in upstate New York by Countess Tolstoy, the youngest daughter of the Russian novelist. Within hours of reaching Reed Farm Mrs. Kasenkina disappeared.

The people at the farm protested that the lady had been kidnapped. The press besieged the Soviet Consulate in New York until the consul general held a press conference, at which he produced Mrs. Kasenkina. The plump middle-aged schoolteacher had been kidnapped, he agreed—but by the Russian émigrés at Reed Farm, who had drugged her and held her captive. Mrs. Kasenkina, looking pale and frightened, mumbled her assent to the consul general's story.

A week later she jumped from a third-story window at the consulate.

Badly injured but still alive, she was taken to the hospital by policemen who had first to drag her broken body away from Soviet diplomats who were trying to pull her back into the building. From her sickbed she pleaded not to be handed back to the Russians. Another Russian schoolteacher, attached to the embassy in Washington, at the same time chose to defect and to ask for asylum.

Incidents such as these did far more to convince people that the Soviet Union was a place run by liars and murderers than any exercise in Cold War propaganda could ever achieve. Nor had Americans any illusions that the Russians were open to reasoned argument. Thanks to the style of Russian negotiations the one Russian word which most Americans knew was *nyet*.

It was against this background of deep-seated suspicion of and hostility to the Soviet Union that the major Cold War policies need to be seen. No politician ever lost by taking a hard line toward the Soviets. Anti-Soviet policies expressed the people's will.

Early in 1946 Truman's military aide, Brigadier General Harry Vaughan, was hoping to help his alma mater, Westminster College, in Fulton, Missouri, by finding a big-name speaker. With the President's help the speaker he found was Winston Churchill. To make the occasion still more of an occasion, the President himself traveled to Fulton to sit on the platform while Churchill spoke. Churchill noted that an "Iron Curtain" had descended across Europe, "from Stettin on the Baltic Sea to Trieste on the Adriatic." And only an alliance of some kind between Britain and the United States would halt the creeping tide of Soviet expansion.

The effect of Churchill's speech was electrifying, and it gained added point when at almost exactly the same time the Canadian government announced the discovery of a Soviet spy network which had operated during the war and whose principal target had been the atomic bomb. What the West would not share, the Russians were prepared to steal if they could, even from an ally.

The Soviet Union was prepared to wage a twilight struggle against the West before the war ended. A week before Roosevelt died and several weeks before the German surrender, American Communists were shocked to be told that they had been following the wrong line. Earl Browder, who had led the CPUSA in an unconvincing show of wartime nationalism, was abruptly ejected, and William Z. Foster was dusted off and brought back as the head of the party. The old banners (inscribed "Class Struggle," "Boring from Within," and "Smash the Wall Street Imperialist War Mongers") were unfurled once more. And the new line, which appeared first in the French Communist journal *Cahiers du Communisme,* must almost certainly have been debated and written out at least a month before Roosevelt's death. So much for the presumed close personal relationship between Roosevelt and Stalin.

A wish persisted in some quarters to reach an accommodation with the Soviets. But it was impossible to establish a close, working relationship with a state which relied heavily on mass murder, slave labor, and systematic lying. The Western democracies were already badly compromised by handing over to the Russians three million people who had managed to escape from Soviet control during the war, either as prisoners or refugees. Hundreds of thousands returned willingly, unaware of what lay ahead of them. Some tens of thousands had fought for the Third Reich and any Allied government would have punished such people. Very large numbers, however, were unwilling to be returned and innocent of wrongdoing. In exchange, the West secured the release from the Russians of tens of thousands of Western Europeans, Britons, and Americans who had fallen into Russian hands. As a result of this exchange, millions of men, women, and children innocent of any crime were murdered, raped, or starved to death in slave labor camps. That was what accommodation with the Soviet Union involved from 1945 to 1947. To a government which ran its country as a charnel house, accommodation meant being permitted to conduct such operations without criticism or interference from outside. It was argued by many well-meaning people that what the Soviets did was their business and theirs alone. But part of the American responsibility, however dimly seen, was to try to bring into existence a world community. A community without a moral sense is a contradiction in terms.

American policy makers were under no illusions about the prospects of even moderate cooperation from the Soviet Union after the war. "I can testify," one high-ranking State Department official recalled, "that there was no time when the danger from the Soviet Union was not a topic of serious conversation among officers of the State Department; and by the winter of 1944–1945 as the day of victory approached, it became the predominant theme in Washington."

The overriding policy interest was to secure Western Europe against Soviet ambitions. But the way in which the war was fought made rational plans impossible. The Army and Navy fought the war much as they wished. As the armies and the fleets advanced, the politicians and the policy planners hurried along behind, trying to tidy things up. The results were predictably hopeless. The United States and Great Britain, for example, "chose Berlin, deep within the zone to be assigned to the Soviet Union, as the center of the Allied Control Authority for the whole of Germany, the city to be divided into national sectors. High school juniors with a history book, a map, and a set of toy soldiers could have devised a better arrangement," decided Herbert Feis.

The fate of Western Europe was more than a matter of cultural and moral congruity with American life. It possessed the largest pool of industrial skills and the largest industrial plant outside the United States. What the policy planners sought was the restoration of a balance of power in Europe as a whole. But there was no powerful Western European state left to counterbalance the postwar Soviet presence in Eastern Europe.

In mid-1946 the deputy chief of mission at the American Embassy in Moscow, George Kennan, transmitted a sixteen-page cable to Washington in which he tried to analyze Soviet behavior in a way that made planning possible. A revised version of the cable appeared in early 1947 in

Foreign Affairs under the title "The Sources of Soviet Conduct." It was signed, as if by an illiterate, with the letter *X*.

The identity of the author was soon widely known. The article was reprinted in *Life* and *Reader's Digest*. It sparked something very much like a serious national debate on the Cold War. Much of the appeal of the Kennan article lay in its combination of short-term caution with long-term optimism.

He saw Soviet power as a ruthless growth, inspired more by fear than by ambition, with deep roots in the blood-drenched Russian past. Its claims to political legitimacy were so fragile that in time it was more likely to decay than flourish. If the West, especially the United States, found a way to counterbalance the political threat posed by the current Soviet leadership, then changes within the Soviet Union might in time lead to a "mellowing" of the Soviet system, said Kennan.

The central idea in the X article was "containment." That is, the political power of the Soviet Union must be contained, and the peace preserved. It was an active verb for a passive policy; it struck the right note.

What Kennan intended was the limiting of Soviet political threats by political means. His suggestion was interpreted, however, as the containment of a military threat by military means. As Walter Lippmann saw, military containment was a snare and a delusion. It called for a prompt American response to every Soviet encroachment; this meant, inevitably, giving the Executive a blank check and slighting the restraints imposed by the Constitution. American strength, moreover, was most effective in the air and at sea. Were Russia an island a policy of military containment might work. But Russia was sprawled across a vast landmass. Any attempt to contain anything so big was likely to fail. "The Americans," wrote Lippmann, "would probably be frustrated by Mr. X's policy long before the Russians were." Such a containment policy would involve dozens of allies; this meant subsidizing puppet states, forcing alliances on wayward and impetuous governments, becoming involved with tribal factions, petty despots, and corrupt legislatures. Instead of concentrating American energies, such a policy would scatter them. Whatever American policy attempted at great cost to organize, the Russian at far less cost would be able to disrupt. Finally, argued Lippmann, a containment policy would make every state threatened by the Soviets as important as every other state so threatened; this would mean, for example, that Britain would be no more important than Burma, and Western Europe would be no more important than any other region under threat. Such a policy, originally aimed at securing Western Europe, would thus promptly lose sight of its purpose. Containment would become an end in itself.

Ironically, Kennan agreed with most of Lippmann's criticisms. But it was too late for regrets. Containment was elevated to a doctrine and became military containment. The United States began to draw a military line around the Soviet Union. Perhaps that would have occurred anyway. The X article conveniently justified attitudes already formed and events already in train.

While the article was being set in type for *Foreign Affairs*, the British government was preparing a message to the American government, informing Washington that Britain could no longer support the efforts of the Greek government in its war against Communist-armed and -led guerrillas.

The White House and the State Department hurriedly worked out a statement of policy, and it bore all the earmarks of ad hoccery. It was not a carefully considered weighing of interests and resources. It was little more than a speech aimed at winning a quick appropriation from the Republican-controlled 80th Congress. Although elevated since into one of the epochal policy declarations of the century, it was so hurriedly pasted together and had so attentive an eye to the present (and almost none to the long term) that the Truman Doctrine speech contained a deeply felt reference to the postwar poultry shortage.

Truman justified aid for Greece on the grounds that it was a democratic country under threat by Soviet-supported guerrillas. Turkey was not a democratic country, and he made no pretense that it was. But should Greece become a Soviet satellite like Bulgaria, the pressure on Turkey from Greece would become irresistible. Greece and Turkey were too closely involved with each other for the fate of the one to be kept separate from the fate of the other. If in pursuit of political stability one of them must be aided, common sense dictated that both must be aided.

Truman oversold the threat to Greece and exaggerated the response it required. But throughout the Cold War complex international political problems were reduced to comic-book terms, presumably to secure public support and Congressional action. It may have been that the people who made policy were themselves inclined at times to see the problems, and the solutions, in simplistic terms. At all events, public support for the Truman Doctrine was overwhelming.

The Communist threat to the Greek regime (headed by an unpopular monarchy) was defeated. But not by American aid. The closure of the frontier with Yugoslavia in 1948, when Tito broke with Stalin, robbed the guerillas of their only secure base camps.

But by this time the Truman Doctrine, with its promise of American aid to any government threatened by Communist subversion, had become in effect the holy of holies in American policy. "President Monroe's hands-off doctrine has been expanded by President Truman to encompass the globe," wrote Freda Kirchwey, almost as soon as Truman acted. It is doubtful that he began with any such intention. His aim was to defend Western Europe. But events and attitudes gave his words a broader meaning, and in time he came to believe that what he had in mind was the entire world, indeed.

During the debate over aid to Greece and Turkey Secretary of State George C. Marshall had returned deeply troubled from a tour of Western Europe. The physical and psychological desolation he had found called out for action, and Marshall was afraid that if the Administration did not do something soon, then Congress would. His opinion of Congressional intelligence was not very high.

Marshall instructed Kennan to produce a set of proposals for European recovery and gave him two weeks in which to do it. It was Kennan's turn to feel deeply troubled. He had been recalled to Washington largely on the strength of his brilliant cabled analysis. He had never exercised responsibility at this level before.

He collected a group of State Department officers of roughly the same age and rank as his own. He had no staff, little time, and half a dozen speaking engagements to fill in various parts of the country during the next two weeks; being a man of unflinching honor, he felt obliged to keep those engagements simply because he had given his word. The two weeks brought day-and-night conferences, hectic journeys to and fro, and Kennan, a sensitive man, was soon exhausted. At one all-night session he had to withdraw in order to regain his emotional balance. Weeping, he walked at midnight all around the State Department building in the dark.

Meanwhile, the Under Secretary of State, Dean Acheson, was combing the department for ideas to go into a speech he was to make on the President's behalf to the Delta Council in Mississippi. On a warm day in early May 1947 Acheson spoke to an audience of seemingly carefree picnickers sitting under the tree on the campus of Delta Teachers College. But they listened seriously and attentively, and Acheson asked them to consider the following: other countries needed to buy $16 billion worth of American goods to repair their economies, but had only $8 billion to spend. What, he asked, would happen to those countries, democracies like the United States, if they were denied the necessaries of life for want of ready cash?

A month later Marshall went to Harvard for the 296th Commencement exercise to receive, in company with J. Robert Oppenheimer and T. S. Eliot, an honorary degree and to make a speech.

Marshall had drawn on the work of Kennan's* group and others, mainly unheralded young men and women in the State, War, Navy, and Treasury departments. They were, and perhaps sensed that they were, lucky to live in exciting times and to have as their superiors men such as Marshall and Acheson, who were receptive to new ideas, whatever their source.

Marshall's address proposed assistance on a scale that was bigger by far than anything proposed before. Yet he made it sound so sensible that hardly anyone raised an eyebrow, at least, not in the United States. News of the Marshall speech set off rejoicing in Western European capitals and especially in Britain.

Even at this late date the Administration was reluctant to affront Russian feelings. With the aim of helping all Europe to recover, Marshall Plan assistance was offered to the Soviet Union and its satellites. The offer was made in sincerity and refused categorically. Formally known as the European Recovery Program (leftists said that the initials ERP really stood for

---

*Kennan's position was a good example of Sod's Law (which states that the bread never falls but on the buttered side). He was credited with the Truman Doctrine, most of which he considered unrealistic, and he was told by his critics that the Marshall speech, most of which he had written, was the kind of thing he should be working on instead.

"Erase the Russian Peril"), the Marshall Plan was an act of enlightened generosity. It was neither sentimental nor Machiavellian. And at a stroke it ended the dollar shortage which had hampered European recovery.

In order to make the best possible use of the billions of dollars ERP made available each year, the recipient countries formed the Organization for European Economic Cooperation. When the Marshall Plan came to an end in the 1950s, the OEEC had provided the groundwork for a new body, the European Economic Community.

That the Marshall Plan was put into effect by the 80th Congress was in large measure a reflection of the esteem in which Marshall was held. He possessed both simplicity of character and an imposing mien. Representatives and Senators tended to regard the President as a man cut from the same cloth as they. But Marshall was held in awe. His devotion to his country was self-evident. He was without vanity, beyond flattery, and unmoved by criticism but attentive to ideas. His abilities as an administrator were of the very highest order. His modesty was such that he refused to write any memoirs because he could not praise himself as memoirs at least tacitly require. When Marshall went to the Hill to argue the ERP case before the Senate Foreign Relations Committee, even the most willful members of that body, noted for its egoists, were on their best behavior. Marshall's character was such that it made other men decorous.

He was also fortunate that the Senate Foreign Relations Committee in the 80th Congress was chaired by Arthur Vandenberg of Michigan. Until recently Vandenberg had been a fervent isolationist. He was liked by many Democrats and admired by most Republicans. He enjoyed nothing so much as helping people reconcile their differences. He had the gift of complete sincerity, even when contradicting himself. For amusement, he wrote short stories, publishing more than 100 of them in various magazines; they were usually about idealistic, heroic youth in conflict with millionaires or unscrupulous politicians. The war and the bomb had made him an internationalist. No Democratic Senator could have done as much for Truman's foreign policy as Vandenberg did. Vandenberg did not make foreign policy bipartisan; the weight of opinion, the pressure of events, and the anti-Soviet nature of the policy were probably more important. But Vandenberg put the matter beyond doubt, speeded actions the White House considered pressing, and relieved policy makers of the frustrations which inevitably occur when the Executive and the Legislative branches are in disagreement.

The Republicans were aware that to have denied Truman's foreign policy outright would have led to slaughter for them at the polls in 1948, for every Communist success would then have been laid at their doorstep and no other. And every month seemed to bring a foreign policy crisis somewhere in the world.

The year 1948 brought the prospect of a Communist coup in Italy. Tensions rose in Berlin, and on March 5 General Lucius D. Clay sent the President a cable which said that war might break out at any moment. There was a crisis in Czechoslovakia. The Communist International had been revived, but was now called the Cominform, dedicated to resisting "dollar imperialism" and Socialism in Western Europe. There was knowing talk these days about shaking the mothballs out of the old uniforms hung in the closet. More than a few people were evidently tempted by the thought of having a showdown with the Russians and destroying their war-making power once and for all.

The President went to Congress to ask for a peacetime draft and for universal military service. "Not since the fateful days of 1939," one journal noted, "had Washington experienced the sense of urgency that gripped it last week."

In April the Czech government was toppled by a coup from within when the Communists, who held a minority of Cabinet posts, seized power from the non-Communist majority. Americans had believed, mistakenly, that since the war the Czechs had enjoyed a free and democratic government. The limitations on its freedom became tragically obvious when the Communists refused to accept majority decisions. And when the majority began to express interest in the offer of Marshall Plan aid, they were ousted.

Hard on the heels of the Czech coup the Soviets denied land access to Berlin to the other occupying powers, ostensibly over a currency reform planned for the city, but obviously to try to force the United States, Britain, and France to abandon Berlin to them. A Berlin airlift was hastily patched together and set in motion.

To repair American military strength to meet the challenges posed by the world's principal land power, Truman stepped up the calls he had been making since 1945 for Universal Military Training. The idea was to give every youth a year of military training either when he graduated from high school or when he reached eighteen. UMT was popular with the public, the press, and the military, but unpopular with Senator Taft, who, as head of the Republican majority policy committee, decided which bills reached the Senate floor. Taft considered UMT militarism, and in principle he was right. Not everyone else liked the idea, either. Some 500 young men in Boston, San Francisco, New York, and Los Angeles burned their draft cards in protest against the UMT proposal and sent the ashes to the President.

In the meantime, the Army made the best it could of what remained of the wartime draft law, which Congress was willing to extend, but it attempted to placate American mothers by exempting men under the age of twenty-one. The result was a draftless draft. In Philadelphia one day in 1947 ten Selective Service doctors, a psychiatrist, and seventy other Army and Selective Service workers carefully examined the day's draft intake from sixteen counties of eastern Pennsylvania. That is, they examined one freckle-faced twenty-one-year old, Edward Francis Mooney. Los Angeles, which had a monthly quota of 790 men, one month found only 170. Denver's quota was seventy-nine men a month; it found only four. Congress had forgotten that the overwhelming majority of draftees under the 1940 Draft Act had been teenagers. The Army fell 20 percent below its authorized strength.

In 1948, with UMT as far away as ever, the Administration turned its efforts to passing a new draft law. In the background, "The dreadful word 'war' has come back into the vocabulary of American leaders," wrote a well-informed journalist. "Secretary Marshall is saying grimmer things off the record than on." In June the 1948 Selective Service Act became law. It raised the authorized active-duty strength of the military to 2 million.

Registration under the new act was expected to bring an outbreak of protest demonstrations. Almost no one protested. Resistance was negligible. And with the act on the statute books, Selective Service officials did the President a favor; they did not draft anyone until after the November election.

Among the host of responsibilities which crowded upon the United States was one of the saddest of all problems, that of Europe's displaced persons. Even after three million people had been handed over to the tender mercies of Stalin, there were millions more who had to be provided for.

It was possible to help large numbers trace friends and relatives. In most such cases it was possible to get them out of DP camps within a year or two of the war's ending. But nearly 1 million were still in camps in Germany in 1947, supported by the United States. The camps could not be disbanded because Germany was still struggling to absorb millions of refugees of German origin driven out of Czechoslovakia, Poland, and Hungary. The only feasible solution was to settle the DPs outside Germany. The most logical place to settle them was in the United States.

Since 1939 as many as 150,000 European refugees had made their way to Cuba in the often vain hope that from there they would find a way into the United States. Thousands attempted to smuggle themselves into ports from Charleston to New Orleans. Most were foiled.

The Administration's answer to the DP problem was to assign half the places on the annual immigration quota to DPs. This was popular but inadequate; and the inadequacy was probably the reason for the popularity. It admitted only a comparative handful into the United States. The problem remained pressing.

Truman established yet another Presidential committee, on Immigration and Naturalization. Its report deplored the racism inherent in a quota system based on national origins; it called for a larger entry of immigrants, on the basis of their skills and family ties; it recommended the entry of 300,000 DPs outside the established quotas. Truman accepted the report's recommendations. But Congress passed the Displaced Persons Act of 1948.

This was a measure Truman signed with manifest reluctance, calling for its speedy revision even as he signed it into law. By various devices it excluded Jews. It charged the DPs against the quotas of their country of origin. Each DP needed a security clearance and the offer of a job before being admitted. This legislation, ostensibly to assist the resettlement of refugees, kept them out. In the first year of the 1948 act's operation a total of 2,507 DPs entered the United States under its provisions.

The DP question was integral with the resettlement of the Jewish survivors of the Nazi Holocaust. Americans agonized so volubly over the fate of the Jews that Europeans wondered why the United States did not settle the problem directly by admitting them *en masse*. The unpleasant truth was, most Americans did not want them. Only 1 person in 100 favored unrestricted Jewish immigration. The solution to the Jewish problem, almost everyone agreed, was the creation of a Jewish homeland—but somewhere else, preferably in the Middle East.

In recent years anti-Semitism had become discreet rather than overt. During the war there had been a rise in anti-Semitism, but after the revelation of the Nazi death camps it became fashionable to be nice to Jews. In 1948 half a dozen anti-anti-Semitic novels appeared, and one, *Gentleman's Agreement* by Laura V. Hobson, although dull and ineptly written, was successful as both book and film. But a residue of anti-Jewish sentiment remained. Some of it doubtless found expression as anti-Communism. Jews, steeped as they were in European Socialism and alert as they were to questions of social justice, were heavily involved all along the left of the political spectrum.

The overall picture had changed to such an extent that the president of Dartmouth admitted that his college set a limit on the number of Jewish students it would accept. He justified it on the ground that a large Jewish presence would provoke anti-Semitic feelings. Dartmouth was not unique in operating a *numerus clausus*; it was unique only in having a president willing to talk about it.

Jewish quotas did not involve anything so crude as asking an applicant outright, "Are you Jewish?" Instead, he would be asked for a photograph, his mother's maiden name, and his father's birthplace, none of which even remotely involved his intellectual ability.

It was not only Ivy League colleges which restricted the number of Jewish entrants. There were few Jewish nurses, schoolteachers, or architects. And during the 1940s it seems likely that restrictions on the number of Jews in professional schools increased rather than decreased. Even so, the United States was becoming increasingly sensitive to all matters involving Jews.

Following the Holocaust, the 5 million American Jews constituted nearly half the world's Jewish population. To most of them, as to most other Americans, the answer to the problem posed by the survivors of the Nazi era was the creation of a Jewish state in Palestine.

When the war ended, 600,000 Jews were already living in Palestine. There were also 1 million Moslems and a sizable Christian community. Although they were one-third of the population, the Jews in Palestine owned only 7 percent of the land. The object of American Jewry during between 1945 and 1948 was to turn this minority position into a Jewish state by whatever means necessary.

They already possessed strong moral leverage on the United States government. The Balfour Declaration of 1917, which "looked with favour" on the creation of "a Jewish national home in Palestine," was concurred in by the Arab powers and the United States. But the Balfour Declaration also stated that this looking with favor was with the understanding that the rights of the Palestinians would not be infringed.

Woodrow Wilson in 1919 declared American support for a Jewish homeland. In 1922 Congress adopted a resolution calling for the establishment of one, without a dissenting vote being cast. Both major party platforms in 1944 had contained planks supporting a Jewish homeland in Palestine.

The number of Jews entering Palestine was meanwhile rising sharply. The British, bound by their moral obligations to the Arabs and by their economic necessity for Middle Eastern oil, attempted to restrict the inflow of Jews. In the wake of such outrages as Belsen and Auschwitz any attempt to interfere with what Jews did or did not do was bound to create a furore. The British found themselves in an impossible position.

An Anglo-American committee issued a report saying that of the 500,000 European Jews waiting to enter Palestine at least 100,000 should be accepted at once. The British government declined to accept this suggestion. And it reduced the number of visas granted each month for entry into Palestine.

To American Jewry this was a policy so base that it justified almost any response, including terrorism. Money, arms, and moral support flowed to a variety of Zionist bodies, from the moderate and pacific to the immoderate and violent. Americans, Jew or Gentile, in 1947 followed with avid interest the journey of *Exodus 1947*. Formerly an old Chesapeake Bay steamer, the *President Garfield*, she sailed from Baltimore in January on behalf of the Haganah and under the command of a young man from Cincinnati, twenty-four-year-old Bernie Marks. Most of the crew were American Jews. *Exodus 1947* picked up 4,500 European Jews and attempted to land them in Palestine. The British forced the vessel to sail back to Germany and forcibly removed the kicking, screaming passengers.

The creation of a Jewish state in Palestine was simply impossible without dispossessing the Palestinians; few were much troubled by that. Arabs were considered to combine the vices of indolence with those of Fascism. It had not been long since photographs of Arab soldiers showed them in German uniforms. The Wehrmacht had contained an Arab Legion. Arabs had been numbered among the Waffen SS. The Grand Mufti of Jerusalem had declared (presumably to the Führer's surprise) that Hitler was "a direct descendant of the Prophet." The British had been obliged to put down a pro-Axis revolt in Iraq. Taking some of the most repellent characteristics of Hitler's Germany, the Arabs appeared to have shunned the few good points, such as industriousness and an interest in sanitation. A typical cartoon expressed the popular view of Arabs and Israelis: it showed an Arab squatting in the middle of a desert called PALESTINE, while standing over him was an energetic young Jew carrying plans marked "Irrigation to make the desert bloom." The Jew gestured in frustration at the lone and level sands stretching far away, and the caption below the squatting Arab read: "He prefers sandcastles."

People who were normally concerned with justice and decency became morally callous. When the King David Hotel was blown up in Jerusalem, killing ninety-one people—Arabs, British, and Jews alike—hardly a voice was raised in protest. When 376 Arabs, mainly women, children, and sick old men, were murdered in cold blood at the village of Deir Yassin, hardly a word about it appeared in the American press. When Arab families fled their homes in terror and Jewish families moved in, this was described in a leading liberal publication as "fitting and just." People who believed themselves true lovers of democracy were for once opposed to the rule of the majority, because the majority in Palestine were Arabs, not Jews. Such was the spirit of the times that even Eleanor Roosevelt's high principles cracked. No Zionist, she was nonetheless deeply moved by the plight of European Jewry. To protests that the creation by force of a Jewish state would be unjust to the Palestinians she replied loftily that having the go-ahead Jews in charge would do the Palestinians good and airily dismissed the protests of the Palestinians with, "We do not always like what is good for us in this world."

Although the President was personally in favor of a Jewish state, the objections of the State and War departments gave him pause. But his partner in a failed haberdashery, Eddie Jacobson, prevailed on him to meet with Chaim Weizmann. When the meeting ended, Truman said, "You can bank on us." Shortly afterward he met with the Chief Rabbi of Israel, who told him, "God put you into your mother's womb so that you could be the instrument to bring about the rebirth of Israel after two thousand years." Truman, a man with a deeply emotional nature, a man who had read the entire Bible twice, a man whose deep interest in history made the past as real as the present in his imagination, burst into tears.

In May 1948 Israel came into existence, under fire. Within minutes of the Israeli declaration of statehood the new state was recognized by the United States. Americans took the survival of Israel so much to heart and warmed so strongly to the Israelis as people cut in the pioneering, resourceful mold of their own ancestors that the creation of Israel did not settle the Jewish question at all. Instead, it became a permanent element in American politics.

Isolationism had become a museum piece, as remote from the present day as a collection of dinosaur bones. Americans were proud of their eminence on the world stage. Anti-Communist internationalism carried all before it. And it was just as nationalistic in its way as the old isolationism had been. Some doughty souls persisted in spreading the gospel of world government, but most regarded them as cranks and eccentrics, if not Communists. An ex-GI named Garry Davis, the son of an eminent bandleader, became a folk hero in France, addressing vast rallies at which he renounced his American citizenship and declared himself "A Citizen of the World." He popped up unannounced and uninvited at meetings of the UN, to demand formal recognition of his new citizenship. Most advocates of world government preferred to tread a less idiosyncratic path to reach it.

In 1947 a variety of world government organizations met in Asheville,

North Carolina, and quickly fell into hot dispute. But they were sufficiently reconciled in the end to form the United World Federalists. It had some 40,000 members and 650 chapters and sincerely believed that world government was an idea whose time had come. After all, since 1940 twenty-three state legislatures had passed resolutions in favor of world government. But this was mere pietism. There really was no serious, widespread desire for world government among the richest, most powerful people in the world. The UWF and its like fatally underestimated the St. Augustine syndrome.*

The publications of Henry Luce were much closer to the sentiments which moved the bulk of Americans who took the country's responsibilities seriously. (Liberal intellectuals and conservatives, whether intellectuals or not, tend to assume that they are the only people who take such matters seriously. While there is a grain of truth in this, there is no more than a grain). They attempted to educate a nation which was prepared to be educated. *Life* ran a lavishly illustrated, ponderously worded series on Western civilization for much of 1947, so that Americans might better understand the priceless social, cultural, and political heritage now in their care. *Time* became so concerned with the United States' image as defender of truth and beauty that it was at one point reduced to grumbling about stamps. "What," *Time* demanded to know, "or who, makes them so ugly?"

It seemed the most natural thing in the world for George Marshall to tell a graduating class at Princeton that if they wished to understand the nature of the present challenge, they should read Thucydides' *History of the Peloponnesian War.* James Burnham had a similar view, yet doubted that the young Americans he met these days were capable of taking their place in history alongside the Athenians of the fifth century B.C.

The desire to understand and to live up to the historical challenge the United States faced made a popular success of six obscure and densely printed volumes from the 1930s, Arnold Toynbee's *A Study of History.* Rediscovered and reprinted in 1947, they were the fourth best-selling book of the year, with sales of 200,000 copies. A one-volume abridgment appeared the next year. It was also a best-seller.

What Toynbee offered was not narrative history but a synthesis which reached out to encompass religion, philosophy, and sociology in the study of twenty-six civilizations. These twenty-six, he claimed, were all that there had ever been. But his definitions were so obscure and so elastic that he could pick and choose much as he liked. What made Toynbee unique among modern historians was that he brought God into his conception of history as an agent of historical change. He offered less a theory of history than a faith, in both humanity and the divine.

---

*St. Augustine, when still comparatively young and leading a life of pleasure and debauchery, was offered the opportunity to repent, change his way of living, and be saved. He liked the idea of salvation and was willing to be saved. But, he prayed, "Not yet, Lord; not yet."

Toynbee became a celebrity. His face peered out from the cover of *Time*. His lecture tour of the United States was a triumph; he was received by rapturous crowds wherever he spoke.

The hope which stirred such people was that in defending the civilization of the West, the United States would itself become one of the great civilizations, entitled to a place alongside the other twenty-six or however many there were, with "Made in the U.S.A." stamped clearly upon it. It was a nationalistic, at times parochial, desire, yet it was no mean or ignoble thing because there was no wish to build the United States up by bringing other nations low.

6
Red Pawns, White Knights

To be a Communist shortly before and after the war called for a combination of personal traits involving both arrogance and humility, calculation and recklessness, cunning and fervor, not required by any ordinary political party. It is not surprising that many people looked on Communists as exotics and held them in both contempt and awe.

The Party relied heavily on deception, but it deceived almost no one except its own members. The turnover of membership was always remarkably high. Every twist and turn in the Party line shook out hundreds, sometimes thousands, of adherents. Party members had few illusions about the hostility the nation at large felt toward them. In the postwar right-wing journalists would insist that to be an anti-Stalinist between 1936 and 1946 "was to court social ostracism." Nothing was farther from the truth. Even at the height of the Popular Front CP members went under assumed names, met clandestinely, learned how to cover their tracks and to avoid drawing attention to themselves. Communist Party members behaved furtively because they believed that it was necessary; some may have overdone it on occasion out of a weakness for melodrama.

The wartime U.S.-Soviet alliance had not brought any fundamental change in the popular temper. When the war ended, two-thirds of the public were convinced that American Communists were loyal not to the United States but to the Kremlin. Nearly 70 percent wanted the Communist Party to be banned.

The popular view of Communists and Communism tended to be the stuff of cheap novels; it was accurately caught in one of the best-selling works of the era, Mickey Spillane's *One Lonely Night:* "Some of them even looked like Commies . . . sharp eyes that darted from side to side, too-wise women dazzled by some meager sense of responsibility, smirking students who wore their hair long, tucked behind their heads." His answer to the Red menace was: "Don't arrest them, don't treat them with the dignity of the democratic process of courts of law . . . do the same thing that they'd do to you! Treat 'em to the inglorious taste of sudden death. . . . Kill, kill, kill, kill!" Millions of people evidently liked this approach, because *One Lonely Night* sold 7 million copies.

Most people actually knew very little about the Communist Party, what it did and what its members were like, except for the few who had darting eyes and long hair. The Party was never as monolithic as outsiders assumed. "Leninist discipline was an ideal rather than an achievement," recalled Granville Hicks, after he had left the CP, "what the party would like to be true rather than what is true." But the structure was such that all important matters remained in the hands of full-time, paid officials, who were usually well removed from the sentiments and concerns of ordinary dues-paying members.

While it pretended to be avidly devoted to "Americanism," the chief issue to excite the CP's attention was no domestic question but foreign policy. And to the Communists the principal foreign policy problem was the security of the Soviet Union. Party members found that on domestic matters there was something resembling freedom of expression; on foreign affairs there was no such thing.

Under Earl Browder the Party was soft on capitalism, to coin a phrase. In early 1945 the Party was supporting UMT. And this was the moment when membership reached its peak, approaching 80,000. Then appeared the letter from Jacques Duclos to *Cahiers du Communisme*, and disaster followed. American Communists believed, rightly, that so important a letter would not have been published in so important a Communist journal without Moscow's approval. But to believe that it was a concealed instruction to get rid of Browder and resume the class struggle was probably to exaggerate the importance of the American CP in the Kremlin's thinking.

The Communist Party of the United States was plunged into round-the-clock meetings. When Browder appeared at the next meeting of the National Committee in New York, he was treated like a pariah—no one greeted him, no one sat next to him, and no one stood as all had stood until recently to greet his entrance by singing "Browder is our leader, we shall not be moved." In 1946 he was expelled from the Party.

The post-Duclos letter upheaval drove up to 30,000 members out of the CPUSA. But a successful recruiting drive made good most of this loss during the next twelve months. Party membership had always been something of a revolving door. Although it had never had as many as 100,000 members at a given time, in its first thirty years of existence 700,000 people had joined the CPUSA, and left it.

During its recruiting drive in 1946–47 it tried to identify with ordinary people by becoming involved in the housing shortage: when people were evicted from their homes, tough young Communists would show up to move them, and their furniture, back in again. Getting closer to the folk, Party members took up folk singing and square dancing. They wore plaid shirts and peasant blouses. Guitar playing was elevated to a revolutionary activity and was taught at Party schools.

While the recruiting drive met with some success, the attempt to act on the Duclos letter by reviving the class war was less successful. Liberal bodies were no longer the soft targets they had once been. During the war American liberals had recovered much of the ordinary patriotic sentiment which it had been fashionable to eschew in the 1930s. They were also alert to Communist tactics, which were no longer novel. When the CPUSA revived the class war, alarm bells sounded all along the left.

Late in 1946 a conference of progressives attempted in Chicago to devise a formula which might link all liberals in united action, whether they were personally antagonistic toward Communism or not. It was soon evident that this was impossible. The pro-Communist faction split away, to form the Progressive Citizens of America. The anti-Communist faction in January 1947 formed the Americans for Democratic Action. The formation of the ADA was an important event because it marked the irreversible transition of the non-Communist left into the anti-Communist left, a development in the making since the Hitler-Stalin pact of 1939 but one held in abeyance by the war. It showed, moreover, that an entire generation of 1930s radicals had come to terms with the Cold War. As one of them concluded, "Since the imperfect tyranny of the West is clearly a lesser evil than the perfected tyranny of the Communists, we have chosen the West." Finally, liberalism, traditionally radical and to the left of center, moved toward the political center and became markedly less critical of the established order and usually supportive of it.

A liberal orthodoxy soon developed regarding foreign policy. It was not necessary to like a foreign government (e.g., Franco's Spain, Perón's Argentina) in order to work with it to create a more stable world; containment was no threat to legitimate Soviet security interests; the alternative to economic and political intervention in another country's affairs was military intervention, and that being so, the former was better than the latter. It was an orthodoxy which extended to the State Department, "and the cryptic designation 'NCL' (for Non-Communist Left) was constantly used in inner State Department circles."

Throughout 1947 the nation went on the offensive against domestic Communism. The rise in CP membership was abruptly halted and thereafter went into steep decline. "The long slow ebb of the American Communist Party had begun."

The most devasting defeat came in the one place where the Communists had gained a serious lodgment, in the unions. Between one-fourth and one-fifth of all CIO members were in unions under Communist influence or control. The CIO's national staff was liberally sprinkled with CP members or sympathizers, and some important state and local CIO councils were under Communist control.

The president of the CIO, Philip Murray, was both a devout Catholic and an unshakable anti-Communist. He tolerated the Communist presence within the CIO for two reasons: first, he was a genuine democrat—if a union freely chose Communist leaders, it had that right; second, a purge might wreck the CIO, leaving the pieces to be scooped up by the AF of L.

But by 1946 Murray's patience and caution were coming to an end. Events were also slipping beyond his control. Anti-Communists were becoming eager to oust the Communists; Communists were at the same time struggling to extend their influence. They attempted to control every union they had penetrated. It was a strategy of all-or-nothing, pressed from a position of comparative weakness. The Communists tried, moreover, to break the CIO's links with the Democratic Party, in the unrealistic hope of swinging much of organized labor behind a third party in 1948. When some Communist union members tried to point out to CP organizers that what they were attempting was impossible they were ignored or forced out of the Party.

No one knew more about Communist tactics than union leaders, who had seen them at close hand for twenty years or more. As a result, once a union decided to purge itself, there was little wasted time or effort. Where effective anti-Communism was concerned, organized labor was vastly more capable than the FBI or the American Legion.

The rank and file had never been responsive to Communist appeals anyway. Unions which failed to expel their Communist or pro-Communist leaders lost their members in droves; that is what happened to the biggest union the Communists ever controlled, the United Electrical, Radio and Machine Workers, whose membership dropped from 500,000 in 1945 to 80,000 four years later. Unions which openly refused to rid themselves of their Communist mentors were expelled from the CIO.

The anti-Communist purge was bitter, not least because those who led it were often men whom the Communists had humiliated in the recent past. Many an old score was being settled.

With the election of the 80th Congress the House Un-American Activites Committee bestirred itself. It acquired a new chief investigator, Robert Stripling, and a new chairman, J. Parnell Thomas. Thomas was a self-made man: born John P. Feeney, he changed his name (adding Parnell, however, so as to hang onto the Irish vote); long a Democrat, he became a Republican; reared a Catholic, he became an Episcopalian. A small man, he elevated himself at committee hearings by sitting on a cushion covered with red silk, which was placed on top of a telephone book. Stripling was an energetic ex-FBI agent who in later life would go on to become rich in the oil business in Midland, Texas.

HUAC enjoyed such overwhelming public support that the rest of Congress left it to its own devices. HUAC appropriation requests were nearly always granted in full. In 1946 the committee was granted the power to subpoena witnesses,* a power unprecedented for a House committee.

*HUAC's subpoenas were printed on pink paper.

Ostensibly, HUAC's various hearings and other activities were undertaken with an eye to proposing legislation. Its chief objective was to see the Communist Pary declared illegal. The committee viewed the Party as a criminal conspiracy, and its hearings were conducted mainly to prove that.

Yet its proposed legislation was strangely cautious. The first Mundt-Nixon bill did not declare the Communist Party illegal but instead required that the agents of foreign dictatorships would have to register with Federal authorities.

Many HUAC hearings, whether by accident or design, elicited no new material on Communist activities but instead amounted to exercises in browbeating and harassment. HUAC was to leave in its wake a trail littered with broken careers, wrecked families, and suicides. Yet most committee members sincerely believed that no honest, loyal person could be harmed by the committee's inquiries. And while they displayed an astonishing naïveté in regard to Communism, and the modern world in general, as Eric Bentley has remarked, it would be "mistaken to write off the Committee as merely gauche, let alone stupid; they were masters of a certain kind of showmanship and public relations."

John Rankin, Thomas's predecessor, had been eager to investigate Hollywood partly, it seems, because like many other people he was troubled by that bogey of the 1930s, "propaganda," and partly because of the prevalence of Jews in the film business. Communism was, in Rankin's mind, older than Christianity and Jewish in origin. Communists, he claimed, had crucified Christ, "then gambled for his garments at the foot of the Cross." But it was not until 1947, with Thomas in the chair, that HUAC opened its hearings on Communism in Hollywood.

HUAC repeatedly claimed to possess a list of "Communist pictures." This fascinating compilation was never published. The most flagrantly pro-Soviet film made in Hollywood in recent years proved to be *Mission to Moscow*, but it was produced by Warner studios, the most right-wing lot in Hollywood. For years Jack L. Warner had employed a full-time investigator to check on the patriotism of his employees. Everyone who worked for him had to have what amounted to a private security clearance. Warner groveled at HUAC's feet and claimed that the wicked Roosevelt Administration had forced him to produce *Mission to Moscow*, a contention refuted by the evidence; Warner was obliged to revise his story. The problem, Warner explained, was that pro-Soviet propaganda was fiendishly subtle. Why, "you have to take eight or ten Harvard law courses to find out what they mean."

Certainly Warner failed to spot the pro-Soviet reference smuggled into *Action in the North Atlantic* by John Howard Lawson.* Two seamen

---

*The most famous line in a Lawson film script was delivered by Pepe Le Moko in *Algiers*, starring Hedy Lamarr and Charles Boyer. But it was seductive, not subversive: "Come with me to the Casbah." The only other noted line by a leftist scenarist was Clifford Odets's "We could make beautiful music together," from *The General Died at Dawn*.

were shown on deck when an approaching aircraft was heard. One seaman said, "It's ours!" The second seaman demurred: "Famous last words." The first seaman pointed upward. "It's one of ours all right." Close-up of airplane—decorated with the red star insignia of the Soviet Air Force.

Ayn Rand was not so easily fooled. She informed the committee that *Song of Russia*, starring the volubly antileftist Robert Taylor, was filled with propaganda. Miss Rand, a Russian émigré, pointed out that *Song of Russia* contained appalling scenes of happy peasants and neat, clean cottages.

Hollywood Communists did try to put pro-Communist references into their films. But the results were hardly a credit to grown men. There was, for example, a character actor of left-wing views who one evening arrived at a friend's house out of breath and exultant. "By golly, I got away with it!" he said triumphantly. He explained to his friend that during shooting of a particular scene he was required to wait for an elevator. "So I press the button and there is a pause and the director says, 'Whistle something and fill in.' So I whistled four bars from *The Internationale!*"

The Communist and leftist scriptwriters proved, in the event, to be no more capable of writing effective propaganda than of writing great films. And it was notable that despite their supposed proletarian sympathies, the working class almost never appeared in their films except to provide comic relief. Working people were not taken seriously in Hollywood until the 1950s, and then they were considered of interest only when they were involved with gangsters.

HUAC's Hollywood hearings divided witnesses into the "friendly" and the "unfriendly." Altogether, nineteen unfriendly witnesses were scheduled to be called, but only eleven were, and of these one, Bertolt Brecht (the sole great talent on HUAC's list), soon left the country. Which left ten.

The Hollywood Ten defied the committee. Being men of words, they were more than a match for the blustering Thomas, who was reduced to impotent gaveling. The committee abandoned the hearings with sixty-eight subpoenaed witnesses waiting to be called. Because the committee was taking a beating in the press, it broke and ran for cover.

The committee was always sensitive where its public standing was concerned. It hung on its own press clippings: this suggests something about why it devoted so much attention to show business. Had it been more seriously concerned with uncovering Communist activities, there were far more promising places to look for it, such as in the labor unions. Its predecessor, the Dies Committee, had betrayed the same proclivity—its first hearing had been on the Federal Theater Project.

Despite losing the public relations battle, HUAC won the legal struggle which followed. The ten scriptwriters based their defense on the First Amendment, arguing that the committee had no right to inquire into their political beliefs. Thomas used to refer lovingly to what he called "the $64 question," which rolled with practiced ease from Stripling's lips all in one

piece:"AreyounoworhaveyoueverbeenamemberoftheCommunistParty?"
The ten claimed that this was no one's proper business but their own.
Congress disagreed. By a vote of 346–17 the House cited all ten for contempt. Following their conviction in a Federal court, the Supreme Court
refused to review their cases.

Meanwhile, a Federal grand jury in New York sitting in New York had
listened to the testimony of Elizabeth Bentley, former mistress of a Soviet agent, one Jacob Golos (which may not have been his real name). During the war Miss Bentley had acted as a courier for her short, fat, balding
Russian lover. Shortly after his death in 1945, Bentley realized that without Golos she was of no evident interest to the Communist Party. From
what were evidently very mixed reasons she visited the FBI. For the next
eighteen months she remained in touch with both the Party and the Federal authorities.

The grand jury hearing lasted from the spring of 1947 to the spring of
1948. Rumors hinting at sensational revelations circulated in Washington
and New York. Then, in June 1948, the grand jury handed down an indictment which merely charged the CPUSA with conspiracy, dating the conspiracy from the renewal of the class struggle following the appearance of
the Duclos letter.

Miss Bentley was deeply offended that the product of her mountain of
testimony should be this unpromising mouse of a charge. She turned to
the press and politicians to ventilate her grievance and to recite her story
once more. The Senate Investigating Committee promptly invited her to
testify.

HUAC was jealous of its standing, taking a decidedly possessive attitude toward revelations of Communist mischief-making. Miss Bentley
and her accusations against a young economist in the Department of
Commerce, William Remington, were exactly what HUAC considered its
own raw materials. She was subpoenaed to appear before the committee.
Another figure who had testified before the grand jury in New York was
Whittaker Chambers. HUAC subpoenaed him also.

Miss Bentley was the object of intensive attention, portrayed in the
press as a glamorous blonde, the queen of spies, alluring and mysterious.
She turned out to be a chinless bespectacled brunette with no more talent
for secret intrigue than a cuckoo. In her years as a spy she had done little
more than fetch and carry. Yet as her story unfolded, it was interesting to
see how her role in events grew with the retelling.

The gist of her story was that during the war she had helped Golos, who
worked for the Soviet trade mission, to establish various spy networks in
Washington. The most important of these was, she said with a straight
face, in the Department of Agriculture. But among those caught in Golos'
web was the Assistant Secretary of the Treasury, Harry Dexter White. "I
was able through Harry Dexter White to arrange that the United States
Treasury Department turn over the actual printing plates [for currency in
occupied areas] to the Russians!" she boasted.

She named forty-two other people employed by the government as Soviet agents. But nearly all proved on examination to be people she had never met, and it appears that she never met White. Yet she began referring to the people she named in familiar terms, suggesting that she knew them well, such as William Taylor at the Treasury. For the next two years he struggled, at considerable cost, to get her to confront him in court and repeat her charges. When the question was finally put to her under oath whether she had ever met William Taylor at the time she claimed he was a Soviet agent, Miss Bentley answered, "No."

Her most serious charges were leveled against William Remington, and he admitted that he had met her and spoken with her. But, he maintained, she had been introduced to him under another name and on the understanding that she was a journalist. The information he had given her was material he would have given any reporter, he said. Miss Bentley claimed she had collected Remington's party dues; on the contrary, said Remington, it was money he gave her because she said she was collecting for a fund to aid refugees from Nazi persecution. As a result of Miss Bentley's claims, Remington was suspended from his job while his loyalty was investigated.

She repeated her accusations on the radio. Remington sued her for libel. The Loyalty Review Board, which had no power to issue subpoenas, invited her to appear and substantiate her accusations. She declined the offer. Remington was cleared of disloyalty. The libel suit was settled out of court for $9,000.

The Senate Investigating Committee, deprived of Miss Bentley's testimony by HUAC's speedy action, had to content itself with questioning Louis Budenz, who had been managing editor of the *Daily Worker* for ten years. Budenz was among the 20,000 to 30,000 Communists who left the Party during the post-Duclos purge of the Browderites. But he fared better than the average lapsed Communist: two days after his break with the Party he was appointed a full professor (of economics and journalism) at Notre Dame. Much of what he had to say was little more than a repetition of Miss Bentley's well-aired accusations before HUAC.

On August 3, 1948, Whittaker Chambers appeared in response to the subpoena served on him. Chambers was a senior editor at *Time* and had written much of the *Life* series on Western civilization. For years he had been regaling his friends and acquaintances with stories about his life in the Communist underground. In 1939 he had told A. A. Berle, Jr., then an Assistant Secretary of State, about Communists and Communist sympathizers he knew or knew of in various government departments. During the war he had told the FBI. Recently he had told the grand jury in New York. Now he was about to tell HUAC. But this time he would be taken seriously.

At first, however, he appeared—like Miss Bentley—unable to live up to the advance publicity (mainly rumor). He dressed carelessly. He was short and overweight, and he spoke in a monotone. The Communists he described sounded like one more Marxist study group of a type known about in Washington in the 1930s and considered harmless. He had said nothing about espionage to Berle back in 1939. He said nothing about espionage to HUAC. The committee, the press, and the spectators at the hearing were soon bored with Chambers's recital.*

But in passing he corroborated Miss Bentley's accusations against Harry Dexter White. White demanded to be heard. Ten days after Chambers's appearance he denied before the committee both Miss Bentley's accusations and Chambers's supporting testimony. His Keynesian economic views, however, were enough to make him an object of suspicion to conservative Congressmen. White concluded his testimony having done little to clear his name so far as the committee was concerned. Three days later White died.

Following Chambers's appearance, a Baltimore newspaperman called one of the people Chambers had named as a member of the Communist network in Washington during the 1930s, a man who had risen far since then, Alger Hiss, currently president of the Carnegie Endowment in New York. Hiss promptly asked HUAC for an opportunity to rebut Chambers's accusations.

Hiss had traveled to Yalta with Roosevelt. In 1945 he had organized the UN's charter writing conference in San Francisco. He was not exactly famous, but not quite obscure.† His impeccable dress, erect bearing, precise and emphatic speech, noble head, and blonde good looks bespoke a man of unusual natural dignity and remarkable intelligence. At his first appearance he overawed the normally taciturn members of HUAC. Sensing another public relations disaster, all the committee members, except one, hurried to shake his hand after Hiss finished denying Chambers's accusations. The committee was prepared to let the matter drop. All but one.

The laggard, who refused to shake Hiss's hand, was Richard Nixon. Hiss had asked to confront Chambers to his face. Nixon and Stripling persuaded the committee to grant Hiss's wish—but it was done out of the public's gaze, in a hotel room in New York. The confrontation was like an episode from a Feydeau farce, with Hiss asking to be allowed to look into Chamber's mouth to see whether he could recognize him by his teeth. Hiss eventually admitted having known Chambers—but as one George Crossley, a free-lance journalist and brazen moocher. Hiss continued to deny that he had ever been a Communist.

In public session before the committee Chambers repeated his assertions. Hiss continued to refute them. Chambers offered a wealth of detail on what he claimed had once been a deep friendship, a friendship which

---

*The world of the anti-communists was a world of reversals and surprises. At his first HUAC appearance Chambers met an old acquaintance, Benjamin Mandel, who had issued him his "Party book" nearly twenty years before, when he had joined the Communist Party. But these days Mandel was the research director of the House Un-American Activities Committee.

†A full-page photograph in *Life* (July 16, 1945) shows Hiss carrying a briefcase. At his feet there is a seventy-five pound fireproof safe with a parachute strapped to it. The same contains the UN Charter. A placard pasted to the safe reads dramatically, "Finder—Do Not Open! Notify the State Department, Washington, D.C."

had ended, he said, when he, Chambers, broke away from the Party in 1937. Two days later Chambers repeated his claims on the radio, saying that Hiss had been a Communist in the 1930s "and may be now." Several weeks later Hiss sued for libel. When Chambers repeated the charge in public, the claim for damages was raised from $50,000 to $75,000.

But the tide of events was now with Chambers. He offered to take a lie detector test; Hiss declined to take one, on various grounds, without actually refusing outright. However well founded his objections may have been, he appeared to be evasive and insincere. As his credibility declined, that of Chambers rose accordingly.

Before HUAC Chambers had listed nine men he had known to be Communists in the government's employment in the 1930s. Hiss was one of the nine. Seven of those remaining had taken the Fifth Amendment when called before HUAC. The eighth, Hiss's brother Donald, admitted that he knew the others but denied knowing that they were Communists. The worst that Chambers had ever said about the men on his list was that they were misguided. But then Hiss's lawyers in the libel suit asked Chambers for proof that what he had said was true, for truth is a defense in a libel suit. Did he have any such defense to offer?

Chambers's answer was to submit a collection of confidential State Department material from a decade earlier: sixty-five typewritten pages and four sheets of paper covered with Alger Hiss's handwriting. Chambers would later claim that he had retrieved this material and microfilm of a further fifty-eight pages of documents from its hiding place in his brother-in-law's New York apartment. And ever a man to keep something up his sleeve, he secreted the recovered microfilm in a hollowed-out pumpkin in the pumpkin patch at his Maryland farm.

Hiss and his lawyers turned the material Chambers had offered for their inspection over to a Federal grand jury which had for some months past been sitting in Baltimore, making a desultory probe into violations of the espionage laws. It had yet to issue its first indictment. Chambers's documents brought the grand jury to life.

They also inspired rumors of a major spy case in the making. Nixon and Stripling, their curiosity excited, asked Chambers if by chance he had anything left over for *them* to see, anything which might substantiate his accusations against Alger Hiss? To encourage his memory, they had a subpoena served on him. One rainy night toward the end of the year, while Congressman Nixon was basking in the warmth of the Florida coast, Chambers led two HUAC investigators out to his vegetable patch and there recovered what should strictly be known as the pumpkin microfilm but is better known to history as the Pumpkin Papers. News of this turn of events was relayed to Florida. The young Congressman made a rapid, highly publicized return to Washington after being plucked from a small boat by a Coast Guard amphibian.

Appearing before the grand jury, Hiss denied almost everything Chambers said or the documents suggested. On the last day of its statutorily set life, the grand jury handed down its indictments. There was a possibility that it might indict Chambers for perjury. But it contented itself with bringing two charges of perjury against Hiss. He could not be charged with espionage because the statute of limitations then ran for only three years. He was charged with perjury when he denied passing documents to Chambers. He was further charged with perjury when he claimed never to have seen Chambers after January 1937.

To HUAC, Alger Hiss was the biggest fish that ever got away. But its involvement with Chambers was not finished. When Chambers saw A. A. Berle, Jr., in 1939 he did so in the company of Isaac Don Levine, a journalist whose career was based on anti-Communism. In December 1948 Levine told HUAC that among the Communists Chambers had mentioned to him was one of Hiss's friends, Laurence Duggan, onetime head of the Latin American Division in the State Department. Duggan had since become head of the Carnegie Institute for International Education. Duggan suddenly found himself being interviewed by the FBI.

At dusk, a few days before Christmas, his lifeless body was found lying in the slush on a Manhattan sidewalk. News of Duggan's death reached Washington several hours later. Congressman Karl Mundt of HUAC called a midnight press conference to talk about Duggan's death. When, he was asked, would the rest of the names Levine was said to have given the committee be released? "We will give them out," Mundt replied, "as they jump out of windows."

Chambers then denied that he had ever named Duggan as a Communist. He had never even met him. Levine bravely continued to maintain that if Duggan was not a Soviet spy, he was at the very least a Communist dupe. He must surely have been guilty of *something*—"the man jumped [because] he couldn't face the music."

Only a few weeks earlier a Justice Department lawyer named by Chambers in connection with the transfer of a car to him from Hiss in the days of their friendship, W. Marvin Smith, jumped to his death from the roof of the department. Chambers had suggested that Smith was in some way involved with the Communist Party.

HUAC appears to have played an important role in the deaths of at least twenty people. The roll of suicides connected with its investigations and hearings is long and sad. Some of those who killed themselves may have been Communists at some time in their lives. Some were probably people of an overly sensitive nature. But some, perhaps most, were certainly innocent of any serious wrongdoing. Indeed, the death toll includes several women never accused of anything; they happened to be married to men who fell foul of the committee. But HUAC always liked to emphasize that fighting Communism was a matter of life or death.

The fight against subversion was too exciting and too rewarding politically to be left to Federal agencies and Congressional committees. More than a dozen state legislatures passed anti-Communist legislation at the end of the war. These laws shared two characteristics—they were impossibly vague, and they carried enormous penalties. More than thirty states adopted loyalty-oath statutes. Three (Maryland, Mississippi, and

New Hampshire) were more ambitious and tried to make the Communist Party illegal. Six states created "little HUACs." The little HUACs convened in Los Angeles in 1948 to exchange ideas and to be addressed by J. Parnell Thomas. He was forced to cancel his appearance, however, because he was suddenly distracted by a Federal indictment charging him with fraud.

The most active of the "little HUACs" was Washington State's Canwell Committee, created in the wake of the Republican victory in state elections in 1946. Washington's Un-American Activities Committee was composed entirely of Republicans. Its chairman, Albert S. Canwell, was a former portrait photographer and deputy sheriff from Spokane, and he was convinced that the University of Washington was harboring Communists.

In the fall of 1947, the university's president, Raymond B. Allen, nervously welcomed the freshman class and told them, in effect, to keep their mouths shut. "You are here to learn how to build intelligently the kind of world you want. [But] if you are here to lead parades and incite riots we suggest you try another field." This get-tough-with-the-freshmen policy failed to appease the Canwell Committee.

Dozens of professors were subpoenaed to appear at public hearings in Seattle. All except one refused to abase themselves by giving the names of university employees they knew or suspected of being Communists or Communist sympathizers. But the attitude of the professors was one of contrition rather than defiance. They spoke freely about their own leftist beliefs and associations, nearly always back in the 1920s and 1930s, when they were young and unformed. The Canwell Committee, which had promised to unearth Communists by the dozen at the university, was reduced to issuing contempt citations against witnesses who had refused to name names.

Three faculty members who were still Communists lost their jobs. Their beliefs were well known. But until the Canwell Committee's inquiry began, these academic Marxists and the university administration had observed a tacit gentleman's agreement not to cause trouble for each other. Although all three had been employed by the university for more than twenty years, not one was a full professor. In the current climate such understandings were no longer possible.

The nature of a democracy is such that once the people lose their sense of proportion, their government, far from standing as a barrier against folly, will add to it. The powerful resources of the state will be misapplied. The cautious procedures of bureaucracy will be turned to witless pursuits. The politicians who recognize the folly for what it is will, in most cases, be reduced to silence and hopes. Although the apparatus of government will go on much as in normal times, carrying out ordinary, unexciting tasks, it will appear to the world at large as being obsessed with the ephemeral and futile passions of the moment, to the neglect of serious work. And when the search for Communists and their secret allies got into its stride, the Executive branch set off, too, in fruitless pursuit of a phantom creature with the double-barreled name, "Loyalty-Security."

Until 1939 the loyalty of American citizens had been taken for granted. The civil service rules of 1884 barred the government from inquiring into the "political or religious opinions or affiliations of any applicant" for employment. The Hatch Act of 1940 rejected the presumption of loyalty. Under Section 9-A anyone who belonged to any organization which was said to advocate the violent overthrow of the government was ineligible for government employment.*

At the height of the wartime alliance with the Soviet Union the Civil Service Commission had ruled that anyone holding Communist beliefs was "potentially disloyal." On these grounds, it declared 563 people ineligible for government employment. By V-J Day nearly 1,000 people had failed in some way to meet the loyalty requirements set by the commission. Despite this screening, conservatives continued to believe that the Federal government was riddled with Communists or fellow travelers, and that the State Department in particular was as well staffed with Communists as the Kremlin.

In 1945 the State Department had been embarrassed when hundreds of its top secret documents were found at the offices of a small liberal publication concerned with Far Eastern affairs, *Amerasia*. A grand jury investigation led nowhere. The three principals involved, including a State Department officer, John Stewart Service, were exonerated of wrongdoing. The practice of leaking secret government material to journals or journalists sympathetic to one's views was not unusual, nor was it necessarily sinister. But the Administration mistakenly prevented a full hearing into the matter. To its critics, the *Amerasia* case was a gift, to be cited endlessly as proof positive that the State Department was under Communist control.

The department was further embarrassed by the discovery that Carl Marzani, employed by it as an economist, had been a Communist Party organizer as recently as 1940 and 1941, when he worked the East Side under the plebeian-sounding name of Tony Whales. And Marzani had perjured himself, to circumvent Section 9-A of the Hatch Act. Altogether, he had perjured himself eleven times. Marzani was not exactly among the wretched of the earth or one of the prisoners of starvation hailed in *"The Internationale."* He was a graduate of Williams and Oxford, and having done his bit for the masses, the upper-middle-class employment which a good job in the State Department represented seemed only fitting. A lie or eleven was neither here nor there.

Since he had gone to work for the department there was nothing to suggest that he failed in his duties or was for an instant disloyal to the govern-

---

*Terrorist outrages at the turn of the century, including the assassination of McKinley, had led to an attempt to define unlawful threats to lawful authority. From this came the phrase "belief in the overthrow of government by force and violence." Not until after World War II was it widely used, however.

ment. But as interest in his past began to develop, he left his job. It did no good. He was indicted for perjury and in time was sentenced to three years' imprisonment.

Civil service rules still protected government employees from "arbitrary dismissal." In 1946 Congress stripped away even this constraint. It passed the McCarran Rider to the State Department's appropriation, under which the Secretary of State was given (whether he wanted it or not) the power of summary dismissal "at his absolute discretion."

The Atomic Energy Act had raised the security issue to a new level of sensitivity by requiring that the "character, associations and loyalty" of all prospective employees of the AEC be investigated by the FBI. The act also gave the AEC the power of summary dismissal over all its employees. The AEC's security operation became the model that other government agencies attempted to copy, whether they had statutory authority to do so or not.

Truman saw the way events were moving. Only three weeks after the election of the 80th Congress he appointed a Temporary Commission on Employee Loyalty, with the clear intention of preempting action by the incoming Congress.

On March 21, 1947, he issued Executive Order 9835 "Prescribing Procedures for the Administration of an Employee Loyalty Program in the Executive Branch of the Government." The grounds for dismissal or for rejecting an applicant for employment were described as "reasonable grounds"—a phrase so vague as to constitute an admission by the lawyers who drew up the proposal that they had no idea how to frame a legal definition of loyalty or security and then to say that those who fell short of the definition might be dismissed or rejected.

Truman nevertheless chose to believe that his measures were superior to anything Congress might have proposed. There can be little doubt that had the President not acted to institute some form of screening the 80th Congress would have set up a program of its own. Years later Truman's EO 9835 would be roundly condemned. It is possible that for his future reputation the President would have been well advised to let Congress enact a measure of its own choosing and refuse to put his name to it. At all events, the new Senator from Wisconsin was asked for his opinion on the President's Executive Order and he praised it as something "definitely needed" on account of "the tremendous number of Communistically inclined employees on the Federal payroll."

EO 9835 established a Loyalty Review Board to hear appeals from those dismissed from government employment because of adverse rulings on their loyalty or as security risks. The FBI was given the task of screening the 2.5 million people on the Federal payroll, plus the 10,000 new employees hired each week. All had to be fingerprinted. Most of the "investigations" consisted of file checks.* But 100 full-field investigations need-

---

*In most cases the FBI simply ran a check on its own files. If nothing untoward appeared, the loyalty investigation form would be stamped "No Disloyal Data FBI Files" and returned

ed to be conducted each week under the Loyalty-Security program. Thousands of similar investigations were being conducted each year by other Federal agencies, such as the military intelligence services, the State Department's Security Division, and the Secret Service. To help the hard-pressed FBI shoulder its new burdens, the Civil Service Commission developed its own investigative branch, 2,000 strong.

But not all the investigators in the world could have done what was required by the Loyalty-Security program. Loyalty is a matter of emotional commitment; security a matter not of what someone did in the past but what they might do in the future. To have determined the depth of emotional commitment, plus the course of future events, called not for an investigator but for a combination clairvoyant-psychiatrist.

The pursuit of the impossible by a bureaucracy armed with formidable powers could have only one result—a reign of fear. Just as predictably, that will-o'-the-wisp known as Loyalty-Security was reduced to the lowest common denominator, conformity. It was a dismal business in every respect. The passion for reform was blunted; the questioning, critical voice which informs all creative thought was muted; people were discouraged from some of their best impulses and were encouraged to give rein to some of their worst—hypocrisy, timidity, cynicism, tale bearing, grudge bearing, callousness.

Government employees who subscribed to *The Nation* or *The New Republic*, owned records by Paul Robeson or read avant-garde literature, practiced yoga, or showed an interest in Eastern Europe, China, or the Soviet Union ran the risk of being secretly denounced and of then being forced to defend themselves against vague accusations made by faceless accusers.

Loyalty hearings were conducted in private. The accused bore all the expenses of travel, witnesses, and lawyer's fees and had no power to subpoena witnesses. If he lost, he might appeal to the Loyalty Review Board, which was composed of twenty to twenty-five eminent men and women, usually lawyers. Sitting in three-man panels, they listened to the appeals. They could only make recommendations; they had no power to restore a successful appellant to his job. But they could, and often did, recommend that an employee who had been cleared at his loyalty hearing should be dismissed.

Among those who suddenly found himself caught up in this world of vague accusations and incomprehensible tribunals was James Kutcher, the legless veteran who had got the first steady job in his life only when the VA hired him as a loan clerk. In 1948 he was abruptly dismissed on the ground that he was disloyal. It was a dull, low-paid job of no importance to anyone except Kutcher. The reason for his dismissal was really that he

to its office of origin. Only when a file check revealed an indication of potential disloyalty (which could be anything from subscribing to the wrong magazine to being named by an ex-Communist witness) was an investigation authorized. The results were then set out on the form, without recommendation on further action. The FBI neither "cleared" nor "charged" those it investigated.

was, as he had been for nearly ten years, a member of the Socialist Workers Party. But he denied the slightest interest in attempting to overthrow the government. As he pointed out, the only time in his life when he had had anything to do with violence was on behalf of, not in opposition to, the government of the United States.

His situation was Kafkaesque right down to his initials. The question was soon changed from whether or not he was disloyal to whether or not the SWP was subversive. But when he raised the matter of the SWP at his Loyalty Review Board hearing, he was told that this was outside the rules under which the hearing was being held. It was enough that the SWP was listed by the Attorney General as a subversive organization.

Such lists went back to the Deportation and Exclusion Acts of 1917–18. The practice was revived during the war, and in 1945 the AG's list carried forty-seven organizations. The AG was allowed to list any body he wished and did not have to give his reasons. There was no legal remedy. Listing was an unanswerable way to taint people with guilt-by-association wholesale. The SWP was a legal party, carried on the ballot in a score of states, yet, Kutcher discovered, he could be dismissed from his job for belonging to it. It was thus somehow both legal and subversive at the same time.

While the Loyalty-Security program was weaving its tragicomic course through many a government agency, the AEC and the State Department were doing some vigorous pruning of their own under their powers of summary dismissal. Along with the military services, they used those powers to dismiss nearly 2,000 civilian employees in 1947–48 on vague charges of disloyalty.

It is doubtful that many of them were disloyal at all. The disloyal are as a rule the people who are incapable of giving themselves to anyone or anything for very long. Outwardly, they are likely to appear conformist, for they will turn and turn again whichever way the wind is blowing.

7

The World Turned Upside Down

Cut adrift from government, Henry Wallace washed up as editor of *The New Republic*. His prestige brought a doubling in its circulation, raising it to 100,000. But after a few months the new editor became bored. Even his weekly column was being written by ghosts, while the editor's attention was increasingly concerned with the Progressive Citizens of America.

The PCA was formed from the remains of several other left-wing bodies when anti-Communist liberals formed the ADA. PCA's founders were a sculptor, Jo Davidson, and a clergyman, Frank Kingdon, neither of whom could be considered a Communist. The PCA's great white hope was Henry Wallace.

He encouraged those hopes by leaving *The New Republic.* He denounced both UMT and the Marshall Plan. He was for a time occupied with fending off questions concerning the farcical "Guru letters"—correspondence dating from the 1930s, written on Department of Agriculture stationery, addressed "Dear Guru" and signed "Galahad."*

The PCA led a stormy life. Its rallies and public meetings were often attacked by American Legionnaires. In Philadelphia the Legionnaires appeared carrying rifles and proceeded to throw stones at the PCA worthies on the platform. In Trenton, Newark, and Bridgeport PCA speakers were silenced by stamping, booing, and shouting in unison. In La Crescenta, California, Legionnaires forced their way into a house were a PCA meeting was being held and occupied it.

Unknown to Wallace and Kingdon, Communists had infiltrated the PCA from the beginning. Since 1945 the Party had been looking for a third party which might run in 1948, under Communist control. And the PCA fitted the bill nicely, provided it could put up a serious candidate for the Presidency.

In January 1948 the PCA held a "draft Wallace" convention at the Ashland Auditorium in Chicago. The delegates had a lumpen-proletariat look; shabbily dressed, they were also usually broke. The delegation from Los Angeles had held an impromptu rally on the train from the West Coast and raised nearly enough money for their return home. At the auditorium Paul Robeson led the convention in community singing while bedsheets were spread in the aisles and $3300, most of it in small change, was collected to help defray the convention's expenses.

The auditorium was shabby and cold. But Wallace was given a fervent reception. They sang "Glory, Glory, Hallelujah!" He called on them to form a new political party—the new Progressive Party, a name honored in myth and memory, harkening back to an older strain of American radicalism.

But Wallace's new party made no sense. Nor did his candidacy. If they did well at the polls, they would help the Republicans capture the White House and strengthen their hold on Congress. If they did badly, the left would be more fragmented than ever. Vanity had something to do with it; Wallace and his followers were engaged in a hopeless cause rather than be without a prominent role of their own to play.

---

*It is thanks to Wallace's interest in the occult that the Great Pyramid, with the eye peering out, appears on the back of the dollar bill. It had appeared on the Great Seal of the United States since 1782. Wallace suggested that it should go on the currency as well, especially including the motto which appears at the base of the pyramid: *Novus Ordo Seclorum.* It would be, he suggested to Franklin D. Roosevelt, a fitting and lasting tribute to the New Deal. Roosevelt enthusiastically agreed. Such was Wallace's luck, however, that in 1948 this alteration of the currency was held against him as a sign that he was not entirely rational.

The Communists who had infiltrated the PCA were similarly self-intoxicated. Any breakaway party of the left which lacked the support of organized labor was doomed to ignominious failure, as they well knew. But the temptation the PCA and Wallace presented was simply irresistible. "We were infatuated," one of them would later write, "with the prospect of a great name like Henry Wallace at the head of a third ticket and we convinced ourselves that the rank and file labor would revolt against its officialdom."

The Communist role became blindingly obvious at the Ashland Auditorium. Kingdon and dozens of others who had brought the PCA into existence left the new party in disgust at almost the very moment of its birth. Naturally, their departure made it all the easier for the Communists to take over the Progressive Party lock, stock, and Henry Wallace.

But Wallace was one of those men with the nature of a salmon—born to swim upstream. He made light of the difficulties which faced him. He called his followers "Gideon's Army—small in numbers, powerful in conviction."*

During its brief existence the Progressive Party was torn by internal strife. It was a typical party of the left; every time it moved, someone walked out. When it held its nominating convention in Philadelphia in July 1948, it was held together only by its hard core of Communists. Norman Thomas, who had spent his entire adult life in left-wing politics, recognized twenty-four Party members personally known to him on the platform committee.

There were more women, more blacks, more veterans, and more people under thirty, more artists and more intellectuals, at the Philadelphia convention than you would find at any major party convention for several decades to come. There was also more than a little self-righteousness in Gideon's Army, and more than a little self-congratulation. To Rebecca West, many of the young people she encountered were "embryo Babbitts, having their fling before they settled down to safe and narrow lives."

The Communists were fatal to the Progressive Party, and essential to it. "If they are ever purged," remarked I. F. Stone, "the Progressive Party will disappear. This is not because the Communists are a majority of the Progressive Party. They are distinctly a minority. But they are fanatics, and they have the virtues which go with the defects of fanaticism. For them politics is their life. They work hard. They bring to the Progressive Party a devotion, an earnestness, a drive no other group can supply."

---

*Gideon figures in the Book of Numbers. He led a small army against the far more powerful Midianites. But the account of Gideon is so apt that I wonder whether Wallace bothered to read all of it. When Gideon asked the fearful to depart, two-thirds of his force left him. When he winnowed the alert from the weary his force was reduced to 300 men. These he equipped with a trumpet, a lamp, and a pitcher apiece. Gideon's "army" marched on the Midianite camp at dead of night, sounding their trumpets, smashing their pitchers, and flashing their lamps. The startled Midianites, thinking themselves surrounded, fled in disarray. Gideon's men never struck a blow. The whole enterprise was a bluff.

And that was the secret of their extensive, but never complete, control over it.

The convention found a running mate for Wallace in the amiable singing cowboy from Idaho, Glen Taylor. Being a United States Senator was the first good job Taylor had ever held. During the Depression he and his family had lived on rabbit stew. Taylor had been a farmhand and a factory worker. His wife begged him not to throw away all that he had won by hard work and sincerity. Yet Taylor was a man in whom conscience was paramount. To him, as to Wallace and others, the Administration's hard-line policies toward the Soviet Union courted an irreparable disaster and really did no good to anyone.

It was the final tragedy of the Progressive Party that there were too few Glen Taylors in it—that is, men who were both radical and anti-Communist. Had there been more of them, they would have been able to reduce the Communist presence to that of a rump—much as anti-Communist liberals had contained it within the Democratic Party in the 1930s. It was a tragedy compounded by the Progressive Party's most notable non-Communist, Henry Wallace. Had he possessed the courage of the original Gideon, he would have cleared from the ranks of his army those who were only going to be a handicap to him in the fight ahead.

Wallace's personal tragedy was not that he led a doomed cause. It was that in the end he descended to the expediency and cynical compromises which he excoriated in other men. He never repudiated his Communist support for the simple reason that he knew his party would be weakened if he did so; that is, he lacked the moral courage to take any but a narrow, short-term view. In the long run, the presence of the Communists would cost him not an election but reputation. He sold his honor for a handful of sure votes and unpaid workers.

In November 1947 Clark Clifford, who had risen rapidly from being the President's naval aide to being one of his closest advisers, presented Truman with a forty-three-page memorandum. The memorandum flatly denied the conventional wisdom, which held that Truman would lose in 1948 if he attempted to win the Presidency in his own right. Provided he campaigned vigorously throughout 1948, Clifford's memorandum argued, there was no reason why Truman should not win.

His campaign began in January 1948, with his State of the Union address. He used it to urge the passage of every piece of economic and social legislation he had requested since September 1945. In many respects Truman was more liberal than Roosevelt. Liberal Democrats, however, continued to convince one another that Truman was not fit to be President and could not win in November.

Fortune had given the President the best campaign contribution he could hope for in the 80th Congress. He was free to damn it as much as he wished. He made the most of the opportunity offered.

He also enacted much of its program between its election in November

1946 and its first session in January 1947. He had cut Federal payrolls, lifted nearly all remaining economic controls, and established the Loyalty-Security program.

When he started campaigning in 1948, the Democrats were desperately short of money, as usual. But chance intervened once more. Truman was invited to speak at the University of California at Berkeley in June, at the commencement exercise. The President accepted and made a leisurely progress from the East Coast to the West Coast by train. Ostensibly it was a nonpartisan trip, with the President merely going out to collect one of the honors typically bestowed on a President of the United States. The distinction was important: nonpartisan trips are at public expense.

During his twelve-day journey the President was able to speak to his fellow citizens—many, many times. The crowds grew larger as he neared the West Coast. When he reached Los Angeles, at what the polls showed to be the nadir of his popularity, more than 1 million people turned out to watch him travel the few miles between the railroad station and the Ambassador Hotel.

Truman's election campaign was based almost entirely on domestic questions. It was aimed at four groups—organized labor, consumers, farmers, and blacks.

His acceptance of *To Secure These Rights* and his order to desegregate the armed forces cemented the support of blacks, who had become accustomed anyway to voting for the Democratic candidate during the Roosevelt years. His attempt to maintain price controls had failed, but it had shown him to be on the side of consumers. And it had been the consumers who had broken under pressure and deserted him during the "meat famine," not the other way round.

The President increasingly concentrated on organized labor and the farmers.

The Labor-Management Relations Act of 1947 virtually assured him of labor's support. This legislation was better known after the respective chairmen of the Senate and House committees on labor, Robert A. Taft and Fred Hartley, as the Taft-Hartley Act. It was feebly derided in the union press as the "Tuff-Heartless Act."

It was a measure with widespread public support. Most people felt that once labor had been too weak vis-à-vis management, but now the shoe was on the other foot. What was needed, people believed, was not legislation which would smash organized labor but something which would curb the irresponsible use of union power to damage the national interest in pursuit of union objectives. Taft-Hartley did not represent an unprecedented approach to labor legislation; it drew on various proposals advanced in recent years. Senator Taft, moreover, was no antiunion extremist; he had eschewed some of the more stringent measures—such as a ban on mass picketing—proposed in the 79th Congress. A majority of Democrats in both houses eventually voted for the Taft-Hartley Act.

But two of the freshman Congressmen disagreed vehemently over this legislation. They carried their fight outside Congress and publicly debated one another. They were John F. Kennedy and Richard M. Nixon, both of whom sat on the House Labor Committee.

Taft-Hartley outlawed the closed shop. It also encouraged the states to ban the union shop. A union which broke a contract with an employer could be sued for damages. The Federal government was given what amounted to an eighty-day injunction to be invoked at its discretion, without having to resort to the courts. Officers of recognized unions were required to swear an oath that they were neither Communists nor Communist sympathizers. Unions and companies were forbidden to make contributions to candidates for Federal office. Secondary boycotts were forbidden. Union accounts came under government scrutiny. All of which amounted, said the unions, to "a slave-labor act."

Truman vetoed it without much ado. It was passed over his veto by increased majorities in both houses.

Although Taft-Hartley became law and although organized labor for decades to come would denounce it, the act was never as formidable as it appeared to be. The ban on the closed shop was never enforced on the docks or in the construction industry, for example. The Supreme Court struck down the ban on political contributions. The number of closed shops was reduced somewhat, but those which survived became stronger than ever, such as the Newspaper and Mail Deliverers Union of New York, where the effect of Taft-Hartley was to make memberships so valuable that they sold for as much as $5,000.

Congress believed that given the chance to reject the union shop, most workers would seize it. It provided for secret ballots to be held under the supervision of the NLRB. In more than 90 percent of the elections which were held the workers voted for, not against, the union shop.

Passage of Taft-Hartley over Truman's veto set off a wave of strikes. But only John L. Lewis managed to find a way to get around it. The 1948 coal miners' contract contained a clause saying that miners would work, provided they were "able and willing." Even the Taft-Hartley injunction would find it hard to take effect against workers not overtly on strike but absent because they were feeling unable and unwilling.

Lewis also attempted to lead organized labor in an organized boycott of the act. But the AFL leadership was not willing to force a showdown. Lewis scribbled a note to William Green, AFL's president, during a meeting which failed to resolve the issue. Lewis had only a few years before led the UMW out of the CIO. Now, in blue crayon and on a torn piece of paper, he scrawled, "Green. We disaffiliate. Lewis."

Truman denounced the Taft-Hartley Act repeatedly—and repeatedly invoked its "national emergency" measures. During its first year of existence he resorted to Taft-Hartley seven times, using it to send seamen, longshoremen, atomic energy workers, and others back to work.

Unions passionately denounced Taft-Hartley, but they refrained from denouncing the President. More than one union leader could sympathize with the President's position. They were men who were not unacquainted with saying one thing and doing another.

The passion directed against Taft-Hartley was nearly all the passion they had left. A reporter who visited Chrysler Local Seven in 1940 made a second visit in 1948:

> The strike photographs had come down from the bulletin boards and had been replaced by idyllic snapshots of the union's annual outings and sports events. . . . The "class-conscious" educational director was gone—ousted in the UAW-wide fight against the Communists. . . . On their desks the new officers had propped the slogan, "UAW Americans for US." They were wearing green jackets and green silk legion caps. In 1940 the flavor of the local was one of street barricades and sitdown strikes; eight years later it was almost like a lodge hall.

Union representatives had taken over the device of superseniority to provide themselves with job security. Arbitrarily fixing their date of employment years before the actual date, they were protected against almost any conceivable layoff short of collapse, and if they were laid off, they would be near the top of the list of workers to be recalled. Superseniority was also granted by companies to their key workers, with the union's agreement. One company granted superseniority to all members of its prizewinning baseball team.

Violent strikes had not disappeared. A ten-week dispute at meat-packing plants in 1948 left three workers dead. It took the National Guard to restore order during strikes in Ohio, Minnesota, and Iowa. In April that year Walter Reuther was standing in his kitchen one evening, taking a snack from his refrigerator, when he was felled by a twelve-gauge shotgun blase fired through the kitchen window.

Because he turned away at the last moment, all unawares, only five pellets of the double-O buckshot struck him, but he effectively lost the use of his right arm. His assailant was never caught, nor was the motive for the murder attempt ever established.

In the current climate of union-management relations the attempt to kill Reuther was pointless. If it was connected with the CIO purge of Communists, it was still pointless. Violence in organized labor had become an aberration. Unions now possessed power and respectability. Working with, but not within, the Democratic Party gave them an opportunity to pursue both those aims at the same time.

Union members and their families had it within their power, if they voted in a bloc, to decide the outcome of every national election because they constituted a third of the electorate. But only half the union members and their families bothered to vote. Despite Taft-Hartley, a sizable fraction voted Republican.

Truman wooed the labor vote and did so with success. But more impressive still was his success with the farmers.

* * *

Farmers are the easiest group to understand in any election. They have only one interest to pursue. Ideology has no appeal to them. Because they are so devoted to a single issue, they shift their vote back and forth between parties more readily than urban workers shift theirs. Historically, no group has been more likely than farmers to support third parties when the major parties have neglected the farmers' overriding political interest—money.

Politicians never neglect the farmers for long. Agriculture is the only business with its own Cabinet minister. It is also the only business with House and Senate committees devoted exclusively to its welfare. And the efforts of these worthies are directed to a single end—putting money into the farmers' hands. Of course, it was not called money explicitly. American farmers lived on faith, hope, and parity. And the greatest of these was parity.

With the help of government loans (parity) farmers' incomes rose faster between 1942 and 1948 than did the incomes of other occupational groups. Starting in 1948, however, the farmers began to lose ground, and the Steagall Amendment, which had set parity at 90 percent for two years after the cessation of hostilities, would expire on December 31, 1948.

Most farm prices stayed high for two years after the war simply because demand stayed high. The farm program was unpopular with many people because of such episodes as the burning of potatoes at a time when millions faced starvation and also because price supports were felt to be propping up nothing more estimable than the farmer's greed.

But parity actually provided a stabilizing force in 1948 when there were bumper crops all over the world. Had American farm prices plummeted, they would probably have dragged down farm prices everywhere, and that in turn would probably have dragged down the rest of the economy. The collapse of farm prices in the early 1920s had been one of the principal causes of the Depression at the end of that decade. Even farmers disliked the price support system, however. They wanted the money but opposed high, inflexible price supports as such.

The Republicans in control of the 80th Congress were obliged to apply themselves to this problem. The 80th Congress duly passed the Agriculture Act of 1948. It was one of the strangest pieces of legislation enacted in recent times. A bill offered by House Republicans had set parity at an inflexible 90 percent. A bill offered by a Senate Republican established parity on a scale fluctuating between 60 and 90 percent. The 1948 act included both provisions. It was less a policy, one scholar remarked, than a shotgun wedding.

At the same time Congress passed a new charter for the Commodity Credit Corporation. In a flourish of conservatism, the CCC was sternly forbidden to buy or lease its own storage facilities. The summer and fall brought record-breaking crops of wheat, corn, rice, soybeans, and peanuts. Commercial storage space was soon filled. The CCC, required by law to buy the farmers' surplus but forbidden by law from erecting its own storage bins, refused to accept the surplus. Only properly stored crops qualified for government "loans" (the loans did not have to be paid back; that was the chief point about parity).

Farmers began to sell their surpluses on the open market, and the price of wheat dropped below the government-guaranteed price. Throughout rural America people turned gloomy. The fat years were over.

The war had brought the second revolution in American farm history. The first, which followed the Civil War, had applied the technology developed between 1840 and 1860 to the newly settled lands west of the Mississippi. The second revolution, of 1939 to 1947, had been based mainly on the wartime labor shortage and the sudden abundance of ready cash and easy credit. The technology developed between the wars, based on intensive applications of chemicals and machinery, was suddenly thrust upon the land. In eight years the productivity of agriculture rose by 35 percent.

The new technology relied heavily on nitrogen-based fertilizers. Used in combination with potash, calcium, and phosphorus, a million tons of nitrogen could increase corn production by a billion bushels. Equally lavish use of urea and antibiotics brought a similar increase in meat production, while it lowered the cost per pound produced.

Farmers were ambivalent about the new technology. Its general effect was to raise their incomes—but in a bumper year, like 1948, it could just as easily bring them down. Corn prices dropped from $2.46 a bushel in 1947 to $1.21 a bushel in 1948. And the Republicans, unfairly, got most of the blame for it because they had kept the CCC from putting up its own storage bins.

No one in the Department of Agriculture, or the Democratic Party, or the CCC, had anticipated the bumper crop of 1948 and suggested putting up new storage facilities. Truman nevertheless used the shortage of bins as a stick with which to belabor the Republicans.

To reporters from the big-city dailies Truman's reminiscences about his days as a poor dirt, or dirt poor, farmer, his boasts about the straightness of his furrows, and the impassioned little speech he would finish with concerning storage bins, were boring. So they did not pay much attention. But the farmers did.

The conventional wisdom had it that the farmers were all Republicans at heart anyway, that he was therefore wasting his time wooing them so intently. But most farmers were registered Democrats or Independents. It was the small towns in farming areas which held the Republicans of rural America, the small town dominated by the small businessmen who serviced the farmer, providing him with his clothes, his tools, his insurance, and so on. It was a distinction overlooked by the press—but not by the President. He saw the farmers for what they were, his natural constituents.

* * *

Liberal Democrats began toying with the idea of trying to persuade Associate Justice William O. Douglas to seek the Democratic nomination. Their attitude was anyone-but-Truman. But they were so out of touch with ordinary Democratic voters that polls showed only 2 percent of Democrats supported a Douglas nomination, while 67 percent wanted Truman.

Polls in the summer of 1948 also showed Truman to be more popular than Dewey or Taft. His anti-Soviet stance was popular. And on the basis of the 1947 election results one authority concluded: "The chances are less than even that the Republicans will win in 1948 no matter whom the Republicans select as their candidate."

But still the Truman-can't-win talk filled the air and the press. The President's critics, right and left, believed that what disgusted them—the White House porch, the departure from the Administration of noted liberals, the commodities speculation indulged in by the President's doctor—would have the same effect on the mass of voters. Yet there was no strong and obvious alternative candidate available. In the end, the nomination was Truman's for the asking.

The Democratic convention, when it met in Philadelphia, was saved from dullness by a bitter floor fight over civil rights. A group of Northern liberals, led by the young mayor of Minneapolis, Hubert H. Humphrey, forced an open vote on a genuinely liberal civil rights plank in the platform. Delegations from the big, industrialized states of the North, where there were large numbers of black voters, reluctantly voted for the plank offered by Humphrey, rejecting a compromise acceptable to the South. Those who voted for the liberal plank had the President's blessing. Clifford's memorandum had told him he could be as liberal as he desired on civil rights; the South had nowhere else to go. Clifford was wrong.

Half the Alabama delegation and all the Mississippi delegation walked out of the convention hall, to catcalls, booing, and shouts of "Good riddance!" The convention was being covered by television and viewed by up to 10 million people. The Alabamians and Mississippians were persuaded by an NBC producer to add to the drama of their walkout by marching to the rear of the hall, where the NBC cameras were placed and there to wrench off their delegate's badges and throw them onto a mounting pile of discarded badges on which a television camera was trained.

By walking out, they were probably doing Truman a favor, rather than the injury they intended. Until this moment large numbers of blacks had preferred Wallace to Truman, whom many blacks considered a Southerner at heart despite *To Secure These Rights* and the order desegregating the armed forces. After the walkout of the Southern delegates, however, the black vote was Truman's.

He attempted to appease the liberal wing of the party by choosing Douglas as his running mate, but Douglas, after some hesitation, declined. Senator Alben Barkley of Kentucky, despite being seventy years of age, promoted his own nomination, and Truman offered no objections. Barkley secured this prize with an effective keynote speech. The only better speech the convention heard was delivered by Truman, when he ac-cepted the Presidential nomination.

The Republican convention was, true to form, a much duller affair than the Democrats'. Republican voters preferred Dewey to the other hope-fuls, but the Republicans had never given the nomination to a defeated former candidate. The New York governor was, moreover, a figure who inspired derision, thanks to his prissy ways and priggish utterances. Al-though he was of average height, the belief persisted that he was short. The proud owner of a huge sheepdog called Canute, it was said that the governor "rode to work." Alice Roosevelt Longworth said cuttingly of his chance of winning in 1948, "No soufflé ever rose twice."

Dewey was a more reasonable, capable, and open-minded man than his critics usually allowed. Even his abilities as an administrator.were turned against him, being cited as showing that he was not a man but an automa-ton. He proved during the primaries that he could be a very effective cam-paigner. Five weeks before the Oregon primary, polls showed that Harold Stassen held a very big lead over Dewey. For once, Dewey campaigned with passion rather than calculation. In three weeks he erased Stassen's lead. Then, in a showdown debate between the two men, the first debate between political candidates ever broadcast live across the country, he tore Stassen to ribbons. Stassen, in a cheap attempt at demagoguery, ar-gued that the Communist Party should be outlawed. Dewey responded with a calm but cogent defense of political freedom and thereby "won" the debate. On polling day Dewey buried Stassen.

At the Republican convention he won the nomination on the third bal-lot. In choosing Dewey, the Republicans had opted for the middle of the road, between Stassen, who tried to portray himself as a liberal, and Taft, who was undeniably conservative. Dewey's instinct for caution had left him the only important politician in the country yet to express an opinion on Taft-Hartley. His running mate was the genial but unexciting governor of California, Earl Warren.

Truman campaigned less against Dewey and Warren than against the 80th Congress ("that worst-ever, do-nothing, no-account 80th Con-gress"). He called it back for what he mockingly called a "Turnip Ses-sion."* The President revived all the proposed legislation which had not been acted on during the past eighteen months which the Republicans convention had included in their party platform. Now, Truman told the Republicans in Congress, put up or shut up.

They did very little during the twelve-day Turnip Session, except au-thorize a $65 million loan to the UN to finance construction of the UN headquarters by the East River. Otherwise, they turned their attention to investigations of Communist activities; which is where Elizabeth Bentley came in. Truman dismissed Miss Bentley et al. as "red herrings," a re-mark which was held against him for years.

*In southern Missouri farmers planted turnips in July so as to have something to eat in the winter.

The Republicans in the "worst-ever" Congress replied that the President had no cause to complain; he was the "worst-ever" President. Insults (however sincere) apart, the 80th was a historic Congress, and a busy one. It had enacted the Marshall Plan; had provided Truman Doctrine aid to Greece and Turkey; had created the Department of Defense and the CIA; had passed a tax reduction bill over the President's veto; had revised the order of Presidential succession; had enacted Taft-Hartley; had made some, if confused, headway, toward flexible price supports; had written the Twenty-second Amendment and submitted it to the states for ratification; and had enacted the Selective Service Act. In all, it had passed more than 1,000 bills.

But the failure to pass a housing bill enabled the President to portray it, with considerable success, as a Congress which had no serious concern with the welfare of ordinary people. For the Republicans, the sweet victory of 1946 was likely to bear bitter fruit in 1948 because Truman was able to hold the 80th Congress responsible for all the unresolved social crises persisting since the war's end. From the Republican point of view it might have been better for them not to have won control of Congress in 1946. The sentiment summed up in "Had Enough?" was still there, but now Truman was able to turn it around.

People were also fed up with government itself, a feeling which both parties attempted to exploit. The 80th Congress established the Hoover Commission, under the direction of the former President, to study government reorganization. Denouncing bureaucracy had become a national pastime, like denouncing John L. Lewis.

This was the first generation to have to live with what people at the time liked to call "Big Government." It was a new growth, and being new, it felt enormous, like a hole in a tooth or an ulcer in the mouth. It had come about during the New Deal and the war. For most people the Federal government had been a remote presence before 1933. In southern Missouri, where the President himself came from, the twentieth century had arrived with the automobile, shortly before the First World War. But the Federal government did not arrive until 1936, in the form of the county agent, the WPA-built library, and the Civilian Conservation Corps. And since then it had rapidly supplanted in importance the combined forces of state and local government. It took one-fifth of people's incomes. And it returned it in the form of Social Security checks, disability pensions, parity payments, matching grants, and the like. Even in a small town in a rural area the Federal presence was unavoidable. Big Government was a force so powerful that even its putative opponents turned to it for remedies. When, for instance, Robert Taft attempted to curb what he saw as the excessive powers of organized labor, he turned to that Federal bureaucracy which he so often and so bitterly denounced and gave it an additional grant of powers.

The Republicans saw themselves, nevertheless, as the natural opponents of Big Government. And it was an issue which was safe—that is, just what Dewey wanted. The Republican Presidential campaign exuded an air of confidence shading imperceptibly into complacency. Dewey acted with more circumspection than McKinley, who had campaigned from his front porch and let the crowds come to him. He was notable for his unmemorable utterances ("Our future lies before us"). When he eventually expressed an opinion on Taft-Hartley, he declared it a valuable piece of legislation—but one that could be changed.

Dewey's campaign was organized to the last minute. Even his lateness was organized. He would appear at a rally ten minutes later than scheduled, to increase the tension, arriving as if from nowhere in a flying column of fast, sleek cars, with sirens screaming, bands playing, flags waving. He would dominate the scene from dramatic entrance to thunderous exit. He was also an accomplished television performer, being coached in how to appear relaxed, how to modulate his voice, how to gaze piercingly into the camera.

Unfortunately for the Republicans they were laboring, as Samuel Lubell observed, "on the wrong side of the birth rate." Between 1900 and 1920 millions of immigrants had settled in the United States, mainly in the big cities of the North. The children of these immigrants had come of age in the 1930s and 1940s, and when they did so, they voted Democratic. They did so not because they admired the jaunty angle of FDR's cigarette holder or because he appealed to their hearts with his fireside chats, but because they were hungry for a place in the world. That meant, for most of them, that the world would have to be remade. Trapped within increasingly ugly, dangerous cities, frightened by high levels of unemployment, still young and energetic, they represented the kind of fundamental social change which is the cause of politics. But the Republicans, as wedded to ideology as the Marxists, never saw the ordinary, undramatic human reality behind the rising Democratic and the falling Republican vote. When Dewey campaigned in 1948, he did not have much to say about social issues not only because he was cautious but because he and his advisers hardly understood what they were.

Truman's campaign was very different in both substance and style. On the Truman train there was bourbon and poker; on Dewey's "Victory Special" it was bridge and cocktails. The President's crowds were often large, but polite rather than enthusiastic. He was a terrible speaker when working from a written text. But when he could be direct and informal, when he abandoned his set speeches, he was jaunty and combative. And on these occasions there came the cries of "Give 'em hell, Harry!"

Dewey, too, found it hard to awaken much response from a crowd. But he could usually count on the Communists-in-government part of his speeches to draw applause, particularly when he promised "the greatest pruning and weeding operation in American history" once he was in the White House.

Truman, however, was not easy to score off, not after the Justice Department indicted twelve top Communist Party leaders under the Smith Act. The indictments could just as easily have been brought in January or December 1948. They were brought in July, at the end of the Democratic Convention. Coming in the wake of the Loyalty-Security program and the

Berlin airlift, they made any claim that Truman was "soft on Communism" look patently absurd.

As the campaign wore on, Truman consistently outdrew Dewey in the towns and cities both visited. The press noticed this, but said it meant nothing. Dewey was going to win, and that was that. The pollsters were of the same opinion and stopped their polling. There was a rule of thumb in American politics that every vote in a Presidential election was settled by October 1.

Anyway, how could any Democratic candidate win without the Solid South? Truman made virtually no attempt to placate the breakaway Southern Democrats. Yet when he campaigned in the South he studiously avoided any reference to race.

The delegates who had walked out at Philadelphia held their own convention, in Birmingham, Alabama. They called themselves the States' Rights Democrats, and they chose Strom Thurmond of South Carolina as their nominee for the Presidency. The States' Rights Democrats insisted that the issue was not race but the growing power of the Federal government. But race was the dominant element because Truman was the first Presidential candidate ever to come out unequivocally for civil rights, and he was obviously prepared to use the powers of the Federal government to that end. Thus, the issues of race and Big Government were inextricably linked.

A copy editor on the Charlotte, North Carolina, *News* found himself struggling one night to fit "States' Rights Democrats" into a headline. Abandoning the struggle as hopeless, he coined the name "Dixiecrats," and to Thurmond's disgust, it stuck.

The threat the Dixiecrats posed to Truman was much exaggerated. They did not represent the South as a whole, as was widely and wrongly assumed. "The seat of the rebellion was the delta of Mississippi, the home of great planters, few whites, many Negroes, as well as the last vestiges of ante-bellum civilization."

The Progressive Party was also less fearsome than it appeared. A special election in the Bronx in February 1948 had been won by a Wallace admirer, Leo Isaacson, the American Labor candidate. It was a sign of Wallace's blindness that he, an Iowan, should take this example of New York radicalism as indicative of sentiments in the nation at large. But that was what he, and much of the press, did.

He strove untiringly to cast himself as the heir of the old Progressive movement. He saw himself as the "Peace" candidate. Much of the electorate saw him as the Communist candidate. He never repudiated Communist support. And he met his avowedly Communist supporters at least once. He began by informing them, "I believe in God. I believe in progressive capitilism." That was the nearest he ever came to drawing a line between him and them. The role the Party played in his campaign became increasingly brazen. "By October they [CP members] were even trying to sell the *Daily Worker* at meetings where Wallace spoke, including, of all places, Houston, Texas."

His campaign was so frantic it made Truman's whistle-stop journeys, in which anything and everything seemed to go awry, appear staid by comparison. "Wallace barnstormed the country in those middle months of 1948 like an impecunious tent evangelist. He scrounged the money in one town to move on to the next." To raise money, the Progressive Party resorted to a tactic which would have stopped the Democrats or Republicans cold—it charged admission to its rallies. But the biggest single source of money was Anita McCormick Blaine, the octogenarian heiress to the fortune reaped by her father. She gave Wallace as much as $1 million from her thoroughly capitalist inheritance.

Wallace's campaign had an upside-down character. Not only did he charge for what others gave away, but he campaigned strenuously in the South not to win Southern votes but to win Northern ones. For another candidate's meetings to be broken up by riots, that was bad; when it happened to Wallace, it was good, because it exposed the warmongers and Fascists. He traveled 50,000 miles, only to prove "beyond dispute that a candidate can travel almost indefinitely without getting anywhere."

Wallace did not run alone on the Progressive Party ticket. In the forty-five states where Wallace got on the ballot, there were other people seeking lesser offices. As a rule, the Progressive Party candidates ran in areas which were traditionally Democratic. This threatened hundreds of incumbent Democrats and was often as good as a guarantee of a Republican victory. The hatred this created within the Democratic Party toward Wallace and his followers lasted for years.

Truman for his part frustrated them by refusing to let them outflank him. On the principal domestic issues—housing, civil rights, medical care, inflation, and Social Security—he was as progressive as the Progressives.

To be a Wallace supporter at times required courage, moral and physical. Progressive Party workers were frequently beaten up or threatened with assault. Academics who openly supported Wallace found it cost them their jobs at institutions as diverse as Northwestern, the University of New Hampshire, the University of Miami, Evansville College, and Bradley University in Peoria. It is gratifying to record, therefore, that when Williams College was given a choice between a left-wing professor who was a Wallace admirer and a gift of $2.5 million, the college kept the professor.

On election day, there was the lightest voter turnout for twenty years. And Dewey got almost exactly the same number of votes Herbert Hoover had received in 1928. But what had been enough then was nowhere near enough now. Nor was Dewey much helped by the hidebound Republican candidates who seemed to have learned nothing in twenty years, while Truman was helped by the presence on the ballot of strong Democratic candidates such as Humphrey in Minnesota, Adlai Stevenson in Illinois, Chester Bowles in Connecticut, and Estes Kefauver in Tennessee.

Truman won by more than 2 million votes and said, "Labor did it." But labor did not do it. He lost four of the biggest industrialized states—New York, New Jersey, Michigan, and Pennsylvania. On the other hand, he carried the farm states of Iowa and Wisconsin, which Roosevelt had not carried in 1944, and cut heavily into the Republican vote throughout the Midwest and Great Plains states.

Gideon's Army collected one vote out of every fifty cast, and that one was usually cast by someone Jewish or black and living in New York. The Progressives set a record for money spent per vote cast, at nearly $3 apiece. The chief effect of the Progressives was to deny Truman 1 million or so votes. Without Wallace, Dewey would probably have lost by a landslide.

So Truman had won. The nation was astonished by what it had wrought. To Democrats—who had braced themselves for defeat—and to Republicans—who had been giddy with the expectation of victory—the world appeared to have been turned upside down in less than a day. The *Chicago Daily Tribune* was appearing on the streets with a big black headline which read: DEWEY ELECTED. It was the best joke of the year, perhaps of the decade.

PART II

THE COLD WAR AS A WAY OF LIFE

8

Used to War's Alarms

In January 1949 snow fell on Los Angeles. Hollywood starlets were popped into swimsuits and hurried out into the snow to make snowballs and be photographed in glorious incongruity. Across the country rolled a Gratitude Train from France, a gesture of thanks for American help during the terrible winter of 1947. The train pulled a boxcar for each state filled with works of art and historic memorabilia such as one of Napoleon's swords. These gifts, offered not by the French government but by the people of France, came to rest in art galleries and museums.

While the Gratitude Train was making its way westward, the Pyramid Friendship Club was making its way in the opposite direction. It began in California. People would show up at a Pyramid party either clutching their contribution in cash or bringing two friends. A new member paid $2 at his (more often, her) first Pyramid party and thereby became a "Number 12." The next night he or she returned, this time with two friends each willing to pay $2 and become Number 12s. The former Number 12 now became a Number 11. If the next night two more eager friends were brought along, there came promotion to a Number 10. And so it went for twelve consecutive nights, by which time the successful player became Number 1, and collected $4,096. The possibility of fraud in such an enterprise did not appear to discourage thousands of people from playing. The law stood aghast and helpless.

By the time the Pyramid Friendship Clubs reached New York the initial stake had risen to $5 and the eventual payoff to $10, 240. Inevitably, after a few months the pyramids collapsed for want of an infinitely expanding base of suckers. Nine out of ten who played the game were left with fewer friends and less money than they had begun with.

In the spring an assortment of liberals, leftists, and Stalinists, plus a

151

number of Russian officials (who denied that they were anything of the kind), met in heated conclave at the Waldorf-Astoria for several days. They were doing so, they maintained, as part of the struggle for world peace. The main attraction for the Americans who attended was Dmitri Shostakovich. The main attraction for the Russians was the opportunity to denounce the United States on its own soil. Even the speakers who were ostensibly scheduled to talk about art and literature spoke mainly about American foreign policy. There were 2,000 people at the conference; dozens of them were intelligence agents, from the FBI, the CIA, the New York Police Department, and the Bureau of Immigration. These latter took advantage of the occasion to make several arrests, which led to the deportation of two of the conference's guests. Outside the hotel pickets patrolled the sidewalks, praying, weeping, and hurling abuse at the conferees whenever they came fleetingly into view.

Of greater popular interest was the death of Margaret Mitchell, author of *Gone with the Wind*. The diminutive Miss Mitchell was struck by a taxi while crossing Peachtree Street in Atlanta. Her untimely death was mourned nationally, and in Georgia the flags flew at half-mast.

In Camden, New Jersey, Howard B. Unruh, a twenty-eight-year-old ex-soldier, brooded about his unpopularity with the neighbors and decided to do something about it. Having filled his pockets with extra ammunition, he took out his Luger and went for a walk through the neighborhood. In twelve minutes he murdered 13 people, including a woman of sixty-three and a child aged two.

On the labor front things were more or less normal: the coal miners were on strike for nearly the entire winter of 1949–1950. Truman invoked Taft-Hartley to force the miners to go back to work. But the miners refused to budge, even though they were told to do so by the UMW. Evidently they were receiving telepathic messages from John L. Lewis. The owners capitulated.

January 1950 brought the biggest cash robbery in American history. The Brink's office in Boston was settling down to counting the money brought in during the day when the five men doing the counting suddenly discovered that they were not alone. The bandits got away with more than $1 million in cash. Had they not been so rudely interrupted, they would have been able to take $2 million in cash.

The early months of 1950 brought three mercy-killing cases which attracted worldwide interest. In all three cases the accused were set free but without their actions being condoned.

People were fascinated and, they said, disgusted over the affair between a Swedish film star and an Italian movie director. Both were married to someone else. What made the affair all the more fascinating was that it resulted in a baby.

On a May night 500 tons of explosive blew up at a pier in South Amboy. For miles around the air was filled with flying debris. Thousands of buildings were damaged. Thirty-one people vanished without trace.

That same summer of 1950 an "odd-looking, snub-nosed little car" appeared on the streets of Manhattan. Only 600 had been imported because hardly anyone believed that such a cheap, noisy, ugly little car could be sold to Americans. It cost $1,300 and was called a Volkswagen.

In Chicago, meanwhile, the automotive ambitions of Preston Tucker had come not only to grief but to trial. He was tried in Chicago for violating the securities laws. He was acquitted. Still, $28 million *had* gone somewhere; surely it had not all gone into making exactly 34 Tucker Torpedoes? Tucker described his acquittal as "A victory for free enterprise."

One November afternoon, while the White House was being remodeled, the President was spending a quiet hour in Blair House. He had been there since 1948.

Suddenly, two Puerto Ricans made a chaotic attempt to shoot their way into Blair House. They killed one guard, and wounded two others, before falling themselves, one dead, the other seriously wounded.

Shortly before Christmas a new record called "Boogie Woogie Santa Claus" appeared. It was instantly and completely ignored. But on the B-side was a number called "The Tennessee Waltz." It soon sold more than 5 million copies. That same Christmas also saw the arrival of "Rudolf the Red-Nosed Reindeer," which was even worse, and even more successful.

In 1951 Boston was held entranced by a young man who balanced himself precariously on a narrow ledge high above a busy street and threatened to kill himself. A crowd gathered and began to chant, "Jump! Jump! Jump!" A passing priest and an attractive blonde talked the young man into being rescued. Several months later an almost identical incident occurred in Louisville, Kentucky. Once again the crowd cried, "Jump!" A priest arrived. So did a blonde. The end result was the same. So was the young man, Louis Tirini, aged nineteen.

In December, New Orient Mine No. 2 at West Frankfort, Illinois, blew up, killing 119 miners in the worst mine disaster since 1928. Federal mine inspectors had informed the owners of the danger of an explosion but had no power to enforce safety standards.

As 1951 turned into 1952, the entire country, and much of the world, was held enthralled by the struggle to save a storm-battered 7,000-ton freighter, the *Flying Enterprise*. The ship's decks and hull had been ripped open during a storm in the Bay of Biscay. Her Danish-born captain, Henrik Kurt Carlsen, lived in Woodbridge, New Jersey, and his defiant spirit thrilled his adopted country. Carlsen was the epitome of the man who pits his will against the sea and risks his life to save his ship.

The passengers and crew were taken off by other vessels when the storm briefly abated. The owners of the crippled freighter urged Carlsen to abandon ship. He replied laconically, "I shall remain until vessel is sunk or saved." A dozen attempts, each hazardous, were made to secure a towline. When a line was eventually secured, "Captain Stay Put" and his freighter were towed with agonizing slowness through heaving seas toward England. Uncounted millions of people waited anxiously for news.

Near Falmouth, on the third day of towing, a sudden torrential storm swept down on the freighter. The towline parted. Once more Carlsen was urged to save himself. Once more he refused. For the past three days he had spent most of his time in the cold and the wetness and the darkness of a broken ship, living on poundcake and Rhine wine. The *Flying Enterprise* began to sink inexorably. With little time to spare, Carlsen abandoned ship. Before he was safely ashore, there was a record called "The Flying Enterprise" on sale in the stores. It was atrocious.

When Carlsen came home, New York Harbor was filled with tootling, whistling, spouting ships and boats. Half a million people cheered him as he drove from the docks to Gracie Mansion to receive a gold medal and have lunch with the mayor.

The year 1952 was also memorable for the chlorophyll craze. At best, chlorophyll was of little use or value. But it appeared in chewing gum, toothpaste, dog food, cough drops, deodorants, and almost anything else that might be chewed, sucked, swallowed, smoked, or smelled. The packaging was invariably a sickly shade of green.

College campuses were enlivened with a new diversion—the panty raid. Adults were appalled and wondered where it would all end. Young men on balmy spring nights raced across campus to bay under the windows of the women's dormitory. Then, to encouraging cheers and excited squeals from the women gathered at the windows, they would brave a shower of water bombs to force their way inside and seize the women's underwear. As a rule, they were content with what they found in drawers.

In the summer California suffered the most severe earthquake to strike the state since 1906. But fortunately it was centered in the sparsely populated Tehachapi Mountains. Power lines collapsed for miles around, thousands of windows were shattered, the walls of the women's state prison were leveled, and in the small town of Tehachapi a dozen people were killed. The quake rocked Southern California. One of the most vivid memories of my childhood is of seeing my 300-pound father sitting in an armchair reading a book at one moment, then seeing him sprawled to his astonishment on the floor a moment later.

In August, Minot F. Jelke III, the heir to a margarine fortune and better known as Mickey Jelke, was arrested and charged with living off the earnings of prostitutes. Scraping along on a $200-a-month allowance from a trust fund while waiting for his twenty-fifth birthday and a $3 million birthday present, Mickey found it hard to make ends meet. When he went into the skin trade, Mickey was too well bred to be an ordinary pimp, hanging around street corners or combing dreary neighborhood bars. He hung around expensive nightclubs, carrying a portfolio of nude photographs of his girls.

Fashion these days turned to the slim and the sleek, which brought a nostalgic revival of interest in the styles of the 1920s. Cigarette holders did not come back, but the "king size" cigarette appeared, more than half an inch longer than the standard size. King size soon displaced standard size in popularity. Women's skirts became tighter and shorter. Men's slacks and now ties became slimmer.

Women's hair was supposed to be both long and short. The short look was in fashion—but not with short hair. The well-coiffed woman grew her hair long, then put it up in a chignon. For women with short hair, however, there was a fake chignon. For a year or two there was a hairstyle in vogue called the Poodle. It required more than 100 curlers and constant attention. The Poodle was short, but inconvenient. The Ponytail, on the other hand, was long, but convenient.

Fashion in the otherworldly did not stand still. For several years there was spate of green-fireball sightings. In 1950 *True* magazine published "The Flying Saucers Are Real," by Donald E. Keyhoe, a retired major in the Marine Corps. Keyhoe claimed the Air Force was ridiculing UFO sightings because it knew where they came from but could do nothing to stop them. The saucers, said Keyhoe, came from outer space. The *True* story created a sensation. Sightings rose steadily, and in 1952 they were being reported at the rate of four a day for the entire year. On the night of July 19–20 extraordinary flashes of light were reported over Washington, D.C., and odd radar returns were recorded. Several airline crews reported strange sights, and Air Force interceptors were scrambled to comb the skies over the capital. They found nothing.

Science fiction had spread to television, most of it aimed—ostensibly, at least—at children. *Flash Gordon* was a tremendous hit, until he was banished from the screen for being an unwholesome influence on tiny minds. *Captain Video; Tom Corbett, Space Cadet*; and, on the West Coast, *Space Patrol* held millions of children entranced on most afternoons.

Science fiction films were also popular. *Destination Moon* showed brave, resourceful Americans making a lunar landing at the end of the twentieth century. *When Worlds Collide* doomed most of the human race to fiery extinction, while a few hundred escaped in a huge rocket to roam the universe, looking for a place to perpetuate the species. *The Day the Earth Stood Still* brought a visitor from outer space whose mission was to warn earthlings to shape up or the rest of the civilized universe would step in and do the job themselves. It was more or less taken seriously

Behind nearly all the science fiction, and probably at the root of the sudden interest in science fiction, stood the atomic bomb and television, the one carrying a threat of doom while opening a new vista of control over natural forces, the other introducing the marvels of the electronic age, with its unprecedented opportunities for communication. And lurking in the background there was the decline in traditional faiths, while the craving to believe in *something* persisted.

Inevitably, there was a sci-fi religion, and its Prophet was L. Ron Hubbard, a writer of science fiction stories. He called the new revelation Dianetics ("the science of the mind"). Its bible was *Dianetics: The Modern Science of Mental Health*. Its followers were legion. The new religion's earliest sacred texts had appeared in *Astounding Science Fiction* magazine, and they offered what read like a parody of psychoanalysis combined with the jargon of the infant electronics industry.

Established science shrugged off such ventures as nonsense, but it was shaken by a work which seemed to straddle both science and science fiction, Immanuel Velikovsky's *Worlds in Collision*. "His book," wrote *Time*, "is causing as much excitement as if it had been co-authored by Einstein and Toynbee." And this was before it had been published.

Velikovsky had been a doctor in Russia, before emigrating to the West in the 1920s. To the scientific establishment, his credentials to pronounce upon important matters of physics and astronomy were weak. Yet Velikovsky maintained that there had been a collision between Jupiter and Venus, which explained several spectacular events described in the Old Testament. He claimed that Venus was a hot planet, with a hydrocarbon atmosphere, when nearly all reputable scientists were convinced its atmosphere was predominantly carbon dioxide and the planet therefore cold. He claimed Jupiter emitted radio waves,an idea reputable scientists derided. Velikovsky made claims like a gold miner set free in virgin territory. Many of his claims were either disproved or remained unproved. But in time it was found that the temperature of Venus was 800 degrees and it was swathed in hydrocarbon clouds. Jupiter was discovered to emit radio waves.

Velikovsky's book aroused such fury in American science that his publisher, Macmillan, dropped *Worlds in Collision* from its list. Macmillan was a major publisher of textbooks and vulnerable to pressure from the academic community. *Worlds in Collision* was snapped up by Doubleday, which produced no textbooks. Scientists who attempted to defend Velikovsky found that it "was enough to cost a man his job, as at least two men discovered." Jacques Barzun dryly observed, "In short, the scientific treatment of the case was successful."

These were years filled with wars and rumors of wars. and the country began to count the cost of its new responsibilites. In broad, crude terms the proper aims of American foreign policy were peace and justice. It was easy to assume that these were as linked as Siamese twins. But Americans would find that in a perverse and imperfect world they sometimes had to choose the one at the expense of the other.

The wartime idea of union with Britain was revived, notably in the pages of *The New Republic*. Associate Justice Owen J. Roberts resigned from the Supreme Court to spend the remainder of his life laboring for Atlantic Union. In 1950 forty Senators went on record in favor of such a link. But it was really an eccentric idea which flew in the face of two nationalisms.

With the ebbing of idealistic internationalism, Citizen-of-the-World Garry Davis returned and asked for his American citizenship back. He was told that like anyone else married to an American citizen, he would have to follow the normal procedures of nationalization, including a residence requirement, a literacy test, and an examination of his knowledge of American history, customs, and political institutions.

That repository of internationalist hopes, the UN, in 1950 flew its own flag for the first time. It showed all the countries of the world in white, without national boundaries, set on a blue disc. To the alarm of the DAR and the American Legion it was decreed that the UN flag should be flown at the same height and to the left of Old Glory. Boycott campaigns against the "Spider flag" of the UN started all over the country. But the League of Women Voters launched a more successful campaign to encourage schools and public buildings to fly the UN flag, and the Agriculture Department mailed out thousands of UN flag kits to sewing circles in towns large and small.

There was still a note of defensiveness about the country's fitness to defend Western civilization. Typical of the current mixture of bombast and impatience was a *Life* editorial with the following headline and subhead:

BELIEF IN AMERICA
It is time for Europeans to assume that
Americans Know the Score and Will do the Job

Many people thought it only realistic to expect that sooner or later the country would be drawn into war with the Soviet Union. A novel by Leonard Engel and Emanuel S. Piller, *World Aflame*, was published in 1947 and anticipated a war beginning in 1950 and raging for nearly a decade. It was a war where both sides used atomic bombs, in which submarine-launched, atomic-armed missiles were fired from far out at sea, nerve gas was widely used, crops were destroyed and vegetation was defoliated from the air, a polio vaccine was developed, and germ warfare was freely practiced. But exactly what the United States and the Soviets were fighting over that justified 100 million dead and every major city destroyed was not spelled out.

Life, perhaps taking its cue from General Marshall, ran "How a Democracy Died" in its issue of January 1, 1951. An account of the Peloponnesian War, it drew a number of dubious parallels between the Athenians and the Spartans circa 400 B.C. and the Americans and Russians circa A.D. 1950. Having started its reader thinking, however, *Life* shortly followed up with "The War We May Fight." This modestly unveiled a daring strategy for defeating the Russians in a total conflict.

But the most extraordinary effort both to excite and to profit by present war fears was the entire issue of *Collier's* for October 27, 1951, called "Russia's Defeat and Occupation 1952–1960." In the course of the war Washington and Moscow and scores of other cities are laid flat. The war turns into a stalemate, until a successful parachute drop in the Urals brings the capture of the Soviets' stockpile of atomic weapons. The Russians, by this stroke virtually disarmed, sue for peace. The occupation which follows is benign and successful. The Russians, liberated at last from Communist enslavement, soon learn how to be peaceful and freedom-loving. In 1960 a new, Democratic Russia hosts the Olympic Games. Everybody is very happy.

At home, the ruined cities are rebuilt, and that provides the opportunity to introduce a little love interest into these weighty matters of war and peace. A pretty Russian engineer ("He looked at her, wondering how a woman in grimy overalls could still be so attractive") and an American banker's son meet in the radiocative rubble of what had once been Philadelphia, and love blooms.

What made this drivel noteworthy was the people who had a hand in it. Allan Nevins, Robert E. Sherwood, Arthur Koestler, Edward R. Murrow, Bill Mauldin, and Walter Reuther were among the eminent men who wrote about various aspects of Russia's defeat and occupation. These were no venal scribblers but serious-minded men, and what evidently prompted them to lend their names and their abilities to this enterprise was the great longing of the present hour—to see Communism destroyed, utterly and finally. This was the objective Americans at midcentury had turned into a secular Holy Grail. That estimable man of good sense and honesty H. L. Mencken, the Sage of Baltimore, called for war against "the Russian barbarians." And for once he was not joking. "My own impression," he wrote, "is that tackling them at once will be easiest in the long run. . . . We'll be able, at worst, to do enormously more damage than we'll have to suffer, and in the end, if we are lucky, there will be something resembling a civilized peace in Christendom."

The American people had come up against the harsh, unwelcome fact of Soviet power and became so obsessed with it that, as Emmet John Hughes aptly remarked, "they came close to losing sight of the world." Every disappointment, every failure, every danger was traced back to Moscow. It did not matter that these were just as likely to be the result of technological change, struggles for national independence, rapid population increases, the revival of old enmities, the emergence of new states, or the decline of long-established powers; the Soviets were considered responsible. Yet had the Russians all become pacifists and vegetarians, many of the problems would have remained.

Americans chafed, furthermore, against the policy of containment. It was too passive and defensive to suit the American temperament. David Riesman made fun of the urge to do *something* in a satire called "The Nylon War." Possibly remembering the remark once made by Roosevelt that the best way to destroy Communism was to drop million of copies of the Sears, Roebuck catalogue over the Soviet Union, Riesman went a step farther. His short story featured a bombardment of American consumer goods, authorized by act of Congress, "to bring the benefits of American technology to less fortunate nations." The Russians, taken by surprise, hold their fire when the planes pass overhead, self-indulgently telling one another that this mad gesture only proves that capitalism really *is* on its deathbed; the Westerners cannot consume any more; they have to give the stuff away. From the sky fall cartons of cigarettes, nylon stockings, yo-yos, chocolate bars, and wristwatches. After softening the Russians up to enjoy the good things in life, the planes begin to drop stoves, refrigerators, washing machines, and steam irons.

The Soviet leadership becomes nervous at this development. It begins to claim that these goods are really the products of Russian industry and the Party in its wisdom has hit upon this novel, speedy system of distribution. The bounty continues to fall from the skies. Instead of being sated, the appetite of the long-undernourished Russian consumer grows with what it feeds on.

Becoming frantic, the Kremlin issues a warning that if these acts of provocation are not halted, the Soviet Union will be forced "to reply in kind." But Americans are not so easily intimidated. Several days later, to their amazement, the people of Seattle are bombarded with vodka and caviar.

Riesman's *jeu d'esprit* was characteristically American in its self-mockery. But during the Cold War satire of this kind was notable for its rarity. The Cold War was usually treated like a death in the family. It was nothing to make jokes about. The playful spirit which helps offset the pomposity and boredom so evident in American life was, for once, severely repressed. Far more characteristic were assertions such as James Burnham's "Peace is not and cannot be the objective of foreign policy." Such was the attitude which increasingly informed American attitudes toward the world outside. Given a choice between fighting a total (and potentially suicidal) war with the Russians and allowing the further expansion of Russian power, 70 percent of the American people chose war.

The most clear-cut expression of the nation's willingness to draw the line against the Soviets was the North Atlantic Treaty Organization, which occupied the Senate for much of 1949. The NATO pact involved a tacit commitment that the United States would go to war to defend Western Europe without waiting to consult Congress. Was NATO Constitutional? The answer was plainly no. The pact was ratified, all the same. A week after the Waldorf Conference concluded its hectic deliberations, the NATO Treaty was signed in Washington amid pomp and ceremony and to the strains of the Marine Corps Band playing "It Ain't Necessarily So."

September 1949 brought news long expected but nevertheless unwelcome. The Soviets had exploded an atomic bomb. It sent a shock wave through millions of Americans. People had expected the Russians to acquire the bomb around 1950, but it was a different matter to have to live with it once it happened. The Soviet bomb helped inflame the war talk and the war nerves we have already seen. The clock on the *Bulletin of the Atomic Scientists* was moved up from eight minutes to midnight to three minutes to midnight.

For the AEC, the Soviet bomb came at a bad time. Trifling incidents, such as the disappearance of several grams of U-235 from the Argonne National Laboratory and the award of an AEC fellowship to a young physics student who was discovered to be a member of the Communist Party, were treated in Congress and the press as threats to national security. When the commission voted to ship radioactive isotopes to Norway for use in medical research, and AEC commissioner who cast the only vote against this proposal, Lewis Strauss, was turned by press and politicians into a Tribune of the People.

The AEC had been intended to be removed from political manipulation. But Senator McMahon successfully pressed Truman to elevate Gordon Dean, the Senator's former law partner, to a seat on the commission and later helped make Dean the AEC chairman when Lilienthal stepped down.

It was against this background of hypersensitivity and political maneuvering that the AEC attempted to decide whether the United States should build a hydrogen bomb. American scientists had been working toward an H-bomb since 1946. The principle employed simulated a process which occurs in stars, like the sun: the fusion of hydrogen atoms to form helium, in the course of which large amounts of energy are released. But while the principle was known, a reliable method for fusing hydrogen atoms was not.

There were both practical and moral doubts among the scientists involved. The AEC's General Advisory Council, headed by J. Robert Oppenheimer, eventually advised against building a hydrogen bomb. Oppenheimer's personal doubts were, he would suggest, shared by others: "In some sense, which no vulgarity, no humor, no overstatement can quite extinguish, the physicists have known sin; and this is a knowledge which they cannot lose." But he was also among the first people to see that if thermonuclear weapons were developed, then national security would inevitably become notional security; no place on earth would be safe, and in a thermonuclear war there would be no limit to the number who might be killed except for the total number of human beings available. A war without survivors was not yet possible, it might not be possible for decades; but it would become possible once thermonuclear weapons, and the ancillary technology of guidance and delivery systems, had been perfected. Oppenheimer saw not the immediate dilemma of whether or not to build an H-bomb before the Russians did, but the problem beyond that—was this the first, inexorable step on the road to the extinction of humankind? If to build the H-bomb was to take that road, what person, what nation, would wish to hurry along it faster than someone else?

Oppenheimer was not a sentimentalist. Nor was James B. Conant, another member of the GAC. Conant and Oppenheimer encouraged one another in their doubts, and when the GAC cast its vote not to recommend construction of the H-bomb, the vote of the six-man council was unanimous.

But within the AEC Lewis Strauss lobbied for the H-bomb. Within Congress Senator McMahon lobbied for the H-bomb. Within the scientific community Edward Teller lobbied for the H-bomb.

The argument broke into public view in November 1949 when Senator Johnson of Colorado during a television interview blurted out, "Here's the one thing that's top secret. Our scientists . . . have been trying to make what is known as the Superbomb." He accused the scientists who opposed construction of the Superbomb of jeopardizing the nation's security by giving that secret away. Johnson, by talking about it on television, was evidently under the impression that he was keeping the secret.

The AEC crushed most of the resistance among scientists by means of an order which read: "All AEC and contractor employees working on AEC contracts are instructed to refrain from publicly stating facts or giving comment on any thermonuclear reactions or the Commission's program of thermonuclear weapons development." This short telegram silenced the most important physicists for the reason that most important physicists worked for the best universities, and the best universities held valuable AEC contracts.

But one of the leading figures in nuclear physics, Hans Bethe, refused to be silenced. He wrote an article opposing the H-bomb for publication in the April 1950 issue of *Scientific American*. The AEC hurriedly decreed that this article jeopardized national security. FBI agents seized and burned thousands of copies of the magazine containing the offending article, and the presses were stopped so that the plates could be pulled before any more could be printed. The Bethe article contained not a scintilla of information not already to be found in other publications. His article was censored for no other reason than its opposition to the H-bomb.

On January 31, 1951, President Truman issued a terse statement concerning the H-bomb. The United States, he announced, would build it.

The Soviet atomic bomb explosion was followed a few weeks later by a political explosion of sorts, the creation of Communist China. Chiang Kai-shek had fled to Taiwan with what remained of his army, who proceeded to dispossess and slaughter the Taiwanese. Americans deeply lamented the "loss" of China, regardless of the fact that it had never been theirs. It was a country for which many Americans felt an odd, sentimental regard. It was, that is, a country they worried about and about which they knew almost nothing.

The China Lobby, an assortment of rich reactionaries (such as Alfred Kohlberg, the leading importer of Chinese lace and the publisher of the right-wing periodical *Plain Talk*, edited by Isaac Don Levine), Republican politicians, and agents of the Chiang regime, labored assiduously to discourage recognition of the new government in Peking. Chiang's brutal and corrupt rule was excused as harsh necessity; his defeat was put down to the stupidity of Marshall and Acheson, who were blamed for denying him guns, ammunition, and aircraft. To the China Lobby, Taiwan was more vital to American interests than Britain. In these years the Atlantic was the Democrats' ocean; the Pacific, the Republicans'.

Early in 1950 the former French colonies in Southeast Asia were granted quasi-independence as the state of Vietnam. Its ruler was the "King of the Nightclubs," Bao Dai. The emperor was installed as leader of a country through much of which he dared not travel. French armies protected his throne against the Communist-led Viet Minh. The United States in turn armed the French. This was a war so detested by the French people that the government of France exempted French conscripts from service in Vietnam.

The Administration hoped to pursue a policy of nonintervention in Asia. It clearly tried to put the Asian mainland beyond the pale of American commitments. Acheson in March 1949 told a British journalist, "Our line of defense runs through the chain of islands fringing the coast of Asia. It starts from the Philippines and continues through the Ryukyus archipelago, which includes its main bastion, Okinawa. Then it bends back through Japan and the Aleutian chain to Alaska." In January 1950 in a speech to the National Press Club Acheson drew the same defensive perimeter.

This was an approach which departed so firmly from the thrust of the Truman Doctrine that *The New Republic* jubilantly announced: THE TRUMAN DOCTRINE IS DEAD. American aid would be provided, Acheson told the National Press Club, only where it was "the missing component." Anti-Communism was not enough. The recipient regime would have to be prepared to win the support of its own people before it could hope to win the support of the United States. This seemed to disqualify Chiang Kaishek, Bao Dai, and the government of South Korea. First, they lay outside the perimeter Acheson had drawn; second, they were not representative enough of their own people to qualify for aid should that perimeter be extended.

Although Acheson was trying to take a second look at American foreign policy, neither he nor the President was in a conciliatory mood regarding the Russians. In March 1950 Acheson traveled to Berkeley, and in a speech ostensibly aimed at reducing tension between the United States and the Soviet Union he demanded that the Red Army withdraw from Eastern Europe and that a UN commission be allowed to enter North Korea to help pave the way for reunification of the Korean peninsula. Truman was meanwhile swearing that he would never set foot in the Soviet Union so long as he was President.

All through the spring of 1950 tensions continued to rise. Acheson traveled the country, making hard-nosed speeches, which were cheered wherever he went. His activity may well have been undertaken partly to refute critics of the State Department. Acheson had few friends or admirers on Capitol Hill.* Nor had he done himself much good by saying, "I shall not turn my back on Alger Hiss." Acheson's law partner was Alger's brother Donald.

Tensions were being raised by the seeming onrush of Communist triumphs—the Soviet A-bomb, the fall of China, the victories of the Viet

---

*Acheson's Congressional appearances were unfailingly tempestuous. After one particularly grueling session before a Senate committee Acheson returned to the State Department looking haggard to find Adlai Stevenson waiting to see him. Acheson greeted Stevenson wryly: "Home is the hunted, home from the Hill!"

Minh. In mid-April Soviet fighters shot down a U.S. Navy plane flying over the Baltic sea, killing the crew of ten. American authorities clashed with Communists in Berlin, Trieste, Czechoslovakia, and Austria. "The rising frequency of protest and reply clearly indicate[s] a hotting-up of the Cold War," observed *Time*. The tension broke on June 25, when the North Koreans crossed the 38th parallel and swept the South Korean Army before them.

The Korean people have the misfortune, shared by the Poles, of occupying a land which sits between two far stronger, and historically belligerent, powers. Korea has been the battlefield of invading armies for more than 1,000 years.

The last American combat forces to leave South Korea had departed in July 1949. They had left behind them a 500-man training mission attached to the South Korean Army. In doing this, the United States had violated the spirit, if not the letter, of its agreement with the UN to withdraw all American military forces. The Russians had withdrawn, or claimed to have withdrawn, all their forces from North Korea in January 1949.

To the President and his advisers the invasion of South Korea was seen at the outset as a test of American will. For two days the issue hung—or appeared to hang—in the balance. The conventional wisdom in Washington was that Truman would try to find a way to appease the North Koreans and Russians. After all, people said knowingly, who would risk World War III for the fate of South Korea? But "At 12:07 Tuesday noon (June 27), when Truman's executive order hit the wires, Washington took a new look at the President. It found that he had fooled them even more than he did on Election Day 1948." Truman's order directed American forces to resist the North Korean attack by air, by sea, and on the ground.

As chance would have it, the Russians had recently walked out of the UN Security Council. The Council speedily ratified the American intervention, ignoring Russian protests that their absence was as good as a veto. Instead of a fig leaf to cover itself in South Korea, the United States had the UN flag.

Questions were raised about the constitutionality of what Truman had done by Executive Order. But Congress settled the question by passing resolutions in the President's support.

In cities and towns across the country anti-Communist ordinances were hurriedly passed. But it was no easy matter to find an outright Stalinist in Birmingham, Alabama, or Houston, Texas, or McKeesport, Pennsylvania. There were, however, people circulating the Stockholm Peace Petition, a pro-Soviet propaganda ploy designed to embarrass the United States by cynical manipulation of the general desire for peace. Peace petitioners were beaten up and harassed in various, invariably petty ways.

When it began, the Korean War was very popular. Few challenged Truman's decision that the United States should stand and fight. Over much of the country the invasion of South Korea brought a sense of relief. It broke the tension which had been building up since the establishment of the Communist government in China. The Washington bureau chief of the *Christian Science Monitor* observed, "Never before [in 20 years] have I felt such a sense of relief and unity pass through the city."

Recruiting stations were swamped with eager, untrained volunteers. The armed services preferred to turn to their trained reservists. These, grumbling but resigned, were put back into uniform. Mothballed ships and planes were uncovered, refueled, remanned, and sent back into action. The Army doubled in size within a few months and was forced to buy back material from Army surplus stores. Items such as shoes, sold a year earlier at $1 a pair, were retrieved at $6 a pair; duffel bags sold for 9 cents were bought back for 89 cents, and so it went.

In an oblique act of homage to the constitutional niceties Truman began referring to the war in Korea as a "police action." The North Koreans were not soldiers but "bandits."

The President's decision was a reflex action; it neither stemmed from a searching look at global policy nor encouraged such a look. And for the first few months the object of the fighting was simply to stay in South Korea. In September, against the advice of almost every authority on the subject of amphibious assaults, MacArthur launched a brilliantly successful attack on Inchon, near the 38th parallel. He cut off the North Korean forces hundred of miles to the south, who were confident they had the American and South Korean forces trapped around the port of Pusan. The Inchon landing was known in Tokyo as Operation Common Knowledge, but it nonetheless caught the North Koreans by surprise. Their army was shattered on the long retreat northward and thereafter became a negligible factor in the war.

Within six weeks all South Korea was regained. The President, the UN, the Joint Chiefs of Staff, the State Department, and MacArthur all were carried forward on the tide of this success to support the unification of Korea by occupying the entire country up to the Chinese border. But MacArthur, in an excess of self-confidence, divided his forces during the rapid drive toward the Yalu River. In this, he offered the Chinese armies an unmatched opportunity—the chance to fight the UN forces piecemeal. Three hundred thousand poorly armed Chinese soldiers were infiltrated deep into MacArthur's rear. Their communications were of the flag and bugle variety. They enjoyed no armor to speak of, no heavy artillery, no air support. Yet tactically they held the upper hand. The Chinese "volunteers" were mainly battle-hardened veterans of the armies which had defeated Chiang Kai-shek. They inflicted a massive defeat on MacArthur's divided forces and sent them in disarray back to the 38th parallel. Had they been equipped with modern weapons and transportation, the Chinese could have turned the defeat into a rout.

Beaten on the battlefield, MacArthur began a propaganda campaign to be allowed to recoup his losses by attacking China itself. He nursed the desire of any career soldier to be allowed to fight again the opponent who had defeated him on their first encounter. Militarily, his position had all the advantages of logic. Politically, it had none of the advantages of sense. The UN resolution which had authorized the American intervention in the Korean War did not authorize war with China. Nor was there anything in Korea which was vital to American interests that could be secured only by war with China. Nor, finally, was there any widespread public support for a larger war—one which would, moreover, run the risk of war with the Soviet Union.

But MacArthur's view did appeal to some people. *Time* continually pleaded for a war with China. At least one draft board, in Montana, refused to draft another man until MacArthur had been given permission to use the atomic bomb on Chinese targets.

The general's propaganda campaign exhausted Truman's patience. He had also lost the President's faith in his judgment by assuring Truman when they had met on Wake Island shortly after the Inchon landing that the Chinese would not intervene in Korea and that if they did do so, they would be destroyed. He sent a message to the VFW convention criticizing the Administration's vacillating policy over the defense of Taiwan. Within four days at the end of November, the *New York Post* noted, "MacArthur has found time to (1) reply to an 'exclusive' cable from Ray Henle, a lesser-known radio commentator, (2) answer an 'exclusive' inquiry from Arthur Krock, *New York Times* Washington correspondent, (3) tell all 'exclusively' to Hugh Baillie, President of United Press, and (4) grant an 'exclusive' cabled interview to *U.S. News and World Report.*"

MacArthur requested permission to bomb the Yalu bridges across which reinforcements and supplies were carried to the Chinese "volunteers." When the request was refused, MacArthur was tempted to resign but chose instead to criticize Administration policy, or the lack of policy.

Traditionally, American generals have been given free rein to fight much as they have preferred to fight, with the politicians making policy after the battles have been won. But Korea was a different war. Its objectives were not physical but psychological, something felt rather than something to be marked out with pins and boundary markers. MacArthur, like the dinosaur, proved unable to adapt to a changed environment.

On April 5, 1951, Joe Martin, the Republican Minority Leader, read to the House a letter from the General, sent in reply to a query from Martin concerning the use of Chiang Kai-shek's forces. MacArthur was scornful of the Administration's decision to keep the generalissimo out of the Korean War and concluded, "There is no substitute for victory."

The letter to Martin was a sensation. It also forced the President's hand.

The growing body of anti-MacArthurites was satisfied that the general had been insubordinate. But although he had used his enormous prestige to air his differences of opinion with the Administration, he had at no time refused to obey orders. Under military law and practice he had done nothing for which he could have been convicted by a court-martial. He had been exceedingly impolitic. For that, he had to go. After several days of anxious discussion Truman called a press conference at one in the morning to announce MacArthur's dismissal.*

The country was thrown into shocked indignation. Flags were flown at half-mast. The Los Angeles City Council adjourned, too sick at heart to conduct the city's business that day. The Michigan legislature passed a resolution which began, "*Whereas*, at one a.m. of this day, World Communism achieved its greatest victory of the decade in the dismissal of General MacArthur. . . ." Thirty thousand letters and telegrams were delivered to the White House on the subject. All but a handful protested the President's action. Across the country there were demands for Truman's impeachment or resignation. Polls showed that at least two-thirds of the nation considered MacArthur's dismissal a mistake.

The general's return was one of the incandescent public events of the postwar, one of the handful of occasions that remained bright in the memory long after the event. What was ostensibly a return in disgrace was turned into a Roman triumph, lacking only enslaved prisoners and cavorting bears. The most astonishing thing about it, however, was that the Administration was an eager party to every aspect of this triumphant homecoming, praising MacArthur handsomely and giving him a costly silver tea service, while it stripped him of his job.

His Farewell Address to both houses of Congress was an occasion of the greatest theatricality, so heightened in dramatic effect that it was hard to believe that it was real. A circle of generals and admirals, glittering with braid, gilt, and silk ribbons, sat in the well of the House. Row upon row behind them were hundreds of Representatives and Senators, many of them old men of flinty character. For the next half hour MacArthur held them, and the nation beyond, rapt. Attendance at the Boston Marathon was reduced by half, and those who showed up brought their radios with them. Ball parks were nearly empty. In bars and homes people fell silent.

MacArthur's speech was short and unsentimental, in the Roman style. But it was deeply felt, and it carried the weight of the nation's past. MacArthur's life had been so inextricably linked with his country's fortunes for more than fifty years—his had been so public a career—that he epitomized America's rise to world power since the turn of the century—epitomized, too, its frustration and bafflement when faced with present constraints. Within that glittering assembly in the well of the House, and

---

*MacArthur stood in the line of eminent American generals who openly disagreed with their civilian superiors. Jackson in 1818 was allowed to undertake hot pursuit into Spanish Florida but told to leave the Spaniards alone. He chose, however, to attack Spanish forts. Monroe was indignant; the public, delighted. Zachary Taylor clashed with Polk over the surrender terms concluding the War of 1846. Polk dismissed Taylor from his command. Two years later Polk was out of the White House, and Taylor was in it. McClellan repeatedly humiliated Lincoln. Only when it became obvious that McClellan could not win battles was he dismissed. "Billy" Mitchell was court-martialed because he quarreled publicly with his superiors over the merits of air power. The only officer at Mitchell's court-martial to cast a vote of "Not Guilty" was General MacArthur, and Congress later declared Mitchell's conviction to have been wrong by awarding him the Medal of Honor.

among the flinty old men, and across the country in homes and public places, emotion rose steadily higher as the general drew toward the end of his speech, and the end of his career, and tears stole silently down men's cheeks. MacArthur closed with the refrain from a song he had first heard as a West Point cadet, that "Old soldiers never die, they just fade away."

Leaving Washington, the triumphal progress continued. "On the day MacArthur rode in triumph down Broadway under clouds of ticker tape, President Truman stood up in his box at Washington's Griffith Stadium to throw out the first baseball of the new season. A sullen thunder of boos rolled across the stands."

On the road, MacArthur gave his views wherever he stopped and was invariably received with acclaim. His principal concern was the fate of the wretched Gismo and the Gismo's even more tawdry retinue. He made glib and slanderous remarks about "Communist influences" in government. He spoke intemperately about "Socialist policies." His wife, more sensitive than he to the effects of such tirades on the luster of his name, asked him to desist. He had the grace and the sense to comply.

The Senate Armed Services Committee and the Senate Foreign Relations Committee were meanwhile conducting joint hearings on the conduct of the war. The Administration's critics were badly discomfited. MacArthur's tactical and strategic mistakes were ventilated. And Acheson, the hated Acheson, spent eight days being interrogated. Intellectually more gifted than his tormentors and more familiar with the issues and problems involved, he smashed their arguments to pieces. "It looks," said one Washington reporter, "like the lions have been thrown to the martyr."

As the Korean War began to settle into a stalemate, loud noises were heard offstage. Early in 1951 the first atomic bomb test conducted on American soil since 1945 rattled windows in Las Vegas, sixty miles from the test site at Frenchman's Flat, and set off burglar alarms. The flash of the explosion was visible in Southern California. In Los Angeles in following months there was a craze for building home bomb shelters.

Test followed test all through 1951 and into 1952. It was evident that the United States was developing battlefield nuclear weapons, a case made by the scientists and resisted by the Air Force which looked with disfavor on any atomic weapon that did not call for a bomber to carry it. No one pressed the case for tactical nuclear weapons harder than Oppenheimer.

More than twenty atomic weapons tests were conducted at Frenchman's Flat and nearby Yucca Flat during the Korean War. All were highly publicized. One test was broadcast live on television. In April 1952 the Army unveiled its first atomic cannon, a gun which fired an eight-inch shell. The arrival of the atomic cannon underscored the rapidity with which atomic weapons had been scaled down to battlefield size—a point no doubt of interest to the Russians and Chinese. Whether by coincidence or not, it was the Russians who, in the summer of 1951, began to suggest that the belligerents in the Korean War might find it to their mutual advantage to seek a negotiated settlement.

* * *

When the Korean War began, the economy was already based mainly on wars past, present, and future. Nearly three-fourths of the Federal budget was spent on the armed forces, veterans, servicing wartime bond issues, and the like. Of each dollar spent, health and welfare programs took less than seven cents. There were extensive Social Security programs, but these were nearly entirely self-financing.

The Cold War was a spur to business. Thousands of corporations became, in effect if not name, civilian dependencies of the Department of Defense, a development mockingly termed "military Socialism."

Radical thought holds that business likes war. News of the invasion of South Korea sent the stock market plummeting. Business had prospered in recent months as never before. GM, for example, had earned $3.68 a share at its wartime peak. In the first six months of 1950 it was earning nearly $20 a share. Most blue chips showed a similar picture.

But while the stock market fell, partly in anticipation of a new excess profits tax, the outbreak of war could not have been more timely for the unemployed. Unemployment had been rising steadily since the fall of 1948, when it stood at 2 percent. In the spring of 1950 it stood at 5 percent. By the end of 1950 it was back down to 2 percent.

Most people at first took the news of fighting calmly. But after two weeks self-restraint began to crack. By mid-July people would buy almost anything they could get their hands on. Stores were rapidly emptied of tires, sugar, nylons, canned goods, and television sets. The retail price index began to rise dramatically. The government's war orders provided an added stimulus to inflation. But Congress rapidly passed a $3 billion tax increase to help pay for the war, and this helped damp down the fire. The Federal Reserve Board put sharp restrictions on consumer credit. Unions were persuaded to exercise restraint in making wage demands.

Although the country proved able to fight the Korean War without serious economic or social dislocation, many people felt uneasy. They knew how to throw themselves and all their productive capacity into a war. But no one, in government or business or the nation at large, knew how to do it halfway or less than halfway.

The central question the Administration faced was whether to build new war plants to produce material for Korea or whether to expand existing plants. A compromise was reached: business was allowed to build new plants and write off the entire capital cost over five years instead of the normal twenty-five. Although not intended to have this result, the fast write-off produced a phenomenal increase in capital investment from 1950 through 1955. By the late 1950s the United States would achieve a "dual economy"—half private, half government-directed; half military, half consumer goods. Thus, although the development was spread over nearly a decade, the Korean War can be said to have brought the Cold War economy to full flower.

The Korean War also, and perhaps not so incidentally, brought the gross national product back, in real terms, to the peak achieved in 1944.

In January 1951 wages and prices were frozen. The Administration began thinking out loud about a tax increase and thought that $10 billion sounded about right. After months of hesitation, and making unhappy faces the while, Congress eventually raised taxes by $5.7 billion. This included increased excise taxes which raised the price of liquor forty cents a fifth and triggered a frantic descent on the liquor stores. An excess profits tax was enacted but was mild compared with its predecessor of a decade earlier. The stock market recovered and for the remainder of the war rose steadily.

9
Whatever Happened to the Fair Deal?

After his 1948 victory, Truman found a new charman for the CEA, an economist whose expansionist views coincided with Truman's Populist instincts. But with the onset of the Korean War nearly all increased production went not into domestic consumption but into the war. Nor could the Fair Deal hope to gain much ground with price controls and increased taxes. Not surprisingly, "For the achievement of domestic reforms, no President worked harder and accomplished less."

He asked Congress to elevate the Federal Security Agency to a Cabinet-level Department of Welfare. Congress rejected this request in 1949 and again in 1950. He hoped to begin a major program of Federal aid to education. In an attempt to placate Catholics, he sent an American ambassador to the Vatican. (Attempting to placate Protestants, he chose a fellow Mason, General Mark Clark.) It did no good. He was roundly berated for according the Vatican full diplomatic recognition, and his aid to education bill was killed by Catholic opposition. He lent his efforts to attempts made by labor's friends in Congress to rewrite Taft-Hartley. But a California Republican, Donald L. Johnson, was able to report to his constituents, in gleeful doggerel:

> The tumult and the shouting die,
> The lobbyists in haste depart,
> Still stands that ancient labor law,
> T-H, intact in every part.

When Truman sent a civil rights bill to Congress, it was, inevitably, filibusted to death in the Senate.

Nor did these initiatives increase his standing with liberal Democrats.

His Inaugural Address, they disdainfully remarked, consisted largely of vitriolic anti-Communism, with hardly a constructive thought to relieve the tedium. Appointments such as putting Tom Clark on the Supreme Court and bringing in J. Howard McGrath to succeed Clark as Attorney General provoked astonishment and dismay. McGrath looked impressive but was irredeemably mediocre. Clark was equally mediocre, and it showed.

The President did enjoy some successes; the most notable part of the Fair Deal to become law was the Housing Act of 1949. It was passed over fierce opposition from the real estate lobby. The President wanted a million units of low-cost public housing, and public housing of any kind was a highly emotive matter. The debate on the act grew so heated that two members of the House Rules Committee, during discussions on the bill, engaged in a fistfight. One of the combatants was sixty-nine; his opponent was eighty-three. The Housing Act of 1949 compromised at 810,000 units. (Fewer than half would ever be built.) And ironically, it took effect just when the evident need for such legislation—the postwar housing shortage—was drawing to an end. In 1950, 1.4 million housing units were completed.

The desegregation of the armed forces advanced, over a guerrilla resistance waged by Army officers. The Air Force, by comparison, made no attempt to thwart the President's directive. A Bristol, Tennessee, housewife in June 1949 received a panic-stricken letter from her airman son: "Mom, this is something I want you or Dad to do quick. They are mixing niggers in the same barracks with us. If everyone's parents write their Congressman for something to be done about it, it will. Mom, please don't let me down. . . ."

The Army Secretary, Kenneth Royall, tried to justify the Army's obduracy by rehearsing the old arguments, including the assertion that blacks were endowed by their Creator with certain innate characteristics which made them unusually well suited for manual labor. Truman replaced Royall with Gordon Gray, who was willing to implement the desegregation order.

In March 1950 Gray lifted the quota which had kept blacks below 10 percent of Army strength. Within three months one-fourth of the Army's recruits were black. With so many blacks now coming into the Army, integration became inevitable—unless the generals wanted to have black units at three times their authorized strength and white units at barely half strength.

The Korean War completed the process. Field commanders demanded trained infantry replacements, quickly, and regardless of color.

Desegregation of the military was not a major concern to most white people, but it was to most blacks. It involved both elementary justice and racial pride. It was also a chance for many young black men to get away from a life of poverty and hopelessness. The middle class generally has never understood how important the military option has been among the poor and the working class.

While it was not overtly a part of the Fair Deal, the desegregation poli-cy deserves to be counted as its most striking success. It was wholly with-in the spirit of the Fair Deal, and it was a large step toward a more just society.

The most lamentable defeat suffered by the Fair Deal was the rejection of Truman's proposal for nationwide, comprehensive health insurance. As a rule, nothing is deader (or duller) than rejected legislation, but the health care controversy was not resolved by the defeat of the Truman proposal; it endured throughout the postwar. The issues it raised were raised again and again. And the number of people affected ran into the tens of millions.

In the late 1940s up to one-half the entire population fell ill in the course of a year. A major study conducted in 1947 concluded: "If allowance is made for forgotten illness or unrecognized conditions, it is not unreason-able to assume that at any given time one person in four needs medical at-tention for some chronic ailment or serious physical defect."

The Administration claimed that there was a doctor shortage; the AMA, that there was a doctor surplus. It was a pointless dispute, depend-ing mainly on how you defined adequate health care. And health is so much a part of the total fabric of society that health standards can be im-proved without training one more doctor or adding one more hospital bed; by improving roads, for example.

Health was (is) in large measure a matter of class, race, and geography. Infant mortality, rheumatic fever, mental illness, heart disease, tuber-culosis, nephritis, diabetes, and pneumonia all were markedly more pre-valent in the lower third of society than in the top third. Health problems involved poverty, neglect (including self-neglect), and lack of education. It was problematical whether offering more medical services would achieve a better result than would a more equitable distribution of exist-ing services. The latter might also do wonders for social mobility. Chronic illness was twice as prevalent among the lower third as among those above them, and chronic illness made it virtually impossible for people to rise in the social scale.

Better organization of health care during World War II, when 40 per-cent of the nation's doctors were taking care of the 9 percent of the popu-lation that was in uniform, had brought about an astonishing increase in the country's health. Wartime prosperity had also put health and medical services for the first time within reach of tens of millions of people for-merly unable to afford them.

Cost had become the worm in the bud of American medicine. It was that which Truman intended to change. In Illinois, for example, the num-ber of tests doctors ordered for hospitalized patients doubled between 1945 and 1950 and were at six times the Depression level. The daily cost of a private hospital bed was $14.65 in 1949, or 50 percent more than the average daily wage. At a time when three-fourths of the nation had no medical or health insurance, the prospect of a serious illness was terrifying, and this was true despite the fact that the nation as a whole spent more on tobacco and alcohol than on health and medical care.

The VA offered a form of Socialized medicine, to the disgust of some VA doctors, whose hearts were with the AMA. The exact figure can never be known, but it seems possible that as few as 20 percent of all VA beds were occupied by patients with service-connected illnesses and nothing else. The remainder, wrote one VA doctor, "are hospitalized for some infirmity not remotely connected with the war or their military service." He recalled an ex-GI who got drunk and wrecked his car and his legs; a man of forty-six who was stabbed in a bar brawl; an ex-WAC who had suffered from bunions since the age of thirteen. After leaving the Army, she eventually decided to have her bunions removed, and the VA obliged, "with Uncle Sam footing the bill." All that any veteran need do was swear that he or she needed medical care and could not afford to pay for it. A grateful nation then stepped in to show its appreciation for services rendered.

Truman proposed to levy a 3 percent payroll tax which, when added to the 2 percent Social Security levy, would provide cradle-to-grave security for all. He proposed, moreover, that the Federal government provide money to private nursing homes and private hospitals to take care of the indigent sick who were otherwise ineligible under the payroll deduction scheme.

The overriding merit of the Truman proposal was that it would cover 20 to 25 percent of the population who could not possibly obtain medical insurance on their present income at rates which they could realistically afford, or could not obtain because of their present bad state of health. *Life* called the proposal HEALTH BY COMPULSION.

But the emphasis of the President's plan was on voluntary cooperation. Each state would run its own program. The Federal government would merely collect the payroll levy and remit it to the states. Each community would create an area health authority, under state supervision. The health authority would sign up the doctors. It was for each doctor to decide whether or not, and to what extent, he would participate in the program. Each patient would be free to choose his own doctor. Each doctor would be free to accept or reject a patient. The doctors who joined the program would decide how they wanted to be paid, whether for each service provided, or so much per patient on their books, or whether to form group practices and put themselves on salary. The hospitals would be run much as they had always been run and would submit their bills to the area health authority.

The AMA resisted the Truman idea in part and in toto. Since 1943 it had assiduously promoted medical insurance (Blue Shield, which paid the doctor's bill) as an alternative to any government plan. Blue Shield collaborated closely with Blue Cross (which paid the hospital bill). The AMA's efforts met with remarkable success. Both Blue Cross and Blue Shield covered only a few million people in 1943. Ten years later they covered 50 million (37 million Blue Cross, 13 million Blue Shield). But insurance paid only part of the total bill. Typically, Blue Cross covered 80 percent of a claimant's hospital bill; Blue Shield, 55 percent of a claimant's doctor's bill. These plans did not provide preventive medicine. Nor did they offer full coverage. The best Blue Shield plan available excluded: mental illness; industrial accidents; dental fillings, inlays, and dentures; optical care; chronic illness which lasted longer than twelve months; and any preexisting medical condition. Comprehensive insurance did not exist because only the rich could have afforded the premiums. If they were rich, they did not need insurance. Most plans also excluded anyone entitled to treatment by the VA or who qualified for workmen's compensation.

By showing that health insurance was actuarially sound, within such limits, Blue Cross paved the way for the large insurance companies to move into the health and medical insurance field. They signed up all the good risks they could find, leaving Blue Cross and Blue Shield to sort through the remainder. Blue Cross had begun with the aim of coverage for all, exclusion of none. By adding more and more riders, Blue Cross managed to avoid the bad risks without overtly repudiating its original philosophy.

As insurance and prepayment plans spread, the demand for hospital services rose accordingly, and people went to see their doctors more often. Any nationwide comprehensive insurance program was certain to increase the demand for health care. Part of the increase would, inevitably, come from people merely seeking attention. But much of it would just as predictably come from those who had a genuine need for prosthetics, drugs, operations, and therapy—a need hitherto suppressed for lack of money.

The AMA denounced Truman's proposed legislation as "Socialism," the next thing to Godless Communism, and a menace to the American way of life. The hostility to government and all its works, however, might on occasion be relaxed, as when the doctors lobbied for and won an amendment to the GI Bill of Rights so that they could take a medical refresher course for up to one year at government expense. Nor did their ideological scruples discourage their zealous lobbying to be allowed to buy, for nominal sums, the vast quantities of surplus drugs, sterilizers, X-ray machines, EKG equipment, surgical instruments, and other interesting items paid for by the taxpayer. To the doctors' horror this treasure trove was sold at giveaway prices to the nation's hospitals and clinics.

The AMA was not as obscurantist as its critics tended to believe. It supported Federal financing for hospital construction. It supported expansion of the Public Health Service. It approved Federally financed medical research. But it opposed the creation of a Department of Health, Education, and Welfare, medical examinations for all school-age children, maternal and child-care services at public expense, and help with catastrophic illnesses, the costs of which ran into the tens of thousands of dollars. It opposed these measures because singly or together they pointed toward a national system of health care.

The nation's medical schools were hard pressed for money. But the

AMA pressured them to refuse Federal aid, because with its foot in the door the Federal government might try to increase the number of schools or the number of places in them. The AMA and the medical schools kept the ratio of doctors to population at 135 per 100,000.

No craft union ever protected the economic interests of its members with greater skill or dedication. It had watched Truman's interest in health care with the deepest suspicion. In 1946 it accused him of a secret desire to turn doctors into "slaves" or at least "clock watchers." Following his victory in 1948 the AMA prepared for the coming showdown by levying a $25 assessment on its members. But because it was a tax exempt, nonprofit body barred by law from lobbying, it cynically claimed that the money, amounting to more than $3 million, was being raised "for a nationwide plan of education on the progress of American medicine, the importance of the conservation of health, and the advantages of the American system in securing a wide distribution of a high quality of medical care."

Until this assessment was levied, AMA members had never paid dues. The AMA had financed itself through subscriptions to its *Journal* and advertisements in it. Thousands of doctors objected to the $25 levy, but they were promptly brought to heel by a threat that anyone who refused to pay this voluntary assessment would lose his AMA membership. This in turn raised the possibility of expulsion from the county or state medical association. If that happened, any doctor was likely to lose his staff appointment at the local hospital to which he sent his patients. He could also expect to lose his malpractice insurance. The theme of the AMA's publicity campaign was that politics should be kept out of medicine.

This educational enterprise was placed in the hands of the San Francisco public relations agency Whitaker and Baxter. In 1945 it had handled the campaign of the California Medical Association against Governor Earl Warren's proposed plan of statewide health insurance. It had succeeded, but narrowly. Warren's proposal was defeated in the state legislature by a single vote.

Truman's plan was supported by the AFL, the CIO, the ADA, the American Jewish Committee, the American Veterans Committee, the NAACP, the National Farmers Union, the Brotherhood of Railroad Trainmen, and Eleanor Roosevelt. Like Warren's proposal, it was popular with most people, but like it again, it would never be put to them for a vote.

The AMA's campaign against "Socialized medicine" raged for all of the second Truman Administration. It cost the AMA nearly $5 million. It was ironic, however, that the first victim of the campaign was the man who had made the AMA what it was, Morris Fishbein, the editor of the *Journal*. Although a doctor by training, Fishbein's gifts were less those of the healer than of the promoter. He was an abrasive, self-important little man whose panting avidity for esteem evoked only scorn and laughter. He alienated the conservative doctors, who loathed "Socialized medicine," and the liberal doctors, who loathed him. When the struggle to defeat the Truman plan began in earnest, they combined, to Fishbein's utter astonishment, to get rid of him as a public relations liability.

The AMA's strategy was to frighten the doctors into frightening their patients into frightening their Congressmen. Doctors' offices sprouted large reproductions of the sentimental painting *The Doctor*, by Sir Luke Fields. Until now it had been best known as the central feature in a laxative advertisement. It showed a wan, comatose, but pretty lad in his sickbed. The parents hovered anxiously in the background. In the foreground sat the doctor, gray-bearded, worried, chin in hand, gazing with tender concern at the inert boy. Whitaker and Baxter improved on the painter's efforts by providing a caption for his work: "Keep Politics Out of This Picture."

Besides spreading the work of Sir Luke Fields, the AMA campaign filled doctors' waiting rooms with stacks of red, white, and blue pamphlets called "The Voluntary Way Is the American Way." Doctors' bills bore stickers which began "As your personal physician . . ." and concluded "Please write your U.S. Senator and Representative." Leaving no stone unturned, the AMA itself got in touch with every Senator and Representative.

The AMA also descended to telling lies about the British National Health Service, then reported them as factual accounts in the *Journal*. There were fantastic tales of patients being diagnosed in batches of twenty or thirty at a time, whereupon one prescription was written for the entire group. When the British Medical Association challenged these stories, the AMA insisted the stories were true but refused to offer a shred of evidence to support them.

In the end, the AMA lobby in Washington defeated the President. It was the most comprehensive legislative defeat of the Truman Presidency and the one with the widest social consequences.

Truman broached an ambitious answer to the problem of agricultural surpluses on the one hand and declining farm incomes on the other. Almost no one was satisfied with the present arrangement.

Yet the farmers had few friends. People tended to regard them with a mixture of envy and scorn. They believed farmers and their families enjoyed a uniquely pleasant way of life; they also believed farmers were fawned upon by government. "The U.S. farmer, the nation's most favored man, could continue his fat income-guaranteed wartime living," was a typical comment on the 1949 farm bill.

To the farmers, life appeared very different, and so did the role of the Federal government. There was widespread anger in farming areas over legislation in 1950 which extended the Federal ban on the employment of child labor (children under sixteen) to agriculture. Child labor on farms extends back millennia; it was also part of the sentimentalized notion of "the family farm." In vain did the farmers argue that work made children into sober, responsible citizens who knew the value of a dollar.

While there was much about farming that was satisfying and pleasant, agriculture was the third most dangerous of all occupations, after construction and mining. But although safety records in those two fields showed a steady improvement, safety in agriculture did not.

Urban dwellers grumbled without understanding such matters, being unaware how dangerous farm work was, how exhausting it remained despite (at times because of) the revolution in agricultural technology, how even simple things, such as electricity, had to be fought for.

When the New Deal began, only 10 percent of American farms enjoyed electricity. When the Fair Deal ended, only 10 percent were without it. The private power companies showed no interest in stringing power lines across sparsely populated areas; the rates they would have been forced to charge would have been more than the farmers could pay. Unfortunately, when the farmers formed power cooperatives, the power companies resorted to every form of obstruction available, from legal harassment to physical intimidation. So far as they were concerned, the farmers could stay in the darkness forever.

The rural electrification program begun under Roosevelt was completed under Truman. Farmers borrowed government money at low interest rates to establish power co-ops. These in turn were allowed to buy power from Federally built dams at competitive prices, to the fury of the private power companies.

Electrification was a profoundly important social development in farming areas between 1935 and 1952. Its chief effect was to break down the farmer's isolation within what was an urban nation, first by bringing him radio, later by bringing him television. Federally financed roads also put him in closer contact with the city. The Department of Agriculture taught him how to farm more efficiently. Bit by bit, the sturdy, independent farmer, needing only a plot of land and a break in the weather, became a figure of myth and legend. Without the cheap fertilizers, the government loans, and the help of the county agent, most farmers would have been lucky to get through more than a year on their own.

Farmer's incomes were extremely unstable, fluctuating by as much as 25 percent from one year to the next. They remained unstable because of man-made, as much as natural, causes. When the supply of a particular farm product fell, prices rose. Farmers would then plant a lot of that, whatever it was, for the next year. This meant that the next year there was too much of it, and prices fell. At this point many of them decided not to plant so much of the product the next year. So the next year its price would probably go up, by which time they had switched to overproducing something else, causing *its* price to go down.

For instance, there were large surpluses of potatoes from 1948 to 1950. Tens of thousands of potatoes were dumped on the government and destroyed. Under parity, however, the farmers were still assured a reasonable, if not a lavish, income. Art Wardner of East Grand Forks, Minnesota, for example sold his potato crop to the government in the winter of 1949–1950; technically he got a government loan on them at a value of $1.46 a hundredweight. On eighty tons of potatoes that came to a "loan" of $2,336. Art thereupon bought the potatoes back, under the farm surplus disposal program, at 1 cent a hundredweight. He wrote the government a check for $16, then fed the eighty tons of potatoes to his cattle. During these transactions not a single spud ever left his farm.

Then, in 1951, there came the inevitable potato shortage. A potato black market developed. When a young couple in Buffalo got married they discovered to their joy that a thoughtful wedding guest had given them a 100-pound sack of precious spuds. Meanwhile, armed guards were patrolling America's largest potato fields.

Unstable incomes were one side of the coin; low incomes were the other. Despite the massive migration from the farms to the cities, there were still far too many farm families trying to get a share of total farm income. Income distribution in agriculture resembled that in an impoverished, preindustrial country; a few rich at the top, many poor at the bottom. In 1952 only one-sixth of Americans in full-time work earned less than $1,500. Among farmers, however, half earned less than $1,500.

Farmers retained an emotional commitment to free enterprise. But neither they nor the politicians who courted their votes and represented their interests ever considered this a realistic possibility. So to many people farmers also appeared to be hypocrites.

There was among politicians a catechism of agriculture which ran: "Thou Shalt invariably promote The Family Farm. Thou Shalt elevate The Rural Life above the urban life. Thou Shalt steadfastly uphold Parity for the Farmer. Thou Shalt blame the Middleman for any economic difficulties which overtake farmers." With this catechism on his lips no politician alive need entertain the least trepidation when soliciting the farmer's vote.

The famous storage bin problem was eventually solved in 1949 by a simple expedient: farmers were given government loans to construct their own bins. It was a simple and effective answer. But no one had thought of it in 1948.

Farm policy was so dangerous an area that it became, like foreign policy, an area where nonpartisanship prevailed, even though farmers voted Democratic by a margin of three to one. The conventional wisdom in Washington was that it had been the farmers, not labor, who had made Truman President in 1948, that they had been won over by Democratic promises of "high, rigid price supports." There was thus no interest in the flexible supports authorized by the 1948 Agriculture Act.

But the law had changed the parity formula for good. It was brought closer to the present time by being based on average commodity prices during the past ten years. The objective remained unchanged, however—to secure for the farmer the same standard of living he had enjoyed during the halcyon years 1910–1914. The aim of parity payments was to make up the difference earned in that golden age and what was earned at present.

There was one alternative to price supports to achieve this aim: direct subsidies. It was an idea mooted at various times. But in 1949 Secretary of Agriculture Charles F. Brannan proposed to guarantee the farmers a fixed share of the national income by paying them a direct subsidy on every basic crop, plus cotton and tobacco.

The Farm Bureau Federation was aghast. Yet USDA officials and agricultural economists in scores of universities had for more than a decade been discussing the idea, usually in favorable terms. But among farmers' organizations only the National Farmers' Union, which represented the poorer farmers, endorsed the Brannan Plan.

It was popular, however, with organized labor, because it held out the prospect of cheap food. Brannan proposed to make direct payments to farmers to make up the difference between what they could get for their crops on a free market and what they needed for a decent standard of living. The government would no longer be saddled with farm surpluses; the food would go straight to market, even if that meant that prices would fall. When viewed in conjunction with the graduated income tax, the effect of the Brannan Plan would have been to put the top half of income groups into a position of buying food for the bottom half, and most particularly, they would be helping to feed the people in the lower half for whom food was the largest single item in the family budget. Considering what taxpayers were already paying for price supports, it is problematical whether the Brannan Plan would have cost any more.

But Brannan mismanaged the presentation of his proposal. He failed to consult the most important farm body in advance, the Farm Bureau Federation. He also antagonized the big farmers by putting an upper limit on the payment to be made in respect of any one crop at $20,000. And he insisted on the need for tight production controls.

He also oversold the possible benefits of his proposal, portraying it as both a defense against economic depression and a barrier to the spreading of Communism. He forfeited public confidence, moreover, by refusing to say what his plan would cost. Estimates ranged from $3.5 billion to $8 billion, and without estimates from the USDA one guess was as good as another.

Opinion among farmers was almost equally divided over the Brannan Plan. But after a year of furious controversy the Korean War broke out, and soon the surpluses, which had encouraged Brannan's demarche, were no longer an important problem.

Truman was temperamentally sympathetic toward ordinary people—small farmers, industrial workers, small businessmen, the elderly, the poor, the obscure. He retained a border Populist's suspicion of Big Business and its friends in Congress. In the last major strike of his Presidency he unabashedly took the side of the steelworkers.

Steel was an industry still run in the style of the Gilded Age. The big steel companies formed an oligopoly which was allowed to set its own rules—an oligopoly made more effective than ever by the government disposition of the wartime, tax-financed steel plants. By its generosity in giving the big steel corporations modern plants at minimal cost, the government had effectively foreclosed any possibility of postwar competition developing in the steel industry.

Steel prices were set not by competition but by U.S. Steel. Its pivotal role was further strengthened by its possession of so much of the country's supply of iron ore that its "competitors" (e.g., Inland, Republic, Bethlehem) depended on its supplies to keep their own plants working at a high level of production.

The steel companies showed consistently high profits. The Korean War only added to their profitability. In November 1951 the steelworkers began negotiating a new contract. They demanded a thirty-cent wage increase and a union shop. The steel companies rejected both demands.

The Wage Stabilization Board intervened but failed to resolve the dispute. When the unions eventually struck, in April 1952, Truman refused to invoke his powers under Taft-Hartley. Instead, he seized the steel plants.

This was the seventy-second time that the Federal government had taken over private business, and without a doubt it was the most popular. Regardless of the issues involved, to most people it was indefensible that anyone should strike so vital an industry in wartime.

A Federal judge ruled the seizure was illegal. The Supreme Court listened before a packed chamber to oral arguments on the issue. For once, chairs were allowed to be set in the aisles of the court and standees were allowed to fill what space remained at the back of the room. After three weeks of deliberation the Court ruled that the seizure was indeed illegal. But the strike was still on—and Truman still refused to invoke Taft-Hartley.

The union permitted a partial reopening of the plants to provide steel for national defense. Yet shortages of critical items appeared; production targets for combat aircraft, artillery shells, and small arms were not met.

Truman summoned Philip Murray, leader of the steelworkers, and the president of U.S. Steel, Benjamin Fairless, to the White House. He demanded that they settle the strike. His leverage was that neither side wanted to be blamed for a catastrophic reverse on the battlefield. Closeted in the Cabinet room for two hours, they emerged with an agreement. The workers got wage and fringe benefits worth twenty-one cents an hour, the companies relented on the union shop, and steel prices were allowed to rise by $5.50 a ton.

The strike had run for fifty-five days. It had cost the nation 17 million tons of steel. It had put more than 1 million non-steelworkers out of their jobs. Yet Truman, convinced that justice was on the side of the steelworkers, refused to act against them as he had acted, in the past, against miners, oil refinery workers, and railwaymen. And he held out against public opinion and the Supreme Court, hewing to his Populist convictions.

The Fair Deal was not a slogan glibly coined but a series of proposals the President genuinely believed in. But the times, the Congress, his own inability patiently to cultivate support, all contrived to frustrate him.

10

Justice on Trial

The American Communist Party continued to stagger from one bout of self-mutilation to the next. In most organizations the ultimate sanction—expulsion—is reluctantly employed. In the Communist Party it was often the weapon of first resort. It was invoked even for such trifling offenses as taking a vacation at Miami Beach, that cesspool of "white chauvinism."

The post-Browder leadership of the Party led it from disaster to disaster. Lemmings could not have done better. And the fierce internal struggles denoted not tight party discipline but a lack of control. Just as petty criminals were once summarily dispatched because it was hard to catch a pickpocket or sheep thief in the act, so the ready resort to expulsion testified to the Party's comparative impotence. It was noteworthy, too, that in the course of these purges it was the working-class members who were likely to be dropped and the middle-class, professional members who were usually retained.

Firmly repudiating anything which smacked of Browderism, the Party became increasingly provocative. Even during the trial of the Communist leaders it helped precipitate a bloody riot in Peekskill, New York. The Civil Rights Congress, one of the Party's principal fund-raising bodies, had scheduled a concert by Paul Robeson. The intervention of the American Legion and the VFW, who beat up the audience before it could reach the concert site, prevented it from taking place. A second concert was scheduled. But instead of seeking to avoid another clash, the organizers prepared for one. "Their advance statements [were] so provocative that they came close to incitement to riot, and many of the men who came in chartered buses from New York city, recruited from the Communist-led Fur and Leather Workers Union, carried clubs." They carried themselves like a military formation and were led by a former Army officer.

More than 500 right-wing veterans, accompanied by brass bands, were on hand to meet them. The veterans attempted to march into the picnic grove where Robeson was scheduled to sing. The "concertgoers" linked arms to check them. The veterans momentarily withdrew but soon charged from out of the gathering dusk, advancing behind a barrage of rocks and bottles. The wavering line of ducking pickets sang "We Shall Overcome," then broke under the veterans' charge.

The veterans smashed their way into the grove, demolished the stage, set fire to stacks of wooden chairs, and, after the fashion set by the SA, burned such vestiges of culture as sheet music. They punched and kicked anyone within reach of fist or boot. Up and down the nearby road they overturned cars and vandalized buses. Nearly 150 people were injured despite (in some cases because of) the presence of 1,000 policemen. For to some policemen the opportunity to beat up a leftist was simply irresistible.

But the real battleground of the domestic Cold War was not in picnic groves and streets. It was in the Federal courts. This was a war fought according to Clausewitzian dicta on strategy: muster a superior force; bring the enemy to battle; destroy his forces by exploiting local superiority; never allow the enemy to rest. Part of the superior force these days consisted of a highly charged atmosphere in which it was impossible with the best will in the world to assure a fair trial to anyone connected with the Communist Party. When the eleven Party leaders went on trial in New York in February 1949,* even lifelong opponents of Communism were deeply troubled. The charges were so vaguely drawn and the country's mood so vitriolic where Communism was concerned that, concluded two eminent scholars, "Conviction was almost a foregone conclusion."

During the trial of the CP leaders hardly a week passed without some new sensation or revelation. Gerhardt Eisler, a German Communist convicted of passport fraud and contempt of Congress, was released on bail of $23,500. Eisler was spirited aboard a Polish ship and jumped bail. An unsuccessful attempt to extradite him from Britain was a matter of such passionate interest that it temporarily pushed the marriage of Rita Hayworth and Aly Khan off the front page.

In a single week in June 1949 while the CP leaders were being tried, David Lilienthal was being interrogated by a Senate committee amid rumors that Soviet agents had penetrated AEC laboratories; the National Education Association was launching a campaign to get Communists out of the schools; the California legislature published a list of supposedly secret Communist sympathizers in Hollywood; Judith Coplon, an employee at the Treasury Department, was on trial for passing secret documents to a Soviet agent; HUAC resumed its hearings in Washington; J. Robert Oppenheimer's brother Frank, himself a distinguished physicist, admitted that he had once been a member of the CP; Morton Kent, a former State Department employee, was described in FBI reports introduced at the Coplon trial as a suspected Soviet agent (several days later, by the banks of the Potomac, Kent cut his throat); and in the first Hiss trial Henry Julian Wadleigh admitted that he had transmitted State Department documents to the Soviets. In Carnegie Hall that same week Oksana Kasenkina appeared, fully recovered at last from her terrible injuries, as the star of a rally on behalf of Western democracy.

Contrary to popular opinion, the CP leaders were charged not with conspiring to advocate violence but with conspiring to form a party which would, at some time in the future, advocate violence. They were not charged with any overt action; they were accused of harboring evil intentions. The central event in the prosecution's case was the reestablishment of the Communist Party in 1945 following the rejection of Browderism.

---

*One of the original twelve was dropped from this trial because of poor health. Earl Browder complained that he deserved to be indicted with the remaining eleven. But he was not overlooked. He was indicted for contempt of Congress for refusing to answer questions before HUAC. When news of this indictment reached him, Browder hastened to Washington to be arrested.

The government argued that the old CP had advocated violent opposition to legally constituted government, that this bad old Party had gone out of existence in 1944, when the Communist Political Association was formed, but that when the CPUSA was reestablished in 1945 there had been a "return" to the advocacy of revolutionary violence.

In effect, the government was admitting that the CPUSA was teaching nothing in 1948 it had not been teaching in 1940, when the Smith Act, under which the members were charged, had become law. So why had they not been indicted then? Or conversely, why were they being tried in 1949? Clearly because the climate had changed; the CP had not; the Smith Act had not. And Truman had taken advantage of that change in the political and emotional climate during his election campaign, when the indictments had been handed down.

The Communist leaders attempted to portray themselves as erstwhile champions of the Bill of Rights. Yet they had applauded, and supported, the Smith Act back in 1942, when it had been used to send a band of Minneapolis Trotskyists to prison mainly on the basis of their reading matter.

For the trial, the FBI compiled three briefs, running to nearly 2,000 pages in all, and provided 184 exhibits. The whole was: "A giant new edition of the brief which Hoover had drawn against the same Communist Party 27 years earlier." To prove its claim that the newly reconstituted Party intended to overthrow the government at some future time, the prosecution case dwelt at tedious length on the writings of Marx, Lenin, and Stalin. It presented thirteen "expert" witnesses—ex-Communists and FBI informants within the Party—to interpret what the sacred texts *really* meant—that is, the government invoked a theory that Communists used "Aesopian language," and what they said was often the opposite of what they meant. Thus, when a Communist claimed to favor peace, he really favored war. When he claimed to be opposed to a violent attack on government, he actually was seeking a violent attack on government. The emphasis placed on language was paramount to the government case, because it was the distinction of the Smith Act that it made words of themselves treasonable.

The prosecution sprang a melodramatic surprise by calling as a witness Herbert Philbrick, for eight years a Communist for the FBI. Philbrick had drifted into the Communist-dominated pacifist youth movement in 1940. In 1941, his suspicions aroused, he contacted the FBI. He had never risen from being a foot soldier in the Party, never did anything of consequence within it, never met any of the eleven leaders on trial. The greatest risk he had run was of dying from boredom. Nevertheless his "exploits" became the basis of *I Led Three Lives*, a turgid television program ground out for most of the 1950s for the edification of a faithful audience of millions.

The trial judge, Harold R. Medina, foresaw that the trial would prove long and difficult. The defendants and their lawyers harried him from the outset, attempting to force him into making errors which would be reversible on appeal or to create so much disorder that the trial would be abandoned. But Medina, like a good general, had in his mind already fought out the battle to come. He prepared himself accordingly. He imposed a rigid discipline on himself, paying close attention to his diet, forcing himself to take a nap each afternoon, giving up his social life for the duration of the trial. He spent many hours studying the 1944 sedition trial of the native Fascists, which had run for eight months before it ended with the death of the judge.

Medina's life was threatened several times. His telephone rang incessantly. His mail was fat with obscene literature. On his way to and from court, and in the courtroom itself, he was mocked and abused. Toward the end of the nine-month trial (the longest in American criminal justice) Medina's nerves were badly frayed, and he began to feel ill. One afternoon, retiring for his nap, he felt the weight of his sixty years, and "When I went out to that little room behind the courtroom I honestly didn't think I was ever going back." But some "tall praying," as he put it, helped.

To Medina, the trial was a head-on clash between Communism and the Constitution, between subversion and Christianity. He was determined to survive. He was also determined that the accused would be convicted—and the convictions would stick.

The established legal doctrine for determining the point at which the advocacy of an idea justifies government intervention (and prosecution) was the doctrine formulated by Holmes and Brandeis of "a clear and present danger." Medina allowed the jury to ignore that doctrine and turned their attention to what he called the "substantive evil" of the alleged seditious conspiracy. Having led the jury into making what was a moral judgment on words and ideas at a time when very few people were able to think coolly about Communists' words and ideas, Medina made conviction nearly as certain as it could be. When the jury returned from their deliberations, they lived up to the judge's expectations. All eleven accused were convicted.

Ten received the maximum penalty for conspiracy, five years. The eleventh, Robert Thompson, received three years—a concession to the DSC he had won for heroism during the war.

The trial made Medina famous; the conviction of the accused made him popular. He appeared on *Time*'s cover. He was inundated with fan mail from thousands of people not noted for their infatuation with elderly judges of the Federal bench. In following years he spent much of his free time traveling the country, delivering speeches on the Communist menace.

The Court of Appeals unanimously upheld the convictions. Not a scintilla of evidence had been offered to show that any of the doctrines the Communist Party leaders had advocated were to be implemented soon, let alone immediately. Thus, Judge Learned Hand, who wrote the Appeals Court's decision, had to go to great lengths (123,000 words) to skirt the "clear and present danger" doctrine which ran through all the relevant case law. He gladly plumbed the metaphysical depths Judge Medina had conjured up and similarly concocted a new doctrine, that of the "grave evil." He looked to current events, such as the Berlin airlift, to prove that a grave evil, which justified the suppression of free speech, existed. This eminent jurist turned for his authority not to the law but to the newspapers.

When the case reached the Supreme Court, only Justices Hugo Black and William O. Douglas shunned the new line of reasoning. The majority of the Court upheld the constitutionality of the Smith Act and decided that the government need not "wait until the *putsch* is about to be executed, the plans have been laid and the signal is awaited." The new criterion laid down was: "The gravity of the evil, discounted by its improbability."* It had become lawful, despite the Constitutional protections of free speech, to punish words and ideas, provided that juries and judges found those words and ideas so repugnant as to consider them evil. One can only regard with amazement the response which the words and ideas expressed by Communists occasioned; the frame of mind was that of the innocent maiden confronted by the notorious seducer and pleading, "Please don't tempt me . . . I'm bound to fall."

The *New York Times* applauded the convictions and justified them partly on the ground that the Communist threat had imposed an onerous defense burden on the country. It acknowledged that the defendants had been charged with uttering words rather than committing deeds. But words "may be thought of, one deduces, as comparable with the fingerprints a burglar leaves on the window sill of the house he is about to break into. It is not unlawful to leave fingerprints, but it is unlawful to break into another person's house." Yet in that case, they ought to have been acquitted, one deduces, because all they were found guilty of was leaving fingerprints.

With this legal victory behind it, the Administration set out in earnest to destroy the Communist Party. Hard on the heels of the Supreme Court decision, the FBI rounded up seventeen "second-echelon" Communist Party leaders in New York. The accused were charged with such criminal activities as attending meetings and circulating petitions.

A similar sweep in Los Angeles netted fourteen "third-echelon" leaders. *Newsweek* gloated, "The score was now 45 Reds in jail, in flight or under arrest."

Smith Act prosecutions continued throughout the Truman Administration's last three years. Six Communists were tried in Baltimore (including a couple expelled from the Party for "defeatism" shortly before their trial began). In Honolulu, there were seven on trial; in Pittsburgh, five; in Detroit, six; in Seattle, four; in Philadelphia, nine; in St. Louis, five. In all, eighty-five CP functionaries were indicted by the Justice Department under Truman. By the end of 1952 forty-four had been convicted, three had been acquitted, and the remainder were either on trial or about to go on trial.

Meanwhile, four of the eleven convicted CP leaders, including Robert

---

*Six years later, in 1957, the Court would, in a calmer mood, reject this metaphysical foray and revert to the "clear and present danger" doctrine.

Thompson, had taken flight. The Civil Rights Congress forfeited $80,000 in bail. The government used the flight of the convicted men as a weapon against the CRC. It demanded to know the names of the donors to the bail fund. The trustees of the CRC refused to comply, and three of them, including Dashiell Hammett, were jailed for contempt of court.

In effect, the Federal government, with the assistance of the Federal courts, was attempting to deny bail to indicted Communists. Formally, the right to bail guaranteed by the Eighth Amendment remained intact. But at the moment, to be identified as a donor to a bail fund for Communists was to invite harassment, investigation, and character assassination. So although the right to bail remained, the realistic possibility of exercising that right had been drastically reduced. McGrath was so eager to prevent Communist defendants from securing bail that he tried to set down rules under which bail should be granted. Federal courts were compliant up to a point, but not subservient. Federal judges overtly rejected McGrath's rules. Bail nevertheless became much harder to secure, not only in cases involving Communists but in such sensitive matters as deportation.

The real issue in the trial of Alger Hiss was not perjury but espionage. And what made matters worse, so the feeling ran, was not simply that the country had been betrayed, but that it had been betrayed at a very high level. A particular picture of Soviet espionage was created, and this picture was an integral part of the spy obsession which colored the trials of Hiss and various other people.

But contrary to the picture most people had of Soviet spies at work, Soviet espionage operations in the 1930s might have been played out by the Marx Brothers; only the corpses were real. In order to save precious foreign currency, for instance, the Center, the Moscow headquarters of all Soviet espionage and sabotage, began counterfeiting dollars to finance its American operations. To float this counterfeit currency, contact was made with various Chicago gangsters, who were willing to do the job, for a price. The plot also involved a noted Nazi sympathizer. This farcical episode concluded in a Chicago courtroom in 1934.

The Center's judgment was notoriously bad, repeatedly turning down or distrusting people who really had something to offer, such as Rudolf Roessler and Leopold Trepper, while accepting all manner of mendacious opportunists and hacks. In works such as *Witness* and *Out of Bondage* the accounts of *konspiratsiyi* verge on the laughable, except for the bloodshed. The achievements recounted, in the few cases which can be verified, are trivial.

It was also an article of faith that the Communist Party was an integral part of the Soviet intelligence system. Such claims were frequently advanced to justify a ban on the Party. Yet according to Alexander Orlov, who literally wrote the book on Soviet espionage in the 1930s (he was the author of the manual used in training Soviet agents), members of foreign

Communist parties were not employed in espionage. This stemmed not from scruple but from an acceptance that they were not likely to be very good at it, and if they were caught, their activities would compromise the parties they belonged to and spoil the real work of those parties, which was defending the Soviet Union.

There were hundreds of fellow travelers and perhaps more than 100 Communist Party members in the government during the New Deal. They were to be found notably in the Agricultural Adjustment Administration, the Works Progress Administration, and the National Labor Relations Board. But far from being engaged in espionage, nearly all were involved in discussion groups. They were generally young, and they were trying as best they could to turn the reasoning of Marxism-Leninism on the overriding issues of the hour, the failure of capitalism, and the rise of Fascism.

During the war Communists and their friends became active in the more sensitive agencies of government, such as the Office of Strategic Services, the State Department, the War Production Board, and the Department of Justice.

In their zeal to be of service and to show the depth of their sincerity, it was inevitable that some of these individuals would lead themselves, or be led by others, to filch confidential material from their agencies. But to this day no one has ever shown that this material made the slightest difference to anything or was even heeded by its ultimate recipients. It would have been treated with respect because to the Center anything stolen was considered genuine intelligence material. The same material, culled from public sources, would be dismissed as the mere gleanings of research. So the intrinsically useless material that Hiss, Remington, Wadleigh, and Coplon were claimed to have handed over may very well have been treated as if it were important simply because of the underhanded way in which it was obtained. There was more than a little role playing and pose striking in the world of *konspiratsiyi.*

It provided the perfect stage for a Whittaker Chambers or anyone else who so thoroughly embraced both arrogance and humility. Chambers saw the development of Communism as the turning point around which all human history revolved. Naturally, that made Communists and ex-Communists the crucial figures of the twentieth century.

In his account, Chambers had been led into the Party from the purest motives. From there, he had been recruited into the Communist underground: "I was in the Fourth Section of Soviet Military Intelligence."* Chambers saw himself as the direct heir of the *narodniki* and was deeply moved by their deeds with homemade bombs and large-caliber revolvers. He looked with contempt on those American Communists who did not thrill as he did to the youthful revolutionaries who had at least succeeded in murdering a czar. Yet despite his attitude of more-revolutionary-than-

---

*A foreigner recruited into Soviet intelligence is not told the truth about whom he is working for. That is an elementary precaution. So either his controller was incompetent, instead of the genius Chambers portrays, or Chambers was gullible.

thou, there is no evidence that Chambers ever struck a blow with bomb or gun.

He cast himself, however, as the man who always chose the hard road: to live when he wanted to die; to choose Communism, which was demanding, rather than Socialism, which was not; to break with the Party when it would have been easier to stay; to go underground rather than remain a mere Party member; to testify against Alger Hiss when he might have saved his highly paid job by hiding behind a legal barricade. Like nearly all ex-Communists, Chambers saw himself as a man different from, and superior to, almost all others—he considered himself brave, simple, dedicated, and one of the most important figures in modern life.

Predictably, when he wrote of the apparatus to which he had belonged in the 1930s, he described it in sweeping terms: "It is hard to believe that a more highly placed, devoted and dangerous espionage group existed anywhere." A stunning claim to set beside the known exploits of the Red Orchestra, the Lucy ring, and the career of Richard Sorge.

Fortunately there are independent accounts of the super-secret agent in action. A former Columbia classmate, Donald Zablodowsky, received a call from Chambers in 1936, after thirteen years without any contact between them. "He told me that he was doing secret work for the Communist Party," Zablodowsky recalled. He asked him to act as a mail drop, and Zablodowsky agreed. The sealed letter which Chambers left at his office was picked up as arranged. Several years passed; then in 1939 the two men met by chance. And Chambers pretended not to recognize Zablodowsky. There were a dozen similar episodes to the Zablodowsky mail drop routine. Chambers went out of his way to appear a man of mystery; the last thing a good spy wants is attention. But Chambers might as well have had business cards printed bearing the legend "SECRET AGENT (Don't ask me any questions)."

Chambers liked to boast of his extraordinarily powerful memory. And the accuracy of his memory became, necessarily, an article of faith where questions of perjury and events long past were involved. On this, as on almost everything else, Chambers was emphatic and dogmatic.

According to his own account, he "disappeared" into the underground in June 1932; this involved his abrupt departure from *New Masses*, and it set off a fluttering of concern in the tight little dovecote of left-wing journalism. But anyone who goes to the trouble of looking up *New Masses* for 1933 will find Chambers's name carried on the masthead in capitals as late as September of that year. His wife, Esther Shemitz, was carried on the masthead as a "Contributor."

Chambers repeatedly stated that he had broken with the Party in the spring of 1937. That was what he told the FBI, twice. But when he confronted Alger Hiss, the date of the break continually crept forward, until it got into 1938. It eventually became very specific—April 15, 1938. This date came to mind only after Chambers had retrieved his hidden documents and microfilm, some of which had dates from February and March 1938.

The spy ring Chambers described as working in the Department of

Agriculture was led, he said, by Harold Ware. Here, too, Chambers was confused by dates. Ware was a dollar-a-year man of known left-wing sympathies. But he had served not under Roosevelt, as Chambers maintained, but under Coolidge and Hoover. When Roosevelt came in, Ware, along with the rest of Hoover's appointees, went out. And at the very time when Chambers identified the AAA as being a hotbed of subversion, it had recently been purged by Henry Wallace, to howls of outrage from the liberal and leftist press.

Chambers repeatedly claimed that he had told all that he knew. But even this is implausible. He claimed to know of an espionage agent in the Bureau of Standards. Yet he never identified him except by the pseudonym "Abel Gross."

At the time he claimed to have been in hiding from his Soviet masters, fearing for his life and the safety of his family, staying awake throughout the night with a revolver close to hand, he put his name in the Baltimore telephone book and his wife got a driver's license.

Nor could he be relied on to tell the truth even when sworn to do so. At his grand jury appearance in New York in October 1948 he had denied any direct knowledge of espionage. At the first Hiss trial he was asked, "Was that answer true or false?" He calmly replied, "That answer was false."

Yet Chambers, whose memory was as flawed as his character, was not making up lies from whole cloth. He imaginatively embroidered the truth, so elaborately that in the end it became impossible for anyone to find it. An anonymous reviewer of *Witness* remarked: "His autobiography has the power of a novel . . . because he organized his life along the lines of a work of fiction." And *Witness* is indeed so laden with Dostoevskian turns of phrase and images that one literary scholar has claimed that large chunks were lifted from the Russian novelist's works. Chambers had written fiction and translated it. But he was to find that the novel in him was his own life.

Much of that life was a rebellion against middle-class existence. And there is nothing more bourgeois than rebellion against middle-class life. In Chamber's case, it showed. The chaos and clutter of Communist Party offices, the untidiness of radicals' apartments were partly the result of poverty, but mainly they were a rejection of bourgeois notions of tidiness. Chambers, the dedicated revolutionary, lived and worked among this clutter, but, he confesses in *Witness*, "I never got used to it."

In later life he developed a passionate interest in the stock market. He took a delight in giving tips to his friends on what to buy and what to sell.

It was all of a piece that Chambers should become one of *Time*'s senior editors. In the Luce publications Communist materialism was endlessly and passionately attacked amid glossy advertisements for glittering material possessions. It was one of the more delightful ironies of midcentury that Communism should stress materialism, and be poor, while capitalism stressed spiritual values, and grew rich.

Time bore the cost of Chambers's lawyers, evidently believing that an attack on a senior editor was tantamount to impugning the integrity of the Luce publications. *Witness* earned Chambers more than $100,000 in royalties. Sale of the serial rights to *Saturday Evening Post* brought in a further $75,000. "No martyrdom," concluded I. F. Stone, "was ever more lavishly buttered."

However unevenly Chambers served the truth, there can be little doubt about the sincerity of his conversion to the Quaker faith. He believed in the need for mystical religion as fervently as he had once believed in the need for Communism. And his spiritual drive did much to commend him to Henry Luce, devout Presbyterian and worried well-wisher at the sickbed of Western civilization.

From 1944 Chambers held one of the most important positions at *Time*, editing the foreign news section. This offered an opportunity not so much to report the news as to use it. Long before the war ended, *Time* regularly preached the absolute incompatibility between the West and the Soviet Union.

It was Chambers, too, who had written the *Life* series on Western civilization. Through these articles there ran the theme which informed Toynbee's *A Study of History*—that if the West were to be saved from moral, social, intellectual, and political collapse, it would have to return to its traditional Christian faith.

Through *Witness* there really move only two figures, Whittaker Chambers and God. At every critical juncture, or when an argument needs closing, God makes a timely appearance. The recovery of the hidden materials from his brother-in-law's apartment, for example, made Chambers swoon. He reached out, to cling to a table and keep from falling when he found himself "in the kind of physical hush that a man feels to whom has happened an act of God." On the verge of suicide when "the Great Case" (Chambers's term, frequently employed) gathered momentum, he suddenly discovered that "the weight of God's purpose was laid on me not to destroy myself." He had a divine mission to bear witness against godless Communism.

When the trial of Alger Hiss opened at the Federal Courthouse in Foley Square, New York, the trial of the eleven CP leaders was well under way in the same building. Each day Hiss and Chambers had to push their way past a singing, chanting line of Communist pickets who broke into a frenzy at the least glimpse of Judge Medina.

Hiss's counsel was a flamboyant, eye-rolling, arm-waving exemplar of the lawyer as dramatic actor, Lloyd Paul Stryker, not at all the type of lawyer you might expect to find representing Hiss, who was so calm, so reflective, so orderly. Stryker's strategy was to defend Hiss by attacking Chambers, portraying him as a pathological liar, a man without moral scruple, and possibly a psychopath. And if these things were true, how could anything he said about Alger Hiss be credible?

Chambers had lied about so many things in his life that Stryker had an embarrassment of riches to choose from. He had lied fluently in youth and in maturity. He had lied under oath, not once but many times. The at-

tack on Chambers's character, or lack thereof, included the revelations
that he stole books from the public library, had lived in a fleabag hotel inhabited by drunks and prostitutes, and when compiling the Foreign News
section at *Time* had taken some of his material from the pages of the *New
York Times.*

The government called Henry Julian Wadleigh to testify. Wadleigh was
a product of the Ivy League and Oxford, had been employed in several
Federal agencies and the departments of State and Agriculture, and for a
time worked for UNRRA. In the 1930s he had been one of those idealistic
young men who had been attracted almost simultaneously to Communism
and to Washington. Although never a Party member, he had, as he expressed it, "collaborated." His collaboration had taken the form of giving
government documents to Whittaker Chambers and others. In all, Wadleigh admitted to handing over some 400 items. Wadleigh's testimony corroborated Chambers's claim that he had been in receipt of government
documents.

But the heart of the prosecution's case was not that Chambers was a
Soviet courier. It was the documents themselves. The prosecution, however, bungled its own case and spent many tedious hours in trying to
prove that Chambers knew Hiss as well as he had claimed. This involved
conflicting testimony over the gift of a rug, various trips involving the two
families, an old Ford transferred from Hiss to Chambers, and a wide variety of domestic details.

Hiss by now had admitted to knowing Chambers but insisted that he
had known him under the name of George Crosley and had never known
him well. The essential matter, however, was not the friendship claimed
on the one side and denied on the other but a Woodstock typewriter on
which, Chambers asserted, Mrs. Hiss had typed copies of the documents
stolen by her husband for transmission to the Soviets.

The Hisses had owned a Woodstock typewriter. Hiss would, in later
years, claim that a duplicate had been made of his typewriter and the incriminating documents typed on this forgery. But such a claim makes no
sense. To make a copy of a typewriter requires access to the original machine; if you have access to the original machine, why take the trouble of
making a copy of it on which to type faked evidence? The material Chambers produced was almost certainly typed on Hiss's machine, whether by
Hiss, his wife, or someone else.

A number of eminent men appeared at the trial to testify to Hiss's spot-
less reputation. To the evident awe of Judge Samuel H. Kaufman, first
Justice Felix Frankfurter, then Justice Stanley Reed appeared for Hiss.
John Foster Dulles, who had chosen Hiss as president of the Carnegie Endowment for International Peace, testified as to Hiss's reputation. But in
the end it did him little good, being derided as "his own theory of innocence by association" and affording the government prosecutor, Thomas
Murphy, with a matchless opportunity. "I dare say Judas Iscariot had a
good reputation. He was one of the Twelve. He sat next to God, and we
know what he did. Brutus, Caesar's friend, I dare say he had a good reputation. He got so close to his boss that he stabbed him. And then Major

General Benedict Arnold. He came from a fine family . . . he could have called George Washington as a reputation witness.''

Throughout his trial Hiss was a picture of composure, taking a lawyer's interest in a complex and interesting case. His serenity was almost unnatural to those who saw it, day after day. "If he was innocent, it could only be the deep well of security in a character of great strength and purity. In a guilty man, certainly, his detachment would be pathological in the extreme.''

It was still more remarkable considering the handicaps under which his defense labored. The documents were the most important part of the case against him; they called for the most minute and expert examination. They were more important than Chambers's testimony, nearly all of which was uncorroborated. But Hiss could not subject the documents to the scrutiny required because it was impossible in 1949 to find a typewriter expert who would risk his career by helping Alger Hiss. The sole expert witness to appear at the trial was an FBI employee. Lacking another expert on whom to call, the defense allowed his assertions about the typewriter and the typed documents to go virtually unchallenged.

But the prosecution made a number of important mistakes in handling its own case. In the end, the jury was deadlocked, eight to four for conviction. *Life* ran a long article on the jury, including a photograph of the jury members, their names and addresses, and a terse statement on how each had voted. The text was hostile to Hiss, the judge, and the four jurors who had voted for acquittal. Richard Nixon demanded an investigation of the judge, "to determine his fitness to serve on the bench.'' Nixon thought that HUAC should investigate the jury deadlock.

In neither the first nor the second Hiss trial was the jury sequestered. They went home each day to face the full force of public and private opinion, which was overwhelmingly hostile to Alger Hiss.

When the second trial opened in November 1949, both sides looked older and grayer than during the summer. Both sides deployed subtler tactics and more intricate cases, with the result that the second trial lasted nine weeks, compared with the six of the first trial. Hiss had also employed a new counsel, Claude Cross of Boston.

Cross made far more of the internal contradictions and inconsistencies in the prosecution's case than Stryker had attempted. He examined the documents with greater care and succeeded in showing that at least some of them had not come from Hiss at all but from Wadleigh. But the typewriter and the stack of documents doomed Hiss. This time Murphy played the physical evidence for all that it was worth. Words and arguments aside, this tangible proof of espionage gave a force and immediacy to the prosecution's case that was well-nigh irresistible.

Hiss was found guilty and sentenced to the maximum of five years on each count of perjury, the sentences to run concurrently. Unflinching, handsome, elegant, poised even to the end, Hiss heard sentence passed and then submitted courteously that he had never been a traitor to his country and claimed that he was the victim of "forgery by typewriter.''

The trials and eventual conviction of Alger Hiss served as a landmark in the Cold War life of the nation; that is why these events have been covered at length here. They were more than a fascinating conflict of wills and words between two unusual men. They were not only the funeral pyre on which were finally burned the dried-up and brittle hopes of left-liberals of the 1930s. The showdown of Alger Hiss and Whittaker Chambers was the great divide in public opinion on the Cold War. The Hiss case was taken, wrongly, as a vindication for nearly every intemperate, extreme criticism of the New Deal; as proof that China had been "lost" to Communism by treachery; as evidence that Yalta, where Hiss had served in a very minor role, had been a betrayal of fundamental American interests; as a revelation that the Federal government was riddled with spies; ultimately, as a demonstration that the United States stood in mortal and imminent peril. From this moment forward no one could be trusted, especially not bright young men of impeccable appearance and unimpeachable background. The conviction of Alger Hiss was used to justify the irrationality and emotional turbulence of the Cold War as a way of life. Hiss had been found guilty. That was a hard, solid fact, as irritating as grit, as immovable as Gibraltar.

The nation was divided into pro- and anti-Hiss factions of irreconcilable bitterness. And that bitterness lingered on for decades, long after the Cold War climate had changed.

Hiss appealed his conviction, arguing that the judge at the second trial had not defined corroboration to the jury. His lawyers also attempted to prove that a typewriter could be copied, right down to its singularities. The cost of Hiss's struggle to clear his name would eventually total $500,000. Most of this cost was borne by his lawyers, out of their own pockets. Hiss resisted every attempt to turn his case into a political trial and to appeal for funds. He abhorred the prospect of becoming a left-wing cause. Even so, a Hiss Defense Fund established by his friends drew donations totaling $70,000.

When Hiss began serving his prison sentence, the *New York Daily News* exulted: RED HERRING CANNED. Congress exacted what revenge it could by passing the Hiss Act, legislation whose sole purpose was to deprive Hiss of his government pension.

The truth about Hiss and Chambers is almost certainly beyond retrieval by now. Neither man told the entire truth; by 1949 it is doubtful whether either of them was able to recall it had he wished. Years after his trials Hiss was identified by Nathaniel Weyl, a former Communist Party member, as having been in the Party in 1934, when both were in the AAA. It seems likely that Hiss drifted into a left-wing group during the early New Deal. It is plausible, too, that what Weyl claimed were Hiss's Party dues were no more than a contribution to one of the many left-wing causes for which funds were continually being solicited.

From these essentially harmless activities Chambers, after the passage of years and aided by his gift for self-deception, was able to concoct a spy network in the way that children with a handful of toy soldiers and a tin helmet can persuade themselves that they are generals in command of great armies.

Knowing that what he had done was foolish and, if it did involve handing over government documents, illegal, but was not harmful, Hiss would have probably felt justified in denying Chambers's exaggerated claims. Yet once embarked on a policy of denial, it was impossible for Hiss to turn back. And at the outset, considering his standing, Hiss's strategy appeared the one most likely to succeed. Under the present circumstances a defense of "Yes, but . . ." would have been no defense at all. He gambled all on success or failure—and lost. His outward calm stemmed, I am inclined to believe, from an unshakable conviction that whatever he had done, however ill-advised it might appear in retrospect, he had done his country no injury. That belief may have been foremost in his mind, even if the details of his actions had become blurred and fragmentary with the passage of time.

All this is surmise, of course. But the four pages in Hiss's handwriting almost certainly came from Hiss. Washington officials have long been in the habit of revealing classified material to outsiders. Much, if not most, of what is classified is trifling, which encourages contempt for classification of all but the most sensitive documents. There is no reason to believe that Hiss, because of his impressive character, would have felt restrained so long as two things were uppermost in his mind: first, that he would do his country no harm; second, that he might be serving a high moral purpose, such as the achievement of peace. In this, he would have been like a figure closer to our own time, Daniel Ellsberg.

Strictly speaking, the guilty verdict on the perjury charges is almost certainly right. The lessons drawn from the verdict were almost certainly wrong. "Hiss is one man," ran a typical comment, widely circulated via the *Reader's Digest*, "but there were those who aided and abetted him . . . and their name is legion. Instead of crushing the seeds of treason, they scattered them in the good American earth. . . . There is a time to plant and a time to pluck up what is planted. The time is now."

The "spy ring" exposed by Elizabeth Bentley was located in the Department of Commerce, under the tutelage of Nathan Gregory Silvermaster. But this, too, appears to have been less a band of revolutionaries than a left-wing study group attracting lost liberals and narrow-minded Communists. Miss Bentley's revelations, moreover, came as no revelation to the Civil Service Commission. As early as 1942 the CSC had identified Silvermaster as a member of the Communist Party "and very probably a secret agent of the OGPU." Silvermaster was left unmolested, but not unwatched, until November 1947, when the Loyalty-Security program encouraged him to resign from government service.

William Remington was also employed by the Commerce Department. In early 1950 his ordeal appeared to be over, following his clearance by the Loyalty Review Board and the out-of-court settlement of his libel case against Miss Bentley. But at the beginning of May HUAC produced two men who claimed to have known Remington in the 1930s, when, they maintained, Remington, recently graduated from Dartmouth, had been a member of the Communist Party. And that was at a time when he was employed by the TVA. Far from being over, Remington's troubles were only beginning. Miss Bentley was once more roused to savage him, but this time she had an ally—Remington's ex-wife.

Ann Moos Remington had herself once been a devout leftist. When she and Remington were married, she had asked him solemnly to promise her that he would not try to become a success; to her, as to many other educated young people in the 1930s, the bourgeois ideals of success could be sought only at the expense of important personal, social, and moral values. The pledge she demanded was one the idealistic young Remington was only too happy to give.

But the marriage had failed, resulting in divorce in 1947. By now Remington was a success and had turned conservative, if not right-wing. Ann Remington was subpoenaed by a New York grand jury to give testimony concerning her husband's former political beliefs and activities. She had long since repudiated her mother's radicalism, her former idealism, and her husband's love. Yet she was moved by ordinary decency to resist the attempt by the grand jury to bring William Remington to grief.

She was bullied into submission by the grand jury foreman, John Brumini, in a manner that shocked Judge Learned Hand when the transcript of the grand jury proceedings reached him. She was questioned closely, and for many hours, until she became confused, hungry, tired, and despairing. She repeatedly asked to be allowed to consult her lawyer and was denied. She repeatedly asked to be allowed to rest but was kept on the witness stand. Brumini taunted her. "We haven't shown our teeth yet, have we? Maybe you don't know about our teeth. A witness before a grand jury hasn't the privilege of refusing to answer a question. . . . You must answer it." Otherwise, he told her, she would be sent to jail and kept there until she "purged" herself. Brumini suggested that she might spend the remainder of her life in prison if she continued to resist.

Bursting into tears, she told them what they plainly wanted to hear: yes, her husband had been a Communist. And how did she know that? Because he told her so.

Appearing before the same grand jury, Remington unequivocally denied that he had ever been a Communist. He was indicted for perjuring himself when he made that denial.

Miss Bentley, meanwhile, had not only appeared before this grand jury but had written a book, *Out of Bondage*, which she termed "my livelihood." Her partner in this venture was none other than John Brumini. When asked during Remington's trial whether Brumini had collaborated with her on her book, she denied it. But asked the same question later, perhaps fearing a perjury indictment, she admitted it.

Miss Bentley's experience as a Communist courier had left her as incapable of telling the true from the false as it had left Whittaker Chambers. The more often she told of her life in the underground, the more important it became, until by the time her book appeared it was she who had been telling Earl Browder how to run the CPUSA. Browder, probably with good reason, considered the suggestion hilarious.

One of the few secrets she claimed to have imparted which might be verified was the date of D-Day. No doubt this would have interested the Russians. But the date of D-Day was set by wind and tide, not by staff officers working months in advance. Even Eisenhower did not know that D-Day would fall on June 6 until the afternoon of June 5.

At the end of 1950 Remington's trial began in the same courtroom where Hiss's first trial had taken place. He was convicted and received a five-year sentence. But his conviction was reversed on appeal. The indictment was suspect for the way in which it had been obtained.

Remington was indicted again. But this time it was not for perjuring himself before the grand jury. He was charged with perjuring himself at his first trial. At his second trial he was convicted on two counts: for lying when he denied giving Bentley classified information and for lying when he denied knowing of the existence of the Young Communist League at Dartmouth during his years as a student. He was sentenced to three years' imprisonment.

One night, while serving his sentence in Lewisburg Federal Penitentiary, Remington awoke while his cell was being robbed by three other inmates. To silence him, the robbers beat him over the head with a brick-filled sock and killed him.

Judith Coplon, a secretary in the Justice Department, was arrested under the Third Avenue el on the Lower East Side with a handbag stuffed with government documents. She was attempting to hand them to Valentin Gubichev, a Russian working at the UN. Like many Soviet espionage operations of the time, this one was amateurish almost beyond credibility. But the myth persisted that Soviet intelligence was formidable.

Miss Coplon's trial began during the first Alger Hiss trial. She was employed in the section of the Justice Department which was responsible for the registration of foreign agents. In the course of her work she handled many classified documents. Her defense was that she needed some of these documents as notes for a novel she was thinking of writing. The remaining documents in her handbag, she explained, were part of the study material she had assigned herself for a civil service examination she was thinking of taking.

Why, then, was she meeting so furtively with Gubichev? She was madly in love with him. But wasn't he a married man with children? She didn't care about that. Then why had she been checking into hotels up and down the East Coast with one H. P. Shapiro, a Justice Department lawyer, under the nom de plume "Mrs. H. P. Shapiro"? Oh, *that* . . . well, they were just good friends.

In the course of her trial Miss Coplon enthusiastically gave her views on W. H. Auden, modern dance, and the state of society. She pleaded repeatedly, "I'm innocent of all charges. I'm the victim of a horrible, horrible frame-up," but allowed that her trial was "a panic" and her counsel "a riot." Convicted, she was sentenced to one to ten years' imprisonment. *Life* solemnly applauded the jury for "a grueling job well done."

The verdict was reversed on appeal because the FBI had violated the established standards of search and seizure when it took Miss Coplon's handbag. The government made a second attempt to send Miss Coplon to jail. She was indicted for espionage.

At her second trial, in 1950, she was once more convicted. Gubichev left for home, and Miss Coplon was sentenced to fifteen years' imprisonment. But the FBI was embarrassed once more, because during the trial Miss Coplon's lawyers forced the bureau to open its files on Coplon and Gubichev. The world at large was provided a brief glimpse of the way in which the slanders of anonymous informers were set down as if they were sound evidence. Of greater moment, however, was the revelation that Miss Coplon had been trapped by wiretapping. There was no Federal law which authorized wiretapping. Nor was there a law which forbade it. But there was a Supreme Court decision which ruled that wiretap evidence was inadmissible in Federal trials. The Court of Appeals once again voided Judith Coplon's conviction, on technical grounds, but declaring, "Her guilt is plain." Of all the figures in the espionage-linked trials, there's less doubt in her case than any, yet Miss Coplon alone went free. Were there such a thing as the music of the spheres, the sound would presumably resemble that of sardonic laughter.

According to an inside account of the FBI, Hoover learned in September 1949, the month of the first Soviet atomic explosion, "that agents of a foreign power had stolen the very heart out of the atomic bomb. . . . . Hoover reached for the intercom telephone. He gave a series of orders to his key subordinates. . . . In essence, Hoover's orders were: 'The secret of the atomic bomb has been stolen. Find the thieves!' "

The idea that there was *a* secret to the bomb persisted, despite the repeated attempts of nuclear scientists to make people understand that there was no such thing. As late as 1951 this idea was still being mooted by no less a body than the Joint Congressional Committee on Atomic Energy, which described the Russians as engaging in espionage for "the secret of the atomic bomb." And the two ideas were inseparable—not only was there a secret, but the Russians had stolen it.

At the end of 1949 a former Army Air Corps major, George Racey Jordan, testified before HUAC that during his wartime service as a lend-lease expediter he had seen entire crates of secret atomic data being shipped by air to the Soviet Union. He had come across detailed plans of Oak Ridge, Tennessee, with an accompanying note on White House stationery: "Had a hell of a time getting these away from Groves—H.H." (Presumably Harry Hopkins.) He had seen a suitcase break open, he claimed, spilling folders of State Department documents which bore covering notes reading, "From Hiss."

But the break in the atomic espionage case came not from Hoover or Jordan. It came when Klaus Fuchs confessed to an MI-5 interrogator in January 1950 that during his years at Los Alamos he had been in the service of the Center. Fuchs's family had taken refuge in England during the 1930s, to escape the Nazis. Fuchs, a brilliant young physicist, had been part of Britain's contribution to the building of the bomb. Tried by a British court, Fuchs was sentenced to fourteen years' imprisonment. Within a few months of his convictinon in May 1950 nine people were arrested in the United States ostensibly in connection with atomic espionage.

The nine were a Philadelphia chemist, Harry Gold, Abraham Brothman, Miriam Moscowitz, Morton Sobell, David Greenglass, his sister Ethel, Ethel's husband, Julius Rosenberg, a Syracuse chemist, Alfred Dean Slack, and Oscar Vago, an engineer formerly in partnership with Brothman. This, on the face of it, was the spy ring which had stolen the very heart out of the atomic bomb.

Four of the nine, however, were never charged with anything remotely involving the bomb. The real offense of Brothman, Moscowitz, Slack, and Vago was that they knew Harry Gold. Slack had once given Gold a sample of an explosive known as RDX from government stores; RDX had been in use since 1917 and was not secret. The hapless Slack was sentenced to fifteen years' imprisonment. Vago was held in jail for two years on a very high bail requirement before being released. The only charge the government was able to bring against him was that he had once told a lie to get his residence visa extended. He had voluntarily confessed to the lie a week after telling it.

Brothman and Moscowitz had once employed Harry Gold. Brothman had also been named by Elizabeth Bentley as someone who had given her information in her days as a Communist courier. Brothman's version was that he had simply been trying to get Russian contracts for the chemical plant he and Miss Moscowitz owned and operated. Unable or unwilling to bring an espionage indictment, the government indicted Brothman and Moscowitz for obstruction of justice because they had not told the entire truth about their relations with Miss Bentley. Each received a two-year sentence and a fine of $10,000.

Harry Gold pleaded guilty to espionage. He had been identified as Fuchs's contact at Los Alamos. And Gold proved to be one of the most cooperative witnesses ever to appear in a Federal courtroom. In recognition of his contribution to the government's case, the prosecution asked that Gold receive only a twenty-five -year sentence. But the judge, James P. McGranery, imposed the maximum the law allowed, thirty years.

Gold had already begun serving his sentence when the trial of Julius and Ethel Rosenberg, David Greenglass, and Morton Sobell began in March 1951 in the same courtroom where the eleven Communist Party leaders had been tried. Sobell's connection with the atomic bomb case was tenuous at best; his misfortunes stemmed mainly from being a friend of Julius Rosenberg's.

Sobell had left hurriedly for Mexico City with his wife and family almost as soon as he he had heard of the arrest of Julius Rosenberg and David Greenglass. His explanation for his abrupt departure was vague and implausible. He made all the arrangements necessary for his departure, but only hours before he was scheduled to leave did he write to his employer asking for an extended leave of absence. He left before receiving a reply. While in Mexico, he traveled under several aliases and attempted to correspond with relatives and friends under a pseudonym.

His hurried departure did him little good and much harm. At what appears to have been the behest of American officials, Sobell was kidnapped and brought to the Texas border by Mexican secret police, with blood caking a head wound where he had been pistol-whipped. Sobell was promptly arrested by American officials.

Having once perjured himself on a security clearance affidavit, Sobell was vulnerable to prosecution. He had been, for a short time, a member of the Communist Party. But he was not charged with perjury. Nor was he directly charged with stealing the secret of the atomic bomb. He was charged with conspiring with Julius Rosenberg to commit espionage.

The case against Sobell consisted entirely of the uncorroborated testimony of a former friend, onetime roommate, and best man at his wedding, Max Elitcher. According to him, Sobell had attempted to recruit him into a spy ring. Elitcher was himself vulnerable to prosecution because like Sobell, he had once perjured himself to gain a security clearance. Nevertheless, the government now accepted him as a trustworthy witness when he claimed that Julius Rosenberg had told him frankly that Morton Sobell was a Soviet agent, engaged in espionage.

At no point was Sobell accused of receiving, stealing, or transmitting classified information. There was no evidence that Sobell had ever committed espionage. There was nothing to link Sobell with the atomic espionage offenses with which the Rosenbergs were charged. Yet Sobell was tried with them.

Sobell and his lawyers believed that the case against him was so weak that it was unlikely to result in conviction. But to take the stand and testify would be to expose himself to damaging cross-examination concerning his Communist past and his former perjury. Sobell's attitude during his trial was oddly fatalistic and passive, and it suggested to one eminent trial lawyer a subconscious desire to be caught and punished for *something*. In which case, he was successful. He was sentenced to thirty years.

The confession of Klaus Fuchs had led to Harry Gold; Gold's confession had led to David Greenglass. But it did so by a circuitous route. During his first interrogation by the FBI Gold completely forgot to mention having met Greenglass in New Mexico to receive the object of the exercise—namely, the secret of the atomic bomb. At a later questioning session Gold was unable to recall the name of his contact. The FBI offered him a list of possible names, and this was reduced to three. From these he picked Greenglass.

Greenglass was already under FBI investigation for having stolen a sample of uranium.* He had also been a member of the Young Communist League in the late 1930s, a fact he must have suppressed on his application for a security clearance.

At Los Alamos, Greenglass had worked in the machine shop where explosive charges were made to special shapes for detonating the first atomic bombs. There were two possible ways of initiating an atomic explosion: either by firing one piece of fissionable material into another to bring about the required critical mass at which a chain reaction would begin or by concentrating the force of an explosion inward, compressing a core of fissionable material until it became critical. The latter method, known as implosion, was employed in the bomb dropped on Nagasaki. Its principles had been known since the 1920s. Yet this was presented to the Rosenberg trial as *the* secret of the atomic bomb. This was the secret that machinist David Greenglass, an enlisted man in the machine shop at Los Alamos, gave to the Soviets by means of crude sketches.

Although the Justice Department and the Federal prosecutor, Irving Saypol, repeatedly stressed the scientific value of what Greenglass had given away, no one from the one agency in a position to give an authoritative opinion was called to offer one. Dr. James Beckerley, director of the AEC's Classification Office, had spent hours interviewing Greenglass. He sat at the prosecution's table throughout the trial. Yet he was never called on to testify.

The testimony David Greenglass and his wife, Ruth, gave against the Rosenbergs could not have been more damaging. As a rule, the courts consider the testimony of an accomplice unreliable. In the Rosenberg case it was treated as if it were unimpeachable.

Greenglass's testimony was corroborated by Harry Gold. But Gold was a strange, emotionally twisted, and reclusive man. He was also a perjurer. At the trial of Brothman and Moscowitz he had lied repeatedly under oath. He was a bachelor, introverted, shy, not known to have ever enjoyed a close relationship with any woman except his mother. Yet during the Brothman-Moscowitz trial he had testified that he was married, was the father of two children, and his mother was a slob. He invented names, ailments, and individualistic quirks for his fictitious family. He consigned his brother, who was very much alive, to a heroic death during the war. He gave one of his imaginary children a broken leg; the other he gave polio. He claimed to own a house in a particular suburb where he had never lived. When lying, Harry Gold was fluent and inventive. Naturally, when his Soviet superiors pressed him to recruit other people, Gold soon obliged by creating an entire network of spies, all of them busy, all of them loyal, all of them nonexistent. He was not a voracious reader, but his taste in literature ran to detective stories and spy thrillers.

Besides being a pathological liar, Gold was a man of impulsive, and at

---

*At the end of the war several Army NCOs were charged with taking uranium or classified documents home with them as souvenirs of the Manhattan Project, but the charges were dropped.

times, compulsive, generosity. He borrowed money at usurious interest rates and lent it freely to other people, unconcerned about being repaid. He volunteered for dangerous medical experiments. At the conclusion of his trial, he thanked the judge, who disregarded the prosecution's plea for leniency. When he received his thirty-year sentence, he refused to appeal it.

At the Rosenberg trial both the judge, Irving R. Kaufman, and the prosecutor knew of Gold's fantasies and perjuries. But the jury never knew.

There is no doubt that Gold was in touch with Soviet intelligence. Orlov later identified him as a Soviet agent. Yet it is astonishing that he was not cross-examined at the Rosenberg trial. Several years later, when he was cross-examined in another security trial, involving Benjamin Smilg, Gold's earlier perjuries came to light, and he recanted parts of the testimony he had given in the Rosenberg trial. Smilg was acquitted.

Gold also told the Rosenberg jury that the Russians had placed a high value on the information passed by Greenglass. To a Senate subcommittee five years later he declared that the Russians had placed no value whatever on the Greenglass material.

The essence of the case against the Rosenbergs was that they had recruited Greenglass into espionage, had given him part of a Jell-O packet and told him that he would hand over secret information to a courier who would identify himself by showing the other half of the torn packet. The courier turned out to be Harry Gold. Julius Rosenberg was the principal figure throughout; Ethel Rosenberg's part was limited to two conversations, plus "moral support" for her husband's treason.

Julius Rosenberg had once been a member of the Communist Party, a fact which he went to such obvious lengths to avoid denying that he might as well have confessed it. As Louis Nizer remarked, "If a trial was heard as a symphony, dissonances and all, the theme of Julius and Ethel's cross-examination would have been the Fifth Amendment."

The Rosenbergs were indicted under the Espionage Act of 1917, which provided the death penalty for espionage committed in wartime. Saypol suggested at the conclusion of the government's case that the Russians had dared begin the war in Korea only because they had broken the American monopoly on the atomic bomb. Following the jury's verdict of guilty, this suggestion evidently shaped Judge Kaufman's view of the sentence appropriate to the crime. He blamed the Rosenbergs for the Korean War and held them personally responsible for the 50,000 American casualties incurred to date. He blamed them for altering the course of history, "to the disadvantage of our country." He accused them of jeopardizing the lives of untold millions in the event of a nuclear war. Under the circumstances, he decided, the only possible sentence was death.

Despite his cooperation with the government, Greenglass, to his evident bewilderment, received a sentence of fifteen years.

The value of the information Greenglass had passed to Harry Gold in no way affected the question of guilt. But it clearly influenced the sentence passed on the Rosenbergs. There was sufficient evidence to convict them. But they were also victims of circumstance. The espionage they had engaged in had been on behalf of an ally, rather than an enemy. It is inconceivable that they would have been sentenced to death had they been spying for France, say, or Canada.

Everything involving the atomic bomb was indiscriminately treated as if it were of the highest importance. Even a skeptical and experienced lawyer could be so dazzled by the glare of the atomic bomb that he pronounced the slow-witted, ineffectual Greenglass as "the man who had scored the greatest coup in the history of espionage," ignoring the facts that the Soviet Union during the 1930s had possessed some of the world's leading nuclear physicists and that even during the war atomic research had been continued in Russian laboratories.

But Greenglass cheerfully maintained throughout his testimony that yes, indeed, it was he who had given the Russians virtually the entire design of the bomb. When the Joint Committee on Atomic Energy questioned him, however, it proved that he knew hardly anything about its overall design. He also proved incapable of remembering anything clearly, and his mental powers were defeated by anything complex. He could not retain mathematical formulae beyond the level of high school algebra and even then was hard pressed. The committee concluded that the bomb had indeed been betrayed, but by scientists such as Fuchs, Alan Nunn May, and Bruno Pontecorvo, all of whom had been cleared by British security. By their actions they saved the Russians eighteen months of effort, the committee decided.

But Dr. Beckerley, who was one of the very few men to have access to everything concerning the atomic bomb, decided that even this overstated the case. He scoffed at the notion that the bomb had been, or could have been, stolen by Soviet agents. Whatever role espionage played, he said, it was a peripheral one. The Russians had come into possession of the bomb for the simple reason that "The Russians have the skills and the plants to make fission materials and bombs."

But the Rosenbergs faced the electric chair because they were not only guilty, but also unlucky. The had been faced by a judge who swallowed entire the prosecutor's emotional and inflated claims on behalf of Greenglass's "espionage coup."

Long after the trial there were many people who refused to believe that the Rosenbergs were guilty. There is to this day a suspicion in some quarters that the government, in a fit of discomfit following the Fuchs confession, had exacted revenge by staging a frame-up. But convictions based on testimony no worse than that in the Rosenberg case are secured in the courts every week. Rare is the complicated trial without gaps and weak points.

To some, the idea that Julius Rosenberg—he of the meek manner, somewhat in awe of his strong-willed wife, vacillating and inept in running his business—could be an important spy was on the face of it absurd. Yet his manner and appearance were more those of the real than the fictional spy; he was highly strung, ordinary in appearance, without serious intellectual interests, and confused in his loyalties.

Throughout the twenty-three-day trial the Communist Party press did not print a single line of reporting on the Rosenberg case. But in the wake of the death sentence, the Party took up the Rosenbergs as martyrs. In death as in life the Rosenbergs were used by the Communists in a cynical attempt to injure their country. The Federal government had meanwhile delivered them to Sing Sing. Nowhere in the Federal prisons was there an electric chair.

The various trials discussed above involved few people, and great principles. They were an essential part of the Cold War as a domestic affair. Without them, the Cold War emotions of distrust and bitterness would not have spread so far or gone so deep. These trials were, in large part, the vindication for behavior and beliefs which ordinary, fair-minded people would never have entertained otherwise. They were an essential part of the atmosphere which sustained the informer, the venal journalist, the character assassin, and the opportunist.

The wave of spy trials had really begun not in the United States but in Canada, in 1946 following the revelations of Igor Gouzenko, a Russian defector, who had exposed a Soviet espionage apparatus which had operated in Canada through the war. Ever since the Gouzenko case the United States had seen one spy case after another. What was disturbing was not that the Russians engaged in espionage against America, but that Americans engaged in espionage for Russia.

The Communists helped spread the poison of suspicion by boasting that for every overt Communist the Party had the loyalty of a dozen secret sympathizers. It was a thesis taken up by the career anti-Communists, such as Herbert Philbrick: "Where Communism is concerned, there is no one who can be trusted. Anyone can be a Communist. Anyone can suddenly appear in a meeting as a Communist Party member—close friend, brother, employee or even employer, leading citizen, trusted public servant."

Any society so imbued with suspicion as to believe that no one can be trusted is surely ripe for any charlatan bold enough, glib enough, and shrewd enough to seize the opportunity offered him.

11

The Long Night of McCarthyism

McCarthy, like Himmler, was a failed chicken farmer. He studied engineering, without success, before he shifted to the more flexible and imprecise study of law. Here he was equally undistinguished but at least was able to finish the course. His lowest grade in law school came in a course called "Legal Ethics."

It does not take professional lobbyists long to discover which of each new batch of Senators and Representatives can be successfully wooed. Real estate interests, impatient to profit from the postwar housing shortage, found in McCarthy their kind of Senator—once bought, he stayed bought.

In the 80th Congress McCarthy and a West Virginia Senator had introduced a resolution calling for the creation of a committee to investigate the housing problem. When the committee was formed, McCarthy was, naturally, offered a place on it. Representative Ralph Gamble of New York, a noted friend of the real estate lobby, was made chairman, at McCarthy's suggestion. But it was McCarthy who took the committee on the road to preach the gospel according to prefabrication and to decry the false promises of public housing.

"McCarthy left no brick unturned to defame every public-housing development he visited. After a trip to the 1,424-unit Rego Park Veterans' Housing Project in New York City, he pronounced the place 'a breeding ground for Communism.' " The McCarthy-Gamble committee played a crucial role in the defeat of the Taft-Ellender-Wagner housing bill which would have provided 500,000 units of low-cost public housing. Many a veteran living in an attic or garage in 1948 and 1949 had fellow veteran Joe McCarthy partly to thank for his plight.

Lustron took to the new Senator from Wisconsin almost from the first, enriching him by $10,000 in return for a pamphlet called "A Dollar's Worth of Housing for Every Dollar Spent." This was one of history's most lucrative literary ventures, worth $1.43 a word. The president of Lustron was so moved by McCarthy's devotion to prefabrication that he covered the Senator's losses at the racetrack. Another real estate tycoon showed similar favor to McCarthy by waiving payment of $5,400 McCarthy lost to him in a crap game.

McCarthy helped Pepsi-Cola win a larger sugar quota at a time when sugar was still severely rationed. Pepsi's lobbyist provided the Senator with an unsecured loan of $20,000.

During the 81st Congress McCarthy kept himself in the public eye by serving on a Senate committee investigating influence peddling, a subject on which he was rapidly becoming an expert. The investigation was highly publicized, and throughout 1949 McCarthy's name was frequently mentioned in the national press.

But his most notable triumph that year was his role on a three-man subcommittee of the Senate Judiciary Committee, investigating the forty-three members of the German SS "Blowtorch" battalion who had murdered nearly 200 American prisoners of war at Malmédy, Belgium, at Christmas 1944. McCarthy was not actually on the committee. He demanded, and was given, the right to "sit in" at its hearings, and these had been called because of agitation in Germany over the death sentences passed on the forty-three SS men. McCarthy also demanded, and received, the right to question witnesses. To the bewilderment of the three committee members, he proceeded to use the privileges granted him as a platform from which to denounce the hearings, which he called "a shameful farce" and "a deliberate and clever attempt to whitewash the American military." The forty-three convicted murderers had been framed. There had been no massacre at Malmédy. The confessions given by the forty-three men had been wrung from them by torture. McCarthy blamed the American, rather than the German, Army for the Malmédy incident.

For German Communists, who were attempting to incite hostility toward the American occupation authorities, McCarthy was a gift from the gods. The Communists and the families of the condemned men succeeded in raising emotions in Germany to such a pitch that in order to prevent an outburst of rioting which might have jeopardized the occupation's success, American officials commuted the forty-three death sentences.

When 1949 gave way to 1950, McCarthy was, like any Senator two-thirds of the way through his term, thinking hard about reelection. One night in January 1950 he dined with several acquaintances, including the dean of Georgetown University's foreign-service school, Father Edmund Walsh. McCarthy confessed to him that he needed an issue on which to base his reelection campaign, and Father Walsh suggested, "How about Communism?"

McCarthy accepted the idea at once, not because it was novel and daring but because it was familiar and successful. It was not unlike telling a man who had made his fortune as a gold prospector to put his money into mining stock. "The government is full of Communists," McCarthy said, thinking aloud. "The thing to do is hammer at them."

Each February, Congressional business slows down for a week or two while Republicans fan out across the country to make speeches celebrating the first Republican President. McCarthy's speechmaking for the Lincoln Birthday weekend was scheduled to open in Wheeling, West Virginia, where he would address the Ohio County Women's Republican Club. As a junior Senator held in some disesteem by the Republican Party leadership McCarthy did not get the choice speaking engagements, but the only speech to be remembered from that weekend was McCarthy's.

Addressing the 300 Republican women assembled in the Colonnade Room at the McClure Hotel, he suddenly brandished a sheet of paper which, he contended, bore the names of 205* known Communists working in the State Department. The naming of names was an essential part in fighting the Cold War at home; naming names brought the enemy to battle. It was thus an irreplaceable element.

---

*The actual figure he cited is the subject of much dispute. McCarthy later offered several other figures when he was pressed for details. But one of his speechwriters, L. Brent Bozell, says in *McCarthy and His Enemies* (Chicago: 1954), p. 45, that the figure 205 appeared in the Senator's rough draft for the speech. And Roy Cohn, *McCarthy* (New York: 1966), p. 2, accepts the figure of 205. But in the end it does not matter greatly; McCarthy's figures were always as hard to pin down as mercury. What matters is not the numbers but their elusiveness.

From Wheeling McCarthy moved on to Salt Lake City and Reno. As interest in his remarks at Wheeling grew, the number of names on the list dropped to fifty-seven. It appears that McCarthy had taken material from the State Department's files on its Loyalty-Security program. By taking different lists from different dates and subtracting those named who had since left government employment, McCarthy was able to arrive at different figures. By the time he returned to Washington to address a Senate which was by now eager to see McCarthy's lists, the number had become eighty-one.

The Senator had inadvertently stumbled upon a famous dramatic device. Perhaps he had at some time seen a performance of *Julius Caesar* where Mark Antony, by brandishing Caesar's will and by putting on a show of reluctance to read out its contents, turns a crowd come to bury Caesar into a mob desperate to know what is in the will.

But McCarthy bored the Senate by raking over eighty-one stale investigations carried out several years before. He continued to refer to "card-carrying Communists," evidently unaware that in 1949 the CPUSA stopped issuing identity cards and told members who had them to get rid of them, to make prosecution of Communists more difficult.

Although McCarthy's efforts had so far led nowhere, they had won him some important allies and admirers. Taft, formerly cool to him, now encouraged him. "Keep talking and if one case doesn't work out," he advised, "proceed with another." McCarthy had also attracted the attention of Alfred Kohlberg and the China Lobby.

Shortly after the Wheeling speech the cartoonist Herblock coined the term "McCarthyism"—he wrote it in crude letters on a drawing of a bucket of mud. The newspaper columnist Max Lerner took up the new coinage and spread it further. To McCarthy's admirers it was the term of opprobrium it was intended to be. But McCarthy loved the sound of it and like to boast, "McCarthyism is Americanism with its sleeves rolled up."

The State Department in these years offered a barn door of a target. Most of the people who had heard of the term "Cold War" believed that the United States was on the losing side of it. And what the War Department had been from 1941 to 1945, the State Department was considered to be at present: "For as long as the war against the Soviet Union is a cold war, our front-line troops are the working staff of the State Department."

Despite repeated purges and investigations, both internally and externally conducted, the department never succeeded in convincing its critics that it was not riddled with security risks. Taft, for instance, never tired of portraying it as being under Communist influence. Yet the man who delighted in being called the Senator with the "passion for facts" never produced the slightest evidence for his numerous slurs against the State Department's integrity. Its corruption was for him, as for many others, an article of faith.

Hard on the heels of the Wheeling speech the Senate Foreign Relations Committee established a subcommittee, chaired by Millard Tydings of Maryland, to make yet another investigation of the State Department.

The subcommittee broadened its scope to include consideration of the charges McCarthy had made against the department. Its hearings were dominated by the Wisconsin Senator. By now the number of card-carrying Communists had dropped to ten.

When the subcommittee issued its report in July, it dismissed McCarthy's assertions against the State Department. McCarthy began to grow desperate. His number of known card-carrying Communists dropped to one.

He announced that he would name "the top Russian espionage agent in the United States." This was to be the name of names. "I am willing to stand or fall on this one," he declared. "If I am shown to be wrong on this, I think the subcommittee would be justified in not taking my other cases too seriously." Several days later, before a crowded and expectant Senate, he gave the name of names—Owen Lattimore. To the few who knew of his existence, Lattimore was the leading Western authority on Mongolia, a prolific writer on Far Eastern affairs, and, on occasion, a consultant to the State Department. Yet here, according to McCarthy, was "Alger Hiss's boss." Lattimore was currently in a hut in Afghanistan. He was soon on his way home, breathing defiance.

Proof? It was all, McCarthy said, in the FBI's files. It was a ploy which might have worked. FBI files were never opened to public examination. But on this occasion Hoover personally inspected the material relating to Lattimore and personally reported to Congress that there was nothing there to support McCarthy's accusation.

The Senator hastily revised his earlier unequivocal statements. "Maybe in the case of Lattimore I have placed too much stress on the question of whether or not he has been an espionage agent," he grandly declared in a four-hour speech on the Senate floor. During his speech, "At frequent intervals he sipped from a small brown bottle of cough medicine." The Senator reduced the problem to the simplest terms. Lattimore, he said, was definitely "a policy risk," and "I believe you can ask almost any schoolchild who the architect of our Far Eastern policy is, and he will say 'Owen Lattimore.' " From the Senate press gallery came peals of laughter.

To save his accusations against Lattimore from collapsing completely, McCarthy brought in Louis Budenz to testify before the Senate Foreign Relations subcommittee. Had Budenz ever met Lattimore? No. Then how did he know that Lattimore was a Communist? Because another Communist had told him so? Were Lattimore's writings pro-Communist? They certainly were. Had Budenz read them? But of course. Which works had he read? Well, he had not read everything. What exactly had he read? It was hard to remember. Yet Budenz unblushingly claimed to be carrying in his head the names of 1,000 Communist agents entrusted to him by the "Chief Disciplinarian" of the CPUSA. It was considered remarkable by some observers that in the many hours he had spent talking to the FBI since his break with the Party, and in the numerous appearances he had made at hearings and trials involving Communists, although he had named many names, he had not once mentioned Owen Lattimore. Following his appearance before the Tydings subcommittee Budenz was interviewed on television and asked to repeat his charges against Lattimore away from the libelproof Senate hearing room. Budenz firmly and repeatedly declined to do so.

The other witnesses McCarthy found to give testimony against Lattimore were Freda Utley and Harvey Matusow. Miss Utley was an Englishwoman who had been married to a Russian. Devout Communists both, they had lived in Moscow until he had been arrested and subsequently executed during the Great Purge, after which Miss Utley became a devout anti-Communist. She turned up at various hearings throughout the 1950s, bearing huge stacks of Communist writings, which she would rummage through from time to time, mumbling irritably that she could not find what she was looking for. She was so hapless and confused that Lattimore considered her an asset to his own defense, as an illustration of the kind of idiocy he was up against.

Matusow had been one of McCarthy's assistants, an investigator for the Ohio Un-American Activities Committee, a consultant on subversion to the New York Board of Education, a paid informant for the FBI, and once upon a time a member of the Communist Party. He had never seen or met Lattimore. But he swore that Lattimore's books were used by the CP to make sure that it was following the correct line laid down by Moscow.

The conservative and aristocratic Tydings, a Democrat loathed by Roosevelt for his consistent record of voting against the New Deal, plainly despised McCarthy. As that estimable figure Henry Stimson remarked, "McCarthy is not trying to get rid of known Communists in the State Department; he is hoping against hope that he will find some." As the Tydings subcommittee's report made clear, by that test McCarthy had failed completely.

Tydings was running for reelection in the fall of 1950, and McCarthy turned his thoughts to seeking revenge. Roosevelt had in 1938 attempted to secure Tydings's defeat and succeeded only in embarrassing himself. McCarthy's adversaries were hoping for a similar result. McCarthy's friends were meanwhile circulating a fake photograph of Tydings and Earl Browder in which the two appeared to be relaxed and exchanging pleasantries. The photograph was the work of the art department of the *Washington Times-Herald* and ran over a caption which read:

Communist leader Earl Browder, shown at the left in this composite picture, was a star witness at the Tydings committee hearings, and was cajoled into saying Owen Lattimore and others accused of disloyalty were not Communists. Tydings (right) answered, "Oh, thank you, sir." Browder testified in the best interests of the accused, naturally.

It is unlikely that many who read the caption understood what "composite" meant even if they noticed it. The photograph was intended to show

Tydings in a friendly attitude toward Browder, and in that it succeeded.

McCarthy gave his support to Tydings's opponent, John Marshall Butler, an obscure Republican lawyer who had never before run for office. Butler beat Tydings. McCarthy got the credit. But the credit really belonged to Butler's campaign manager, a Chicago public relations man named Jon M. Jonkel. By conducting his own poll of public opinion, Jonkel learned two things: first, almost no one had ever heard of Butler; second, hardly anyone had an opinion about the Tydings's subcommittee. Shrewdly, Jonkel did not claim, as McCarthy claimed, that the hearings were a "whitewash." He played instead upon the theme that there was a *doubt* about the honesty of the hearings. Tydings was vulnerable, moreover, because like Voorhis and La Follette, he had become a power in Washington at the expense of his home base.

The same fall McCarthy threw his support to the opponents of Senators Scott Lucas of Illinois, Claude Pepper of Florida, and Frank Graham of North Carolina. Lucas, who was the Senate Majority Leader, Pepper, and Graham all went down to defeat. McCarthy was credited with unseating no fewer than four Senators in a single election. From this moment on the Senate treated him gingerly.

Yet Lucas had been defeated mainly because he was the victim of a scandal involving the Democratic machine in Chicago, Graham was beaten by racism, and Pepper was beaten by George Smathers, who ran a campaign of such scurrility that it became a legend in its own time, a sort of McCarthyism without McCarthy. The same fall McCarthy had traveled to Missouri to campaign against Thomas C. Hennings, Jr., who had won the Democratic Senatorial primary by attacking McCarthyism. The Missouri Senatorial election was the only one in which McCarthyism was the issue, and Hennings won. Over the next few years this obscure freshman Senator defied and denounced McCarthy, and his career was never harmed by it.

But when the Senate convened in January 1951, there were few Senators prepared to take the chance. "Certainly few had seemed more securely ensconced than Millard Tydings. Joe had got him; *ergo*, Joe could get you."

McCarthy used his new position of strength to do something only one other politician had dared do: he impugned the honor of George Marshall. Senator William Jenner of Indiana, the sole competitor McCarthy ever had for last place on the poll conducted periodically among Washington journalists, had in the summer of 1950 called Marshall "a front man for traitors . . . a living lie." McCarthy followed suit a year later with a 60,000-word review of Marshall's career that blamed every major calamity to have befallen the United States in recent times on a single individual—Marshall. Even the Marshall Plan was considered part of the Communist conspiracy; by financing Socialist governments in Europe, it paved the way for an eventual Communist takeover. Marshall, said McCarthy, "would sell his grandmother for any advantage."

Throughout McCarthy's histrionics, which now became increasingly reckless, there ran a deeply self-conscious streak. He referred to himself in the third person. He never stopped performing. Joseph and Stewart Alsop went to interview him. They found the Senator "with his heavy shoulders hunched forward, shouting instructions to some mysterious ally. 'Yeah, yeah. I can listen but I can't talk. Get me? You really got the goods on the guy?' The Senator glances up to note the effect of this drama on his visitors. 'Yeah? Well, I tell you, just mention this sort of casual to Number One, and get his reaction. Okay? Okay. I'll contact you later.' This drama is heightened by a bit of stage business. For as Senator McCarthy talks he sometimes strikes the mouthpiece of the telephone with a pencil. As Washington folklore has it, this is supposed to jar the needle of any concealed listening device."

To many who saw the McCarthy performance at close range he was not a fanatic at all; he seemed to know that he was performing and expected them to recognize—and accept—it. To him it was all part of the political game. Nothing personal.

McCarthy's protean accusations also made it impossible to come to grips with them. "Card-carrying Communists" became mere "policy risks" at a moment's notice. People called "traitors" on the Senate floor became no worse than "stupid" and "degenerate" in his public speeches. "Joe was noticeably braver," two journalists remarked, "when he stood on the solid, libel-proof floor of the Senate."

In person, the Senator was belching, balding, heavy-drinking, poker-playing, race-going, disheveled, and a woman-pawing slob. He was a walking caricature of all the masculine virtues celebrated on toilet walls. He loved to be considered tough and ruthless. Yet there were persistent, unsubstantiated rumors that he was a homosexual. He married late in life, and his wife did not bear him a child; their child was adopted. The Senator's weak interest in women, except to paw them at parties when other people were looking, may have stemmed not from inversion but from impotence. As Richard Rovere noted, "there was no doubt that he was full of bodily afflictions commonly associated with an afflicted psyche. He was a mass of allergies. His hands trembled incessantly. His stomach ailments were unending. . . . He had bursitis, troubled sinuses and was accident prone."

He had been shy since childhood, and despite his fame and brash manner, he remained nervous with people he did not know well. He found it impossible to sit still for long, to concentrate his mind for long, or to pursue a complicated line of thought. He bolted his food and gulped his drinks. He also had a nervous twitch which set his head bobbing uncontrollably.

Yet he was, in a sense, a man who had triumphed over a host of difficulties and disabilities. His shrewdness, his daring and his willpower had carried him over obstacles which would have stopped almost any other intending demagogue. McCarthy possessed the all-American gift: he was a superb promoter of himself. He was also the most accessible politician in Washington. Each day a table was set aside for him at the Grill Room of the Carroll Arms Hotel. Throughout lunchtime he presided over his rag-tag court, consisting of his personal assistants, an assortment of hangers-on, often East Europeans looking for protection in exchange for tips, plus a sprinkling of misfits, sycophants, and job seekers. Anyone might gain entry to this motley court, and one observer was moved to reflect that a genuine Soviet agent would have found it incredibly easy to get close to the country's most famous anti-Communist.

McCarthy's voting record, interestingly, paralleled the House voting record of Vito Marcantonio, the noted left-wing Congressman from the East Side—opposition to Point Four; opposition to the Voice of America; opposition to foreign military aid; votes in favor of big reductions in the Marshall Plan; votes to cut foreign aid. In general terms, McCarthy by coincidence voted the straight Communist Party line on foreign policy.

Yet he remained throughout the darling of the Hearst press. He was courted by Texas millionaires, who took to his buccaneering style. They bought him Cadillacs and took him hunting white-winged doves.

His most clamorous admirers, however, were the ordinary people who flocked to his rallies, "moon-struck souls wearing badges or carrying placards identifying them as the Minute Women of the U.S.A., Sons of I Shall Return, members of the Alert Council for America, the Nationalist Action League, We the Mothers Mobilize, the Republoform, and so on." After they had fervently sung "Nobody Loves McCarthy but the Pee-pul, We Just Love Our Joe," the Senator, braced with several stiff pulls at the whiskey bottle, would make his entrance, invariably a few minutes late. He entered in a cloud of alcohol fumes behind a flag-carrying honor guard. Everyone would recite the Pledge of Allegiance. Then, to thunderous applause, McCarthy would step forward to make his speech, lugging a bulging briefcase, which he placed at his feet or on a chair at his side. His first sentence was always "Well, it's good to get away from Washington and back here in the United States."

During his speech he would reach down and rummage in the briefcase, overflowing with "documentation," for an item he needed. He took his time, searching conscientiously, before standing up and waving a piece of paper, announcing, "I hold in my hand proof." It was the Wheeling gambit, played out over and over again.

A year after Wheeling 1,200 hundred Republicans filled Washington's Uline Arena to celebrate Lincoln's Birthday. No more speaking engagements in Triple-I League towns for the Senator this year. Now he shared top billing with Senator Taft. *Time* reported: "Lincoln got the homage, Taft got the respect, but McCarthy got the cheers."

McCarthy was by this time more than a political figure. He had become a force in national life. As the number of his admirers increased, the number of those willing to clash publicly with him dropped sharply. Truman, however, never failed to denounce him. He even used the occasion of dedicating the new Washington headquarters of the American Legion to make several pointed remarks about character assassination. The Legionnaires were noted for their admiration of McCarthy. He also called

McCarthy a liar and challenged him to bring a suit for libel and slander. *Time* was characteristic of the vacillation the Senator's career seemed to encourage. After helping promote him for several years, the Luce publications began to find his methods distasteful. He was finally put on the cover. But the portrait, however, was unflattering, not like the images of sagacious but kindly business tycoons who often graced the cover. And the accompanying text called him a liar, a demagogue, and an unwitting ally of the Communist cause.

McCarthyism appeared to sweep all before it. It is worth remarking, however, that although it did incalculable harm, it never eliminated critical thought or critical expression among those who were capable of either.

It is undeniable that the road to McCarthyism was paved with Truman's good intentions. Instead of preempting a Red scare Truman's action encouraged one. If there was not a serious problem of Communists-in-government, why screen millions of people for loyalty and security? The hunt for subversives was favored with the Presidential seal. Truman heartily despised McCarthy. But the President proved in this instance to be among those defenders of liberty who carry their wounds in their backs.

Under the program authorized by EO 9835, 4.75 million people were fingerprinted and subjected to FBI file checks. Full-field investigations were made on 26,000 people. Charges of disloyalty were brought against 9,000. Only one in three of these demanded a hearing; the rest stole quietly away. The standards employed, always vague, became increasingly subjective. And in the wake of Remington's perjury conviction the basis for dismissal was changed from "reasonable grounds" to "reasonable doubt." Several hundred people cleared under the earlier standard were promptly dismissed as a result. Hundreds of others chose to resign rather than go through another round of hearings.

To screen tens of thousands of applicants who each year sought jobs in sensitive agencies, the government turned to the polygraph. But the machines did not detect lies; they detected changes in physiological responses, however caused. Less than half of all the polygraph operators in the country had been properly trained at the time the government began resorting to lie detectors. When the National Security Agency employed its first six, all were graduates of a notorious diploma mill in Chicago. One operator was reported to be in the habit of turning on the examinee and screaming at him, "Goddammit, you're lying! I know you're lying, the machine says so!" This was meant to shock the examinee into telling the truth. It was more likely to send his blood pressure soaring. And then the machine did indeed purport to show that the poor wretch was lying. In time the NSA's program became so disreputable that it put the entire polygraph business at risk. In time the worst abuses were gradually eliminated. But the tests were of dubious reliability even when properly conducted, because despite tens of thousands of lie detection tests and tens of thousands of full-field investigations, the Loyalty-Security program did not unearth a single spy.

Yet there were Soviet agents at work in the government. Judith Coplon passed a security investigation. Joseph Patterson, employed by the NSA, passed government documents to foreign agents and was caught only because the documents were missed. At a later date two young mathematicians employed by the NSA defected to the Soviet Union.

Overseeing the program was the Loyalty Review Board, a body detested by liberals and, paradoxically, by McCarthy, who never forgave the LRB for having cleared Remington.* The LRB was headed by a courtly Republican lawyer, Seth Richardson. He himself expressed serious doubts about the methods the board was expected to follow and once remarked, not entirely in jest, that when it came to determining a person's loyalties, you might as well throw dice as hold a hearing.

There was, for instance, a Jew who was secretly accused of wanting to burn the Bible and of associating with people who mailed postcards inscribed "Save the Rosenbergs." He was also accused of criticizing the American Legion and of associating with a "Miss E" who read the *Daily Worker*. He secured a hearing and hired a lawyer and at heavy cost to his nerves and his savings was able to show that where the charges were not clearly false they were at least fatuous. Of the "reliable" sources who condemned him, not one appeared. But of the "known Communists" he was reported to associate with, one proved to be an employee of the FBI.

Another government employee was accused of being a member of the Communist Party while a student at UCLA. But he disproved the claim that he had attended Party meetings by producing bus schedules, maps, and his class attendance record. The meetings were held in East Los Angeles, he had no car, and the bus service was poor. During the hearing he was questioned closely about his sex life. and was asked such pertinent questions as "What do you think of female chastity?"

A proofreader in the Government Printing Office, who never handled classified material, was one day abruptly informed that he was being suspended without pay because "It is charged that you continued sympathetic association with a known Communist, read Communist literature and made pro-Communist statements." He admitted that he had once known a Communist, back in 1933; the man worked in the same printing plant as he. The pro-Communist statements were evidently remarks he had made back in the days when he was an isolationist, but he had been a La Follette Progressive at the time. He admitted that he had looked at the *Daily Worker*, but from curiosity, not conviction; he was not a regular reader of the paper. At his board hearing no witness confronted him. The board found against him.

---

*After the LRB had gone out of existence, the Supreme Court would rule that its legal safeguards were inadequate and that the board had exceeded its powers. *Peters* v. *Hobby* 349 U.S. 831 (1955).

A low-level employee in a government agency was accused of engaging in "left-wing" talk. At his hearing the agency's security officer repeated this accusation and was asked to substantiate it. He answered that the accused had referred to some people being "second-class citizens." In what context? He had said, the security officer explained, that "he would rather be a second-class citizen in Mississippi than a first-class citizen in Russia." The board found against him also.

James Kutcher was meanwhile continuing to fight for reinstatement in his job with the VA. His case provided a melancholy commentary on the pettiness of powerful men, notably in the VA and the Justice Department. But elsewhere he was treated with sympathy. He traveled around the country to address the NAACP, Baptist conventions, the AFL, the CIO, Methodists, social workers, teachers. Even the American Legion took Kutcher's side in his struggle with the LRB.

But Congress extended the Loyalty-Security program right down to where the poor and the obscure were gathered, in the Federally financed public housing projects. The heads of all families in public housing were required to swear that no member of the family residing with them was a member of any of the organizations on the Attorney General's list. Kutcher's septuagenarian parents were thus faced with a choice between perjuring themselves or evicting their legless and only child from the family home. Kutcher challenged the housing project's eviction notice in the courts.

At a higher level of government employment was O. Edmund Clubb, brought back to head the China desk at the State Department after closing the U.S. Consulate in Peking in April 1950. One day in January 1951 Clubb was handed an interrogatory by the department's legal officer. It was a splendidly tortuous document in which he was accused, among other things, of possessing " 'pink' tendencies in 1934–1935," of showing "a marked preference for some Communist principles in the early 1930s," and of becoming "100% pro-Red in 1940." These allegations were made by secret accusers, and Clubb was ordered to provide a complete account of all his political opinions since 1928. The sole specific charge against him was that he had delivered "a sealed envelope" to the offices of New Masses in 1932.

The implication was that the envelope contained classified material. But Clubb had fortunately saved his diary for 1932. The envelope had merely contained a letter of introduction to someone employed on the noted Communist periodical. He had stopped by to deliver it out of a spirit of curiosity and courtesy, not because he was engaged in conspiracy. This, however, was disputed by someone who had worked on New Masses in 1932—Whittaker Chambers. Clubb was suspended from his job.

In vain did he demand to be allowed to face his accusers. The LRB was awed by Chambers's uncorroborated testimony. When it came to naming names, Chambers, following the Hiss conviction, was in a class by himself. In vain, too, did Clubb produce thirteen witnesses to rebut the accusations made against him. The board decided that although there was no proof of disloyalty, Clubb was a security risk.

Clubb appealed the board's decision and was upheld. But his career was effectively ruined. And to be cleared once was not the end of the matter. John Stewart Service, for example, was investigated and cleared five times until, on the sixth attempt, the effort to dismiss him succeeded. To Clubb, after a year of interrogatories and hearings, "I felt that the government of which I had long been a part had been disloyal to me." His name cleared, Clubb resigned. Of course, McCarthy thereafter cited Clubb as one more Communist he had driven out of the State Department.

The system of interrogatories, hearings, and appeals was time-consuming and expensive. That alone made many decide not to fight. Each time the interrogatory arrived it brought suspension without pay, and even a successful challenge would take two to three years before the issue would be decided. But it is to the lasting credit of the American bar that it was graced with lawyers willing to take such cases for nominal fees, sometimes for no fee at all. And in the Hiss and Rosenberg cases the defense lawyers had borne their clients' costs. There were very few bright spots in the domestic Cold War. But the conduct of these lawyers, who made themselves the champions of impoverished pariahs, with no prospect of eventual reward, was surely one of the brightest.

The mainstay of the Loyalty-Security program was the government's body of paid witnesses. They also turned up at various HUAC hearings, at deportation proceedings, and before state and local bodies valiantly rooting out subversion. Wherever accusations were anonymously laid, there was a good chance that its source was a kept witness.

The best-paid of the witnesses was Louis Budenz, employed by Notre Dame and later by Fordham. Budenz had for many years been a radical union organizer before becoming a Communist in 1935 at the age of forty-four. By 1945 he was managing editor of the *Daily Worker*. But he was disenchanted with Communism, was silently fingering a rosary while at work, and his daughter was secretly receiving religious instruction from Monsignor Fulton Sheen. Following his break with the Party, Budenz augmented his professorial salary by lecturing and writing on Communism. He was also in heavy demand as a professional witness, and this alone was worth $10,000 a year.

Harvey Matusow, who, like Budenz, testified at the Lattimore hearing, was interviewed to see if he would be useful to the government side in the prosecution of the "second-string" Communist leaders. He asked if he stood much chance of being called as a witness. The young Assistant U.S. Attorney who was interviewing him, Roy Cohn, replied, "I think you'll make as good a witness as Budenz." To Matusow, this was high praise indeed, "because in the witness world Louis Budenz was regarded as the witness's witness."

By his own admission Matusow was an unprincipled opportunist. He decided that with the domestic Cold War at its peak there was only one place for a sensible ex-Communist to be these days—on the witness stand. His new mentors coached him in his new career, they taught him how to make a dramatic accusation, how to use the press, how to float a libelproof smear, and, a point of considerable importance, how to make his career as a paid witness last.

The professional witness, if he or she were to succeed, needed a personal publicity ploy. Philbrick had led three lives. Bentley was "the Red Spy Queen." Chambers had the Pumpkin Papers. Budenz had a Catholic's answer to Communism. Paul Crouch combined Communism and the armed forces. Matusow was much younger than all these people, and he turned his comparative youth to account by setting himself up as the expert on Communist corruption of American youth. Soon he was testifying that high schools and colleges were infested with Communists and their ideas, that the Party was rewriting beloved nursery rhymes and infiltrating the Boy Scouts.

He testified at twenty-five trials, deportation hearings, and LRB hearings. He identified 180 people as being known to him as Communists. He was courted by the president of Queens College, the superintendent of the New York school board, and the New York commissioner of police. He testified at the Lattimore hearing. Throughout these various appearances he lied, and lied and lied, as he later confessed.

Another of the 100-odd witnesses kept by the government at $34 a day, plus expenses, was one Mrs. Marie Natvig. She swore on oath that a newspaper publisher from Erie, Pennsylvania, was known to her as a member of the CP during her own years as a member. But the truth was, she had never been a Communist Party member, nor had the man she accused. She eventually confessed her perjury, as did the third of the paid witnesses, Lowell Watson.

Even where perjury was never proved or confessed the testimony offered by some of the witnesses inspires disbelief. Paul Crouch, who was almost as busy a witness as Budenz, was given to making incredible claims, such as a close friendship with Stalin or being treated on equal terms by generals of the Red Army's General Staff at a time when Crouch was a private soldier in the Red Army. Before becoming a paid witness, Crouch was a menial, earning eight-five cents an hour. After becoming a witness, his fortunes changed dramatically. He was treated as a celebrity, feted wherever he went, in heavy demand as a speaker. He was likely to turn up anywhere. He even appeared at Congressional hearings on Hawaiian statehood. The islands, he swore, were under Communist influence.

In one sense, these witnesses were among the most privileged figures of the domestic Cold War—they alone were above the Loyalty-Security program. They were the only people in government service who were exempted from the need for security clearances.

The paid witnesses supplemented their Federal income by performing similar services for the states. During the Canwell Committee hearings on subversion at the University of Washington, Melvin Rader, a philosophy professor, found himself accused by a black ex-Communist, George Hewitt, of being enrolled in a Communist Party summer school in New York in 1939 or 1940. Rader insisted that he had never been east of the Rockies prior to 1945.

Hewitt, who also claimed to have been a confidant of Stalin's, was employed by Alfred Kohlberg, when not busy testifying. The charges he made against Rader were supported by another kept witness, Manning Johnson.

The Canwell Committee ruled that Rader had perjured himself when he denied Hewitt's claims under oath. But Rader, with the assistance of an enterprising newspaper reporter, was able to account for every week of the summers of 1939 and 1940. The reporter won the Pulitzer Prize. A perjury indictment was brought against Hewitt, who had meanwhile hurried back to New York. The Canwell Committee proceeded to destroy most of the evidence it had collected concerning Rader, particularly the evidence which had supported his contention that he was innocent.

Nero had erected statues to paid informers. Without going that far, the Federal government went to considerable lengths to maintain the reputations of its kept witnesses. The Immigration and Naturalization Service attempted to intervene in the case of Hewitt's perjury indictment. He was, after all, one of its star performers at deportation hearings. But such intervention was superfluous. When the attempt to extradite Hewitt reached the New York courts, the judge before whom the case was argued adopted an extraordinary approach to weighing the issues. The *Daily Worker* was offered in evidence of Hewitt's Communist past. He refused to look at it. "I never saw the *Daily Worker* and I hope I never will." The district attorney who was ostensibly arguing the case for extradition put most of his energies into arguing against it. The judge finally decided that to send Hewitt back to Washington would be to send him "to eventual slaughter" because the entire state was under Communist control.

The Rader fiasco had at least one positive result—it finished the political career of "Communist Fighter Al Canwell," as his campaign literature described him. He repeatedly ran for Congress, with a consistent lack of success. He created the American Intelligence Service in Spokane and a Freedom Library. In a tiny office, beneath a large portrait of Joe McCarthy, he spent years grinding out his newsletter *Vigilante*.

Hewitt died shortly after the attempt to extradite him failed. But Manning Johnson was thoroughly discredited by this and other episodes. He testified at more than twenty trials before Justice Felix Frankfurter ended his career as a paid witness by calling him what he was—"a professional perjurer."

Not all the scoundrels were working the right side of the street. Paul H. Hughes managed to trick $10,000 from anti-McCarthy liberals in exchange for what he claimed was damaging evidence against the Senator. The documents he produced were shown to be forgeries. Hughes later appeared at Harvey Matusow's trial for perjury and, on the basis of the testimony he offered against Matusow, was himself indicted for perjury. But he was never brought to trial.

The House Un-American Activities Committee continued along its established course, its membership changing somewhat from election result to election result. J. Parnell Thomas went off to Federal prison for putting five women on his payroll and then sharing their salaries with them. Three HUAC members, by contrast, found the committee to be a stepping-stone to the Senate. Karl Mundt, Richard Nixon, and Francis Case were all elected to the upper chamber in 1950.

HUAC hearings would never again be as turbulent as they had been during the proceedings starring the Hollywood Ten. The people who appeared these days were markedly less defiant than their predecessors. They had learned that to defy the committee outright was to risk going to jail, a fact that was not well established in 1947 but one beyond a peradventure from 1950 to 1952. In the week the Korean War began Congress had set a Cold War record of a kind: it cited forty-three persons for contempt because they had refused to answer the question "Are you now or have you ever been a Communist?" Contempt citations had rarely been employed by Congress, and then only after much earnest debate. But now they were being issued wholesale. The contempt laws were like the conspiracy laws—a tacit admission of failure. It was beyond the wit of the nation's legislators, many of them lawyers by training, to devise laws which protected both the individual's right to freedom of expression and association and the nation's right to survive in peace. Bad laws were turning prosecutors into persecutors, investigators into character assassins. But HUAC and its admirers far from standing against this danger either ignored it or rushed to embrace it.

When HUAC resumed its hearings on Communism in Hollywood it found that most of the people it called were cowed and cooperative. They named names. Even people who had defied the committee only a few years before, such as Edward G. Robinson and Edward Dmytryk, were now eager to be helpful.

The committee succeeded in making one of its sternest critics, the *New York Times*, dismiss three of its staff members because they had once been Communists. The *Daily News* fired two of its reporters after they invoked the Fifth Amendment during their appearance before the committee. A fiction editor at *Collier's* was fired for what the committee considered his Communist-front activities. After Louis Budenz denounced Angus Cameron, an editor at Little, Brown as a Communist, Cameron was fired. Little, Brown similarly rejected a novel, *Spartacus*, by Howard Fast, which it had accepted before Fast's left-wing associations became generally known. No other publisher would consider the novel after that, and Fast was forced to publish it himself. Lee Pressman, general counsel to the CIO until forced out by Philip Murray, admitted to HUAC that he had been a Communist in the 1930s, during his time with the AAA. To purge himself, he named names, dozens of them.

Whether because of McCarthy or because of its own efforts, by 1952 HUAC hardly ever confronted a hostile witness. The most it encountered were people who invoked the Fifth Amendment, over and over again. These persons it was pleased to refer to as "Fifth Amendment Communists."

Swearing was an essential part of the loyalty mania. And what the State Department was to the nation, the local school was to the community. By 1952 thirty states had imposed loyalty oaths on teachers, in addition to any other loyalty oath imposed on all state employees.

If, as a result, there was an increase in loyalty among teachers and students, there was no outward sign of it. What was noticeable was acrimony, bitterness, and confusion. The orgy of oath swearing produced litigation, not loyalty.

Almost anything could spark trouble. At Oregon State a biology teacher was dismissed for suggesting that Lysenko's theories ought to be read before being condemned. A professor at a distinguished Eastern university admitted to a Congressional committee that he had been a Communist nearly twenty years before. But he invoked the Fifth Amendment when asked about the activities of other people. Although he had tenure, the professor was dismissed for "intellectual arrogance before a Congressional committee." Faculty members who were similarly unforthcoming before Congressional committees were fired from a number of the better colleges and universities, such as Harvard, Temple, Michigan, California, Washington, NYU, and Rutgers, as well as from such less esteemed institutions as Emporia State Teachers College.

State institutions were always vulnerable to pressure from state legislatures. It was sad but not surprising that President Allen of the University of Washington congratulated the Canwell Committee on the "integrity" of its proceedings, which we have seen included perjured testimony and the destruction of evidence. A debate by two professors at the University of Michigan on "Capitalism v. Communism" was banned by the university authorities; they were afraid that in the course of the debate someone might say something favorable about Communism.

Private institutions were not free from harassment. Temple University in Philadelphia, a place noted for its liberalism and independence, had as the head of its philosophy department Dr. Barrows Dunham. Called to appear before HUAC, he answered only those questions which he believed the committee had a right to ask. He was fired by the trustees for failing to do his part "to preserve the freedom of our society."

In Illinois the state legislature hired J. B. Matthews, onetime Methodist missionary, longtime organizer of Communist fronts, to spearhead an attack on the University of Chicago, considered by Illinois conservatives the Kremlim's major outpost on the North American continent. The legislature accused the university of harboring an "avowed Communist," a professor by the name of Pooche. The university had no professor by that name, or any like it. Matthews questioned the university's president, Robert Hutchins, at length on the activities of an eminent left-wing emeritus professor. Why, Matthews wanted to know, had the university given so dangerous a man so eminent a distinction? Matthews proved not to know that "emeritus" simply meant retired, and that once an emeritus always an emeritus. Hutchins used Matthews's ignorance on this and other matters as a source of comic relief. The legislators and their ace Communist hunter were laughed out of town, without unearthing a single subversive student or professor. But in its report the legislative committee solemnly announced that the Communist Club at Roosevelt College was probably full of Communists or, at the very least, some of the members held Communist views.

In 1949 New York State adopted the Feinberg Law, a piece of legislation in direct descent from the discredited Lusk laws of 1921. The Feinberg Law, however, had a slightly nutty flavor all its own. It proposed to root out Communist influences in the schools, even though, as the law itself acknowledged, "the propaganda disseminated by Communists in classrooms is frequently so subtle as to defy detection."

The Feinberg Law charged the New York Board of Regents with responsibility for compiling a list of subversive organizations. Virtually any organization could be listed, without any proof being required that it was subversive; membership in a listed organization was ground for dismissal. The Supreme Court in 1952 upheld the Feinberg Law.* Scores of teachers were fired under the Feinberg Law simply for invoking the Fifth Amendment.

New York was as vigilant as any state when it came to battling subversion. It was distinguished, furthermore, by being the only state to enact a security-risk statute. The New York Civil Service Commission was empowered to dismiss any employee who filled a "security position" or was in a "security agency" if he was felt to be a risk. Thus, paleontologists employed by the Department of Education learned that they held security positions because they knew the location of all the state's caves. The New York City Department of Sanitation was a security agency, because an outbreak of disease might lower the city's defenses against attack. The Probation Department was another security agency, but no reasons were ever given for this; perhaps they were too secret to be revealed. In time one-third of all state and four-fifths of all city employees were covered by security-risk legislation.

In Detroit there was an intensive search for subversion among city employees. As a result, the city unearthed an insubordinate assistant water engineer who was reputed to hold radical views. He was fired—for insubordination.

---

*The Supreme Court in 1967 finally decided that the Feinberg Law was unconstitutional after all.

The obsession with loyalty in the schools opened up a particularly rewarding field for the pursuit of patriotism at a profit. There was, for instance, big, fat Allen Zoll, a practiced hand at creating organizations, most of them nasty. In 1948 he had established the National Council for American Education (a name easily confused with both the National Education Association and the American Council on Education). Zoll wrote off in all directions in search of sponsors whose names would add luster to the NCAE's brand-new stationery. He netted a famous general, a famous editor, a famous Senator, and ex-heavyweight boxing champion Gene Tunney.

The NCAE was soon publishing pamphlets by Allen Zoll ("Internationally known sales consultant") on such topics as "REDucators at Harvard," "They WANT Your Child," and "Progressive Education *Increases* Delinquency." These pamphlets sold at prices from 16 to 20 cents each and in batches of 10 to 1,000. Membership in the NCAE sold for whatever the traffic would bear, from $5 to $1,000. Thousands of people subscribed to the NCAE's monthly bulletin.

Zoll's office was dripping with early-American kitsch, including a huge picture of Betsy Ross stitching the flag. Zoll was for several years ardently supported by parents' action groups locked in conflict with liberal schoolteachers and administrators.

Then there was Pro-America. Shortly after the war the elderly relict of Theodore Roosevelt was passing through Seattle when the docks came to a standstill because of a strike. Outraged that workers should have the power to shut down a big port, she organized her society women friends to take up the cudgels. Calling themselves Pro-America, they agitated among middle-class women all over the country to set up Pro-America chapters. These combined talks on the Red Menace with the usual round of garden club activities. But along the West Coast the Pro-America chapters distinguished themselves by harassing the local school board or college.

In California there was hardly a college or university which did not feel vulnerable. Occidental, Mills, Pomona, and Stanford threw themselves on the mercy of the Tenney Committee, established by the state legislature after the model of HUAC. In effect, they sought the Tenney Committee's blessing and petitioned it, protesting their keen desire "to collaborate with the Committee in a cooperative, long-range preventative plan to eliminate Communist Party members from the faculties of California institutions of higher learning, and to take steps to prevent infiltration of faculties by Communist Party members." Each campus appointed an intellectual "Security Officer" acceptable to the committee.

The University of California attempted to preempt the Tenney Committee and the state legislature by imposing its own loyalty oath, reasoning that a bitter pill would be more easily swallowed than one forced down by law. The Regents also summarily banned two speeches the British Socialist Harold Laski was scheduled to deliver at UCLA.

Faculty members at the university had already sworn an oath imposed on all state employees to uphold the constitutions of California and the

United States. They resented being singled out for special treatment. But although a few academics opposed the proposed oath on grounds of principle, it was resisted mainly because it violated the hallowed ground of tenure.

In 1949–1950 tenure at the University of California was still tribal in character, consisting of unwritten practices and unspoken agreements, deriving their authority from custom. The dismissal machinery created as an appendage to the new oath took no cognizance of this "system." Most of the anguish which seized the various UC campuses was not over a matter of conscience at all. Principle was one thing, but tenure was something else again.

There was brave and heady talk of mass resignations. But in the end a compromise was effected. In all, far fewer than 1 percent of the UC faculty lost their jobs, whether by resignation or by dismissal, as a result of the oath controversy. But the university had been embarrassed and its good name sullied. The American Association of University Professors was asked by faculty members at Berkeley to make an investigation. The AAUP agreed to do so and in time censured the university administration. But the censure resolution was not passed by the AAUP until 1956, when it was safe to do so.

In Southern California, meanwhile, the obsession with subversion in the schools had passed its apogee. In Los Angeles the Board of Education had given control over all hiring and firing of teachers and administrators to the counsel of the Tenney Committee. A Los Angeles woman who was convinced that the United Nations Educational, Scientific and Cultural Organization was a Communist front managed to get UNESCO Christmas card sales banned from the public schools. In Pasadena (where the three Rs of education were reported to stand for Rich, Reactionary, and Republican) the city was in turmoil for a year over curriculum changes proposed by the new superintendent of schools, Willard Gosling.

Far from being a radical educator, Gosling was one of the most highly regarded school administrators in the country; that was why he had been offered one of the best school jobs in the country. Pasadena's schools were well supported, almost free from delinquency or vandalism, and were academically distinguished. But Gosling's style of administration was so detached that to the school board his directives appeared to issue from the stratosphere. Behind every change he proposed they began to detect hidden motives because he never made his thinking clear to them. Given the current climate, hidden motives meant only one thing—he was trying to introduce Communist ideas into the schools.

Before long a corps of self-appointed educational vigilantes was harrying the baffled Gosling. His chief tormentor was a local osteopath who maintained that the curriculum changes were "leading to Socialism, and there isn't much difference between Socialism and Communism." When the issue was joined, the school board, instead of supporting Gosling, took the part of his tormentors. Gosling, by now the object of national attention, was forced out of his job after only a year.

It was in episodes such as this that the domestic Cold War was fought out in the neighborhood, the community, the schools. And a dreary, silly business it usually was.

The principal legislative monuments to the domestic Cold War bore the name not of a Republican, such as McCarthy, but of a Democrat, Nevada's Senator Pat McCarran. He was a man who would normally have been one more among hundreds of forgotten Senators.

McCarran was detested by his fellow Senators as heartily as McCarthy or Jenner. But seniority had brought him since his election to the Senate in 1932 to a position where he was conceivably its most powerful figure.

His state was the poorest in the Union and the most sparsely populated. It possessed the social structure of a medieval state or an underdeveloped country: a few rich at the top, many poor at the bottom, and not much in between. Lacking a strong middle class, Nevada lacked the constraints of bourgeois morality. It was notable for only three things: legalized gambling, easy divorce, and legalized prostitution. It is unlikely that Nevada was capable of electing any Senator better than McCarran.

The Senator was moved deeply by his faith in four causes—gambling, silver, Spain, and anti-Communism. As a young man he had spent many happy days tending a flock of sheep given him by his father. But as he grew older, the need to earn a living drew him into a career in law. His interest in sheep never faded, however. Late in life he used his considerable powers to force an exception in the immigration laws so that hundreds of Basque shepherds might freely enter the United States to tend the sheep of Nevada.

The basis of McCarran's power was his chairmanship of the Senate Judiciary Committee, to which nearly half of all Senate bills were referred, and his chairmanship of the Senate Appropriations Committee, which controlled appropriations for the departments of State, Justice, and Commerce. He was also chairman of the subcommittee established to oversee the Marshall Plan. Few Senators would risk a clash with him, because through the Judiciary Committee he held a veto of the small, but highly prized, Federal patronage they possessed—the appointment of Federal judges, attorneys, and marshals. His power over appropriations made the White House fear to cross him, despite his anti-New Deal, anti-Fair Deal, pro-isolationist attitudes. He was, in the view of one close observer, "a greater threat to his party's program than the combined forces of the Dixiecrats and the Republicans."

McCarran admired only one foreign leader—Franco. Although Spain was excluded from the Marshall Plan on the ground that it was a Fascist state, McCarran won a $62.5 million loan for Franco, without conditions. Even democratic states such as Britain and France were obliged to meet various conditions before they received American assistance.

In 1950 McCarran introduced the Internal Security Act. This measure was in large part based on the Mundt-Nixon bill, which had been passed two years earlier by the House, only to fail in the Senate. The Administration had since then attempted to head off the Mundt-Nixon bill by introducing its own measure which would intern "dangerous persons" during periods of national emergency, an idea which earned for the President and his advisers the sobriquet "concentration camp liberals" from the *Chicago Tribune.*

McCarran adopted the idea of interning "dangerous persons," plus various parts of the legislation proposed by Mundt and Nixon, to form the basis of the Internal Security Act, otherwise known as the McCarran Act. This legislation declared by fiat that Communism was by its nature "a clear and present danger to the security of the United States." It was already a crime to engage in any overt act which aimed at the destruction of the government by violence; the McCarran Act went a step further and made it a crime to "agree with any other person to engage in any overt act which would substantially contribute to the establishment within the United States of a totalitarian dictatorship." The McCarran Act created the Subversive Activities Control Board which would determine whether an organization should be required to register itself as "a Communist-action organization," the members of which would be denied passports and contributions to which would be denied tax exemption. Out in the deserts of Arizona, New Mexico, and, appropriately, Nevada, camps were established of wooden huts and barbed wire. They stood ready to receive the tens of thousands of "dangerous persons" who would be rounded up during a national emergency.

When the McCarran Act was passed it was no secret that Truman intended to veto it. House members for their part waited impatiently for his veto message to arrive. When it did, they scanned it quickly then began shouting, "Vote! Vote!" In fifteen minutes, without a word of debate, the House overrode his veto by 286–48. Senate liberals attempted to filibuster the McCarran Act to death. They failed utterly. The Senate voted for it by 57–10.

Scores of municipalities passed "little McCarran" acts. These came mainly in two varieties—registration and "run 'em out of town." Communists and fellow travelers were ordered to leave Jacksonville, Florida, and McKeesport, Pennsylvania, within forty-eight hours by local ordinance. In New Rochelle, New York, and Los Angeles they were ordered to register at the sheriff's office. In Miami the anti-Communist ordinance was drawn so broadly that if it were interpreted literally, it had become a crime to say anything concerning politics which was subsequently proved false. In time nearly all the "little McCarran" laws were found by state and Federal courts to be so vague that they violated the due process of law.

The Subversive Activities Control Board began its work in April 1952. With the aid of the Criminal Division of the Justice Department it attempted to prove that the CPUSA was a Communist-action organization. The legal definition of such a body was so elastic that it made defense extremely problematical. The Justice Department's lawyers, on the other hand, were forced to spend hundreds of dismal hours reciting the history and ideology of the Communist Party. This was not a good idea. The defendants knew that history and ideology far better than the government lawyers, and they made fools of people on whose tongues Marxist dialectics lay as clumsily as Chinese poetry might.

The hearing plodded solemnly along for eighteen months. The SACB then ruled, without cracking a hint of a smile, that the Communist Party of the United States of America was indeed a Communist-action organization. It was therefore an agent of the Soviet government. The CPUSA was ordered to register itself forthwith. The Party refused to do any such thing.

During its time-consuming hearings, the SACB questioned John Gates, one of the eleven convicted CP leaders. During his six days of testimony he was asked if it were true that Party members were required to take a pledge to defend the Soviet Union. Gates replied that the only pledge he and his fellow Communists had ever taken was the Pledge of Allegiance. The Pledge of Allegiance was soon amended to include the words "under God" so as to make it unpalatable to Godless Communists.

While the SACB had been arguing dialectics with Communists, McCarran had been turning his attention to Owen Lattimore. The Senate had obligingly created an Internal Security Subcommittee, attached to McCarran's Judiciary Committee, following passage of the McCarran Act, and the Senator was made chairman of the subcommittee, which was soon hotly engaged in the pursuit of subversives.

In December 1950 one of McCarthy's investigators, Don Surine, received a tip that several filing cabinets of material from the Institute of Pacific Relations were stored in a barn near Pittsfield, Massachusetts. The IPR was an association of national councils in the United States, the United Kingdom, Canada, Australia, France, New Zealand, the Philippines, India, and Japan. Its major activity was the publication of scholarly, or at least well-informed, books and articles on Pacific affairs. Among its publishing ventures was the magazine *Amerasia*. The institute had attracted some radicals and Communists to its conferences. There were several notable Communist sympathizers among those who contributed to the IPR's funds. But it could not by any stretch of the imagination be seriously considered a Communist front, except by people like McCarran and McCarthy. It was the IPR's misfortune, as well, that its most prolific author had been Owen Lattimore.

Following the recall of General MacArthur, his intelligence chief, Major General Charles A. Willoughby, had returned to the United States. Among Willoughby's effects were four footlockers which contained material detailing the work of the brilliant espionage ring created and run in wartime Japan by Richard Sorge. But as a spy story it was old news. What made the material in the footlockers of immediate interest was that four of the members of the Sorge ring had been members of the IPR.

But the material in the barn near Pittsfield was as interesting as a collection of galoshes. It consisted of correspondence, manuscripts, and internal memoranda stored there by a thrifty former secretary-general of the IPR who was trying to save money on storage costs. Nevertheless, the files in the barn became the object of much secretive coming and going, clandestine meetings, and cryptic conversations. Surine examined the dusty filing cabinets at dead of night and then conferred with J. B. Matthews, the Hearst newspapers' authority on every aspect of the Communist menace.

HUAC was also tipped off on the IPR files. The contents of the cabinets were surreptitiously pored over, photostated, and eventually taken away—all without benefit of subpoena or search warrant.

The agents of McCarthy, HUAC, and Hearst had engaged in breaking and entering, stealing, and transporting stolen property across state lines. When the owner of the barn discovered what was happening, the plotters nervously dropped everything in McCarran's lap.

The stolen material was smuggled back into the barn. The McCarran subcommittee issued a subpoena. The filing cabinets were lugged out of the barn in the middle of a snowstorm, placed aboard a truck, and given an armed escort from New York to Washington. The press was jubilant and expectant over this procession and what the seized filing cabinets might reveal. What they did not yet know was that the FBI had long since gone through all the IPR's files, at the institute's invitation, and had found nothing untoward.

But McCarran attempted to use the seized material to prove that, on the contrary, the IPR had been a nestbed of Communist agents, under the direction of that master spy Owen Lattimore. Elizabeth Bentley was trotted out once more to testify that the IPR was under the control of Earl Browder, forgetting that she had claimed she controlled Earl Browder.

Lattimore was questioned at exhausting length on the entire contents of the IPR files. He failed to remember them down to the least detail; this was also true of articles and letters he had written more than ten years past. The Justice Department, ever solicitous regarding the wishes of Senator McCarran, brought a lengthy indictment of the professor, charging him with perjury at a dozen places in his testimony. Lattimore was not accused of anything which might be settled by objective proof or concrete evidence, however. The perjury charges were based on Lattimore's repeated claim that he had never been sympathetic toward Communism and had never sought to advance Communist interests.

The law on sympathetic encouragement of a possibly illegal enterprise is another venture into the realm of metaphysics. Nor had any democratic country ever attempted to define "Communist interests." Lattimore's lawyers, in their defense brief, asked the courts to consider this question: "Did President Roosevelt promote Communist interests when he furnished lend-lease to Russia?"

McCarran's subcommittee began to take an interest in the Secretariat of the United Nations. It labored diligently to portray the UN as little more than an outpost of the Center. There was not much that could be done, however, about the Russians assigned to serve at the UN. The subcommittee had to content itself with pestering the Americans attached to the Secretariat.

This was pressure that the UN could not ignore. The United States provided it with nearly half its income. The UN's permanent bureaucracy found it politic to appease this powerful subcommittee, even if this meant making a mockery of the idea that the UN transcended narrow national interests and obsessions. Ten members of the Secretariat were suspended from duty; three were fired outright. The Secretary-General, Trygve Lie, resigned in disgust over these incidents. The UN's General Counsel, Abraham Feller, one of the subcommittee's particular targets because of his sponsorship by Alger Hiss, jumped to his death from a twelve-story window.

The Justice Department was responsible for immigration; to McCarran that entitled him to set immigration policy. After 1948 the liberal immigration lobby had succeeded in creating enough converts on the Senate Judiciary Committee to have the 1948 Displaced Persons Act amended over McCarran's opposition. A new Displaced Persons Act was passed in 1950, allowing an additional 100,000 DPs to enter the country. Several hundred thousand refugees in other categories were also permitted entry.

McCarran made a well-publicized tour of the DP camps, finding them filled with Communists. Passage of the 1950 Act was an unwonted, bitterly resented rebuff to his *amour propre*. For the next two years McCarran sought his revenge. In 1952 he got it, with passage of an omnibus immigration bill, the McCarran-Walter Act of 1952. This severely limited immigration from any area under Communist control. It altered existing quotas. It gave the President power to exclude anyone whose entry could be considered "detrimental to the interests of the United States." Special procedures were enacted to hasten the expulsion of aliens deemed undesirable. The McCarran-Walter Act (Francis Walter, chairman of HUAC and a Republican Representative from Pennsylvania) was so comprehensive and so stringent that the Attorney General had to pass on whether foreign seamen were subversive before they were allowed to leave their ships while in American ports.

McCarran's approach to immigration policy had been prefigured in the Internal Security Act, which had banned any alien who had ever been "affiliated" with "any branch, affiliate or subdivision" of any "totalitarian party." Ellis Island was soon chockablock with hundreds of Germans and Italians (and very few Russians). The detainees were often people eminent in their professions; unfortunately they had belonged to some organization or other in Mussolini's Italy or Hitler's Germany, such as the war bride who had been in the Hitler Youth when a child or the conductor who had led the orchestra at La Scala when the opera house was part of the Fascist state.

The best-known victim of the capriciousness of immigration policy in these years was a German war bride, Ellen Knauff, who fell foul of the bureaucracy of the Immigration Service. She arrived in New York in August 1948 aboard the ironically named USS *Comfort*. She spent the next year uncomfortably on Ellis Island, virtually a prisoner, without being told why she was being detained.

Released on bond, she fought her case in the courts. She was suddenly seized without warning, and an attempt was made to put her on a plane out of the country before anyone noticed. This failed by minutes. But she was taken back to Ellis Island. The Justice Department all the while refused to give any reason for its adamant opposition to her entry into the United States.

When her case was brought to the President's attention, one of his assistants was instructed to look into it. Justice Department officials refused to let the White House see the files. Truman chose not to press the matter further. It was an episode which demonstrated the limited control Truman himself exercised even within the Executive branch when issues of loyalty and security were involved.

But Mrs. Knauff had at least one very powerful ally—Francis Walter. She had the support, too, of Irving Dilliard, the editor of the *St. Louis Post-Dispatch*. Dilliard had made her case famous throughout the country. Walter had raised it repeatedly in Congress. After more than two years Ellen Knauff was finally granted a hearing before a board of immigration inspectors. She was confronted with three people she had never seen before, all of whom claimed that someone else had told them that Ellen Knauff was a spy. The board ruled that she was a security risk. She was once again locked up on Ellis Island.

No evidence was ever offered to show that she had been a spy. Mrs. Knauff was convinced, however, that much of the hearsay testimony was based on lies deliberately spread by a woman who had once been in love with her husband. In November 1951 the Board of Immigration Appeals ruled in her favor, and she was allowed to enter the United States. It had taken three years and three months. She was another victim of the domestic Cold War who had to rely heavily on the devotion of her lawyers.

Mrs. Knauff was not the only war bride to be detained for more than a year because of unsupported accusations made by anonymous informants. But she appears to have held the record for endurance.

The State Department from 1947 had been fighting the Cold War with passports and visas, chiefly by denying them. It was a popular policy at home, the cause of resentment and laughter abroad. When the department in 1948 refused to issue a passport to Leo Isaacson, who was planning to travel to Europe to attend a left-wing conference, the *New York Times* applauded. The great liberal newspaper took a stern line with those people who had somehow acquired the idea that being free meant being free to travel. "It is nothing of the kind. No citizen is entitled to go abroad to oppose the policies and interests of his country, and this, on the record, is the purpose of the conference which Mr. Isaacson proposed to attend . . . the State Department acted wisely and within an intelligent conception of individual rights in seeing to it that he did stay at home." If a member of Congress could not get a passport, who could?

The time was so out of joint that even the ACLU defended the restrictive policy on passports and visas. The State Department had a responsibility to protect the United States against clear and present dangers, the ACLU averred, "and under present circumstances perhaps also against dangers which are neither wholly clear nor demonstrably present." This formula moved I. F. Stone to wonder, "Is this defending civil liberties or doing psychic research?"

Thousands of people were affected by the State Department's passport policy, most of them obscure but some of them intellectuals and artists of international reputation, such as Rockwell Kent and Paul Robeson. Visas were denied to many thousands more, including Pablo Picasso, the Italian novelist Alberto Moravia, and the distinguished Anglo-Catholic writer Graham Greene. As an undergraduate at Oxford twenty-five years earlier Greene had been, for one month and mainly as a joke, a Communist. Charlie Chaplin, resident in the United States for forty years, left for Europe in possession of a reentry permit. No sooner had he quit American soil than he was told that the permit would not be honored if he attempted to use it. Paul Dirac, a Nobel prizewinner in physics, was not allowed to come to the United States to give a speech. One of the world's leading physicists, Marcus Oliphant, the head of the Australian Academy of Science, was denied a visa to address a conference of physicists.

Linus Pauling was repeatedly denied a passport. But in 1954 he won the Nobel Prize for Chemistry. It would have been embarrassingly too much like Soviet practice to stop him from traveling to Stockholm to collect his prize. Scientists jested bitterly, "Win the Nobel; win a passport."

Another joke had it that the only place in the United States where an international meeting of scientists could be held was Ellis Island. International scientific bodies began to shun the United States. The International Congress of Genetics, scheduled to convene in America in 1953, changed its mind and met in Italy. The International Congress of Psychology similarly shifted its venue to Montreal. The International Astronomical Union was invited to meet in the United States but declined the invitation specifically because of the visa policy.

No scientific body wanted to expose its speakers or its delegates to humiliation at the hands of bureaucrats working from suspect files and to appease powerful but ignorant politicians. Many estimable bodies for years did not consider meeting in the United States for much the same reason they did not consider meeting in the Antarctic—it was not a serious possibility.

12

Lighten Our Darkness

When the war ended, there were only six commercial television stations on the air and a set cost $500. The screen was sicklied o'er with a pale cast of green. To make the picture look more like a picture and less like a radar set, cabinets were designed to block the upper and lower tangents from sight. But the sides remained decidedly bowed until 1950, when the rectangular cathode tube was perfected.

Throughout the late 1940s there was no television in most of the United States, but there were sets everywhere. Hundreds of thousands of people, perhaps millions, bought one before they had ever seen a program. A million sets were sold in 1948; 7.5 million in 1949. Nothing, it seemed, could interrupt the growth of TV, not even blank screens. The sale of sets grew at an annual rate of 500 percent for nearly a decade.

By 1953 half of all homes had a TV set. The cost of most models had dropped to around $200. Screens ranged in size from seven inches to fifteen. Reception in most areas remained poor. But TV was a passion, a craze, a social event, and a new focus for family life. Even the Federal Communications Commission in its ineptitude failed to blunt its appeal.

The FCC had so completely botched the political, commercial, and technical problems television raised that in 1948 it was forced to stop granting licenses to new stations while it tried to make some sense out of the mess it had created. The FCC had forced 120 licensed stations into twelve channels. They were, predictably, beginning to run into one another on the airwaves. For three years no new stations began operating. Many a proud new set owner discovered that all he had to show for his money was a kind of electronic venetian blind because all that his set picked up for most of the time was flickering interference.

The FCC had listened to the entreaties of RCA and other major radio and TV manufacturers. They already had a large investment in equipment which would work only in the lower part of the radio band. The FCC had obligingly granted licenses for television broadcasting only in that part of the spectrum despite expert advice that it did not offer sufficient room for expansion. In 1951 the FCC reluctantly agreed to do what it should have done in the beginning—put all new television broadcasting in the ultrahigh-frequency range.

The FCC was also embarrassed by CBS's claim to have perfected color TV. RCA had based its production on black-and-white sets. All NBC's programming was based on black and white. Were CBS to begin color broadcasts, RCA's multibillion-dollar investment in sets and broadcasting might be wiped out. The FCC had for twenty years been deferential to RCA, which had dominated radio broadcasting. It decided to grant broadcast licenses only for black and white.

Television was economically dependent on radio for nearly a decade. Capital costs were high, and the market still comparatively small, if rapidly expanding. Radio's profits offset television's losses. A ruthless, cutthroat element crept into radio programming because of this burden. Anything not commercially successful was abandoned without hesitation. Discussion programs, current affairs documentaries, serious drama, classical music, educational programs—all were cast overboard in the pursuit of higher profits. Radio was already declining in popularity. This frantic groping for the lowest common denominator helped push it farther down the slope.

Television was also dependent creatively on radio; it lifted most of its program formats from established radio successes. The formats—crime shows, situation comedies, dramas, Westerns, etc.—were so fully developed that all television need do was provide the scenery.

But television's news documentaries borrowed not from radio; they took their cue from the *March of Time* films produced by Time-Life in the 1930s and 1940s. The style was pithy, dramatic, and aggressive, relying on quick cutting from scene to scene, with wildly contrasting pictures shown rapidly, one after another, to the accompaniment of a hard-hitting text full of short, adjectival phrases. It was a style which inevitably eschewed depth or subtlety. Its objective was not really to inform but to grab the viewer's attention and hold it. In time, this style seeped from the news documentaries into news broadcasts as more and more film was shot for them.

Although people wanted television, that did not necessarily mean that they did not want radio. For some things, such as the news, people for a long time continued to put their trust in radio. Radio was also the source of a major innovation in popular culture: the advent of the disc jockey. Until the 1940s records were rarely played on the air. But the courts gradually rejected the opposition put up by the record companies. And in the search for maximum profits to sustain TV's losses the disc jockey programs became radio's bread and butter. DJ programs were cheap to produce and attracted huge audiences, which in turn raised advertising revenue. Radio commercials had also been limited to three and a half minutes each hour before 1946. By 1950 the limit had been raised to nearly ten minutes.

Despite taking over successful program formats, television programs in the early years as a rule ranged from the dull to the dreadful. Yet if the network programs were bad—badly written, badly lit, badly acted—local programs were invariably worse. Local stations tried to give their offerings a regional flavor (polka bands in Milwaukee, Dixieland jazz in New Orleans). But most local TV programs were simply feeble copies of what the networks offered. Yet people watched it all, indiscriminately, in something like rapture.

The first truly successful television program, in terms of giving its audience something they found wholly satisfactory, was *Howdy Doody*, which made its debut in 1948. Howdy was a freckled, shock-haired, inanely grinning puppet dressed in checked shirt and jeans. For millions of children, of whom I was one, the age of television began with Howdy and Uncle Bob.

For most adults the first star of TV was Milton Berle. A flop at thirty-nine, Berle was the hottest property in show business at the age of forty. On Tuesday nights from 1949 through 1952 attendance at movie theaters, already low, dropped still lower. Berle specialized in the witless joke, the abrasive personality, and taste which never rose higher than the vulgar.

Much of what he offered was warmed-over vaudeville. Yet he was the first comedian to exploit the possibilities of immediacy and physical action which television offered.

In some ways the most successful of the early shows was *Today*. During its first two years it was perennially on the brink of extinction. But in 1952 one of the show's staff members stepped into an elevator and was confronted by a chimpanzee sucking on a baby's bottle. The monkey soon afterward appeared on the show under the *nom d'artiste* J. Fred Muggs. The monkey stole the show and made the program.

"Women proposed to him; advertisers fought for the right to use his picture in their supermarket flyers; Chambers of Commerce sought his good offices; actresses posed with him; officers of newly-commissioned vessels demanded that he christen them." Muggs appeared as the guest of honor at an I Am an American Day rally in Central Park; an honor indeed—Muggs was from Cameroon.

The year 1952 also saw the arrival of *Ding Dong School*. It began as a local program (the exception to the rule) in Chicago. Within months it was taken up all over the country. Its star was a plump middle-aged schoolteacher, Frances Horwich, who got the job by mistake; it was supposed to have gone to a lady named Horowitz. Mrs. Horwich sat on a hassock, addressed her preschool audience as if they all were present and correct, and led them in a constructive half hour of finger painting, paper cutting, and drawing, talked to several dolls and puppets, presented her three goldfish named Wynken, Blynken, and Nod, and never lapsed into the frenzied, factitious behavior common to children's shows. Throughout the 1950s *Ding Dong School* had one of the biggest and most faithful audiences in television.

But the biggest success among adults and children alike was a puppet show, *Kukla, Fran and Ollie*. The script was vestigial. Nothing ever seemed to happen. It was so low-key that it was something of a miracle that the program registered at all. Yet, wrote a critic who began by scoffing only to find himself watching with interest, it had "an odd, narcotic pull."

The most successful show of all, however, made its first appearance in October 1951. Called *I Love Lucy*, it was a phenomenon. For a show designed purely for entertainment it set a record that was unmatched. Episodes of *I Love Lucy* were shown again and again for years after their first showing. It was less a program than a cult, drawing the faithful every Monday night.

In the daytime there were the soap operas, indistinguishable from those on radio. The real star of daytime television, however, was food. There were cooking programs on every day of the week.

That first TV set provided tens of millions of people with one of those never-forgotten moments in life. It carried a sense of wonder and excitement.

One man recalled years afterwards:

I sure can remember when we got our first set. The first thing I saw was a give-away program. Happy Jack Somebody. He had a mustache. . . . It was "Queen for a Day!" That was it, Happy Jack [Bailey], a man with a mustache. And it was like that for several weeks: rush home to see it. The next stage was you watched everything while you were at home but you didn't rush home. From then on I watched only when I had the time. It was a week, maybe longer, when I'd race home. The next period lasted a couple of months and I'd sit in front of the thing every night, shove the kids out of the way so I could watch it. I'd like the shows the first few times, then I couldn't stand it. . . . We bought it because it was like buying a new car, maybe more so. It was new and different. . . . I wish I felt about television now like I did when I bought my first one. I spent $420 on that first set. Now I wouldn't spend $150.

Television arrived almost simultaneously with the affluent working class—the first generation of blue-collar workers able to afford middle-class pleasures. They enjoyed security, property, and leisure on a scale unthinkable for workers in the 1930s. It was the working class and lower middle class that provided the mass market on which the rapid growth of television was based. The better educated took to television more slowly.

In working-class neighborhoods business at the taverns slumped when television came into the area. Fighting fire with fire, tavern owners installed television sets, and the customers came flocking when a sporting event was on. For many people, in fact, the first TV set they ever watched regularly was in a bar. But, as one bartender lamented when watching the screen, "people forget what is the prime purpose of a bar, which is to drink."

What people wanted from television was entertainment. Television quickly became the prime leisure activity of most Americans. But to say that it took over people's leisure time is probably to misconstrue what was happening. Television may have created most of the leisure time it consumed. Chores and other inevitable activities were speeded up, whereas they had once helped kill time. Some of the time spent unnecessarily on sleep was now spent in front of the TV set. There was no longer the same incentive to linger over dinner to help fill up the evening. No one had heretofore considered cutting the lawn, sleeping, eating, and talking leisure activities.

People also listened less to radio, went to movies less often, and read less fiction. But the demand for information—for nonfiction books—rose strongly throughout the postwar years.

Radio had for a long time been damned as a corrupting influence on the young; adolescents were said to listen to the radio too much and to have their minds turned toward sex and violence as a result. As television viewing spread, these criticisms were directed increasingly at television. Given the nature of much of the programming—Westerns, crime shows, tales of horror—violence was an integral part of the entertainment. But there was one notable change: the trend on television was toward fatal violence, a shift from the fist and the foot to the gun and the knife.

* * *

Within the story of television's success there was a human tragedy in the classic mold. Edwin Howard Armstrong was a man destined to see his creations enrich others, while he fell into financial straits. But in the end his was the case of the man who stood against the powers of a great corporation in an age when the corporation, with help from the state, had no compunction about crushing the eccentric, the awkward, and the rebellious, even if he were a figure of genius.

As a young man Armstrong had invented the regenerative circuit. This device ws the heart of all modern radios. But as often happens with major inventions in modern times, there was a rival claimant, and the rival had the backing of AT&T. The Supreme Court had ruled in favor of the rival, Lee De Forest, in a decision which showed that the Court had simply become confused by the technical arguments involved. To his fellow radio engineers Armstrong was and remained the inventor of radio.

His inventive genius was fecund. He was a rich man, drawing huge royalties from his many patents. Nearly all this income was poured into the development of frequency modulation—that is, FM. His ideas on FM were flatly contrary to every received view on the subject. For many years his work in this field was scorned as impossible, and his severest critics were the engineers employed by AT&T and RCA.

By an ironic stroke Armstrong was one of the biggest stockholders in RCA. To finance his researches on FM, he sold large blocks of his RCA stock, and from one of these sales he financed the construction of a 400-foot transmitter. All this time he was ridiculed by RCA, which had a large investment in radio based on amplitude modulation—AM.

Armstrong was combative by temperament. Big, balding, energetic, he threw himself into arguments and litigation with hardly a second thought. Yet he was also thin-skinned. He suffered terribly when things went against him.

He also had a generous and expansive nature. Appointed professor of electrical engineering at Columbia, he asked for a salary of $1 a year and never bothered to collect it. The university provided him with laboratory space, and Armstrong paid to equip it and paid his assistants out of his own pocket. He had spent more than $1 million on developing FM. Yet when the war began he put all his patents at the government's disposal. FM radio sets, which were static-free, unlike AM, which was crackling and easily upset, went into millions of American tanks, planes, ships, and jeeps, and helped give American armed forces the best combat communications in the world.

During the war Armstrong threw himself into radar research. While everyone else was working on pulse radar, Armstrong went his own way and developed continuous wave radar, which is to this day the basis of all long-range radar. This was another of Armstrong's "impractical" ideas.

When the war ended, Armstrong resumed the fight for FM. But the entire radio industry was based on AM. RCA tried to buy Armstrong off for $1 million. He refused to sell his FM patents. There were forty FM stations in operation and 500,000 FM sets in use.

RCA and CBS and the major radio manufacturers pressured the FCC to restrict FM to a new section of the radio band, 88–108 megacycles; this would make those FM stations and FM radios useless, because they all had been designed to operate in a lower part of the band. The FCC's chairman was Paul A. Porter, a noted Washington lawyer, an activist in the ADA, and champion of many a liberal cause. Porter had once been legal counsel to CBS. In the face of expert testimony that there were no technical reasons for shifting FM to a narrow part of the radio band, that was what Porter did. It was a body blow to the development of FM.

This might have proved fatal had there not been a sizable army of supporters for FM—veterans. They had learned from experience with military FM sets that it was a far better system than amplitude modulation. Not only was there the eternal and maddening static to put up with on AM, but in a music broadcast a third of the notes, notably those in the upper and lower registers, were simply lost. To tens of thousands of young men "high fidelity" became something of a passion. By the early 1950s hi-fi zealots had sprouted everywhere. They were considered slightly eccentric. But a number of small companies began to produce radio and record equipment for this devoted and knowledgeable market, a market, moreover, which the major manufacturers claimed did not exist. They had argued for so long that people actually liked the muddy sound of AM and did not mind listening to static that they appear to have convinced themselves that what they said was true.

Armstrong enjoyed no part in the eventual success of FM. RCA, seeing that FM was unstoppable, began to chip away at Armstrong's patent rights. From its laboratories came FM transmitters and receivers which its engineers maintained, to no one's surprise, were substantially different from his. Armstrong sued. The suits dragged on. In the meantime, his patent rights expired. As his patents ran out, so did his income.

RCA offered him $2 million to drop his suits. Armstrong refused. His health had broken down. So had his wife's. The strain on him grew unbearable, and his marriage collapsed. While his wife was recuperating in Connecticut from a serious illness, he wrote to her, "Lord have mercy on my soul." Dressed in his hat and overcoat, he stepped out of a window of his apartment, thirteen floors above a Manhattan street. His body was found the next morning.

It was decided that AM really was not so good after all. It was not good enough for television, anyway. Today all television sound is transmitted on Armstrong's "impractical" FM.

"In the large cities," wrote Paul Lazarsfeld in 1948, "there is a movie house around almost every corner." By 1952 it was probably still there. It also stood a good chance of being closed down.

The best year in the history of the movies had been 1946, when receipts topped $1.5 billion. After that the only place to go was down. Hollywood had been doing little more than break even in the domestic market; most of its profits came from foreign countries. In 1947 the British, in one of a series of desperate moves to shore up their economy, put a 75 percent tax on the net receipts of foreign films.

The State Department did what it could to help the studios by forcing the French, who were pleading for American aid, to reserve 70 percent of their screen time for American films. The British knuckled under to the extent of 40 percent, the Italians agreed to 65 percent. Thus, the Americanization of European popular culture was not left entirely to chance and Sam Goldwyn. In the best imperial style it combined profit with propaganda.

As if it did not have troubles enough, the film community was shaken by periodic scandals. Robert Mitchum and two lovelies were caught smoking marijuana. Mitchum went to spend thirty days in the Los Angeles County Jail. The jail shortly thereafter was graced with the presence for four months of a noted film producer, Walter Wanger. He was there because he shot a man he believed to be the lover of his wife, the actress Joan Bennett. On his release from jail Wanger produced a prison picture.

Troubled by falling profits, HUAC, and the emergence of television as a rival attraction, while scriptwriters were preparing to go to prison, while red ink appeared all over the accounts, while disaster lurked around every corner, shutting down one theater after another, Hollywood in the late 1940s began turning out many of the best films it ever made.

There were "problem pictures" by the dozen. Subjects barely hinted at before the war were suddenly all over the screen. Bigotry, insanity, drug addiction, adultery, alcoholism, juvenile delinquency, crooked politicians and brutal policemen, disabled veterans, miscegenation, anti-Semitism, and mental retardation—all were considered suitable for treatment. The economic crisis brought a shift toward realism because it was cheaper to portray than fantasy. But it could not have occurred without an equally profound change in mood among producers, directors, and writers.

The films of 1947–1952 are full of romantic disillusionment. They are heavily atmospheric, characterized by low-key photography, stark contrasts of light and shade, bleak interiors, cloudy or wet exteriors, headlights weaving wildly through the night, and unflattering close-ups. These were films which caught the anxieties and neuroses of contemporary urban life in all its defensive cynicism, sexual confusion, and emotional vulnerability.

This style, later termed *le film noir* by French *cinéastes*, was also accompanied by a fascination with violence, blood, and cruelty. The pat explanation was that the war had inured people to horror. There had been violence in the war films, gangster films, and Westerns of the 1930s. But it had been routine, part of the formula. Screen violence these days turned sadistic and orgiastic. It often involved a psychopathic element, and there was, in fact, a new type of screen villain—the psychopath, a character not in rebellion against moral constraints but emotionally dead to their existence.

Le film noir improved American films, despite the often cheap attempt to enliven the plot by killing someone. But the new style did nothing to stem the flight from the box office.

While the movie theater on the corner was closing down, however, there was something new opening up on the outskirts of town—the drive-in. These spread rapidly and appealed mainly to the young. Between 1946 and 1951, 3,000 drive-ins were opened. They attracted huge numbers of adolescents every night of the week. It was assumed, however, that they were not there necessarily because they liked movies. The drive-in was known as the "passion pit."

In its struggle against television and falling receipts Hollywood opted for defense in depth. The studios tried to save themselves with a technological innovation, three-dimensional movies. The first of the new genre was *Bwana Devil*, released in 1952. The depth of the 3-D movies was entirely a matter of optics. Scripts were written to provide excuses for lions to leap out from the screen, for spears to be thrown at the viewer, and, in one Western, for the bad guy to spit in the audience's eye. It soon became boring. Before long 3-D was said to stand for "Dead, dead, dead."

While the movies lost most of their audience, a new audience for innovative, high-quality films was coming into existence. In 1946 there were a dozen "art" theaters, mainly in New York. By 1953 there were more than 200, all across the country. There were hundreds of film societies, enrolling anything from a few dozen members to the 5,000 members of Cinema 16. There were film societies attached to museums, universities, colleges, and local art theaters. Educated, critical, knowledgeable, and enthusiastic, here was an audience ready-made for filmmakers who wanted to make intelligent and original films. As people of imagination had for thousands of years turned naturally to poetry or music as their natural medium of expression, so thousands of young men and women now tried to put their ideas and emotions onto film.

The more glamorous parts of show business—radio, television, films—were part of the front line of the Cold War (along with the State Department). Writers, actors, directors, and producers were vulnerable to pressure because entertainment in America is largely under the control of nervous businessmen. And the resentments which are commonly nursed by the obscure and bumptious for the famous and well-paid were cloaked these days with the American flag. Rarely has there been a nastier case of rank envy masquerading as patriotism.

The HUAC hearings in Hollywood and the defiance of the Ten had set the scene. In 1951 the Hollywood Ten, as unregenerate as ever, began serving their one-year sentences for contempt. The Motion Picture Alliance for the Preservation of American Ideals (the patriotic front of the studio heads) operated a blacklist which spread far beyond those questioned by HUAC. At least 300 people were blacklisted by the studios. Leftists were also purged from the Screen Writers Guild and the Screen Actors Guild.

Destroying someone else's career was a game anyone could play. All you had to do was publish a list of names or, as it was termed, "cite" their involvement in what were, or could be construed as, pro-Communist activities. Three ex-FBI agents, who had worked as researchers for *Plain Talk*, in 1947 went into business for themselves by publishing *Counterat-*

*tack.*Calling themselves American Business Consultants, they offered not only this four-page weekly "Newsletter of Facts on Communism" but also an anti-Communist security service to big business, at $5,000 a year.

ABC's clients included General Electric, Du Pont, Metropolitan Life, Reynolds Tobacco, and several major New York department stores. The service consisted mainly of planting informers within the work force. "The firm had little difficulty in obtaining informers," recalled Harvey Matusow, who worked for ABC. To encourage prospective clients of the need for this service, *Counterattack* would run a series of articles on subversion in a particular industry or business. Shortly thereafter the leading companies in the field would be visited by ABC's salesmen.

In 1950 *Counterattack* turned its attention to radio and television. It published a special report called *Red Channels.* This report was the subject of excited speculation even before it appeared. Nor could the timing have been better: *Red Channel* appeared three days before the invasion of South Korea. It cited 151 persons as having "helped Communism."

Published as a paperback book (with a cover showing a red hand closing around a microphone), it was snapped up immediately. Few people ever saw a copy. Most of the 151 people it cited never saw it. Yet it was treated by radio and television executives as if it were holy writ; they swore by it.

The idea that radio and TV were hotbeds of subversion was on the face of it preposterous. Two of the most popular radio commentators, Westbrook Pegler and Fulton Lewis, Jr., were among McCarthy's most devoted admirers. On radio McCarthy was nearly always given the benefit of the doubt. Since 1945, moreover, the liberal commentators who had often given luster to the coverage of the war, had been fired almost to a man. *Red Channels'* list was absurd for another reason: it read like a roll of honor. Among the 151 people it cited were most of radio's most gifted and admired figures. But ABC was absolutely serious. In *Counterattack* it warned:

In AN EMERGENCY (at any given time) IT WOULD REQUIRE ONLY THREE PERSONS (subversives) one engineer in master control at a radio network
one director in a radio studio
one VOICE before a microphone
TO REACH 90 MILLION AMERICAN PEOPLE WITH A MESSAGE

There was another blacklist in operation, although not as well known as *Red Channels.* This was compiled by the American Legion and circulated mainly among studio executives in Hollywood. The Legion backed up this initiative by organizing picket lines at cinemas and theaters featuring works involving people they considered subversive. *Death of a Salesman*, for instance, was picketed because the Legion considered Arthur Miller a fellow traveler.

The Legion's Americanism Commission also published a biweekly called *Firing Line*. Supposedly intended for circulation among post commanders, copies of it nevertheless appeared regularly in Hollywood and up and down Madison Avenue, where Legion posts were thin on the ground.

By the fall of 1950 *Red Channels* was taking its toll. Jean Muir, the very popular star of a very popular radio show, was dropped from her program. The "Singing Lady," Irene Wicker, lost her television show. Philip Loeb, a character actor in the interminable and highly popular radio program *The Goldbergs*, was dropped. For Loeb, who had seen his substantial salary swallowed up by private care for his mentally retarded son, this was the last in a sequence of personal disasters. With the aid of a fistful of pills Loeb killed himself in a New York hotel room.

The McCarran Internal Security Subcommittee encouraged the blacklisting mania by holding hearings in 1951 on what it billed as "Subversive Infiltration of Radio, Television and the Entertainment Industry."

But blacklisting was mostly a private affair. Almost anyone might be cited if they protested the Rosenberg death sentence, circulated a petition opposing development of the hydrogen bomb, were involved in civil liberties activities, spoke a good word for the Hollywood Ten, criticized Senator McCarthy, or raised money for causes or people most of the country disliked. Blacklisting was done with a show of scrupulous care; every citation had a source. Dozens of bodies, from HUAC to the Los Angeles County Board of Supervisors, had held hearings on subversion in recent years. Anyone who had been named during one of these hearings was considered fair game. Right-wing publications of impeccable militancy were also accepted as being authoritative sources. To be cited in *Counterattack* or *Firing Line* as an individual who had "helped Communism" was considered proof enough. So these various sources reproduced each other's citations; to be named in one was to be named in half a dozen or more. The result for the individual concerned was a list of citations which looked long and damning, even though its origin might be a single isolated and misrepresented event.

Blacklisting went from the passive to the active with the arrival of Laurence A. Johnson, owner of four supermarkets in the conservative city Syracuse, New York. It began with the recall to active duty of Johnson's son-in-law, a member of the Marine Reserve, to fight in Korea. Johnson's daughter, Eleanor, suddenly took a personal interest in the struggle for the world. The housewives of Syracuse began to receive lengthy extracts from *Counterattack* and *Red Channels* in envelopes addressed to the "Lady of the House."

Eleanor carried the fight down to the Syracuse Kiwanis Club. "My husband, a veteran of World War Two," she told the assembled Kiwanians in July 1951, "never received a penny for being a member of the Inactive Reserves. When he was recalled to active service last October it meant leaving the small town on the Hudson where we'd been so happy, the company in which he'd been found to be a valuable asset, my small but interesting teaching position at Vassar College, all our plans for the future. And I know that Jack detested military life. He's very un-military about hanging up his clothes." She quoted from one of her husband's letters, so that they might understand his plight. "I have not been sick," he wrote, "which is a blessing in this land of loose bowels and bodies. The flies go from the dead Gook 20 feet away to the fish heads he left behind, to my C rations, so I'm glad my stomach is strong."

"Well," concluded Eleanor, "my stomach isn't that strong. It sickens me to know of those banquets engineered by Red sympathizers on radio and television to raise funds for their henchmen, and the do-nothing patriotic citizens who discuss the rights and wrongs of the world over a dinner table while my quiet, unassuming Jack eats his lunch surrounded by dead Chinese." She appealed to the Kiwanians, as she had appealed to the American Legion, the Rotary Club, and the housewives of Syracuse to do something to rectify this situation. Syracuse Post No. 41 of the American Legion rallied to her call by establishing its own Un-American Activities Committee. And Laurence A. Johnson, father-in-law to quiet, unassuming Jack, threw his supermarkets into the fight.

Shortly thereafter Leonard A. Block, president of the Block Drug Company, was amazed to find in his mail a letter which began:

DEAR SIR,
    Is [actor's name] who appeared on your "Danger" program last night the Communist Fronter [of the same name] who also appeared on the Civil Rights Congress Show? . . . Is [actress' name] who also appeared in the same show the same [actress] who was mentioned in *Counterattack*?

Johnson's letter concluded with a veiled threat, visible to all but the totally blind:

    If you plan to continue the use of Communist Front talent wouldn't it be a good idea if you were to send a representative of the Block Drug Company. . . . Perhaps we could work out a questionnaire to give to the people who buy from our cosmetic displays. A questionnaire could be drafted reading, for instance, as follows: Do You Want Any Part of Your Purchase Price of Amm-i-Dent to be Used to Hire Communist Fronters?
    YES/NO
                                Very truly yours,
                    VETERANS ACTION COMMITTEE
                    OF SYRACUSE SUPERMARKETS

Through such tactics Johnson terrified the networks and the sponsors. Whatever their private opinions, the prospect of highly publicized confrontations in supermarket aisles made the blood of important executives run cold. Once a business was identified as being sympathetic to Communism, the cost could run into millions. Johnson soon amassed a drawerful of fawning letters from browbeaten tycoons.

The blacklisters' success was nowhere more evident than at CBS. Because it packaged most of its own shows, CBS was more vulnerable than its rivals. Virtually everyone on one of its programs had been hired in the first instance by CBS.

Fred Friendly and Edward R. Murrow wanted to commission a short piece of music to accompany the opening and closing titles and credits on *See It Now.* Friendly went to see the vice-president in charge of programs to approve the cost of the commission. "When the vice president asked me what composer we had in mind," Friendly recalled, "I handed him the names of three well-known modern composers listed in order of preference. He glanced at the top name and asked, 'Is he in the book?' "

"I don't know, but I'm sure 'Music Clearance' has his number."

"I know," said the vice president, "but is he in the book?' "

"I started to ask the secretary for a telephone directory when the vice president pulled open a drawer in his desk and said, 'This is the book we live by.' It was a pamphlet called 'Red Channels.' "

Shortly after the appearance of *Red Channels* CBS had imposed a loyalty oath on all its employees. In 1951 it created an executive-level post of security officer, a position derided by resentful CBS employees as "the Vice President in charge of treason."

Among the various protégés of Laurence A. Johnson was Harvey Matusow. Another was Vincent Hartnett. Following his discharge from the Navy, Hartnett had been first a magazine writer, then a program packager for an advertising agency. He soon grasped the opportunities offered to any resourceful young man who set himself up in the business of "clearing" names, a kind of subindustry of the major business of citing names. By clearing a name, he would be sparing sponsors and networks a possibly nasty shock.

Hartnett began by charging $20 for each name he cleared—that is, he looked through all the relevant publications and blacklists to see if the name had been cited anywhere. As business grew, unit cost dropped to $5. Hartnett's business was conducted under an appropriately vigilant name, Aware, Inc.

As his operations expanded, Hartnett was inevitably drawn into the affairs of the American Federation of Television and Radio Artists—he was a thorn in AFTRA's side. The organization was badly split over what stance it should adopt toward Aware, Inc. Some members thought it best to cooperate with Hartnett, who was not a member of AFTRA, while the majority detested the idea. AFTRA elections were fought mainly over Hartnett and Aware, Inc. The anti-Hartnett candidate who topped the poll was John Henry Faulk, a comedian who specialized in Southern homilies and carefully homespun wisdom. Aware, Inc., shortly thereafter made seven "charges" against John Henry Faulk.

For example, there was the claim that "A program dated April 25, 1946 named 'John Faulk' as a scheduled entertainer (with identified Communist Earl Robinson and two non-Communists) under the auspices of the Independent Citizens Committee of the Arts, Sciences and Professions (officially designated as a Communist Front)." The "program" in question was not exactly a conclave of left-wing conspirators; it was a dinner to celebrate the first anniversary of the United Nations. The guests included the members of the UN Security Council, the Secretary-General, and the Secretary of State and was sponsored by a dozen bodies including the American Bar Association and the YMCA.

In its vagueness and studied evasion of the truth this example was typical of the methods employed by the blacklisters. It was a style which commended itself to Laurence Johnson. He gave his name, time, and money to support Hartnett and Aware, Inc.

Faulk categorically denied all seven charges and their inference that he was a subversive. It did no good. His principal employer was CBS. And the blacklist reached far beyond New York. When things began to go badly for him there, he became interested in a $100,000 job he had been offered in Minneapolis. But suddenly the offer was withdrawn. Faulk was reduced to begging for work as a stand-in at $10 a day.

Between them Johnson and Hartnett ended Faulk's career. He sued them for libel. He was almost alone among the victims of the blacklists in that he fought back. But his lawyer, Louis Nizer, asked for $10,000 for out-of-pocket expenses; it would be a long, hard, ugly fight. Faulk's suit would have failed had not Ed Murrow put up $7,500, not as a loan, Murrow insisted, but "as an investment in America." It was to be seven harrowing years before Faulk would get his day in court.

There were others who were even less fortunate. The gifted black actor Canada Lee was a nearly man: he nearly made it as a violinist, nearly made it as a prize fighter, nearly made it as an actor. But his name was mentioned at the second Coplon trial. After that he was cited *ad nauseam*. He was destroyed, without ever being shown to have done anything harmful, let alone illegal. He made strenuous—and for a man of spirit, unendurably degrading—efforts to establish that he was a devout anti-Communist. It changed nothing. He was untouchable. In penury and despair he killed himself.

Several days later John Garfield, one of the most admired actors of the current wave of heavily atmospheric films, died at the age of thirty-nine. Garfield's leftist politics had exacted a heavy toll. Denied work, hounded at every turn except by the women who loved him, he fell into a spiral of depression and drunkenness which ended only when his heart burst. The funeral parlor where his body lay was mobbed by distraught fans. Not since the death of Valentino had there been such scenes of grief over the death of an actor.

The Hollywood studios were busy filming anti-Communist action pictures. There was *Conspirator*, starring Robert Taylor, who had put on a flawless demonstration of long-distance crawling for the benefit of HUAC. In *Conspirator* he played the role of a Communist Party member who murders his devoted, loving wife simply because Moscow thinks she is becoming overly inquisitive. There was also *My Son John*. This was an American tragedy concerning a pillar of the American Legion who discovers that one of his sons has been hanging around with Communists and fears that the lad may have been seduced into becoming one. The son always was a little strange—he never cared much for football, unlike his brothers, he used long words, and he was rude to the priest. And there was *Big Jim McClain*, with John Wayne playing a fearless investigator from HUAC sent to Hawaii to stamp out Communism down at the docks.

The entertainment world jumped through hoops to keep out of the way of HUAC and the blacklisters. For every individual who breathed defiance there were dozens who groveled. By 1952 there were very, very few who refused to be cowed. Among the few, notably, was Lillian Hellman. Before HUAC she spoke freely about her own beliefs and associations but refused to discuss those of other people; she invoked the Fifth Amendment on their behalf. Because she was a woman, because she caught HUAC by surprise, and because the law was ambiguous on the legal point she had raised, she got away with it.

Dashiell Hammett, with whom she had lived for thirty years, was less fortunate. He was one of the directors of the Civil Rights Congress. He refused to give the names of people who had contributed to the CRC bail fund. He did not know any names; he had never been inside the CRC office. But he reasoned that even had he known any names, he would not have given them; his resistance was entirely a matter of principle. Instead of invoking a defense of ignorance, which he might honestly have done, Hammett simply refused to answer HUAC's questions on the ground that they were improper. At the age of forty-eight he had managed to get himself into the Army during the war. His health had been seriously impaired during his service in the Aleutians. It did not improve during the year he spent in a Federal penitentiary.

In these diverse ways was entertainment made safe for democracy at the height of the domestic Cold War.

13

The World Turned Right Side Up

Truman's last two years in the White House were a time of scandals, public scorn, and legislative failure. Ever since the winter of 1950 when the Korean War bogged down nothing seemed to go right. The last genuinely popular move the President had made was the decision to fight in Korea. A year later even that was no longer popular; on the contrary, it was bitterly regretted by many. Nor were there any important legislative triumphs to point to; instead, almost every important Fair Deal proposal had been rejected.

So for two years the country had a lame-duck President, one who was, moreover, held in considerable disesteem. In mid-1951 only one-fourth of those polled approved of his leadership. Later that year 60 percent agreed with the statement that Korea was "an utterly useless war."

The Internal Revenue Bureau (not yet a Service) was tainted with corruption. It reflected on Truman's appalling lack of judgment where other people were concerned. The corruption was further aggravated by Tom Clark, the Attorney General. Clark had installed one of his protégés, Theron LaMar Caudle, as head of the Justice Department's Tax Division. Caudle proceeded to work on the principle that Justice is blind. When the payoffs to tax commissioners and IRB agents became known, Caudle testified, Clark had tried to stop further investigations into corruption among the tax men. But by that time Truman had put Tom Clark on the Supreme Court.

Clark's successor, J. Howard McGrath, attempted to dissuade a Federal judge in St. Louis from pursuing his inquiries into corruption in the tax office there. When the judge protested publicly against this attempt to obstruct justice, Attorney General McGrath replied by calling the judge "a damnable and contemptible liar." Unhappily for McGrath a log of his telephone calls showed that his repeated claims never to have called the judge were simply untrue.

By the time the tax scandals of 1951 had closed, more than one hundred IRB officers, including six regional collectors, were fired. Truman also found it politic to accept McGrath's resignation.

Even before the tax scandals broke the President had been discomfited by the Congressional inquiry into the activities of the "five percenters"—people in or out of government who helped business win government contracts in exchange for 5 percent of the contract's value. Two Army generals were both abruptly relieved, and there were questions raised concerning Truman's poker-playing crony and military aide Major General Harry Vaughan.

General Vaughan admitted to having received a deepfreeze from a lobbyist. In fact, he admitted, he had received seven deepfreezes. He distributed six of them to good friends—including Mrs. Truman, Chief Justice Vinson, and the Secretary of the Treasury, John Snyder—and kept only one for his own use.

The worst of the various scandals, however, affected the Reconstruction Finance Corporation. Once one of the ornaments of the New Deal, it had gone rotten, like a fish, starting from the head. The RFC never recovered a penny on such major investments as the $37.5 million lent to Lustron. Lustron was but one of dozens of ventures which gave off a putrid smell and from which there was no repayment of capital, no payment of interest, merely a large loss to be covered by the taxpayer.

The RFC scandal reached into the White House. One of the President's aides, Donald Dawson, spent many uncomfortable hours trying to convince the Senate Banking Committee that although he had acted as a go-between for people seeking RFC loans, he had had nothing to do with whether they actually received them. Truman loyally supported Dawson.

Just as he backed up E. Merl Young. Mrs. Young was a White House stenographer. She was also the proud owner of an $8,000 mink coat, the gift of a lawyer whose clients happened to be seeking loans from the RFC.

The RFC scandal involved both major party chairmen. The Democratic National Committee's chairman, William Boyle, had for some time enjoyed a very large income based on doing nothing at all, as he explained it, for people who were moved by incredibly generous impulses. The President expressed his total confidence in Boyle. Guy Gabrielson, the chairman of the Republican National Committee, claimed to have done even less than Boyle, in exchange for which *his* friends gave him $25,000. Before long both party chairmen had chosen to resign.

Even the Vice President's staff was touched by the RFC affair. Alben Barkley's personal secretary was another who had been generously rewarded in exchange for doing nothing.

Truman, in the feudal style of the machine politician, considered loyalty the highest form of honor. And in his attempts to defend the indefensible he turned on the press, the men who insisted on bringing bad news or asking awkward questions. In these last two unhappy years he became thin-lipped, angry, confused, and self-righteous. He became uncharacteristically evasive. The popular view that Truman was always forthcoming was belied by his conduct in these last two years in power.

Even in foreign policy he could hardly put a foot right. Typical was his appointment of General Mark Clark to be ambassador to the Vatican. It was a Cold War demarche, for no state was more hostile to Communism than the Vatican. With the United States currently making anti-Communist alliances around the globe it was a logical step and one which the President expected to be popular at home. Instead, it brought an outcry from Protestants. And if, as many suspected, it was a cheap bid for the Catholic vote, it was wasted; the Catholics were to be found mainly in the big cities, and they had voted Democratic for ages.

As 1952 drew near, the question of whether Truman would run was a greater mystery than whether General Eisenhower would. Truman appears to have toyed with the idea of running again, but his wife was against it; so, *sotto voce,* was much of the Democratic Party. The President also faced strong opposition from Senator Estes Kefauver of Tennessee.

Kefauver had been elected to the Senate in 1948 after ten years in the House. By defeating the incumbent backed by the Crump machine in Memphis, Kefauver was viewed as a reformer. By refusing to be antagonistic to labor or blacks, he was viewed as a radical. Crump, in his folksy way, had compared Kefauver to a raccoon—seemingly innocent but full of wiles and cunning. In an attempt to turn this taunt to advantage, Kefauver for a time campaigned in the company of a pet raccoon kept in a cage. It was a smelly, frightened, bad-tempered creature, winning few friends and endangering fingers. Kefauver abandoned it. He settled for a coonskin cap. Atop Kefauver's lanky, bespectacled frame and for a man of his aloof and professorial manner, it was both sad and laughable at the same time.

In 1950 Kefauver introduced a Senate resolution to establish a committee which would investigate organized crime. Its claimed authority was the Federal power to regulate interstate commerce. Crime, the committee's brief implied, was not a local or a state affair but a national one.

The committee's hearings were a sensation from start to finish. When they moved to New York for two weeks, they were televised. For millions of people the Kefauver hearings became compulsive viewing. It was the fifth, not the first, time that Congressional hearings had been carried on TV. But there had been nothing like this before. The cast included Frank Costello's hands (he refused to allow his face to be shown); a dapper, but heavily sweating, brow-mopping William O'Dwyer; the buxom blond consort of the murdered Bugsy Siegel, Virginia Hill; an ex-waitress who arrived swaddled in mink and diamonds; and gravel-voiced Jake "Greasy Thumb" Guzik. The crime committee hearings outdrew Milton Berle.

They concentrated on gambling, which Kefauver portrayed as the lifeblood of organized crime. His other thesis was that crime in America was controlled by a national crime syndicate, the Mafia. In the course of these events he became a hero to many people. He was named Father of the Year for 1951. On a poll of the best Senators he came second only to Paul Douglas of Illinois. He was awarded an Emmy for his contribution to television.

But there was little love for Kefauver within the leadership of the Democratic Party. His committee moved from city to city, not so much uncovering crime as publicizing criminal activities already known. The city officials were nearly always Democrats. And because big-time gambling could not exist without corrupt politicians and crooked policemen, it was inevitable that Kefauver would embarrass both the police chiefs and the politicians who appointed them.

In Illinois, for example, the committee's hearings in Chicago coincided with two brutal gangland murders. Public suspicion fell on the Democratic candidate for sheriff of Cook County as being somehow implicated in these killings. When the candidate for sheriff went down to defeat, he took the rest of the Democratic ticket with him, including Senator Scott Lucas, the Senate Majority Leader. Lucas blamed Kefauver for his defeat, for not having the sense to stay out of Chicago until after the election. For the remainder of Kefauver's career Scott Lucas intrigued against him within the Democratic Party in Illinois.

The Kefauver Committee unearthed little that was new. Local crime commissioners, grand juries, police chiefs, and police reporters had already examined most of the evidence he introduced to a shocked, fascinated public. Nor did the hearings lead to a major offensive against organized crime. Only three of the forty-five persons the committee cited for contempt were successfully prosecuted. Indirectly, however, it led to a strengthening of the Internal Revenue Bureau's use of the tax laws to bring major criminals to justice, which helped send nearly 900 crooks to prison or put them on probation and brought the recovery of $336 million in back taxes and penalties.

On the strength of his sudden celebrity Kefauver began to seek the Democratic nomination for President. To many Democratic Party leaders, though, in running for the nomination he had been running all over them. They refused to lie down and play dead. Kefauver had the support of no major segment of the party. In the first primary of 1952 he beat Truman at the polls. Truman was not a man to take a philosophical view of that. While Kefauver went from primary to primary, winning twelve of the thirteen he entered, the President and the party leaders were looking for a candidate.

In their discussions one name surfaced more often than any other—Adlai Stevenson of Illinois. He was the successful governor of one of the biggest states. He was energetic and in good health and had never offended anybody who mattered in the party. That he was divorced was regrettable but not fatal to his chances. More serious was the fact that two-thirds of the voters had never heard of him. What was more, Stevenson said that he did not want the nomination.

He felt honor-bound by pledges already made to his friends to run for reelection as governor in 1952. When those friends and admirers began a Stevenson-for-President campaign, they received no encouragement from Stevenson. Privately, he was disgusted by the recent scandals.

Yet the more he resisted, the more ardently he was pursued. The draft Stevenson movement faltered, but it refused to take his no for an answer. When the convention opened, Stevenson was credited with only 41½ delegate votes, to Kefauver's 257½. Yet the party leaders from the big cities and the whole of the Southern bloc were too hostile to Kefauver, and controlled far too many votes, for Kefauver to stand any chance of winning the nomination. The choice which faced Stevenson was stark—either accept the nomination or make it useless by refusing it. Not wishing to be remembered as the man who ushered the Republicans into the White House in 1952, Stevenson accepted the nomination with misgivings. As a concession to the South the nomination for Vice President went to Senator John Sparkman of Alabama.

The Democratic Party proceeded to fall in love with Adlai Stevenson after the knot had been tied. But, they wondered, was he *too* witty, *too* bright, *too* thoughtful for his own good on polling day?

The Republicans were faced with a reluctant candidate of their own. Most Republicans wanted a winner; this meant they wanted Eisenhower. Admittedly, there was nothing to show that he was a Republican; he just seemed like a Republican. Sherman Adams, the governor of New Hampshire and one of the growing body of Eastern Republicans involved in the draft Eisenhower movement, wrote to the county clerk in Kansas, where Eisenhower maintained his permanent address. Had the general ever registered a party preference? He received a prompt reply.

Mr. Eisenhower has never voted in this county as far as I know.
. . . Dwight's father was a republican and always voted the republican ticket
up until his death, however that has nothing to do with the son as many differ
from their fathers of which I am sorry to see, the multitude believes in going
into debt and see how much money they can spend, it has become a habit and
will sink this nation into bankruptcy.
I don't think he has any politics.

The general's name was entered in the New Hampshire primary. But he
remained in Europe, commanding NATO's forces. The absent Eisenhower beat the present Taft, who campaigned, despite his age, in the New
Hampshire snow. In the next primary, in Minnesota, Eisenhower's name
was not on the ballot. He nevertheless came in second to that native son
and inevitable candidate Harold Stassen. Nothing daunted by the challenge of spelling his name properly (which produced such variants as
"Izenour" and "Isenhowr"), almost everyone could write "Ike." One
way and another, he received nearly 100,000 write-in votes.

Prominent Republicans were beseeching him to return and run for
them. Many of these supplicants had never met Eisenhower. But those
who had were invariably impressed. He was a man of complete self-
assurance. Accustomed to command, accustomed to accommodating rival points of view, accustomed to success and power, he spoke with unmistakable authority. He carried himself erect. His blue eyes were pene-
trating and alert. His gestures conveyed an impression of strength. Eisenhower had presence. Yet he had no craving for power. Although the idea
of becoming President gradually appealed to him, it never became a soul-
consuming appetite.

Truman still admired Eisenhower. When the general resigned his command in May 1952, he requested that he should also be allowed to resign
his pay and privileges, which are granted a five-star general for life. He
also waived his pension.* Truman acceded to Eisenhower's request. But
unknown to him, he ordered that all the general's pay, privileges, and
pension be restored on the day following the election should Eisenhower
run and lose.

Although he was clearly the country's political favorite, Eisenhower's
political beliefs were mainly a matter of speculation, except for the fact
that he favored the foreign aid program. And despite his being the preferred choice of most Republican voters, Senator Taft had a clear lead in
committed delegates.

Taft was regularly voted among the best Senators. Against the common run of Senate Republicans he shone like a good deed in a naughty
world. He was not devious. He worked conscientiously. He was extremely intelligent, in a conventional way. He would stand up for a principle, as

*Not that he would be reduced to penury. The IRB had ruled that the $625,000 he received
for *Crusade in Europe* would be taxed as a capital gain rather than income. He thus collected
$500,000 after taxes, instead of the $150,000 to $200,000 any ordinary writer would have
cleared. Other generals wrote their memoirs, and they paid income taxes on what they received.

he did in his criticism of the Nuremberg trials as being little more than the retribution of the victors. Like most politicians, he understood interests, not economics. He detested Federal bureaucracy. He lauded business, large or small. When government officials presented their arguments in economic terms, Taft, who was reputed to be clearheaded if nothing else, would counter with ideology.

In foreign policy he was extremely critical of such initiatives as the Marshall Plan and NATO. He saw the dangers in overcommitting American strength or of misapplying it. Many of his criticisms were sound. But Taft also tried to have things both ways. He was an unswerving anti-Communist and had no desire to see the Soviets make a meal of Western Europe. Yet he continually attempted to reconcile the old isolationism with the new internationalism. Invariably, he succeeded only in confusing himself.

On domestic policy he favored public housing, within limits; he also favored Federal aid to education, within narrower limits. He was never either as illiberal or as high-minded as he was variously portrayed. Nor was he above the flummery of politics as the art of finding the lowest common denominator. At the 1948 Republican Convention he had sought to inspire confidence by passionately embracing the trunk of a baby elephant named Little Eva, his mascot in his bid for the Presidential nomination.

Taft was ardently pro-Zionist and deeply anti-Semitic. He called for unrestricted immigration into Palestine. He also wrote the head of the Taft School on reports that the number of Jews being admitted was creeping up. "You must enforce the quota," he sternly enjoined.

He attempted to refute the story that he had encouraged McCarthy to keep bringing up names. But it was Taft himself who had told three reporters about it, and all three had quoted exactly the same remark.

His passion for facts, evinced in a willingness to plow through reams of statistical material, gave him a reputation as an intellectual. Yet he never showed an unusual interest in ideas. Nor had he any evident interest in art, literature, or science. His sole interest was in being a Senator—except when he was interested in being President. By 1952 he could think of almost nothing else.

The prize was within reach, or so it appeared, well before the convention opened. Yet Taft was in command of a decidedly clumsy and amateurish campaign organization. A myth current at the time had it that the Taftites were the professionals and the Eisenhower men the amateurs. The truth was exactly the opposite.

Taft's supporters were insistent that the clamor for Eisenhower did not come from *real* Republicans but from Democrats in disguise. And it was true that among Republican voters there was an almost equal division between those who were pro-Taft and those who favored Eisenhower. Independents, however, preferred Eisenhower to Taft by two to one, and millions of Democrats were willing to vote Republican if that was the only way they could vote for Eisenhower.

The split within the Republican Party was to a large extent a split between Eastern and Midwestern Republicans. It was a division based not only on personalities but, more important, on differences in outlook. The Midwesterners were more rigidly conservative on spending and social welfare and were isolationist compared with the Atlantic-facing Easterners.

Because Eisenhower's support was broad and his own narrow, Taft could make sure of the nomination only if he did not make a mistake on the way to claiming it—or have one made for him. His supporters in Texas ruined him.

When precinct conventions to choose delegates for the Republican National Convention were held in May, there was no hint of the tumult to come. There were comparatively few regular Republican voters in Texas. Yet the state was given as many delegates as New Jersey. The party's executive committee in Texas was dominated by Taftites. Most regular Republicans in Texas were Taftites.

When the precinct conventions opened, the weaker faction—that is, the Eisenhower faction—turned to independent voters for support. The welcome that was extended was so broad, in fact, that even Democrats were made to feel at home. Under Texas law anyone could participate in a precinct convention simply by making a pledge to support that party's nominee in the fall. For many a Texas Democrat the prospect of voting for Eisenhower posed no crisis of conscience at all.

When the voting began at the precinct conventions, the Taft supporters, who had anticipated a jolly time, were trounced. They then denounced the proceedings as a farce or a fraud, or both, and walked out to set up their own conventions, sometimes on the lawn outside. Eisenhower later noted laconically, "All over Texas that day meetings broke up in fist fights."

The convention opened in Chicago with indignant Taft supporters parading through the streets under banners reading, "Thou Shalt Not Steal." But by this time the Eisenhower camp had been shouting, "Steal!" for more than a month and, with the aid of the overwhelmingly pro-Eisenhower press, to greater effect.

Taft held a lead in delegate strength of more than 100 votes. By most calculations he was within 75 votes of the nomination. The convention machinery was in the hands of his supporters. But the floor was worked with greater skill by Eisenhower's "amateurs." They brought the issue of seating the rival Texas delegations to an issue on the convention floor. The uncommitted delegates from several big states voted for the pro-Eisenhower slate. The nomination at that moment slipped through Taft's fingers.

Taft's supporters began to drift away even before the first ballot was taken. To chants of "We Want Ike" the general received 595 votes, 9 short of victory. Minnesota suddenly changed its votes and gave them, 19 in all, to Eisenhower. The chants changed to "We Got Ike."

For second spot they got Richard M. Nixon. This was mainly because Eisenhower wanted someone who had a reputation for harrying the Reds.

He chose Nixon because of his role in the downfall of Alger Hiss and because of his comparative youth. Indeed, had there been a medal in 1952 for hunting Communists, it would have probably gone not to McCarthy but to Nixon, who was known as "the man who put Hiss behind bars."

Nixon's election to the Senate in 1950 had been based on harrying the Reds, or at least the Pinks; his campaign literature referred to his opponent, Congresswoman Helen Gahagan Douglas, as "the Pink Lady." Elections in California that year were entirely dominated by the Communist menace. Edmund G. Brown ran for attorney general, and won, on a campaign whose theme was that Brown would turn the AG's office into a center for fighting Communism. James Roosevelt ran for governor, unsuccessfully, on a platform that he would get more money from the legislature for fighting subversion than his opponent would get. So Nixon's 1950 campaign was not unusual in its barrel scraping. Liberals, however, never forgave him this victory, which ended the career of "the most courageous fighter for liberalism in Congress."

But to Eisenhower, Nixon was the best choice the party had to offer for the second spot. Within two months Nixon was to give him the worst moment of his political career and threatened to turn the easy march on the White House into a swift descent into oblivion.

Nixon's admirers and supporters (mainly business executives) had decided that their champion owed it to his country to spread his message everywhere, not only in California. He was clearly a young man destined for great things, with a little help from his friends. One hundred of them pledged to pay $200 a year apiece into a fund for the Senator's use. Instead of campaigning in California each six years, he would be able to campaign everywhere, all the time. The fund was not a secret; Nixon made public mention of it several times. But in the middle of the election campaign it was suddenly "discovered." The small and vocal liberal press, plus the entire Democratic Party, was in an uproar. Once he was attacked, it was Nixon's nature to counterattack. He rounded on his critics, calling their references to a "slush fund" a Communist smear designed "to make me relent and let up on my attack on the Communists." When Nixon's campaign train pulled into Eugene, Oregon, there was a melee when pickets descended on it carrying placards reading, "Shhhh! Anybody who mentions $16,000 is a Communist" and "No Mink Coats for Nixon—Just Cold Cash."

To Eisenhower and his aides the Nixon fund was a potential catastrophe. They were frightened to keep him on the ticket, terrified of forcing him off. "There is one thing I believe," Eisenhower gloomily confided to Sherman Adams. "If Nixon has to go, we cannot win." True to his nature, Nixon took the burden of decision out of their hands by taking the offensive on a broad front.

He bought half an hour of national television time. He put his finances, his wife, and his dog, a spaniel named Checkers, on public show. The accompanying recital of personal rectitude, delivered at times in a tear-choked voice, was probably the most pathetic performance by an American politician in this century. By turns contrite and aggressive, Nixon struggled to achieve the common touch by pointing to his wife's cloth coat and to the dog, a gift from an admirer to his two young daughters. Whatever the outcome of this crisis, he vowed, he would not give up the dog.

People had never seen anything like it. It was novel, and it was a success. There was no denying its emotional impact. Many of the people who saw it were affected by the sight of a promising young man struggling desperately to save his career, and they ignored the cheap ploys. Their impulses were generous, and Nixon got the benefit of the doubt.

Even Eisenhower, watching the performance in a Cleveland hotel, was moved, and his fate was as involved in the outcome as Nixon's. "We could hear that the crowd of 13,000 people in the auditorium downstairs was also carried away," wrote Sherman Adams. "They were cheering and shouting their approval. . . . As [Eisenhower] worked thoughtfully on his talk, he could hear the crowd downstairs that awaited him stamping its feet in rhythm and roaring, 'We Want Nixon! We Want Nixon!' "

But back in Los Angeles the man of the hour was convinced that the speech had failed. The tensions of the past few days overwhelmed him. He broke down in tears.*

Eisenhower sent an enthusiastic telegram from Cleveland, but it was delayed in the torrent of messages pouring in from all over the country. Nixon was tempted to take himself off the ticket. But in response to his appeal that the people should give their judgment on his future, more than 2 million letters and telegrams were sent to the Republican National Committee. They ran in Nixon's favor by a margin of 350–1. There was also more than enough money stuffed into envelopes to cover the $75,000 the telecast had cost. Nixon was sent scores of dog collars, handwoven dog blankets, a dog kennel, and enough dog food to feed Checkers for a year.

The speech was important for several reasons. A success at the time, it became an embarrassment later, when viewed dispassionately. It was not a classic in the sense of being timeless and universal; it was a classic example of tastelessness. But the broadcast kept Nixon alive politically. It also marked the first (though hardly the last) time that television played a crucial role in politics.

It had been present on the fringes of the campaigns of 1940, 1944, and 1948. But 1952 was the first year there was a television election. Its most obvious impact on party politics was the decision of both major parties to hold their conventions not only in the same city but on the same site, the Chicago Amphitheater, in response to the networks' promise of more comprehensive coverage. Broadcasting schedules also helped set the conventions' schedules. And just as radio had cut convention speeches from two or three hours to a maximum of sixty minutes, so television cut them still further to a maximum of forty minutes.

Convention reporting made celebrities of television reporters. The CBS anchor man at the 1952 conventions, Walter Cronkite, became a TV star.

---

*In his account of the Checkers speech Nixon agrees that tears were shed, but not by him—by admiring television directors, sound engineers, and cameramen.

And what it did for Cronkite, television could do for politicians. It had made Kefauver a national figure. Now it made Stevenson known throughout the country almost overnight.

The idea of using television to sell candidates as it sold cornflakes had been canvassed among Republicans in 1948. But Dewey had stiffly shunned the idea of being the actor in his own commercials. Eisenhower was persuaded that this was an idea whose time had come. But he felt uneasy about it. Between takes he sat with his brother Milton. The General shook his head in rueful reflection. "To think," he said, "that an old soldier should come to this!"

Television had another, more general effect. In 1952 it generated added interest in the election. That meant a high turnout on polling day. As a rule that would be good news for the Democrats, bad news for Republicans. But given the extraordinary interest in Eisenhower, these cases had been reversed.

Yet he traveled the country by train and campaigned as if he were facing an uphill struggle. In 1950 the Republicans had campaigned on what they termed "The Three Cs," blaming the Democrats for "Communism, Confusion, and Corruption." In 1952, Karl Mundt suggested, they should change the mixture to "Korea, Communism, and Corruption," and they did.

Under this not-very-inspiring banner and calling for a "Crusade" (harkening back to the Crusade in Europe, but the relevance of this term to domestic life was never made clear), Eisenhower went from state to state on a train called the Look Ahead, Neighbor Special. As a speaker he was dull. But as a man he was imposing and sincere. The crowds that gathered to hear his leaden utterances were frequently more deeply moved than those that the quick-witted Stevenson addressed.

Eisenhower made more references to the New Deal than Stevenson, repeatedly promising not to attack its programs of social welfare and economic management. He bluntly told an audience in Worcester, Massachusetts, "Anyone who says it is my purpose to cut down social security and unemployment insurance, to leave the ill and aged destitute, is lying." In Harlem, he vowed that if a recession ever seemed imminent, "the full power of municipal government, of state government, of the Federal government will be mobilized to see that it does not happen. I cannot pledge you more than that."

His farm policy consisted almost entirely of a promise to keep parity at 90 percent. For most farmers that was all they wanted to hear. The Democrats were stymied. A frustrated Stevenson complained that Eisenhower was "making off in broad daylight with the Democratic farm plank."

The general also played the anti-Communist with vigor. Anti-Communism was an essential part of the amorphous Crusade. In more than thirty campaign speeches he portrayed the government as being infested with Soviet agents. Once elected, however, he would root them out. Yet it appears that the issue of domestic Communism had passed its peak as a political appeal. So far as domestic Communism was concerned, it came almost at the bottom of the list of voters' concerns.

But Eisenhower's anti-Communist utterances and the choice of Nixon as his running mate meant that McCarthy had been outflanked. At the Republican Convention McCarthy had been treated like a hero. His attacks on Marshall, who had made Eisenhower's career a progression to the summit, had pained Eisenhower deeply. "Towards Senator McCarthy, he had a sense of loathing and contempt that had to be seen to be believed," one of his advisers remarked.

Dewey and others urged him to avoid Wisconsin. But a majority of his advisers voted that suggestion down, at the urging of Governor Walter J. Kohler, Jr. Kohler also persuaded them to persuade the candidate to delete a passage in praise of Marshall from his speech. Eisenhower appeared on the platform with McCarthy, criticized him obliquely, and supported him indirectly by calling for the election of all Republican candidates.*

Eisenhower's repugnance for what he considered "politics" was only heightened by such episodes. He made it clear that having to embrace the likes of Jenner and McCarthy was part of the price of public service and that he found the embrace distasteful.

On Korea, the candidate had little to say until late in the campaign. Part of his difficulty was that Eisenhower agreed, in public and in private, with Truman's decision to fight. Emmet John Hughes, a lifelong Democrat who joined the Eisenhower staff because he believed that another Democratic victory would mean the end of the two-party system, drafted a speech for Eisenhower which turned the Korean issue to the Republicans' advantage. He put into Eisenhower's mouth the words "That job requires a personal trip to Korea. I shall make that trip. I shall go to Korea!" Delivered in Detroit, this utterly pointless promise had an effect that was electrifying.

Stevenson had begun his campaign by being reluctant to run against Herbert Hoover. He did so only in the later stages, after he made little headway running against Eisenhower. The Democrats' slogan was: "You Never Had It So Good." They suggested that "It" would all go aglimmering with a Republican President.

Stevenson put up a cheerful fight against what he knew were daunting odds. And although he was not enthusiastic about Truman's offers of help, he tried not to let it show. Truman went his own way, by train, taking on all comers. In Massachusetts he ignored the pleas of the local Democratic powers (that is, the Kennedys) and enjoyed himself thoroughly by denouncing McCarthy in the one state where McCarthy was probably more highly regarded than in Wisconsin.

Stevenson also accepted that he was opposed by what he termed "a one party press in a two party country." On election day he received 27 million votes to Eisenhower's 32 million. Under the circumstances it was a very creditable showing.

---

*Nixon, by contrast, always handled McCarthy as if he were a package of explosives. He never saw McCarthy alone. As a rule, he arranged for his lawyer, William P. Rogers, to be present. He thereby had a defense against McCarthy's using his name or twisting his words.

Eisenhower's victory was attributed variously to Korea or Communism or Corruption. Among people in the media and up and down Madison Avenue the smart belief was that television had "put Ike over." But the fact was, Eisenhower was the most popular political figure to have appeared on the national scene for a generation. His television appearances were nearly always atrocious; the star was wooden, stumbled over his lines, and improvised with painful self-consciousness. Eisenhower won because he was Eisenhower. Every TV station in the country might have burned down; he would have won anyway.

Korea, Communism, and Corruption were also comparatively unimportant when set alongside his personal appeal. A majority of people wanted him in the White House regardless of the issues, regardless of the merits of his opponent. His appeal cut across lines of party, class, or religion. He ran 5 million votes ahead of Congressional Republican candidates.

In Wisconsin, McCarthy ran behind every other Republican on the ticket. He retained his seat in 1952 because he was the incumbent and it was a Republican year. The same was true in Indiana, where Jenner narrowly missed being defeated.

A month after the election Eisenhower kept his promise. He went to Korea. He was there for three days. Truman grumbled irritably that it was a cheap exercise, which it was. But having made so simple and firm a promise, Eisenhower had to keep it. There was nothing he could learn in a hurried tour of the combat zone that would break the stalemate. Yet he resented Truman's attacks, just as Truman was disgusted with Eisenhower's refusal to defend General Marshall in order to appease the McCarthyites in the Republican Party. The press exaggerated their mutual coolness as a feud. It never became that. But their estrangement was unfortunate because both were men of honor, intelligence, and courage. Political rivalry was unhappily allowed to magnify the imperfections of each in the eyes of the other.

Truman nonetheless ordered that the President-elect's son, Major John Eisenhower, be brought home from Korea to attend his father's Inauguration. When the President-elect announced that he would wear a homburg instead of a silk hat, there was grumbling in the White House that it was for the President to set the style, not his successor. But Truman appeared in a homburg.

Eisenhower's dazzling ascent from obscure lieutenant colonel to General of the Army in fewer than ten years had given him a reputation for being unbelievably lucky. His luck prevailed again on Inauguration Day. The dripping gray skies parted in the nick of time to provide him with a sunny swearing in.

As soldiers since the time of Pyrrhus have known only too well, it is often better to have a lucky general than one who is merely excellent.

PART III

ROCKING!

14

The End of Two Joes

New York opened 1953 by greeting the biggest, most luxurious liner built in Europe since before the war. The Italian liner *Andrea Doria* arrived to the tooting of steam whistles and fireboats spouting arcs of water.

Much of the country was entranced by the coronation of Elizabeth the Second, and the networks staged a $1 million race to be the first to show film of the event on American screens. Television brought another sensation when, at the end of a song sung by Julius La Rosa on *The Arthur Godfrey Show*, Godfrey turned to the startled singer and told him that he had just been fired.

It was also the year when the UFO "contactees" began to come forward. The first person to claim personal contact with extraterrestrial beings was George Adamski, who was well placed for such an experience. He ran the snack stand on Mount Palomar. Adamski reported that he had been accosted in the desert by a man with dazzling blonde hair shortly after he saw a spaceship touch down. To his surprise, he found that he and the stranger were able to communicate telepathically. The stranger identified himself as a Venusian and shyly asked Adamski not to take a photograph. He wished to travel incognito. His mission, however, appears to have been an issue of public concern—the testing of atomic bombs. Having met one extraterrestrial being, Adamski began to run into them everywhere, especially in bars. After Adamski, the deluge. Contactees grew so numerous that they began an annual festival at Yucca Valley, California, and they attracted paying visitors by the thousands. One contactee ran for the U.S. Senate on a platform of intergalactic harmony and won 171,000 votes.

In the fall there was the kidnapping of Bobby Greenlease, the six-year-old son of a wealthy elderly GM distributor in St. Louis. Robert C. Green-

257

lease offered the abductors a "blank check" for the release of his son. The number the kidnappers put on the blank check was $600,000. The boy had been taken by Carl Austin Hall and Bonnie Brown Heady. Both came from solid and successful middle-class families, had married well, and had slid into the gutter, which was where they met. Hall was a drug addict. Mrs. Heady, after twenty years of marriage to a successful livestock broker, had turned prostitute, at an age when most prostitutes are thinking of retiring. She and Hall collected the ransom, which was delivered in tens and twenties stuffed into an army duffel bag. But when they went to pick up the money, Bobby Greenlease was already dead. In fact, they had dug the boy's grave before kidnapping him. Shortly after collecting the ransom, they had a drunken quarrel. Hall broke away on a spending spree which led to his capture. Mrs. Heady was arrested hours later. But one mystery remained. Why was only $292,000 recovered? Hall and Heady, who were executed, maintained to their deaths that they had spent only $8,000. Where was the missing $300,000? The police of St. Joseph, who made the arrests and dug up the dead boy's body from under a bed of chrysanthemums, said they hadn't a clue.

In 1954 three Puerto Ricans, two men and a woman, entered the gallery of the House of Representatives on a February afternoon in the middle of a dull debate on Mexican immigration. Then Lolita Lebrón, Rafael Cancel Miranda, and Andrés Figueroa shouted, "Puerto Rico is not free!" unfurled a Puerto Rican flag, and opened fire with their German automatic pistols on the Representatives below. By the time the trio had been overpowered five Representatives lay in the aisles or were slumped over their desks, bleeding from bullet wounds.

On March 1 a thermonuclear explosion at Bikini surprised the men who had designed it by producing a yield of ten megatons. The fireball was twenty-eight miles in diameter. Sailing seventy-one miles away, presumably out of danger, was a Japanese fishing boat inappropriately named *Lucky Dragon*. A fine radioactive ash rained steadily down on the boat and its twenty-three crew members, dooming several to painful, lingering death and the others to a lifetime of illness.

During the summer people were diverted by the strange, sad death of Montgomery Ward Thorne, grandson of Montgomery Ward and heir to millions. At the age of twenty the young man was found dead in a dingy room, killed by the combined effects of morphine and alcohol. He was survived by a strong-willed mother and a strong-willed fiancée. What gave this unfortunate affair widespread interest was that the deceased youth had left two wills—one leaving all to mother, the other leaving it to the fiancée. And the circumstances of the death were so odd that the coroner could not decided whether to rule it a murder, an accident, or a suicide.

For much of this year the French staggered from calamity to catastrophe in Indochina. While government and the press agonized over whether the United States should intervene, so did many ordinary citizens. Thousands wrote to the President and Congress to say, "Please don't." And in a poll which asked, "What would the United States gain from fighting in Asia?" the most common response was: "Nothing."

In Cleveland the biggest crime story since the trial of Bruno Haupt-mann in 1935 kept the nation enthralled for several months. A successful young osteopath, Sam Sheppard, was charged with the murder of his young and pregnant wife. The motive for the crime was said to be a pretty twenty-four-year-old lab technician. Sheppard was convicted at the end of a sensational trial and was sentenced to life imprisonment. His mother took her life.

A television broadcast at the end of 1954 to publicize Disneyland set off *the* craze of 1955—Davy Crockett. Crockettiana proliferated, stimulated by "The Ballad of Davy Crockett," and a turgid ballad it was. But mil-lions of fake coonskin caps adorned small heads, and the price of a genu-ine coonskin rose from 25 cents to $5. One publisher alone sold 2 million Davy Crockett books in 1955. The Disney-style Crockett was brave, clean, smart, and honest; the real article had, naturally, been a back-woods scoundrel with a preference for cheap whiskey and the ill-gotten gain. When Disneyland opened in the late summer of 1955, it was a tre-mendous success, given the kind of press and television coverage normal-ly reserved for Presidential inaugurals.

The crime story of the year was the murder of Serge Rubinstein. The very hated, very crooked playboy-swindler-financier was found strangled in the silk sheets of his bed in a swank Fifth Avenue apartment. It was a story which had everything—missing millions, lots of pretty girls, a but-ler, an infamous victim, and literally dozens of people with a motive for the crime.

Twelve Russian farm managers arrived to tour American farms. They were treated like celebrities every mired step of the way on their travels through the Midwestern corn belt, one of the most conservative parts of the country.

In 1956 the United States had its own royal romance leading to a royal wedding. Grace Kelly of Philadelphia married Prince Rainier III of Mona-co.

A young housewife in Pueblo, Colorado, Virginia Tighe, excited much of the civilized world by claiming to have made contact with her earlier human form, a young lady of Belfast, Northern Ireland, named Bridey Murphy. Bridey had died in 1864. Mrs. Tighe was able to reestablish con-tact with the aid of an amateur hypnotist, Morey Bernstein. Bernstein's subsequent account, *The Search for Bridey Murphy*, was one of the best-sellers of the decade. There was also a best-selling record in which Mrs. Tighe, under hypnosis, made incoherent remarks in a decidedly Irish brogue. Bridey Murphy set off a new wave of interest in the occult. There were "Come as You Were" parties in which the guests arrived dressed as what they believed were their earlier selves. A youth in Shawnee, Okla-homa, left a note saying that he intended "to investigate the theory in per-son," then killed himself. Psychiatrists who practiced hypnosis were pes-tered by large numbers of people demanding to be "taken back." In pub-lic libraries, every book on hypnotism was on the waiting list. Bernstein left the hurly-burly of Pueblo for the solitude of Greenwich Village. Alas, every effort to substantiate the existence of Bridey Murphy failed. And

Mrs. Tighe's Bridey speech was tainted with Americanisms such as "real red" hair and "an awful" spanking. She also mispronounced Irish names, calling Sean "See-an," for instance.

There was a national outcry when six young marines were drowned one night in a swamp at Parris Island, South Carolina, during a march that was being conducted to punish recalcitrant recruits. The court-martial of the staff sergeant involved, Matthew C. McKeon, was the most publicized military trial since Billy Mitchell's. McKeon was charged with drunkenness while on duty and culpable negligence. There was considerable anger over this affair, until McKeon at his court-martial showed himself to be no sadist or bully but a sober and remorseful young man who had made a tragic misjudgment. He was found guilty of simple negligence, spent three months in the brig, and was allowed to remain in the Marine Corps as a private.

At 11 P.M. the band was playing "Arrivederci, Roma." The gangways were congested with baggage to be unloaded at New York in the morning. On deck, passengers took a last casual stroll in the moonlight. The *Andrea Doria* was nearing the end of her voyage. Suddenly the Swedish passenger liner *Stockholm* appeared on the starboard side and in seconds had cut a thirty-foot gash in the side of the Italian ship. The *Stockholm*'s bow was unusually sharp and strongly reinforced for cutting through ice. The wound in the *Andrea Doria* went deep and proved fatal. Luckily this mishap occurred on one of the world's busiest shipping lanes. A dozen vessels were soon on the scene to rescue the passengers of the stricken ship. Fifty were known dead or were never accounted for, but 1,670 others were saved.

The Olympic Games in Melbourne came in the immediate wake of the Hungarian uprising. When the Soviet and Hungarian water polo teams met, the water was crimson. Romance bloomed between American hammer thrower Harold Connolly and Czech discus thrower Olga Fikotova, and many millions were delighted to see young love overcome Cold War divisions. To help get Olga out of Czechoslovakia, the Secretary of State himself took up the case. "We believe in romance," declared the normally flinty John Foster Dulles. "That is our principle." These efforts were crowned with success. Harold and Olga, gold medal winners both, were married to national rejoicing.

The year 1957 began with a fire which spread through Malibu, fanned by hot winds blowing in from the desert. The fire raged for the best part of a week, burning 40,000 acres and razing sixty luxurious homes. In the summer Hurricane Audrey destroyed the town of Cameron, Louisiana, killing 300 people.

For a decade New York's "Mad Bomber" had been leaving his handiwork in movie theaters, telephone booths, and the New York Public Library. In a last desperate attempt to flush him out, the police finally let the city know that a bomb-planting lunatic was in its midst. Enamored of seeing his name in print, the bomber began writing letters to the newspapers. One of these led to his arrest. He proved to be an elderly bachelor,

George Matesky, of Waterbury, Connecticut, and he had a grievance against Consolidated Edison.

In Japan a local court tried U.S. Army Specialist 3rd Class William S. Girard of Ottawa, Illinois, for killing a Japanese woman who was scavenging for scrap metal on a firing range. Millions of people joined in Girard's protest against his being tried by foreigners. His fate occupied the front pages of newspapers for weeks. He was found guilty of manslaughter and tactfully given a suspended sentence.

In the fall the Edsel appeared. It was a $250 million investment which flouted fashion—it had no fins.

Millions of people came down with Asian flu, which first appeared in Hong Kong and rapidly spread throughout the world. Before it had run its course, it killed 70,000 Americans.

When the new Administration took office, Korea was less like a war than a running sore. It would not clear up of its own accord, and neither side could do much with it.

MacArthur was still traveling, still speaking out, and claiming that he had a plan for ending the war but refusing to divulge it. Years later he claimed that he had revealed it to the President-elect. He suggested laying a belt of radioactive waste behind the Chinese armies, cutting them off from food, ammunition, and hope of escape. They would either die or surrender.

Eisenhower's thoughts were moving along similar lines. He proposed to end the war by making a major offensive which would break the stalemate through the introduction of tactical nuclear weapons. Through various channels he made the Soviets and the Chinese understand that he was prepared to end the war this way, even if it led to making atomic attacks on military bases inside China. The threat was kept vague. But that may have only made it more effective. What is more, the Russians and the Chinese were as tired of the war as was the United States.

The Russians had already signaled a willingness to moderate the tensions between themselves and the West. In October 1952 the 19th Congress of the Communist Party had made a shift which one scholar described as "a shift from 'cold war' to 'cold peace.'" Nor were Eisenhower's terms for ending the war onerous: a restoration of the status quo ante bellum and the return of prisoners of war. The unification of Korea could wait, angry murmurs of protest within the Republican Party notwithstanding. The moderate terms Eisenhower accepted may have been as important as the threat of tactical atomic warfare. But more important than either of these was the death of Stalin in March 1953.

Within three weeks of Stalin's death there was an agreement on the exchange of sick and wounded prisoners. And this exchange was obviously only a prelude to a general prisoner exchange, which would mean an effective end to the fighting.

The Republican Administration was able to wind up the war on terms which no Democratic Administration would have dared seriously propose, if only for fear of McCarthy and his followers. By July the fighting had become fitful and desultory. The POWs were returning home in the thousands each week. The condition of many of these men caused anger. It contrasted tellingly with the health of North Korean and Chinese prisoners in UN hands. But more disturbing yet was the refusal of twenty-three Americans, and an Englishman, to be repatriated. They chose to go to China.

The war was heartily disliked long before it drew to an end. Few men came back to a hero's welcome. But there was one who did—Major General William F. Dean. During the retreat to the Pusan perimeter in the early days of the war Dean, then a brigadier general, had fought on foot, carrying a bazooka to attack North Korean tanks at close range. He led a band of green troops in a delaying action which had gained valuable time. In captivity he had been tortured, yet his spirit had remained unbroken. He made an unsuccessful attempt to kill his guards, after which he expected to be killed in turn. He returned to the United States expecting to be court-martialed for allowing himself to be taken alive. Instead he rode down Fifth Avenue through billowing clouds of ticker tape, and in Washington he received the Medal of Honor.

Dean was a modest man. He accepted his sudden celebrity with good grace. He was seen as a new kind of hero for the new age—the man who would die rather than yield to Communist torture or indoctrination. This was comic-book stuff. But underneath he was a man of the noblest type. He had been betrayed into captivity by two South Koreans. When they in turn were captured by their own government, Dean pleaded with Syngman Rhee to show clemency toward them. He also appeared in defense of a Marine Corps pilot who, under torture, had signed statements that the United States had waged germ warfare in Korea.

While the war was drawing to its close, so were the lives of Julius and Ethel Rosenberg. They resisted every attempt to induce them to confess, in the knowledge that confession would probably have spared their lives. When it was put to Ethel Rosenberg that she might yet be saved from the electric chair because of her sex, she considered it a proposal "in which I shall live without living, and die without dying." She made a Roman reply to this idea: "No power on earth shall divide us in life or in death."

While their lawyers filed motions and appeals, requests for clemency, and requests for stays of execution, the Rosenbergs pinned their hopes not on the courts but on aroused public opinion. Even so, theirs was the most carefully considered case in American legal history: 112 judges considered their case on twenty-three separate occasions.

The publicity campaign was largely taken over by the Communist Party, which had shown no interest in the Rosenbergs until they appeared likely to die. But it is fair to say that large numbers of people who were not Communists disagreed with the verdict, or the sentence, and protested at the behest of conscience, not Communism. There were "Rosenberg Trains" carrying demonstrators to Washington. There were twenty-four-hour vigils in front of the White House. There were scores of motorcades, rallies, and lengthy petitions. The Pope twice appealed for clemency.

But so far as Eisenhower could see, the Rosenbergs had received a fair trial. They had been properly convicted. He was troubled at the thought of a woman being executed.* Yet he had an irrational fear that to spare her would mean that henceforth the Soviet Union "would simply recruit their spies from among women."

On June 19, 1953, insisting on their innocence to the end, the Rosenbergs were electrocuted at Sing Sing. Their attorney, Emmanuel Bloch, had ruined his health in his efforts to save them. Several weeks after the electrocution Bloch died.

Many who were convinced of the Rosenbergs' guilt considered the sentence excessive. As the remarks at the trial suggested, it was passed in anger and in response to the public temper. The attempt to pin the blame for the Korean War on the Rosenbergs was irrational and splenetic. Their feckless, amateurish venture into espionage could not remotely compare with the villainy of a Fuchs or a Philby. They had achieved nothing of note in their entire lives. Ethel was a failed singer. Julius was lackluster as both an engineer and an entrepreneur. But in the belief that they were dying for a principle, believing, too, that they had done no harm, they turned a brave face to death. They joined a painfully long line of misguided good people who have died for wretchedly bad causes.

It had taken the Soviets four years to catch up with the American atomic bomb. It took them less than a year to catch up with the H-bomb. So much for the security the H-bomb provided. The more anxiously the country sought security, the less it appeared to find.

The Soviet H-bomb was detonated in August 1953, only weeks after the Korean War ended in a general truce. Democracies are as prone to seek scapegoats for their disappointments as other nations. The scapegoat of the failure to achieve security through the H-bomb was J. Robert Oppenheimer.

He had made important enemies in the Air Force by helping to break down its monopoly on delivering atomic weapons to their targets. He had struck the Strategic Air Command a further blow by arguing, within government and in the pages of *Foreign Affairs*, for an effective system of air defense. This flatly refuted the SAC doctrine that bombers would always get through. Finally, Oppenheimer had opposed one of the Air Force's most cherished projects, the atomic-powered airplane. The project was not dropped, but it never got beyond the study stage.

Oppenheimer also had a number of enemies in Congress. His attitude toward people not as clever as himself was dismissive. Nor had his relations with Lewis Strauss improved during Strauss's tenure as chairman of

---

*The last woman executed on the order of a Federal court had been Mary Surratt, for her role in the assassination of Lincoln.

the AEC. Strauss had arranged for Oppenheimer to become director of the Institute of Advanced Study at Princeton. He evidently believed that this plum appointment would make Oppenheimer beholden to him. But Oppenheimer believed that it was a job he had won on merit and was beholden to no one.

Oppenheimer was unusually vulnerable. He was intellectually gifted and he had been friendly with Communists and leftists before the war. During the war he had failed to report for eight months a clumsy attempt to recruit him into Soviet espionage. At the time he was the head of the Manhattan Project. When he did report this incident, he did it in such a garbled fashion that it became impossible to investigate it properly.

The new Administration introduced a new standard in the Loyalty-Security program. Employment from now on had to be "clearly consistent with the interests of national security." This dictum was so broad and so vague that it became impossible to make a defense against it. As a consultant to the Atomic Energy Commission Oppenheimer was as much subject to this new standard as anyone.

Throughout 1953 his views on air defense, disarmament, and weapons research had been countered with a propaganda offensive from the Air Force and its friends. This culminated in an anonymous article which appeared in *Fortune* in May 1953 under the title "The Hidden Struggle for the H-Bomb." Oppenheimer was portrayed as a man whose judgment was so thoroughly bad that from his high place he had put the security of the country in danger. The author of the article was Charles J. V. Murphy, an aide to Secretary of the Air Force Thomas Finletter. When it became evident a few months later that the Soviets possessed an H-bomb of more advanced design than the first American model, Murphy's strictures appeared undeniable. In September *Time* carried an article which portrayed Oppenheimer and Lilienthal as fuzzy-minded do-gooders; Lewis Strauss was shown as the hardheaded man who was saving the nation.

In November 1953, against this background of recrimination and anxiety, J. Edgar Hoover received a letter which concluded, "based upon years of study of the available classified information, more probably than not, J. Robert Oppenheimer is an agent of the Soviet Union." This was no poison-pen letter written by a crank; it came from William L. Borden, an executive with Westinghouse and until recently the executive director of the Joint Congressional Committee on Atomic Energy.

Oppenheimer had been under intensive scrutiny for eleven years. His telephone had been tapped, his mail opened, his home and office bugged. He had been questioned by the FBI and Army Intelligence on more than a dozen occasions. The security file on Oppenheimer was a stack of reports four feet high. The Borden letter added nothing to what was already known. Yet it could not be ignored. For one thing, there was Borden's standing to consider. For another, both McCarthy and HUAC had been shown copies of this missive. Eisenhower ordered that a "blank wall" be placed between Oppenheimer and all classified information. This made Oppenheimer's consultancy nugatory.

He was informed that the AEC intended to terminate his security clearance. Although his consultancy had but a few months to run before his contract with the AEC expired, Oppenheimer chose to fight to retain his security clearance; he considered its revocation a stain on his honor.

The AEC attempted to justify its action by setting out twenty-four "charges." The first twenty-three items covered well-traveled ground— that is, his known and rumored left-wing associations of the 1930s. But they were not the kinds of charges any court of law would have considered specific or actionable. The twenty-fourth, however, was specific enough: Oppenheimer was charged with opposing the development of the H-bomb. Here was a leaf from the Soviets' book—to punish a scientist for having given advice unwelcome to powerful men. The twenty-three preceding charges were all concerned with events predating Oppenheimer's employment with the AEC and were evidently included to suggest a treasonable motive for number twenty-four.

At the hearing, the AEC's lawyers had access to top secret material; Oppenheimer's were not only not given clearance to see this material but on three occasions were ordered to leave the room while secret material was discussed. Edward Teller, touted in the press as "the Father of the H-bomb" (as Oppenheimer before him had endured being called "the Father of the A-bomb"), appeared and in a single sentence cut Oppenheimer down. Teller had chafed at Los Alamos, where he had been obliged to work under Oppenheimer's direction. Teller wanted a laboratory of his own and, thanks to his careful cultivation of the Air Force and his ardent advocacy on behalf of the H-bomb, had secured one, at Livermore, California. His evident ambition had made him unpopular with other scientists. Now he cut himself off even further. "If it is a question of wisdom and judgment, as demonstrated by actions since 1945," he told the three-man panel, "then I would say it would be wiser not to grant clearance." This suggestion, that Oppenheimer was a security risk, was fatal to Oppenheimer's hopes.

Borden appeared at the hearing and, ironically, made no impression whatever. He brought nothing to show that Oppenheimer had ever been a Soviet agent. His accusation was simply disbelieved. "It was as if the match that had ignited the fire had been snuffed out. Yet the fire burned on."

On June 29, 1954, only two days before Oppenheimer's consultancy was due to expire, the three-man panel issued its report. They ruled that all the evidence showed Oppenheimer to be discreet and loyal. Yet, by a vote of two to one, they decided it would be in the national interest to revoke his security clearance. The dissenting vote came from the only one of the three who was a scientist.

When the news of the adverse recommendation reached Congress there was spontaneous applause in the House. The AEC accepted the panel's recommendation by a vote of four to one.

The Oppenheimer case was important for several reasons. But its most telling consequence was that it discredited the Loyalty-Security program.

The standards of proof and the nature of the charges were so slippery that, in effect, anything was permitted to be used to destroy people's careers. Political ambition, personal gain, security mania, petty frictions took the place of evidence and objectivity. Norbert Wiener was moved to reflect wryly on Oppenheimer's ordeal: "Any scientist, participating in what has become a floating crap game, must expect to get slugged occasionally."

There had been thousands of Loyalty-Security hearings before Oppenheimer's. But they had been of interest only to those involved directly and those solicitous of the state of civil liberties. The Oppenheimer hearing was followed by much of the educated part of the population, and they were appalled at the spectacle it presented. Because of Oppenheimer's invaluable service to his country, and because the finding that he was both extremely loyal but somehow a security risk was fatuous in the extreme, hardly anyone who was interested in this case was satisfied with the result. Within a few years it would prove almost impossible to find anyone in government or the scientific community willing to defend the hearing or the report.

Eisenhower had wasted no time in reorganizing the Loyalty-Security program. Three months after his Inauguration he had supplanted EO 9835 by issuing Executive Order 10450. This abolished the Loyalty Review Board. Henceforth each agency of government ran its own screening program, and there was no one to whom appeals could be made. The Loyalty-Security program had formerly applied only to "sensitive" agencies; now it applied to all agencies. Dismissal had been based on "reasonable doubt." From now on employment in government had to be "consistent with the national security"—which meant whatever anyone wanted it to mean.

Even before the new program had begun, the Postmaster General, Arthur Summerfield, a successful Chevrolet dealer with an eighth-grade education, was happy to report that the great housecleaning was well in hand. The Administration, he said, was "rooting out the egg-heads."

In his first State of the Union message the President announced that under EO 10450 more than 2,200 "security risks" had been dismissed from government employment. He was pressed for details. How many were subversives? How many were secret Communists? The figures began to change almost from day to day. Yet however they were juggled, it gradually became evident that fewer than 2 percent had been dismissed for anything to do with security. Most were alcoholics, people who did not pay their bills, homosexuals, people with mental illnesses, chronic liars, incompetents, and the like. It turned out that EO 10450 had provided a marvelous opportunity for agency heads to get rid of their misfits, who had formerly been protected from dismissal by civil service regulations.

The Administration was eager to have some anti-Communist legislation to its credit. So were both parties in Congress. The Republicans wanted to deny collective bargaining rights to unions with Communist officers. The

Democrats wanted to make it a crime to belong to the Communist Party, a measure supported by such stalwarts as Senators Humphrey, Fulbright, and Lehman. The bill they supported failed of passage only because the Administration did not want to see the Democrats get the credit for having made Communism a criminal offense. The Republicans countered with the Communist Control Act of 1954. This barred Communists from running for public office. The effect was to outlaw the CPUSA as a legitimate political party. The act declared that Communism, in and of itself, was "a clear, present and continuing danger to the United States."

More popular still was the Loss of Citizenship Act of 1954. To all the penalties already provided for under the Smith Act this new measure added loss of citizenship—the punishment traditionally reserved for those convicted of treason.

The Administration also moved against "Fifth Amendment Communists." Under EO 10450 any government employee who invoked the Fifth Amendment could be dismissed. Herbert Brownell, the Attorney General, sought to limit the Fifth Amendment still further. He asked Congress for legislation which would give immunity from prosecution to any witness before a Congressional committee, at that committee's discretion, and the witness could then be compelled to testify or else face an indictment for contempt. Congress passed the legislation. The Supreme Court upheld it. Congress also tried to have the last word on the Rosenberg case. It made peacetime espionage an offense punishable by death.

The new Administration never tired of reminding the country that it was being more vigilant than the Democrats had been. In November 1953 Brownell told the Executive Club of Chicago that Truman had knowingly promoted a Soviet spy, Harry Dexter White. Nine times in the course of his speech he called White a spy.

Truman called Brownell a liar. All that there was against White was "derogatory information"—that is, secret accusations by people whose veracity had never been openly put to the test.

Under Brownell's direction the Justice Department made strenuous efforts to send Owen Lattimore to prison. When Federal Judge Luther Youngdahl threw out the principal charge (that Lattimore had perjured himself when he denied that he was "a sympathizer or promoter of Communist interests") on the ground that it was too vague, the Justice Department brought pressure on the judge to make him disqualify himself from the case. Youngdahl refused to be browbeaten.

At the State Department John Foster Dulles had installed as security officer an ex-FBI agent, Robert Walter Scott McLeod, with the rank of Assistant Secretary. McLeod's name quickly became a byword for misguided zeal. Before long he was an embarrassment even to an administration proud of its anything-goes approach to fighting the Communist menace. When Congress in 1953 passed the Refugee Relief Act, to provide a haven to people fleeing from Soviet rule, Scott McLeod was made responsible for administering the act. It permitted 209,000 refugees to enter the United States. But McLeod let only 58,000 of them do so.

The new Administration never lacked for willing hands to help it in the great struggle. The American Legion found that the Girl Scouts had fallen under "un-American influences." This was because there were several favorable references in the 1953 Girl Scout *Handbook* to the UN and no mention of the Constitution. The Girl Scouts rallied under this challenge and decided that henceforth in order to win a "My Government" merit badge, a Scout would be required to recite the entire Bill of Rights from memory.

The Texas state legislature made it a felony to be a Communist. The punishment was twenty years' imprisonment. Governor Allan Shivers signed the bill reluctantly, in disagreement not with the principle but with the penalty. He thought it should be death.

In New York a loyalty oath was imposed on anyone who applied to fish in the city's reservoirs.

At the State Department Dulles was not content to let the entire burden of vigilance rest on Scott McLeod's willing shoulders. He took a personal hand in the matter of John Patton Davies. Davies had been in trouble since 1945, when as a member of Joseph Stilwell's staff he had made critical reports about Chiang Kai-shek. Under the Truman Loyalty-Security program he had endured, and been cleared by, eight hearings. Dulles called for another review of the Davies case. He was cleared for the ninth time.

Dulles dismissed him, anyway, ending twenty-three years of service on the ground that he personally found Davies lacking in "judgment, discretion and reliability." John Stewart Service, in trouble since the *Amerasia* affair, had similarly survived six hearings, plus a grand jury appearance. But under Dulles and EO 10450 he was summarily dismissed. And there were others who survived repeated hearings only to be worn down in the end.

Elderly leftists, who had not engaged in political activities for decades, found themselves under the new dispensation fighting attempts to deport them. Most were people who had arrived here as children. They had no substantial ties in most instances with the countries to which the Justice Department was attempting to deport them. Often they were persecuted because they had refused to become informers. An eighty-three-year-old man from Rochester, New York, was faced with deportation when he refused to inform on his son, who was a Communist. A former editor of the *Daily Worker* refused to turn informer, and denaturalization proceedings were started against his wife. Another man was acquitted under a Smith Act indictment; in revenge the Justice Department attempted to deport his wife and arrested her. Fifteen editors or former editors of radical newspapers faced deportation or denaturalization.

The people who endured these harassments were placed on "supervisory parole," which meant that they were required to report to Federal authorities in person each week, to submit to periodic psychiatric examination, and to give information under oath concerning all their activities and associations. Little appeared in print about this shabby wave of persecution, even though it involved hundreds of people. One reporter who did investigate their plight was moved to remark in sorrow, "The suffering in terms of broken families and disrupted lives is beyond the most sympathetic imagination . . . [and] people are afraid to look, lest they be tempted to help, and bring down suspicion on themselves."

And for James Kutcher things went from bad to worse under the new order. He was still jobless; he and his parents faced eviction; now he was informed that his sole source of income, his disability pension (which had cost him both his legs), was being revoked as part of the government housecleaning of Communist influences.

Disability pensions were revoked for dozens of Communists who had been wounded on active duty. The old-age pensions of elderly Reds, such as William Z. Foster, were stopped, and repayment was demanded of all the pension money already received. A career Party official serving time in Atlanta under a Smith Act conviction had an income of $88.10 a month, from his Social Security check. He kept $10 and sent the remainder to his wife. Although he had paid Social Security contributions for more than twenty years, his pension was stopped. The blow fell not on him but on an old woman who had no other means of support. Such was the human face of antisubversion.

Kutcher's case, however, began to attract widespread interest. He used it to demand a hearing, which the VA granted. The case against him, he was solemnly informed, was that he was "giving aid and assistance to Communist China and North Korea." How he was doing this was not explained. The hearing was run by a chairman appointed by the VA who set out the principle he proposed to follow: "I will make the rules as I go along." It was decided that the VA had been justified in taking Kutcher's pension from him. But from humanitarian—some believed public relations—motives it would be restored.

More famous than Kutcher was Lieutenant Milo J. Radulovich of Ann Arbor, Michigan, who held a commission in the Air Force Reserve. He was suddenly relieved of his commission on the ground that he was a security risk; to wit, he maintained a close relationship with persons "said to have been associated with Communists." The persons in question were his father, an immigrant from Serbia who subscribed to a left-wing Yugoslavian newspaper, and his sister, who had participated in demonstrations against the Smith Act and who sometimes attended social functions organized by the Labor Youth League. Edward R. Murrow put the Radulovich case on *See It Now*. There was a national outcry. Tens of millions of people until this moment had no idea how petty and witless the Loyalty-Security program could be. The Air Force was shamed into restoring Radulovich's commission.

There was a similar case eighteen months later. The number two man in the 1955 graduating class at the Merchant Marine Academy was Eugene Landy. He had won a scholarship to Yale Law School. He was an outstanding athlete and an accomplished debater. But on graduation day he alone of his class did not receive a commission in the Navy Reserve. The

Navy had ruled that Landy was a security risk because he maintained a close relationship with a known Communist—his mother. She had been a CP member from 1937 to 1948. She had broken with the Party in response to pleading from her son. Nationwide hoots of derision persuaded the Secretary of the Navy to award Landy his commission.

The longer the Loyalty-Security program ran, the more embarrassing it became. It reached a low of inanity when, at about the time of the Landy affair, the case of Wolf Ladejinsky came to a head. Ladejinsky's misfortunes stemmed from his being born in Russia and being brought to the United States while still a child. He left behind him scores of uncles, aunts, nephews, cousins, nieces, with none of whom he retained any contact. Over the years he had become an international authority on agricultural development in underdeveloped lands. Ladejinsky worked for both the departments of State and Agriculture. Scott McLeod, employing the "standards" set out in EO 10450, cleared Ladejinsky.

The Agriculture Department, employing the same criteria, decided he was a security risk. There was not a shred of evidence to support this contention, as the Secretary of Agriculture, Ezra Taft Benson, was forced to admit when pressed to produce it.

The Loyalty-Security program fell into disuse. There was a change in the atmosphere, but the change was partly brought about by growing skepticism over the entire business of screening people for loyalty and security—a skepticism which owed much to the cases briefly discussed above.

In its first three years the Eisenhower Administration dismissed 10,000 people as security risks. To its discomfiture half of them proved to be people hired under the Eisenhower Administration. And in 1956 the Supreme Court undercut EO 10450 by ruling that only individuals employed in sensitive agencies could be dismissed as security risks. This took more than 80 percent of all government employees out of the purview of EO 10450. Eisenhower, normally very careful not to exceed the strict limits of Presidential power, had in his "housecleaning" overstepped the Constitution.

The Republicans enjoyed wafer-thin margins of superiority in both houses of the 83rd Congress. In the Senate McCarthy became chairman of the Committee on Government Operations, which did not much interest him, and chairman of its Permanent Subcommittee on Investigations, which did. The subcommittee was empowered to investigate all operations of the Executive branch.

Until now McCarthy had been a free-lance, accountable to no one, responsible for nothing. Now he had to build up a staff, or at least find new staff members. His investigative apparatus had consisted of freebooters much like himself; one of them unfortunately turned out to be both a homosexual and a former Communist. (This individual, in fact, was the only Communist McCarthy ever found by his own efforts.) He also received tips from a handful of low-ranking civil servants, whom he grandiloquently called "the Loyal American Underground." Their loyalty was to McCarthy rather than their superiors or the President. McCarthy's principal investigator was Don Surine, a former FBI man.

To strengthen his staff commensurate with his new powers, McCarthy hired Roy Cohn to be chief counsel to the subcommittee. Not yet thirty, Cohn's credentials were, for McCarthy's purposes, positively sterling: as an Assistant U.S. Attorney he had been involved in the prosecutions of the CP leaders, the Rosenbergs, and William Remington.

Cohn in turn hired twenty-six-year-old G. David Schine to be the Subcommittee's "Chief Consultant." Schine's credentials consisted of a pamphlet, *Definition of Communism*, printed at his own expense, which graced every room of the extensive chain of Schine luxury hotels. He had been educated at Phillips-Andover and Harvard, but scholarship was not his strongest suit. In only a few pages he managed to misdate the Russian Revolution, the founding of the Communist Party, and the first Five-Year Plan. He confused Stalin with Trotsky, Marx with Lenin. His little pamphlet offered a hilarious profusion of wrong names, wrong dates, and badly jumbled history. But it is not risking much to suggest that neither Cohn nor McCarthy ever noticed that Schine knew almost nothing about Communism.

In search of something to investigate, the team of Cohn and Schine fastened on the various information programs conducted overseas by the Federal government, notably the State Department's information agency. The agency attempted to shake them off by issuing a directive which banned all materials, including paintings, by "any controversial persons, Communists, fellow travellers, et cetera." The reference to controversial persons excited criticism and was dropped, but the et cetera category remained in force.

There was a problem posed by materials which had been acquired back in the days when information policy attempted to offer a rounded view of the United States, including criticism from the American left. Fearing that McCarthy might descend on them at any moment, agency staff began to destroy incriminating books. At this juncture Cohn and Schine got wind of the book burning and decided to make a tour of Western Europe to investigate the information program. Their vigilance extended to the leaden novels of Howard Fast and the works of Dashiell Hammett, whose subversive masterpieces included *The Maltese Falcon*, *Red Harvest*, and *The Thin Man*.

In the panic which gripped the Voice of America the head of the agency was fired one day, when it seemed McCarthy was after his scalp, and rehired the next day, when it became evident he was not. Seeking guidance on which works the program should include and which it should avoid, agency staff turned to McCarthy and Co. rather than the State Department. It was quicker—and safer—that way.

VOA and the International Information Agency were vulnerable to these onslaughts because they had been created from the wartime Office of War Information. The OWI had been falsely but effectively portrayed as a Soviet outpost on American soil. A VOA radio engineer, Raymond Kaplan, wrote to his wife, "Once the dogs are set upon you, everything you have done since the beginning of time is suspect." Kaplan then killed himself.

Theodore Kaghan, in charge of the Public Affairs Division of the U.S. High Commission in Germany, had never hidden the fact that in his student days he had associated with members of the Young Communist League. He had been screened and cleared under the Loyalty-Security program. But Cohn and Schine, who were roundly mocked in the press, were desperate to turn up at least one Communist before their not-so-grand tour ended. They picked Kaghan to be their fall guy.

He was hauled before the McCarthy subcommittee three times. Nothing was offered in evidence to suggest that he had been, was, or might ever be disloyal. Yet the State Department offered him a choice—resign or be fired. Because the government would pay to bring his wife, his children, and his furniture back from Germany if he resigned, Kaghan resigned.

In acquiring new staff members, McCarthy took J. B. Matthews on as staff director of the subcommittee. It was a decision which was unpopular with the rest of the subcommittee. Despite his twenty years as an avowed anti-Communist Matthews made other people nervous; he managed to be both naïve and reckless. McCarthy insisted on having him, however, and McCarthy soon had cause to regret it.

The July 1953 issue of *American Mercury* appeared with an article by ex-missionary Matthews called "Reds in Our Churches." It began, "The largest single group supporting the Communist apparatus in the United States today is composed of Protestant clergymen." There were, by his reckoning, no fewer than 7,000 Protestant clergymen who had been recruited into the Communist conspiracy.

Matthews's article outraged conservative politicians, to whom clergymen were sacred. Religious leaders—Protestants, Catholics, and Jews alike—made impassioned protests against Matthews's unsubstantiated assertions to the White House.

At last Eisenhower bestirred himself. And McCarthy, for once finding himself isolated, moved to shed Matthews. The race was on to see who could cut Matthews down first. The White House won by minutes, with a statement expressing the President's repudiation of the Matthews article. McCarthy was ten minutes late with his announcement that Matthews had resigned. This was the first major public setback the Senator had suffered. Ironically, he had had nothing to do with the offending article. McCarthy was a victim of guilt by association.

After the Matthews debacle there were hopes the President would at last bring his towering prestige to bear against McCarthy and provide leadership to the anti-McCarthyites. But Eisenhower continued to believe that for a President to wrangle with a Senator was worse than futile: the Senate would rally to the beleaguered Senator and thereafter seek ways to

obstruct the White House. If McCarthy was to be brought down, he reasoned, it was for the Senate to do it. He brushed aside the pleas of his
staff to take the initiative. "I just will not—I *refuse*—to get into the gutter
with that guy."

But by the spring of 1954 he was prepared to defend any member of the
Administration McCarthy attacked. Even Mamie had changed in her attitude. Once friendly toward Mrs. McCarthy, she now snubbed her. "If Eisenhower could have had his way," Sherman Adams noted, "he would
have ignored the Senator completely." But that spring matters moved
beyond the point at which Eisenhower could continue to hold back.
McCarthy chose—or was led by his staff—to make a frontal assault on the
very institution within which the President had come into man's estate—
the United States Army.

At the time he attacked the Army the tide had already turned against
McCarthy. In March, with the strong wind of the Radulovich broadcast
behind them, Murrow and the *See It Now* team had presented two programs on the Senator. In the first, they showed him in action and offered
no commentary. What they showed was nothing new. It was thirty minutes of film selected from extensive footage shot during the previous
three years. CBS refused to advertise the program, so Murrow and Fred
Friendly paid for the advertisements themselves. To Murrow television
was meant to be a public service. He told his staff, rightly, "We are going
to be judged by what we put on the air; but we shall also be judged by
what we don't broadcast."

In the second program *See It Now* showed McCarthy's subcommittee
in action, persecuting a bewildered middle-aged black woman, Annie Lee
Moss, who held a low-grade clerical job in the Defense Department. Her
name was similar to that of a woman of known left-wing associations. As
it dawned on the subcommittee that the woman they were hounding was
the wrong woman, McCarthy, making no apologies for what he had done,
hurriedly left the room.

For millions of people these two broadcasts were a revelation. They
had never seen McCarthy in action before this. Here he was shown in de-
vastating close-up, smirking, bullying, lying, twisting people's words, and
utterly unfeeling.

McCarthy demanded air time for rebuttal. He appeared armed with
maps, pointer, and lectern and launched into a pseudo-academic analysis
of the Cold War which was like a parody of itself. This soon began to bore
him. He turned to hurling accusations at Murrow and CBS, which was
more his style. The dissolute life had ravaged McCarthy's never-hand-
some features. His hairline had beaten a long retreat from his forehead.
His face was heavily caked with makeup, and a new hairline had been
created, unconvincingly, by resorting to eyebrow pencil and a hairpiece.
He looked like a melodrama villain. He behaved like a melodrama villain.
For those with an eye for such things, it was a priceless performance.

These broadcasts made Murrow a national hero. At the White House,
the President embraced him.

McCarthy had meanwhile taken a sudden interest in the U.S. Army Signal Corps research facility at Fort Monmouth, New Jersey. It proved to be Fort Monmouth's unhappy lot that back in 1942 and 1943 one of its civilian employees had been Julius Rosenberg. Eleven years after the event McCarthy, Cohn, and Schine declared that it was alive with Soviet spies. In a futile gesture of appeasement the Army suspended thirty-seven of its Fort Monmouth employees on grounds ranging from the trivial to the laughable.

McCarthy was also busy investigating training pamphlets used by G-2, the agency loosely termed Army Intelligence. McCarthy decided that the pamphlets were so laden with Communist propaganda they could have been written only on orders from Moscow. The major general in charge of G-2 soon found himself back in command of an infantry division.

But while this was going on, the Army had deprived the Senator of the inimitable services of G. David Schine, a loss McCarthy seemed prepared to bear, but not so Roy Cohn. With McCarthy's assistance, Cohn secured for Schine a range of privileges beyond the imagination of the ordinary draftee. But the Army balked at giving Schine a commission.

While the struggle over the elevation of G. David Schine was under way, McCarthy's attention was drawn to an Army dentist named Irving Peress, inducted under the Doctor Draft Law despite some unusual declarations concerning his past associations and beliefs. Peress represented another little lunacy of the combination of bureaucracy and Cold War vigilance. The Army needed Peress; Peress did not need the Army. But if the Army sternly refused to take people who had been, or might become, attracted to unorthodox or unpopular ideas, then it was likely to lose large numbers of people whose education and skills it happened to need. Peress was drafted, and a blind eye turned to his left-wing beliefs. The Doctor Draft Law provided, moreover, for rapid promotion; this was meant to make it more palatable to doctors and dentists. Peress was routinely promoted from captain to major.

Having stumbled across Peress, who was now out of the Army, McCarthy attempted to portray this promotion as being either a threat to national security or part of the Communist plan to take over the world. "Who promoted Peress?" became a battle cry of the McCarthyites for the remainder of the decade.

The Army refused to dignify this farce by allowing Brigadier General Ralph Zwicker, commander of the post where Peress had been stationed and thus nominally responsible for his promotion, to appear before McCarthy's subcommittee. McCarthy managed to create such a furor that Zwicker, a much decorated soldier, eventually appeared, to be informed by Tail Gunner Joe that he was "A disgrace to your uniform."

This time McCarthy had gone too far. Conservative Republicans turned against him in large numbers for the first time. The American Legion and the VFW for the first time openly criticized him. Right-wing newspapers began to carry unflattering comments. And the President came to the defense of the Secretary of the Army. Even Nixon criticized McCarthy, although indirectly. It became obvious that McCarthy was trying to get even with the Army for refusing to grant Schine a commission. And the Army said flatly that this was exactly what had happened: that he had sought to secure special treatment for Private G. David Schine.

McCarthy categorically denied having done any such thing. Thus was joined the issue which for eight weeks occupied television screens as the Army-McCarthy Hearings. The ostensible aim of the hearings was to discover who was lying—the Army? McCarthy? Or both?

They were not as riveting a daytime drama as the Kefauver hearings had been. To many people, possibly to most, the issues were obscure. But here was the Senator as Murrow had tried to portray him, completely unbuttoned. The Army had hired a courtly, elderly Boston lawyer, Joseph N. Welch, to put its case and defend its honor. Gentle, quizzical, and sprightly, he became the hero of the hearings. He made fun of McCarthy, often so cleverly that McCarthy did not realize that he was being guyed. But most of the time the viewers got the joke.

When McCarthy, baffled by Welch's composure and tactics, attempted to smear one of Welch's young assistants, the old man had, and seized hold of, the matchless opportunity this presented to show McCarthy for the character assassin that he was.

Throughout the year opinion polls showed a steady drop in support for McCarthy. The Republican National Committee told him that it would not be using his services in the fall elections. Candidates in Wisconsin and Maine who did run with McCarthy's backing were trounced.

The Army-McCarthy Hearings ended inconclusively. But in the Senate Ralph Flanders of Vermont decided that the time had come to introduce a censure resolution which condemned McCarthy for his "habitual contempt of people" and, more to the point, his contempt of the Senate. A Select Committee was set up to inquire into McCarthy's conduct and make recommendations concerning the resolution.

This was the opportunity the Democratic Minority Leader, Lyndon B. Johnson, had been patiently awaiting for several years. It had been at Johnson's prompting that the Army-McCarthy Hearings had been televised, an idea inspired by his conviction that McCarthy, with only one already well-worn card to play, could not survive prolonged public exposure. Johnson had also been very careful in choosing the three Democrats who sat on McCarthy's subcommittee and had dissuaded McCarran from claiming a seat on it. Johnson took still greater care in choosing the Democrats who sat on the Select Committee. Not one had ever spoken out publicly against McCarthy; not one had a powerful personal enemy in the Senate; not one was up for reelection in 1954. The Republican leadership made its selections employing the same Johnsonian principles.

The Select Committee recommended that McCarthy be censured on two counts: for obstructing a Senate subcommittee which had been investigating McCarthy's labyrinthine finances and for being rude to General Zwicker.

McCarthy proceeded to drive the nails into his own coffin. Given an opportunity to save himself by making an apology, he spurned it out of hand. He preferred instead to go on the offensive and suggest that the entire Senate was now under Communist influence. Why else, he demanded, would it be trying to censure him?

His admirers never lost heart or voice. More than 3,500 of the faithful convened at what the Senator liked to term "the so-called Constitution Hall." Admittance was gained by tickets printed "Admit One Anti-Communist." A body calling itself Ten Million Americans for Justice circulated petitions which in a single day netted more than a million signatures in support of McCarthy. One of the masterminds behind this massive petition was G. Racey Jordan, who spent much of his time these days traveling the country to warn of the dangers of fluoridation, revealing that this was but one more plot hatched in the Kremlin.

While the censure resolution wound its way through the Senate, McCarthy was in and out of the U.S. Navy hospital at Bethesda, Maryland. Shortly before the Christmas recess he appeared in the Senate Chamber, right arm in a sling,* to demand that his fellow Senators stop talking and get on with the censure vote.

Everett Dirksen of Illinois made one final plea for Joe, invoking the spirit of Christmas. The censure vote was passed by 76–22. Every Democrat but one voted for it; that one was John F. Kennedy. He alone proved beyond the blandishments of Lyndon Johnson who lined up the Democratic vote for censure. And Johnson broke his own long silence. He equated McCarthy's speeches with the legends scrawled on toilet walls.

The censure resolution appeared to break McCarthy's fitful spirit. His drinking grew worse, his spells in hospital longer, his appearances in the Senate or on his committees increasingly rare. When he did appear, he was usually treated as a pariah. He showed up now and again at rallies, to ask, "Who promoted Peress?" He played the stock market and lost heavily.

In May 1957, in something approaching obscurity, he died. His body was returned to Appleton, Wisconsin, for burial. He received a funeral befitting a hero, not a man in disgrace. To his followers, he had not simply arrived at man's fate; rather, the Communists had finally gotten Joe; heartbroken, he had died prematurely, his noble task unfinished, the State Department still under the Kremlin's control. McCarthy dead, McCarthyism was not yet buried.

For American Communists the first few years following the death of Stalin were not without interest. The armistice in Korea and the ensuing "thaw" in the Cold War favored by the new Soviet leadership resulted in a moderate line. The result was known sardonically as "Browderism without Browder."

For instance, the Party now offered the Catholic Church, "an out-

---

*McCarthy, being McCarthy, explained that his arm had been operated on. This came as news to the staff at Bethesda. They had been treating him for bursitis.

stretched hand . . . in the fellowship of common struggle for our mutual goal of peace, democracy and security to all." In 1954, at about the time of the McCarthy censure vote, the Party launched a glossy new publication aimed at adolescents, *New Challenge*. It combined Communist stock-in-trade (*e.g.*, articles opposing the draft) with articles such as "How a Wonderful Day Got Started" (on the origins of Mother's Day).

But the new moderation did not much impress the new Administration. In 1956 the Justice Department attempted to put the *Daily Worker* out of business. Tax liens were secured against the paper amounting to $400,000. For a newspaper with an annual deficit of $200,000, one which stayed in business only as the result of frantic fund drives every few months, one which had never shown a profit, Brownell's stroke was incomprehensible. What was more, the *Daily Worker*'s financial mainstay was not Soviet Intelligence but the CIA. It took out thousands of anonymous subscriptions each year. The CIA considered the *Daily Worker*'s survival an important part of the Cold War. So long as the paper existed it provided an increasingly skeptical public with concrete proof that the Communist menace was still in business.

The Justice Department raids on the run-down *Daily Worker* offices brought cries of alarm not only from the ACLU but also from the fervently anti-Communist Committee for Cultural Freedom, because the paper had become the sole bright spot within the CPUSA. It was the only Communist newspaper in the West, for example, which printed Khrushchev's secret speech to the 20th Party Congress in Moscow in which the crimes of Stalin were admitted and condemned. Defying the Party leadership, the paper was also unique in its criticisms of the brutal Soviet repression of the Hungarian revolt.

In 1958 the *Daily Worker* managed to frustrate the Justice Department in the courts, only to close down thanks to rifts within the Party. The Justice Department for its part was deprived of its principal weapon, the Smith Act. By late 1956 a total of 114 Communists had been convicted under its provisions. A dozen more were under indictment. But then, in the case of *Yates* v. *United States*, written materials were ruled not to be adequate evidence of incitement to illegal acts.

On the day it handed down the Yates decision the Court also handed down two other important rulings: *Watkins* v. *United States*, which ruled that it was not illegal to advocate the overthrow of the government "as an abstract principle divorced from any effort to instigate action to that end," and *Sweezy* v. *New Hampshire*, which curbed the efforts of states to harass teachers because of their beliefs. The Yates and Watkins decisions also abandoned the doctrine of "evil intent" which stemmed from the trial of the eleven CP leaders.

In *Nelson* v. *Pennsylvania* the Court struck down most of the anti-Communist legislation passed by the states, ruling that subversion was a field which Congress had preempted for Federal law. The total effect of these decisions was to gut the Smith Act. The convictions so laboriously secured were struck down on appeal. The act itself fell into disuse.

Except for the shadowboxing of the Subversive Activities Control

Board, the attempt to prosecute the Communist Party out of existence was over. And just as it had once shown that the only people it could lead astray were its own members so the Party now demonstrated that no one could do it more harm than itself. The revelations of Stalin's crimes, the dawning realization of Soviet anti-Semitism, the bloody activities in Hungary, caused thousands of people to leave the Party each year. Between early 1956 and late 1957 Party membership dropped from 22,000 to 8,000. In the next year it dropped to 3,000.

The few who remained were elderly, often unable or unwilling to pay their dues, devoid of energy, ideas, or interest. They were the Fosterite rump, with nowhere else to go. What the Federal government could not achieve in a decade of trying the Party did for it with ease. "For all intents and purposes," concluded a study of the Party, "as these lines are being written in late 1957, the American Communist Party is dead."

15
McCarthyism—An Appraisal

Citizens of the Soviet Union lived their lives at the mercy of a bureaucracy that was fearful, unimaginative, and capricious. It was dangerous to express unorthodox political views. Almost every aspect of everyday life was touched by politics, so it was easy to make a mistake and excite unwanted attention. In the Soviet Union artists and intellectuals who opposed this tyranny against the human mind and spirit were driven to expressing their true opinions obliquely—to cast their work as fairy tales, allegories, and parables.

The most striking feature of McCarthyism is the extent to which it made the United States ape nearly every repellent aspect of Soviet life. In its American form the result was heavily diluted: no slave labor camps; no mass murder; no scientific torture conducted by police doctors. Russia was a vast prison to all but the comparative few who were allowed to leave; America was not a prison except to the comparative few who were not allowed to leave. The wrong political attitudes brought not 15 years in a labor camp but 12 months in a Federal penitentiary, that is, unless you happened to be an official of the American Communist Party and were found to be reading evil literature and thinking evil thoughts—then your sentence was five years.

In the Soviet Union books were periodically rewritten to conform to the changing political climate. So were textbooks in the United States. During the 1930s the great American capitalists had been portrayed as Robber Barons, the great diplomats as imperialists. In the McCarthy era they were suddenly transformed into society's benefactors and states-men. Besides the self-censorship practiced by such worthies as Samuel Flagg Bemis of Yale and Louis Hacker of Columbia on their own published work, there was probably far more self-censorship on work not yet published. Writers kept one eye on their notes, the other on the American Legion or some similar self-appointed body. And that is how censorship also worked for the most part in the Soviet Union: writers censored themselves.

It was in the Soviet style that the only important theatrical work to attack McCarthyism, Arthur Miller's *The Crucible*, was safely set in the seventeenth century. *The Caine Mutiny Court-Martial*, a notable Broadway success based on the best-selling novel, was equally allegorical from what might be considered the opposite point of view; it was reverential toward authority, even when that authority was perversely exercised.

The film *On the Waterfront* was principally concerned with the morality of informing on others. It is not too much to say that it is a defense of the informer. Both its director, Elia Kazan, and the script-writer, Budd Schulberg, had appeared before HUAC and named names.

In the Soviet Union scientists were expected to make their findings conform to the political orthodoxy; this was not the case with all findings or with all scientists, but it did happen from time to time. And it also happened in the United States. In 1953 the National Bureau of Standards tested a battery additive called AD-X2 and pronounced it "worthless." The Secretary of Commerce, Sinclair Weeks, thereupon fired the director of the NBS, Dr. Allen Astin. The bureau's research standards were unacceptable, declared Weeks, "because they discount entirely the play of the market place." This was the capitalist analogue of Soviet research standards which discounted the play of Marxism-Leninism.

These were miserable years, in fact, for much of the scientific community. Oppenheimer's hearing was only the best known of scores, possibly hundreds, of such hearings. Whatever its good intentions, the Loyalty Security program was not conducted in a dispassionate spirit but in an atmosphere of distrust and hysteria. And on no group did the program have a more deleterious impact than on scientists. Vannevar Bush in 1954 described them as being extremely despondent. The security hearings had revealed, he believed, a deep distrust of science as a good thing and of scientists as good people.

What made McCarthyism so difficult to resist was its ability to fasten on almost anything. The color red was so terrifying that thirty-four states made it a felony to display a red flag. The Cincinnati Reds legally changed their name to the Redlegs. The Harvard Russian Club changed its name to The Slavic Society. When his horror comic empire was under attack, William Gaines decided that his critics must be Communists. The pubescent readers of his publications were soon challenged on the inside pages of their favorite comic to face up manfully to the question: "ARE YOU A RED DUPE?" This was accompanied by several hundred words on the Cold War and a few quotes from the *Daily Worker* to provide the ring of authentic Communist duplicity.

If there was something you disliked or something which threatened to cut your income, the thing to do was to denounce it as being part of the Communist conspiracy. But a prize of sorts was called for by the attempts to portray fluoridated water as a vital step in the Kremlin's master plan.

There was, for instance, a small town in Massachusetts, whose town council decided after reading of the happy results of fluoridation in Newburgh, New York, to fluoridate its own water supply. There was only perfunctory discussion; it all seemed very simple. But only days before the necessary equipment was due to be installed a pamphlet began to circulate in the town. Under the title *Americanism Bulletin* it offered twenty-five reasons why fluorine was dangerous. These ranged from the prospect of a drunken water engineer pretending to add fluorine but really adding arsenic, thus killing off the entire town, to fluorine as a cause of breast cancer, to fluoridation being "probably a plot of the world planners."

The entire town was immediately gripped by fear. At any other time such a pamphlet would have been laughed off as the work of a crank. But the temper of the times was such that it was taken seriously. At a town meeting the issue was put to a vote, and fluoridation won, narrowly. But this only sent the anti-fluoridation camp into a frenzy. They held meetings of their own to denounce fluorine as "rat poison." People drove for miles to other towns to bring back "pure" water. There were rumors that all the town's goldfish had died in their bowls. A woman who had spoken in defense of the fluoridation plan was denounced in the street as a Communist.

A secret town-wide referendum was held. This time the antifluoridationists won. Common sense and the weight of the evidence were rejected. There was a rational antifluoride case to be made. The main drawback was that there was not yet enough information on the long-term effects of fluoridated water. It might, for instance, help save the teeth of children but harm the kidneys of the elderly. Yet the debate was not conducted in rational terms; it was, instead, shrill and hysterical. In the nation at large only 7 percent of those polled in 1952 opposed fluoridation. Yet in hundreds of American communities fluoridation was rejected for no other reason than the incredible claim that it was somehow connected with Communism.

And this leads to what made McCarthyism so shameful: it was not something forced on a long-suffering people; it was something they accepted and often encouraged. In one way or another it involved millions of willing participants. To the efforts of the state, private bureaucracies added their own. Bar associations, large business corporations such as Bell Telephone and General Electric, state medical associations, private colleges, and universities—all demanded proof of loyalty (that is, conformity). Doctors, scientists, schoolteachers, engineers, professors, social workers, librarians, telephone operators, bookkeepers, actors, movie directors, radio announcers, scriptwriters, union officials, and many others were required to make positive assertions of loyalty to the state at the behest of private employers.

In the early 1950s 20 percent of the entire labor force was subjected to loyalty or security screening. An estimated 10,000 lost their jobs in the process. In all, some 20 million Americans were affected by Loyalty-Security programs. Not a single Soviet agent was ever unearthed as a result of the thousands of hearings and investigations.

Rank amateurs set themselves up in business equipped with nothing more complicated than some index cards, some stationery, a telephone, and *Appendix IX*, which was a list of 22,000 names compiled for the Dies Committee by J.B. Matthews. Supposedly only for the use of the committee, "enough copies managed to get into the hands of private anti-Communists to make it the Bible of the postwar Red-hunters." And Matthews kept this list of ostensible fellow-travelers and Communist fronters up to date. By 1952 there were 35,000 names on the revised version of *Appendix IX*.

But the reason for the pervasive character of McCarthyism was not that it was amenable to amateur Red hunting or that it could masquerade as a normal form of public protest, as in the fluoridation affair. It required no public or overt activity at all. A blind eye or a cold shoulder could do just as well. The *American Review of Soviet Medicine*, for example, was a learned journal with no political stance whatever; it consisted entirely of translations of articles which had first appeared in Soviet medical journals. It was interested in factual accounts of medical problems and procedures, the effects of drugs, developments in medical equipment, and so on. But starting in 1947, no one was willing to be seen with it. Within eighteen months of Truman's order on Loyalty-Security the *Review*, which had been mailed in plain brown wrappers during those eighteen months, was forced out of business, because its subscribers had taken fright. The destruction of a learned journal, which would have been done in a totalitarian state by fiat, was brought about in a free country by free people.

Nor was it true that the Soviets never gave anything important away in their publications. For example, the official journal of the Soviet Academy of Sciences in 1950 carried an article by one A.G. Lunts on the application of symbolic logic, or Boolean algebra, to computer circuitry. None of the Americans working on computers in the early 1950s appears to have seen this article. So for the next five years American scientists and engineers expended considerable effort on problems which Lunts had already solved.

As liberals discovered, it was not enough to move over to the center of the road to avoid the Cold War backlash against anything identified with left-of-center politics. A careless remark which criticized the prevailing order, subscription to the wrong publications, friendship with people who retained left-wing opinions, and a man's livelihood could be put in jeopardy. *The New Republic* abandoned its anticapitalist, antistatist position, yet its circulation dropped from 97,000 in 1948 to 24,000 in 1952, and it was forced to close down its New York office.

For individuals of a critical cast of mind and a sensitive nature this was a brutal time. Gentle, scholarly F.O. Matthieson, one of the ornaments of Harvard but denounced as a fellow traveler, rented a room on the twelfth floor of a Boston hotel. He wrote a brief note: "I have taken this room in order to do what I have to do. How much the state of the world has to do with the state of my mind, I do not know. But as a Christian and a Socialist, believing in international peace, I find myself terribly oppressed by the present tension." It was early spring 1950. Matthieson removed his glasses and plunged from the window.

The most impressive feature of McCarthyism was how thoroughly it permeated American life. It was less a political than a social phenomenon. McCarthy did not create it; he stumbled across it. With the instincts of a born opportunist, he provided it with a voice and a name.

It was because it went so deep in the fabric of society that McCarthyism was a source of lasting shame. The Red Scare of the Palmer era had produced far more bloodshed and far more horrifying examples of persecution. But that had been the work of a handful of officials and right-wing vigilantes. It had been a narrow, essentially political persecution. The sense of shame which attaches to McCarthyism, however, arises from the fact that in large ways or small, tens of millions of people collaborated with McCarthyism; not infrequently they denied they were doing anything of the kind.

Behind their fears was a fear of difference and an unthinking obsession with national unity. The world for which Americans felt themselves responsible was proving more dangerous, more complicated, and more intractable than they had ever expected. The confidence which stood so high during and at the end of the war could not continue indefinitely. It began to crack. In their desperation to retain the sense of unity of purpose which had been so powerful in wartime they groped toward the lowest common denominator—anti-Communism.

Behind the loyalty oath was less a fear of disloyalty than a demand for conformity—the outward and visible symbol of national unity. It was not subversion as such that was dreaded; it was heresy. Very few people genuinely believed that their neighbors or co-workers were aiding the Soviets, but they were uneasy if their neighbors or co-workers were different from them. It was not treason that was looked for; it was having the wrong attitude.

Americans struggled to defend "Americanism." But when you got down to it, this Americanism consisted of little more than the status quo. Such a frame of mind was at odds with the traditional American admiration of new ways, new beliefs, the welcome given to the novel and innovative. The conformist, timid spirit which motivated McCarthyism was a spiritual betrayal of what was best in American life—openness, generosity, optimism—and a triumph of all that was deplorable. In their hearts many people understood that. Hence the enduring legacy of shame.

How easy it was to despise Communists, who flip-flopped back and

forth with every twist in the Party line. But what can you say, for instance, about the thousands of professors at the University of California
who signed a loyalty oath they despised for no more exalted reason than a
desire to hang onto their jobs? Hundreds of thousands, possibly millions,
of free men and women crawled for the sake of comfort and convenience.
When Communists truckled to the Party line, it was, perverse though this
may seem, for the sake of what they genuinely believed was a higher truth
and a better world. Intolerance, conformity, and ultimately expediency—
these were the mainstays of McCarthyism.

The last-ditch defense of McCarthyism was that although it might result
in an occasional injustice, it was better that one man lose his job, or his
self-respect or his reputation, than that the entire nation be put at risk.
McCarthy may have gone about things in the wrong way, the argument
went, but what he was trying to do was essentially right. That argument
made sense only if the menace he attacked (scores of Communists betray-
ing their country to a foreign power from within their own government)
was a real menace, not a sham. It is evident now, as it was to those who
kept their heads at the height of the Cold War, that it was a phantom.

McCarthy was a man bent on self-destruction. It was to be expected,
moreover, that he would spend his time chasing shadows, being incapable
of substantial achievement. He stumbled across a situation not of his
making and exploited it without scruple; he could be so ruthless, I suspect, because he never fully understood what he was doing. He provided
an outlet to the pent-up rage which the New Deal, the end of isolationism,
and the setback of 1948 had provoked in the Republican Party. His forays
provided a catharsis. It was noteworthy that his strongest appeal was to
traditionally Republican voters, on traditionally Republican issues.

The issue of Communists-in-government was never very convincing to
large numbers of people. Two interlocking polls conducted in mid-1954
asked people to list political matters which troubled them. Fewer than 1
percent listed Communism. And only 8 percent rated McCarthy more
highly than Hoover or Eisenhower as the man best equipped to deal with
American Communists. This suggests the very limited political nature of
McCarthyism. The polls also showed considerable intolerance toward the
rights of Socialists and Communists to speak in public places, to hold jobs
in schools or colleges, or to have their writings placed in public libraries.
There was an attitude toward civil liberties in general which was dismaying. But this was an attitude which reflected conformism, rather than anti-
Communism. Nearly half those polled agreed that recent years had seen a
decline in free speech.

It is tempting to portray these years, roughly 1947–1955, as a period of
unrelieved intellectual darkness and moral cowardice. The result would
be graphic and easy to grasp. But although American life was badly tainted with suspicion, conformity, distrust, and petty spite, the victories of
McCarthyism were, in the end, limited victories. Honor, badly dented,
was not destroyed.

The British economist Barbara Ward and her husband found during a three-month tour of the United States in early 1954 that there was wide-spread evidence that McCarthyism had cast a pall over American life. "We found in most areas saddening proof of the harm done in neighborly relations and to the unconscious trust of local communities by irresponsible smear campaigns, by denunciations of supposed nonconformists and the exploitation of such things for political purposes," she wrote. But "it was, again and again, derived from the angry comments of American men and women pointing to this or that abuse in their own experience . . . *and denouncing it in the strongest terms."* (My italics.)

What foreign critics of the United States, and many Americans, did not notice was that while millions of people succumbed to McCarthyism, millions more rejected it completely. And they could make themselves felt.

For much of 1952 and 1953 the *Boston Post* led a campaign to have works by Communist authors or favorable to Communist ideas banned from one of that city's few prestigious public institutions, the Boston Public Library. The mayor helpfully proposed a compromise: that the works in question bear large red tags. Two of the library trustees agitated for the BPL to "clean up" its holdings. But the majority of trustees stood fast and rejected censorship in any form.

Following the Gosling affair in Pasadena, the city commissioned a survey to discover exactly what was going on in the schools and what the citizens thought needed to be done. Nearly 1,000 Pasadenans were enrolled as investigators and pollsters. The books which had been termed subversive were actually read, by informal discussion groups of concerned parents. There were scores of survey subcommittees, hundreds of meetings and discussions. One fact emerged as plain as a pikestaff—there was not a trace of subversion in the schools. Pasadena had better schools, they began to understand, than almost anyone had believed. And the taxpayers were not hostile to the school board; on the contrary, they were willing to pay handsomely for good schools and good teachers. The school system was not faultless. But it was extremely sound. And in the course of making this extensive survey, which in time involved tens of thousands of people, the wounds opened during the Gosling furor were closed.

Similarly, the upper-class suburb of Scarsdale, New York, was embroiled in dispute over books in the public library by reputed Communist sympathizers such as Howard Fast. Scarsdale was possibly the most Republican town in America, subversion-proof if ever a town was. But friends and neighbors began to snub each other because of the book issue. Town meetings became angry and poisonous. In the end, however, good sense and reason prevailed. Out of the heated debates and community involvement came a reassertion of democratic self-confidence. The disputed books stayed where they were.

The *Educational Reviewer*, a publication instrumental in the censorship of textbooks, functioned for five years. Its reviewers were on the lookout for anything "collectivist" or infused with "propaganda." But when they attacked the leading economics textbook of the postwar years, Paul Samuelson's *Economics*, on what were ideological grounds, the counterblast from the nation's economists, of all shades of opinion, was so strong that it blew the *Educational Reviewer* right off its self-erected perch.

Federal courts bowed to the prevailing winds of conformism. Yet a Federal judge in Hawaii acquitted thirty-nine longshoremen charged with contempt because they refused to answer questions from HUAC on their political beliefs.

In mid-1951 a jury in Salt Lake City, a place of thoroughgoing conservatism, awarded a $25,000 libel judgment to the National Farmers' Union because the Farm Bureau had called it "Communist-dominated." In Pennsylvania a doctor, Alexander Solosko, was discovered by a neighbor to read *The New Republic*. Before long a local feed salesman was regaling church suppers with fervent denunciations of the doctor as a Communist. Dr. Solosko sued for slander and won a $10,000 judgment from a local small-town jury.

Scientists, although harried, usually refused to be cowed. The American Association for the Advancement of Science, for example, had its own answer to the attempt to smear Edward U. Condon. In 1953, when McCarthyism was at its peak, the AAAS elected him its president.

That same year the Cabinet considered introducing a law similar to the British Official Secrets Act as part of its package of anti-Communist measures. The idea had a strong appeal. But Eisenhower "felt that the climate of American opinion at the time ruled out any attempt to put through such legislation."

It was in the fall of 1953, with people presumably terrified to speak their minds, that a group of Socialist litterateurs and scholars began publishing a radical periodical, *Dissent*. At almost the same instant I. F. Stone, one of the liveliest, most honest men ever to grace American journalism, began publishing *I. F. Stone's Weekly*. Although it was a radical newsletter of small circulation, it stayed alive in the teeth of the storm. Stone obtained a second-class mailing permit without difficulty. And he found 5,000 subscribers, the number he needed to stay in business.

Although approximately one academic in three was to some degree intimidated during the McCarthy period, by 1955 loyalty oaths were rapidly falling into disuse on American campuses. By 1956 it was possible for the students at Princeton to invite Alger Hiss to address them, and despite howls of rage from alumni, the university administration let the speech go ahead as planned.

In 1957 a genuine Russian master spy *was* eventually discovered. He called himself Rudolf Ivanovich Abel, but this was almost certainly not his real name. Abel's career and capture were of some interest. But two features were particularly remarkable: he had no contact with the American Communist Party, and instead of reviling him, most Americans seemed to have a certain sympathy for him. He had an American appeal: the solitary, dedicated man, performing an exacting and dangerous job year after year, without complaint, in the service of his country; he was brave, resourceful and intelligent. His stoical acceptance of a long prison sentence and his unassuming nature provoked admiration.

There remain only two things to be said about the Cold War as a domestic phenomenon. First, despite the excesses of word and behavior, Americans were for the most part committed to the right cause—the defense of democratic freedoms—even when they served that cause badly. Secondly, for all the deep emotions which were stirred up there was at no time a serious danger of the country's sliding into Fascist tyranny. A country with a long history of liberty will no more turn rapidly into a totalitarian state than a historic dictatorship will rapidly become a true democracy.

16
The Other-Directed Organization Man in the Gray Flannel Suit

Suburbs are as old as antiquity. The archaeologist Sir Leonard Woolley, who dug up the remains of Sumerian civilization, "found evidence of suburban developments in 'Greater Ur' beyond the built-up area—scattered buildings as far as the temple of al'Ubaid, four miles away." But postwar American suburbs were different from any that had gone before because costs were kept down, putting suburban dwellings within reach of most people. In the postwar years suburban life was democratized.

Previously, a suburb had comprised from a few score to a few hundred houses, placed in a parklike setting, shunning straight lines and uniform design. The entire point of suburban life had been the pleasure of living in a setting characterized by space, greenery, calm, and light. Such suburbs had rarely boasted more than 3,500 inhabitants. And despite the postwar boom, some of the older communities, such as Riverside, Illinois, and Bronxville, New York, did manage to keep their populations below 10,000. But the vast majority were swamped and their original charms obliterated.

The rural ideal was proclaimed in the name of many a subdivision: "Park Forest," "Pinewood," "Sweet Hollow," "Point-O-Wood," "The Ridge," "Smokerise," "Victorian Woods," "Crystal Stream." The trees had been torn down, the hollows filled in, the streams made muddy, yet their names liveth forevermore.

Fields were buried under concrete. An entire town was put up within a year, with wide streets, freshly painted houses, and, here and there, a sapling supported by a post.

Formerly a family looking for a new home would buy a lot from a developer and then find a builder to put up the house. Now developer and builder were likely to be one and the same. The new house would gleam with factory-made parts and standardized fittings. These helped to keep costs down, but at the expense of graciousness. Technically, however, the new house might be an improvement on its predecessors, with an open plan to generate a sense of spaciousness, large windows to let in plenty of light, dry-wall construction, simplified heating, and ease of cleaning.

The cheapness of many suburban developments was, of course, relative. And after 1950 the construction industry tried to avoid low-cost housing. Builders were more interested in middle- and upper-income homes, where more value could be added to each unit, a policy known as "more house for the money." The postwar had also seen the flowering of the exurbs, the belt beyond the suburbs. The exurbanites were the people who stayed on the train each night when the suburbanites got off. The areas where they lived (commonly twenty to fifty miles away from the city) had most of the characteristics of the prewar suburb but were yet more expensive, more arcadian, and more exclusive.

The tendency to build bigger, more expensive houses meant that the average house built in 1956 was 25 percent bigger and 40 percent more expensive than its 1950 counterpart. This inevitably put homeownership farther than ever beyond the grasp of low-income families. But the builders considered the policy a success. Millions of young families had moved out to the suburbs around 1950. For a veteran and his wife and baby a two-bedroom house had been acceptable. But by 1956 they needed a three-bedroom house. They were ready to move. The builders were ready to receive them.

The first suburbs had been based on a house style known loosely as the Cape Cod, on account of its steep roof. But almost everyone also wanted a picture window and to have all the rooms on one level; this was a type of house commonly found in California and was called the Ranch style. The result from 1948 to 1953 was the construction of several million Cape Cod Ranch houses. Then came a new opportunity for stylistic chaos—the split-level. This was seized with both hands.

Builders themselves were often sensitive to complaints that their subdivisions were monotonous and tasteless. Some of them began to mix basic house types so that only every fifth or sixth house repeated what had gone before. Streets began to curve. Pastel shades, light-colored bricks, expanses of stone greeted the eye. Enlightened developers attempted to coax a genuine sense of community into existence by providing schools, playgrounds, swimming pools, tennis courts, and community centers.

It is true that few suburbs ever created the tribal loyalties which were often found before the war in city neighborhoods. Yet it was not unusual for people to feel that they belonged to their suburbs and to slight the nearby city, to identify with Sherman Oaks or Shaker Heights, rather than with Los Angeles or Cleveland, for example.

Ties to the city were further weakened, and those to the suburb to that extent strengthened, by the advent of the suburban shopping center. A few pioneering centers had been built before the war, like Country Club

Plaza in Kansas City, Missouri. But these were experiments. The shopping center as a familiar, taken-for-granted institution dates from the late 1940s and early 1950s.

To European architects such as Victor Gruen the suburban shopping center was a twentieth-century agora, a new form of the European city square, yet something uniquely American. It offered a counterweight to the formlessness of suburban life by offering a community core. The ideal center, Gruen urged, would contain more than stores; it would have the offices of doctors and dentists, gymnasiums, auditoriums, restaurants, churches, movie theaters, and playgrounds.

Much of the pioneering work done on such centers in the postwar took place near Detroit, at the Eastland and Northland centers. To help shoppers find their cars, the parking lots were named after animals (it is easier to remember a giraffe than a number). The principal tenant at the two centers was the department store J. L. Hudson. And the company was so enlightened in its approach that it declined to spoil the overall architectural effect by putting its name on its buildings.

The first generation of shopping centers provided architects and planners with a variety of challenges. Some of their solutions were highly ingenious. Service areas were made almost invisible to the naked eye. Traffic was controlled almost subliminally. Money was coaxed from pockets by electronic wizardry, by changing the balance of positive ions in the air—an effect which makes people more active; in a shopping center the main activity is spending money.

Shopping center developers were often patrons of modern art. They also tended to favor fountains. Many provided gardens. The shopping center also played a role in helping round out the externals of suburban living, even though they hardly ever became important centers of cultural activity.

In time, as the tracts filled up, people began to look beyond the immediate satisfactions offered by a roof, a lawn, and a plate glass window. "At first they advertised Park Forest as housing," wrote William H. Whyte, Jr. "Now they began advertising happiness."

There was a strong element of self-selection in these early postwar suburbs, self-selection by race, age, status, military service, and family size. Most of the families were young, white, and on their way up from a lower-middle-class job. And the blue-collar workers among them were not, outwardly, very different.

By the early 1950s suburbia was usually considered classless. That is, most people assumed that it was all of one class. For several decades there had been a figure dear to American hearts called the Common Man. In a society which had classes but hated to admit it, the Common Man was a way of referring to the majority of people without drawing attention to the fact that they were lower class. But if now everyone was middle class, America had in its own way achieved the Marxist ideal of a one-class society; which means in effect a class*less* society.

Thanks to the redistribution of income achieved in recent years by union wage demands on one side and the progressive income tax on the other, the peaks had been eroded and the valleys filled in. The consumer society had leveled tastes and advertising had encouraged the lower classes to demand the goods long enjoyed by those above them. The middle class set the tone of national life: the schools were in the hands of middle-class teachers, molding the next generation of citizens and consumers; the middle class took the lead in politics; the media were overwhelmingly middle class in outlook and standards. The middle class, went the current belief, enjoyed not only superiority of numbers but a natural superiority of manner.

Because the lines were becoming blurred, it was becoming hard to think clearly about class or to go on believing that classes still existed. There was the rise of new occupations to contend with. Where did a computer programmer fit into the old ranking of occupations? Old jobs were also taking on new names, designed to uplift but more likely to confuse— "supply specialist" for stock clerk, "maintenance engineer" for janitor.

But comforting mythology to one side, at least half the population remained by every objective criterion working class as that expression has been traditionally understood. Skilled, semiskilled, and unskilled workers, paid wages, not salaries, constituted more than half the working population in the 1950s, and they well knew their place. When asked if they were middle, upper, or lower class, a majority of respondents said they were middle class. But when asked if they were upper, middle, or *working* class, more than half put themselves in the last category.

Different scholars discerned different numbers of classes. W. Lloyd Warner found six; Richard Centers found four; August Hollingshead found five. But what these various studies showed beyond any question was that there were really two middle classes and two working classes. A bank manager is a member of a different class from a mere bookkeeper; a skilled diemaker lives a very different life from an unskilled bootblack. And a major study conducted in Chicago in the 1950s showed that two-thirds of that city's population was not middle class by any stretch of the imagination; this finding was probably true of most big cities.

Although the postwar saw a remarkable rise in white-collar employment there was never any shortage of dirty, menial work to be done, and in absolute terms there were more blue-collar workers in the late 1950s than in the late 1940s. The percentage of the work force engaged in manual labor actually rose by 1 percent.

Where class was involved, the work done was the bottom line. It was comforting to believe that "if the worker earns like the middle class, votes like the middle class, dresses like the middle class, dreams like the middle class, then he ceases to exist as a worker. But there is one thing the worker doesn't do like the middle class: he works like a worker." And that nearly always meant work which was dull, dirty, and disesteemed.

Class reached down into childhood, so that children quickly learned their place, and everyone else's, in the schools, organizations for the young, patterns of dating, sexual behavior, and leisure activities. But unlike other nations (notably the British), Americans had classes without choking on class antagonisms. "Like Molière's M. Jourdain who had been using prose without knowing it, Americans live class in the same kind of ignorance." And, as C. Wright Mills remarked, class consciousness was not felt everywhere with equal force: "It is most apparent in the upper class."

Among the lower half of the population class consciousness was less sharp than it had been in the 1930s. And this was despite the fact that the characteristic sorrows of working-class life—economic insecurity, sexual promiscuity, high levels of drunkenness, family breakup, mental illness, and illegitimacy—endured. But they were made more bearable by the sustained postwar prosperity which brought a dramatic improvement in living standards for most of the working class. Before 1939 to be working class was by definition to be poor. But now a range of incomes, from affluence to near starvation, had developed among American workers.

The war years had seen the only substantial redistribution of income in American history. Income shares remained largely static after 1945. But the large increase in real wages and fringe benefits which set in around 1951 brought a taste of security and comfort to tens of millions of working-class families for the first time—health insurance; paid vacations; plenty to eat; a decent car; good furniture; a trailer; a savings account. Young, ambitious working-class couples rapidly acquired the trappings of middle-class life, while inwardly retaining their working-class identity. And for those who wanted to work their way up the status and class ladders there were opportunities to do so.

Ever since the First World War there had been powerful structural forces promoting social mobility—the rapid increase in white-collar clerical jobs; the difference in the birthrate between social classes; the emergence of new occupations; the drop in the number of inheritable jobs; the easing of guildlike restrictions on access to skilled jobs. By the principal index of social mobility—a shift from manual to nonmanual work—opportunity abounded.

Yet mobility also means that some people slip downward. One-third of the sons of professional, proprietarial, and managerial men spent their lives as blue-collar workers.

Although Americans liked to believe that the United States was unique in the opportunity it provided for people to rise, mobility rates were much the same for all industrialized countries. In each generation one-third of sons stood higher on the social scale than their fathers, while one-fourth stood lower. The rest were on a par with daddy.

Even though the rise in the number of white-collar jobs opened up a wide range of new opportunities, the reality was often more disappointing than the raw figures would suggest. Most of these clerical jobs were filled by women, working for low wages. Factories were meanwhile coming to resemble offices in their layout, just as offices were beginning to resemble factories. Vance Packard observed, "Many white-collared office workers—billing clerks, key-punch operators—are actually machine attendants; manual workers in any honest nomenclature." The work called not

for a high level of skills or intelligence, but for a high tolerance of tedium.
Many of the gains were illusory or self-delusory. And the class barrier which had long been the hardest to cross—between the lower and the upper middle classes—was becoming formidable. The ticket across was now a college degree. Chairmen of the boards of big business who had come up from being messenger boys and machinists were, in the 1950s, the last of their kind.

Yet the dream of individual business success would not disappear. Ironically, such dreams were cherished less among the lower middle class, who tended to view such prospects realistically, than among the working class. The middle-class aspirant was likely to want to break into one of the learned professions; his working-class counterpart was likely to want to start his own business. But most workers accepted that the odds were against them and, whatever their hopes to the contrary, against their children as well.

Behind the enduring dream of individual success stood a staunch belief in social mobility as being in itself a social good. It seemed positive in a Darwinian way. Melvin Tumin, however, noted four undesirable social consequences of the mobility ladder: social fragmentation—the arrivistes were resented by those already there, while those who tried to rise and failed were filled with resentment, all of which drew the class lines more sharply; work lost its dignity—all that mattered was money, the pursuit of which became the chief end in life, and that in turn demeaned life itself; political reaction—those who succeeded became unyielding defenders of the status quo, believing (wrongly) that because it worked for them, it would work for everyone else; and the diffusion of insecurity—with so many going up and so many coming down, it became impossible for people to believe in unchanging values and identities, so they surrendered to status anxieties and fashionable beliefs.

Anxieties over status gained added force from the frequency with which people moved. A reporter returning to the United States from abroad was struck by it. "Does anyone stay put anymore?" he wondered. "In Odessa, Texas, we found that out of 70 high school students 66 were born some place else; most of them had lived in at least four different homes. In Greenville, Mississippi, we were invited to a farewell party for a young couple moving to Walla Walla, Washington. Only two of the 16 people present could call Greenville their home town."

To the three currents of migration which had prevailed during the Depression (from east to west, south to north, country to city) the postwar had brought a fourth, from city to suburb. Each year one-fifth of the population moved house. But most did not move far. Fewer than 3 percent moved to another state. Most did not even move to another county. And the few who did cross state and county lines were often students who left home to go to college, young men entering the armed forces, and people moving fewer than twenty-five miles, say from the Bronx to Teaneck, New Jersey. The one-in-five figure was often adduced to suggest that Americans were rootless. It showed nothing of the kind.

But all this shifting about did make expressions of status more important than they would have been otherwise. Status was itself an idea Americans wore more easily than the idea of class; talking about class seemed radical, almost un-American. But status was somehow more democratic; it could be acquired and altered, whereas class was in large part inherited and seemed unalterable.

A wide range of goods and services was provided less as goods and services than as a form of reassurance—that is, as status symbols. Within large corporations the windows, the desks, the carpets, the doors, the secretaries, and the toilets were assigned with a devout attention to rank which seemed natural in the court of Louis XIV but sorted oddly with the manufacture of turbines or paper towels. For instance, mahogany desks outranked walnut, "and walnut outranks oak. The man who is entitled to wall-to-wall carpeting is likely to have a water carafe. . . : An executive with a two-pen desk set clearly outranks a man with a one-pen set. At one broadcasting company, executives above a certain rank, and only they, are entitled to electric typewriters for their secretaries."

There was also the Cadillac Phenomenon. Before the war Cadillacs had cost four times the price of the average car. By the mid-1950s they were less than twice the price of the average car, and the more available they became, the more the demand for them increased. The Cadillac had become *the* car for the arriviste and was blatantly advertised as such. There was a waiting list, which grew steadily longer. Each year 150,000 Cadillacs were made, and 90,000 orders went unfilled. Cadillac advertisements were considered crass by the fastidious, but they probably drove Jaguars, Mercedes, or Rolls-Royces anyway.*

Nor was there any way of getting out of the status race at home. In upper-middle-class suburbs the value of a house could often be derived simply by calculating the distance to the country club. A house which stood a good chance of having a golf ball come crashing through the picture window was a home to be coveted.

To add to their snob appeal many houses were advertised in Franglais. One Florida builder advertised entirely in French, except for the price. Many a new homeowner craved antiques, not from a love of beauty but from a love of snobbish display. It was not unknown for these passions to extend to portraits of distinguished-looking strangers, dressed in period clothing and dead a century or two, to be passed off unblushingly as direct and eminent ancestors.

There was a boom in private clubs, reflecting general prosperity, a revived interest in golf, and the suburban desire to maintain, or to taste, distinctions of class and status. "The classic situation is for a city to have two or three country clubs: top status for the elite, middle class for the strivers and the minority club for the Jews." As a rule the top clubs—e.g., the Burlingame in San Francisco, the Country Club in Brookline, Massa-

---

*Inevitably, Cadillacs were nowhere more conspicuous than in Texas. This was said to have given rise to the following exchange: "Y'hear Zeke got a new car?" "Nope. What kind he get?" "Dark blue."

chusetts—spurned golf tournaments, banned business discussions, disdained to publish membership lists, served plain food, and were at pains to avoid display. In all these matters the middle-class clubs did exactly the opposite.

As country club membership became less exclusive, gin rummy displaced bridge as the most popular card game in the clubhouse. The high tide of togetherness made the country club a place for the family and discouraged hopes of sexual adventure as an off-course pursuit. All the while the number of courses opening each year failed to keep pace with the rising tide of new golfers arriving at the links.

In the end, although people felt more at ease with ideas of status than with ideas of class, the sum of someone's status symbols gave you a very accurate account of their class. And it was class which remained the bony structure of American society. High status and high class nearly always went together anyway because although raw naked money had a vulgar side, high status never came cheap.

But class distinctions showed up even in humble pleasures. Out in the suburbs, where the middle-class norm was assumed to prevail, the professionals were more likely to attend plays and concerts than managers and supervisors, who were in turn more likely to play golf.

There were also suburbs and suburbs. In some the homes cost $50,000 or more. In these, the teachers, policemen, and other essential workers were imported from somewhere else. There were also tracts where the homes cost less than $12,000. And while the middle-class aura clung to suburbia, as the 1950s wore on, it became the skilled and semiskilled workers who moved in the largest numbers into suburban subdivisions.

There was a common belief that when these working-class families did make the move to suburbia, they somehow became middle-class in their values. But this was exaggerated. There was no marked increase in church attendance in working-class suburbs, these families did not start to vote Republican, they did not take a permissive attitude toward child rearing, and they did not begin to entertain on a larger scale, even though they had acquired middle-class comforts. The wives were likely to be more status-conscious than the husbands, but the husbands did not surrender the overt working-class domination over women for middle-class attempts at parity. As incomes rose, so did living standards. But the main differences of class did not change markedly by the move out to suburbia.

There was a tendency, however, in working-class suburbs, as in middle-class suburbs, for a matriarchy to set the tone of affairs. This came about by default. The men played hardly any part in the daily life of the community. They did little more than sleep when they were there. The community, such as it was, centered on the women. If within the family the women were also likely to prevail (far more true among the middle than among the working class), this was not because the women were viragoes but because the men were absent.

There was also an undercurrent of restlessness among American women in the 1950s. It was encouraged by the rapid increase in economic independence as more and more married women went to work. It was further encouraged by rising levels of education and better understanding of birth control. The possibility of being something other than breeders was for the first time presented to the majority of women. But this groundswell of discontentment could find few outlets in the 1950s. Indeed, it was hard to express precisely what was wrong.

There was also a growing disenchantment with suburban life, and much of the hostility this inspired was directed against the most obvious target—suburban women. They were informed that they were domineering, their children spoiled, and their husbands emasculated.

But these women were more to be pitied than censured. The frequent moving forced on families in which the husband was employed by a large corporation was harder for the wife and children to bear than it was for the man. He was moving within the same company; a ready-made set of co-workers, and sometimes old friends, awaited him. But the wife's milieu, the neighborhood, was utterly new; so was the children's milieu, the school. The husband's life had continuity; the wife's was fragmented. He was surrounded by people; she was alone for much of the day. The husband could develop deep roots within his profession; it was the wife who bore the burdens of transience.

Not surprisingly, business began to take a serious interest in the wives of managers and junior executives. The corporations wanted to see their executives of the future married to women who were adaptable, gregarious, and willing to accept the fact that their husbands belonged to the corporation. American women proved remarkably adaptable. The wives of management could, like their husbands, get along with almost anyone. They possessed a vital asset termed "group-mindedness."

Yet beneath the bland, harmonious surface there were some very strong emotions being held in check, especially when a man was moving up the corporate ladder faster than the others in his age-group. His wife and often his children were forced to abandon people they had become accustomed to calling their friends. And there was the resentment, however politely veiled, of those left behind.

Wives were meant to be ego massagers and sounding boards, and there were some heroic performers among them. But they were also often bored to distraction by the manufacturing of widgets and the merchandising of rubber ducks. Suppressed boredom was another source of tension.

There was the nagging awareness that the company was pushing their husbands to success or failure; either possibility held out a better-than-average chance of heart disease, ulcers, a nervous breakdown, possibly a premature death. Yet wives could not help being ambitious for their husbands.

Assuming that her husband did succeed, there was a fair chance that not only would he leave his old friends behind but he would leave her behind, too. "The socially retarded wife has become the great sorrow of the corporation, and partly its responsibility," wrote William H. Whyte, Jr. The socially retarded wife was likely to reach for the bottle or the tranquilizers. Given all these strains and pressures, it does not seem remarkable that in Bergen County, New Jersey, a practicing psychiatrist found that a third of his patients were upper-middle-class women in their presumed prime of life, aged twenty-five to forty-five.

Companies began to take a very close look at the wives of their management applicants. The young wife was judged by such matters as what she made for breakfast, how much she drank, and the cut of her clothes. By the mid-1950s many business corporations were trying to involve the wives in company activities, to create a sense of identity, of being part of "the IBM family" and the like. There were company swimming pools, golf courses, picnic grounds, and dinners where, thanks to the company's kindness, "togetherness" might be pursued. And in the end, unable to fight or flee the corporation, most women came to accept it, like the galley slaves who were taught to kiss their chains.

Life for working-class women was still more onerous. Their daily life was more rigidly fixed than that of middle-class women. When they were asked to describe their lives, the word most often used was "dull." Even their weekends—a break which middle-class women looked forward to—were dull. The white working-class wife spent her day in a round of drudgery, was insecure and lonely, succumbed to wild shifts in emotion, and looked upon the world at large and her husband with deep apprehension, for she felt that she had no control over either and any assertiveness on her part would lead to rejection. To her husband she was an object for sexual gratification, rather than a person desired out of love. She was constantly worried about money and had no money to call her own. Thinking was arduous, and imagination something best left to children. The extent of her ambition was to have a house, a husband, and two or three children. She was sympathetic toward those in trouble or beaten down by life; she was passive, sentimental, kind, and well-meaning; she had an addiction to television and women's magazines; she believed that what was new was invariably better than what was old; and her tastes reflected the combined powers of advertising and natural banality.

The fact that marriages, whether in the working or the middle class, usually survived these disappointments and limitations is something to be marveled at. But the cost was undoubtedly high. When Irwin Shaw's *Lucy Crown* and John O'Hara's *Ten North Frederick* both stood high on best-seller lists in the spring of 1956, Max Lerner was moved to reflect: "They are both symptoms of the obsession of contemporary American novelists with the theme of marriage as a kind of hell." And divorce rates stayed high after reaching their peak in 1947. By the mid-1950s there was one divorce each year for every four marriages; there were perhaps as many cases again of desertion ("the poor man's divorce"). The usual result of divorce, desertion, or separation was a drop in living standards for both parties and a rise in the number of families headed by women.

While women were being accused, falsely in my view, of becoming masculine, men were undoubtedly drifting away from traditional externals of masculine display. Sales of cosmetics for men continued to soar.

Men began spending as much money on haircuts as women spent at the beauty parlor—that is, $500 million in 1956. A barber was no longer a mere cutter of hair; he was now a "hairstylist." Until about 1950 a man had his hair cut short or regular, assuming he was a regular guy. But the most popular style five years later was the Crew Cut. There were variations on the theme, but the end result was unfailingly meant to be a youthful look regardless of age. "The Crew Cut is the big brother of what was once ridiculed as a G.I. haircut," wrote Herbert Mitgang, "but was carried into civilian life, with a dash of nostalgia, by millions of now-graying men." Second in popularity was the Butch, one step down from a Crew Cut but one step up from a shaved head. For the more rakish there was the Detroit, short on top, but with full length at the sides and back, and there was the Madison Avenue, short everywhere but neatly parted. Styling was in heavy demand from men under the age of forty-five. Older, unregenerate types continued to walk into the barbershop and demand "a haircut."

As women went off to work and the servant shortage showed no sign of abating, a new servant class arose—husbands. They cooked, cleaned, did the laundry, and performed a variety of household chores their grandfathers knew nothing about. With the growth of the middle class there was a spreading of casual, democratic middle-class domestic arrangements. And with men doing so much more around the house it is possible that the real force behind the extraordinary postwar demand for laborsaving appliances came less from wives than from husbands. A woman did not have to tell her husband how useful a dishwasher or a mixer would be. He already knew.

To a visiting British anthropologist it appeared that America, while retaining the appearance of a patriarchy, had in fact become matriarchal. The mother stood for kindness and freedom. It was mother who held the family together. In films, usually the women were the strong characters; the men, unless they were private detectives, were likely to be amiable incompetents. At school, most of the teachers were women. The moral universe of children was shaped mainly by women, with the result, it was said, that Americans of both sexes grew up with "feminine" consciences and confused emotion regarding sex differences and sexual behavior. The men were passive and sensitive; this was presumably bad for them and worse for the women.

Ever since the war years, when Philip Wylie had vilified "Momism" in *A Generation of Vipers*, American women had received a bad press.* Yet they were really no better and no worse than American men. And if the essential element of the supposedly "feminine" conscience is a close awareness of other people's feelings, it is an odd "fault" to condemn.

---

*There was a wartime jingle which cautioned Army officers from risking attacks where casualties might be high:

American soldiers are not like any others,
Because only American boys have mothers.

A Yale professor, Stanley Williams, on an exchange year at the University of Uppsala in the early 1950s, found that he could draw an attentive audience of thirty Swedes to his lectures on American literature. His wife lecturing in a nearby hall about the American kitchen drew an equally fascinated audience of 300. In the 1950s the glory of the American home was its kitchen.

Before 1945 most kitchens had been small antiseptic cubicles, except in upper-middle-class homes, which often had a full-time, live-in servant. But as houses grew bigger following the war, the kitchen grew rapidly. Some house designs were based chiefly on a colorful, spacious, laborsaving kitchen. The appeal of kitchens could not have been greater because this was the one place where the entire family could be expected to be gathered regularly.

The sale of kitchen furniture rose strongly every year. In the first postwar decade appliance sales increased by 1,000 percent. Modern kitchens virtually eliminated stooping and stretching. Water at the desired temperature came from a single faucet. As they became more useful, kitchens also tended to be more attractively decorated.

The object of all this attention was ostensibly the preparation of food. But in this regard the picture is very mixed. Eating was becoming both better and worse. The middle ground was contracting. Junk and convenience foods (bolstered with vitamin pills; a tacit admission that they were not eating properly) slid down more and more throats in larger and larger quantities every year. At the same time there were millions of people who began to take a serious interest in food—food that looked good, tasted good, and was good for them. These millions discovered that eating has an artistic side.

Cookbooks, meanwhile, went from being a minor to being a major branch of publishing. Television cookery programs draw huge audiences of the faithful, including some who did not cook but had an interest in eating. Among some zealots cooking became a cult; among others it became an outlet for a highly competitive spirit.

Behind the new fascination with cooking there was, at least in part, a rejection of the contemporary emphasis on convenience and standardization. There was also something ironic in the preparation of time-consuming dishes in a kitchen designed principally to save time. The preferred style of cooking among serious cooks was French—sort of. But German, Mexican, Chinese, Italian, Greek, and Jewish were also explored.

"You might also say," Eric Larrabee noted, "that for many *not* eating has become a hobby." One of the manifestations of the postwar food obsession was dieting. There were certainly many more diets available than there were national or regional cuisines.

To those who found food a bore and a chore their best friend was the deepfreeze. Until the 1940s deepfreeze lockers were rented for a dollar or two a month. After the war the price of a deepfreeze dropped to around $300. Millions were sold each year. They ruined the taste and texture of meat, fruit, and vegetables by forming large ice crystals inside them. But most people appeared not to notice as they tucked into the soggy result. And by the 1950s the deepfreeze business held the whip hand over much of American agriculture. Soils were specially tailored for crops which were scheduled to be frozen. The biggest frozen food company, Birdseye, laid down restrictions on the fertilizers to be used and the crop strains to be planted, because some strains froze more easily than others. The pea crop was almost entirely controlled by the frozen food companies, as was true of most of the bean crop.

Instant coffee, made by processes which removed nearly all the aromatic oils which give coffee taste and body, was another great success. So, too, was the frozen chicken, full of water and with the texture of wet cardboard.

The same blandness spilled over into drink. Until the 1940s most liquor drinkers preferred straight whiskey. By the 1950s blends were preferred. Scotch remained the high-status whiskey, yet the more esteemed blends tended to be the lighter varieties. Dark rum was drunk only by eccentrics; smart people drank the light, insipid varieties. These were further deprived of what little taste they possessed by a large infusion of sweet, sticky Coca-Cola. There was an increase in sales of vodka that was astonishing. Before 1946 few Americans had ever drunk vodka. By 1956 it was ubiquitous. Its appeal, like that of the light rums, was that it did not have a strong taste, but the desired effect was in no way diminished.

This widespread acceptance of blandness reflected an underlying absence of taste combined with a longing to appear to have taste in abundance. The result was a pursuit of mere stylishness of the most fleeting kind. Preferences abounded, based on nothing more than momentary impulse and permanent status anxieties. But taste, based on education and thought, was as rare as ever. The fundamental lack of self-assurance made itself most plainly evident in people's homes. A generation earlier it was only the upper and upper middle classes which employed interior decorators. By the 1950s interior decoration was an accepted, ordinary middle-class service. It was ideal for people who had acquired money and leisure faster than they were acquiring a sense of color, line, and proportion. It was a service essential to people who were unsure of themselves and defensive about it. Hiring someone else to choose your carpets and rearrange your furniture appealed, moreover, to the modern penchant for self-improvement without your actually going to a lot of trouble. The usual result was something impersonal, neutral, without idiosyncrasy or strong effects, yet it was also likely to offer the benefits of convenience, simplicity, and utility.

The same blandness appeared to extend to social relations. The object of conversation was agreement, not thought or the play of wit. Contradiction was considered in bad taste. "The motive of curiosity about ideas, the play of the mind, is not accounted a social possibility. But subversion is," remarked Jacques Barzun.

This blandness, eschewing strong preferences, avoiding sharp differences of belief, was part of the tepid lake of conformity which appeared to seep in everywhere. There were communities where simply to wear a beard was to excite suspicion; a bearded stranger would be asked by the local police for identification.

Paradoxically, Americans were not complacent about conformity. It troubled them deeply. No society can exist without conformity in many matters, large and small. To be much the same as other people was not a new way of living. But what was new was the frequency with which people complained that perhaps it had gone too far. Almost no one defended it. No one liked to be accused of it, even if they had to admit that it was true. Even the *Reader's Digest* ran an article critical of conformity.

The loss of domestic help gave encouragement to the trend of informality which had emerged during the war. And the influence of the California way of life, with its emphasis on the out-of-doors, provided a further push in that direction. The patio and the backyard barbecue became the hub of social life for much of the year.

Television drew people away from many of their prewar leisure activities, but there was one notably resistant diversion—cardplaying. Five times as many decks were sold in 1950 than had been sold before the First World War. Two nonfiction best-sellers in a single year concerned canasta ("the Argentine rummy game"). It was claimed that cardplaying retained its appeal in this bland, conformist time because it offered face-to-face competition without the courting of personal hostility; there was excitement without risk. But mainly it appeared to provide a chance for people to get together at a time when traditional small groups (sewing circles, book discussion groups, etc.) were in decline.

In this fabled "nation of joiners" two adults out of three did not join anything, and the most common voluntary associations were not social organizations but professional bodies. Besides, the most avid joiners were not the WASPs, who set the tone of national life, but Jews and Catholics.

Most people enjoyed some solitary pursuit, such as fishing, and this was probably the most popular masculine activity away from the home. At home, there was an avidity for do-it-yourself not seen since frontier days. Modern houses were built so as to encourage additions—attics, carports, garages, patios, swimming pools, barbecue pits, extra bedrooms, a workshop. They simply cried out to be built. And built they were. Before the war few men had ever painted their own homes. In the 1950s two-thirds of all the house paint sold was bought by the amateur house painter. Roughly 60 percent of all wallpaper was put up by amateur paperhangers. Military service or high school "shop" provided much of the male population with the rudimentary skills demanded of the basic tools. New tools also helped the budding D-I-Y artist: rollers instead of brushes; self-adhesive tiles; quick-drying, nonsmelling paints. And there were millions of women who were happy to lend a hand; after working in wartime defense plants, they were not daunted by working with tools. By 1956 D-I-Y was a $6 billion-a-year business, ten times what it had been in the 1930s. Rare was the suburban home these days that was ever actually finished.

There was a comparable, and possibly more lucrative, boom in arts and crafts, from painting to pottery, needlepoint to flower arranging. And in the suburbs, gardening became *de rigueur*. One sociologist found that it had "all kinds of linkage to the status structure. People may garden because they feel they have to. . . . As one overcommitted suburban housewife finally admitted: 'I really hate gardening; we both do. My husband never plays golf anymore and we do nothing all weekend but work in the garden. I mean work!' " Not all suburbs were like this, but doubtless there were many where it had taken root. And the visiting sociologist noted, "A sloppy and inept garden is *visible.*"

When the suburban family was not barbecuing, cardplaying, painting, hammering, or gardening, there was time and attention left over to be lavished on pets. America had as many dogs, cats, and pet birds as voters, to say nothing of the 600 million tropical fish in captivity in the United States in 1957. They were sold by 3,000 shops; 3,000 pet hospitals looked after them. There were fashions in pets as in every other diversion, and the mid-1950s saw a craze for owning poodles. This did wonders for pet beauty parlors. Pets had become a $3 billion-a-year business. The national capital of petdom was Beverly Hills, which boasted a dog for every man, woman, and child. If you included cats, there were considerably more pets in Beverly Hills than there were people.

It was inevitable that the rising tides of income and leisure would set one of the greatest seagoing nations in history to messing about in boats on an unprecedented scale. From 1947 onward there was a boom in marinas; they were built at the rate of 1,000 a year. And each year they grew bigger and more expensive. The cost of boats was brought within the reach of most families, thanks partly to the use of new materials such as fiberglass and the popularity of build-your-own-boat kits. By 1957 as many outboard motors were sold each year as had been sold throughout the 1930s. And the lure of the water washed across class boundaries. Outboards were most popular among working-class families; the middle and upper classes preferred to sail.

With people spending so much time in the open, dress became increasingly casual. The sale of slacks and sports coats rose dramatically. The 1950s also brought Bermuda shorts. Sales of short-sleeve sports shirts overtook the sale of long-sleeve white dress shirts. When people did go formal these days, they went the whole way; sales and rentals of formal wear rose. There was something of a totemic appeal to the charcoal gray business suit. This drab, inelegant garment was worn with a somber tie and heavy wing-tip shoes. It was so popular among the upper middle class that it became in effect a uniform. Thus, in men's clothing there was both a movement toward formality and a movement toward informality. Once again the middle ground contracted.

The postwar prosperity which financed these changes in styles of leisure and dress was sustained by the insatiable appetite of American consumers, whose appetites were whetted by advertising, status anxieties, and an ordinary love of comfort. It seemed they would buy almost anything. Yet there was really a "standard package" of middle-class consumer goods, David Riesman noticed, and these goods were to be found in the homes of the middle class wherever they lived. Their children were reared to be avid consumers of the same goods, and the result was a sameness of styles and goods which overset regional and local variety.

Behind the eagerness to buy stood a willingness to borrow. And it was not only the middle class that borrowed heavily. William Attwood, who came back to the United States in 1955 after nine years in Europe, overheard a counterman in Louisiana complaining. "He had a 1955 car, TV and hi-fi, and his wife had just bought a new deepfreeze. 'But if I had to pay cash,' he complained, 'I couldn't buy a carton of cigarettes.' "

Many a family of proud homeowners had only $1,000 or so of equity in the home they "owned." People moved house so often that the real estate business was not so much selling property as providing a complicated housing service which gave clients the comforting illusion of belonging to a stable, property-owning class. Most houses being built in the mid-1950s were not being constructed to last a lifetime, *i.e.*, sixty to seventy-five years, but to last for twenty-five to thirty-five years. They were made for rapid depreciation and fast turnover.

Modern apartments were even more flimsily built. They transmitted sound from one unit to another as easily as dogs pass fleas. Not only were walls thinner than ever, but ceilings were lower, furniture was lighter, cushions, carpets, and drapes less sound-absorbent than before, and the sound of television sets boomed out all day and far into the night. Yet these flimsy dwellings, whether apartments or houses, made sure that the demand for credit would remain high for a long time to come because no one buying one of these was buying a home for life.

Money, in fact, appears to have been the principal obsession of postwar life. Many people, possibly the majority of adult men, spent far more time thinking about money than about their families, their work, or their sex lives. The more people earned, the more desperate the money obsession was likely to become. *Harper's* in July 1952 carried a poignant article called "Going Broke on $10,000 a Year." The author hid behind the pseudonym Jay Taylor. He was earning what amounted to three times the average income.

At first glance, Jay Taylor was well-off and could afford to live much as he pleased. And yet, he said, "I am forced to live by standards which I did not set, cannot afford and must adhere to under a code as rigid as that of Moses." He was expected to live in an expensive house, wear expensive clothes, entertain lavishly, make generous donations to private charities, pay premium prices to the doctor and dentist, and make sure that his wife dressed well. Should he fail to play his allotted part in life's drama, people would notice; he would lose his chance of promotion at work; and by the standards of his family, his friends, and ultimately himself, he would be counted one of life's failures. The brunt of this Mosaic code was borne by the Taylor children. They were dressed at the thrift shop, ate a lot of hamburgers and hot dogs, and played with secondhand toys. When not feeding filet and lobster to others Mr. and Mrs. Taylor lived on spaghetti. He did not run a car, could not afford to drink for pleasure, and had no savings. Each year he slid a little deeper into debt.

During his extended sojourn at Park Forest, Illinois, William H. Whyte, Jr., noticed the same phenomenon—an outward and visible show of affluence, an inward, invisible shortage of hard cash. And Bruce Bliven, visiting Anaheim, California, in 1956, to see the newly opened Disneyland, also found that most of the people he met lived comfortably but really did not own very much.

As the Taylors and millions of other young suburban families found, they enjoyed the comforting illusion of freedom. Thanks to the high level of employment, they could try to make more money by sending their wives to work. Thanks to the easy availability of birth control information and material, they could have more children, or not have any. If they wished to forsake extra money and children, they could enjoy more leisure time together. Outwardly at least, suburban families were free to choose the life-style which suited them best. But the pressures of conformity, the suspicion of anything genuinely different, the Mosaic code involved in working for a large corporation, the lack of ready cash—all made it unlikely that they would do so.

Besides, the ideal of the suburban family was not uniqueness but "togetherness." The term had been around for decades. But it was revived by *McCall's* in 1950. It soon became part of everyday speech. It conjured up impressions of family harmony, and personal satisfaction. But in search of a definition *McCall's* ran a contest, which drew tens of thousands of entries, and failed to find one.

As reconstructed from advertisements, the typical American of the 1950s, an eminent historian discovered, lived a nightmarish existence. He was assailed by constant anxiety. He was fundamentally dishonest. And he was as shallow as a pauper's grave. "He read books to make conversation, listened to music to establish his social position, chose his clothes for the impression they would make on his business associates, entertained his friends in order to get ahead, and held the affection of his wife and children only by continuous bribery." The historian would have preferred to dismiss this portrait as a fantasy, but advertising these days was said to be based on very reliable surveys of human behavior. "Yet if their analysis was correct, the American people were decadent and depraved."

The picture was deliberately overdrawn. It nevertheless touched a sore point. Tens of millions of Americans went through the 1950s feeling vaguely dissatisfied with their private lives. It was a dissatisfaction made harder to bear by the hopes which people had clung to so fiercely during the war—the hopes of a new age in the postwar, an age in which life would take on a new meaning and be filled with creative satisfaction. Peace, men and women believed, would be wonderful.

"But was this, at last, the real life to which I had been looking forward since childhood?" wondered John Keats. "To live in a barracks instead of a town and be a function instead of a man? Such apparently was the fate of millions of my generation who . . . returned to an America of mass housing, mass markets, massive corporations, massive government, mass media and massive boredom."

That archetypal figure of the new age, *The Man in the Gray Flannel Suit*, who dominated the best-seller lists of 1955, similarly bemoaned his fate. When he came back from the war, recalled Sloan Wilson's creation, "all I could see was a lot of bright young men in gray flannel suits rushing around New York in a frantic parade to nowhere . . . pursuing neither ideals nor happiness. . . . For a long while I thought I was on the sidelines watching that parade, and it was quite a shock to glance down and see that I too was wearing a gray flannel suit."

And his fictional wife, Betty, added her own gloss on the past ten years: "All I know is that I lived in the belief that everything would be marvellous after the war, and that we've both been half-dead ever since you got home. . . . We've learned to drag along from day to day without any real emotion except worry. We've learned to make love without passion. . . . All I know how to do nowadays is to be responsible and dutiful and deliberately cheerful for the sake of the children."

The most powerful American play of the first postwar decade was Arthur Miller's *Death of a Salesman*, with its tale of a mediocre man whose pursuit of success leads inevitably to failure and despair. It has been said that each night when Willy Loman shuffled across the stage middle-aged men sat in the darkness beyond the footlights, silently weeping. And *The Man in the Gray Flannel Suit* carried much the same emotional impact for the married middle-class veteran in his thirties or early forties who had come home unwounded, slightly idealistic, and believing that "money doesn't matter."

A decade later he had two or three children. The job he was doing was hardly worth the life of a serious man. He and his wife were tense for much of the time. And money now mattered desperately. It had become the point around which almost everything else revolved. They *needed* rather than wanted a bigger house, they told each other. They *owed* each child a college education. Ironically, in Sloan Wilson's book the sole character who is free from this money obsession is a multimillionaire with a bad heart. It is fair to say that money was the ruling passion of life in the prosperous postwar, much as jobs had been during the hungry Thirties.

By 1957 it was obvious to almost everyone that suburbs were not and would never be the arcadian refuge from city life that so many had hoped for. Yet the idea lived on that at least in the small towns older, less materialistic values still prevailed. Once again the myth ran far ahead of the limping reality.

An intensive study of a small town in upstate New York in the 1950s showed a community which was overtly stable, enjoying deep roots in the past, possessed of a strong sense of community identity. The townspeople were hardworking, frugal, sober, democratic, and optimistic. Yet only one-fourth had been born in or near the town. Another one-fourth had moved in since the war. Sober and industrious the community was; deep-rooted it was not. Like Troy, its cultural remains were deposited in layers reflecting succeeding historical eras, but even then each layer was heavily larded with cultural importations from outside. It had never been autonomous at all.

The farmers and businessmen of the town were extraordinarily devoted to their work. But this devotion was not really economic; it was a form of self-avoidance. Life was not, as they liked to insist, endlessly rewarding. It was filled with self-doubt and petty frustrations. By working intensively, they were able to avoid facing the truth for most of the day. Rural and small-town life was not, on this evidence, so very different from life in the suburbs.

There was also a pervasive sense of loneliness. It was fashionable to blame this on the rise of the cities. But it had been equally true long before the cities had spread very far. The land was so vast and communities so scattered that loneliness had long been characteristic of American life. What was dismaying was that patterns of loneliness seemed to endure even when people were brought into close contact. It was further aggravated by the ordinary human response of people who find that they are not liked by others—withdrawal. They withdrew physically when that was possible. But in suburbs and small towns it was not possible, so they withdrew by means of alcohol, pills, or narcotics.

As if these strains and disappointments were not enough, recent decades had added rapid technological change, gigantism, standardization, and bureaucratization, all of which militated against the individualistic, the autonomous, and the idiosyncratic. Most people felt they had lost any real control over their lives and were at the mercy of powerful, impersonal forces. In itself, this was not necessarily new; the same catalogue of complaints could have been produced in the 1880s about the consequences of industrialization. What was new, and chilling, was the persistent emphasis on the claims of the community against the autonomy of the individual. There was nothing to show that it led to greater happiness.

If anything, the evidence suggested the contrary. There was a major study which closely examined an entire suburb for five years. Here was "a community rich in all the means ordinarily thought of as contributing to mental health. Life here is *not* nasty, short or brutish. The setting is physically spacious. Time is purchaseable in plenty, at least in the sense that reprieve from menial tasks and labor . . . can be bought with relative ease. Institutions generously endowed, intelligently managed . . . are not only present or available, but consciously dedicated to those ends and procedures that the mental hygienist recommends . . . yet no forcing of the data, no optimism, no sympathy with aims can lead us to suggest that the mental health of the community is sensibly better than elsewhere or that after all this effort it is being sensibly improved."

As Herbert Gans found, living in the third Levittown to be built, between Philadelphia and Trenton, life there unfolded within a homogeneous community, but this did not mean that children grew up shielded "from such unpleasant realities as alcoholism, mental illness, family strife, sexual aberration or juvenile delinquency, which exist everywhere." Suburbs provided, at most, a very limited escape from the tensions, the loneliness, and the alienation of modern life.

So to this extent there was no great change. Yet it was claimed that a profound change was occurring in the American character and that where it could be seen most graphically was out in the suburbs. For this was the natural habitat of the Organization Man and his Other-Directed cousin.

This was a path trodden once before, in the 1920s when an attempt had been made to develop a theory of suburban personality. Suburbanites had been described as "a chosen people separated from their fellow city-men by the strength of a particular group of inner attributes." But the theorizing of the 1950s was more ambitious than this early effort because it attempted to relate alterations in character to deep structural changes in the whole of society.

David Riesman's Other-Directed personality, described in *The Lonely Crowd*, took as its starting point changes in population and consumption patterns. *The Organization Man* of William H. Whyte, Jr., was the product of the all-embracing, mature Organization.

The Other-Directed personality was distinct from its Inner-Directed predecessor, which had looked to an internalized set of beliefs for its guidance. The Other-Directed individual had no such set of beliefs and looked instead to other people. The Other-Directed personality was therefore friendly in manner, while knowing nothing of friendship; free with money, but emotionally bankrupt; eager for praise, stung to the quick by criticism.

All this was a change from the nineteenth-century individual who had known his own mind, had been sure of his beliefs, and had pursued his own way through life whatever the cost. Riesman acknowledged that there were still some Inner-Directeds about. There were also some people who were Other-Directed in some parts of their lives, but Inner-Directed in the rest. Yet he had few doubts that the Other-Directed was the coming man.

He was the result of a society in which population growth was slowing down and of an economy whose emphasis had shifted from production to consumption. The Other-Directed personality, racked with status worries, was if nothing else a devout consumer, endlessly open to suggestion. For not only did he look to his acquaintances for guidance, but he took many of his cues from the mass media. Not for him the Inner-Directed's Puritanical traits of thrift and postponed gratification. What he wanted, he wanted Now!

The social mainspring of the Other-Directed life was not competition but cooperation. "The peer-group becomes the measure of all things; the individual has no defenses the group cannot batter down." Other-Directedness was evident, Riesman claimed, in a growing number of children. "The assumption [is] that the other-directed child is almost never alone, that by six or seven he no longer talks to himself, invents songs, or dreams unsupervised dreams." As the child grew up and went to school, whatever pockets of individuality remained would be surrounded and wiped out.

The Other-Directed personality was both manipulator and manipulated. The ideal work was work with people, not with things or ideas; in sales, advertising, or personnel, rather than in design, production, or testing. And the prevalence of manipulation as a way of life gave rise to a concern with sincerity. There was no higher compliment than to call someone "sincere." In *The Hucksters*, Frederic Wakeman's best-selling autobiographical novel based on his year's servitude at a major advertising agency, the hero cultivates his sincerity and parades it when it is needed.

William H. Whyte, Jr.'s, Organization Man bore many of the characteristics of the Other-Directed. He, too, was cooperative rather than competitive. Of course, how well he cooperated had a bearing on his success within the Organization. So he cooperated to the best of his ability, possibly a shade more noticeably than the next fellow. His aim, though, was to be a "team player."

The Organization's reason for existence was not to make money; it was to make people happy. It made the workers happy by providing them with jobs. It made the consumers happy by providing them with goods and services. Again the emphasis was on people. Among college graduates going to be interviewed for jobs in big business the preferred field was personnel. Whyte at times had the impression when he talked to college students preparing for careers in business that they were preparing for the ministry. All they talked about was of being of service to others.

He was convinced that the Organization Man was fast becoming the predominant American character type. He did not simply work for the Organization. He belonged to it body and soul. To him, the Protestant Ethic, with its emphasis on the individual, was an anachronism. The Organization Man did not resist the bureaucratization of American life, the aptitude tests, the Harwald Group Thinkometer; he welcomed them all with open arms. And everyone, he sincerely believed, should belong to something. People who did not belong would be unhappy and ineffective because it was only through the Organization that the world could be changed.

By the Organization Whyte did not necessarily mean big business. To his eye there was little difference between the young men who went to work for U.S. Steel and most of those who went into law, journalism, teaching, or most other fields. For there, too, it was the Organization which mattered—the big law firm, the big newspaper, the school district, or college.

The language Riesman and Whyte introduced, and some of their ideas, were rapidly absorbed. They illuminated various corners of American life usually left in the shadows. But although the American character may have been modified, it does not appear to have changed greatly. The Americans described by De Tocqueville more than 100 years ago would seem strange, exotic creatures had the American character changed profoundly during the intervening years. But what is most remarkable about them is how contemporary they seem.

As for the cohesion of American society in the postwar, the fact is the vast majority of people were not rootless; the vast majority of marriages did not end in failure. It seems impossible that the majority of women were overbearing or the majority of men spineless. Most people were, in most aspects of life, responsible and reasonable. The spreading of huge organizations, the rapidity of technological change, the rise of suburbia, the standardization of life posed new challenges, but for the most part people coped with them. That may not be very dramatic. But it is the truth about daily life as most people knew it and lived it.

Sorrow, frustration, self-doubt, occasional feelings of loneliness and futility, flashes of self-contempt, fear of failure—these are a part of everyday life, and always have been. They have been remarked upon here to complete the picture, not to darken it for effect. There was also kindness, thoughtfulness, and love, openly expressed, accepted without embarrassment, as part of daily life. But this nearly always went unnoticed. The 1950s brought much furious, hostile writing about suburban life, the role of women, the state of the family, and the desire for security. And these criticisms have tended to color our view of these years, just as they tended to influence opinion at the time. But much of this critical literature is simply unfair and wrongheaded. It is often little more than the scorn of the educated and sophisticated for ordinary people doing ordinary things. Life in the 1950s, as most people knew it, was a better life than they, or almost anyone else, had ever known.

17

Sex—Plain and Fancy

"As the week nears its end a festive desperation shivers across the land," wrote an observer in 1957. "There is no defeat more catastrophic than a good book on Saturday night." Romance was as integral to the American way of life as success, self-improvement or free enterprise.

For those who were not married (and for some who were) the date offered the semblance of romance, publicly flaunted. Among adolescents the date was the all-important ritual: it provided the appearance of freedom and denied freedom's possibilities of experiment, risk, and adventure. There was control without a chaperone. The date was as formal as a Noh drama while appearing to be informality itself.

And dating patterns were becoming more, not less, rigid. Adolescents in the 1950s had taken to "going steady," a phrase usually referring to high school students, but equally true of many college students. Going steady was a progressive relationship, moving from steady and exclusive dating with one person to wearing the other's class ring to being pinned with a fraternity pin. Being pinned was one step short of an engagement and called for a party.

Such behavior, one bemused elder was moved to reflect, was appropriate to small towns and rural areas; it was not what anyone would expect among the young people of a sophisticated, predominantly urban nation. Going steady also managed to combine most of the drawbacks of marriage with few of its pleasures. It appealed strongly, however, because it took most of the anxiety out of dating. But parents disapproved of going steady. The Catholic Church agitated against it. In parochial schools recalcitrant couples were expelled. The fear which priests and parents did not like to express was that if two young spent most of their free time together, they would inevitably start to have sexual intercourse.

American dating patterns were meant to promote proximity without intimacy. And that, some psychologists believed, would induce deep-seated sexual anxiety, leading to impotence in men and frigidity in women. Young people aged fifteen to twenty-one were fully mature physically, were given ample opportunity to arouse each other sexually, yet were heavily discouraged from following such arousal to its logical terminus. The result was a nation of people who grew up confused and unhappy about sexual relationships.

Whether they were miserable or not, nothing seemed to diminish interest in the subject, especially among the young. Student spring riots in the 1950s took as their theme and reason sex rather than goldfish partly perhaps because of the tremendous increase in coeducation. Before 1946 most college girls were in girls' colleges. But now they were on the other side of the campus or in the building next door. Young men stormed the girls' dormitories to seize their lingerie. At some colleges the favored chant of the besieging force was: "Drop your panties!" But Princeton students were more explicit: "We want sex! We want sex!"

Panty raids and going steady had little appeal for lower-class youth. They engaged in sexual liaisons earlier than their middle-class counterparts. Their experiences also tended to lack finesse. Gangs of juvenile delinquents often held a "gang bang" or a "circle jerk." Groups of a dozen or more gang members would while away part of a summer's evening in a secluded spot in the city park in these pursuits. "Sometimes," one reporter found, "a boy and girl may give an exhibition in the center of the circle while group masturbation goes on."

Sex seemed to be becoming increasingly casual, lacking in emotional involvement. "Don't get involved" had once meant don't get, or get someone else, pregnant. But now, remarked David Riesman, it appeared to mean don't be jealous, don't take it too seriously. And "marriage manuals," once suffused with invocations to romance, had become like mechanics' handbooks.

Formal barriers to prurience crumbled, despite the resistance offered by the Post Office, the Hays Office, and the local police department. The Post Office regularly seized and burned publications with such titles as *Sunshine and Health*. But it found it was fighting a losing battle when it got into court. Completely naked women had to be dark-skinned to appear in ordinary, respectable magazines, e.g., *National Geographic, Holiday*. Not until the 1950s did even the girlie magazines show full-frontal views of naked white women. The only place they had been openly on view was in the nudist publications, which operated on the pretense that nudism was a religion of the body; the number of nudist magazines bought far exceeded the number of nudists. And serious practitioners of the cult were usually considered cranks. Naked women had to be regarded as exotica or eccentrics instead of what they were—desirable. It was a transparent hypocrisy, as many an adolescent who had a cache of *National Geographic* or *Modern Sunbathing* was well aware.

There were also the millions of photographs of naked women which passed from hand to hand each year without ever being openly on sale. Then there were the little telescopes which, when extended to the light, showed a naked girl at the far end. There were millions of "French decks"—playing cards with fifty-two or fifty-four naked girls shown in color. There were cocktail glasses made with lucite stems. As you drank from the glass a naked female was slowly revealed in the stem. And then there were the calendars, millions of them, which offered a glimpse of breasts and thighs in grubby offices and neighborhood taverns.

Sexual titillation was around every corner, yet when *The Moon Is Blue* was scheduled for release in 1953, it was denied the seal of approval of the Motion Picture Production Code because it contained not nudity but such words as "virgin," "seduction," "mistress," and "pregnant." Scores of movie theaters refused to show it. The Roman Catholic Legion of Decency condemned it. And in the dozens of cities where it appeared it was a tremendous success.

Three years later *Baby Doll* was released. Although it was burdened with a half-baked plot, it showed flashes of engaging idiosyncrasy. It contained a lot of heavy breathing, and there were lingering close-ups of thumb-sucking. But there was no overtly sexual behavior. The idea somehow began to circulate that it was a film of amazing carnality. Huge crowds turned out to see it.

At about the same time *Tea and Sympathy*, a play concerned with repressed homosexuality, was running on Broadway. It ran for two years. The play culminated in therapeutic coitus between a married middle-aged woman and a shy, sensitive teenager.

In Hollywood, where the Production Code was breaking down, the moment was ripe for the advent of *the* sex symbol of the postwar. Her career had really begun during the war when her husband went into the Merchant Marine and she went to work as a parachute packer. From this kind of war work she moved to another, in the "dope room" at the Radio Plane Company in Van Nuys, spraying "dope" (liquid plastic) on cloth used in airplane fuselages. She was not popular with her fellow workers. First, because she was given an "E" certificate for her zealous over-reaching of production targets. Secondly, because when a *Yank* photographer visited the plant to do a story on women war workers, he spent three days taking photographs of Norma Jean Dougherty busily spot welding, packing parachutes, and spraying dope. Another photographer noticed the resulting pictures and launched her career as a model. By 1950 she was a starlet, little more than a plaything for short, aging movie producers. But her naked body appeared on the most famous calendar shot of the century. She turned a few tiny parts into electric moments on celluloid. By the mid-1950s, as Marilyn Monroe, she was a star. Her appeal was unique and universal, combining desirability with vulnerability.

December 1953 saw the publication for the first time of *Playboy*, the creation of Hugh Hefner, former circulation manager of *Esquire*. The resemblance to *Esquire* was more than somewhat. But *Playboy*'s sexual line was more explicit. In its first few months it sold a modest 70,000 copies per issue. But by 1956 circulation had risen to 500,000. *Playboy* was the most impressive magazine publishing success of the postwar. It had none of the crudeness of the older girlie magazines. Its nudes were airbrushed and touched up so that they had bodies which were antiseptic, poreless, creaseless, hairless; almost like plastic, but with nipples and a smile. *Playboy* was glossy and carefully catered to appeal to status-worried males; the glossiness and the unreality of the girls made it acceptable inside the home. But the idea that it was daring was also cleverly promoted, and this made it appeal to large numbers of college students. Its best-known feature, the "Playmate of the Month," was taken from *Esquire's* "Lady Fair." It inspired a joke about a nation of young men growing up in the belief that normal girls had a staple in the navel. *Playboy*'s first "Playmate of the Month" was the rising Marilyn Monroe.

Published erotica became increasingly explicit and ever more available. Pornography was such a wide-open market—so much money, so little effort—that it was one enterprise which mobsters did not mind sharing with others. The market was so big, they realized, that it was beyond the control of organized crime. The profit on pornographic books, photographs, films, magazines, playing cards, and sexual bric-a-brac commonly ran above 1,000 percent.

Just as sustained postwar prosperity democratized such pleasures as golf, boating, and pedigree dogs, so it spread pornography. Affluence also increased anxiety, as a by-product of the scramble for success and the need for status display. Sexual obsessions are usually a manifestation not of a lively sensuality but of anxiety. Pornography and sexual experimentation were further encouraged by the democratic feeling that people had a right to pursue such interests, that they might miss something important if denied them. And given the dissatisfaction many people evidently felt in their sex lives, it was inevitable that this right would be exercised even if it proved to be expensive and even if it proved to be demeaning. The postwar saw the democratization of publications traditionally considered pornographic and practices traditionally considered perversions. Whether the result was a happier, healthier sexuality is open to question.

If anything, the characteristic confusion of sexual emotions seems not to have abated. Attitudes toward sex veered from the prudish to the lascivious within a single work, whether a novel, play, film, or news story. Sexual maladjustment may well have been on the increase, although there is no way of determining this statistically. There are only impressions. But Polly Adler noticed in her final years as a madam that "people's peculiarities were intensified. They seemed to get more and more off the beam. Whore-houses always drew twisted people who were unable to satisfy their desires normally. But now it got so that I began to think of a patron who wanted the simple, old-fashioned methods as a 'truck-driver.' "

People were also increasingly open about their aberrations. In 1952 George Jorgenson, Jr., of the Bronx had undergone a "sex change" operation in Copenhagen. His sex had not actually been changed; he had simply been castrated and given injections of the hormones which produce secondary female characteristics in women but have a much less decisive effect in men. Physically, Jorgenson was little more than a eunuch, of which there have been thousands. Yet Jorgenson's "sex change" operation was the second biggest news story of the year, surpassed only by the election of Eisenhower to the Presidency. Under the name Christine, Jorgenson returned to the United States the next year, clicking along in high heels and swathed in a heavy fur coat, and proceeded to reveal (almost) all in a series of well-paid articles.

Despite the fascination with Christine Jorgenson, there was a loathing of homosexuality in America which bordered on panic. Men were silently terrified and disgusted by homosexual impulses in themselves. Women despaired lest their sons or husbands show homosexual tendencies, for what could they do if their emotional rival was not another woman but a man? American life, with its approval of manliness only in its crudest forms, made of homosexuality a kind of sexual un-Americanism.

But every large city in the country had a sizable homosexual community, a world unto itself, with few links to heterosexual society. It was a world within which homosexuals found employment, friendship, a social life, sexual partners, and innocent amusements. New York in the 1950s was said to have a homosexual community numbering at least 100,000. The actual figure might easily have approached 200,000. There were gay bars, apartment houses, and offices, and some public beaches had been virtually commandeered by homosexuals in bikini-style briefs.

Urban, bourgeois homosexuals disdained "drag" balls, riotous parties, most gay bars, or anything that conjured up the "flaming faggot." They despised male prostitutes, degenerates who cruised the lavatories, and female impersonators, But naturally, as with the heterosexual middle class, lapses were not unknown and hypocrisy was commonplace. The homosexuals who were blatantly effeminate were generally those who held low-paying, low-status jobs. It was among the lower orders too that most of the "sadi-masies" were to be found, in company with the fetishists. Gay society was brittle, artificial, and as thoroughly conformist as white middle-class suburbia. It was as obsessed with status, and there was the same yearning to belong and to be admired.

There was an unmistakably more tolerant attitude toward homosexuals as the 1950s wore on, albeit grudging and tentative. Several states began to rewrite their sex laws to exclude most homosexual acts between consenting adults. In literature, in films, and on the stage, homosexuals were treated with far more sympathy than had been possible before the war. Homosexuals also made themselves increasingly visible, by forming their own organizations, publishing newspapers, and holding conventions. A generation earlier such activities would have been stopped by local police and courts. But these days they were harassed and threatened, not stopped.

Whether there was more homosexuality than in the past, or whether it was simply becoming more visible, is doubtful. Many people were convinced that there had been an increase. Certainly men's interest in women's bodies appeared to have undergone a suggestive change. Around World War I men had considered a woman's legs the most sexually arousing sight, and this was true up to World War II. But from the war years onward the emphasis shifted to breasts, the bigger the better. It was attributed to the strains of modern living, a longing for the comforts mother had offered.

The on-going postwar prosperity was meanwhile drawing women out to work and giving them more money to help make themselves more attractive. It provided appliances and homes which spared them the drudgery their mothers had endured, drudgery which had made them old by the time they were thirty-five. And prosperity gave a margin of economic independence which encouraged a varied, active sex life. More than ever women were able to use their sexual allure to manipulate men. And power, like sex itself, is an appetite which grows with what it feeds on. Women, it was said, with more than a grain of truth, were becoming more demanding—of everything, from a second car to simultaneous orgasm. Men were rumored to be impotent on a massive scale. Certainly the sale of double beds remained constant, while that of twin beds doubled between the late 1930s and late 1950s. Men complained that the battle of the sexes was over—the women had won.

Yet women hardly ever felt sexually triumphant. They often succeeded in making themselves appear sexually desirable and in their manner seemed sexually accomplished. But it was frequently a masquerade. Their show of sexuality was a substitute for a sexuality they either did not feel or felt but could not gratify. And their ignorance on the subject could be stunning, even where their own bodies were involved. Millions of American women believed that there was such a thing as vaginal orgasm, and they went to see doctors and psychologists to ask why they had never had one. This hoary myth,* created by Freud, was accepted as fact without a shred of objective evidence to support it. American women continued to believe the sex manuals (written in most cases by men) which spoke in glowing terms of vaginal orgasm.

The year 1948 had seen the publication of *Sexual Behavior in the Human Male.*The year 1953 brought *Sexual Behavior in the Human Female.* These two works by Dr. Alfred Kinsey and his associates were commonly held to have ushered in a new era of frankness concerning sex and accuracy as to what people did, with whom they did it, and how often it was done. Kinsey was to be blamed, or credited, depending on your point of view, for the sexual permissiveness of the postwar, much as Dr. Benjamin Spock was to be blamed, or credited, for permissive methods of child-bearing.

Kinsey's temperament was that of the archivist or collector rather than the scholar. As a boy he collected stamps. In maturity he collected irises and lilies. He bought thousands of secondhand books on a wide variety of subjects. His search for gall wasps resulted in a collection of 4 million specimens. When he donated it to the American Museum of Natural History, it was the largest collection of anything ever to come the museum's way. Kinsey was a collector of recordings of classical music, and he bored his assistants with programmed "concerts" from his collection. In middle age Kinsey set himself the goal of collecting 100,000 individual sex histories. This was one collection which defeated him. At his death he was 82,000 short of his target.

Behind Kinsey's passion for collecting things there went, as often happens, only a fitful interest in the contents of the collection. Most of the books he bought, for example, went unread. But "he always answered that if an individual collected anything widely enough, in time it would have some value." And there was one type of request to which Kinsey always responded positively. Any autograph collector who asked for his signature got it from fellow collector Kinsey.

Kinsey was a professor of biology at the University of Indiana. He was drawn into collecting sex histories as a result of his counseling students who were confused about sex and given to thinking that their difficulties were unique. Kinsey had a close friend in the president of the university, Herman Wells, and throughout its trials Wells was a staunch defender of the Institute for Sex Research, which Kinsey founded and the Rockefeller Foundation funded. But when the first report was readied for publication, Wells became nervous. The year *was* 1948; Indiana *was* a state university, beholden to the legislature; the topic *was* sex. He begged Kinsey to look for a medical, not a trade, publisher. In this way, he hoped, the re-

*A myth definitively demolished by the only twentieth-century masterpiece of sex research, William H. Masters and Virginia E. Johnson, *Human Sexual Response* (Boston: 1966), pp. 66–67.

port's appeal would be confined to doctors, psychologists, marriage counselors, and the like. He also asked Kinsey to exercise what control he could over the publication date and "not to publish anything during the 61 days the Indiana legislature would be in session or immediately before it began."

Sexual Behavior in the Human Male was brought out by a reputable medical publisher, and the first edition of 5,000 copies, instead of disappearing quietly, was sold in the first week. Over the next few years more than 250,000 copies of the first Kinsey report were sold. It was, at first glance, the most unlikely best-seller of the century: long; crammed with figures and tables; turgidly written; little advertised. But it enjoyed a word-of-mouth success that no amount of money could have bought. And it profited from combining an old interest, sex, with a modern approach, scientism.

Kinsey, his assistants, his admirers, intoned endlessly that Kinsey was "a scientist." And every criticism of his work was parried with the reply "unscientific." But there were two yawning chinks in this armor. First, there was the elaborate array of charts, graphs, and tables to give the work the appearance of mathematical precision and minute detail. But even had all the figures been accurate, the effect would have been misleading; in itself it would have been neither science nor scientifically arrived at. Kinsey made the mistake common to modern academics of considering mathematics synonymous with science. But whether it is or not depends on where the numbers came from and where they are going. The second error, and one which a genuinely rigorous intellect would have confronted squarely, was the inherent lack of representativeness in the figures on which the reports were based.

Neither Kinsey nor any of his assistants was a statistician. Yet the statistical difficulties involved in his first report were so daunting that there were no more than twenty statisticians in the world capable of resolving them. Kinsey, in his innocence, does not appear to have understood what the difficulties were. He also inflated his figures by referring throughout the text to the mean, rather than the median; whether from a poor understanding of what he was doing or whether he knew only too well is impossible to say.

Although he was trained as a biologist, by the time he began collecting sex histories the normal prudence a training in scientific method is supposed to reproduce was wearing thin. The fever of the collector was far more evident. He simply could not resist a good history, no matter how unrepresentative it was. He once made a journey of 1,500 miles to obtain the sex history of a man who claimed to have had sexual contacts with hundreds of children, hundreds of adults, and a variety of animals, and to be able to masturbate to orgasm in 10 seconds flat from a flaccid start. This last, he demonstrated. The hero of the male report was clearly "the scholarly and skilled lawyer" who claimed to have averaged more than thirty orgasms a week for thirty years. Christine Jorgenson was invited to the institute, where Kinsey took her history. Doubtless these were interesting cases and had a place in sex research. But they did not belong in a sample of 10,000 men. The man in the Southwest was one in a million—which is exactly why Kinsey drove 1,500 miles in wartime, on priceless tires, and hoarded gasoline rationing coupons to collect it. Christine Jorgenson was 1 in 10 million. And if the "scholarly and skilled lawyer" was telling the truth, he was probably the only one of his kind in the nation.

Kinsey was fascinated with deviants. Both reports are heavily overweighted with homosexuals, prostitutes, drug addicts, bestialists, and convicts. In the *Male* report Kinsey acknowledged that it under-represented men over fifty, men in unskilled jobs, black men of any age or occupation, single adult men, men who lived in rural areas, men who worked in factories, male adolescents, and male children. What remained? Middle-class, married white men aged twenty to forty-five living between Chicago and Boston and in or training for managerial or professional occupations. Most of Kinsey's respondents came from Illinois, Ohio, and Indiana. Should anyone offer an opinion poll claiming to represent the weight of public opinion on any important subject but based on a sample in which half of the respondents were college graduates, were nearly all white, aged twenty to forty-five and resident chiefly in the Midwest, the poll would be tossed aside as being worthless. But Kinsey's figures, far from being dismissed, were taken to be nothing less than true.

Both reports carried an air of self-congratulation, and this may have helped convince people of their authority; they were as dogmatic as the Bible. And there was, in the *Male* report, a touching faith in people that was almost ingenuous. For example, in the securing of histories from deviants, "The underworld requires only a gesture of honest friendship before it is ready to admit one as a friend." To secure histories from prostitutes (people to whom time really *is* money) and the poor, Kinsey paid for them. Yet he bravely maintained that the prostitute and destitute did not really offer their histories in exchange for money, but because "they have faith in scientific research projects." Here is Kinsey the Scientist on his method for telling whether a respondent was telling the truth: "As well ask a horse trader how he knows when to close a bargain!" In other words, it was not science but "horse sense." And his principal assistant, Wardell B. Pomeroy, claimed: "Not remembering accurately could be dealt with statistically; the errors one person might make were offset by errors another might make in the opposite direction." But this is true only in a very carefully drawn sample; in the kind of sample Kinsey employed, errors are more likely to compound one another.

Kinsey believed that diversity (e.g., 100 Harvard graduates, a sprinkling of policemen from Kansas) was as good as representativeness. But the essential statistical element was what he referred to as "statistical sense"; naturally, he had it. It was a gift, something like perfect pitch. It enabled the Scientist (Kinsey) to cast his eyes on the data and tell the general from the particular, the trivial from the vital, and wring from a mere collection of facts the truth. Kinsey tried to describe "statistical sense" at some length, but like any great art, it proved very difficult to put into words.

A group of eminent statisticians, with the blessings of the American

Statistical Association, evidently apprehensive that Kinsey's dubious methodology might spread on the strength of Kinsey's popular success, made a close study of the *Male* report. They cast doubt on its conclusions "because of possible inaccuracies of memory and report. . . ." All that Kinsey's method involved was to collect and lump together reported, as opposed to recorded, behavior. The two might differ enormously. Not surprisingly, the statisticians decided: "Many of the most interesting and provocative statements in the book are not based on the data presented therein, and . . . much of the writing in the book falls below the level of good scientific writing."

But there could be no denying Kinsey's real achievement—the collection of 18,000 sex histories. They were his strongest card. No one else had anything like them. He deserved praise for his perseverance, courage, and vision. He knew that he had for once collected a mass of material unlike anything anyone else had ever acquired. It was unfortunate that his background, his temperament, and the need to secure grants to keep his institute going led him to misuse what he had gathered. In the end the collector gave way to the promoter, as the scientist had given way to the collector.

In the second report, *Sexual Behavior in the Human Female*, Kinsey and his co-workers managed to repeat most of the major errors of the earlier volume. The range of respondents in the sample was drawn more narrowly than before: a mere 3 percent had never been to high school (the national figure was 40 percent); three out of four were college graduates; one in four was Jewish; half were aged twenty-nine to thirty-nine; one in five had at least a master's degree; and they lived in urban areas of Indiana, Ohio, Pennsylvania, New Jersey, and New York in most cases. There were the same sweeping judgments on Freud, social mores, primitive tribes, the "normal" (which is scorned), and the "natural" (which is praised), the rise and fall of civilizations, and the brilliant achievements of Dr. Alfred C. Kinsey.

As in the first work, there were also sensible comments on the relativity of sexual practices. In its exploration of the wide variety of sexual behavior an individual might experience in the course of a lifetime and in its inquiries into the wide range of any one sexual activity Kinsey's work broke new ground. But this was not what people took from the reports. Some of the figures (e.g., that a third of adult males had engaged in homosexuality) became part of the folk wisdom of the educated middle class. Doctors, psychiatrists, and sociologists for years invoked Kinsey's figures as if they were true, rather than open to serious doubt. And the general effect of these works may well have been to impair, rather than to advance, research into sexual behavior. Ignorance, openly acknowledged, is less an impediment to learning the truth than is a falsehood which is widely accepted.

Kinsey's figures may or may not be accurate. No one knows how closely they come to presenting a representative picture. Certainly Kinsey never knew. And the use of the same figures over and over again in different forms is so exhaustive that it suggests an attempt to still not the doubts of the critics but the doubts of the author.

The publication of the *Female* report was surrounded with intense public interest. The next year, 1954, Congressman Carroll Reece of Tennessee took it into his head to investigate the major foundations. The Rockefeller Foundation had a new president, Dean Rusk. The *Female* report was more venomously attacked the *Male* report. Much of the hostility was irrational. Obscurantists such as Reece considered sex research a threat to female chastity. When the institute applied to the Rockefeller Foundation for renewal of its grant it was turned down, after fifteen years of support.

But by now the reports were legendary. Kinsey was credited with the postwar sexual revolution. Yet that revolution would have occurred had Kinsey stuck to gall wasps. Greater honesty and openness about sex were the result of social and economic forces. The anonymity of urban life which spread as urbanization spread, the revival of a hedonist ethic in the twentieth century and its democratization, the invention of the automobile, the growing economic independence of women, the dissemination of birth control information, the rising level of education among women— such were the forces at work. And one of their consequences was the Kinsey reports. They made it possible for him to collect 18,000 histories and to publish the results. Kinsey did not cause the sexual revolution; the sexual revolution caused Kinsey.

Americans were more willing to discuss their sex lives with strangers (interviewers) than their incomes, which they considered "too personal." There was a strong connection between sex and money in that the wartime and postwar prosperity, by providing extra income, encouraged people to have an extra child. The baby boom which began during the war continued into the late 1950s. It was not due to big families becoming bigger but to many couples having three children instead of two and many others having two instead of one. There was also a marked decline in the percentage of childless couples. It is pushing the evidence too far to attribute all of these extra births to the nation's economy. The most that can be said is that a nation's birthrate is influenced by social morale. As this changes, so does the image of the "ideal" family. In 1941 the popular ideal family had two children; in 1955 it had four.

The most striking rise in fertility was not among the uneducated and poor but among young college-educated couples. This group had traditionally been among the last to have children. Most college-educated people are still studying or only at the beginning of their careers when in their mid-twenties. But the war appears to have destroyed the traditional inhibitions by putting heavy responsibilities on young men. Returning to face a choice between marriage and college, they had taken on both. They had gone a step farther by having children, too. By the mid-1950s the war veterans were approaching middle age, but the example they had set was being followed by other young men.

Unhappily, the baby boom also meant an abortion boom and a sharp increase in illegitimacy. Abortion, because it was nearly always illegal, was another important aspect of sex about which it was impossible to collect accurate information. The most thorough and responsible investigation made of abortions in the 1950s concluded that the number of induced abortions each year was between 200,000 and 1,200,000.

It was a painful paradox that abortion and illegitimacy should be increasing at the same time that people were becoming markedly better informed about contraception. What had been termed "race suicide" in the 1920s was known in the 1950s as "planned parenthood." Before the war the most popular form of contraception had been the douche, which was also the least effective method available. By the mid-1950s the douche had slipped to fourth place, surpassed by the condom, the diaphragm and rhythm.

Condoms were especially popular among Jews, the rhythm method among Catholics. Condoms had been widely used during the war mainly to protect against venereal disease. Rhythm had been little understood and little practiced before 1939; it required both an awareness that birth control was possible and a modicum of self-discipline and education to practice it. The Catholic Church sanctioned rhythm without actually approving of it, in tacit recognition that a new generation of Catholics had come to maturity. Even so, the proportion of Catholics resorting to forbidden (and more effective) methods such as condoms and diaphragms rose from one-fourth in 1939 to one-third in 1955. And many of the transgressors were regular communicants.

The postwar also saw a remarkable increase in voluntary sterilization. Before 1946 vasectomy was rare, the subject of rumor and bad jokes. In most cases it was performed on mental patients in state hospitals. But by 1957 up to 100,000 men each year had vasectomies. The number increased year by year, even though this operation, simple and painless as it was, was of a character to make almost any man feel nervous.

Sex was always more than a matter of having children. In the postwar it became part of the standard package of goods and services expected of middle-class American life. Much of it was tame, glossy, vicarious, was pursued not to make the spirit burn more brightly but to bask in the reflected glow of an attractive partner, prominently paraded. It was endlessly worried over and provided harmless amusement in Hugh Hefner's excursions into hedonism portentously titled "The Playboy Philosophy," in which you could almost see the furrowed brow, hear the scratching of the head.

Among the lower half of the population, class was at least as important as any other factor in determining how often people had intercourse, how likely they were to have children, how much or how little gratification they derived from sex, and the number of children they were likely to have.

In the suburbs there were other constraints. There was a common impression that suburbia was a place where people hopped from bed to bed, fought that old devil ennui by swapping wives and organizing group sex on Saturday night. But life in most suburbs was life as it is lived in a goldfish bowl. You still had to face the neighbors on Monday morning. And the chances of conducting an affair without being detected ranged from very bad to much worse. No doubt there was a lot of sexual frustration, which expressed itself in the voracious appetite for printed pornography and sex films.

There were also, among middle-aged, middle-class men, sizable numbers who lost interest in sex after their children were born. They concentrated on their jobs. "Repeatedly," remarked two scholars studying business executives, "they see sexual relations as limiting, frivolous and unreal." And their wives were supposed to accept this. For the many women who did not bloom sexually until they reached the age of thirty this must have been a painful form of neglect to have to endure.

Most people expected far more from their marriage partners than their parents and grandparents had expected. They expected excitement and romance. As such expectations rose, so did disappointment. Before long it was smart to believe that the family was on its last legs.

The prosaic truth was that the divorce rate leveled off after 1947 and then dropped slightly. By the late 1950s it was almost exactly what it had been in 1940. There were fewer than 10 divorces per year for every 1,000 married females. Of all the people ever divorced, 96 percent had been divorced only once. When divorced people remarried, and most of them did, they stayed married—perhaps because they now had more realistic expectations. In 1940 only 1.4 percent of the entire population comprised people who had been divorced; by 1960 the figure was 2.5 percent. The increase was the cumulative effect of a high, but hardly catastrophic, divorce rate spread over twenty years. Marriage had not lost its appeal; if anything, it was more popular than ever. The family still represented for the vast majority of people the ideal of human harmony. Once almost every community had had a considerable body of elderly spinsters and bachelors. By the 1950s, however, unmarried people over the age of thirty were becoming marginal figures in American life. Neither marriage nor the family was about to disappear. Both were becoming more difficult to sustain. Yet of those who tried the overwhelming majority succeeded.

18
Rockin' to a Brand-New Beat

Between the wars Hollywood and Tin Pan Alley had gone a long way toward making the popular culture of the world something with an American look and an American sound. But in the 1950s, in only a few years, a comparative handful of singers, musicians, and recording studios did far more, with far less. In two-and-a-half-minute outbursts they conveyed the insistent, youthful energy of American urban life; it was music strident, sex-obsessed, and as knowing as only adolescence can be. They called it rock 'n' roll.

In those years between the wars America had created a new time of life—adolescence. Before World War I nearly all youngsters entered the adult world at the age of fourteen or fifteen, when they went to work. From that moment on they were expected to support themselves; often they were expected to support their parents as well. But by the 1920s secondary education was keeping most people in school up to the age of seventeen. Youth was being prolonged. The shortage of jobs in the 1930s prolonged the age of irresponsibility still further. Between fourteen and twenty there was neither childhood nor adulthood. There was adolescence, and much of its energies went into fighting off boredom.

The movies provided excitement and escape. So did music. The Depression, however, put the recording business flat on its back. The war revived it. In the first year after the war the record business saw its turnover double, from $100 million to $200 million. It appeared set for great things. But suddenly the rising sales curves leveled off. And attendance at movie theaters was dropping spectacularly. There was evidently something lacking in the appeal of movies to the young.

But some young people, to the surprise of the record companies, and the dismay of their parents, began to show a liking for black music. This was known as race music, presumably to distinguish it from real music. As a market for it developed, the mocking name was dropped; now it was called rhythm and blues.

Most of the black music came out of the South, where the music native to most whites was not the Child ballads but "hillbilly" songs, with whining vocal styles, sodden lyrics, and a simple, emphatic rhythm. Hillbilly music was ridiculed, but the overall sound was undeniably distinctive. In the 1940s that sound merged with the sound of "Western" music, whose apotheosis was the singing cowboy. The result was Country and Western.

These were fertile years for popular music; throughout the first postwar decade musicians were seeking new sounds wherever they might be found. The record companies were looking for new markets. And black musicians were pouring out of the South as demand for their music spread.

Each year scores of them traveled to Chicago to cut a record and hope for the lightning to strike. An enterprising young white businessman, Sam Philips, who liked black music, decided to save their having to make so long a journey. He opened a recording studio, Sun Records, in Memphis, which provided all the facilities close to the source.

Black music tended to follow one of two lines: religious ecstasy or sexual ecstasy. The lyrics of the latter were based on black slang, understood by blacks but not by many whites. As the appeal of black music grew, to get the records into the record stores or onto the air, the sexual material had to be defused. Like jazz in its original meaning, rockin' and rollin' originally stood for copulation. By 1950 it had been transformed so that it seemed to refer to dancing. And by 1952, when a young Cleveland disc jockey, Alan Freed, started a rhythm and blues program called *Moondog's Rock and Roll Party* that was all it meant. Freed had been running a classical music record program until he happened on a record store where he discovered white teenagers dancing enthusiastically to big-beat rhythm and blues records. After two years of mounting success Freed in 1954 took the gospel of rock 'n' roll to New York.

By then it was ready to break across the nation. In 1953 a Country and Western singer with a blond cowlick and an unmistakably white man's voice, Bill Haley, had made the *Billboard* charts with a song called "Crazy Man Crazy." It was the first, if modest, success of the new genre. Haley brought together the styles of c & w and r & b; the result was termed rockabilly.

Early in 1954 a black singer, Joe Turner, recorded a new kind of up-tempo blues number, "Shake, Rattle and Roll." "Not many people in the pop music audience heard Joe Turner's record, but more than a million bought Bill Haley's cover version on Decca." The Haley version prudently dropped the original sexual allusions. The next year Haley and the Comets went on to yet more resounding success with "Rock Around the Clock." For most people this was when rock 'n' roll began for them; this was the first rock 'n' roll number they had ever heard.

The blacks who were meanwhile moving north and west out of the South found that the record companies of New York and Los Angeles were waiting for them. It was ironic, but the "sound of the city" as one historian of rock 'n' roll has termed it, was predominantly the sound produced by blacks and whites from the rural South. And back in Memphis Sun Records had taken a chance on a young truck driver who came in one day to cut a record as a gift to his mother. Sun, like many a small record company, earned its bread and butter by letting modest talents and no-hopers pay it to let them cut their own records. Sam Philips did not have to beat the bushes for a potential star. With a little bit of luck the star might simply walk in off the street. All that Philips had to do was recognize him when he arrived.

He knew what he was looking for. "If I could find a white man who had the Negro sound and the Negro feel," he would say, "I could make a billion dollars." The truck driver was, to the trained ear, as unpromising a

prospect as Florence Foster Jenkins. He fluffed even the most simple lyrics. His voice was uncertain. He could not hold a tune for long. He mumbled. He also had what Sam Philips was looking for.

The truck driver came from Tupelo, Mississippi. Born in extreme poverty, little educated, unmistakably working-class, he had listened to the
music of poor blacks since childhood. He imbibed, too, something of the
nonstop style of the white revivalist preachers at the local Assembly of
God church—men who spoke in tongues, preached hellfire and brim-
stone, sang fervently and loudly, and never stopped moving. The raw
nervous energy of the white man's religious fervor and the heavy beat and
sensual vitality of the black man's music fused in this earnest young man
with the unlikely (to non-Southern ears) name of Elvis Presley. And that
was what Sam Philips had been listening for; that was the sound, however
crude, however unpracticed. The only thing he was wrong about was the
billion dollars. Presley helped make him rich, but not that rich.

Presley's early style was so "integrated" that from his first few records
he was widely assumed to be black. It was also hard to place him. *Billboard*'s charts contained three categories: pop, c & w, r & b. Rock 'n' roll
spread across all three, borrowed from all three.

Until the advent of rock 'n' roll the popular music market had been
dominated by adults. In recent years they had shown a preference for sy-
rupy, sentimental ballads. The change in taste had led to the breakup of
most of the big bands during the 1940s. The brassy, full-blooded sound
had suddenly lost most of its audience. Popular music had gone insipid.
Nor were the record companies entirely enthusiastic about rock 'n' roll.
But it did wonders for record sales.

The long period of stagnation was over. Between 1954 and 1960 record
sales tripled. In these years the tastes, such as they were, of adolescents
came to dominate the record business. But in that six-year period something happened to rock 'n' roll. It rapidly lost its authenticity. The recording studios began to "make" rock 'n' roll. This meant that they made it
tamer, more bland, less objectionable. Unlike other styles in popular music, it never had an opportunity to mature in the course of live performance. Much of the rock 'n' roll sound was impossible to achieve outside
the recording studio, as disappointed fans discovered when they attended
live rock 'n' roll concerts. But the music did have a measure of authenticity few music styles have ever enjoyed; rock 'n' roll not only reflected the
interests of the adolescent subculture but became an important part of it.

Its rites were celebrated several times each week on national television.
The service was called *American Bandstand*. It began as a local show in
Philadelphia in 1952. But in 1957 it acquired a new host, Dick Clark, and
became a national institution. It offered minimal entertainment for the
viewers, but for those in the studio it offered a dance party. Watching other people dancing to records should have being the most boring thing on
television except for the test patterns. But it proved to be one of the most
popular.

American Bandstand had a natural, spontaneous air. It was, in its way,
completely genuine, and in its austerity it had a classical grace. The regu-

lars who appeared at the studio several times each week became its stars. Who was dating whom; who was showing an interest in whom; who was wearing what—these things provided the drama. Dick Clark was perfectly cast. He did not intrude. Neither did he patronize. He made no attempt to identify with adolescents. He was self-effacing, allowing the show to find its own way. And its secret was that it allowed the teenagers who appeared to be themselves. *That* was something the viewing audience could identify with—people their own age, with interests like their own, doing something they enjoyed, and doing it naturally, spontaneously.

In its harsh, strident, sensual period, rock 'n' roll did not last very long. There were outcries from parents. Presley's movements were so overtly sexual that many adults blinked in disbelief. When he appeared on the *Ed Sullivan Show*, the cameras showed him only from the waist up. But this sexual appeal was a crucial aspect of the music. To teenagers, physically mature but sternly enjoined to control themselves, sex was a subject of intense and immediate interest. American mothers were scandalized by Elvis Presley. Yet the boy was devoted to his own mother and in person was shy, sincere, kindhearted, eager to please, and very polite—the kind of son many a mother would be proud to call her own. His was also the triumph of character over poverty. When he became rich, the first major purchase he made was to buy his mother a house of her own.

Presley was beyond any doubt the biggest show business success of the postwar. His appeal to young people of the working and lower middle classes was astonishing and enduring. In some ways it was also endearing, because it was really harmless, yet gave much pleasure to large numbers of people. It provided a measure of excitement to people whose work was often dull and dispiriting.

Elvis Presley's success was not entirely spontaneous; in fact, it was heavily promoted. No teenage fan need be without comfort day or night. On rising, she might pull on:

> some Elvis Presley bobbysocks, Elvis Presley shoes, an Elvis Presley skirt and an Elvis Presley blouse, an Elvis Presley sweater, hang an Elvis Presley charm bracelet on one wrist, put an Elvis Presley handkerchief in her Elvis Presley purse and head for school, where she might swap some Elvis Presley bubblegum cards before class, where she would take notes with an Elvis Presley pencil. After school she might change into Elvis Presley Bermuda shorts, Elvis Presley blue jeans (which were not blue but black, trimmed in white and carried Elvis's face on a pocket tag) or Elvis Presley toreador pants, and either write an Elvis Presley pen pal (whose address she got from an Elvis Presley magazine) or play an Elvis Presley game while drinking an Elvis Presley soft drink. And before going to bed in her Elvis Presley knit pajamas, she might write in her Elvis Presley diary, using an Elvis Presley ball-point pen, listen to "Hound Dog" a final ten times, then switch off the light to watch an Elvis Presley picture that glowed in the dark.

Littering her now-darkened room were her Elvis Presley guitar, stuffed hound dog, cologne, playing cards, dolls, busts, pillows, comb, belts, gloves, T-shirts, necklaces, lipsticks, photographs, buttons, and records.

It was possible to get a good-sized collection of Presleyana started at almost any five-and-dime store in the country in the late 1950s. For the housebound nearly all these treasures were available by mail. Presley's appeal was not limited to teenage girls. Millions of teenage boys copied his hairstyle, his clothes, his sullen, sensual, lower-class look. If, to the critical eye, the result looked artificial, so was the genuine article. There was a standard sort of good looks: dark for men, blond for women. Thus, Marilyn Monroe, dark-haired by nature, was bleached blond; Presley, whose hair was fair, was blackly dyed.

In the few years, roughly 1955–1958, when Presley and rock 'n' roll were at their most distinctive, they faced bitter hostility. "The pop music business," wrote one music critic, "having scraped the hillbilly barrel and blown the froth off the mambo craze has taken over rhythm and blues, known to the teenage public as 'cat-music' or 'rock 'n' roll.' The commercial product, whether by Negroes or whites, only superficially resembles the prototype. It has a clanking, socked-out beat, a braying, honking saxophone, a belted vocal, and, too often, suggestive lyrics. . . ." *Life* grimly intoned, "Up to a point the country can withstand the impact of Elvis Presley." But what, *Life* worried, was the meaning of all those screaming girls and Presley's gyrating pelvis?

Rock 'n' roll concerts were often forbidden. In Bridgeport, Connecticut, the police even banned rock 'n' roll dance parties in private homes on the grounds that the music was so exciting it threatened the maintenance of the peace. A rock 'n' roll concert at the National Guard Armory in Washington featuring Bill Haley and the Comets ended in a fracas. The trouble quickly spread to surrounding streets, and passing cars were stoned. In Jacksonville, Florida, a Presley concert ended with a warrant being sworn out against him, in which he was charged with corrupting the morals of minors. Wherever Presley appeared the local clergy were likely to make a protest.

A rock 'n' roll concert at Asbury Park, New Jersey, in July 1956 resulted in a riot which sent twenty-five teenagers to hospital. The mayor banned rock 'n' roll music from the town's dance halls, and Jersey City canceled all the rock 'n' roll concerts scheduled to take place there. There were riots and bans in a score of California communities, including San Jose and Santa Cruz. In San Antonio, Texas, a city ordinance removed rock 'n' roll records from jukeboxes on city-owned property. In 1958 Alan Freed was on the road with a touring rock 'n' roll show, just as the protests were beginning to die down. But a riot broke out in Boston. Freed was indicted for "inciting the unlawful destruction of property." Four towns where the show was due to appear promptly banned it.

The *Denver Post* had already handed down what many adults would accept as the definitive statement on the merits of rock 'n' roll: "This hooby-dooby, oop-shoop, ootie-ootie, boom-boom, de-addy boom, scoobledy goobledy clump—is trash." A million parents said, "Amen."

But to many a radio station rock 'n' roll came as a blessing undisguised. Before 1947 half of all radio programming was music broadcasts, from hillbilly to classical. With the decline in radio listening the primacy of music in American popular culture was threatened. And radio appeared to have no future at all. From 1947 to 1955 net profits fell alarmingly every year.

In the meantime, however, records had been revolutionized. Peter Goldmark, no lone pioneer tinkering away in his basement but the inventor-in-residence at CBS, had created the long-playing record. No longer were four or five minutes of music scratchily recorded on each side of a heavy, brittle disc. Goldmark's LP contained up to 300 grooves per inch and played at 33⅓ rpm. That meant that up to fifty minutes of music could be recorded, with much greater clarity, on each side of the new records.

RCA countered by producing a 7-inch record with a big hole in the middle to be played at 45 rpm. It was in no respect competitive with the LP; in most ways it was inferior. But this feeble riposte had one important, unintended consequence: it was an ideal method for putting a hit song within the reach of adolescents at a retail price of seventy-five cents or so.

By the mid-1950s popular music had become a very big business. The new record markets opened up by the LP and the 45, the rise of rock 'n' roll, the radio DJ programs, the astute promotion of the Top 10, the Top 20, the Top 40, and the arrival of the transistor radio pulled radio back from the abyss. And even when its audience had been shrinking and its profits falling, hardy souls had been opening radio stations. Each new entry aimed at some narrow segment of the total radio audience; to that extent radio offered a wider variety and cultivated its audience more closely than television ever attempted. By 1957 and 1958 radio was very profitable. It had become a central feature in American popular culture. Thanks to the arrival of the transistor, it was all too often inescapable.

Goldmark's LP had by now become essential to the craze for high fidelity, along with the FM tuner invented by Armstrong and magnetic tape recording invented in Germany but perfected in the United States. The 78, which felt and shattered like a dinner plate, had become a curio almost overnight. As the record business grew, it divided. The 45 captured most of the popular music market; the LP took most of the jazz and classical music market. LPs also put a lot of literature on disc—plays, poetry, prose. The best offering was Dylan Thomas read by Dylan Thomas. There was also T. S. Eliot reading T. S. Eliot and Colette reading Colette. High culture was far from neglected in the record boom, although popular music raked in most of the profits.

Adults gradually came to terms with rock 'n' roll, but few of them ever liked it. Middle-class and upper-class parents remained convinced that it was somehow unhealthy and dim-witted. Their fears were wildly exaggerated. Adolescence was still a comparatively recent development, and it was a prolonged identity crisis, strung between childhood and maturity. Rock 'n' roll was the first thing to come along which adolescents could feel was theirs alone, and the more parents agitated against it, the more their own it became. Ownership in turn creates a vested interest. It encourages self-definition even—perhaps especially—when what is owned is something abstract. Far from being a disruptive influence, rock 'n' roll was a conservative force.

The atmosphere of sexual frenzy which rock 'n' roll generated, the riots, the hysteria of teenage girls, the lower-class, street-corner boy aura of the performers, all helped persuade adults that young people were depraved. For that, they blamed comic books.

Comic books had begun in 1934, offshoots from the newspaper comic strips. They were not very successful until 1939, when Superman began whizzing around Metropolis. By 1954 comic-book sales were estimated at 60 to 100 million copies a month. Each book sold was assumed to pass through half a dozen small, and sometimes not so small, pairs of hands.

The most successful comic-book figures were those cast in heroic mold, such as Superman and Batman, offering elementary plots in which the good invariably defeated the bad. But mainly they offered action, which increasingly meant violence. The Korean War did wonders for the fortunes of war comics. More violence. But the Korean War also saw the appearance of something else—horror comics, also known as "the creeps."

By now the advertising in comic books ran strongly to such items as air guns for boys, breast developers for girls. Little wonder that all parents could see in them was sex and violence.

There was an unmistakably nasty element to many of the post-1950 comics. There was hatred of women which expressed itself in fantasies of cruelty, involving white-hot pokers, knives, chains, whips, saws, razor blades, guns, clubs, and axes. Women were commonly shown being branded or blinded. Limbs were hacked off, sending gobbets of blood flying. Rape, torture, and murder were not incidental—they were what the stories were about.

By far the most successful purveyor of horror comics was William Gaines. His father, Max Gaines, had let Superman slip through his fingers but profited anyway from turning out comic-book versions of Bible stories. Max Gaines's publishing dictum was: "I don't care how long it took Moses to cross the desert, I want it in three panels." He also laid down strict rules for his comic books: "Never show anybody stabbed or shot. Show no torture scenes. Never show a hypodermic needle. Don't chop the limbs off anybody. Never show a coffin, especially with anybody in it." On taking over his father's business shortly after the war, William Gaines proceeded to break all of his father's rules. One of his stories, for example, "Foul Play," featured a baseball player who put poison on his spikes to slide into, and murder, a player on another team. The dead player's teammates discover the villain's deed, trap him, kill him, dismember him, then take his dripping portions out to the ball park. There, by the light of the moon, they disport themselves, using the deceased's limbs for bats, and what appear to be his brains, heart, and genitals mark first, second, and third base.

Gaines thought up many of the plots for his horror comic stories. In his personal life he had always been shy around women. Fat and shortsighted, he had never had a date in high school. His first wife was a second cousin. He had a deep distrust of women, and shortly before he turned to producing horror comics, his marriage had failed. Some years later he married again. That marriage also failed. The treatment of women in his comic books was unspeakable.

Dismayed and outraged by the material their children were reading so avidly, parents turned on the comic-book publishers. Senators, local dignitaries, clergymen, psychiatrists, teachers, and youth workers began to organize and press for reform. In some communities comic-book sales were banned to persons under the age of eighteen, but such bans were unenforceable. Under pressure, however, the wholesalers began to drop horror comics.

When sales slumped, Gaines lost interest in them. He was also a man whose feelings were easily wounded. And now his fellow comic-book publishers, who had copied his formats without hesitation when they were profitable, began to shun him. They self-righteously banded together to form the Comic Magazine Association of America in May 1954. They pointedly excluded Gaines from membership. They wrote out a "Code." Then they hired a retired judge to enforce it.

Gaines, meanwhile, gave one of his editors the opportunity to produce a humor magazine with the format of a comic. The result was *Mad*, a publication completely unique. Throughout the conformist 1950s it offered a satirical, skeptical appraisal of American life which was badly needed. It developed an almost faultless eye for the pompous, the false, and the pretentious. In the middle of the age of blandness arose a publication that was positively subversive of bourgeois complacency. *Mad* ridiculed everything and everyone. Astonishingly, it prospered from the first. It sold mainly to teenagers and people in their twenties.

Youthful fashions appalled and baffled parents who, only a generation earlier, had themselves dressed outlandishly, given the chance. Ties were now so slim they merged imperceptibly into the string ties favored by cowboys. Pants were pegged, although not so sharply as on the zoot suits of the war years. Shirt collars were so big that they arched upward before turning down. Hair was greasy and worn in the style known as DA (for Duck's Ass). The essential item in youthful garb was the jacket, with narrow lapels and one button or four rather than the conventional two or three. Jackets came in a single shade, like passion pink or baby blue. A rock 'n' roller might well sport a black leather motorcycle jacket with at least a score of gleaming studs. Formal wear consisted of a white sports coat. Sports shirts were brightly patterned and usually worn open well down the sternum. Shoes with thick rubber soles were favored, as were engineer's boots, with heavy metal zippers. A young man these days was likely to look as if he owned both a motorcycle and a switchblade knife, when there was a good chance that he possessed neither. Not surprisingly, "tough" these days meant "the best."

Language itself was an important part of the assertive adolescent subculture. To have sexual intercourse was to "go all the way." To be excited was to be "all shook up." Money was "bread." Anything interesting was "far out." To do something for the sheer pleasure of it was to do it for "kicks." To "make like an alligator" meant to "drag ass"; this in turn meant to move slowly. And there were the additions which added nothing to what was said but provided audible pauses and punctuation, such as "like" and "y'know?"

Wherever people met or wherever an event was held, that was "the scene." An automobile, regardless of length, was a "short" or an "iron." Clothes were "vines" or "threads." Someone supercool was "hippy." Where you slept, that was your "pad." Much of this language derived from the slang of jazz musicians. By the mid-1950s it was the patois of the young. And if you happened to meet with anything or anyone beyond description, there was an expression for that, too—"something else."

In the fall of 1955 James Dean, a young actor of definite, but definitely limited, talent died in a two-car crash near Paso Robles, California. He was admired for his surly manner. He was twenty-four at the time of his death. He had barely been buried before his grave was vandalized. A Dean cult sprang into existence, and it was decidedly occult in nature. Tens of thousands of adolescents refused to believe that James Dean was dead. Tens of thousands more accepted that he had been killed but believed deeply in his reincarnation. Long after his death newsstands carried James Dean magazines. In the record stores there were upwards of a dozen James Dean songs on sale. Among moviegoers under the age of twenty-five he was the number one movie star.

For those who seriously maintained that there was something profoundly wrong with the nation's young people the Korean War had been a godsend; not so much the war as the twenty-three soldiers who refused repatriation and the stories about the thousands of otherwise healthy young men who had died in captivity from "Give-up-itis." An Army doctor who had been taken prisoner reported his dismay at what he witnessed: "It was their almost universal inability to adjust to a primitive situation. . . . This reaction was partially the result of the psychic shock at being captured. It was also, I think, the result of some new failure in the childhood and adolescent training of our young men—a new softness."

If young people at times appeared bewildered and confused, it was not surprising. Their elders were equally baffled by the modern world. And there is no denying that there was much in midcentury life that was repellent to any independent spirit or critical mind. That, however, could be said of almost any period in history.

What did appear to be new was a variety of emotional despair which, like polio, seemed to concentrate on the young. Alienation had historically been attached mainly to adults, most particularly to workers. It was, moreover, something inflicted on people, in Marxist theory, by the workings of capitalist society. But now, wrote Kenneth Keniston, a psychiatrist employed at Harvard, "Alienation, once seen as imposed *on* men . . . is increasingly chosen *by* men as their basic stance toward society." No longer was it found mainly in the lower level of society; it was spread liberally from top to bottom. And among American youth, he maintained, it had become a way of life—"an explicit rejection of the values and outlook of American culture."

Keniston's uncommitted youth did not simply reject American life, however. In itself such a sentiment would not necessarily have meant very much. But theirs was a rejection which went beyond the general arrangements of American society. It ruined their relationships with other people, and among those they rejected they included themselves. They believed in nothing and no one. Their "participation" in life consisted of making observations. In their conviction that life was inherently meaningless they resembled the French existentialists, who were the *dernier cri* of intellectual fashion shows in the late 1940s. But except for having read one or two of Camus's novels (which the author vehemently insisted were not existentialist at all), they had no acquaintance with existentialism as a rule. Their bleakness was their own. They took a gloomy relish in ideas of struggle leading to failure. Theirs was the power of negative thinking.

To the alienated individual only the present matters. The past is irrelevant, the future uncertain. Feeling becomes more important than knowledge or is exalted as a superior form of knowledge. The emphasis on the present is an incentive to adventure, but the uncommitted are passive by temperament. The adventures thus become internal, made possible by drugs, alcohol, or casual sex.

To the uncommitted, *they* were the world's realists; the rest of humanity consisted of varying types of human gullibility. Traditional ideas of success were a sour joke when the individual had no evident influence on his environment. Traditional ideas of community, identity and commitment were laughable when compared with the power of technology. This bleak outlook marked a break with the traditional exuberance of American youth; it would last, furthermore, beyond the 1950s.

Parents naturally agonized over their wayward young. Where had they gone wrong? No one could seriously contend that American parents were not concerned with their children. American homes were, as the phrase had it, "child-centered." This was especially true in the suburbs, where, thought William H. Whyte, Jr., "a term like filiarchy would not be entirely facetious." It became popular to blame the problems on permissive methods of child rearing. But it is doubtful that in general terms relationships between parents and children altered greatly between the 1930s and the 1960s.

Nor were the majority of adolescents rebellious or alienated. More than 80 percent believed in an omniscient God. Almost as many believed that the most important lesson for people to learn was to obey authority. Nearly half sternly resisted the idea that man descended from the apes. They did not worry very much about important social or political questions. What they did worry about was their bodies: they were too thin or too fat, too tall or not tall enough; their skin was bad, or their posture was. They lived in dread of being rejected by the opposite sex. When they did raise their eyes to contemplate the world around them, they were censorious and conformist—just like mom and dad.

The old bohemian life, self-infatuated, trailing its artistic pretensions like a beggar's cloak, had been swallowed up by the Depression. It was one thing to choose a life of poverty; it was another to have it thrust upon you by the collapse of Wall Street. It was one thing to starve for one's art; another to have the Works Progress Administration find you a wall to paint on and give you a weekly stipend to buy groceries.

Traces of the old bohemia appeared fitfully in Greenwhich Village into the 1940s, in the form of a handful of survivors from the heady days before 1929. Otherwise, it had gone for good.

Yet in the midst of prosperity there was a sudden increase in the number of people who chose to be poor. In the age of conformity there were people who chose to flirt with starvation rather than conform. Rejecting incentives to succeed, they chose to fail. Most of them were in their late teens or early twenties when the war ended. Within them there moved a new sensibility, harkening back to the old bohemian impulse, inchoate but irresistible.

For Jack Kerouac, descended from Indian and French Canadian stock, reared in a Catholic environment, it was a sensibility steeped in sadness and suffering. For Allen Ginsberg, descended from Central European Jews who had made good in America, it was freedom: the freedom to be a poet and a homosexual.

Kerouac called himself a "strange, solitary, crazy Catholic mystic." He decided early in life to be a writer, and in 1950 his first novel appeared, *The Town and the City*. It was very sub-Thomas Wolfe and flashed its sensitivity in all directions. Kerouac had been a student at Columbia, on a football scholarship, during the war. When his knees gave out, so did his scholarship. He drifted into a new kind of twilight, furtive existence then beginning to appear, an existence which did not yet have a name.

He gravitated toward life among the broken, the rejected, the scorned, as unerringly as a nun interested in social work. Kerouac had a longing to believe in something but found nothing to believe in, except unhappiness, of which there was never a shortage among the drug addicts, blacks, prostitutes, migrant farm workers, and petty thieves whose company he began to keep. In his restlessness he began to crisscross the country by car and bus, taking journeys whose only purpose was movement itself.

While at Columbia he had met Ginsberg. And Ginsberg, like Kerouac, had become fascinated with the fringes of criminal life. In 1948, during his last year at Columbia, Ginsberg became involved with a six-foot redhaired hooker and two of her hoodlum acquaintances. On what was intended as the first leg of a journey to Mexico the car they were in (stolen and heavily laden with other stolen property) was approached by a police car. The driver of the stolen vehicle, one "Little Jack" Melody, panicked. A ninety-mph chase followed. It did not last long before it ended in a spectacular crash. Ginsberg escaped almost unharmed from the wreckage. Papers left in the car, however, soon led the police to his apartment. The New York press worked this humble material into a mammoth crime ring. And Ginsberg first came to public attention as the ring's brilliant adolescent mastermind.

The other three went off to prison. Ginsberg's middle-class family, friends, and professors succeeded in getting him committed to the Columbia Psychiatric Institute for treatment. When he was released, he contrived to meet William Carlos Williams, the famous doctor-poet of Paterson, New Jersey, Ginsberg's hometown. Williams encouraged him, praised his poetry, and helped strengthen his resolve to go his own way in life.

But it still took several years before Ginsberg screwed up the courage to break with the comfortable bourgeois life. Until he did, he toiled within it as a market researcher. But his mind made up, he presented his employers with a memorandum on how he could be replaced by an IBM machine. No one ever embraced advanced technology more ardently than this scruffy rebel. His employers took his advice. They kindly gave him a letter explaining that Mr. Ginsberg was the victim of technological progress. With this letter he was launched, on the $40-a-week unemployment compensation it brought him, as a full-time poet and prophet.

The twilight world where middle-class dropouts such as Ginsberg and William Burroughs (of the adding machine family/fortune) merged with the fringes of crime and hucksterism had a name by the 1950s. It was conferred by Kerouac, who in turn had picked it up from a friend of Burroughs's, Hubert Huncke. He was the other man in the crashed car with Ginsberg, "Little Jack" Melody, and the red-haired hooker. One day in the late 1940s he remarked to Kerouac, "Man, I'm beat." In Kerouac's mind there flared a vision of furtiveness and freedom. To be beat meant to be beaten down. But it also meant bop music, hipsterism, sexual promiscuity, drugs, cheap wine, and being responsible for nothing and to no one.

The world at large first encountered the Beats in John Clellon Holmes's article "This Is the Beat Generation" in *The New York Times Magazine* in November 1954. Holmes and Kerouac had been friends. During the early years of this friendship Holmes had written *Go*, the first Beat novel, a plodding autobiographical account of Beat life. It was a life which centered not on Greenwich Village but on Times Square. To the early Beats the Village was fake, literary, co-opted, a place for licensed jesting. As Holmes described it in *Go*, the Beats lived in "a world of dingy backstairs 'pads,' Times Square cafeterias, be-bop joints, night-long wanderings, meetings on street corners, hitchhiking, a myriad of 'hip' bars all over the city, and the streets themselves." They "dug" jazz, mainly of the "cool" variety. A few were confirmed drug addicts. But most stopped at marijuana and Benzedrine. When the latter could not be obtained as pills, Benzedrine inhalers were cracked open and the reeking, sodden paper inside extracted. Rolled into a ball, the Benzedrine-soaked paper was washed down with anything from Coca-Cola to cheap muscatel. It was a habit which was easy to support and more or less effective. But Kerouac became so hooked on Benzedrine inhalers that he developed thrombophlebitis in his legs and spent the last years of his life in considerable pain as a consequence.

In 1956 Ginsberg secured his reputation as an outré poet with the publication of *Howl*. It possessed demonic energy and chutzpah. *Howl* began with a scream of protest: "I have seen the best minds of my generation destroyed by madness." It went on to be thoroughly outrageous, celebrating assorted delights, such as being "fucked in the ass by angel-headed motorcyclists." Ginsberg's reputation spread rapidly from East to West, and the poet soon followed where his reputation had created audiences. In California there were high hopes for "this new prophet of the open fly."

In Los Angeles in the fall of 1955 a poetry reading was arranged featuring Ginsberg and Gregory Corso, whose claim to attention was that he had never, ever put a comb to his hair. Corso had been nurtured in various foster homes and several penal institutions and, with the assistance of Beat-struck students at Harvard, had completed his education in Widener Library.

During the reading one of the auditors drunkenly challenged Corso to a fistfight. Ginsberg jumped up and issued a challenge in reply. "All right," he said. "You want to do something big, something brave? Well, go on, do something *really* brave. Take off your clothes!" Unbuttoning his own shirt, Ginsberg continued to taunt the by-now bemused drunk. "You're afraid, aren't you?" Ginsberg said. He hurled his shirt in the man's face. "You're afraid," said Ginsberg, dropping his trousers. He took off his underpants, bent down and removed his shoes and socks. Completely naked, he danced a triumphal jig. The drunk was shocked into speechless sobriety. The audience, ostensibly hip and unshockable, were angry, but not with the drunk—with Ginsberg. It was an episode, however, which spread the Ginsberg legend still further.

The focus of the Beat scene shifted to the West Coast, but without ever losing its New York connection. In 1956 Black Mountain College in North Carolina disbanded. Much of what was left of its faculty and student body went west, and the *Black Mountain Review* continued to publish. The *Review* became an important outlet for Beat writers.

San Francisco suddenly found itself the center of a poetry "renaissance." This infuriated the local poets who saw the *arriviste* Beats get most of attention.

Since writing *The Town and the City*, Kerouac had crossed the country by bus half a dozen times, always writing, lugging a duffel bag which grew heavier with unpublished, and what must often have seemed unpublishable, manuscripts. But eventually one of them, *On the Road*, which had been rewritten half a dozen times, was published. It made Kerouac and the Beats famous overnight. The 1957 appearance of *On the Road* put the Beats firmly on the map of public consciousness.

It threw a narrow but dazzling beam on a corner of American life. Many people were astonished to find that an alternative life-style existed in American society. The Beats asserted the spiritual against the material, the visionary against the rational, the spontaneous against the carefully thought out. The Beats tapped the vein of anarchism which does not run very far below the surface of American life. Americans were fascinated because the Beats also tapped something else—the American love of the bizarre, the scandalous, and the different.

The Beat life was something new to its time, yet typically American. It began in a vision of freedom. It ended in a cry of despair. It was an adventure simply to hurl yourself on a continent which passed for a country. "I felt like a million dollars," exults the first-person narrator of On the Road. "I was adventuring in the crazy American night." The road was everything. "Our battered suitcases were piled on the sidewalk again; we had longer ways to go. But no matter, the road is life." ". . . we said quick good-byes . . . and stumbled off towards the protective road where noboy would know us." ". . . the road must eventually lead to the whole world. Ain't nowhere else it can go, right?" Yet there was, in the end, only "the raggledy madness and riot of our actual lives, our actual night, the hell of it, the senseless nightmare road."

There had been people similar in their lives and beliefs to the Beats back in the 1920s and 1930s. But there had been no attempt then to embrace in one set of values the saintly with the criminal. There had not been the "cool" attitude toward sex which was both more and less than promiscuity. Nor had there been the present infatuation with Oriental mysticism.

Central to Beat life was the rejection of work as everyone else understood it. (As Beats understood it, "work" meant to copulate. A job was a "gig.") It was shunned not so much from laziness as from a rejection of a capitalist economy. Roughly two-thirds of the Beats appear to have come from middle-class homes. Some came from upper-class homes. Many had at least a year or two of college behind them. However employable they may have been, they chose to be poor. And there were odd jobs to be had for short periods and at odd hours: as mental hospital attendants, art gallery guards, meter readers; waiting on tables, working on construction sites, fire watching. For Beat women there were jobs to be had driving cabs, washing dishes, or an income might be made from homemade pottery, jewelry, or candles. Those willing to accept the risks could turn to selling marijuana or shoplifting. The more attractive Beat women could pick up ready money as B-girls or from unvarnished prostitution. Some Beat men were also known to hustle (or "sell trade") for two or three evenings a week. Enough could be earned in a good summer to finance a trip to Greece or India or North Africa in the winter. But in general, it was fair to say that confronted with the "Permanent War Economy, the Beats have responded with the Permanent Strike."

Most Beats were men. Like the population at large, one-tenth of Beats were black. Bisexuals were not uncommon, but homosexuality, its joys sung by Allen Ginsberg, remained a minority persuasion.

Beat parties were widely assumed to be little more than orgies. But most consisted of listening to poetry or jazz, or both combined, and drinking beer or cheap wine. Beats tended to despise dancing, considering it an activity for the "squares." As the Beat mystique spread, hordes of crypto-Beats, part-time Beats and pseudo-Beats appeared. Their parties featured bongo drumming and energetic dancing—until the police arrived.

Following the appearance of *On the Road*, Beat life was reported as if it were the discovery of life on another planet. Yet most Beats were not publicity seekers. What they principally wanted was to be left alone. Some wore beards, some wore sandals, but most dressed like the working-class men of the run-down neighborhoods where they lived. They made no effort to draw attention to themselves. The Beat Madonna wore leotards or toreador pants, perhaps a pair of large earrings, but no make-up, and she wore her hair long. When Beats wore badges such as beards, it was to identify themselves to other Beats, not to attract the notice of squares.

The average level of education among Beats was higher than the national average. They never voted but were better informed on politics than most people who did. A generation earlier antimaterialistic young people had been left-wing radicals. Yet the Beats were deliberately antipolitical. "Beats suffer not from apathy," Ned Polsky remarked, "but from political antipathy."

Outcasts by choice, they welcomed those outcast at birth. They romanticized blacks the way middle-class radicals in the 1930s had romanticized the working class. "At lilac evening I walked with every muscle aching among the lights of 27th and Welton in the Denver colored section, wishing I were a Negro, feeling that the best the white world had offered was not enough for men, not enough life, joy, kicks, darkness, music, not enough night," says Sal Paradise, the narrator of *On the Road*. "I wished I were a Denver Mexican or a poor overworked Jap, anything but what I was so drearily, a 'white man' disillusioned. . . . I was only myself . . . wishing I could exchange words with the happy, true-hearted, ecstatic Negroes of America."

In Beat circles there was considerable cachet to having a black friend or, better still, a black bed partner. Much Beat language was taken from blacks' slang. And the "authenticity" which idealistic college students before the war had looked for among the lumpen proletariat, the Beats were inclined to seek among the outcasts of the outcast—the hipsters, most of whom were black. These were the poor who preyed on the poor, as thieves, pimps, drug peddlers, and stickup artists. White middle-class hipsters were laughably tame compared with the original article, much as white middle-class radicals had been tame compared with worker-revolutionaries who had blood or dirt on their hands.

There were "cool" hipsters and "hot" hipsters. The cool ones were aloof and sardonic. The hot were passionate and talkative. Beats were often able to switch from being one to the other as the occasion demanded. Behind their infatuation with hipsters was evidently a craving for excess;

almost anything was better than the smooth, bland, efficient, complacent world which called itself the American way of life. The appeal of hipsters was augmented by their involvement in two nonbourgeois subcultures: jazz and junk (from Benzedrine to heroin). Beats were also into jazz and junk, and these shared interests with the hipsters provided a tie. But most white Beats shrank from violence—although it was cool to have friends who did not.

Beatness was largely a style, yet it was a style which could vary widely as between individuals. Ginsberg was a very American type of mystic, for instance, full of optimism, energy, and plans. In some ways he was almost a caricature of Jewish hustle. He loved to act as broker between the dropouts and the Establishment. He was constantly in touch with the Beat scene in Los Angeles, New York, and San Francisco. He oozed sympathy and kindness. Corso was not as gifted a poet as Ginsberg, yet he possessed a grain of talent. He despised straights or squares and provoked them with his wise-guy, street-scuffler manner. He cultivated a nice line in deadpan put-ons which baffled and irritated the polite middle-class audiences who showed up at his poetry readings. Corso would launch into a disquisition on "fried shoes" or would reveal his vision that "All life is a Rotary Club." Kerouac was neither apathetic nor antipathetic to politics; he was, in fact, a fervent anti-Communist. He astounded his Beat friends by telling them that he was going to vote for Eisenhower. Voting was odd enough, but voting for *Eisenhower?*

With discovery came derision. There was both deep interest in and deep hostility toward the Beats. They had opted out from the Cold War and the American way of life. That smacked of treason. But the Cold War and the American way of life could be dreary and stifling. It was not hard to detect in some of the criticism a note of envy.

A San Francisco newspaper columnist, Herb Caen, added the Yiddish diminutive -*nik* to coin the belittling term "Beatnik." It stuck, to the intense disgust of the original Beats. Before long suburbanites began throwing "Beatnik" parties.

Beat literature was mocked. It lent itself to mockery. Kerouac, like Balzac, pretended that he never changed a line and claimed to have created "spontaneous prose." It was reminiscent of the "automatic writing" of the 1920s, which was supposed to tap the unconscious. Kerouac, however, was a serious and dedicated writer, his pretensions apart. The trouble with most of his writing is that it is simply dull. Ginsberg had the poetic gift, plus an engagingly anarchic sense of humor. Some of Corso's poetry is effective. But Beat writing tended in most instances to be not simply incomprehensible but bad and incomprehensible.

Only one established writer gave the Beats his (unsought) blessing, Norman Mailer. But the Beats' favorite writer, Henry Miller, would have little to do with them. Mailer's benediction, moreover, had nothing to do with admiration for Beat writings. He considered the Beats of social, not literary, importance.

With two friends Mailer in 1955 founded the *Village Voice*. There was serious disagreement from the start. "They wanted it to be successful. I wanted it to be outrageous," said Mailer. The Beats were outrageous, so he showered them with praise.

Old-style leftists hoped, briefly, that the Beats would prove to be a generation of new young radicals. On acquaintance they disliked what they found. "Their onslaught on the Air-Conditioned Nightmare, as Henry Miller—their John the Baptist—called it, sounds very like the griping of soldiers who do not intend to mutiny," complained one sorely disappointed old Socialist.

Hardly had they been discovered than the Beats were commercialized. A bad Kerouac novel, *The Subterraneans*, was turned into a worse movie. Suburbanites studied the film seeking clues on how to run their "Beatnik" parties; they wielded foot-long cigarette holders and wore black leotards, berets, and paste-on beards. The New York Beat scene shifted away from Times Square down to Greenwich Village just as a night spot, the "Colledge of Complexes," opened, to cater to the tourist trade and to run an annual "Miss Beatnik" contest.

Fame brought the fellow travelers, orphans of the storm, phonies and Beat careerists flocking. Beats in the three major Beat communities numbered only 4,000 to 5,000 at any given time. Yet the number of people who sampled Beat life at some time or were strongly influenced by it ran into the hundreds of thousands. Most of these people were under thirty. The Beats were important for another reason: in the 1950s they were the only rebellion in town.

19

Crime—Organized and Otherwise

Crime paid, most of the time, in the prosperous postwar. By the late 1950s for every 100 reported crimes there were 14 reported convictions. Crime was democratic and ubiquitous. There were rich criminals and poor, violent criminals and criminals who would faint at the sight of blood, criminals who acted alone and criminals who acted in concert. Crime was a pervasive reality of everyday life; at some time almost everyone was in some way touched by it.

There was no criminal class. Criminals were drawn from every class. White-collar crime, which usually meant stealing from one's employer, flourished, from stealing stationery to embezzling $1 million or more. A firm of management consultants, whose clients included hotels, airlines, banks, hospitals, major retailers, and government agencies, was able in a

CRIME—ORGANIZED AND OTHERWISE

single year to unearth $60 million worth of unreported white-collar crime. There had developed, said Norman Jaspan, the firm's president, "a new kind of thief. Generally a member of the middle or upper class, he rarely has financial cause to steal. Often the product of a college education . . . in the last decade he has become America's most resourceful and successful crook. He is the thief in the white collar." And he was stealing upwards of $2 billion a year.

The sums taken by some individuals made legendary bank heists look trifling by comparison. Mrs. Minnie Clark Mangum, for example, surpassed the Brink's robbers by a clear margin. As assistant treasurer of the Commonwealth Building and Loan Association of Norfolk, Virginia, she lifted $3 million over several years in the 1950s, using nothing more unwieldy than a fountain pen. She gave most of what she stole to needy friends and relatives and her favorite charities. Mrs. Mangum did not consider herself a crook.

To the white collar criminals, what they were doing was not crime at all. Yet there remains the fact that a free, democratic society is held together by trust, not coercion. White-collar criminals are violators of trust. And when trust breaks down, anarchy threatens. Forced to choose between anarchy and tyranny, people nearly always chose tyranny. In terms of the damage done to society the white-collar criminal may well be a more deadly menace than the racketeer.

But it was the racketeers who excited the greater measure of public interest. Americans had long been fascinated by organized crime. After 1945 organized crime flourished as never before.

Its mainstay was gambling. In annual turnover, gambling in the 1950s was said to be the sixth biggest business of the coutry, after food, steel, automobiles, chemicals, and machine tools. Considering that gambling was illegal in nearly every state, this was an all-American success story—of rampant success in the face of heavy odds.

Before 1933 illegal gambling was mostly a small business operation; a cozy affair involving only the bettors, the neighborhood bookmaker, and the local police. But when the twenty-first Amendment dried up the income from bootlegging, mobsters began to move in on illegal gambling. It was a soft target; the bookies could hardly turn to the law for help. By the Second World War the mobsters controlled nearly all illegal gambling, and they were richer than they had ever been during Prohibition.

The Depression, far from making people gamble less because they had less money made them gamble more because gambling offered hope. The numbers, in operation for several decades, suddenly became wildly popular. On a nickel bet a lucky player could win up to $25—as much as most people took home from work each week. The numbers also provided a training ground; many a postwar racketeer began his life in crime as a numbers runner.

After the war sustained prosperity and the rapid spreading of middle-class incomes made gambling a very big business and one of the least dangerous of criminal activities. The police would hardly ever countenance crimes involving drugs or violence, but gambling, which appeared to hurt no one, was another matter, and a profitable one for the police, too. In the late 1940s Harry Gross, a New York bookmaker, was able to build up a bookmaking empire involving 400 employees and 200 policemen. Gross paid out what he called the "standard in the trade," which ranged from $2 a week to the policeman on the beat, $40 to the sector radio car crew, $15 a month to each police sergeant for every horse parlor in his section, $50 a month to each lieutenant, $100 a month to each captain, and $650 a month to the chief inspector. Gross was also generous with gifts of fur coats, TV sets, watches, suits, and cases of liquor. In all, he was paying out $1 million a year for police protection, which included tips of impending raids so that he could remove his records in good time.

Gambling not only prospered; it was transformed. Before the war it was only in decadent Europe that respectable people wanted to be seen gambling, preferably at Monte Carlo. There had been gambling ships anchored offshore from American coasts in the 1930s. But the moment a photographer appeared the customers would shyly hide their faces. The newly affluent Americans of the postwar were a different breed. They not only gambled but wanted to be seen to have gambled.

Gambling became a status symbol, and as life became safer and more comfortable, and often dull, gambling provided a vicarious outlet for the dangerous impulses constrained by middle-class life. This new middle class, hungry for excitement without risk, eminence without struggle, had the time and the money to travel (and the inclination: travel was another part of the status display). The crooks obligingly provided a place for them to go. It was, fittingly, a place built on sand—Las Vegas.

Boulder Dam, built during the New Deal, had brought a reliable water supply to southern Nevada and thus helped keep Las Vegas alive. But it took a racketeer to put the place on the map. The crooks discovered Las Vegas in the course of a bloody little war between the legal Continental Press Service, which carried race results, and a rival operation set up by former Capone henchmen to provide a wire service from the West Coast. The war brought to prominence one Benjamin Siegel—better known as Bugsy, on account of his lunatic tirades when his temper snapped.

Nevada, as has already been mentioned, was free from bourgeois morality. It tolerated both gambling and prostitution. The wire service ran through Las Vegas, the biggest town in Clark County, which in 1940 had a population of 16,000. It did not look like much. But Siegel had a visionary's eye. The state's total revenue from gambling was a paltry $30,000 a year. Yet, moved perhaps by an unerring talent for spotting human weakness, he saw this dreary, arid, cheerless spot as a place where a gambling heaven could be built to draw the suckers from every state in the Union, provided the setting was made alluring.

When the war ended, Siegel contracted with a Phoenix construction company to erect the Flamingo Hotel (later, and invariably, called by Siegel, "the fabulous Flamingo Hotel"). It was scheduled to cost $1.5 million. But Siegel approached it the way Louis XIV approached the construction of Versailles: only the best would do. It was built of concrete, in a climate where plaster would have sufficed. Every bathroom had a private line to the sewer. Plumbing costs alone ran to $1 million. Expensive hardwood was imported. Marble displaced humble stone. At a time when millions of people could not get a house built because of the shortage of materials, Siegel was able to find steel, copper, pipes, fittings, wire, tiles, nails, screws, and glass in any quantity he wanted. The cost of the Flamingo, however, took off. Siegel made numerous trips to the East Coast to raise money from his friends. The Flamingo had cost $6 million by the time it was finished, and Siegel had sunk his entire fortune in it.

"On the evening of December 26, 1946, Siegel donned a white tie and swallowtail coat, and with Virginia Hill on his arm, flung open the doors to his 'fabulous Flamingo Hotel.' The hotel was not yet finished, but the theatre, casino, restaurant and lounge were spanking new and ready for action. . . . It was a flop from the beginning. Bugsy's specially chartered Constellations were grounded by bad weather in Los Angeles, and only a few of the invited celebrities showed up . . . the casino went into the red the very first night." Bugsy threw one of his fits.

In its first two weeks the fabulous Flamingo lost $100,000. Siegel closed it down and waited for the hotel rooms to be finished. The local fraternity of small-time gamblers regarded these events with glee.

In March 1947 the Flamingo opened for a second time. For three weeks it steadily lost money. But then the customers began to arrive. The hotel filled up by summer. The casino began to make a clear profit of more than $10,000 a day. Bugsy's vision had been vindicated. His fellow racketeers began to look at Las Vegas in an wholly new light. They also took another look at the man who had put Las Vegas on the map.

A year after the Flamingo had proved itself to be a money spinner Bugsy Siegel had recouped his fortune. He was the most powerful man in Las Vegas. Sitting on the couch in Virginia Hill's Beverly Hills home, quietly reading a newspaper like a man without a care in the world, he was riddled with bullets by someone standing at a nearby window.

In following years Las Vegas outgrew Bugsy's wildest hopes. Dozens of casinos sprang up along "Glitter Gulch" and the streets abutting it. Not all of them were run by mobsters, but most were. And under the tutelage of Meyer Lansky, who stood in relation to the mob bosses much as Cardinal Richelieu had stood in relation to Louis XIII, the crooks learned how to make their casinos pay with a minimum of trouble from local, state, or Federal authorities. Lansky already provided a massive layoff betting operation for bookies. It seemed only natural that he should guide the Las Vegas operation.

Each new casino tried to be more lavish than its predecessors. Each was designed to keep the customers' thoughts on the action. No clocks on the walls marked the passage of time. No door or window betrayed the location of the sun or moon. There was nowhere to sit down except at the tables. And nothing was allowed to interfere with the rattle of dice or the sibilant murmur of cards being shuffled. On one occasion a crap player suffered a fatal heart attack. He was rolled out of sight under the table until the ambulance arrived, while the play went on all around, and above, him.

Las Vegans liked to joke that there were only three things to do in their town, and two of them were drinking and gambling. Much of the local economy rested on prostitution, itself the second biggest illegal enterprise in America.

Prosper though it unmistakably did, all was not well in Nevada. Las Vegas and Reno had the largest police forces of any towns of their size in the entire Western world. Las Vegas could boast the world's highest suicide rate—fifteen times the American national average. The juvenile delinquency rate was, in a place where juveniles were comparatively rare, more than twice the national average. A city of 64,000 in the late 1950s, it had more than 13,000 reported crimes a year. As a ratio of crimes to population this was probably an all-time record. And whatever the mobsters brought, it did not include peace and quiet. But for solid, sensible business reasons killings connected with gambling were prudently arranged to take place outside Nevada.

Most Nevadans appeared content with the heritage of Bugsy Siegel. Tourists provided the state with three-fourths of its revenue, and that revenue rose strongly from year to year; so too did population. Clark County, so sparsely populated back in 1940, by 1960 had 200,000 residents. It had grown at seven times the national rate, and nearly all because of gambling. Boulder Dam had brought the water. Bugsy Siegel brought the people.

From May 1950 to May 1951 the Senate's Special Committee to Investigate Crime in Interstate Commerce had unfolded, for the benefit of both the American people and the presidential ambitions of Senator Kefauver, a panoramic view of crime in America. The televised hearings were a national education on the subject of corruption. The committee possessed a very powerful tool in its endeavors: an Executive Order from President Truman authorizing it to examine income tax returns.

The Senators could be seen to be shocked, but it is doubtful that they heard anything in public that they had not already heard in executive session. The people at home, however, were shocked. Most people who had played the numbers or patronized prostitutes had never felt themselves to be part of a vast criminal enterprise; but that was how the Kefauver hearings portrayed them.

Gambling was the lifeblood of organized crime. The committee put its turnover at $17 to $25 billion a year. This was little more than a guess, and probably a highly inflated guess. Yet it seems beyond dispute that the money involved in gambling ran into the billions of dollars each year.

The hearings showed how deeply entrenched gambling had become in everyday life. In some small towns it was open and accepted, even though no one dared to suggest that the laws against it ought to be repealed. In

Havana, Illinois, however, the townspeople protested when Governor Adlai Stevenson in 1950 attempted to put the gamblers out of business. A third of Havana's annual budget was covered by raiding the gambling houses each month and fining the operators. "With the gambling fines cut off," the mayor lamented, "the next year is going to be tough."

The Kefauver Committee went from town to town, publicizing rather than investigating local crookedness. In Chicago it subpoenaed Captain Daniel A. Gilbert, a figure celebrated in the Chicago press as the "richest cop in the world." On a policeman's pay the enterprising Captain Gilbert had managed to accumulate a fortune of nearly half a million dollars. He modestly attributed most of his wealth to making lucky bets on prizefights and football games.

In Tampa the committee encountered a sheriff nicknamed "Melon Head." He was hard pressed to explain an equally remarkable feat—how he had saved $128,000 in nine years out of a salary of $7,000 a year. But he found the going difficult because he was cursed with an almost total inability to remember past events.

In Kansas City, Missouri, there stood the Last Chance Saloon, a place of considerable fame in that region. The saloon was built exactly over the Missouri-Kansas state line. Whenever there was a raid all the equipment and customers were moved across the line into the opposite state. For some inexplicable reason there had never been a joint raid conducted by the Kansas and Missouri police.

In Detroit, the committee found, Ford had contracted with a notorious racketeer for the shipment of its automobiles. There were also Ford agencies which were owned by well-known crooks.

In Saratoga Springs, New York, the gamblers could call the police each night and request help. A police car would soon appear to pick up the night's takings and escort them to the bank for a nominal fee of $10.

The committee managed to make life miserable for racketeers if it achieved nothing else. Joseph Bonnano (better known as Joe Bananas), for example, spent almost a year driving around the country, from one small town to another, with his wife and children. Like dozens of his fellow gangsters who were driven to the same extreme, Bonnano was trying to keep out of a subpoena's way.

In the end none of the committee's legislative recommendations became law. But a new income tax code did make life miserable for bookmakers. It required them to register their occupations and pay a $50 license fee. They were also required to pay 10 percent of their gross in taxes. The penalties for violation were steep. For several years bookmakers kept their heads down. The existing tax laws were also enforced more rigorously against known crooks. Hundreds were prosecuted, and hundreds of millions of dollars recovered in back taxes and fines.

The enduring legacy of the Kefauver hearings was to make the myth of the Mafia part of American folklore. "A nationwide crime syndicate does exist in the United States," Kefauver flatly stated. It was an idea encouraged by numerous sensation-mongering journalists. But with the imprimatur of a Senate committee "investigating" crime its validity appeared unassailable. Kefauver conceded that there was no single individual who oversaw this vast criminal conspiracy. Nevertheless, "Behind the local mobs which make up the national crime syndicate is a shadowy, international criminal organization known as the Mafia."

Kefauver's contention was reminiscent of the newspaper stories of the 1920s which repeatedly attempted to pin the responsibility for bootlegging on the "Mafia Grand Council of America." There was organization in crime, but that was not the same as an organization of crime. Kefauver overstated the case. J. Edgar Hoover, for reasons of his own, understated it.*

What organization there was dated from the 1928–1931 Castellamarese War, when two gangs were fighting for control of rackets in New York. One gang was mainly Sicilian in origin; the other, mainly southern Italian. The war proved to be costly in blood and treasure to both sides. As often happens, the war was concluded with a truce and the creation of a peace-keeping body. This body was known to outsiders as the Mafia. But to those on the inside it was commonly known as La Cosa Nostra—Our Thing. There were local variants—e.g., in Buffalo, The Arm; in Providence, The Office.

Cosa Nostra embraced the 4,500 to 6,000 gangsters of Italian or Sicilian origin. Nearly half the membership was located in New York, enrolled in five crime "families." The remainder were distributed in nineteen other families in other cities. The various families formed a permanent commission to arbitrate disputes and to formulate general policy. This body was the Commission.

A top family was headed by a "Don." The remainder were headed by a mere "Boss." The Commission was composed of from nine to twelve Dons and Bosses. This provided a structure which was stable, yet rigid. Below the Commission were regional and big-city councils.

But the family was from first to last the essential unit. A family might have as few as twenty members. Some had as many as 500. Each family was virtually autonomous within its territory. The Commission had no power to become involved in internal affairs.

The existence of the Commission, the councils, the families, the Dons encouraged the myth of an all-powerful, all-encompassing Mafia. So, too, did the late emergence of the Italians on the urban scene. They had arrived in America after the Irish and the Jews, each of whom had turned to crime when they found the channels of advance restricted to only a few at a time. As opportunities for advancement improved, however, the Irish and Jews began to shun crime as a career, leaving the field to the incoming Italians.

*The FBI's record against organized crime was undistinguished. Had national pressure forced any administration to charge the FBI with smashing it, as it had long ago smashed amateur bank robbers of the Dillinger variety, it would almost certainly have failed. Hoover appears to have sensed that. He chose to maintain that the Mafia, or the Mob, or the Syndicate, did not exist.

But the southern Italians and Sicilians, although they got most of the attention, remained a decided minority within the total number of persons involved in organized crime. And this remained true long after the formation of the Commission. Detroit was in the hands of a Jewish mob. Irish gangs controlled the docks of the major East Coast ports. Organized crime in Cleveland was a Jewish preserve. It was a Jew, Abe Reles, who had founded the most dreaded organization of all, Murder, Inc. Sometimes when Italians began careers in crime, they found it expedient to take Irish names: Jimmy Plumeri became Jimmy Doyle; Thomas Eboli became Tommy Ryan. In San Francisco and New York a sizable part of organized crime was controlled by Chinese gangs.

The Commission no more ran organized crime in the United States than the United Nations Security Council ran the world. There were striking parallels to be drawn between these two bodies, with the Mafia being analagous to the UN. There was strong local autonomy, with each family exercising a jealous watch over its sovereign prerogatives. There was a weak central organization which relied on a few strong families to bring pressure to bear against recalcitrant members. Now and then the Commission, like the Security Council, was able to settle a dispute. But if two parties were determined to fight, it was really powerless to stop them. Wars were rare, not because the Commission exerted pressure but because they were more costly in muscle and money than the possible gains could justify. Also, of course, the postwar generation of mobsters was more sophisticated and less trigger-happy than the warlords of the Castellamarese War had been.

As Ramsey Clark remarked following his term as Attorney General of the United States: "There is no one massive organization that manages all or even most planned and continuous criminal conduct throughout the country. There are hundreds of small operations that engage in organized criminal activity—car theft rings, etc—scattered throughout the nation." Every Cosa Nostra family in the country could go out of business; there would still be organized crime—in plenty.

In time, stability and success weakened the family element within the crime families. In the beginning, back in the 1920s or 1930s, they had been based on a collection of brothers, brothers-in-law, cousins, nephews, fathers, and sons. By the mid-1950s it was unusual for a father to be able to bring in his son to succeed him. Crime families were becoming business organizations, with the distinction that the business was illegal. But even that was changing.

Gangsters already provided services for which demand was always strong: gambling; prostitution; narcotics. Through loansharking they provided credit. By taking over unions, they could provide a grasping employer with cheap labor. When they began to look for investments in which they could place their rising gains from illegal services they turned, naturally, to the provision of other services—that is, they do not appear to have considered investing in IBM or opening factories. In the growing service economy no business consultant could have given them sounder advice. Gangsters' money in the 1950s was being poured into hotels, bowling alleys, parking lots, restaurants, and Las Vegas.

Yet the old ways died hard. A New York mobster named Carmine Lombardozzi was able to get control of a Wall Street brokerage house. He proceeded to use it to float stock frauds. Joseph Profaci, for a time the Boss of Bosses in New York, was seemingly no more than a prosperous small businessman, the owner of the Mama Mia importing company. Profaci was convicted of selling adulterated olive oil.

The impression that organized crime was more highly organized than was really the case was accompanied by an equally exaggerated belief that it was fantastically profitable. This was true for a comparative few. But some estimates of the profits of organized crime were so high that they would have provided a net income of $1 million a year for every mobster in the country, including the lowliest foot soldier. Where could these presumed billions be salted away each year? Las Vegas was the biggest single mob investment, and by 1963 every mob-owned casino and hotel there could have been bought for less than $300 million. Very few mobsters lived ostentatiously. The majority lived in ordinary middle-class homes in unexceptional neighborhoods. "There is big money in organized crime for a few," concluded Ramsey Clark, "but for most it is dangerous, hard, dirty work for uncertain middle class incomes."

It was the irresistible lure of easy money that led the mobs into the dope business. In 1948 the then Boss of Bosses, Frank Costello, decreed that heroin was too hot to handle. The Federal Bureau of Narcotics was far more feared than the FBI. Many of the family heads found narcotics repugnant and agreed to follow Costello's lead. But heroin simply proved too profitable and some families, such as the Accardo family in Chicago, already dealing heroin, could not kick the habit. It proved impossible even in families where discipline was supposed to be strict to keep low-ranking members from dealing on the sly.

The heroin problem added to the tensions which constantly threatened to plunge the five New York families into another Castellamarese War all through the 1950s. Several attempts were made to depose Costello, including an assassination attempt which left the putative hit man dead and his intended victim slightly wounded. Costello covered one of his flanks by reaching an understanding with the head of Murder, Inc., Albert Anastasia.*

On October 25, 1957, Anastasia went to the barbershop of the Park-Sheraton Hotel. For once, while his boss's head was swathed in towels, Anastasia's bodyguard took a walk. What followed was an example of scrupulous adherence to the hit man's code: "You do not kill a man in his own home; you do not kill a man in front of his family; you do not hit him in a church or in any other place of worship; you do not torture a man;

---

*At his appearance before the Kefauver Committee Anastasia was asked to name one job he had held between 1919 and 1942. After racking his brains for several minutes, he finally replied, "I don't remember."

and you do not rob him. Other than that, he's all yours.'' In front of a dozen silent and terrified witnesses the hit man, Jack "Mad Dog" Nazarian, shot Anastasia in the head while he lay back relaxed in the barber's chair, breathing heavily through damp, steaming towels.

Two weeks later, to resolve the question of succession to Anastasia's territories and to put an end to the simmering unrest over Costello's leadership, the Commission met in Apalachin, New York, at the home of Jack Barbera. The meeting was also supposed to settle the heroin question, the mobsters' own version of Prohibition; no one was supposed to touch the stuff, but the ban was proving to be unenforceable.

In the wake of the Anastasia killing the atmosphere was tense. Everyone came well armed and with half a dozen bodyguards. It was no cozy gathering but an unwonted display of muscle. The New York State Police stumbled on it by a fluke. For a week thereafter the press was filled with sensational accounts of fat middle-aged mobster millionaires running into the woods, tearing their $1,000 vicuña coats on barbed wire, ruining their $100 alligator-skin shoes in the mud of plowed fields. The Apalachin gathering broke up before it could settle anything and the Anastasia killing led in time to more killings, spawning a gang war which flared up sporadically for another five years.

The spreading drug trade carried organized crime still further afield. When it was discovered that narcotics addiction was spreading rapidly among adolescents, there was shock and alarm. It was not most teenagers who were at risk, however, but a comparative few, and those few mainly black and living in Chicago or New York. The drug racket set off a powerful sentiment of revulsion, but one which had confused effects. When *The Man with the Golden Arm* appeared in 1956, the Motion Picture Alliance attempted to show its disapproval of drug addiction by refusing to issue a seal for the film. At the same time *A Hatful of Rain*, a serious play concerning an addict, was playing to full and enthusiastic houses on Broadway.

Dispassionate consideration of the drug problem was bedeviled by the marijuana issue. There had for decades been horrifying tales concerning its effects: it led to murder, rape, insanity, destroyed the lungs, attacked the brain, made men impotent, and women insatiable. Until the 1940s pamphlets published by state and local authorities gave credence to these stories. But in 1944 a Committee on Marijuana established by Fiorello La Guardia concluded four years of study with a report which rejected these absurd claims. Marijuana, said the report, was not a drug of addiction and impaired neither health nor morals when consumed in moderation. It was a stimulant, but no more a menace to society in its effects than alcohol.

Yet hardly had the old myths been overturned than a new one arose. Now marijuana smoking was said to be the straight short road to heroin. So when *The Alice B. Toklas Cookbook* was published by Harper's in 1957, the famous recipe for marijuana brownies was excised (it appeared in full in the English edition).

Despite the strictures, and precautions, the use of marijuana spread rapidly. It was heavily and successfully propagandized by the Beats, whose most enduring legacy was probably to turn on middle- and upper-class white youth to marijuana smoking. Before this time it had been confined almost entirely to jazz musicians, blacks, and a few Mexican-Americans. And when in the early 1950s an eighteen-year-old girl was arrested in California on a "drug" charge for smoking marijuana, she sent a chill down the spine of middle-class parents, because she looked exactly the kind of well-bred girl who did not do such things. What was more, she claimed that in smoking marijuana she found a sense of community with others. To the Beats, that made her one of their own. For hundreds of thousands of young Americans smoking marijuana became part of their spiritual search.

The resort to chemical stimulants had been further encouraged by the war. Benzedrine ("Bennies") was widely used by soldiers, sailors, and airmen during night operations. Benzedrine tablets were also used to arouse men on the verge of combat. In time Benzedrine became a commonplace aid to college students, hipsters, Beats, and tired businessmen.

Atop this spreading network of sniffing, gulping, and smoking stood heroin, because the people who sold the one were also likely to sell the other. No direct connection was ever shown between the use of lesser stimulants and the hard drugs. Yet such a connection was assumed to exist.

So long as there was a strong demand for heroin, mobsters would try to provide it. In the early 1950s a kilo of high-grade heroin could be bought in Marseilles for $2,500. Diluted and repackaged, it would bring, on the streets of New York, as much as $30,000. But the fact that such a thing was possible at all was in large part due to a bureaucratic mistake.

Few people remembered it, but hard drugs had for a short period been legal in fifteen states. The principal Federal narcotics law, the Harrison Act of 1914, was really a revenue act. It did not forbid doctors to prescribe anything, nor was it intended to. The Harrison Act simply demanded that the doctors keep accurate, detailed records of all drug prescriptions.

The United States possessed tens of thousands of drug addicts at the time the Harrison Act was passed. Narcotics clinics were established in more than a score of major cities. Almost without exception they were successful. Addicts were given free advice, prescriptions, and information. The drug traffic in states where such drugs had been illegal dropped sharply. There was a comparable drop in drug-related crimes. Very cautiously, the clinics began to report cures.

Then, in 1921, the Prohibition Bureau, the body responsible for enforcing the Harrison Act, issued a four-page pamphlet based on a report on narcotics written by a committee of the AMA. The committee recommended that addicts be confined during treatment. The Prohibition Bureau's pamphlet seconded this recommendation. The pamphlet had no legal force, yet it soon shut down every one of the clinics. The people responsible for them took the bureau's advice as a command because at that time it wielded Draconian powers and at times wielded them with stunning clumsiness. Doctors working at the clinics disagreed with the bureau recommendation on confinement. But they were not prepared to fight out the issue with the AMA.

After 1921 states and municipalities unfailingly took the approach that drug addiction was a crime, instead of seeing it for what it was, a personality disorder. Every serious attempt at reform was handicapped by the Federal Bureau of Narcotics, which, with the passage of time, acquired a vested interest in the continued criminalization of drug abuse. The FBN had powerful friends in Congress and a wide measure of public support. If anything, most people appear to have supported ever more rigorous measures and to have rejected every suggestion of a more flexible approach. The 1951 Boggs Act was characteristic of this view. It set stiff mandatory sentences for second and third offenders. Presumably aimed at dealers rather than at addicts, in practice it bore down on the addicts who supported their habit by selling small quantities of drugs. It had no appreciable impact on drug traffic; it affected merely the luckless addict, who went to prison for ten years or more.

The drug trade was handed to criminal elements on a plate. They grasped it with both hands. In the 1950s it seems likely that it became the most profitable of all criminal enterprises. It demonstrated, moreover, the ability of organized crime to keep pace with social trends.

Organized crime was able to shift and turn as the occasion required because it was hardly ever interrupted. Local police and politicians proved to be venal in almost every city; not all or even most policemen and politicians, but enough. The FBI posed no inordinate threat; the initials, mobsters joked, stood for "Fumbling Bunch of Idiots." Hoover's men were excellent record keepers but indifferent crime fighters. The Treasury and the FBN were far more effective, but they were engaged in the fight against organized crime on a very limited scale.

Because racketeers had to spend only a small part of their time and energies on staying out of prison, they were able to concentrate on expanding their operations. Besides the drug scene, for example, there was the record business. In the late 1940s three major companies, Columbia, RCA, and Decca, virtually controlled the record business. Mobsters already had an extensive involvement in jukebox businesses. It appeared only logical for them to start putting money into some of the many small record companies which were started in the 1950s. They took no part in the running of the business. The were content to take their share of the (sometimes impressive) profits the small companies earned.

Labor unions, especially in areas where a rational industry-wide union was difficult to create or control, continually offered opportunities for mob infiltration.

The irresistible postwar demand for vicarious sexual experience created rich opportunities for the production and sale of pornography.

And then, as has been described, there was gambling. Yet gambling, like pornography, was so vast an enterprise that much of it was outside criminal control. Indeed, the most successful gaming entrepreneur was a man whose name was wholly free from scandal, William F. Harrah, of Reno and Lake Tahoe.

Harrah was remarkable for his reliance on social science research. At one time he employed a psychiatrist to explain to him what it was that gamblers were *really* looking for. He contracted with Stanford Research Institute to advise him on where to find extra customers.

Harrah opened his first casino in Reno in 1946. He prospered by making it more comfortable and more respectable than rival establishments. Looking for somewhere conducive to expansion, he preferred Lake Tahoe to Las Vegas. The lure of Lake Tahoe was that it was suitable for entire families. There was more to do than drink, gamble, and fornicate. Tahoe in the late 1940s was a small, beautiful, sparsely populated place with some of the clearest water and cleanest air in the world. As Harrah prospered, the town became more and more hideous. The lake and the air were ruined.

Harrah overcame his principal problem—bringing people up from the Pacific coast—by paying to have the width of the highway doubled in some places, by providing a cheap bus ride, and by offering a free meal and a free drink on arrival. He spent a lot of money to advertise his club without mentioning that its chief function was gambling. He also made gaming more democratic by going after the moderate-income people who were accustomed to riding buses. All over Northern California the bus stations contained a Harrah's "Information Desk," looking much like Traveler's Aid, staffed by clean-cut youngsters whose job was to steer people toward Lake Tahoe. As many as twenty buses a day hauled the customers up into the Sierra Nevada from Oakland. They kept coming even in dead of winter, through howling blizzards. One Washington's Birthday, when a heavy mantle of snow covered the ground, fifty-nine busloads disembarked at Harrah's halls. The customers not infrequently arrived in the early-morning hours. Harrah's operated not only year-round but for twenty-four hours a day.

The atmosphere within was as aseptic and tidy as an operating theater; there was no hint of extravagance; this was what the doctor ordered, for this dull, clean setting was designed to overcome those feelings of guilt which the social scientists and the psychiatrist told Harrah gambling inspired in ordinary people. Harrah's club had the insipid Disneyland atmosphere long before Disneyland was built.

Gambling, like prostitution, pornography, and drugs, was part of the rapid postwar increase of life-at-secondhand. These simulacra of risk, sexuality, and spirituality were the reverse face of security and prosperity because too often security and prosperity produced only blandness, tedium, and self-loathing. It was on this basis of human frailty that organized crime rested. Tens of millions of ordinary, usually decent people made it profitable; so profitable that it was worth organizing for.

But whether there was, as much of the nation believed, a massive rise in crime after the war is open to question. Crime waves are notoriously easy to concoct. When Jacob Riis and Lincoln Steffens were rival reporters on rival newspapers, the *New York Evening Sun* and the *New York*

Evening Post, they tracked down every lurid crime they could find and wrote it up in the most sensational fashion, each striving to outshine the other. When they both were in form at the same time, New Yorkers found themselves in the midst of a terrifying crime wave.

FBI crime reports depended on figures from thousands of police forces. Standards of bookkeeping varied widely from force to force and could alter sharply from one year to the next. The New York Police Department, for example, reported a 254 percent increase in crime between 1950 and 1951. This occurred not because crime had suddenly doubled but because the police had found a new and more accurate way of recording it.

Undoubtedly crime increased in the postwar. But its magnitude was distorted by the remarkably low levels of crime during the war years, a period when tens of thousands of the young men most likely to take up criminal careers had been otherwise occupied.

While the war had seen a drop in adult crime rates, it had also seen an astonishing increase in juvenile delinquency. And the adolescent gangs which appeared toward the end of the war were the most terrifying since the turn of the century. A reformed gang leader held the war responsible: it had glorified violence, yet had found no role for those under eighteen. But if the Army was not interested in a fourteen-year-old with a zipgun or a switchblade knife, the Deacons or the Zombies were.

Juvenile gangs were hardly an innovation. Gang fights and gang beatings had been part of life in New York for as long as anyone could remember. But after 1945 the beating was likely to be only the beginning of things, not the end. Postwar gangs turned to outright torture and cold-blooded murder. This made them different from their predecessors, who, if they killed someone, had done so more or less by accident.

Some of the worst gangs were spawned by the brutal, ugly housing projects which increasingly defaced the big cities. Fort Greene Houses in Brooklyn was proudly described by city authorities as the world's biggest housing project; it was "home" to 30,000 people. But to Harrison Salisbury it was "A $20,000,000 slum." The projects created murderous juvenile gangs, he decided, because "They are fiendishly contrived institutions for the debasing of family and community life." Fort Greene was home to two of the toughest gangs in North America, the Chaplains, who were black, and the Mau Maus, who were Puerto Rican. They hardly bothered with fighting other gangs. They fought the police.

The typical gang was run by a president and his war counselor. This latter combined the roles of Secretary of State and Secretary of Defense. His function was to conduct an aggressive foreign policy.

New York's fighting gangs followed geographical rather than racial lines. A project that was predominantly black would produce a black gang. A mainly Puerto Rican street would produce a Puerto Rican gang. But where a project or neighborhood was integrated so, in most instances, were the gangs.

Contrary to popular impression, most adolescent gangs were not fighting gangs. They were defensive alliances of juvenile delinquents. They were an outgrowth of the security mania the rise of the fighting gangs inspired.

A fighting gang would be heavily armed; its armory could involve rifles, pistols, zipguns, shotguns, switchblades, kitchen knives, hunting knives, razor blades, Molotov cocktails, car radio aerials, tire irons, lengths of chain, pieces of pipe, broken bottles, axes, crowbars, or automobiles driven with deadly intent.

New York's fighting gangs drew most of the publicity, but every major city had at least a handful of fighting gangs in its slum districts. The gangs of Los Angeles were as dangerous as those of New York; in 1957 they were credited by the Los Angeles Police Department with 8 murders and more than 200 aggravated assaults.

For the gang member who survived—that is, for one who did not go to prison for a long spell, was not crippled for life, or blinded—there was a logical progression from juvenile violence to adult violence. And it seemed impossible to put the gangs out of business—they reflected the obsessions of the world at large only too well: the security mania and the resulting efforts to arm, fight, negotiate, strike truces, and draft available young men into the armed forces.

Then, suddenly, the fighting gangs appeared to vanish overnight. "By 1957," Claude Brown recalled, "the fight thing had just about gone." Claude at thirteen had been a member of a "bopping" gang and close to death with a bullet in his back. Much of his childhood was spent in training schools.* and in fighting. But now "A man didn't have to prove himself with his hands as much as he had to before." Fighting had been supplanted as an activity for tough young men by heroin. The questions about a newcomer to the neighborhood had been: "How good is he with his hands? Does he carry a knife? Or a gun?" Now they were: "Is he strung out? Is he dealing? Who's his connection?"

A young addict from 100th Street wrote a psalm for himself at about this time:

Heroin is my shepherd; I shall always want.
It maketh me to lie down in gutters;
It leadeth me beside still madness;
It destroyeth my soul.
It leadeth me in the paths of hell for its own sake.
Yeah, though I walk through the valley of the Shadow of Death,
I shall fear no evil, for heroin art with me;
My syringe and spike will comfort me.

*During his stay at the Wiltwyck School for Boys, not far from Hyde Park, the boys were taken once a year "to the nice old rich white lady's house." And at the age of twelve he was astonished. There was plenty to eat, and the house was enormous. So where were all the cockroaches? After all, "it wasn't like roaches to hide when there were lots of people around eating food and stuff. That's why Mama didn't like roaches—they were always coming around and showing off when company came."

Thou puts me to shame in the presence of mine enemies.
Thou anointest my head with madness; my cup runneth over with sorrow.
Surely hate and evil shall follow me all the days of my life.
And I will dwell in the house of misery and disgrace forever.

Among those who studied juvenile delinquency at first hand it did not appear to have increased so very much; much of it was simply the spreading of behavior formerly confined to the lower class to middle-class youth, and in doing so it became visible for the first time to much of the middle class. Rock 'n' roll was one more example of the spreading of lower-class dress, speech, interests, and manners to middle-class youth. Comic books, television, and rock 'n' roll all were held by middle-class parents to account for juvenile delinquency.

Definitions of delinquent behavior varied from state to state and town to town, making it hard to tell exactly what was happening. There was, for example, the "juvenile delinquent" aged seven who was sent to jail for "lewd and immoral conduct." He had put his hand up the skirt of a five-year-old.

In the mid-1950s some 400,000 children and teenagers, aged ten to seventeen, were convicted of delinquency each year by juvenile courts. Although this figure was large in absolute terms, it represented only 2 percent of this age-group. And some of the offenses committed by juveniles, such as repeated absence from school, entering poolrooms, and "associating with immoral persons," would not have been considered offenses in criminal courts.

The convicted JD would, after two or three convictions, in most states be sent to a training school. The best training schools were in the more prosperous states, such as New York, Michigan, Illinois, Minnesota, Ohio, and California, and in Washington, D.C. They were, almost without exception, horrifying.

In a typical training school there were students living in cottages under the care of cottage parents. Difficult students were transferred, for their and the community's good, to adjustment cottages. There they were under the care of supervisors, who exercised various tools of control. Some students spent long periods in meditation rooms. Among the students were numerous postgraduates, who had returned for further training. Such was the way the training school presented itself. But cottage meant cell block; adjustment cottage meant punishment block; the meditation room was solitary; a supervisor was a guard; and the tools of control consisted of whips, paddles, blackjacks, and fire hoses. There was also a technique known as rice polishing. This consisted of forcing a naked youth to crawl on his hands and knees across a floor strewn with rice. It was extremely painful and, repeated several times, ripped open the palms and took the skin off the knees. "Runaway pills" were another favorite measure. These were large doses of laxatives given to retrieved runaways—"to help them keep running."

In the late 1940s there were 30,000 inhabitants of training schools, which were really prisons for the very young. Another 40,000 to 60,000 were in jail at any given time, awaiting sentence.

Assuming that there was an increase in juvenile delinquency in the postwar, even if the size of the increase was often exaggerated, the reason was a social mystery. During the Depression juvenile delinquency appears to have decreased sharply. With the war, and the return of prosperity, it rebounded. Evidently economic hardship bore a more complex relationship to juvenile crime than was conventionally believed.

Now it was said that delinquency was not the result of hardship as such but was, instead, the response of lower-class youth to a society which created desires the lower class was unable to satisfy on a small income. Within the bounds of class-delimited desires (e.g., a flashy car, flashy girl, flashy clothes, which the middle class would find vulgar and trashy), the juvenile delinquent was not a rebel at all. He was a conventional adolescent. But frustrated by want of money or want of esteem, he turned to unconventional behavior. Mere rebelliousness or poverty was not the cause of delinquency.

Delinquent subcultures also varied with the neighborhood. The immediate environment both encouraged delinquency and shaped its character at the same time. Some neighborhoods were notable for juvenile violence; others for theft; still others for adolescent prostitution; and some for a combination of these. The mixture depended on population density, racial makeup, the degree of poverty, and the character of the surrounding area. Delinquency patterns in a lower middle-class white neighborhood, for example, would almost invariably differ from those in a poor black neighborhood.

It is possible that besides the impact of brutalizing, impoverished neighborhoods, the high rate of population turnover in some areas added to juvenile crime. Between two comparable areas the one with the lower mobility rate was also likely to have the lower rate of juvenile delinquency. Young people needed both community as well as personal ties.

When delinquent boys were paired with nondelinquent boys, matched by age, intelligence, ethnic origins, and neighborhood, there were some notable differences: the delinquents lived in the slummiest parts of the slums, led more unstable home lives, were more likely to have parents who were insane, alcoholic, physically handicapped, or convicted of a crime. The delinquents came from larger families and had looser family ties. The nondelinquent boys came from homes which were equally poor but more stable, more proud, more independent, and more loving.

Disturbing as the increase in delinquency was, more troubling still was the viciousness which often accompanied it. Every year produced some new and sickening example which defied comprehension. In 1954, for example, four adolescents were arrested in Brooklyn and charged with a list of unspeakable crimes against old men and young girls. They had kicked one man to death. They had tortured another by burning the soles of his feet with lighted cigarettes and then slowly drowned him. They confessed to their crimes and related their methods of torture with evident cold-blooded pride.

The day of the psychopath appeared to have dawned. It created interest in the work of Robert Lindner, whose *Rebel Without a Cause* was a pioneering study of criminal psychopathy. Lindner saw two environments where such behavior might be expected to flourish: on the frontier and in the modern city. He found that "psychopathy is more wide-spread today than ever before in the history of our civilization; that it is assuming more and more the proportions of a plague; that it is today ravishing the world with far greater ill-effect than the most malignant of organic diseases; that it represents a terrible force whose destructive potentialities are criminally underestimated." It was a Hobbesian vision of the war of all against all.

While it frightened most people, it was welcomed by Norman Mailer. ". . . the bohemian and the juvenile delinquent came face to face with the Negro and the hipster was a fact in American life. . . . It can of course be suggested that it takes little courage for two strong 18-year-old hoodlums to beat in the brains of a candystore keeper. . . . Still, courage of a sort is necessary, for one murders not only a weak 50-year-old man but an institution as well, one violates private property. . . ." It is, moreover, part of the psychopath's pursuit of love. "Not love as the search for a mate, but love as the search for an orgasm more apocalyptic than the one which preceded it." Mailer hailed this new social type as the potential savior of the nation.

This chapter began by suggesting that only one crime in seven resulted in conviction. But given the number of unreported crimes, the true figure could well be one in twenty or thirty. Most of those who were convicted went to prison. (The distinction between jail and prison is this: jail is where you are held before and during trial; prison is where you go after being sentenced, if the sentence is a year or more). Well aware that the odds were heavily in their favor but that they have ended up in prison anyway, most prisoners are, and bitterly agree that they are, the failures of the criminal world.

But their deepest grievance is not their bad luck. It is that society is punishing them for behavior which is no more anti-social than things many thousands of people do every day. And these are people usually treated as if they were honest and law-abiding; e.g., the dishonest advertiser, the expense-account padder; the man who pressures a poor and nearly illiterate family into buying an expensive encyclopedia; the man who secretly interferes with young children. Most prisoners are as ready to wash their hands of society as they are ready to believe society has washed its hands of them.

Yet the postwar saw a rapid increase in prison reforms. There was, in the immediate postwar, a fashionable desire among prison authorities to attempt rehabilitation and to take risks if necessary. This was the (short-lived) era of the New Prison. Its models were Jackson State Prison in Michigan and California's San Quentin. "The New Prison has abolished stripes, the lockstep, the ball and chain, the shaved head, the water cure and the dehumanizing silence," wrote an admiring reporter. "The New Prison no longer exploits its inmates for private profit; it no longer works them to make them pay for their own keep. In New Prisons inmates enjoy radios, books, magazines, newspapers, visitors, letters, baseball games, motion pictures and toilets. They learn to read and write; they learn trades. They eat better food and sleep on better beds than their miserable forerunners. . . . The purpose of the New Prison is rehabilitation, not punishment."

Much of what the state prisons attempted had been tried in the Federal prison service, which was always more enlightened. Among criminals the most highly regarded prison in the country was the Federal correctional facility at Danbury, Connecticut. Ironically, the most dreaded prison in the country was also run by the Federal prison service—Alcatraz. It was the most secure lockup in any Western nation. Alcatraz made no attempt to rehabilitate the men it held. They were considered incorrigible. Penologists, reformers, and criminologists wanted to see it closed down. The notion of men being locked up and left to rot indefinitely was both cruel and absurd.

By way of contrast, they pointed to Chino, the California State Institution for Men, opened during the war, as an example of what could be achieved. Chino was an "open" prison, holding 1,500 minimum-risk prisoners. A female equivalent of Chino was opened in the Tehachapi Mountains. A medium security prison was opened at Soledad. The Deuel Vocational Institute was established for juveniles who were too tough for their families to cope with but too young to go to prison. The California Medical Facility was established to care for prisoners who were senile, blind, tubercular, physically handicapped, or psychotic. In these years California probably led the world in penal innovation.

At Chino the prisoners wore no drab and humiliating prison uniform but ordinary clothes. At night they slept in pajamas hand-made at Tehachapi. Their families could visit them to stroll the spacious, pleasant campuslike grounds and picnic under the plane trees, instead of being forced to hold tense, brief meetings under the eyes and within earshot of prison guards. The prison superintendent, Kenyon J. Scudder, greeted each new busload of arrivals and personally showed them how easy it was to escape.

Dozens of minimum-security prisons were established in other states on the Chino pattern. It was an idea whose worth was proved again and again, with certain types of prisoners. But ultimately a shortage of money, nerve, and interest made itself felt. Minimum-security prisons, which could have held at least half the nation's prisoners without undue concern, never held more than 2 or 3 percent.

The era of reform came to an end, moreover, in a wave of prison riots which broke out in the early 1950s. There were major riots in the top security prisons of Arizona, California, Georgia, Idaho, Illinois, Indiana, Louisiana, Massachusetts, Michigan, New Jersey, North Carolina, Ohio, Pennsylvania, and Utah. In a dozen state penitentiaries there was not one riot but several. More than twenty prisoners and guards were killed; the number of injured ran into the hundreds.

The New Prison revived the old, enduring conflict within prisons between Custody and Rehabilitation. It probably attempted to change too
much too soon, although change was long overdue. Most prison wardens
and prison guards saw their role as keeping the inmates inside. But to the
reformers prison is a place for salvaging human wreckage. Prisoners soon
become adept at exploiting the conflict between custodians and reformers. As a result, tensions build up throughout the prison.

It is also the case that prison work is done, for the most part, by the
prisoners. They do the cleaning, the cooking, the record keeping, and
most of the maintenance. Within the New Prison more and more responsibility was placed on the shoulders of the inmates.

When the custodians decided that the reformers had gone far enough
and attempted to reassert their control of the prisons, the result was riots
and bloodshed. Yet not all the reforms were undone. The prisoners of the
mid-1950s were better treated, in an admittedly crude sense, than the prisoners of the 1930s. To the extent that a society's treatment of its prisoners
is a rough index of what kind of society it is, the improvement was the
sign of a more humane America, even though much remained to be done.

20

Toward Little Rock

Race relations at midcentury were turbulent not only because blacks
for the first time since Emancipation had enjoyed something approaching
full employment, not only because they had moved by the million from
the rural South to the urban North, but also because they had undergone
an important change as a people. The young adults, aged twenty-one to
forty, of the first postwar decade were psychologically different from
their parents and grandparents. So far as their feelings and attitudes were
concerned, they were the inhabitants of a different wortld.

In slavery black people had lived in a world made by white men. They
possessed only the most fleeting vestiges of their ancestral culture. There
was no black community worth speaking of; ignorant, illiterate, immobilized, they were isolated mentally and emotionally from any but the handful of people known to them personally. Even in the Northern cities
where thousands of free blacks lived unmolested there was no national
black community with an identity of its own.

For a decade after Emancipation black people continued to live in a
world made by white men; the pattern of black life remained one of passivity and dependency.

But by the First World War a deep change had worked its way into black life. Something approximating a black subculture had come into existence. It took root in the big cities. By the Second World War a wide range of black community institutions, not least the black press and black colleges, had developed. Black service organizations, churches, sporting bodies, and the like marked the beginning of the end of the suffocating paternalistic ties which had characterized race relations even under slavery. Black children were for the first time being reared in a black world.

It was still a weak and ramshackle structure. And the strains of being born black were debilitating. Among young men examined for Selective Service blacks were twice as likely as whites to suffer from high blood pressure. On average, black men died ten years younger than whites.

Black life was full of petty, tension-creating humiliations, and these were hardly noticed by whites unless, like Ray Sprigle and John Howard Griffith, two enterprising reporters, they darkened their skins and passed for black. Sprigle and Griffith learned what it was like to search with a bursting bladder for a toilet blacks were allowed to use, to be unable to find a place to spend the night or cash a check, to be threatened simply for looking at pictures of white female movie stars prominently displayed in front of a movie theater. Places to rest, eat, drink, or sleep became, in their travels, like oases in the desert. And they learned to endure the "hate stare," directed at them for no other reason than the color of their skin.

To be black, intelligent, and sensitive was perhaps the worst condition of all. That often meant growing up with both a hatred of whites and a contempt for one's own people. No bright young black boy or girl was unaware of the failings of the black people around them. "Some of the most energetic people of my generation," James Baldwin wrote, "were destroyed by this interior warfare."

Black people often went to extraordinary and humiliating lengths to get rid of, or lighten, their blackness. Hair was painfully straightened, then slicked down with glossy pomade. Skin was virtually bleached with expensive cosmetics. And blacks would try to shuck off their ancestral ties with slavery by affecting to be anything but American—Arabs, or Ethiopians, even, in the case of two people I knew in El Paso in 1960, Seminole Indians ("We were never defeated"). But in the end there was no escape. "I was forced to recognize that I was a kind of bastard of the West," said Baldwin.

Yet the world was changing, and so was the West's place in it. The domination exerted by the whites of Western Europe and North America was being challenged, often with success, but more important, the self-confidence which had characterized the white man's rule was crumbling. And the world itself was moving in a clumsy, dangerous way in the general direction of a world community. American blacks began to see that in the world at large most people were not white.

They also saw, in the struggles for national liberation in Africa in the 1950s, that black men could challenge white men and win. They began to understand that nonwhite people were important figures on the great stage of history. They became for the first time self-conscious participants in the drama. And to embrace history is, for a time at least, to anesthetize self-doubt. In its early stages it is a liberating experience, freeing the personality for action.

Blacks had, of course, been aware of Africa. But usually it had evoked only deep feelings of shame, for it was the Africa portrayed in films, radio programs, and textbooks—a continent inhabited by grunting, spear-throwing savages, people whose idea of Western Union was a hollow log, drinkers of human blood, with bones through their noses and grotesque scars on their bodies, people who were dirty, naked, brutal, and diseased. The sole exception to this embarrassing picture was the Ethiopians, who had never been enslaved, who were Christians, and who had fought the Italians to a standstill.

But after 1945 there was a new Africa and a new African: the man who fought for freedom. Intelligent, articulate, brave young African leaders emerged during the liberation struggles. Africa, so long a source of shame, began to be a source of pride.

Racial pride had led a few blacks who might have passed for white to spurn that opportunity. Ray Sprigle knew two who were ordered out of the Jim Crow section of a train by the conductor, who admonished them, "You can't ride with these niggers. It's against the law." But it was not until about 1950 that a positive sense of identity began to make large numbers of blacks take pride in their blackness. And it could lead to sharp conflicts between parents and their children, inhabitants of different mental worlds. The parents of Claude Brown, for example, had come up to Harlem from South Carolina before the war. But they never lost their fear of "Mr. Charlie." They had evidently never heard of the Emancipation Proclamation or Abraham Lincoln, Claude Brown decided. His mother believed strongly in voodoo, and his grandfather would reminisce for hours about his happy days working on the chain gang.

Part of the struggle for a new identity was to get "Negro" spelled with a capital N. In Louisiana, when black people registered to vote, they would enter "Negro" in the box which asked "COLOR?". Registration officials would scratch it out and write in "Black." But the struggle for the capital N and the use of "Negro" was successful. Then there came a reaction against "Negro." It was a term from the days of slavery and forever reminiscent of "Nigger." But it would be some time yet before they came to prefer to be called blacks, for blackness suggested something dirty or evil. And too often it was employed by white people to add injury to insult ("black bastard"). Publishers, for instance, were pressured by civil rights groups to change "Little Black Sambo" to "Little Brave Sambo." Stephen Foster's songs were rewritten to exclude "darkies" and replace them with "chillun." In New York City the liberal school board removed *Huckleberry Finn* from school libraries and classrooms because of its unwelcome references to Nigger Jim.

Yet old habits remained hard to break. Even in enlightened Southern circles black people were termed "Niggers" for a long time to come. It was claimed, in excuse, that regional speech patterns made it difficult for Southerners to pronounce "Knee-grow."

The emerging sense of black identity was not uniform. Nor did it heal the deep rifts within the black community. There were sharp class conflicts among urban blacks. In some respects the sense of common identity appears to have been more complete among the blacks of the South. But that was partly because the South offered a clear-cut target on which to focus their minds and energies: segregation. In the North the challenges were more subtle, involving job discrimination, police brutality, housing problems, and the welfare system. The impact of these differed from class to class.

But there was no denying the fact, said Louis Lomax, a black journalist, that blacks were becoming more "tribal," that although still divided, they were less divided than before; through soul food and soul music, through a sudden sense of worth, they felt a mystical union despite the old antagonisms, which had long set the educated against the uneducated, the prosperous against the poor, the rural against the urban. Before, all that had bound them had been a common color and common suffering; now they were joined by color, suffering—and something else.

Among the young the new sense of community and identity was carried by black slang. Claude Brown recalled how thrilled he was the first time he ever heard one black man address another as "baby," in 1951. "I think everybody said it real loud because they liked the way it sounded. It was always, 'Hey, baby. How you doin', baby?' . . . it seemed to be the prelude to a whole new era in Harlem. . . . This was the beginning of the 'soul' thing too."

With the new sense of identity there went a second look at blackness itself. In 1955 James Baldwin wrote of his father, who had died in 1943: "He knew he was black, but he did not know he was beautiful."

The high demand for labor in the postwar transformed the black community. Just as wartime manpower shortages had put blacks into factories in large numbers for the first time, so the burgeoning service economy opened up hundreds of thousands of low-paying white-collar service jobs, creating black sales clerks, typists, telephone operators, and the like. A black middle class was rapidly coming into existence.

It would follow whites into the consumer society. It had the same obsession with status and display. Much as the white bourgeoisie had done for centuries, so the black bourgeoisie now began to pin most of its hopes for its children on higher education. Education was widely accepted as the nostrum which would bring blacks up to the level of whites, but it could bring only some blacks up to equality with some whites.

The black bourgeoisie, like the white, tended to become more conservative the more it prospered. The most conservative black people were the doctors, "who are generally opposed to any tendency towards socialism, especially 'socialized' medicine, which would benefit the Negro masses." wrote an eminent black scholar.

Yet the black bourgeoisie was not entirely like the white. In some respects the sizable postwar black middle class was very different from the much smaller black middle class which had begun to emerge in the 1930s. Prosperous blacks before the war were painfully conventional in outlook and behavior. But the new entrants into the black middle class in the 1950s—who arrived in sufficient numbers to make it seem more like a class and less like a coterie—were traveling fast. They had not had time to shed their lower-class traits. Nor did they seem likely to do so. The new black consciousness made it seem important not to lose the language, dress, and manners of the street. These new entrants to the bourgeois life did not look to black college presidents and civic leaders for their models; they looked to black athletes and entertainers. Although most of them held modest jobs, a few had come into a lot of money in very short order. The virtual impossibility of blacks' inheriting money from generation to generation gave rise to a joke among blacks: "Anybody with money can belong to Negro society, no matter where he stole it."

The pervasiveness of lower-class speech and behavior made it difficult for whites to accept the emerging black middle class or even to see it. At the same time the black bourgeoisie was regarded with deep distrust by the mass of blacks.

This black middle class demanded the right to compete with whites for better jobs, for admission to the better colleges, for commissions in the armed forces, and for political appointments. Yet there was a deep, if rarely admitted, fear of genuine competition, where blacks would have to accept success or failure according to the same standards of competence and conformity expected of whites.*

Black people had a consoling belief that they already enjoyed parity of a kind; there was, they believed, an important structure of black businesses operating successfully within the white man's economy. It was a myth. Not one major industrial enterprise was owned by blacks or run by blacks. Many of the more prosperous black businesses were dependent on white financial institutions. And nearly all the money spent in supporting black businesses came from employment provided by whites. It was only on a minor scale and for unusual reasons that any black business was very prosperous. Black undertakers, for example, were often the richest men in a black neighborhood. Death provided one occasion when a black man could show himself to be equal with a white man. Even very poor black people would diligently put a few cents away each week in the "burial society."

Unlike other ethnic groups, blacks did not develop an extensive network of small businesses, providing jobs, however poorly paid; skills, however rudimentary; incentive, however often thwarted. Not only did black people fail to cultivate an authentic, deeply rooted petit bourgeoisie of small shopkeepers and manufacturers, but they never developed a tra-

*Not for some years would a way be found to gain access to the desired jobs or into the better colleges and universities without having to compete with whites—that is, through affirmative action.

dition of thrift. As a consequence, they were permanently vulnerable to
the ups and downs of the national economy. They were quickly forced
into economic dependence on the state.

Even in crime the blacks fared badly. They were allowed to work the
outer—and most exposed—reaches of the narcotics and numbers rackets,
but they never got into organized crime. When some ambitious individuals attempted to set up black organizations, they were killed. Even in Harlem the big. money from crime found its way into white hands, even
though black hands had collected it.

Among lower-class black families even the most conventional kind of
ambition could seem terrifying. When young Claude Brown told his mother that he wanted to be a psychologist, she was gripped with fear. To her
an ambitious son was bound to bring only trouble and grief, on both him
and his family. In South Carolina, where she had been reared, ambition
had led to a lynching. She thought he would be better off as a janitor or
waiter. Yet throughout the black community, which now covered the entire nation, there were tens of thousands of young men like Claude Brown
coming of age every year. The mere presence of a black middle class was
a demonstration that it was possible to rise without being as athletic as
Jackie Robinson, without being as intellectually gifted as W. E. B. Du
Bois, without boasting the musical talents of Louis Armstrong, or without
combining all three gifts, like Paul Robeson.

Insecure and conservative as it was, the black bourgeoisie had only the
most fitful commitment to raising the position of the black masses. Most
of its energies went into defending the crumbs it had won for itself. Yet
the fact that a black middle class had arrived offered hope to anyone who
could raise his or her eyes above the level of the street.

Blacks moving into the twenty-four largest cities in the 1950s almost exactly equaled the number of whites moving out. Blacks were often a generation behind whites in social and economic changes; they had been
twenty to thirty years behind in the shift from agriculture to industry, in
the shift from blue collar to white collar, in the shift from rural to urban
areas. But by the late 1950s they were as urbanized as the white population. Yet they were still a generation behind because the whites were
streaming out to the suburbs. It would be another generation before large
numbers of blacks would do the same.

The exodus of whites eased the dreadful overcrowding of black neighborhoods. As the whites left, block after block of the central city became
black. Racial segregation suddenly became impossible to sustain. But it
was not because of any rapid upsurge of racial tolerance. It was the ordinary effect of supply and demand: the more blacks there were in a neighborhood, and the fewer whites, the more blacks wanted to move in, and
the more the remaining whites wanted to move out. If, in time, there were
only a few token whites living in what was now a black neighborhood,
then the area would be as segregated as ever.

Although the worst of the housing shortage was past, blacks remained more segregated than any other racial minority. Not even the black bourgeoisie could escape. Whatever their class, black people were forced to live together. At the same time the black bourgeoisie had a vested interest in keeping the black population concentrated in a limited area because this secured a stable clientele for local black businesses, churches, and politicians.

Black neighborhoods continued to grow throughout the 1950s as the migration from the South continued. But for many who made the journey there was only disappointment. Being opposed to de jure segregation did not mean that the North embraced de facto integration. Many a black family discovered when they moved to Detroit, or Cleveland, or Chicago, or Newark, or Gary, or New York that they had no more contact with whites than they had ever had. But the city offered jobs paying three or four times anything available to a black worker or sharecropper in the South. And many blacks actually felt safer in the ghetto of a big Northern city, secure at least from the violence of hostile whites, whether Kluxers, the sheriff, or an angry employer. It seems ironic now that blacks should have fled to the central cities seeking safety.

And there were some notable instances of resistance to the influx of blacks into formerly white neighborhoods. In the summer of 1951 a black veteran named Harvey E. Clark, Jr. attempted to move his family into a modest apartment in Cicero. The mayor and the police chief chose this moment to leave town. The apartment complex into which the Clarks moved was mobbed. Their windows were smashed, their door was beaten down, and their furniture was dragged outside to be burned. After three days of rioting Governor Adlai Stevenson quelled the disturbances by sending in the National Guard.

Two years later a black mail carrier, Donald Howard, moved his wife and two children to Trumbull Park Homes, a public housing project near the South Side of Chicago. The project was immediately under attack each night by angry crowds numbering in the thousands. The project became like a bomb site, littered with broken glass and shattered doors. Four attempts were made to burn it down. Night after night hundreds of police stood guard. The Howards cowered behind barricaded doors and windows for nine months until, their nerves frayed beyond endurance, they moved out.

In Miami the city authorities attempted to ease population pressure in the black ghetto by building a housing project only for blacks on the northwest city boundary. A six-foot-high concrete wall was build around the project, which was called Liberty City. Local developers built several apartment buildings close to the wall, tried to rent them to whites, and failed. They then offered the apartments to blacks, who accepted with alacrity. There followed a series of bombings, one of them involving an explosion with 300 pounds of dynamite.

How bizarre and embittered the housing issue could be was demonstrated in Louisville, Kentucky, when, in 1954, Carl and Anne Braden bought a new house in their own name and promptly sold it to a young electrician named Andrew Wade. The Bradens were white; Wade was black. The Supreme Court's ruling on racial covenants had not made it any easier for blacks to find a decent place to live in Louisville. And even though blacks in Kentucky constituted fourteen percent of the registered voters Louisville's schools, parks, restaurants, swimming pools, and rest rooms were still thoroughly segregated.

As soon as it became known that the Bradens had sold the house to Wade, a mob surrounded it. A few nights later a cross was burned on the lawn, and rifle shots were fired into the house. A rock crashed through the picture window wrapped in a note which read, "Nigger get out." One Saturday midnight, six weeks after he moved into it, Wade's house was blown up with dynamite. Only by a stroke of luck did Wade, his wife, and their child escape with their lives.

The Bradens and the Wades repeatedly demanded an investigation of these events. When the police eventually bestirred themselves, the investigation turned into an inquiry concerning the Bradens' political opinions (they had joined the Progressive Party in 1948) and some of the literature found in their home. The local prosecutor had a theory that the Bradens had carried out the bombing; it was all part of a Communist plot to stir up racial strife in the hitherto happy city of Louisville, where black and white had long lived together in great harmony. When it developed that one of Andrew Wade's white friends was sharing an apartment with a seventy-nine-year-old retired riverboat captain who had once run for mayor of Cleveland on the Communist Party ticket—well, that only proved the theory was true.

The former riverboat captain, the roommate, and Carl Braden were jointly tried under Kentucky's 1921 antisedition statute. It was the first time the act had ever been employed in a prosecution. During the trial nine ex-Communist witnesses were brought to Louisville to examine the literature taken from the Bradens' home. They said that it was exactly the kind of thing that a Communist would read. Outside the courthouse an excited mob chanted, "Hang the nigger lovers!"

The local prosecutor and his aides enjoyed the proceedings hugely. They had found real live Communism flourishing in Louisville and were now heroically stopping it dead in its tracks. But the jury recommended mercy, and the judge imposed a mere fifteen years on the defendants, instead of the maximum allowed, twenty-one years.

Carl Braden spent only seven months in prison. It took that long to raise his appeal bond, and during his appeal the Kentucky antisedition law was superseded by the Nelson decision. The Braden affair was a remarkable combination of racism and McCarthyism. Louisville prided itself as being one of the most enlightened and well-governed cities in the border states.

Despite every possible discouragement, the migration from South to North continued. Yet the ghettos to which black families moved would have made almost anyone else think twice about migrating. By almost every criterion of social cohesion Harlem, the South Side, Watts, Roxbury, Hunter's Point, were disaster areas. As a whole, the black ghettos within the big cities were far above average in the incidence of illegitimacy, venereal disease, juvenile delinquency, drug addiction, mental illness, and homicide. They were usually below average for suicide, but self-destruction can take various forms without ever appearing in the "suicide" statistics.

Through these ghettos, new or old, large or small, a terrible sickness spread rapidly during the 1950s until it became a part of ghetto life; it became as pervasive as soul language and soul food. It was what Claude Brown discovered when he returned home from Wiltwyck in 1950; something had happened while he was away. "Horse was the new thing, not only in our neighborhood but in Brooklyn, the Bronx, and everyplace else I went, uptown and downtown. It was like horse had just taken over. Everybody was talking about it. All the hip people were using it." And by the mid-1950s "Harlem had changed. . . . Heroin had just about taken over Harlem. It seemed to be a kind of plague. Every time I went home somebody else was hooked, somebody else was strung out. People talked about them as if they were dead. . . . It was like a plague, and the plague usually afflicted the eldest child of every family, like one of the first born with Pharaoh's people in the Bible." Heroin spread fear. People armed themselves with guns, clubs, axes, and knives to protect their homes and their property from drug addicts. Heroin spread death, from overdoses and drug-related killings. Black families had lived with poverty for generations. But the need for money had suddenly become a killing matter. Adolescents would murder their parents to get the rent money to pay for a fix.

It was a terrible burden for a community which was fragile to begin with. The central social institution of human life, the family, existed in a weakened form among black people. Marriage had been a rarity among blacks for most of their history in America. Not until the end of the Civil War were the majority allowed to legitimize their unions and their offspring. Yet by 1917 the vast majority of black adults were married and their children were being reared in stable families.

In the 1920s and 1930s the shift from the countryside to the cities and the northward migration began to tear black families apart once again. After dropping for fifty years, the proportion of illegitimate births began to rise. After World War II the rise in illegitimacy not only increased sharply but took a new turn. No longer was it typically a case of the young girl seduced and abandoned; it was more likely to be a woman who already had children bearing yet another child by one of a succession of casual lovers. Families headed by women came close to the number of those headed by men.

Black women enjoyed various advantages over black men: they had been less damaged in their self-respect by slavery; they were more acceptable in white homes; they usually did better at school; and, more than anything else, they found it much easier to find work. As a result, black women tended to be more at home in a white-dominated environment, could adjust to it better, and could take better advantage of whatever opportunities it offered, whether it was earning a living by honest work or relying on welfare.

This black matriarchy created ambivalent feelings in black men. They were wounded in their pride. Yet these women were so resourceful and enduring that they compelled respect for their toughness—a characteristic rightly admired by anyone hard pressed to survive.

Despite the growing sense of black identity and despite the rapid urbanization of the black community, blacks were not remotely as well represented in politics as their numbers would justify in a democratic state. There was not a single black Senator. In the House, black members represented less than 2 percent of the whole. No big city had a black mayor. There were no black governors.

In the black ghettos of the North much of the male population not only failed to vote but could not vote, thanks to felony convictions. The women had most of the votes, and they tended to cast their ballots as the preachers suggested. In most cases that meant voting for the status quo, for the few blacks who had been able to make an accommodation with the local white power structure. And in Atlanta, which boasted the most fully developed black middle-class community in the nation, in continual contact with a comparatively enlightened white civic leadership, the black leadership was allowed to deal only with the lower levels of the white power structure.

So blacks had to make their demands felt obliquely, wherever they were, rather than directly. Their principal political pressure group was not a party but the National Association for the Advancement of Colored People. Founded in 1910 in the aftermath of a bloody race riot in Springfield, Illinois, the NAACP was created by whites. But it had promptly merged with an all-black body, the Niagara Movement. In 1910 the National Urban League was founded, also by whites. It concerned itself with the welfare of the growing black population in the cities of the North and sought to help those making the rapid transition from life in the rural South. Interestingly, the Urban League, which was presumably closer to the ordinary black people of the ghettos, was considered more moderate than the NAACP, the emphasis of which was on working through the legal system. The NAACP attacked segregation head on and for that was considered militant.

By the 1950s it had established itself beyond any doubt as the chief body engaged in the civil rights struggle. Yet it did not arouse much enthusiasm among the majority of blacks. It is even doubtful that the majority of blacks had ever heard of it.

In 1950 the NAACP's Legal Defense Fund decided to concentrate on reversing the 1896 Supreme Court ruling in *Plessy* versus *Ferguson*, which had upheld the principle that separate but equal facilities satisfied the

Constitution. The next year the NAACP carried the struggle into the enemy's strongest camp. It held its annual convention in Atlanta, the first time it had met in the Deep South since 1920.

A few months later, on Christmas night 1951, the executive secretary of the NAACP in Florida, Harry T. Moore, was assassinated along with his wife when their home was bombed. Moore was the first NAACP organizer to be murdered. He would not be the last.

A campaign of anti-NAACP terrorism raged throughout the South over the next decade. In most Southern states NAACP membership was cut by half. In Mississippi membership dropped from 22,000 to 8,000 in fewer than three years. But despite the attacks and the attempts at intimidation, the NAACP in the mid-1950s began to overprint its literature with the legend "The Negro shall be free by 1963"—the 100th anniversary of the Emancipation Proclamation. It took heart from the frantic attacks being made on it because they suggested that its efforts were beginning to pay off.

The Legal Defense Fund was deeply engaged in a five-pronged attack on segregation as the weakest link in the chain—education. It was the heart of the NAACP's case that to be separate was to be inherently unequal. By taking up segregation in the public schools, it was also taking the issue at its most emotive. Injustice is one thing; injustice involving children is another.

Throughout the 1940s the Supreme Court struggled with the *Plessy* versus *Ferguson* ruling as it applied to higher education. Each time it laid stress on the need for the provision of facilities to be truly equal, not a sham. But Federal courts were also showing themselves increasingly responsive to claims involving civil rights. The Legal Defense Fund thus had reason to believe that the moment was ripe for a comprehensive challenge to *Plessy* versus *Ferguson*, even though the Supreme Court would probably have preferred for the issue to go away. The five cases the fund took up were selected with care. It had what appeared like a winner in Clarendon County, South Carolina.

In 1948 the parents of children enrolled at Scott's Branch School, Summerton, South Carolina, had held a meeting at St. Mark's African Methodist Episcopal Church to discuss some of the school's shortcomings. The average class size was 100 plus; there was no auditorium, no science classes, no vocational training, and only two toilets to serve more than 600 children. The school was also without water, which had to be brought up in a bucket from the home of a minister who lived at the bottom of the hill. There were schools which were in a more desperate plight—e.g., where there were no toilets and the class size approached 200. The parents of the children sent (or condemned) to the Clarendon County schools decided to petition the school board. They asked for facilities equal to those in the nearby white school.

The school board replied solemnly that conditions were equal as they stood. The parents turned to the NAACP for advice.

The Legal Defense Fund took up the case not because it was highly sensitive to injustice. Injustices in the education of black children were as common as could be. The Summerton case was ideal because it was appalling. It became known as the Briggs case in honor of the first name on the list of petitioners. By virtue of the alphabet Harry Briggs, Jr., aged eight in 1949 when the case was filed in Federal District Court, was vouchsafed a tiny niche in American social and legal history. By the same instrument, however, his father lost his job at a local filling station.

Harry Briggs, Sr., turned to sharecropping. But when he took his cotton to be ginned, he was repeatedly turned down. He finally found a gin operator who took a robustly pragmatic view: "If the NAACP was cotton I'd gin it for money."

But sharecroppers, like farmers, need credit to get from one harvest to the next. No bank in Clarendon County would give credit to Harry Briggs. While the case wound its way through the courts, he was forced to leave South Carolina in search of work. In Florida he got a job driving a truck. His wife stayed behind in South Carolina, working as a motel chambermaid. But when it became known that she was *the* Mrs. Briggs, she was fired. She too was eventually forced to leave the state because no one would employ her.

As for the Reverend Joseph A. De Laine, who organized the parents to petition the school board in the first place, there was more drastic retribution. His house was burned down. So was his church. He was ambushed by armed men and beaten up. His wife lost her job as a teacher.

Meanwhile, in Topeka, Kansas, 1,000 miles away, the local NAACP was looking for a black plaintiff willing to challenge the Board of Education of the crazy-quilt system of segregation and integration in the Topeka schools. It took courage to sue the school board because most black people feared for their jobs. But the NAACP was convinced that the board had the power to integrate the city's grade schools any time it chose; only it would never do it until forced. The law said that up to the seventh grade black students could not go to school with whites. The law also said that from the seventh grade on this was exactly where they would go to school, with whites.

The NAACP found a very reluctant plaintiff, the Reverend Oliver Brown; his reluctance made him all the more desirable in the eyes of the NAACP lawyers. No one could consider him a firebrand. He was not even a member of the NAACP.

In 1951, with the Briggs case still in the courts, Oliver Brown's nine-year-old daughter, Linda, was enrolled in the fourth grade at Monroe School, which was more than two miles from her home. She had to make her way through the railway yards to reach it. Only five blocks away from her home was Sumner grade school. She repeatedly asked her father to explain why she could not attend Sumner School. Oliver Brown was hard pressed to provide a coherent explanation of segregation and integration in the Topeka school system. Linda continued to walk through the railroad yard each morning to catch the bus which took her to Monroe. But the school schedule did not match well with the bus schedule. She often arrived well before school opened. On winter mornings she could be seen on the pavement outside, jumping up and down while she waited, trying to keep warm. Her father "came to the conclusion that this arrangement was anything but satisfactory."

He agreed to sue the school board. The Federal District Court rejected his suit to enroll Linda at Sumner grade school. He appealed to the Supreme Court, which had recently heard from Briggs et al. It sent that case back to South Carolina for a report on the facilities provided in the schools there, black and white. There was also another case on appeal from Prince Edward County, Virginia, another from Delaware, and a fifth from the District of Columbia. The Court took the Brown case under review.

In 1952 the NAACP's flock of school segregation cases appeared, or reappeared, before the Supreme Court and were listed after *Brown* versus *Board of Education of Topeka*. Brown did not come first alphabetically; that distinction still belonged to Harry Briggs, Jr. But *Brown* versus *Board of Education* was the northernmost case available, and as Justice Tom Clark later explained, it was given precedence, "So that the whole question did not smack of being a purely Southern one."

The Truman Administration decided at the last moment and after considerable disagreement to file a brief on behalf of the plaintiffs—after the November election. Initial arguments were heard in December 1952.

Despite the monumental setback of the Plessy ruling, the Supreme Court had increasingly become the black people's last hope for equality. Congress was stymied by Southerners whenever race was involved. City and state governments were hostile or indifferent. The Executive branch, usually well meaning, was immobilized by fear of outrunning public opinion. To secure the most basic rights in housing, military service, voting, employment, criminal justice, and schooling, the black population found itself turning again and again to the Supreme Court. There was nowhere else to go.

With the school cases making their way to the Supreme Court the governors of South Carolina, Georgia, and Mississippi—Herman Talmadge, James Byrnes, and Fielding Wright, respectively—became apprehensive. If the Court struck down the Plessy case, they announced, they would close the public schools of their states.

All the same, school districts throughout the Deep South suddenly began to build modern schools for black students. Emergency bond issues were passed with little ado, and the money was quickly spent on new classrooms, stadiums, roads, books, and staff, all in the hope that the Supreme Court would take notice.

But in many a Southern community where blacks heavily outnumbered whites, there was a white school built since the war largely with money from blacks. They could not vote. But that did not exempt them from paying taxes. Of course, where whites were in the majority it was argued that each race should pay for its own schools out of its share of the tax revenues. This, it was said, was what separate-but-equal *really* meant.

But no one could deny that there had in recent years been a dramatic narrowing of the gap between the black and white schools in most Southern counties. It was being closed so rapidly after 1945 that expenditures per pupil and salaries per teacher would, on current trends, be identical for each race in 1963.

The postwar South had developed a remarkable commitment to education. Mississippi in the early 1950s, for example, was the poorest state in the Union. Yet in expenditure per pupil it ranked twenty-seventh. Education was something for which Southerners of both races were willing to make sacrifices. Under the threat of a Supreme Court decision striking down *Plessy*, Southern legislatures showed that they were prepared to make even greater sacrifices for the education of black children than anyone had ever thought possible. But the South had had fifty years in which to demonstrate its sincerity where separate-but-equal development was concerned. Its response had been sham, lies, and evasion. The ordinary practices of Southern school districts since 1896 provided the opponents of *Plessy* with more than enough evidence.

Between the initial oral arguments in the *Brown* versus *Board of Education* case and the reargument a year later something important intervened, the death in September 1953 of Chief Justice Fred Vinson. Truman had hoped that in selecting Vinson he had been putting a conciliator on the Court. It was a vain ambition. Vinson was outshone by half the members of the Court and was a decidedly undistinguished judge. The quarrels only seemed to get worse. In 1952 four out of every five decisions were published with dissenting opinions. The sole area in which the Vinson Court advanced, albeit cautiously, was in civil rights. Under Vinson the Court showed itself willing to require genuinely equal treatment of the races.

Vinson's sudden death occurred at a critical time for the Court. "It has no fixed left, center or right. It is not moving forward or back or even in well-defined circles," noted *Time*. "Assuredly it is not standing still. It wanders unguided over the infinite and orderless sands of fact." It was a bench without the strong sense of moral purpose which had guided the Court during its best periods.

To widespread surprise and dismay Eisenhower announced that he had chosen Earl Warren, the governor of California, to succeed Vinson. The dismay appears to have extended to Eisenhower himself.

Shortly before the 1952 Republican Convention Warren's support had been secured with a promise that Warren would be given a place on the Supreme Court should a vacancy arise. What Eisenhower had never anticipated was that the first vacancy would be for the Chief Justice's chair. Brownell was dispatched to California to plead with Warren to accept an appointment as an Associate Justice, allowing Eisenhower to elevate one of the sitting members of the Court. Warren refused to budge. It was Chief Justice or nothing. Eisenhower and Brownell swallowed hard and honored their promise.

"Earl Warren," wrote John Gunther shortly after making his acquaintance in 1947, "is honest, likeable and clean; he will never set the world on
fire or even make smoke; he has the limitations of most Americans of his
type; he is a man who has probably never bothered with abstract thought
twice in his life."

Although Warren was a Republican appointee and assumed to be conservative, his conduct in the recent University of California loyalty oath
controversy made some liberals wonder if he were not, at heart, really
one of their own.

As Gunther suggested, Warren was not a complex man. Events would
prove he was neither a doctrinaire liberal nor an intellectual. Nor was he
an amiable cipher. Warren believed passionately in justice, as distinct
from believing in the legal process as the instrument of justice. He formed
no judicial theories worthy of the name. Nor did he have a love affair with
the Constitution which blinded him to ordinary reality, as happened to a
number of great Justices. His mind moved quickly to a single point in deciding a case: is this the right result? Thus, he made only cursory attempts
to have his decisions conform with past decisions or established judicial
doctrine. Even when they agreed with his opinions, many lawyers and
judges disliked the way he got there. To a rigorous mind it appeared untidy and sometimes quixotic. Warren was more like a Biblical lawgiver, a
tribal elder, or a Platonic guardian than a man in the tradition of the great
American judges from Marshall to Frankfurter. When pressed to choose
between the demands of a hard but entirely legitimate law on the one hand
and those of elementary justice imperfectly expressed on the other, Warren would opt for the latter. While Roger Taney, the great scholar of the
Constitution, for instance, had decided against Dred Scott, Warren would
probably have set him free, on the grounds that slavery was evil.

What Warren brought to the Court in 1953 was what it most needed:
moral purpose. He gave it a sense of direction and an encouragement to
act boldly which no Chief Justice more concerned with the Constitution
and legal precedents would have possessed or so directly expressed. Had
Warren been more of a lawyer or more of a judge, he would have been
less of a Chief Justice.

It is rare for any man with Warren's temperament to rise high in a common law system. His receptiveness to nonlegal arguments would have
given him a reputation as one of the wild men of the lower bench and
would have kept him there. Only the American system of political
appointment to the highest bench could have produced a Warren. And the
Supreme Court could probably afford only one Warren a century.

Only three months after being sworn in, Warren sat with the rest of the
Court to hear reargument in the case of *Brown* versus *Board of Education*
et al. The history of discrimination written by the opposing sides reflected
much expense and little learning. The NAACP brief was the work of eminent historians and legal scholars, but it was riddled with *suggestio falsi*
and *suppressio veri*. The defendants' brief achieved the same result without going to the same amount of trouble. Its emphasis instead was that the
Plessy doctrine needed to be given more time in which to prove itself. The

black schools were of a low standard, the defendants argued, because they were in rural areas where the white schools were not very good either.

The amicus curiae brief submitted by the Attorney General on behalf of the plaintiffs took the Cold War as its theme: segregation made the United States appear hypocritical in the eyes of the world.

The Legal Defense Fund offered a novel type of evidence—the testimony of social scientists. Their argument was that segregation did serious psychological harm to children, and this was a denial of the equal protection clause of the Constitution. A black psychologist, Kenneth B. Clark, described an experiment he had performed. Two dolls, exactly alike except that one was painted white and the other black, were shown to black children. When asked to choose the "pretty" doll, they invariably chose the white one. When asked to identify the "bad" doll, they pointed to the black one. It was also shown that through the third grade black children performed as well as white children. But between the third and sixth grades their IQ scores fell sharply. It may have been no more than coincidence, but it was at about the third grade age of seven or eight that black children began to learn what racial discrimination was.

Whatever the Supreme Court's decision, it seemed certain to plunge the South into crisis. The least that the Court could be expected to do was to demand equality between black and white schools. But it was doubtful that Southern legislatures would have appropriated the money required to comply with a court order. Nor was it evident that school boards could be forced to make the necessary expenditures, especially not in places where the accepted method of raising money for new schools was by bond issues submitted to the voters for their approval.

As the spring of 1954 wore on, an unusually large number of reporters from black newspapers appeared at the Supreme Court building each Monday, when Court decisions were handed down. The press room became crowded. This was where reporters usually waited to collect copies of the decision, delivered by pneumatic tube while it was being read out in the chamber above. But on Monday May 17, 1954, the eighteenth day of the Army-McCarthy Hearings, the journalists were told to put their coats back on and follow the press officer upstairs. They dutifully trooped after him.

The audience in the Court chamber was packed, tense, and alert. The atmosphere was charged with a sense of historic moment. Warren read the opinion. It was short as major decisions go, only ten pages. "We come then," he read tonelessly, "to the question presented: Does segregation of children in public schools solely on the basis of race, even though the physical facilities and other 'tangible' factors may be equal, deprive the children of the minority group of educational opportunities?" Warren stolidly read on. "We believe that it does." Grown men, including a famous journalist, wept silently. The decision read, the Court rose. In the well of the chamber the lawyers of the Legal Defense Fund embraced one another in high emotion.

This moment of history had taken only fifteen minutes. The decision was unanimous, all nine Justices concurring. Had Vinson lived, the decision might well have been the same because it had been in the making for a decade. But it would almost surely have been a split decision. It was Warren's achievement to secure unanimity. A split decision would have made enforcement more difficult. And it was going to be difficult enough. So the Court postponed the question of enforcement until another day.

The wheels of justice had ground too slowly to benefit Linda Carol Brown from the decision which bore her name. At about the time Warren became Chief Justice she had gone on from Monroe grade school to junior high, which was integrated.

Meanwhile, Robert "Tut" Patterson, a boyish-looking thirty-three-year-old ex-paratroop officer and the father of two small daughters, had dropped in on a school board meeting in Indianola, Mississippi, one evening because he had nothing better to do. What he heard made him angry. The meeting was concerned with the school segregation cases about to be decided by the Supreme Court. One old man was incredulous. "You mean I may have to send my grandchildren to school with niggers after we built that good nigger high school?" Returning home, Patterson found it impossible to sleep. He went and sat in his bathroom. Through the night he wrote heartfelt letters to local newspapers and politicians. "Dear Fellow American," they began, "I attended a meeting on the elementary school issue and when I left I was confused and ashamed. It seems a great danger is hanging over the heads of our children—Mongrelization. . . . I for one would gladly lay down my life to prevent Mongrelization." He concluded, "The people of America must call all of their resources and stand together forever firm against Communism and Mongrelization."

Tut Patterson's letters did not draw much response. Even after the Brown decision was handed down, there was no immediate upsurge of anger. Most Southerners had not been aware such a decision was pending. Those who did had braced themselves for the worst. The question of enforcement had been postponed for another year. And what could anyone do?

In mid-July Patterson and thirteen friends and acquaintances, representing the reputable elements in town, organized themselves as the Indianola White Citizens' Council. Patterson was given membership card number one. In Indianola the school issue could not have been more urgent, because there were 2,000 black schoolchildren to 700 white.

The White Citizens' Councils spread rapidly throughout the Delta and across the Black Belt, where in most counties blacks substantially outnumbered whites. As in Indianola, council membership was drawn mainly from the natural civic leadership of small-town America—lawyers; doctors; small businessmen; bank officials. These kept their distance from the lower-class types who gravitated toward the KKK. They looked instead for recruits down at the Rotary Club, the Lions, the Kiwanis, the Chamber of Commerce.

The White Citizens' Councils attracted men who were prejudiced but believed they were not, who despised blacks, yet were convinced they were not hostile to anyone. They were men like Patterson himself, a prosperous farmer whose pleasant, spacious home was surrounded by the hovels of his black workers ("my nigras," as he termed them). "I'm living," he would declare, "crammed right in the middle of 35 nigra families. I'm completely integrated." They were men like Gilbert Wilkes of Charleston. He only taught his children what everybody already knew, "that God chose members of the white race as his chosen people, and then colored the others." And men like Judge Tom P. Brady, a pillar of white society in the Mississippi Delta, the owner of the courtly manner and white-painted mansion of the Southern seigneur.

A week after the formation of the first White Citizens' Council the judge, who was a founder member of the council, addressed the Sons of the American Revolution in nearby Greenwood. His speech became the basis of *Black Monday*, a slight volume with heavy consequences.

Black Monday circulated throughout the Deep South in the mid-1950s. It was a catechism of outrage. The frontispiece carried the likeness of Jefferson and Stalin and a Biblical injunction: "Choose ye this day whom ye will serve." There was a pretentious, if short, bibliography at the back ranging from *The History of the Decline and Fall of the Roman Empire* to the *World Almanac*.

The judge began by warning the reader, "The popular concept of a superior race has no place in this treatise." But he soon forgot himself: "In spite of his [the black man's] basic inferiority. . . ." And he offered such insights as: "The social, political, economic and religious preferences of the negro remain close to the caterpillar or the cockroach. This is not stated to ridicule or abuse the negro. There is nothing fundamentally wrong with the caterpillar or cockroach. It is merely a matter of taste. A cockroach or caterpillar remains proper food for a chimpanzee." From his evidently wide historical research the judge concluded: "Whenever and wherever the white man has drunk the cup of black hemlock, wherever and whenever his blood has been infused with the blood of the negro, the white man, his intellect and his culture, has died."

The learned judge had enjoyed the benefits of a Yale education. He offered a list of white geniuses to demonstrate the unrivaled brilliance of white civilization. His list included the illustrious name of Alexandre Dumas.

Despite the formation of the White Citizens' Councils, despite the distribution of scurrilous racist literature, of which *Black Monday* was by no means the most odious example, the year following the Supreme Court's first Brown decision was comparatively calm—deceptively so. This would later encourage arguments that had the Court ordered immediate and complete compliance, then the South, caught unprepared, would have done as it was told, that by waiting a year before issuing a decree on enforcement, the Court allowed the opposition to organize itself. But the reason for the calm was that the South was waiting for the other shoe to drop. The Brown decision enjoyed strong public support in every region of the country except one. The South neither accepted nor was prepared soon to accept the end of segregated schools.

In the border states there were dozens of instances of spontaneous compliance, where the school board chose not to wait for the enforcement decree. Local courts took the Brown ruling at face value and were prepared to enforce it as it stood. When white mothers in West Virginia picketed a recently desegregated school, a local judge ordered them to stop interfering. If they did not do so, he warned, "I'll fill the jail until their feet are sticking out of the windows."

On May 31, 1955, little more than a year after its first Brown decision,* the Court handed down its ruling on implementation. It was cautions to the point of circumspection. It did not compel school boards to present plans for desegregation within a specific time limit. Instead, it called for "a prompt and reasonable start toward full compliance." It ruled that desegregation must proceed, however, "with all deliberate speed."†

By seeking refuge in vagueness, the Court was attempting to avoid setting off a social calamity pitting black against white at the schoolhouse door. It was an acknowledgment that bloodshed might well follow any attempt to hurry the pace of desegregation. Yet to many blacks it appeared that what had been given with the right hand had been taken back with the left.

In Constitutional law it was universally accepted that a civil right was a personal and present right—that is, it was possessed by each individual. He or she could demand that it be honored at once. A white man could demand his rights here and now; a black man, said the Court's second Brown decision, would have to wait. The Legal Defense Fund had won on principle. It lost on implementation.

The black struggle for justice stood at a crossroads. It appeared in danger of losing its way and its momentum. But suddenly it became direct, it became visible, it took to the streets.

No one planned or intended this to happen. Yet the times were so arranged that when it did happen, it seemed almost inevitable. It was important that the struggle move out of the courtroom. For it to succeed, it needed to involve the mass of black people, and it needed large numbers of whites to become involved as well. The quiet, polite, orderly, seldom-glimpsed proceedings in the courts sought justice such as the law can provide. But beyond that was true social justice, and that required a change in the mass of white people. Either they must lose their racial prejudice, which was too much to expect, or they must become sufficiently ashamed

---

*In that intervening year Justice Robert Jackson died. He was replaced with John Marshall Harlan, whose grandfather had enjoyed the distinction of being the sole dissenting voice in *Plessy v. Ferguson;* in his dissent he made the observation "The Constitution is color blind."

†A phrase first used in a Supreme Court decision of 1911 by Oliver Wendell Holmes. He may have remembered it from a line in Francis Thompson's "The Hound of Heaven," invoking "Deliberate speed, majestic constancy." Wherever it came from, it was of shaky force and meaning in legal parlance.

of prejudice to defend it halfheartedly—to become ready, in a word, to compromise it. This was possibly the most important work of the black protest movement: that although it involved hundreds of thousands of blacks, it also reached tens of millions of whites.

Insofar as anything so multifarious can be said to have a beginning, the protest movement of the 1950s began in December 1955. There had been civil rights demonstrations before. But they had involved only a handful of people. Their activities were usually reported on the inside pages. But this time there was a massive increase in scale. A dog twice the size of any other dog is merely a big dog. But a dog 100 times average size has become a different animal completely. A sufficiently large increase in scale is a change in kind. And that is what happened now.

It began not in the comparatively safe North but in the comparatively dangerous South, in Montgomery, Alabama, the proudly self-styled "Cradle of the Confederacy." It was on the steps of the State Capitol that Jefferson Davies had been sworn in as President of the Confederate States. Ninety-four years later across the handsome square which fronted the capitol building stood the Dexter Avenue Baptist Church. It had a black congregation and a young pastor recently called to his first church, Martin Luther King, Jr.

King was a serious young man of twenty-six in 1955. Sensitive and highly strung he was rarely at peace with himself. In his youth he had twice attempted suicide. Yet he was one of the few young black men of his generation to have been reared in a comfortable, stable home. He had never experienced the poverty, squalor, vice, or diseases of most black families. Both his father and his grandfather were substantial figures in the black bourgeoisie of Atlanta.

King's Montgomery congregation was drawn largely from the black teachers and other professionals connected with Alabama State College. It was a church where the ecstatic, chanting, hand-clapping emotionalism of most black churches was shunned. The pastor, like most of his parishioners, was a member of the NAACP; like them again, he was sober, softly spoken, and immaculately dressed in somber good taste. This was possibly the last place, with the last pastor, anyone would expect to become the hub of street confrontations. Yet it happened; it came about, moreover, in connection with a pair of tired feet and an empty bus seat—the most humble materials with which anyone ever started an era of civil turbulence.

In Montgomery, as in nearly all Southern cities, black bus passengers seated themselves from the rear forward; white passengers seated themselves from the front back. Black passengers often had to board through the front door to pay their fare, dismount, and enter again through the rear door. Some bus drivers (all white) considered it the height of hilarity to drive off before the blacks had reached the rear door after paying their fare. More galling still was having to stand while "white" seats in front were empty or, when the white seats were full, having to surrender a "Negro" seat to a white passenger.

In the spring of 1955, shortly after King's arrival in Montgomery, a fifteen-year-old black girl, Claudette Colvin, refused to give up her seat to a white passenger. She was dragged from the bus, put in handcuffs, and taken to jail. There was talk of a bus boycott, but none materialized. Then, on December 1, Rosa Parks, a black seamstress employed at the Montgomery Fair department store, wearily sat down on a seat immediately behind the last row of "white" seats. When the bus filled up, she was ordered by the driver to give her seat to that model of chivalry and good manners, a white man. Three other black people sitting near her stood up. Mrs. Parks remained seated. She received the Claudette Colvin treatment.

But since that episode racial tension had been at a high level all across the Deep South, ever since the broken body of a fourteen-year-old black boy, Emmett Till, had been dragged out of a Mississippi creek. The boy, on vacation from Chicago, had thoughtlessly whistled at a white woman. Blacks fumed in impotent rage at the murder and the evident lack of interest in bringing the murderers to book. With feelings running so high the arrest of Rosa Parks provided all the spark that was needed to ignite an explosion.

Although she was only a humble seamstress, Mrs. Parks was also prominent in Montgomery's black community. She had for a time been executive secretary of the local NAACP branch. When news of her arrest became known, black leaders began telephoning one another. An emergency meeting was held the next day at the Dexter Avenue Baptist Church. It was decided to launch a bus boycott.

Some 15,000 black people rode the Montgomery buses each day. They depended on the buses to carry them to work, to the stores, or to school. For the boycott to be effective it would have to be well organized. But to take effect at all, it would have to be well known. Neither King's church nor the local NAACP had contact with more than a small part of the total black population of the city. Telephone calls were made by the hundreds, and handbills were hurriedly cranked out on a few mimeograph machines for posting on telephone poles, fences, and store bulletin boards. But it was as promising as attempting to bail out a boat with a teaspoon. Fate, however, made a timely intervention.

The *Montgomery Advertiser* came into possession of one of the handbills. To show the good white people of Montgomery what the dastardly, treacherous blacks were up to, the handbill was reproduced in full on the front page the morning the boycott had been called. And the reasons set out in the handbill, which seemed trivial to the white journalists at the *Advertiser*, seemed compelling to them. The boycott was 90 percent effective on its first day.

In the first few weeks there was a collective leadership to make the decisions. And while other people were assertive, King was diffident. He was younger than the other boycott leaders. He was a newcomer to Montgomery. But his superior education, his polished middle-class manner, and his obvious sincerity brought more and more responsibility into his hands. The boycott was a very public affair. Of the potential leaders to choose from, King looked right and sounded right for this particular crisis. For once a local black leadership was not fragmented by internal rivalries.

The boycott was run by the Montgomery Improvement Association, which was specially created for the purpose; the very name had a bland, bureaucratic ring, as if the MIA were a body devoted to improving the streets and installing playgrounds.

At a meeting of more than 1,000 spellbound boycotters at the Holt Street Baptist Church, King held out his vision of what they might achieve: "If you will protest courageously, and yet with dignity and Christian love, when the history books are written in future generations, the historians will have to pause and say, 'There lived a great people—a black people—who injected new meaning and dignity into the veins of civilization.' This is our responsibility." It was typical King rhetoric—one eye on dignity; the other on history.

These mass meetings, which went from church to church throughout the boycott, brought together the local black middle class with large numbers of lower-class blacks. For the moment, at least, they were literally shoulder to shoulder. The meetings were religious and political at the same time.

The white people of Montgomery confidently expected the bus boycott to be a nuisance, nothing more, which might run for a few days, perhaps as much as a week. It was inconceivable that black people could organize anything effective. And when the weeks turned to months without a break in the boycott, that was attributed to the presumed intervention of Communists, Jews, and other outside agitators from the North. The boycott was certainly effective. It not only deprived the bus company of most of its income but also hurt the downtown stores. Its impact carried into the suburbs, where middle-class white women, married to the men who ran Montgomery, had to struggle along without their maids, seamstresses, cooks, and nannies. There were many who helped the MIA by driving into black neighborhoods to pick up their servants either because they refused to do without them or, in some instances no doubt, because they found it intolerable that elderly or middle-aged domestics should have to walk miles to work.

And some people really did walk for miles. But not everyone could walk up to ten miles a day. As the boycott bit deeply, car pools were organized. The boycott would probably have failed without them. But even after the car pools were organized, some people continued to walk, to make their protest evident.

The white people of Montgomery were merely discommoded by the bus boycott. Yet the longer it wore on, the more fearful they became. They had been convinced that they could control "their" blacks. When it became clear they had deluded themselves, they retaliated.

King was arrested on a charge of driving at thirty miles an hour in a twenty-five-mile zone and was put in jail. There, for the first time in his life, he encountered at first hand the degradation commonly inflicted on the poor, uneducated, and black. It made a deep impression on him. And such experiences—of which he would know many more in coming years—provided King with credentials which ordinary black people recognized.

A few days after his release on bail and while he was addressing a meeting, King's home was bombed. The coolness of his wife, Coretta, saved both her life and that of their child. An angry mob formed within minutes around the shattered house. King arrived and preached an impromptu sermon. "We must love our white brothers," he exhorted. "No matter what they do to us, we must make them know we love them." By his eloquence and presence he was able to send them peacefully away.

King and nearly 100 other people in the MIA were indicted for conspiracy. Black people waiting on the sidewalk to be picked up by the car pools were arrested and charged with vagrancy. The car pool drivers were continually hounded by the police for offenses both real and imaginary.

With expenses running as high as $5,000 a week the MIA seemed likely to disapper under an avalanche of unpaid bills. But the boycott had made it world-famous. Just as the city of Montgomery bestirred itself to try to crush the boycott, money began to flow in to keep the MIA going—to pay the lawyers, buy food, pay the rent, pay the printers, pay for gasoline, pay the telephone bills. Altogether, $250,000 arrived, unsolicited, in small bills and modest checks, from every state and from dozens of foreign countries. The MIA found that it had enough money to keep the struggle going for more than a year.

Yet the pressures on King were beginning to tell. He developed a morbid interest in dying a martyr's death. At one of the mass meetings, in a state of nervous collapse, he begged to be struck down on the spot by a merciful God. To horrified screams of "No! No!" the distraught King was gently led away from the pulpit. Although he preached a gospel of love, he had to struggle valiantly within his own heart not to succumb to hatred of the white men who hated him. In this struggle he weakened at times and in one such moment applied for a license to carry a gun. He was relieved and thankful when his application was denied.

In March 1956 King and the other pastors involved in the MIA were tried for conspiring to hinder lawful business activities, "without just cause or legal excuse." Convicted, they were jubilant. The struggle had now spread beyong seating arrangements on the Montgomery buses. Had the city wished to make a few minor concessions on seating, the boycott could have been promptly settled. But the city had decided that the boycott was really a trial of strength and proposed to fight it out on that basis. The conviction of King and the others was taken by whites as a victory over a dangerous new development.

But while the conspiracy convictions were being appealed, four black women filed suit in Federal District Court protesting that segregation in local transportation violated the equal protection clause of the Constitution. The court agreed. In November 1956 the Supreme Court upheld the lower court's decision. The bus company capitulated without further struggle. Four days before Christmas 1956 black passengers boarded the Montgomery buses for the first time in more than a year, and the bolder spirits among them sat down next to whites.

For the first week there was only minor unpleasantness. Then a black teenage girl was beaten up by several white men when she descended from a bus. A pregnant black woman was wounded by gunfire when the bus she was riding was ambushed. Sniper attacks on buses led to an end of night services. The homes of two ministers prominent in the MIA, Ralph D. Abernathy and Robert Graetz, who was white, were bombed. Four black churches were blown up. A black-owned gas station was set ablaze. Another attempt was made to murder Martin Luther King by blowing up his home.

Yet the gunshots and the dynamite could not reverse the victory the blacks had won. In time Montgomery learned to live with it. It reverted to being another sleepy Southern town, cocooned in conforting memories of its once-glorious past.

With the boycott won the MIA went out of existence. But from its ashes rose the Southern Christian Leadership Conference, whose proclaimed aim was to secure the end of segregation on public transportation in the South. Its president was Martin Luther King, Jr. The real aim of the SCLC would prove, under his leadership, to be continuation of the struggle for civil rights by means of the massive, nonviolent style introduced in Montogomery.

King had brought off what no black leader had ever managed, something often talked about but considered impossible: a direct, large-scale confrontation in the streets without bloodshed. His gift was to have shown that black people could protest actively, visibly, volubly, and directly without flirting with suicide. He borrowed from Gandhi, but he did so creatively; he made the tactics of passive resistance applicable to American circumstances. He had also tapped the sentiments of ordinary black people and drawn them into the struggle. This was the other, possibly more important side to his achievement.

His effect on black people was electrifying. "For some 50 years, Negroes had been expecting a leader. Now, as King's image rose on the horizon, Negroes of all ranks and creeds pooled their psychic energy and projected it onto King, anxiously asking themselves, anxiously asking King, with every gesture, every glance: 'Art thou he who should come or should we seek another?' "

On May 17, 1957, three years after the first Brown decision, King led a Prayer Pilgrimage to Washington. At the Lincoln Memorial 35,000 black people staged the biggest civil rights rights demonstration the country had ever seen. Almost every prominent black leader was there. But it was King, the youngest of them all, not yet thirty, who was the object of every eye, whose words carried the greatest weight.

At any such event King hardly ever failed. Although he possessed a PhD, he was not a scholar. He was not an intellectual but a preacher, with an education in theology. He was a poor administrator, but he possessed a good eye for recognizing administrative ability in others. He was able to inspire young men of talent to enlist in his cause. He was able to persuade others to reconcile their differences. He was immensely dedicated and selfless. Yet his greatest single art was his oratory.

When he returned to Montgomery after the Prayer Pilgrimage, he was arrested once again on a petty charge. But this time, when he appeared happy to go to jail, the city went to considerable trouble to deny him his wish.

In September he was autographing books in a Harlem department store when he was approached by an elderly black woman. "Are you Mr. King?" she asked. He replied affably, "Yes, I am." "Luther King," she declared, "I have been after you for five years." From her dress she pulled an ornate letter opener. With a quick motion she plunged it deep into King's chest.

It was ironic that King's closest brush with death came not at the hands of a white Southern racist but in an encounter with a mentally deranged middle-aged black woman in Harlem. The letter opener's tip touched King's aorta. A sneeze would have killed him.

King, who preached nonviolence, lived close to violence as a youth and as a man. He was hailed for having shown that effective nonviolent protest was possible. Yet organized black protest had nearly always been nonviolent, not from ideology but from necessity. It was not so much an ethical choice as a tactic dictated by circumstances. It was the only form of protest which was not suicidal. King had done something remarkable all the same: he had ushered in the age of massive public confrontations.

Before *Brown* white Southerners used to remark, apropos of the NAACP, "What we need is a white man's organization." After *Brown* hardly a month passed without another white man's organization being formed. Literally dozens of "protective societies" were created. The total membership ran into the hundreds of thousands.

There was an Association of Catholic Laymen, the Pond Hollow Segregation Club, the Virginia Defenders of State Sovereignty and Individual Liberties, the National Association for the Advancement of White People, and scores of others. But far out in front were the White Citizens' Councils. Beginning in July 1954 with fourteen members, the councils two years later boasted 250,000.

The second Brown decision spread the councils rapidly through the Black Belt, where the soil was rich, the people usually poor. It had been the Black Belt plantation aristocracy that forced the South into the Civil War. A powerful, willful minority of white Southerners based in the region had kept effective power in the states of the old Confederacy ever since. Outside the Black Belt the Citizens' Councils had a very limited impact. In northern Alabama, for example, there was not one council. But in central Alabama, virtually the heart of the Black Belt itself, the councils were many and powerful. Here, in a swath from Louisiana to South Carolina, where the land was flat and rich, a plantation economy dependent on slave labor had flourished for 200 years. Its legacy in the middle of the twentieth century was a white minority terrified of being swept away by the black population which dwarfed it.

This was an area, and there were others in the Deep South, where the windows in white neighborhoods bore signs reading:

Preserve State Sovereignty
And Our Bi-Racial Society
CITIZENS' COUNCIL

When the council movement was at its peak, filling stations in Mississippi sold tens of thousands of front license plates which announced, MISSISSIPPI—THE MOST LIED ABOUT STATE IN THE UNION. And along the Gulf Coast the councils put up signs saying, WHITE SOLIDARITY MEANS WHITE BEACHES.

The councils decided to drop the word "White" from their name, evidently hoping to refute the critics who said that they were racist. The membership, if not the name, remained avowedly white.

The council message was pushed hard. Starting early in 1957, a weekly television program, *Citizens' Council Forum*, began broadcasting, as a public service, on eighty stations from Texas to Washington, D.C. The program was billed as "The American point of view with a Southern accent."

Council members liked to see themselves as the leaders of a national revival of conservative politics, not provincial, single-issue defenders of Jim Crow. They loved to pretend that far from being hate sessions, CC meetings were a form of "town meeting" democracy. But "In practice," one skeptical observer discovered, "they more closely resemble vigilante meetings."

To black people the rise of the councils came as a distinctly nasty surprise. Many informed blacks had expected that after the first Brown decision had been handed down it would be carried into effect, however reluctantly, by decent, reasonable Southern middle-class whites who were law-abiding and responsible. They never anticipated the Citizens' Councils.

For every council member who attended meetings and paid his dues there were perhaps half a dozen fellow travelers. Even after the councils passed their 1956 peak, they remained very powerful in much of the Deep South. Few politicians could be elected without their endorsement. Where race was an issue (and it was in most Southern elections), governors, mayors, police chiefs, Congressmen, Senators, and safety commissioners deferred to the councils even if they did not embrace them outright. In Mississippi for several years the most powerful figure in the state was said to be no elected official, no multimillionaire, but William J. Simmons, who was in charge of the Mississippi Citizens' Councils' publicity and propaganda department.

When the Falstaff Brewing Corporation purchased an NAACP life membership as a gift for one of its most successful salesmen, the councils organized a boycott of Falstaff. Beer sales fell precipitately. Falstaff flew one of its vice-presidents to Jackson, Mississippi, to negotiate a surrender. It was rumored that he offered a large payment in cash. The councils generously let Falstaff off with an apology and a statement critical of the NAACP. Other major corporations were similarly brought to heel.

But the councils were at their most ruthless where black people were directly involved. When, for example, fifty black parents in Yazoo, Mississippi, petitioned the local court to have their children enrolled in the white school, the Yazoo Citizens' Council put an advertisement in the *Yazoo City Herald*. The advertisement carried the names and addresses of the fifty petitioners. In less than a week the number of people with their names still on the petition dropped to two. The black plumber established in town for twenty years was forced out of business. The price of a loaf of bread to any of the original fifty petitioners jumped from 20 cents to $1. The black grocer could no longer get supplies from his wholesalers or credit at the bank. The black housewife who went to buy food for her family was turned away at the cash register by the store manager, who told the cashier, "This nigger woman's one of the ones that signed the petition." Economic boycotts such as this spread, with the CC's help, far beyond Yazoo City into other communities where black parents petitioned for desegregated schools.

But boycotts cut two ways in areas where blacks were in the majority. Counterboycotts of businesses owned by council members in South Carolina put a stop to such tactics. It was also claimed that some canny individuals had gone to see the local bank manager with a story that they had been approached by the NAACP. "But what I really need is a loan," they said, "not one of those petitions." They got the loans.

While the councils were making most of the running, the KKK managed to break into a dogtrot. The Klan had stagnated since the death in 1949 of Dr. Green. But in 1955 the "U.S. Klans, Knights of the Ku Klux Klan, Inc." received a charter from a Georgia superior court, and the KKK was back in business. The U.S. Klans claimed title to the old Invisible Empire. But there were rivals. Imperial Wizards and Grand Dragons seemed to pop up everywhere without warning. In Alabama there were six rival Klans. There were another six in South Carolina and four more in Florida. And despite the charter, there were several rival Klans in Georgia.

The various Klans never had more than 100,000 members between them. But they had the moral, if that is the word, support of much of the white working class of the South. Klan motorcades regularly wound their way to rebel yells and honking horns through small towns on a Saturday night. Klan rallies drew thousands of enthusiastic spectators. Traditional Klan activities revived.

In Camden, South Carolina, a white teacher was flogged for an alleged remark critical of segregated schools. In Charlotte, North Carolina, an attempt was made to blow up a black school as a publicity stunt. In Stanton, Alabama, a white sawmill worker was flogged because it was rumored that he had a friendly attitude toward blacks. The home of a white doctor in Gaffney, South Carolina, was blown up after the doctor's wife wrote a magazine article praising the civil rights movement. In Maplesville, Alabama, 100 sheeted men rampaged through the black section of town beating up terrified blacks. On a September night in 1956 six Alabama members of the "Ku Klux Klan of the Confederacy" racked their brains to devise a test in which the newest member of their band, one Bart A. Floyd, could prove his fitness for promotion. They decided that the best measure of his readiness would be to throw a scare into a black man. They bought some turpentine and razor blades, drove around until they came across a young black handyman named Judge Aaron, and kidnapped him. They drove Aaron to a small, dirty hovel fashioned from cinder blocks. There they stripped Aaron naked. They forced him to crawl on his hands and knees for them. Then they beat him up and asked for his views on "the race problem." The Exalted Cyclops of the Ku Klux Klan of the Confederacy, Joe Pritchett, turned to Floyd and commanded, "Do your duty." Floyd unsheated a razor blade. While the others held the bleeding Judge Aaron to the ground, Floyd castrated him. To prolong the agony of his writhing, pain-racked victim, Floyd drenched the gaping wound with turpentine.

The Klan had no monopoly on violence. Emmett Till was taken away from the home of his grandparents in Money, Mississippi, at two o'clock in the morning by Roy Bryant and his half brother J. W. Millam. It was Bryant's wife at whom the boy had wolf-whistled. Three days later his body was recovered from the Tallahatchie River. It was so badly damaged from the beating he had received and from the gunshot wounds in his head that the boy was identified by the ring he was wearing. His mangled remains were patched up by a mortician and put on display at the Temple of Church of God in Christ on Chicago's South Side. Thousands of grim-faced black people filed past the coffin in stifled rage.

The murder of Emmett Till created an international furor. The white people of Mississippi were puzzled. Why should there be such a fuss over one insolent black boy? One man, thoughtfully sipping a Coca-Cola in Sumner during the trial of Bryant and Millam, nodded in the direction of the Tallahatchie. "That river's full of dead niggers."

Throughout the trial Mississippi lived in an atmosphere of terror. Congressman Frank Smith, driving home to Greenwood one night, found hundreds of people milling in the streets. "The wild rumor had spread that 'hundreds of cars of Chicago niggers' were en route to take the accused killers out of jail and lynch them." And this may have been part of the perennial fear of Southern whites—that one day blacks might do to them what they had long been doing to blacks. In the event, to national and international outrage, Bryant and Millam were swiftly acquitted.

At least three other blacks were the victims of race-inspired murder in Mississippi in 1955. In front of the courthouse where Judge Brady (later elevated to the Mississippi Supreme Court) presided, Lamar "Ditty" Smith, who was attempting to register black voters, was shot dead on an August afternoon. Two dozen people witnessed the killing. Three men were identified as the murderers. The local grand jury refused to indict them.

In Belzoni, Mississippi, the Reverend George Lee was making strenuous efforts to persuade his parishioners to register to vote. He was found dead in his car in the early hours one morning. The sheriff decided that the large metal fragments scattered profusely throughout Lee's face and head were dental fillings. The FBI identified them as coming from bullets. The coroner's jury ascribed death to "causes unknown."

Similar crimes occurred elsewhere, with similar results. In East Texas, for example, Perry Dean Ross of Tatum drove over to Longview one Saturday night in 1955. Parked across from a jukebox parlor filled with dancing black teenagers, he raked the flimsy structure with rifle fire. A young boy was killed; two girls were seriously wounded. At Ross's trial the district attorney delivered an impassioned plea that Ross, whom he was prosecuting, be set free. Convicted, Ross was given a suspended sentence.

At Rock Quarry prison camp near Buford, Georgia, forty-one black prisoners in 1956 in desperation broke one another's legs with twenty-pound sledgehammers in protest against torture and beatings inflicted on them by their guards. The Georgia legislature investigated. It found the camp to be a model penal institution, praiseworthy in every respect. The leg-smashing incident, it decided, was nothing but a wicked attempt to give a good place a bad name. This was the same prison camp where thirty-one black prisoners had in 1951 severed their Achilles' tendons with razor blades in an attempt to draw attention to conditions.

Episodes such as these shocked public opinion at home and abroad. And to judge from them, nothing appeared to have changed for the better in race relations. Yet, observed Harry Ashmore, an Arkansas newspaper editor, "With far more provocation [e.g., *Brown*] than existed a generation ago when such affairs were commonplace, there has not been a single lynching in the grand manner—the sort of fiesta where an entire community gathers, children and all, to watch the crosses burn and the limp body sway at the end of a rope."

This reflected the rapidity with which the South had been tamed in a generation, not by force but by rising incomes, rising levels of urbanization, industrialization, and education. As these increased, protest sought to stay within the law. But at the same time the desegregation issue was twisting and poisoning Southern politics for another generation. After the first Brown decision politics in the South once again was reduced to an exercise to see who could "holler nigger" loudest.

The Brown decision came at a crucial moment. In the 1940s the Bilbos and the Rankins were clearly on their way out. A number of liberal Senators and Representatives were elected from the South. But in 1950 two liberal Senators, Claude Pepper of Florida and Frank Graham of North

Carolina, were defeated by adamant segregationists. That same year Herman Talmadge won a four-year term as governor of Georgia principally on the race issue, and James Byrnes became governor of South Carolina. Talmadge and Byrnes led the opposition to any change in the Plessy doctrine.

No state was more diehard and comprehensive in its resistance, however, than Mississippi. In the U.S. Senate the leader of the knee-jerk segregationist faction was the man who had succeeded to Bilbo's seat, James O. Eastland. Although not as fatuous as the unlamented Bilbo, Eastland was known, nonetheless, as "a thin-lipped, hating man."

The Brown decision came at a time when the South was torn between the attractions of politics which involved more than race and politics which involved nothing but race. After 1954 every one of the eleven former Confederate states became obsessed with thwarting the Supreme Court. And in 1956, 101 Senators and Representatives issued a "Southern Manifesto." The 19 Senators and 82 Representatives pledged themselves to devote their energies to reversing the Brown decision. The manifesto repudiated violence and cautioned against "disorder and lawless acts." Yet it was noteworthy that so many elected officials should encourage overt resistance to what was plainly the law of the land.

The Southerners in Congress in these years understood far better than most of the people back home that the South had lost much of the weight it had long carried in national politics. Truman had won without the South; so had Eisenhower. The manifesto was a gesture. It altered nothing.

It was to the states that angry Southerners had to look, as they had looked a century earlier, for politicians who would defy the Federal government. They did not look in vain. Virginia provided the theory and the vocabulary. The theory was termed "Interposition." It might have been gleaned John C. Calhoun's wastebasket. An elderly Virginia country lawyer, William Olds, came across two Interposition resolutions dating from the 1790s, one from Virginia, the other from Kentucky. For his services to segregation Olds was made a circuit court judge.

The gospel of Interposition was zealously propagated by the *Richmond News-Leader*, edited by James J. Kilpatrick. His thesis was older than the retrieved resolutions. Kilpatrick said that blacks were less civilized than whites. Regardless of what the Constitution said, "the Negro race, as a race, has not earned equality." Like other segregationists who affect a tone of reasonableness, Kilpatrick's thesis assumed that blacks, simply because they were black, were inherently inferior to whites. It was no great intellectual challenge for him therefore to ignore the Civil War and its outcome. The states, he wrote repeatedly and at length, had a legal and moral right to interpose themselves between the Federal government and their citizens. It was secessionism, but without anyone's firing on Fort Sumter or giving up Federal matching grants. "Enthusiastically, Southerners, who love legalisms, debated interposition, for no one knew precisely what it meant."

In South Carolina the expression had barely surfaced before fifty-two leading citizens had formed themselves into "The "Committee of 52" and demanded that the state legislature "interpose the sovereignty of the State of South Carolina between Federal courts and local school officials." Tens of thousands of respectable white South Carolinians eagerly added their names to the committee's petition.

Interposition became, in practice, the consolidation of school authority in the hands of state officials and then the use of that authority to close the schools rather than comply with Federal court orders. Enough locked schools, it was fondly believed, would force a reversal of Brown much as determined drinking had brought the repeal of the Eighteenth Amendment.

When Virginia's voters in January 1956 approved a tuition plan which would pay to educate children in private schools if the only alternative open to them was education in integrated public schools, they were scolded by Senator Harry Byrd. He was a man of immense prestige in the South. Nothing less than "massive resistance" would do, he said. The tuition plan was duly held in abeyance, and school closure laws were swiftly enacted.

Massive resistance became the watchword of the bitter-enders. Virginia was not, on the face of it, a likely candidate to lead resistance to desegregation. The proportion of blacks in its population was much the same, at 22 percent, as in next-door Maryland, where there was low-grade evasion, not outright defiance. There were entire counties in Virginia where black people were comparatively rare. The University of Virginia had been integrated in 1950. But in the southern and eastern counties, which provided most of the political leadership, blacks constituted nearly half the population.

Byrd may also have put himself at the head of the forces of resistance because his hold on the Democratic Party machinery in Virginia was slipping, and the Republicans had recently taken three Congressional seats which had long been part of the Byrd fiefdom. Whatever the reason, one of the handful of Southern politicans who could have helped to secure an accommodation with reality chose to do precisely the opposite.

Mississippi's contribution to Interposition was the establishment of the State Sovereignty Commission, to "do and perform any and all acts and things deemed necessary and proper to protect the sovereignty of Mississippi and her sister states from the encroachment thereon by the Federal government or any branch, department, or agency thereof." The commission hired press agents. It financed the Citizens' Councils. Through a corps of paid informants and agents provocateurs it harrassed the civil rights movement.

The legislatures of Alabama, Arkansas, Florida, Georgia, Louisiana, and Virginia established similar bodies. For kept witnesses and self-styled experts on Communism, fallen on hard times with the demise of McCarthyism, the State Sovereignty Commission and its ilk provided a new lease on life. Like McCarthyism, massive resistance was a scoundrels' charter.

The Court had struck at the South. The South struck back through the courts. Shortly before his death Justice Jackson had foreseen that the Brown decision would produce "a generation of litigation." Dozens, scores, eventually hundreds of lawsuits were filed to challenge, but, most of all, to delay, enforcement of the Brown decision. *Brown*, remarked one observer, was "the greatest thing that has happened to the legal profession since the invention of the ambulance."

The Court had provided encouragement to resistance even as it struck down *Plessy* v. *Ferguson*, one of its most famous and far-reaching decisions. Given a different set of judges and an altered climate of opinion, the segregationists reasoned, *Brown*, too, could be struck down one day.

The Court's famous Footnote 11 to the Brown decision was another weak spot. The footnote made reference to the evidence offered by social scientists. It was clearly offered to support the reasoning behind the Court's decision; it was hardly crucial to the decision. Yet it provided a handy stick with which to attack it because it appeared to put sociology in the place of law. Clark's doll test, moreover, was of dubious value at best, as other psychologists were quick to point out. Footnote 11, instead of making the Brown decision more effective, made it less acceptable. And *Brown* needed all the help it could get.

The use of evidence from social scientists called forth a response in kind. There was an outpouring of "scientific" racism on a scale unknown since the era of Social Darwinism in the late nineteenth century.

The Court's second Brown decision contained a reference to Federal judges and "their proximity to local conditions." Many Southerners clutched at this straw and proceeded to erect inflated hopes on it. The forty-eight Federal district judges and their ten immediate superiors on U.S. Courts of Appeal were almost without exception men who had been born, reared, educated in the South. They were by temperament and upbringing men of sober habits and moderate to conservative views. Doubtless as ordinary mortals some among them believed that segregation was morally right. And although they held lofty positions, they were not remote from community sentiments; their wives and children were especially exposed; the local political machinery was probably in the hands of their friends.

A judge who set his face flatly against prevailing sentiments on race would soon discover their force, as Judge J. Waties Waring found. The Clarendon County schools case had been filed in his court. He found in favor of the plaintiffs. He had been raised in Charleston, South Carolina, stood high in Charleston society, and was on good terms with all the people who mattered in that city's affairs. But an unpleasant divorce, plus his rulings in cases involving blacks, had far-reaching effects. His upper-class friends shunned him. He and his second wife were forced to resign from every club and society they belonged to. A cross was burned on their lawn. Rocks crashed through their windows. Their telephone rang all night long with abusive, scurrilous calls. Where had Waring, reared as he had been, developed his liberal views on race?

On the bench itself. Until he became a Federal judge, the only blacks he had seen had been subservient menials. Suddenly he was faced by black people who were proud, articulate, and brave. And the anger against injustice which moved them moved him. When he retired from the bench in 1957, feeling against Waring remained so high that he and his wife left South Carolina.

Despite the pressures on them, the Federal district judges of the South without exception strove to uphold the Supreme Court's directives on desegregation. The Federal courts at all levels made it clear that sooner or later they intended to secure compliance.

The upper South and the border states began to accommodate themselves to the Brown decisions. Little Rock, Arkansas, was typical of hundreds of school districts. Only six days after the first Brown ruling the school board issued a statement declaring, "It is our responsibility to comply with Federal Constitutional requirements, and we intend to do so when the Supreme Court outlines the method to be followed." After the 1955 enforcement ruling Little Rock began making plans to begin desegregation at the fall semester, 1957.

But there was violence, in Hoxie, Arkansas, in Sturgis, Kentucky, and in Mansfield, Texas, to prevent integration. It failed in Hoxie and Sturgis, but it succeeded in Mansfield. The worst trouble flared in September 1956, in Clinton, Tennessee, where Frederick John Kasper, a confused bohemian admirer of Ezra Pound, succeeded in raising a mob of angry whites to a murderous pitch.

In New York, where he had been educated at Columbia, most of Kasper's friends had been Jewish or black. By the time he reached Clinton, however, he was a perfervid anti-Semite and racist. He went from door to door, pleading with people to resist desegregation. The Clinton school board was confident that it had prepared the ground for desgregation, and it had—among the middle class. But Kasper was working his way through lower-class neighborhoods, cultivating the very people the school board had ignored—the Holy Rollers; the agricultural laborers; the tenant farmers; the unemployed.

When Kasper was arrested for inciting a riot, a baying mob 3,000 strong filled the courthouse square to demand his release. More than 40 good men and true were hurriedly pressed into service as special deputies. A call was made to the governor for speedy assistance.

In a showdown that was straight out of a B picture the Clinton forces of law and order (one sheriff, six policemen, and the special deputies) were about to clash with the mob, who outnumbered them by nearly 100 to 1, when the sun went down. The mob was simply waiting for the cloak of darkness. Through the fast-gathering dusk came the sound of sirens. Twenty Tennessee Highway Patrol cars pulled into the square, tires squealing, sirens howling, lights flashing, at the last moment. Nearly 100 heavily armed state troopers jumped from the cars and formed a line in front of the mob. Losing their nerve, Kasper's admirers scurried away into the welcome darkness.

The National Guard arrived a few hours later, in tanks. The next week black children were enrolled in the Clinton schools. Kasper was charged with sedition. A local jury set him free.

Many believed that it was a mistake to attempt integration with small children; that it would work best if tried from the top down, starting with the colleges and universities. But when Autherine Lucy was admitted to the University of Alabama by Federal court order, rioting erupted on the campus. To chants of "Keep 'Bama white," it spilled onto the streets of Tuscaloosa. Miss Lucy and the NAACP expected the Federal government to enforce the court order. It was a hopeless hope. Neither Eisenhower nor Brownell intended to intervene. The university expelled Autherine Lucy, on the grounds that she was the cause of the disturbances.

The problem with attempting integration from the bottom up, on the other hand, was that in places like Clarendon County, South Carolina, it could be achieved only by putting white children into predominantly black schools. In Clarendon County there were 285 white schoolchildren, and 2,800 black. Integrated schools there would have been, in effect, black schools with a sprinkling of whites, whose presence would have been only a token.

Even where the schools were desegregated the result was not necessarily integration with whites. The newly desegregated school often organized its classes according to "ability groups." Almost without exception the top groups were virtually all-white; the bottom groups virtually all-black. After school the white children went home to white neighborhoods. The black children went back to life in the slums.

If it was problematical to integrate black children, what of black teachers? Hard as it was to make parents accept that their children would have to go to school with blacks, it was impossible to make them accept being taught by black teachers. And the qualifications of black teachers often were inferior by any standard to those of their white counterparts, whose own abilities were not as a rule very impressive. Yet if the schools were integrated, many of the South's 75,000 black teachers were in danger of losing their jobs. For black communities in the South that would have been a cruel blow. Black teachers constituted most of the educated segment of those communities.

The forces of resistance to Brown by 1957 had found a way to make a show of compliance without actually complying. They discovered the pupil placement plan. Ten states passed pupil placement legislation. These statutes said not a word about black students or integration or Interposition or massive resistance. All they said was that pupils would be assigned school places after taking into account such factors as health, safety, scholastic aptitude, transportation problems, class size, sociability, home environment, intellectual compatability, and economic parity. All these boiled down into one word—homogeneity. And the Supreme Court confessed that it could find nothing unconstitutional in these laws. Simply to read them without knowledge of their context is to see only a tender concern for the welfare of the students.

All that black parents need do to enroll their child in a predominantly white school was to submit themselves and the child to searching personal inquiries, time-consuming interviews, and any number of tests. There were many forms to be filled in, long delays to be patiently endured, and many petty irritations to enliven the proceedings. And if the application failed, there was still a fair, time-consuming, expensive appeals process to invoke. Some school districts shrewdly permitted a handful of black schoolchildren to be placed in white schools under the pupil placement plan. This made it almost impossible to challenge them in court.

Three years after the first Brown decision, in the seventeen states with segregated schools in 1954, fewer than 62 percent of black children were even now at school with whites. Only in the District of Columbia had the schools been fully integrated.

The Supreme Court had not ordered integration anyway. It had simply banned discrimination. And in practice there was a wide difference between integration and desegregation. Integration suggested a student mix which reflected the population mix in the surrounding area. The schools which admitted black students between 1954 and 1957 usually admitted only a handful and had no intention of admitting more. Such schools were desegregated, but they were not integrated.

White Southerners were beginning to tire of making overt protests. And among young middle-class Southerners there was something like indifference. They would neither rally to the massive resisters nor raise a finger to help blacks. It was an attitude which would spread far afield in coming years.

There was deep anguish all the same over the steady erosion of Jim Crow's rule. It was not proximity as such which made white people afraid. Whites had lived with blacks, been nursed by them, worked alongside them, slept with them. "Integration has always worked well around here," a light-skinned young Southerner remarked to James Baldwin, "after the sun goes down." White infants were fed at black breasts when no black man could stand at a white man's urinal.

Harry Golden made mock of the inherent lunacy in the Jim Crow laws. He offered his Golden Vertical Negro Plan as the solution to the desegregation crisis. Whites stood next to blacks at store counters, Post Office windows, and bank teller's cages without a whisper of protest. The problem evidently arose when black people sat down. He suggested that the state legislatures pass laws to provide the schools with desks but no seats. "Since no one in the South pays the slightest attention to a vertical Negro, this will completely solve our problem."

Jokes aside, what desegregation threatened was not proximity but loss of status. Segregation had been based on an unshakable belief in the inferiority of blacks, without acknowledgment that the white man was in large part responsible for the low condition in which blacks lived and had to rear their children. What was remarkable was that most black people were honest and decent despite these degrading conditions. But it became impossible, thanks to the belief in black inferiority, to raise the status of blacks without lowering the status of whites. Status is so important a factor in people's lives that any sensation of downward movement triggers feelings of panic and fear.

The schools were at the center of the struggle. But the real issue was education in its broadest sense. It would take a long time. During the drive to put the NAACP out of business James Harris of Yalobusha County, Mississippi, returned home one night and found a note tacked to his door: "You is getin to smart trin to vote. Mr. Harris. Have yore name took off the Books—Real soon like—an straiten yore friens."

Blacks could could not rise very far until the whites rose with them.

21

The Religion of America Is Religion

There was more of a turning toward religion in the prosperous postwar than there had ever been during the hungry Thirties. It began, however, during the war. But it continued unabated for more than a decade after the war's end. Enrollments at seminaries rose remarkably. Church membership remained high. In a 1954 survey 56 percent of men and 69 percent of women claimed to have been to church or to have taken part in a religious service in the preceding month. In another survey half those polled claimed to go to church each week.* There was also a boom in church construction. The value of new construction rose from $76 million in 1946 to $868 million in 1957.

"Surprising as it may seem," wrote one observer, with more than a grain of truth, "Catholicism, Protestantism and Judaism are stronger in the United States than anywhere else in the world—in number of *active* adherents, in financial support, and in support of missionary enterprises."

Churches stood high in popular esteem. Asked to rate five institutions for trustworthiness—radio, newspapers, schools, government, and churches—the churches came first by a wide margin. Behind faith in the churches stood a deep and widespread faith in God. Nine Americans out of ten accepted the divinity of Christ. Nearly two in three believed in the existence of the Devil. Even among supposedly wayward, rebellious youth there was a nearly total trust in priests, rabbis, and pastors.

*True figures on churchgoing are impossible to establish. There is a strong tendency for people to overstate their actual churchgoing because it is generally considered a "good" thing to do. The best guess is probably 35 to 40 percent attended church regularly, another 30 to 35 percent went irregularly, and the remainder never went at all. Churches keep no attendance records and are themselves reduced to guesswork.

Religion was an integral part of popular and middle-brow culture. Radio stations paused not only for station breaks but for a minute of religious meditation. Millions of plastic figures representing Jesus, Mary, and Joseph, singly or in family ensemble, appeared on car dashboards. Popular songs frequently carried a religious message. Football games began with a prayer. Railway dining car menus carried a prayer on the back, in three versions—Catholic, Protestant, and Jewish. The Advertising Council devoted millions of dollars of air time to exhortations for people to go to church ("The family that prays together, stays together"). Best-sellers had religious themes. In 1948, for example, the biggest seller of the year in fiction was not *The Naked and the Dead* but Lloyd C. Douglas's *The Big Fisherman*, which outsold Mailer's novel by three to one. In the ten years following the war the demand for Christmas cards with religious motifs doubled. Religious love, religious obsession, religious figures appeared in the work of serious young writers of the 1950s such as John Updike and J. D. Salinger. They appeared onstage in Arthur Miller's *The Crucible* and Archibald MacLeish's *J.B.* They found poetic expression in the works of Phyllis McGinley, John Ciardi, and Robert Lowell. On the screen, religious epics such as *The Robe* and *The Ten Commandments* attracted vast audiences at a time when movie attendance was in a steep decline. The *Revised Standard Version of the Bible* was published in 1952. Within a year it had sold 26.5 million copies. The result of fifteen years; labor by a learned committee, it took advantage of the advances in Biblical knowledge and Oriental language study since the turn of the century. It was more accurate than the King James Version, and less powerful; it was clearer and less imaginative. There was no more passion in it than the minutes of a committee meeting might hold. Its God was a God who issued memos. These, collected, formed the Bible.

When Harvard in 1953 picked a new president, Nathan Pusey, an obscure academic administrator currently in charge of Appleton College, Wisconsin, he set his mind to reviving the Harvard Divinity School as the first order of business. The Divinity School very soon raised $5 million.

Throughout the Cold War there was a conviction that religion would both improve the world and help secure American leadership of it. Piety became a form of nationalism. It was irresistible to conservative politicans, and in that form it had little to do with faith as such. J. Edgar Hoover counseled parents, "Since Communists are anti-God, encourage your child to be active in the church." The American Legion conducted a "Back to God" campaign. "Today there is a suspicion in the air," reflected Roy Eckhardt, "that it is somehow un-American to be an atheist, or to talk up atheism publicly."

Atheists and agnostics were discriminated against. In a dozen states they were barred from becoming notary publics. In most states an agnostic couple could not adopt children. And brave, rare, and foolhardy was the political candidate who would dare say publicly that he did not believe in God.

The separation of church and state in which Americans were likely to take deep pride was less than met the eye. That separation had never been clearly defined in law and tended to reflect the temper of the times. There was as much cooperation as separation. American churches in all probability gained more from tax exemption than did churches in European countries which had church-supporting taxes. Prohibition had been in large measure a concession to the power of the clergy. Religious agencies were even permitted to screen refugees seeking entry into the United States and to decide on their acceptability. The Pledge of Allegiance had been rewritten to include "under God." There was a proposed Constitutional amendment introduced in Congress several times after the war which would have had the Constitution declare, "This nation recognizes the authority and law of Jesus Christ, Savior and Ruler of Nations. . . ." "In God We Trust" had been on U.S. coins for decades; in 1957 it began to appear on every greenback. The previous year Congress made those four words the official motto of the United States. The President and the Secretary of State made a public appearance to celebrate a new postage stamp which, in red, white, and blue and for only eight cents, announced, "In God We Trust." Politicians flocked to "Prayer Breakfasts." The President's Inaugural Parade had featured an item termed "God's Float."

Following his election Eisenhower himself joined a church for the first time in his adult life. He attended service irregularly. Yet in his campaign he had announced, "I am the most intensely religious man I know. That doesn't mean I adhere to any sect. A democracy cannot exist without a religious base. I believe in democracy."

The first Cabinet meeting of the new Administration opened with a prayer, delivered by Ezra Taft Benson, the Secretary of Agriculture, who was one of the Twelve Apostles of the Mormon Church. The Cabinet voted to continue the practice of praying at each meeting.*

Religious passion these days tended to be dull, bland, standardized. The postwar religious "revival" appeared to plunge few souls into religious ecstasy, transformed comparatively few lives, produced no masterpiece of religious thought or art. There was less a religious revival than a revival of interest in religion. And when all was said and done, "the most widespread of all devotions in America is hedonism, the worship of pleasure." An eminent divine was skeptical about the claimed religious revival among college students: "Secularism is too widespread for one to be able glibly to conclude that colleges are more Christian in atmosphere than in 1900."

Some of the growth in church membership and Sunday School attendance reflected increased population rather than an increase in belief. Much of the rest was due to counting children as church members, a practice unusual before 1900 but increasingly common thereafter. High rates of population mobility also led to many people being counted twice.

---

*It was claimed that the Cabinet at first had trouble adjusting to the new way of doing business, that at the end of one session one member slapped the tabletop and said, "Goddammit! We forgot the prayer."

The rise in church attendance was a reflection of increased leisure time. When an Indianapolis department store gave its workers Monday off, instead of a day in the middle of the week, many more of them began going to church on Sunday because they now had Monday free for resting or catching up on their chores.

There was also a strong desire to belong to something. Religious affiliation had long been an important source of self-identification among first and second-generation Americans. Their children and grandchildren found at mid-century that the struggle for an individual identity was as intense as ever, constantly under threat from bureaucratization and conformity.

Behind the revived interest in religion stood "the cult of reassurance—a sort of alliance between religion and depth psychology." In the late 1940s one work appeared for three consecutive years among the ten best-selling nonfiction works, *Peace of Mind*, by Joshua Loth Liebman, "the Radio Rabbi." Its flavor is conveyed by its chapter headings: "Some Truths That Psychiatry Adds to Religion," "How Religion and Psychiatry Parallel One Another." For the millions of people who bought the book there was a new set of commandments, which began, "Thou shalt not be afraid of thy hidden impulses."

The 1950s brought *The Power of Positive Thinking*, by Norman Vincent Peale, the minister of a fashionable Presbyterian church in New York. The very title became a cliché. Peale offered an irresistible combination of Couéism and Christianity, but with an American touch: when you pray, he urged, pray *big*. It was a work with patriotic fervor and old-fashioned boosterism—and shrewdness. Peale assiduously mined a deep, rich vein: feelings of inferiority; lack of self-confidence; low self-esteem. Yet when the pietism and chauvinism were peeled away, there remained a core of sensible advice on a wide range of anxieties.

There were scores of books like *Peace of Mind* and *The Power of Positive Thinking*; so many that it was a moot point whether the search for reassurance actually comforted anyone for any longer than the time it took to read one such book and move on to the next. Trudging through such works may, in the case of the skeptical, only have deepened the depression.

One theologian began to feel that the "peace of mind" and "positive thinking" cults were God's judgment on Christ's ministry. They were hollow compared with the Christian faith of repentance, sacrifice, and redemption, he argued. Yet people took to them by the millions. Would they have done so had not their churches failed them?

Christianity was, moreover, a challenge to the material order. It was in a critical stance toward a society obsessed with money and possessions. Yet the peace of mind and positive thinking schools of theology preached a message of adjustment to the status quo. As any serious person knows, some things are hardly worth adjusting to.

Clergymen liked to see themselves as moral teachers and spiritual leaders. But they were usually content to reflect the moral impulses of the secular conscience. There were, indeed, religious writers who urged the adoption of "societal religion," in which American churches would support the state at every opportunity and "teach Democracy." The churches not only helped people to define themselves but already played an important role integrating the individual with society. And these two socially important functions—identification and integration—appear to have become more central to American religion at midcentury than belief in any creed.

Since the turn of the century the psychological, mystical, and theological elements of religion, long distinct and separable, had been so intermixed that they had become indistinct and inseparable. Religion in the process became diffuse, unified, easily accessible, and without its sharp corners, cutting edges, and bitter traditional disputes. There was a strong strain of quietism in American religion at midcentury, and religious retreats proliferated.

The religious life seemed to have moved from worship to "service." It had gone from the altar to the office. Much of the life of a church in an American town or city in the 1950s did not look like the practice of religion—or anything particularly spiritual—to people whose religious upbringing dated from before 1917. Drive-in churches, storefront churches, church-run community centers, youth associations, and paid religious lobbyists—these all were characteristic of present-day churches and a far cry from the parish church of 1900.

But clergymen were determined to move with the times. "Persons of cultivated taste and education," they were informed, "find that the techniques of worship are hopelessly antiquated." Although the ceremonies changed slowly, the setting was drastically altered. Church buildings adopted modernistic architecture. The church itself became the set for a religious play, the stage for a religious dance. Interiors were brightly lighted; bold colors were lavishly employed. And while churches were built in huge numbers, huge churches were hardly ever built. Religious buildings became cozy and familiar, instead of imposing and remote, useful for more than solemn religious ceremony.

With this toning down and opening up there went a budding spirit of ecumenism. The same was happening in Europe. But there ecumenism took matters of "faith and order" to be the principal order of business. In America the interest was instead on common approaches to religious work and community service. Protestants, Catholics, and Jews stopped fighting one another. But where they cooperated was on the fringe activities, where religion merged with the secular and nondenominational.

And all the while religious faith was trickling away into the tepid sea of modern relativism. There was a religious program on radio called *This I Believe*. Listeners found that there was plenty of "Believe" and no end of "I," but very little "This." Rather than holding to a particular faith, Americans of the 1950s possessed a faith in faith itself.

* * *

No decennial census ever asked a question of religious beliefs or practices. But in 1957 the Current Population Survey did. It was not concerned with how often people went to church or synagogue. Instead, it bluntly asked, "What is your religion?" The answers were: 66.2 percent Protestant, 25.7 percent Catholic, 3.2 percent Jewish, and the remainder belonged to either some other religion or none.

Jews and Catholics were most heavily represented in the Northeast. The Midwest, South, and West were overwhelmingly Protestant. Catholic and Protestant birthrates were almost identical. The Baptists were outbreeding the Catholics. Episcopalians were more highly educated than Jews. But Jews made more money than Episcopalians.

Outside of Utah all the states with the highest proportions of church members were in the Northeast. Those with the lowest proportions were in the West and Southwest. The most urbanized areas, as a rule, had the highest proportions of church membership, belying the belief of country people that the cities were havens of Godlessness.

There were nearly 300 Protestant denominations. Most had fewer than 10,000 members. The denominations had evolved mainly from sects. Yet they did not stand halfway between sects and churches. They were, instead, a uniquely American form of religious grouping, based on voluntary membership and evangelical worship.

It was not always easy to tell what it was that one denomination believed that set it off from the rest. And in the case of Unitarians it was difficult to say what they believed at all. Unitarians, it was reported, believed that there was, at most, one God. There was an attempt to define the major differences in prosaic rather than theological terms: "A Methodist is a Baptist who has been to high school; a Presbyterian is a Methodist who has been to college; an Episcopalian is a Presbyterian who has gotten into Society; and a Catholic is an Episcopalian who has gotten religion."

The fastest-growing denomination in the postwar was the Southern Baptists. They increased at three times the rate of population growth. By the end of the 1950s they had nearly caught up with the Methodists, who were the largest of the Protestant denominations. In the South, where the Episcopal Church was the church of the upper class, a fast-rising family would be tempted to join it. But in recent years the Baptist and Methodist churches of the South had fallen into line with the new wealth and rising status of their parishioners. They offered more formal services, richer vestments, and more imposing places of worship, attempting to staunch the flow.

There had long been little to choose between Baptists and Methodists in the South except for sprinkling versus immersion. But after 1945 the Methodists became increasingly liberal in both theology and social attitudes; more like their Northern coreligionists. The Baptists tended to cling to the old ways and the old faith. They were expected to save others and thought nothing of stopping a passer-by to ask, "Are you saved?" Southern Methodists had long been equally fervid, equally evangelical. But the postwar generation of young Methodists appeared to find the old style distasteful. They also appeared to consider life on earth at least as important as life hereafter.

The Methodist Church, with its 12 to 13 million members, was usually felt to be quintessentially middle-class, somehow "typically American" in its adherents' optimism, energy, and smugness. They boasted a long tradition of social action and proudly recalled their part in the Abolition and Prohibition movements. For Methodists, the "Social Gospel" was as old as the Hebrew prophets of the Old Testament. And it was this side of their heritage which began to spread to Methodists in the South when other influences, such as urbanization, secondary education, and postwar prosperity, took hold in that region.

Yet it was the Southern Baptists who enjoyed the greater success. They were skillful proselytizers. The extreme autonomy of each congregation offered a powerful appeal. No policy adopted by the Southern Baptist Convention was binding on any congregation without the congregation's consent. That is, the convention could be as liberal on race as it wished; the congregation could remain as conservative as *it* wished. The Southern Baptist Convention meeting in St. Louis in June 1954 gave its blessing to the Brown decision. The Methodists followed suit a few weeks later. But while there was racial moderation at the top, there was stubborn resistance at the bottom. This was true of many Methodist congregations as well. The leading Southern Baptist preacher, Billy Graham, held integrated revival meetings and preached that Christianity was color-blind. His popularity remained undimmed. But when an ordinary, obsure minister spoke out for desegregation, he was likely to find the collection plate coming back light.

Dan Wakefield visited a Baptist church in a small Southern town a week after the minister had preached a sermon on why desegregation was better than closing the public schools. The collection plate passed twenty worshipers before it reached Wakefield. Glancing down, he saw that it contained a solitary nickel. In Palestine, Texas, a young Baptist minister shook hands with a black man on a downtown street. This, and teaching a Bible class for black children, led to his dismissal. Jubilant, one parishioner at the meeting to fire the minister held up a hand and shouted, "*This* hand has never touched a nigger."

It was this unyielding quality which lay behind the Southern Baptists' appeal. They were as militant and as dogmatic as the Roman Catholic Church. They made few concessions to the liberal sentiments which prevailed in postwar Protestantism. Baptists alone had the true Scripture; they alone understood the word of God. It was this exclusiveness which kept the Southern Baptists out of the National Council of Churches. With millions of Southerners moving north in recent years, the Southern Baptist Convention moved with them. It held several of its annual meetings in Chicago.

These years also saw a pentecostal revival. It had the usual forms— speaking in tongues, prophesying, miracles. But more than anything else it was a healing revival. In hundreds of tents and auditoriums each week the sick were restored to perfect health through the intervention of the Holy Ghost. This was the point toward which the entire service—possibly eight hours long—had been directed. When the sick were assembled and every head was bowed in prayer, the minister would raise his arms and cry "God, do it now!" This healing revival was separate from the fundamentalist revival, but it probably succeeded for much the same reasons that fundamentalism did.

Despite the appeal of fundamentalism, there were, by the late 1950s, younger, more liberal Southern Baptists who wanted to see a centralized structure, peaceful coexistence with the other major Protestant denominations, and a stronger sense of social responsibility. These reforming impulses could not make much headway for a long time, however. The Citizens' Councils were able to organize much of the lay opposition to ministers of moderate views. The reformers had to move slowly and circumspectly to move at all. Business probably did more to bring about desegregation in the South, close observers believed, than the churches.

Ironically, the second largest gathering of Baptists was the National Baptist Convention. It was black. In the 1950s it had some 5 million members, 25,000 ministers, and more than 20,000 churches. It was the largest black church body in the world and the largest black organization in the United States.

The black Baptists were the reverse of the white Baptists. Here it was the bottom that was radical, and the top conservative. It was the Baptist congregations of Montgomery and their until-then-obscure young pastors who had organized the bus boycott. "We Shall Overcome," the unofficial but universally known anthem of the civil rights protestors, was based on a Baptist hymn which began:

> I will overcome, I will overcome,
> I will overcome someday.
> Oh, if in my heart I do not yield
> I will overcome someday.

Black churches were accustomed to providing a (very limited) outlet for political protest at the neighborhood level. The NAACP had close links with black churches. A fifth of its chapters were headed by ministers.

It was claimed that black people were "overchurched." There was a church for every 200 black churchgoers, twice the ratio of churches to the churchgoers among whites. But in the South, where black newspapers were very few and generally inferior to the black newspapers of the North, when blacks wanted to know what was happening in or to their community, they turned not to the press but to the church down the street.

The black church was also one of the very few social mobility ladders available to an ambitious young man. It was a help to be born a minister's son. James Baldwin's father was a preacher; so were Martin Luther King, Jr.'s, Adam Clayton Powell's and Paul Robeson's. Four very different men, and all destined to rise.

Yet, as we shall see, until the advent of the Black Muslims white people tended to take a slightly amused, rather superior view of religion as it was practiced among blacks. They mistakenly saw it as a harmless emotional release. "The faith may be described as childlike, but the ends it serves are often sinister," cautioned James Baldwin. "Religion operates here as a complete and exquisite fantasy of revenge: white people own the earth and commit all manner of abomination and injustice [but] God is not sleeping and vengeance is not far off."

The Catholic Church was clearly the largest single religious body. Yet more than a third of all those it claimed as members were children under thirteen or lapsed Catholics. Some were so far lapsed they were atheists and agnostics. But once exposed to the faith in childhood they were considered members of the church forever, short of excommunication.

Tightly organized and found mainly in the big cities, Catholics were able to make their presence felt out of proportion to their numbers. Any city with at least 10,000 Catholics would have half a dozen Catholic churches, a Catholic school or two, and probably a Catholic hospital. There was every chance that the Catholic community would be well represented at city hall and on the police force. In organized labor, if there was any ideological influence at all in the 1950s, it was not Communist but Catholic, the product of worker priests and Catholic labor schools.

The Catholic Church's influence spread well beyond the circle of its adherents. It was able to limit the dissemination of birth control information and devices. It made divorce difficult in many states. It lobbied successfully for aid to Franco. It lobbied successfully for the withholding of recognition from some Communist regimes.

In the United States the Catholic Church was under the control of an Irish-descended priesthood. In the 1950s there was not one bishop with an Italian name, or an archbishop. In part this reflected the earlier arrival of the Irish immigrants, in part the readier willingness of the Irish to accept celibacy.

The Irish preeminence produced a Catholic Church which was activist in the Irish tradition. In American Catholic communities the priests were community leaders, not remote, autocratic figures. A noted French Catholic layman found the result distasteful: "He [the Irish Catholic] has introduced gangsterism into the Church along with a taste for 'arrangements.' It was he who brought in the habit of playing bingo for money in churches." Certainly American Catholic literature tended to be undistinguished compared with the European variety. Its theology was derivative; its standards of education were unimpressive. "The choice between humility and comfort must be made," the Frenchman sternly warned. "The

American Catholic clergy has opted for gold-rimmed spectacles—the number of American priests wearing gold-rimmed spectacles is unimaginable—arrogance, ecclesiastical pride and well-pressed clothes, beer parties and bingo games in the churches.''

In *Morte D'Urban*, one of the finest novels of the postwar, J.D. Powers presented a memorable portrait of the priest-as-hustler. Father Urban has a gift for it. He is in wide demand as a speaker; he hobnobs with the rich, charms *grandes dames*, and is a shade brighter than the ordinary priest. But fate has perversely made him a member of a poor and obscure order. And because his success inspires envy, he is assigned to a forlorn outpost in the wilds of Minnesota. The gift, however, is immune to cold and ice. He turns this dreary spot into a new kind of retreat—a deluxe golf course. After all, he reasons, not only are golfers numerous and their numbers rapidly growing, but like other mortals they stand in need of spiritual comfort.

Father Urban has faith, but it is chiefly faith in getting ahead. He turns his order into a success without giving much time to theology or prayer. He glad-hands his way from state to state (usually traveling first class), dining well, drinking well, to spread the good news about the order and its unique retreat, "with a shrine of Our Lady below Number Five green."

Throughout the 1950s one of the premier television performers was Monsignor Fulton J. Sheen, notable for bringing many a prominent ex-Communist or well-known figure such as Clare Boothe Luce into the fold, in a blaze of publicity. The monsignor did not appear at some ungodly hour but in prime time, eight to eight thirty each Tuesday evening. The show featured dramatic props—a statue of the Virgin and Child, candles, Sheen's gorgeous bishop's garb— but there was no music. Sheen told Bible stories, offered moral uplift, kept things moving right along with jokes and humorous anecdotes. But most of all, there was the piercing eye, the long, elegant, jabbing fingers. It was a bravura thirty minutes of dramatic poses, purple oratory, and comic-strip theology. In 1952 the monsignor received an Emmy for being that year's "Outstanding Television Personality." His show ("sponsored by God") ran for five years. Its most remarkable achievement was that for nearly two years it held its own against *I Love Lucy*.

Despite the popularity of a Sheen or the high visibility of Catholics, they tended to be distrusted by the Protestant majority. Paul Blanshard's *American Freedom and Catholic Power* sold steadily throughout the 1950s, reaching sales of 250,000. It was a work which attempted to prove that Catholicism was, by its very nature, a threat to civil liberties and suggested that it made a truly humane society impossible.

Certainly the fact that so many of McCarthy's most smitten admirers were Catholics fanned suspicion. And Protestants found repugnant such church doctrines as that which made it a duty for the Catholic Church to persecute all "false religions", such as their own. To liberal-minded Catholics doctrines of this kind were an embarrassment.

The Catholic Church was especially disliked for its pronouncements on

sex. The strict Catholic view was that the purpose of marriage was pro-
creation, that intercourse for the sake of pleasure cast a husband as a pa-
ramour and his wife as his mistress. Should the erring husband go further
and attempt to use a condom, the wife was instructed to resist him as strenuously as if he were a rapist and she a virgin. The Catholic Church opposed sex education in the schools; this to many educated people seemed
irredeemably obtuse. And despite considerable evidence to the contrary,
Catholic priests decided that the United States faced disaster because it
was not breeding sufficient numbers of people. It was "faced with a threat
of decline," thanks to birth control. "In our large cities the situation is
acute . . . only seven persons are being born to replace ten now in existence." It was confidently predicted that unless something drastic were
done the U.S. would have a population of 40 to 50 million in 2050.

Catholic writers could be pugnacious and provocative. John T. Flynn's
The Road Ahead, of which one million copies were distributed, repeatedly accused the Protestant churches of harboring revolutionaries and pro-
mulgating Socialism. If Flynn's intention was to promote interfaith bitterness, he succeeded. And Catholics too often cast themselves as being
more anti-Communist than anyone else; during the Cold War this was the
ultimate in moral smugness.

Although Protestants tended to dislike and sometimes despise Catholics, it was unusual for them to know very much about them. There was a
Roman Catholic world which remained terra incognita to all but a handful
of non-Catholics. Besides Catholic colleges, parochial schools, hospitals,
and the Knights of Columbus, which everyone heard of, there were Catholic welfare agencies, veterans' organizations, Catholic Boy Scouts,
Catholic professional and fraternal associations, Catholic leagues of policemen and firemen, Catholic newspapers, and a Catholic Youth Organization which enrolled several million members.

Nor was the Catholic Church as uniform and monolithic as most people
believed or as its leadership liked to pretend. Much of the medieval doctrine which so exercised Blanshard had been quietly allowed to lapse, if it
had not been specifically renounced. But there was no denying the strongly authoritarian streak which held many of the poor and uneducated in
thrall to their priests.

What excited the most widespread concern, however, was the Catholic
Church's attempts to secure state aid for parochial schools. In many communities in the 1950s there was a deep tension when Catholics who were
influential at city hall or in the school board "pushed Bible reading, encouraged graduation exercises in churches, asked the school system to
sell property to the churches at reduced prices and urged that children be
released in school time for instruction in religious centers."

For their part, Catholics resented what they considered "double taxation." They vented their annoyance by blocking programs to improve the
public schools, strove to defeat school bond issues, and lobbied against
Federal aid to education. At the same time they were increasingly dismayed by the growing secularity in the public schools, which made them
less suitable than ever for Catholic children.

What to Catholic parents might appear as no more than a reasonable infusion of religious instruction into nonreligious subjects could be enough to inspire the deepest suspicion among non-Catholics. This was a parochial school arithmetic question: "If it takes 40,000 priests and 140,000 sisters to care for 40,000,000 Catholics in the United States, how many priests and sisters will be needed to convert the 120,000,000 non-Catholics in the United States?" The objection most non-Catholics had was not that there was religion in the schools but that in Catholic schools religion permeated everything.

Catholics liked to imagine that the parochial schools were a sacred trust handed down from Mother Seton, whose Sisters of Charity undertook to educate poor girls. But the parochial schools as an alternative to the public schools dated only from the 1880s. By the 1950s Catholic education involved nearly 10,000 elementary schools with 3.5 million students and 2,400 high schools with nearly 700,000 students. Yet more than half of all Catholic children were being educated in the public schools.

The Catholic Church pressed, with some success, for state-aided ancillary services, such as the provision of free textbooks and school buses. Catholic schools were also tax-exempt and were accepted by state authorities as an alternative educational system under their compulsory education laws.

The Catholic schools had traditionally operated on the principle that God had outlawed segregation long before *Brown* reached the Supreme Court. Even so, there were some parochial schools, notably in Louisiana, which were segregated. In most Southern states Catholic activities, such as retreats and Cana conferences, were restricted to whites. Even black priests were barred. There was also informal evasion of church policies on race. In Louisville, Kentucky, for example, the Catholic churches were on record as opposing segregated housing. But after the Bradens sold the house to the Wades, no Catholic priest who would admit that the house was in his parish could be found.

The overall record of the Catholic Church on race, however, was distinctly better than that of most Protestant sects. Nor was it noticeably more illiberal and authoritarian than fundamentalist Protestantism. Finally, there were thousands of Catholics who disliked censorship, authoritarianism, and reaction. As it had been for centuries, the Catholic Church was a more diverse and flexible institution than most non-Catholics ever acknowledged or understood.

Jews faced an identity crisis as severe as that faced by blacks. American society was so open and so secular that a unique identity required constant care and attention. For Jews this was made more difficult by their success.

The Jewish immigrants who arrived before World War I had put their energies into the prosaic business of survival. They had worked as peddlers and seamstresses. Their children, on reaching maturity between the wars, had struggled to become self-employed petit bourgeois—shopkeepers, tailors. The third generation, coming to maturity in the postwar, entered the professions; they were accountants, lawyers, doctors, dentists, academics. In only three generations the Jewish working class had almost disappeared. Jewish labor leaders found themselves running unions in which few Jews were left. By the 1950s American Jews were almost entirely middle class. Yet success had done nothing to resolve the ancient question "Who is a Jew?"

Between the wars Jews had been torn between Jewishness and Judaism. Jewishness, in which American Jews would maintain their identity by creating a secular and national subculture, never appealed strongly to young Jews, however. But Judaism , which sought identification through religion, flourished. Hundreds of tiny Orthodox synagogues in the old, run-down Jewish neighborhoods in the central cities closed down each year. Out in the suburbs and in the better city neighborhoods hundreds of prosperous new synagogues, Conservative and Reform, were meanwhile being opened. Orthodoxy enjoyed a postwar renaissance in Jewish schools, colleges, and universities. The all-day schools (yeshivas) where the curriculum was divided between Jewish and non-Jewish subjects had a strong appeal among upper-middle-class- Jews and never lacked students.

When Jews became upper-middle-class, however, they were likely to blend in with the rest of the upper middle class. They moved out of Jewish neighborhoods, gave their children Anglo-Saxon names, joined non-Jewish organizations, disregarded dietary laws, and put up a Christmas tree each year ("for the children"). In short, the more successful, the less Jewish.

There was a strong undercurrent of antagonism in Jewish communities, usually along class lines. The upper middle class tended to consider those below them "separatists" —that is, still residents of the ghetto, mentally, if not physically. To lower-middle-class Jews and the handful of working-class Jews the Jew in the upper middle class was a goyish Jew, hardly Jewish at all.

Yet the Americanizing influences had a strong effect on all Jews, regardless of class. As they moved up the social scale, Jews stopped haggling over prices, stopped playing cards, and started to play golf. Those willing to risk rejection might take their vacation at a non-Jewish resort. If they were accepted, the vacation was a success, and their status back home went up a notch. Upper-middle-class Jews became Masons, but they retained their memberships in B'nai B'rith. And the zeal of rich Jews to give money away resembled the potlatch ritual of the Kwakiutl Indians in which "The more a man gives away the higher his status and the greater the mortification of those who have been outdone."

Since they were an urban people, it was natural that when other ubanites fled to the suburbs, Jews would follow the same path. In a sense the existence they pursued was less Jewish. But in the suburbs they seemed to compensate by making the synagogue their social and religious center to a degree not known back in the cities. They sought out their fellow

Jews and in some respects may, paradoxically, have led a more overtly Jewish existence than ever.

When Park Forest, thirty miles south of Chicago, opened in 1951, it held 2,000 families at first, several hundred of them Jewish but widely scattered throughout the development. There was no synagogue, no kosher food store. Yet within a year there was a B'nai B'rith lodge, a Jewish Sunday school, a chapter of he National Council of Jewish Women, and a Board of Jewish Education. Even the Jews who held aloof from these organizations socialized almost entirely with other Jews. During the day, Jew and Gentile mingled freely. But at night each stuck to their own.

A Jewish community such as this had a self-conscious Jewishness that was of a strain unknown to Jewish communities before the war. Children no longer assumed their Jewishness. They were carefully taught it.

Surburban Jews were likely to observe far fewer sacred rituals, from eating only kosher foods to lighting Hanukkah candles, than their parents. Their parents had probably observed only half as many sacred rituals as their grandparents. On the face of it, Jewish religious observance was threatened with extinction within two generations. But what had happened was that a low, minimal level of observance had been reached. This was clung to tenaciously. Compared with traditional Jewish practices, it was vestigial and debased. Yet it remained crucial to the maintenance of a separate identity.

The sacraments which were retained were the least demanding: lighting candles on Friday night; observing the major holidays. Although visited infrequently, synagogues were well supported. For millenia Judaism had been a way of life; it had centered on the home. Most of the sacraments were performed there, by each Jewish family. But in postwar suburbia Jews looked to the synagogue and the Talmud Torah to teach their children what it was to be a Jew.

Synagogue membership in the 1950s stood at a record level. Many a suburban synagogue had a waiting list. Attendance figures rose steadily. Yet, remarked a noted Jewish scholar, "The synagogue in America no longer represents a community of believers. Nothing in the way of belief or practice—not even the belief in God or the practice of the most elementary mitzvot—may be taken for granted among synagogue members . . . it has become 'normal' for Jews, and even for synagogue members, to believe in and observe nothing in particular. . . " In this, Jews had much in common with midcentury Christians.

Although most Christians were probably unaware of it, the range of religious belief and practice among Jews was as wide as the range between Roman Catholics and Unitarians. In some synagogues all the prayers were in English and the music was provided by Mozart. In others the men kept their hats and the entire service was in Hebrew. Some Jews worshiped a personal God. To others the idea of a personal God was absurd.

The postwar saw the intermarriage of Jews and non-Jews for the first time on a large scale—another impediment to the search for identity, another rupture with the traditions of Judaism. Among Jewish immigrants intermarriage had been almost unheard of. Among their grandchildren it was not unusual. And the children of such unions were likely to be reared as non-Jews. The combination of intermarriage and the low fertility rate of Jews meant that the already small proportion of the population that was Jewish was likely to grow still smaller.

Jews were conscious of their comparatively small numbers. No matter how high they rose, they always felt vulnerable. Anti-Semitism certainly had not vanished, but it had become far more polite, far less vicious. Nowhere was it more polite than in the upper reaches of American business; nowhere was it more effective. Some 15 percent of the graduates of Harvard Business School were Jewish, for example, but in the Advanced Management Program, where the students were chosen by the companies, not by Harvard, only .5 percent were Jewish. This .5 percentage usually came from Jewish-run companies. Hard as it was to get into the country club, it was harder still to get into the boardroom.

Racial covenants also kept Jews out of the better neighborhoods. When Richard Nixon bought a house in Washington after being elected to the Senate, for instance, he agreed as a matter of course never to sell or rent it to "persons of Negro blood or extraction or to any person of the Semitic race, blood, or origin. . . ."

Long into the 1950s hotels in resort areas from New England to Nassau had signs prominently displayed at the reception desks reading, "No Jews Allowed" or "Christians Only." Hotel advertisements read, more discretely, "Protestant church nearby" or "Discriminating Clientele." But year by year the signs came down.

The Ivy League discarded the quota system, although Jewish students tended to be limited somewhat by policies of "geographical preference," which gave an advantage of students from west of the Mississippi and south of the Mason-Dixon line. There was also strong preference shown to black applicants. A black student with slightly above average qualifications would probably be accepted ahead of a Jewish applicant with an A minus average and College Board scores in the 700 range.

It was sad and ironic that blacks, toward whom Jews had shown much sympathy long before it was fashionable to do so, tended to hate Jews. It may not have been their Jewishness that was hated, however, but the fact that they were white. "Just as a society must have a scapegoat, so hatred must have a symbol. Georgia has the Negro and Harlem has the Jew," said James Baldwin.

To Harlem blacks the Jew was "Goldberg." He owned Harlem: he was around every corner; he ran the business where you worked and owned the tenement where you lived. Half the teachers in the New York public schools were Jewish. The only way to get out of Harlem was to get a job in the garment district. But Goldberg owned the garment district. Jews were hated because they made money, hated because they were different, hated for keeping to themselves. Much of the anti-Semitism of blacks was of the well-known traditional kind, right down to "Them goddamned Jews killed my Jesus, too!"

Jews were sensitive toward blacks because of their own folk memories of slavery, memories recalled each Passover. But in their hearts many Jews despised blacks. Certainly they had no more desire to live next to a black family than had Gentiles. Where their homes and children were affected Jews were as capable as anyone of practicing discrimination. In the late 1940s Jews began going to vacation on Fire Island each summer in large numbers, to the rage of the long-term, predominantly Gentile residents. Then, in the 1950s, homosexuals began flocking to Fire Island. The Jews and Gentiles stopped being unpleasant to one another. They put up a united front against the inverts.

The way in which Jews regarded themselves and were regarded by others was transformed by the creation of the state of Israel. But it added yet another complication to the question "Who is a Jew?" There had been a Jewish nation for 2,000 years without a Jewish state. Suddenly, there was a Jewish state. This revived another old question: "Is it good for the Jews?" Most thought it was, but a minority of thoughtful Jews disagreed.

Jews whose immigrant ancestors had come from Eastern Europe and Russia were considerably more pro-Israeli than those descended from German Jewish immigrants. Zionism had not carried much appeal to American Jews until the advent of the Third Reich. Even after the war many Jews continued to argue that Judaism was a religion, that American Jews could have only one national allegiance. The American Council for Judaism remained entirely Jewish but profoundly anti-Zionist.

Yet most Jews felt that they had little choice: Israel had to be preserved—first, as a home for survivors of the Nazi Holocaust; second, as a potential refuge should such massive persecution ever occur again; third, as a country which would welcome Jewish refugees from Communist countries—a role the United States had chosen not to accept.

In the first ten years following the war the amount of money privately raised for Israel totaled $1.4 billion. It was money from American Jews which financed the resumption of large-scale immigration to Israel from Europe and North Africa in the 1950s. Jewish groups also lobbied the American government with considerable success to provide economic and military aid to the fledgling state.

The ongoing struggle to help secure the survival of Israel had a positive effect on American Jewry. "Bonds for Israel," said Harry Golden, "have done as much for the Jewish middle class in America as they have done for Israel itself. Within a short time the Bonds for Israel fellows have molded the rawest of raw material into men of prestige and status; in short, *leaders*."

After 1945 American Jewry constituted the largest cohesive Jewish community in the world. Yet before the war it had been possible in the main to ignore it. After 1945 that community made its presence felt. It had been able to retain its unique character at the same time that it had become middle class. Educated, articulate, and highly organized, American Jewry was a remarkable, and unusually self-critical, success.

22
Everybody (well, almost) Liked Ike

Twenty years out of office had left the Republicans woefully naïve about the economic realities of the world's most intricate economy at midcentury. Having mouthed the clichés and platitudes of business at its least enlightened for as long as they could recall, most Republican politicians held their own words in reverence and felt it their destiny to turn those words into deeds. The result was a painful series of accommodation to awkward reality.

"When Joseph M. Dodge, Eisenhower's first Budget Director, revealed in detail the facts and figures of the government's financial predicament at the first Cabinet meeting in the Hotel Commodore in New York before the Inauguration," Sherman Adams recorded, "most of us were stunned." Dodge put the overall problem in terms of family finances (reflecting a certain innocence in the Budget Director); so debts were portrayed as four times the size of annual income and there was "never more money in the bank than was needed to cover one month's living expenses."

Unsophisticated as they were, the conservatives who took office under Eisenhower were not of the reactionary ("A spell of unemployment keeps the workers in their place") type. The chief characteristic of the Eisenhower appointees was a devout belief in price stability. Only Communism was worse than high inflation, and might follow it. Forced to choose between inflation and recession, they would have opted for recession with hardly a second thought. This outlook colored economic policy throughout the Eisenhower years.

Since the last Republican government there had occurred a profound structural change: the public sector had been transformed. The new Administration was loath to admit that the new role of government, at the very center of the economy, was not the result of New Deal wickedness but the natural result of the Second World War and the Cold War. In 1953 nearly 90 percent of Federal spending went for wars past, present, and to come. The "creeping Socialism" which Republicans denounced so hotly took approximately 4 percent of the Federal budget, in Social Security, health, welfare, education, and housing expenditures. Short of massive disarmament there was little room to cut back government spending after the Korean armistice.

Yet during his election campaign the one pledge Eisenhower had made most often was a promise to balance the budget. When in February 1954 he presented the first wholly Republican budget for twenty-one years, it contained a projected deficit of $3 billion.

The Administration wasted no time in scrapping the vestigial wage and price controls imposed because of the Korean War. But monetary controls became more stringent and remained so for the remainder of the 1950s. The Republican way of fighting inflation was to prevent it from getting started.

The Council of Economic Advisers, a body regarded with suspicion by conservatives in and out of Congress, was allowed to go out of business. But then the Administration discovered that it needed the CEA or something like it if it intended to have an overall view of where the economy was going. The CEA was revived, and Arthur Burns, "an economist's economist" and a man who detested inflation, was installed to run it. Burns was, moreover, an authority on the business cycle. The ghost of the Depression stalked the offices of Republican politicians. Burns was critical of Keynesian economics. Under his guidance the CEA concentrated on preventing inflation, aiding small business, and improving government statistics.

In the two years after the Korean armistice Federal spending dropped by 35 percent. But the drop in government demand was offset by a $5 billion tax cut. There was only a brief, mild recession. Wall Street prices rose steadily and continued to rise until the fall of 1957.

For two decades the Republicans had denounced "confiscatory" tax rates on income. Once in power they cut the top rate—by 1 percent. The excess profits tax from the Korean War was promptly repealed. The scandal-ridden RFC was put out of business. Some of its functions were taken over by a new entity, the Small Business Administration. Some of the changes effected smacked of revenge against the New Deal; but it was a timid, circumspect revenge in most instances, such as changing the name of Boulder Dam back to Hoover Dam and passing the Twenty-second Amendment. Republicans who had hoped to dance a triumphal jig on Franklin Roosevelt's grave were sorely disappointed.

Yet there was no mistaking the change of tone in economic matters. Many of the people the new Administration brought to Washington "seemed to believe in no function for government except perhaps the collection and distribution of mail." They stayed for a year or two, then returned to their companies bursting with damning anecdotes about governmental bureaucracy.

The president of General Motors, Charles E. Wilson,* Eisenhower's choice for Secretary of Defense, came to stand as the crass nonpareil of the new breed. He got off to a disastrous start. During his confirmation hearings he appeared unable to understand why he was expected to divest himself of his GM stock. To help make the point clear, one of the Senators asked him to imagine a situation where he would be called on to make a decision which would lower the value of GM stock. Wilson replied, "I cannot conceive of one because for years I thought that what was good for our country was good for General Motors, and vice versa." This ut-

---

*There were two Charles E. Wilsons who served in high office between 1940 and 1957, and they were further confused by one being the president of GM and the other of GE. To prevent confusion, one was known as Engine Charlie and the other as Electric Charlie.

terance was promptly and unfairly and memorably distorted, so that Wilson was assumed to have said, "What's good for General Motors is good for the United States." Nor did he endear himself to the proud Senators and Representatives on Congressional committees by loftily addressing them as "You men."

The new Administration made good on one of the President's most important campaign pledges: the states were allowed to take possession of what they misleadingly termed "tidelands" oil. Strictly speaking, it was offshore oil. It was not limited by the reach of the tides. Louisiana, for instance, claimed the right to oil twenty-seven miles out in the Gulf.

Since the 1930s, when large amounts of recoverable oil were found offshore from a dozen coastal states, the Federal government had claimed the oil as a national resource. The Supreme Court had never faced the issue of ownership squarely and made a definitive ruling. But it had nullified the claims of coastal states to exploitation of the waters beyond the low tide mark.

Oil companies and the coastal states lobbied intensively from 1947 on to secure a Federal quitclaim at least as far as the three-mile limit. Inland states lobbied with equal vigor against a quitclaim. The Submerged Land Act of 1953, passed by the first Congress since Hoover's day in which Republicans were in control of both houses of Congress, settled the issue. The coastal states were given exploitation rights from the low tide mark to the continental shelf. In some areas that was more than ten miles out at sea. Congress had made these lucky states a gift worth billions of dollars in royalties. In Texas, Governor Price Daniel rose to the occasion by commissioning the seven lawyers who had worked on Texas's claims to offshore oil as admirals in the Texas Navy.

Oil interests usually did well under the Eisenhower Administration. Depletion allowances were extended to nearly 100 minerals, including sulfur, coal, iron ore, and clamshells. But oil and gas accounted for more than 80 percent of the mineral depletion allowances actually allowed, and they enjoyed the highest rate, 27½ percent. The value of this tax concession was calculated at $2 billion a year. Oil companies operating outside the United States also enjoyed the depletion allowance, even in places like Saudi Arabia, where it was no easy matter to drill a dry hole.

The private power companies did not fare as well under the new dispensation, although they had stronger ideological claims on Republican politicians. Two generations of businessmen and conservative politicians had burned with indignation at the rise of the public power companies. On each side of the power divide the opposition was known as "those bastards." It was not so much a fight over the price of electricity as a head-on clash between opposing views of society and government. The great symbol of all that was involved was the TVA.

By the 1950s the TVA was primarily concerned with generating and selling electric power. Flood control came a distant second. To the alarm and disgust of the private power companies roughly 70 percent of the population approved of the TVA; an institution which the power companies had tried to portray for nearly twenty years as a threat to the nation. Yet the Republicans simply could not leave well enough alone. The result was a bitter fight over a deal whose details were so complicated that hardly anyone could keep them straight in his mind for more than ten minutes at a time. Everyone, however, knew the name of the fight: Dixon-Yates.

Edgar H. Dixon was the president of Middle South Utilities. Eugene Yates was president of the Southern Company. They proposed to build a steam plant in western Tennessee under government contract for $120 million. The plant would provide power for the AEC's new facility at Paducah, Kentucky. The TVA would have been happy to provide the AEC with the power it needed. But the new Administration refused to let it build a new steam plant to do so.

Eisenhower had tried to use the TVA in his election campaign as an example of the "creeping Socialism" with which the country was threatened. The bankers who had been brought into the Bureau of the Budget nursed wistful fantasies about selling off the TVA's power plants and restricting its activities to flood control and navigation. And this idea appealed very strongly to Adolphe H. Wenzell, on loan to the BOB from the First Boston Corporation for a trifling $10 a day, plus expenses.

Both Memphis and the AEC were asking for more power than the TVA could provide without building new steam plants. The challenge, as Wenzell and his colleagues saw it, was to help Memphis and the AEC without helping "creeping Socialism." The solution, they decided, was for the AEC to award a contract for a new steam plant to be built by the private power companies, and any surplus power not needed by the AEC could be sold to the TVA, which the TVA in turn could sell to Memphis.

The TVA responded by offering to build a steam plant which would provide as much power as the proposed Dixon-Yates edifice to free enterprise but at two-thirds the cost. To show that they were not really doing this for the money after all, Dixon and Yates cut the price of their plant by 25 percent. The President ordered the AEC to sign a contract with Dixon-Yates. It was an order of dubious validity and little sense. Nor did it say much for the legendary love of competition which was supposed to be the heart of free enterprise. It also turned out that among the directors of the Southern Company was none other than Bobby Jones, a man of the highest personal integrity, but nevertheless a friend and golfing partner of the President's.

By this time Eisenhower found himself attempting to explain actions and decisions about which he was being misled by his own appointees. When he ordered a complete report on the affair, he received a document which covered everything except the role of Adolphe H. Wenzell. And this was noteworthy not only because Wenzell had put the Dixon-Yates deal together, but because the financing of the Dixon-Yates contract, involving a commission of $4 million, was to be handled by the First Boston Corporation.

When the scandal broke, first in Congress, then in a press which was generally reluctant to embarrass the Administration, Memphis decided to build its own steam plant. This left the AEC with a contract to buy more power than it needed and no one to sell the surplus to. Eisenhower ordered the AEC to revoke the Dixon-Yates contract on which the ink was hardly dry. Dixon-Yates sued the government for $3.5 million in cancellation costs. When the case finally reached the Supreme Court in 1961, the contract was held to have been invalid, thanks to the secret and dubious role of Adolphe H. Wenzell.

The private power interests lost an even more important fight in their struggle to stop the Saint Lawrence Seaway. For 200 years the United States had chosen to act as if the Saint Lawrence did not exist. The Erie Canal had been built on that assumption. But since the Wilson Administration the Federal government had moved, in fits and starts, toward the idea of building a seaway along the Saint Lawrence, and in 1941 it had reached a tentative agreement with the Canadians for a joint venture.

Since the war Canada had enjoyed high growth rates in both its economy and population. It rapidly outstripped the energy resources available in the eastern third of the country. In 1951 the Canadians decided that if necessary, they would build the Seaway themselves. They urgently needed the vast amounts of inexpensive hydroelectric power it would provide.

Nearly every American town and city on the Great Lakes wanted the Seaway. The cost of American participation, $1 billion, was trifling as such projects go. The engineering problems were not daunting. Yet Congress, over Truman's protests, refused permission for American participation.

The private power and utilities interests opposed it. So, too, did the railroads, the East and Gulf Coast port authorities, the East and Gulf Coast longshoremen, coal mine operators, and coal miners. Eisenhower himself could not see the merits of the Seaway. If the Seaway were built, it seemed certain that the Canadians would have to build it alone. But the Canadian government prudently left open the option for American participation should the United States change its mind.

If there was only one Cabinet member whose judgment Eisenhower respected, it was that of his Secretary of the Treasury, George M. Humphrey, lately president of the Mark A. Hanna Company and the Iron Ore Company of Canada, which was developing iron ore fields in Labrador and Quebec. The Seaway also had a strong lobby in the steel industry. Through Humphrey that lobby had access to the Presidential ear.

The iron and steel men wanted the high-grade, low-cost Labradoran ore. The fabled Mesabi range was beginning to run out of its richest and most accessible deposits.

Humphrey discovered that he had an ally in Sherman Adams. These two men, whom Eisenhower trusted above all of his advisers, broke down the President's objections. With most of the people in the states affected in favor of the Seaway, with the Canadians about to begin digging, and with the intervention of the President, decades of Congressional resistance were swept aside in a matter of weeks. In May 1954 the President signed the Saint Lawrence Seaway Act. "Throughout the Midwest and in northern New York the victory was celebrated by speeches, parades and the ringing of bells."

Eisenhower's supposedly conservative administration was, inevitably, a reflection of the President; it was thus an enigma; both more and less than it seemed. It was neither as liberal as right-wing Republicans often claimed nor as witlessly stuck in the mud as the Democrats liked to believe. The Federal Security Agency became the Department of Health, Education and Welfare. Social Security coverage was widely extended. The first civil rights legislation since Reconstruction was passed by a reluctant Congress under the Administration's prodding. Had Truman achieved these things, Democrats would have considered him a strong and effective President. But because they were done under Eisenhower, there was scant praise for them in either party.

He moved cautiously, less for tactical reasons as from the dictates of his own temperament. He encouraged Congress to amend Taft-Hartley, but shrank from grasping the nettle himself. His appointment of a former president of the plumbers' union as Secretary of Labor was a token of his goodwill toward labor. But when the President declined to make a public stand to amend Taft-Hartley, his Secretary of Labor resigned.

Republicans were decidedly unenthusiastic over the new, Cabinet-level Department of Health, Education, and Welfare. Health and education were all right. But *welfare*? Under a Republican Administration? To make the unpleasant more palatable, Eisenhower appointed a rich Republican from Texas, Mrs. Oveta Culp Hobby, as his first Secretary of HEW. Mrs. Hobby, the publisher of the *Houston Post*, combined the skills of an experienced administrator with the social outlook of Calvin Coolidge. When, for example, a proposal was made to expand Social Security so that payments to retired workers were based on a statutory right rather than on the level of past contributions, Mrs. Hobby saw it as "a criminal raid on the Social Security Trust Fund."

More telling was the polio shambles. In 1955 the polio vaccine developed by Dr. Jonas Salk at the University of Pittsburgh was pronounced a success; it was more than 90 percent effective and produced only minor side effects. Salk overnight became a national hero. Honors rained down on this modest, retiring man who could not profit directly from his work. The pharmaceutical companies would, on the other hand, make a profit of $1.50 per injection, even though they had contributed not a dime to Salk's researches.

The Salk vaccine involved taking a live polio virus and killing it in formaldehyde. The pharmaceutical companies were told how to do it, then left to enforce production standards on themselves. Demand for the the vaccine immediately outstripped supply. The vaccine had been pronounced a success by HEW, and the pharmaceutical companies encouraged to begin production before any provision had been made for mass distribution. An ugly little black market in polio vaccine developed. Mrs. Hobby fatuously declared that "no one could have foreseen the demand."

Suddenly the entire program was halted. Vaccinated children were being killed and crippled by live virus which had not been destroyed back in the laboratory.

Mrs. Hobby resigned. Eisenhower had accepted her in order to get HEW through Congress; the moment she became a liability he got rid of her without compunction. Vaccine production was resumed under tighter supervision. The President got an emergency appropriation from Congress to ensure that no child would be denied the vaccine because his or her family was poor; and had Congress not provided the money, he intended to spend the President's Emergency Fund. By the end of 1955, 8 million children had been vaccinated. Polio, which had struck down 55,000 people each year, had been brought under control.

The Old Age and Survivors Insurance fund enjoyed its only major overhaul under Eisenhower. In 1950 its benefits had been stretched to include the self-employed. In 1954 farmers were brought in. In 1956 the permanently and totally disabled were covered. By the time Eisenhower left office nearly 90 percent of the labor force and their dependents were covered by what was now OASDI (Old Age, Survivors and Disability Insurance).

Candidate Eisenhower had opposed "Socialized medicine." President Eisenhower, however, proposed that the medical insurance companies provide comprehensive coverage to nearly everyone and that the government should in turn reinsure the companies against losses on that coverage. The leading insurers tentatively accepted this proposal, but the AMA fought it tooth and nail, considering it only the entering wedge of Socialized medicine. The proposed legislation died in committee.

By the end of his first term the President had shaken off the trammels of conservatism to such an extent that he asked Congress for $2 billion for aid to education; asked for a huge increase in Federal assistance to medical research; and offered a housing bill which conservative Republicans allowed to pass only after reducing it by half.

It seems probable that had Eisenhower enjoyed the measure of support in Congress which he enjoyed in the nation at large, he would have been a much bolder President. He was free of the ideological constraints which gave right-wing Republicans tunnel vision. He thought concretely, in terms of people who were hungry, sick, homeless, or uneducated. But the narrow Republican majority in the 83rd Congress allowed him little room for maneuver. And from 1955 onward he found himself relying increasingly on the Democratic leadership in Congress to get anything important enacted.

Eisenhower did not find this as uncongenial as almost any other Republican President would have done. He disliked partisanship, and he despised most right-wing Republicans. He believed, rightly, that for the Republican Party to stop being the minority party it would have to cover the political center. That the party remained weak despite Eisenhower's popularity reflected its refusal to follow his lead. Much of the Republican Party preferred instead to hew to its principles, yet these principles nearly always served to defend some important privilege or a frankly economic interest. So Eisenhower, who had no interest in either ideology or the care and protection of rich men's money, was thus repeatedly written off within his own party as not being a *real* Republican at all but a Democrat at heart.

His relations with important Democrats were relaxed and pragmatic. The Democratic majority in the Senate, under the guidance of Lyndon Johnson, never attempted to humiliate the President. Sam Rayburn, the Democratic Majority Leader in the House, showed Eisenhower respect and, at times, admiration. The President for his part never attempted to vilify the Democratic leadership. It was characteristic of the Eisenhower style that he was able to launch the biggest, most expensive public works project in history and hardly anyone noticed that was what he had done. It was called the Federal Interstate and Defense Highways System. He brought it to fruition over strong resistance from the states.

The roads were needed. One complaint written in 1954 ran: "The United States is now an eight-cylinder nation with four-cylinder roads. . . . The road system is strangling the nation, physically and economically." But the states maintained that roads were for them to build—or not. State highway departments, moreover, were an important source of patronage. The idea of Federal accountants examining the books was enough to make strong men feel faint.

The Senate Roads Subcommittee quietly smothered Eisenhower's proposal to spend more than $40 billion to construct and improve 41,000 miles of highway. His suggestion that construction be financed by a Federal Highways Commission, which would be authorized to sell tens of billions of dollars' worth of bonds looked to conservatives like an attempt to increase the national debt without actually admitting it; which it was. Opposition to the highways project stopped it dead.

But by some astute lobbying in the states; by a successful campaign to secure public support; and by sweetening the pill (fewer controls, more money), the states were induced to think again. In 1956 the Interstate Highways and Defense Act became law. It committed the Federal government to pay 90 percent of the $1 million-a-mile cost. Federal safety standards had to be observed; otherwise, state highway departments were left to their own devices. Financing came from a Federal gasoline tax.

The road program was exceptionally popular. Not until the 1960s were there widespread doubts about proliferating roads and disenchantment with the automobile. The Federal highway program was the mainstay of the road construction business. For twenty years it provided employment to hundreds of thousands of people. At the end of that time the United States had the finest system of highways in the world. Every major population center in the country was included, regardless of cost or distance. But typical of everything positive Eisenhower accomplished, it was taken for granted.

In his own mind the President knew what he wanted and where he stood on the political spectrum: "When it comes down to dealing with the relationship between the individual and his government, [I am] what I think we could normally call liberal; when we deal with the economic affairs of this country [I] believe in being conservative." As an expression of political centrism it could hardly be faulted.

He knew only too well how his ideas of economic conservatism went down with some of his supporters. He amused the Cabinet one morning by telling them of a letter received by the Republican National Committee. A carbon copy of the letter had been sent to his mother-in-law. The writer was disgusted with the "New Dealers" in the new Administration, the worst of whom were George Humphrey and Dwight Eisenhower.

The President was always more interested in foreign than in domestic matters. He was an unwavering, unequivocal internationalist. Possibly his strongest convictions on any political questions were his faith in mutual security and programs of economic assistance. The Republican 83rd Congress and much of the Republican Party could not have been less interested.

Indeed, much of the country, and many Democrats, disliked what was popularly and dismissively termed "foreign aid." America, they believed, was once more being had.

Yet this was a subject close to the President's heart. A lifetime in military service had left him with a passion for peace. Mutual security was one crusade on which he never hesitated to use the powers of his office or to spend his personal prestige. Economic assistance was the one program for which he was willing to risk an open clash with Republican leaders in Congress. Nor was he reluctant to press for changes in the immigration laws to allow 250,000 refugees to enter the United States outside the quota.

Programs of military and economic assistance were, to his mind, a defense of American interests, not a frittering of American strength. Taft's hositility to foreign aid was one of the factors which turned Eisenhower the general into Eisenhower the candidate. It was his good fortune, moreover, that Taft died only six months after the Inauguration because Taft's hold on the Republican right wing, suffused with isolationist nostalgia, was likely to become mixed with Taft's disappointment at defeat. The honeymoon between the Senator and the President was rapidly coming to a close when Taft died.

The President still had to endure for another six months the threat of the Bricker Amendment. Senator John Bricker of Ohio was the chubby, silver-haired, baby-faced, thick-headed darling of Republican troglodytes. A vain and ambitious man, Bricker had for years nursed Presidential ambitions.

When the 83rd Congress convened, Bricker introduced a Constitutional amendment which would have had the effect of giving the states the power to ratify treaties. This was the Republicans' intended revenge for Yalta. For his first year in office the President's energies were often spent in fighting the Bricker Amendment. Unfortunately it enjoyed strong support in both the country and Congress. On its introduction in the Senate sixty-four Senators put their names down as cosponsors. It appeared an odds-on bet to be passed into law.

Yet Eisenhower fought the Bricker Amendment to a standstill, using coercion, flattery, the pork barrel; all the grubby political tools the President normally disdained. In February 1954, with strong assistance from the Democrats, the Bricker Amendment was put to rest.

Not only did Eisenhower have to conduct his foreign policy largely in spite of his party in Congress, but he suffered a further handicap within the Executive branch. The Republican Party could call on few men of notable ability and imagination to serve in the new Administration. Such men are always in short supply and high demand. But it was an index of the desperate plight of the Republicans that their "natural" choice for Secretary of State was John Foster Dulles.

"Whether expanding at philosophic length upon his estimate of the Communist challenge, or responding at legalistic length to a specific question of policy," wrote a close observer of the two men, "Dulles apparently made one consistent impact upon Eisenhower: he bored him." * It may have been a relief to Eisenhower that his Secretary of State was constantly in motion; he was forever on the move, without getting very far.

Dulles brought to international politics the very mixed vices and virtues of the corporation lawyer. His client was now the United States. The opposing lawyers—that is, the governments of other nations, including those of America's allies—were there to be outwitted. To his admirers, of whom there were millions, he was a man of the highest principles and gifted with the keenest intellect.

Yet the melancholy truth is that Dulles was never much concerned with the pursuit of truth or justice—the natural inclinations of a first-rate mind and a first-rate character. Instead, he occupied himself with trying to think of ways to discomfit the Soviets.

Because the Democrats had been the party of "containment" the Republicans could not resist casting themselves as the party of liberation. Dulles burned his fingers on this hot potato several times; he simply could not leave it alone. Containment went against the American grain; it seemed passive and defensive. Talk of a "rollback" of Communist power had much greater appeal. It was language which went down particularly

---

*There was an appraisal which ran: "Dull, duller, Dulles."

well in areas where the Republicans were weakest—the big cities, which held sizable voting blocs of Eastern European stock.

Dulles's language had an inbuilt tendency toward escalation. Beginning with "rollback," he moved on to "instant retaliation," which in turn gave way to the more awesome "massive retaliation." In the meantime, he was trying to hurl defiance at the Soviet Union while justifying cuts in the defense budget. But his language, evidently intended to awe the Russians, was more likely to make them feel apprehensive.

The "policy" of massive retaliation did not exist anyway. No sooner had Dulles coined the phrase than Eisenhower denied that there had been any change in defense policy. Dulles backed away from his brainchild, claiming that he had been misunderstood. This was the Dulles style in full flower: ever bolder assertions, followed by ever wider evasions.

But the popular demand for a rollback would not die down. And even within the government hopes were wistfully raised from time to time of being able to foment revolt in Soviet satellites and setting Chiang Kai-shek loose in a massive invasion of the Chinese mainland.

Eisenhower found himself trying to conduct foreign policy despite Congressional Republicans. Dulles was nevertheless permitted to ruin the opportunity to settle the Indochinese war from 1954 to 1956. The British, French, Chinese, Soviets, and the Vietnamese were prepared to make a long-term settlement. Dulles refused a full and responsible part for the United States in any agreement that could have been reached. Despite the Viet Minh's victory over the French, blind to the essentially nationalistic character of the struggle, he could see no legitimate Communist claim to rule any part of Indochina.

The Republicans had not yet recovered from the supposed "loss" of China. Dulles and Eisenhower may have been fearful of the cry being raised that they had "lost" Indochina. At all events, Dulles strove to put the United States in a position where it made a viable settlement impossible while it accepted no responsibility for the consequences of what it had done. To Dulles's legalistic mind this was a triumph. But had his intention been to sow trouble for the future to reap, he could hardly have done better.

The running of the State Department did not interest him. He gave Scott McLeod free rein to conduct what amounted to a campaign of terror. It was under Dulles that the denial of passports and visas reached its Cold War apex. Dulles personally involved himself in the efforts to prevent American journalists and academics from traveling to China. It was the kind of low-grade pettiness normally left to low-ranking bureaucrats. Yet it was one more venture which appealed to Dulles's niggling nature.

To America's allies the Secretary of State was both a mystery and an irritant. He sanctimoniously lectured them on their unreliability and the next week would demonstrate his ability to turn on a dime. At various times he was in favor of recognizing the Communist Chinese government, and opposed to it; opposed to German rearmament, and in favor of it. In every case he was guided by expediency.

Dulles's forceful character impressed Eisenhower, even when the monologues bored him. But the President found that he could not expect new ideas on foreign policy to come from his Secretary of State. He was forced to look elsewhere, mainly to himself.

In December 1953 the President addressed the UN. He offered to provide fissionable material and nuclear technology, free, under UN aegis, to other countries. Eisenhower's Atoms for Peace proposal was his own idea, one readily accepted by the rest of the world. In time it led to the creation of the International Atomic Energy Authority. He also directed Dulles's own department to establish the United States Disarmament Agency.

Before traveling to Geneva in 1955, he appointed a study group under Nelson Rockefeller to think of some bold proposal he could present at the summit conference. Rockefeller and his assistants met for several weeks at Quantico, Virginia, making Dulles apprehensive. "He seems to be building up a big staff" Dulles complained to Sherman Adams. "He's got them down there at Quantico and nobody knows what they're doing." Rockefeller's team provided Eisenhower with what he was looking for— the "Open Skies" proposal. By allowing the United States and the Soviet Union to make regular flights over each other's territory, it would have encouraged stabliity by precluding fears of a surprise attack. The world in general thought it an excellent idea; the Russians in particular thought it impossible.

The President also moved far ahead of his party and his Secretary of State in his efforts to reach a *modus vivendi* with the Soviets. Dulles was a man of the Cold War; it appealed to his nature—his love of bluff, move and countermove, denunciation and moralizing. But to Eisenhower the Cold War was a burden which had to be borne and, if possible, made less dangerous. On the one hand, he believed deeply in mutual security; on the other, he believed that lasting peace required mutual understanding.

Eisenhower was lucky in his foreign policy. He was lucky that he came to the White House after the Communist victory in China, the last major Communist gain of the immediate postwar; lucky that the Korean War had been fought to a stalemate; lucky that Western Europe was on its feet again; lucky that the Soviets had already acquired the atomic and hydrogen bombs, which they were bound to acquire at some time. The crowning stroke of good fortune was Stalin's death in March 1953. The Cold War thawed considerably thereafter.

Eisenhower was also lucky in that the press rarely embarrassed him or tried to trip him up. The only question not raised in the American press concerning the coup d'état in Guatemala in 1954, for example, was, how extensive was the American role? The regime of Jacobo Arbenz was democratically elected, and very left-wing, but not actually Communist. The CIA planned and financed the coup. Arbenz escaped with his life and ample proof that the United States had overthrown his government. Yet the President was not asked a single question at any of his press conferences about Arbenz or Guatemala. Instead, the coup was portrayed as a semicomic affair, described as "a 12-day civil war." The American role was portrayed as that of mediator between warring factions of Communists and non-Communists. No President before or after Eisenhower had such a tame press eating from his hand. And self-censorship is the most effective censorship of all.

But he was too astute a man to leave everything to chance. He covered one important flank by appointing Clare Boothe Luce as ambassador to Italy. Unfortunately her brashness and self-importance got the better of her diplomacy. She succeeded in making her country look ridiculous to educated Italians, who had for years been telling one another that the United States was absurd. The right-wing Italian politicians whom she openly supported found, moreover, that Mrs. Luce's favor was fatal at the polls.

Although Eisenhower's appointees tended to be regarded with incredulity abroad, his popularity in foreign lands remained very high for almost the whole of his Presidency.*

Arthur Larson, one of Eisenhower's advisers and speech writers, found after moving into the White House that much of the Republican Party remained stolidly in the grip of two fantasies. The first was that the two major parties could be reconstructed along ideological lines, with all the conservatives in the one and all the liberals in the other. The second related and more fantastical of the fantasies, was that the Republicans would then win most elections. In vain did the President labor to disillusion them.

There was a stirring of life among conservatives in the 1950s which inspired exaggerated reports of a "conservative revival." In 1955 it gained a reputable and regular national organ with the founding of *National Review*. Although it sold 50,000 copies a week, the *National Review* lost money. But its losses were made good by its publisher, William F. Buckley, Jr., with aid from dozens of his friends and acquaintances.

Buckley properly disliked the blandness and conformism of the age. It seemed to be a time lost to principle, imagination, and daring. The Republican Party was as capable of political leadership as Caligula's horse. Eisenhower was not a true conservative. American conservativism, Buckley and his friends decided, would have to look elsewhere for nourishment.

Many of the criticisms Buckley made were sound. But it became evident that Buckley et. al. had nothing to offer but criticism. They were not thinkers but columnists. Their conservatism turned out to be as undistinguished as the thoughts of Senator John Bricker. They offered little but virulent anti-Communism and routine attacks on governmental waste and

---

*It was reported that Nixon was astonished to discover during a trip to Cambodia in 1954 that Eisenhower was known and revered in the most remote villages. Each mention of the President's name drew ecstatic shouts of approbation. Dwight, however, sounded much like "dwaiekt," meaning free; and "Iekendowah" was the name of the local beer.

inefficiency. What fundamental ideas they advanced could usually be traced back to Burke, not Buckley.

Compared with the conservatism of the 1930s, that of the 1950s was remarkably English. "It is less individualistic. . . . It is less absolutist. . . . It is less optimistic. . . . It is more traditionalist. . . . It is less materialistic. . . . Finally, it is more conservative in principle and purpose," decided Clinton Rossiter.

While right-wing Republicans frothed and grumbled, Eisenhower was meanwhile reminding party leaders to take note of his age and the limits of ordinary human frailty each time the question of the 1956 election was raised. It was perhaps this consciousness of his mortality which encouraged his many and lengthy absences from the White House.

By a stroke of irony he was on vacation in Denver when, on the first Saturday in October 1955, he suffered a massive heart attack. When the New York Stock Exchange opened on Monday, the Dow-Jones took its biggest plunge since October 1929, shedding nearly thirty-two points in a day. Most people assumed that he would not run for reelection in 1956.

Eisenhower's heart attack was the biggest domestic news story since the death of Franklin Roosevelt. It became a public education on heart disease. The United States became the most heart-conscious country in the world. The President recuperated at Fitzsimmons Army Hospital in Denver while the scar on his heart healed. In mid-November he returned to the White House, looking like a man who had never been ill in his life.

It was doubly ironic that illness had given him the resolve, formerly wanting, to run again. To have bowed out of public life on account of sickness would have been a wound to his proud nature. And withdrawal from the scene was made even more intolerable by the evident lack of any Republican who could have run in his place in 1956 and been sure of victory. Even within the Republican Party there were more doubts about Nixon's fitness for office in the light of his mean, vindictive nature than there were about Eisenhower's fitness for the Presidency in the light of his questionable health.

When the Republicans met at the Cow Palace in San Francisco in 1956, there was nothing to get excited about. There was far more of interest on the Democratic side.

Kefauver once again tried to take the Presidential nomination by running up a long string of primary victories. But Stevenson fought him on equal terms. He attempted to emulate Kefauver's calculated folksiness. The aloof Stevenson began plunging into crowds. He traveled with a Country and Western group in tow. He donned silly hats. But Stevenson was what he was: an upper-class intellectual. Leaving a small town in Florida, he turned to a journalist traveling with him and asked what he thought of the new style. It had its merits, the journalist replied, but was not a complete success. "When you are shaking hands in a supermarket," he explained, "and a little girl in a starched dress steps out of the crowd and hands you a stuffed alligator, what you say is, 'Thank you very much;

just what I've always wanted for the mantelpiece back in Libertyville.'
What you don't say is what you actually said: 'Jesus Christ, what's
this?' ''

Stevenson and Kefauver were neck and neck in the primaries until they
reached California. Stevenson won there by a two to one margin. Kefauver quit. Averell Harriman, with the support of Truman, challenged Stevenson for the nomination. But a visiting British peer found that the rich
Democrats he met in Georgetown took it for granted that Stevenson
would be nominated and that he would lose, if only because he would
have less to offer the second time around. "He can't be a virgin twice,"
they said.

For the first time in American history there was more interest in who
would secure the second spot than in who would gain the first. Nixon had
to fight off several attempts to keep him off the ticket. On the Democratic
side, when the convention opened in Chicago, there was only one declared candidate for the Vice Presidential nomination, Hubert Humphrey.
But Senator John F. Kennedy had gone to remarkable lengths to draw attention to his "availability." It was also evident that Kefauver, having
given up hope of first place, was willing to take second.

When Stevenson left the choice of his running mate to the convention,
Kefauver had a tactical advantage over the opposition because he was the
only contender with a large personal following present on the floor. Kennedy was also anathema to much of the Midwest because he had been one
of only four Democratic Senators to vote against the Agriculture Act of
1956, which set price supports at a rigid 90 percent. Kefauver had favored
more rigid, and higher, support prices.

But Kefauver in turn was anathema to the South. So the Democratic
Convention provided the nation with the remarkable spectacle of Southern delegations voting en masse for a Roman Catholic from New England.

Although he was no longer a virgin liberal, Democrats fell in love with
Stevenson all over again. The fact that he was doomed to defeat cast a
slightly perverse, romantic charm over his candidacy. He was hailed as
the greatest orator the party had seen since William Jennings Bryan. But
when read on the cold page some twenty years later, his speeches give off
goodwill rather than power of expression or depth of thought. There are
some lively anecdotes and well-turned phrases, but little that is memorable.

The convention gave him Kefauver for a running mate. Neither man
ever warmed to the other during the campaign. Stevenson revived his earlier, hardly noticed call for a ban on nuclear testing. This time Eisenhower
took note of it, to dismiss it out of hand. The press criticisms of Stevenson for making an issue of fallout suggested that fallout was holy.

Stevenson found his task considerably harder than in 1952. It was impossible any longer to portray Eisenhower as a threat to the social gains
of the past generation. The President was not considered so forceful a

figure as he had been portrayed in 1952, yet he was held in a deeper affection. He was felt to stand above politics. On election day there was no contest to speak of. But the Democrats won control of both houses of Congress, just as they had done in 1954.

Eisenhower's victory was more a national victory than the victory of 1952. In the South, the Brown decision pushed many thousands of life-long Democrats into voting Republican because the Democrats identified themselves ever more closely with the civil rights struggle. At the same time large numbers of blacks voted for Eisenhower. In the spring of 1956 he had allowed the Justice Department to send a civil rights bill to Congress, where it died in the Senate. But blacks took notice.

Eisenhower's effortless reelection reflected an instinctive and unshakable popular trust. He appeared as natural to the 1950s as Roosevelt had appeared to the 1930s

Shortly after his second Inauguration the President was twice asked by reporters if he regretted having won reelection. There were persistent rumors that he was beginning to find the job beyond his true desire and his abilities, that he was casting around for a decent opportunity to retire and turn the White House over to Nixon.

Although the press generally held the President in high esteem, the Washington press corps did not. These questions reflected their wishful thinking. To critical journalists, the President appeared irredeemably banal, his appointees disastrous. Nor did he endear himself to thinking people by making cheap gibes, such as defining an intellectual as "A man who takes more words than are necessary to tell us more than he knows." It contained a grain of truth, but also a hint of hostility. Anti-intellectualism seemed particularly unedifying on the lips of the former president of a great university.

Eisenhower was considered an amiable, easygoing, reliable man of simple character. Then, when his press conferences were televised for the first time, people were surprised to discover that he was a forceful, authoritative figure. He was not by any means a simple man. For all the lofty talk about religion he was not religious at all. He was more at ease with a sophisticated, worldly individual like Churchill than with a provincial such as Taft. He spoke glibly about selling the TVA, yet when Republicans in the House cut HEW appropriations, he called them fools and grumbled privately that were they facing reelection, they would "lose the vote of every liberal in the country—and that includes me."

His spontaneous utterances could evoke yawns, yet he took pains over his speeches. They are as good as Stevenson's, and he proved to be a more memorable phrasemaker.

He had spent his adult life in the Army, yet he looked upon war as a crime against humanity, as his "Chance for Peace" speech delivered shortly after taking office in 1953 reflected:

Every gun that is fired, every warship launched, every rocket fired signifies, in the final sense, a *theft* from those who hunger and are not fed, those who are cold and are not clothed. . . . The cost of one modern bomber is this: a modern school in more than 30 cities. . . . We pay for a single fighter with half a million bushels of wheat. We pay for a single destroyer with new homes that could have housed more than 8000 people. . . . This is not a way of life at all, in any true sense. Under the cloud of threatening war, it is humanity hanging from a cross of iron.

This General-for-Life detested military show, military wastefulness, and armaments themselves. His strongest disappointment in office was that there was no reduction in the level of armanents. This failure troubled him long after he left office.

He was a man of honor. Yet he appeased McCarthy, indirectly. He could accept Richard Nixon as his running mate and putative successor, yet disliked and distrusted him.

His idea of leadership was not to seize a banner and run with it in the hope that others would follow, but to persuade, to conciliate; most of all, to await the right opportunity. He had more practical experience of leadership than most of his critics would ever possess. He recognized and lived within the limits of the possible. He could not have won over his opponents within his own party by browbeating them in public or chastising them in private. They would, instead, have been encouraged to work harder to frustrate him.

Although he found ordinary politics distasteful he enjoyed being President. But he felt that the powers of the Presidency had grown in recent years to exceed the limits set out in the Constitution. Congress, by comparison, had become weaker than intended. This limited view of Presidential power was taken by his critics to be proof of his weakness as President. They were wrong. Eisenhower's conception of the Presidency reflected a shrewd judgment that there were serious practical as well as Consititutional checks on the Executive. His successors were destined to rediscover that fact for themselves, over and over again, much as humanity itself at times shows a tendency to rediscover the wheel. Truman's entire Presidency, in fact, can be seen as a seven-year itch brought on by failure. It had been Truman rather than Eisenhower who had sat in the Oval Office saying, "Do this, do that," only to find that nothing happened.

Eisenhower spoke in terms of crusades, but in truth led none and sought to lead none. He saw his responsiblity as upholding the law, which meant first and foremost the defense of the Constitution. If the American people wanted to remake the country's social, political, racial, and economic character, then they could elect representatives who would pass the necessary laws. Yet Eisenhower and his advisers could not help thinking out loud about new initiatives. Nothing came of them. The President reserved his energies for foreign policy, where he did believe that he had a responsiblity to educate, to lead, and to cajole.

Within the self-imposed limits of Eisenhower's leadership he was remarkably successful. His party and the nation were deeply divided when he took office. Yet not only were the disgraceful McCarthy days buried in due course, but for the rest of his Presidency they stayed that way. Foreign policy was conducted with minimal risks despite Dulles's bellicose talk. Most Americans dislike the foreign aid program, but they were led to accept it as a national responsibility. Nowhere had Eisenhower in his first term made a bad situation worse; and many a bad situation had been made better. Some of his appointments were dismal, yet he kept his appointees in nearly all cases on a short rein.

Eisenhower's style was like Jonathan Swift's prose—that is, something so plain and direct that it appeared to have no style at all. Yet the very directness, the lack of ornament gave it, to those not prejudiced, an immediate appeal. It had the ring of truth. It inspired trust. It was not daring or eye-catching. But after the nadir of the Cold War and the excesses of McCarthyism it was a balm the nation stood in need of, as his popularity demonstrated.

23

The Hand That Cradles the Rock

Emmet John Hughes clearly recalled the President in one of his rare outbursts denouncing the Brown decision: "I am convinced that the Supreme Court [has] *set back* progress in the South *at least 15 years*—if you remember you may also be talking about school *dis*integration . . . and the fellow who tells me you can do [moral] things by *force* is just plain *nuts*." Arthur Larson had much the same recollection.

Yet after leaving the White House, Eisenhower claimed that he had agreed with the Court's decision, and that was Adams's recollection too.

Eisenhower saw his function as the upholding of Supreme Court decisions, not the making of public pronouncements on whether he agreed with them. He deplored segregation. During his first year in office he had involved himself in the desegregation of hotels, restaurants, and theaters in the District of Columbia. When the Department of Health, Education, and Welfare was found during Mrs. Hobby's tenure to be providing financial support to scores of segregated facilities, Eisenhower became angry and ordered the support to be stopped immediately. The Assistant Secretary of Labor, J. Ernest Wilkins, was black and during his superior's absence sat in for him at Cabinet meetings, becoming the first black man to participate in such meetings. The Navy was the least integrated of the services when Eisenhower took office. When the Navy's foot dragging was brought to his notice, he directly ordered the Secretary of the Navy to bring it to an end.

Yet so far as the struggle for equality in the nation at large was in question—that is, where the President could command very little obedience—he would have preferred to stand aside. The Supreme Court had made that impossible.

There were also a dozen lawyers in the Justice Department who were attempting to break down the Administration's resistance by boring from within. They occupied themselves by drafting proposed civil rights laws which would establish a legal basis for broader Federal intervention in civil rights cases. They were encouraged, discreetly, by Herbert Brownell.

There was nothing important that the Attorney General could effect, however, against the President's wishes. But when Eisenhower's heart attack appeared to rule him out for reelection in 1956, Brownell asked the Cabinet for its approval of civil rights legislation submitted to Congress in Brownell's name. The Cabinet reluctantly agreed. When Eisenhower recovered, he, with equal reluctance, allowed the proposed legislation to go forward.

A civil rights bill was certain to be passed by the House. Two had been passed in the lower chamber under Truman. Neither ever reached the Senate floor.

Brownell began not with one bill but with four. When they reached Capitol Hill in the spring of 1956, they had been combined in a four-part omnibus bill: first, the creation of a national Civil Rights Commission; second, the creation of a Civil Rights Division in the Justice Department; third, a grant of powers to the Justice Department to intervene whenever civil rights appeared in danger of being violated; and fourth, a grant of power to protect voting rights. Brownell's bill was approved by a large margin in the House on the eve of the 1956 conventions. But no one expected it to be passed by the Senate. Even Eisenhower's acceptance speech to the Republican convention made not a single reference to blacks, civil rights, or the racial struggle. The nearest he came to recognizing the most important domestic issue of the time was an innocuous remark in passing: "Now, in all existing kinds of discrimination there is much to do." He made specific reference to discrimination against Indians, against migratory farm workers, but there was not a word about discrimination against black people.

During the campaign, however, desegregation became the principal political and social issue in dispute. And under the continued goading of the Democrats Eisenhower began to argue for Brownell's bill as if it were his own.

Brownell's sincerity is beyond doubt. He repeatedly urged the President to support a Federal antilynching law. To the South, any such legislation would have been both a moral and a political indictment—a declaration that the Southern states would not or could not enforce their own laws against murder.

When the 85th Congress convened in January 1957, Brownell was back with his civil rights bill. This time he had a powerful ally in the Senate— Lyndon B. Johnson. For years Johnson had opposed civil rights legislation, but he had never said a word against blacks. He had refused to sign the "Southern Manifesto." As a young schoolteacher he had taught Mexican children. In his campaigns for office he had actively sought the support of Texas Mexicans. Like Truman and Eisenhower, he was neither hostile toward racial minorities nor deeply indignant at their lot.

Yet he set about making the Brownell measure into the Johnson civil rights bill of 1957. He had his eyes not on justice but on the 1960 Democratic Presidential nomination. To win it, he would have to break out from being typecast as only another Southern Senator—that is, a Populist of sorts (more or less liberal) but on race just another bigot. To get the bill onto the Senate floor and to prevent it from being filibustered to death, he had to resort to cosmetic surgery and dentistry.

The bill's teeth consisted of Title III, which empowered the Attorney General to secure Federal court injunctions to force the pace of desegregation in the public schools. Johnson removed the teeth. At the same time he altered the occasionally emotive tone of the bill to make it less repellent to the South and spent many hours talking to Southern Senators. The day was not far off, he convinced them, when a civil rights bill would be passed over their opposition. And when that day came, Northern liberals would get their revenge by making it a bill which bristled with teeth and claws. Surely it made sense to pass a weak bill now to preempt a worse later?

To Brownell and the White House, Johnson's surgery on the Civil Rights Act of 1957 had gutted it. But even without Title III the bill's passage in September 1957 was a signal achievement, one which in years to come the Republican Party was proud to acknowledge. It was the first Federal civil rights legislation since 1875.

It did not create new rights. But it did much to secure rights which were denied, particularly the right to vote, and extended Federal powers to effect compliance with school desegregation. To the 35,000 black people who had come to Washington in the summer on the Prayer Pilgrimage it was the realization of their hopes, for that was what they had come to Washington to pray for—passage of the bill.

In the late spring of 1953, when the Korean War had been moving toward a cease-fire and the new Administration was tasting the first heady delights of power, Little Rock's new superintendent of schools, Virgil T. Blossom, made a trip to New York in search of advice. The enlightened voters of Little Rock had recently approved a $4 million bond issue for new school construction. Blossom had never handled a bond issue of such a size back in Fayetteville, where he had been superintendent for twelve years. He went to Wall Street to learn how to deal sensibly with so much money.

While sitting in the outer office of a noted Wall Street broker, he leafed idly through one of the magazines lying on a table. His eye was abruptly taken by a photograph of a young black man who gazed with longing at the Supreme Court Building and the legend inscribed above the glistening marble columns: EQUAL JUSTICE UNDER LAW. The Court, said the text accompanying the picture, had recently begun to consider the case of *Brown* versus *Board of Education of Topeka*. The cutline below the photograph asked: "Will the Court have the courage?"

Blossom received the guidance he sought, but the bond issue had suddenly become of secondary importance in his mind. He was far more deeply concerned with the photograph. He returned to Little Rock filled with foreboding. He confessed his anxieties to the school board. They made light of them.

A year later the Court showed that it had the courage. And the day after the Brown decision the Little Rock Board of Education decided that it would not resist or evade the Court's ruling, much as it regretted it.

Blossom wanted to integrate the schools from the bottom up, beginning with the youngest and least prejudiced children. But this was considered impractical, first, because the younger the children involved, the more ferocious the parental opposition to be expected; second, because black and white children lived in very different neighborhoods. To send a handful of children of either race all the way across town to integrate the schools there seemed both an insult to common sense and unfair to the children involved. Given the lower standards of the black schools, it might even be said to be a form of discrimination against the white children who were forced to attend them. For these reasons it was decided to integrate the schools from the top down.

Thanks to the bond issue, two new high schools would be opened in the 1957–1958 school year. Central High School, which was regarded as one of the best high schools in the United States on the basis of its National Merit Scholarship results, would be integrated. So would one of the new high schools. The existing all-black high school would become a junior high. To integrate the entire school system from top to bottom would take as much as ten years. This was not because the school board was being evasive but because it wanted integration to be accepted with a minimum of protest. Once the high schools had been integrated, the junior high schools would follow. The elementary schools would be integrated last of all and on the basis of earlier success.

Blossom's integration plan was applauded within and outside Arkansas. He appeared to have found a way to make the unpalatable palatable. He was voted Little Rock's "Man of the Year" for 1955. He began to screen black applicants for admission to Central High in the fall of 1957.

But Mrs. Daisy Bates, the head of the NAACP in Arkansas, did not like the Blossom plan. He offered integration piecemeal and slowly; she wanted it now, and she wanted it complete. She marched twelve students, one from each grade and all of them black, into his office one morning in January 1956 and demanded that they be enrolled in various white schools for the spring semester. Blossom refused her demands.

The NAACP filed suit in Federal court charging that the twelve students had been rejected solely on account of their race, in defiance of *Brown.* The court disagreed. It found that Blossom's plan was in compliance with the doctrine of "all deliberate speed," in the light of local conditions. The NAACP appealed and lost on appeal.

Of the several hundred black teenagers eligible to transfer to Central High only eighty applied. After talking to them soberly about the problems they might face, Blossom found himself with seventeen applicants. When the fall semester of 1957 drew near, eight of these withdrew, leaving only nine.

By this time Little Rock had become a magnet for bigots and erstwhile demagogues. The Citizens' Councils suddenly became active in Arkansas. Governor Orval Faubus came under pressure from diehard segregationists. But most people kept their nerve and reason. When the Citizens' Councils got an initiative on the Arkansas ballot in the November 1956 two candidates for the Board of Education ran on a white supremacy platform. Both lost heavily.

Yet these setbacks only spurred the fanatics to redouble their efforts. The Capital Citizens' Council, drawing most of its support from the skilled working- and lower-middle-class sections of the city, began an intensive propaganda campaign. Its rallies gave proof of its growing public support. The city was alive with rumors of impending violence.

A new organization suddenly appeared—the Mothers League of Central High School. The mothers had only one interest to pursue—keeping Central High white.

It now became evident that Blossom's plan had contained a deadly flaw. Desegregation had been held up for a year longer than was necessary, and in that time the segregationists had been able to mount a virulent campaign against his plan. The year's delay was to await the completion of Hall High School, located in the upper-middle-class neighborhood of Pulaski Heights. Hall High would be all-white; its students would be drawn mainly from Central High. It was a step characteristic of desegregation in years to come: the upper-middle-class citizens in the community, usually the best educated and most responsible people in town, were all in favor of it—for other people's children.

In Little Rock this abdication of responsibility was further compounded in 1957 by the city's changeover from a mayor-alderman system of government to a city-manager system. The present administration was a lame duck. Thus, Little Rock's civic leadership, elected or informal, was not directly affected by whatever happened at Central High.

As the rumors of violence spread, Blossom sought help from the Federal District Court and from Faubus. The city was not prepared to take responsibility. The court said that it could not; the governor, that he would not. Faubus was not a segregationist. He had integrated the Arkansas Democratic Party. He derided massive resistance and the "doctrine" of Interposition ("Everybody knows state laws can't supersede Federal laws"). Blossom found him serious, broad-minded, and exceptionally intelligent. Faubus agreed with him that peaceful desegregation of the schools was possible. But Faubus could see no reason why he should end his political career solely to make sure that nine black children went to school with whites.

Several days before the fall semester began the Mothers sought a temporary injunction in Chancery Court against desegregation of Central High on the ground that it would lead to bloodshed. The plaintiffs assured the court that students were arming themselves with knives and guns. Faubus testified that this was so. Yet he offered not a scintilla of proof. Nor did the Mothers. And the Little Rock police chief, Marvin Potts, said that he knew absolutely nothing which might suggest that black and white adolescents were preparing to slaughter one another in the corridors of Central High. The Chancery Court nevertheless granted the injunction.

The Federal District Court swiftly nullified it. Meanwhile, *Birth of a Nation*, widely shown in the 1920s but rarely seen since 1939, was playing to appreciative audiences in downtown Little Rock. And Marvin Griffin, archsegregationist governor of Georgia, appeared at a Citizens' Council dinner in the city. To a chorus of rebel yells and defiant cheers he urged the people of Little Rock to resist desegregation on the following Tuesday, September 3, when school opened.

Faubus found himself boxed in. He had promised not to use the power of the state to force desegregation on an unwilling community; he had also scorned the idea of interposing the state between the Federal government and the schools. The state legislature in recent years had striven diligently "to combat the legend that Arkansas is filled with moronic, jughappy mountaineers." It had discovered the Yankee tourist long before the Deep South, giving rise to its unofficial motto: "One Yankee tourist is worth about twice as much as a bale of cotton and is about twice as easy to pick." Little Rock's Congressman, Brooks Hays, was hardworking, unassuming, moderate, and devout. In the *Arkansas Gazette* Little Rock possessed one of the few good newspapers between Cleveland and California. But if there is one basic educational skill common to every successful politician, it is simple arithmetic. There were more people opposed to desegregation than in favor of it, and Faubus could count. On Monday, September 2, he called out the Arkansas National Guard. By nightfall a cordon of green-clad men ringed Central High School.

The next morning the white students arrived for class. None of the black students appeared. The white citizens of Little Rock rejoiced, believing they had won. Faubus announced that the Guard was at Central High not to prevent integration but to prevent trouble.

He was attempting to ride two horses at once. For an instant he seemed to have carried it off. But on Wednesday morning everything went wrong. A black student arrived at the high school, alone, bewildered, yet determined to do what was expected of her. Elizabeth Eckford, tall, slender, only fifteen, a pretty girl with glasses, tried to enter Central High.

Until that moment Little Rock ("City of Roses") had seemed an unlikely place for a historic confrontation over desegregated schools. It had a smaller proportion of black students in its public schools than many another border state city which had desegregated its schools, such as Wilmington, Baltimore, Louisville, and St. Louis. If trouble came, it seemed more likely to strike Nashville, which had scheduled desegregation for the same week as Little Rock. Frederick John Kasper had been agitating the citizens of Nashville these past few weeks to "Throw a lit stick of dynamite" rather than allow black students into white schools.

Trouble certainly came to Nashville. A mob advanced on the elementary schools under Confederate flags and banners provided by the KKK. Nashville planned to integrate from the bottom up. With fists, rocks, and flying bottles, the black first-graders were dissuaded from going to school. One of the Nashville grade schools was razed to the ground by a huge bomb. Kasper was arrested.

But events in Nashville were overshadowed by those in Little Rock. Faubus had not wanted a showdown. If anything, he wanted the Federal government to intervene before he was forced to choose between the law of the land and the law of the ballot box. Even while the National Guard was taking up position around Central High, the governor was hoping, like Mr. Micawber, that something would presently turn up. Nor was he the first governor to act in this way. In Texas, Governor Allan Shivers had sent the Texas Rangers into Mansfield during turmoil over desegregated schools—and the schools stayed white.

But Mansfield did not have a school desegregation plan approved by a Federal court. When the Arkansas National Guard surrounded Central High, Mrs. Bates and the NAACP had gone back to the court. The black students scheduled to enroll at Central High had been told to stay at home until the court made its ruling. But the family of one of the nine, Elizabeth Eckford, did not have a telephone. When the other eight students were reached on the morning of Wednesday, September 4, Elizabeth Eckford was already on her way to school. The car sent to intercept her missed her by minutes.

As she approached the school, a cry went up from the small, ragtag crowd which had assembled without expecting much to happen. "A nigger! A nigger! They're coming! Here they come!" Elizabeth Eckford walked up to one of the school doors. A National Guardsman, wordlessly, pressed in front of her and barred the way.

Confused and alone, she turned around. The crowd, jeering and threatening, formed a gauntlet behind her. With extraordinary dignity she made her way through it, trying not to show her fear, trying not to cry. When she reached the nearest bus stop, she sat down and began to sob quietly. A white woman, her heart moved by the sight of this lone, inoffensive young girl being hounded by a screeching mob, sat down beside her and tried to comfort her. "What are you doing? You nigger lover!" protested someone in the crowd. "She's scared," said the woman. "She's just a little girl." When the next bus arrived, the unknown white woman got onto it with the girl and saw her part of the way home.

The next day the photograph of Elizabeth Eckford walking past her tormentors appeared on the nation's front pages. It caused an outcry against the city of Little Rock. Much of the nation and half the world was now emotionally engaged in the struggle at Central High. It could no longer be settled locally or quietly.

Yet Eisenhower refused to intervene publicly. He preferred to try behind the scenes to persuade Faubus to withdraw the National Guard. But at the moment the young national guardsman had barred Elizabeth Eckford's way the power of the Federal government had been challenged. This was an issue no President could ignore.

Brooks Hays offered his services as an intermediary between the governor and the President. A meeting was arranged at Newport, Rhode Island, between them. At the end of it Eisenhower's impression was that Faubus would back down; Brownell's that he would not. Federal District Judge Ronald N. Davies ordered desegregation to proceed. Faubus condemned the court's ruling, told the nine black students to stay at home, and withdrew the Guard.

On Monday, September 23, Little Rock was the news capital of the world. Hundreds of journalists gathered at Central High. No other city of comparable size had become so famous so quickly. An angry crowd filled the streets near the high school, chanting, "Two, four, six, eight! We ain't gonna integrate!"

The nine black students slipped into the school by a side entrance. When the mob outside learned that they had been deceived, they stormed the school, trying to fight their way past state and local police, who covered every door and ground-floor window. When the police found that they could not control the riot, the students were removed from the school. Mrs. Allen Thevenet of the Mothers League then toured the building and returned to placate the seething mob with the happy news; "We went through every room in the school and there was no niggers there."

The next day the mob came back, stronger than ever and better armed. Faubus, whose predictions of violence had helped bring it about, crowed in self-congratulation. This time Eisenhower decided to intervene directly.

In the late afternoon a battalion of 101st Airborne Division paratroopers pulled up in trucks and jeeps at Central High—only two months after the President had said that he could not imagine any circumstances in which he would use the Army to enforce a court order.

Faubus not only had got himself into a position from which he could not back down but had put the President in the same position. And now all his hopes of postponing the desegregation of the Little Rock schools until after the 1958 gubernatorial election had vanished. From this time on Faubus, to keep himself in power, broke faith with the moderates who had elected him in 1954. He increasingly threw in his lot with the Citizens' Councils. Faubus had come to office in 1954 as a ray of hope. He turned into a pall of despair. In 1957 eight new major plants had been built in Little Rock. In 1958 and 1959 there were none. Consumer spending dropped sharply. So did migration to the city. Rental vacancies rose by 20 percent; home sales slumped. After a decade of progress Arkansas suffered a decade of stagnation. People left the state in droves. Its population in 1960 was nearly one-fourth below that of 1950. Only the Citizens' Councils appeared to have gained. After the Little Rock showdown they became a force to be reckoned with. CC mail after September 1957 carried the slogan "REMEMBER LITTLE ROCK!" Beneath was a drawing of a soldier shepherding two little white girls at bayonet point toward a classroom with black figures in it. "Remember Little Rock!" became a rallying cry in the fashion of "Remember the *Maine!*"

Under the strain of events Marvin Potts committed suicide. Mrs. Bates and her husband, who had spent twenty years and all their savings on their newspaper, the *Arkansas State Press*, lost everything. Their home was the target of attempted arson and bombing, hurled excrement, and a barrage of bricks, bottles, and rocks. All the parents of the nine black students were fired from their jobs. After twenty years in Congress Brooks Hays was defeated when he ran for reelection. Dozens of threats were made to kill Virgil Blossom, his wife, and his daughters. When he returned home one night, an attempt was made to assassinate him. The bullet failed to penetrate completely the door of his car.

But the arrival of the paratroopers had irrevocably decided the outcome of the desegregation issue: the black students would attend Central High. The soldiers behaved with commendable restraint, good humor, and good sense, under the command of Major General Edwin Walker. Faubus ranted inanely about soldiers bayoneting innocent citizens, freely shedding the rich blood of patriots, and molesting girls in their locker room, all of which was nonsense. But the governor was off and running for 1958.

Five attempts were made to blow up Central High School. At least thirty fires were set in lockers and wastebaskets. A stink was raised by students urinating onto hot radiators. The nine black students were kicked, punched, spat at, and insulted. They bore their ordeal with stoic courage, and none asked to withdraw; not even Thelma Marshall, who suffered a heart attack during one assault on her.

The paratroopers remained for the rest of the school year. Eight of the black students were graduated from Central High in due course; the ninth transferred by mutual agreement to a private high school in New York for her senior year. The nine were superior students; all went on to college.

In the nation, most people supported Eisenhower's intervention. Even in the South one person in three supported his action. It was, however reluctantly undertaken, one of the epochal Presidential initiatives of the postwar, because it committed the Federal government to an active role in the gathering revolution in race relations, the most important single social issue of the time. After Little Rock there could be no turning back.

PART IV

FALLING SHORT

24

The Rockets' Red Glare

The fall of 1957 was enlivened by a party thrown by movie producer Mike Todd and his actress wife, Elizabeth Taylor, for 18,000 close friends at Madison Square Garden. The festivities were self-financing: Todd had sold the party to television. There was a cake that weighed a ton and stood eleven feet high. There were ballons and bands. But as parties go, it was a disaster. Waiters shook down guests panting for a glass of "free" champagne. There was too little food and too great a multitude. No miracle forthcoming, starving partygoers in formal wear straggled out of the Garden in search of hot dog vendors. The gifts and prizes Todd had bought were looted before they could be given away. Fiasco followed fiasco, and as they mounted, Todd snarled and cursed at the ubiquitous cameras.

Three days before Thanksgiving the President suffered a stroke. His resilience was such that within a month he had recovered.

The nation threw itself into the hula hoop craze of 1958. It began with the use of bamboo hoops in Australian gym classes. The American hoops were made of plastic and cost $1.98 each. Millions were sold. Children learned to use a hula hoop in about fifteen minutes. Adults seemed to take several hours.

A train filled with communters left the tracks and plunged into Newark Bay, New Jersey. More than 50 people were drowned.

Anti-semitic outrages occurred in Peoria, Brooklyn, Atlanta, and elsewhere. Most of the targets of the vandals and bombers were synagogues.

In Rome a new Pope was elected, John XXIII.

A spate of Martian jokes produced a new catch phrase: "Take me to your leader."

Fire swept through a Chicago parochial school, killing three nuns and eighty-nine children. It was the worst school fire in three decades.

Harvey Lavan Cliburn, a wavy-haired young pianist from Kilgore, Texas, became a national hero by winning the Tchaikovsky piano competition in Moscow.

In Los Angeles the Dodgers were playing baseball in the Coliseum, with a towering fence compensating, sort of, for the absence of left field.

In Caracas the Vice President's motorcade was attacked by an angry, rock-throwing mob. Americans were shocked. Even allowing for Communist agitation, many people found it disheartening that people in other countries should fear and hate the United States. Nixon's coolness during this attack won the praise it deserved. On his return to Washington 100,000 people were on hand to greet him.

In the Great Plains states nineteen-year-old Charles Starkweather and his fourteen-year-old girlfriend, Caril Ann Fugate, went on a killing spree through Nebraska and Wyoming. They left eleven dead in their wake.

In Beverly Hills Cheryl Crane, the fourteen-year-old daughter of Lana Turner, stabbed to death her mother's lover, a truculent creep by the name of Johnny Stompanato. The deceased had been a small-time hoodlum before moving on to the less dangerous pastime of beating up women. The trial of Cheryl Crane was a gift from the gods to American newspapers. They made the most of it.

When winter arrived, Oswego, New York, was buried under five feet of snow.

When the new year began, there was a new regime in Cuba. Fulgencio Batista, after scooping up the national reserves of gold and foreign currency, fled to the Dominican Republic, leaving Cuba to Fidel Castro and his guerrillas. Castro's idealism exerted a powerful romantic appeal, one which had inspired a dozen Americans to fight beside him. Within a month of his accession to power, however, American goodwill turned to indignation as dozens, then scores, and eventually hundreds of Cubans who had served the Batista government were executed. Often there was not even the form of a trial. Men were dragged from their homes to be murdered in the street under the eyes of their wives and children. The top Batista leadership had escaped. These victims were lowly functionaries, police spies, informers, and sometimes simply people unlucky enough to have the wrong name or the wrong relatives. They were tortured, were kicked, clubbed, bayoneted, or shot to death in an orgy of revenge.

The worst storm of a terrible winter swept the Midwest, killing more than 100 people.

Castro came to the United States in the spring. Huge crowds turned out to see him in Washington, New York, and Boston.

The craze of the year came from Britain: cramming as many people as possible into a phone booth. According to the British rules, once the booth was filled, someone had to make a phone call. The record was claimed by thirty-two short, thin students at Modesto Junior College in California.

Earl Long, the governor of Louisiana, was spirited away to a Texas mental hospital. He made a dramatic escape eight days later. He held a press conference from a motel bed to deny his wife's charges that he was a satyr. At sixty-four, he said modestly, he simply was not up to it. "How can an old man take care of three or four women?" he asked plaintively.

In September 1959, Nikita Khrushchev arrived in America. His tour was an exquisite combination of the useful and the ludicrous. Whenever important foreign visitors arrived in Washington, their national flag was festooned from the Capitol to the White House. But this time no one dared droop the Hammer and Sickle the length of Pennsylvania Avenue. The Catholic Church was deeply troubled by the visit. Cardinal Spellman decreed that an extra three Hail Marys should be said each day in the parochial schools to ward off possibly dire effects. The Archbishop of Washington warned Washington's Catholics to avoid Khrushchev's presence. When the Soviet Premier's plane landed at Andrews Air Force Base a skywriting plane hired by anti-Communists made a large white cross in the sky over Washington.

Khrushchev was not allowed to visit Disneyland, on the grounds that the Anaheim police could not guarantee his safety. In Southern California no one wanted to run the risk of being accused of being helpful to a known Communist. Mayor Norris Poulson greeted Khruschev to Los Angeles with a speech which in its entirety ran: "Welcome to Los Angeles, the City of the Angels, the city where the impossible always happens." No Los Angeles newspaper printed a schedule of his travels. He journeyed down nearly empty streets. Yet Khrushchev was more politely treated elsewhere, and many people found him direct, impulsive, and unpretentious. His spontaneity was his charm.

As people prepared for Thanksgiving, they pondered the question "Are the cranberries safe?" A weed killer, aminotriazole, had proved to be a carcinogen in rats, but not before cranberries treated with it had reached the market. It would take the consumption of 15,000 pounds of contaminated cranberries to start a cancer in a human being. But nobody was taking any chances.

Television's first original program format, the quiz show with huge cash prizes, provided the new medium with its first major scandal. The programs were very popular. They were also very crooked. The best known and most popular of the ten currently on the air was The $64,000 Question, a show that loved incongruities—the little old lady who knew all about baseball, the marine captain who was an authority on French haute cuisine (and who was the first $64,000 winner). In 1957 Time had put QUIZ CHAMP VAN DOREN on its cover. Charles Van Doren appeared on Twenty One and beat all comers to win more than $200,000. He was so personable that people wanted to see him win. He was also a consummate actor. On some questions he snapped the answer right back; on others he agonized aloud, clenched his fists, bit his lip, or rolled his eyes before giving the correct answer in the nick of time. When the scandal broke, Van Doren, who taught at Columbia, was the center of attention, not because he had won the most money, which he had not, but because he was the classic figure of tragedy—the gifted man brought low by a defect in his character. Not only had he won dishonestly, but he had compounded venality with perjury by lying to a New York grand jury. But he came to his senses before a Congressional committee. He confessed everything.

While the quiz show scandal was unfolding, so was radio's payola scandal. Disc jockeys had been bribed into playing certain records. That cleared up the mystery of how some of them got on the air.

When the year drew to a close, the 1950s were over. A distinguished historian gave the decade the back of his hand in an article called "Goodbye to the Fifties—and Good Riddance." He mordantly declared, "Probably the climate of the late Fifties was the dullest and dreariest in all our history."

At the start of 1960 eleven Yale students were expelled after a 14-year-old nymphet named them (and twenty other young men) as her hurried partners at a sex orgy in a Yale dormitory.

In Los Angeles Dr. Bernard Finch was charged, with his mistress, Carole Tregoff, with the murder of Mrs. Finch.

Two airliners blew up, killing seventy-six people. In each disaster the bombers were among the dead, having insured themselves heavily in advance. This was a variant on a caper first broached by John Gilbert Graham of Denver in 1955. He had put his mother and a bomb aboard a United Airlines DC-6. The bomb exploded, killing Mrs. Graham and forty-three other people. Graham attempted to collect $37,500 in insurance.

Charlotte Ford, daughter of Henry Ford II, demonstrated that conspicuous consumption was very much alive. She threw a $250,000 coming-out party. It was as public an affair as the Mike Todd bash except that the waiters were polite, there was enough food, and the presents were not looted.

Jack Paar, who had created a new form of television entertainment, the late-night chat show, fired himself on camera after losing an argument with NBC concerning a joke about a toilet. In television circles Paar was esteemed as a thinking man. Looking straight into the camera, he dolefully announced, "There must be an easier way to make a living. I am leaving the *Tonight* show." Whereupon he stood up and walked out of the studio. Three weeks and a second thought later Paar was back. Thereafter live shows were taped by the networks before they were shown.

The craze this year was the trampoline. Scores of trampoline parlors opened for the benefit of those who did not have a trampoline at home.

In California the saga of Caryl Chessman (a name so obviously symbolic that even a third-rate novelist would have rejected it) drew to its close. After eleven years on San Quentin's Death Row and a score of appeals, stays of execution, and judicial reviews, plus a best-selling book, a change in public opinion about capital punishment in kidnapping cases, and a movie based on the book, Chessman had become a cause. There was a record called "The Ballad of Caryl Chessman," which sold well; the refrain ran, "Let him live, let him live, let him live." In foreign countries there were "Save Chessman" clubs. The number of executions each year had been dropping steadily for decades. But Chessman raised the issue of capital punishment in a new form: he had killed no one. His death sentence had been passed under California's "Little Lindbergh" law, which made kidnapping a capital offense.

Most people and most state legislatures still favored the death penalty in principle, but they also disliked it in practice. Chessman played on this revulsion with remarkable astuteness. Eight times he was given a date for execution. Eight times he won a reprieve.

Chessman fascinated people, moreover, because of his psychopathic nature. He was portrayed as a "criminal genius." He was a hipster. He protested his innocence to the last, claiming to know the identity of the real "red-light" bandit for whose crimes he had been convicted and claimed that he had the proof. Yet his evidence was never offered for inspection. In his own account, where he presumably was being completely honest, he encouraged the assumption most people held that he had been convicted of raping his victims. He had, instead, forced them to fellate him.

He had been sent to Chino to serve one of his earlier sentences. The only use made of the gun towers there was as aircraft observation posts during the war. Of the 250 men who scanned the skies, recorded Kenyon Scudder, "only one betrayed our trust, and he proved to be one of our worst mistakes." That one was Caryl Chessman. He not only used his role as a sky watcher to escape but needlessly involved another man for no apparent purpose except to get him into trouble.

Yet many people became convinced that in his struggle to save his life Chessman's character had been reformed. The warden at San Quentin, Clinton Duffy, was opposed to the death penalty, was a man who believed in rehabilitation, and was widely considered a good judge of other men. But he remained skeptical of the claims that Chessman had reformed. He called him "A very arrogant, mean, hating individual, resentful of authority, and he did not change. . . . He was not rehabilitated." Governor Edmund G. Brown was similarly convinced that Chessman had not changed. But he found the death penalty repugnant in the extreme. He pleaded with the California legislature to repeal it. The legislature declined. In May 1960 Chessman kept his ninth rendezvous with death.

Khrushchev and Castro paid return visits to the United States. This time Washington treated them as unwelcome guests. But as they came to attend meetings of the UN, they could not be kept out. They were not allowed to leave Manhattan. Khruschev pounded his UN desk with his shoe. Americans loved it.

Dr. Tom Dooley came home to die. As a young Navy doctor at the time of the partition of Vietnam he had treated thousands of the refugees moving south. Discharged from the Navy, Dooley had gone back to Southeast Asia for the International Rescue Committee. He established a hospital in Laos. Dooley was no saint. He had a cocksure manner and a prickly personality. He spent more time raising money than practicing medicine.

During a previous tour of the United States he had raised nearly $1 million and been operated on for a malignant melanoma in his chest. The cancer had spread to his spine. At the age of thirty-four he was dead.

These were the years of the sack dress for women and the sack suit for men. Properly called the chemise, the sack dress harkened back to the 1920s. There was also a revival of the slouch suit of of the 1930s for women; comfortable, loose-fitting, usually worn with the jacket unbuttoned and a simple but expensive blouse underneath, it was both nostalgic and pleasant to wear. It had a certain elegance, which could rarely be said for the chemise. The ultimate really did look like a sack—the Hawaiian muumuu. This shapeless garment had been foisted on Hawaiian women by American missionaries in the nineteenth century as an anti-sex device. Tourists innocently stumbling across it in the 1950s found it colorful, inexpensive, and comfortable. They brought it back to the mainland with missionary fervor.

But the general sheath look aimed at a slender ideal. Shoes became pointed, heels tall and narrow. Doctors lamented the tortures inflicted on toes. The National Safety Council issued warnings about the stiletto heel. No one paid the least attention.

Men's clothing also aimed at sleekness. First came the Ivy League look, with narrow trousers, adorned at the back with useless buckles, and jackets with narrow lapels and unpadded shoulders. Then came the Continental look, with still narrower trousers, cuffless and unpleated. Jackets had peaked lapels, two buttons, and high square shoulders. Ties became ever slimmer, collars less pointed.

Everyone wanted to look slim. In a single generation dieting had become part of the American way of life. One theory blamed it on the camera, for having altered men's conception of feminine beauty. Robustly built bodies may be very attractive in the flesh, but they are not photogenic. Medical research also made people weight-conscious by showing that on average slim people lived longer than fat people. Finally, there was the midcentury image of the streamlined as the very model of modernity. Whatever the reasons for it, there was one crash diet after another. Food fads multiplied; food mythology spread faster than influenza in January. Millions of people took themselves off to the gymnasium for repairs. One entrepreneur alone claimed one million clients at his chain of establishments. These were not exactly Spartan; they featured chrome-plated equipment, bright carpets, Muzak, and smiling, unflagging salesmen. And the bikini, popular on European beaches since the war, finally succeeded in America, suggesting that the dieting and exercising had not been entirely in vain.

There was a new style in nightclub entertainment; small, unpretentious, offering satirists rather than naked women or comics dealing in stereotypes and jokes about genitals and toilets, the clubs featured a new brand of humor that was more pointed and more intelligent than the old, being based on the study of human character. And like the American character at midcentury, it was nervous, knowing, self-mocking, self-aware. In the hands of Mort Sahl, Lenny Bruce, Tom Lehrer, Elaine May, and Mike Nichols, it sought to tell the truth as well as jokes.

There was a new dimension in home entertainment—width. Just as people finished paying for the hi-fi set, stereo arrived. Home movie cameras were becoming commonplace in American homes, part of the standard package of consumer goods.

Camping became a major form of recreation. The call of the wild induced 12 million Americans to go camping in 1960. But it was wilderness without solitude. The lone trekker was regarded with pity and awe. The vast majority of campers crowded into areas where there were other campers to talk to at night.

The intellectual avant-garde amused itself by taking up Zen Buddhism. It was a fashion deriving from the writings of the Beats.

Children amused themselves with Barbie. Following her debut in 1958, Barbie became in a few years the most popular doll of all time. There was a national fan club. Barbie received 500 letters a week. There were millions of little Barbies in tiny hands, and all those millions of Barbies needed clothes—lots of them. Constantly. Barbie could be had for a trifling $3. But Barbie's complete wardrobe cost more than $100, and the wardrobe grew and grew. Barbie also wore wigs.

These were the years when the station wagon came into its own. Until the late 1940s the station wagon was considered a novelty designed for gentlemen farmers. By the late 1950s it was one of Detroit's most popular products, taking 15 percent of the market. It was a staple of the suburban life.

Baby-sitting had meanwhile become a business with an annual cash turnover of $1 billion. And on this base stood the prosperity of the nation's nightclubs, its restaurants, its movie theaters, its dance halls, and the theaters of Broadway. The baby-sitting boom grew from the conjunction of postwar fecundity and postwar prosperity. It was not unknown before 1945, but not until about 1950 did the practice become widespread and the term "baby-sitter" came into common usage. It reflected the rise of suburbia in the postwar, when millions of young married couples moved away from the people who had traditionally looked after the baby while the parents went out for the evening—that is, the grandparents.

Baby-sitting quickly evolved its own etiquette: the sitter was entitled to ransack the refrigerator; the sitter was entitled to play the radio or watch television; the sitter was not entitled to play the record player unless she brought her own records; the sitter was driven to and from work or else had to be given taxi fare. By the late 1950s half of all teenage girls were baby-sitters. Sitting had become an important part of the social training of American girls. But they faced competition from adults. The nation's champion sitter was Ione Marshall of Los Angeles; in her thirties, she earned $400 a month plus expenses. Most girls settled for approximately seventy-five cents an hour plus a full refrigerator.

Jittery Americans had doubled their cigarette consumption since 1940. By the late 1950s they were smoking 2,500 cigarettes a year per capita.

But they were becoming worried about the effects. Before 1951 filter tips had accounted for less than one percent of cigarette sales. By 1960 they accounted for half. The filters were virtually worthless.

In the home, soap was replaced by detergents. The cleaning mainstay of centuries was toppled in less than a decade by this German innovation.

Salt Lake City in 1958 tried a new approach to the problem of downtown parking—"the garage on stilts." This five-story structure was opened to jeers and skepticism. Wise men agreed that it would never work. What other city, they asked, would want to build huge parking structures in the middle of town?

The latest hazard to unwary drivers was the radar speed trap. Motorists considered it underhanded and unsporting. Rumor had it that a collection of ball bearings or a thick layer of tinfoil in the hubcaps would dazzle the radar screen with electronic snow.

It was with matters such as these that ordinary, everyday life in the late 1950s was concerned.

The American Century lasted, like the Thousand-Year Reich, all of twelve years, as Americans discovered in October 1957. The world's leaders in boosterism found they had let slip the propaganda coup of a generation. In large part it was due to Eisenhower's indifference to publicity stunts. Khrushchev, on the other hand, was a born showman.

The Russians picked up the idea of putting an artificial satellite into orbit from accounts in the American press. Until then all their missile development work had been aimed at military purposes. The United States Navy, however, planned under Project Vanguard to put a satellite into orbit in late 1957 or early 1958 as part of the American contribution to the International Geophysical Year. Vanguard was delayed because of its complicated design; it was intended to carry half a dozen scientific measuring devices. The Russians saw that if they hurried, they might beat Vanguard into orbit. And because it was, as Khrushchev recognized at once, a propaganda coup, all that mattered was for the world to know that they had done it. Sputnik 1 carried nothing but a small, simple, rugged radio transmitter.

In September the Russians claimed to have successfully launched an intercontinental ballistic missile. No one paid much attention. It was always difficult to know what to make of Soviet boasts.

On October 4 Americans got up and were stunned to learn that the Russians had put up an artificial satellite. It could be picked up on the radio, giving out a monotonous "beep . . . beep . . . beep." People listened in awe and apprehension. No one doubted that it marked the beginning of a new epoch—which was thrilling—but the Russians had got there first—and that was unsettling.

Several weeks later the Russians dropped the other shoe: they put a dog in space.

With the Sputniks drawing eyes heavenward there was a new wave of UFO sightings.

To help reassure an anxious people, the President went on a national tour to make soothing and optimistic remarks at televised rallies. Yet the nation remained convinced that it had suffered a setback.

The truth was, although no one in America could have seen it at the time, that this was really another stroke of Eisenhower's luck. The Soviet missile scientists had deep misgivings about what they had done. For the sake of short-term political and propaganda advantages the Soviet Union had made a very costly long-term economic mistake. They had begun a competition they could not afford, and the United States could; they had started a race they could never hope to win, and one the United States could therefore hardly lose; and for the next decade a large part of the small base of advanced industry and many of the most gifted engineers the Soviet Union possessed would be drawn into this folly. The Soviet space program was a brake on the Soviet economy; the much more sophisticated American economy, by contrast, would profit from the space race because it was capable of turning its technological spin-off into commercial products very quickly. Khrushchev, in his zeal to beat the United States at *something*, had dug a bottomless money pit. He had also provided the United States with something which almost everyone agreed it needed in the late 1950s—a challenge.

Meanwhile, of course, Americans were reeling from Sputnik shock. In Cabinet meetings Arthur Larson, elevated to the directorship of the USIA, was pleading for a chance to strike back: "My pet project was the orbiting of a satellite that was inflated to a huge reflecting balloon, plainly visible to the naked eye in many parts of the world. I pictured remote jungle tribes hailing a new deity in the heavens. . . ."

Americans had little excuse for being taken by surprise. In recent months the press had been filled with stories about ICBMs and artificial satellites. Both the Army and the Air Force had protested the leisurely pace of missile development. And on September 8, 1957, one of the Army's missile experts said flatly in a story in the *New York Times*, "The Soviet is likely to beat the United States in placing a satellite in orbit around the world."

Having seized the propaganda advantage, the Russians rubbed it in when they put Laika into orbit, consigning the poor dog to death and doing nothing for science. Rumor had it cows were next on the schedule, which would result in the herd shot round the world.

Vanguard—an amusing name considering that it was trying to catch up—made its first ascent. It reached a height of fifty feet before it fell back on its pad at Cape Canaveral and vanished in a fireball of exploding fuel.

On January 31, 1958, the Army's Jupiter C put a thirty-pound satellite, Explorer, into orbit. Khrushchev called it a "grapefruit." Americans for years to come were shamefaced that their missiles and satellites were smaller than the Russians'. It was a kind of masculinity contest.

The Russians put a missile into orbit around the sun, they sent back the first pictures of the far side of the moon, and when Khrushchev made his first American visit, they sent up a missile designed to crash into the moon's visible side. It was a project with no scientific value. It was meant solely to raise a cloud of dust.

In the wake of Sputnik 1 Eisenhower appointed James R. Killian, Jr., of MIT to fill the newly created post of Special Adviser to the President for Science and Technology. Until this moment the United States had been without a science policy or the means of making a science policy.

A Scientific Advisory Commission had been created during the Korean War to provide advice to the President. But it had been wrecked in the clashes between the scientists and the State Department over passports and visas. For five years the Executive branch had no means of incorporating the advice of scientists in policy making, except for scientists in government employment. The OST henceforth provided scientific advice much as the CEA provided economic advice. Thought was seriously given to creating a Cabinet-level Department of Science and Technology.

Fortunately science in the United States remained free from central control and direction, despite the Sputniks, despite the new structures. A comparative handful of key figures in fifteen to twenty locations (major government laboratories, leading universities, important industrial research departments) were in constant communication with one another and in touch with the principal developments in scientific research and applied technology. This informal network was both an early-warning system and a recruiting office. Its invaluable strengths were its flexibility and its enthusiasm, strengths which could only be vitiated by bureaucratic control.

Eisenhower recognized that. Much as Roosevelt had done during the war, he kept out of the scientists' way. But he made sure that the money they asked for was forthcoming. For the remainder of his term in office the Federal budget was heavily in the red mainly because of increased spending on missile development and the rapid growth of the National Aeronautics and Space Administration, established in 1958. Within a few years NASA was outspending the AEC.

The new agency planned to put a man into orbit in early 1962. The Army claimed that with the Jupiter missile and a bit of imaginative engineering it could do the same thing in 1959. And just think of the publicity, urged the head of its missile development program, Wernher von Braun. Without Project Mercury, however, NASA would have little to aim at for nearly a decade. The Army's plan was rejected.

In April 1959 the first American astronauts were introduced to a nation eager for heroes and heroic adventure. *Time* rhapsodically hailed them: "Seven men cut out of the same stone as Columbus, Magellan, Daniel Boone, Orville and Wilbur Wright." All of which was pure hyperbole. These were no lone pioneers or visionaries. They were middle class, clean-cut young Organization Men. The organization happened to be the Air Force, the Navy, or the Marine Corps. They wore their hair short, they all were trained pilots, and they all were accustomed to doing as they were told. Every one of them had spent his entire adult life on the Federal payroll.

Project Mercury intended to orbit one of them in three years' time, but *Newsweek* glumly prophesied. "A Russian astronaut is very likely to get into orbit first in 1961."

NASA was already looking beyond Mercury at a far more ambitious goal. Beginning in 1959, the agency began to lobby Congress and the White House for a project to put a man on the moon by 1970. NASA had no doubt that it could be done. The only question seemed to be whether the man would be an American or a Russian. It was a measure of the publicity success of Sputnik that an opinion survey in ten countries in 1960 showed that in nine of them most people expected the Soviet Union to be the world's leader in science by 1970. But in the tenth country, the United States, most people were confident that given another ten years, they would leave the Soviets behind.

Yet there remained the nagging sensation that at the moment the Russians were ahead. This opinion was strenuously encouraged by generals, who were embittered at the shabby treatment given the Army's missile program. "Informed people agree," wrote Lieutenant General James M. Gavin, who resigned in protest as head of research and development for the Army, "that the Soviets are ahead of us technologically. . . . There is, for example, the 'missile lag.'" General Maxwell Taylor, who resigned as Chief of Staff of the Army, wrote sourly of "the Missile Gap." As early as December 1958 *Newsweek* had adopted the phrase and wrote: "The words 'missile gap' have become commonplace." And for some time to come the nation had to endure long, hand-wringing articles over the presumed technological shortcomings of the United States which, it was said, posed a threat to the country's survival.

But the Administration repeatedly denied that a missile gap existed. Then in 1960 the new Secretary of Defense, Thomas S. Gates, Jr., reversed the theme: the gap, formerly said not to exist, was now being closed, he announced.

It had first become evident during the war that the military was not mentally prepared to fight a modern war. This was not because they lacked modern weapons, for they did not, but because they had only the haziest idea of how to use them. Radar, jet aircraft, rockets, and proximity fuses were gifts which civilians dropped into military laps. Generals had only the most rudimentary ideas about tank warfare; admirals had simplistic ideas about submarine hunting. It had been civilians—as a rule, civilian scientists—who taught the men in uniform how to fight a mid-twentieth-century war using the weapons produced by advanced technology. And just when the military men began to get the hang of it, the atomic bomb, designed and built by still other civilians, brought the war to an end and undid much of what had recently been learned.

But one lesson stuck. The military establishment in the postwar turned to civilian scientists for guidance on how to fight, or prevent, war in the nuclear age. The Air Force, with the help of Douglas Aircraft Corporation, in 1948 established the RAND Corporation (from Research and Development) in Santa Monica. At the time of Sputnik 1 RAND still worked mainly for the Air Force. But its staff had grown from 60 to 1,000. Widely believed to be eccentric, individualistic, and nonmaterialistic intellectuals, they were, tweed jackets aside, Organization Men, well paid and ambitious. Those who had arrived in the "think tank" business sported a blackboard in their offices, much as executives above a certain rank elsewhere had a good carpet and a water carafe. RAND was supposed to be sufficiently independent to offer objective advice, but sufficiently close to have that advice taken seriously, a relationship, it was said, comparable to that of a mistress who is supported in style but not slept with.

By the late 1950s there were more the fifty think tanks in business, and more opened each month. What they sold was advice. The advice business, like the shoe business, was moved by fashion. In 1956, for example, it was almost impossible to sell advice on arms control; five years later it was the hottest thing on the market.

Another American innovation was the "summer study." Each summer, when the academic year ended, each military service would bring together a collection of the best scientific minds it could round up and invited them to thrash out a major military problem. Some of these summer studies, such as Vista (combat and combat support in Western Europe) did not simply add to existing policy; they made policy by altering military thinking. There were dozens of summer studies, many of them secret.

But think tanks and summer studies represented only a very small fraction of the much larger research and development effort. Some $11 to $12 billion a year was being spent on R & D in the late 1950s; that was approximately 3 percent of the GNP. Most of it went into development, which accounted for more than twice the money spent on research. Industry claimed to account for seventy-five cents of the R&D dollar, and the universities accounted for another ten cents. But government was putting up most of the money spent by industry and the universities by contracting with them to do research and development of interest to it. What it was interested in mostly was weapons.

Before the war nearly all Federal research was concerned with growing things. After 1945 it was concerning with destroying them. It did not, however, find itself forcing its attentions on a reluctant scientific community. Federal money was lusted after. Since the turn of the century scientific research had grown rapidly in scale and moved away from the workbench to the laboratory. In effect, by the 1950s it had become socialized because only the taxpayer could afford to finance the facilities required. And it was big science which most of the best scientists wanted to pursue.

It would be wrong to give the impression that all government-financed R&D was concerned with weapons or that all such R&D was on a huge scale. R&D expenditures at the National Institutes of Health, for instance, increased tenfold in the 1950s, from an admittedly small base. And the Office of Naval Research was held in something like affection by many scientists for the enlightened way in which it made grants, even for small-scale projects of no evident use to the Navy. Federal generosity was such, in fact, that the government provided more money for research in the humanities and the social sciences than the universities provided. Federal R&D money had another positive effect. Much of what the Defense Department was buying, and much of what NASA would need in the years ahead, was so advanced that it was virtually handmade, involving thousands of man-hours from skilled labor and the use of very expensive, very precise tools. It seems probable that government-financed R&D was raising the standards of American engineering to a very high level.

Yet in the aftermath of Sputnik 1 most people felt that there must surely be something seriously at fault. The most obvious target for criticism was the duplication of effort: the United States seemed to be attempting to do too many things at the same time, under the aegis of huge bodies which had come into existence since the war—the CIA, the AEC, the Defense Department, and now NASA.

American science and technology, however, was at its strongest when it was allowed to express most fully the diversity and energy of the nation as a whole. America was rich enough and stable enough to afford failures which would have crippled almost anyone else. It thus accepted risks others would shun and won rewards to match the risks. It apparent profligacy and recklessness were an inextricable part of its strength. In the long run the American way, characterized by duplication and multiplication, was more likely to produce a successful result—and thus be cheaper, in the end—than a concentrated effort, which ultimately fell short.

Nor, as was suggested earlier, was American science as fragmented as sometimes appeared. To the informal network of key scientists and science administrators there had been added, in 1950, the National Science Foundation. It had no military division, which represented a success for the scientists who resisted the importunings of Congress. The NSF concentrated on the support of scientific education and basic research. It sought out research which it believed deserved encouragement and then let contracts or made grants which would provide it. The NSF was a typically American creation—informal, open, and openhanded.

Nor was science a stranger in the corridors of power. "The plain fact is," wrote an authority on public administration, "that science has become the major Establishment in the American political system: the only set of institutions for which appropriations are made almost on faith, and under concordats which protect the autonomy, if not the cloistered calm, of the laboratory." Of the sixty-three civil service departments in the Federal government in 1958 there were twenty-six headed by a trained scientist or engineer; this compared very favorably with nine headed by economists and eight headed by lawyers. There was also a rich sprinkling of scientists in the civil service "super grades"—that is, specially created positions which were remarkably well paid, designed to attract men and women of outstanding ability into long-term government service. The scientists who were recruited into the upper reaches of government, furthermore, were not as a rule interested in administration; they were interested in policy making. And because they were not usually thought of as being bureaucrats, their opinions were as a rule seriously considered by Congress, the White House, the press, and the people who *were* bureaucrats.

The danger was not that government would ignore scientific research but that it might abuse it by turning it to cruel, trivial, or ignoble ends. That danger was somewhat offset by the refusal to put science under centralized control; there was a score of patrons, all disbursing government money, but according to their own needs and interests. For the present the cultivation of science in America was as enlightened as the patronage of art had been in Renaissance Italy.

The most important field for basic research in the postwar was in the most humble, least prestigious of the natural sciences, biology. Its achievement was the unraveling of the biochemical basis of life and reproduction, bringing about one of the most portentous discoveries in the history of the human race.

There had been a suspicion since about 1940 that deoxyribonucleic acid (minute quantities of which are present in every human cell) might carry the body's genetic code. But geneticists continued to devote their energies to the traditional questions, such as "How are blue eyes transmitted?" Not until about 1950, when physicists and biochemists began to take an interest in genetics, did the emphasis of the questions change to "What tells the body to make eyes at all?"

The average human body is composed of approximately 1,000,000,000,000,000 cells. Each contains a blueprint for the entire structure. And after 1945 physicists began to take an interest in the workings of human cells. Theirs had long been the most glamorous field in science. But after the first few atomic explosions physics lost some of that glamor. In a slightly defensive way, the physicists themselves were attracted toward the study of life processes, as if to repair an uneasy conscience. Out of this came a book, *What Is Life?*, by the physicist Erwin Schrödinger, which inspired a young English physicist, Francis Crick, to take up biochemistry and to speculate about DNA.

At about the same time, and working toward DNA studies by a different route, was James D. Watson. After graduating from the University of Chicago, Watson applied to Harvard and Caltech for graduate work and was turned down by both. He took his doctorate at the University of Indiana, under a noted geneticist, Salvador Luria. Watson became obsessed with the idea that there was a genetic code and that it could be cracked. With his ambition as his only guide, Watson wound up in a roundabout way at Cambridge, in the same laboratory as Francis Crick. To those around them both seemed destined to be scientific second-raters. They nevertheless announced that they were after "the secret of life." It was the kind of remark out of fashion since the passing of the scientist in silk hat, spats, and kid gloves.

Watson was not a brilliantly original thinker. But he brought an American sense of urgency to the search. And Crick, who was something of a dilettante, knew enough physics, mathematics, and chemistry to build, rebuild, and build yet again the model of the DNA nucleus as they teased out its secrets. In harness, Crick and Watson did a remarkable job of following up research possibilities pioneered by Linus Pauling. It created some ill feeling in scientific circles. But this is really the way in which science has advanced in the twentieth century and is the main reason why secret science is nearly always inferior to the open variety.

Pauling, who had himself been torn between physics and biochemistry and had opted for the latter, had made a crucial discovery in 1950. He found that fibrous proteins had a helical—that is, a spiral or coiled—structure. The coil promptly became the key conceptual tool employed by Crick and Watson. In 1954 the importance of Pauling's work was acknowledged when he was given the Nobel Prize.

But two years earlier, in 1952, Crick and Watson were eagerly following Pauling's researches and planned to meet him when the great man traveled to London. To their amazement the closest to London that Pauling got was the departure lounge at Idlewild Airport. The State Department, then under Dean Acheson, who cultivated the impression that *he* never knuckled under to McCarthyism, had revoked Pauling's passport.

Pauling, however, continued to publish his researches. And at a critical juncture he took a wrong turn. Crick and Watson spotted the mistake almost at once. They also drew on the work of two young English scientists, Maurice Wilkins and Rosalind Franklin, to fill in parts of the structure. In the late spring of 1953, after eighteen months of feverish work, and only one jump ahead of Pauling, Crick and Watson unraveled DNA. It was not one helix, they announced, but two—one inside the other.

They had guessed that the secret of how DNA worked was to be found in its structure, and their guess proved right. In time, DNA and RNA (ribonucleic acid) were synthesized in the laboratory, which for better or worse opened up extraordinary possibilities in genetic engineering. Crick, Watson, and Wilkins received the Nobel Prize. Rosalind Franklin had died while still young and unrecognized. Watson finally found a way to get into Harvard. He was made professor of molecular biology and biochemistry.

It would be some time before many people realized that the biological revolution had already taken place. But they were more than prepared for rapid advances; they expected them. There was also a sentimentalized aura around medical research, an aura bolstered by the introduction of polio vaccines.

The biological revolution brought major advances in surgery. Before 1945 open-heart operations were rare. When risked, they nearly always proved fatal. But a new technique developed for "blue" babies brought a rapid reduction in mortality rates, as did the advent of the heart-lung bypass machine. By 1960, 5,000 open-heart operations were successfully carried out each week.

In the 1950s it became possible to remove entire sections of damaged or badly clotted arteries and replace them with seamless synthetic tubes. These years also saw the development of the pacemaker, to regulate faltering and erratic heartbeats. Dialysis machines, which saved the lives of tens of thousands of kidney patients each year, were perfected,. And a score of new diagnostic tools were also perfected, with profound consequences for the treatment of illness.

But what people noticed most was the victory over polio, which provided an object lesson in class distinction and emotionalism as factors in medical research. Polio afflicted mainly middle-class children, who were more likely to have access to swimming pools than lower-class children. Tuberculosis, on the other hand, was more common among the lower classes and afflicted five to ten times as many people as polio struck down each year. The cost to the national economy of polio was $70 million a year in the mid-1950s; of tuberculosis, $800 million. But no one got very excited about TB. So while hundreds of millions of dollars were spent each year on polio research, only a fourth as much was spent on TB research. Social considerations reached right into that orderly, aseptic haven of reason, the laboratory.

Salk's vaccine was far from ideal. But despite its shortcomings (three shots instead of one, the risk of using a live virus, its effectiveness against only one of the three polio viruses), it was considered priceless. A better vaccine, developed by Dr. Albert Sabin of Cincinnati, was close on its heels, but no one would wait for it. The eradication of polio became a national cause in the 1950s, and by 1960 it had been achieved for all practical purposes.

Following this spectacular triumph the National Foundation for Infantile Paralysis, one of the most successful fund-raising bodies in the history of medical research, changed its name to the National Foundation, nothing more, and turned its attention to other ailments. Doctors heaved a sigh of relief. The NFIP had done more than support research; it had helped polio-stricken families by paying part of their medical bills. The doctors had agitated against this assistance as "an ominous precursor of socialized medicine."

Despite the sanctified nature of biomedical research to most people, it remained the poor relation of research and development spending. The biological revolution was sustained with only 3 to 4 percent of total R&D money.

The application of the wonders scientific research wrought was the advanced technology of the postwar. Its effect on society was pervasive, it pace accelerating. Until 1900 the time lag between scientific discovery and practical application had been several decades. By the 1950s it was down to a few years.

Much technology had been developed independently of scientific research, through tinkering, individual inventiveness, or mere idle curiosity. Some of the most important tools of the modern age (typewriters, steam engines, pumps, microscopes) were developed by people who had no interest in basic scientific research. But tinkering and individual invention would no longer suffice. Most inventing these days was done by organizations and for organizations—business corporations mainly, but also government and universities. Nor was it necessarily done in laboratories; much of it was conducted in offices, with pen, paper, and computer. This only speeded up the exploitation of research results because most of it was conducted for commercial reasons.

The most important new tool was the computer. It had roots trailing back into the nineteenth century but for all practical purposes dated from the early 1940s and a wartime project on controlling naval gunfire. In 1946 the University of Pennsylvania, financed by a wartime Army Ordnance Corps contract, produced the first modern computer, ENIAC (Electronic Numerical Integrater and Computer). ENIAC was not really one machine but a dozen, which took up most of the floor space of a very big room. It had a memory of twenty-seven "bits"—that is, it could absorb twenty-seven very specific items of information at one time and use them to provide answers to very simple, straightforward questions. ENIAC sweated out each answer through 18,000 vacuum tubes. It resembled a megalithic dinosaur, possessing an enormous body and a minuscule brain.

Five years later, working on the construction of the H-bomb, John von Neumann, a Hungarian refugee, built a computer with a memory of 40,000 bits and capable of correcting the information fed into it. Von Neumann called his creation the Mathematical Analyzer, Numerical Integrator, and Computer (MANIAC).

Within two years, in 1953, General Electric introduced the first commercial computer. It was believed that there might be a market for computers, but no one was certain. Some optimists thought that several hundred might eventually be sold. By 1960 there were more than 1,000 in operation and thousands more on order.

The computer was itself the chief expression of the electronics industry which had sprung up since the war. Radar had provided it with a base, television provided it with work, but the humble transistor lay at its heart. The transistor was developed in 1947 and 1948 at the Bell Telephone Laboratories.

The early transistors were expensive, but smaller and more reliable than the vacuum tube. Their first commercial success was in hearing aids. Even though a transistorized aid cost $200, four times the usual cost, within four years of their introduction they had captured 99 percent of the market. The cost of a transistor had meanwhile dropped from $10 to little more than $1. From 1957 onward they swept through the radio industry.

In 1960 the sale of electronic products was more than $11 billion and rising fast. In little more than a decade it had grown from a comparatively small industry to the fifth largest in the country. That it had grown so quickly was thanks to lavish government support. Three-fourths of all scientists and engineers involved in electronics were working on defense projects. But the principal effects of this rapid growth were felt in American society. There was hardly a home or a business that was not, or was not about to be, directly affected.

In some areas the electronics boom had made or remade a community; as in "Silicon Valley," the area between San Francisco and Palo Alto, or along Route 128, the girdle of concrete to the west of Boston, which by 1960 boasted a "new industrial complex signifying the union of higher education, R & D, engineering services, electronics and the defense budget."

Americans had good reason to be proud of American science since the war. Until 1945 the United States had been a net importer of scientific knowledge. In the years since then it had played a part in scientific research in keeping with its wealth, power, population size, and intellectual resources.

Before the war, thought I.I. Rabi, a Nobel prizewinner in physics, the United States had produced only one undeniably first-rate theoretical physicist (presumably Josiah Willard Gibbs). From 1901, when the Nobel awards began, through 1944, a total of seventeen awards in physics, chemistry, physiology, and medicine went to Americans. In the same period Western Europeans, whose numbers were approximately the same as those of the United States, collected 100 awards. Britain and Germany, both much smaller countries, each won more Nobel prizes. But after 1944 Americans dominated the Nobel awards, and that domination only seemed to grow stronger with the passage of time. In medicine and the natural sciences it took approximately half the prizes each year and often took most of them.

Similarly, before 1945 a scientist who wanted a first-rate instrument for his laboratory would in most cases have ordered it from Europe. By the mid-1950s his laboratory would be full of American-made scientific instruments. So would the laboratory where his European counterpart worked. In the 1950s one of the fastest-growing branches of industry was thus the manufacture of scientific instruments, where employment doubled during the decade from 40,000 to 80,000.

In the meantime much of science had become Big Science—e.g., the big national laboratories, the multimillion-dollar projects. Big Science depended on public money; this dependence created an urge to secure publicity, to create a strong public image. The pursuit of public relations was hardly in keeping with the caution, sobriety, and modesty of the scientific method. The worst features of scientific research—an emphasis on personalities, the overstatement of results, premature publication—would be encouraged, and the best features slighted. Alvin Weinberg, the director of Oak Ridge National Laboratory (a Big Science establishment), pointed to this and other dangers, such as a tendency to spend money in the place of thought because money was easier to come by. Yet history, he believed, "will find in the monuments of Big Science—the huge rockets, the high-energy accelerator, the high-flux research reactor—the symbols of our time just as surely as it finds in Notre Dame a symbol of the Middle Ages."

American science flourished not only because money was being poured into it but because between the wars it had attracted large numbers of bright, ambitious young men from lower-middle-class homes—that is, from families where to become a scientist was to take a large step upward. The typical research scientist who came to maturity between 1945 and 1960 had attended a small liberal arts college in the Midwest or on the Pacific coast and came from a modest, hardworking Protestant family, possibly farmers. Young men at the prestigious Eastern colleges, in contrast, were not much attracted to science. To most of them the laboratory was a step down, not up.

Despite their prosaic origins, scientists were widely regarded as remote, rather otherworldly, figures. At the same time there was a romantic assumption that they had chosen to accept a stern intellectual discipline out of love of humanity. Humanitarianism was not, however, what motivated all but a handful of scientists. The satisfactions of their work were individualistic, and their reasons for taking up science were personal. Their attitude was that if what they were doing was of benefit to society, then that was society's good luck.

The impression that scientists were remote and otherworldly probably discouraged some young people who might have been attracted to careers in science. Antiscience attitudes were found to be as commonplace among adolescents of marked scientific aptitude as among those who had no such bent. The resulting loss of talent was considered as extensive as that caused by poor science teaching or poor science facilities in the high schools. Students had a very ambivalent view: a positive one of scientists as benefactors of mankind; a negative one of scientists as people who were odd and led dull lives.

Adults were susceptible to the same attitudes, and there was often a note of hostility, most remarkably among people who were highly educated. There was a strong antiscience strain in the works of esteemed intellectual writers such as Aldous Huxley and T. S. Eliot, for example. To the English writer and scientist C. P. Snow, the result was dismal. He lamented, "The great edifice of modern physics goes up, and the majority of the cleverest people in the Western world have about as much insight into it as their neolithic ancestors would have had."

But to many of those who served the traditional, mainly literary culture of the West, science and technology were spending too much time in bad company. So much so that they had become synonymous in the minds of people such as Edmund Wilson with mass destruction, soulless mechanization, and indifference to the needs of the human spirit. And to ordinary people science and technology meant automation, which meant loss of jobs.

If people had mixed feelings about science in the modern era, it was because science in the modern era had produced mixed results. But too often was the good ignored or taken for granted, while the bad was certain to be sensationalized.

At the human level, where science and technology bore down on individuals directly, American science in the postwar could offer some remarkable sights. A noted Swiss journalist watched in fascination while young Americans in the Santa Susana Mountains of California were strapped into tiny sleds and shot vertically into the air, risking broken backs; on the other side of the continent, in Johnstown, Pennsylvania, they were swung on large pendulums until they passed out; in the Mojave Desert a powerful sledge spun them in circles, causing nausea, giddiness, and intense muscular pain; at the University of Michigan they were shaken by sound waves so powerful they temporarily lost their hearing; at Princeton another sound wave experiment destroyed their sense of balance; in Dayton, Ohio, they were frozen; at Eglin Air Force Base in Florida they were baked in an oven; they bailed out of aircraft more than ten miles above the earth at the risk of losing their fingers and toes; in San Antonio they were put into pressure chambers, and when the air was expelled, their blood began to boil and their skin blistered. "Why," he . asked, "do they permit themselves to be so tormented? No tyrant has condemned them to it. No regime wishes to extort confessions from them . . . they do so of their own free will. For they have been told, 'You are the vanguard. You are the pioneers, the patrols on the frontiers of human capacity and endurance.' " And so they were.

25

The Bombs Bursting in Air

William Attwood, home after nine years in Europe, set off to cross the country and, leaving New York by the Pulaski Skyway, was shocked by a sign announcing that the Skyway would be closed during an enemy attack. He reflected, "Here was tangible evidence of the war nerves we had never seen abroad. We drove on, all set to record other manifestations of the national jitters. But when we returned to New York three months later, our notes told a different story. . . If the jitters exist, they are harder to find than uranium in your back yard." Alexander Werth, living and teaching in Columbus, Ohio, in 1957 and 1958, found that people sometimes talked about a future nuclear war, but no one seemed able to take it seriously because they could hardly imagine what it would be like. New Yorkers, on the other hand, in a typical combination of bravado and civic pride, boasted that their city was "Target A."

The prospect of nuclear devastation appeared remote because Americans had no experience of modern warfare on their own soil and in their own cities. Even during the war hardly anyone except officials had taken air-raid drills very seriously. The old habits died hard. In May 1955 a flight of SAC bombers approached San Francisco Bay from the Pacific and were not properly identified. The Air Force sounded "Warning-Yellow" —which meant that an attack was imminent. Sirens blared throughout Oakland. Only 15 percent took any notice of the alert. The rest refused to believe, or were simply unaware, that there was a civil defense emergency.

Yet now and again there was the prospect of an accidental nuclear disaster, and people took *that* seriously. In 1958, for instance, an atomic bomb slipped from a B-47 flying over South Carolina. The triggering mechanism was unarmed. But the impact exploded the TNT in the bomb, shattering a nearby house. It was news which sent shivers down many a spine. Assurances that there had been virtually no chance of the entire bomb's being detonated were taken with the well-known pinch of salt.

There was also increasing anxiety over the effects of radioactive fallout. In the late spring of 1957 Congress spent ten days holding hearings on fallout, and by the tenth day a new term had entered everyday speech— strontium 90. This was an entirely new element, something unknown in nature, the product of the H-bomb.

The British Atomic Energy Authority, meanwhile, let it be known that according to its calculations, the nuclear and thermonuclear tests already conducted would create 50,000 cancer cases; for every megaton exploded in future there would be another 1,000 cases. Cancer was a reality almost everyone could understand and be frightened by.

The AEC strove energetically to make light of these fears. Chairman Lewis Strauss (described by cartoonist Herbert Block as "the Chairman of the Atomic Energy Good News Committee") blandly maintained that continued atmospheric testing was essential; otherwise the United States would not be able to learn how to make "clean" (less radioactive) bombs. Dr. Willard Libby, the only scientist on the AEC, admitted that strontium 90 was a danger to life—but on the same order that cosmic radiation is a danger to people who live on mountaintops.

The Federal Civil Defense Administration printed and distributed a million copies of a pamphlet, *What You Should Know About Radioactive Fallout*. As the pamphlet described it, fallout was something which would be created during an enemy attack. Only in passing was fallout as a by-product of testing in the upper atmosphere mentioned; it was promptly followed by this reassurance: "By the time [the radioactive particles] reach the surface of the Earth—perhaps days or even months later—most of their radioactivity has been given off harmlessly into the air." The text suggested that people several hundred miles from an area attacked with H-bombs would be safe, and so did the accompanying maps. But in fact, wind patterns over the North American continent would have brought radiation sickness to people 1,000 miles away from a major attack along either coast.

At the end of the 1957 Congressional hearings the Livermore Laboratory, presided over by Edward Teller and devoted to the production of thermonuclear weapons, issued more good news. The clean bomb (96 percent less radioactive than the first generation of fusion weapons) was close at hand.*

Despite the outpouring of good news, people remained apprehensive. The British writer Nevil Shute in late 1957 published *On the Beach*, which described the last days of human existence following a thermonuclear war fought in 1963. The nations of the Northern Hemisphere succeed in destroying one another but in the process create an enormous radioactive cloud. Drifting southward, it kills all the vegetation, all the animal life, and all the people in its path. The Australians await its arrival, knowing that they will be the last of the human race to live and die. *On the Beach* was an enormous popular success, and nowhere more than in the United States. It was serialized in scores of big-city dailies; for many of them it was the first time they had serialized a novel. The film version was equally successful when it appeared shortly before Christmas 1959.

The government, however, was reluctant to take civil defense seriously. The most comprehensive defense policy review of the 1950s, the Gaither Committee Report, was delivered to the President at the end of 1957. It argued that development of the ICBM made a shelter program an important part of the strategic deterrent. The Administration was also urged to build up the nation's conventional forces, so as to increase its ability to fight a sizable war without having to make it a nuclear war. Eisenhower remained skeptical about both these ideas.

The Federal Civil Defense Administration remained little more than a public relations office throughout Eisenhower's Presidency. It urged the cities and states to act, showering them with advice but always short of money. The FCDA tried to enlist the churches. Belief in God, clergymen were informed, "will fortify people against mass hysteria" during a thermonuclear attack. "After the disaster the demand for sacramental rites or ordinances will be multiplied beyond all expectations . . . the clergyman is ideal to group ministrations, such as to hysterical groups. . . . Mass burials will occupy many hours." Sermons on thermonuclear warfare were encouraged, and clergymen were asked to allow their churches to be used for civil defense training.

Most governors, most mayors, and most clergymen in the end chose not to promote civil defense strongly. There was a lack of money; there

---

*One of the first people to have warned of the dangers radioactive fallout posed to health had been Edward Teller, in the *Bulletin of the Atomic Scientists* (February 1947).

was also a disinclination to add to public alarm. When an effort was made, it was usually small. A New Hampshire town appropriated $50 for civil defense and blew the entire sum on whistles. In parts of Texas civil defense drills were practiced diligently, but as a form of protection against tornadoes.

Only in New York, following the election of Nelson Rockefeller as governor in 1958, was there an active campaign to provide every home in the state with a fallout shelter. And in the next few years people began to take steps on their own. By 1961, 5 percent of American families had made structural alterations or additions to prepare their homes for a thermonuclear war, and 20 percent had at least gone to the trouble of stocking up with extra food, first-aid kits, and other emergency supplies.

The H-bomb was not simply built. It was sold. Its development was a story with sudden dramatic shifts, a villain, a hero, and a happy outcome. The villain was J. Robert Oppenheimer. The hero was Edward Teller, who gazed balefully at a menacing world from behind an encroaching hedge of eyebrows and found himself hailed as "the Father of the H-bomb."

According to the semiofficial, AEC-inspired version of events retailed in *The Hydrogen Bomb* by James Shepley and Clay Blair, Jr., the United States had sat dumb, fat, and happy on its nest of A-bombs, listening to soothing, bad advice from its scientists who said that the Soviets were years behind, when the Russians exploded their A-bomb. The only thing to do then was to begin work on the H-bomb. But American scientists, incredibly, resisted. They were mesmerized by the wicked Robert Oppenheimer.

All might have been lost. But in the nick of time there arose a hero who, scornful of the obstacles in his way, brought the nation to its senses. "It was an accident bordering on the miraculous," wrote Blair and Shepley in suitably awed tones, "that the nation had working in its atomic weapons laboratory, where he could pit both his knowledge and determination against Dr. Oppenheimer, a man like Edward Teller."

But the turnaround had really been effected by the Korean War. The scientific opposition to building the H-bomb collapsed overnight. The invasion of South Korea confirmed what the fervent anti-Communists had claimed about the nature of Soviet power—that it was expansionistic, opportunistic, and a permanent threat to peace. Hans Bethe, for example, had been as opposed to the H-bomb as Oppenheimer, but his contribution to it was almost as important as Teller's.

The H-bomb had an influential admirer in William L. Laurence, the science reporter of the *New York Times*. He rhapsodized over it as having made peace "inevitable. It has achieved the realization of one of mankind's most cherished dreams—the abolition of wars of aggression." He was afraid, however, that the United States might be behind the Soviets in the development of the H-bomb. Heroic measures had saved the day, but to gain a lead on the Russians, the United States needed atmospheric testing, and plenty of it; otherwise, its security would be in peril (which did not quite square with the H-bomb's having made peace "inevitable").

The strategy of deterrence itself had a hero, but no one as famous as Teller. Deterrence was in large part the brainchild of RAND's Albert Wohlstetter. In the early 1950s the Air Force had asked RAND to study the placement of its bases overseas. But Wohlstetter and his assistants chose to concentrate on the reasons for putting a string of strategic air bases overseas. They decided that it made little sense. The bases were, and would remain, highly vulnerable to Soviet attack. Far better, they argued, to keep the bulk of SAC at home, to keep a portion of its strength continually airborne, and to take other measures which would minimize the effects of a Soviet first strike at American strategic air power. The policy Wohlstetter recommended was to retain sufficient force to absorb a first strike and still be able to devastate the Soviet Union. Like most important ideas, it was simple and obvious—once someone else had thought of it. The bases study made RAND's reputation and became the basis of strategic deterrence into the 1960s.

In the meantime, an attempt was made to present nuclear war as a reasonable proposition. People were encouraged to look on the bright side. Teller, in *Foreign Affairs*, urged them to recognize that a war fought with H-bombs need not necessarily be suicidal, that it could, in fact, be won, provided the proper steps (e.g., lots of deep shelters) were taken.

A study group set up by the Council on Foreign Relations was wrestling with the same problem, and it came up with a similar answer. Its conclusions were written up by Henry Kissinger as *Nuclear Weapons and Foreign Policy*. This was a work within whose sober prose moved a yearning for heroic action and scorn for whatever was negative, including the doctrines of containment and deterrence. "Mastery of the challenges of the nuclear age will depend on our ability to combine physical and psychological factors, to develop weapons systems *which do not paralyze our will* [my italics]." Kissinger considers the possibility of limited war being fought along the arc stretching from Turkey to Korea. He deplores the "lesson" of the Korean War summed up in the phrase "Never again." Along this arc, he insisted, was the very ground on which to fight the Soviets and/or the Chinese and defeat them decisively. They would find themselves fighting American-supported armies defending their hearths and homes. "Moreover, if we utilize nuclear weapons there will be an inherent upper limit to the number of troops that can profitably be employed in the threatened areas. Thus, if we could develop forces capable of conducting limited war and of getting into position rapidly, we should be able to defeat the Soviet Union or China in local engagements despite their interior position." What was needed, he admonished, was not fewer nuclear weapons but more of them, and in much greater variety. Anyone who shrank from the high casualties which tactical atomic weapons would produce was "a defeatist."

The study group which produced this clarion call to the nuclear battlefield could not have been more impressively formed; it was an Eastern establishment body of the first water. It included, besides McGeorge Bundy, several generals, a Rockefeller (David), several past and future Secretaries and Under Secretaries of the military services. There was, in the late 1950s, a growing desire in defense circles to fight a limited war, and win it. Kissinger et al. thought that the key was to resort to tactical atomic weapons.

Far better known, however, was Herman Kahn's *On Thermonuclear War*. This too struck a robustly optimistic note. "Despite widespread belief to the contrary, objective studies indicate that even though the amount of human tragedy would be greatly increased in the [post-thermonuclear-war] world, the increase would not preclude normal or happy lives for the majority of survivors and their descendants." The thing to do was get ready. There must be plenty of deep shelters and big stockpiles of such necessaries as $100 million worth of radiation counters. Kahn also beat the drum for the small, winnable war: "We must be *willing* [my italics] to fight wars on a local and limited basis." And he, too, deplored the wrong lesson being drawn from the Korean War. He felt that a democracy which was not prepared to fight limited wars had a very limited future.

William Attwood discovered that even among the men who built the weapons, at Los Alamos, there was an optimistic air. In fact, "these men struck me as being more relaxed—you might even say happier—than most of the Americans we had been talking to on our trip . . . their work has a kind of purpose and direction which gives meaning to their lives."

Yet far from regarding the H-bomb as an inestimable contribution to peace or thinking of battlefield atomic weapons as offering a wonderful way to give the Communists a thrashing if used intelligently, many people regarded the entire business with horror. A mock thermonuclear attack on sixty-one cities in June 1955 was resisted by thirty people in New York who refused to take shelter. They held a prayer vigil across from city hall while the sirens brayed around them. They were arrested and tried. The judge who passed sentence told them they were "murderers."

In 1957 a group of pacifists and nonpacifists meeting in New York established the Committee for a Sane Nuclear Policy, better known as SANE. Its members included John Hersey, Norman Cousins, Erich Fromm, and Walter Reuther. It was, predictably, considered a Communist front; after all, were not many SANE members also members of the United World Federalists, a body the right wing had long regarded with the deepest suspicion? Within a year SANE had enrolled 25,000 members in 130 chapters. But Senator Thomas Dodd, whose career was based, like J. Parnell Thomas's, largely on shrill anti-Communism (and, like Thomas's, was destined to end in ignominy because he too was a crook) began to campaign against it. SANE, said the Senator, was taking its orders from the Kremlin. Although he produced not a scrap of evidence for his assertions, Dodd was able to stop SANE's rapid growth.

The year 1957 had also seen the first Pugwash conference. This came about in response to an appeal from Bertrand Russell and Albert Einstein for the scientists of the world to put the interests of humanity above the interests of governments. The conference was financed by Cyrus Eaton, the Cleveland industrialist who had made several million dollars out of trade with Communist countries. It was held at his summer home and birthplace, Pugwash, Nova Scotia.

Individuals began to make protests on their own initiative. The British in 1957 conducted a series of H-bomb explosions at Christmas Island, 1,000 miles south of Hawaii. A British Quaker named Harold Steele prepared to sail into the test area. But the British government was able to prevent him setting sail from Japan in time to reach it.

Steele's idea, however, fired the imagination of others, notably Albert Bigelow, a wartime destroyer captain from Connecticut. Like Steele, Bigelow was a Quaker. His revulsion against nuclear weapons had been sharpened by his role as host to two young women from Hiroshima during their visit to the United States for plastic surgery. When the AEC announced a series of H-bomb tests in the South Pacific in the summer of 1958, Bigelow decided to sail his ketch, the *Golden Rule*, a thirty-footer with a rakish look, into the test area. His crew consisted of several pacifist volunteers.

The Justice Department attempted to intervene but found that there was no law to stop Bigelow from sailing wherever he wished on the high seas. The AEC hurriedly passed a "regulation" which made it a crime for any American citizen to enter the Eniwetok test area without its authorization.

Under the 1946 Atomic Energy Act, AEC regulations had the force of law on American soil and over American citizens. But Bigelow for the life of him could not see how any AEC regulation could supplant international law on the high seas. There was nothing in the Atomic Energy Act which gave the commission title to rule the oceans of the world.

When Bigelow reached Hawaii, the Federal District Court in Honolulu granted an injunction to the Justice Department to prevent him from sailing any further. Convinced that the AEC regulation was invalid, Bigelow ignored the injunction. Well beyond the three-mile limit, the *Golden Rule* was overhauled by a Coast Guard cutter and towed back to Hawaii. Bigelow and his crew were convicted of "criminal conspiracy" and "criminal contempt of court." They spent the next sixty days in jail serving their sentences.

But while tied up in Honolulu, they had met Earle Reynolds, an anthropologist who had once worked for the AEC. Reynolds was an authority on radiation and its effects on human growth. He, his wife, his two children, and a Japanese crew member arrived in Hawaii on the last leg of a round-the-world cruise which had begun, by chance, a year earlier in Hiroshima. After attending the trial of the Golden Rulers, Reynolds felt a moral duty to sail in their place. It meant, he realized, the likely loss of his academic career and banishment from doing work which he deeply loved.

Reynolds and his family set sail. Several days later they were intercepted close to the test area. The US officials involved in the case appear to have tried to ensure that Reynolds's yacht was ruined in a manner which would have made it impossible to claim compensation, and the yacht constituted all he owned. At Reynolds's trial the judge conducted the proceedings less on the basis of law than on patriotic sentiments. A Federal Court of Appeals ordered a new trial. But Reynolds once more faced a judge who turned legal matters into Cold War polemics and ruled accordingly. Reynolds was given a two-year prison sentence. But in December 1960 Reynolds was saved from going to jail when another Court of Appeals ruled that the AEC regulation was invalid. Reynolds was broke, but free.

Ironically, it was neither he nor Bigelow, both men of conscience, who were hailed for protesting against the nuclear arms race. That accolade went to Claude Eatherly, whom we last encountered in the proposed invasion of Cuba, in which Eatherly's role was to drop bombs on innocent Cubans in downtown Havana. In the years since that aborted foray, Eatherly had fairly raced along the road to ruin.

Yet suddenly, in the late 1950s, he found himself hailed as the principal figure of moral protest against the atomic age. Eatherly had flown ahead of the aircraft which dropped the atomic bomb on Hiroshima. He had reported on the weather and the visibility over the target. He had been 300 miles away at the time of the explosion and had seen nothing of it. Yet there was a common belief that he had dropped the bomb and, stricken with remorse, he had become the first Hiroshima casualty. He was assailed by nightmares; his marriage had collapsed under the burden of guilt he carried; he had attempted suicide; he supported nineteen poor children in various countries out of his small disability pension; he had robbed a store to get hold of money to give to worthy causes but, being a saintly man at heart, could not follow through and fled, leaving the money behind. Eatherly was celebrated in the American and European press. A movie was about to be made based on his life. Then the bubble burst.

Eatherly, "the Hiroshima Pilot," was a petty thief, a pathological liar, and a mental patient. The VA, which was said to be persecuting him, had instead repeatedly shielded him from the consequences of his crimes. His marriage had failed, and he attempted suicide; but in each instance the fault was his. He had spent a year in prison in New Orleans for a series of swindles. And after burglarizing a post office, he faced the prospect of a Federal indictment. He proceeded to commit several lunatic robberies in order to get back into a mental hospital and avoid spending up to ten years in a Federal penitentiary. The Texas press unwittingly stumbled across Eatherly and proceeded to swallow him whole. Well-meaning people across the country and around the world were soon persuaded that Eatherly was being persecuted by the VA and the Air Force. They had found this saintly man to be a moral atom bomb, ran the legend, and, not recognizing the higher sanity he represented, had locked him up in a mental hospital. The truth was, he was neither a Dreyfus nor a lunatic.

But it was possible for Eatherly to become a cause célèbre at just this juncture because of the sudden sensitivity which millions of people felt toward the threat posed by thermonuclear weapons. Among scientists there had been mounting hopes of a deceleration in the arms race since the death of Stalin. Western scientists began to urge their governments to take the first step; to many of them that meant a suspension of atmospheric tests. This was the idea which Stevenson had tried to raise in 1956 and which Eisenhower had rejected as being hardly worth consideration. But the public was interested, and that interest was fanned by the vigorous dispute among scientists over fallout. Linus Pauling was the nominal leader on one side of the argument; Teller, the nominal leader on the other. The longer the debate went on, the more repetitious the arguments became, and the more public opinion shifted.

Eisenhower was among those who began to change their minds. But his hopes of effecting a test ban agreement were strongly resisted by the AEC and the Department of Defense. The AEC appears to have gone so far as to falsify its own reports in its opposition to a test ban. It claimed that underground tests could not be detected over long distances. To prove it, it produced a report on one of its own underground tests and asserted that it had not been detected beyond 250 miles. The test had actually been detected 2,300 miles away by AEC monitors.

Since the war the American policy toward atomic energy had tried to combine control with cooperation. The principle adopted had been to share knowledge and materials so long as they were put to peaceful uses. The world could not be kept from the atom, but it was hoped to keep from atomizing the world. Eisenhower's "Atoms for Peace" proposal was a perfect expression of the American policy, which was to educate people in the constructive uses of atomic energy so that they would be educated away from its uses for destruction.

It was the most enlightened policy possible, but perhaps also a trifle naïve. It was late in the day when Eisenhower turned his attention to the unpeaceful atom. And then he found the path to a Test Ban Treaty impassable. Not only was there suspicion on both the American and the Soviet side, but American scientists kept finding ways to set off explosions either deep belowground or high in the atmosphere, which frustrated the inspection systems the treaty writers kept devising. But still the public clamor mounted. Strontium 90, it was said, fell to Earth, was absorbed by grass, which in turn was eaten by cows, and arrived on the kitchen table in the milk. The menace of the nuclear arms race had finally got home.

In November 1958, with deep misgivings but in response to public demand, the governments of the United States and Britain took the first step. They stopped their atmospheric tests and invited the Russians to follow suit. The Russians, still far behind in nuclear weapons technology, replied by setting off ever bigger, ever dirtier explosions.

26
Was Johnny Really a Functional Illiterate?

Paratroopers, it developed, could make sure that Little Rock's schools were desegregated. But they could not make sure that they stayed open For most of the 1958–1959 school year they were closed. Still, the Central High Tigers played all their football games, with the governor's blessing. In late July 1959, however, Faubus was finally ordered by a Federal District Court to do nothing to "to impede, thwart, delay or frustrate" the desegregation plan. The schools opened once more, ringed by police and soldiers.

An irate mob descended on Central High to the accompaniment of a new version of "Dixie" blaring from a sound truck:

> In Arkansas, in the state of cotton,
> Federal courts are good and rotten.
> Look away, look away, look away,
> Dixieland!

There were rebel yells, piercing bugle calls, and ungrammatical chants of "One, two, three, four—Throw them niggers out the door!" Police, wielding nightsticks, and firemen, gripping high-pressure hoses, broke up the mob as it made a rush for the school. Inside, the handful of black students went to class, while outside, the protestors, bloodied, drenched, and frustrated, fled down nearby streets.

In various towns in Arkansas, Tennessee, and Virginia the schools were shut rather than accept desegregation by court order. When this happened, the encyclopedia salesmen swarmed into town.

School closures stirred deep and bitter emotions wherever they occurred. But by 1958 national attention on education had shifted from race to space. Americans became convinced the Russians had stolen a march with Sputnik because Russian education was better than American education. It was an almost predictable turn of events because Americans loved to berate their schools.

On the face of it, the schools showed a picture of substantial progress since 1945 in the face of severe difficulties—low teachers' salaries, cramped classrooms, juvenile delinquency. Between 1940 and 1960 the median school years completed by people over the age of twenty-five rose a full two years, from 8.6 to 10.6.

But education is perennially susceptible to changing fashions in popular anxiety. "Now Russian is the rage," grumbled Jacques Barzun, "and thousands are taking it up who will never progress beyond bungling."

The Russians, it was said, were turning out much larger numbers of scientists and engineers than the United States. What went unrecorded was the woefully low standard of training of many of those Russian engineers. There was a widespread alarm at the shortage of scientists and engineers in the United States. What was remarkable, however, was that a nation with a genius for engineering and science should be paying its graduates in the natural sciences less, on average, than the average graduate in law, business administration, dentistry, or public administration. That may have helped account for the shortage.

But most people preferred to blame the schools. Since 1955 they had been reading, and arguing about, *Why Johnny Can't Read*, by Rudolf Flesch. It became one of the biggest best-sellers of the 1950s. Its thesis was that hordes of youngsters were being turned into functional illiterates by wrongheaded teachers.* "The teaching of reading," pronounced Flesch, "—all over the United States, in all the schools, in all the textbooks—is totally wrong." Virtually the only country in the Western world where remedial reading courses were offered was the United States, but this was because the United States was virtually the only place where reading problems were found on a large scale. The thorn in Flesch's side was the word method of reading instruction, in which the meaning of each word was memorized, an abandonment, as he saw it, of the superior method of alphabet-phonics in which children are taught to break every word into its component sounds and from the completed sound to recognize its meaning. The word method was not reading, Flesch maintained, but "word guessing."

What made *Why Johnny Can't Read* such a success was not the weight of argument alone. Flesch provided the anxious parent with exercises for teaching children to read by the alphabet-phonics method at home. It combined an attack on the schools with self-improvement, while offering a "togetherness activity." It could hardly fail.

Right-wing zealots were meanwhile protesting that what was lacking was a bracing dose of patriotism in the textbooks. The twenty-three Korean War turncoats were attributed to the lack of compulsory American history courses in the high schools.

But more germane was the mounting chorus of criticism directed at the education of American teachers. Most of them were drawn from the lower middle class. In itself this was no bad thing, but too many were drawn from the least imaginative, least ambitious, least able, and most narrow-minded elements. In consequence, the values advanced in American classrooms were nearly always trite and vulgar. The average—that is, the mediocre—was held to be the ideal.

David Stevenson, who had taught at two teachers' colleges, said flatly, "There is no hope for the American school because the American teachers' college is hopeless." Low salaries, shabby campuses, and weak li-

---

*In 1960 that part of the population over twenty-five that really *was* functionally illiterate (unable to read beyond a fifth-grade level) was 8.4 percent.

braries did not wreck these institutions. But laziness, pettiness, lying, cheating, adamantine ignorance, and a deep contempt for serious learning did. All were characteristic of the teachers' colleges where he had taught. Such places were refuges for people undistinguished in intellect or character. The teachers who were trained there were able to deal only with ignorant students; the schools which employed such teachers produced no other kind.

A study of nearly 211 prospective elementary teachers showed that "nearly 150 had a long-standing hatred of arithmetic." Another study showed that of 370 teachers fewer than half were able to place ¼ among 5/16, 1/2, 3/16, 3/8 and 7/16. It was not unusual for high school mathematics teachers to have trouble with problems no more difficult than this. They relied on memorized answers.

On the Selective Service Qualification Test students majoring in education were far behind the rest. More than half of all other students reached a passing grade. Among education students only one in four did so.

The best teachers were usually those who had done well in college. Yet the best college graduates were on occasion advised not to take teaching as a career; they would become bored easily, were introverts, where extroverts were needed, were not democratic enough, making them impatient with slow learners, and might become too enthusiastic about the subject matter when "we don't teach subject matter, we teach children."

What was wrong with teachers' training could in large measure be traced back to the turn of the century, when the better universities refused to accept responsibility for educating teachers. Since then teachers' training had been considered rubbish by American intellectuals, and those responsible for it had become defensive and anti-intellectual in response. In recent years Harvard and Columbia had attempted to narrow the breach, but with no general success. Through such programs as the Master of Arts in Teaching they found themselves in a tragicomic position: they were trying to make education intellectually respectable.

Yet one way or another the nation at large was determined in the aftermath of Sputnik 1 to raise the educational standards in the public schools. During the next four years the number of states which required teachers to hold certificates approved by the NEA jumped from eighteen to forty-three. The National Science Foundation provided money for high school science teachers to go back to college. This was, in effect, a remedial science program, offering an opportunity to learn what they might have learned earlier had they not been forced to take so many education courses. A wide variety of summer schools for teachers flourished and were generously financed. The aim of almost every such program was to raise the intellectual standards of secondary education.

Yet serious doubts remained. The teachers of the late 1950s were, on balance, better educated than their predecessors. But the aims they held out to students, like the aims they held for themselves, do not appear to have risen much, if at all. In the increasingly standardized, certified, bureaucratized teaching profession it appeared impossible that teachers could bring to learning a sense of excitement and discovery. Yet the teachers could hardly be blamed for bowing to the prevailing forces of the age.

The schools inevitably reflected all the virtues and all the defects of the society around them. They were in large measure shaped by the powers of money and class.

America spent lavishly on education. When foregone earnings are included, the cost of education from kindergarten through graduate school in the late 1950s was approximately $35 billion a year. When counted in this way, most of the cost of education was being borne not by the taxpayers but by the students and their parents, belying the assumption that most education was free. It also happened that among the top 5 percent of high school graduates—that is, the intellectual cream—half did not go on to college. The reason they did not was lack of money, in most cases. Yet nothing could have been more shortsighted because in strictly economic terms education paid one of the best returns available. On a college degree it amounted to nearly 10 percent a year for life, and on a high school diploma it was 12 percent.

There was nevertheless a strong resistance to every attempt to extend Federal aid to education. As we have seen, the Catholic Church opposed such aid. So did the U.S. Chamber of Commerce, in the belief that it was fighting "collectivism." Southern state legislatures opposed Federal aid to education lest it provide added leverage for desegregation. So while aid to education bills were passed by the House, they died in the Senate.

Yet by a number of routes Federal money found its way into the schools. Since 1917 the Smith-Hughes Act had provided Federal aid to vocational training in agriculture, home economics, trades, and industries. In 1957 Washington began to finance housing for college students; in 1959 it did the same for student doctors and student nurses. The Impacted Areas program begun during the war to help school districts under pressure from a large influx of Federal employees' children provided several hundred million dollars each year to several thousand schools. There were also programs which provided free milk and subsidized school lunches. But the most important source of Federal aid was due to Sputnik. Congress in 1958 passed, at the Administration's urging, the National Defense Education Act. By the early 1960s the Federal government was providing aid to education in various ways at a cost of $3 billion a year, ten times the level of Federal assistance in 1945.

Technology also came to the aid of the schools. Teaching machines began to appear. These allowed children to learn at a pace which matched their abilities. More important, however, was television. It was a boon particularly to adult education. In the late 1950s, 500,000 willingly got up before 6 A.M. for lectures on mathematics, political science, chemistry, history, and so on, offered by *Continental Classroom*. New York University's *Sunrise Semester* began as a new type of correspondence course, with reading and writing assignments geared to televised lectures. Before long the formally enrolled were outnumbered by the merely enthralled. And a television course on classical literature turned long-neglected masterpieces such as *The Red and the Black* into unexpected best-sellers.

Closed-circuit TV proved invaluable as a teaching aid in medical schools, where it carried close-up views of operations in progress. It also proved its worth in drawing, zoology, and electrical engineering classes. Nearly 300 colleges and universities by the early 1960s had set up their own television stations. Beyond this there was what was termed educational television, but it was based on the larger community rather than the local college. Such stations in San Francisco, Boston, Chicago, Pittsburgh and Detroit, were run for love, not money. Viewers voluntarily contributed money; the staff worked on a shoestring. When WGBH's studio in Boston burned down, more than $1 million was soon given to the station to build a new studio. But the fond hope that educational television would bring enlightenment to the uneducated proved to be in vain. Educational television was more likely to provide stimulation and amusement for the already well-educated.

With the aid of Ford Foundation money television entered the public schools of fifteen cities in 1957. Four years later the Midwest Program on Airborne Television Instruction began transmitting programs from high-flying aircraft for six hours each school day to an area bounded by Detroit, Milwaukee, Louisville, and Cincinnati. Television held out the (not-always-fulfilled) promise of reducing the cost of instruction and possibly easing the postwar shortage of teachers.

To some extent the interest in televised instruction was a fad. So, too, was the post-Sputnik obsession with gifted children, variously defined as anything from the top 10 percent to the top one-tenth of 1 percent. But whether they were 1 in 10 or 1 in 1,000 they were considered too important a national asset to waste. Harvard's former president, James B. Conant, wanted to see intensive, intellectually demanding programs set up for them in the high schools. Admiral Hyman Rickover preferred instead that twenty-five "national" high schools be built and the little geniuses be assigned to them.

The television quiz shows had unearthed a dozen precocious youngsters who awed uneasy adults who could not remember just where Tierra del Fuego was located or had forgotten how to find the square root of 1,000. Robert Strom, a ten-year-old from St. Louis, had devastated the adult opposition on two shows and collected $224,000. But he may have been admired more for his sudden riches than his intelligence.

John Hersey's 1960 novel *The Child Buyer* both mocked and lamented the current excessive interest in the young and gifted. Barry Rudd, a child prodigy, resists attempts being made to sell him to United Lymphomilloid, a large corporation grown rich and powerful on defense contracts. The corporation is working on a secret project involving the nature of human intelligence. "I had a problem," Barry explains to a skeptical Senator Skypack. "My problem was that I didn't like being for sale." The Senator is shocked to his patriotic core. "You mean your problem is that you wanted to chicken out on the national defense. That's more like it," he retorts.

Education had become a passion. It was both the ladder of success and, for the millions enrolled in adult education courses, a stimulant. It was both the hope of the nation and the cause of despair. It had never been better; it had rarely been worse. More than anything else, however, it was in demand.

The baby boom of the 1940s flooded the schools in the 1950s. For William Attwood and his wife the results were dismaying: "Almost everywhere we went we found harried, underpaid teachers, bulging classrooms, and principals who frankly admitted that under present conditions a high school diploma meant little more than a certificate of attendance."

The crush reached down into the kindergartens. In 1940 fewer than 20 percent of five-year-olds were in kindergarten; by 1960 the figure was 55 percent, and rising.

Even before the baby boom hit the schools, they had been swamped with veterans. Although 2.3 million ex-servicemen had used the GI Bill to go to college, 3.4 million had used it to go back to high school or, in some cases, grade school.

A decade after the war ended the country was still short of classrooms. Up to 1 million students were deprived of full-time schooling as a result. There was also the shortage of teachers and the presence of several hundred thousand teachers who were still using emergency credentials granted during the war.

Despite what these shortages suggested, American communities were pouring money into their schools. Expenditures on education far exceeded increases in enrollments, rising from $2.34 billion in 1940 to nearly $14 billion in 1960. As a percentage share of the GNP the public schools took 3 percent in the 1950s, compared with 2 percent in the 1940s. There was virtually no increase in the number of public schools between 1940 and 1950. But in the 1950s their numbers rose from 25,000 to 36,000. Not since the turn of the century, when secondary education had been put within the reach of most children, had there been so much growth.

Within these 36,000 schools there was, Conant discovered when he set out to examine the public schools in the late 1950s, a remarkable variety. And the great divide in American education was class. It was seen at its most graphic in the differences between the suburban high schools and those in the central cities. In a suburban high school 70 to 90 percent of the graduates would go on to college. In such a school, moreover, there was constant pressure on the staff to raise their educational standards because middle-class parents wanted their children not only to go on to college but to go to the prestigious college. The suburban high school's criteria of success were: how many of our graduates go to college and, which college? At the inner-city high school twenty miles away the criteria of success were: How good is the football team and how good is the marching band? The difference also showed up in expenditures per pupil. At a high school in Evanston or Scarsdale they were likely to run close to $1,000, while at a high school on the South Side or in Harlem they were probably under $400.

Conant discovered another aspect of class difference: nothing was as rare as a truly comprehensive high school. A high school would be either nonvocational (in which case it was in a small town or a suburb) or vocational (downtown). In rural areas, on the other hand, public schools offered an education which was neither vocational or nonvocational. It was fragmentary.

The big-city vocational high school was most tellingly portrayed in Evan Hunter's best-selling novel, *The Blackboard Jungle*. "This is the garbage can of the educational system," an older teacher informs a newcomer. "Every vocational school in the city. You put them all together and you've got one big, fat, overflowing garbage can. And you want to know what our job is? Our job is to sit on the lid of the garbage can and see that none of the filth overflows into the streets. That's our job." He adds, not altogether cynically, that the vocational high school had been invented by the white middle class to keep adolescent riffraff occupied so that respectable white women—wives and daughters—might go about their business safely.

Hunter's unflattering view of these schools was borne out by events in some of them. Under the social pressures of the postwar even good schools could quickly go bad, as happened to P.S. 210, John Marshall Junior High School, in Brooklyn. Until 1950 it had a good reputation. By 1958 it was a dangerous place for adults and children alike. There were more than twenty arrests each week on school property for crimes extending to rape and murder. The principal, George Goldfarb, was twice brought before grand juries to give testimony about events at his school. The third time he received a subpoena he went up to the roof of his apartment building and jumped to his death.

As Evan Hunter's (autobiographical) hero found to his surprise, the students he was asked to teach knew that they were in a bad school; knew that they were the garbage consigned to this particular garbage can. And it was one of the unspoken purposes of all schools to teach adolescents their class roles.

At a station labelled "high school" there are several types of inspection and the main belt divides into smaller belts which diverge slightly from each other. From some of the belts the children, now become youths, are unceremoniously dumped down chutes into the outside world, while the other belts, labelled "college preparatory," "commercial," "vocational," toll steadily on. The young people are inspected not only for brains and learning ability, but also for skin color, pronunciation, cut of clothes, table manners, parental bank account. Strangely enough, they are not inspected for moral integrity, honesty, or other qualities which go under the name of "character."

Thus, W. Lloyd Warner. The chance of going to college depended principally on how much money a student's parents had. So, in fact, did his chance of finishing high school. There were substantial out-of-pocket costs amounting to several hundred dollars a year for any student who wanted to participate in several school activities, such as playing in the band or running on the track team. Adolescents also needed money to take part in social activities and be accepted by their peers.

The postwar high school was much closer to the community in which it was placed than its prewar predecessor had been, and it reflected that community's nature. In suburban communities and small towns the schools were open to continual pressure from middle-class parents, the most articulate, best-educated people in the community. They forced changes in the school curriculum, opening it up to the social sciences.

The curriculum was constantly being torn up by the roots to see how it was doing. But it remained in its essentials much as it had been for decades: geared not to the majority, who did not go on to college, but to the minority, who did. If anything, the postwar high schools outside the inner cities increasingly became prep schools. This was the great unresolved issue in secondary education, and much of the unrest in the public schools, among students, parents, and teachers, could be traced to it.

Even the vocational high schools had an identity crisis. The number of blue-collar jobs had virtually stabilized, yet the number of vocational schools grew from year to year. And as their fearsome reputations spread, their graduating students began to run into hostility from unions and employers, fearful that they might be recruiting adolescent cut throats.

Meanwhile, curriculum reform was being influenced by important developments in educational psychology, through the works of B.F. Skinner, Jerome Bruner, and Omar Khayyam Moore. Although they advanced ideas which were at times in conflict, they shared a strong, and characteristically American trait: they were all unblushing optimists.

In his most influential work, *The Process of Education*, Bruner asserted: "Any subject can be taught effectively in some intellectually honest form to any child at any stage of development." Among American teachers in the 1950s this one sentence became something of a rallying cry, an article of faith, and a philosophy of education.

Moore's experiments at Yale and Rutgers supported Bruner in that they proved that given the right environment, even small children could perform challenging mental tasks. Moore succeeded in teaching children whom standard tests showed to be of less than average ability to read and write as well as the average. He showed that under the guise of playing, children could, in fact, teach themselves; for example, by "playing" with a typewriter, they became increasingly literate and articulate.

Skinner worked directly in the "behaviorist" tradition dating from the work of John B. Watson at Johns Hopkins during World War I. Watson had tried to explain all human behavior by tracing it to physical, mechanical, and observable causes. By controlling the stimuli to which people are subjected, he maintained, their responses could be controlled. Watson's argument meant that for learning purposes all people were identical at birth. Those who believed in the uniqueness of the individual and the reality of inner promptings found this a deplorable proposition. Yet it was also a democratic one—with impressive antidemocratic potential.

Skinner beavered away along these lines for several decades in a Harvard basement with rats, pigeons, and boxes. The result was a body of work which, one skeptic admitted, was "of an intelligence virtually unparalleled in our time for vivacity, subtlety, strength and confidence to the point of pig-headedness."

Finding a teaching machine developed by the Navy in the 1920s, Skinner spent much of his life perfecting both the machine and the theory which justified it. A student who answered a quetion correctly was "rewarded" with an opportunity to answer the next question. The student kept pressing buttons until he or she came up with the right answer. The machine kept score of wrong guesses. It was claimed that the machine "reinforced" the student's knowledge, which had been acquired from the teacher or a textbook. But teaching itself was part of what the machine offered by presenting questions which were easy to answer and incorporating extra snippets of information in the questions themselves.

"The simple fact is," Skinner loftily declared, "that as a mere reinforcing mechanism, the teacher is out of date. This would be true even if a single teacher devoted all of her time to a single child. . . ." He forecast a time when teaching machines, simple in design and inexpensive to produce, would be in almost every classroom.

Simon Ramo, who was both a pioneering engineer and a multimillionaire businessman, also anticipated the age of the teaching machine, but operating in a somewhat different fashion (and with fewer pretensions), in a package involving film, slides, tapes, and television. He expected a new type of specialist to come into existence, the "teacher-engineer," who would carry the new technology into every school.

Although the new day heralded by Skinner and Ramo did not dawn as brilliantly as they expected, it made an impact. The typical classroom had changed very little since the 1850s. It contained desks, or chairs and tables, of heavy, dark wood, and nothing else except a map or a poster, and the teacher. In the late 1950s the industrial-technological revolution arrived, bringing projectors, tape recorders, TV sets, slide projectors, and teaching machines. Walls became movable. There were language laboratories with tape machines, microphones, and headsets. In a few years there would be computer terminals in some classrooms. And as the machinery poured in, the teachers became still more receptive to new ideas about the nature of teaching and the process of learning.

The climate was right for the adoption of the "Direct Method" of foreign language instruction, and hundreds of school districts tried it. This was the method by which millions of Western Europeans—notably the Scandinavians, the Dutch, and the Germans—learned to speak English fluently and almost without an accent. It eschewed memorization and emphasized constant practice in the spoken language. But it suffered the same fate as Progressive education a generation earlier: it was misunderstood and misapplied. Discredited, it was dropped. The best chance Americans had ever had to break a long tradition of complacent monolingualism was lost.

Other innovations, however, fared better. Team teaching, pioneered at the University of Chicago's Laboratory School, was avidly taken up. It offered an opportunity to alleviate the effects of the teacher shortage and in some subjects appeared to improve the quality of instruction. What group practice was to medicine, team teaching was to the schools.

The most radical innovation in teaching came in mathematics. There was almost unanimous agreement among parents, teachers, and school boards that something had to be done. A close observer, who had once been a teacher, remarked, "As one nears the question of instruction in mathematics, a striking change comes over the school terrain . . It is apparent that a great plague has struck this part of the world . . . this is the country of the dead—and the long dead, too."

A group of reform-minded school administrators established the School Mathematics Study, comprised mainly of eminent mathematicians. The result of nearly a decade of deliberation was the New Math, which began to enter the schools around 1960. The numbers stayed the same, but almost nothing else did. No longer did the little scholars add and subtract. Now they were busy "exchanging" and "regrouping." Parents were baffled. So were many teachers of the math. They did not find it easy in middle age to have to learn to think in terms of Cartesian products, strict inequalities, null sets, and so on. But high school students did not know any better. Whether in the end they actually learned any more from the new method than from the old is doubtful. Math by any other name was still for most students a brain-racking ordeal.

There was one set of number facts teachers swore by, even in *The Blackboard Jungle*: "He had a tool now, one tool. A magnificently powerful, overwhelmingly miraculous tool, a tool no one in all his years of preparation had ever thought to tell him about. . . . He now knew the average IQ of his students."

Teachers and school administrators loved IQ scores. For the most part it was stark naked scientism. A genuine Stanford-Binet test took approximately one hour, with a specially trained examiner dealing with one child at a time. Rare was the school that was willing to spend that kind of time and money. Yet there was a strong demand for IQ tests, so tests there were—second-rate, mass-produced, mass-administered, cheap. Costs were kept down by administering only one or two such tests in the course of twelve years, the fact that IQ is unstable and can change dramatically in children in the space of two years being ignored. Despite the poor reliability of most IQ tests, the results were treated as the Holy Writ of secondary education. And the correlation between IQ scores and social class was, in some schools, nearly perfect for the entire student body.

Testing of all kinds made rapid advances as a consequence of the doubling in a decade of college admissions. Before the war scholastic aptitude tests had played only a minor role in admission to the better colleges. In the early 1940s there were three applicants for every two places at Ivy League colleges. But by the late 1950s there were four or five applicants for every place. And most of these had done very well in high school or prep school. One effect of the reliance on aptitude tests was that graduates of the public schools took half the places available, compared with only a third prior to 1945.

By the mid-1950s the number of College Entrance Examination Board SATs administered each year was twenty times the numbered administered in the early 1940s. Average scores rose steadily, but not spectacularly—except at the elite colleges. At Harvard, for example, the freshman class in 1959 had a median mathematics SAT score of 691. Only three years earlier the median had been below 600. Students were evidently becoming more accomplished at taking standardized tests, and those who did well at them had hit on the straight , short path to the Ivy League.

John Gardner, the head of a great educational foundation, regarded it all with a sardonic eye. "Geniuses used to be rare. Today, thanks to popular interpretation of test scores, every elementary or secondary school has its quota."

Over and above everything else, the high school diploma became the minimal educational goal that was considered respectable, whereas a generation earlier it had been a prize sought by the minority. It had become the passport to a white-collar job, if a modest one. Not to have one was to carry a stigma, even if you were famous and adored. To Marilyn Monroe, despite her success, it seemed shameful not to have a high school diploma. It is doubtful that before 1945 anyone cared *that* much about not having one.

The most obvious feature of American higher education in the postwar was its size. The number of college students per 1,000 people was greater than in any other country. Colleges and universities found that growth could be neither escaped nor delayed. They were in the position of fat people who go on diets and still gain weight.

The University of California, for instance, decided in the early 1950s that UCLA was growing too quickly to maintain its academic standards. By raising its admission requirements, it forced thousands of California high school graduates each year to apply elsewhere. Enrollment rose sharply at Long Beach State and San Diego State partly as a result. But they too had to raise their admission requirements to avoid being swamped. Enrollment in junior colleges throughout Southern California soared. At the end of the 1950s the University of California prepared to open two new campuses, at Riverside and Irvine. Even before they were opened, they were deluged with applications from the graduates of junior colleges. The wheel had come full circle.

Higher education was as much in demand in California as garbage pick-up and tap water. But the rest of the country did not lag far behind. The percentage of eighteen to twenty-one year-olds attending college rose from 15 percent in 1940 to 40 percent in 1960.

The most striking aspect of the boom in higher education was not in the colleges, however; it was in the graduate schools. There was an unprecedented demand for PhDs. In the 1930s some 2,500 to 3,000 PhDs were awarded each year. But by the late 1950s the figure topped 10,000 and was still rising strongly. Nor were the new PhDs being churned out by diploma mills. The majority came from highly esteemed institutions such as Harvard, Columbia, the University of California, and the University of Michigan. With the colleges groaning under the pressure of rising undergraduate enrollments no young man or woman with a freshly minted doctorate need worry about finding a job. Even with more than 10,000 new doctorates entering the market each year it was argued that this was not enough.

Rapid growth in the postwar enlivened the byways of higher education. Summer schools, known only on a modest scale before the war, attracted 1 million students a year by the mid-1950s. Similarly, junior colleges had been a fringe phenomenon before 1945. By 1955 dozens of them were opening every month. There were 500 already in operation, ranging from All Saints Episcopal Junior College in Mississippi, which had 19 students, to Los Angeles City College, which had 10,000. Two-year colleges were mainly to be found in the Midwest, South, and West. Uneasy at the implications of the term "Junior" they took to calling themselves "Community" colleges. In California, moreover, nearly 70 percent of their graduates, such as I, went on to gain a bachelor's degree.

There was higher education aplenty. But how good was it? Most people would probably have answered, "Not very." Conant tartly observed: "The mere holding of a bachelor's degree has almost no significance. . . . In the United States we have a hierarchy of institutions granting the first degree, and a tight conspiracy of silence as to the existence of such a hierarchy."

Jacques Barzun, teaching at Columbia College, was despairing at what he saw, and Columbia was one of the best colleges in the country. Each year he met hundreds of young men and women—energetic, lively, curious, sensitive, open and honest, but possessing "no knowledge that is precise and firm, no ability to do intellectual work with thoroughness and despatch . . . many of them cannot read accurately or write clearly, cannot do fractions or percentages without travail and doubt, cannot utter their thoughts with fluency and force. . . ." They had been encouraged to be creative without first learning the disciplines of the trained mind.

At the better colleges the 1950s saw a decided fondness instead for popular culture. "A knowledge of comic strips, jazz, baseball, Westerns and soap opera is occasionally *de rigueur* if one is to be up to date," noted David Riesman. He attributed it to "a kind of late love affair with the U.S., accompanied by a rejection of Europe." Perhaps it was only playfulness. Yet there seems a good chance that the students concerned were likely to have known very little about Europe and to have preferred Pogo to Proust.

Compared with their European counterparts, who were selected more rigorously, most American college students were in their first two years doing remedial work. Those two years were spent in catching up with the graduates of the lycèe, the Gymnasium, the sixth form. Admiral Hyman Rickover confessed to being baffled. "There is no valid reason," he insisted, "why our bright children should be forever forced to trail Europeans by two or three years."

The high schools took the blame or had it forced on them. Whitney Griswold, president of Yale, was moved to marvel at the transcript of one young applicant whose last two years of high school comprised two courses in English, two in choral singing, two in physical education, and one each in American history, typing, speech, journalism, personality problems, and marriage and the family. As the dean of a Midwestern university described it to a visitor, he was continually being asked to accept credits for impossible subjects—that is, he said wryly, for subjects which were "*in*-credible."

The wringing of withers extended all the way from the badly prepared freshmen to the PhD candidates. The central feature of the doctorate was the dissertation. This piece of original research was the presumed take off point for a career of scholarship. Yet more than 80 percent of those awarded the PhD never published anything again. The degree had become little more than the ticket to a job. Its chief educational value was that it provided an opportunity for the university to offer advanced instruction to the candidates, toiling over research which was hardly ever of a very high standard. And as everyone with experience of graduate school could testify there were Doctors of Philosophy who could not read, write, or do mathematics much above the level of the average high school graduate. Robert Hutchins remarked, "One of the most remarkable features of American society is that the difference between the 'educated' and the 'uneducated' is so slight."

In large part this did no more than reflect the wide variety in American education; it was not simply a lowering of standards. More did indeed mean worse. But as with food, it also meant better. Engineering, for example, was characterized by low standards in most state colleges and polytechnics. The first two years consisted of remedial work, chiefly in mathematics. Only the students who went on to graduate school could be assumed to possess more than a barely adequate degree of skill. Yet at such places as MIT, which set exacting entrance requirements, the standards were very high. And competition to get into the better colleges and universities was, in almost all fields, intense. Admissions officers had more applicants of every kind to choose from. There can be little doubt that there were more students of outstanding ability enrolled in college in 1959 than there had been in 1939. Trained intelligence, as expressed in the number of doctors, lawyers, scientists, academics, engineers, and architects, was being produced faster than the population was increasing. Those who could not get into Harvard or Yale or Princeton or who could not meet the standards for training in one of the learned professions could still work for a degree in something else, somewhere else.

Nor, after Sputnik, was any student with at least average ability denied the chance to go to college. Under the rubric of "National Defense" hundreds of millions of dollars of Federal money was funneled each year into fellowships and low-cost student loans. The colleges and universities and state legislatures were also moved to adopt the principle that no able and willing student should be kept out for mere want of money.

The sudden rush of riches, in both bodies and cash, did not, as was often assumed, invariably drag down standards. No doubt in some places and some subjects that was the result. But the percentage of students preparing for the learned professions remained at 6 to 8 percent. This was the same percentage of college-age youth enrolled at British and European universities, where the primary purpose of university education is professional training or general preparation for a career in government service.

American higher education itself was overwhelmingly devoted to vocational training. It was a fact the colleges and universities did not like to stress. They preferred to cultivate a more romantic idea about what they were doing. The vast majority of their students, however, were training for subprofessional white-collar careers, in teaching, business administration, journalism, and physical education. People who were uninterested in collecting a degree but were there to seek education were hard to find.*

Tenuous as the pursuit of learning may have been as the *raison d'etre* of American higher education, it was only in the postwar that the best American universities were finally accepted as being on a par with the best in Western Europe. Even Harvard at its tercentenary in 1936 did not enjoy a reputation comparable with that of Oxford, Paris, or Heidelberg. Twenty years later no one would have seriously contested its standing.

Meanwhile, a new cultural elite had come into existence. It was based on the more prestigious universities. It was, Daniel Bell remarked, a decidedly "liberal culture, receptive to ideas, critical in its outlook, and encouraging of (sometimes nostalgic for) dissent."

The nostalgia was doubtless partly drawn from fond memories of the 1930s, when radical ideas had flourished among the young; partly it was inspired by the conformity of the college campus of the 1950s. These days the most popular courses were not those which tended to take a critical stance toward society, such as economics and sociology, but those which emphasized the individual. At the University of Michigan the most popular course was in abnormal psychology; at Chicago it was "Culture and Personality." Harvard in 1946 had created the Department of Social Relations. Within two years it was the university's third largest department.

*I am the only person I know who did not bother to collect his or have them sent by mail.

There was a veritable boom in psychology. The armed forces had provided employment for thousands of psychologists and sociologists during the war. In the postwar period business was happy to hire them, to work in personnel, to administer psychological tests, to conduct motivation research . The number of PhDs in psychology doubled every five years between 1945 and 1960. It was the only social science to attract as many exceptionally bright students as the natural sciences.

This concern with the personal over the political was lamented by their professors, who had been students during the exciting days of the New Deal, the Popular Front, Spain. Yet it was a concern which was, in its own way, just as idealistic and probably less self-righteous. Instead of trying to save the world, they sought to know themselves.

Since the inception of universities in the Middle Ages, their function, in good times and bad, had been to create, preserve, and transmit knowledge. A university had succeeded in its obligations to society and culture to the extent that it managed to strike the right balance among these three. But after 1945 the flow of Federal riches upended the equation—first, by tilting the emphasis toward the research side, second, by making academic research concentrate largely on science and technology.

Up to 1945 the universities were becoming, decade by decade, centers of vocational training. But after 1945 not only did humane learning become a fringe activity, but it lost all chance of ever becoming anything else. Western intellectuals, whether literary or academic, had been obsessed since the 1920s less with truth and learning than with power.

That obsession with power became the obsession of the universities. Power over other men, power over nature, power over other nations— these were the concerns of the teaching and research of colleges and universities in the postwar. To that extent the continuity with the traditional, romantic ideal, with its emphasis on learning as the enrichment of the mind and the purification of the spirit, had been broken. Yet the new love was one which paid, and paid, and paid.

Government money was not forced on academics. It was pursued with an avidity which would have done credit to John D. Rockefeller. Getting the grant became at least as important as the subject of the research proposed. Accomplished grantsmen were treated deferentially by university administrators. "Almost any program of study and research that can be financed can be introduced in some American university," said Robert Hutchins in disgust.

The war had created, in the phrase of Clark Kerr, the president of the University of California, "the Federal grant university," a phrase echoing the land-grant college of nearly a century earlier. It was, he remarked, a revolution which had passed almost unnoticed. By 1960 $1.5 billion of Federal money went to the universities each year, an increase of 100-fold over 1940. Approximately half this largess was connected with research involving national defense.

Industries based on advanced technology snuggled up to the Federal grant university. Even before the Riverside and Irvine campuses had a single complete building to call their own, new industrial laboratories were sited near them. The AEC led the way by establishing five very big, very expensive national laboratories and locating them in carefully chosen regions so as to draw on the universities in each region for scientific talent.

By 1960 the link between national defense and higher education was such that any serious attempt to sever it was likely to impair the nation's security. And the universities accepted that on their own they could never have financed the equipment needed for large-scale scientific research.

In the first ten years after the war the government had provided more than $500 million for university laboratories. The result was the construction of hundreds of excellent research sites, each filled with the best equipment available.

Even during the 1930s there had been a atendency for scientific research to take precedence over all other academic activities. But this outpouring of Federal money settled the issue once for all.

The other major effect of Federal money was that it reinforced the attractiveness of the better universities. This was a perfect illustration of the Matthew Effect.* They got more of the gifted students and the outstanding academics than ever before. In turn those universities became still better at securing grants. The top twenty academic institutions receiving Federal money saw their share of the total rise from 32 percent in 1948 to 61 percent a decade later. Of the nearly 2,000 colleges and universities in the United States approximately 100 received 95 percent of all Federal money, whether for research, graduate fellowships, or grants for buildings and equipment. And even among the favored, some were far more favored than others. The University of California received more than $150 million a year, the University of Iowa $7 million.

By 1960 the Federal government each year was providing 10,000 fellowships and traineeships. More than 100,000 students took out Federally-financed loans. There were nearly 300,000 students entitled to GI Bill money, mainly from the Korean War. There were also 7,000 foreign students being educated on American campuses courtesy of the State Department.

Despite so much Federal money and the emphasis on science, there did not, in the end, appear to be any sizeable increase in the production of scientists. The long-term upward trend remained the same from the 1920s through the early 1960s. In terms of growth there was a more notable impact on the social sciences, which accounted for 20 percent of Federal money. The NDEA provided the fellowships which saw thousands of budding economists, psychologists, and anthropologists through to their PhDs.

There were other unexpected consequences of Federal money. The natural sciences had long taken a disproportionately large share of the

*The Matthew Effect derives from Matthew XIII, 12: "For whosoever hath, to him shall be given, and he shall have more in abundance . . ."

brightest students. But now Federally financed science fellowships creamed off the best graduate students in science into research projects. This left their less gifted contemporaries to take positions as teaching assistants. The same happened in other fields also—the better students got the fellowships; the rest got the teaching jobs. TAs tended to be the poor students, in both senses.

There were remarkably few instances of intellectual subornation, considering the amount of money the government provided. But they were not unknown, although very rarely did they come to light before the mid-1960s. MIT was one of the favored recipients of Federal grants, and in 1950 the CIA financed the establishment of the Center for International Studies there. Among the center's notable productions was a work purporting to be scholarly and objective, *The Dynamics of Soviet Society*, published in 1953. Its authors were Walt Rostow and other members of the center. Its thesis was that the Soviet Union was an expansionist, imperialistic power whose sole reason for existence was the conquest of the world. The book concluded that America's historic responsibility was the frustration of this ambition, whatever the risks. The CIA was so deeply involved in the production of this work that there were two versions, one of them classified. The principal theme and the stirring conclusion, however, were not kept secret.

Some academics found these developments deeply repellent. "At some of our major universities," said David Riesman, "the social sciences are as wrapped up in the defense effort as the physics and chemistry departments are: the atmosphere of Cold War of some leading departments, whose faculty have frequent contact with the CIA or the RAND Corporation or other like agencies, is quite different from that in a traditional Ivy League college."

Even scholars engaged in unclassified research had to submit to Federal security screening and to swear a loyalty oath if they wanted government money. Not a few failed to qualify or refused to submit to the swearing and screening.

However difficult to assess, the effects of Federal largess—which was usually administered in as benign, as mannerly, and as enlightened a fashion as was humanly possible—were pervasive. They involved the instruction of undergraduates, the caliber of the faculty, the atmosphere and nature of research, the availability of funds for research outside the sciences, and the prestige of the institution. It is impossible to conclude that the results were wholly good or wholly bad. But it was the case that in the end Federal money was tied to conceptions of the national interest which were at times extremely narrow. And to that extent the universities had failed to serve the real justification for their existence.

27

At the Back of Our Minds

The upsurge of education and prosperity set off a postwar pursuit of culture so ardent that culture hardly stood a chance. Appropriately, the most successful Broadway production of the 1950s concerned an ignorant flower girl who learned to pass herself off as a cultivated lady after a six months' crash course.

The number of concertgoers, museum visitors, readers of serious books, art-film devotees, dancers, singers, musicians, painters, opera lovers, sculptors, playgoers, poets, actors, and collectors rose faster after 1945 than did population or national income. And these new "culture consumers," an estimated one-sixth of the population by 1960, were markedly different from their prewar predecessors: they were much younger, and most were male.

In the postwar years Americans spent more money on tickets to plays, concerts, and the opera than they did on tickets to sporting events. The sale of musical instruments doubled between 1948 and 1957. Billions of dollars were poured into the arts by private patrons and government agencies. And for every prize offered, a score of eager hands reached out. As the number of grants, awards, commissions, and fellowships proliferated, the number of budding painters, musicians, writers, and sculptors in need of patronage seemed to grow even faster. America had democratized culture more than any society since Periclean Athens. There were millions of practitioners, tens of millions of consumers.

It began with children, and the first place in the sudden increase of output and consumption went to music. The number of children learning to play an instrument quintupled, from approximately 2 million at the end of the war to 10 million by the early 1960s. And during the 1950s the explosive popularity of rock 'n' roll inspired still more millions of young adults to take guitar in hand.

It was not only popular music which throve. While rock 'n' roll was on the rise, so was traditional music. The music of the seventeenth and eighteenth centuries was rediscovered. There was also a sudden interest in the atonal music of twentieth-century composers. Never was there so much music making. Besides the many thousands of amateur bands and amateur choirs, there were 1,000 symphony orchestras, ranging from the excellent to the execrable. These professional and semiprofessional orchestras performed before tens of millions each year. There were 250,000 professional musicians, but most found it impossible to earn a living from their art; while demand was great, it was not infinite. Despite the hardship and discouragement they faced, tens of thousands of young adults each year tried to begin musical careers.

For the player who was content to remain an amateur there was a new kind of recording, MMO—Music Minus One. One played the missing part oneself, accompanied by the rest of the ensemble, who were on the record.

The *Saturday Review of Literature*, for decades an important cultural force in American life, accepted the fact that its readers were as interested in music as in literature. In 1954 it changed its name to the *Saturday Review*.

Music was not simply available. Thanks to Muzak and the jukebox it was inescapable. Movies had music from opening credits to THE END. Sporting events began, ended, and were accompanied with marching rhythms and crashing chords.

On the stage the musical had achieved parity with the play as an entertainment, and surpassed it in popularity. Until the arrival of *Oklahoma!* in 1943 the American musical had usually been feeble and derivative. But *Oklahoma!* brought an infusion of vitality and exuberance to the musical stage through the introduction of dance. Throughout the postwar period *Oklahoma*'s format of athletic dancing combined with show-stopping song reigned supreme.

Before 1945 music departments were a rarity in American colleges. Academic deans were not easily persuaded that music was really one of the liberal arts. They tended to consider it not a branch of humane learning but an estimable craft, like carpentry. But by the 1950s the pressure on the colleges became irresistible, and within a decade hundreds of college music departments came into existence.

By the 1960s the colleges had become an important source of musical scholarship, the fount of new audiences, and an important venue for concerts and recitals. This merged with a larger development: the local college or university had become, in many a town, city, or state, the center of local cultural life. It provided the plays, concerts, lectures, poetry readings, and art exhibitions not otherwise available. Perhaps one reason why American communities were so willing to support higher education was the colleges' eagerness to share their cultural offerings with the community.

But the communities did not simply sit back. More than 100 towns and cities between 1948 and 1961 created arts councils to promote cultural activities. The councils provided patronage for scores of new orchestras and museums. These had for decades been the toys of a handful of rich local worthies. But in the postwar they began to find another, broader base in thousands of middle-class patrons and subscribers.

With the rise of the arts councils went a passion for building multipurpose arts centers. The first opened in St. Paul in 1954. It combined galleries and concert halls with museums and theaters. The arts center became an important feature of many of the urban redevelopment programs which cleared huge tracts of land in downtown areas.

The showcase of these centers was Lincoln Center in New York. In 1956 the New York Philharmonic was told that its lease on Carnegie Hall would not be renewed in 1958. The Metropolitan Opera was meanwhile complaining about its decaying home on Thirty-ninth Street. And the president of Fordham University was wondering out loud to Robert Moses whether the university would ever be able to afford a downtown campus. Moses pulled these separate concerns together and razed eighteen square blocks in mid-Manhattan to provide the Lincoln Center, plus a campus for Fordham, plus 4,400 luxury apartments, plus a new home for the American Red Cross. Lincoln Center cost nearly $200 million by the time it was finished. But by the time it was finished nearly every city in the country wanted such a center (scaled down) of its own.

The ardor for culture was, on the face of it, positive and inspiriting. Yet serious men expressed serious doubts. Culture was ubiquitous, but had it not been cut down to fit the average man, instead of raising him to a higher level of sensation and perception? Music written in passion had become aural wallpaper. Was this a love of music or a fear of silence? The language of Shakespeare was half-heard, a diversion at best, instead of being weighed and savored. Paintings were bought with an eye to how well they might complement the furniture. Sculpture was sold, and bought, as "a conversation piece" or to fill up the empty space near the untouched piano.

There was ample encouragement to consume culture as fun or background, not as an assertion of the human spirit. Cultural totems were flaunted as status symbols, like the pig's bladder of the Morris Men. As a consequence of being ubiquitous and accessible, culture seemed likely to dull, not sharpen, that inner sense to which it appealed.

The Great Books, which appeared from 1945 to 1952, were characteristic of this debased culturalism. The books themselves had been available, in most cases, for centuries. The fifty-four volumes of the Great Books offered 443 works by seventy-six famous authors, from Plato to William James. This enterprise in Philistine vulgarity had cost $2 million to launch; the money did not go to royalties (the authors were conveniently dead) but to the financing of *The Syntopicon* ("collection of topics"). *The Syntopicon* comprised the Great Ideas culled from the Great Books. All told, there were 102 Great Ideas, each of which was set out in a plodding essay penned by Mortimer J. Adler. Most of the works had not appeared originally in English. The Great Books offered them in translations which ranged from the adequate to the awful. But all the translations had one shining merit—they had cost next to nothing, being old and often out of touch with modern scholarship.

The money had gone to pay committees of academics for many hours of cerebration over *The Syntopicon*. The entire enterprise reeked of the hustle and the hype. Peddled like vacuum cleaners from door to door by salesmen on commission, it was a venture which had not so coincidentally enriched William Benson, a former advertising man since elevated to the U.S. Senate. The University of Chicago also had a heavy involvement, in the self-serving and profitable belief that it was elevating the minds of the masses.

For years to come, in hundreds of thousands of ordinary American homes the expensive set of Great Books sat silently gathering dust. The men who had written them would probably have been horrified. And the men of culture who had filleted, tidied up, and trimmed the great literature of the past provided a classic example of the distinction Max Weber had drawn between the men who live for ideas and those who live off them.

Another instance of confusing democratization of culture with debasement of cultural artifacts was the third edition, unabridged, of Webster's *New International Dictionary*. It appeared in 1961 to high anticipation. In the twenty-seven years since the second edition a profound change had occurred. Either educated people had stopped believing that language required precision in order to be most useful, or they preferred to keep that belief to themselves. In the second edition warnings such as *slang, incorrect*, and *illiterate* abounded. The third edition took the anything-goes approach. This, the editors decided, was closer to the spirit of language as a living, man-made creation. This, however, suggested in the work they produced not a new belief but the absence of any belief.

The only line the editors were prepared to draw was to omit one common word, "fuck." It was an omission probably made not for reasons of scholarship but with a high regard for sales. There was a $3.5 million investment to consider—even if language was "a living thing."

The English language was further menaced by the steady abandonment of clear, forceful, and elegant speech for the pomposities and false eloquence of jargon. Here, too, it was often the supposedly educated who were among the worst offenders. Lionel Trilling wrote, "A spectre haunts our culture—it is that people will eventually be unable to say, 'They fell in love and married,' let alone understand the language of *Romeo and Juliet,* but will as a matter of course say, 'Their libidinal impulses being reciprocal, they activated their individual erotic drives and integrated them within the same frame of reference.' "

The war had been a friend to art. With fewer things to spend their money on, people began buying pictures. With fewer entertainments available, they began visiting art galleries and exhibitions.

The Works Progress Administration was gone, but new patrons appeared. Pepsi-Cola began a competition which by the late 1940s was attracting the work of thousands of artists each year, in pursuit of prizes worth tens of thousands of dollars. Pepsi's contest was taken seriously: art museums offered space; art critics provided publicity. It spawned no geniuses. But the contest spread interest in art, and that nearly always turns out to be helpful to serious artists.

Art galleries opened in unprecedented profusion and actively sought artists whose works they could show. A new body of art critics arose, favorable to modern art. A new crop of art publications came into existence. In San Francisco a young Canadian, Douglas MacAgy, took control of the California School of Fine Arts and turned it into a bastion of abstract and nonrepresentational painting and sculpture. It was for a decade both the best and the best-known art school in the country.

The Museum of Modern Art in New York had entered the postwar in possession of what was probably the richest collection of modern painting and sculpture in the world. Until 1939, however, there was not a strong popular interest in modern art. But by the mid-1950s the demand for MOMA's circulating stock was intense. "Where no museum existed, women's clubs, libraries and other organizations were sending for the exhibits . . . small, isolated and relatively poor communities were going to the expense of bringing the most controversial art to their people."

Responding to strong foreign interest, the State Department in 1949 sent a collection of seventy-nine oils and thirty-eight watercolors by contemporary American artists on a world tour. Foreign audiences were usually impressed. But Congressmen at home maintained that the collection was little better than junk and that the paintings gave evidence of a Communist master plan "to control art in the United States." It would be another decade before the State Department risked sending another exhibition of American art abroad.

But while government patronage lagged, a new source of support developed—colleges and universities. They offered the artist the very mixed blessings of security. Art departments with a dozen to a score of teachers were not unusual. Ben Shahn described the new dispensation: "It's become a kind of super WPA, without a pauper's oath." To attract first-rate art teachers, the colleges began to drop the restrictions which had helped promote provincialism. In 1950, for example, Harvard lifted the ban which for 314 years had prevented its art students from sketching naked women. "The students requested permission to draw and paint nudes," reported the *New York Times*, "because they were tired of painting apples and landscapes."

Provincialism proved more resistant elsewhere. Although the art boom resulted in a remarkable increase in the number of pictures bought each year for the home, reproductions of Renoir, Rembrandt, and Van Gogh did not sell well. "I wish they did," said the executive at Sears, Roebuck in charge of buying pictures. "Our best seller is called 'Fiery Peaks.' It's a picture of the Cascade Mountains either at sunset or sunrise, you can't tell which, and the sky is bright orange." Sears's most popular artist went by the name of Huldah. The buyer explained, "She paints pictures of Parisian women with big black eyes and frilly things around their necks and we sell them in very fancy Edwardian frames." There was not a strong interest in abstracts, he commented. "Our experience shows that people like realism."

The artists themselves had moved since the war from the ersatz Parisian atmosphere of Greenwich Village and taken up residence along Tenth Street, in the area between Grace Church and St. Mark's-in-the-Bouwerie. They had their studios in a neighborhood of low brick buildings, which housed pawnshops, foreign-language clubs, cafeterias, liquor stores, poolrooms, small factories, and run-down warehouses. It was an area stolid in a poor, lower-class way. Yet this colorless, lifeless neighborhood, with nothing overtly artistic about it, became the artistic center of the United States and thereby the most important part of the planet for a working artist between 1945 and 1960. It was to this dreary stretch of urban ugliness that Jackson Pollock, Mark Rothko, Robert Motherwell, Clyfford Still, Willem De Kooning, Arshile Gorky, and most other important American painters gravitated. The only external sign which suggested that this was the artists' quarter of New York was the shimmering presence among the pawnshops and liquor stores of a dozen bright, modernistic little art galleries.

The artists in the studios nearby worked these days with a self-confidence American artists had never before enjoyed. The United States had become the center of the international art scene. American modernists had learned from European refugees during the war. When the refugees returned home in 1946 and 1947, their confidence in European culture was badly shaken. American art became dominant. But this was not entirely a victory on merit. Too often it was neither technically superb nor imaginatively brilliant. Even successful artists were likely to be weak at drawing and brushwork.

Yet American abstract art became increasingly independent and aggressive; it was no longer in thrall to European models and techniques. Abstract art carried everything before it. Its Parthenon was MOMA, whose director, Alfred H. Barr, Jr., articulated the credo of the new faith: "Since resemblance to nature is at best superfluous and at worst distracting it might as well be eliminated." There were nonabstract artists of considerable reputation still at work, such as Edward Hopper, Andrew Wyeth, and Jack Levine. But in the 1950s abstract art was so predominant as to be synonymous with "American art." Its most flourishing field was Abstract Expressionism, a term first used in Germany in 1919 but revived by *The New Yorker* in 1946 to describe what was happening up and down Tenth Street.

Although Abstract Expressionism became uniquely American, it was not entirely American. The leading teacher of the school was Hans Hofmann, a German who had arrived in the United States in 1934. He was already middle-aged, but a painter's painter. Abstract Expressionism was informed,moreover, by the ideas of the Surrealists, such as Fernand Léger and the poet André Breton, who spent the war years in the United States, and by the geometric style of the Dutch painter Piet Mondrian.

The central element in Abstract Expressionism was a new conception of space: that it was for the artist to create the space he needed to achieve his effects. The most important exponent of this approach was Arshile Gorky (who died, tragically, by his own hand in 1948 after most of his life's work was destroyed in a fire). "Every time he stretches canvas," Gorky maintained, "he [the artist] is drawing a new space." The other reason for Gorky's impact was, as a critic observed, that he was, "the first American to paint pictures that did not look like provincial adaptations of European styles."*

Most Abstract Expressionists had worked for the WPA. In painting

*This "American," however, happened to be an immigrant from Armenia.

murals, they had become accustomed to covering a large space. Now, with the ideological encouragement provided by Gorky's theories, they began to turn out canvases which were enormous by traditional standards. Their canvases also had a flat look about them. They tried to provide space, instead of trying to enclose it as paintings had done for centuries. On this flat expanse the paint became assertive and drew the viewer's attention to itself. Canvas and paint had become as important as design or subject matter. As a result, these paintings had a physical presence, a "feel" to them that was new.

Of course, to the artists themselves there was no such thing as Abstract Expressionism. Each artist saw himself as going his way. Styles varied widely, from Pollock to Motherwell, Rothko to De Kooning. And artists such as Pollock and De Kooning changed their style over the years.

Pollock was the most famous, and generally, but mistakenly, assumed to be the most accomplished, exemplar of Abstract Expressionism. Prematurely bald and highly strung, he was a tormented and energetic man who was able, through hard work, to pour his agonies and energy onto canvas. The paintings he executed between 1947 and 1953 are undeniable in their vigor and uniqueness. One series consisted of six canvases, each nine feet high and seventeen feet long, hardly the thing to hang on the living-room wall. Pollock would walk around the canvas, which lay on the floor, splashing house paint from a gallon can, casting it down from the top of a step-ladder, smearing it, dribbling it, anything but brushing it on. Pollock's "gesture painting" puzzled even his admirers, such as Peggy Guggenheim, who had given him his first one-man show back in 1942 and supported him for nearly a decade after. Yet his canvases had one characteristic which only the greatest artists have ever been able to capture— movement.

In 1953 he went back to using a brush, turned to painting human figures once again, began to drink himself to death, but was overtaken first by a fatal car crash in 1956.

De Kooning was by a clear margin the best painter of the group. After arriving in America at the age of twenty-four as a stowaway, he learned his craft in poverty and obscurity. Not until he was nearly fifty did De Kooning make his name. In 1953 he showed a sequence of seven paintings called "Woman." Several portrayed faces and torsos which were hideously distorted as if they had been ripped open to spill entrails and viscera onto the viewer. In others the woman appeared to be torturously held in bondage or to have been whipped and left bleeding. Throughout whatever vile ordeal had been visited on them these women grinned inanely; heedless of disfigurement and bondage, they were apparently attempting to offer their bodies for sex. The savagery of these seven paintings was not only intensely felt, but skillfully painted. The furor they aroused made De Kooning famous. By 1960 he had become the most admired painter in the United States. The lifelong rebel had rapidly become the grand old man.

While Pollock and De Kooning were carrying Abstract Expressionism forward at one extreme by putting gesture onto canvas, Mark Rothko and

Barnett Newman were experimenting with fields of color. And between these extremes, the one active, the other reflective, stood Clyfford Still, whose canvases were buried under thick layers of paint, up to an inch deep. The paint was then gouged or made to appear as if ravaged by fire. Still's paintings had a three-dimensional character; they were forceful and crude. A Still canvas looked less like something painted than attacked.

Rothko and Newman reduced painting to its simplest elements of space, line, and color. Rothko's canvases particularly had an air of austerity and purity. This was *art pour l'art*, and it made no concessions to the viewer's interests or expectations.

It appears in retrospect that success came quickly to Abstract Expressionists. But it did not appear so to the artists at the time. In 1951 eighteen of them picketed the Metropolitan Museum of Art and demanded that it take notice of their work. They organized their own exhibitions at a storefront on East Ninth Street.

The combination of abstraction and geometry which characterized the new style lent itself particularly to sculpture, notably to the work of Alexander Calder. His fluid mobiles—abstract designs cut from metal and hung on wires to move with the breeze—brought American sculpture to the international eminence which Pollock's canvases had gained for American painting. Calder's work, moreover, won for ordinary metals an equal place with richer ores and polished stone. Calder and his contemporaries hardly ever worked with marble or gold or silver; they were happier with iron and steel. Welded metal sculpture had been essayed in the 1930s. But not until the 1950s and the creations of David Smith was it esteemed. He cannibalized old machinery in search of raw materials. His works were abstract, and they were huge. Like the best of Pollock's paintings, the best of Smith's sculpture conveyed a sense of restless energy and movement. And within welded metal sculpture there was a fascination not with beauty or balance but with power, cleverness, and organization. In this they evoked the spirit of the age.

The artists who continued to work in the realist tradition lacked the glamor of the abstract painters but had a wider appeal. Edward Hopper continued to pursue his own bleak vision, uninfluenced by anyone. His paintings conveyed the remoteness and the loneliness of American life as seen in its plain, functional streets and houses. His was a deceptively simple craft of remarkable honesty and intensity within a narrow range of technical skills and an even narrower vision.

The most accomplished of the realists was Andrew Wyeth. Like Hopper's, his best work conveyed a sense of loneliness within a setting which offered no comfort, no illusions, no alternative. There was great beauty in his paintings, however, arising from his extraordinary skill. There was no joy in a Wyeth painting, but a sense of mastery so complete that it could quicken the pulse.

The Social Realist school of art popular in the 1930s had virtually died out. But painting as social criticism lived on in the work of Jack Levine. He had an infallible eye for the absurd and pompous. His "Welcome

Home," showing a returning general gorging himself at a banquet table while surrounded by sleek, rubicund tycoons of ineffable crassness, evoked cries of patriotic rage when it was included in an exhibition of contemporary American paintings sent to the Soviet Union in 1959.

By 1960 the impetus which had sustained Abstract Expressionism since the war had begun to die out. It was no longer daring or novel. The works of Pollock were little more than a decade old, yet they opened up no new directions. They were based partly on European ideas but mainly on American gusto. The ideas Abstract Expressionism represented had been taken as far as they could go. The next generation of American artists found itself having to start almost from scratch.

The new art shunned gesture. It was detached, sardonic, "cool." It fixed on identifiable objects, but of the most banal variety—cigar boxes, flags, targets, Coca-Cola bottles. In the work of Robert Rauschenberg and Jasper Johns, who were pioneers in this new style which derived from comic books and collage, the line between painting and sculpture was blurred. The canvas shared its space with other objects—plaster heads, stuffed animals, rusting junk. No one knew quite what to make of it, not even the art critics. For want of any more expressive name the new style was termed Pop Art, not on account of its popularity (which took a long time to develop) but on account of its adoption of the artifacts of popular culture.

Pop Art was a revolt against Abstract Expressionism and a return to American provincialism. It was anonymous and explicit and, sometimes, amusing; Abstract Expressionism had been impersonal, obscure, and serious. The new style was derided in some quarters as a new Ashcan School, thanks to its love of junk, physical and metaphorical. Yet its practitioners attracted intense attention, which was transformed into money, lots of it. To a large degree their sudden riches were inevitable. Pop Art exploited both modernism and provincialism at the same time.

Postwar prosperity and the obsession with status combined in the art boom to create an astonishing demand for obscure, outsize, often feeble works of art, provided they came from a famous hand, living or dead. Tickets to major auctions were as coveted as tickets to the heavyweight championship. At a Parke-Bernet auction in the winter of 1958, for example, 5,000 people were turned away, and of the 2,000 lucky ticket holders half had to follow the auction via closed-circuit TV in an adjoining room. The hunger to buy a little piece of fame became so indiscriminate and mindless that even vandalism paid: a New York art dealer in 1959 bought a Renoir canvas for $28,500, cut it into ten pieces, and sold them for $5,000 each.

When Peggy Guggenheim returned to the United States after twelve years abroad, she was astonished and dismayed by what she found. She had spent much of her life and her fortune on the patronage of American modern art. But art had become one vast business of buying and selling. Few people who bought paintings seemed to care about them. Art was bought for reasons of snobbishness or to avoid taxation or in the hope of making a profit on resale. "Prices are unheard of. People only buy what is the most expensive, having no faith in anything else. Some merely buy for investment, placing pictures in storage without ever seeing them."

When the Metropolitan Museum paid more than $2 million for Rembrandt's "Aristotle Contemplating the Bust of Homer," Louis Kronenberger was moved to reflect on the crowds who flocked to view it: "I watched them and their 'Ahs' were chiefly for the price and not the picture: they stood in vulgar awe as before a jeweller's window ablaze with huge diamonds."

The success of American art did not, in the end, appear to have transformed interest in art into a deeper appreciation of the values art represented. Nor did it appear to have produced a genius. There was nothing inherently wrong with commercial success or popular appeal. Great painters from Rubens to Picasso have enjoyed both. But there was too little that served the human spirit in even the best postwar art. Humanity itself was held in low regard. Abstract art was built on theories of art rather than on beliefs concerning life and death. Energy and movement were prized for themselves, but there was no sense of purpose, no sense of direction.

For a European architect at midcentury an American Grand Tour had become an essential part of his education. Superficially, at least, high artistic endeavor seemed inevitable in American buildings; there was both overflowing prosperity and an openness to new ideas. And of the four most important architects practicing between the end of the war and the 1960s three—Ludwig Miës van der Rohe, Frank Lloyd Wright, and Walter Gropius—lived and worked in the United States. The fourth, Le Corbusier, came to the United States on two occasions.

There was one point on which these four masters agreed: that the machine dominated the age. Their responses to this perception, however, were very different. Wright recoiled from it and developed a cult of individualism. Miës's buildings bore witness to the machine by employing machine-made parts of remarkable refinement and purity of line. Like Wright, Le Corbusier was repelled and resorted to a calculated primitivism. Gropius embraced the machine's characteristics of anonymity and interdependence; he made architecture a collective activity.

The most influential of the four was Miës. He had arrived in the United States from Germany in 1938, at a time when Americans were ready for a major shift in architectural styles. The boom in construction during the 1920s had left the country with thousands of buildings, public and private, which were big, dark, expensive and overornamented. Miës and Gropius brought to American shores the International Style developed in Germany between 1910 and 1930. It was a style whose obiter dicta were: "Less is more" and "Form follows function." It derived its force from an attachment to bright surfaces, straight lines, and a fascination with modern technology.

It was only in the United States, the center of advanced technology at midcentury, that such a style could be carried to its limits. In a sense, however, the wheel of modern architectural aesthetics had come full circle. Gropius, practicing at the Bauhaus during the First World War, had been inspired by photographs of American factories and grain elevators, while Le Corbusier's brainchild of the 1920s, Radiant City, was frankly based on that Chicago innovation, the skyscraper.

The International Style, as developed in Europe between the wars, was comparatively modest in scale. But in 1941 Sigfried Giedion's seminal *Space, Time, and Architecture* appeared in print. Giedion was the most influential critic of architecture of his time. He argued that American architecture needed to develop a monumental style appropriate to the country's size, wealth, and power but based on modern ideas of space and light. American light is different from the dazzling light of the Mediterranean and the constantly changing light of Northern Europe. From 1945 American architects followed Giedion's ideas, and no one did more to realize them than Miës.

Appropriately, his most important early commissions were executed in and around Chicago. He designed an entire campus for the Illinois Institute of Technology, built between 1942 and 1952. It had the look and the feel of a factory. It was laid out on a grid pattern. Its shapes were taken from the basic figures in geometry. It was austere, mathematical, shining. As an example of rational planning according to the strictest principles it was flawless. Yet the result was cold and remote. It appealed to the mind, not to the emotions. But to many a young architect Miës's work was a welcome alternative to the anarchy which had prevailed in architecture for the past century. It seemed to offer an antidote to the personal expressionism which, in most instances, had nothing much to say.

While still a young man, Miës hit on an idea which had to wait for thirty years before he could give it concrete expression: that the external beauty of a building did not arise from the balancing of light and shade but from the play of reflections over its surface. This was to prove a doctrine which, unlike the ideas advanced by individualists such as Wright and Le Corbusier, other architects could build on. The first mature realization of the Miësian ideal was 860 Lake Shore Drive in Chicago. This comprised two identical twenty-six-story apartment buildings finished in 1951. They appeared to be rectangular glass boxes made from thousands of identical windows held in a black steel frame. To ensure that the uniformity—that is, the purity—of his creation would not be ruined by the individualistic impulses of the apartment tenants, their leases banned venetian blinds and stipulated that their own curtains could be hung only on the inside of the gray curtains already installed. The result was a pair of buildings resembling two enormous sets of mirrors, enlivened by reflections of the ever changing sky. The result was the most stunning architectural effect in a generation.

The other hallmark of the Miësian style was the structural steel frame. Lighter and more delicate than reinforced concrete, it lent itself to extensive prefabrication. And although prefabrication was not very successful in domestic architecture, it became an essential element in the apartment and office blocks built from the late 1940s onward. Aluminum, moreover, steadily supplanted steel.

The Miësian glass-curtain wall became the dominant architectural motif of the age. It set the character of the UN Secretariat, designed by a committee of architects headed by Wallace K. Harrison. It set the style of Lever House, built in New York in 1952 to a design by Gordon Bunshaft of Skidmore, Owings, and Merrill. Lever House was popular with both architects and public. It influenced office building architecture for a decade. But the Lever House idea was rarely copied in full because at its base was a garden, for the enjoyment of all; it was not a building designed to wring the last measure of economic advantage from the space it occupied. In 1958 the Miësian ideal was carried a step further by the master and his protégé, Philip Johnson, in their design of the Seagram Building in New York. Like Lever House, the Seagram Building gave away some of its space, to show off the structure to its best advantage. The ideas it embodied were admired and copied, but usually in a penny-pinching, compromised way.

Some of the prettiest and most gracious designs to issue from Miës and his admirers were for houses. Using brick, local stone, and wood, working on a modest scale, they built houses for themselves and their friends which were among the most beautiful creations of American architecture of the twentieth century, such as Philip Johnson's house in New Canaan, Connecticut, the Farnsworth House designed by Miës in Plano, Illinois, and the house owned by the architect Marcel Breuer, also in New Canaan.

But Americanized International Style was, by 1961, discredited. As pioneering work often is, it was aped rather than followed. Cheap-jack attempts at the glass-curtain wall could be seen scattered throughout the business districts of the suburbs, reflecting nothing but caution. Domestic suburban architecture was full of straight lines which led nowhere and, instead of being rational, made no sense whatever.

Hardly anyone by the 1960s liked modern architecture. Yet our buildings reflect what is at the back of our minds in regard to the space around us. This bastardized, compromised architecture caught only too well the craving for greatness compromised by mere bigness; the desire for order, with a resistance to discipline. And brought face to face with the result, many people disliked it intensely. One observer remarked, "I would not be surprised if modern architecture is aggravating the problem [of mental illness]."

The fault was often not the architects'. In many modern buildings the architect had less to say about the final design than the engineers, the contractors, and the mortgagees. But the architects had not helped matters by abandoning the largest single sector in construction, family homes.

Local government also did what it could, usually through its zoning practices. Taxation was another useful device for penalizing beauty. The

Seagram Building was one of the most handsome structures raised in New York between 1945 and 1961. It was not a high-rise, high-rent building like the ugly solid office buildings surrounding it. The city tax assessors ruled that Seagram was being unfair. Rental income was the usual basis of tax assessments. But Seagram did not generate as much rental income as it might have done had the company taken the proper grasping attitude. The assessors chose to tax the building according to its replacement value. Seagram each year paid an extra $400,000 in taxes as the price of beauty.

But the most important contribution to ugliness made by public bodies was in housing. Peter Cooper Village, built in New York shortly after the war, for example, embraced every possible mistake. Placed on seventy-five acres of land near the East River, between fourteenth and twentieth streets, it comprised a dull, mechanical layout of eighteen tower blocks. These housed 24,000 people in 9,000 apartments. Peter Cooper was intended to be a community. But it had no shops or schools—that is, the natural foci for encounters between neighbors. With a population density of 350 people a square acre it managed to be utterly impersonal. There was no cultural life to speak of; even at the best of times its park and ten playgrounds were joyless and uninviting. Yet despite its dreariness, and thanks to the importance of New York and because America was in these years the center of architectural innovation, Peter Cooper Village, a horrible example if ever there was one, was copied, not only across the United States but throughout the world.

While modernism came to be associated with ugliness in much contemporary architecture, the products of industrial design, where personal taste played an essential part, filled American homes with elegant objects. Yet because these were often useful and prosaic, such as the tulip glass or the subtly shaded carpet, they were taken for granted. A pretentious office building excited more notice than a beautiful table. A garish piece of junk sculpture such as the 1957 Chrysler Imperial awoke sentiments of pride in its owner, while a well-designed mixer, lamp, or settee would receive only passing attention. An industrial designer spelled out the law: "Form follows sales."

Some Americans began to become increasingly aware of, and concerned with, such matters. Around 1960 some of the better newspapers set out to educate people by offering specialized reporting on architecture, urban planning, and environmental issues. George McClure of the *St. Louis Post-Dispatch*, Allan Temko of the *San Francisco Chronicle*, and Ada Louise Huxtable of the *New York Times* were notable for writing what amounted to columns of criticism on physical change. At times much of what they wrote read like art or drama criticism; at other times, like social history.

They articulated much of the reaction against the bastardized International Style which proliferated throughout the 1950s. It was a reaction which brought some notable conversions. Eero Saarinen, whose design of the General Motors Design Center outside Detroit had been hailed as one of the architectural glories of the 1950s, ostentatiously turned his back on his earlier work. In the six years before his death Saarinen worked energetically to bring back flowing forms—in the Ingalls Hockey Rink at Yale, in Dulles Airport outside Washington, in the TWA Terminal at Idlewild, and in the "Gateway to the East" arch to be set soaring alongside the Mississippi at St. Louis.

A young Nisei architect practicing in Detroit, Minoru Yamasaki, was carried by the tide of reaction to international fame. In the Reynolds Metal Building, constructed in 1958, and in the Community Center at Wayne State University three years later, he introduced overhanging upper stories, whimsical exterior decoration, screens, diamond shapes, triangles, arches, and columns attached to the upper floor but not reaching to the ground. (This last was the one nonutilitarian feature Miës included in 860 Lake Shore Drive). Yamasaki's first big commission, for the St. Louis Airport terminal, featured three intersecting barrel vaults of concrete.

Concrete itself, smooth-surfaced for more than a decade, was increasingly shaped to produce coarse or variant textures. Aluminum, instead of forming smooth, shimmering sheets, was, as at Alcoa's new Pittsburgh headquarters, stamped to create glittering multifaceted facades.

The late 1950s also saw the sudden popularity of West Coast architects who for more than a decade had been designing individualistic houses and other small buildings in a line of descent from Spanish colonial styles. Their buildings were in harmony with their settings, were picturesque, yet balanced, and made loving use of natural materials. Yet California's architecture had matured before it became fashionable; it could not lead American architecture out of its impasse and was too closely suited to the California climate and terrain to be exported to Cleveland or Boston.

Now, in his last years, the greatest American architect was rediscovered, for the third or fourth time. Long famous, he suddenly became popular. With straight-edged, cold, aloof buildings going up Frank Lloyd Wright's softer, warmer-looking structures were finally seen for the humane and generous creations they were. But Wright no longer had anything much to say. If anything, his repeated claims that his designs were "organic" had become tiresome, and there was a quirky element to his latest work that was hard to take seriously. His design for the Solomon Guggenheim Museum of Non-Objective Art (a title so ponderous it sounds like a comic novelist's parody) discomfited even his staunchest admirers. It appeared less a museum than a cenotaph built to memorialize the creative genius of Frank Lloyd Wright. The paintings on the walls sloped away from the viewer. The construction, like much postwar building work, was slipshod. Designed in the shape of a corkscrew or spinning top and made of reinforced concrete, it would, the architect liked to boast with a straight face, survive a nuclear attack. It would bounce like a spring, he maintained, but would not collapse.

Some of the most venturesome architecture in the country began to appear on college campuses. The Air Force Academy at Colorado Springs, designed by Skidmore, Owings, and Merrill, was a triumph of Miësianism. MIT and Yale, by contrast, put out the welcome mat for architects looking to break with the formalism of International Style.

Churches resisted modern architecture for as long as they were able.

Religion is largely an emotional matter, and straight lines and cold surfaces tend to chill faith in anything except mathematics. But by the late 1950s, with the emergence of flowing shapes and rough textures, the churches were able to accept modern architecture. They soon found that they liked it. Wallace K. Harrison's design for the First Presbyterian Church in Stamford, Connecticut, finished in 1958, was a far cry from the UN Secretariat. The church was shaped like a fish (if a very stylized fish). Its surfaces were mainly old wood and stained glass. As light streamed in through the glass, the inside of the building seemed to glow with color and life. Yet there was also a note of restraint and nobility to the clear and simple lines of the structure. It was a building that refuted doubts that modern architects could design churches which would add to the powers of faith.

There was a similar development in the schools. Their traditional architecture had been dominated by squares and rectangles. But in the 1950s, inspired largely by the school architecture of California, the old order was banished. Much of what was best in postwar architecture was to be found in the new schools, which had an invigorating sense of light, space, and freedom. Imagination was indulged, producing domes, shells, hyperbolic parabolas, and curvilinear walls.

The accepted school design of 1960 was a one- or two-story structure, based on a finger plan, with landscaped courts, plazas, patios, or gardens filling the space between the various units. The massive heap of a school, three or four stories high, dark, cramped, and stolid, the dominant design for more than a century, was stone dead. A school was now expected to be a place of light, space, and bright colors. The modern school was also a triumph of modern industrial design, for it was safer, with more resistance to fire and fewer stairs, than its predecessor. It was cleaner and healthier without being dull. It is probable that it was more useful as a building and much happier as a place of learning.

Modernism finally reached even the most conservative institutions, the banks. An odd reversal had occurred along the way. Architects had become so interested in the extra-aesthetic questions of design that they talked less of beauty than economy, while supposedly hardheaded executives were often as entranced by prestige as by profits. They willingly spent millions to acquire a building of striking originality or charm, as Seagram and Lever had done or as Johnson's Wax did when it commissioned Wright for its headquarters in Racine, Wisconsin. And the banks were eager to shed the traditional, forbidding image which clung to them. They turned to the architects for help. In the new banks everything was (or was made to appear) up front. Bars, cages, heavy doors were banished—or at least out of sight. New bank exteriors had lots of glass and few metal shutters. Facades looked whimsical or fragile, instead of forbidding and austere.

The most lasting and important result of the architecture of the postwar was that it brought light and space into American buildings. And whatever name was given to it, the current style was the architecture of the age of technology, in both appearance and construction. The key to modern designs was tension; it was "designed into the structural members which make modern buildings possible." The glass-curtain wall was feasible only when the walls no longer bore the major load of a building's weight. A large glass window in a Gothic cathedral had required massive buttresses and walls to support it. It was because the walls carried so much weight that pre-twentieth-century buildings were dangerous once they topped twelve stories. But gradually there appeared the elements that made possible an architecture based on metal in tension: the I and H beams; reinforced concrete; plate girders; skeleton frames; a variety of metal trusses; suspension cables.

The tension these innovations created was close to the surface, yet the result was to make the surface light and more varied than ever. Here was a revolution in construction, and it was almost inevitable that the possibilities it opened up would be more fully and more rapidly exploited in the United States than anywhere else. Because although the new structures were based on metal in tension, the nineteenth-century American innovation the balloon-frame house had employed exactly the same principles, but using wood instead of metal.

Structures based on tension rely on the balancing forces within themselves. This is exactly how human beings are made. What holds our bodies together is the constant interplay between muscle and bone. We are able to move because of the elastic tension between tendons and sinews. An architecture based on the interactions of opposing forces is more alive and, in a sense, closer to nature than the architecture of the past.

Paradoxically, this may be the principal reason why so much of the new architecture was so unattractive—it was too new. Not enough time had passed for architects, government, and people to know how to make the best use of it.

The Word enjoyed so great a boom that employment in "printing, publishing, and allied industries" rose by 50 percent between 1946 and 1960, to reach nearly 1 million. The most obvious manifestation of this growth was the spread of the paperback.

Launched in the American market in 1939 by Pocket Books, paperbacks did well during the war and phenomenally well thereafter. The emergence of the "quality" paperback in the 1950s added respectability to popularity. By 1960 paperbacks had been thoroughly democratized; they offered something for everyone. And by this time nearly ten paperbacks were being sold for every hard-cover adult trade book.

Paperbacks accounted for the gigantic sales of best sellers. The best-selling novel of the postwar, *Peyton Place*, sold 10 million copies—95 percent in paperback. The paperback tapped an enormous market for mystery fiction; this enabled Mickey Spillane to rack up multimillion-copy sales on a series of books ideal for reading while moving the lips. But more popular still was Erle Stanley Gardner. Of his prodigious output ninety-one works sold more than 1 million copies apiece. Mysteries were the most popular form of reading matter, apart from newspapers. Forty percent of American adults claimed to read them regularly, almost the same percentage that claimed to go to church regularly.

The paperback also found a large new market for serious writers such as William Faulkner and James T. Farrell. Both were more or less rediscovered in the postwar, thanks to paperback editions. In 1945 Faulkner was the author of seventeen books, every one of which was out of print.

Other developments helped transform publishing. While Book-of-the-Month Club membership peaked in 1947 at 920,000 and thereafter declined, there was a rapid expansion of book clubs. Every kind of interest was catered for. Publishers brought out hundreds of made books, or nonbooks, each year, cobbled together by editors, as part of a series, rather than the work of a single author. There was also the emergence of the coffee-table book, a status symbol encountered with increasing frequency in middle-class homes, as weighty and as subtle as a brick.

In the first postwar decade publishers brought out fewer new titles each year than in the prewar years. But sales were higher. The book business grew from $500 million in 1952 to $1.2 billion in 1961, while the prices of books rose hardly at all. Nonfiction steadily supplanted fiction, causing alarm for a time in a score of publishing houses which had for decades buttered their bread with the income from novels. It was not that novels invariably sold badly these days, but they sold very well or not at all. And the best-selling novels were often so dull that they probably chilled interest in the genre. There was, moreover, a fresh appetite for facts. By the late 1950s the nonfiction best-sellers each year outsold the fiction best-sellers by a two to one margin. Cookbooks, Bibles, gardening manuals, and dictionaries now provided the butter, and books for juveniles were developing into an important source of income. Meanwhile, religious books, which had provided an average of four major best-sellers in each year up to 1955, had slid back so far that in 1960 they provided only one.

By this time publishing had lost many of its traditional, cottage-industry characteristics, and the number of titles published annually had begun to rise dramatically. The proliferation of titles threatened to make it virtually impossible even for the discerning reader to find the good when it was so crowded by the indifferent. Yet the stature of American books had risen. The old taunt "Who ever reads an *American* book?" had lost its sting. One-tenth of the output of American books went for export, and for scholarly publishers, such as Princeton University Press, up to a quarter of their output each year went abroad.

Perhaps the most disappointing feature of postwar publishing was the poor state of fiction. At the end of the war there had been a sense of high anticipation among the people working in art and literature that a literary flowering was at hand, that the decade following this war would be as fruitful as the 1920s had been. But as early as 1950 that illusion had been shattered. It had not survived the housing shortage, which made even cold-water flats hard to find; it had not survived the spiritual vacuum of the Cold War; but more deadly still was the rapid increase in opportunities to make a comfortable living without doing serious work. "A writer isn't a writer anymore," complained one participant-observer, "he's a *Time* writer, a *New Yorker* writer, a Hollywood writer, a television writer. . . . The employment policy nowadays, I am informed, is to get them young, preferably before 30, so that you can build them quicker and tighter into the institution. Sound corporate policy."

While literature was falling into desuetude, literary criticism flourished. By the mid-1950s literary critics enjoyed more power and status than practicing novelists and poets. But, remarked a visiting Frenchman, the standard of American literary criticism was exceptionally high. Its practitioners were steeped in both American and European literature; their range was far wider than that of their European counterparts, who were likely to be familiar only with the works produced by their countrymen.

American literary life also became in the postwar largely a Jewish affair. Jewish writers and critics arrived in such numbers that they dominated the foreground of American literature. At least in New York literary life became Jewish for all practical purposes. According to another participant-observer, Seymour Krim, it consisted in large part of self-mutilation and mutual destruction. Jewish literati were tormented by an awareness that the literary tradition to which they were attempting to make a contribution was not theirs and never could be. And the Gentile literati seemed to be no better off; they felt like epigoni compared with the giants of the generation preceding them—Hemingway, Faulkner, Fitzgerald. The giants seemed to be standing on *their* shoulders, instead of the other way round.

Postwar writers typically showed themselves to be both arrogant and insecure, traits common to bright adolescents. There was a strong sense of competition with both the quick and the dead. But the chief problem they confronted was: what had they to say? And the answer was: not much. Which they knew only too well. That awareness made their boasts shrill, their lamentations unmoving. Life on the literary magazines, such as *Dissent, Partisan Review*, the *Kenyon Review*, was hardly the path to high achievement. Yet such toeholds on the literary life were clung to in frenzy and savagely defended. And always there was the talk. Too many aspirants to literary immortality were, literally, wasting their energies in bars, at dinner tables, and on little magazines, where they worried at other men's work instead of getting on with their own. Rather than learn to become artists, they chose to pretend they were geniuses.

The glory of American literature became less and less the novel, which became overblown and self-indulgent, than the short story. Working within the discipline of an accepted form, modern American writers performed brilliantly, and they carried it forward as an art, albeit a minor one.

The literary scene was afflicted by the dullness which seemed to seep in everywhere. There were bitter disagreements, and hardly any good scraps. But in January 1958 Dwight Macdonald provided one. That month's *Commentary* carried his twelve-page review of James Gould Cozzens's turgid melodrama *By Love Possessed*. Cozzens had been practicing his craft, to good reviews, for three decades. In 1948 his novel *Guard of Honor* had won the Pulitzer Prize. For some reason inexplicable except as chauvinistic puffery *By Love Possessed* was hailed as a masterpiece. Serious men such as John Fischer of *Harper's* thought that it ought to net Cozzens the Nobel Prize for Literature. As Macdonald demonstrated, to a thunderous chorus of protest, it was a work pretentious in style, confused in ideas, and weak in characterization. It was built on sand, most of which seemed to have been cast into readers' eyes.

Two years later there was a still more extensive uproar over a far better book, Vladimir Nabokov's *Lolita*. This was one of the finest novels written in the postwar. It was, naturally, deplored as salacious trash, and widely read for the wrong reasons. *Lolita* depicts the passion of Humbert Humbert, self-styled "nympholept," for certain girls aged nine to fourteen. Not all young girls, Humbert explains, are nymphets. They are a decided minority, possessing a rare combination of vivacity and sexuality. But Humbert is a connoisseur; he can spot a nymphet under a shapeless sweater, calf-length skirt, bobby sox and saddle shoes. Nabokov hedges slightly, however, by arranging matters so that Lolita is no virgin when Humbert meets her and it is she who seduces the middle-aged, but receptive, narrator.

Lolita is written with remarkable skill and verve. It is one of the funniest novels in postwar fiction. Its depiction of sexual passion is both convincing and strangely nonerotic at the same time. Yet the idea of a middleaged man having sexual intercourse with a twelve-year-old girl shocked reviewers into silence when it did not move them to vitriolic rage. The *Baltimore Sun*, the *Christian Science Monitor*, and scores of less admired papers refused to review it, even though it was one of the few important novels to appear in the 1950s. A reviewer in *The New Republic* greeted it as "Probably the best fiction to come out of this country . . . since Faulkner's burst in the Thirties." But when *The New Republic*'s editors saw a copy of the novel, they were moved to write a front-page editorial which denounced, "this story of the two-year rape of a pre-adolescent . . . this obscene chronicle of murder and a child's destruction."

Lolita, published in 1958, marked the turning point in popular attitudes toward sex in literature. *Lady Chatterley's Lover*, suppressed for thirty years, was brought out in an unexpurgated edition by Grove Press the next year. Grove Press expected expensive and protracted litigation, and knew that such a work was illegal in most states, but calculated rightly that after *Lolita* a change in attitudes had been effected.

If there was a single unifying thread in the literature of these years, however, it was less sex than the power obsession of the modern world. It dated from the war years, and in post-1945 war fiction the struggle was seen less as a fight for democratic values than as a collision between vast bureaucracies. This thread ran through Norman Mailer's *The Naked and the Dead*, Thomas Heggen's *Mister Roberts*, James Jones's *From Here to*

Eternity, Herman Wouk's *The Caine Mutiny*, and Cozzens's *Guard of Honor*. In each, the individual is flattened within the military machine— the supreme expression of power and violence. The organization becomes everything, the individual nothing.

The most political and class-conscious of these novels, *The Naked and the Dead*, has no heroes, but it sports a villain, the fascistic General Cummings. "You can consider the Army," he informs the liberal, serious, doomed young Lieutenant Hearne, "as a preview of the future."

James Jones's *The Thin Red Line*, which offered the most convincing view of combat in the South Pacific, carried much the same message. One of the principal characters, a gin-sodden master sergeant, informs an awestruck private, "There's no choice for anybody. And it ain't only here, with us. It's everywhere. And it ain't going to get any better. This war's just the start."

Heggen tried to make a joke of the foolishness of it all, while Cozzens and Wouk rather liked the idea of men finding purpose in their lives by submitting to the organization.

In 1961 there came the novel which gathered up this thread and gave it a genuinely contemporary twist. Set in wartime Italy at an Army Air Corps base, it was ostensibly a war novel. But it was just as much a novel about the postwar world. It concerned the inherent lunacy of organized power whose real purpose is nothing more than destruction. The novel's title, *Catch-22*, passed into everyday speech as an expression meaning "There's no escape from this lunacy—this is how things work."

Joseph Heller's novel was not a work of literary merit in the strict sense. Although it is replete with jokes, much of the humor is labored and footling. Most of its characters are literally unbelievable. So is most of the action. Nor is there any plot to speak of. Parts of it are lackluster. But it captured perfectly the spirit of an age which turned reason on its head, when, for example, the Communist Party was being financed by the FBI, and the *Daily Worker* was kept in business by 3,000 paid-up subscriptions from the CIA; when the Army drafted Peress because it needed dentists so badly that it could not afford to look too closely at whose side they were on; when it was necessary to explode dirty H-bombs in the peacetime atmosphere in order to make them clean enough for wartime. Behind such examples of illogic stood the logical imperatives of bureaucracy.

Catch-22's achievement was that it caught the spirit of the age. It portrayed at full length the manic nature of what C. Wright Mills termed "crackpot realism." Instead of sighing over contemporary life, Heller laughed at it. And by 1961 large numbers of people had grown tired of pretending that two and two made seven. College students particularly, who had known nothing of the war but had been raised on the lunacies of the postwar world, devoured *Catch-22*. It was borne to success by a new generation, disenchanted, angry, self-knowing, irreverent.

28
Jam Today, Jam Tomorrow

There was no escaping the Organization. Still, the mature bureaucracy which most people knew best was not government or the military but the business corporation. Economically, the great corporations wielded influence that was immeasurable and profound. Politically, they wielded more power than most people ever realized. Although the biggest 500 corporations employed less than 10 percent of the nation's working population, they played a central and possibly decisive role in the economy. The corporate model became the paradigm for nearly all large organizations. The corporate style of recruitment, promotion, and employee relations; the corporate ideals of cooperation and stability; the corporate cultivation of public relations—all had a deep influence on American life and values. A few hundred large corporations were a far more important social force than the tens of thousands of medium-sized businesses which employed more than half the work force. One contemporary observer was moved to reflect, "The organization is more important than who owns it or who works for it. It has a life of its own. It began as a mere legal person. In has acquired a social personality."

In the meantime, it had become the setting for a way of life whose Baedeker was *The Organization Man*. Some writers wrote critically about its sticky embrace, but there were business novels which invested the large corporation with the kind of romantic aura which until now had normally been reserved for a sacred calling or patriotic sacrifice—e.g., Howard Swiggett's *The Durable Fire*, Cameron Hawley's *The Lincoln Lords*. In the Hawley novel Lincoln Lord is offered a college presidency after his company has gone to the brink of collapse. He refuses the offer and humbly confesses, "I *need* the company."

He was one of the new breed, the men to whom the company was everything partly because they had not made it; it had made them. This was the postwar generation of business executives who had taken over running the creations built up by an earlier generation of men more or less with their own hands, shaped to their vision of the world. But since about 1920 "management control," as opposed to owners' control, had spread rapidly through big business. By the 1960s there was not one major corporation in twenty in which the majority of shares were in the hands of the founders or the founders' families. Nor did the new presidents, vice-presidents, and chairmen of the board have to look to the profits to assure themselves of a large income; few owned as much as 1 percent of the voting stock of their companies. "Corporation executives," wrote A. A. Berle in 1959, "are not capitalists seeking profits. They are seeking careers, in a structure offering rewards of power and position rather than profit or great wealth." They were almost indistinguishable from ambitious civil servants or career military officers from the service academies.

Business corporations were simply too big to be handed down from generation to generation like a successful foundry or department store. Not only was an enormous amount of property owned in the postwar by legal fictions, but the corporations themselves were being acquired by still larger legal fictions—pension funds, insurance companies, big banks. By the 1960s it was doubtful whether even the chief executives of most top corporations were able to exercise property rights, as they were traditionally understood, over the company's property. Ownership, which was diluted when stock ownership became widespread, had become further diluted by management control and was by now so far removed from immediate and tangible concerns that it was almost invisible. The ownership of property, in short, had become virtually as remote in much of the American economy as it had become in most Communist countries.

There was hardly an executive of a major corporation who had ever, in that beloved phrase redolent of the rolltop desk and the kerosene lamp, "met a payroll." And there was an underlying uneasiness about these men. They were conscious that they were a new breed. They tended to be defensive and insecure. They were impatient of criticism. They were, in comparison with the men who had built the corporations they worked for, a lesser breed. They were not men of enterprise and risk but were, "recruited from the grab-bag of middle class life, [lacking] the assured sense of self-justification which the older class-rooted system provided." Yet to justify themselves, they clung to the language of laissez-faire capitalism, little caring that the creature had expired. From time to time they stood on its carcass to beat their breasts and lament, as one steel executive did in a letter to a businessman-scholar who had given a speech on changing attitudes toward Socialism since the war: "What do the Socialists have to gain any more? They have won. . . . Ownership of our firm is so widespread as to be properly designated public. . . . Our actions and decisions are based on all kinds of social and and economic considerations. If this is capitalism, Norman Thomas should love it." Possibly the nearest thing left to a big capitalist was the manager of a pension or insurance fund—and the money he had to invest, or not to invest, belonged to other people. As capitalists, however, they were on the cautious side, and there was a shortage of venture capital throughout the postwar.

The thing to be these days was not a capitalist but an "executive." In the corporation becoming an executive was everything; it was the sorting of sheep from goats. The young executive was a man on his way up. But odds were that he got a hefty shove from dad to get him started. Two-thirds of all executives these days were the sons of men who had themselves been executives or small businessmen or engaged in one of the better professions. If a boy from a poor family managed to go to college and studied something useful, such as engineering, law, accounting, or business administration, and afterward applied for a job with the corporation, his social background would not, however, spoil his chances of getting the job or of becoming an executive. The American social system was based on class, not caste; people could move from class to class, instead of being branded with a caste for life. The business corporation was happy to accept upwardly mobile young men, provided they were white, preferably Protestant, and had college degrees.

The corporation provided a comfortable living. In 1950 the dominant group among the top 5 percent of income earners were the self-employed, who accounted for nearly half. Ten years later the self-employed doctors, farmers, small businessmen had fallen far behind. The dominant group now was the salaried professionals and managers.

As they moved up the corporation ladder, the rising executives found that whatever specialized knowledge they had striven so hard to acquire, it was of less and less relevance. Mergers and diversification were so commonplace that few executives could remember all the operations their corporation was involved in. What mattered in the higher reaches was not the mastery of a body of knowledge but an all-purpose ability at administration and, more important at times, "personality"—that is, the right kind of personality.

The personality required was not particularly forceful or energetic. Big business executives were remarkable for their passivity. No matter how much they were paid, few were allowed to make decisions on their own. The largest sum of money most could spend without prior authorization was more likely to be $100 than $1,000. Vance Packard encountered a man responsible for an operation with a yearly sales volume of $2 million who was not allowed to spend more than $10 a year.

The complete absorption in their work had a further narrowing effect. Their range of friends and acquaintances was narrow. The constraints of geographical and social mobility limited emotional involvement with other people and other places. The executive was likely to find the sexual demands of his wife an unwelcome distraction from the demands of his work. She was expected, however, to organize her own life and interests to further his career. Even his relaxation was dictated by his work—he played the right games, whether golf or bridge, at the right places, with the right people. The consequence of such a life was a personality with little sentimentality, and no passion; trained, disciplined intelligence, and no interest in ideas. There was success, but often of a dispiriting kind.

To their own eyes, however, the successful businessman was a figure cast in heroic mold. The dedication to hard work was seen as a creative commitment. In Sloan Wilson's *The Man in the Gray Flannel Suit* the businessman-as-hero, the president of United Broadcasting Corporation, loses his self-control momentarily: "Somebody has to do the big jobs! . . . This world was built by men like me! . . . You people who just give half your minds to your work are riding on our backs." In Cameron Hawley's *Executive Suite* the fast-rising young executive hero looks out over the factory town, mentally stripping the roofs from the workers' houses, to peer inside.

Don Walling felt suspended in space, yet tied to the hive of the earth by the awed realization of his new-found responsibility. They were his . . . all of them . . . the uncounted thousands, born and unborn. If he failed them there would be hunger under those roofs . . . the belongings of the dispossessed would stand in the streets. . . . Don Walling accepted his fate. He would expect no thanks . . . he would live in loneliness . . . but the Tredway Corporation would go on. There would be jobs and paychecks. There would be no hunger. The belongings of the dispossessed would not stand in the street.

To the men who ran the big business corporations, business was the bedrock, the fount, and the capstone of American life and all that that suggested—political democracy, economic prosperity, individual opportunity, the endless struggle to secure social justice. And it was they who kept the economy in good running order, the economy on which all else depended.

But while they were prone to take a flattering view of business and to admire the corporation for which they worked, they were also given to deep personal insecurity. Military service, an experience common to most able-bodied men aged twenty-five to fifty, had instilled in them an acute sensitivity to rank, and the corporation, like all mature bureaucracies, was many-layered and precisely graded. Status was a constant concern. Not only was it important to have high status, but it was vital that others should know it. An article in the *Wall Street Journal* in 1957 began with this information-packed heading:

STATUS SYMBOLS
Pigskin Tile, Carafes,
Free Autos Tell Rank
Of Company Executives

Rivalries Wax Hot, Leading
Many Firms to Formalize
Signs of Corporate Caste

Marble Walls & Sea Horses

When Crown Zellerbach built a new twenty-story headquarters, it was designed with the status-symbol problem firmly in mind. The building manager proudly announced, "We'll be able to arrange the walls so that offices for executives of equal rank can all be built within a square inch of one another in size." At Standard Oil of Ohio the brass spittoons of an earlier generation of executives had given way to water carafes and trays. Drapes, carpets, desks, the number and size of windows—such were matters about which grown men could be deadly serious. Executives' secretaries were called assistants; managers' were called stenographers. Executive assistants got electric typewriters; stenographers got manual machines. The executive who had really arrived had a secretary who had her own secretary. One Midwestern firm attempted to nip the worm in the bud by giving its new building four glass-curtain walls so that all windows were of equal size. But the building had corners, a point it had overlooked. When the building was opened, the rivalry for a corner office—with two windows—was intense. Most companies simply accepted the great status race. Some actively encouraged it. And the few that would have liked to have put a stop to it realized it was impossible, because although their executives may have been willing to give up the trappings of status, the executives' wives were not.

Possibly the biggest growth sector within big business following the war was in vice-presidencies. By the mid-1950s there were a quarter of a million business VPs. Corporations which had managed with two or three during the Depression now had a dozen to a score. The Bank of America had 146. (Hershey Chocolate, however, continued to go its own eccentric way, never advertising and turning out chocolate without the assistance of a single vice-president.) In *Executive Suite* there is reference to a fictitious company which has thirty-two vice-presidents, "in order that no client need feel slighted." But with hundreds of thousands of VPs ("When everybody's somebody, then nobody's anybody") a hierarchy became necessary. A host of prefixes sprang up: senior, executive, administrative, first, second, third, regional, field, or assistant.

Status obsessions did not simply grip individuals. The corporation had its own status to consider. In the mid-1950s Chrysler was forced to effect drastic economies. The corporation fired one-third of its office workers. Thousands of clerks, secretaries, managers, and executives were dismissed, but the production and sales workers were left alone. There was no drop in production or sales. "Nevertheless, Chrysler was not one to show that an empire could function half-clothed." When, around 1960, it had regained its economic feet, it proceeded to build up its force of office workers to what it considered a level in keeping with its standing as one of the top 100 corporations in the United States.

"The social strains of the last ten years," Daniel Bell remarked, "have *not* been over property but over status." Workers and executives alike looked for one thing more than any other in a job—security. Before the war people had been interested almost entirely in cold cash. But by 1960 the wage was no more important than the package containing the pension plan, the medical insurance, the bonuses, the expense account, the company car, and the paid vacation.

The corporation itself was concerned with security. Power mania and prudence alike inspired the urge to merge, the desire to diversify. Modern management thinking was to move from a single product to coverage of the entire field of which that product was a part. Thus, Continental Can saw its field as packaging. It moved from the production of tin cans to all areas involved in packaging, investing in steel, glass, paper, and plastics. Another impetus to diversification was the size of postwar profits. In many cases they were too big to be turned back entirely into one's own plant because either the market could not expand fast enough to absorb the increase in production or, if it did, the result might be such market domination that it would lead to years of antitrust litigation. One way and another mergers and diversification helped raise the survival rate of big business corporations engaged in manufacturing to 99 per cent. Among all industrial and commercial concerns the failure rate was only 5 percent in the 1950s, compared with 12 per cent in that fabled era of business prosperity, the 1920s.

The corporation no longer provided a paycheck. Secure, big, benign, it offered a way of life. It provided workers and executives alike with a host of luxuries and necessaries—sports facilities, dances, charm schools, travel, beauty parlors, evenings out, theater tickets, meals, cars, prizes, clergymen, psychiatrists, and an opportunity to contribute to charity. The big business corporation in the postwar was a combination of welfare state, modern bureaucracy, and medieval feudalism.

Immediately following the war big business conducted various public relations campaigns to persuade people that it had been falsely blamed for the Depression. No one appears to have been much impressed. But around 1950 business stumbled upon the higher ground of "the Gospel of Social Responsibility." It dropped its pointless attacks on the New Deal. And the motto of corporate enterprise was no longer "The public be damned," but "The public be cultivated."

Justice Brandeis had taught that business was or ought to be a public service. That was precisely what business claimed to be from the early 1950s. And when Theodore Levitt, a Chicago business consultant, began publishing articles in *Harvard Business Review, Sales Management,* and *Advertising Age* in the late 1950s telling businessmen that social responsibility was no concern of theirs, they were outraged. These publications were promptly inundated with letters of protest from business executives.

Public relations became an important corporate exercise. In 1947 there had been 35 colleges offering courses in public relations. In 1955 there were 267. It was a development which drew the sardonic gaze of John Kenneth Galbraith:

> The rise of the public relations industry, which draws its clientele overwhelmingly from business executives, shows that business achievement is no longer of itself a source of acclaim. . . . [He] must be a statesman, a patron of education, or a civic force . . . some intellectual or artistic facet must be found. A businessman who reads *Business Week* is lost to fame. One who reads Proust is marked for greatness.

To demonstrate their concern with the fate of American society, businessmen leaped onto various nonpolitical hobbyhorses. At well-publicized dinners and lunches they came out foursquare for bigger metropolitan government, better mental health facilities, better public schools, and more money for medical research.

The modern corporation executive was proud of both his corporation and the role of American business in the economy. Yet he fought shy of ever speaking of capitalism; he preferred to talk about "free enterprise," the "price system," or the "competitive system." The very term "capitalism" seemed in the 1950s to refer to another age. Certainly no one would have been prepared to sacrifice his life and that of his family in defense of a privileged elite living on profitable investments. And the current reality was one of pseudocapitalism, a creation heavily dependent on government.

At the best of times the majority of Americans had never admired capitalism. But there was no hostility toward business as such, which was generally taken to mean small business. Big business, however, evoked ambivalent feelings of admiration for its money and power, and suspicion that it misused them. During the 1930s a new term of abuse had come into use, "bankster." But after 1945 public antagonism toward big business declined sharply. Large corporations were no longer the property of a few families, always an emotive issue. The postwar prosperity dispelled the need to find and pillory economic villains. But most important of all, people had become accustomed to bigness. Even that much-maligned New Dealer David Lilienthal, a man business executives had loved to hate, was now singing the praises of big business because it *was* big. Yet it was not that most people had begun to think highly of big business. They had instead stopped thinking badly of it. Three people in four were prepared to concede that the good things big business did outweighed the bad. Only one in ten thought the bad outweighed the good.

There was one notable exception to the avoidance of "capitalism," and that was in the expression "People's Capitalism." It was an idea revived from time to time under one rubric or another. At midcentury it was prompted in part as a counterweight to the appeal of highly centralized Marxist/Socialist ideas of economic justice. It was, moreover, a way of having bigness while paying lip service to individualism. It had little to do with raising investment capital. In the 1950s 60 percent of capital was internally produced by business corporations, from undistributed profits and depreciation allowances. Another 20 percent came from banks, as credit expanded. Pension funds and insurance companies provided most of the remainder. Individuals directly provided approximately 5 percent of business's capital requirements.

The brokerage houses, led by Merrill Lynch, were the principal architects of People's Capitalism. They got rid of their former style of business, which featured advertising that proclaimed OUR CUSTOMERS HAVE YACHTS. In the late 1940s and early 1950s Charles Lynch revolutionized the brokerage business by democratizing it. Commissions were kept low. The atmosphere of the brokerage house became informal and unintimidating. By the time of his death in 1956 Charles Lynch had built Merrill Lynch into the biggest brokerage in the world, with more than 500,000 customers.

Corporations also tried to encourage People's Capitalism, through employee participation plans. These encouraged employees to buy the company's stock. The New York Stock Exchange promoted the cause by launching the Monthly Investment Plan in 1954. This aimed to double the number of shareholders, then approximately 7 million. But MIP brought in only 150,000 new investors. By the late 1950s, however, the number of shareholders had risen to 12 million—thanks to the sudden popularity of mutual funds.

But People's Capitalism still embraced only 8 percent of the population, not much of an advance on the 1937 figure of 6.6 percent. The main beneficiaries of People's Capitalism were the brokerage houses, whose branch offices spread rapidly into nearly every town of 50,000 people or more. The brokers encouraged speculation, then raked in millions of low but risk-free commissions.

Stock ownership varied widely. In San Francisco, one adult in four owned stock; in Mississippi, it was one in thirty. Even at its height People's Capitalism was very limited. Almost half the $400 billion in stock owned by individuals in 1961 was held by 1 percent of the nation's taxpayers, who were less than one-half of 1 percent of the entire population. There were nearly 15 million stockholders, nearly all of whom held tiny amounts of stock.

The only windfalls the stock market shook down, furthermore, fell on those holding stock options. This innovation was introduced in the late 1940s. The stock option was reserved for the top executives of the top corporations. It provided a wonderful way to sudden riches because it cut two ways. The executive entitled to buy the company's stock at a guaranteed price did not have to exercise his option. If the stock dropped in value, he was free to ignore it. But in all probability the value of the stock would have gone up, if only because of inflation. So the second attraction was that he could make a handsome profit by buying at the guaranteed price, then selling at the market price and paying only the capital gains tax, at 25 percent, on the difference. Considering the way the wind was blowing, the phrase one writer coined to describe prevailing economic realities was "Executive's Capitalism."

But business was willing to share more of its riches than it had ever been. Part of the Gospel of Social Responsibility was "Thou Shalt be Generous." The chosen vehicle for this generosity was the tax-free foundation.

There had been only 10 foundations in 1900; 16 more were founded in the following decade, 75 more in the decade after that, nearly 200 in the 1920s, 300 in the 1930s. In the 1940s some 2,500 foundations were established. In the 1950s there came another 10,000. By the early 1960s there were 15,000 institutions in the United States whose sole justification for existence was to give away money; in nearly every case it was money made by business. The combined worth of these foundations was approximately $20 billion.

There had been a remarkable reversal in attitudes. Jacques Barzun recalled a conversation he had held on V-J Day with a famous corporation lawyer: "To my arguments showing the logic and necessity of gifts to educational, artistic and scientific establishments, he opposed the law, the outcry of stockholders, and the jealousies of directors with diverse allegiances. He predicted that capitalism would have to be overthrown before such gifts could be authorized.'' Contacts with foundations and universities also appeared to work a remarkable effect on businessmen. As David Riesman noticed, there was "a tendency for the [professors] to appear worldly-wise, practical and even cynical, whereas the trustees have been the high-minded, 'academic' ones."

Once the foundation was in operation, it had to get down to the serious business of giving money away. Julius Rosenwald, who had given away his fortune to support schools and colleges for blacks, once remarked that it was easier to make $1 million than to distribute it wisely. It was easier, moreover, to give $1 million for a big project than to give a grant of $10,000 to an individual. The foundations thus gave added impetus to a growing tendency for intellectual effort to be supported where it involved teams of workers and to be slighted where only an individual was involved. The result was to support mediocrity, for the basis of nearly all collective effort is the average ability of the group. It was also inevitable that many a small idea would be turned into a major project because that was the only way to get the grant.

As the foundations grew and spread, their image changed. Before the war they were widely believed to be reactionary, and founded on a tax dodge. After the war they were widely assumed to be radical, and founded on a tax dodge. The foundation which came in for the most intense criticism was the Ford Foundation. Congressional investigations during the 1950s attempted to blame it for the "loss" of China and the outbreak of the Korean War.

Ford's problems were a consequence of its being the biggest foundation in the world. No other, not even the Rockefeller Foundation, approached it in wealth or in range of interests. Established in 1936, Ford led a quiet life until 1949. It then came into the estates of both Henry Ford and his prematurely dead eldest son, Edsel. The foundation found itself awash with cash—the one thing it already had in abundance. It was currently accumulating dividend income faster than it could find good ways to spend it.

The foundation inherited huge blocks of Ford stock. This saved Henry's and Edsel's children from paying several hundred million dollars in inheritance taxes. The foundation was appraised for tax purposes in the early 1950s as being worth $412 million. But on the basis of the Ford Corporation's earnings its stock holdings were worth $2.5 billion. And now the dividend income began accumulating so rapidly that the urge to give money away became feverish. The foundation, accustomed to spending a million or two a year on local projects, such as the Detroit Symphony and the Henry Ford Museum, had to dispose of more than that each week.

The other major foundations had already carved out niches into which they directed their largess. Rockefeller fostered medical education and research; it was Rockefeller money which underwrote the laboratory at Cambridge where DNA was unraveled and the New York laboratory where it was first synthesized. The Duke Foundation enriched the Methodist Church and Duke University. The Carnegie Foundation promoted international understanding. When Ford began to splash out, it had no narrow range of interests to pursue. But it chose to concentrate on education. It dumped half a billion dollars in accumulated dividend income on the colleges and medical schools in a vast, indiscriminate giveaway, favoring the very bad and the very good alike. It boosted teachers' salaries for one year. It financed the Fifth Year Program for high school and college teachers who wanted to update or upgrade their education. It underwrote educational television. It funded another Adlerian enterprise (an attempt to classify and index all human knowledge; Adler was in the grip of Maimonideism) which flopped. It played Santa Claus to the classroom by showering audiovisual aids on grade schools and high schools. It financed adult education programs. The results were at best mixed. Many of the projects Ford financed were characterized by "a distinctively American combination of organization at the top and anarchy at the bottom."

In 1950 the Ford Foundation brought in a new president, Paul Hoffman, who until recently had been the principal administrator of the Marshall Plan. The foundation discovered that it had now taken the world as its province. Ford was soon training social workers in India and librarians in Turkey. The East European Fund provided help to 100,000 East European refugees who entered the United States in the early 1950s. A Ford program subsidized Soviet exiles who wrote scholarly monographs on Russian society, history, and culture. Ford financed the Chekhov Publishing House, which by 1960 was the biggest Russian-language publishing house outside the Soviet Union. It offered Russian classics and published Western works in Russian. Ford provided millions of dollars for foreign scholars to visit the United States, and millions more were made available to Americans engaged in study abroad. It financed foreign-language dictionaries in exotic tongues. It subsidized the Council on Foreign Relations.

Hoffman brought in Robert M. Hutchins, the all-purpose wunderkind of American higher education and controversialist by vocation. Hutchins in turn encouraged the foundation's multifarious involvement in education. His own private preserve within the foundation's sprawling estate was the Fund for the Republic, which cost a trifling $15 million. Its brief was the defense of the Bill of Rights. Normally nothing might have appeared more anodyne. But in the early 1950s that was a brave cause.

The Hearst press and *The New Yorker*, a couple odd enough to make almost anyone rub his eyes in wonder, attacked the foundation for harboring the likes of Hutchins. Ford dealers were harried by outraged patriots, who informed them that they were Communist dupes. The upper-class liberals who sat on foundation boards were horrified to learn that the fund under Hutchins's management succeeded in spending a third of its money simply on administration.

Ford's failures were seized on with glee. In 1953 Hoffman was induced to resign. In 1959 Hutchins was allowed to set up the Center for the Study of Democratic Institutions at Santa Barbara with what was left of the Fund for the Republic. Hutchins was not really an intellectual by nature, any more than Henry Luce was a publisher, Morris Fishbein a doctor, or Billy Graham a theologian. Hutchins, like them, possessed but one real gift, the all-American gift—he was a promoter.

After it announced that it intended to give away vast amounts of money, the Ford Foundation was never short of ideas. They arrived with the post each day. There were proposals to irrigate the Sahara, to plant flowers all along the U.S.-Canadian border, to melt the icecap at the South Pole, the merits of this last idea being that the earth's tilt would be corrected and the planet would then enjoy days and nights of exactly twelve hours' duration.

The most extraordinary growth industry in the postwar was advertising. There were people such as Vance Packard who believed that it had become one of the principal determinants of values and behavior, putting it on a par with the church, the school, the home, and the state.

Advertising expenditure grew in real terms by nearly 250 percent between 1948 and 1960. Running at an annual rate of $12 billion, it equaled the national expenditure on elementary and secondary education. Advertising after the war grew considerably faster than did increases in sales volume.

Behind this development lay a profound change in business activity. Before 1945 the biggest part of business had been production. But starting in the late 1940s, the chief problem of most business was not producing things but selling them. Business turned its attention to "want creation."

The twin of want creation was debt creation. And judged by the rise of personal indebtedness, want creation was a success. Between 1946 and 1959 private debt rose by $375 billion; over the same period, and to howls of protest, Federal debt rose by $13 billion. Consumer indebtedness rose three times faster than personal income, so by 1960 the average American family "was taking on about $750 installment debt alone each year—and paying it off at the rate of $650 a year." This burgeoning installment debt was probably what sent many married women out to work. For the finance companies, this was a golden age. In the first postwar decade Seaboard Finance, for example, grew by 50 percent a year. The finance companies, comparatively small when the war ended and not much admired, by the late 1950s had become major financial institutions.

The changing emphasis from production to consumption had varied results. Within the big business corporations the men who were experts in production lost their old dominance. Now the top men were coming up through finance or marketing. There was also a new social type at the center of economic life. Producers, whether workers or executives, are expected to be active figures, but consumers are passive. The traditional masculine characteristics are associated with production; the traditional female characteristics with consumption.

Another result of this change of emphasis was that it encouraged profligacy on an unmatched scale. Economists had long acknowledged that in a mass-production economy the unit cost of production will go down and the unit cost of distribution will go up. Even before the war it may have been that costs of distribution exceeded costs of production. This was a trend which stimulated the rapid development of the service industries because almost every phase of distribution is a service. But it also spawned wastefulness. The package bore much of the burden of making the sale. Many purchases were believed to be made on impulse. Packages therefore became increasingly elaborate, colorful, and eye-catching. Store displays featured unusual shapes and bright colors. The packaging business by the late 1950s had an annual turnover of $25 billion. Divided by the number of American families, this meant the average family was spending $500 a year on packaging, nearly all of which was promptly thrown into the trash can. The throwaway civilization had arrived.*

But there remained a Puritan streak to the American character which made many people uneasy about profligacy and want creation. They had a sneaking contempt for advertising. It was an occupation regarded much as stock brokerage had been regarded up to 1929: "glamorous, financially rewarding and somehow not quite honest."

It was also a nerve-racking business, for those who succeeded at it. The average advertising executive died ten years younger than the average man. It was also a business notorious for the disenchantment it bred among its practitioners. In Frederic Wakeman's *The Hucksters* everything they touched seemed flat, stale, but profitable. "Huckster—that was a good name for an advertising man. A high class huckster who had a station wagon instead of a pushcart."

Yet they flattered themselves with the thought that they were really on the side of the consumers. They maintained that they were giving people the information they needed to spend their money wisely. The head of an advertising agency, Otto Kleppner, articulated the Gospel of Social Responsibility as it affected advertising. First, he said, advertising was a form of communication between people. Second, "The function of advertising is to help create and distribute the better values a business offers in competition for the buyer's selection." But the prosaic truth was that advertising existed to sell the stuff, whether it was good, bad or useless, ugly or pretty, safe or dangerous, wanted or not. It was seriously maintained by some advertising men that their work was a form of folk art. But the "folk" had nothing to do with it. Glossy though it often was and talented though some of its writers and artists were, the fact remained that advertising had no noble or artistic aim such as the elevation of the spirit or the enrichment of the mind.

One thing the advertising people claimed to understand, however, was human nature. Between 1945 and 1960 advertising discovered the social

---

*Its model was the Mad Hatter's Tea Party. The Mad Hatter went from cup to cup, so that he always had a fresh cup of tea without having to clean the last cup he drank from. The end result was a table littered with dirty cups from which no one else would drink, and the Hatter ran out of tea.

sciences. There were tens of thousands of pyschologists, economists, and sociologists eager to be of service. From the marriage of the ad men and the social scientists issued "Motivation Research."

It had been an article of faith for decades that the most important part of an advertisement was the copy. But that was challenged. The traditional belief had been that the way to sell something was to show how useful it was. That, too, was disputed. Modern advertising became more and more visual, less and less verbal. Instead of selling utility, it sold status.

Symbols were better than words, one expert decreed, because "There is no work called for, no mental effort." There was anyway a deep distrust of words and a dread of difficult or long words.

Motivation Research had a pervasive effect on nearly all postwar advertising. It may also have been something of a self-fulfilling prophecy, helping bring about the conditions it claimed to find. The style of postwar advertising was to worship youth, blur sex roles, adore the new, deride the old, emphasize the casual and informal, portray leisure activities as adventures in self-expression, and, ironically, foster a craving to be different from other people.

Motivation Research made advertising more sophisticated. It approached people as they were, acting from mixed motives, dissatisfied with themselves, open to suggestion. But the principal instrument of advertising remained the eternal resort of the servile—flattery.

Because women spent most of each day performing boring, disesteemed housework, advertising aimed at women showed them being adored and marveled at by their husbands and children for being so thoroughly competent. Instead of suggesting that a new appliance would give her more time to gossip with neighbors or put her feet up, advertising showed it giving a woman more time to spend with her children. The sale of deepfreezes was not associated with economy or convenience. It was based on appeals to the insecurity of people who still had strong memories of the Depression, who had fears about the food running out.

The bulk of Motivation Research consisted of blinding glimpses of the obvious spiced with a little sub-Freudian guesswork, e.g., that a lighter is a symbol of sexual potency, that a man considers his automobile his mistress, that salt is suggestive of semen. Women did not buy cosmetics; they bought hope. Men did not buy tobacco; they bought masculinity. A liking for soup started in the womb. And so on. It all seemed fairly harmless until 1957. Then James Vicary began "subliminal advertising" in several New Jersey movie houses. During each film a second projector flashed "Coca-Cola" and "Eat popcorn" onto the screen so rapidly and so dimly that the letters could not be detected even by people who were looking for them. Consumption of soft drinks and popcorn at the movie houses rose by 15 to 50 percent. Vicary modestly suggested that his advertising affected only people who were already wondering whether to have a Coke or eat some popcorn. There was a frisson of alarm, however, that he might have found a new, sinister, and irresistible method of brainwashing. But subliminal advertising proved to have only a very limited use. No one was likely to be motivated to go out and buy a new car or book a world cruise while they were at the movies.

Advertising men discovered, or rediscovered, social class. When W. Lloyd Warner's *Social Class in America* was published in 1948, it created a greater stir along Madison Avenue than on campus. "It came to be regarded as a milestone in the sociological approach to the consumer. The book became a manual. . . ." What the advertising agencies learned about class they applied to status. Advertising became, on the face of it, antidemocratic. It appeared to be aimed at the top 10 to 20 percent of the population. But it was really attempting to yoke the aura of upper-class and upper-middle-class life to its clients' products, which were usually uninteresting even if they were useful. The one thing to be avoided in advertising was ordinary life in all its drab, commonsensical reality. It happened, too, that some things sold better when their price went up, making them seem more glamorous.

Advertising did not create snobbism; that has an ancient history. But it did much to shape the expression of snobbism in the postwar. And new status symbols, such as credit cards, were continually appearing to be heavily promoted and exploited. In some fields the advertising men were at times too successful. People drove furniture manufacturers to distraction in the 1950s by looking and looking and looking and then being frightened of buying. Why? Because they wanted to have something that was in good taste, and it had to match their status aspirations. But they were thoroughly bewildered as to what good taste was in furniture and which furniture suited their status, thanks to furniture advertising. Inevitably, too, the successful status symbol contained the seeds of its own destruction, which might be termed the Duke of Plaza-Toro Syndrome.* Cadillacs had become so much the symbol of the arriviste that it became fashionable to be able to afford one but to drive something else. Monsignor Fulton J. Sheen, for instance, in the late 1950s switched to a chauffeured Mercedes-Benz.

By 1960 Motivation Research was beginning to fall into disfavor. Some agencies had never believed in it. Motivation Researchers tended to be as gifted at casuistry as any Jesuit. If something sold, they had an explanation. If it did not sell, they had an explanation. Advertising people were like spies, avid to claim credit for anything that worked. Again like spies, they had powerful masters to satisfy, much to prove, and few ways to prove it. Motivation Research gave ground to a new fashion, Operations Research. This involved gathering vast amounts of data. The computer had arrived.

The heart of all advertising was still merchandising, however. And the industry which most fully exemplified the problems involved was automobiles. It relied heavily on Motivation Research and "planned obsolescence." This meant making things that looked good but were not designed to last. It was the throwaway civilization at its least edifying and the utter

---

*"When everybody's somebody, nobody's anybody."

negation of one of the few qualities which Veblen felt the human race could count to its credit, "the instinct of craftsmanship."

It had taken Detroit only four years to catch up with the demand for cars following the war. And after the Korean War ended and the economy cooled down slightly, Detroit caught a chill. People had money to spend but did not seem to have the inclination to replace the cars they had recently bought. The automakers responded by selling "more car per car." Automobiles grew longer and heavier, were equipped with automatic transmissions, power steering, power brakes, and bigger engines. Obsolescence was speeded on its way by the more rapid changing of body styles. At Ford styling was taken away from engineering and became a separate department. George W. Walker, a noted dress designer, was brought in to head it at a salary of $200,000 a year. Walker was known as the Cellini of Chrome.

Car styles became bizarre and freakish. For unblushing vulgarity the cars of the 1950s are in a class of their own. But the method appeared to have worked. In 1955 automobile sales reached a record 7.4 million. Then in 1956 they dropped, and they dropped further in 1957, and in 1958 they fell to 4.7 million. The automakers had made a monumental blunder: they all were trying to sell the same three or four cars. Despite the bizarreries of styling, what they offered was too much alike. Meanwhile, at the top and bottom of the scale imports rolled in to fill the sections of the market they had left uncovered.

To the picture of sameness there was a historic exception. There was one car that was intended to be utterly different. That was the Edsel, a name arrived at after 6,000 other possibilities had been discarded. The Edsel was based on the most elaborate pretesting and market research and was accompanied by the most brainstorming, ulcer-making advertising campaign of the decade. And in the end nearly every important decision involving the Edsel was made with almost no regard for the results of the research or the advice offered by the advertising agency.

The purpose of the Edsel was to give Ford owners something to trade up to as they moved up the social scale. At present they had an unpleasant tendency to ignore the Mercury and to buy an Oldsmobile or a Pontiac instead. The Edsel was intended to batter down their resistance by offering them the most innovative styling of the time—an oval grille, gull-wing taillights, push-button transmission. But the Edsel turned into the biggest business failure of the postwar. It probably arrived two years too late; it would almost certainly have done better in 1955, when the market was at a peak, than it did in 1957, when the market was in a severe slump. It also received an advance buildup that no car could have lived up to. And the bold styling misfired—the oval grille looked astonishingly like a chrome-plated toilet seat.

The net loss on the Edsel was $350 million. Some 110,000 Edsels were sold, so the loss was approximately $3,200 a car. Ford might have done better by giving away 110,000 new Mercurys to ex-Ford owners to see how they liked one. The Edsel passed into folk history, once it was no longer in production. Years later the sight of an Edsel rolling down the street could cause a twinge of nostalgia. It had become an object of wry, mocking affection.

The general effect of advertising appears to have been that it cheapened popular culture. More than $1 billion a year was spent on television commercials by 1959. No one seriously maintained that this produced better television. Programs became worse as pressure from advertising increased. There was a perpetual search for the lowest common denominator. Advertisers were given to petty tyrannies over the content of programs. One cigarette company ruled that no one on its programs could be seen smoking a cigar or a pipe, chewing tobacco or gum, or doing anything which might be mistakenly assumed to be as satisfying as smoking a cigarette. Views of public places had to include cigarette vending machines. Nor would the advertisers risk offending possible consumers. One sponsor decreed: "No material shall give offense, even by inference, to any organized minority group, lodge, or other organizations, institutions, residents of any state or section of the country, or a commercial organization of any sort. . . . There will be no material for or against any sharply-drawn national or regional controversial issues."

Advertising interests were sufficiently powerful not only to ruin the landscape with billboards but to induce the government to subsidize billboards and put penalties on developers who planted trees along the roadside. Advertising was also heavily dependent on the taxpayer. The Curtis Publishing Company, whose stable included the *Saturday Evening Post* and the *Ladies' Home Journal*, had a mail bill of approximately $4 million in 1950. But the true cost of delivering Curtis publications was $19 million. The difference between these figures covered Curtis's annual profit three times over. The *Reader's Digest* was in the same position; all its profits were made possible by lavish government support of its operations. And that other bastion of free enterprise, *Time-Life*, in 1960 was subsidized by the taxpayer to the tune of $20 million a year.

The production cost of *Time* and *Life* was forty cents a copy. The income from sales amounted to thirteen cents a copy. Thus, the primary business of the Luce empire was not selling magazines or publishing news. Its primary function, as a business, was publishing advertising. That was true of nearly all the major, glossy periodicals. They sold advertising, and the taxpayer financed it.

Ironically, advertising itself stood in need of public relations. Its press agent was the Advertising Council, which had begun operations back in 1942 as the War Advertising Council. Its aim then had been to help sustain wartime morale. After 1945 it broadened its responsibilities to include public service campaigns initiated by nongovernment agencies, such as the American Red Cross, the Road Safety Council, the Community Chest. Each year it made tens of millions of dollars' worth of advertising available free of charge—a fact the council was proud to advertise.*

---

*A cartoon in the *Saturday Review* parodied the result, showing a radio which blared: "Herbert's, the clothing store for better prices and greater savings, where wise shoppers go for double-their-money-value, the store preferred by millions of happy buyers, FORGOES ITS COMMERCIAL to bring you an important public announcement—Drive Carefully."

* * *

Although the buccaneering days were over, the world of business still had a dramatic aspect, with villains and heroes, bold strokes and scandals. When *Time* in 1955 chose as its Man of the Year GM's president, Harlow Curtice, it had hardly fastened on a deathless name. But what was being celebrated was less the man than business prosperity. A prospering economy seemed at least as important in holding Communism at bay as a healthy Christianity. Business itself was the real hero now.

The corporate style was not going to breed men in the heroic mold. The best that could be made of Curtice's successor at GM, Frederic Donner, was: "a taciturn thoughtful financial man who has spent most of his life poring over charts of statistics and astonishing his colleagues with his photographic memory." Not even the new industries, such as electronics, brought forth a new Ford or Rockefeller. There was, instead, Thomas B. Watson, the man who had created IBM and whose motto "THINK" hung on IBM walls around the world. To his admirers he was "the greatest salesman in the Universe." But almost no one outside business had ever heard of him. Endicott, New York, was to electronics what Detroit had been to the automobile. Hardly anyone, in business or out, had ever heard of Endicott.

But two heroes cut from the old bolt of cloth managed to capture the public imagination. One was Henry Kaiser; the other, Robert Young.

The war had turned Kaiser from being only another millionaire businessman into a national figure. He was the man who built the Liberty ships. On the basis of his wartime reputation and experience he went on to make cars, steel, aluminum, cement, houses, and building products. He ran a major insurance company and one of the best health and medical plans in the country. He owned several big construction companies and some of the busiest construction consulting companies in the world. In ten years his worth rose from several million to an estimated $600 million in 1951, and more than 90 percent of his fortune had been built up since V-J Day.

Kaiser was something of a Populist. His health and medical program was one expression of that element in his nature. His determination to break into the automobile industry was another. Kaiser was fascinated by Henry Ford, regarding him as a man of the people who had failed the people because Ford had not produced the genuinely simple and inexpensive car the ordinary man needed; Ford had not produced an American Volkswagen. Kaiser set himself the task of succeeding where Ford had failed. Kaiser would build the People's Car. Nearly all of Kaiser's assistants were against it. Trying to compete with the Big Three, starting from scratch, was to slide down the razor blade of life. But like Lincoln, Kaiser outvoted them.

He found a partner in Joseph Frazer, a manufacturer of agricultural machinery. When stock in Kaiser-Frazer went on the market, the new company had no assets to speak of except a lease on Willow Run. But thanks to Kaiser's prestige, the first stock offering was hugely oversubscribed. So was the second. More than $50 million was raised without difficulty. But for once Kaiser had made the mistake of not thinking on a sufficiently large scale. To break into the car business, he should have raised at least $250 million. He was surrounded, furthermore, by men who knew shipyards, cement, dams, and aluminum from start to finish but who knew no more about cars than how to drive one.

Kaiser's undercapitalization and his lack of expert knowledge left him vulnerable from the moment he began operations. He simply could not risk a strike. As a result, he suffered the worst of both worlds—endless wildcat strikes and endless, expensive concessions. Kaiser remained determined to sell his cars at a low price, no matter how much they cost. He lost money on every car he made.

In 1953 Kaiser Motors went out of business. The following year a still-smarting Kaiser visited Hawaii and fell in love with it. He moved there and began remaking it, building everything from hotels in remote areas to entire towns. Past seventy, he put all his passionate nature into this new love; it was certain to be his last.

Meanwhile, Robert Young had made himself famous as the man who had made it possible for train passengers to cross the country without having to change trains. Hogs did not have to, Young's advertisements pointed out, so why should people? Young overcame decades of bitter jealousy and petty spite between the railroads involved. He was described by John Gunther as one of "the ablest, brainiest and most ruthless men in the country." In the mid-1950s Young, who liked a fight and loved publicity, set out to wrest control of the New York Central Railroad from its very proper, very conservative board of directors, after they had decided by a vote of 15–0 to decline his invitation to make him their chairman. Young announced that he was going to fight the "powerful interests" on Wall Street; that is, the same interests he had recently offered his services to. Young had been trying for nearly a decade to get onto the Central's board. With a loan of $10 million from two Texas oil millionaires and seven mailings to Central shareholders Young tried to gain control of enough shares and enough proxies to oust the current board. The board fought back with a lavish publicity campaign and seven mailings of its own. "Some shareholders, overwhelmed by attention, signed the proxies of both sides with an indiscriminate sense of power." Young promised a dividend of $10 a share and spoke cryptically about a revolutionary train which was going to reverse the Central's fortunes, "Train X." To something like national rejoicing, when the proxies were opened Young won.

At the first meeting of the new, Young-controlled board he presented the shareholders with a bill for $1,308,733.31. This was the cost of his successful proxy fight.

The Central was run more efficiently, but there was no miraculous recovery. Central shares never paid a $10 dividend. In 1958, three years after taking over the Central, Young took a double-barreled shotgun and killed himself. The railroad business was in a long, steep decline. Nothing Young could have done would have reversed that. But a sense of failure, probably exaggerated by the very public course of his career, combined with his mercurial temperament to produce a suicide.

There was one other business hero in the postwar. The path he followed, however, was more that of an Edison than a Ford. He combined the genius of the inventor with the skills of the businessman. This was Edwin H. Land.

Shortly before the war and not yet thirty, Land created the Polaroid Corporation of Cambridge, Massachusetts. Polaroid was based on his invention of a thin, flexible sheet of material which polarized light. Incorporated in sunglasses, it earned Land a multimillion-dollar fortune. At Polaroid he was president, chairman of the board, and director of research. He was also a visiting professor at MIT and, following Sputnik, a member of the newly formed President's Science Advisory Committee.

By this time he had become famous for his invention of the fifty-second camera. Land's patent lawyers protected the process which made this camera possible by erecting a structure of 268 separate, interlocking patents. The secret was in the paper backing of the film and, with the formula for Coca-Cola, was one of the best-kept secrets in the business world. Every camera expert had confidently predicted that the Land camera would prove a failure. The pictures were of indifferent quality, and who cared about how quickly they were going to see their pictures anyway?

By 1959 Land's Polaroid camera had a sales volume of $65 million, growth was running at 15 percent a year, and Polaroid stock had risen from $12 a share in 1951 to more than $100. Polaroid also had the most positive image of any business. Land despised planned obsolescence. The camera was continually improved. But every functional improvement was designed to fit existing Land cameras. Some innovations were made available at no cost to owners of old models.

Not only were there business heroes, there were hero stocks and hero companies. The most romantic stock offering of the postwar era came when Ford went public in January 1956. Some 10 million shares were put onto the market. A million people clamored to buy without knowing what the asking price would be. Only 300,000 would-be purchasers came away with Ford stock, at $64.50. However desirable their stock may have been as an investment, these lucky 300,000 were second-class shareholders. Unlike people who held shares in other major, publicly held corporations, they would never be able to remove the top management, as the New York Central's shareholders had done. At least, not for as long as the top management was named Ford. Ordinary shareholders held Class A shares, which sounded impressive. The Ford family held Class B shares, which sounded far less impressive. But the Class B shares were unique: they were less than 12 percent of total Ford shares and were entitled to 40 percent of the total voting power of Ford shares. No one seemed to mind. But during the next five years Ford stock languished. The lucky 300,000 had nothing to show for their purchase—except a little bit of history and legend.

General Motors represented the corporation as hero. It was deeply respected by businessmen and people who were interested in administration and organization. GM had turned one of the neatest tricks of corporate life—it had decentralized successfully, in an age when centralization seemed irresistible. Each of GM's thirty-five divisions had a wide measure of autonomy in designing, producing, and selling its products. Ten policy-making bodies coordinated overall operations. But the ten bodies were highly flexible and pragmatic. At the top of the structure was a president who could, as Harlow Curtice frequently did, offer advice and ideas at every level of operations. The people at the lower levels were encouraged in turn to take up their problems and suggestions with the people at the top. It was the most adaptable major manufacturing corporation in the United States and a model admired all over the world.

GM's success was largely due to the brilliance of its organizational arrangements. It owned so many of its suppliers, moreover, that it may have earned more money selling parts to itself than it made by selling cars to others. GM was also admired for the seriousness with which it took the Gospel of Social Responsibility. Considering that it had the power to make a town, that was no trivial matter. During the 1950s GM literally made the town of Warren, Michigan, whose 1950 population was 727. Its population in 1960 after GM placed several plants there was 89,246.

The three issues which excited public concern were business size, competitiveness, and honesty. This was a change from the 1930s, when there had been only one issue, business failure. The arguments over size, competition, and ethics were arguments over success—that is, had success been achieved at too high a cost for the good of American society?

Most businesses were small. Of the more than 4 million businesses in operation in the 1950s at least three-fourths could be considered small on the basis of turnover and number of employees. Small businessmen felt aggrieved for much of the time. There was relentless pressure toward bigness in labor and bigness in business. Industry-wide labor contracts meant that there was almost nothing to discuss at the local level. Once a national agreement was reached it was presented to small business by the union local on a basis of take-it-or-leave-it.

The small businessman found that he had become a socio-economic curiosity. By a quirk of fate he had fallen heir to a body of values that were more agrarian than commercial. He represented independence, self-reliance, risk taking, personal integrity, hard work, personal thriftiness, personal property, and the worth of the individual. Business above him had moved on to other business, pursuing the benefits of scale, security for employees, minimal investment risks, the separation of ownership and control.

Small business found itself in a world where $500,000 was harder to raise than $25 million because only big business would try to raise this later sum, and big business hardly ever failed, but small businesses folded every day.*

As business grew, it became more concentrated. But absolute monopoly was extremely rare. The classic model of free competition threatened by wicked monopolies was as outdated as the bookkeeper with a steel pen and an eyeshade. The chief menace to economic efficiency and free competition was oligopoly—the domination of a market by a handful of large firms. The chemical industry, for instance, had been controlled by three companies before the war; it was controlled by seven in the postwar—and more completely controlled than before.

Competition had been curbed when the Reconstruction Finance Corporation was liquidated. The RFC, for all its faults, had financed new businesses, not only small ones but new entrants in steel, automobiles, and aluminum. Big business lobbied for years to have the RFC wound up. John Kenneth Galbraith was convinced that the RFC had done more to help competition than all the antitrust legislation ever passed, and the attitude of big business suggested he was right.

The cost to the economy of oligopoly and the vestiges of monopoly was calculated at $35 to $40 billion a year in 1960. This was equal to the defense budget and accounted for nearly 10 percent of the GNP. That was the difference in price between the way things were and the way they would have been had competition not been restrained.

Businessman nevertheless extolled competition, and they were not being cynical. They acknowledged that a truly free economy would drive some businesses to the wall. But optimists that they were, they were convinced that it would be somebody else's business, not their own, which would go under.

They also argued that if there was no truly free economy, that was as much the fault of the unions as anyone. The biggest single cost of production and distribution was labor. But in the major industries, and many minor ones, there was no free market in labor. With the active help of government the unions prevented the price of labor from dropping. And when the market attempted to correct excesses by cutting production and employment, the government stimulated demand.

Business also resented the antitrust laws. The law said that business must compete. At the same time no one was allowed to win the competition.

But however much businessmen complained, it was undeniable that business was as prosperous in the 1950s as it had ever been in the 1920s, the long-lost Golden Age. And there were fewer worries. "Many officials privately confide," reported the *New York Times* in 1961, "that many

*But not all "small" businesses had trouble raising capital. Bank of America, Chase Manhattan, Humble Oil, Weyerhaeuser Timber, and other billion-dollar corporations had no problems. They were not listed on any stock exchange, however, so legally, and especially so far as the SEC was concerned, they were still small businesses.

companies can now operate in the black at 45 percent of capacity, against 60 to 70 percent two decades ago."

Business was given a sharp boost thanks to the fast tax write-off. A company would be allowed to retain $1 million, for example, on the taxes it owed. The concession would run for five years. It was thus tantamount to a five-year, interest-free loan of $5 million. In the sixth year the business began to pay the $5 million of accumulated back taxes, and it had 45 years in which to repay that sum. This amounted to $111,000 a year. It need only put that $5 million in tax-free municipal bonds at 4 percent per annum to pay its taxes and collect a risk-free $89,000 each year. But it was more likely that the company would put the $5 million back into the business, where the net rate of return on invested capital was likely to be more than a trifling 4 percent.*

Until 1955 consumer demand was so strong that business had little need to worry about profit levels. It could sell almost all it produced and at a high price. But from 1956 onward a buyers' market began (fitfully) to emerge. And around 1960 the Western European and Japanese economies began to make inroads.

It was the industries which were the most highly concentrated (steel, electric machinery, chemicals, automobiles) that were best placed to maintain their high profit levels. The less concentrated (furniture, textiles) saw their profit levels fall drastically. The corporations which could control their prices were, on average, 50 percent more profitable than those which could not. In the more highly concentrated industries, moreover, wages tended to be higher than average, so workers enjoyed some of the benefits of oligopoly. The control of these industries was such that they were able to raise prices even when demand for their products was dropping.

Steel succeeded at this better than any other industry. After the Korean War the demand for steel dropped. According to the textbooks, that meant that the price of steel would fall and the wages of steelworkers would come down. Instead, both prices and wages in steel rose sharply. This evident anomaly came about thanks to government intervention. And the government involved was solidly Republican. A strong union, a powerful industry leader (U.S. Steel), and the Administration, each pursuing its own interests, together repealed the effects of market forces on steel prices and wages. The productivity of the steel industry was lower than that of most manufacturing industry. By paying itself far more than it earned, steel was responsible for nearly half of all the inflation of the 1950s, so great was the disparity and so central its role in the economy.

The Administration avoided a steel strike in 1956 by buying off the in-

---

*The tax laws could also be very kind to big business executives. For instance, Section 1240 of the Internal Revenue Code of 1954 reads much like any other dull tax provision. But it was actually written with a single taxpayer in mind, Louis B. Mayer, president of MGM. It saved him nearly $2 million. Section 2055 (b) (2) was written for the benefit of another taxpayer, Gerard Swope, former president of GE and a widower. It saved him $4 million in taxes on the estate of his late wife.

dustry. Steelworkers got an extra 62½ cents an hour; the companies raised prices by an average $21 a ton. At the next election year, 1960, the steelworkers were back for more. Once again the industry was bought off, after a twenty-seven-day strike. And the Republican candidate labored diligently to portray himself as the man who had settled the dispute.

The chief trouble with steel was that the industry leader, U.S. Steel, was not its lowest-cost producer. At the same time U.S. Steel was one of the most advanced examples of administered prices. These were a recent development. Such prices ignored the laws of supply and demand. The industry decided what level of profit was a fair return on investment, then set its prices accordingly.

In the early 1950s U.S. Steel thought that 8 percent was a reasonable target. But after a few years it decided that to be fair to its stockholders it should be as profitable as major manufacturers in other industries such as chemicals and automobiles. Here was another development outside classical economic theory. Large corporations no longer sought to maximize profits. They set target prices, geared to target profits. The result was price stability (of sorts) in between the setting of targets. General Motors and Du Pont, two of the most effectively managed corporations in the country, were pioneers in this development. They set their sights on a net return of 20 percent.

Competitiveness was further compromised by outright dishonesty. The Gospel of Social Responsibility, devoutly believed in by thousands of businessmen, was, for business as a whole, a public relations exercise. Business is of its nature neither moral nor nonmoral. It is an ordinary necessity—providing goods and services—in every society. When it is not allowed to operate openly, it flourishes furtively, usually with the connivance of authority. Business can be run by bureaucrats, tycoons, or peasants, with varying costs in efficiency. It arises in both free and unfree societies. Those who are skilled at business have cause to be proud, but the pride attaches to the skill, not to the mundane business of buying and selling. Businessmen occasionally flatter themselves with the thought that they are society's good servants because they provide essential services. But these are services in high demand. If this man is not willing to provide them, someone else is. And no one goes into business in order to make a sacrifice. People go into business with hopes of making money or finding security. They seek to serve their own interests first. Business was obliged to set up a system of moral constraints because there was no such system inherent in the activity itself. Business has no moral aim, only moral, or nonmoral, or antimoral, effects. The paroxysms of embarrassment which enlivened business life from time to time in the 1950s came about because of the unfavorable publicity they created, the price of which was not blushes but hard cash.

Even the seemingly irreproachable were caught out. Sears, Roebuck spent $250,000 in the mid-1950s bribing Teamsters' leaders not to organize its workers. Continental Foods, Whirlpool, A&P, Food Fair, and dozen of other big employers did the same, to the disadvantage of their workers and the benefit of their stockholders. *The New York Times* paid off union leaders for several years to save the Sunday magazine section. The Hearst press, always keen on principles, bribed an ex-convict named Harry Gross for ten years to make certain that its supplement, *The American Weekly*, was delivered. Hearst also bribed Gross into agreeing to a below-scale wage increase in 1954 and 1955 for its platform workers.

One electric supply company of Newark, New Jersey, was pursuing an interesting approach to industrial procurement—hookers. The company was soliciting the goodwill of its dealers by offering them the attentions of a busty prostitute and several of her acquaintances. The company was not prosecuted for transporting women across state lines for immoral purposes; instead, the Justice Department chose to prosecute the hooker, even though the traveling expenses of her friends had been paid out of the company's sales promotion budget.

In 1959, three years after the activities of the hooker came to light, Ed Murrow made a documentary called *The Business of Sex*. It depicted the widespread use of prostitutes by major corporations. It created a furor, and many people adamantly refused to believe that Murrow's picture was accurate. There was a common disinclination to believe that reputable businesses would stoop to tawdry, ethically shabby practices. When Martin Mayer wrote his book on Wall Street, he went into raptures over the Stock Exchange. "Is the Stock Exchange honest? It is incredibly self-denying, almost absolutely honest. It is honest beyond the imaginings of the ordinary businessman; honest in word, thought and deed."* In his book on advertising Mayer praised advertising as an honest business and the biggest agency, J. Walter Thompson, as the very model of business integrity. This was at a time when several thousand people were each month making reports on their spending to a consumer research panel run by a lady named Emily Rogers. For twenty years Mrs. Rogers and her panel had been collecting these reports. Each Christmas there was a card from Mrs. Rogers. When a baby was born, there was a telegram of congratulations. But Mrs. Rogers was really a man named Wallace Flynn. There was no disinterested consumer research panel. This hoax was perpetrated by J. Walter Thompson.

Meanwhile, officials at the TVA were marveling at the persistency with which identical bids kept appearing for TVA contracts, identical down to one-tenth of a cent in some cases. For secret, competitive bidding it was a coincidence bordering on the miraculous. There was another intriguing fact. The average price of electrical goods in the stores had risen by 5 percent over the past ten years. But the average prices the TVA was asked for by its suppliers had risen by 50 percent. In May 1959 TVA officials made a routine announcement that they had received seven bids for conductor cables. The lowest bid was for $194,438.24. That was also the highest bid. An alert young Tennessee journalist spotted the apparently casual

---

*But in the revised edition published a few years later Meyer manfully admitted error. The superlatives had been overdone, he acknowledged, in light of recent revelations of an impressive variety of shady practices on the Stock Exchange and along Wall Street.

item. It was soon brought to the attention of Estes Kefauver. With both the press and the Senator hot on its trail the price-fixing conspiracy of the electrical industry collapsed.

The conspiracy had been in existence for eight years. It involved annual sales of electrical equipment worth an estimated $1.75 billion, running from tiny insulators costing $2 each to massive turbine generators costing up to several million. The electrical industry was burdened with overcapacity, and the industry leader, GE, had set its target prices to produce a net return of 20 percent. To maintain its prices at a time when demand was falling, something had to give. What gave was competition.

To the Organization Men in the electrical industry negotiation was more appealing than competition anyway. Yet despite their outward sobriety, a subversive craving for melodrama seems to have seized them. They adopted code names such as Joe Number One. The price-fixing formula (which gave GE 39 percent of the market, Westinghouse 35 percent, and the remainder shares ranging from 7 to 11 percent) was called "The phases of the Moon." Meetings were held at a Milwaukee bar called Dirty Helen's. The attendance list for conspiratorial meetings was "the Christmas Card list." Meetings were referred to as "choir practice."

At an exclusive resort in Ontario one GE vice-president, W. F. Oswalt, considered it demeaning to engage directly in conspiracy with executives from less exalted corporations. He kept to his cabin, and a messenger scurried back and forth, conveying the views of the other conspirators.

What doomed the conspiracy to failure was the old Adam, the competitive instinct. A range of bids would be agreed on. But once someone knew what the lowest bid was supposed to be, it became increasingly difficult to put in a higher, plainly hopeless bid.

Thirty-two corporate defendants and fifty-two individual defendants were indicted. For the first time in seventy-one years the criminal sanctions of the Sherman Act were applied. In the 1,500 antitrust cases prosecuted up to 1961 more than 90 percent had been brought on civil indictments. The few convictions secured on criminal indictments had been settled with fines. But when the electrical conspiracy indictments were still in the offing, four executives of a Midwestern hand-tool manufacturer were given thirty-day prison sentences for price-fixing. One of the four committed suicide on the way to prison. A wave of fear ran through the electrical industry. Yet the reputable press chose to ignore, or at least decently to bury, the news of both price-fixing conspiracies right up until the sentencing of the electrical industry's "Unlucky Seven"—the men from the electrical companies who received thirty-day sentences.

In vain did Fred F. Look, president of one of the indicted companies, protest, "No one attending the gatherings was so stupid he didn't know the meetings were illegal. But it is the only way a business can be run. It is free enterprise." The fines imposed on the corporate defendants totaled $2 million. The Unlucky Seven were, to a man, pillars of the community: sober, industrious, involved in church and charity work. The corporations maintained that these men were low-ranking functionaries whose misguided zeal had led them to betray the corporations' normally high standards. But for low-level functionaries they boasted some imposing titles, which may not have meant much, and were paid as much as $135,000, which did. The Federal judge who passed sentence refused, he declared, to be so naïve as to believe that the top executives in the electrical industry had not known what was going on.

How honest, then, was big business? How well had the major corporations and the Organization Man been able to reconcile the conflicting demands of competition and security? "Many of the defendants *Fortune* interviewed before and after sentencing looked upon themselves as the fall guys of U.S. business. They protested that they should no more be held up to blame than many another American businessman, for conspiracy is just as much a way of life in other fields as it was in electrical equipment. 'Why pick on us?' was the attitude."

A survey of 1,700 business executives and senior managers questioned during the electrical industry conspiracy trial found that to a man they disclaimed any belief in pursuing higher profits without regard to social and ethical consequences. But they were not prompted by a stern sense of moral propriety. About 99 percent of them simply believed that good ethics was good business. This was not morality but public relations. Each man claimed that he was honest, but he had deep misgivings about the next fellow. He it was, went the refrain, who padded the expense account, conspired to rig prices, hired away his competitor's best employees, took advantage of inside information to make a killing on the stock market at someone else's expense and sponsored misleading advertisements. Four men out of five claimed that they knew of unethical practices within their industry, including the employment of prostitutes, deliberate deception, and the substitution of poor work, poor materials, and poor designs in place of the good work, good materials, and good designs the customer had already paid for.

Deplorable as such practices were, however, they hardly compared with the prevalence of corruption and brutality of business in the nineteenth century. Business claimed too much for itself in the Gospel of Social Responsibility. At the same time it was not likely to be any more honest than society and government required it to be.

29

State of the Union Business

Real family income was lower when Truman left the White House than when he entered it. The Eisenhower Administration, by way of contrast, was able to raise annual family income by $1000 simply by controlling inflation. From the frequent expressions of concern, however, anyone would have been excused for thinking that inflation was raging at a high level and was about to go out of control. This hypersensitivity regarding inflation was the legacy of the price spiral from 1946 to 1948. Over the next twelve years inflation averaged 2 percent a year, and the GNP rose by nearly 4 percent. This period, from 1948 to 1961, was one of the most remarkable instances of price stability in the twentieth century.

Conservatives, meanwhile, wrung their withers over the national debt. Yet what mattered was not the absolute size of the debt but the economy's ability to service it. In those terms net public debt had fallen dramatically, from 125 percent of the GNP in 1946 to 60 percent in 1960.

There was a price to be paid for stability, however. From 1953 to 1960 the economy operated well below its capacity. Some $200 billion, almost what it had cost to fight the war, was lost to production through a low level of demand. And in 1957 the economy faltered badly. Prices rose by 4 percent in a year. This set off cries of alarm over "runaway inflation." More alarming was the emergence of a novel development not accounted for in the economic conventional wisdom: inflation had gone up, and so had unemployment. To its surprise and chagrin the United States found itself with the worst of both worlds: inflation and recession at the same time.

No one knew just what to make of this unexpected hybrid. In the past, extreme fluctuations in private investment (the business cycle) had made the economy unstable. But these days government expenditures were twice as large as business investment, and government spending was assumed to be more stable. But in practice, government spending since 1945 had, thanks to changes in government policy and the Korean War, fluctuated more widely than private investment. The Administration's dilemma was further aggravated by the economic recovery of Western Europe and Japan. In the late 1950s Americans were wounded in their pride to learn that other countries were rapidly building up their gold reserves and that America's reserves were, as a result, rapidly shrinking.

The Administration was of three minds about how to cope with the recession: it could increase Federal spending, it might try to stimulate consumer demand by cutting taxes, or it might follow the Micawber school of economics and wait for something to turn up. Ideologically, the Micawber method was the one best suited to the Administration's outlook. During the 1958 Congressional elections Eisenhower stoutly defended it as a policy the country both needed and wanted. Whether doing nothing was needed is open to dispute. Whether it was wanted is not. Republican candidates were trounced at the polls. Their strength in both House and Senate fell to its lowest since 1938. At a subsequent press conference the President was asked if there was anything ordinary people could do to help pull the country out of its slump. Evidently he still had not decided on a major change in policy because he answered, "Buy." "Buy what?" asked the reporter. "Anything," said the President. But there was no real drop in consumer demand during this recession. "Customers suddenly started robbing the supermarkets blind to the tune of a quarter of a billion dollars' worth of goods a year. In southern California arrests for supermarket shoplifting soared fifty percent within a few months."

The automatic stabilizers of government spending prevented aggregate demand from falling very low. So the country stood in little danger of plunging into another depression. And consumers did their allotted work. There was a steady rise in real personal consumption, "a rise which rarely faltered, and on an annual basis never declined from 1946 through 1961—a remarkable historical phenomenon." The Administration was therefore right to think that not a great deal was required. It tardily administered several modest stimulants. But in real terms Federal spending fell from 1957 through 1960, the very time it most needed to be sustained. Real output actually increased by more than 2 percent a year despite this foot dragging. This, however, was only half the rate of growth under Truman; a fact the unions and the Democratic Party made much of; a fact which increasingly became a social and political issue.

For business, the recession marked the end of an era in which it had prospered sufficiently to be able to buy off strikes. Now major strikes broke out nearly every month and often ran for weeks on end. In 1959 Atlantic and Gulf Coast ports were shut down by a thirty-three day longshoremen's strike. That summer the steelworkers walked out. Eisenhower hesitated for three months before invoking Taft-Hartley. After 116 days production of steel resumed.

The effect of the recession on the unions was to shake them out of nearly a decade of torpor. For these few years, from 1957 through 1960, they recovered some of their old militancy. The recession awoke the unions and the country into an awareness of the most intractable economic problem of the postwar—that is, the persistence of a level of unemployment considerably below depression levels but considerably higher than the Employment Act of 1946 had envisaged.

The hard-core unemployed (defined as those without work for more than fifteen weeks) averaged 500,000 from 1947 to 1957. But within less than a year the figure had tripled, to top 1.5 million. In following years it remained stubbornly above the 1 million mark, seemingly invulnerable to any government measure. The overall unemployment rate from 1957 stood at 6 to 7 percent, twice the level considered normal for a full employment economy, in which allowance has to be made for people changing jobs, falling ill, or coming onto the job market for the first time.

Despite the high level of unemployment, the country had never been more prosperous, nor had employment ever been so secure. The result was a paradox. For 80 percent of the nation, they had never had it so good. For the remaining 20 percent, things were as bad as ever; perhaps worse, for in the midst of such prosperity unemployment may have been felt more keenly.

The past decade had seen enormous upheavals in the job market. The aircraft industry had employed 1.3 million people, mainly women, at its wartime peak. In the space of two years more than 1 million people had to leave it. The decline in shipbuilding was still more dramatic. Employment in the shipyards fell from 1.4 million in 1943 to 85,000 in 1949. The Korean War and the permanent war economy raised employment in both aircraft and shipbuilding in the early 1950s. Employment in construction doubled in the first postwar decade. In state and local government it had risen sharply, while in mining and agriculture it had dropped just as sharply.

The war had brought large numbers of women into the job market for the first time, and throughout the postwar rising numbers of married women took full-time employment. Population increased by 15 percent in the 1950s, and the work force increased by 8 percent. Most of the 8 percent was made up of women. Their employment signified, moreover, the shift in the economy from the production of goods to the provision of services because most of them found employment in stores and offices.

Not only had the corporations found a way to maintain their prices despite falls in demand, but the unions had managed to keep the cost of labor from falling despite the increase in unemployment.* This was at a time when labor costs accounted for more than half the price of goods or services.

To workers, of course, that was the way things ought to be. Money was the reason most people went to work. All that most people owned was their labor. Fear of unemployment pervaded American life. Even though people were continually told that they enjoyed an easier life than their parents or grandparents (doubtless true), they actually put in more work for what they received. The number of hours worked each week had dropped from the pre-World War 1 average of fifty-four to an average of fourty-two in the early 1950s. But increases in longevity since the turn of the century had raised the number of years worked in an average lifetime from 32.1 to 41.9.

The seniority system, intended to increase security of employment, for some people had precisely the opposite effect. They were never able to hold a job long enough to acquire even this modest measure of job security. In most industries seniority did not mean much short of ten years. And during the recession even fifteen years' seniority was not enough to save some auto workers' jobs. In most industries the loss of seniority, however caused, meant the loss of health insurance and company pension rights.

Work itself held out fewer satisfactions even for those who were able to hang onto their jobs. What people strove for now, whether they wore blue collars or white, was the achievement of a successful, admired life-

---

*Western governments use different methods of measuring unemployment. But in the United States the government itself used different methods, one at the Bureau of Labor Statistics, the other at the Census Bureau, and got two different results. In every year covered by this work the Bureau of Labor Statistics' rate was lower than the Census Bureau's rate. But both rates probably undercounted the true number of unemployed and made no proper allowance for the underemployed.

style. The work people did was only a part of that life-style, and not always a very important part. It was the life-style which decided how people regarded themselves and were regarded by others. This was why many workers and many middle-class salaried employees fought doggedly over such matters as fringe benefits and differentials. Minor matters of status became vital, while serious questions about the integration of life and work were ignored.

Workers in manufacturing industries were likely, meanwhile, to resent their boring work and lowly status. They took refuge in fantasies about one day owning a farm or small business; not to get rich, simply to get away. There was, they knew, virtually no chance of rising from the shop floor to management. For the time being they guarded their jobs, and the unions considered job security almost as important as wages and fringe benefits.

The unions were ostensibly stronger now than they had ever been. In November 1952 the longtime heads of the AFL and the CIO, William Green and Philip Murray, both died. The AFL's new president was George Meany. Walter Reuther became head of the CIO. They were men of a new breed: labor leaders who had spent only a small part of their lives working for wages. They had made their careers in labor politics, not labor. The ideological and personal animosities which had kept the two major congregations apart were now a thing of the past. Within six months of their election Reuther and Meany signed a "No-Raiding Pact." Jurisdictional disputes still occurred, but less frequently and with less of the old venomous spite. Two years later the two bodies merged. Reuther, who headed the smaller body, became vice-president of the AFL-CIO, with Meany as its president.

The merger did not create perfect labor unity. It produced a body with a strong resemblance to the major political parties—a coalition, that is, of factions large and small pursuing common interests, opposing common foes. The factions, however, could fight bitterly between themselves. Yet they offered a united front against the constant threat of antilabor laws from a Republican Administration.

Polls showed people had mixed feelings about unions: they supported labor's right to organize but also supported right-to-work laws. There was "a national sentiment of being pro-labor without being pro-union." So despite their increasing power and sophistication, American unions continued to feel insecure. Taft-Hartley outlawed closed shops and encouraged right-to-work legislation. By 1961 twenty-five states had passed such laws. But six had chosen later to repeal them. Right-to-work legislation had its deepest impact in the South, where only 15 percent of the work force was organized.

Insecurity was also stimulated by the decline in union membership. After reaching 17.5 million in 1956, union membership fell to 16 million by 1961. It was the biggest blue-collar unions, such as the UAW and the Steelworkers, which lost most heavily.

Management, however, was rarely a threat any longer. On the contrary, the unions since the war had proved a valuable source of labor stability. An agreement with a major union was a binding agreement. The union would enforce it. When clashes occurred between labor and management these days, they had nothing to do with the old class antagonisms. They were over automation.

GE's policy of "Boulwareism" took most of the bargaining out of collective bargaining and remained a curiosity, little copied elsewhere. Yet it could be very effective. In 1960 the company broke a strike by the International Union of Electrical Workers in what a labor reporter described as "The worst setback any union has received in a nationwide strike since World War II."

It was more characteristic for a corporation to hire social scientists to help it deal with absenteeism, high labor turnover rates, lagging productivity, and vandalism in the washrooms. Some companies took to holding an attitude survey among the workers every two or three years, not so much to learn what the workers were thinking as to raise morale. Simply by conducting the survey, the company appeared to be taking an interest in the workers as human beings, and being human, they were flattered.

The catchwords of industrial relations were "communications" and "human relations." The personnel department was (at least to outsiders) one of the very few glamorous areas of business. The new approach embraced aptitude testing, counseling, attitude surveys, and sociometry. For the best part of a decade there was a craze for "role playing." This was intended to give executives, managers, and supervisors a chance to see things from the other fellow's point of view by pretending for a couple of hours, or a couple of days, that they *were* the other fellow.

The influx of women into the factories during the war had done wonders for personnel counseling. In the postwar it seemed utterly logical to employ staff psychiatrists, as Du Pont and Kodak did, or full-time social workers, as Hughes Aircraft and Raytheon did. The presence of large numbers of women made management sensitive to what were really human problems, affecting men as well as women.

The unions were often of two minds about these developments. Management's concern for the welfare of workers seemed too good to be true. Was it trying to wean the worker away from his union? The answer seems to be no. Business was not concerned with human relations as such. Its aim was to raise productivity. What it wanted was a contented work force and a malleable one. Aptitude testing, for example, was used to weed out putative liberals and radicals.

Labor leaders remained suspicious of management's intentions, even if there was far less of the old hostility. They were also perpetually disappointed by labor's failure, even after the great merger, to carry its maximum political weight. They discovered the ingrained resistance of many union members to being coached at the ballot box. Besides being workers, they were husbands, fathers, mothers, wives, veterans, Catholics, Protestants, immigrants, blacks, Puerto Ricans, well paid, and badly paid; that is, they had competing loyalties and interests. Even at its most highly organized, labor could deliver no more than a third of the labor vote, and often far less than that.

The unions helped select candidates, financed them, provided volunteer workers for them. But except in a very few localities, they could not elect them. In a close race the union vote might tip the scales. But in a close race everyone who makes a sizable effort on behalf of the winner can (and almost certainly will) claim to have elected him. The competing claims cancel out.

Liberals for their part were somewhat disenchanted with the unions by the late 1950s. Union membership had failed to liberalize American workers, confounding the high hopes of the 1920s and 1930s. It was a failure that was especially graphic in the South. The mob which hounded Autherine Lucy off the University of Alabama campus contained a strong delegation of United Rubber Workers. Teamsters were found baying outside Little Rock Central High. In Georgia the Imperial Wizard of the United Klans was Eldon Lee Edwards, a paint sprayer at the GM plant in Atlanta and a paid-up member of the UAW.* In a Tennessee plant an attempt to organize the workers was stopped in an hour when the management circulated a photograph of Walter Reuther handing a check to Roy Wilkins for an NAACP fund drive. Below the picture was written: "This is what happens to your union dues."

Many thoughtful people were deeply disappointed by labor's inability to live up to the high (probably exaggerated) promises of an earlier time. The main criticism was that organized labor had become concerned entirely with higher wages and better fringe benefits for their members and heedless of the public good. Union business had become business unionism. Labor leaders had become interchangeable with corporation executives in their salaries, life-style, and outlook. No one could any longer seriously describe the major unions as organizations of, by, and for the working class. The extent of the change from the tear-gas days of the late 1930s was exemplified by the election of George Meany to head the AFL-CIO. "It may interest you to know," he told a reporter, "that I am President of this great organization that has such tremendous power and I never went on strike in my life, never ran a strike, never ordered anyone else to go on strike and never had anything to do with a picket line."

The leader of the biggest union in the country, James R. (for Riddle) Hoffa, was wont to talk about "the labor business." His fellow union heads were his "friends in the labor business." And to men such as Meany and Hoffa it made perfect sense for the unions to match the big business organization: to grow as big, as powerful, as diversified, as bureaucratic. By the 1960s 40 percent of all union members were concentrated in the seven biggest unions.

The unions lost their original impetus in other ways. The International Ladies Garment Workers Union, long one of the most radical and idealis-

*Lord Kinross, visiting Atlanta, met a black teacher who remarked wryly: "Hitler could at least use a brush."

tic of unions, had become something of a family business. David Dubinsky in his youth and middle age had built it into a widely admired body. But then his only child, a daughter, got married. Dubinsky's son-in-law was swiftly installed as manager of an ILGWU local.* At the next union convention he was elevated to a vice-presidency. Half the ILGWU members were black or Puerto Rican. But the union executives were Jewish. Hundreds of thousands of dollars of ILGWU money went to Jewish causes, including Israel. A derisory $200 was given to CORE. Most of the union's money came out of the earnings of poorly paid black and Puerto Rican seamstresses. When the NAACP drew up a list of what it considered racist practices in the union (owing as much to the workings of oligarchy and nepotism as to anything else), the ILGWU leadership did not even deign to reply. Once a union like the ILGWU had been a ladder; now it was a lid.

Much of the lost drive of the union movement was inevitable. Union membership could not rise indefinitely. Half of industrial wage earners were organized; excluding farmers and the self-employed, one-third of the work force belonged to unions. There was little the unions could do to improve on this. Large numbers of workers simply did not want to join a union. To try to organize them against their will would be self-defeating.

Unions had not only pressed up against the inherent limits of membership but also reached the limits of collective bargaining. The GM contract of 1953 which tied wage increases to increased productivity was the logical extension of Charles E. Wilson's earlier idea of tying wages to the cost of living index. The UAW had accepted Wilson's original proposal with deep misgivings only to discover that it protected workers' living standerds during the Korean War bout of inflation. But once wage increases were made contingent on productivity increases, there was less and less for unions and management to negotiate because in the current atmosphere even fringe benefits had become cut-and-dried matters. Although this pattern of labor-management relations was most fully developed in Detroit, by 1960 it had spread to most of manufacturing industry.

Free collective bargaining was further circumscribed by government intervention. Any strike involving steel, shipping, the railroads, food supplies, electric power, coal, or oil brought in the government. And the list of industries it considered crucial grew steadily throughout the 1950s and into the 1960s.

The bane of the labor unions was racketeering. It tarnished the image of labor and made the rank-and-file membership apathetic. Some unions were reduced to trying to bribe members to attend meetings by offering door prizes, free movies, guest speakers, and free drinks. There were union meetings which appeared to the naked eye to be nothing but parties.

---

*Dubinsky's principal assistant in the postwar was none other than Jay Lovestone, formerly the head of the CPUSA. Lovestone proved invaluable as a conduit for CIA money and advice to anti-Communist unions abroad.

There were other unions which took the opposite approach: members who did not attend meetings were fined.

Nor did union militancy make much sense when union pension funds were heavily dependent on the success of business. To have attempted a revival of the old confrontations would have excited the fears, and the resentment, of middle-aged and elderly union members.

The unions' own private welfare state had developed rapidly since the creation of the UMW's health and welfare fund. The Teamsters established a union medical center. The Amalgamated Clothing Workers Union owned Amalgamated Life Insurance, which provided comprehensive coverage to 500,000 workers and their families. The railroad unions had a tradition of running their own insurance programs. The ILGWU had its own health centers. There were union-paid social workers, union-owned resorts, union-financed housing projects. But pride of place still attached to the string of UMW hospitals in the hills and valleys of Appalachia.

The UMW health and welfare fund had an almost spirtual importance to Lewis and the people around him. The fund drew its inspiration from the VA, which during the war had shown how far modern surgery, prosthetics, and physiotherapy could go in restoring terribly injured men to something like a normal life. In the late 1940s the UMW's annual casualty list ran to 12,000 permanently and totally disabled miners. Each year a thousand miners were killed and another 50,000 were injured to a degree short of total disablement. To cope with such a flow of casualties, something drastic was required. And the hospitals were able to boast some astonishing successes, such as the miner who endured thirty-two operations to his crushed and twisted body. After years of medical attention he became a county sheriff.

Royalties to the health and welfare fund mounted faster than inflation. They went from a nickel a ton in 1947 to forty cents a ton in 1960. Unhappily, much of the money was wasted. The hospitals were not well run. Spurious claims on the program and overly generous pension programs proved major impediments to further progress.

Union welfare funds also proved to be a wonderful opportunity for peculation. Fund administrators were given wide latitude in handling the huge sums. It was not uncommon for a fund administrator to become an insurance broker, and thereafter to steer the fund's business his way. Because the funds were so new and because they grew so quickly, union officials had no time in which to work out proper systems of accounting and disbursement. They considered their work well done when they wrung a welfare fund from management. They found themselves with a fund and few ideas on how to manage it. The rank and file were still more bemused. Welfare funds involved insurance and investment questions—areas few workers understood or were interested in exploring.

By 1961 there were 152,000 union welfare and pension plans. The only Federal legislation affecting them was self-enforcing. In effect, union welfarism amounted to a thieves' charter. So no one was surprised to learn that unions proved hospitable to thieves.

Racketeers had got into them a generation earlier, when the repeal of

Prohibition caused them to cast around for new opportunites. The crooks found that a number of the smaller unions were so fragmented and chaotic (e.g., Hollywood unions) that they were easy to penetrate. Those were the days before the Teamsters became powerful and well organized.* Until the 1940s they were much as they had been at the turn of the century, but using trucks instead of horses. The racketeers found the Teamsters vulnerable at nearly every turn.

From 1940 onward, however, the Teamsters became highly organized. In fewer than twenty years they grew into the largest union in the country. In 1960 there were 1.7 million members. Most of this growth was at a time when most unions were having trouble holding their membership levels. The secret of the Teamsters' astonishing growth was its contracts; negotiated on a regional basis by Dave Beck in the 1940s, on an interregional basis by James Hoffa in the 1950s. Their negotiating skills brought first Beck and later Hoffa to the top of the union.

Beck was moved by a deep craving for respectability. He became a power in the state of Washington. Making the most of his impeccable anti-Communism, he was able to become a member of the Board of Regents of the University of Washington. After several years he became president of the board. He lusted after civic awards and received them by the armload. His reputation in the early 1950s was of a man without fear and above reproach—honest, bright, dedicated to the welfare of others. Beck was second only to Walter Reuther among labor leaders in public esteem.

But rumors of corruption began to swirl around Beck in 1954 and 1955. By 1956 the Senate's Permanent Subcommittee on Investigations had received so many reports of wrongdoing that its chairman, John L. McClellan of Arkansas, and its chief counsel, Robert F. Kennedy, began to devote much of their time to the Teamsters' affairs. Beck and Hoffa, who was by now his principal aide, were so confident in their power and public standing that they contemptuously refused to cooperate with the Senate's inquiries. It was the kind of overweening behavior which invites retribution. The Senate considered the Teamsters' conduct a challenge to its power. It responded by creating a Select Committee, under McClellan, to investigate union corruption. In trying to show how tough they were, Beck and Hoffa sowed the seeds of their own destruction.

The AFL-CIO had a rule which prohibited union officers from pleading the Fifth Amendment to a Congressional body. Beck and Hoffa resorted to the Fifth again and again. The Teamsters were thereafter expelled from the AFL-CIO.

McClellan's committee ranged far beyond the misdeeds of the Teamsters. Its hearings were televised and were watched by an audience of tens of millions. The most sensational episodes arose during the hearings in Chicago, where gangsters controlled the restaurant workers' unions. Bars and restaturants had been blown up or burned down; recalcitrant

*Full name: the International Brotherhood of Teamsters, Chauffeurs, Warehousemen and Helpers of America.

owners who refused to pay bribes or interfered with union organizers were tortured, terrorized, and murdered.

Elsewhere the unions of carpenters, bakers, and dairy workers proved rife with violence and venality. Corruption took many forms. One official of the United Textile Workers spent $2,564.64 in union funds on tickets to *My Fair Lady.* He had gone to see it, in the company of his family and friends, no fewer than twenty-four times. Beck's dishonesty was equally eccentric and more comprehensive. He used union money to buy five dozen diapers for a niece with several children. He looted a trust fund set up to provide for the widow of one of his closest friends. Beck eventually went to jail for stealing $1,900 which had been realized from the sale of union property. He was succeeded as union president by Hoffa.

Hoffa wore dark, ill-fitting suits, cheap ties, white cotton socks, and old, scuffed shoes. His fellow Teamster bosses, by contrast, wore mohair suits, silk shirts, expensive ties, bench-made shoes, and diamond-studded cuff links. Hoffa was a complex man. He fascinated Robert Kennedy. During the hearings he would stare malevolently at the young counsel for the best part of an hour; then, to Kennedy's astonishment, Hoffa would smile and wink at him.

Until these hearings Robert Kennedy had pursued an easy, superficial course through life. But the destruction of Hoffa, who came to represent an evil threat to national life, stirred Robert Kennedy's hitherto-untouched sense of moral outrage. Pierre Salinger, whom the committee had hired as an investigator, recalled, "One night Bob and I left our offices in the Senate Office Building . . . as we passed the Teamsters' Washington headquarters . . . he saw a light burning in Jimmy Hoffa's office. 'If he's still at work, we ought to be,' said Bob. And we went back for another two hours." As Kennedy discovered, there was virtually no crime which the Teamsters, under Hoffa, would not commit. And Kennedy's frustration knew no bounds when what appeared to be a foolproof case against Hoffa failed for want of foresight to produce the expected conviction.

The Select Committee's hearings marked a turning point not only for Robert Kennedy but also for his elder brother, John. The television coverage brought something priceless for an ambitious politician: national recognition.

As public alarm mounted, it became inevitable that either Congress or the President would introduce labor legislation before the 1960 election. Eisenhower, the noted "do-nothing" President, made a national television address to urge the public to turn the present sense of outrage into support for the Landrum-Griffin Act, a bill aimed specifically at union corruption. When the bill appeared in the House, 430 of the 434 Representatives eligible to vote on it did so. Landrum-Griffin was one of the three or four most acted-upon pieces of legislation in the twentieth century.

It was believed that the major objective of the bill was to break Hoffa's power. In this, it failed. McClellan was deeply disappointed that the bill's enforcement provisions were too weak. Despite four years of hearings, in which a tale of murder, arson, beatings, and torture, kidnappings, black-mail, and extortion was told, organized labor was still resistant to Congressional control. The victims of the thieves and killers were, in nearly every case, ordinary working people; usually union members.

30
Eat Up . . . and Swallow Hard

Back in 1939 a young graduate student at Columbia had scoured the lower Midwest in search of a small farming town still isolated for the most part from the intrusions and excitements of the twentieth century. His aim was to study it much as other anthropologists were studying the fast-disappearing primitive communities of the South Pacific, Central Africa, the Amazon basin, and remote parts of Asia. He eventually found what he was looking for, in the southeast corner of Missouri. To protect the privacy of its people, Carl Withers gave it the pseudonymous name of "Plainville."

Fifteen years later another graduate student from Columbia arrived in town, to see how much change had occurred. He found it had been transformed. The great world had beaten a path to this small, unprepossessing place; there were television sets in almost every home, and a major highway had been built only a few miles away. In fifteen years incomes had doubled or tripled. For a few they had quadrupled. The people of Plainville had joined the consumer society; they were no more resistant than anyone else to the appeals of modern advertising. Their appetites and interests were almost indistinguishable from those of people in the cities. One subject dominated their lives—money.

Back in 1939 Plainville farmers had grown a little of this, a little of that, raised a few chickens, bred a few cows, and looked on "book farming" with suspicion and contempt. By 1955 they had learned to specialize, and whatever the county agent or the nearby agricultural college was ready to teach, they were willing to learn.

Farming had become more than ever a business. Like business everywhere unit size had grown and grown. The average farm by the 1960s covered 330 acres, double the size of the average farm of the 1930s. Some 3 to 4 percent of all farms accounted for half of all farm acreage. These were agriculture's equivalents of the large corporations. An agribusiness farm covered, on average, more than 4,000 acres.

In the mountain states the average farm was nearly 1,300 acres; in the

Great Plains it was closer to 500, reflecting the different types of farming according to region. But everywhere the trend was toward bigger and bigger farms. As the size of farms grew apace, the value of agricultural land rose rapidly. The assets of farmers tripled in little more than a decade, while their liabilities rose at a comparatively modest 10 to 15 percent a year. In terms of capital investment per worker American farms were, by the late 1950s, more "capitalistic" than big business.

In agriculture, the farmers had learned, scale paid. An acre of corn grown on a quarter section (160 acres) cost $61 an acre in 1960; on 640 acres the average cost of production dropped to $54. Not surprisingly, the top one-fourth of all farms were by now growing three-fourths of the nation's food.

Even farmers who owned only modest-sized farms were able to enjoy the benefits of scale, thanks to farming cooperatives. The co-ops were an essential feature of agriculture. They promoted self-sufficiency at the same time they advanced mutual aid. Co-ops flourished after the war. They not only marketed the farmer's crops but provided such essential services as electric power, telephones, fire insurance, and irrigation. There were co-op banks, health clinics, artificial insemination stations, and grazing associations. There was hardly a farm family that did not belong to at least one co-op.

Did urbanites but know it, many of the most popular food products on supermarket shelves were provided by farmers' co-ops: Sunkist oranges; Land O'Lakes butter; Norbest turkeys; Ocean Spray cranberries. By 1961 the co-ops boasted a turnover of more than $10 billion a year, a membership of more than 7 million, and some 10,000 active co-ops. What had once been dismissed as an eccentric experiment had become, in its entirety, a very big business. And one of the consequences of the rivalry between marketing co-ops and the chain stores was that it helped keep food prices down. In this one area at least free enterprise and open competition was cutthroat.

Large-scale farming was continually spurred by advances in agricultural technology; that technology in turn was spurred by large-scale farming. It was no accident, moreover, that the most prosperous farming areas were invariably those in close proximity to the most highly industrialized areas.

Harvested cropland fell steadily during the 1950s. But the productivity of the acreage remaining went up by nearly 30 percent. Two teenage boys in Prentiss, Mississippi, Lamar and Linden Ratliff, set out to demonstrate what the chemical revolution could do. Throughout 1955 they diligently cultivated what they termed "God's Little Acre." They applied thirty-eight tons of manure and a ton of concentrated fertilizer, plus another ton of ammonia nitrate. The average yield of corn per acre in the corn belt was 60 bushels. Lamar and Linden produced a world-record yield of 304 bushels an acre.

But even as Lamar and Linden toiled away, the productivity revolution in American farming was over; it had taken place in the early 1940s. After

1946 farming productivity rose by 3.3 percent a year, above the national average, but below the productivity gains achieved in air transportation, railroads, electricity, gas, chemicals, coal mining, and textiles. It was assumed that technology was bringing prosperity to the farms. But technology had no friends, no favorites. While it rewarded some, it made hundreds of thousands of marginal farms hopelessly uneconomic. Where the land was suitable and credit available, modern farming technology could produce prosperity. But to the farmer on poor land, who was uneducated and whose credit was poor, it was a disaster. The prosperous farmer could not raise his products for less than the poor farmer and undercut him at the marketplace. Here was the other half of the Matthew Effect.*

It is unfeeling not to acknowledge the enormous social costs of the success of American agriculture between 1940 and 1960. Hundreds of thousands of farm families were pushed off the land and into the cities, regardless of whether they were capable of adapting to city life. Families were shattered. Lives were destroyed.

Most people, however, were less concerned over what agricultural technology was doing to poor farming families than what it was doing to the land and the diet. "To find a diet free from DDT and related chemicals," wrote Rachel Carson in sardonic vein, "it seems one must go to a remote and primitive land, still lacking the amenities of civilization." Her book *Silent Spring* expressed her deep pessimism over what the massive application of chemical agents was doing to the natural order. Her fear was that one year there would come a spring unlike any other—it would arrive in utter, unnatural silence. No birds would sing; no bees would drone among the flowers; no flies would buzz at windowpanes. There would be only the stillness of death. Miss Carson was both an eminent biologist and a gifted writer. Her book sold more than 1 million copies, and after its appearance Americans began to take a lively interest at last in what they were doing to their natural environment.

Americans had never lost their slightly romantic, idyllic attitudes toward the life lived close to nature. The family farm remained an object of veneration. And despite the advent of agribusiness, 90 percent of all farms in 1960 could still be considered family farms.

The nostalgia for the "real" values of rural life inspired the creation of hundreds of rural museums where, for a small price, "One could see a lumber camp, a country lawyer's office, an Amish farm, or a cotton plantation." And there were people such as the "Cleveland business executive [who] purchased the right to live on a farm for a week during the blackberry season. He had not picked berries for 35 years. He was willing to pay for the opportunity."

The artifacts of rural culture began in the late 1950s to flood into urban homes—cowboy boots, blue jeans, stetsons, kerosene lamps, gingham tablecloths, and Amish dolls were being turned out in huge quantities for a population which wrinkled its noses at the smell of manure. Among the

*". . . but whosoever hath not, from him shall be taken away even that he hath."

middle class there was an outburst of enthusiasm for anything in the style usually (and usually inaccurately) called American Colonial. It might with equal justice have been termed Rustic Colonial. From hundreds of thousands of urban walls there stared the frozen, work-worn faces of Grant Wood's "American Gothic." It was a picture which inspired feelings of affection and mockery. Meanwhile, in smart boîtes from Manhattan to San Francisco a folk music revival was in full swing, and smart people took up square dancing.

No one could deny that farm life was rich in pleasures. But for the most part life on farms and in rural areas remained what it had always been— hard. The most obvious sign of how hard it was was the poor state of health of the rural population. Congress had attempted, through the Hill-Burton Act, to provide almost every small town in rural areas with a hospital or a clinic. But there is more to health than hospitals. By almost every index the farming population was considerably more susceptible to illness, injury, and accidental death than the urban population.

Most other major distinctions between the two populations were rapidly being obliterated. Rural life and urban life shaded into each other. Most people living in rural areas were not farmers, anyway, or members of farming families. After the war the most common occupation in rural areas was some kind of blue-collar work, such as being a mechanic or an electrician. Not only was the rural population mostly nonfarm, but the nonfarm rural population was almost indistinguishable from the people who lived in the suburbs which were spreading deeper and deeper into what had for centuries been farmland.

By 1960 only 8 percent of the nation lived on farms. This low figure was partly due, however, to a new definition of the farming population, as well as to the fact that the Census Bureau stopped asking, "Do you live on a farm?" The bureau henceforth decided who lived on a farm and what constituted a farm. The new definition weeded out the people who had a second home where they grew a few vegetables to take back to their apartments in the city. It recognized at last that "People who live on farms do not necessarily farm for a living, and that those who farm for a living do not always live on farms."

With the drop in farming population there was an accompanying drop in the political power of farmers. By the late 1950s the Farm Bloc was a shadow of what it had been twenty years earlier. The aging Farm Bloc Senators and Representatives who remained were few. The new men from rural constituencies had a broader outlook and no seniority. Any concessions they sought for agriculture could be won only with the help of politicians from the cities. With the decline in the Farm Bloc there inevitably went a decline in the power of the very conservative, and often obstructive, Farm Bureau Federation. The FBF was still bigger than all other farm interest groups combined. But much of its membership of 1.5 million "farm families" was made up of people who were not farmers at all; they were, instead, the families of small-town grocers, filling station operators, hardware store proprietors, and bankers. FBF placards could be seen posted on the windows of businesses up and down Main Street in hundreds of Midwestern towns.

As the farm population shrank and its political power dwindled, it became much like the rest of the country, for better or worse. Outwardly there were some distinctions of manner, dress, and speech. Inwardly, however, they were not so very different from city dwellers and suburbanites. Farm machinery was sold more successfully when presented in bright colors (rationalized, in concession to the Puritan conscience, as an aid in identifying parts). Muzak appeared in both farmhouse and henhouse. Pickup trucks began to appear "with whitewall tires, quilted plastic upholstery, half-foot foam rubber cushioning, heavy chrome trim, and such non-Puritan colors as flame red, goldenrod yellow and meadowmist green, with some two-toning."

Nothing did more to integrate country life with town life than the coming of electricity. Before 1940 only one farm in three had electricity. By 1960 even the poorest farm in the most remote area probably had it. Electricity brought much of the new technology with it. It also brought television and radio. It brought kitchen appliances as well as electric milking machines. In various ways it broke down the farmers' age-old isolation from city life.

The sturdy independent farmer, needing only his land to live on, had become a figure of myth and legend. Take away his supply of nitrogen fertilizers, government loans, bank credit, and gasoline, and almost every farmer would go broke within a year. The vice-president of the National Federation of Independent Business, Ed Wimmer, portrayed the farmer as he appeared to the critical eye of his fellow small businessman:

> He gets up in the morning, puts on his chain store pants, shirt, socks, shoes and cap. He picks up his chain store milk bucket and goes out to milk a subsidized cow. He pours the milk into a can that came from Sears Roebuck or Montgomery Ward, loads it onto a truck run on Sears Roebuck tires and Standard Oil gasoline. He sells the milk to National Dairy or Borden, and takes his money to Kroeger or some other chain and buys his food. His wife cooks it for him on a chain store stove and serves it with chain store utensils. After supper, instead of reading the Bible, he looks at the pictures of the pretty girls in the catalogue. Later, he crawls into his chain store bed, turns off his chain store radio, sets his chain store alarm clock, and rests his head on a chain store pillow. And do you know what Sears and Montgomery Ward have done to show their appreciation? They are printing their catalogues on slick paper.

In 1960 there were 3.3 million commercial farmers—that is, individuals and heads of families who relied on farming for their livelihood. Almost everyone connected with agriculture felt that that was 1 million too many. For two-thirds of farm families farming provided a good living. But for the bottom third it offered only grinding poverty combined with a lot of hard work.

The farm population dropped by 20 percent between the end of the war and 1960 (which accounted for a sharp overall drop in the number of self-employed). But this was not nearly sufficient. It was also the young who went and the old who remained behind. The better-educated were more likely to take their chances in the city than the worse-educated. In Plainville many young men had returned at the end of the war and with the aid of the GI Bill had enrolled at the local agricultural college. They learned new methods of farming. But when their GI Bill money ran out, few stayed in Plainville to apply what they had learned.

In 1959 the average age of farm operators was fifty. And of the farms which sold less than $2,500 worth of farm products each year 400,000 were run by someone over sixty-five. Farming on so modest a scale was little more than a hobby for the nominally retired.

Ironically, even as the drift from the land ran its course, the farm surpluses continued to pile up. "Where the population was once thought to press relentlessly on the food supply, now the food supply presses relentlessly on the population." It also bore down on prices. Had there not been a hungry Europe to feed in the late 1940s and the Korean War in the early 1950s, the postwar could easily have witnessed a major financial collapse in agriculture.

Up to 1951 farm prices increased in step with increases in the price of manufactured goods. But after 1951 their paths diverged. Net income in constant dollars per farm fell from $3,551 in 1947 to $2,545 per farm in 1957. It was the good fortune of many farmers that there was a nonfarm income available to supplement what the farm earned. A wife or daughter might teach school; the farmer himself might own a filling station; his son might live on the farm but work in town as a mechanic. The nonfarm income of farm families was almost equal to what they earned from farming.

Farmers found that in common with the rest of the self-employed the consequence of a fluctuating income (other than a deep sense of insecurity) was that they paid more income tax than people who earned as much as they but did so more stably. The difference over a six-year period in the 1950s on an income that averaged out at $5,000 a year could be as high as 40 percent.

Many a farmer was, as the saying had it, "land rich, cash poor." Between 1940 and 1961 the value of all farm assets rose by $119 billion, while mortgage debt rose a trifling $8.5 billion. It was a paradox, but a man worth a quarter of a million dollars might find it difficult to pay his bills. With the value of the average farm rising by 10 percent a year throughout the 1950s there was a large capital gain to be made by any successful farmer who chose to sell and a virtually paid-up mortgage for those who did not.

But these riches did nothing to solve the farm problem and probably made it more intractable. Depending on the region and the type of farming involved, a farm capable of producing at least $10,000 in farm products each year (the minimum needed to provide an adequate family income) in 1959 required a capital investment of $60,000 to $135,000. For the 1 million marginal farmers what farm program or poverty program would ever provide them with capital on that scale?

With perfect logic, farm surpluses were blamed on surplus farmers. In practice, however, marginal farmers consumed nearly all they produced. The little they could afford to sell was neither here nor there in the total market. Farm surpluses were produced by superior organization and advanced technology, not exactly the principal features of twenty acres of badly drained land being worked by a black sharecropper in South Carolina. To prise the bottom third of the farm population off the land would have resulted not in less food (the successful farms would have promptly taken up the slack) but in longer welfare rolls.

The Republican Administration when it turned its mind to the critical problems posed by agriculture promised, in effect, to leave them alone. This amazing promise was accepted in farming areas with the wildest enthusiasm. Compared with American agriculture in the postwar world, *Catch-22* was a portrayal of stark realism.

The Republicans came into office on an often-repeated promise that they would "get the government out of agriculture." Comes the hour, comes the man. In this case, Ezra Taft Benson. In his youth he had sought English converts to the Mormon faith in the wet and dreary streets of Newcastle. In maturity he had been a county farm agent and had taught agricultural economics. His energetic salesmanship had made him the ideal public relations agent for the Idaho potato. In his age, however, as one of the Twelve Apostles of the Mormon Church, he looked forward to a life of spiritual concerns. When approached by Eisenhower to accept appointment as the new Secretary of Agriculture, Benson was deeply reluctant. "I told him," said Benson, "that I was not sure that a minister of the Gospel belonged in the Cabinet." But Eisenhower countered "by asking in return if a position of responsibility in the government was not a spiritual job."

There was as much ideological fervor in the Agriculture Department under Benson as there was in the State Department under Dulles. He really did hope to get the government out of agriculture. Worse, he kept trying to find ways to do it. It was not a popular thing to do, despite the chorus of bucolic cheers. "Benson has a talent for making enemies," concluded *Time*, "and a genius for keeping them." Farmers loved to hate him. For one thing, he provided a useful scapegoat on which to work off their frustration over falling farm incomes. For another, Benson relished telling them that government subsidies, in any form, were indefensible. His descriptions of the evils of Socialism were enough to curdle any patriot's blood. And the miserable sinners, clutching their parity checks, squirmed with all the torments of the self-damned, because they could not fault his moralistic strictures. When at a corn-picking contest in Sioux Falls, South Dakota, in the fall of 1957 Benson made his usual speech on the wickedness of price supports, anger carried the farmers away. The dignified, bespectacled, erect, and immaculate Secretary of Agriculture was pelted with some of America's agricultural surplus. Attempts were made to lay hands on his person. Five farmers were arrested.

"Enveloped in a kind of celestial optimism," in Sherman Adams's phrase, Benson pursued a vision in which price supports would be reduced year by year and large parcels of productive land would be retired each year, until in the end supply matched demand and a decent living was made possible for all who lived by farming. That was how the government would get out of agriculture. It is fair to say it was the stuff that dreams are made of.

Benson found that no administration could foist on farmers any program that most of them opposed. As other administrations had learned long before, the only way government intentions ever became translated into action was for the farmers to run the program. The position of farmers was unlike that of any other group of citizens. Local farm committees, composed of private citizens, were allowed to spend public money on what was plainly private enterprise. The members of these committees were not chosen by the Department of Agriculture or by the public at large. They were chosen by farmers. After taking office, Benson tried to limit the power of farmers to implement (or impede) farm policy. All that he was able to do was end the formal links between the Farm Bureau Federation and the Agricultural Extension Service. It had almost no effect on how things were actually done.

While the new Administration was getting the government out of agriculture, Federal farm programs rose from little more than $1 billion in 1952 to more than $7 billion in 1960. Most of this money was spent on shoring up farm incomes. Farmers remained among the most adamant opponents of Socialism or anything that smacked of the welfare state, William Attwood found on his travels. But "When we asked [a farmer] if he did not regard subsidies as socialistic, he replied: 'We're not for subsidies. We're for parity.' There seemed no point in asking him to define the distinction." However it was dressed up, parity was an income supplement. And by 1961 parity payments amounted to $5.2 billion a year, a welfare program bigger than the British National Health Service.

Parity represented a new kind of Socialism. It was ostensibly intended to help the poor farmer, and in 1956 the typical small farmer enjoyed price supports worth $109. The farmer in the top 25 percent of farm incomes got supports amounting to $1,993, on average. In typical American fashion parity had turned into a system not to help the poor but to reward the successful. Efficiency was encouraged; sentimentality got nowhere. It was Socialism with a competitive impulse.

In 1954, under Public Law 480, Congress attempted to provide a large export market for farmers, underwritten by the taxpayers. It was, admittedly, a very enlightened experiment in self-interest. By the late 1950s PL 480 accounted for a quarter of all agricultural exports. It permitted foreign countries to buy American farm surpluses at very favorable prices using their own (overvalued) currency. The United States promptly lent half the money back to the country involved. Another slice was given as a grant for economic development. Some of the money was made available as loan capital to private enterprise in the country. The remaining slice, about 20 percent, was retained by the United States. It financed the study of American students in the foreign country, underwrote cultural exchanges, and could be spent on anything that seemed likely to promote good relations.

Under PL 480 nearly $2 billion in surplus food was given away for famine relief. Another $2.4 billion worth of food was given to supplement the diets of poor people overseas; food worth $1.3 billion was given to the poor at home. Nearly $2 billion in food was bartered abroad for strategic raw materials. PL 480 was flexible, enlightened, and well administered. The only trouble was that there was not enough legislation like it.

Ezra Taft Benson was meanwhile trying to reduce price supports from a high and rigid 90 percent to something more adaptable and modest. But it proved impossible to agree to anything lower than 82.5 percent, and the surpluses continued to mount inexorably. For three years, 1954–1956, Benson and the White House strove, at times nearly in desperation, to secure Congressional approval of a soil bank. If America's farmland was so embarrassingly productive, then less of it ought to be harvested. That was simple common sense. Under the acreage reserve scheme eventually wrung from Congress there was to be prompt retirement of land presently producing the four most plentiful crops—wheat, corn, rice, and cotton. The land set aside under the Soil Bank Act of 1956 would continue to pay, via the Treasury, but would henceforth grow only grass and trees.

So there was the farmer who used to harvest twenty bushels of wheat an acre from fifty acres. Ten acres had been retired. In the bank was a stiff, green government check for $2,000 or $3,000. But with the extra cash he could now afford some better seed, some more fertilizer, more intensive irrigation, more effective spraying. The next year he harvested twenty-five bushels an acre from forty acres. He produced as much wheat as ever.

Nor did he have to plant trees and grass on the retired ten acres. There was nothing in the law to prevent him from growing feed grains if he wished. And many wished. By 1961 there was a livestock surplus, thanks to the rapidly rising supply of cheap feed grains.

Harvested crop acreage nevertheless dropped from 336 million acres in 1956 to 288 million acres in 1960. And by this time the government had nearly $10 billion in surplus crops in storage. The surpluses continued to arrive with every harvest. When the silos and storage bins were filled, the surplus was put in old Liberty ships moored in the Hudson River.

The efforts to curb farm production went against the grain with many farmers. Most were content to breathe defiance. But Stanley Yankus, who ran a small farm in Michigan, went out and planted thirty-five acres of wheat just as he had done for years, instead of the fifteen acres the government allowed him under the 1956 act. He was fined $253 for every illicitly sprouting acre. In disgust Yankus sold his farm and emigrated to Australia, a country built by the intransigent.

There was a rich and famous (among farmers) figure named Jack A. Harris who chose to defy the cotton allotment system. He was already rich in cotton allotments, holding 5,000 acres' worth. But Harris rented another 4,600 acres of land near Gila Bend, Arizona, and planted every single outlawed acre with cotton. The Federal government honored ambition on this scale with an equally imposing fine: $965,595. But Harris had calculated that he could produce 2¾ bales an acre, which he could sell at the government-supported price of thirty-four cents a pound. That would cover all his production costs plus a $1 million fine. Because of bad weather, he suffered a small loss when he might as easily have turned a modest profit. In all events, Harris was a hero to his fellow farmers.

Cotton exemplified the overriding importance of scale in successful farming. It was, in fact, the difference between riches and nothing. A twenty-acre cotton allotment was almost worthless. But a man with twenty cotton allotments could make a lot of money.

With a fistful of allotments in his hand he could get enough credit to buy enough machinery and fertilizers to work every allotment to the point of exhaustion. This, in turn, opened new possibilities for enrichment, as Billie Sol ("it's pronounced *soul*") Estes of Pecos, Texas, discovered.

Billie Sol had been born poor. He had since become a millionaire. He was a Church of Christ lay preacher, a teetotaler, a nonsmoker, and a crook. Hardly out of knee pants, he got his start in business by operating a housing swindle based on government loans at 2 percent interest for constructing grain storage. Under the guise of building storage facilities he built ramshackle prefabricated homes, which he sold at exorbitant prices during the housing crisis. For this business acumen the United States Chamber of Commerce chose him as one of the nation's most promising young men of business.

By the late 1950s Billie Sol was working half a dozen major swindles. But now that he was rich, he longed to be respectable. He set his sights on becoming an elder in the Church of Christ. The people of Pecos, however, looked on his religious ambition less tolerantly than on his business practices. Billie Sol had to use some crude tactics to secure his elderhood over strong local opposition. Then he sought election to the school board. What Pecos thought of him is suggested by the fact that the richest man in town was beaten by a write-in candidate.

In the course of his pursuit of respectability Billie Sol repeatedly clashed with the local newspaper, the *Pecos Independent and Enterprise*. In the comic-book revenge style of Scrooge McDuck he started his own paper, the *Pecos Daily News*, to put his enemies out of business. It was a fatal move. The *Independent* knew far too much about Estes's manipulation of cotton allotments and his funny fertilizer business.

Estes held 3,000 acres of cotton allotments. That much cotton needed a lot of fertilizer. But Billie Sol maintained that he had lots of fertilizer. So much, in fact, that he was able to raise $22 million on his imaginery fertilizer empire. But the cotton allotments were really the basis of it all. When Billie Sol's creation came crashing down, the first and most valuable asset the government seized was his collection of cotton allotments.

Meanwhile, the *Independent* had drawn attention to Billie Sol's affairs. The Agriculture Department began an investigation. Interest quickened when the principal investigator was found in a ditch riddled with bullets.

A local coroner ruled that death was due to suicide, and the local police declared the case closed. It was, however, an exceptionally thorough suicide; the deceased had evidently shot himself at close range five times with a bolt-action rifle. The deceased also had a masochistic streak because he had first given himself a tremendous pummeling, which left him with a cut over one eye, extensive bruises, and brain concussion.

Billie Sol Estes's pursuit of respectability* led eventually to a long term of repentance in a Federal institution.

While getting the government out of agriculture, the Republican Administration signed the checks for $40 billion in assistance to farmers. Almost two-thirds went in parity payments. The rest went into helping make farmers more productive. Agricultural experiment stations produced new breeds of sheep and hogs, new crop strains, new techniques for pest control, all at taxpayers' expense. The Department of Agriculture charged the farmers nothing. The government also took the lead in the struggle to stop soil erosion. Washington, so often and so loudly assailed, was the strongest single force behind the application of modern technology in agriculture. Federal agencies had educated the farmers to use it, either through the Extension Service or in the land-grant colleges, and then provided the loans or subsidies to finance it. The Federal government was also a major and generous landlord. The Bureau of Land Management rented out 180 million acres in the public domain to cattle and sheep men for less than two cents an acre a year. That was less than was spent on these lands for weed and pest control. To have removed the government from agriculture would have been like taking the spine out of a fish.

Farming offered a life full of uncertainty and hard work. But while many left the land each year and while there was a surplus of farmers, farming retained much of its traditional appeal. There was the 4-H Club, encouraging the young to stay on the land and learn to become good, serious farmers. There was also the county agent, whose job it was to help all farmers, including the inefficient ones, stay in business. When the states began to try to reduce structural unemployment, they set up vocational training programs for young adults. The surplus of farmers notwithstanding, two-thirds of their trainees were trained for agriculture.

The one farming problem that most people were interested in was the price of food. They were convinced that it was rising by leaps and bounds. In real terms throughout the 1950s it was becoming cheaper, and food's share of the average family's budget dropped from 30 percent to 24 percent.

What was happening was that tastes were changing. Americans in 1959 ate far less starch and far more fish, fresh fruits, and green vegetables than in 1945. The fastest-growing section of the food business was in "fancy" foods—tinned lobster bisque, instant vichyssoise, Jordanian al-

*He was an ardent Democrat. In 1956 he tried to curry favor with Stevenson with a plan to train thousands of parakeets to chirp "I like Adlai." Once trained, the birds would be released in the downtown districts of the major cities. To his rage this masterstroke was turned down.

monds, rum babas, and so on. Unfortunately there was also a decline in the quality of the ordinary ingredients in the average diet to offset what might have been mistakenly considered a more educated national palate.

Produce became dull to the papilla and uniform in appearance, caught in the millstones of farm technology and chain store marketing. Tens of thousands of small farms began to sell their produce directly to supermarket chains. They became, in effect, contract growers, working exclusively for the chain. Appearance became vital, taste unimportant; cost was the basis of the relationship, and uniformity essential to its maintenance. The chains did not want produce where the good, the bad, and the ugly were mixed together. Housewives would start picking through the entire selection when that happened. Oranges had to be unblemished, no matter how thick the skin required. Tomatoes needed to withstand rough handling, so they were bred to have hard, rubberlike skins. Green vegetables became tough with fiber, but were less perishable as a result. Corn was perfected so that it had kernels in shells that were like plastic.

In a generation American farmers presided over a revolution in taste. Most Americans, far from their national roots in mud and manure, no longer knew anything about meat or milk, fruit or vegetables, or cared.

31
The California Phenomenon

During the war 1,000 people had moved into California every day, to work at aircraft plants and shipyards, to pick crops and pack parachutes. When the war ended, they faced an uncertain future. The aircraft plants laid off more than half a million workers. The slipways were idle. What should the war workers do? "Better that they go home and rake leaves with which they are familiar," ran the advice offered by native Californians, "than that they stay here and rake leaves they know nothing about."

In the week following V-J Day 417 cars "loaded with furniture, bedsprings, mattresses, baggage, children, dogs and goats passed through the Arizona border station on the backward swing to Oklahoma and Kansas." It appeared that the advice was being taken. California newspapers carried delighted stories about the Grapes of Wrath migration in reverse. To many Californians, surveying their crowded schools and colleges, their busy streets, the lengthening lines at the factory gates, it seemed a boon devoutly to be wished.

Each month 3,000 or 4,000 people, usually with a tidy nest egg built up from wartime savings, moved east. But at the same time there were

15,000 to 20,000 people, drawn from all over the country, pouring in across the Arizona border. California was simply irresistible. It offered:

> A unique way of life which is physically the most comfortable and attractive way of life of any region in the U.S. It differs radically from the life lived by most Americans and, because it contains an answer to many basic problems of modern living, it may radically influence the pattern of life in America as a whole. This California way of life flourishes chiefly in the southern half of the state. There the people live half indoors and half out. They dress for comfort rather than social elegance. They spend much of their lives in automobiles, think nothing of driving 20 miles on a routine shopping trip. . . . Their enormous automotive mobility and the decentralization of their shops and playgrounds have tended to unmake conventional city life.

It was a life-style with enormous appeal. Asked to choose their favorite vacation spot, Americans from the early 1940s to the late 1950s regularly chose California first, Hawaii second. A tenth of all Americans wanted to move to California to live. No other state inspired more than 1 percent to want to change their residence. But California also inspired envy and derision, especially among New Yorkers and upper-class Easterners. It was considered a ridiculous place, full of sunshine, quackery, movie stars, and instant religions. As Fred Allen described it, California was "A great place to live—if you happen to be an orange."

To foreigners, it was a place to marvel at. "California is for the United States what the United States is for the rest of us, a clean new world," exulted Luigi Barzini, ". . . the empty slate on which to start writing anew. . . . To be in California now is a thrilling experience, like being in Virginia or Massachusetts before the Revolution."

The chief attraction of California was assumed to be its climate. But more likely it was the chance to earn more money. Just as America had suffered from a labor shortage almost from the time the Pilgrims landed at Plymouth Rock, which pushed wage rates well above European levels and thus exerted a strong pull on European workers, so California grew so fast after the war that it suffered a labor shortage which pushed up wage rates and attracted workers from elsewhere. Behind its rapid growth there was a shift in manufacturing from the North and East to the South and West—a shift under way since World War I. In the South it was the western part (Texas) which prospered most; in the West it was the southern part (California) which did best. The bulk of manufacturing was still to be found in the Chicago, Baltimore, Boston triangle. But its old preeminence had gone.

The westward migration was also bound up with the migration to the cities. When asked in 1956, "Which city do you think you would most like to live in?" more Americans chose Los Angeles than any other.

The streets were not paved with gold, even in the Golden State. But most of the migrants found they had moved up the social scale, from unskilled to skilled working class, from lower to upper middle class. The higher standard of living, the sunshine, the open spaces, and the clean air appear to have had a liberating effect on people fleeing the dark, cold cities east of the Mississippi.

The only development which might have spoiled everything—massive economic collapse—never happened. The Cold War rained down riches on the state. By 1960 its share of prime defense contracts exceeded the shares of New York and Texas combined. Nor did any state benefit more from the developments of advanced technology. Places such as Palo Alto and Pasadena flourished, while Youngstown and Wilkes-Barre languished. California and Texas prospered from the Cold War, but possibly at the expense of Michigan and New Jersey.

The 1950s brought a revival of the aircraft industry, thanks to the Cold War and the rapid growth of commercial aviation. By 1958 there were more people producing aircraft and aircraft parts than there were producing motor vehicles and equipment. The revived aircraft industry in turn created hundreds of thousands of other jobs in the production of electrical machinery, electronics, scientific instruments, and fabricated metals. Southern California had a climate that was unrivaled for the testing and storage of aircraft. So it enjoyed most of these benefits.

The state's biggest business, however, was not manufacturing but agriculture. It prospered throughout the postwar. The Bank of America, partly because it involved itself heavily in promoting California's agricultural development, rose on the back of this prosperity to become the biggest bank in the world. Credit could, and often did, make the difference between a prosperous farm and one which simply got along from year to year. As the farms flourished, so did the bank. California farmers were also a powerful force in the state. They were strong enough to wring from the state legislature several massive irrigation projects which literally made the desert bloom. Much of the irrigated land was given over to cotton. By the mid-1950s it was the biggest cotton-growing state by far.

And all this time the people kept coming. Its appeal to Iowans was, for some unexplained reason, remarkably strong. Long Beach was known as Iowa's principal seaport. In the first postwar decade the country grew by 20 percent; California's population grew by 50 percent. Of the fifteen largest cities in the 1950s, fourteen lost population. Los Angeles (to some, the anticity) alone grew bigger.* A fifth of all postwar housing starts were in California. It had plenty of clean, comfortable new housing at a time when Chicago, Philadelphia, and Detroit had huge housing deficits.

California also boasted the most advanced development of the consumer society and the service economy to be found anywhere in the world. By the 1950s it alone accounted for half of all the annual increase in service employment. States such as Illinois, New York, and Ohio simply contained too much of the old-style economy to move rapidly into the new one. The contrast between California and the rest of the country became

---

*Los Angeles's indiscriminate, sprawling growth moved pranksters to erect signs out in the desert and up in the mountains reading: LOS ANGELES—CITY LIMITS.

so glaring that in 1955 a reporter from the East reported back: "California is no longer a place. It is an event."

Far from being the haven of half-wits which the consoling fantasy of Easterners often suggested, California had the most highly educated adult population in the country. And those who moved there were, as a rule, better educated than those already there. A study of teachers showed, moreover, that California's teachers were, as a group, more emotionally stable than their Eastern and Midwestern counterparts. The state enjoyed an unprecedented infatuation with education. "Everyone is taking a course in something," reported a professor. And, as Christopher Ricks discovered on a journey through the state, "In California universal higher education is closer to realization than anywhere else in the world."

The state's distinctive architecture was an outgrowth of its warm climate, its brilliant light, and its Spanish heritage. Its domestic architecture blurred the distinctions between indoors and outdoors and exerted a strong influence far beyond the state. Many of the improvements in school architecture throughout the United States in the postwar reflected the designs of Richard Neutra, California's most important architect.

The state's appeal was especially powerful among the young. Yet it also attracted large numbers of retired people. The average age of Californians was several years above the national average. To the young, California meant freedom, nowhere more so than at the beach, and there the name for freedom was surfing.

Until the 1950s surfing had attracted comparatively few followers and offered unlimited dangers. Surfboards were made of wood, were expensive, heavy, and deadly. But the 1950s brought the lightweight, inexpensive, foam-filled fiberglass surfboard. This launched the biggest beach invasion since the Normandy landings. From Santa Monica to Newport Beach, hugging the twisting shoreline the whole of the way, ran the world's first "surfurbia."

By 1961 it was evident to almost anyone with reasonable eyesight that something had gone wrong with the promise that California had held out only twenty years earlier. The freeways of which the state was so proud (free because the state earned so much from offshore oil royalties that it could dispense with tolls) had ruined much of the landscape and spoiled the once-pellucid air. Californians fell out of love with the automobile, even though they had no choice about living with it. In San Francisco an irate citizenry put an end to freeway construction within their city, and its last freeway, the Embarcadero, opened in 1959 unfinished. It is still unfinished.

The chaotic character of local government was another important reason for the despoliation of California. In both Northern and Southern California nearly all the postwar growth was concentrated in "slurbs" (sleazy plus suburb). Local government was in the hands of more than 2,000 special districts. These were political subdivisions given responsibility for essential services such as police, fire, water, roads, and sewage. It was not unusual to live in half a dozen different special districts, so often did they overlap, and to pay taxes to all. Yet because they had no political life or civic meaning, the citizen was effectively no citizen at all. The government provided was not government either, only the mere provision of a service, like dry cleaning. In this civic vacuum the land developer and the real estate speculator got rich. Parks became freeway intersections. Lakes became dumping sites for sewage. Billboards fouled every prospect. And for mile after dreary concrete mile the cheap, standardized, overpriced houses covered the foothills, the plains, and the once-pretty valleys.

Yet nothing slowed California's growth. By the early 1960s it had caught up with New York as the largest state in the Union, and would soon surpass it. No politician and no political party could afford to ignore what was or would soon become the largest single reservoir of votes. There, too, however, California was to offer the nation a mixed blessing. Its first native son to become a truly national politician was Richard M. Nixon. A high-ranking Republican told Theodore White how Nixon had been chosen for the Vice Presidential nomination in 1952: "We took Dick Nixon not because he was right wing or left wing—but because we were tired and he came from California."

California enjoyed the melancholy distinction of possessing the big city with the highest suicide rate in the country, San Francisco. Its people were five times more likely to kill themselves than New Yorkers, twice more prone to self-destruction than the people of Chicago. No one knows exactly what suicide statistics say about a city or a country. Nor can they be ignored.

Looking around them, Californians in 1960 saw what they had wrought in a single generation. Most of it was ghastly. They had succeeded in turning one of the loveliest places in the world into a collection of eyesores. The clean air and sparkling water of the 1930s had been replaced by smog and a repellent-looking soup. Where there had been vistas which ravished the eye there were ribbons of concrete sprouting a tangle of wires, poles, and billboards. They had taken, and given back nothing. The drive to bring industry and people to California had succeeded only too well. They had created "one vast Pittsburgh, with palms."

But starting in the early 1960s, Californians began to take note of what they had done. Saving what remained became for tens of thousands of them a crusade. And despite the damage done to it, California remained the most emulated, the most glamorous state in the Union.

While the West Coast boomed, so did the South. Its growth was largely at the expense of the Northeast and the mid-Atlantic states. Textiles, traditionally a low-wage, labor-intensive industry, relocated to Virginia, the Carolinas, and Georgia. But the biggest stimulus to the South's growth was the Federal paycheck: Washington accounted for more than 10 percent of total personal income.

Only in the South did cities (other than Los Angeles) grow. The region was making up for lost time. In catching up with urbanization, the South unfortunately followed in exactly the same steps. Houston, Dallas, Atlanta, Birmingham, and Miami were well on their way to developing rotting inner cities and suburban sprawl.

What California was to the West, Florida was to the South. Its main attractions were its climate and coastline. And by the late 1950s Florida had supplanted California as the preferred vacation spot.

Florida attracted people rather than manufacturing, and many of the people were over sixty. Most of the 3,000 people who moved into the state each week were retired. They brought with them a steady flow of Social Security and pension checks. They were not invariably elderly, however. A sizable number were under fifty, retiring after twenty or thirty years' service in the armed forces or with Midwestern police or fire departments. Between 1940 and 1960 its population doubled, from 2 million to 4 million. Brevard County, the site of Cape Canaveral, was the fastest-growing county of the 1950s. With the population boom went an economic boom. By Southern standards Florida was a rich state with lots of tourists, low taxes.

In the 1950s there was a strong land boom, which stirred unhappy memories. The Florida land boom of the 1920s had, when it collapsed, helped bring about the Great Depression. But this time the Federal government played a large part in the land boom. It was financed with checks from the VA and the FHA. Florida also built up a viable industrial base but limited it to light rather than heavy industry.

The South's astonishing postwar growth resembled elephantiasis: it struck the extremities first. Florida boomed; so did Texas. And Texas's neighbor, Oklahoma, profited hugely from the exploitation of oil and natural gas, at the expense of coal mines in West Virginia and Pennsylvania. Texas also had some powerful friends in Washington. One-fourth of the state's income was provided by the Federal government. Defense industries and military bases sprang up all across the state in these years when Lyndon Johnson ran the Senate and Sam Rayburn ran the House.

Rapid growth brought daunting social problems. When the cities grew, so did the slums. As tension mounted, so did violence. It was Houston that had the country's highest murder rate, not New York.

Nor was Texas much admired outside Texas. John Gunther drew a wounding comparison: "California compares to Texas as Paris, say, compares to Albania. . . . Texas is a kind of intellectual vacuum . . . an artist in Texas is as rare as an icicle in the Sahara. . . . California literally swarms with poets, artists, men of science."

Texas's much smaller neighbor to the west, New Mexico, enjoyed a thriving tourist trade, plus the riches of natural gas and oil exploitation, plus the munificence of Uncle Sam. Sadly, however, too much of the Spanish charm was unnecessarily abandoned in the scramble for money, and the plight of the state's Indians was not notably improved by this sudden outburst of prosperity.

* * *

There were two more states at the end of the period than at the beginning. About 80 percent of the country favored statehood for both Alaska and Hawaii. Politically, their fates were linked. Hawaii was expected to send mainly Democrats to Congress, Alaska to send mainly Republicans. Neither party could secure admission of the one without tacitly accepting the admission of the other.

The difficulty was posed by Hawaii. A handful of conservative Republicans were convinced the islands were lock, stock, and piers in the hands of Harry Bridges and the West coast longshoremen—that is, under Communist influence. It was a conviction shared by a number of Southern Democrats. Senator Eastland solemnly informed a television audience that to allow Hawaii to send Senators and Representatives to Washington would be to expose Congress to Communist manipulation. CBS was even persuaded to offer fifteen minutes of valuable air time to a Congressman whose stated aim was to prove that getting Hawaii into the Union was "a major objective of the Communist conspiracy."

What really aroused Southern opposition, however, was that Hawaii was a multiracial society (although not as much so as outsiders often assumed). Still, the Pentagon wanted to see Hawaii admitted to the Union. So did the Democratic majority in Congress. The White House, on the other hand, wanted to see Alaska become a state.

In 1958 with the admission of Alaska the flag gained its forty-ninth star. Almost as soon as the new banner was unfurled, it was obsolete. Congress wasted no time after Alaska's admission to vote in Hawaii.

When the news reached Honolulu, people poured joyously into the streets. Homes, offices, and businesses stood deserted amid the revelry. Strangers embraced each other ardently. Church bells pealed among the palms. Ships at anchor whooped their sirens. Exploding firecrackers filled the downtown streets with smoke. For the next two days Hawaiians celebrated. No children went to school. No factories toiled. An enormous bonfire blazed day and night on Waikiki Beach. The hotels dispensed free champagne. At the Hawaii Statehood Commission, which had worked toward this day for more than ten years, the staff closed their office and went out to join the celebrations. On the way out they put a sign on the door reading: GONE OUT OF BUSINESS.

32
All Adrift on a Turning Tide

Throughout his tenure in office Eisenhower remained remarkably popular. But in the fall of 1957 bumper stickers began to appear in the Southwest reading, "Ben Hogan for President (If We've Got to Have a Golfer in the White House, Let's Have a Good One)." By the spring of 1958 the undercurrent of impatience in the national temper was unmistakable. Sputnik was to blame. So was the recession. So was the integration crisis. Out in Columbus, Ohio, Alexander Werth found a deep sense of unease among his students. There was a feeling the country may have already passed its peak while they were coming to maturity; the future was paradoxical—it offered danger combined with dullness.

Allen Drury's 1959 best-seller *Advise and Consent* caught the mood in an interior monologue: "In his own lifetime he had seen America rise and rise, some sort of golden legend to her own people, some sort of impossible fantasy to others . . . rise and rise and rise and rise—and then, in the sudden burst of Soviet science in the later fifties, the golden legend crumbled, overnight the fall began, the heart went out of it. . . . " And who was responsible for this calamity? Everyone. "Nobody could stand forth in America and say, 'I am guiltless. I had no part in this. I did not help bring America down from her high pinnacle.' "

At the White House, the President became obsessed with balancing the budget before he left office; George Humphrey agonized aloud that if taxes remained at the present levels, there would be a depression "that will curl your hair." The budget obsession reflected in part the rigid views of the new Budget Director, Maurice Stans, a political hack appointed to high office on the strength of his ability to raise large sums of money at campaign time. "Negativism was triumphant," wrote Arthur Larson, who saw it at first hand. "Postpone, delay, or better still don't do anything."

Throughout 1958 and 1959 the Rockefeller Panels, a privately financed, public-spirited series of inquiries by eminent men and women from various walks of life into major national and international problems, published their findings. Running through the panels' reports was a very pessimistic strain: the country was failing to give of its best. That so much wealth and so much freedom should produce so little that was clearly excellent was a depressing mystery. Where, they worried, were the manifestations of greatness freedom ought to produce? Where the works of individual genius? Where the elevated taste? The intellectual daring? Throughout these sober reports runs a yearning for excellence that is touching.

But to ordinary people what appeared to be missing was not brilliant achievement so much as an exciting way of life. Everything was so much safer, tamer, duller than it had been twenty-five or thirty years earlier. This was the inevitable result of standardization and bureaucratization. To a visiting Swiss, "The USA has become more bureaucratic than most European countries." For anyone familiar with Europe there could be no more damning indictment.

There was no denying the extraordinary growth of bureaucracy since the war. Most people, however, mistakenly blamed it on Washington. The Federal government had grown rapidly during the New Deal and the war. But after V-J Day its numbers leveled off abruptly. Between 1946 and 1960 state and local government, on the other hand, doubled in size. And it was at the state and local level that government was closest to the people.

In 1960 Congress held public hearings on the country's poor morale. It portentously termed them "Hearings on the National Purpose." The President had meanwhile created a Presidential Commission on National Goals. The commission's members were solemnly instructed to find some.

The result, *Goals for Americans*, was the kind of dispiriting report for which committees are noted; as anodyne as a lullaby. The first goal was to secure the primacy of the individual. But all that it could recommend to achieve this was more—more equality of opportunity, more money for education, more housing, more jobs, more technology, and more basic research, more support for the arts, more help for the poor, more aid to other countries, and more vigilance in the defense of freedom. To pay for all these, and more, required more rapid economic growth. The commission aimed at 5 percent.

There were some estimable concrete objectives: reform of the tax system, a space program that did not degenerate into a celestial private Olympiad between the United States and the USSR, nuclear disarmament, and a test ban treaty. But the commission was in difficulties from the start. Only twice in Western history has a committee produced a masterpiece: the King James Version of the Bible and the United States Constitution. And these had been possible because the committees that wrote them were already informed by a strong sense of purpose. They did not have to seek it out like a felon in hiding. Moreover, the Presidential commission repeatedly invoked the word "equality," but every one of its ten members was male, and every member was white. However worthy its recommendations might be, they were not the work of a body which could hope to generate widespread public support.

For the President himself these were unhappy times. Even the fabled Eisenhower luck appeared to be running out. His principal assistant, Sherman Adams, was in trouble over a vicuña coat, an Oriental rug, and hotel bills amounting to $3,000—all of which had been paid for by a New England industrialist, Bernard Goldfine. These items had been put on Goldfine's income tax returns as business expenses, so the real benefactor of the Adams family was not so much the industrialist as the taxpayer.

Adams's frosty, no-nonsense demeanor earned him Eisenhower's trust and intense dislike elsewhere. He was known as "Sherm the Firm" and "the Abominable No-Man." At the first meeting of the White House staff he had set down the ground rules like a principal addressing the new freshman class: no smoking in the corridors, no feet on executive desks, and no loitering in the secretaries' offices.

Despite his reputation for being an unfeeling man, Adams responded to a plea from his old friend Robert Frost to try to secure the release of Ezra Pound from St. Elizabeth's Hospital. Pound was finally set free in April 1958, just as the Goldfine scandal was breaking.

Eisenhower at first refused to let Adams go, saying, "I need him." But the uproar did not die down. Eisenhower was satisfied that Adams was an honest man. But it was not so much his honesty as his judgment that was in dispute, and in his dealings with Goldfine, Adams had shown appalling misjudgment. For that, he had to go; in the fall of 1958 he went.

Eisenhower was transformed. For the next two years he acted with vigor and a sense of urgency. He took the initiative in domestic matters and, following the death of John Foster Dulles in May 1959, began to run his own foreign policy. He had few qualms any longer about vetoing legislation he disliked. Within the Executive branch his presence was felt as it had never been in Sherman Adams's time.

But he carried less weight with Congress, where both houses were controlled by the Democrats and all eyes were fixed on the 1960 election. Two of Eisenhower's appointments failed. He nominated Clare Boothe Luce to become ambassador to Brazil. Senator Wayne Morse of Oregon chose to make a long, emotional, personal attack on Mrs. Luce, using her past utterances to portray her as a mendacious, vindictive, and foolish person; her idea of serving the nation was the diligent protection of the comforts of the rich. Over the years the loquacious Mrs. Luce had offered a host of hostages to fortune. Senator Morse paraded them one by one across the Senate floor. Stung to the quick, this vain but sensitive woman demanded that her name be withdrawn even though her appointment was almost certain to be confirmed.

The second rebuff came when Eisenhower nominated Lewis Strauss to be Secretary of Commerce. Kefauver used the nomination hearings to rehearse the Dixon-Yates affair. But far more damaging was the opposition raised by Senator Clinton Anderson. He had served as chairman of the Joint Committee on Atomic Energy. Anderson was one of the most capable and modest men in the Senate. He described Strauss in so many words as a liar and a braggart. There were the most bitter and protracted nomination hearings in memory. Yet Strauss's nomination would have succeeded had it not been for Strauss. Charged with serious errors of judgment, he became arrogant and self-righteous. Under close questioning he became evasive. Congress was full of lawyers. It knew an evasive witness when it saw one. Strauss's nomination was narrowly rejected by the Senate.

It seemed only natural to blame the current downbeat atmosphere on the recession. The nation's pride and joy, its economy, was falling short, and other nations, notably the Russians, appeared to be catching up. It is not often that even sophisticated people become exercised over the figures of productivity growth. But from 1958 to 1960 that was what happened. "Growth," an astonished observer recorded, "is fast becoming a hallowed word alongside Democracy and Motherhood."

Since the Civil War productivity had grown at an annual rate of 2.3 percent. If that figure seemed small, it was worth recalling that over the same period no other country had done much better. Since V-J Day the United

States had continued to grow at the same rate as in the past. But suddenly everyone decided that was not good enough. The ruling passion had been fear of inflation. Now it became growth. Economic growth became the principal object of fiscal and monetary policy.

In part the current obsession with growth was an offshoot of the sudden concern for the economic development of non-Western nations. Attempts to aid scores of newly liberated nations in their struggle to achieve modern economies in the space of decades rather than centuries concentrated people's minds on the nature, the forms, and the consequences of rapid economic growth. Inevitably, however, it was an effort distracted by the claims of the Cold War. Walt Whitman Rostow's *The Stages of Economic Growth*, published in 1960, combined both an analysis of the process and impassioned Cold War polemics.

Sober men were heard to insist that the country needed to double its growth rate if it ever hoped to satisfy its needs and aspirations, regardless of what other were doing. But most people appear to have been worried about the Soviets. Their economy was growing at nearly 6 percent a year in the 1950s, with only 1 percent inflation.

Growth rates became a species of spectator sport. Always the Russians were on the verge of catching up. But given the fact that the Soviet economy in the late 1950s was, at most, half the size of the U.S. economy, it would take until the end of the century for the Russians to draw level, and two or three bad years (harvest failures) in a row and they would be set back so far that it would take them 100 years. But Khrushchev, being Khrushchev, threw himself into the spirit of competition. He boasted to Walter Lippmann that within a generation the Soviet Union would be more productive than the United States. When that happened, he suggested modestly, the Russians would be the natural leaders of the world. But Americans would find that situation intolerable and in their envy would launch an attack on the Soviet Union. Khrushchev's bombast probably did more to popularize and legitimize economic stimulation than the entire school of Keynesian economists combined.*

This competitive element was probably unavoidable and in its positive aspects well worth having. It affected Eisenhower, who was so immune to either criticism or flattery that he took no interest in public opinion polls on his popularity at home. But he was always anxious to know how he stood with people overseas. Cabinet meetings, which were held infrequently, were likely to be turned to "the battle for hearts and minds" in foreign lands.

Most people thought the United States was losing the Cold War. The 1958 best-seller *The Ugly American*, by William Lederer and Eugene Bur-

---

*Khrushchev's most famous boast was directed to Adlai Stevenson: "We will bury you." At least, that was what he was reported to have said. But this was evidently a mistranslation which would have been more accurately rendered as "We will be present at your funeral." That is, Communism would outlast capitalism. That was the view of the scholar serving as Stevenson's translator at the time. Herbert J. Muller, *Adlai Stevenson* (New York: 1967), p. 216.

dick, hit the right sour note. The novel involves, for instance, an important conference on providing tactical nuclear weapons to America's Asian allies. But the conference is in danger of failing because one of the senior U.S. delegates keeps nodding off at critical moments. Why is he so exhausted? Because his energies are being drained each night by a Chinese woman doctor who is both torrid in bed and a secret Communist. In the end the delegate's answers to "tough" questions become listless and hesitant. The Asians lose faith in the strength and determination of their American allies and thereby lose the will to defend themselves from Communism.

The hero of the book is Homer Atkins. He looks ugly, but beneath that unpleasant exterior beats a big heart for all the ordinary people of the world. Homer and his wife are down-to-earth types. They literally force the people of the semimythical land of Sarkhan to stand tall. How? By making their brooms two feet taller, so that they no longer have to bend over.

The Ugly American sounds a single note from beginning to end: the Russians are winning, the Russians are winning. Their biggest victory to date was their conquest of China. (The next year, 1959, the Chinese ordered the Russians to get out.) Lederer and Burdick carefully counted every soul won for Communism since the war and with gloomy relish measured every square mile of territory conquered since 1945. More than 8,000 people responded by writing to them asking what they could do to help restore America's prestige in the world. Lederer thereupon published a citizens' handbook with the insulting title *A Nation of Sheep*. Americans were urged to pitch themselves into the struggle by adopting yellow orphans, writing stern letters to Congressmen, by reading *The New York Times* or *The Washington Post* every day, by making sure that the women's club schedules a few talks on foreign affairs, by finding a foreign pen friend and writing regularly, and by inviting foreign students into their homes. Americans were losing the Cold War, ran the argument, not for lack of energy or goodwill but from ignorance of foreign nations and their problems.

Yet during the 1950s Americans went out into the world as never before. In ten years the number of Americans living abroad had tripled, to reach 1.5 million in 1960. Since the war tens of millions of Americans had gone to Europe or Asia in uniform or as tourists or on business. But there was no denying the desire to do more. Their competitive spirit once aroused, Americans hate to lose, whether the stakes are a few dollars or the destiny of the human race.

Typical was a young Air Force pilot who was offered a strange, dangerous, and exciting new job. He later recalled:

> It is difficult to describe what I felt at that moment. I was [one of many who] believed that the Cold War was a very real war, with real objectives and that since the stalemate and compromise in Korea, the free world had been losing that war. . . . The discovery that the government of the United States had conceived an intelligence operation so bold and daring restored much of my

faith. . . . I was amazed. And intensely proud, not only of being chosen to participate in such a venture but, even more, proud of my country itself for having the courage, and the guts, to do what it believed essential and right.

So Francis Gary Powers began to fly the U-2.*

It was less than a secret that these remarkable aircraft were making reconnaissance flights over the Soviet Union; far above the operational altitude of Soviet fighters, higher even than any Soviet antiaircraft missile could reach. The Soviets could put a Sputnik in orbit but could not shoot down the U-2. Twice in 1958 *Time* carried veiled, and gloating, stories about what the U-2 could do and probably was doing.

The Russians tracked these flights with feelings that are not difficult to imagine. The first complete crossing of the USSR was scheduled by the CIA for May Day 1960. Powers was chosen to fly it.

The Russians celebrated May Day by shooting him down. After several years of embarrassment the art of Soviet missilery had caught up with the aviation genius of Lockheed. Powers floated down to Soviet soil by parachute, armed with a large silk sheet overprinted with the Stars and Stripes and a message in fourteen languages: "I am an American and do not speak your language. I need food, shelter, assistance. I will not harm you. I have no malice toward your people. If you help me, you will be rewarded."

Eisenhower denied the real purpose of the flights. The U-2, he maintained, was merely a weather reconnaissance aircraft off course because of bad weather or faulty navigation. When the Russians produced Powers alive and contrite, the CIA's cover story, mouthed by the President, was discredited. Khrushchev blustered and played the incident for all the melodrama in it. He overplayed his hand, however, when he attempted to make Eisenhower grovel. The President had expressed his regrets that such flights were necessary but refused to apologize for having authorized them. Khrushchev then refused to meet with Eisenhower at a summit conference scheduled to open in Paris. The conference was abandoned, amid shrill agonizing that a wonderful chance to advance world peace had thereby been lost.

In the end, the Powers affair did the country no appreciable harm. Many Americans were, like Powers, thrilled to learn that their government had been prepared to take risks, not to threaten another country or to threaten peace, but to break through the wall of Soviet secrecy. By a very large margin Americans believed—the shrill voices aside—that the Administration had handled the U-2 incident properly. But crude notions of what honor may require prompted a bloodthirsty attitude toward the unlucky Powers; some felt he had had a duty to commit suicide rather than allow himself to be captured. Although he had the means, he had no instructions to take his own life. His death would have been pointless. Indeed, it might well have put the U-2 flights in the light of a callous esca-

---

*For Utility-2. An earlier version, the U-1, had been scrapped.

pade and Americans would have appeared less like heroes than fanatical kamikaze types, so mentally unstable that they could be driven to self-destruction by Cold War frustrations.

Undaunted by the collapse of the Paris summit, Eisenhower pressed on with his travels. In the winter of 1959 he had journeyed around the world on a trip to India. He intended to make clear America's growing interest in the fate and problems of the non-Western world. He was also moved by a profound longing to leave the world in a more peaceful state than he had found it on taking office. In Greece, Iran, and Pakistan he was met by tumultuous crowds. In India he was received like a savior.

After India had come a triumphal springtime progress through South America. After the U-2 affair he traveled to the Far East. But there the country he most wanted to visit, Japan, America's principal Asian ally, was denied him. Japanese leftists rehearsed street clashes on such a scale and of such ferocity for Eisenhower's proposed visit that it would almost certainly have resulted in bloodshed and killings. So the journeys which ought to have raised America's prestige—journeys undertaken to show the United States cared about the fate of other peoples—came to a sadly anticlimactic end. The Eisenhower luck really had run out.

Having passed the Twenty-second Amendment to spite the dead Roosevelt, the Republicans in Congress brought to an end the Presidency of the living Eisenhower. Had there been no Constitutional bar, he would probably have run again, thought his closest advisers. Had he run again, there is little doubt, despite the current sense of disenchantment, that he could have beaten any of the likely Democratic candidates.

Eisenhower made an attempt of sorts to prepare Nixon to succeed him. He suggested that the Vice President's ambitions might be better served by doing a real job for a few years, such as being Secretary of Defense. Besides, no Vice President had ever reached the White House except over his boss's body. Nixon ought, by rights, have been able to succeed to the Presidency, except that the Republicans were still, after eight years of a Republican Administration, the minority party. And Nixon was still Nixon, belying the periodic reports of the emergence of "the new Nixon," as if he were a Detroit product, to be restyled in accordance with changes in fashion and marketing strategy every few years.

The doubts which clung to Nixon refused to go away. An attempt to name a Whittier street in his honor was beaten back by a storm of local protest. When the Vice President revisited his alma mater, Whittier College, only two students would shake his hand. The trustees of Duke, where he had studied law, voted to award him an honorary degree; the faculty vetoed it.

To liberal Democrats Nixon was a man so devoid of principle as to be a threat to Constitutional government. Stevenson described America under a future Nixon government as "Nixonland—a land of slander and scare, of sly innuendo, of the poison pen, the anonymous phone call, and hustling, pushing, shoving—the land of smash and grab." Yet there were many people who believed that this very ruthlessness would make him a strong and therefore effective President.

His foreign tours added to his reputation for toughness. He had kept his nerve during the attack on his motorcade in Caracas in 1958. His combative nature led him to engage in a testy exchange with Khrushchev in a model American kitchen at an exhibition in Moscow of American goods. They swapped barbed remarks around the dishwasher and the garbage disposal over America's foreign bases and Russian exploits in space. It was the kind of puerile clash of egos which grown men are likely to regret the next day. Instead, this trifling episode was puffed into the "Kitchen Debate," and Nixon was declared the victor by the American press. Until this time the Vice President had trailed the leading Democratic Presidential contender, John Kennedy, by a large margin in the polls. Overnight he closed the gap. And by the end of 1959 he had a lead of 53–47.

On January 2, 1960, Kennedy announced that he was running for the Presidency. He had been running for it since the 1956 Democratic Convention. In the intervening three and a half years he had become a national figure. His book *Profiles in Courage* had sold more than 1 million copies. He had spoken at Democratic dinners and rallies in almost every state. He knew almost every county chairman in the party. He had helped raise money for hundreds of Democratic candidates, many of whom had since been elected.

Kennedy was celebrated for his style: urbane, witty, relaxed, yet energetic. He was a complex man; the more that is known about him, the more there is that defies explanation. The sophisticated and educated felt him to be one of them, unlike the homiletical Eisenhower. Yet it was Kennedy who was given to writing to a correspondent, "God never permits prayers to go unanswered." This news was contained in a letter whose glutinous style matched that of Norman Vincent Peale platitude for platitude. He never ate meat on Friday; he knelt childlike by his bed each night to say his prayers; during critical moments in his carreer he would make a sudden visit to church. Yet Cardinal Cushing described him as "a man who wore his religion lightly." One of the most striking Kennedy traits was the sense of aloofness; part of him was always hanging back. It appears to have extended even to his religion. He was religious, yet somehow aloof even in his faith.

His evident lack of political commitment led to gibes that he was "the Democratic Nixon." In return he expressed only scorn for liberal Democrats, whom he termed "wild-eyed ADA people." Kennedy was also regarded with suspicion because of his, and his family's, close ties with McCarthy. The future Senators had met in the South Pacific during the war. Kennedy took McCarthy out for a ride in PT 109 and let him fire the machine guns at empty beaches. Kennedy later introduced McCarthy to his family. McCarthy dated Patricia Kennedy and took Robert Kennedy onto his staff. At Hyannisport the Senator from Wisconsin played shortstop on the Kennedy softball team, "the Barefoot Boys." Joe Kennedy liked Joe McCarthy and in 1952 contributed $3,000 to his reelection campaign.

During the Senate vote to condemn McCarthy John Kennedy was in the hospital for a serious operation. He was the only Democratic Senator not to vote for the resolution. It often happens that Senators vote without being present; several did so on the McCarthy resolution. Had Kennedy wished, he could have paired his vote. But he chose, in effect, to put family and friendship above what was largely a matter of conscience.

To the"wild-eyed ADA people" his book, with its theme that there had been politicans who put principle before expediency, was so at odds with his own conduct that some people doubted he had written the book at all. Critics whispered that he ought to show "less profile, more courage."

While seeking the Vice Presidential nomination in 1956, he had sent an emissary to ask the blessing of the *grande,dame* of the wild-eyed ADA people, Eleanor Roosevelt. She refused to give it because of the Senator's refusal to make even a gesture against McCarthyism. Kennedy then went to her in person. She found him charming—and evasive. She turned him down once more.

Yet Kennedy was not notably less courageous than most politicians, and during the fight for the St. Lawrence Seaway he had accepted risks for the sake of principle. Kennedy voted for the Seaway. His fellow Senator from Massachusetts, Leverett Saltonstall, a man whose integrity was never questioned, voted against it. Boston was opposed to the Seaway. Kennedy agonized over his vote and lost sleep over it. But he finally voted for the national rather than the narrow interest. Boston newspapers for years to come described him as the man who had ruined Boston.

Within his own party Kennedy was considered too young, too rich, too independent, and in too much of a hurry. Should he become President, would the men who ran the party, usually twenty years or more his senior, be eased out to make way for brash young men in the Kennedy mold? they wondered. Two of the party's most powerful men, Truman and Rayburn, openly disliked him, Truman because he despised Joe Kennedy and all that he stood for; Rayburn because Congressman Kennedy had been a playboy and had scorned Rayburn's leadership.

The conventional wisdom when Kennedy announced his candidacy was that the Democratic convention would result in a deadlock: Hubert Humphrey was favored by liberal Democrats but'was not well known outside Minnesota; Stuart Symington was esteemed by those who knew him, but few did; Lyndon Johnson was too much a Southerner for Northerners to accept; Kennedy was too young and a Catholic; Stevenson was a two-time loser.

Most calculations were based on the assumption that the primaries would prove inconclusive, as they had proved in 1952 and 1956. But to Kennedy it was as plain as the writing on Nebuchadnezzar's wall that he could win the nomination only in the primaries; he could never win it at the convention.

His religion was the most daunting obstacle he faced; greater even than his youth. It was the principal issue in his campaign from its outset and remained so to the end. Yet Kennedy was opportunist enough to play both sides of the religion issue; it was not simply a barrier to his hopes; with a little dexterity it could be used as a vaulting horse. Once the primaries were under way, he used his religion to exert pressure on the Democratic Party leadership. Should he be denied the nomination because of it, he said, the Catholics would stay home in November and the Democratic candidate would lose. Thus, when it was convenient to say so, there was no Catholic voting bloc such as Protestants claimed; when it was convenient, not only was there such a bloc, but it would decide the outcome of the November election.

The struggle for the nomination led to some strange gyrations over the 1957 Civil Rights Act. While Johnson was trying to identify himself with it, hoping to woo Northern support, Kennedy would have nothing to do with it, in an effort to curry Southern esteem.

Kennedy's most important source of strength was not his charm, his style, or his money. It was the Kennedy organization. Alone among Democratic aspirants he commanded what no politican outside the White House had ever before enjoyed—a national network of effective, intelligent, loyal lieutenants. There were hundreds of them, known to Kennedy personally or to some member of the Kennedy family. When the first important primary got underway, in Wisconsin, Kennedy boasted a fully staffed headquarters at work in eight of the state's ten Congressional districts. Humphrey, from next-door Minnesota and boasting many friends and admirers in Wisconsin, had only three.

The Kennedy organization had contacts everywhere. As a rule the Kennedy workers were young, well educated, and highly motivated. They offered the kind of help mere money cannot buy. The Kennedy legions stood outside the regular Democratic Party, working with its local organs where possible but prepared to work outside them if necessary. As each primary approached, the local corps of Kennedyites were augmented by an influx of Kennedy workers arriving from out of state, supported in turn by drivers, typists, and pollsters. "The Kennedys were not only the richest family to make politics their business; but they were by far the most sophisticated. They were able to demand full value for every dollar spent." In the 1960 primaries Joe Kennedy spent as least $1.5 million on his son's behalf. By comparison there was the Spartan campaign of Hubert Horatio Humphrey.

The Wisconsin primary, which Humphrey expected to win, proved inconclusive. The next major contest was West Virginia. Humphrey opened his campaign there with unpaid campaign debts of $17,000. Kennedy had a large and comfortable plane to carry him around the state. Humphrey had an aging bus.

Yet Kennedy found himself involved in a desperate fight for survival. He had entered his name in this primary because polls showed him to hold a 70–30 lead over Humphrey. But after the Wisconsin primary the voters of West Virginia discovered that Kennedy was a Catholic. West Virginia was the most Protestant state in the country. Kennedy's large lead vanished, but once committed, there was no turning back.

West Virginia made a deep impact on Kennedy. At the age of forty-two, campaigning to become President of the United States, he knew almost nothing about poverty and hardship. In West Virginia he came face to face with them for the first time in his life. "He climbed back into the car after a visit to a jobless miner's shack visibly moved," Theodore Sorensen recalled. "He shook his head in dismay and said nothing."

The entire country appeared in the course of this campaign to have discovered Appalachia. It was as much of a revelation to the journalists from Washington and New York as it was to the Senator. What they had stumbled upon was southern Appalachia, which extends from West Virginia down to central Alabama. The postwar economic renaissance which had revitalized much of the South was piecemeal and patchy. For the most part it had missed southern Appalachia. The region's poverty was thus thrown into stark relief when seen in close proximity to the flourishing parts of the South. An overlay of new highways, spreading urbanization, and forests of television antennas gave a superficial impression of modern life. But the ruling forces throughout the region were ignorance, poverty, and disease.

The West Virginia primary would make or break Kennedy's progress to the convention. No effort was spared. Within the Democratic Party rumors circulated for years afterward that the primary had been bought; the going price of a county sheriff—the key figure in the local political structure—was said to be $1,000.

The night the votes were cast Kennedy sought distraction in a soft porn film called *Private Property*. But he had trouble keeping his mind on this tale of a concupiscent housewife who is by turns raped and seduced as the opportunity arises. Kennedy kept slipping out to the foyer to call Bobby in Charleston, West Virginia. By the time the film ground to a halt he knew that he had won the state by a large majority.

After that the rest of the primaries were comparatively easy. He arrived at the Los Angeles Sports Arena with enough delegate votes already committed to him to win, if nothing went wrong. He had learned some valuable lessons from the fortunate failure of 1956. He had a system of communication and control on the convention floor that his rivals could only envy; they had no hope of matching it.

Stevenson's supporters managed to pack the galleries, and they began a demonstration whose fervor made it appear spontaneous but whose prior organization makes clear that it was not. The delegates on the floor went about their business unmoved by the uproar over their heads.

Lyndon Johnson was in the position of a man standing in a rainstorm hoping to be struck by lightning. Although he enjoyed enormous political power, he could boast only a handful of delegate votes. He had insisted tirelessly for months past that he was not a Southerner at all but a "Westerner." But even his appearance was against him. He was tall (six feet three inches) and big (220 pounds), and "he dressed like a riverboat gambler: dark silk suit, monogrammed shirt, French cuffs and those long-pointed collars."

He had burnished his liberal credentials by getting the 1957 Civil Rights Act through Congress. He also turned back, in the Senate, three bills passed by the House and aimed at curbing the authority of the Supreme Court. The bills were blatant attempts to punish the Court for its liberal rulings on civil rights and civil liberties. Johnson's brilliant gifts as a negotiator and political tactician were rarely more splendidly employed than in his defense of the Court. But hardly anyone knew about it.

Johnson spoiled whatever slender chance he might have had by not entering the West Virginia primary. Had he entered the race, his accent and his style might well have beaten Kennedy. Such a victory would have knocked the strongest contender out of the race and given Johnson a win in the North—more or less.

Kennedy made no mistakes at the convention. He won on the first ballot and proceeded to dumbfound his closest aides by offering the second spot to Lyndon Johnson. Kennedy tried to placate them by saying, "He'll never accept it." But to Kennedy's surprise he did accept it. Some of Kennedy's principal assistants, such as Kenneth P. O'Donnell, knew nothing of the offer until after Johnson had accepted it. To placate O'Donnell Kennedy contrived a face-saving explanation about putting Johnson on ice by taking him out of the Senate, where he would be a hard man to have to deal with.

Kennedy had reason to be embarrassed. His ploy had backfired. He wanted Johnson's support, but without Johnson; he wanted Texas in November, not Johnson in January. To flatter Johnson's huge ego by offering him a nomination he, Johnson, had already said he did not want would cost nothing. Or so Kennedy believed. But Johnson appears to have been hoping for at least the second spot on the ticket for as much as a year before the convention. By becoming Vice President, Johnson would at last lay down the Southern cross. This would make his hopes of becoming President someday, say about 1968, realistic at last. Kennedy, thinking only of his own long term interests, overlooked those of Lyndon Johnson, as viewed by Lyndon Johnson. Outsmarted, and pressed by Pierre Salinger for the true story of the Johnson nomination, Kennedy said dismissively, "The whole story will never be known. And it's just as well that it won't be."

Ten days after the Democratic Convention concluded its business, the Republicans, meeting in Chicago, gave their nomination to Richard Nixon. For once the Republican Convention was more dramatic and intriguing than the Democratic. Eisenhower's massive presence had pulled together the right and the moderate wings of the Republican Party. Nixon, confident of his hold on the right wing, made a play for the moderates. He offered the Vice Presidential nomination to Governor Nelson Rockefeller, a man who never concealed either his Presidential ambitions or his impatience with the reactionary elements in the Republican Party. Nor did he make any pretense of his contempt for Nixon. He curtly rejected the offer.

As the nominee of what was the minority party Nixon could not afford to see the liberal Republicans drift away and vote for Kennedy or else stay home on election day. Without informing his staff, Nixon left the convention and flew to New York to wrest from Rockefeller a peace treaty which was supposed to reconcile their ideological differences. Rockefeller generously allowed Nixon to abase himself. The Republican Presidential nominee thereby found himself riding two horses and possessed a certain hold on neither.

To a candidate such as Kennedy an opponent such as Nixon was a gift from the gods. Kennedy understood only too well that he could not win by his own efforts. He could win only if Nixon did something to lose because although Nixon represented the minority party, Kennedy represented the minority religion. Nixon produced a series of blunders of which the "Compact of Fifth Avenue" was but a foretaste.

He forced a strong civil rights plank into the Republican platform. This was intended to win black votes in the North. Then, once the convention was over, he scorned his own civil rights plank. This was intended to win white votes in the South.

The South was well worth cultivating, but not in this manner. Southerners were willing to be persuaded that the most natural party for them was the one most opposed to any extension of Federal power. Eisenhower had won nearly half the Southern vote in 1956. Nixon would find that some of his most enthusiastic audiences were below the Mason-Dixon line. And their zeal at times carried him away. After receiving a rapturous welcome in a thriving town in Mississippi, he tried to respond in kind: "I note the tremendous progress of this city. The mayor was telling me that in the 12 years he has been mayor, you have practically doubled your population. Where has that progress come from? That progress has not come primarily from government, but it has come from the activities of hundreds of thousands of individual Mississippians. . . ."

Kennedy repeatedly challenged Nixon to a series of debates. Against the unanimous advice of his staff Nixon accepted Kennedy's challenge. He had begun his political career by beating Jerry Voorhis in debate. And after standing up to a Khrushchev, what had he to fear from a Kennedy? Up to now Nixon's campaign appeared to be doing better than his opponent's. Kennedy even drew a poor crowd at a Labor Day rally in Cadillac Square in Detroit organized by the UAW.

A month before the first debate Nixon banged his right knee against a car door. The injury became badly infected. Nixon spent two weeks in the hospital. He had pledged to campaign in every state. It was a promise which made some sense in the beginning. After he had lost two weeks, it made no sense at all. Nixon announced he would honor his pledge. He proceeded to wear himself out. When he appeared for the first debate, he looked ghastly.

Radio listeners could not find much to choose between Kennedy and Nixon. What was on offer was not exactly an interview and not quite a debate. It was more like a press conference. Instead of addressing each other, the candidates gave long-winded answers to journalists' questions. Most of what they had to say was taken almost verbatim from their printed campaign literature. And that was what the radio audience heard.

But the television audience believed that Kennedy had won the argument. His youthful vigor, his assured manner, his physical presence came over very strongly. Nixon, looking haggard and saturnine, provided the perfect foil.

The remaining debates were anticlimactic. The general effect of the debates was to raise the stature of both men. Nixon was only a few years older than Kennedy and no more experienced in politics. The debates convinced the country that they both were capable of being President.

But Nixon continued to undo himself. His campaign strategy was no strategy at all; it avoided making hard choices. By trying to campaign everywhere, Nixon kept himself on the brink of nervous collapse. His speeches lost their resonance. He fluffed even his standard homilies. He lost his temper in public. And he alienated the journalists who traveled with him. But the newspaper publishers remained loyal to the end. Only one in six endorsed Kennedy; the rest endorsed Nixon.

Kennedy, however, won the admiration of the journalists. It showed in the reporting on his campaign. He won them over by being both open and subtle at the same time. Crowd counts were often disputed by reporters. At one Kennedy rally the staff claimed a crowd of 35,000. A skeptical reporter wanted to know how they had reached that figure. Pierre Salinger, explained Kennedy, "counts the nuns, then multiplies by 100." The reporters sitting around him burst into laughter. It was a disarming answer, and it probably killed any future story about inflated crowd counts in the Kennedy campaign.

The religious issue remained the most serious obstacle Kennedy had to surmount. A group of 150 prominent Protestant clergymen and laymen met to draw up what amounted to an anti-Catholic manifesto. Among the moving spirits in this venture was Norman Vincent Peale. The group called themselves Citizens for Religious Freedom, and their manifesto said, very politely, that the nature of the Catholic Church was such that any Catholic President would be bound to obey the wishes of the Vatican. Kennedy's staff read this pronouncement with dismay and foreboding.

The candidate had been invited to address a meeting of Protestant ministers in Houston. Against the unanimous advice of his staff he accepted the invitation. His appearance at the meeting combined defiance and reasonableness in exactly the right proportions. His answers to the questions from an audience which clearly did not like him were models of brevity and responsiveness. He showed that he had no horns, no tail, no cloven hoof. It was a bravura performance and, on film, was shown up and down the country in the last three weeks of the campaign.

In these closing stages Martin Luther King, Jr., was arrested, with fifty-two other people, for sitting in at the Magnolia Room of Rich's Department Store in Atlanta. The fifty-two were promptly released on bail. King was sentenced to four months' imprisonment at hard labor. Kennedy called Mrs. King to express his concern. Robert Kennedy called the judge to ask him to reconsider. The next day King was released on bail. These actions did not mean much to white voters. But among blacks they had an electrifying effect.

Kennedy's campaign was remarkably lucky: the issues were handed to him. The missile gap had been around for three years, ever since Sputnik. The growth issue had been a subject of widespread concern for several years. And there was an aversion to the crudities of Massive Retaliation as a strategy for the nuclear age that had exercised thinking people for five or six years now. Moreover, *Goals for Americans*, the work of Eisenhower's commission, might have served as the Democratic Party platform. Even the head of the USIA, George V. Allen, an Eisenhower appointee, was lamenting that American prestige was on the decline. When Kennedy said that he wanted to get the country moving again, there came a national chorus of agreement. That was the mood. He embraced it wholeheartedly, but he did not create it; he exploited it.

Kennedy was also far luckier than Nixon in his choice of a running mate. Henry Cabot Lodge, whom Kennedy had displaced as Senator from Massachusetts in 1952, campaigned languidly and ineptly. Johnson ran for the Vice Presidency as if it were the best job in the country. But he mainly worked on delivering Texas, which Eisenhower had carried in 1956. At the end of the campaign Johnson and Lady Bird traveled to Dallas. When they entered the Adolphus Hotel, a crowd of hysterical, screaming right-wing protesters swarmed across the lobby and jostled them. Johnson, instead of hurrying his pace, slowed down. Television viewers throughout Texas were treated to the sight of a respectable, middle-aged white woman being pushed and reviled while her husband tried to protect her. Was there a heart unmoved?

Nixon's misfortunes dogged him to the end. Winding up one of his press conferences, Eisenhower was asked to give an example of "a major idea of [Nixon's] that you adopted." The President, bringing the conference to an end and thinking of the press conference scheduled for the next week, said, "If you give me a week, I might think of one." This immediately passed into legend as the political insult of the decade when it was meant as no such thing.

Eisenhower was willing, and at times eager, to campaign for Nixon. Had he been set to it, he might well have put Nixon in the White House. But Nixon, to Eisenhower's bemusement and irritation, kept the President's involvement to a minimum. What Eisenhower did not know was that his wife and his doctor had begged Nixon not to jeopardize the President's fragile health. It was also a request which met with the dictates of Nixon's nature. Should he win, he wanted to win on his own.

The result of the most exciting Presidential election campaign of the century was that two-thirds of eligible voters went to the polls. This was the highest measure of popular participation in a Presidential election in the country's history.

His religion cost Kennedy an estimated 1.5 million votes. Voting in the 1960 election demonstrated that group identification along religious or ethnic lines remained strong despite suburbanization, strict controls on immigration, and the decline of minority cultures.

Unlike almost every other successful Presidential candidate, Kennedy ran behind (often far behind) the Congressional candidates of his party, and had he won the debates with Nixon as decisively as legend suggests, then he would surely have beaten Nixon at the polls by more than 100,000 votes. Contrary to most assumptions, he had no unusual appeal to young voters. But Harry Truman was mystified by the closeness of the Kennedy triumph. "Nixon is a shifty-eyed, goddamn liar," he protested, "and people know it. I can't figure out how he came close to getting elected President in 1960. They say young Kennedy deserves a lot of credit for licking him, but I just can't see it. I can't see how the son of a bitch carried one state."

The Democrats for once outspent the Republicans in a Presidential election. They went $4 million into debt and probably considered it a bargain.*

Nixon had reason to believe that he had in fact been robbed. The rest of us call it stuffing the ballot box; politicians call it the fast count. On election night, with Illinois hanging in the balance, Kennedy called Mayor Richard Daley of Chicago to ask how things appeared to him. Daley answered cryptically, "Mr. President, with a little bit of luck and the help of a few close friends, you're going to carry Illinois." In Texas as many as 100,000 nonexistent voters cast votes for the Kennedy-Johnson ticket. But Nixon refused to challenge the election result in the courts. This strange, complicated man had shown faultless discretion and patience following Eisenhower's heart attacks. And now, when his supporters and aides urged him to challenge the result, he told them to desist: "Our country cannot afford the agony of a Constitutional crisis—and I damn well will not be party to creating one."

Eisenhower brought fifty years of public service to a close. Three days before Kennedy's swearing in the President delivered his Farewell Address. It proved to be the only memorable Farewell Address since Washington's. Two new dangers had arisen, he warned his countrymen, which made more difficult than ever the ceaseless struggle for liberty. The first was "the conjunction of an immense military establishment and a large arms industry [which] is new in the American experience. The total influence—economic, political, even spiritual—is felt in every city, every state house, every office of the Federal government. . . . In the councils of government we must guard against the acquisition of unwarranted influence, whether sought or unsought, by the military-industrial com-

*There is an axiom which holds that the only expensive election is one that has been lost; it is only extravagant when you get nothing in return for your money.

plex. The potential for the disastrous rise of misplaced power exists and will persist." This was hardly the sentimental leave-taking the nation expected. There was astonishment. Eisenhower continued to surprise people, however, because people continued to underestimate him.

The second threat, and related to the first, he continued, came from the Federal government's domination of research. The spirit of free, disinterested inquiry would not flourish long when "a government contract becomes virtually a substitute for intellectual curiosity." These days, he said, respect for science and its powers stood so high that public policy might eventually become "the captive of a scientific-technological elite."

He expressed a deep sense of disappointment that during his eight years in office there had been no appreciable movement toward a more peaceful world. There had been only the absence of war.

With Eisenhower's departure from the White House in January 1961 the 1950s finally came to an end. But there was a sense of anticipation in the air. The last time the atmosphere had been like this was when the war ended.

PART V

LIGHTNING ALWAYS STRIKES THE HIGHEST PEAKS

33

Bliss was it in that [false] dawn to be alive,
But to be young was very heaven

When 1961 began, a radar tower sixty-five miles off the New Jersey coast was pounded to pieces by heavy seas. Twenty-eight Air Force officers and men went to their deaths. The first fatal crash of a Boeing 707 on a commercial flight came at Brussels Airport, killing the eighteen members of the United States ice skating team. At their third trial Dr. Finch and Carole Tregoff were convicted of murder.

One morning, returning home after a fruitless search for steady work, a black part-time janitor named Douglas W. Johnson, fifty, spotted a sack lying in a Los Angeles street. The sack contained exactly what he needed: $240,000 in small, untraceable bills. Johnson had a wife and three sons to provide for. Yet without hesitation he set about returning the money to its rightful owners. He called the FBI and told them, "I've got something here you might be looking for." The money had fallen from a Brinks armored car. Brinks gave Johnson a reward of $10,000. His friends and neighbors treated him to a torrent of abuse. Thousands of vitriolic letters arrived, most of them from outraged blacks. His three sons were hounded at school. Johnson's envious fellow janitors harassed him. He was repeatedly informed that only a moron would have done as he had done. One of his sons ran away from home. Despairing, Johnson said, "I wish I'd let that money sit in the street and rot. I wish I'd thrown it down a sewer." Yet when news of his fate spread, his mailbox was once again filled to overflowing. A telegram addressed to THE HONEST COLORED MAN WHO TURNED IN A FORTUNE was promptly delivered to him. He was praised from far and wide for his integrity.

At the age of sixty-one Ernest Hemingway, placing both barrels of a shotgun into his mouth, ended a life which had illuminated an era.

In July 1961 Wilfredo Roman Oquendo, waiter and naturalized Ameri-

573

574 A DREAM OF GREATNESS

can citizen, returned to his native Cuba. He inaugurated a new form of travel. He hijacked ("skyjack" had yet to be coined) an Eastern Airlines Electra. An enormous crowd cheered him on his arrival at Jose Marti Airport. They mistook him for the first Russian cosmonaut, Yuri Gagarin, whom they had been assembled to greet.

In August the East Germans drove an ugly, twisting wall across Berlin. In September the biggest hurricane on record, Carla, cut a swath of devastation from the Gulf Coast to Kansas, driving nearly half a million people from their homes. Massive evacuation kept the death toll down to fifty. In the fall extensive searches failed to find Michael Rockefeller, youngest son of Nelson Rockefeller, who had vanished while looking for primitive art among some of New Guinea's fiercest tribes.

Denver's baffling wave of big robberies was finally explained. The robbers were thirty-five Denver policemen. They enjoyed advantages denied the average burglar, such as being able to return openly to the scene of the crime and under the pretense of collecting evidence destroy it.

An enormous fire fanned by Santa Ana winds blowing off the desert ravaged Bel Air. Nearly 500 luxurious homes were razed or badly damaged. Their owners—movie producers, Nobel prizewinners, big business executives—were forced to seek temporary accommodation. They were described as "The richest refugees since the Russian revolution."

The year 1962 brought the first national newspaper, the *National Observer*. It was well written and had a handsome appearance. But it appeared only on Sunday.

In February John Glenn made three orbits of the earth. By the time he splashed down the country had regained much of its battered pride. Glenn, clean-cut, smiling, fair-haired, and modest, became the embodiment of the nation's refusal to concede first place to the Russians in anything that was positive and exciting. All the astronauts were taken to New York to be given gold medals by Mayor Robert Wagner. Nearly 3,800 tons of paper rained down on them in the most tumultuous welcome the city had ever given. Not even Lindbergh had been received with greater rapture. Seattle opened its Century 21 World's Fair. The heritage of the fair was an impressive Space Needle and a monorail.

The Dodgers finally moved into their permanent West Coast home, Dodger Stadium in Chavez Ravine. As ball parks went, it was the most advanced structure yet seen. But in Houston work had already begun on the *ne plus ultra* of postwar stadiums, the Astrodome.

The launching in July of Telstar was a national and international event. Telstar was the world's first communications satellite, able to relay television signals across the ocean.

At the age of sixteen Marilyn Monroe had attempted to kill herself. Twenty years later she succeeded. Born a bastard, reared an orphan, she died a suicide. Her appeal had been her unique combination of sensuality and vulnerability. It might have been for her that Thomas Hood had written:

One more Unfortunate,
Weary of breath,
Rashly importunate,
Gone to her death!

Take her up tenderly,
Lift her with care;
Fashioned so slenderly,
Young, and so fair!

She soon became the object of a cult. Painters turned out Monroe portraits, often with bizarre and surrealistic elements. Red roses always graced the entrance to her crypt. Joe DiMaggio had instructed a Los Angeles florist: "Twice a week—forever."

On a lonely road near Plymouth, Massachusetts, a mail truck was held up and robbed of $1,551,277, most of it in small bills.

Robert A. Soblen, convicted of spying for the Soviet Union and sentenced to life imprisonment, fled the United States while free on bail of $100,000 during his appeal. Soblen and his brother had been admitted as refugees from Lithuania in 1940. They repaid their new country by betraying it. His brother had committed suicide after being caught. Soblen's ultimate betrayal was of the people who had put up bail for him. He fled to Israel. On the plane returning him to the United States he stabbed himself with a steak knife. When the aircraft landed in London, Soblen was taken to the hospital. When he lost his fight against being deported to the United States from Britain, he fled from life itself with a handful of barbiturates.

In Boston elderly women living on their own were living in terror. A man who strangled and raped his victims had killed six women in less than a year and assaulted a dozen more.

The fall saw the release of *The First Family*, with Vaughan Meader imitating President Kennedy's flat, nasalized Massachusetts accent. The record sold 3 million copies in the first month of release, making it the fastest-selling record of all time.

When the Christmas shopping season came around again, the New York newspapers were struck again. This time the strike ran for 114 days. Its legacy, however, was *The New York Review of Books*. It was not expected by its creators, Barbara Epstein and Robert Silvers, to outlast the newspaper strike.

When 1963 arrived, so did the "Mona Lisa," aboard the *France*. When unveiled at the National Gallery, the smiling lady was visited by the President and his wife. A million people later stopped by to take a look for themselves.

The winter proved to be the worst in living memory. There were rumors that a new ice age was beginning. The intense cold killed hundreds of people.

Hardly had the snow and ice cleared before the Marine Corps Commandant, General David Shoup, announced the discovery of a memorandum from Teddy Roosevelt addressed to the marines of 1908 suggesting that all marines should be able to walk fifty miles in three days. To show how far they had progressed since then, a group of Marines went out and walked fifty miles in a single day. So did Robert Kennedy. With the President's encouragement the fifty-mile hike became a craze. Boy Scouts, young men in derbies, adolescents, senior citizens, and aspiring politicians hit the road. The *San Francisco Call-Bulletin* gave Kennedy credit for fulfilling one of his campaign pledges: "He's surely got the country moving again."

Philharmonic Hall opened at Lincoln Center to great expectations. There was only one thing wrong with it: the hall was not harmonious. Reviews of concerts were divided into reviews of the performance and reviews of the acoustics. In a desperate move sound reflectors were hung from the ceiling. The striking effect this produced was forgivingly called "clouds" by some, damned as "surfboards" by others.

The USS *Thresher*, a fast, nearly new attack submarine, nuclear-powered and deep-diving, broke up while underwater 220 miles east of Boston. She sank in 1,400 fathoms of water, taking 129 men to their deaths. It was the worst submarine disaster in history. Across the United States flags hung at half-mast. Along the New England shore there was a somber air, and in New London, Connecticut, and Portsmouth, New Hampshire, where most of the dead men's families lived, entire towns were plunged into mourning.

Two women were killed by botulism traced to canned tuna fish. America's garbage cans were soon heavy with tins of unopened tuna.

New Hampshire began operating the only legal sweepstakes in the nation. Twice a year, on the basis of races at Rockingham Park, the state offered a top prize of $50,000. The lottery was intended to provide several million painlessly raised dollars each year for the schools.

In the fall a nervous Joe Valachi was regaling the McClellan Committee with an inside account of "Our Thing"—La Cosa Nostra.

An explosion at the Indianapolis State Fairgrounds Coliseum during an air show killed 66 people and injured 400.

One of the biggest robberies in history, a $3 million jewelry theft in Manhattan, went farcically awry. The robber assigned to steal a getaway car flagged down a 1951 Ford and ordered the owner to get out. After the man had run away, the robber discovered that the car had a standard transmission, which he did not know how to operate. While he was struggling with the gears, police sirens were heard and the robbers took to their heels. Construction workers at a nearby site promptly hauled the car away and divided the stolen jewelry among themselves.

These were years when the First Lady in the land was also the first lady of fashion. Her bouffant hairdo was described by its creator, Mr. Kenneth, as "Uncontrived fullness." Whatever it was called, it took half the country by storm. Women spent hours teasing their hair into uncontrived fullness before spraying it with lacquer until it became as brittle as a bird's nest.

Jacqueline Kennedy also helped prolong the life of the chemise or shift dress. It was already a simple, shapeless garment, little more than an envelope into which to slip a body. Mrs. Kennedy took her shifts one step further by wearing them neckless, sleeveless, and usually in a single bright shade.

Hostess gowns, which reached to the floor, had been worn by few people in the 1950s. But in the early 1960s they were worn by millions. The hostess gown was an expression of the trend toward simplicity and comfort. So were leotards, more commonly known as tights. Until recently they had been associated with dancers or crypto-bohemians. Skiing, introduced young women (and young men) to the merits of the stretch pant. One admirer pronounced gratefully: "The development of stretch pants is really more important than the discovery of the ski." The biggest news in cosmetics was eye makeup—lots of it. At first glance it appeared that the women of America were taking a terrible beating.

American men were themselves trooping off to the beauty parlor, although they continued to pretend that they were simply going to have their haircut. But hair was not being cut; it was being "styled." They could also have their eyebrows and eyelashes tinted, their hair permanently waved, and enjoy a "facial," a manicure, and a shampoo.

The early 1960s saw the folk song boom reach its peak. In its wake it left millions of guitars in millions of pairs of hands. High schools offered guitar classes. Guitar sales doubled every few years. A guitar was portable, and anyone could learn to play a few chords in two or three hours. Every little folk song told a story. Few of the numbers to achieve popularity were genuine folk songs. They were, however, based on songs which were. "Tom Dooley" had begun life as a ballad concerning one Tom Dula, hanged at Statesville, North Carolina, in 1868. "Michael" was a commercialized, folked-up version of a pre-Civil War black spiritual originating among slaves who were transported each day between a plantation on the Georgia coast and their offshore island slave quarters.

In folk songs the words were meant to be heard; in rock 'n' roll it was the beat that mattered. Folk music concerts ("hootenannies") played to packed, hand-clapping audiences, mainly on college campuses. The concerts provided background music to the rising chorus of youthful protest against the Bomb, conformism, and racial injustice. The folk song movement by 1963 had merged with political and social unrest, which took for its anthems "We Shall Overcome" and a union song from the 1930s, "We Shall Not Be Moved." It was a movement that produced a singer of incandescent brilliance, Joan Baez, and a songwriter of unique sensibilities, Bob Dylan.

The really popular music these days produced a new dance, the Twist. It spread out from Philadelphia, and cafe society jumped to its feet. The Twist involved no touching, minimal use of the feet, and considerable agitation from the knees up.

The early 1960s also saw the arrival of the California sound. It sang the joys of surfing, and the Beach Boys were its prophets. A thousand miles from any ocean American teenagers vicariously celebrated a world of pounding waves, physical daring, and carefree golden girls.

And *then* came something bigger still—the Beatles. These four young Liverpudlians were wretched musicians but among the best songwriters of the twentieth century. They also gave back to popular music something it had lost—the sound of authenticity. What they sang, they had written—all of it. They were working-class, unpretentious, and offbeat. They sounded original and noncommercial, even though they drew heavily on American musical styles.

To say that by 1963 there was no escape from popular music is a simple statement of fact. Transistor radios carried the sounds along the street, to the irritation of many and the bliss of the comparative few, who were young and oblivious.

A Hungarian living in Brazil labored for seven years to translate *Winnie-the-Pooh* into Latin. In 1961 and 1962 it appeared on many best-seller lists. The translator, Alexander Lenard, was as baffled as anyone that *Winnie-Ille-Pu* should sell nearly 100,000 copies in a dead language to a nation notoriously monolingual.

There was in these years a spreading awareness of the emergence of Pop Art. Roy Lichtenstein's huge cartoons, Claes Oldenburg's idiosyncratic "soft" and plastic sculptures trod the borderline between art and parodies of art and suggested that no such line existed. A painter named Wayne Thiebaud became famous for painting wedges of pie.

For a year there was a craze for adult coloring books. The themes involved the Kennedys, Khrushchev, sex, alcohol, or business. There was a revival of the yo-yo. In some cities, such as Nashville, more yo-yos were sold in a few months than there were inhabitants to play with them. There was a craze which arrived from England for passing a piano through a hole twenty centimeters in diameter. First the piano had to be worked over by a team of six "reducers."

There was a new diversion: creating Tom Swifties. The original Tom Swift stories written before World War I by Edward Stratemeyer had a charming knack for coining the inadvertent adverbial pun. The new Tom Swifties included: "You have the charms of Venus," Tom murmured disarmingly; "I lost my crutches," Tom lamely explained; "I have plans for the South," said John Kennedy darkly.

These were the years of the key club. Men's clubs had long been exclusive, and there were scores which remained so. But democratization and status scrambling produced a new kind of club, open to anyone but pretending to be exclusive. The first of the key clubs was the Gaslight Club in Chicago. The nubile young waitresses were for decoration only. Customers (members) who propositioned or fondled them were deprived of their keys and banished. Any girl who gave out her telephone number was similarly ejected. The atmosphere was seemingly lubricious, but the old Adam was kept under heavy wraps. The clubs offered an illusion of sexual excitement without the problems of sexual involvement. The Playboy

Clubs advanced the art to its highest form and enrolled more than 1 million members at $50 a key—not exactly cheap but not expensive either.

Standardization moved on, giving us all more numbers to remember. Everyone now had a ZIP code. The Zone Improvement Plan was intended to speed the delivery of first-class mail, a boon desired by business, which generated 75 percent of all first-class mail. "In other words," *Time* explained, "the new system will speed the delivery of the letters (and bills) that nobody is in a hurry to get."

In the name of progress telephone exchange names were dropped and replaced with seven-digit numbers. To the telephone companies' surprise, people liked the old exchange names and resisted progress. An Anti-Digit Dialling League arose in San Francisco to oppose "creeping numeralism." But probably apocryphal was the subscriber who was reported as saying, "Give me LIberty or take the blinking phone out."

Every administration begins in mystery and ends in disappointment. But the Kennedy Administration began in deeper mystery than most. The comparative youth and inexperience of the President, his aides, and many of his appointees prompted Kennedy's best biographer to write that it "would probably be a no-nonsense type of administration, run by men young, dedicated, tough-minded, hard-working, informed, alert, and passionless. The place would be quiet, taut, efficient—sometimes, perhaps, even dull."

The makeup of the new regime was unusual. It relied heavily on academics and free-lance intellectuals. "Kennedy has picked a college faculty rather than a Cabinet," wrote a political reporter. It appeared a daring and novel approach to government. But it was not so much a deliberate choice as a necessity imposed on Kennedy by the limited nature of his circle of friends and acquaintances—that is, the people whom he could induce to take up government service. The people he knew best were journalists and politicians. Few of them wanted to give up their jobs to become bureaucrats. Academics, on the other hand, were much easier to lure away. His limited circle meant that the two most important appointments in his government, State and Defense, went to two men he had never met on the recommendation of a third, Robert Lovell, a Republican with whom he had only a slight acquaintance.

At forty-three Kennedy was the youngest man ever elected to the Presidency, although not the youngest President; Theodore Roosevelt had inherited the job at the age of forty-two. Kennedy's approach to politics was pragmatic. Every conversation with him, reported Theodore White, led to a view of the world in which some men led other men. Men whom others held in esteem were likely to seem hollow as Kennedy described them, while obscure political operators were lauded for their nuts-and-bolts ability. To Kennedy, politics came down to personalities, not to major forces or crucial issues. What mattered first of all was the handful of men who exercised leadership. Political ideas, political institutions, political programs were of interest only to fill in the details. Politics was a matter of who had power and what they did with it.

By the time he reached the White House the new President had developed a dazzling bravura style. Large chunks of it were sham. Its hallmark was vigor (mockingly known as "vigah"). Kennedy campaigned in the cold of New Hampshire without hat or overcoat and was incensed when a reporter gave his secret away: the candidate wore thermal underwear. The Kennedy image was carefully cultivated and protected. His eyes were becoming progressively weaker, necessitating larger and larger typefaces for his speeches; he wore glasses, but never in public, and he refused to be photographed with them. He was going deaf in one ear, suffered a severe adrenal insufficiency, had a bad back, and walked with a limp from an injury to his right knee. Even the White House lawn was expected to look vigorous under the new administration. When the lawn began to sport bald patches, the President ordered that they be painted green.

Kennedy culture was both widely admired and wildly overrated. The young President's idea of a well-spent evening was to throw a party, with lots of good-looking women doing the Twist. For relaxation, he liked to watch Westerns or adventure films. One of his particular favorites, however, was *Roman Holiday*. Kennedy was a man of remarkable intelligence, yet ideas quickly bored him. The conversation he enjoyed most was political gossip.

For a Roman Catholic of Irish descent he was remarkably British and Protestant in dress and demeanor. The Eastern Republican establishment could accept him (whatever its reservations about his father) in a way that was impossible with that upstart Californian Quaker Richard Nixon, who shared much of their ideology. Despite his patrician air, Kennedy possessed some of the instincts of the Boston ward politicians he disdained. When McCarthy's widow remarried, for example, her new husband needed a job. Kennedy appointed him to the Civil Aeronautics Board, although the appointee's only previous contact with aviation had been as a passenger.

Kennedy's style cast such a befogging glow that his cornball pieties were overlooked, pieties which in any other politicians would have been mocked without mercy. He actually liked to quote Knute Rockne on the great game of life: "When the going gets tough, the tough get going." Eisenhower used to skip the annual Presidential Prayer Breakfast when he could. Kennedy never missed one.

The Kennedy style succeeded because it was comprehensive and because the principal actor played his part with conviction. Even his reading was vigorous—1,200 words a minute. Speed reading, a curiosity known only to a few, suddenly swept the country. The Presidential rocking chair, a comfort to his painful back, did wonders for the somnolent rocking chair business. This humble piece of furniture, long redolent of the sedentary and aged, all at once seemed youthful and dynamic. Used furniture stores, attics, sheds, and garages were combed for long-abandoned rockers.

The more people saw of the Kennedy style, the more they liked what they saw. Between the election and the Inauguration a musical based on the Arthurian legends, *Camelot*, opened on Broadway. Before the curtain went up on the first night $3 million had been taken at the box office. And as the country proceeded to fall in love with a man it had only narrowly elected President, so it adopted the mental scenery of the fabled Camelot for the world around him. And because his was more than a one-man show, the same aura surrounded his glamorous young wife, his cerebrating assistants, and tough young brother Bobby.

At thirty-five Robert Kennedy was the youngest man ever to sit in the Cabinet (not that it sat often; six times in three years).* The President's first choice for Attorney General was Abraham Ribicoff, governor of Connecticut. But Ribicoff did not believe the country was ready for a Jewish Attorney General, especially not when the Justice Department was in the forefront of the civil rights struggle. He accepted appointment as Secretary of Health, Education and Welfare.

Within days of being sworn as Attorney General, Robert Kennedy created a "Hoffa Unit" within the Justice Department. It took priority over all other business. Henceforth Hoffa found himself confronting a superior force: one with more money, more lawyers, and a determination equal to his own. If necessary, the Attorney General could call on the President for support and expect to get it. As Hoffa's chances of remaining at large began to dwindle appreciably, tongues began to loosen. Yet paradoxically, Hoffa's stature among trade unionists rose, much as the efforts to deport Harry Bridges had made his grip on the West Coast docks unbreakable. Hoffa was not an intellectual, like Reuther. He was not an ideologue, like Meany. He was simply a hard-as-nails son-of-a-bitch. Rank-and-file Teamsters admired him for that.

Besides his determination to break Hoffa, Kennedy also brought to Justice a determination to make life miserable for mobsters. Thus, Louis Gallo was prosecuted for making a false statement on a VA loan application. Joseph Aiuppa was prosecuted under the Migratory Birds Act for owning too many mourning doves.

Regrettably, Robert Kennedy in his youthful brashness and toughness was unable to spare the fragile and frightened Marilyn Monroe. There appears little doubt that he conducted an affair with her, belying the image of devoted husband and father. In classic fashion he slept with her, tired of her, then dropped her. At times the most manly thing is to leave a woman alone, no matter how strong the physical attraction she exerts. A strong man will; a weak man cannot. Her suicide was an embarrassment and a threat. A thirty-six-year-old woman died in unusual circumstances,

---

*The fewest number of Cabinet meetings of any President, with the exceptions of James Garfield and William Henry Harrison.

yet there was no coroner's inquest. Great public powers seem to have been turned to squalid private purposes. The Kennedy image of selfless service and faultless rectitude in the use of power perhaps made the Nixon camp blink in disbelief and wonder how the trick was done.

But for the present there ran throughout the country a fresh stirring of the spirit. Every mood was heightened: the uneasiness was sharper; the excitement more exhilarating. The New Frontier promised the fulfillment of the postwar's brightest hopes. The hour appeared perfect to reach for the crown of immortality. "If other nations falter in greatness," wrote Theodore White in 1961, "their people remain what they were. But if America falters in greatness and purpose, then Americans are nothing but the off-scourings and hungry of other lands." Thus the challenge. What the response? Kennedy certainly saw the challenge in much the same terms as White. He greeted a gathering of artists and scholars at the White House by saying, "If we can make our country one of the great schools of civilization (like Athens) . . . then on that achievement will surely rest our claim to the gratitude of mankind." And being what and who he was, Kennedy was determined his country would succeed. In his attitude, he stood for a new generation, millions strong. He was part of a new leadership elite. They, like he, had come into their own while comparatively young.

These men, in their late thirties and forties, were a new force in society and politics. The shared experiences of Navy wardrooms and Army messes had dissolved the prejudices natural to young men of upper-class stock. The old arrogance was absent. There was a new outlook, relaxed, unaffected, direct, unemotional. There was concern for the weak and the poor that was not perhaps very deep but free of sentimentality and condescension. Their approach to politics acknowledged the rights of Jews, Catholics, and blacks to share political power. Digby Baltzell, a scion of the Philadelphia Main Line, fell into conversation during these bracing New Frontier days with an upper-class friend who had, by chance, been at wartime Navy OCS with John Kennedy. Like Kennedy, he had spent two years in the Pacific during the war. He told Baltzell, "I love everything about the New Frontier, and whatever Kennedy does, whether I agree with it or not, seems a part of me and my generation."

In Kennedy's Inaugural Address men such as this, and the society they were about to lead, can be found behind the words, between the lines. It was a speech comparable with Pericles's Funeral Oration for the Athenian dead. The President was ostensibly addressing himself to foreign policy. Yet it was as much a speech about America, as Pericles in praising the dead described the living.

The Inaugural Address, pared to the bone, describes America in 1961 as it was and as it wanted to be. The content of the speech is this:

> We are a free people, who choose their own leaders, and we have chosen change. Life has altered greatly since the founding of our Republic: we have acquired a peril (the Bomb) and a hope (the eradication of poverty).

We are a religious people. We worship God, not the state.

A new generation of Americans has come to power. I am one of that generation. We know what war is like.* Yet we are not afraid to take risks to defend our liberty. We are a brave and fearless people.

We are true to our friends in other countries. We hope that they recognize, as we do, that their freedom as well as ours depends on mutual trust and cooperation.

We are not an imperialistic, colonial power. We are generous by nature and will help emerging nations because we are a very moral people.

We are jealous of our position in the Western Hemisphere, and we will defend it.

We believe in the United Nations. We would like to see it strengthened.

We must do what we can to avoid a nuclear holocaust. But we must also remain strong. Weakness is always a temptation to one's adversaries. At the same time we recognize the need to slow down the arms race. It is not only a menace; it is a waste of our resources.

We would like other people to join with us in the wonderful adventures science has placed within our grasp—the exploration of space, the eradication of disease, the exploitation of the earth's wealth. We are a cooperative people who are happy to be partners with others in ventures such as these. Because ours is a society so open and generous that we are glad to welcome even those who are our adversaries.

Such adventures will take a long time to reach fruition. But we are prepared for the long haul. We are an enduring people.

I cannot do these things on my own. It is for you, my fellow citizens, to carry them to completion. Success or failure is in your hands rather than mine. After all, this is not a dictatorship.

We live in challenging times. We must pit our energies against tyranny, poverty, disease and war. We are too intelligent and alert to want to waste our strength on ignoble ends.

Are you, then, willing to accept this challenge to greatness?

We live in an exhilarating but dangerous age. I love it. I believe that you love it, too. And by rising to this challenge, we can change the world; in doing so, we will find ourselves.

Are you, the people of America, willing to pull your weight?

Are you, people of the world, willing to join with us in the defense of human liberty?

Only the best will do—my best, your best. We will not settle for the second-rate.

The only reward we seek is a clear conscience. History will judge us. We do not believe simply in the present moment. We are God's humble servants.

Such is the speech stripped of its poetry, its power, and its rhetoric. Here are the contents or guts of the speech. It was an oration which gained its effects not by eschewing platitudes and clichés but by holding a mirror to the face of American society.

It contained echoes of Lincoln and, oddly, enough, of Eisenhower's first Inaugural Address. It leaned heavily on the poetic device of parallel-

---

*In 1961, 40 percent of all adult American males had seen military service.

ism: a balance of thought conveyed by a balance of sentence. This literary stroke was developed in early Hebrew literature and was carried directly into English in the King James Version of the Bible ("So when this corruption shall have put on incorruption, and when this mortal shall have put on immortality. . . ." "Our Lord has gone up to the sound of a trump; with the sound of a trump our Lord has gone up"). The speech drew on yet another Hebrew literary device, assonance. And these two elements, parallelism and assonance, have informed the literary and moral imagination of English-speaking peoples for centuries.

Kennedy's Inaugural Address thrilled and moved the nation because it rang true and because it was nourished by roots which ran deep in the national culture. No one could find anything novel in what Kennedy said. But the expression was at once both lofty and immediate. This was the most admired political utterance of the postwar and the most inspired Presidential address since Lincoln's little speech at Gettysburg. Here, in 1,000 polished words, an entire people saw themselves. And the tone was exactly right: self-confident, self-aware, commanding, enthusiastic, positive, and high-minded. When their new President said proudly, "I do not believe that any of us would exchange places with any other people or any other generation," he hit the very heart of the American experience since 1945.

The bravura Kennedy style sprang from a craving for action. When he reached the White House, he found a plan awaiting him for the invasion of Cuba. Eisenhower might well have called it off at the last moment, in response to his innate caution and distaste for starting anything he could not be sure of controlling. Kennedy, however, was moved by a desire to show his mettle.

The idea behind the invasion was that the Cuban people were opposed to the Castro regime. Therefore, the United States ought to invade the island.

But what was there, an observer might have asked, that might drive the Cubans into a defense of Castro's government? An American invasion of Cuba would probably do that as fast as anything could.

The attack on Cuba was the worst-kept military secret since Hitler prepared to invade Poland. On April 10, 1961, Walter Lippmann spent the day at Khrushchev's villa at Sochi on the Black Sea. The two men ate, drank, swam, played badminton, and talked. Khrushchev said in an offhand way that Cubans armed and supported by the United States were about to invade Cuba. The project, he said, would fail. This was less than two weeks before the invasion. Four days after Lippmann's conversation with Khrushchev *Life* carried a story, complete with photographs of the invasion force, on the Cubans in training. The invasion was inept, compromised for want of air support (although four Americans died flying combat aircraft for the hapless Brigade 2506), and no secret. Yet Kennedy emerged from this seriocomic disaster with credit by unequivocally accepting responsibility for it.

Several weeks later he gave the country something more laudable to shoot for than toppling Castro. He asked a joint session of Congress to commit the United States to put an American on the moon. The program which NASA had been touting for the past two years had finally found a powerful friend in high places. To Kennedy it was a project which would give to the ages a lasting symbol of American determination and ingenuity. It gave the present a goal to be achieved, "within this decade." This could be taken to mean 1970 if 1969 proved too soon. James Webb, the head of NASA, held out the tantalizing prospect of a moon landing as early as 1968, when Kennedy might reasonably be expecting to end his Presidency. Without showing much enthusiasm for the project, Congress approved the $20 billion the President asked for.

Nor was there notable excitement among American scientists. The space program was overwhelmingly an enterprise for engineers and pilots. The moon program had comparatively little scientific value compared with scores of other, far less expensive ventures.

Yet ordinary people thought it a wonderful idea. Shortly before the President's address to Congress the Russians, to American chagrin, had put Major Yuri Gagarin into orbit. It was to be nearly a year before John Glenn matched this feat. Scheduled to go into orbit on December 20, 1961, Glenn endured ten postponements, on account of bad weather or mechanical malfunction in the rocket or capsule. Two months later, to enormous national relief and rejoicing, he made three orbits of the earth. When he splashed down after five hours in space, Americans had recovered their self-esteem and optimism where space was concerned. In May 1963 Leroy Gordon Cooper, Jr., made a twenty-two-orbit flight to conclude the Mercury program. Four million New Yorkers turned out to welcome him. Cooper's flight was the longest to date in space and did more than any other to vindicate the space program with the American people and Congress alike.

The American approach to space stood in telling contrast to the Soviets'. It was as open as it could be. And Khrushchev realized as soon as the President and Congress committed the United States to putting a man on the moon that his bluff had been called. When the President met the Premier at Vienna in the summer of 1961, Khrushchev blandly suggested that the United States could afford to be first on the moon. The Russians would be along later. This was taken at the time to be no more than another piece of wily Khrushcheviana, merely a devious attempt to lull the Americans into complacency.

But the new administration was, if nothing else, eternally vigilant. The President took up the defense doctrines and attitudes his predecessor had avoided. While in the White House, Eisenhower had been careful not to show the least partiality to the Army. Yet his emotional ties to it were so strong that he never attended the Army-Navy game while President because he could not have kept his feelings to himself and shown the proper even-handedness.

Sport aside, however, he was content to see the strategic weapons systems available in the 1950s decide the military posture of the United States. These systems almost without fail left the Army far behind. They reflected the heritage of the Second World War, when American forces had excelled in the air and at sea. Eisenhower also understood, as a long-time planning and operations staff officer should, that the kind of military force one commands will help determine the nature of the fights one will take part in and may even decide whether one will fight at all. To Army generals such as Maxwell Taylor the defense policy of the 1950s was nothing but "air-atomic fetishism." Taylor and others who called for a policy of "flexible response" were struggling to defend the interests and outlook of the Army. But the language they employed was Kennedy-style language: "It should be made clear that the United States will prepare itself to respond anywhere, at any time, with weapons and forces appropriate to the situation." Taylor's all-embracing "National Military Program of Flexible Response" was like *Goals for Americans*; instead of making hard choices, it called for more, of everything. This, too, was in the Kennedy mode. At home that meant, as the Gaither Committee had recommended in 1957, more resources for air defense and a national fallout shelter program.

Kennedy accepted the Gaither/Taylor recommendations. They were activist. They required that the President educate the nation on thermonuclear realities. Shortly after taking office he began to beat the civil defense drum. Some (millions) came running.

In May 1961 the Federal government received several thousand queries concerning civil defense. In October the number of monthly queries topped the 100,000 mark. The Russians also added to the President's educational efforts by exploding a 30-megaton H-bomb, then a 50-megatonner, and Khrushchev announced the good news that a 100-megaton weapon was under consideration.

The biggest deterrent to building a shelter was cost. A sturdy little shelter, properly equipped, ran to more than $1,000. For $2,500, including freight and installation, one could buy a ready-to-wear shelter which had a window painted on one wall showing a sylvan scene. The fake window was equipped with a genuine screen. This could be lowered at night and then raised in the morning to greet the new (and radioactive) day.

Most people who heeded the call did their own digging. There was a nationwide run on sandbags, flashlights, and periscopes. Hucksters did a roaring trade in "anti-radiation pills" and "anti-radiation salve." These were likely to be aspirin and cold cream. There was a nifty but worthless "anti-radiation suit." It cost $21.95. Thousands were sold. In Boston, bargain hunters were offered shelter for a mere $4.50. Those who sent in their money received a crowbar good for lifting manhole covers.

Some 20 million families, representing nearly half the population, took at least a few modest steps to prepare themselves to survive a thermonuclear war. They stored food or other essentials. Millions of people made structural changes to their homes or built shelters. There were some home shelters that were capable of surviving anything short of a direct hit. People would proudly show the dinner guests around the family fallout shelter. William Walter of Olympia, Washington, put up a sign outside his, reading, "He who lasts, laughs." The President himself, building a large new house on Rattlesnake Ridge in the Virginia hunt country his wife loved so much, ordered a bomb shelter to be dug deep below his future home.

An Austin, Texas, hardware dealer, Charles Davis, raised a national moral furore in his backyard. He armed himself with four rifles and a pistol to defend his hole in the ground. The shelter had a door four inches thick. "This door," he declared, "isn't to keep radiation out. It's to keep people out." And should some improvident intruder get to the door before he did, Davis had a supply of tear-gas grenades on hand to smoke him out. The Reverend L.C. McHugh, an editor of *America*, gave Davis his blessing. Squatters in another man's shelter, he wrote, were "unjust aggressors." They were to be "repelled with whatever means will effectively deter their assault." The howls of rage which the priest's "Ethics at the Shelter Doorway" provoked were loud enough to penetrate four inches of wood.

The President asked Congress for $700 million to launch a national shelter program which would eventually cover the entire nation. Group shelters, authorities agreed, had every advantage over family shelters. The government had already created a signal system, CONELRAD (Control of Electromagnetic Radiation), which would provide communications in the event of a nuclear attack. When the sirens sounded, commercial broadcasting would cease. Everyone would be expected to go to a shelter—if he could find one. But lacking that, Americans might prefer to build one of their own.

The Post Office distributed 30 million copies of a reassuring pamphlet called *Fallout Protection: What to Know and Do About Atomic Attack*. More than 4,000 were mailed back to the government in protest. *Fallout Protection* was filled with togetherness illustrations of mom, dad, and junior first building, then happily occupying their own shelter. But the community shelter was made to appear even more enticing; built under a school playground, it was used in preattack days as "an after school hangout where . . . gregarious teenagers . . . can relax with sodas and play the jukebox."

From 1961 on, one frequently came across a public place marked with black and yellow signs to show that it was a fallout shelter. Most of these places were already given over to some other use (subways, office building basements). But somewhere nearby there was a store of emergency food and medical supplies.

In this fashion hundreds of thousands of community fallout shelters came into existence. When they were combined with the private shelters, there was by late 1963 room for more than 100 million people to take cover. Nearly all shelters, public or private, were useless. They offered a greater or lesser degree of protection against fallout, which would contain the heaviest radiation. But most would not stand up to the blast of a hydrogen bomb or the rubble which would rain down on them. There was only one place, RAND and other bodies agreed, which was safe: deep underground. That was where government and military shelters were located. Herman Kahn suggested that America's best hope of winning a thermonuclear war might rest not with SAC but with SUC—the Strategic Underground Command.

The shelter craze lasted for two years before people wearied of it. But in the summer of 1963 shelter salesmen found the pickings were lean. And Portland, Oregon, once one of the most praised participants in the Federal civil defense program, became the first city to abandon the civil defense idea as a futility bordering on a hoax. Ever since 1945 civil defense had been impeded by bickering among local, state, and Federal authorities. Even the Kennedy Administration, with its commitment to civil defense, was unable to devise a coherent policy and make it stick.

The new Administration inherited the self-imposed United States-British moratorium on all types of nuclear testing. It chafed at this self-denying ordinance. In August 1961 the Soviets pushed American patience to its limits when they exploded a hydrogen bomb in the atmosphere. Two months later the United States resumed underground testing. The President authorized preparations to begin for a resumption of atmospheric testing. Tens of thousands of women marched in protest through American cities to picket city hall or the Federal building in what they termed "the women's strike for peace." Many of them brought their babies with them and carried placards protesting against milk laced with strontium 90.

The President did his duty to the farmers by issuing an announcement that it was safe to drink milk. He went on television in a somber mood to say that unless the Soviets agreed to an enforceable test ban, the United States would go ahead with a program of explosions in the upper atmosphere. In July 1962, true to the President's word, a one-megaton H-bomb was exploded 260 miles above the central Pacific. The flash momentarily bathed Hawaii in a burst of light brighter than the noonday sun. For the next seven minutes the night sky glowed, first a brilliant lime green, then a passionate pink, finally an ominous red. As far away as New Zealand the sky appeared to be burning. To an awed spectator, "It was as if someone had poured a bucket of blood onto the sky." Among the hundreds of thousands of people who witnessed these thermonuclear pyrotechnics there was a feeling of stupefaction and impotent despair.

Within a single year four end-of-the-world books appeared, and all sold well. *Triumph*, by Philip Wylie, *Fail-Safe*, by Eugene Burdick and Harvey Wheeler, *Red Alert*, by Peter George, and *Two Hours to Darkness*, by Anthony Trew. Of the four, *Fail-Safe* was the least cataclysmic: only Moscow and New York were obliterated. In the others, everything—well, nearly everything—disappeared. In time *Red Alert* became the basis of one of the best films of the 1960s, *Dr. Strangelove: or How I Learned to Stop Worrying and Love the Bomb*. But it was *Fail-Safe* that played most effectively on the mood of the moment. First as a novel, then as a film, it reminded people that an all-out thermonuclear war would probably occur not from design but by accident. If that was meant to be a consoling thought it was a remarkably cheerless one.

The conservative revival of the 1950s had flared up not only in the United States but also in Western Europe. It brought to power Macmillan, De Gaulle, and Adenauer. But it was conservatism without a Burke or an Adams. "I have heard its critics argue cogently that it has no philosophy," said Clinton Rossiter. Yet whatever American conservatism may have lacked in ideas, it appeared ready to substitute for with passions. It was perennially on the brink of hysteria. Inevitably some of its adherents lost their balance and fell into attitudes of fanaticism.

In 1961 Americans for the first time became aware of the existence of a semisecret body, the John Birch Society. Stanley Mosk, the attorney general of California, laughed it off as an organization of "wealthy businessmen, retired military officers and little old ladies in tennis shoes." But to most people as time went by it became no laughing matter.

The Birch Society was the creation of Robert Welch, who operated a successful candy business in Belmont, Massachusetts. Welch ("Candy Man of the Year" in 1947) had been on the board of the National Association of Manufacturers. Three former NAM presidents graced the National Council of the John Birch Society. It also boasted a former Commissioner of the IRS, T. Coleman Andrews, whose personal ambition was to see the abolition of the income tax. Welch was proud of his longtime record as an anti-Communist and liked to brag, "I am a good friend of J. B. Matthews. Of course, I have the benefit of J.B.'s files."

Welch appears to have realized just how far the Communist conspiracy had gone only when Robert Taft was denied the 1952 Republican Presidential nomination. The scales had at that moment fallen from his eyes. Taft would have routed the Communists from government. Yet Taft was denied the chance to do so. Welch put two and two together.

For the next five years he devoted his spare time to the study of Communism, and in December 1958 he called eleven of his friends and acquaintances to a two-day harangue at an Indianapolis hotel. On the third day the John Birch Society was created. It bore an uncanny resemblance to the small, secret, revolutionary political party created more than fifty years earlier by one V.I. Lenin. The two-day lecture became the *Blue Book of the John Birch Society*. John Birch was not himself a member. He was, in Welch's view, the first American killed in the Cold War. A Baptist missionary sent to China, John Birch had in 1945 been shot to death by Chinese Communist soldiers. The circumstances surrounding his death were vague and open to doubt. Yet this was the obscure young man whom

Welch claimed to admire more than any other figure in the recent past. John Birch enjoyed the merit of being a fundamentalist. That was Welch's own brand of religion.

To the Birchers the hour was ever late. Two-thirds of the world were already in the greedy hands of Communists. Another 7,000 "newly enslaved subjects" fell into their clutches every hour. "What is not only needed, but is absolutely imperative," Welch announced, "is for some hardboiled, dictatorial and dynamic boss to come along." After a careful survey of the possible candidates for the job he confessed that in the end he could see only one man who, for all his faults, would fill the bill, and bravely shoulder the burden.

Within three years of its founding the Birch Society enrolled as many as 50,000 members. Its annual income approached $2 million. Membership was concentrated in and around a dozen major cities, notably Los Angeles, Boston, Memphis, and Atlanta. At Birch Society headquarters in Belmont there was a full-time staff of 40 at work. Several dozen traveling "coordinators" were out on the road recruiting new members, selling Birch literature, and organizing new chapters. Two Southern California Congressmen were members. Welch, who suddenly became famous in 1961, spent the next two years traveling back and forth across the country, addressing large crowds wherever he stopped.

Rumors circulated meanwhile about a Welch "letter" so long that it was really a book, with the title *The Politician*. In this work Welch identified Eisenhower as an agent of the Communist conspiracy, in company with Earl Warren and Harry Truman. *The Politician* was the uncut version of the truth. It was so powerful that it was to be read only by the leadership; it was more than the mass of followers could be expected to grasp. In little exercises such as these Welch demonstrated that Lenin had rarely had a more conscientious student.

But the rumors grew insistent, and in 1963 Welch allowed *The Politician* to be published. It sold 100,000 copies without ever appearing on a list of best-sellers. And it *was* explosive because the Birch Society contained many people who were as opinionated and as cantankerous as Welch, and *they* refused to believe that Eisenhower was a Communist agent; maybe Harry Truman was, maybe Earl Warren was, but never Eisenhower. Welch was to become the biggest cross the Birch Society had to carry.

This is briefly and roughly the true faith as presented by Robert Welch:

In January 1953 the entire Communist world was on the brink of collapse. The Russians had no deliverable atomic bombs. All they had were a few static test devices assembled from stolen American parts. In Korea the Chinese armies propping up the beaten North Korean regime were being chewed to pieces. Chiang was poised to invade the mainland of China, which was seething with unrest. The Middle East was free from Communist influence. Western Europe had regained its feet, and Eastern Europe was on the brink of revolt against Soviet repression. Stalin was soon to die, plunging the Soviet leadership in crisis. "The sad truth is that this great tyranny was actually saved, in this period of great vulnerability, by just one thing; by the inauguration on January 20, 1953, of Dwight David Eisenhower as President of the United States." Eisenhower was bluntly described as "the most completely opportunistic and unprincipled politician America has raised to high office."

Welch coined the term "Comsymp" for Communist sympathizer. And Comsymps seemed to pop up everywhere. They ran the National Council of Churches, the U.S. Army, the AMA, the U.S. Chamber of Commerce, and the White House. The Birch Society, whose views were shared by far more people than were members, was opposed to the UN and all bodies associated with it, foreign aid, U.S. government savings bonds, the TVA, NATO, the graduated income tax, urban renewal, Social Security, fluoridation, the PTA, mental hospitals, and parity payments. The Birch Society created its own front groups, which included the Committee Against Summit Entanglements, the Committee to Impeach Earl Warren, and College Graduates Against Educating Traitors at Government Expense. To the despair of librarians, airline executives, and television producers, Birch Society members took a keen interest in the local library, the publications offered to airline passengers to while away the flight, and TV programs. Birchers had no qualms about disrupting meetings at the local school or library and turning them into angry debates on Communism. Where they could not gain control of a meeting, they made it impossible to continue with it.

An entire community could be thrown into turmoil. In the winter of 1960–1961 the *Santa Barbara News-Press* ran two articles critical of the activities of the local Birch Society. Santa Barbara found itself in the grip of a new cold war. Heretofore the Birchers had gone unchallenged because almost no one had known about them except people who were sympathetic to them. But now old friends cut one another on the street. Every civic association was divided into pro-and anti-Birch factions. Every public question was turned into an argument over the Birch Society. "An anti-Communist phone service was set up. By dialing 5-0858 or 6-5064 a troubled citizen could get a quick hypo of canned patriotism, sponsored by a pizza parlor."

In scores of towns and cities Birchers enthusiastically organized boycotts of goods from Communist countries. When the Jewel Tea Company began selling Polish hams ("slave labor merchandise") its stores were picketed until it stopped. A drugstore chain was made to rue the day it began selling brooms made in Hungary. The most effective tactic was developed by Birchers in Miami in 1962. They started the Card Party. Stores all around the city were visited by a "Committee to Warn of the Arrival of Communist Merchandise on the Local Business Scene." Then if the store began to stock goods from Communist countries, members of the committee paid a second visit. In their wake were hundreds of little cards hidden among the shelves of merchandise reading, "Always buy your Communist goods from . . .," with the name of the offending store filled in. The Card Party idea quickly spread across the country. Many stores capitulated without the semblance of resistance. An Indiana retailer was so effectively harried that he publicly burned a consignment of 700 wicker chairs made by Bulgarian "slave labor."

After scoring triumphs such as these, every Birch Society member was expected to complete the Triple M (for Member's Monthly Memo). This was a detailed account of exactly what he or she had done in the month past to fight Communism. The Triple Ms were sent on to Belmont for scrutiny at the highest level.

Welch's power over the Birch Society was absolute. He was not required to account for how the society's money was spent. He was not required to run for reelection; in fact, he was never elected to head it. He could expel any member at any time without offering an explanation or chance of redress. To people of a certain type this kind of behavior was true leadership, and therefore irresistible. Major General Edwin A. Walker, who had commanded the soldiers sent to Little Rock Central High School, was suspended from his command of the 24th Infantry Division stationed in Germany when he began to distribute Welch's publications among his troops. Walker became a hero to the radical right when he resigned his commission, the better to save the nation. Retired military officers provided a major source of Birch Society members and supporters. The most thoroughly Birchite town in America was Coronado, California, a few miles from San Diego. Coronado was a popular retirement town for retired military men and one place where it was impossible to buy a Polish ham. Welch's authoritarianism also appears to have attracted large number of Catholics. To the dismay of liberal Catholics Welch claimed that half of all Birch Society members were Catholic communicants.

Beyond the formal membership there is little reason to doubt that there were hundreds of thousands, possible 1 or 2 million, Birchsymps. The Birch Society's success, moreover revealed a very large, untapped market for right-wing literature and right-wing speakers. No one ever went broke fighting the Communist menace.

By 1962 there were at least twenty major radical right organizations. Their membership was in the region of 300,000. Their annual budgets topped $20 million. The total number of sympathizers revolving around these bodies was probably in the region of 5 to 10 million. As fringe groups go, this collection had gone far in only a few years. It roped in unconstructed isolationists, McCarthyite leftovers, crypto-Fascists, and the simply bewildered.

Scores of business corporations, including such giants as GM and R. J. Reynolds, were running anti-Communist education programs for their employees. Some were "in-plant," on company property; others were at "schools" of anti-Communism, with the company paying tuition and expenses. Some programs were avowedly Birchite. But most claimed only to be teaching "Americanism."

One of the biggest savings and loan associations, Coast Federal, went a step further and proselytized its customers to enlist in the fight against

Communism. Coast Federal had thirty-eight anti-Communist lecturers on its payroll, to educate its employees and savers alike.

Hundreds of blue-chip firms such as 3-M, Alcoa, and Goodyear, were wont to show their workers Birchite films, such as *Communism on the Map*, a minor masterpiece of its genre. Boeing distinguished itself by hiring as the house authority on Communism a lecturer whose stock speeches included one which maintained that African delegates to the UN were cannibals and witch doctors.

There was a program run by the Foreign Policy Association which offered a history and analysis of Communism that was not paranoid or frantic, and hundreds of business executives enrolled in the FPA course each year. But this sober inquiry was the exception, not the rule.

The largest following among the radical right could be found trailing behind the Reverend Billy Joe Hargis of Tulsa. He offered a combination of right-wing radicalism with religious fundamentalism. His Christian Crusade dated back to 1947. But it was not until the years from 1959 to 1961 that it made an impression. In the meantime, Reverend Hargis had made his name known by trying to send Bibles to Russia by balloon.

And then there was Dr. Frederick Charles Schwartz, Australian Doctor of Medicine, honorary Doctor of Theology from Bob Jones University, and part-time Baptist preacher. Arriving in the United States in 1957, Dr. Schwartz teamed up with W. E. Pietsch, a radio evangelist of some note during the 1930s. Pietsch had incorporated his Christian Anti-Communist Crusade in Iowa a few years before he met Schwartz and had been touring the nation as its principal performer, to no evident effect. Pietsch died in 1960. Schwartz took control of the CACC. Under new management it flourished mightily. Working out of Long Beach (a second home to Iowans) Schwartz and his "faculty" barnstormed the country. In each town they visited they set up a three-day school on Communism. Every school ended with a rousing rally of the faithful.

Schwartz's bigger rallies appeared on television, with big business picking up the tab. Schwartz fascinated many business executives. He was plainly a man of education and intelligence. They flocked to lunches at which, for a price, the doctor with the funny accent would reveal the inner secrets of the Communist threat. He avoided some of the popular ideas of the radical right, such as the repeal of the income tax and impeaching Earl Warren. But he became so nettled at being told repeatedly he was some kind of nut that he decided the mental health movement was part of the Kremlin's conspiracy.

By 1963 the CACC under Schwarz had a budget of more than $1 million a year. His book *You Can Trust the Communists* had sold more than 1 million copies. He claimed to have more than 5,000 "study groups" digging up Communist influences on the local scene. His road show had the biggest sponsors and the biggest star attractions, such as Pat Boone, Senator Dodd (in his youth an FBI agent), and Herb Philbrick. At Schwartz's 1962 Madison Square Garden Rally Boone emotionally declared, "I have four lovely daughters. I would rather have Cherry, Debbie, Wendy and

Laurie be lined up and shot down before my eyes than for them to grow up in a Communist United States," while the police sat among the crowd leafing through their free copies of *I Led Three Lives*.

In most areas the true faith was available at the touch of a button and a twist of the dial. Hundreds of radio and TV stations each week carried such programs as *The Dan Smoot Report* and *Manion Forum*. Dan Smoot was a former FBI agent whose programs were sponsored by D. B. Lewis, a Los Angeles manufacturer of dog food and founder of ORFIT (Organization to Repeal the Federal Income Tax). Clarence Manion was a former dean of the law school at Notre Dame.

The Smoots and the Manions were looked on with condescension or contempt by the critical. But 1959 saw the formation of a new body which sent a frisson of apprehension around the country. Robert Bolivar DePugh, a drug manufacturer from Norborne, Missouri, while out on a duck hunt with a few friends began to wonder how people might fare if forced to leave their homes and live in the wilderness. Why would they do anything so drastic? Because the Russians had invaded the United States. DePugh and his friends decided to train themselves to be guerrillas. They called themselves the Minutemen.

In 1962 DePugh claimed that there were 25,000 trained Minutemen, ready for combat. Their wives were kept from feeling neglected by being assigned to screen textbooks and children's literature for Communist influences. According to DePugh, who was a Birch Society member, "If you left me naked in the desert I could make gunpowder." The Minutemen evaded Federal laws against private armies by doing without a formal chain of command, uniforms, and pay. Even their monthly dues were optional. But the prospect of right-wing fanatics armed to the teeth and in training for combat made many people uneasy.

The atmosphere was such nowadays that it did not take much to spark some new form of radical right protest. When the news got out in 1961 that four Yugoslavian officers were in training at Perrin Air Force Base near Dallas, incensed Texans promptly called a "National Indignation Convention." In fewer than two months the NIC carried off rallies in ninety cities. And it proved to be capable of working up its indignation over almost anything, including a report that peat moss currently for sale on Long Island had originally been dug from Russian soil.

Texas was always ripe for the radical right. As early as 1953 Houston had boasted an all-female, ultra-right group called the Minutewomen. They zealously raked over the schools, the churches, the libraries, and any organization interested in civic or social reform. Houston grew spectacularly from 1945 to 1963, and so did its right wing. The same was true of Dallas. In both cities there was no escaping the radical right. It dominated local press, radio, and television. The churches of both cities were noted for their pastors being cut from the same cloth as Billy Joe Hargis. Their school boards were invariably dominated by the superpatriots. And anywhere in the country that there was a right-wing school board the students were certain to be treated to a showing of one of the strangest film successes of the postwar.

The film was only forty-five minutes long. The camera work was poor. The editing was worse. And the cast consisted entirely of amateurs. Yet more than 10 million people saw *Operation Abolition*. It showed the HUAC hearings in San Francisco in May 1960 and was concerned chiefly with the events of May 15 ("Black Friday") when the San Francisco police turned fire hoses on a chanting, singing band of several hundred protesters inside city hall. The police made sixty-eight arrests (mostly students, mostly from Berkeley), and the arrested were charged with inciting a riot. The film's narrative was written and delivered by Fulton Lewis III, son of Fulton Lewis, Jr. The protesters were described as "Red dupes." Their singing constituted a "Communist riot."

What *Operation Abolition* actually revealed, however, was not the face of the Red menace unmasked but that the ice was cracking: American youth was beginning to assert itself over major issues in American life. Nor was it a movement confined to the left. The right-wing Young Americans for Freedom came into existence in 1960 and within a few years enrolled nearly 30,000 members. The YAF turned its attention to Young Republican clubs. In the best Leninist fashion it bored diligently from within.

Their elders, meanwhile, had found a politician to their liking, Senator Barry Goldwater of Arizona. Conservative Republicans took to him as they had taken to no one since the death of Robert Taft. Goldwater was partly Jewish. But he was a man who spoke their language, denouncing Federal matching grants to the states as "a mixture of blackmail and bribery." The UN Secretariat was full of Red spies ("Get the US out of the UN and the UN out of the US" was almost as appealing as "Impeach Earl Warren"). Foreign aid was a "giveaway." The United States had to continue nuclear testing. The Federal government had to get out of education, agriculture, urban renewal, and Social Security. Rich and poor alike should pay income tax at the same rate. Thus ran the creed.

This sudden efflorescence of right-wing politics came in the middle of the New Frontier. It was bound up with the sense of flux and drift which gripped the country around 1960. It also reflected the bitter disappointment conservatives felt after eight years of Republican government under Eisenhower, a disappointment compounded by Nixon's defeat. And ideologues that they were, conservatives were still suffering from the collapse of the old certainties during the Depression. When a deeply rooted faith is shattered, people do not simply stop believing in something. Instead, they are likely to believe anything.

As the new administration settled down to its business, not the least of its pleasant surprises was that the President and his Vice President got along amicably, even though they were two men who could never become close friends. The gulf between them was too wide. In attitudes and behavior they had little in common. When Jacqueline Kennedy gave birth to Patrick Bouvier Kennedy, who died shortly after birth, Johnson sent the President a telegram: "Name that boy Lyndon Johnson Kennedy and a heifer calf will be his."

The Vice President's dissatisfaction at the powerlessness of his office was turned into a deep resentment not against the President but against the President's brother Robert Kennedy. Johnson felt that he was usurping the Vice President's rightful place as the second man in the Administration. Johnson's own position was further compromised by the revelations about his former protégé Bobby Baker, who had in short order gone from being an obscure Senate functionary to being a millionaire and big man about town.

Nothing seemed to go right for Johnson these days. When, in a lordly gesture, he invited a Pakistani camel driver, Bashir Ahmed, to visit the United States, the camel driver not only accepted the invitation but proceeded to charm everyone he met with flowery compliments and peasant folk wisdom. Johnson, whose ego was enormous, found himself upstaged by an illiterate middle-aged camel driver who could not speak a word of English.

Kennedy, too, found that victory had its frustrations. During the campaign the two domestic issues which concerned him most were Federal aid to education and raising the minimum wage to $1.25 an hour. To get important legislation of this kind through Congress meant dealing with the House Rules Committee, chaired by Virginia's elderly and conservative Howard W. Smith. Almost nothing ever reached the House floor which Smith did not approve of. Eisenhower had lived with this cantankerous nuisance. Kennedy characteristically refused to contemplate doing so.

With the assistance of Sam Rayburn he sought to increase the size of the Rules Committee, from twelve to fifteen members. By adding two liberal Democrats, plus a Republican, he would be able to rely on an eight to seven majority for his programs, or so he calculated. The Rules Committee was enlarged, but only after a bitter fight and a close vote (217–212). In the process the President stirred up deep resentment in Congress against the White House for involving itself in what most House members considered House business. As a result, most of Kennedy's major legislative proposals made very little headway on Capitol Hill even after the Rules Committee fight had been won.

Kennedy was bound to have a difficult time of it in any event. His narrow margin of victory, and the 1.5 million votes lost on account of his religion, had cost the Democrats twenty House seats. A genuinely New Frontier Congress, under the control of liberal Democrats, simply did not exist to pass New Frontier legislation.

Yet Kennedy stymied did not mean Kennedy at a standstill. He had a sure gift for the grand gesture. The issues of the campaign had come ready-made, but he had made them his own. He did the same with the Peace Corps. He embraced it so completely and it seemed so much in his own spirit that it was often assumed it was his idea to begin with. But it had first been mooted by Harvey Swados, a novelist and journalist, in *Esquire* in September 1959. "Why Resign from the Human Race?" was Swados's question to disenchanted, restless college students. The campuses were stirring but without any evident sense of direction. Swados proposed that the Class of '60 volunteer its skills, its enthusiasm, and its labor to aid people in underdeveloped countries. Swados, *Esquire*, and a handful of volunteer workers operating out of a tiny office in Cambridge, Massachusetts, who went by the name of Volunteers for International Development, were snowed under with correspondence after the article appeared. VID had been mentioned by Swados as the kind of thing he had in mind. Young people from every state demanded that it make use of them. So when the President called for Peace Corps volunteers, he knew that he would get them, by the tens of thousands.

His main pledge had been that he would get the country moving again. To most people that meant a commitment to speeding the rate of economic growth. To the President and others a vibrant American economy was the bedrock of both the country's welfare and its role in the world. The Soviets and the Chinese for the moment at least appeared to the non-Western world to have found a shorter, more direct path to economic maturity than anything the United States had to offer. Walter Heller, the chairman of the Council of Economic Advisers under Kennedy, recalled with wry amusement the time when the President " 'ordered' me not to return from an international economic meeting in Paris until I had discovered the secret of European growth."

The economy was stimulated and revived noticeably by 1963. But what was especially noteworthy was that a rapid economic upturn brought only the most gradual drop in unemployment. Yet the President found, to his surprise that the unions had by now come to accept a high level of joblessness. After a meeting with the top leadership of the AFL-CIO he is reported to have said to an aide, "And where is the pressure from the left?"

When he turned his attention to the nation's military posture, which he had strenuously criticized during his campaign, he found that the United States was much stronger than he had allowed for. There was a shortage of ground troops. but nothing that an extra couple of divisions and better organization of existing resources could not take care of. Robert McNamara, installed as Secretary of Defense, admitted that there was no missile gap after all. But the truth was that there was indeed a missile gap— and the Russians were on the unpleasant side of it. Shortly before the 1960 election the USS *George Washington* from underwater launched two Polaris missiles at targets more than 1,000 miles distant and struck them both. The subsurface-launched missile not only worked but worked a revolution in modern strategic warfare. It would be the very core of the nation's strategic deterrent—its assured second-strike force—for the next generation. The Russians set to work copying the Polaris weapons system. It would take them more than a decade to catch up with it.

The first year of the Kennedy Presidency passed in an atmosphere of crisis; it contained more incident and drama in a single year than Eisenhower had managed in eight. Some 50,000 soldiers were hurriedly shifted to Germany during one Berlin crisis; more than 75,000 reservists were called up during another. The American mission in South Vietnam was rapidly built up from a few hundred men to several thousand. From Castro there came demands for 500 tractors in exchange for the 1,200 prisoners taken at the Bay of Pigs. The wall went up in Berlin, Khrushchev and Kennedy met in Vienna and managed to show that summit meetings could make problems worse rather than better. In this electric atmosphere of crisis and posturing *Newsweek* warned the country in September 1961, "We stand on the brink of war." The average citizen was left to wonder where it would all end, and in case it did, perhaps the shelter program really was a good idea. Young Gail Pitts solemnly told her friends in a Denver cafeteria what many people felt: "I want to be around when it's all over."

As 1961 gave way to 1962, there was a perceptible drop in tension. The recalled reservists became restive. At Fort Bragg, North Carolina, they went on a hunger strike.

The President appeared to thrive on the atmosphere of crisis. His idea of normality in matters of state was never to leave until tomorrow a stone that could be turned over this minute. And after the bland Eisenhower regimen many people found the exciting new approach much more to their taste. Looking ahead to 1964, Kennedy had every reason to feel confident, whether he faced Goldwater or another new Nixon.

Nixon set about the first of his comebacks by running for governor of California in 1962, although in one TV broadcast he blurted out that he was "running for governor of the United States." The old habits died very hard. The theme of Nixon's campaign literature was that the incumbent, Edmund G. Brown, was aiding the Communists. When this ploy at last backfired, it was followed by a son-of-Checkers television appearance in which Nixon attempted to show that it was he, not Brown, who was being smeared these days. He brought on his wife and children to look grieved at some of the things being said about him in the Brown camp. It was a performance rancid with self-pity. After Brown defeated him with consummate ease, Nixon called his "final" press conference. He rambled incoherently for twenty minutes before concluding sourly, "Just think what you're going to be missing. You won't have Nixon to kick around anymore."

After this debacle Kennedy expected to face Barry Goldwater in 1964. Considering that Goldwater would represent a minority of a minority, Kennedy had every reason to believe that he would be in office until 1969.

34
Room at the Bottom

Americans were realistic enough to admit that poverty and social classes existed. But they considered them an implied criticism of the American way of life. As a consequence, the poor were always under-counted, poverty was always on the verge of extinction. In 1929 Herbert Hoover chose his Inaugural Address to give the happy news that poverty was about to be abolished. Within three years millions of people were queueing in the streets for free soup and bread. In 1960 the editors of *Fortune* said that there were fewer than 1 million poor people left in the United States and by 1970 there would be none at all.

There was more to this than willful blindness. Poverty was hard to see because it had changed its face. The poor did not curl up on the sidewalk and die there, as they did in Calcutta. Hideous and obvious diseases such as yaws were no longer encountered except in remote parts of the South. And the wide spread of affluence had jumbled matters so thoroughly that paradox took over: "More people die in the United States of too much food than too little." There was a well-educated New York vagrant of clean, sober habits who had learned how to live in the big city without a regular income, without a home, and without having to beg. One lesson that Henry Shelby had learned since falling from a comfortable middle-class job into the gutter was: "Nobody starves in America."

But poverty and misery were not entirely invisible. They were the stuff that afternoon television was made of. Misery shows, in which the audience was asked to thrill to the hardships other people suffered and to iden-tify with them as they identified with the participants on quiz shows, were a tremendous success. On this level, where poverty was made trivial, larded with sentimentality, and at the same time kept remote, people could deal with it; it was poverty as entertainment.

The principal reason why the poor were assumed to be few and growing fewer was that hardly anyone bothered to look for them. The handful of people who bothered to seek them out had no difficulty unearthing mil-lions of poor people. But these investigations had no impact until, in 1963, Michael Harrington's *The Other America* was published. He had been ac-tive in various Catholic social welfare programs. He had lived in poverty among the Bowery bums he sought to help, had risked life and limb in neighborhoods middle-class whites would not dare to enter on foot. Har-rington reported on poverty from the trenches and called it "the failure of the great society." Nothing less would do, he maintained, than to declare "a war on poverty." But what took the country by its ears was the figure he gave for the number of Americans living in poverty—50 million. Mid-dle-class Americans blinked in astonishment.

Yet his claim had to be considered seriously because he offered an array of figures drawn from government publications and a theory which made the figures, and the social reality they represented, intelligible. What made the poor poor, said Harrington, was not money. Someone with a little money and a lot of motivation was on his or her way up. Such an individual was escaping the "culture of poverty." Harrington defined the poor not by income but by spiritual defeat. People who had given up the struggle to defend their self-respect, to assert their rights, to make decisions and accept responsibility had not even the willpower to cling to the lowest rungs of the welfare state. People such as this had been crushed; they would remain crushed. And no one truly cared about the poor, said Harrington, because few people were willing to believe the poor constituted a major social problem.

The culture of poverty which he portrayed was pervasive and tenacious. Once anyone was caught in its grip there was little chance he would ever break free. Its roots were deep in American society. Technological advance seemed only to drive those roots deeper. New groups of poor came into existence every few years. These were people whom welfare state measures, minimum wage laws, and public health programs would never reach.

Those above them cherished a consoling belief that the poor were responsible for their own plight, that they had failed to meet the ordinary and reasonable demands of life. Their poverty was therefore the result of their weakness of character. But the drunken middle-class misfit who fell into the gutter was the rarest of the poor. Nearly all those who lived in poverty had been born in poverty. They had grown up knowing no other way of life. Without education and self-confidence there was no realistic way for them to rise.

The welfare state had an upside-down character, Harrington discovered. It was remarkably good at helping the handful who showed some ability to help themselves. But it was hopeless at reaching down to those at the very bottom. The Matthew Effect was alive and well among America's poor. In the end, he concluded, "The poor get less out of the welfare state than any group in America."

Much of the attention Harrington's book aroused was, naturally, devoted to quarreling with his figures. But no one any longer seriously argued as the editors of *Fortune* had that the poor were half of 1 percent of the population. One estimate, based on the 1960 Census and setting the parameters of poverty and deprivation at $2,000 to $3,000 for an unattached individual and $4,000 to $6,000 for a family of four or more, concluded that 20 percent of the nation was poor and another 20 percent was deprived. So 40 percent of the people were ill-housed, ill-clothed, and ill-fed. One authority on the subject put the poor at 32 million. The most convincing effort to count the poor, however, arrived at a total of 34.5 million in 1963. This was nearly 20 percent of the nation. The standard it employed was Spartan: 70 cents a day for food, $1.40 a day for clothing, transportation, housing, heating, and all other necessities. Besides these 34.5 million living on less than $2.10 a day, there were a further 15 million who were seriously deprived—badly housed, poorly dressed, unable to afford sufficient heat in winter, unable to afford to eat properly, and so on. Altogether, these various studies tended to confirm Harrington's claim that up to one-fourth of all Americans lived in the culture of poverty or in very close proximity to it.

It was a picture which had showed no evident improvement since V-J Day. The war years had seen a substantial change in the distribution of income and some redistribution of wealth. In the postwar there was no further equalization of incomes, and wealth was redistributed back toward the prewar pattern. The distribution of income was remarkably unequal when compared with some countries, such as Sweden and Australia, but it compared very favorably with that in most industrial democracies, such as Canada, Japan, and France.

Although some 2 percent of poor families did escape from poverty each year, the number of unattached individuals living in poverty rose steadily from 1945 to 1963. So little had changed. If the poverty line were set at a family income of 50 percent or less than the median family income, then the poor remained at one-fourth the population from 1945 to 1963.

Nearly half the poor were children under eighteen. The United States was in the unusual position for an industrialized country that in 1960 one-third of its population was under the age of fourteen. Current divorce rates meant that many of them would grow up in poverty or deprivation. Current unemployment rates meant that many of them would stay there when they became adults. The percentage of unemployed young people, ages fourteen to twenty-four, rose from 5 percent in 1953 to 12.6 percent in 1960. And these figures probably underestimated the true amount of youth unemployment.

The family was under considerable strain, often for reasons having nothing to do with the family as such: the shift to the cities; the growing economic independence of women; changes in the divorce laws; changes in people's expectations; increased physical and social mobility. And when these or other pressures proved too much and families broke up, some, if not all, of a family's members were likely to be plunged into a harsh economic struggle.

The rapid increase in the proportion of the population aged sixty-five and over was another large source of poverty. Nearly 10 percent of the nation comprised people sixty-five or older. For many of them, if not for most, Social Security was not enough to cover their needs. These were the first generation of beneficiaries to retire under the 1935 Social Security Act. As a result, their pensions were small. The Kennedy Administration acknowledged the existence and the increasing importance of the social problems the aged faced. A President's Council on Aging was created. HEW set up the Office of Aging. The Senate created a Special Committee on Aging. The Public Health Service began to spend large amounts of money on medical research concerned with health and medical problems particularly associated with the elderly.

By 1963 there were more than 2 million in receipt of Old Age Assistance, a welfare provision added to the 1935 Social Security Act. These were welfare cases of a new type: mainly middle-class, white, people who had known little or nothing of poverty until they retired, when employment, savings, and health had run out.

What the poor had in common, regardless of differences of race, age, and location, was their lack of education. Two-thirds of the poor were in families headed by someone who had no more than a grade-school education. And the chances of this pattern's being broken were very small because the fastest-growing welfare program was Aid to Families with Dependent Children. In 1963 this involved 1 million families and 3 million children. The AFDC (later ADC) program was growing at nearly 10 percent a year, and nearly half the parents qualifying for assistance had themselves been reared on welfare. This, too, was part of the culture of poverty, generation after generation being born and raised in dependence on the state, knowing no other way of life.

The daunting growth rate of ADC made it, inevitably, the most fiercely attacked of all welfare programs. It was regarded as one more case of liberal humanitarianism gone mad. The program had begun modestly in 1935, growing out of the Mothers' Aid Program. It aimed at keeping families together. Congress thought it was simply extending a helping hand to those traditional figures of tender concern, the bereaved widow and her little orphans. If mothers and children could be kept together, then perhaps something resembling ordinary family life might be maintained and the children saved. The reality was a different matter: 1 million deserted black women and 3 million abandoned or illegitimate children. And in the meantime OASDI had taken responsibility for helping widowed women and orphaned children.

The ADC family of 1963 faced no shortage of troubles, most of them beyond the help social workers could provide: drunkenness; bad teeth; weak lungs; nervous disorders; mental illness; unsanitary housing; child beating; child molestation; exposure to violent crime; proximity to drug addiction. ADC added to these troubles by breaking up families. If an able-bodied man was present in the home, the ADC check was absent from it. A man knew that if he left home, at least his children would probably be fed.

Among the tens of millions of urban poor there was no group more deserving of pity and care than the ADC children. By 1963 many were the third generation in their families to be reared on welfare. They would grow up to be the least educated of the urban poor, and they would be the least likely young adults to find employment. In time they would breed a fourth generation on welfare.

Because ADC had a bad name, the name was changed, to Aid and Services to Needy Families with Children. But the old name still stuck. So did the old scorn. Congress nevertheless broadened the provisions of ADC so that unemployment of parents became sufficient grounds to qualify for assistance.

OASDI remained the biggest single welfare measure in operation despite the rapid growth of ADC. In 1963 it provided assistance to 13 million people, roughly one-third of the poor. The Federal government also provided large amounts of indirect assistance in the form of transfer payments and government expenditures on schools, job training programs, and public works. The effect of transfers and government spending was to raise the incomes of families below the $3,000 mark by approximately 50 percent. Assistance provided by friends, relatives, and private charities was worth a further $21 billion. Thus, in one way and another, enough money reached the poor and the nearly poor to keep them from falling into Asian depths of destitution and starvation.

Much of the New Deal's drive toward a complete welfare state had been lost in the exigencies of wartime. Truman's Fair Deal had been stymied on its major reforms. Eisenhower had launched several new programs, but without much enthusiasm. The Kennedy Administration by way of contrast brought a strong emotional commitment to social justice. In part it reflected traditional Democratic concerns. But it also expressed the spirit of more—more of everything.

By the fall of 1963 social welfare's share of GNP had virtually doubled over the 1945 level of 4 percent. Welfare, plus education, plus health, accounted for a fifth of the GNP, or $100 billion a year. The price tag was picked up in roughly equal parts by local, state, and Federal government and the private sector. There was a rough division of labor: Washington carried most of the welfare burden, state and local government took care of education, and private citizens and agencies paid most of the health bill.

Federal programs were remarkably uneven in their effects, being based in most cases on matching grants. By refusing to put up its share of the money called for, any state could deny its citizens the welfare benefits Congress had provided for them. Medicaid, for example, created in 1960 under Eisenhower, allowed the states to establish stiffer criteria for qualification than Old Age Assistance allowed. As a result, four generous states (California, New York, Pennsylvania, and Massachusetts) by 1963 accounted for nearly 90 percent of total Medicaid disbursements.

In 1961 the food stamp program was revived after nearly twenty years. There were even now more than 13 million schoolchildren receiving free or subsidized lunches. Congress supported the food stamp program for the same reason it supported the free lunch—the farmers favored it.

But in its efforts to expand the welfare system the Kennedy Administration found itself frustrated time and again by Southern opposition. The South stood to benefit more than any other region from an expansion of welfare programs. This, however, was the self-mutilating revenge of the South for the Administration's firm commitment to civil rights.

At first glance it appeared that the Federal government had it within its power to end poverty in America. "The United States has arrived at the point where poverty could be abolished at the stroke of a pen," wrote one optimist in 1962. "To raise every individual and family in the nation now below a subsistence income to the subsistence level would cost about $10 billion a year. This is less than two per cent of the gross national product.''

This, however, took insufficient account of the complexity of poverty. A slum neighborhood with high levels of crime and low levels of education, bad housing and bad roads, prostitution and drug addiction would soon soak up larger welfare payments and leave nothing positive to show for it. Sex and drugs would cost more; the absentee landlord would be enriched the more; the bars and poolrooms would do better business; the pawnshops might fall on bad times. The brutal truth was that government retraining programs and investment incentives would not do much good unless the original inhabitants were moved out of a slum neighborhood. But under the new Administration such programs were launched, welfare payments were raised, and in an air of optimism it began tackling the poverty problem.

The Federal government had failed to get the country out of the Depression. There was no reason to believe that in the years since then it had learned a great deal about the elimination of poverty.

Fair-minded, compassionate people ought to have been able to admire the welfare system. It sprang from a sense of responsibility to others. It enabled the successful in life to help the unsuccessful without the bad odor of charity. Yet the welfare system was thoroughly despised—by those who paid for it, those who administered it, those who were dependent on it.

As welfare expenditures rose, so did public revulsion. In 1961 Newburgh, New York, became famous by deciding to take a stand against welfare. The town's experience since the war was typical of hundreds of other towns: Newburgh's black population had tripled, and the number of poor whites had also risen appreciably. Most of the blacks and the poor whites had arrived from the South and the border states. They were unskilled, uneducated, and often unemployed. Newburgh did not have a large downtown area, and what it did have rapidly became a slum. By 1961 it was spending more on relief payments than on police and fire services. Relief accounted for one-third of the city budget. The council and the city manager, Joseph McD. Mitchell, decided to put a halt to rising welfare costs.

A new welfare code was enacted. It cut off relief to any unmarried mother who bore another child. Able-bodied males on relief were obliged to work for forty hours each week for the city. Welfare checks had to be collected from the police.

Newburgh brought into the open the latent hostility which enmeshed the welfare system and those it supported. Even in New York, which had the most enlightened welfare administrators of any city, welfare workers were called "investigators." Welfare had become, in effect, part of society's system of policing the poor. Presumably ignorant and illiterate recipients for their part often showed themselves gifted at evading or avoiding the trammels of modern bureaucracy more successfully than the middle class. A few demonstrated an ingenuity and imagination which might have been better spent. Neither side in the welfare system trusted the other. They fought a guerrilla war which smoldered unnoticed for years at a time before, as in Newburgh, it burst briefly into flame.

Under Mitchell's direction the pace of welfare investigations was accelerated. Prosecutions for welfare fraud rose sharply. And mail poured into city hall from all over the country, praising Newburgh's stand and making contemptuous allusions to "them," the "welfare chiselers," or "the black bastards."

Newburgh's brave new world came to an ignominious end. Federal and state authorities paid most of Newburgh's relief bill, and they ruled that the new code was invalid. Mitchell's charges were shown to be, in many instances, highly exaggerated. He was forced to resign as city manager. He became East Coast organizer of the John Birch Society. Public support turned to embarrassment when the highly publicized effort to put able-bodied men to work produced, after diligent investigation, only one able-bodied man.

In the beginning, Newburgh's praises were sung on the Senate floor. In the end, a baseball player introduced to a Florida crowd as coming from Newburgh was greeted with derisive laughter and chants of "Welfare! Welfare! Welfare!"

Efforts to help the poor, like the efforts to harass them, were full of irony and paradox. Everyone despised the public welfare system; everyone admired the private welfare system. The private welfare state was one where only death was certain; taxes could be held at bay or avoided. Untaxed income in the form of school fees, cheap loans, training grants, free season tickets, and the like created a new world of privilege. And because the money spent in the private welfare state was tax-exempt, the true cost was passed on to other, less privileged taxpayers who had to rely on and also finance the public welfare state. Then there was the private tax-exempt pension scheme. In 1963 such private plans covered 24 million people and held reserves of nearly $70 billion. There were also programs which provided death benefits, cash sickness benefits, company cars, houses, planes, vacation resorts. What the public and private welfare states had in common was that in each the many were supporting the few.

The most galling paradox poverty presented was pointedly expressed by James Baldwin: "Anyone who has ever struggled with poverty knows how extremely expensive it is to be poor." Or, as a book by David Caplowitz expressed it more concisely, *The Poor Pay More.* A run-down tenement cost more to keep warm than did a comfortable, properly insulated suburban home. The corner store in a poor neighborhood charged higher prices than did the stores out at the suburban shopping center, where volume was high and competition keen. The poor had to buy the small, expensive size, rather than the large, economy size. When goods were on sale, the poor did not have the time and energy to shop around for bargains. They were prey to loan sharks and usurers. They were susceptible to high-pressure selling methods which often left them with unwanted, expensive, badly made products. Heavy and repeated borrowing was a feature of life among the poor. Caplowitz surveyed several hundred poor families. "It is of interest," he remarked, "that none of the respondents had any difficulty understanding the word *garnishee*. This may be one long word that is better known among the poorly educated than by the better educated."

Extra money was not saved, for the good reason that it was likely to be stolen or extracted under pressure. Surplus money, like surplus food, was promptly consumed. It was hardly a profligate's attitude to life. Eliot Liebow integrated himself into a poor black neighborhood in Washington in 1959 and 1960. He reported:

> Portable consumer durable goods, such as watches, radios, television sets or phonographs, are sometimes looked at as a form of savings. When Shirley was on welfare, she regularly took her television set out of pawn when she got her monthly check. Not so much to watch it, she explained, as to have something to fall back on when her money runs out toward the end of the month. For her and others, the television set or the phonograph is her savings, the pawnshop is where she banks her savings and the pawn ticket is her bankbook.

To outsiders the world of the poor appeared static and indolent. Yet there was considerable mobility among the poor. Poor farmers moved into the cities and gave up the land but not poverty. Migrant workers traveled from one end of the country to the other and, far from being shiftless, were searching for brutally hard work. The poor could be as mobile as suburbanites. In slums populated not by blacks but by whites, James B. Conant found, "It is not uncommon in such a school to have a turnover of the entire enrollment in one school year." The culture of poverty was such, however, that all this movement led nowhere.

It was a life that managed to be both dull and turbulent. The poor were madder, sicker, drunker, and more violent than the rest of us. And they saw that there was no realistic way out of poverty except for a few. Most of the time they were therefore withdrawn and passive toward a world they could not influence, and their repressed frustrations were turned against themselves and those within their reach. Where an opportunity of escape did present itself, the poor were too ignorant in most cases to see it or too insecure to seize it. To a poor woman something as mundane as the local PTA can appear formidable. And in the United States the ideology of classlessness was itself a handicap. By denial of the reality of classes there has been no incentive for explicitly class-based organizations to take root. This has been a mixed blessing.

The poor took the same contemptuous view of themselves that others took of them. And in their psychological isolation they had fewer friends, fewer interests, and fewer pleasures, even cheap ones, than the people above them enjoyed. The bottom 25 percent simply did not participate in the national life. One side of this isolation was the willingness with which they accepted other people's views. Another was their aversion to the polling booth.

The best opportunity for escaping the culture of poverty was for a husband and wife to work. But the percentage of working wives rose hardly at all among the poor and the deprived in the postwar. It was the income groups above them which produced the remarkable increase in the percentage of working wives. They became increasingly common as one moved up the income ladder. In the top fifth nearly half of all wives were at work in 1963. For many American families the wife's income made the difference between poverty and adequacy, between adequacy and affluence, between sickness and health, between misery and happiness.

In the land of opportunity, nonwhites discovered, there is always room at the bottom. Mexicans, Puerto Ricans, and Indians made up much of the bottom 25 percent. They, in company with millions of poor whites, found room for themselves. Often it was out in someone else's fields.

No one sought work more assiduously than migrant farm workers. No one was more badly paid when they found it. On the Friday following Thanksgiving Day 1960 CBS shocked the nation by showing *Harvest of Shame*, a harrowing documentary on migratory labor made by Murrow and Friendly. Having stuffed themselves on Thursday, Americans were ripe for shaming on Friday. To the many millions who had simply assumed that the misery portrayed in *Grapes of Wrath* was by now a thing of the past, *Harvest of Shame* was an emotional bombshell.

They discovered that contrary to comforting illusion, mechanization had not put an end to "stoop labor." Nor was it about to do so. Sugar beets, tobacco, lettuce, grapes, and many other crops could be picked by machine, but they also needed to be pruned and thinned. Selective chemicals killed some weeds growing in with certain crops, such as wheat, but were too powerful to use on delicate green leaf crops, which had to be weeded by hand. Nor was there a machine which would harvest potatoes one day, pick grapes the day after, and gather nuts the day after that. The delicate touch of the human hand and the discriminating vision of the human eye were, and would long remain, essential in harvesting. There were more than 2 million migrant agricultural workers because they were needed.

The largest domestic source of migrant labor was Texas-Mexicans. Second came blacks from the South. Third came Puerto Ricans. Finally came 100,000 poor whites. Half a million braceros came in each year under Public Law 78, an agreement reached in 1941 with the Mexican government. Canada and the British West Indies also sent thousands of migrant farm workers to the United States annually.

State employment agencies were heavily engaged in this traffic. When winter drew to a close in New York, employment officials surveyed New York farmers on their estimated labor needs for the summer. A report would then be sent to employment officials in Florida, who would begin recruiting migrant labor to travel to New York in four or five months' time. Wisconsin had a similar arrangement with Texas. In all twenty-two states where agriculture was heavily dependent on the migrants, state officials were involved in their recruitment. The typical migrant farm worker of 1961 did not bundle his wife, children, and cooking pot into his beat-up pickup truck and drive off in hopes of finding work somewhere down the road. He usually knew exactly where he was going and had a good idea of what he would find when he got there.

But it remained a life of hardship and insecurity. Injured farm workers fell outside the workmen's compensation system. Unemployed farm workers were not entitled to unemployment insurance, except in Hawaii. Outside New York State public assistance involved both need and a residence requirement. Few migrants stopped long enough in one place to qualify.

There was an attempt in Northern and Midwestern states in the 1950s to guarantee by law a modest but reasonable standard of housing, working conditions, health conditions, and transportation for migrants. But in almost every instance enforcement was left to the operators of the migrant labor camps. The typical camp had too few toilets, too little floor space for each worker, a shortage of hot water, and wretched provisions for laundry. Child labor, moreover, almost unknown in industry or the retail trades, was a common practice, regardless of child labor laws.

The only migrants to benefit noticeably from legal safeguards were the braceros covered by PL 78. They were guaranteed forty hours of work a week, and in 1959 their minimum wage was raised, over furious protest from the farmers, to the princely level of 50 cents an hour. The bracero paid no rent. But from his $20 a week $1.75 was deducted each day for food and insurance. He received $7.45 in cash, out of which he had to provide for his family and try to save something to live on between harvests. PL 78 indentured the bracero to the farmer for the length of his stay in the United States. He was not free to move from farm to farm or camp to camp as he chose.

The braceros undercut every effort to raise the wages of domestic migrants and to improve working conditions. Nor was the bracero program popular with the Mexican authorities. It stood as an open admission of Mexico's enduring poverty; more tellingly, it pointed up the failure of Mexico's "revolutionary" government to secure a decent life for the Mexican people. Even American farmers were known, now and then, to have pangs of conscience over the bracero program, such as the farmer who told a Senate subcommittee, "We used to own the slaves. Now we rent them from the government." In 1963 the House, to widespread surprise, refused to renew PL 78. But that did not keep the Mexicans from coming.

Even when the bracero program was at its peak, as many as 1 million Mexicans were arrested and sent back across the border each year. The farmers wanted the Mexicans; the Mexicans wanted the work.

There was a noticeable aversion to sending Mexicans back at harvest time, regardless of how they got here. But when the harvest was in, the human roundup began. The farmer who had been unable to tell a legal from an illegal alien in early September would on the first of November be able to point out scores of illegal aliens to the Border Patrol, known to the Mexicans as *La Migra*. The Border Patrol for its part was so attuned to the farmers' needs that on one occasion several thousand Mexicans about to be deported at El Paso were "paroled" to the local farmers until the crops were harvested.

Almost everyone felt pity for the migrants, domestic or Mexican. It was not much of a life, most people agreed, to follow the crops from state to state for seven or eight months a year. From mid-January to mid-April there was virtually no work to be had on the land anywhere in the continental United States. Work, when it was available, meant a week here, a couple of weeks there, a month somewhere else if you were lucky. In between there was—nothing. A family which had at least one member who worked twenty-six weeks out of the fifty-two had had a good year. But the worst part of the migrants' life was not the traveling or the hard work or the miserable camps. It was the abysmally low wages. A Congressional committee concluded: "The plight of the agricultural migrant, as demonstrated by his wage rates, is almost beyond belief."

The growers were blamed, for being greedy. Consumers were blamed, for wanting cheap produce regardless of the human cost. But the productivity of migrant labor was so low that the wages they received were not necessarily due to wicked exploitation. In strictly economic terms it is debatable whether they were actually underpaid.

Mexican-Americans were associated, in most people's minds, with migrant farm labor. But by the early 1960s most Mexican-Americans were as urbanized as other Americans. Four million strong, they were the second largest racial minority in the United States. Most were to be found in California and Texas. They were usually scorned. The stereotypical Mexican-American was: in daily life, lazy and emotional; in power, corrupt and cruel; in personal relations, quick with a smile and quick with a knife.

Mexican-Americans shared with blacks a deep identity crisis. "The Mexican-American thinks of himself as both a citizen of the United States and a member of La Raza." The struggle to maintain a distinctive identity led those in San Antonio to call themselves Latin Americans, those in Albuquerque said they were Spanish Americans, while those in Los Angeles preferred to be known as Mexican-Americans. But about 1963 sizable numbers of the young began to call themselves Chicano, derived by dropping the first syllable of Mexicano. The name had been known in Mexican-American neighborhoods since the war, but was rarely used until now. Its appeal lay in the slightly aggressive assertion of identity it conveyed.

But wherever they lived and whatever they called themselves, Mexican-Americans rarely felt secure. The Border Patrol, which carried out a thankless task for the most part with patience and compassion, had extraordinary powers. A Border Patrol officer could flag down a carload of Mexicans in Milwaukee and demand to see their visas or proof of citizenship. And the McCarran-Walter Immigration Act of 1952 had launched Operation Wetback. This was a wide-ranging three-year roundup which had extended as far north as Spokane. The Special Mobile Force of the Border Patrol was encouraged to spread fear throughout the barrio. Thousands of Mexican-American families were roused by a knock on the door in the middle of the night. People were tracked down in movie houses, taken from schools, seized in the street. By the time it ended Operation Wetback had resulted in 3.8 million deportations. By keeping down the number of illegal aliens in the United States, the Border Patrol was, indirectly, helping raise the wages of those legally here. But the real heritage of Operation Wetback was that for the next generation *La Migra* was hated and feared.

Although they never attracted the attention devoted to black people, Mexican-Americans were commonly assumed to be as poor as blacks. Until the war this was probably true. But in the postwar their living standards rose remarkably. There was something resembling a middle class of up to half a million people. This middle class was based on the 200,000 Mexican-American veterans who came home with new skills, new ambitions, and new claims on American society. With the aid of the GI Bill and encouraged by a spreading sensitivity among white people to questions of racial and social justice this group of ambitious young men were able to win for themselves more in two decades than their parents had accomplished in a lifetime. With success, they began giving Anglo names to their children.

But in the barrios the brooding sense of injustice and the consoling atmosphere of passivity were as strong as ever. Mexican-Americans had a consoling myth. Most of California, New Mexico, Arizona, and Texas was rightfully theirs under Spanish land grants. They cherished the old court records, the ornate scrolls with elegant writing, the faded, stained, brittle old maps. But how had the Spanish obtained these vast tracts of land in the first place if not by dispossessing the Indians? In this quasi-historical, quasi-moralistic revery, in which they were the victims of an injustice instead of equal parties to the perpetration of an injustice, the Mexican-Americans consoled themselves and did little to improve their lot. They remained far weaker than their numbers justified. Even in El Paso, where half the population was of Mexican birth or ancestry, they enjoyed little political power. Poverty and education were partly to blame. But so was a deep aversion to politics. One observer remarked, "The only thing most people in Mexico get from the government is trouble."

But the growing Mexican-American middle class was beginning to assert itself in politics. In 1960 it made a national impact for the first time. *¡Viva Kennedy!* offices were established throughout the Southwest. In Texas, where the race was very close, their votes were especially important.

* * *

There was a second Spanish-speaking minority which the United States endured rather than assimilated—the Puerto Ricans. By 1963 there were nearly 1 million Puerto Ricans living in the United States. The overwhelming majority lived in New York.

Before 1945 comparatively few Puerto Ricans had ever left their island. But unscheduled carriers flying war surplus aircraft had cut the air fare to New York by two-thirds. Some flights offered a trip from San Juan to New York for as little as $35, until several such flights ended at sea instead of at Idlewild. On the nighttime thrift flights out of San Juan every passenger would be Puerto Rican. And they looked less like pilgrims journeying to the land of hope than refugees forced to flee a land being sacked: the planes were crammed with the old, the young, the poor, crying babies, a handful of cheap possessions tenaciously clung to. The passengers were tense, nervous, and bathed in sweat. Yet nothing could deter them. Throughout the 1950s and into the 1960s they arrived in New York at the rate of 1,000 a week.

Each week some 200 to 300 Puerto Ricans made the journey home. The shuttling back and forth was so intense that one of the candidates for governor of Puerto Rico in 1960, Luis Ferré, conducted part of his campaign in New York's Puerto Rican neighborhoods.

Large sections of the city had become Puerto Rican. East Harlem was Spanish Harlem, or El Barrio. It covered the area from Third Avenue to Fifth Avenue and from 116th Street to Ninety-sixth Street. By the 1960s this was one of the most densely populated places in the world: 300,000 people in one square mile. A single block on East 100th Street held more than 4,000 people. The police considered it the most violent, crime-ridden, doped up block in the city.

The population pressure forced Puerto Ricans to move farther west. They spilled over into neighborhoods which had been Irish and Italian for fifty years or more. The more they spread toward the Hudson, the more they impinged on areas long occupied by the white middle class. The liberalism of neighborhoods which were proud of their tolerance when they were almost completely white and middle-class was severely strained.

The other area into which the Puerto Ricans pressed was that traditional beachhead for newcomers, the Lower East Side. When Jews and Italians removed themselves to Mount Vernon and Darien, Puerto Ricans moved into the old neighborhood.

The tension in these Puerto Rican communities was almost palpable. The strains of poverty were exacerbated by an acute consciousness of class and color. White skin and straight hair were highly prized. Class and status were determined by such matters plus length of residence in New York and fluency in English. Even within a family differences of skin color or and knowledge of English created deep conflicts.

The Puerto Ricans, like blacks and Mexican-Americans, sought to identify themselves by adopting a distinctive name. Before 1945 middle-class Puerto Ricans had called themselves Hispanos, to set themselves apart from the comparative handful of lower-class Puerto Rican immigrants in the city. But by the 1960s the lower-class types were calling themselves Hispanos. The new, preferred usage was Latino. "Puerto Rican" had itself become a name like Mudd; this led the Commonwealth of Puerto Rico to hire an advertising agency to remake the island's image.

As they struggled to learn English, the Puerto Ricans created "Neoyorquismos" (New Yorkisms). They were eloquent in their own way at evoking life in El Barrio: bigchot (bigshot), broque (broke), chipe (cheap), despose (dispossess), jolope (holdup), raquet (racket), rilif (relief), tofe (tough), and trobel (trouble).

Despite the language barrier (they joked bitterly that they were illiterate in two languages), the Puerto Ricans were able to escape from poverty more easily than blacks. They were notably more enterprising when it came to setting up a business or taking advantage of an opportunity to go to high school or college or learn a trade. Their biggest problem was not language or color but the absence of birth control. The burden of having too many children to feed, clothe, house, and keep healthy while their total income was still small destroyed many Puerto Rican families, kept earnings low, and finally threw entire families onto the welfare rolls.

A Puerto Rican self-help organization, composed principally of.Puerto Rican social workers and schoolteachers, was set up in the 1950s. It was called Aspira, and it encouraged Puerto Ricans to take as their models the Jews and Italians who had preceded them into the Lower East Side thirty to forty years earlier. These were people who had made it up from the very same mean streets. Aspira urged Puerto Ricans to stop taking contemporary blacks as their models of how to survive in the city. But the Puerto Ricans seemed incapable of emulating the Jews and the Italians; not even in crime, for which some whites liked to believe Puerto Ricans had a natural affinity. When Puerto Rican gang members, of the kind portrayed in *West Side Story*, a musical notable for introducing questions of social justice on the musical stage, left the gang behind, there was no Puerto Rican mob for them to move into. So they settled down to marriage, grinding poverty, and more children than they could afford.

Not only were the Puerto Ricans not the criminals white people took them to be, but they were not the Christians either. The true faith of a majority of Puerto Ricans was spiritualism rather than Catholicism. The Catholic confession was the gloss on a pre-Christian belief in spirits, particularly possession by spirits of the dead. There was not a choice made between Catholicism and spiritualism; the religious Puerto Ricans usually believed in both. But many preferred to keep their belief in spiritualism to themselves. This enduring paganism, however, was a reflection of how far Puerto Ricans remained from assimilation into American society.

The smallest of the racial minorities, the Indians, grew rapidly in the postwar. The 1960 Census counted 508,000 Indians, but the true figure was probably in the region of 600,000.

Two-thirds of the Indian population lived on reservations or considered the reservation their home. The remainder lived in cities, more accurately, in Indian slums, such as the Chippewa slum in Minneapolis, the Navajo slum in St. Louis. Indians moved to the city for the same reason that black sharecroppers moved from Alabama to Chicago and Puerto Ricans moved from San Juan to New York—because there were jobs there: dirty jobs, hard jobs, badly paid jobs, but better than nothing. On the reservations unemployment rates were beyond anything white people had ever known. In the winter of 1962–1963 these were typical unemployment rates on Indian reservations: 72.5 percent among the Blackfeet of Montana; 71.1 percent among the Hopi of New Mexico; 86.1 percent among the Choctaw of Mississippi. Even among the Five Civilized Tribes of Oklahoma unemployment stood at 55 percent.

Since 1945 Indians had undergone experiences similar to those of black people: a return of the young men from wartime military service, an upsurge of assertiveness, followed by a dramatic increase in high school and college enrollment, accompanied by a growing sense of identity and an increase in expectations.

Some 25,000 Indians saw wartime military service; another 50,000 left the reservation to work in war production. Indians in uniform were invariably called "Chief" by the rest of the platoon or company. But they were also regarded as bloodthirsty by nature and incredibly brave. The war's effect on the Indians was revolutionary. For the first time large numbers of Indians had a chance to travel and to earn a decent living, to acquire an education, and to live away from the reservation. The old tribal culture disintegrated. Yet paradoxically, by 1963 there was more tribalism among American Indians than there had been in 1945. The new assertion of tribal identity was fueled with the passions of the young.

Indians, again like black people, had meanwhile found there was a place where they could fight for their rights: in Federal courts. They had no faith in Congress, or the Executive branch, or state government. Officials concerned with Indian affairs were usually powerful only when it came to telling the Indians what they could not do or could not have; their powers to help were severely limited.

At the end of the war the Bureau of Indian Affairs acquired a new Commissioner, Dillon Myer. The bureau decided it was time to stop treating Indians like children (wards) and to introduce them to the bracing air of citizenship. The war had shown that Indians could work regular hours and serve the state like everyone else. They did not have to live on reservations. If they could cope with life in a barracks or a boomtown, they could cope with life in the cities.

Congress put its blessing on this change in policy by means of a concurrent resolution. In 1953 it followed up with Public Law 280. This act granted the states authority to assume criminal jurisdiction over Indian lands, whether the Indians living on the land liked the idea or not. In later years further legislation transferred even more of the Federal government's responsibility to the states, which found themselves bearing most of the burden of education, social welfare, and the protection of reservation property.

The catchword for the BIA's current policy was "termination." No one knew exactly what termination meant, however. Some programs were terminated by mutual consent; others over angry protests. The new policy unfolded in some questionable ways. In the case of the Unarillas termination consisted of firing the land-use expert who was helping the Indians preserve their lands and replacing him with a former real estate salesman. Where termination ended an expensive but necessary program, the states were invariably reluctant to keep it going. Several reservations were put out of existence; the land was sold; the money was divided up. But whatever termination meant for the Indians, the BIA never showed any interest in terminating itself.

In the end, the new policy failed. The Indians and the states, for very different reasons, refused to cooperate. When this attempt to push the Indians off the reservations and into the factories failed around 1960, the BIA tried another approach. It would bring the factories to the reservations. And there were a few local success stories: a pickle factory in New Mexico, an electric toothbrush factory in Montana, a diamond-cutting shop in Arizona, and so on. But the number of Indians employed in these ventures remained small. Every reservation had a sizable body of grown men with not enough work, not enough self-respect, too much time on their hands, and too much to drink.

Termination in the end, like every Indian policy before it, ended up as a license to steal. Little wonder that Indians felt their situation was hopeless. Under termination nearly 3 million acres of Indian land were sold off, nearly always under a pretext of necessity and nearly always over the objections of the Indians. And nearly always white men profited handsomely as a result.

The fate of the Iroquois typified what Indians endured in the postwar. They had been among the first to make a successful transition to urban life, without breaking their links with the reservation. The heroic engineering of the Gilded Age had created a demand for a new kind of worker—one able to work high above ground on a skyscraper's skeleton or on the towers of a suspension bridge, oblivious to both mortal danger and the thunderous din of riveting. Seamen, accustomed to climbing about in the riggings of tall-masted sailing ships, were recruited. But then it was found that Mohawk Indians, one of the five principal tribes of the Iroquois nation, which was strung along the Canadian and American banks of the St. Lawrence, possessed the agility of mountain goats, a lofty indifference to both heights and danger, and a stolid disregard for noise.

Jobs in high steel became the economic mainstay of the Caughnawaga reservation of the Mohawks. In Brooklyn a Mohawk neighborhood developed. Here the riveting gangs spent most of the spring and summer. Their wives came with them, bought beads and thread from the five-and-dime, and made Indian souvenirs to be sold at the weekend. The Mohawks had reached a *modus vivendi* with the white man's world.

But the 1950s brought the St. Lawrence Seaway. The lands of the Iroquois Confederacy were coveted by Washington and Albany. A lengthy round of court cases was set in motion. The Seaway also revived questions of jurisdiction over the Indians. Did Indians have to pay income taxes? When taxes were deducted from the paychecks of Indians working on the Seaway, the hereditary chiefs of the Iroquois appealed to Eisenhower, as a fellow sovereign head, to put a stop to this practice. When he declined to intervene, they tried to take the matter to the UN General Assembly for action.

Until now the Indians living along the St. Lawrence had been unmolested on their lands because the surrounding area was sparsely populated and economically moribund. The Seaway brought dams, roads, aluminum plants, shipyards, docks, locks, a GM factory, trailer parks, and housing projects right up to the borders of the reservation. And when the New York State Power Authority under Robert Moses had to choose between taking land owned by whites and land owned by Indians, it took the Indians' every time. It took it forcefully and without consultation, armed as it was with sweeping powers of eminent domain. As the Tuscarora Indians living near Niagara discovered, no reservation was secure from the cupidity of state officials. When the Federal courts refused to uphold the guarantees they believed the Federal government had extended at the time their reservation was created, the Tuscaroras' land was saved at the last moment by a ruling from the Federal Power Commission.

The only place where Indians felt secure was in Oklahoma, which was where a third of all Indians lived. There the Indian influence was pervasive. There was no overt discrimination against them. Oklahoma governors, judges, legislators, and businessmen often were, and were often proud to be, partly Indian. One, Charles Curtis, part Kaw, had been a Vice President of the United States (under Hoover). Will Rogers had been part Cherokee. Indians who were poor or deprived in Oklahoma were not uncommon; this was the inevitable result of two centuries of greed and injustice by whites who took the land by force. And so even even in Oklahoma the early 1960s saw the same revival of tribalism which was under way along the St. Lawrence Seaway and elsewhere.

Ironically, the Federal government was partly responsible for this revival. The old habits were hard to break, but it showed itself increasingly willing to listen to the Indians' demands for justice throughout the postwar. The Indians Claims Commission, created in 1946, adjudicated Indian claims running into billions of dollars. By the end of 1963 it had settled 50 claims for nearly $100 million and was considering a further 430.

There is an inescapable sadness that touches every aspect of life among the poor. But worse is the numbing fatalism:

> Not that they starve, but starve so dreamlessly,
> Not that they sow, but that they seldom reap,
> Not that they serve, but have no gods to serve,
> Not that they die, but that they die like sheep.

35

Cities of Wretched Nights

America had become a nation of cities. Yet the more the cities grew, the more endangered were the principal pleasures and justifications of the civilized—that is, city-based—life. The sense of community, the cultivation of a high artistic life, the development of tolerance, and the encouragement of diversity, the stimulating atmosphere—all were under threat. America's major cities were probably less violent than most of the great cities of the past. Even at their most flyblown and untidy they were doubtless cleaner and healthier than London and Paris in the nineteenth century. Yet American cities were becoming noisome and repellent. The typical American city of 1963 was a place in which civilization lived as a fugitive; it took an effort to find it. The city as a whole was likely to be a bleak and cheerless place.

However, it remained a population magnet. In the 1950s more than half of all Americans lived in only 162 (or 5 percent) of the country's 3,150 counties. Even this figure understates the degree of concentration. Nearly 70 percent of the nation lived in and around cities. The remaining 30 percent were linked to the urban areas economically, socially, culturally.

To deal with this concentration of population, the Census Bureau and the Bureau of Labor Statistics in the late 1940s abolished the crude idea of the city. In its place they put the Standard Metropolitan Statistical Area (eventually shortened to SMA). An SMA comprised a core city of 50,000 or more people, the county or counties in which it was located, the contiguous counties which were closely tied to the core city. The ties involved phone calls, trips to the city for cultural pursuits, commuting to the city to work, and so on. The SMA provided a more realistic, if dully bureaucratic, picture of the city than did the old reliance on legal boundaries. Chicago, for example, claimed a population of 3.6 million within the city limits. But its true population, according to the new criteria, was nearly 5.5 million. In the Los Angeles SMA there were fewer than half of all Angelenos within the rambling city limits and paying taxes to the city on which they depended for so much.

Since 1900 nearly 75 percent of all population growth had taken place within the SMAs. Some, such as Scranton, Pennsylvania, Wheeling, West Virginia, Jersey City, New Jersey, and St. Joseph, Missouri, had lost population since 1945. But most had gained, and heavily. New SMAs were also coming into existence. In 1950 there were 168; in 1960 there were 212.

Each SMA was a confederation of from a few to a few score municipalities and incorporated districts. Each member of each confederation was jealous of its petty privileges and autonomy. Numerous attempts were made from 1960 to 1963 to turn the many into the few. They were invariably rejected by the voters. In Seattle three attempts at consolidation were defeated. In St. Louis the figure was four. In Memphis, Chattanooga, and San Antonio consolidation of the city and county seemed likely to succeed, had the support of civic leaders and local politicians, yet was stopped at the ballot box.

Since the turn of the century political scientists and civic reformers had been pressing the case for a general-purpose government to run an entire metropolitan area. But not until 1957 was it ever attempted, in Dade County, Florida, which was dominated by Miami. It was an experiment which was followed with keen interest. But by 1963 matters had not changed much. The twenty-six cities and towns within Dade County were operating much as before; each had its own policemen and firemen, water supply, sewage disposal, and housing program. All twenty-six levied and collected local taxes. The metropolitan government was limited to drawing up long-range plans, developing the seaport, and running the traffic courts.

Within the central or core city there was usually a government which was both honest and weak. A book such as Lincoln Steffens's *The Shame of the Cities* became impossible to write by the 1960s. The trend in local politics in the postwar was toward the apolitical, the nonpartisan, the middle-class cult of the public good. The technicians, the experts, the chaste guardians of civic virtue were steadily ousting the bad old bosses and the political machines which had dispensed charity, sentimentality, and fear in roughly equal proportions. As the lower class moved up socially, so it cleaned up its politics to come closer to the WASP methods of good government. What corruption remained was more likely to be found at the lowest level of the political ladder rather than at the top and in the state legislature rather than in city hall.

The postwar cities did not so much grow as sprawl. And along the East Coast one sprawling SMA ran into another. The result was termed megalopolis. This unlovely creation could be seen clearly from the air, as a seemingly endless built-up area of concrete and dirty air unfolded below. The first megalopolis was formed in the 1950s. It ran from New Hampshire to Virginia. It was dominated by Boston, Hartford, New York, Philadelphia, Baltimore, and Washington. To the estimable Lewis Mumford it was a development in human history which any sensible man could regard only with horror. Megalopolis was neither a new form of city life nor the culmination of the city's promise. It was, instead, the anticity: the death of civilized life.

To a large extent megalopolis was the inevitable result of the automobile. And by the early 1960s the automobile was being widely condemned as the principal villain in the urban crisis. It suddenly became modish to try to get the automobile out of the downtown area; if that was not possible, then to get it out of sight. There was a spurt of interest in pedestrian malls. Pomona, California, Kalamazoo, Michigan, and Miami Beach, Florida, by 1963 had opened widely admired malls and put the pedestrians' cars underground. Sidewalks were widened. Roads gave way to small parks. For the first time since the Model T town planners had a clear picture of the car's proper place in the scheme of things, it came second.

Meanwhile, at city hall the postwar had brought a remarkable change in the city's links with other power structures. Until 1945 most cities were independent. A handful were supported by the state legislature. But during the Depression the cities had enjoyed a taste of Federal largess. By the late 1940s, as their problems mounted, they were hooked.

The 1949 urban renewal act marked the end of the cities' independence. Here was a partnership the Constitution had never foreseen. The institutions it called for had to be developed ad hoc and from the humblest materials. But by 1963 there was hardly a city in the United States that did not look to Washington, and not to the state legislature, for advice, sympathy, and, most of all, cash. The Federal government provided the cities with their hospitals, airports, and highways.

The Eisenhower Administration disliked this development but could not do much about it. As a concession to its conscience, however, it created the Federal State Action Committee. This body spent two years diligently looking for places to cut Federal aid to the cities. Its only specific recommendation was to eliminate Federal grants to waste treatment plants; this would get the government out of garbage.

The New Frontier, on the other hand, was based on the cities. Policy toward them became activist. Large numbers of Americans, moreover, having rediscovered poverty and their attention having been caught by the clamor of the civil rights struggle, turned their minds at last to the state of their cities and began to talk about the "urban crisis."

Kennedy hoped to tackle the problems comprehensively through a new entity, a Department of Urban Affairs, which would pull together the various strands of the Federal-city connection. He made no secret of is intention to appoint Robert C. Weaver, an authority on housing and a black man, to head the new department. To the disappointment of blacks Congress refused to pass Kennedy's legislation, and he was thus denied the opportunity to appoint the country's first black Cabinet minister.

The term "the slums" was falling out of fashion. Yet the slums endured. During the Kennedy years there was an urban slum population of 12 million. Most slum dwellers were black or brown.

The ethnic makeup of the slums had changed markedly over thirty years. These were now "slums of despair." They were the end of the line for the people who had moved into them since 1939. Before the war the slums had teemed with immigrants. They had then been "slums of hope." The people who had crowded into the Lower East Side around 1910 had believed their children would get out even if they did not. But the slum dwellers of 1961 had no such expectation.

There was not a single major city that was slum-free. America's cities differ widely in their history, their forms of government, their cultural and ethnic character. Yet there was one thing all of them had in common in the early 1960s—a rotting core.

Every city with a population of 150,000 or more had a skid row. In Chicago, New York, Los Angeles, Detroit, and San Francisco the skid row population numbered some 5,000 to 10,000 homeless men. Everyone knew where the local skid row was located. It was invariably adjacent to the central business district, like a gypsy's curse on capitalism. It was an area of fleabag hotels, sad-looking pawnshops. striptease joints, and barber colleges.

Skid row was not, contrary to the popular view, full of alcoholics. Many of its inhabitants did not drink. The most common denominator of skid row dwellers was not drink but poverty. Many were missing a limb or were blind, were over sixty-five, were foreign-born, or were mentally disordered. Usually a sizable number were middle-aged workmen who labored hard for low wages but were unable to find or to keep a steady job. Most of the people on skid row had landed there through some misfortune—bereavement; a mental collapse; an accident. Nearly all were white, and the vast majority were male, although in several skid rows up to a third of the denizens were female. In American society the skid row dweller was among the lowest of the low; these were the most neglected and most despised people of all. No black sharecropper in Mississippi endured a more dangerous or more miserable life.

Slums were more varied than they appeared to most outsiders. Boston's West End, for instance, appeared to city hall, to tourists, to urban renewal experts, and to people in the better parts of the city as a slum. But to the people who lived there it was merely a low-income neighborhood. It was a cohesive community. Its problems arose from lack of money. The life in the West End was similar to life in a middle-class suburb, except for the affluence. Gossiping, feuding, friendship, communal enterprises, the give-and-take of a stable community proceeded in much the same way. The neighborhood was not unusually troubled by crime, disease, or mental disorder. The struggle most people faced was a battle with poverty, and most of the crime, mental illness, and physical breakdown its people were prone to could be traced to lack of money. But the planners at the urban renewal authority did not see that. They were unable to grasp that what they were dealing with was not really a slum but a working-class neighborhood that was as viable, given a chance, as almost anything they might create for these same people.

But in Chicago there was a poor neighborhood which learned to stand up to the planners and defend itself. Its people were black; their tutor was Saul Alinsky. The neighborhood was called Woodlawn, a place long lost to woods, where the lawns were by now the stuff a suburbanite's nightmares are made of. Woodlawn was a large, vaguely defined area south of the University of Chicago campus. Its population of 100,000 was composed mainly of black people who had moved in since 1939. By the late 1950s a pleasant middle-class neighborhood had become a slum. The planners moved in to remake it. But this shattered hulk of a community suddenly roused itself.

With the help of Alinsky's Industrial Areas Foundation, whose aim was to provide the poor with middle class techniques of communal self-help,

The Woodlawn Organization was formed in 1950. This was a confederation of organizations already alive and well in Woodlawn—the thirteen churches, the three businessmen's organizations, the various block clubs, and so on. TWO directly involved more than 30,000 people. It was "the first instance in which a large, broadly representative organization has come into existence in any Negro district in any large American city."

TWO devised and enforced a business code of practice. This put an end to short weights, overcharging, usurious interest rates, and rigged cash registers. The streets were cleaned up by a city government which had suddenly found itself confronted by a highly organized voting bloc which it could not afford to ignore. Adolescents were drawn into many TWO projects. Juvenile crime rates dropped.

TWO became sufficiently powerful and articulate to win important concessions from the urban renewal authority. Woodlawn remained a cohesive neighborhood. But there was only one TWO. Elsewhere the policy toward the slums was to send in the bulldozers. Urban renewal had become an irresistible force. Insofar as bureaucracy can take up a cause, urban renewal had become a cause.

It was built largely on an early, impressive success—Pittsburgh. In 1945 Pennsylvania had passed the first urban renewal act. During the next ten years it was used principally to save Pittsburgh, notably the Golden Triangle section. The main reason why Pittsburgh was able to revitalize the dirtiest, murkiest, most unhealthy part of town, to clear the skies above and the two rivers below, to revive economic life, and to attract new investment was that it was based on the cooperation of private enterprise. The businesses involved, moreover, were not local small businesses, but large national corporations who had their headquarters or a large investment in the city. Scores of cities looked on Pittsburgh's success as proof that the thing could be done.

But the Housing Act of 1949 contained a fatal flaw. It was written into the legislation by Robert A. Taft, who believed in public housing but did not believe the Federal government had any right to get into the city-saving business. Title 1 of the 1949 legislation attempted to straddle these separate stools of Taftism. It encouraged private participation in slum clearance and rewarded private investment in housing on the cleared slum sites. The inevitable result was that urban renewal became a program in which the builders put up new housing for the middle class and evicted the poor in order to do it. Taft appears never to have grasped what he was doing.

Subsequent legislation built on Title 1. The original hope that urban renewal would stop the rot and save decaying neighborhoods became fanciful at best. The original aim of urban renewal was not to raze huge tracts of land but to save this street, tear down that street, provide new community facilities, such as playgrounds and off-street parking, and by such discreet and relevant measures save the neighborhood. The name, the Housing Act of 1949, suggested that the act was meant to build housing. But its real purpose was to try to save the cities. Indeed, between 1949 and 1963 it destroyed considerably more housing units than it built or authorized to be built. More than 1 million units were destroyed, and fewer than 350,000 low-cost public housing units constructed.

Meanwhile, notices such as this were arriving in thousands of homes every week:

> The building in which you live is located in an area which has been taken over by the———Redevelopment Authority according to law as part of the Federal Center Project. The building in which you now live will be demolished after you have been relocated and the land will be sold for public and commercial development according to the———Redevelopment Plan presently being prepared.

For many recipients this was the first that they had heard of urban renewal. And that, as a Marxist would say, was no accident. Because redevelopment involved negotiations among city, state, and Federal authorities, plus private interests, secrecy was considered important. "Outside" (public) involvement was considered "interference." First, the local government created an urban renewal agency and directed it to draw up an urban renewal plan. This would be done with the aid of state officials and private enterprise. Then the local authority approved the plan. After that the Federal government approved the plan. With the plan finally agreed upon, a public hearing was held. Every objection raised was treated as an idiotic menace to several years of work. Because the plan was already fixed and a large bureaucracy had come into existence whose *raison d'etre* was the plan as it stood, the public's protestations were viewed as a threat to the entire project. They had to be beaten down, ignored, or evaded. The hearings were a form of democracy and a mockery of its substance. Armed with the power of eminent domain granted by the 1949 Housing Act, the urban renewal authority could, and usually did, take the land and send in the demolition crews.

The cleared sites were sold to private developers for 33 percent of whatever it had cost the city to buy and raze them. The Federal government paid the city the remaining 67 percent. After that the developers were left alone to proceed with the construction of whatever type of structure the plan had called for—office blocks, shopping centers, high-rise apartments, and so on. Low-cost housing came last on the list of priorities. And by 1963 housing, which had provided the overt justification for the 1949 act, was no longer in short supply. The 1950s had seen a 25 percent increase in the housing stock. Four out of five housing units were sound in 1963, an astonishing improvement in a generation. In 1939 only 40 percent of American homes had enjoyed adequate plumbing, heating, and running water. Although there were some areas with too much housing and some with too little, housing as such was no longer a major social problem.

This remarkable improvement in the quality of housing was due not to the development of suburbia but to the improvement of urban housing.

By the 1960s 90 percent of all urban dwellings were up to standard. It was in the rural areas that most of the nation's dilapidated housing was to be found. The Housing Act of 1949 had the foresight to provide Federal money for the amelioration of rural housing.

As the renewal projects spread, so did opposition to them. The power of eminent domain had traditionally been held to apply only to land needed for public use. But in 1954 the future of the entire urban renewal program was saved when the Supreme Court, overruling a Federal District Court, decided that governments could take someone's property in order to sell it to someone else who would put it to private use in pursuit of "a public purpose."

Urban renewal ground on, although it ground exceeding fine and very slowly. From the creation of the urban renewal authority to the completion of the project ten years or more would pass. This time lag had one common result: it made all that was bad about urban renewal far worse. And the private developers lost their initial enthusiasm. The large profits they had anticipated were certainly possible, but they did not look very impressive when spread over ten to fifteen years.

Despite the criticisms, urban renewal authorities convinced themselves they were succeeding. Their idea of success was quantitative. It was based on the number of slum blocks cleared. Judged by the number of cleared sites awaiting the developers, Newark in 1961 was considered "one of the most successful renewal programs in the country." Similar triumphs were to be viewed in New York, Chicago, New Haven, Philadelphia, Norfolk, and Baltimore.

Newark was typical also in the way its urban renewal authority strove tirelessly to avoid building low-cost public housing. The city was determined to build middle-income housing. As a result, Newark's worst slums were left alone. They were so bad that no one would want to live in such an area even after the old buildings had been torn down. The city learned its lesson the hard way, by first clearing the North Ward and then finding it very difficult to find a developer for the area. "We took an awful chance," a rueful official later explained, "by guessing at what redevelopers wanted. Then we had to go around peddling vacant land. Now we let the developers *tell* us where they want to build."

Urban renewal did produce some positive results. In cities where historic preservation societies were involved in the planning at an early stage—Philadelphia, New Haven, Washington, Little Rock, Mobile, and Providence—some parts of the program were carried out with sensitivity, imagination, and enthusiasm. And in Philadelphia, where much of the white middle class chose to fight rather than to flee, white families began to move back into neighborhoods long considered black. South of Rittenhouse Square white families were buying homes, renovating them, and creating a cohesive community close to the city center.

New Haven was the city which, by the 1960s, was considered the showcase of urban renewal. Under the aggressive leadership of Mayor Richard C. Lee, New Haven had the highest per capita urban renewal expenditure of any city. Much of New Haven had been transformed. It also enjoyed several advantages absent in a city such as Chicago, however: a comparatively small and well-educated population, a comparatively small belt of slums, and an unusually energetic mayor.

New York offered an example of urban renewal at its worst. By 1962 New York alone accounted for one-third of all urban renewal spending. No one believed more deeply in urban renewal than Robert Moses. No one was better at getting money from Washington. And no one had cruder ideas on city planning.

In every city urban renewal projects had one result that was admired at city hall—they provided a new, and possibly fruitful, tax base. Much of the downtown area was, in most cities, owned by tax-exempt bodies (churches, schools, colleges, foundations), and middle-class families were fleeing to the suburbs. Urban renewal projects had another common, but less admired, characteristic: their costs mounted horrendously. One of the highly touted benefits of urban renewal was that for every dollar of the taxpayer's money spent, private enterprise would put up another $3 to $4. The actual figure turned out to be 30 to 50 cents.

But the ultimate failure of urban renewal was not exaggerated promises or cost overruns. It was the misery it caused. Urban renewal authorities did not get rid of urban slums and blight. They simply tore down the already-inadequate housing stock of the poor, then forced them to move to somewhere else in the city. The families and small businesses forced to move away were never able to move back to the old neighborhood because they could not afford to live there now that it was taken up with middle-class housing. The reason they had lived in the old neighborhood had been that it was cheap. Having been forced to leave it, they moved into another poor neighborhood elsewhere in the city, making all *its* problems worse.

Enforced immobility in the old slum or ghetto had been bad. This enforced mobility was far worse. And because 75 to 80 percent of all those displaced were black, blacks called urban renewal Negro removal.

When the Kennedy Administration took office, it inherited the urban renewal program. Thanks to the sluggishness of most projects, only 100 had been completed since 1949. Another 1,200 were being planned or had actually begun, in more than 600 cities. The Administration found itself supervising a program whose successes were far outnumbered by its failures. Yet the program was due to reproduce itself on a scale ten times greater than what had been achieved so far. Several billions had been spent; in the future spending would run to the tens of billions. So far 600,000 had been moved out; in future another 3 to 4 million would be forced out of their homes.

The Kennedy Administration made no attempt to rethink the urban renewal program. Instead, it applied its usual solution—more. Congress in 1961 passed a new Housing Act. This was the biggest such measure since 1949. It provided an extra $2 billion for slum clearance, authorized an extra 100,000 low-cost housing units, and offered inexpensive loans to elderly homeowners who wanted to renovate their homes. Altogether, the Housing Act of 1961 provided an extra $5 billion for urban renewal without correcting any of its principal defects.

The construction of 810,000 low-cost housing units originally called for in the 1949 legislation was unlikely ever to be reached. In 1949 Taft had confidently expected that public housing would in a few years account for 10 percent of housing starts. By 1961 it accounted for 1 percent. And in the interim resistance to public housing had become adamantine. It had never been popular. The hero of Ayn Rand's turgid best-seller of the late 1940s *The Fountainhead* was an architect who made his grand gesture on behalf of the individual by blowing up a brand-new, low-rent housing project with dynamite.

Yet poor housing had long been considered a major cause of crime, juvenile delinquency, drug addiction, prostitution, alcoholism, sex offenses, broken families, and mental illness. Housing reform therefore appeared to be one initiative an enlightened government might take that was sure to do some good. Housing reform was portrayed as one of the most moral and progressive ventures open to local government. It had been a crusade among social workers since the late nineteenth century.

But every attempt seemed to result in failure. Postwar housing projects were usually called self-contained. That sounded good. But the reality was not. "Self-contained" meant isolated, cut off from the life of the city, fragmented, remote, sterile, anything but pleasant. There was also a deliberate, self-conscious effort made by city planners to separate the highrise blocks of the public housing projects from the surrounding streets. Even when they were not erected in a slum, the nice new blocks soon found that they were located in the middle of one as the housing nearby dropped in value, was left to neglect, became blighted, and eventually turned into a slum.

Nearly every project was proudly "open occupancy." That meant mainly black occupancy. What followed was glibly ascribed to racism. But prejudice as such was not the main element in subsequent events. Economic and social factors played a more important part. What the respectable people in a neighborhood wanted to know when a project was opened was: will my property lose its value? What will happen to the schools? Will the streets be safe at night? Respectable and stable people, whether black or white, began to move out if they could afford to before anyone had moved into the new project. It was already well on its way to being set in a slum. Once that happened, its isolation was complete.

The projects were a stunning disappointment to the reformers. "Once upon a time," one of them remarked, "we thought that if we could only get our problem families out of those dreadful slums, then papa would stop taking dope, mama would stop chasing around, and Junior would stop carrying a knife. Well, we've got them into a nice new apartment with modern kitchens and a recreation center. And they're the same bunch of bastards they always were."

To the people who lived in one, a project was more like a cheap hotel than a home. It was treated accordingly. There was no security of tenure. A small, mimeographed notice from the housing authority could put a family on the streets in very short order.

Size of family (preferably big) and size of income (preferably small) got people into a project. Or rather, the family got into the project. No one was housed individually. When a marriage broke up, the entire family had to leave the project. An entire family could also be cast out if one of its members was ruled "undesirable" by the housing authority. In New York up to 200 families a year were evicted on these grounds. Nor dare a family allow its income to rise very far. If it exceeded the rather modest limits set by the housing authority, then the family would be required to move somewhere befitting their exalted new status.

The projects were based not on the harsh dictates of martinets but on laudable humanitarian principles. The lower the family income, the higher the priority on the waiting list. There was no rejection of a family on account of race, religion, or ethnic origin. Unhappily, the result of these principles was that every project became a collecting station for the poor, the desperate, and the mentally disordered. Poverty always draws lines which are sharp and deep. The people in the projects were cut off from ordinary life—that is, the kind of life where along with the sorrows there is also a sense of hope, steady work, a sense of community, and a variety of opportunities for diversion and enlightenment. Every society has a sizable number of people who have been broken by life, for one reason or another. The projects collected them. The income rules kept them together. It was the very nature of the projects to discourage any attempt to break out of the culture of poverty and dependency.

It is possible that the projects also made the condition of slum life worse. The only cohesive element in the lives of the people living in the projects was that they were in families. Outside, in the surrounding streets, they left behind the rootless and restless. The streets became the province of the abandoned women and the abandoned children—the prime raw material for prostitution and drug addiction.

"The projects in Harlem are hated," wrote James Baldwin. "They are hated almost as much as the policeman, and this is saying a great deal. And they are hated for the same reason: both reveal, unbearably, the real attitude of the white world, no matter how many liberal speeches are made."

There was one last mockery to "low-cost public housing": it was not cheap. In fact, it was often expensive. Units in a major project in 1959 and 1960 commonly involved a capital cost of more than $13,000 each. There were projects where unit cost reached $20,000. It would have been much cheaper to have bought or built houses for $11,000 to $12,000 and simply given them to the top priority families on the waiting lists.

New York was the urban crisis writ large, plus something extra. It was both the richest city in the world and the most generous. It attracted the lion's share of the country's most talented people, including the talented bums. But while the city was rich, many of its people were poor. In 1962 the Teamsters' Research Department applied the Bureau of Labor Statistics' definition of a "modest but adequate" standard of living to the population of New York. Half the city's families fell below the BLS standard.

Throughout the postwar the city saw a building boom, mostly in roads and office buildings. Whole sections of mid-Manhattan were completely rebuilt between 1945 and 1963. But behind this feverish activity was a sense of impermanence; it was typified by an earlier venture, Rockefeller Center, which was finished in 1939. This apparently permanent and monumental work was located on land leased for a mere ninety-nine years.

Behind the postwar New York building boom moved the bulky figure of Robert Moses—"Big Bad Bob" to his critics, "The Builder" to his many admirers. No high farce is complete without a larger-than-life villain. Moses was the villain of the massive failure that was New York's urban crisis.

He had come to fame and power in the 1920s as the man who provided parks and beaches for the masses. He installed the plebeian pleasures— tennis courts, picnic tables, barbecue pits. These may have appeared tame by the 1960s, but before the war they were imaginative and extremely popular. And to hurry families out to the parks and beaches, Moses built the "parkways" radiating from New York. After the war his passion for roads (the passion of a man who never learned to drive) led to the building of six expressways through the city. They served as the models for urban expressways in scores of major cities.

Moses's great power rested on the pillars of public esteem and the public authority. The latter was a device imported from England in the 1920s. It was a nonpolitical body created expressly to achieve some specific public purpose. It was financed by bonds instead of taxes and ran for a fixed, but sometimes renewable, term. Moses converted the humble public authority—in this instance, the Triborough Bridge Authority—into a power within a power. By the 1950s no mayor dared fire him, no politician dared cross him.

His trump card was public opinion, more precisely, public adulation. He threatened to resign so often that Mayor La Guardia had a pad of resignation forms printed with Moses's name on them, leaving only a blank space for the date. It was the people of New York, whom he despised, bullied, and condescended to, who made Moses great. If they found themselves with a city they disliked, they could thank themselves for much of it, for much of what they disliked had grown from the vanity and shoddy taste of Robert Moses.

Almost to the end of his life, however, he basked in the favor of the city establishment. The New York Times, the Archdiocese of New York, and the Chase Manhattan Bank alike fawned on him. Nor was Moses ever a man to spurn the goodwill of the rich. When the Lincoln Center site was being cleared by the urban renewal authority, one of the buildings to be razed was owned by Robert Kennedy and three of his sisters. The building was bought for $2.5 million, or $62.88 a square foot. The building next door, owned by some less august personages, was condemned under eminent domain and compensation was made at a rate of $9.58 a square foot. The Kennedys had declared that their building was worth only $1.1 million shortly before these events and had paid taxes on it on that basis. Somehow it more than doubled in value when it had to be sold.

Moses was at home where big money was concerned. Much of his hold over local politicians stemmed from his control over the influx of money from Washington and Albany for new roads, bridges, and public housing. To fire Moses would have been to jeopardize billions of dollars and tens of thousands of jobs. No mayor lacking an interest in martydrom and exile would take the risk.

Thanks to Moses and the network of friends he had built up, the city got highways, bridges, and parks. It got the UN. What it needed, and continued to do without, were schools, hospitals, libraries, and a better subway system. Bridges were regularly repainted. Schools were not.

Throughout the 1950s Moses dominated public housing in New York. His contempt for the poor, the black, the brown, and the otherwise disesteemed was reflected in the result. It also reflected his zeal for urban renewal. The Moses methods were developed in New York and emulated elsewhere. Viable, cohesive neighborhoods were gutted for no more exalted an end than the enrichment of a handful of city politicians, insurance brokers, demolition contractors, and parking lot operators. A neighborhood could be destroyed for the sake of a road and a parking lot. All around there would stand a barren expanse of rubble and dirt. The adjoining residential streets had been turned into a choked slum, filled with the recently dispossessed.

Ordinary working-class and lower-middle-class sections of the city were rapidly turned into sinks of crime, despair, and disease, thanks to Moses and his greedy friends. Title 1 housing in New York became so open to peculation under Moses' reign that even organized crime became involved in public housing.

In classic fashion, Moses overreached himself. He attempted to crush the ego of the one man to come to power in New York who was able to stand up to him—Nelson Rockefeller. The Rockefellers were so rich that no one in New York would make an open challenge to them. They were powerful, too, in Washington and in the informal network of power which was loosely termed the Eastern Establishment. In a 1962 showdown with Governor Nelson Rockefeller, Moses played his trump card. He threatened to resign all his state posts. Rockefeller promptly did what no one else had ever dared to do—he accepted Moses's resignations, then made them stick.

But even to the end Moses's critics were inclined to give him credit for being a man of "vision." This was because he worked on a large scale. Yet it was not vision; it was vanity. He was building monuments to himself. His taste was trite and his "vision" naïve. There is little reason to

suppose that 100,000 years from now anyone will know of or care to remember Big Bad Bob. Like the achievements of Ozymandias (remembered only because a poet memorialized his vanity), all Moses ever built
would one day turn to sand. Vision would have aimed at beauty or nobility or kindness.

Moses's failure was not wholly personal. It was played out again and
again by other people. The same lack of imagination, the same ludicrous
self-importance could be found all over the city. And bad conditions
make good books. In 1961 Jane Jacobs's *The Death and Life of Great
American Cities* was published. It was concerned mainly with New York.
It did for the urban crisis what *The Other America* had done for the poor.
It lit as if by lightning something both murky and obvious at the same
time.

Mrs. Jacobs described the worst results of city planning. The emphasis
on open spaces had produced sterility. The infatuation with grass had produced parks people were afraid to use. Diversity had been diminished. It
was assumed that people hated cities when large numbers of them actually liked city life; they loved its variety, its excitements, its crowds, its
bustle. But the crowds and the bustle were the very elements the planners
wanted to get rid of. There was a preference for uniformity and neatness.
The unspoken dislike of diversity suggested an unspoken dislike for people as they are.

Humanity, however, is wonderfully stubborn. People struggled to retain their identity as they fought to maintain their dignity, and the two
were really inseparable. As Nathan Glazer and Daniel Moynihan discovered, the most important fact about the New York "Melting Pot" was
that it never happened. Ethnic groups *were* assimilated. But they kept
their separate identities. Similarly in Chicago, there were in the 1950s
more than eighty community newspapers in circulation each week. They
had a combined circulation of 1 million copies. Had the planners been
right in assuming a natural decline in local differences, the number and
circulation of such newspapers would probably have been dropping. But
since 1910 the number of such newspapers had doubled and their circulation had risen 800 percent.

Although they were in crisis, the cities did not actually fall apart. But
they were becoming increasingly unpleasant and dangerous. This was not
least because the heroin plague had claimed upwards of 100,000 victims,
half of them in New York.

Attitudes toward the drug problem remained complacent until about
1960. What eventually aroused concern was not that drugs of addiction
are inherently evil (they are an attack on the integrity of the personality)
but that the crime rate was increasing sharply. Drugs were a convenient
explanation. By 1963 the average addict needed $10,000 a year to support
his habit; that is, he needed to steal goods worth $50,000. In New York,
drug-related crime, from stealing to fencing, provided employment for
more people than did construction, said Mayor Wagner.

Yet there was hardly any evidence that drug addiction increased the total crime rate. Law-abiding citizens did not start taking drugs and then begin mugging passersby or breaking into other people's houses. Most addicts were juvenile delinquents when they began taking dope. As drug addiction spread, the incidence of some categories of petty crime rose. But this was not enough to have an appreciable effect on overall crime rates. The laws addicts broke were usually the laws against drug abuse. And delinquency was more likely to lead to addiction than addiction was to lead to delinquency.

Down on the block in Harlem, Claude Brown noticed that it was not the career criminals who became addicts. The typical addict was someone who turned to drugs as an alternative to crime, then resumed his criminal career to support his habit. The crimes were almost always petty, often pathetic. The successful criminals usually avoided dealing in dope, lucrative as it was, because dealing was too close to use. It was only a matter of time before one led to the other.

It took a long time before there was a widespread recognition of either how evil heroin was or what the heroin plague was doing to American society. In 1955 an admired Federal judge, Charles E. Wyzanski, Jr., in charge of the trial in Boston Federal District Court of a heroin dealer, passed sentence saying, "This . . . offense is to me exactly the same as bootlegging, except instead of liquor it happens to be drugs, and I have no more moral view with respect to drugs than with respect to liquor." By 1963 it was impossible to encounter a view such as this openly expressed anywhere on the Federal bench.

One of the reasons for the very gradual recognition of what heroin was doing to the ten biggest cities was the altered character of most drug addicts. Before the war addicts were predominantly white and over twenty-five; after the war they were predominatnly black and under twenty-five.

Not only was the use of hard drugs increasing, but so was the ingestion of amphetamines, which profoundly altered moods and emotions. Pills sold for ten cents retail but could be purchased in bulk from the manufacturer for as little as one and a half cents. Most of the hands clutching these pills were young and white.

It fell to New York, finally, to enjoy the melancholy distinction of "boasting" the only hospital in the world devoted exclusively to the treatment of adolescent drug addicts. This was Riverside Hospital on North Brother Island in the East River. It became an addicts' hospital in 1952. It stood no chance of keeping up with the post-1952 increase in adolescent drug addiction.

As the cities fell deeper and deeper into a slough of drugs, blight, and rubble-filled sites, the flight to the suburbs never slackened. But by 1963 enough time had passed in some suburbs for decay to make itself evident there, too. William Dobriner wrote:

Walking down Levittown streets in the spring of 1962, one is struck by the differences in character and mood of the neighborhoods. Ten years of families coming and going—ten years of change. The 1950 newness has been worn away by the decade. Many of the brave saplings died; few were replaced. Some streets are almost treeless now. . . . As a group, the Cape Cods seem tired. New, they were quaint and had charm. . . . Now, individualism, indifference, neglect, and taste good and bad have changed the balances. Do-it-yourself paint jobs; vivid red, aqua, chartreuse, cerulean and pink trims. Jerry-built dormers stagger out of roofs. The expansion attics are all fully expanded. You see a half-finished carport, patched concrete, broken asbestos shingles, grime and children's fingerprints ground into a peeling light-blue door, a broken picket fence, a dead shrub, a muddy trampled lawn, a torn plastic "storm window" listlessly flapping at an attic window, open garbage cans left permanently at the curb, a rusting hot-rod huddled in the dry weeds next to the carport.

When many of the Levittowners moved up, they soon moved out. And when they moved out, other people from the city moved in behind them. By 1963 there was a range of suburbs covering the entire social spectrum, allowing for very subtle shades of distinction. The suburban life-style remained largely a matter of class. In a working-class suburb, weekends brought visits from city-dwelling relatives out for a day "in the country." In middle-class suburbs weekends brought a round of parties for friends or business associates. When a family began to feel that the surrounding social ethos did not suit what they were or what they intended to be, they moved to another suburb. Far from being classless, suburbia brought a constant sifting of wheat from chaff.

By the 1960s few people retained any of the earlier illusions about the bucolic nature of suburban life. Suburbs were not exactly urban, but they were not rural either. Nor had the city been escaped. The suburban family depended on the nearby city for jobs, entertainment, and many consumer goods. Their car provided the vital link and helped spoil the suburb as it had helped spoil the city. "Instead of having buildings set in a park, we now have buildings set in a parking lot," wrote Lewis Mumford.

For the majority of people who lived there, suburbia was neither spacious nor gracious. The typical suburban home covered 1,200 square feet, on a 60-foot by 120-foot lot. Set back 25 feet from the sidewalk, the house left a strip 10 feet wide down each side of the house. Here the master and his family could stroll.

Rare was the suburban house that was ever declared finished. In the vast majority something was being added—a bedroom, a garage, a fence, a carport, a rock garden, a swimming pool, a patio, a barbecue pit, a window, a utility room, a fireplace—or something was being renovated—the driveway, the garden, the roof, the interior, the exterior, the paint, the tiles, the carpeting. In most cases the work was being done by the householder, using his own or rented tools. Men who spent their weekdays engaged in paperwork or selling things spent their evenings and weekends busily occupied with a simulation of "real" work.

The chief concerns of suburban life ran to the banal, like the obsession with crabgrass. To its critics, suburban life was amiable and shallow, a sad comedown for the descendants of people who had not long before tamed a continent, hewed to exacting principles, and worked themselves to death, but lived intensely. Young adults these days were made uncomfortable by talk of principles, and disliked intensity.

Suburban life produced a host of minor, nagging disappointments. Taxes, for example, were not necessarily lower than they had been back in the city, and lower taxes were often among the reasons for making the move. But the suburbanites wanted the amenities of city life—roads, schools, trash collection, streetlighting. Having to develop them from a very small base often proved more expensive than the same services back in the city.

Yet suburban life continued to offer escape to millions. The air was cleaner. The streets were safer. And "they" (the blacks) were hardly ever seen. Most suburbs remained entirely white. This was achieved without doing anything overtly racist. Black people could not afford to buy a house in a middle-class suburb, and the few who could afford it probably preferred to live in the city, although not necessarily in a black neighborhood in the city.

Hardly anyone said openly that one reason why they moved to the suburbs was to escape from blacks. But almost everyone knew this was so. Then, in November 1962, a black handyman forced his way into a house in Westport, Connecticut, strangled a middle-aged woman, and raped her fourteen-year-old daughter, while the husband and father was working in his office in New York. A wave of fear swept through the upper-middle-class suburbs ringing the major cities of the Atlantic seaboard. Perhaps there was no escape after all.

There was one wholly unexpected feature to the postwar rush to the suburbs. Millions of people decided to live in the desert. In the postwar they fanned out to set up home in the burning sands of Arizona, New Mexico, and Southern California. It was an act of sun worship unprecedented in any Christian country. The population of Phoenix quadrupled between 1950 and 1960. Smaller communities, such as Antelope Valley, California, grew from little more than 10,000 inhabitants to 100,000 in the same period. Entire towns were created in two or three years, such as Salton City, which was sited by the Salton Sea. Other communities sprang up around man-made lakes. Besides the sun, the other common feature of these desert communities was the golf course. Once the standard package of creature comforts was available, then clean air, dazzling sunshine, and low humidity lured Americans into some of the most inhospitable spots on earth.

Behind the development of the various suburbs, whether set in the sands or among rolling green hills, there moved the not-so-invisible hand of the Federal government. The FHA, which insured 5 million new houses between 1945 and 1963, always gave preference to the suburbs over the cities. And this set the pattern for most lenders. While city districts were starved of mortgage money, a new suburb would be awash with it.

Ultimately there was one fatal flaw to any Federal-city policy aimed at resolving the urban crisis: the suburbs. Neither the central city nor Washington could force the suburbs to cooperate. Yet much of the most energetic part of the population of the metropolitan areas lived in the suburbs rather than in the city. And it was the drive, the intelligence, the social stability and the professional skills of the suburbanites which very possibly made the difference between a policy which might work and one certain to fail.

Ironically, there were large numbers of suburbanites who actually preferred city life. But they earned too much to qualify for public housing (in the unlikely event that they were interested in it), yet could not afford the nice, new, expensive apartments being built under the urban renewal program. If they were ever to own their own home, they had no choice but to leave the city. With them went much of the commitment to a civilized life which would have helped make the cities decent places to live.

There was a widespread but mistaken belief that the central city had by 1963 been abandoned to the rich and the poor. Most cities, however, were still mainly inhabited by families and individuals in the middle-income range. But what had altered was the balance. The ordinary, orderly people were a statistical majority. But they no longer dominated city life and lived in cohesive neighborhoods within the city. The population of the central cities grew by 11 percent during the 1950s. All this increase was accounted for by increases among the poor, the unskilled, the uneducated.

"For better or worse," wrote *Time* in 1960, "suburbia is the U.S. grass roots." A third of the nation now lived there. It was, moreover, the third which did most of the nation's work, earned most of its money, enjoyed most of its creative talents, and had the most secure hold on the future. This was both the good news and the bad news. And had the flight to the suburbs not been quite so comprehensive, Americans in the postwar, instead of facing an urban crisis which plainly got worse year by year, might have finally got around to making American cities as pleasant to live in as the best cities of Europe.

36
Sound Minds in Healthy Bodies?

American medicine was a paradox. It boasted the most advanced medical techniques in the world. It also had one of the most backward systems for providing medical care to be found in any industrial democracy.

Apart from the extreme absolutes (one is either alive or dead), health is really a matter of comparatives: some people are healthier than others; each individual is more, or less, healthy than he or she was in the past. The overall standard of health and medical care can be estimated, moreover, by comparing infant mortality rates and longevity rates between populations.* High infant mortality, for instance, is characteristic of countries where the diet is nutritionally inadequate, the drinking water is impure, epidemics are frequent, and public places are unsanitary. These factors also have an impact on the figures for longevity. In order to compare like with like, however, it is more sensible to compare the U.S. figures with those of other industrial democracies, rather than with countries such as Chad and Paraguay.

When the war ended, the United States had the lowest infant mortality rate of any advanced country; one dramatically lower when compared with the rate in those countries recently fought over. But by 1963 the U.S. rate was markedly higher than that prevailing in the British Isles, Denmark, Finland, the Netherlands, Austria, Switzerland, Norway, France, and Sweden. These countries had a rate of 15 to 20 deaths per 1,000 live births. In the United States the rate was 25/1,000. With approximately 5 million births a year in the United States the difference between the American and Western European rates was 25,000 to 40,000 lives a year.

There were also parts of the United States where death rates were astonishingly high for an advanced country. On skid row the death rate was nearly 75 persons a year for each 1,000 inhabitants. This was six or seven times the national rate. "Death rates of this magnitude are found only in a few of the most backward and poverty-stricken nations in the world," wrote one dismayed observer.

Such conditions were plain for anyone to see. And they were not beyond help. American medicine possessed the skills to save 50,000 to 100,000 lives each year with existing means. But it did not do so for one reason—money. Babies could not pay. Nor could the inhabitants of skid row.

A short-lived television program, *That Was the Week That Was,* ran a mock commercial for the AMA ("the Anti-Medicare Association") which provided a scale of fees: "The immediate cure, at $500; the long convalescence, at $200; and, for people of limited means, the lingering death, for $3.98."

Americans were certainly willing to pay for medicine and health care. Expenditures on health rose fourfold between 1945 and 1963. Most of the

*Until the 1960s medical statistics were so unreliable that the only commonly accepted figure was: "One out of one will die." Medical statistics collected by the National Office of Vital Statistics were no better than the collecting bodies (usually state agencies) which provided them. The agencies in turn relied upon local physicians, JPs, coroners, police forces, hospitals, and priests. There were doctors who could not make accurate diagnoses, coroners who could not spell, hospitals with chaotic files. And the NOVS changed its definitions from time to time. Such a change could, and often did, result in a marked increase or decrease in the figures for an illness. A new definition of diabetes in 1948, for example, increased the incidence of diabetes by 50 percent. The figures on infectious diseases, such as smallpox, were usually reliable. Those on other diseases, such as cancer and heart disease, were not.

increase was taken up by hospital care. Hospital staffing had doubled since 1945, and hospital workers these days expected to be well paid. Gone forever were the badly paid cleaners, nurses, and lab technicians. Offsetting the increase in hospital costs (up 500 percent between 1939 and 1963) was a drop in the average hospital stay from fourteen days to ten days. But offsetting *that* was a rapidly expanding and expensive medical technology. Drugs and treatments unknown back in 1945 were commonly available in 1963—cobalt bombs (for cancer patients), heart catheterization, psychotropic drugs, dialysis, heart-lung machines, and so on. The hospital of 1963 was probably air-conditioned and offered more space per bed. So straight cost comparisons were probably a little unfair.

The income of doctors in private practice had also risen by 500 percent since 1939; the consumer price index over the same period had risen by a mere 125 percent. Few doctors any longer made house or night calls. They were probably more skilled than their predecessors. They were also more skilled at collecting their fees, charged for advice once given free, made out (and charged for) many more prescriptions, and, thanks to the increase in hospitalization insurance, more frequently packed their patients off to the hospital. They also had more patients.

Blue Cross had spread so rapidly that by 1963 it covered nearly 35 percent of the entire population. The insurance companies covered a further 30 percent. The remaining 60 million kept their fingers crossed.

It was often asserted that the United States was short of both hospital beds and doctors. But both increased in step with postwar population growth. In absolute terms it is impossible to say that there were too few; but at the same time one can say with certainty that there were never too many.

The principal problem, however, was not numbers but maldistribution. The Northeast, for instance, had nearly three times as many doctors per capita as the Southeast. And the doctors of the Southeast, maximizing their scarcity value, earned far more money than their counterparts in the much richer Northeast.

Surveys consistently showed a close relationship between health and income. What they mainly showed was that the poor fell ill more often, and remained ill much longer, than those who were well-off.

Despite the drawbacks of maldistribution, health standards did rise throughout the postwar. The idea of health care as a right even took hold. And controversial public health programs, such as fluoridation, gradually overcame local resistance. By the end of 1963 nearly 50 million people lived in areas where sodium fluoride was added to the drinking water. This was one public health measure which benefited everyone because the rich were as likely to neglect their teeth as the poor. When fluoridation was put to the vote, it usually lost. But when it was introduced without fuss or ado as part of a larger public health program, it was nearly always accepted.

Surgery made remarkable advances. In 1954 a team of doctors at Peter Bent Brigham hospital in Boston made the first successful kidney transplant. In 1957 Dr. C. Walton Lillehei and two electronics experts perfected the first heart pacemaker. Two silver-plated wires were put into the patient's chest and stitched to the surface of his heart. Outside the chest, the wires were connected to a small battery.

In 1953 Dr. Charles A. Hufnagel of Georgetown University Medical Center made the first replacement of a heart valve with an artificial valve. A few years later Dr. Michael E. DeBakey at Baylor University began to replace failing arteries with lengths of Dacron tubing.

Following the war Americans became remarkably health-conscious. And after Eisenhower's 1955 heart attack people began in large numbers to take a serious interest in heart disease. Although they continued to smoke, they also began to worry about the effects of smoking.

People were fascinated with their own bodies. They often disliked what they found or thought they found. On average, the women of the early 1960s were five pounds lighter than the women of the late 1930s; men were five pounds heavier than their predecessors. And it seemed that every other person, male or female, was on a diet. There was, for instance, the famous Metrecal liquid diet.* There was also an array of low-calorie soft drinks, artificial sweeteners, sugar-free canned fruits and desserts, high-protein diets, low-protein diets, a diet based mainly on liquor, and several diets which never touched the stuff. A middle-aged English doctor, Barbara Moore, was a noted vegetarian. She did wonders for the popularity of vegetarian diets when she walked across the United States, covering 3,387 miles in eighty-five days in 1962.

In their pursuit of good health Americans wasted at least $1 billion a year on quack medicine. Old people were especially susceptible to the snares of charlatans. Tiny incomes were frittered away on useless nostrums such as Queen Bee Jelly or the infamous Spectro-Chrome machine peddled by Dinshab P. Ghadiali until the Federal government caught up with him. This device cost several hundred dollars. It consisted mainly of colored light bulbs. Thousands of them were sold to the gullible. Anything which smacked of medicine and science made otherwise sensible people lose their critical sense. "Even the fake doctors in the headache remedy ads are responded to as if they might possess some medical knowledge," concluded two researchers studying television viewing habits.

For much of the postwar there was a fierce controversy concerning a claimed cancer cure, Krebiozen. It was produced by Dr. Stevan Durovic and came from the pancreas glands of horses. When Dr. Andrew Ivy, a physiologist at the University of Illinois, supported Durovic's claims for this drug, he was fired. The FDA insisted that Krebiozen was useless. Most doctors regarded it was but one more addition to a long line of false cancer cures. Durovic's evasiveness about the manufacture of Krebiozen and its chemical composition did nothing to allay the skepticism of the

*During the 1960 election campaign Kennedy had maintained that 17 million Americans "go to bed hungry each night." A skeptical Republican countered, "Most of them on Metrecal."

doctors or the FDA. Tens of thousands of cancer sufferers, however, clamored for Krebiozen, and they got it. Durovic opened a clinic in Mexico, a few miles from the U.S. border.

It must be admitted that on the face of it there was no reason not to believe that a single drug might cure a wide range of cancers because the 1940s had brought a revolution in pharmacology. Antibiotics which were effective against numerous bacteria strains had emerged. Penicillin was, for most people, the antibiotic they knew best. It had been known before the war. But it, and other antibiotics, had been manufactured in very small batches. Then, in 1944, a Department of Agriculture laboratory in Peoria discovered a way to produce penicillin in huge quantities. The D of A made its patents available without charge to the drug companies. This spurred competition. The wholesale price dropped from $20 per 100,000 units 1945 to 2 cents per 100,000 units in 1952.

In the meantime, the first effective treatment for arthritis and rheumatism, cortisone, had been developed at the Mayo Clinic. Cortisone was not a cure. But, like insulin, it made a tremendous difference in the lives of those who needed it. And soon thereafter a variety of antibiotics (in the parlance of the time, "wonder drugs") was developed in a sudden flaring up of research successes: streptomycin came from a reasearcher at Rutgers; a chemist at Yale discovered Chloromycetin; a drug company developed Aureomycin; yet another drug company found Terramycin. The 1950s brought tranquilizers from France, and polio vaccine from Salk and Sabin.

It became possible to treat some forms of cancer by chemotherapy, a line of research intensively explored at the Sloan-Kettering Institute after it found that nitrogen mustard (the feared "mustard gas" of World War I) could slow the progress of leukemia and relieve Hodgkin's disease. By the 1960s more money was being spent on chemotherapy than on all other types of cancer research. The trick was to find a way to poison the cancer without killing the patient.

What the pharmacological revolution offered was relief and hope of yet greater relief. People would pay and pay and pay to get their hands on the wonder drugs. In the process the drug companies became rich and powerful. The three most profitable companies listed on the New York Stock Exchange in the late 1950s were drug manufacturers. Their after-tax profits were 35 to 50 percent of invested capital. Drug companies in general were twice as profitable as industry as a whole.

The government was one of the drug companies' best customers. It was brought to the attention of Senator Kefauver that three companies had submitted identical, but supposedly secret, bids on a major drug contract. A senior executive of one of the companies involved tried to explain what had happened to a Senate subcommittee chaired by Kefauver: "I had not the faintest idea.̄ . . . Actually I was astonished that they [the other companies] also bid $17.24."

The drug companies worked out pricing arrangements among themselves. Patent disputes rarely came to court. Instead, the disputants would arrange to share the market. There was no price competition in the drug business. There were administered (and very high) prices, instead.

To millions of old people living on Social Security and troubled with arthritis, diabetes, gout, asthma, Addison's disease, or some other painful and debilitating ailment, antibiotics at thirty to forty cents a pill were often as costly as food or rent, and as essential. The very high profits of the drug companies were based on the unfeeling exploitation of the weak and the pain-racked. The retail price of many antibiotics was not three or four times cost, which would have produced a reasonable return on invested capital, but ten to twenty times cost.

The president of one major drug company told the Kefauver subcommittee that drug prices had to be kept high, even if this involved curbing competition, because there simply were not enough sick people available to assure all the drug companies an attractive return on capital. "We can't put two people in every bed," he complained, "where there is only one person sick."

One of the devices employed to help compensate for the comparative dearth of sick people was to educate doctors to prescribe by trade names rather than by generic names. Prednisone, for instance, was available at three cents a tablet. When bought by arthritics as Meticorten, it cost thirty cents a tablet. And for the person holding a prescription saying Meticorten, it was that or nothing.

The drug companies attempted to justify their pricing practices by intoning the magic word "research" over and over again. But most of the major drug discoveries on which they made their highest profits had come from Britain, France, and Germany. What passed for research was likely to be nothing more than an attempt to modify something sufficiently to take out a patent on it, think up a new trade name, and then sell it for as a high a price as possible.

The government agencies involved tended to accept such practices without demur. The traditional position of the Patent Office had been that no one could patent "a product of nature." But drugs were evidently an exception. Most of the antibiotics occurred in a natural mold. What the chemists did was to extract and purify them. The Patent Office would then complaisantly grant a patent. It was comparable to allowing the coal companies to take out a patent on coal.

The head of the Food and Drug Administration's Antibiotics Division from 1953 to 1961 was Dr. Henry Welch. He was also editor of two medical journals which were fat with drug company advertising. He described his editorial work as being simply a pleasant diversion undertaken in return for what he called "honorariums." During his seven years in Washington these nominal payments added up to $287,000. He was also a man whose word was highly esteemed by some. When he made a little speech on the merits of a new line of antibiotics, Pfizer promptly ordered more than 250,000 reprints.

When the FDA did put up resistance to the drug companies' claims, they would go to remarkable lengths to overcome it, as the thalidomide episode demonstrated. Thalidomide was a sedative developed in West Germany. But it entered production in 1956, the year when Miltown (meprobamate) appeared on the American market. The German manufacturer of thalidomide had close ties with the American producer of Miltown. Not until 1960 was a U.S. license sought for thalidomide. Dr. Francis Kelsey of the FDA's research staff was assigned to rule on the license application. She became suspicious of thalidomide's claimed safety record. For two years she fought to keep the drug off the American market. The FDA's power to keep dangerous drugs from commercial sale had been steadily eroded over the preceding fifty years, and Dr. Kelsey found herself fighting a lonely battle. Pressure was brought on the FDA to have her fired. The ancient techniques of *suppressio veri* and *suggestio falsi* were lavishly used on behalf of thalidomide. Only when thousands of hideously deformed children were born as a result of thalidomide's being prescribed in Western European countries was the issue decided in Dr. Kelsey's favor.

Kefauver had meanwhile labored to secure passage of a bill which would halt the worst practices of the drug business. Kennedy, however, was averse to any controversial legislation not initiated by himself. The Kefauver hearings had aroused the opposition of the drug companies, the AMA, and the nation's pharmacists. Fate, in the form of the thalidomide scandal, saved Kefauver's efforts from petering out.

First, however, the White House and the Senate Republican leadership had arranged at a secret White House meeting to destroy Kefauver's bill by reducing it to an innocuous charade. When that venture failed, as it did in a dramatic confrontation on the Senate floor, the Administration offered a bill of its own. It was cosmetic rather than regulatory legislation. But by now Kefauver had so aroused public opinion with the help of the thalidomide affair that he was able to put some of the enforcement provisions of his own bill into the new bill.

The testing of new drugs would in future be more closely controlled. Use of generic rather than trade names was encouraged, although it was not required. Complete records of side effects had to be kept. Minimum standards of manufacture were established. The worst excesses of drug advertising were curbed. When the bill was signed into law by the President in 1962, a few months before Kefauver's death, Kennedy tried to avoid inviting Kefauver to the signing cremony.

This churlish behavior aside, Kennedy was far from being indifferent to the need for better health care, especially for the elderly. He seems almost to have anticipated the case Michael Harrington would make that the best step anyone could take to help the aging poor would be to offer them adequate medical and health care. This single step would alleviate untold misery.

In its final year in office the Eisenhower Administration had tried to help those over sixty-five by creating a new welfare program, Medical Assistance to the Aged. A week before Kennedy's Inauguration the White House had been the scene of the first ever President's Conference on Aging.

Illness spread fear among the aged. Up to sixty-five two-thirds of the population had some form of health or medical coverage. But over sixty-five the figure dropped to one-third. And most of the elderly relied on small incomes which had little or no prospect of rising very much. Meanwhile, their insurance coverage was being eroded by a rising tide of riders in the wake of each illness.

It would be wrong to suggest, however, that old age was nothing but a period of sickness and terror. Those who had provided amply for their old age could, if they chose, go on a vacation ended only by death. From 1960 onward, retirement communites were established in areas with warm climates, such as Florida, the Southwest, and Southern California, to cater to the rapidly growing numbers of retired people. (They were increasingly known by the euphemistic and bureaucratic-sounding name of "senior citizens.") Thirty miles south of Los Angeles, for example, Ross Cortese created Rossmore Leisure World. Here was a $150 million town built from scratch. To enter it, one had to be at least fifty-two years old. The average age of the 12,000 inhabitants was sixty-one. Each house was equipped with ramps as well as stairs, with sit-down showers as well as tubs, and with electric sockets three feet above the floor to eliminate stooping. Medical care was included in the price of the house. A full-time medical staff and a fully equipped clinic were available around the clock.

The President committed himself early in his Administration to securing adequate medical care for the 11 million Americans over the age of sixty-five in 1961. The Medicare bill he submitted to Congress provided 90 days of hospital care, a further 120 days of nursing home care. The AMA once again slipped off its white coat, donned the flag, and swore on its wallet that "Socialized medicine" was about to destroy the country.

Kennedy did not limit himself to asking Congress for Medicare's passage. This was one of the very few occasions when he felt a personal, emotional commitment to a piece of legislation. He traveled the country to campaign for it. He got his Cabinet members to campaign for it. And when the bill was on the verge of passage, the AMA made a counterproposal. The AMA's alternative was a bill to be administered by each state. It was based on a declaration of "medical indigency" and a means test. The recipient of the benefits provided would not be allowed to own more than $300 in cash and would have to sell his car, mortgage his home to the state, and possess little more than the clothes he wore.

Kennedy's Medicare legislation was largely self-financing. It was tied to increased Social Security contributions. But it could not be wholly self financing. No mandatory, comprehensive medical insurance program could ever hope to work without a large increase in costs. Open a free hospital, and within a week every bed will be filled. This is not because people suddenly come down with imaginary ills but because relief is now available for the real ills that until now went untreated. And in a country where the bulk of medical practice was based on the outlook and values of commerce there was such a variety of fees combined with the ordinary variety of illnesses that no one could say what the cost of a genuinely comprehensive medical insurance program would be. Complete care on a fee-for-service basis would inevitably lead to a rapid rise in costs and a steady decline in the standard of care provided. Medicare was a compromise between a national health service on the one hand and free enterprise medicine on the other. It involved the worst aspects of both and the best aspects of neither. But under the circumstances there was not much else the President could do.

Thanks to the AMA's opposition, Medicare lost anyway. It was rejected by the Senate on a vote of 52–48. "The President," noted Theodore Sorensen, "never got over the disappointment of this defeat."

At present most of the Federal government's spending on health went into the Public Health Service programs. In 1945 the PHS had spent $65 million. In every year since then Congress had appropriated more money for the PHS than the White House had asked for. In 1963 its appropration was $1.6 billion. Over the years the emphasis of PHS work had shifted from communicable diseases to chronic illnesses, such as cancer, heart disease, and arthritis. Its research arm, the National Institutes of Health, had become one of the world's foremost centers for medical research.

Since 1946 the Hill-Burton Act had provided Federal grants to cover up to 33 percent of the cost of new hospital construction, especially in rural areas. By the 1960s this legislation had provided nearly 250,000 new hospital beds. But there remained a chronic shortage of beds in nursing homes and mental hospitals. Hill-Burton's scope was gradually expanded until, by 1963, it not only aided hospital construction but also financed diagnostic centers, rehabilitation facilities, and nurses' training.

The sudden concern with the fate of migrant farm workers resulted in the 1962 Migrant Health Act. This provided Federal grants to state and local agencies to provide a reasonable minimal level of health care to migrants and their families. The PHS was authorized to set up clinics which would offer them immunizations, X-rays, dental care, pre-and postnatal care, and emergency medical services at no, or a nominal, charge. Migrant workers' camps were as a rule located in areas where doctors were scarce to begin with. Many of the PHS clinics were mobile. What the legislation provided was far from lavish. The standard of health care it offered was what most people in the cities and suburbs took for granted. Yet to the migrants it was "a Godsend. Seldom has so little in public funds gone so far to relieve physical suffering and illness," said one Mexican-American.

Another development which relieved people—mainly women—from untold heartache was the advent of the contraceptive pill. It put a stop to most, but far from all, unwanted pregnancies. When in 1960 Enovid and Norlutin became widely available, they were not cheap, at fifty cents each. But demand was so keen that unit costs over the next three years dropped spectacularly. The pill was at first prescribed as a corrective for menstrual disorders. But most women used them mainly as a contraceptive. Unwanted pregnancies were further curbed by the growing popularity of vasectomy among middle-class men. By 1963 nearly 50,000 men each year were sterilized by this simple surgery.

It would be some time, however, before such measures began to take effect. Meanwhile, as many as 1 million women were being aborted each year. In New England states contraception was discouraged by law, and in Connecticut all contraceptive devices were banned. "Late every night in Connecticut," wrote Time, "lights go out in cities and towns and citizens by tens of thousands proceed zestfully to break the law."

But it was no laughing matter that up to 5,000 women each year died as a result of abortions which verged on torture and butchery; the most painful and dangerous abortions were often those which were self-inflicted. The majority of abortions were carried out by doctors, at serious risk to their careers. Every state banned abortion except where the life of the woman or child was at risk, and only a handful of states allowed even this measure of discretion. Nowhere in the United States could a woman who had been impregnated during rape secure a legal abortion.

The pointless cruelty exacted by the laws on contraception and abortion was put in its most damning light in the case of Mrs. Sherri Finkbine of Scottsdale, Arizona. Mrs. Finkbine had taken thalidomide during pregnancy.

Although it never appeared on sale in the United States, thalidomide was easily obtained in England. Robert Finkbine had bought some in London as a substitute for sleeping pills. What he did not use he brought home with him. Sherri, who had already borne four children and was carrying a fifth, used the remaining thalidomide.

When her doctor learned of her self-medication, he recommended an abortion. Mrs. Finkbine went to court to ask for an order which would allow her to follow her doctor's advice. She was turned down, twice. She was not furtive or shamefaced about her predicament. Her behavior and demeanor throughout were those of a responsible, intelligent woman. And in her search for an abortion she became famous. Millions of people applauded her honesty and courage. But there was nowhere in the United States where she could be legally aborted. She flew to Sweden in a blaze of publicity. There she was safely aborted. The fetus was grotesquely deformed.

Mrs. Finkbine brought to a head an issue that was long overdue for serious public debate. In the next few years the demand for reform of abortion laws—almost entirely written by men and fiercely defended by celibates—became irresistible.

More than half of all hospital beds were occupied by mental patients. The treatment of the mentally ill ranged from the enlightened to the horrifying. The preferred approach was to get the out of mind out of sight.

Mental illness was prevalent among the aged. But no one could feel easy knowing that at any given time an estimated 6 to 8 percent of the population was suffering from serious mental illness. Admission rates to mental hospitals after 1945 rose dramatically. By 1963 they were nearly double what they had been in 1945. It was only an equally dramatic rise in release rates that kept the hard-pressed mental hospitals from collapsing under the strain.

Nearly every one of the country's 600 mental hospitals was seriously overcrowded. The VA had 40 mental hospitals with 65,000 beds for neuropsychiatric patients, and these hospitals were considered comparatively small. The 9 state mental hospitals in California averaged 3,000 patients apiece. New York's 18 had an average of 4,300. The Georgia State Hospital at Milledgeville held 10,000 patients.

The VA mental hospitals were far more highly esteemed than the state hospitals, many of which were places of fear. But the VA hospitals enjoyed a number of unique advantages. The would-be patients, often actively aided by friends, family, and Congressman, were trying to get in, not stay out. A potential patient presenting himself for examination was, as a rule, hoping the doctors would find something wrong with him; preferably severe and preferably "service-connected." Having succeeded in obtaining a good (that is, bad) diagnosis, the patient did not have much interest in getting better; not unless he wanted his disability pension to be reduced; and, à la Catch-22, for that he would *have* to be crazy. On the other hand, if his condition grew worse, his pension would rise.

However deplorable the conditions in the state mental hospitals in 1963, they were, in nearly every case, considerably better than they had been in 1946, when spending on mental patients was, on average, $1.25 a day. This was one-fourth the average daily expenditure on "charity" patients in the general hospitals. One enterprising state had reduced spending on its mental patients in 1946 to 43 cents a day per patient.

But in the postwar mental illness became a fashionable cause. The statistics were lovingly retailed. There was a certain frisson in the air when a meeting was told that one person in four needed to see a psychiatrist. Those assembled looked around them half-jokingly. The interest in mental illness was encouraged by Mary Jane Ward's best-selling autobiographical novel *The Snake Pit*, which became a very popular film. W. H. Auden's 1948 Pulitzer prizewinning poem was called *The Age of Anxiety*. The 1946 Harper Prize novel *Wasteland*, by Jo Sinclair, consisted of a patient's conversations with his psychiatrist. The book's hero appeared to be psychoanalysis. There was a spate of films dealing with mental patients and mental hospitals: *Woman at the Window; Random Harvest; Now, Voyager; Lady in the Dark*. But a documentary made by John Huston, *Let There Be Light*, concerning soldiers whose minds had been deranged by combat, was never never publicly shown. Mental illness movies were still in vogue in 1963. That year saw the release of *Lilith*. But the best such film of this period was *The Three Faces of Eve*. For some reason the mental patients portrayed in films were nearly always women.

In discovering mental illness, Americans found Freud. Since the 1920s they had embraced Freudian psychoanalysis more ardently than any other nation. But they were highly selective, taking the parts they liked and ignoring the nasty bits. They chose to overlook, for example, Freud's claims that children were innately aggressive and sadistic.

The central element in Freudian thought was sexual development.

Freud's highly ramified conception of sexual energy, or libido, was the basis of most of his ideas on personality formation. It was strong medicine, positing penis envy among girls, suppressed longings for intercourse with the parent of the opposite sex, and extremely powerful anal-sadistic impulses.

American Freudians, such as Karen Horney and Harry Stack Sullivan, repressed the sexual side of Freudianism in order to make psychoanalysis more acceptable to American patients. Where Freud had been bleakly pessimistic about the human condition, his American followers were markedly optimistic. They kept the Master's emphasis on unconscious motivation and employed the techniques of free association. But where Freud had stressed the libido, they preferred to talk about "disturbed human relationships."

"After the war," wrote Betty Friedan, looking back in exasperation, "Freudian psychology became much more than a science of human behavior, a therapy for the suffering. It became an all-embracing American ideology, a new religion . . . which made a virtue of sex, removed all sin from private vice, and cast suspicion on high aspirations of the mind and spirit." Crypto-Freudianism was taken up in the mass media and the schools. Its text was "Biology is Destiny." The physical differences between men and women were so great, girls were repeatedly told, that it was only common sense for the world's work to be divided—and for women to take the duller portion.

Yet for men as well as women, psychoanalysis in America became little more than another technique for adjustment. It was no longer what Freud had envisaged—a tool for emotional growth. Simone de Beauvoir found that "Psychoanalysts are all the rage in America, psychology is a favorite topic of conversation among intellectuals and cultured people." At the same time, she remarked, it was not a challenge to the world as it was but a means of escaping decision, risk, and responsibility.

There was never a shortage of people willing to try psychoanalysis or almost any other form of therapy. During his 1955 travels William Attwood frequently encountered people who were, and who freely admitted to being, tense and anxious. "And I cannot forget the pathetic remark," he wrote, "of Abigail Adams, a part-time actress who killed herself while we were in Hollywood. 'My trouble is that I stay up too late, I drink too much, and then I take too many sleeping pills.' It could have been her epitaph—and that of more than a few Americans we met."

There were 20,000 acknowledged suicides each year in the early 1960s. There were, in addition, an estimated 100,000 other suicides which were put down to accidents, alcoholism, or natural death. And for every successful act of self-destruction there were believed to be many attempts which failed.

Americans these days were very different, thought Daniel Bell, from their ancestors described by De Tocqueville. The old boldness of spirit and avidity for praise "has been replaced by an anxious inferiority, fearful of censure and desperately eager to please."

But for that anxiety relief was at hand—tranquilizers. A French drug company engaged in 1950 in a search for a new antihistamine found that one of its experimental drugs was making its volunteer subjects drowsy. It switched its attention to this unexpected development, and in 1953 it put what was to become only the first in a long list of tranquilizers on the market.* It was chlorpromazine, sold under the trade name Thorazine.

Tranquilizers were an utterly unexpected development, one of the few complete surprises of modern science. Equally surprising was that within three years some 20 million ostensibly normal Americans were resorting to them regularly. This was in addition to the tens of millions of prescriptions filled by druggists each year for drugs derived from the snakeroot plant *Rauwolfia serpentina*, which were prescribed for hypertension.

By the late 1950s tranquilizers were prescribed from the cradle nearly to the grave, for tiny hysterical infants and for overwrought geriatrics. For the drug companies the arrival of tranquilizers was like stumbling across the Mother Lode. Tranquilizers were not being gulped down simply in the big cities where life was at its most hectic but were consumed across the entire country much as other drugs were consumed. Doctors were happy to prescribe them. One patient in three had no manifest organic disorder when he went to see the doctor. For decades this had annoyed the nation's doctors, in part because there was little they could do. Now, however, the doctor could do something more than shrug his shoulders; he could, and would, prescribe a tranquilizer.

They were used to inhibit bed-wetting, premenstrual tension, arthritis, colitis, asthma, delirium tremens, and nausea. People swallowed them to alleviate homesickness, to make a visit to the dentist, or to help them get along better with others. Women who were frigid took them. So did nymphomaniacs. Yet there was something about tranquilizers which left the Puritan conscience uneasy. It was all too easy—take a pill, forget your troubles. This, wrote one reporter, "is an affront to popular morality." Yet they seemed more defensible—perhaps because they were prescribed by doctors—than that traditional tranquilizer alcohol.

The drugs were especially popular in mental hospitals. They were the reason for the sharp increase in release rates. Tranquilizers were undeniably better than the barbiturates they replaced, which had often made patients insensible or severely agitated. Tranquilizers also reduced the reliance on insulin shock and lobotomy, the two most radical and least defensible methods for dealing with the mentally ill. Mental hospitals had for decades been violent and dangerous. In a few years tranquilizers made them comparatively calm and safe, for patients and staff alike. By 1963 most locked wards had been abolished.

Yet tranquilizers were only a stopgap. They were not a cure. There was a danger that the easy availability of tranquilizers could, in the long run, put research into mental illness into a state of drowsiness.

---

*A case could be made for adding television to the list of tranquilizers. It was adopted equally rapidly by mental hospitals as the tranquilizer. And mothers commonly turned on the TV set to keep the children quiet.

But for the present the widespread concern with mental illness was working a major improvement in popular attitudes. Of all those in distress the mentally ill deserve sympathetic help the most and are the least likely to receive it. But the war had brought an upsurge of concern for psychiatric patients. The hundreds of thousands of apparently healthy young men rejected for military service on neuropsychiatric grounds made psychiatrists, psychologists, and the nation at large aware for the first time of the true size of the mental health problem. There were also more than 2,000 conscientious objectors assigned to work in mental hospitals. Nearly all of the COs were white, middle-class, and college graduates. They were stunned by the conditions they found. True to their responsibility as educated people, they founded the National Mental Health Foundation in 1946. For the next decade it was the only national body to lobby for better mental hospitals and more humane treatment of psychiatric patients.

There was, meanwhile, an enormous public demand for psychiatric services. It brought forth a marked increase in supply. In Manhattan the number of practicing qualified psychiatrists tripled between 1947 and 1957.

New Haven had had only three practicing psychiatrists back in 1947. A decade later it had more than twenty. When a private, low-cost psychiatric clinic opened in New York in 1955, it was prepared to treat 500 patients a year. It received 500 applications a month.

One of the most careful large-scale community mental health studies ever conducted found that in mid-Manhattan those it classified as being well comprised only 18.5 percent of the population; 58.1 percent showed mild to moderate symptoms of mental illness, and those it termed impaired accounted for the remaining 23.4 percent. On the face of it the last figure was astonishing. The authors themselves were taken by surprise. Yet evidence from other studies in New York suggested this finding was approximately right. Their breakdown may not have been applicable to the entire country. But it appears likely it was applicable to the entire city. The mentally impaired, the survey found, were usually over forty, were divorced or widowed or had never married. Isolation appeared to be a prime cause of mental illness. Mental health was best among the young and the married.

These findings confirmed those of another important study, conducted in New Haven, which had found an almost complete correspondence between class and mental illness. High status and a low degree of mental illness went together; so did low status and a high degree of mental illness. Class was equally important in diagnosis and treatment. The lower class had nearly all those diagnosed as psychotic or schizophrenic. The middle and upper classes held nearly all those diagnosed as neurotic. The lower class got electric shocks, lobotomies, and group therapy. The others got psychoanalysis. Although it would be unfair to describe the social reality of mental health as providing a system in which upper-middle-class psychiatrists provided ineffective treatment to large numbers of lower-class patients, this description would not be entirely inaccurate.

Among the millions of people who knew at first hand the grief that mental illness causes families was the President. His sister Rosemary had spent nearly all her life in psychiatric institutions. The Kennedy family took an active part in the effort to improve the treatment of the mentally ill.

In 1963 Congress passed the most important mental health measure since 1947, when it had established the National Institute of Mental Health. The 1963 act provided half a billion dollars to train teachers for mentally handicapped children, to build community mental health centers, and to create new facilities for the mentally retarded.

Money, however, could do only so much. It might ease the overcrowding. It might encourage research. It might provide new forms of treatment. And all these were needed. But equally important was public education. On that score attitudes in 1963 were certainly more enlightened than they had been in 1945.

37

The New Knowledge Society

The postwar saw the emergence of a new type of society, one logical from the point of view of various trends since the turn of the century, yet often novel and surprising even so. The first sage of the new society was Norbert Wiener.

He had entered Harvard at the age of thirteen as a boy genius. Unlike most such prodigies, he grew up to become a genial and endearing man and one who fulfilled his early intellectual promise. During the war his mathematical brilliance had been applied to the problems of controlling antiaircraft fire. As one of those men who took all knowledge for their province, Wiener found it only natural to cultivate the friendship of doctors at the Harvard Medical School. And their interest in the human nervous system proved to be proceeding in parallel with Wiener's growing interest in mechanisms of self-correction and automatic control.

Wiener and his colleagues on the fire-control project began to meet regularly with several of the doctors to explore the boundaries between two separate areas of knowledge. This was a decided break with the modern tendency for special knowledge to drive scholars apart. The result was that Wiener and a Mexican doctor, Arturo Rosenblueth, found themselves playing midwives to the emergence of a new specialty, one which embraced communications and control, whether in machines or living organisms. They took the Greek word for steersman, *kybernetes*, and introduced the world to cybernetics.

Wiener's thesis that there were important analogies between the control of machinery and the control of the nervous system was one of the most simple important ideas of the twentieth century. Many of the most difficult problems posed by electrical switching devices were overcome by the understanding of how the synapses work in the nervous system. On the other hand, a variety of nervous disorders became explicable as the state of electronics advanced.

Wiener was not alone in the rollback of these frontiers, as he readily acknowledged. The bundle of interconnected concerns known as cybernetics, servomechanisms, and information theory, was being explored during the 1940s by other thinkers in Europe, the Soviet Union, and the United States. But it was Wiener who was the first to pull the various elements into a coherent and tractable body of thought. When new ideas were needed, he thought of them. When new words were called for, he coined them. And as his mind raced ahead to examine the possibility of constructing what he called "the ultra-rapid computing machine," he made the most important connection of all: the simplicity of the nervous system. It was all or nothing, yes or no, go or stop. It operated on bursts of positive and negative charges of electricity. And that was how a computer would work best.

Even as Wiener and Rosenblueth and their colleagues were sitting around talking after dinner on those wartime Saturday evenings, the computer was moving toward realization. A student at MIT in 1936, Claude Shannon, had already anticipated some of Wiener's ideas. Shannon's master's thesis had explored the similarities between on-off circuit switches and the yes-no paradigm which makes all logical thought possible. It was a remarkable advance on existing ideas about constructing machines which would simulate human thought processes.

The first true computer to be built was ENIAC, which appeared in 1946. It was constructed at the University of Pennsylvania in response to an Ordnance Department request for a machine which would compute ballistics data. But ENIAC was not completely operational until the war ended, by which time it was a temperamental thirty-ton behemoth covering 150 square feet of floor space. The importance of ENIAC, however, was that it validated a number of important ideas about how a computer would, and ought to, work. Its principal tool, like that of human beings, was language. And it was a language of yes or no, go or stop, open or close.

But ENIAC was too underpowered to meet any but the simplest demands made on it. At this very moment, however, there appeared a crucial new device. Bell Telephone Laboratory was at its peak between 1940 and 1955. From BTL's Solid State Physics Group there issued in 1948 the ideal replacement for the fragile, cumbersome vacuum tubes which had made ENIAC so unreliable and so elephantine. Bell's researchers had developed the transistor.

The story of the transistor was typical of inventions in the postwar. It was the creation not of an individual but of a group. It was developed not in a makeshift laboratory or someone's garage but in a very big, lavishly equipped laboratory. Inventing the transistor did not cost very much. Development costs, however, ran into the tens of millions of dollars.

Transistors did not replace vacuum tubes outright. Instead, they opened up new fields for exploration where vacuum tubes were too expensive, too fragile, or too inefficient and too cumbersome. But in effect, it was the transistor which made the postwar electronics boom possible.

The research group, directed by William Shockley (who won the Nobel Prize for Physics), involved not only physicists but chemists, metallurgists, and mathematicians. It was research in the style of the Organization Man. Literally dozens of people were involved in the development of the transistor. Some were engaged in basic research; others had a limited and practical goal to pursue. Shockley, in charge of the project, had to ride both horses at once. Having discovered the transistor effect (in which power fed into one circuit will flow into another circuit and in so doing will amplify the power of the second circuit), Shockley and his team proceeded to invent devices which made use of it. Bell spent a fortune on producing a reliable transistor; the early models were handmade and so fragile that a slammed door would knock them dead.

But once perfected, the transistor raised the efficiency of electronic equipment by a factor of 100. This was still a far cry from the efficiency of the human brain, which operates more than 10 billion cells on less electricity than is needed for a penlight. Compared with the brain, the most efficient computer was a profligate and wastrel. But the transistorized machines had one distinct advantage over the brain—speed. Nerve endings cannot transmit more than 100 impulses a second. An electronic circuit can be used more than 1 million times a second.

The transistor also cut the cost of computing and brought a radical reduction in the size of computing machines. Bell also established the binary system of computer language as the basis for all future machines. In binary language every number was reduced to a collection of ones and zeros. Each letter was made up of seven "bits" of information, so a program of 1,000 words took 7,000 bits.* The machine had to be told what to do with painstaking care "as if one were addressing an idiot child."

Yet computer languages proliferated as different manufacturers began to produce a variety of machines to fill a variety of needs and claim a particular segment of the total market. In a brave attempt to preclude the world of computing from reliving the Tower of Babel experience the Federal government in 1960 pressed for the development of a common high-level computer language. The result was COBOL (Common Business-Orientated Language). It was a help. But it was not the last word on the subject.

By the 1960s it was becoming evident that computers were going to be as successful as television had been. In 1959 there were 400 big computers in operation. In 1960 there were 4,000. Orders for 10,000 more were waiting to be filled. Many business executives were eager to buy or rent them.

---

*There is a well-known method of reading by means of binary digits. It breaks down each letter into six bits. It is called Braille.

The computer was stylish and sophisticated. It was suggestive of celerity, efficiency, modernity. But all too often the executive wanted the computer because it appeared to be the kind of item his corporation ought to have—that is, it was the large corporation's status symbol. It would be some time yet before most businesses had thought through what it was they needed a computer to do. For the present, marveled one reporter, there was the spectacle of "businessmen bringing their records to [a rented IBM computer] in the same way women bring their wash to the corner laundromat."

The age of automatic control had arrived. Its name was coined by a Ford vice-president, Del Harder, in 1946; it was "automation." The term entered popular speech in 1954 when Walter Reuther used it in a speech to the CIO called "The Automation Revolution." It was thereafter accepted as amounting, in effect, to a second Industrial Revolution.

Mechanization had for the past 200 years increasingly substituted for the work of muscles. Automation would substitute for the work of the nervous system. It transferred the control function, traditionally the prerogative of human beings, to automatic devices. The reins led, ultimately, back to human hands, but the distance involved had widened enormously.

Self-regulating mechanisms were not entirely new. Dutch windmills continually adjusted themselves, for example, to keep their blades to the wind. But the conception of feedback and self-regulation as the organizing principle behind a wide range of productive activities was a new and portentous development for the economy and for human society.

By the 1960s almost everyone had heard of automation. Many people feared it. Yet it was, or appeared to be, the most logical course of development for an advanced economy to follow. Machines had for a long time been used to make other machines. What was happening was a shift to machines which ran machines. This conjured up visions of the workerless factory. In the traditional factory the raw materials had been brought to the machine; this was then set to use them, was run for a while, readjusted, then run again, readjusted, left idle, reset, and so on. For each hour of running time it was not unusual for as much as ten man-hours to be spent on machine tending. If it did nothing else, automation appeared certain to destroy millions of jobs.

The 1957–1958 recession, which sent a cold wind through American labor, and the stubbornly high level of unemployment served constantly to remind people that the government was unable to fulfill the implied promise of the 1946 Employment Act. It was only for a few months in 1953, when unemployment fell to 3 percent, that there had been genuine full employment in the postwar. The unskilled bore most of the burden of the high rates of unemployment of the late 1950s and early 1960s. Yet even when their numbers dropped, their wages rose. The American economy of the early 1960s saw skilled jobs going begging for men and unskilled men going begging for jobs.

But exactly how much unemployment there was remained a mystery.

The noted Swedish economist Gunnar Myrdal took the official figures as rock bottom, added to them all those in the armed forces (on the grounds that people in uniform were economically underemployed), added an estimate for those who would have sought work had they not been discouraged by the high level of unemployment, and concluded that 13 percent of the adult population was wasting its time.

The chief difficulty was that the United States had developed a large and growing force of people who were structurally unemployed. And each year there were several hundred thousand people who entered the job market looking for work when there were simply no jobs for them. They were either too young or too old; they had no skills or the wrong skills; they lived in one part of the country, and the one job they might fill was in another part.

The economic remedies of Keynesianism could do almost nothing to help people such as these. Even during an economic boom it was doubtful they would be offered work. The 1957–1958 recession made economists and the labor movement aware for the first time of the existence of the structurally unemployed. But nothing the Kennedy Administration did or could do was likely to have much effect on the overall pattern of unemployment. And with every shake-out of labor the unemployed became, in effect, more unemployable.

Misery always seeks a scapegoat. Automation was blamed for the persistence of a high unemployment rate from 1957 onward. Historically, new machinery has not created widespread unemployment. Recessions and depressions were the result of fluctuations in the business cycle. And the Luddites were the exception among workers; most had accepted the truth of the old adage, "Machines make jobs." But modern servomechanisms were so advanced they either made no jobs at all or created jobs no ordinary worker might fill.

Some unions were recalcitrant toward modernization. Painters' locals in the 1950s banned the use of spray guns. The Typographical Union banned automatic typesetters. But most unions took a more moderate and accommodating line. Organized labor was far more worried about women entering the job market, competing with men and working for low wages. And enlightened labor leaders acknowledged that with most population growth occurring among the under-eighteens and the over-sixty-fives, a shrinking portion of the population was forced to become increasingly productive simply to keep the economy from faltering. The only way out of this dilemma was "to equip factories with every labor-saving machine and process known to American technology, and to invent more such." That is more or less what happened between 1950 and 1963. Of the old economic triad of land, labor, and capital, the one which increased most rapidly was capital. To a considerable extent it became a substitute for labor. Rising capital investment was responsible for most productivity gains after 1950.

The rapid increase in capital investment meant a rapid diffusion of the newest technologies. But it could vary sharply from industry to industry and even within an industry. General Motors, for example, was prepared to suffer long and costly strikes to maintain its right to allocate labor as it saw fit and to introduce new machinery. Chrysler, on the other hand, made concession after concession over automation. And its production standards fell. Eventually Chrysler was reduced to sending a management team over to GM to learn how to make automobiles at a profit. The people at Chrysler had forgotten how it was done.

In most industries by 1963 labor and management had arrived at a compromise over automation. Nowhere was there a more fruitful mechanization compact than in the coal mines. Most unions had known for decades that in the modern world they faced a choice between grudging mechanization or rapid mechanization. And "The fact that the UMW threw its weight [behind rapid mechanization] probably had more far-reaching consequences . . . than any comparable decision reached by a major union in large-scale industry in the postwar period."

Once he had secured the health and welfare fund for coal miners John L. Lewis, the bad boy of American labor, had one last constructive move to make. He ardently embraced advanced technology. Even in his old age he was a man of courage and vision. His faults were the same as ever—arrogance, querulousness, vanity, rodomontade. He was not a skilled union administrator, and like many another autocrat, he created a vacuum around him, which evil men would later occupy. He failed the UMW by doing nothing to ensure that its affairs would be entrusted to men of strong character and integrity after his death.

But Lewis saw clearly that mining coal was not a fit job for a man. The job was, and would always be, dangerous, dirty, and despised. Coal towns were not, and would never be, decent places for women to live and children to grow up. Coal was properly cut by machines, not by men. The fewer people involved in mining, the better. Lewis not only saw mining in this light but had the moral courage to act on what he saw. He was unique among labor leaders. He actively embraced the idea of massive unemployment within his own union.

He took a gamble on the future, choosing to believe that the men thrown out of work would eventually find better jobs and that their children at least would have a better prospect before them than following their fathers down the mines.

Between 1945 and 1960 coal mining was transformed. The rates of death and injury were halved. Mining became more productive while it became much safer. The "coal mole," the endless conveyor belt, the mining jeep, and the roof bolt worked this transformation. The coal mole (or continuous miner) bored directly into the coal face, tearing out such huge quantities of coal that the mines became choked with the stuff until the endless conveyor belt arrived to haul it away. The mining jeep proved as versatile belowground, where tunnels ten miles long were not uncommon, as its namesake was above. The roof bolt was a steel pin up to fifteen feet long. Driven through the soft slate ceiling of a mining tunnel, it fixed the treacherous slate against the more rigid geological structures above. The groaning, splintering pit prop of evil memory was a thing of the vanished past.

Employment in coal mining fell by 50 percent in a decade. Output doubled in the same ten years. The miner of the early 1960s was four times as productive as the miner of 1950. And a ton of coal cost less in the United States than in any other industrialized country. Coal had been forced to run hard simply to keep up. Even then it lost its primacy as an energy source to other fuels. The railroads switched from coal burners to diesels. Homes were heated by fuel oil and natural gas. But at least coal mining did not lose ground by resisting mechanization. And Lewis made sure his miners were the highest-paid workers in industry.

He also brought about an unprecedented identification of interests between workers and their employers. The UMW held cash reserves of $100 million. Under the prompting of Cyrus Eaton, the eccentric Cleveland millionaire, Lewis put the miners' money back into the coal industry. And taking a thoroughly capitalist approach, the UMW put inefficient mines out of business. In its zeal it at one point resorted to breaking strikes called by UMW locals.

But the miners remained loyal to Lewis. They knew why they had the highest daily wage in industry. More than 65,000 miners were drawing monthly pensions from the health and welfare fund to add to their Social Security benefits. Tens of thousands more were receiving medical care at the UMW hospitals.

Lewis was strenuously attacked, however, for the 100,000 miners who had been put out of work. Was it not his responsibility to bring about a better life for *all* miners? It was a criticism that had to be met. The fact was that competition from other energy sources was going to lead to unemployment in the mines regardless of what Lewis did. He had seen the choice which had to be made and had the courage to make the right, if unpopular, decision. Had thousands of miners lost their jobs because of sagging demand for coal and because of high coal prices owing to poor productivity, not only would there have been a high level of unemployment in mining, but there would have been nothing positive to show for it. Lewis had not invented mining. He had not invented unemployment. He was not responsible for modern technology. But he was able to draw the right conclusions from the inevitable developments in all three.

Walter Reuther showed a similar willingness to grasp the nettle automation and from it pluck the flower money. In 1950 he signed a contract with GM which cost the corporation $1 billion. In time this proved a bargain because it gave GM a free hand to introduce modern technology. But when the Korean War upset all the UAW's calculations on the contract, Reuther had no qualms about demanding a revision, even though it had several years left to run. In return for another $200 million GM was allowed to keep control over production standards without interference from the union.

In time even Harry Bridges came to terms with the late twentieth century. The docks were undeniably overmanned. A generous welfare fund was set up for the West Coast longshoremen. In return, the ILWU gave up its "witnesses" (men paid to sit around the docks watching other men load and unload ships). The shipping companies bought the right to introduce containerization. And should the longshoremen then go on strike their welfare fund would lose $14,000 a day. A dock shutdown was henceforth in part a strike against the longeshoremen's own pensions. By the 1960s the "respectability" which Bridges had mocked in "bourgeois" labor leaders had caught up with the old radical.

Everyone accepted that automation was by now throwing thousands of people out of work each week; 4,000 according to the Bureau of Labor Statistics; 40,000 according to the president of U.S. Industries, John Snyder. Even if the larger of these figures were the true one, the number of people affected each year amounted to less than 3 percent of the labor force. Yet it was a figure which put many people in fear of losing their livelihoods. Modern technology had long occasioned a mixture of pride and exasperation. In Karel Capek's play of the 1920s *R.U.R.* and the Charlie Chaplin film of the 1930s *Modern Times*, the machines crushed and debased the human spirit, and hardly a voice was raised to say that this was not necessarily so.

As automation spread, so, here and there, did resistance to it. The first strike caused by automation was probably the 1956 shutdown at Westinghouse, normally a company with an admired record of industrial relations. The 1959 railroad strike; the strikes at Ford and GM in 1962; the 116-day steel strike that same year; the 114-day newspaper strike in New York in 1962–1963, all were partly strikes over technological unemployment. Flight engineers, afraid they would not be needed on jet airliners, went on strike in 1961, grounding most commercial aircraft for a week and reminding the United States of how dependent it had grown on its airlines.

Wherever automation appeared in business, it increased the sense of insecurity, raised in-plant tensions, and threatened to sour labor relations. It was at times a galling reminder to those who chose to strike of how low their place was in a modern plant. When Gulf Oil's refineries at Port Arthur, Texas, were struck for ten weeks in 1961, production dropped by no more than 30 percent. Nearly 4,000 workers were on strike. Yet 300 supervisors and managers kept the refineries working at 70 percent of capacity without any undue strain.

There was silent resistance to the new machinery, but how much is impossible to tell. Its most typical expression was a refusal to work the machinery at full stretch, even if this meant making less money. Daniel Bell observed, "If conspicuous consumption was the badge of a rising middle class, conspicuous loafing is the hostile gesture of a tired working class." But this kind of resistance was not new. It was, moreover, a poky, hole-in-the-corner, defeated type of resistance.

Automation was considered a menace particularly to workers employed in manufacturing. Yet it was more applicable to clerical work than to processes of production. And during the Kennedy years the long-term decline in manufacturing employment came to an end. Between 1960 and 1963 it actually added 1 million jobs.

The computer was as likely to do work that had never been done before as it was to eliminate a job. Much of the impetus behind automation was less a matter of raising profits than of doing what had to be done. The task the new machinery was used for was too big, too dangerous, or too complex for people to do.

But there were jobs which were threatened. The major unions came to terms with automation without actually liking the terms. They concentrated their efforts on maintaining the living standards of their members. Union leaders, furthermore, were usually patriots of the deepest dye. When the House in 1961 held hearings on the effects of automation on employment, the representatives of labor were as zealous in their defense of American technology as the businessmen who testified. Everyone agreed that the United States held a technological lead over the rest of the world, including the Soviet Union, and that lead had to be maintained.

In their efforts to maintain workers' living standards the unions began to develop the idea of the-job-as-property. It was an approach pioneered by the West Coast longshoremen. They agreed to accept technological unemployment in exchange for a guaranteed income for every worker so displaced. After twenty-five years on the docks a longshoreman was entitled to a company pension until he qualified for his Social Security retirement pension. The principle was that the job was owned not by the company but by the worker. If it was taken away from him, he had a right to compensation. This was one of those revolutionary ideas which took hold without a revolution. That was only possible, however, because of a profound change—the development of the service economy.

In the early 1960s the United States was moving, all wise men agreed, from being an industrial to being a "postindustrial" society, which was at other times known as the technological society. The new order was defined as one in which more than half of all economic activity took place in the service sector. Some time in the 1950s the United States crossed that boundary. The line may have been crossed as early as 1947, according to some analysts.*

At all events, from about 1950 on employment in the production of material goods remained stable. Employment in the provision of services grew rapidly. By 1960 it accounted for all the increase in employment of the preceding ten years. It was a development characterized by the rise of

---

*My own inclination in this regard is on the side of caution because it is not easy to tell a service worker from a production worker. So it makes no sense to be dogmatic about absolute categories or precise dates. In a department store a salesclerk is a production worker. In insurance, most of the office staff consists of production workers. In communications, telephone operators are production workers. In the postwar, it was production workers such as these, rather than car workers or welders, who were most threatened by automation and the development of the service economy.

television. In 1960 more money was spent on TV service, parts, and installation than on TV sets.

The coopers and the barbers offered an example of the long-term trends. In 1880 there were more than 50,000 coopers busily making barrels and fewer than 50,000 barbers snipping hair. Both coopers and barbers looked forward to a secure future. But by the time of the Second World War there were 250,000 barbers and fewer than 1,000 coopers. And this change had come about in no more than the working life of the average man. These days nearly every man wore his hair short. Hardly anyone had a need for wooden barrels. Changes in fashion and changes in technology had remade the world as far as coopers and barbers were concerned. And those forces—the vagaries of fashion, the rapid growth of advanced technology—were the wellsprings of the modern service economy.

By the early 1960s the United States was remarkable for possessing the most productive economy in the world yet a mere 19 percent of its working-age population (ages fifteen to sixty-four) was actually employed in industry. In the world's original industrial country, Great Britain, the figure was 35 percent (and was one of the reasons for that country's permanent economic sluggishness).

Productivity rose steadily, while the number of workers engaged in manufacturing things remained much the same from 1946 to 1963. When industry did take on new employees, it was to fill service rather than production jobs. By the 1960s, consequently, one-third of all employees in industry wore white collars rather than blue.

But the distinction between collar colors was blurred. The biggest part of the service sector was retail trade. The work of retail clerks was becoming remarkably similar to the work of traditional blue-collar workers, thanks to the modern organization of retailing in discount stores and shopping centers. Customer contact was reduced to a minimum. Opportunities for advancement were few. Pay was low. Status was lower. And elsewhere in the service economy the same phenomenon could be seen, of people wearing white collars but engaged in work that had all the disadvantages, except the dirt, associated with a blue collar.

The service sector covered all of the most rapidly expanding parts of the postwar economy—trade, finance, real estate; professional, business, and personal services; government. It accounted by the 1960s for more than half of all employment and GNP. For the first time in history there was a nation where most workers produced no tangible things, such as Cadillacs or cauliflowers or coal.

Urbanization and automation alike promoted the growth of service industries. Jobs in the service sector were, as a rule, less demanding physically than jobs in the goods sector, and half of them were thus filled by women (compared with 20 percent in the goods sector). The service sector also created more opportunities for part-time employment and for workers over sixty-five. Although many service sector jobs were dull, they were likely to offer more scope for human contact than jobs in manufacturing. Firms in the service sector also tended to be much smaller than firms in manufacturing. For these reasons service sector employment probably offered greater job satisfaction.

Service sector employment also tended to be less susceptible to fluctuations in the business cycle and therefore more stable. Wages, working conditions, and salaries were more flexible than in manufacturing. But service occupations were not shielded from automation's effects. In New York City alone between 1957 and 1961 some 30,000 elevator operators were thrown out of work by a new generation of fully automated elevators.

Unions managed to organize approximately half the workers engaged in the goods sector. But they had organized little more than 5 percent of those in the service sector. The Retail Clerks International Association was decidedly an exception to the rule. It grew from a membership of 100,000 in 1940 to 400,000 in 1960. But it was recruiting members who, as has already been said, wore white collars but did blue-collar work.

The self-employed offered a similarly mixed development. As a proportion of the work force they shrank from 22 percent in 1940 to 13 percent in 1960. But nearly all this shrinkage was due to the decline in the number of farmers. Among the self-employed of the traditional professions—law, medicine, architecture, journalism, accountancy, and so on—there was a rapid increase, in response to growing demand for professional services. Excluding farmers, there were actually more self-employed in 1962 than there had been in 1948, a reflection of the growth of the service sector. In this regard the scope for individual initiative and responsibility, far from narrowing, may have been expanding.

The foundation of the new service economy and the technological society was to be found in a profound, yet little-remarked development. Trained intelligence was the true source of the power and riches of the Western world. The economic value of rational thought and rational organization was no sudden discovery. Yet the rapid diffusion of basic intellectual tools, the democratization of education in the first half of the twentieth century, had remade economy and society. By the 1960s knowledge had become a primary economic resource, cultivated as assiduously as farmers had for millennia cultivated their fields. Every year was expected to yield a new crop of ideas, products, and services. That was how a modern economy grew, either through the introduction of a new product or service or because an old product or service had been put to new uses or was now being created in a new way. Behind the ceaseless search for novelty and innovation was the human mind, probing, tinkering, experimenting, thinking.

"The post-industrial society is a society," wrote Daniel Bell, "in which business is no longer the predominant element but one in which the intellectual is predominant." Doubtless to most intellectuals—a breed noted for their defensiveness—this came as news indeed. But what Bell said was not that most people were becoming intellectuals; rather, the style of the new society, its interests, its values, its approach to problems, would be increasingly set by those who were.

The growth of Research and Development showed the way that things were going. Before the war it was a small-scale, almost incidental, adjunct of business. In 1963 government support for R&D was nearly $15 billion. Most of this money was not spent on science but on technology (roughly, exploiting the already known). The proportions between research and development were approximately 1:10. Although many scientists believed the amount spent on basic research was far too small, at $1.5 billion it was four times the total amount spent on R&D in 1940. R&D had become another secular cause. Government put up most of the money for it. Private industry spent most of the money. And so fashionable was R&D that a lot of it looked suspiciously like PR.

The three leading growth industries of the postwar were all based on the cultivation of brains—electronics, R&D, and education. The biggest growth in employment occurred in the service sector, where the minimum standard usually required was a high school diploma and where college graduates were commonplace. Between 1947 and 1963 the number of "professional and technical persons" in employment more than doubled.

The demand for a literate and numerate work force had been building up strongly for a century. Since the Civil War the fastest-growing occupational group had been clerical workers. In 1865 1 worker in 160 did clerical work; by 1950 the figure was 1 in 8. Two-thirds of all service sector workers now had a high school diploma. Then, in the 1950s the growth of clerical workers stopped abruptly. They began to increase at the same rate as the population. But the number of engineers, chemists, mathematicians, and other technicians increased by 60 percent in only ten years. The development marked the shift to an economy which rested on advanced and rapidly advancing technology.

This was a development which created a new breed of millionaire. The new millionaires formed a group that was not large but was important. Most of them were comparatively young, that is, under forty-five. They had no business experience to speak of, and most had not set out to become rich. But they became so, thanks to modern science and technology. The Cold War had made them because it had remade the economy to reward brainy young men who had a way with electronics. The richest of the new breed was David Bakalar. In 1960, at the age of thirty-five, Bakalar was worth an estimated $150 million. He was founder, president, and resident genius of Transitron Corporation in Wakefield, Massachusetts. Most of the new breed were remarkably inconspicuous consumers. They had never anticipated becoming rich. They had instead expected to have to live on a college teacher's salary. Sudden riches hardly ever turned their heads; they had more important things to think about.

The Cold War had also remade the prospects for academic scientists. They found themselves facing a wide range of opportunities to earn a second income, to the resentment of their colleagues in the humanities and social sciences. The long-standing cleavage between the scientists and the rest of the faculty was made wider than ever.

The new knowledge elite commanded a high price. "When the Census Bureau purchased its first electronic computer, it found that it also had to hire a young engineer to keep the blasted thing going," recalled Herman Miller. "He was paid a base salary that nearly equalled that of the Director of the Census. With overtime payments, he earned more than the Secretary of Commerce."

The "men of knowledge" could also be found in abundance in that presumed bastion of the working class the union hall. There was hardly a major union in the country that by the 1960s did not boast a highly paid staff of lawyers, public relations men, editors, accountants, statisticians, research directors, education advisers, and pension fund administrators.

In fact, the men of knowledge were to be found almost everywhere—in the unions, in government, in business. Not all benefited equally. The Matthew Effect determined that the rich grew richer and the poor lagged behind. In textiles, for example, in 1962 there were 3 scientists and engineers per 1,000 workers. In aircraft there were 101 per 1,000. It was IBM, however, which really set the style of the new order.

The glamor stocks of the age were those of companies based on advanced technology. Polaroid, for instance, rose from a humble $4 in 1952 to $261 in 1960. Similarly, 100 shares of IBM in 1950 had sold for $21,000. In 1963 the same shares were worth $330,000. IBM almost never fired anyone. And since 1939 no one had been laid off through lack of work or because of company reorganization. Depending on one's point of view, IBM was either disgustingly paternalistic or incredibly enlightened in its labor relations. Any employee with a grievance had the right to see the president or the chairman of the board. Every regional division of IBM held a "Family Dinner" each year. The corporation also provided luxurious recreational facilities for all its employees and an impressive model of the private welfare state.

Contrary to popular belief, IBM did not simply rent its machines. What an IBM contract offered was machine services—use of the equipment, plus an education on how to use it. IBM represented the service sector at its most highly developed. Any number of corporations had the knowledge to build computers, and for some operations there were far better computers available than those made by IBM. But IBM built itself into the biggest company of its kind in the world by offering the best customer service bar none. And to a considerable degree IBM educated the nation and much of the Western world to what the computer could do, how best to use it, how to think in its terms. Under the 1962 Manpower Development and Training Act the Administration set a target of training 130,000 people each year in skills which were important in a modern economy. That same year IBM alone trained 100,000 people to operate computers.

At the pinnacle of the new knowledge economy was perched the space program. It had comparatively little to do with basic science. It was mainly an exercise in advanced technology. As a collective enterprise it was the most complicated endeavor Americans had ever attempted short of fighting a war. Not even the largest corporation could boast more than a tiny fraction of the skills demanded. John Glenn went into orbit inside a Mercury capsule built by a prime contractor, McDonnell Aircraft, which in turn had been serviced by more than 40,000 subcontractors and suppliers. The capsule was no bigger than the average family car.

The principal manpower problem McDonnell had faced was not the hiring of a handful of geniuses to run the operation from the top down, nor was it finding thousands of skilled workers to bend metal and mold plastics. It was finding the tens of thousands of people in-between.

The postwar economy called for a different work force from any that had ever existed: masses of people with a secondary education. As their education rose, workers became more adaptable. And that suited the American way, which eschewed the long, arduous apprenticeship. The typical American skilled worker had acquired some training in school, learned another skill in the armed forces, taken a correspondence course, and picked up yet another trade through on-the-job training. By the 1960s the United States had the most tractable, adaptable, and educated work force in the world. They were prepared for the emerging style of working life in which many millions of people would have to learn how to do half a dozen jobs before they reached retirement age. They would have to learn to work with advanced technology, instead of being awed by it. The key to their adaptability was the rapid increase in the level of general education. The typical worker of 1940 had not gone far beyond the eighth grade. In 1960 his son went to work and had a high school diploma. Even laborers and domestics these days had two more years of schooling than the laborers and domestics of 1940.

Education paid dividends for everyone, including blue-collar workers. In 1959 a high school diploma was worth an extra $1,200 a year to a bricklayer, $1,000 to a bus driver, $900 to a carpenter, $800 to a fireman. And within a given trade the better jobs and the weightier responsibilities were entrusted to the better-educated workers.

Education had become possibly the most important single element in productivity growth in the modern economy. Since World War I incomes had risen three times faster than capital investment. But behind this rapid increase in earnings was an investment in people—in their health, their skills, their education. This intangible capital had created the world's healthiest and most flexible work force. And *that*, more than anything else, had made the United States the richest country in the world per capita in the early 1960s.

According to the calculations of Edward F. Denison, the increased level of education accounted for nearly one-fourth of all productivity gains between the late 1920s and the late 1950s. Increases in knowledge added a further 20 percent.

The pursuit of knowledge, from a grade school education to the applied technology of the space program, had become one of the country's biggest concerns. In the late 1950s the pursuit of knowledge in its various forms was estimated to account for one-third of the GNP. And even then there was broad scope for advancement because the economic cost of basic educational deficiencies such as illiteracy took $100 billion a year off the nation's potential growth.

Throughout the period of this book knowledge appears to have increased much faster than either population or gross national product. In the 1950s, according to the most thorough calculation made, knowledge was increasing by approximately 10 percent a year. Not all this yield was plowed into the economy. In fact, there is no direct evidence to show that new knowledge raised productivity across the board, even though it undoubtedly raised productivity in parts of it. But the new knowledge, the new technology did not simply go into making more goods. They produced better goods, more complicated and expensive goods. They impelled a more rational and effective organization of work. They created new services or made existing services more sophisticated. The result was that work of all kinds was being done more intelligently than ever.

The influx of new knowledge remade some old established businesses. Half of Du Pont's sales involved items no one had heard of before the war. In the 1950s one-fifth of everything sold by General Foods consisted of items which had not existed only ten years earlier. In 1955, 75 percent of Corning Glass' business was in products unknown in 1940. Developments such as these were commonplace throughout business and the economy. And they were only the beginning.

The new knowledge society was wonderfully productive. It poured forth material goods and everyday comforts in abundance. Yet it posed a sharp challenge to self-esteem. By emulating human functions normally associated with the mind, modern machines threatened to reduce human beings to the status of interchangeable things.

The claims made for automation, however, were often exaggerated. It was often claimed that computers were about to simulate the workings of the brain. Yet how the brain worked was still largely a mystery. Then the machines were built. And *their* characteristics were blithely described as being analogous to those of the brain. In time, someone would pronounce that they had discovered that the machines worked "exactly like our brains." The glazed-eye credulity with which such claims were accepted offered a dismaying indication of how far human beings had fallen in respect for their own gifts.

The advent of cybernetics and information theory encouraged the development of another snare for the uncritical: that the central problem in the human condition was poor communications. As concern with communications increased, as it became an academic discipline of sorts, as it infiltrated fashionable thought and chatter, language itself appeared to crumble. Never had ordinary speech been so vague and vacuous, filled with fake eloquence and jargon so pompous it appeared to be parodying itself. The notion that bad relations between people and countries arose from poor communications had been in vogue before now. But cybernetics and information theory were taken as scientific proofs that this was so.

They also had the effect of inspiring a variety of hopeless intellectual ventures. For instance, there was a fruitless search for "Mechanical Translation." On a half-digested diet of cybernetics, information theory, and computer programming hundreds of well-meaning pioneers wrestled themselves into a state of baffled exhaustion. They took the word as the basic unit of language. The basic unit of language, however, is the sentence—that is, thought is conveyed not in separate words but in organized collections of words. In English alone the number of intelligible sentences of twenty words or less is approximately 10^{50}. Before the zeal for MT was over, hundreds of highly skilled translators might have been recruited and trained.

It took time for the inherent limits of computers to become widely understood. But in the meantime, computer engineers had coined the acronym GIGO, for "Garbage In=Garbage Out."

The principal danger the machines posed was that they worked so fast and in so complicated a fashion that they at times behaved unpredictably. If a computer did something it was not expected to do, then it had in effect added something of its own. This was so even though it would probably be possible in time to unravel what the machine had done and describe how it had done it. There was almost no possibility of machines becoming more subtle than human intelligence. The danger, Norbert Wiener pointed out, was that they would transcend human performance. The lag between the speed of the machine and the speed with which the mind could follow what was happening was increasing rapidly. During this reaction time the machines were in effect beyond human control. And the demand was for machines which worked faster and faster. As such machines appeared, continuous human control slipped out of people's grasp.

Wiener also feared that automation, to which he had contributed so extensively, would bring as much social distress as it did liberation from drudgery. The new machine could depreciate average human intelligence much as the machinery of the Industrial Revolution had depreciated ordinary physical labor. Millions of people who had found a tolerable place in life by their performance of routine mental tasks might before long be made useless in an economy in which electronic devices kept books, did billings, and wrote letters.

Wiener attempted to alert the labor movement to his apprehensions. But except in two officials of the CIO he was able to awaken neither concern nor comprehension. The future he tried to describe to them appeared less real than a contract, a jurisdictional dispute, a strike, or a pension fund. He fell into a pessimistic mood regarding the future of automation. "We can only hand it over to the world that exists about us, and this is the world of Belsen and Hiroshima."

It was partly in reaction against the knowledge-based society and the service economy, in which everything appeared to run on straight lines, in which the rational, the uniform, and the dead level appeared to be triumphant over the eccentric, the unique, and the playful, that there was a rapidly growing celebration of the irrational. Its most eager recruits were to be found among the young. Obsessions with the occult and fantastic, with astrology and drugs have traditionally been characteristics of nations in decline, where self-confidence has been destroyed and a sense of purpose lost. Yet although it was fashionable to believe that was exactly what was happening at present, there was little evidence for such a view beyond the conditions themselves. They came about for various reasons, including the democratization of vices formerly practiced by the very few, the spreading of affluence and leisure time, the rise in availabilty of inexpensive books, increases in self-awareness, and the workings of fashion.

America was still a country of extraordinary optimism and energy. Much of the cult of the irrational was no more than skin-deep; it smacked of playacting; it was in large part a yearning for the color and idiosyncrasy which the major forces in modern life were certainly eroding. But in that regard it was unlike nearly all other cults of the irrational, which have been fascinated with death, and was instead a stubborn, perhaps irrational fight for life.

38

Moving Ahead While Sitting Down

Throughout the Kennedy Administration one issue dominated all others on the domestic scene—civil rights. And white Americans were now acutely sensitive to the cries for racial justice. Having become exercised over the urban crisis, they could no longer ignore the plight of urban blacks. As the civil rights struggle in the South degenerated into street clashes and bloodshed, they could no longer plead ignorance of the fate of Southern blacks. Torn though they were between their dislike of blacks and their love of justice, they were at last prepared to see that what the civil rights struggle involved was a national challenge, not a sectional one, that it *was* their business after all.

Rarely has any downtrodden people been forced to assert themselves from so weak a position as the black population of the United States. It was not that they were poor; many people have been poorer. Nor was it that they were uneducated; most poor people have been no better educated. Nor was it that they were discriminated against, brutalized, and held in contempt. History is full of examples of the despised and ignorant redeeming themselves (the British were once slaves to the Romans, the name Slav once meant slave, and so on). The principal disability of American blacks was the absence of social cohesion. They were a shattered people. Their condition in this respect was not growing any better and may well have been deteriorating.

Since 1945 the percentage of American families headed by women had remained steady at about 9 percent. Among nonwhites, however, the figure rose from 13 percent to 25 percent. Each year there were undoubtedly thousands of black people who were starting on what time would prove to be successful careers and successful private lives. But for the black population as a whole the fragmentation factor was getting worse, not better. The reason was that the black family, never very strong, was now a broken reed. Nearly one-fourth of all black marriages by the 1960s had been dissolved. Nearly one-fourth of all black births were illegitimate. For most of the postwar, there was a close correspondence between changes in the rate of unemployment among nonwhite males and the number of ADC recipients. But in the early 1960s the unemployment rate of nonwhite males dropped considerably, and the number of ADC cases continued to rise. More than half of all black children were being raised on welfare.

Lengthening welfare rolls helped give edge to the popular fear that blacks were heavily outbreeding whites. "One high government official called the Census Bureau of few years ago," Herman P. Miller reported, "and wanted to know when Negroes would constitute a majority in the United States." But while black women were 40 percent more fecund than white women, it took fifteen years for blacks to go from being 11 percent of the population to being 12 percent. It had taken thirty years to rise from 10 percent to 11 percent. And in the early 1960s the black birthrate leveled off. Although they had long had a higher birthrate, blacks had also suffered a much higher infant mortality rate. The blacks who survived childhood still died ten years earlier on average than their white counterparts.

Crammed into a big-city ghetto, most black children in the North faced a life that was likely to prove Hobbesian—that is, brutish, nasty, and short. Even in the most liberal city in the country, New York, everything appeared to go from bad to worse. There was no legally enforceable segregation in the city. There was a state FEPC and a city Fair Employment Practices Law, an Open Occupancy Law, and a variety of social service agencies designed to help the poor and uneducated secure their rights. Yet liberal New York was also the site of Harlem, one of the least cohesive and most dangerous communities on earth. In liberal New York between 1946 and 1962 entire schools became almost completely black and Puerto Rican. While the nonwhite children were being crammed into the public schools, white parents in a state approaching panic were hurriedly shifting their children to parochial and private schools. In 1962 it was not hard to find a public elementary school where white children appeared only in token numbers. In the whole of Manhattan, 75 percent of the children in public elementary schools were black or brown.

There were almost identical conditions in other big cities. When black

ghettos spread, the resulting housing patterns created de facto segregation. The ghettos themselves showed considerable variety; there was no
mistaking Watts for Hunter's Point, the South Side for Harlem. Some
ghettos were clearly worse than others. Some were much blacker than
others.

Segregation, the focal point of black protests since 1954, was not an issue that captured the hearts of most urban blacks. They had a number of
more immediate concerns to deal with—unemployment, low pay,
wretched housing, police brutality, exploitation by rapacious landlords,
cheating shopkeepers, the heroin plague, and crime rates far above those
in white communities. But the NAACP and nearly all other black organizations slighted these concerns, arguing that they were due to poverty and
class structure as much as to race. They devoted themselves to destroying
Jim Crow.

It hardly seems surprising that urban blacks were therefore susceptible
to all manner of charlatans, not the least of whom was Adam Clayton
Powell, Jr. This ordained minister and Congressman used his pulpit in the
Abyssinian Baptist Church of Harlem to demand equal opportunity for
blacks in crime. He considered it unfair that Italians should have control
of nearly all the city's organized crime. White people were aghast. But
black people tended to admire Powell even for his vices. It was reported
that an erstwhile contender for Powell's seat in Congress once railed
against him to a Harlem crowd, "Adam Clayton Powell is a disgrace.
He's a Congressman and a minister of the Gospel. But he keeps an expensive apartment in New York and another in Washington. He spends his
evenings in nightclubs and with all kinds of women. Every time you turn
around he's off to Europe. And about the last place you'll ever find him is
in Congress." Came a voice from the crowd: "Man, that's what I call living!"

Powell's hold on his district was so strong that in 1962 he did not make a
single speech for reelection, no Vote for Powell posters appeared, not one
piece of Vote for Powell literature was printed. He defeated the combined
vote of his opponents by 40,000 ballots.

America's urban blacks not only were underrepresented in Congress
but were badly represented, and not just by Powell. They were slighted
by black organizations, which were heavily engaged in the struggle in the
South to end desegregation. Unemployment rates were more than twice
those of the urban white population. Black families were collapsing at an
accelerating rate. The resulting tensions kept emotions close to flash
point. In the 1950s Washington had become the first major city to have a
black majority. On Thanksgiving Day 1962 a high school football game at
District of Columbia Stadium turned into the worst race riot since the Detroit riot of 1943. The football game was between the public schools' top
team, Eastern High School, and the championship team of the Catholic
League, St. John's. Eastern was nearly completely black; St. John's was
nearly 100 percent white. St. John's won the game. But moments before
the final whistle blew, a fist fight broke out between the players on the
field. There had been racial scuffles in the stands during the game. Now,

however, hundreds of black youths charged the St. John's cheering section, brandishing chair legs, pieces of lead pipe, broken bottles, and knives. White girls were stripped and assaulted. Priests who tried to help them were clubbed to the ground. By the time police had cleared the stands more than 100 people were on their way to hospital.

Bad as conditions were in the cities of the North, they had not improved much for blacks in the South. Yet the South had by now lost its singularity. It had been a region dominated by one occupation, farming; one crop, cotton; one political party, the Democrats; one creed, fundamental Protestantism. As each of these was supplanted and the South's singularity diminished, the region's ability to resist the demands for racial justice became fragmented.

The most debilitating singularity had been the dead hand of one-party politics. But Southerners had long been afraid that a two-party system would lead to a competition for black votes; in some counties that would have led to the election of black officials. By 1960, thanks to Eisenhower's extraordinary popularity and Nixon's willingness to reap the political benefits of racism without actually endorsing it, the South had become nearly a two-party region. In doing so, it had moved close to the national mainstream. It could no longer avoid confronting its racial dilemmas squarely, along with everyone else.

Even in its racism the South was not as monolithic as outsiders took it to be. The Citizens' Councils never took root in North Carolina or Florida ("the bright spot of the South"). At the other extreme there was Mississippi. "Northerners, provincials that they are, regard the South as one large Mississippi," wrote Vladimir Orlando Key, Jr. "Southerners, with their eye for distinction, place Mississippi in a class by itself."

Ironically, the most racially enlightened city in the United States was not in the liberal North but in the dreaded South, Atlanta ("the city too busy to hate"). Atlanta was different largely because William B. Hartsfield, who was mayor from 1938 to 1961, had spent two decades wooing the black vote. Hartsfield did not do much to improve the condition of Atlanta's blacks, and it is questionable that there was much that he could have done. But he did do one thing that counted—he made it easy for blacks to vote.

Hartsfield had the support of Atlanta's leading business, Coca-Cola, and its president, Robert W. Woodruff. By the 1960s government in Atlanta was based on business, the good-government elements of the white middle class, and the black population. The white working class was overlooked in this arrangement, but no one made a fuss about it because it helped produce a quiet life for everyone. Not that the blacks enjoyed full equality in Atlanta. They did not. But neither were they ignored or kept down by brute force. And even the appalling Georgia state legislature declined to interfere with this *modus vivendi*. The legislature in 1958 wrote a new Voter Registration Act in order to make it harder than ever for blacks to vote. But in Fulton County, dominated by Atlanta, blacks found it as easy to vote as it had ever been.

Atlanta's arrangement was also made possible because the city could boast "the largest number of educated Negroes in the nation." And from Morehouse College ("the Negroes' Harvard") there emerged a steady stream of earnest young black men and women who were hardworking, politically moderate, and socially responsible.

Meanwhile, the South was not only undergoing a slow and painful moral revolution but literally becoming a cleaner, healthier place. Long the most self-conscious region of the country, it finally got around to doing something to smarten up its appearance. And when self-consciousness turns to self-improvement, it is an unmistakable sign of a positive change under way within. In the late 1940s, under prompting from the TVA and the University of Tennessee, a community improvement contest was launched in Knoxville. The idea spread rapidly throughout the South in the next decade. It combined reforming zeal with the competitive spirit. The object was to make the South—especially the rural South—a cleaner, safer, more pleasant place in which to live. Rusting junk was cleared from the entrances to farms. Old fences were replaced. Muddy lanes were given hard surfaces. Houses by the hundreds of thousands were treated to long-overdue repainting. Sagging roofs were repaired. Lawns were landscaped. Tens of thousands of signposts appeared along minor roads. Eyesores of every kind were screened or eliminated. The measures were, in themselves, not remarkable, perhaps. But cumulatively they indicated the growth of a new and more realistic sense of civic pride. By 1961 the South looked better than at any time since 1861.

Southerners were also becoming receptive to outside pressures, thanks to a more sophisticated view of the damned Yankees. These were now seen to come in two varieties. There was the good damned Yankee and the bad damned Yankee. The former arrived in the South hungry for candied pecans, French-fried shrimp, and Southern-fried chicken. Every night he slept contentedly at the new motel on the outskirts of town. He politely kept his opinions to himself. The bad damned Yankee, on the other hand, brought his own food, slept in his car, and fumed volubly over matters which were none of his damned Yankee business.

By the 1960s tourism was worth more to some Southern states than agriculture. The damned Federal government (and it *was* widely damned) was responsible for much of this. It promoted tourism through such diverse measures as the Interstate Highway Program and the Department of Commerce handbook called *Your Community Can Profit from the Tourist Business.* This offered practical advice, e.g., "Tourists perk up when geological formations are called 'faces,' when a narrow valley becomes 'the pass,' when rocks become 'painted,' or when a cliff is called 'Devil's Leap.'"

Another factor making the South less resistant to change was the declining proportion of blacks to whites. Although there were several score Southern counties and several dozen towns where blacks were in a majority, in the South as a whole blacks had been only 25 percent of the population in 1940. Thanks to the postwar migration to the North and West, by 1960 that figure had dropped to 20 percent. Southern cities were also learning to compromise by emulating the Northern pattern of de facto segregation. In 1963 Albany, Georgia, showed how far this development had advanced in a short time. It repealed all the segregation ordinances in the city code. Nothing changed.

Everything connected with the struggle for racial justice continued to flirt with danger, however. An English journalist invited to an "Integration Party" (where blacks and whites of both sexes mingled freely) in New Orleans in 1961 wrote home: "It was as secret as a Resistance Party in Paris during the German Occupation." Yet those who marched and demonstrated now had the satisfaction of knowing that they themselves bore the danger. Witless attempts to crush the black population of the South by creating a climate of terror, where violence was nearly always random and its victims obscure, was on its way out. The last lynching had taken place in 1959.

With white people becoming increasingly concerned about the fate of black people, the blacks themselves were becoming assertive and articulate. It is only by effort that human beings learn the value of anything. It was essential that blacks struggle for equality in order to learn how to exercise democratic rights soberly. The civil rights struggle was a school for the nation's black population. White Americans, moreover, were never going to respect black people until they stopped shuffling their feet and saying, "Yassuh." Before whites could accept the idea of black equality, American blacks had to assert themselves. To give it credibility, the black protest movement needed a sharp cutting edge. The polite, well-educated lawyers of the NAACP were invaluable. But they were, in the term of philosophers, a "necessary but not sufficient condition." Enter the Black Muslims. Respectable black leaders took one look at them and turned away in horror.

Black secret societies had been in existence since the late eighteenth century. There had been black Masons and Odd Fellows. By the late 1950s the biggest black fraternal order, the black Elks, had a membership of 500,000 enrolled in 1,000 lodges. The black Elks provided an interesting example of an organization that was working-class in membership but decidedly middle-class in outlook.

In recent years, as blacks began to develop an interest in their African roots, they became in a roundabout way, interested in Islam. This was despite the role of Arab slave traders. In part, however, this development was a rejection of the white man's religion and was encouraged by the discovery that the Prophet's first muezzin had been a black man named Bilal. There had been Muslims among the slaves brought to America. And the consolations of religion being, like the consolations of sex, one of the few permitted forms of emotional release allowed blacks, religious cults flourished under slavery and later. In 1913 one Timothy Drew, calling himself Noble Drew Ali founded the Moorish Science Temple in Newark. Male members added "el" or "bey" to their names and were allowed to wear eye-catching red fezzes. Noble Drew Ali's following grew to 30,000, and he regaled them with sermons which described in thrilling detail the imminent destruction of the white man. But destruction reached Timothy Drew first. Success and sudden riches gave rise to leadership struggles which featured violent deaths and mysterious disappearances. Among the murdered was the founder.

When the Moorish Science Temple was breaking up around 1930, another Muslim cult arose, in Detroit. Its mentor was Wallace D. Fard. He identified himself to the Detroit police as "The Supreme Ruler of the Universe." In 1933 the Supreme Ruler vanished without trace. But the torch had been passed to his elect, one Elijah Poole, a sharecropper recently translated from Sandersville, Georgia. Before becoming Elijah Muhammad, he had already been Elijah Karriem, Gurlam Bogans, Muhammed Rassouli, and Elijah Muck Mudd. Now, however, he was the Messenger of Allah (Allah being W. D. Fard) and "The Lost-Found Nation of Islam in the Wilderness of North America" had been placed in his care.

Late in life, he explained to a politely skeptical white interviewer that Fard's appearance on earth had been the realization of both the Second Coming of Christ and the Koran's prophecy of the coming of the Mahdi. "I was in the presence of God [Fard] for over three years," he said solemnly, "and I received what I am teaching you directly from his mouth. I believe I am the first man commissioned by the face of God, in person. If I am lying I will give you $10,000."

For two decades Elijah Muhammad's followers were few. Wartime resistance to fighting the white man's battles put him and other Muslims in prison for counseling draft resistance. In prison, however, they found a new source of devotees. It was in prison that they also found Malcolm Little, who was sentenced in 1946 to a 10-year term for burglary. This was a rigorous sentence to impose on a 20-year-old first offender whose crimes had not involved violence or threats of violence. Fast-talking, quick-witted Malcolm Little had a girlfriend, though, and she was obviously white. She was his partner in both bed and burglary.

While incarcerated in Massachusetts's Concord Prison, Malcolm Little, petty thief, scam artist, and street hustler, discovered "the natural religion for the black man." When he was paroled in 1952, he was a fervent Muslim. He left his "slave name" Little behind him and replaced it with an X. There were at present fewer than 1,000 members in Elijah Muhammad's temples. During the next ten years, thanks largely to Malcolm X's extraordinary energy and charisma, the Black Muslims enrolled tens of thousands of followers and won hundreds of thousands of sympathizers, in the black ghettos of the North. The faith was spread far afield through Elijah Muhammad's column in the Pittsburgh *Courier*, a black weekly which circulated from Cleveland to Miami. But in 1959 the *Courier* abruptly dropped the column. It drew more mail than anything else in the paper, but the tone was evidently too inflammatory for the paper's new owners. Undaunted, the resourceful Malcolm X began a Black Muslim newspaper in the basement of his East Elmhurst, New York, home. Within a year he had made *Muhammad Speaks* into a successful newspaper. By 1962 there were sixty-nine temples in twenty-seven states, a membership of approximately 50,000, and a collection of Muslim businesses worth $10 to $20 million.

The Muslims were by now well known, but not as the Nation of Islam. Eric Lincoln, a black scholar, had coined the term "Black Muslims" back in 1956, and it stuck. In the fall of 1959 CBS showed a documentary called *The Hate That Hate Produced*, and millions of white Americans were stunned by what they saw. They were shown what appeared to be a private army, entirely black, armed to the teeth, fanatical, highly trained, ready to fight to the death, and utterly obedient to the will of one man— Elijah Muhammad. And this was a man who preached that the white man was the Devil and his time was up.

The private black army was the Fruit of Islam, a corps of strapping black working-class men in their twenties. They were charged with keeping order in the temple. But they were portrayed as a Black SA. The reckless language of Malcolm X, which was filled with apocalyptic visions, also made the flesh creep. *Time* described the Black Muslims as "members of the brotherhood of Negro supremacists that is dedicated to the extinction of the white race." In June 1962 a Boeing 707 crashed at Orly Airport. Atlanta was plunged into a state of grief it had not known since Sherman sacked it. Most of the 132 people aboard the plane were prominent Atlantans on a cultural pilgrimage to Europe. Malcolm X heard the news in Los Angeles and exulted to a Muslim congregation 1,500 strong: "A very beautiful thing has happened. . . . God has answered our prayers in France . . . we will continue to pray and hope that every day another plane falls from out the sky . . . . We call on our God—He gets rid of 120 of them at one whop."

Such grisly rodomontade provoked white apprehension and anger. Yet it provided an emotional release for lower-class blacks whose pent-up bitterness was almost certain to turn self-destructive if not harmlessly discharged elsewhere. The Black Muslims were dealing with the lowest of the low. They took the people no one else would take—the drug addicts, the pimps, the prostitutes, the felons, the alcoholics, the muggers, the rapists, the murderers. They were remarkably successful, often succeeding in rehabilitating people considered beyond reclamation. There was no one so wicked that they would not try to save him or her for an orderly, responsible life. Successful criminals avoided the Black Muslims. But the drifters, the losers, the emotionally bewildered who comprised much of the prison population were open to persuasion.

A sympathetic white man at one point in conversation with Malcolm X mentioned "white stereotypes" about blacks. No, said Malcolm, "Most of the things white people say about the Negro that are bad are not stereotypes; they're true." Nor did Elijah Muhammad spare his black followers, reminding them of their faults even as he told them that they were "the Most Powerful, the Most Beautiful and the Wisest" people in the world. He told them to "Wake up, clean up and stand up," or they would never be free.

While preaching the evil nature of everything associated with white people, the Black Muslims strove for an ideal that one might have sworn had been taken wholesale from the Protestant Ethic, with its emphasis on hard work, self-discipline, abstinence, honesty, and self-respect. Much of the Black Muslims' appeal arose from their belief in patriarchy and a close-knit family life. They offered a movement that was as much social as religious. And they provided a ladder to be grasped by upwardly mobile lower-class blacks who yearned to leave their shame and poverty behind them by acquiring the middle-class virtues of mutual help and individual self-improvement. But to educated middle-class blacks the Black Muslims were an embarrassment, gullible followers in thrall to a crooked leadership.

The Black Muslims preached extreme racial separation. This reflected an almost desperate desire to create a unique and strong sense of identity. Muslims refused to vote, rejected integration, refused to be drafted, and, most important of all, categorically rejected Christianity. They affected only contempt for the white man's scientific skills and mastery of technology as being merely "tricknology." They possessed a land hunger that was astonishing for so urban a body, but this was essential to their sense of nationhood. In their struggle for identity they cast aside nearly all the common characteristics of lower-class dress and behavior. They dressed with a sobriety that made Brooks Brothers appear vulgar by comparison. They did not smoke, drink, swear, gamble, sing, dance, or countenance sex outside marriage. Blacks were said to crave pork. The Muslims gave up pork. The stricter the observance, the greater its appeal to some people; the more complete the proscription, the greater its authority.

To become a Black Muslim was to be reborn. The new adherent's past no longer mattered. The X in someone's name signified the past ("ex-") being put aside and the unknown being accepted. Male Muslims were expected to visit the temple twice a week, to eat only one meal a day, and to spend their spare time selling *Muhammad Speaks* and "fishing for the dead" (recruiting new members). By 1963 anyone passing through the downtown section of any major city was likely to be stopped by a politely spoken, neatly dressed, clean shaved, close-cropped young black man and asked to buy a copy of *Muhammad Speaks*. Its circulation was 600,000 copies. And this was the principal occupation of the Fruit of Islam beyond the temple door, not looking for trouble but selling newspapers. The Muslims were never as ferocious as they made themselves appear. "They are on the whole a conservative and peace-loving lot," remarked someone who knew Malcolm X well. "They expect that Allah will bring their enemies low for them."

But fantasies of revenge provided the staple of temple sermons. Malcolm X used to conjure up visions of a vast armada of jet bombers circling the globe, piloted by black men, dropping atomic bombs on all the white man's most prized accomplishments, on white neighborhoods and white businesses. He also liked to enliven his sermons by picking up the Bible, throwing it to the ground, then kicking it back and forth while asserting that white people had tails.

The Black Muslims offered a playlet called "The Trial." For years it thrilled temple congregations. It featured a black man in whiteface indicted for every ugly crime imaginable; there was no perversion too base, no crime too horrendous. An all-black jury carefully weighed the evidence. After due deliberation, which took two or three minutes at least, they found the defendant guilty on every count, plus several more which had occurred to them during their deliberations. A black judge pronounced sentence on the now-quaking and tearful wretch. Dragged to his feet by several burly black policemen, the defendant sobbed uncontrollably that all he ever wanted to do was to "help the nigras." He was taken away for execution to ecstatic applause.

Worship in these temples was not like the practices of Islam elsewhere. There were lectures rather than prayers; there was personal exhortation rather than worship of Allah. All who came for the services were carefully searched for drugs, guns, knives, cosmetics, liquor, cigarettes, or anything other than a handkerchief and comb. In the mosques of Islam the worshipers use prayer mats. Black Muslims were seated.

Although they did not involve themselves directly in the civil rights movement, the Black Muslims believed that they had played as important a role as the NAACP and the Urban League, CORE or the SCLC. They had redeemed the least-educated, least-organized elements of the black population. They had been a powerful force for black solidarity and identity. They had kept pressure on moderate civil rights groups which would have been far less bold otherwise. And in truth, the principal enemy black people confronted was not white society but black backwardness. No one tackled that issue more directly than the Black Muslims. The violence, self-loathing, the pointless promiscuity, the misery, self-pity, apathy, and drug addiction were the heritage of more than 300 years of brutalization. Once these had been set right, then the majority of whites would have to accept blacks as equals, even if the two races retained many of their cultural differences.

In Malcolm X the Black Muslims offered an example of all that was expected of an adherent. He was as abstemious as a Mormon elder. He was a devoted husband and father. He worked himself to the brink of nervous exhaustion. He possessed boundless physical courage. He was scrupulously honest. No one could intimidate him; no one could buy him. Although he was given to inflammatory language, in the last few years of his life he began to moderate his views on the wickedness of white people and in his personal contacts with them was open and courteous. He was one of the very small number of people who are able through strength of character to become a moral force. His growing fame, his spreading influence, his unswerving rectitude, and his increasing independence of mind put severe strains, however, on his relationship with Elijah Muhammad and his court. Malcolm was also becoming impatient with Elijah Muhammad's personal habits. The former sharecropper's pretty young secretaries were remarkably prone to becoming mysteriously pregnant.

But for the moment the Black Muslims maintained a united front. And respect for them grew steadily in the ghettos. "Negroes who do not join the Muslims do not join in criticism of them," noted Morroe Berger. To the civil rights groups, however, they were a constant irritant. Whitney Young once complained that Malcolm X had never found anybody a job or a place to live, yet was on television more often than Johnny Carson. Moderates such as Young resented Malcolm both for his celebrity and for his easy rapport with the lower-class blacks they had never been able to organize. For his part, Malcolm resented the acceptance of the moderates by the white press and politicians as the natural leaders of American blacks. It was they who were invited to the White House or to see Bobby Kennedy, never Malcolm.

This was inevitable. Being slighted by the respectable was part of the Black Muslims' success. They had rounded out the spectrum of black protest. At one extreme were the black leaders who tried to work with the white majority. In the middle were the leaders of direct action and nonviolent protest, such as Martin Luther King. And at the other extreme were Elijah Muhammad and Malcolm X. By shadowboxing, by appearing to be utterly intractable and militant, they did much to make the black protest of the early 1960s credible. What moved white society to accept accommodation on race was less a love of their fellow men and women than a very sensible desire to head off a potential disaster. The Black Muslims served as both lightning rod and early-warning system.

Before the late 1950s black protest was nearly always organized from the top. But suddenly black college students began to act on their own initiative. In 1958 NAACP Youth Councils in Kansas and Oklahoma decided to hold sit-ins at public facilities in protest against segregation. In 1959 several thousand black college students marched on Washington.

The students' protest was partly an expression of impatience with the black bourgeoisie, the very class they were preparing themselves to enter. But they wanted it to be a genuine middle class, not one that was obliged to dine at Jim Crow restaurants, was forced to live in poor black neighborhoods, was cut off from the better colleges, and lived outside the mainstream of national life—all in exchange for a fistful of crumbs. They did not want to marry whites or live next door to them. But they wanted far more from life than a black ghetto with comforts. Between black college youth and the black bourgeoisie the generation gap was more than a gap; it resembled a chasm.

By 1960 there were almost as many nonwhite college students in the South as there were in the rest of the country: 92,000 compared with 99,000. And these 92,000 students daily rubbed up against the humiliations imposed by Jim Crow statutes and customs. It appears inevitable in retrospect that someone one day would, like Rosa Parks, say, "Enough." But no one anticipated what happened. On February 1, 1960, Joseph McNeill, a freshman at North Carolina Agricultural and Technical College, asked for something to eat at the lunch counter of the Greensboro bus terminal. He was told to go away.

The following day McNeill was back, accompanied by his roommate, Ezell Blair, Jr., and two other students. All four belonged to the NAACP's Greensboro Youth Council. But what they did was their own idea. They sat at the lunch counter for more than two hours. Then they went outside and recited the Lord's Prayer. They vowed to keep coming back "Until we get served."

The national press picked up this story from a local stringer. It described their action as a "sit-down strike." Within a month this form of protest had captured the imagination of black college students throughout the South. It was possible within a few hours to organize a protest of this kind. There were sit-ins at lunch counters, supermarkets, libraries, theaters, and department stores. There were stand-ins, kneel-ins, lie-ins, and mass marches.

From Norfolk to New Orleans freshly written signs went up on lunch counters: "Closed for Repairs" or "Closed Indefinitely." But one enterprising restaurant put up a sign reading, "Open to Members." The only qualification for dining at this exclusive new eating club was a white skin. When a contingent of demonstrators from black Knoxville College sat in at a downtown lunch counter, the cook twitted them by lining the lunch counter with tempting slices of watermelon.

Most of those brought face to face in these confrontations were ordinary, decent, well-meaning people, able to relate to others and to sympathize with their predicament. Protesters, waitresses, assistant managers, cooks, and hired guards were more likely to be shy and embarrassed than to be aggressive and willful. It was not uncommon for the waitresses and the guards to be apologetic about the regulations they had been told to enforce. And some openly applauded the protesters for their moral courage.

But there was also intimidation, especially in the Deep South. On occasion tempers on both sides snapped. Efforts to provoke the demonstrators at times succeeded. This was inevitable. The black students had both the idealism and the impatience of youth. Their courage was a rebuke to their elders, and as the protests spread, some of the demonstrators were very young indeed, as we shall see. A black journalist of distinction wrote: "There is nothing more humiliating to a Negro man who cleans cuspidors and bows before the patrons in an all-white barber shop to see a Negro child, head high, face well scrubbed, walk though a howling mob and flying bricks to go to school. He hates himself."

The sit-ins were only the beginning of the new wave of protest. When white resistance stiffened, the students looked for other ways to step up the pressure. Boycotts began and picket lines were formed. And Joseph McNeill and Ezell Blair, Jr., turned for advice to Dr. George Simpkins, president of the Greensboro NAACP. He in turn directed them to the decidedly militant Congress for Racial Equality. CORE had spent more than a decade polishing the tactics of nonviolent direct action.

In the meantime, the NAACP found itself in an increasingly difficult position. It had committed itself to a very clear-cut strategy; it had seen that strategy vindicated, but now it was under intense pressure to abandon it in favor of a different strategy which had not yet been vindicated by events. The NAACP found it impossible to remake its approach and stayed close to its established ways. It never involved large numbers of uneducated, unskilled blacks in what it was doing. It fought for them, not with them. As the pace of protest increased, large numbers of NAACP members became restless. And one of the NAACP's founders, W. E. B. DuBois, resigned in 1961. He joined the Communist Party, moved to Ghana, and died there in 1963 at the age of ninety-five.

Some NAACP officials looked with undisguised envy on the raw energy and fervor of the black masses now being tapped by such diverse bodies as the Black Muslims and the Southern Christian Leadership Conference. The head of the NAACP in Philadelphia, Cecil Moore, felt that even without claiming them as NAACP members, "My basic strength is those [hundreds of thousands] of lower class guys who are ready to mob, riot, steal and kill." And this was how whites saw them, even though the victims of black violence are nearly always black and the rage that most black people feel is self-destructive rather than a threat to whites.

The bitter confrontations and street clashes brought a swift change in attitudes toward the NAACP. Middle-class white Southerners began to treat the NAACP with something close to respect. You could not talk sense to those wild college students. But the polite, well-groomed preachers and lawyers from the NAACP were people you could deal with man to man. "Southerners now dream about the days of the NAACP," wrote Harry Golden in 1963 from his South Carolina vantage point, "when all they had to do was file an answering brief in a courtroom."

But as pressures intensified, the rifts between black organizations became irreparable. There was a struggle for power, there was a profound disagreement over strategy, but most of all, there was a bitter class conflict between the long-established middle-class bodies and the new lower-class ones. CORE, however, occupied the ground between these two. It had been formed in 1942. Its leadership was by this time middle-aged and middle-class. Yet it believed deeply in the tactics of confrontation.

One of CORE's founders, James Farmer, had been the NAACP's program director in the 1950s. But his ideas favoring mass action were unwelcome to his fellow NAACP executives. In February 1961 he resigned from the NAACP. He returned to CORE as its president. Three months later the Freedom Rides began.

Another militant body, the Student Nonviolent Coordinating Committee, had meanwhile emerged. SNCC was an offshoot of the sit-ins and came into existence with the help of the Southern Christian Leadership Conference. In theory it was a confederation of youth groups But it was in practice composed of several hundred Atlanta college students who were prepared to organize direct action anywhere in the South, including the most dangerous and benighted communities in Alabama and Mississippi. Instead of making elaborate preparations, SNCC volunteers would show up in a town without advance notice, would announce their presence, and would then begin to organize for action on the spot. SNCC adopted a policy of "In jail, no bail." This put hundreds of young demonstrators behind bars. There they continued with their protest. They sang fervently and did a lot of defiant chanting. Many of them, male and female alike, maintained that they had been beaten, and occasionally tortured, by irate jail guards and local sheriffs.

CORE's major activity was the Freedom Rides. Farmer had been on the first Freedom Ride back in 1947. He decided to run another, in May 1961. Segregation had been illegal on interstate buses since 1957. But the Supreme Court and the Interstate Commerce Commission had recently extended this ban to all the facilities involved in interstate transportation—the rest rooms, the lunch counters, the ticket offices, the waiting rooms.

Farmer and James Peck were the first to volunteer to take a bus ride into the South to test the recent rulings. With eleven other volunteers they left Washington on May 4, destination—New Orleans. There was no segregation on the buses; black and white sat side by side. In Charlotte, North Carolina, one of the group attempted a shoe-in and was promptly arrested. He had not intended to make a protest. His shoes simply needed a shine. At other stops along the way the remaining twelve Freedom Riders held shoe-ins in honor of their arrested colleague. In Rock Hill, South Carolina, there came the first brush with violence. Several demonstrators were beaten up. Among them was Albert Bigelow.

There was no trouble in Georgia. But in Anniston, Alabama, the bus was attacked and set on fire. Boarding another bus, the Freedom Riders reached Birmingham on Mother's Day. As they descended from the bus at the Trailways Station, they were clubbed down, beaten up, and severely kicked by a mob of hysterical white men. Peck was the most badly hurt. He spent several hours on an operating table at the Hillman Clinic. He suffered serious internal injuries, and it took fifty-three stitches to sew up the wounds in his face and head.

The Freedom Riders blamed the melee on the Birmingham commissioner of public safety, Eugene "Bull" Connor. But Connor held Mother's Day responsible. Most of his men were off duty that day, he maintained, visiting their mothers. No bus company was willing to carry the Freedom Riders any further. They flew from Birmingham to New Orleans, their bus journey abandoned.

Two weeks later the second Freedom Ride, involving mainly college students, was under way. When the students reached Montgomery, they were met by several hundred irate white men and women. They were beaten, clubbed, and kicked. One black student collapsed under a hail of blows from a baseball bat. Three black bystanders watching the riot unfold crumpled to the ground, streaming blood, their faces ripped open by flying bricks. They were then smashed about with a heavy garbage can as they sprawled helplessly on the sidewalk.

Only when the riot lost steam for want of fresh victims did the Montgomery police intervene. They fired several volleys of tear gas to disperse the crowd. As the acrid gas drifted through the downtown streets, it mingled with the smoke from the Freedom Riders' meager luggage which had been rifled and set on fire. Among the twenty who were taken to the hospital by ambulance was John Seigenthaler, a young Justice Department lawyer who had been sent by the Attorney General to make a report on what a Freedom Ride was like.

That afternoon 400 U. S. marshals arrived in Montgomery. They were under orders to maintain public order. The Freedom Riders, bandaged but showing the resilience of youth, appeared as honored guests at the First Baptist Church. Martin Luther King arrived to greet them and to introduce them to his excited, but apprehensive, congregation, who packed the church, occupying every pew, filling up the aisles. When night descended, so did a crowd of white people. They surrounded the First Baptist Church and raised threatening voices.

The black congregation several times sang what was by now the anthem of the civil rights movement, "We Shall Overcome." The whites worked up their anger to a murderous pitch. In between them and the church stood a slender ring of heavily outnumbered marshals. It was only with extreme difficulty that Robert Kennedy was able to persuade the governor of Alabama, John Patterson, to send units of the Alabama National Guard into Montgomery. Overawed and outnumbered, the mob dispersed in compliance with a proclamation of martial law in the city. King, the Freedom Riders, and the congregation were at dawn led safely from the church.

When the Freedom Riders resumed their progress several days later, the scene outside the Montgomery Trailways terminal was unprecedented in the annals of public transportation. More than 1,000 National Guardsmen lined the surrounding streets and patrolled nearby rooftops. The bus carrying the twelve Freedom Riders also carried seventeen reporters and a squad of rifle-toting soldiers. It was escorted on its way by twenty-two highway patrol cars, each carrying several armed troopers. Two battalions of National Guardsmen covered the front and rear of this convoy. Three U. S. Army reconnaissance aircraft and two helicopters patrolled the flanks. This implausible armada rolled along the road to Jackson at fifty miles an hour to the sounds of Caribbean calypso music.

The Freedom Rides led the Interstate Commerce Commission, under prompting from the Justice Department and the White House, to take an active part in enforcing its antisegregation rulings. Within the space of a few months in the summer of 1961 Jim Crow signs were removed from thousands of toilets, drinking fountains, waiting rooms, and ticket counters.

The Justice Department's show of strength at Montgomery had another salutary effect: outbreaks of violence at racial demonstrations dropped sharply. Freedom Riders were henceforth arrested rather than beaten up. But violence was not completely unknown. In November five black students—two coeds and three young men—arrived in McComb, Mississippi ("Camelia City of America"). They went to the lunch counter at the bus station and politely asked to be served. A crowd quickly formed at the bus station. To shouts of "Kill 'em! Kill 'em!" a dozen young white men hurled themselves at the five stolidly seated blacks, fists flying, scrambling over upturned tables and chairs to reach their quarry. The five fled from the bus station under a torrent of kicks and blows and found refuge in a nearby black hotel.

By the end of 1961 CORE had sent nearly a score of Freedom Rides into the South, bearing nearly 1,000 riders of both races. At the moment CORE was first among equals in the civil rights protest movement. And under CORE's tutelage, and that of SNCC, several thousand blacks, mainly high school and college students, had gone willingly to jail. Rather than being a means of putting the protesters on ice, this development amounted to a jail-in.

No matter how splenetic they were about race, there was no one in the South—well, almost no one—who would openly admit to defending inequality. What they were defending, they insisted, was racial *difference.*

That hardy perennial from the nineteenth century, scientific racism, was once more dragged out for the edification of the credulous. It retained the usual earmarks of a pseudoscience—shifting definitions, unexamined assumptions, tautology, conspicuous omission, slipshod experimentation. Nor had the objective altered one whit: to prove the innate inferiority of black people. Had they been as hopelessly inferior by nature as the racists maintained, however, it ought to have been very easy to prove it.

The most celebrated figure among the new scientific racists was no biologist or geneticist but a retired airlines executive who had once written a book about Theodore Roosevelt. Carleton Putnam had been trained as a lawyer. As a psychologist, anthropologist, biologist, and sociologist he was entirely self-taught. This did not dissuade him from pronouncing dogmatically on the work of eminent academics such as Franz Boas and Gunnar Myrdal. He blamed them for foisting on a credulous world the ridiculous notion that blacks were innately equal with whites. Putnam took as his mission in life the exposure of what amounted to a conspiracy among liberal intellectuals to pollute the blood of the white race and enfeeble it. He considered it highly revealing that both Boas had Myrdal were foreigners to America's shores.

Boas, Myrdal, and others could, in fact, no more prove the innate equality of whites and blacks in regard to intelligence. Controlled, dispassionate, and replicable studies of racial intelligences would be very difficult to perform under any circumstances. To attempt them in the mid-twentieth century, when the issue was so emotive, was simply impossible. And not only because they were so contentious. Intelligence testing was crude and inexact. But Putnam was nothing loath to commit himself on the issue of racial intelligence. He denied categorically in his masterwork *Race and Reason* that he was a racist. "Personally, I feel only affection for the Negro," he confessed.

Putnam in 1959 wrote to Eisenhower and Attorney General William Rogers to reveal to them the shocking Boas-Myrdal conspiracy and to give them his considered views on the Brown decision. For some reason the President and the Attorney General declined to enter into correspondence with him on these matters. His letters to them, however, were reproduced in newspapers throughout the South, for nothing, usually alongside an editorial which commended the author for his brilliance. In the North, the Putnam letters appeared as paid advertisements and often were not far removed from editorials which berated the author's stupidity. Some Northern newspapers, such as the *Washington Post* and the *Los Angeles Times*, flatly refused to accept the letters at any price.

Expanded into *Race and Reason*, Putnam's efforts produced a best-seller. The state of Louisiana purchased 5,000 copies for distribution in the public schools. Southern politicians praised it fulsomely. On October 26, 1961, the state of Mississippi celebrated "Race and Reason Day," and Putnam was feted at a banquet in Jackson by 500 leading citizens who had paid $25 each to dine with him. *Race and Reason* sold 150,000 copies— and never appeared on any list of best-sellers. Although it did not have much of a plot, it did not skip the most important best-selling ingredient, sex. But this interesting activity took some curious twists and turns under Putnam. When black men had intercourse with white women, the very foundations of Western civilization were riven with tremors. Yet when white men slept with black women, no evident harm was done to anyone or anything.

By the time *Race and Reason* appeared in 1961 the Citizens' Councils were a spent force. They were by this time so racked by factionalism that it is surprising that they retained any strength at all. And they were as helpless as the Communist Party when it came to collecting members' dues. In Louisiana the councils had become so raucous and disreputable, flirting openly with anti-Semitism, that they were severed from the parent body. In Alabama the Citizens' Councils were wrecked by the irresponsible antics of Asa "Ace" Carter. After the official council movement ejected him, he set up competing organizations of his own. In Georgia the councils were stubbornly independent. Only in Mississippi did they retain anything resembling their original impact. There they were nourished by large subsidies from the Mississippi Sovereignty Commission.

The councils continued to cling to their tatterdemalion hopes of one day becoming a force in national politics. And it is true that although they were principally concerned with race, they had in recent years cast a wider net. They attracted doctors who were eager to resist socialized medicine, business executives who were opposed to the labor movement, and small-town lawyers who were pursuing their own political ambitions.

In 1962 the councils broached their last notable initiative. They launched "Freedom Rides North." Several hundred unemployed blacks were put aboard Northern-bound buses clutching a one-way ticket and $50 for expenses. An especially favored destination was Hyannisport, Massachusetts. This was a tawdry attempt to embarrass the Kennedys. The first arrival was greeted by Edward Kennedy in a PR counterstroke. But then three dozen more blacks arrived. They all were homeless, nearly broke, unskilled, and uneducated. Hyannisport, Washington, New York, and the other places to which the councils were sending these poor wretches had nothing to offer but welfare, instead of the jobs and homes which cynical council organizers had promised awaited them. It was as cruel a stunt imaginable this side of physical violence. Those who organized it must have known that the only possible result of their venture was human misery. But they preferred to congratulate themselves on their cleverness, boasting that they had helped to rid the South of some of its "surplus" blacks while showing up the hypocrisy of the North.

In the fall of 1959 Little Rock had finally come to terms with reality. It desegregated the high schools. The real test of the doctrine of interposition came a year later, in 1960, when grade schools in New Orleans were scheduled to admit a handful of black children.

The main force behind the effort to integrate the New Orleans schools was the local Federal district judge, J. Skelly Wright. For four years the school board had refused to submit a desegregation plan. The judge drew up a plan of his own. He proposed to desegregate from the first grade up, one grade a year.

The Louisiana legislature immediately went into round-the-clock sessions to pass Interposition legislation. Governor Jimmie H. Davis (composer of "You Are My Sunshine") swore that he would go to prison before a single black child sat in a white classroom. Davis was bluffing. Leander H. Perez was a tougher proposition. Perez was an oil millionaire and the political boss of Plaquemines and St. Bernard parishes, close to New Orleans. He detested black people and made no secret of his feelings. It was Perez, not Davis, who led white resistance to desegregation in Louisiana.

The Citizens' Council of New Orleans was also spurred into action. It staged a score of impassioned public meetings. At one of them "a group of children, half of them in blackface, the others unpainted, were called on stage and instructed to kiss and neck with abandon, demonstrating 'the perils of the future.' "

On November 14, 1961, four black girls were enrolled in the first grade at two formerly all-white schools. The next day the streets of New Orleans were snarled by hundreds of rioters, who overturned and set fire to parked cars, attacked black passersby, and laid down a barrage of hurled bricks and bottles. The state legislature cut off appropriations to pay the salaries of the teachers at the two schools. The teachers reported for work every morning. The school board, however, decided to close the schools for two weeks to allow passions to cool. When the schools re-opened, there were crowds of white women at their gates, screaming like harpies and hurling abuse at tiny, frightened six-year-olds. They turned hysterical at the handful of white parents who continued to bring their children to the now-desegregated schools.

Before the school year ended in mid-1962, the state legislature had backed away from interposition. Judge Wright, the school board, and the Kennedy Administration made it clear that they would fight the issue out to the end. And no one, not even Governor Davis, was ready to go to jail for the sake of making a gesture.

The year 1962 brought the desegregation of the parochial schools of New Orleans. But in the fiefdom of Leander H. Perez the parochial schools remained as segregated as ever. When a few black students came in, all the white students walked out, without exception. They stayed out even after the blacks had been withdrawn. One of the schools involved was razed by a bomb blast. And Prince Edward County remained true to the shabby faith of massive resistance. The public schools had been closed in 1959. They were still closed four years later.

The brightest aspect of the ongoing struggle to enforce the Brown decision was probably the courage of the black children involved. Some were carefully chosen by black leaders to serve as pioneers. But this was far from being the rule. "Many of these pioneer children have not been hand-picked," reported Robert Coles, a psychiatrist who studied them closely, "or particularly able or bright—not natural leaders, chosen for that reason to lead their race into white schools." Some chose themselves, moved by bravado. Yet nearly all, including those who came from appallingly fragmented and unhappy homes, proved emotionally committed; they were determined not to fail.

"In my experience," said Coles, "even two- and three-year-old Negro children have already learned the indirection, the guile needed for survival. They have also learned their relative weakness, their need to be ready to run fast, to be alert and watchful. They have learned that white children, as well as adults, are big, strong and powerful."

Contrary to the popular view among white people, these children did not come from the homes of black militants. Most black people, moreover, were gradualists. Very few clamored for the complete and immediate integration of their children in white schools. They nearly always felt a deep apprehension about pushing the pace of change too rapidly for the good of their own children and their own community. In Charlotte, North Carolina, for example, the black community agreed that it would ask for the desegregation of one of the town's five white schools. But it intended in this to put enough black students into the one school to make it really integrated, not simply desegregated. The school board followed its own plan and desegregated all five schools at once, giving each a token handful of black pupils. This satisfied neither the black people nor the white people. But it headed off Federal intervention.

When one extrapolated from the pace of desegregation of Southern grade schools between 1954 and 1964, it appeared that all Southern grade schools would not be desegregated until A.D. 9256. The South had found a way to live with *Brown*—token compliance. So by 1963 the student of American society was treated to the fascinating spectacle of comparative calm descending on the schools of the South, while there was rapidly increasing anguish in the school districts of the liberal big cities of the North.

Black parents were as exercised over the schools as whites. Both sets of parents were angered by the poor educational standards in the schools their children attended, whether they were the same schools or not. White parents in the North, however, were also frightened that the influx of large numbers of lower-class black and Puerto Rican children was exposing their children to unusual hazards not normally considered part of secondary education—the juvenile stickup artist collecting other people's lunch money at the point of a knife, the adolescent drug peddler, the pubescent rapist. White parents who did not remove themselves from the city did the best they could to remove their children from the public schools. In 1963 it was the white faces in many a New York and Chicago classroom who represented the token presence. There were not enough white children left in many inner-city public schools for there to be genuine racial integration. All across the United States, when white parents these days talked about "the school problem," what they really meant was "the blacks in the school problem." Private schools and parochial schools had only to open their doors, they flourished.

The fears white parents entertained were far from being groundless. But they were often exaggerated. Integration, or desegregation, doubtless ruined some schools. But there is no reason to suppose that this was inevitable. Central High School in Kansas City was one of the first all-white schools to be desegregated in the wake of the first Brown decision. Until then it had never sent more than 15 percent of its students on to college. Very few won college scholarships. By the 1960s Central High was nearly 50 percent black. More than 40 percent of its graduates went on to college, and scores of them each year won college scholarships.

Among black parents in the North school integration was likely to be as important as it was in the South. "Having a white child sit next to my Negro child is no guarantee that mine will learn," conceded Isaiah Robinson, chairman of the Harlem Parents Committee. "But it is a guarantee that he will be taught." There was also a conviction among black parents that only when their children went to school with white children would those schools be properly supported. There was a certain naïveté to this view, however. The white children in the public schools of the inner cities were overwhelmingly those from working-class and lower-middle-class homes. Their parents were rarely articulate, well educated, prosperous, or highly organized. They were nearly as powerless as the black parents.

As their anxieties mounted, black parents began to demand transfer programs, which would make it possible for students to switch freely from school to school. When New York made such transfers available in

1961, however, those who made the most effective use of them were not black parents transferring their children to predominantly white schools but white parents taking their children out of predominantly black ones.

Looking for another panacea which would solve the difficulties of integrating Northern schools, black parents and white liberals began to canvass the possibilities of busing. This was a desperate expedient. No one really liked the idea. It was patently unfair to the children who were to be shuttled back and forth in an attempt to remedy a long history of injustice in which they had played no part at all. But it is nearly always the weak and the poor who have to pay the price of society's mistakes.

More than 7 million students were presently being taken by bus each day to elementary and secondary schools, mainly in rural and semirural districts. There were hundreds of school districts where busing accounted for a third of the annual budget. Busing as such was not a novelty. Here it was accepted as a harsh necessity imposed by distance. It was nevertheless disliked by parents. Nor were the bused students happy about starting life as commuters. There was also evidence which suggested that bused students did more poorly at school than students who walked there, and the longer the journey, the worse the academic performance. Inevitably, the students bused over long distances had the worst attendance records.

Unfortunately it appeared to be beyond the wit of anyone to be able to devise a better solution to the dilemma posed by de facto neighborhood segregation on the one hand and court-ordered school integration on the other.

After Autherine Lucy had been driven off the campus of the University of Alabama by a rampaging mob in 1956, the all-white colleges and universities of the South had been left untroubled for five years. A few half-hearted attempts were made to enroll a black student here and there. But none of these led anywhere. In January 1961, however, in the last days of the Eisenhower Administration, two very bright black teenagers from Atlanta, Charlayne Hunter and Hamilton Holmes, secured a court order which ordered the University of Georgia to grant them admission.

For eighteen months the university had being trying to concoct plausible reasons why these two academically superior students failed to qualify under its less-than-daunting admissions requirements. The state legislature wrung its hands over the threat to higher education posed by 2 black faces among 9,000 white ones. But here was no rural high school to be shut down and its students scattered. This was the alma mater of many a state legislator. It was the place where they wanted their own sons and daughters to be educated. On January 10 Charlayne Hunter and Hamilton Holmes enrolled at the university.

On the night of January 11, 500 to 600 hysterical students and off-campus riffraff laid siege to Charlayne Hunter's dormitory. The white girls in the dorm had until now been polite and somewhat diffident toward her.

But in response to the frenzy swirling around them they turned vicious and mean. The young gentlemen outside were chanting, "One, two, three, four. . . . We don't want no nigger whore." A hail of bricks, stones, and bottles shattered the dormitory windows. Exploding firecrackers seemed to fill the night air with sound of gunfire and the acrid smell of cordite. After the riot had run its uninspired course, the state police arrived. They led a weeping Miss Hunter from the campus. Both she and Hamilton Holmes were informed in the morning that they had been suspended from the University, "for your own safety." The rioters believed that they had succeded as the earlier mob had succeeded five years before at Tuscaloosa. They were wrong.

A week later Charlayne Hunter and Hamilton Holmes were back. They had a new court order. The university administration was ordered to protect them. They stayed on at Georgia until they were graduated in June 1963. Three months later Miss Hunter married a white journalism student she had met at Georgia, Walter L. Stoval III. This only went to prove, Southerners wisely told one another, what was bound to happen when blacks were allowed to study with whites. Charlayne and Walter Stovall decided to live in New York.

While the integration of the University of Georgia was moving toward its anticlimax, the state of Mississippi was the scene of lively events. It had as its governor a leading personal injury lawyer, Ross Barnett. He won election in 1960 on his third attempt. He succeeded by virtue of running the most fervently racist campaign of the half dozen contenders on the ballot. He found himself in charge of the poorest state in the Union, with an average personal income that was half the national average. Mississippi contributed less per capita to, and received more per capita from, the Federal government than any other state. Strictly speaking, patriotic Mississippi had contributed not so much as a dime to the nation's defense since World War II.

Poverty breeds paranoia. Instead of a front license plate, many cars carried a sign that read, MISSISSIPPI: MOST LIED ABOUT STATE IN THE UNION. With its rapidly shrinking population base, thanks to the eagerness of black people to get out, the state had lost two Representatives since 1940. It was a state whose people felt cornered and desperate.

In 1958 a young black man named Clennon King applied to the University of Mississippi for admission. He was forcibly committed to a mental hospital, to derisive laughter from whites. "Any nigger that tries to get into Ole Miss *must* be crazy."

The next year Clyde Kennard, a black ex-paratrooper, applied to the university. He had studied at the University of Chicago for three years. He returned to Mississippi after his father died to help his mother run the family chicken farm. In September 1959 he made a formal application at the Ole Miss campus in Oxford. He was turned away. Fifteen minutes later he was arrested for speeding. Kennard disregarded this veiled threat. He made another application. This time he was arrested as an accessory to the theft of three bags of chicken feed worth $25. The youth who was accused of stealing the chicken feed was not prosecuted. He was not even fired from his job, even though the victim of the alleged theft was his employer. Kennard was given a jail sentence of seven years. While in Parchman Penitentiary he was found to be suffering from cancer. He was taken from prison for an operation. On his return to prison the postoperative treatment his doctors prescribed was denied him. In the summer of 1963 Clyde Kennard died, at the age of twenty-nine.

But by this time there was a black student at Ole Miss, James Meredith, a slight, shortsighted ex-Air Force Staff Sergeant. Meredith's ordeal was not without cost. He emerged from it convinced that he was the agent of supernatural forces, a man who was infallible, and one of the toughest men in the world. Superman Meredith could match Mississippi self-delusion for self-delusion.

He returned to his home town of Kosciusko, Mississippi, after nine years in the Air Force, driving an air-conditioned Cadillac with Japanese license plates. He drove slowly past the police station so that they would know that he was back. "I returned to my home state," he declared, "to fight a war." He enrolled at Jackson State, an all-black college, while he pondered how to destroy white supremacy in Mississippi. The election of John Kennedy finally made the way clear, although by now Meredith was dangerously close to graduating at Jackson State. Days after Kennedy's Inauguration Meredith applied to enter the University of Mississippi for the spring semester starting February 6.

In his attempt to get into Ole Miss, Meredith turned to Medgar Evers, secretary of the Mississippi NAACP, for support. Evers was by all accounts a remarkable person. Walter Lord described him shortly after they met: "A wiry young man of immense energy, a quick smile and the most impressive set of teeth since Theodore Roosevelt. Sitting in his cluttered green office, practically welded to the telephone, he seemed involved in a million things all at once, and delighted to be in them all."

Evers had come back to Mississippi after wartime military service and went with five other young black men to vote in the 1946 elections. They were forcibly held away from the ballot box by a gang of gun-carrying white men. Evers joined the NAACP. He spent most of his life thereafter registering black people to vote. Some of his co-workers were tortured; some were murdered. Others fled the state. But Evers remained there, organizing, talking, investigating, registering, covering 40,000 miles a year, never showing the least concern for his own safety. When Meredith sought his help, Evers did not hesitate.

The University of Mississippi fought Meredith, Evers, and the NAACP in the courts for eighteen months. In those eighteen months, however, the Kennedy Administration, through the Justice Department, became wholly committed to securing Meredith's admission.

Barnett and Ole Miss administrators clung fondly to a belief that the government would back away from a showdown at the last moment on the eve of the 1962 fall elections. When this piece of wishful thinking began to fall apart, Barnett, who had seemed eager to go to prison in defense of segregation, suddenly lost his appetite for martyrdom. When he was indicted for contempt of court, in fact, the prospect appeared to fill him with dismay. But hoping to confront Meredith face to face, Barnett had himself appointed a deputy registrar at Ole Miss. Meanwhile, he had begun secret negotiations with the Justice Department for a face-saving formula which would allow him to back down from his stridently expressed, but no longer tenable, public position.

A new champion suddenly stepped onto this sorry stage—Major General Edwin A. Walker, USA (Ret.). With the crisis at Ole Miss coming to a head Walker appeared on radio station KNKH in Shreveport, Louisiana, to make an emotional appeal to the people of Mississippi: "It is time to move. We have talked, listened and been pushed around far too much by the anti-Christ Supreme Court. Rise to a stand beside Governor Ross Barnett. Now is the time to be heard. Ten thousand strong from every state. Rally to the cause of freedom. The battle cry of the Republic: Barnett, yes; Castro, no. Bring your flags, your tents and your skillets. It is time. Now or never. The time is when and if the President of the United States commits or uses any troops, Federal or state, in Mississippi. The last time in such a situation I was on the wrong side. That was in Little Rock, Arkansas, in 1957 and 1958. This time I am out of uniform and I will be there."

Barnett was trying, unknown to Walker, to arrange a little charade. He would stand in a doorway, heroically barring James Meredith's way. Then half a dozen Federal marshals would draw their handguns and point them at the brave governor of Mississippi. Whereupon, solely to prevent violence and bloodshed, Barnett would bow to this show of Federal force and would stand aside to let Meredith pass. Robert Kennedy rejected this script. He proposed a different compromise. Meredith would move onto the Oxford campus on Sunday evening, a day sooner than was expected, and Barnett could stay away. Unaware of Barnett's machinations, the students of Ole Miss were singing his praises:

> Never, never, never, No-o-o Never, never, never.
> We will not yield an inch of any field.
> Fix us another toddy, ain't a-yielding to nobody.
> Ross is standing like Gibraltar; he will never falter.
> Ask us what we say, it's To hell with Bobby K.
> Never shall our anthem go from Colonel Reb to Ol' Black Joe..

On the afternoon of Sunday, September 30, 1962, Meredith arrived almost unnoticed at the University of Mississippi campus in Oxford. The Citizens' Councils were making radio appeals for Mississippians to go to the governor's mansion and there to "form a human wall" to protect Ross Barnett from being kidnapped by Federal marshals. Then rumors began to spread that the marshals had arrived at Ole Miss. As night fell thousands of people streamed toward the campus, many of them carrying lead pipes, lengths of chain, rocks, and knives.

President Kennedy went on television to appeal to the people of Mississippi to accept the rule of law. It was too late. The riot had started.

At first the few score U.S. marshals on the campus were merely heckled ("Nigger lovers," "We don't want Bobby Kennedy") and occasionally jostled. But there was no undue difficulty in keeping control. Suddenly Ross Barnett ordered the state Highway Patrol, which was covering the entrances to the campus, to leave the scene. Within minutes the darkened university was swarming with men in rough workman's clothing. These were not simply malcontented students.

The marshals, most of whom were taken from the Border Patrol (that week the Texas-Mexico border was virtually unguarded), formed a line in front of the Lyceum, the main administration building. They very soon found themselves fighting to save their lives. The other targets of the mob's fury were newsmen. Two people were killed during the rioting, a twenty-three-year-old jukebox repairman who was killed by a sniper's bullet, and a French reporter from *Agence France-Presse* who was shot at close range in the shrubbery. A *Newsweek* reporter narrowly missed being murdered. Several other newsmen were severely beaten up.

The line of marshals braved repeated showers of bricks, bottles, birdshot, bullets, and stones which rained down out of the darkness. Each attack left several marshals prostrate on the ground or nursing fresh wounds. An attempt was made to shatter their line by driving a bulldozer into their ranks. It was halted by an act of great courage and daring. The marshals defended themselves by firing volley after volley of tear gas. Striding back and forth in the darkness beyond the range of the gas grenades could be seen the tall, slim figure of Major General Walker, resplendent in a large white Stetson, offering the rioters moral encouragement but little tactical advice.

The line of marshals began to waver after several hours of fighting. Their ranks were suddenly stiffened by the arrival of a troop of National Guard armored cavalry, sent under orders from the President. When the leading jeep screeched to a halt in front of the Lyceum, its windshield was decorated with six bullet holes.

At 1:30 on Monday morning the marshals ran out of tear gas. A score of them were out of the fight from serious injuries; one had a bullet in his throat. The marshals expected to be overrun at any moment. The prospect was set for hand-to-hand fighting, in which event the dead were likely to run into the dozens. As the mob gathered itself for the final triumphant rush, four buses drove onto the campus at high speed, and 200 airborne MPs jumed out with rifles in their hands and bayonets fixed. By dawn the rioters had melted away.

After a comparatively peaceful night's sleep James Meredith awoke to begin his first day as a student at the University of Mississippi. The rioters had never realized that he was only a few hundred yards from the Lyceum. Meredith noticed that the car which had brought him from Millington Naval Air Station on Sunday was now riddled with bullet holes and its windows were smashed. He and his guardians placed blankets over the shredded upholstery and proceeded toward the pockmarked administration building. There Meredith at last enrolled as a student at the University of Mississippi. At nine o'clock he went to his first class. Tears poured freely down his cheeks. But this was not from emotional release. It was the effect of the lingering tear gas.

In following weeks a new crop of license plate legends could be seen on cars in Mississippi: FEDERALLY OCCUPIED MISSISSIPPI. KENNEDY'S HUNGARY. BROTHERHOOD BY BAYONET. BEAT LI'L BROTHER. Defiant bumper stickers flourished. A turgid, mournful ballad celebrated what was by any measure the most serious clash of state and Federal power since the Civil War:

> They came rollin' down from Memphis
> And droppin' from the skies,
> With bayonets for our bellies,
> And tear gas for our eyes.
>
> Some resisted them with brickbats,
> While others ran and hid.
> Some tangled with the marshals;
> Who can blame them if they did?

But Mississippi had evidently had enough of violence and the disgrace that it brought. The focus of the struggle to integrate higher education in the South had shifted elsewhere, to Alabama. The University of Alabama seemed prepared to repeat the course of events which had disrupted and disgraced the University of Mississippi. The new governor of Alabama, George C. Wallace, appeared to have made it inevitable.

In 1958 he had lost the gubernatorial race to John Patterson, who had run a single-issue campaign—race. Following his defeat, Wallace informed his friends of his strategy for the 1962 gubernatorial election. "John Patterson out-nigguhed me. And boys, I'm not going to be out-nigguhed again." In 1962 his principal opponent was James "Big Jim" Folsom, formerly a friend of Wallaces's and also a former governor of Alabama. Folsom was currently drowning in alcohol. Wallace modified his campaign strategy slightly. He came out unequivocally against race mixin' and strong drink. Folsom might have won, however, had he not appeared on television so drunk that when he attempted to introduce his family, he could not remember his children's names.

Wallace concluded every campaign speech with a pointless promise: "As your governor I shall refuse to abide by any illegal Federal court order, even to the point of standing at the schoolhouse door in person." Taking office, Wallace delivered an Inaugural Address that was by turns mystical and segregationist. It contained several cryptic references to "the unit of one" and "the unit of many." He also had a deep interest in mongrels. And he concluded on this defiant note: "In the name of the greatest people that have ever trod this earth, I draw the line in the dust and toss the gauntlet before the feet of tyranny. And I say, Segregation now! Segregation tomorrow! Segregation forever!"

As governor, Wallace ran Alabama in Populist fashion. State revenues were spent almost entirely on schools, roads, and hospitals. Textbooks were provided free. A pioneering antipollution program was begun to clean up Alabama's streams and rivers. State welfare programs were rapidly expanded and benefits raised. On every issue but one Wallace was a man for whom a liberal could cast his or her vote without hesitation. But Wallace had vowed, "I'm gonna make race the basis of politics in this state, and I'm gonna make it the basis of politics in this country." For years afterward Wallace was still trying to make good that pledge and see how far it would carry him. Yet he proved to have no more desire to languish in a Federal prison than fellow Governor Ross Barnett.

In June 1963 a Federal court ordered the University of Alabama to admit two black students to the summer session. Wallace was specifically ordered to avoid "physically interposing his person to block the Negroes." The Administration showed that it had learned its lesson at Ole Miss. This time there were hundreds of paratroopers waiting next to dozens of helicopters at Fort Benning, Georgia, little more than an hour's flying time from Tuscaloosa. The campus was cleared of outsiders by court order. University officials and community leaders were drawn into the scenario by earnest young Justice Department lawyers. A force of 300 marshals was immediately to hand, but stayed discreetly out of sight. The short, dark, moonfaced Wallace stood in the doorway of the administration building and read a short, bombastic proclamation while several marshals, the two students, and Assistant Attorney General Nicholas Katzenbach politely waited for him to finish. Wallace stood aside, and the two black students went in to be enrolled. There was now no segregated college or university left in the South.

Wallace, however, continued to interfere with integration of the public schools. In the fall he sent the Alabama National Guard to surround several schools which were scheduled to be desegregated. The President invoked his powers as Commander in Chief and sent the Guardsmen home.

Through the racial confrontations of these years moves the shadow of Martin Luther King, Jr. King was a tragic figure, cast in the mold of classic Greek drama—the great man with the flawed character. His was a life devoted to moral ends, yet he repeatedly betrayed his wife. He counseled direct action, but in a crisis his own nerve was liable to desert him. Most of all, however, was the aura of doom which apppeared to cling to him. His presence was huge, yet streaked with the deepest pessimism. As one observer wrote after meeting him, "An air of incipient martyrdom, of precariousness and fragility, hangs over him."

King loathed any kind of unpleasantness; he was by nature shy, diffident, and sensitive. One reason why he chose to remain a Southern black leader was that he had no stomach to challenge the NAACP and the Urban League for the loyalty of Northern blacks. Before 1963 he made no attempt to become a national black leader. Nor was he ever comfortable about making the grand gesture. He was fiercely rebuked by young black activists for not taking a Freedom Ride. But among his natural constituency, the churchgoing black people of the South, his position was unassailable. When a local black community body sent a Macedonian call to the SCLC, King never failed to respond. Usually within a few days he would appear in person to organize, to galvanize, and to offer his person.

"I got on my marching shoes!" he would exult to a packed, excited congregation in a local church. Shouts of joy would come back in response to this declaration. "I woke up this morning with my mind stayed on freedom," he would shout. "Preach!" came the response. "I ain't going to let nobody turn me around!" Someone in the congregation would shout back, "Let's march, brother!" "If the road to freedom leads through the jailhouse," King would say evenly, "then, turnkey, swing wide the gates!" his voice rising with each word. The congregation would shout, "Amen" and "Praise the Lord!" He would look down seriously, studying this face here, that face there. "Some of you are afraid," he would say. "That's right," they admitted, "that's right." "And some of you are contented. But if you won't go"—their protesting voices mingled with King's own—"don't you hinder me!" The organ would break gently into the strains of "We Shall Overcome." Hesitantly at first, then with rapidly growing power and feeling, the simple melody would be taken up. To the swelling chords from the organ King would hurl his defiance at an imperfect world. "We will march nonviolently. We shall force this nation, this city, this world to face its own conscience." "Oh, Lord!" they cried. "We will make the God of Love that is in the white man triumph over the Satan of segregation that is in him." "Yes, we will!" they shouted in agreement. "The struggle is not between black and white." "No, it isn't!" "It's between good and evil!" "That's right, that's right!" "And when good and evil have a confrontation, good will win!" "Yes, Lord." "For God is not dead. I know because I can feel Him. . . . " And here they would complete the line for him, knowing it well from an old black spiritual . . . "deep in my soul," they shouted back. And then he would lead them outside, domestics and pastors, garbage collectors and college graduates, arm in arm, to face the hard-faced policemen, the fire hoses, the snarling dogs, the beatings, the clubs and the tear gas, and, for many of them, the rest of the night in a jail cell. From 1959 through 1963 this scenario was played out in dozens of small Southern towns. But in 1962, when King tried it on a large scale for the first time, in Albany, Georgia, he was roundly defeated.

King did not so much choose Albany as stumble upon it. Two young SNCC workers had tried to organize a protest against the race-baiting style of news reporting which graced the *Albany Herald*. As a result, the Albany Movement was formed. It took for its model the Montgomery Improvement Association. A Freedom Ride was run from Atlanta to Albany. A sit-in was mounted at the train station. During these demonstrations dozens of people were arrested. King received a Macedonian call for help. The day after his arrival in Albany he lead a march through the streets.

But his mind was fixed on another tactic. Until now mass action had meant organizing 300 or 400 demonstrators. King decided to go for an unprecedented (in the United States) leap in magnitude. He would organize thousands of demonstrators. Within two weeks he had sent thousands of people, young and old, into the streets. He had filled the jails to overflowing. He had also brought a revolution in demands. Until now civil rights protesters had demanded comparatively modest, concrete gains—integrated public facilities, the right to vote, better schools. King started demanding white recognition of the entire black community. He demanded that local government hire sizable numbers of black for responsible jobs, the creation of permanent biracial commissions, regular and serious consultations with black community bodies, and unbiased reporting of racial affairs in the press.

Week after week for most of 1962 King could be found organizing and leading mass marches on the Albany city hall, the public library, the parks, the swimming pools, and the *Herald*. The Albany police responded to this new and unexpected leap in magnitude by refusing to be panicked. They arrested the demonstrators for illegal assembly and conducting unlawful parades. But they made the arrests with remarkable restraint and good humor. The Albany chief of police, Laurie Pritchett, was no gimlet-eyed, malicious caricature of a Southern sheriff; instead, he was affable, easygoing, and fair-minded. The Justice Department watched Albany closely. But it made no move to intervene.

In August 1962 King gracefully accepted defeat. No failure, however, was ever more public. Television had covered the events in Albany so doggedly that in Georgia the three national networks were known as the Negro Broadcasting Company, the Colored Broadcasting System, and the Afro Broadcasting Corporation. King sensibly refused to brood over this defeat. He turned his attention elsewhere. With the instincts of a born commander of men he used the lessons of a defeat to prepare the way for a far more important victory. King decided to take on the most dangerous and the most segregated big city in America—Birmingham, Alabama.

In 1963 its population of 350,000 was composed almost equally of blacks and whites. Despite this—perhaps because of it—Birmingham was unyielding on segregation. "Whites and blacks still walk the streets," reported Harrison Salisbury. "But the streets, the water supply and the sewer system are about the only public facilities they share. . . Telephones are tapped, or there is fear of tapping. Mail is opened. Sometimes it does not reach its destination. The eavesdropper, the informer, the spy, have become a fact of life. Volunteer watchmen stand guard 24 hours a day over some Negro churches. Jewish synagogues have floodlights for the night, and caretakers." To blacks, it was the city of "Bombingham." And the homicide rate was so high that it was dubbed by journalists "The Murder Capital of the World." But city officials preferred to call it "The Magic City," in recognition of its extremely rapid growth early in the century. And incongruously in light of the frequency with which the churches there were attacked, Birmingham had the highest ratio of churches to population of any city in the United States.

Birmingham gave up its professional baseball team rather than allow it to play integrated teams in the International League. The Metropolitan Opera no longer traveled to Birmingham because blacks were relentlessly barred from the Municipal Auditorium; some of the Met's top singers these days were black. Rather than comply with court orders to desegregate its parks and swimming pools, Birmingham closed them down.

In the vanguard of the last-ditch defenders of segregation stood Eugene Theophilus Connor, whom everyone called Bull. The jowly, thickset police commissioner had a baleful countenance partly because he wore a glass eye. In his youth he had been employed to bellow out baseball ticker readings in a poolroom.. That experience established his speaking style for the rest of his life. He had become a local celebrity by serving as a perfervid and highly ungrammatical baseball commentator back when Birmingham still had its team. Largely on the strength of this celebrity he had run for public office and been elected. Nor had the old habits been left behind. He once announced that it was his responsibility as police commissioner to make sure that "Nigras and whites will not segregate together" in public places. This was entertaining enough in its time. But the South was changing, and so was Birmingham. By 1963 the white people of the city had become tired of Bull. He ran for mayor and lost heavily. He was a lame-duck commissioner of public safety, hanging onto his job while the city government was being reorganized, and Birmingham was ripe for change.

Or so it appeared to the Reverend Fred Lee Shuttlesworth, the forceful young head of the local SCLC affiliate, the Alabama Christian Movement for Human Rights. To most people, including most of Martin Luther King, Jr.'s aides, Birmingham was as unyielding as ever. But Shuttlesworth persuaded King that this was the place, and now was the time.

In retrospect, King decided that in Albany he had scattered his forces over too broad a front. In Birmingham the demonstrators concentrated their protest on the white-owned businesses downtown. Their first set of targets was the half dozen stores with lunch counters. King and his assistants scheduled the protest demonstrations to begin on Easter Sunday, 1963. Easter is the second-busiest shopping period of the year, after Christmas.

On the Wednesday between Palm Sunday and Good Friday King, his closest assistant, the Reverend Ralph D. Abernathy, and Fred Shuttlesworth, appeared with the blind singer Al Hibbler at a rally in a black neighborhood. They declared their intention to lead a march on Good Friday. They asked if there were 250 volunteers who were prepared to go to jail for at least five days. "Who'll go to jail with me and Martin and Al Hibbler?" asked Abernathy at the end of a rousing peroration. Scores of people stepped forward eagerly, from tiny children to gray haired septuagenarians, hands upraised. Al Hibbler led them in several fervently sung choruses of "I'm on My Way to Freedomland."

On Good Friday King, usually dapper but now dressed in work shirt and blue jeans, led his hymn-singing volunteers into the streets of Birmingham. They were met by Bull Connor, hundreds of policemen, a score of snapping police dogs, and firemen wielding hoses so powerful that they could strip the bark from an oak tree. That first day King, Abernathy, Shuttlesworth, and Hibbler were arrested, in company with 50 of their marchers. Although the leaders were in jail, the marches continued unabated. No sooner was one group arrested than another took to the streets to protest their arrest. So it continued, day after day.

After a week in jail King was released on a bond of $300. He was then free to open the second phase of his campaign. He made the biggest gamble of his career. He decided to send what amounted to a children's army out to face the high-pressure fire hoses, the dogs, and the police batons. Had any of these children been killed or seriously injured, the responsibility would have been squarely on his shoulders and his conscience. And the death of a child might easily have stopped the protest movement or at least discredited it.

Nevertheless, he spent two weeks recruiting children aged six to sixteen. They were given some rudimentary training in local churches on how to protect their heads, eyes, and genitals. They were taught to resist provocation. They were organized in units from the size of a platoon (50) to the size of a battalion (750). In all, there were 6,000 children who were ready to march.

They debouched from the churches, singing "We Shall Overcome." The police arrested them by the dozen, by the score, finally in the hundreds. And still they kept marching from the churches. The police ran out of patrol wagons and had to commandeer school buses. On the first day of the children's crusade one group almost reached its goal, the steps of city hall, failing by a mere fifteen feet. By nightfall there were 959 children in the Birmingham jail.

The next day the police did not wait for the protesters; they set an ambush for them. Five hundred black people tried to leave a church and found that the police had them besieged. In the surrounding streets hundreds of other black demonstrators were being clubbed to the ground. Some were savaged by the dogs. Fire hoses sent black youngsters spinning on their backs in the streets. A nation which had followed recent events in Birmingham with grim interest was shocked by what it saw now. Television brought them unforgettable scenes of white men, their faces flushed and twisted into expressions of hatred, zealously attacking unarmed children and their mothers.

The children who were already in jail were kept standing for hours on end in pouring rain. Girls who asked for aspirin were given strong laxatives instead, then placed in cells which had no toilets. Other girls were forced to scrub filthy corridors on their hands and knees, equipped only with toothbrushes. But with the jails filled to overflowing the police stopped making arrests. They concentrated instead on dispersing the marchers.

King now launched the third phase of his plan. He sent his marchers into the streets several thousand strong. Heavily outnumbered, physically tired, and sensing impending defeat, the police lashed out with renewed fury. Every clash now seemed liable to lead to massive bloodshed. Connor took fright and at last admitted in effect that the situation was beyond his control: he called on Wallace for help. The governor promptly sent almost the entire Alabama Highway Patrol into Birmingham.

There was little doubt among any of those involved in the street skirmishes that a bloodbath was in the making. At this point the Justice Department made a last-minute effort to reduce the murderous tensions in the city. The biggest business in Birmingham was United States Steel. Federal officials persuaded the steelmen to use their influence with the city's white establishment to urge it to negotiate with King. Robert Kennedy at the same time used his influence with King to urge him to accept this chance to negotiate with the city establishment. The UAW and the National Maritime Union stepped forward to provide bail money for the hundreds of demonstrators in jail.

A four-point peace formula was agreed upon: customers' facilities in downtown stores were desegregated; the stores would hire black sales assistants and clerks; all jailed demonstrators were to be released; biracial committees were created to remedy black grievances.

Irate whites attempted to sabotage this settlement. A bomb destroyed the home of King's brother, the Reverend A. D. King, but fortunately injured no one. Another bomb blew up the A. G. Gaston Motel, in an attempt to assassinate King, who was staying there. Irate blacks responded to these outrages by rioting in the streets, smashing store windows, and setting fire to parked cars. Two people were stabbed during the melee, and policemen and firemen were attacked.

The rioters were not the neatly dressed, well-behaved protesters who had trooped out of the churches to go to jail. Here was no band of young idealists ready to turn the other cheek. This was a mob of angry, frustrated lower-class black men needing only an excuse and the cover of darkness to seek revenge on a society which despised them. Had the riot not been quickly halted, there would have been corpses littering the streets. King and Abernathy defused it by touring the bars and poolrooms in the worst black neighborhoods at dawn. King diffidently apologized for taking their attention away from their pool games and beer. But then he became stern and commanding. He delivered a terse and emphatic sermon on the stupidity of violence. His sincerity, his presence, and his fame overawed them. After that Abernathy, using a pool cue to keep time, led these unhappy young men in singing "We Shall Overcome." When darkness fell, the city braced itself for another outburst of violence. But there was an uneasy peace, and it held.

Birmingham remained a dangerous place, however. Its importance was that here the conscience of millions of white Americans had been deeply stirred. That was the complete vindication of King's strategy and victory enough. He had proved that the most segregated city in America could be pushed and hauled into an accomodation with its black population.

Unhappily this and other positive developments were clouded by bloodshed. Racial confrontations had raised passions to a killing pitch.

There were cowards skulking in the bushes, waiting to gun down men who were unarmed and unprotected. The 1950s had been the decade of the character assassin. The 1960s were turning into the decade of the sniper.

While Bull Connor and his men were wrangling in the streets with black children, a white substitute postman from Baltimore, William L. Moore, aged thirty-five, set off from Chattanooga on a Freedom Walk into Mississippi. He bore a wild hope that he would be able to call on Ross Barnett and make him see sense. Moore pushed a supermarket cart carrying his spare clothing, his toiletries, and handmade signs which read, "Equal Rights for All—Mississippi or Bust" and "Eat at Joe's —Both Black and White." On April 23, 1963, Moore crossed from Tennessee into Alabama. His feet were already swollen and blistered. He sat down beside United States Highway 11 and took off his shoes to nurse his feet. From the underbrush less than fifty yards distant someone fired at him with a .22-caliber rifle. The bullet struck him in the head, killing him instantly.

Less than two months later, on June 11, just as Birmingham was returning to normal life, Medgar Evers, who had been called "the Negro most feared by the segregationists of Mississippi," returned home at midnight from a mass meeting at a nearby church. When he bent to open his front door, a bullet fired from across the street struck him below the right shoulder blade, passed through his body and shattered the front window of the house. Evers collapsed in his doorway, dying from his wound, while his wife and three children rushed to the door.

The funeral parade in Jackson degenerated into a riot. Angry blacks roamed the streets, crying, "We want the killer! We want the killer!" A hail of rocks, bottles, and bricks rained down on the police, who began to draw their guns. Suddenly a young Justice Department lawyer, John Doar, walked into the middle of the street separating the black rioters from the white policemen. He risked bullets from one side and brickbats from the other, but Doar stood his ground and urged the rioters to stop disgracing the memory of Medgar Evers and sullying the cause to which he had dedicated his life. An anonymous black teenager ran into the street to stand beside Doar and share his fate. As if thunderstruck, the rioters desisted at a stroke.

By order of the President, Medgar Evers was given a soldier's funeral. He was buried at Arlington with full military honors. His murderer was apprehended. He proved to be Byron de La Beckwith of Greenwood, Mississippi.* Around Greenwood he was known as Delay, and he "talked nigra" incessantly. Delay was a tobacco salesman, a member of the Sons of the American Revolution, and one of the most extreme racists in a very racist town. But the more he "talked nigra," the more tobacco it helped him sell; it was that kind of place, and he was that kind of man. He was convicted of murdering Medgar Evers. He went to prison for two years.

---

*The Beckwiths were an old Delta family. But Byron had by chance been born on the West Coast when his mother was visiting there. For the past thirty-eight years he had lived in Greenwood. But the Jackson *Clarion-Ledger* announced his arrest with this headline: *Californian is Charged with Murder of Evers.*

Only hours before Evers was murdered the President had gone on television to talk to the nation about civil rights. Until this moment he had never appeared to be moved by this issue, unlike Robert Kennedy. But this time the President spoke with unmistakable sincerity and fervor. He had at last seen that this was not a political issue to be weighed carefully but a moral issue of the first importance. It might have to be resolved bit by bit. But there was no more urgent item of national business. One speech does not, of course, make a convert. But for once the Kennedy reserve was absent. Much of what he said was extemporized. His conviction was beyond a peradventure.

The next day he submitted to Congress the most sweeping civil rights legislation since Reconstruction. He wanted a ban on discrimination in public facilities (mainly hotels and restaurants), the Justice Department to be allowed to act on its own initiative in pursuing the desegregation of public schools, and Federal authorities to be granted wide-ranging powers for the protection of voting rights. The most contentious section of the Kennedy bill was Title II, which affected public accommodation. The Administration tried to make it acceptable to Congress by excluding small establishments (referred to in Congressional debates on the bill as "Mrs. Murphy's boardinghouse"). But Congress still found it very hard to swallow.

Blacks found the bill wanting (inevitably). But they acknowledged that it provided a wider range of desegregation measures than any legislation that would have been conceivable before 1961. To a considerable extent this legislation represented the fruits of the protest movement since the day when Joseph McNeill was turned away from the Greensboro bus terminal's lunch counter.

Bayard Rustin suggested organizing a massive march on Washington to support the bill. This was an idea first broached by A. Philip Randolph back in 1940 to demand a national Fair Employment Practices Commission. Randolph was still, as he had been then, the head of the only important black union, the Brotherhood of Sleeping Car Porters. He was inclined to be arrogant and aloof ("St. Philip Randolph"). He had a disconcerting tendency to flit from one project to another, losing interest long before matters had been carried to fruition. Yet his prestige remained so high that when he agreed with Rustin that a march should be organized and issued a call for the realization of his own twenty-three year-old dream, he received an outpouring of enthusastic support from nearly every black and civil rights organization in America.

The March on Washington was called for August 28, 1963. There was deep trepidation in the capital as to what might develop when 250,000 mainly black demonstrators assembled in what was in spirit largely a Southern city at a time when feelings concerning race were running high. A single incident could lead to a disaster. Yet the Administration was by now so far involved in the struggle that it was unthinkable for it to do anything but cooperate with the marchers.

When they arrived in Washington, they descended on the Reflecting Pool, chanting, "Pass that bill! Pass that bill! Pass that bill!" To the tens of millions who followed the events of that day on television and to most of those at the scene (25 percent of them white), it was a joyous and thrilling occasion.

But matters were not as harmonious as they appeared. James Farmer preferred to spend the day in a Louisiana jail repeatedly refusing to be bailed out. He did not consider the March on Washington sufficiently militant to justify leaving his cell. Up on the speakers' platform John Lewis of SNCC was busy rewriting his speech to meet the objections of Patrick A. O'Boyle, the Catholic Archbishop of Washington. He had seen Lewis's proposed remarks and threatened to walk off the platform if Lewis uttered them. Under intense pressure from the other speakers Lewis removed his more extreme observations. He nevertheless criticized police brutality, and the most he could say in favor of Kennedy's proposed legislation was: "We support this bill with great reservations, because it is too little and too late." When he turned away from the microphones, the other black speakers reached to shake his hand. The white speakers were staring intently at the clouds passing overhead.

The sweltering heat and humidity left many of the marchers inert on the grass or listlessly sitting on the rim of the Reflecting Pool, paddling their feet in the tepid water. They became listless and speaker followed speaker and cliché followed cliché. But finally there came Martin Luther King, Jr. If the March was Randolph's vision, its voice was King's.

For six years he had been polishing one particular speech in his writings and public appearances. By now it did not contain a wasted word or an oratorical effect which had not been proved repeatedly. Yet King delivered the definitive version of the speech with an exquisite balance between the ease that comes from practice and the emotion that comes from freshness. To the vast majority of those who listened to him the result was one of the most thrilling public utterances of the postwar.

King's address within fifteen minutes transformed an amiable, elephantine attempt at lobbying into a historic event. The success of his speech was not to be judged by its impact on the blacks who were there but on the whites who were not. In this electric moment Martin Luther King, Jr., galvanized the conscience of the white majority. He began by surveying the century that had passed since the Emancipation Proclamation. And over and over he intoned, "One hundred years later. . . " Each time he found that nothing much had changed. He termed the promises of human dignity and equality in the Declaration of Independence and the Constitution "a sacred obligation" which had proved to be, for black Americans, a bad check—"a check which has come back marked 'insufficient funds.' " This thrust brought the crowd to its feet roaring its agreement.

King praised the "veterans of creative suffering," the veterans of the protest marches, the sit-ins, the Freedom Rides, the jail-ins, and he appealed to them: "Go back to Mississippi, go back to Alabama, go back to Georgia, go back to Louisiana, go back to the slums and ghettos of our Northern cities, knowing that somehow this situation can and will be changed." Then he began to invoke the theme of his short address: "I have a dream." It rolled out rhythmically, melodiously, yearningly, and each time it served to introduce a vision of racial justice and social harmony expressed in straightforward, specific images. King's vision was at one and the same time Utopian and believable, attainable but elevating. It would not be realized easily or quickly. Much of the nobility of the aims he held out arose from the frank acceptance that it would be hard to achieve them. And when King finished speaking, there was a tingling along the spine and scalp. He found himself looking down upon a sea of upturned faces, many of them shiny with tears.

An hour later, at the White House, the President greeted the March leaders warmly. He praised the "deep fervor and the quiet dignity" the marchers had shown.

Little more than two weeks later, on Sunday September 15, Birmingham's Sixteenth Street Baptist Church, one of the most active churches during the protests back in the spring, was swarming with black children attending Sunday school. Shortly before 10:30 A.M. a powerful explosion rocked the building. Walls and ceilings crashed down. Lying in the rubble and brick dust lay nearly twenty badly injured children and four little girls, aged eleven to fourteen, who were dead.

When news of this outrage spread through the city, embittered, grieving black people rushed into the streets and engaged in rock-throwing clashes with crowds of working-class whites. The police cleared the blacks from the streets by firing shotgun blasts over their heads. But one black youth of sixteen was killed by being shot in the back by shotgun fire. Another black youth riding his bicycle was murdered by a gunshot fired at point-blank range from a passing car.

The bombing of the Sunday school was the fifty-first racial bombing Birmingham had suffered since the war. Not one of the fifty preceding blasts had led to an arrest and conviction. But Bombingham had no monopoly on bomb outrages. Between January 1956 and July 1963 not a single month had gone by without a racial bombing somewhere in the eleven states of the Old Confederacy.

The year 1963 was the high point of the civil rights protest movement. There were civil rights marches, rallies, sit-ins, boycotts, and picket-lines in at least 115 Southern cities. More than 20,000 people went to jail. But with this peak of racial protest there also went a dozen racial killings connected with the protests and thirty-five race-connected bombings.

Far from intimidating the protest movement, the killings and bombings spurred it to ever-greater militancy. As the civil rights movement became a rallying force among the black working class and the black unemployed, it began to drift away from nonviolence. The rioting of blacks was derisory when compared with the violence inflicted on blacks by whites. But the readiness of lower-class blacks to fight back, to riot and rampage was dismaying to leaders such as Martin Luther King, Jr.

The influx of lower-class blacks into the civil rights movement brought another change: civil rights organizations became almost entirely black in leadership, if not in financial support. Henceforth the civil rights movement was characterized by black leadership, a truly mass following and a militant style.

The identification with African liberation movements merged with this militancy. During a debate in the UN General Assembly in February 1961 over the murder in the Congo of Patrice Lumumba, some sixty black men and women raced into the chamber and attacked startled UN guards to bloodcurdling screams of "Lumumba!" The ensuing brawl lasted less than fifteen minutes, but it was broadcast live on telvision. White viewers stared in open mouthed disbelief.

As blacks turned increasingly militant, whites began to fear them. And this was so even though their consciences had been touched. On the other hand, blacks never lost their distrust of whites, as young whites who marched and picketed with them discovered to their confusion and un-happiness. By the time of the March on Washington, the most integrated public action in American history, whites were barely tolerated within the various black civl rights groups. With growing success and self-confi-dence the hostility which blacks had contained for centuries at last burst its bonds. It was inevitably turned against the white people nearest to hand, and this was so even though they were marching, singing, and pro-testing alongside blacks for racial justice. At civil rights rallies in Harlem white supporters were not even allowed to enjoy such simple delights as passing the collection bucket. They were baffled, their feelings were hurt, and many of them longed desperately to be accepted by blacks. They took up black slang, and in 1963 words such as "wasted," "busted, " "nitty-gritty," and "fox" were spreading rapidly among white teenagers and college students.

Among most white people there was an ambivalent mood. Blacks had a moral right to decent jobs, decent housing, and a chance to get ahead. Hardly anyone disputed that. But whites had a deep personal aversion to close contact with black people. Nor was there much support for legisla-tion which would enforce equality. Most white people clung to old stereo-types (blacks smelled, blacks laughed a lot.) Nearly half the white people questioned in a major poll believed that blacks were inherently less intelli-gent than whites.

Following the March on Washington, the Administration's civil rights bill made slow progress on Capital Hill. Passions in the South remained high. In Thomasville, Georgia, a movie theater showing PT 109 put an ad-vertisement in the local paper to entice people to see it: "See the Japs al-most get Kennedy." Among black people, however, he was admired more than any President since Lincoln. Recent years had brought a change both in the country's conscience and its public commitments. An elderly laundry worker in Detroit expressed the prosaic and concrete terms in which blacks approached the issue of racial justice: "He [Ken-nedy] has done more for the Negroes than any President I know. He forced Wallace to get away from that door."

Americans had long suffered from an uneasy conscience over race. But for nearly all their history they had avoided facing the issue squarely. The Civil War was the first grand exception. The civil rights movement of a century later was the second.

39

Endings and Beginnings

America was unique in that in no other country did every important social problem eventually find its way into the courts. As a result, legal thought both as one of the intellectual pillars of Western civilization and as a powerful instrument in social development evolved more imaginatively and responsively in the United States than anywhere else. The law was actively involved in the struggle to create a better society, and this had been so since the turn of the century. The reformist impulses of the Warren Court were not a break with the past but the flowering of a tradition.

In the postwar the Supreme Court was heavily involved in the struggle for racial justice, the efforts to improve criminal law, the intervention of government to secure individual rights and dignities, the domestic Cold War, the effort to protect individual privacy against the depredations made possible by advanced technology, the defense of individual conscience, the reform of state and local government.

For most of the postwar the Court tended to be deeply divided on important issues, and this remained true under the Kennedy Administration. After the new President had appointed two Associate Justices, Arthur Goldberg and Byron R. White, they often wound up on opposite sides of a decision. Throughout the early 1960s the Court turned out a remarkably high percentage of five to four rulings.

The liberalism of the Warren Court was usually exaggerated in the press and elsewhere. Some of its important rulings were markedly illiberal, and the Chief Justice himself was often to be found in disagreement with Justices Black and Douglas. Following the attempts in 1958 and 1959 to curb the Court by Congressional action, its decisions in cases involving subversion showed a falling off in reforming zeal. In other areas, however, the Court continued to act boldly.

Since the war the Court had been petitioned repeatedly and in vain to rule on apportionment in state elections. But until 1960 nearly every state was undisturbed in its cynical violation of its own and the United States Constitution. In 1961 the Court issued a writ of certiorari to bring before it a Tennessee case, *Baker* v. *Carr*, and the next year Tennessee was ordered to stop violating its own laws, which called for reapportionment every ten years. Tennessee's state politicians had put themselves above the law since 1900. Matters were not much better in most other states. *Baker* v. *Carr* corrected a long-standing violation of fundamental justice by persons sworn to maintain the integrity of the law. This decision sent tremors of dismay throughout rural America and the South. The Court's ruling of one-man, one-vote was at least as important in the long term as the Brown decision. It meant that the urban areas would for the first time enjoy something approximating their proper place in state legislatures. At a stroke a century of social change caught up with state government, and offered it a chance to be revitalized. At the very least this was an important step in making sure that the world's leading democracy remained democratic and did not fall into the habit of allowing officeholders and vested interests to ignore the Constitution.

A few months after *Baker* v. *Carr* the Court handed down another decision which fanned widespread resentment—*Engel* v. *Vitale*. The New York State Board of Regents had composed a "nondenominational" prayer to be said by schoolchildren at the beginning of each school day: "Almighty God, we acknowledge our dependence on Thee, and we beg Thy blessing upon us, our parents, our teachers and our country." School boards in other states adopted it. It struck exactly the desired insipid note. The ACLU, however, found it unpalatable. Jewish parents found it offensive. Methodists found it too vague. Lutherans protested that it made no mention of Christ. In 1959 the parents of five children challenged the prayer's legality. Under what power, they asked, were bureaucrats authorized to compose prayers to be recited on tax-financed property? The Supreme Court ruled that the prayer was unconstitutional.

Protestants and Catholics alike were aghast. Prayer in the schools became the second most contentious issue in education, after desegregation. And much as Eisenhower had accepted the Brown decision without public comment, so Kennedy accepted this decision and refused to say anything about it. But Eisenhower had been reviled by liberals for his silence; Kennedy's silence raised not a whisper of protest that he was being cowardly or was failing to provide leadership.

In 1963, in *Abingdon School District* v. *Schemp* / *Murray* v. *Curlett* the Court banned the reading of Bible passages as part of religious exercises in the public schools. To outraged parents and politicians here was the irrefutable proof that the atheistic Supreme Court had let Communism into the schools and forced God out. The House failed by a narrow margin to amend an appropriations bill so as to purchase "a copy of the Holy Bible for the personal use of each Justice." A motion to have "In God We Trust" prominently inscribed above the Speaker's desk was unanimously approved. There were 146 attempts, in House and Senate, to amend the Constitution to allow prayer in the public schools.

The Court was remaking criminal justice, usually to the consternation of police and prosecutors, by raising the standards of local and state criminal law to the much more exacting standards of the Federal law. In 1961 the Court ruled, in *Mapp* v. *Ohio*, that evidence seized illegally could not be used in criminal prosecutions. It imposed a stringent rule on the use of confessions, a tacit acknowledgment that many confessions had in the past involved coercion. *Mapp* flatly invalidated any confession in which intimidation could be shown to have played a part.

The year 1963 brought another landmark case, *Gideon* v. *Wainwright*, which offered a remarkable example of how the Court worked and how far it was prepared, under Warren, to go in the effort to secure justice for the poor, the obscure, the uneducated, and the defenseless. In 1962 the Court received a petition *in forma pauperis*, from one Clarence Earl Gideon, Prisoner #003826, at Florida State Prison, P.O. Box 221, Raiford, Florida. The petition was crudely printed in pencil, more like a communication from a child than from a man aged fifty-one.

Gideon's life had been a long round of petty thefts followed by spells in jail. But like many an ex-convict, he knew more about the legal system and the medieval, Latinized language and stately rituals of the courts than most college graduates would ever know. The childish lettering spelled out stilted phrases such as "Comes now the Petitioner. . . ."

Because Gideon was a pauper, he was not required to file forty printed petitions. The single crude copy would do. Nor did he have to pay a $100 filing fee. He did not have to pay anything at all.

Gideon's claim was that he had asked for counsel at his trial, had been denied a court-appointed lawyer, and, as a result, had been convicted of breaking into a poolroom of Panama City and robbing the cigarette machine. He was currently serving a five-year sentence for the conviction.

As the law stood at the moment, it stood squarely against Gideon. During the war the Supreme Court had ruled in the case of *Betts* v. *Brady* that to be denied a lawyer in a criminal case was not in itself a denial of due process of law. Gideon did not mention *Betts*. He concentrated on his own case. He did not have the help of a lawyer for only one reason—he was poor. And because he did not have a lawyer, he had been convicted. "If the petitioner would of had attorney there would not of been allowed such things as hearsay, perjury or Bill of attainer against him. . . . It makes no difference how old I am or what color I am or what church I belong to if any. The question is I did not get a fair trial. The question is very simple." No lawyer could have put the issue more plainly.

The Court granted a writ. It appointed a lawyer to argue Gideon's case for him. To be chosen by the Supreme Court to represent a destitute defendant is one of the most prized distinctions in the legal profession. It is an honor reserved as a rule for the most successful—that is, richest—lawyers the nation can boast. The Court may select almost anyone, and no matter how busy or distinguished he may be, he will almost certainly take the case and be satisfied with nothing more than traveling and printing expenses and a rare chance selflessly to serve the ends of justice. For Gideon the Supreme Court chose Abe Fortas, in time destined to become an Associate Justice.

Until 1962 *Betts* had required lower courts to provide counsel only in special circumstances—that is, for defendants who were mentally ill or illiterate or otherwise incapacitated. The transcript in Gideon's trial showed that the judge and jury had tried to be fair to the defendant. But they had followed the Betts ruling, and the grizzled, white-haired, prematurely aged Gideon had not known which questions to ask, had no idea of the rules of evidence involved, and was unaware of several lines of defense which were open to him All this was evident from the transcript. To a lawyer's eyes the case against him was astonishingly weak. Yet the prosecution had not been forced to exert itself to secure his conviction. Gideon's defenselessness took care of that.

For twenty years the Betts rule had presented tens of thousands of defendants each year from demanding and being offered counsel. And for those twenty years lawyers and judges alike had criticized the rule. Among the three Supreme Court Justices who had dissented from it back in 1942 was Hugo Black. On March 18, 1963, with obvious relish, Black read the Court's decision in *Gideon* v. *Wainwright*. This time the ruling was unanimous. *Betts* was wrong. Anyone forced to defend himself in a criminal trial without the aid of counsel had been denied due process of law.

On August 5 Clarence Earl Gideon was retried in Panama City. This time he had a court-appointed lawyer to defend him. This time he was acquitted.

Under Warren the Court was not the harmonious body the term "the Warren Court" suggests. In cases involving subversion the division of opinion was often bitter and irreconcilable. Arguments became so heated, it was reported, that one famous Justice scoffingly asked another, "How did you get out of law school?" To which the other replied, "And how did you get *in?*"

The Court steadily narrowed the scope of the Nelson and Watkins decisions. As a consequence, a retired Yale Divinity School professor, Dr. Willard Uphaus, spent nearly all 1960 in New Hampshire state penitentiary. Dr. Uphaus had refused to give the New Hampshire attorney general a list of the names of all those who had attended a 1954 World Fellowship summer camp, on the grounds that to do so would be to expose them to "public scorn" and possibly to official harassment.

In 1961 the Court delivered two five to four decisions affecting the Communist Party. One upheld the Smith Act, the other the Internal Security Act of 1950. The Court found that the CPUSA was not a legitimate political party but a conspiracy controlled by a foreign country. Communist Party members were therefore obliged to register as agents of a foreign government. Communist Party officials were arrested. They were charged with violating the Subversive Activities Control Act. The Cold War still had a little life left in it.

But it was no easy matter these days to become a Communist. A potential Party member was expected to fill out a lengthy questionnaire, to undergo a background investigation, and to be vouched for by three Communist Party members of proved reliability. It was probably easier to get into the FBI. The Party had lost its former élan. "The Communists have gone respectable. They can no longer be easily identified by their advocacy of free love, pie-in-the-sky promises and street corner oratory," wrote one observer.

The Cold War was a shadow of its former febrile self. One frosty February morning in 1962 Colonel Abel was exchanged at the Glienicker Bridge in Berlin for Gary Francis Powers.

And these days they really *were* teaching Communism in the schools. In

Florida and Louisiana it was required by law. The American Legion and the NEA were busily turning out classroom materials which explained the principal ideas of Marxism-Leninism. The courses were designed, however, to put Communist beliefs and Soviet history into the worst possible light. But this was probably unnecessary. Marxism-Leninism contained a built-in antidote to its propagation among the young—dullness and pomposity. Even in the Soviet Union and China it had to be combined with a host of other activities, such as camping and sports, to be sold to youngsters. On its own it was indigestible stuff.

Americans were, with the exception of the fringe groups along the radical right, bored to tears with the issue of domestic Communism. When Whittaker Chambers died in July 1961, there was barely a ripple of popular interest and considerable confusion as to exactly who he was and just what he was famous for. Chambers, however, remained a man of mystery even unto the grave. It appears likely that he died a suicide—and true to his nature tried to fake a natural death.

His body was cremated with remarkable haste. Despite his return to the Christian faith—an event shouted from the rooftops—there was no funeral service. The doctor who signed the death certificate had received a call from Chambers to tell her that he was feeling very ill, but then he insisted that she should not drive over to see him because it was nearly midnight. It was later shown that at the time of this telephone call the telephone at Chambers's farm was disconnected and had been so for several days. Another curious circumstance was that Chambers was first cremated, and then the coroner was notified that Chambers was dead.

Between her husband's death and his rapid journey to the crematorium Esther Chambers collapsed from an overdose of barbiturates. She was in a coma for three days. *Witness* had closed with a retelling of the Greek myth of Philemon and Baucis, the elderly and devoted couple who showed kindness to the god Mercury, not knowing his true identity. Their only wish in life was that neither should be forced to grieve for the other. They lived to a very old age, and when death came for one of them, it came for both. Where they fell, two tall trees sprang up and at their tops their branches touched. The closing pages of Chambers's posthumously published *Cold Friday* also contain this admission: "The only thing about dying that seems to me really insupportable is that my wife should not go with me." The circumstances of his death, his wife's collapse, and these twice-stated views suggest strongly that Chambers and his wife had entered into a suicide pact. It was wholly within Chambers's nature to want to die in a different manner from the run of humanity and to try to arrange it so.

For some of the victims of the Cold War hysterics of a decade earlier time had brought a measure of justice. A seven-year legal struggle culminated in an eleven-week trial of Vincent Hartnett, Aware, Inc., and Lawrence Johnson. Every one of Hartnett's accusations against John Henry Faulk was shown to be false. Lawrence Johnson, the Syracuse supermarket owner, died during the last week of the trial; he choked to death on his own vomit one night in a motel bedroom. Faulk was awarded damages of $3.5 million. On appeal this was reduced to $550,000. Johnson was not, it turned out, the millionaire he had been reported as being and did not leave a large estate. For Vincent Hartnett, a mousy, nervous little man who was by now a poorly paid teacher in a parochial school, the case meant that he would spend the rest of his life sharing his small salary with John Henry Faulk.

In 1962 Linus Pauling received a second Nobel Prize. The State Department had treated him like a menace to the nation; the Nobel Committee gave him the prize for Peace.

The following year the AEC bestowed its highest honor, the Enrico Fermi Award, on J. Robert Oppenheimer. President Kennedy associated himself with this act of atonement by announcing that he would personally make the presentation at a White House ceremony on December 2.

There were times these days when the United States appeared to have exchanged its concern with Communism for an avid concern with sexual diversion. And here too the Supreme Court played a central role. In 1957 in *Roth* v. *United States* it had removed the "clear and present danger" test of obscenity and substituted for it a doctrine of "social utility." Was the publication in question seriously attempting to say something, or was it simply trying to titillate base desires? In the years following the Roth decision the Court made dozens of decisions which struck down obscenity convictions but rather than develop its thinking further merely made reference to *Roth*.

In 1961, emboldened by its successful defense of *Lady Chatterley's Lover*, Grove Press brought out the literary work by an American writer which had the biggest underground reputation of the age, Henry Miller's *Tropic of Cancer*. In 1963 John Cleland's 200-year-old minor masterpiece, *Fanny Hill*, at last appeared openly on sale. It, too, had an impressive underground reputation which assured it of success. But it also deserved its success, being far better written and more convincingly imagined than nearly all the arousal literature currently gushing from the printing presses. In several important respects it was, in fact, far better than the average serious novel being published these days.

Traditional sexual morality was not abandoned overnight. And much of it was not abandoned at all, although it was very unfashionable to say so. In this confused situation it was inevitable that there would be snares and that the unwary would stumble into them. When a professor of biology at the University of Illinois, Leo F. Koch, made the unexceptional observation in a letter to the campus newspaper that sexual intercourse between emotionally mature college students did no harm, he was fired. When the astonished Koch demanded a hearing, he was denied one. The president of Vassar, Sarah Gibson Blanding, ruled that Vassar students who had sexual relationships with men would be expelled. This set off furious arguments among college students and their parents, university administrators, and educationists all across the country.

The year 1962 saw the publication of *Sex and the Single Girl*, by Helen

Gurley Brown. It was chiefly a do-it-yourself guide for young women who wanted men but not marriage. Its style was lifted wholesale from *The Power of Positive Thinking*. The content was also pitched at the earlier work's level of intellectual distinction. There were numerous enthusiastic references to sex and some equally discouraging references to marriage. Yet her own triumph, as the author saw it, was to have lived a life filled with male friends, admirers, and lovers until at the age of thirty-seven she had snagged a rich movie producer who owned a simply gorgeous house on 100 lovely acres south of glamorous San Francisco. All this, she modestly admitted, without being beautiful or clever.

Sex and the Single Girl sold more than one million copies. It was written for the millions of secretaries, nurses, teachers, bank tellers, and salesgirls who lived and worked in the big cities. These women were, many of them, still young, vibrant with life, economically independent, but without any one man to call their own. The book contained handy hints, such as the type of perfume to put on one's bosom and how to do it (douse a small cotton pad, stick it in your bra); there was sensible advice on how to save money, rent an apartment, learn to cook, and buy clothing. The principal theme, however, was that marriage was not the normal and inevitable desire of a single woman of the 1960s. This was a far cry from that 1930s best-seller *How to Live Alone and Like it*.

The change involved was far more than a matter of sex. The condition of women's lives was changing for both the better and the worse. The most important single change was their economic independence. This was a powerful encouragement to independence of mind. So were an extra couple of years of schooling. And so was the development of contraceptives which allowed women to enjoy intercourse regularly and with different partners without fear of an unwanted pregnancy. Any of these three changes would have been remarkable. Coming within a single generation, they were certain to breed confusion and anxiety as well as greater freedom and a wider awareness of the possibilities of life.

Betty Friedan's 1963 best-selling *The Feminine Mystique* attempted to describe this confusion and anxiety as an acute crisis of identity. Women had been fooled by women's magazines and other guides, she maintained, into thinking that they would feel fulfilled as wives and mothers. They had thrown themselves into these roles only to discover that they were bored. They then assumed that their dissatisfaction was their own fault. Besides, who were they to take issue with geniuses such as Freud, who had understood them better than they understood themselves?

Women's colleges, Mrs. Friedan said, were the last institutions anyone would have expected to hold women down. Yet in recent years they had stopped educating their students on the assumption that they were the intellectual equals of men. Instead, they had begun to prepare them for "feminine" roles. College education became available to more and more women, but there was no sizable increase in the number of women doctors, lawyers, engineers, scientists, and college professors. One does not have to be a female or a feminist to see that outdated attitudes were losing the nation the full intellectual contributions of thousands of gifted young women every year. Well might Mrs. Friedan ask, "If an education geared to the growth of the human mind weakens feminity, will an education geared to feminity weaken the growth of the mind?"

Yet there was an undeniable increase in the self-awareness of women after the late 1950s. It was both less dramatic and more portentous than the old feminist struggles. The feminists of 1900–1920 had been few, comprising a handful of remarkable individuals. The feminists and crypto-feminists of the 1960s were ordinary, and their name was legion.

The other notable feature of the stirrings of sexual freedom and women's liberation was that both involved chiefly people under the age of thirty-five and often those who were markedly short of thirty. There was a growing assertiveness among young people, and it was most evident among college students. The United States was literally growing younger. The 1950s were the only decade in the twentieth century when the American people's median age dropped, from 30.2 years to 29.3.

Older people—that is, those who had reached maturity in the 1930s—were inclined to look with pity and scorn on the present college generation. They remembered with nostalgic joy the running battles they had fought in the teeth of bourgeois and academic disapproval for their literary and artistic heroes—Hemingway, Fitzgerald, Picasso, Joyce, Eliot, D. H. Lawrence, and Duchamp. They were prone to lament that there were now no giants and heroes to be fought for by passionately committed students against pigheaded professors. And the result, when they graduated, was inevitable. "They don't sell out," said Louis Kronenberg. "They are exultant volunteers."

To David Riesman, looking at the Class of '55, it was a decent group of young people, very self-aware and well meaning—and hopelessly dull. There was no evident concern with excellence or greatness. Instead, there was a deep yearning for cozy, suburban security, relieved by the right kind of hobbies and social activities. The Class of '31 was not much impressed with its offspring. But there was very little open conflict; conflict was not nice.

When, six years later, the Class of '61 was canvassed, it described itself as being both ambitious and cooperative. It also considered itself fun-loving, idealistic, easygoing, and cautious. Few admitted to being dominant or forceful, but few people really are. Few admitted to being rebellious. When they were given a choice between working for money, working to pursue creative or original ideas, or working with people, money came a distant third to creativity and people. The brightest students (except those who were Jewish) tended to show the least interest in money and possessions. Most of the Class of '61, however, was plainly heading for routine, secure, uncreative employment.

Even the outlets for their evident idealism were directed through large organizations. A month after his Inauguration President Kennedy issued his call for Peace Corps volunteers. They came forward at the rate of 200 a day. For six months it was the most admired idea among the young.

Then, at the end of September, Margery Jane Michelmore, one of the first volunteers to complete training and be sent overseas, wrote down on a postcard her impressions of Nigeria. She lost the card before she could mail it. Her impressions consisted principally of descriptions of poverty and squalor in Ibadan.

This humble postcard was blown up into an international incident. The Nigerian press, its nationalistic sensibilities stung to the quick, printed Miss Michelmore's remarks in full as a shocking example of American imperialism and white supremacist attitudes.

This incident soon died down, but with it went the hazy romantic glow in which the Peace Corps had been launched. It demonstrated how naïve and unprepared many of America's idealistic young people were. They had reached adulthood without ever seeing the poverty, disease, and despair in which most of the human race lived. They were ignorant of the true condition of life of most of the poor people within their own country. It was doubtful that they were capable of doing much to improve living conditions of the poor elsewhere. Yet the Peace Corps was an excellent school for the volunteers. It provided them with an education they badly needed. It heightened their awareness of their own strengths, weaknesses, and privileges. And it held out to them the priceless gifts of adventure and travel.

Never had such gifts been more precious. The conformism of most college students was so extensive that at times it appeared to have blotted out everything else. Yet there was beneath the bland surface an astonishing restlessness. Of all those who started college 60 percent were not there on graduation day. Dropout rates had always been high on American campuses. But the emphasis on securing a college degree was so strong in the postwar, and the economic pressures on students so much lighter than they had ever been, that the dropout rate was widely expected to fall. Instead, it remained very high.

The restlessness of college-educated youth showed itself in other ways as well. Jack Kerouac was credited with launching the 1960s' "Rucksack Revolution" thanks to his novel *The Dharma Bums*, which was based on his acquaintance in the 1950s with Gary Snyder ("Japhy Ryder"), erstwhile dropout, student of Zen Buddhism, and poet, who, all his possessions crammed into a rucksack, wandered off to the high mountains to pray, write poetry, and smoke marijuana. As the 1950s wore on and gave way to the 1960s, college students by the tens, then the hundreds of thousands each year began to smoke marijuana. High school students were meanwhile experimenting with glue sniffing, seeking intoxication from the volatile solvents which went into quick-drying glues.

Most of the rebellious young people were the offspring of the middle class. They were in many cases as adept at role playing as their parents. They were likely to be self-conscious, alienated, and arrogant. To that old radical Paul Goodman they were just the offspring the Organization Man deserved. Yet who could blame them for wanting to reject an adult world in which, to any critical mind, the vast majority of jobs were dull, most forms of leisure were satisfying neither to the intellect nor to the imagination, and where a bland liberal philanthropy obscured the complex issues of social justice and political action?

In these years a psychiatrist at Harvard, Kenneth Keniston, was struck by the growing sense of alienation among the bright young men around the Yard, by the loss of commitment and conviction. Their alienation was not entirely a personal matter, he believed; it was created by the conditions of American life. Americans said proudly that they had adjusted to rapid social change. And that was true, Keniston admitted. But that was not to say they had adjusted successfully. The 1950s gave young Americans too little to believe in or care about deeply.

But starting around 1960, and for no evident reason, rebelliousness came out of the closet. The "silent generation" suddenly broke their silence. They screamed their protest against American life on picket lines, in sit-ins, and on Freedom Rides. In San Francisco, college youth from the Bay area confronted HUAC and sat in at city hall. There was a revival of liberal faith. There was also the formation of the right-wing Young Americans for Freedom. During the annual air-raid drill in New York 300 students at CCNY in 1960 refused to take shelter. At Brooklyn College 150 students staged a protest meeting against the drill. At Harvard that December 1,000 students held an emotional rally in favor of nuclear disarmament. At Berkeley 3,000 students turned out for a rally against the draft.

During the following three years tens of thousands of college students engaged in overt dissent. They protested against everything from racial injustice to dorm regulations. And their protests became increasingly political. In 1963 fifty-nine college students defied the State Department and traveled to Cuba. Having flaunted the Executive branch, they were in no mood to be intimidated by the Legislative branch. HUAC ordered them to appear to be questioned (that is, chastised). To their horror and amazement the members of the committee found themselves to be held in the most thoroughgoing contempt. Worse, they were mocked to their faces, considered not worth taking seriously.

It always comes as a shocking surprise for the self-important to discover that to other people they are figures of low amusement. One student cheekily told an elderly Congressman to put out his cigar and watch his manners. The witnesses broke into laughter at the committee's rituals. The witnesses answered the committee's questions with wisecracks, scratched themselves, yawned, sniggered, and waved to one another. They were insolent and infuriating as only the young can be. The committee's members were baffled. They had called these hearings in order to flush the Communist menace into the open only to find themselves looking—with openmouthed disbelief—into a yawning generation gap.

The hearings degenerated into an inconclusive farce, with Capitol policemen and youthful spectators giving demonstrations of all-in wrestling in the aisles of the Caucus Room. The committee, observed Murray Kempton, "had an extraordinary moment of sympathy from journalists who are normally their enemies but would not in this crisis be traitors to their age group.''

Almost unnoticed, in 1962 thirty-five student leaders meeting at Port Huron, Michigan, had formed the Students for a Democratic Society and issued a manifesto, "The Port Huron Statement," which rejected much of the existing social and educational order. SDS rapidly became a breeding ground for student activists and a focal point of student unrest.

As youth turned active, youth turned violent. Throughout the spring and summer of 1963 adolescents and young adults clashed with police at dozens of colleges up and down the East Coast. In the fall, following a debutante party on Long Island, a group of upper-class adolescents vandalized a Southampton mansion where they had been staying during a debutantes' coming-out party.

Clashes, whether caused by clear-cut political protest or political nihilism, had for so long been on the decline that many people had grown accustomed to assuming that political violence was dead, apart from racial protests. When V. O. Key, Jr.'s famous study *Politics, Parties and Pressure Groups* appeared back in 1947, it had contained an entire chapter on political violence. By the time the fourth edition rolled off the press in 1958 that chapter had shrunk to a page and a half.

The sudden upsurge in political clashes was not limited to the United States. All over the world the annual number of protest riots and demonstrations doubled between 1958 and 1962. In the United States the principal cause of protest was still racial injustice. But behind the rise in political violence as a whole there was a much wider-ranging dissatisfaction with the American social and political order. HUAC had provided only a sample of things to come. Politically and socially in 1963 the United States stood on the brink of a major shake-up.

In 1963 the biggest single enterprise in the new knowledge society was education. There were 50 million Americans enrolled in some kind of school. Millions more were taking correspondence courses, attended adult education classes, or were in trade schools. There were nearly as many full-time students as there were full-time workers. Allowing for nearly 3 million teachers and school administrators to complete the figures, "we can easily say that more Americans are involved in learning and teaching than are involved in anything else," wrote Richard Scammon and Benjamin Wattenberg.

Since 1945 the number of teachers in the elementary and secondary schools had doubled. Their salaries had tripled. The size of college and university faculties had also tripled. The amount of money spent each year on school construction rose from $224 million in 1946 to $3.8 billion in 1963. School construction had been one of the major props in the postwar building boom. In 1963 education took 6 percent of the GNP; this was twice its share in 1946.

After Sputnik 1 went up, the supply of teachers went up twice as fast as the increase in school enrollments. There was still as classroom shortage. But it had eased dramatically, and in light of the postwar baby boom it was an accomplishment that it had eased at all. Education in America now offered an instructive picture. The defects of American education from the grade schools through the colleges were manifest to anyone who cared to examine them. Yet no underdeveloped country had ever pinned more of its hopes for the future on education than did the rich United States. The result was an education system that was full of hierarchies, contradictions, dubious practices, and vague criteria. Yet nowhere in the world was there a system that was as open to talent, as fair, as generous, or as interesting. In American education there was a place for everyone, from the intellectually awesome to the plodding and dim-witted. No student capable of doing the work required need any longer lose the chance of a college education for lack of money. The chief glory of American education in 1963 was its diversity. Only a society that was both rich and intelligent would have ever created so democratic a system of schooling.

And America in 1963 certainly was a rich country. But what it had, it worked for. Despite glib assertions to the contrary, Americans worked as hard as ever. In manufacturing the workweek in 1963 was exactly what it had been in 1933. There were many people who worked a few hours less each week than before the war, but there was no appreciable increase in their leisure time.

What had increased was time away from the job. But what most people did in the time made available was usually to take flight from ease and to do other work—on the car, on the house, on the garden. And thanks to the recent increases in longevity, most people did more work in a lifetime than their parents and grandparents had done. It was also likely that people in the upper ranks of the employed—the professionals, the executives, the owners of small businesses—worked at least as hard as their forerunners had done. There was nothing to suggest that they spent any more time away from work than the most lead-bottomed Victorian entrepreneur.

The growth of large organizations and the more rational organization of work meant that even in middle-class occupations most jobs were rigidly structured. White-collar workers had no more control over what they did than blue-collar workers. And the bunching and ordering of leisure time meant that nearly everyone went on vacation at the same time, exactly in the way that the organization of work made sure that nearly everyone went to work at the same time and went home at the same time. Weekends and holidays were not as a rule expansive, carefree periods of leisurely relaxation; they were more likely to consist of a snatching at fleeting pleasures while caught up in a crowd.

Meanwhile, the diversions of the rich were trickling down, were being democratized. This was especially true of travel. The result, however, was something less than the Grand Tour. In 1957 a useful little paperback written by New York lawyer Arthur Frommer appeared on newsstands. It was called *Europe on $5 a Day*. For the first few months it sold modestly.

But in the early 1960s it sold steadily at the rate of 3,000 copies a week. *Europe on $5 a Day* did not bother with descriptions of Notre Dame by moonlight or how much to tip the sommelier. It offered, instead, listings of inexpensive hotels, pensions, cafes, and restaurants. Scores of once-tranquil bistros were made (and on occasion ruined) thanks to Frommer's listing. The success of his guide marked a profound change in the tourist trade. European travel had at last come within reach of the lower middle and prosperous working classes, within reach of college students, within reach of the elderly living on fixed incomes—within reach, that is, of the vast majority of Americans.

Europe on $5 a Day both encouraged them to go and helped them make contact with ordinary, everyday Europeans. All too often had the American abroad been holed up in the local Hilton, worn his money on his back, been seen only in the most expensive stores and restaurants, and been screened by his wallet and his timidity from European life.

Within their own country Americans nowadays were discovering once again the America they had not made, and they sought in it a spiritual escape from the America they had. In the early 1960s more than 16 million people went camping each year. But wilderness was no longer paradise enow. Most of the campers took with them an array of creature comforts that even Cleopatra might have envied. There was a selection of cooking equipment that was ingenious, lightweight, and not too expensive. Every year the air mattresses became more comfortable, the sleeping bags softer; the tents were easier to put up; the trailers grew roomier. Few people actually sought solitude. Camping was especially popular with young couples and families. It was an escape from urban noise and grime, from irritating distractions such as the telephone, and from boring work. By bringing people in contact with the grandeur of the natural world, it must certainly, in those capable of responding to it, have heightened the sense of wonder and quickened the sensation of being part of all life. It was also an experience which served to remind these millions of the fact that their magnificent country, possessed of some of the most inspiring and dramatic vistas on earth, was being despoiled. From about 1960 onward Americans began increasingly and noticeably to show concern for the land which really belonged to no one and to everyone.

Travel and camping offered escape, and this as much as anything was the secret of their appeal. Yet the most popular form of escape sat in nearly every living room. And by 1963 color TV, after advancing slowly for years, was considered a technical and popular success. Television was becoming increasingly contentious now that the early novelty had worn off and large numbers of people viewed it with a critical eye. Kennedy's choice as chairman of the FCC, Newton Minow, in 1961 told the National Association of Broadcasters that they were filling the screen with trash and as grown men ought to know better. This came at the NAB's annual convention and took some of the festivity out of the festivities. But Minow dared them, if they disagreed with him, to spend an entire day watching television. Some of what they saw, he conceded, would be imaginative and stimulating. But most of it would prove to be "a vast wasteland."

Most people nevertheless liked television. They cheerfully agreed that they were probably wasting their time watching it (the average set was on five hours a day). They made no objection to the commercials as such; what they disliked was the interruption. Most people said they were prepared to give up their cars, their refrigerators, or their telephones before they would give up television.

Yet they looked back to a golden (and somewhat mythical) age of TV when programs had been more exciting. What had really been lost was not so much excellence as novelty. In the first postwar decade televison had been experimental. With very few exceptions it had been undistinguished. The most common complaint in the early 1960s was not directly to do with the caliber of what was being offered now; it was that there was too much violence. The proof of this was there before one's eyes every night.

At the same time television was becoming blander than ever. After Edward R. Murrow's departure from CBS to accept an appointment from President Kennedy to become head of the United States Information Agency, the brighest exception to this remark, the CBS News Department, took a dive. Fred Friendly described the change years later: "I was subtly influenced to do controversial subjects in a non-controversial manner." And that was the rule at CBS and elsewhere for a long time to come.

Popular culture for the young was similarly atrophied. Following his return from the Army in 1960, the king of rock 'n' roll, Elvis Presley, was nearly all pop and hardly any rock. As he grew older, he softened his style to cover a broader swath of the market. By 1963 he was the all-American boy—polite, soft-spoken, religious, generous to a fault. "Compared to Elvis, Jack Armstrong was a Communist."

Then four young Liverpudlians with an abysmal pun for a name, the Beatles, in 1963 started turning rock 'n' roll audiences frantic. *Time*, however, demonstrated that the adult ear was, when it came to the music of youth, as tinny as ever: "Their songs consist mainly of 'Yeh!' screamed to the accompaniment of three guitars and a thunderous drum." But what the youthful audiences had heard was the sound of authenticity—raw, youthful fervor. The Beatles wrote and performed their own songs, and some of their songs were brilliant.

Bourgeois sensibilities were being more seriously affronted by Leonard Alfred Schneider, better known as Lenny Bruce. Bruce's entree to American nightclubs was made possible by Mort Sahl, who had developed a style of satire that took today's newspaper headlines as its starting point. Because there was not much overt dissent in evidence in the late 1950s, Sahl's jokes appeared daring. Yet he was waspish rather than witty. His style of working an audience was both intimate and insulting. Instead of trying to be funny, he tried to find a sensitive nerve. Status obsessions, middle-class pretension, suppressed desires, neuroses—these were his raw materials. But Sahl lacked the nihilistic daring of Lenny Bruce.

Bruce's life was a squalid mess from start to finish. Yet he had developed a sense of humor that was based on a moral vision—"funny being equivalent to vital, strong, ethnic, honest and soulful," one of his biographers said. "Funny guys were the guys who told the truth." Inevitably that took Lenny Bruce into deep waters—race, politics, drugs, Jewishness, theories of comedy, death, religion. He wanted to be thought of as a writer and thinker and not as a man who told jokes.

Bruce was a strange, God-haunted agnostic. For a time he dressed as as a priest, chartered a church for himself, and proceeded to solicit money for a leper colony in British Guyana. It was a swindle, of course. Yet he sent the colony nearly a third of the $8,000 he tricked out of well-meaning middle-class matrons. His first nightclub success was built around a routine called "Religion, Inc."

He became notorious for using language that everyone over the age of eighteen knew and understood, but which most people did not like to hear in public places. Sniggering dirty jokes, jokes about cripples, about minorities, about people with speech impediments were all right. But say "cocksucker" and audience would be outraged. Lenny Bruce shunned jokes about cripples and minorities and speech impediments; he did not seek the easy laugh by resorting to stereotypes; he talked about what real people were like and what real people did; and he used the real language that they used: he said "cocksucker." He was arrested in San Francisco in 1962 and tried for obscenity at the very time the President of the United States was freely using the same kind of language in the White House and on the telephone. Kennedy, like Bruce, used it for comic effect.

Bruce's Jewish upbringing shaped much of his humor. It also pointed up the gulf between himself and many of the people he offended. The arresting officers frequently bore Irish surnames. When he was arrested and tried in Chicago, the jury was entirely Catholic; the judge was Catholic; so was the prosecutor, and so was the assistant prosecutor. On Ash Wednesday the entire jury appeared with ashes on their foreheads. So did the judge, so did the prosecutor, and so did the assistant prosecutor.

Lenny Bruce was important because he personified a new awareness. His vision probably frightened him as much as it frightened anyone. It sprang from an awareness of the fatuities, the pretenses, and the dangerous absurdities of postwar life. Intellectuals, creative artists, and political radicals have long taken an almost proprietorial interest in exposing the fake, the hypocritical, the bizarre, and the cruel. But Bruce possessed few of their characteristics. He had intellectual yearnings (falling in love with long words, such as "anthropophagous"). His free-associating style was creative after a fashion, but avoided the discipline of form. Like the political radicals, he considered conventional politicians charlatans, and the established political order a vast confidence trick in which the strong and the clever did whatever they liked to the weak and the credulous.

By the 1960s there was an audience ready for Lenny Bruce. There was, as we have seen, the restlessness and alienation of middle-class college-educated youth. There was a sense of drift and of falling short. There was a powerful desire for change and daring. Bruce was a product of the postwar. He embodied the alienated self-awareness of young college-educated adults. Not only did he embody it, but he helped carry it farther. It was an awareness that was wise to itself, a self-aware awareness. And it had a deeply nihilistic strain, which Lenny Bruce recklessly pushed.

His artistic integrity made him impossible to ignore. He saw that it would eventually destroy him. The cost of nihilism is suffering; it begins with pain and ends in despair. The savagery of his routines came from the truth in them. People *did* do these things; they *did* use these words; they *did* have these desires. To pretend otherwise was a lie. And they did pretend otherwise. The laughter his routines provoked carried the shock of recognition, and self-recognition at that. It was not the usual self-indulgent safe laughter other comedians created. It was laughter which was keener, too, for the awareness of danger behind it. But the only person in danger was the comic himself. His character had never been very strong. He had been using drugs for years. Now as the burdens on him grew, so did his dependence on drugs. He could not give them up, nor could he abandon his vision of humor as a moral enterprise.

After his death at the age of forty from a drug overdose it became fashionable to consider him a martyr to bourgeois hypocrisy and to blame his death on anything but drugs and on anyone but himself. But it is not always the strong—the Solzhenitsyns—who become the moral beacons of their time. Often the great servants of the truth are the men whose characters are badly flawed, the Martin Luther Kings, the Lenny Bruces. Had Lenny Bruce been able to fight his addiction, he would have been able to fight the harassment of police and politicians. He could not have been silenced. By this time too many people wanted to hear what he had to say; too many believed that what he had to say was important.

Lenny Bruce's most complete obsession was sex. So by now was the country's. While he was being hounded for making fun of sexual behavior and neuroses, the United States was sending into space huge, gleaming, phallic rockets, asserting American power and skill. Much of the emerging space machinery had clearly sexual overtones which colored its language—thrust, coupling, penetration, entry, and reentry.

The Americans of 1963 were proudly the first space generation. In a few years NASA had grown from little more than a few offices to an operation which employed more people than most Cabinet-level departments and had far more money to spend. Its budget in 1963 was more than $4 billion. Nearly all its efforts were directed to a single aim—to put an American on the moon.

NASA had briefly been headed by a scientist. But as the agency's purpose became clear and momentum gathered behind it, the scientist was replaced with a political figure skilled in the ways of Washington bureaucracy, James E. Webb. NASA became an organization of engineers rather than scientists.

There was no longer any question about the seriousness of the American commitment to the space program. Space and missiles had become the basis of a new industry, one which in 1963 had a turnover of $12 billion. And an American astronomer, Fred Whipple, made a bet of $1,000 that an American would land on the moon by 1970. An eminent Austrian physicist, Hans Thirring, bet that it would not happen. It would be as easy, he said, to level the Rocky Mountains.

40

The Lightning Strikes

The Kennedy Administration set about conducting the nation's business in an atmosphere heavy with mutual admiration and self-congratulation; typical of any group of men who have climbed to the top of the greasy pole. But they never stopped telling one another and themselves how clever and stylish they were. Many and flattering were the comparisons they drew between themselves and their predecessors. The hallmark of the Kennedy Administration was vanity. Yet for all their cleverness and stylishness, for all the talk of vigor and selflessness, they showed remarkably little ability to effect positive change.

From 1957 to the summer of 1963 the economy grew at less than 2 percent a year in real terms; this barely kept pace with population growth. Unemployment remained above 5 percent for the entire time. In 1960 it had touched 8 percent, and the sharp rise in unemployment in the months before the election may well have played as large a part in Kennedy's victory as anything that he or Nixon did. But the rise in unemployment also made the President's problems at home more difficult when he took office. There had been an underlying trend in the direction of increased unemployment since 1946. By making economic growth a central issue in his campaign and by promising to get the country moving again, the President had in effect committed himself to reversing that trend.

He also inherited a balance of payments deficit, which alarmed Eisenhower because there was no room for it in his simplistic economic views. Kennedy was not much better prepared to deal with it. Much of this deficit was unavoidable once the economies of Western Europe and Japan had revived and so long as the United States maintained heavy commitments abroad. Recovery had brought new strength to foreign currencies. Foreign governments no longer clung desperately to every dollar that came their way. They chose to exchange their surplus dollars for gold. Throughout the whole of the Kennedy Administration there was the intriguing sight of serious, sensible men wailing piteously over America's dwindling gold stocks. They attached a totemic significance to gold which went far beyond its mere utility as an economic regulator. And instead of moving toward what was really needed—international monetary reform—they held endless and pointless meetings on how to protect America's stock of gold bars.

The President, for all his urbanity and quick-wittedness, came to power with a grasp of economics which might have been taken from a Chamber of Commerce pamphlet. Yet during his years in the White House he became, by fits and starts, a Keynesian of sorts, under the tutelage of the excellent economists he brought into his Administration. Microeconomics bored him. But macroeconomic theory appealed strongly to his activist temperament.

When he took office, Kennedy had an intense dislike of deficit spending. He believed stoutly that a sound economy was one with a balanced budget, and a balanced budget was the mark of a sound economy. He was convinced that deficits could be justified only when a shortfall in one year was covered by a surplus in another. His mentor at this point might have been thought to be George Humphrey, rather than the eminent Harvard economist Seymour Harris or the new, Keynesian chairman of the CEA, Walter Heller.

Kennedy put Harris on the Federal Reserve Board. Under Heller the CEA for the first time in ten years had a chairman who was committed to the spirit of the 1946 Employment Act and had the confidence of the President. Heller believed in the creation of "social capital" by putting money into education, training, and health. He was representative of a new breed of American Social Democrats who, unlike their European counterparts, were free from the burdens of an ideology which might or might not be pertinent to the present day. American Social Democrats were free to concentrate their minds and energies on concrete problems. Heller was to prove the most effective chairman the CEA ever enjoyed. Effective in this case meant being persuasive. and he set himself the task of educating the President and, through the President, the nation.

He taught the President and Congress to look at the economy rather than at the budget. Was the *economy* in balance? Was it working at or near to its full potential? If it was falling short, how much was *that* deficit costing the country each year? Every major issue in fiscal policy was then related to a model of the American economy working at 95 to 100 percent of its capacity. The natural emphasis of this approach was put on economic growth; its obvious objective was the achievement of a full employment economy. In making this approach persuasive, Heller prepared the ground for tax cuts and tax incentives.

He did not work alone, however. A generation of first-rate economists had come to maturity since the war. In the early 1960s the United States almost certainly had more of the leading economists than the rest of the world combined. Not until this time, under the Kennedy Administration, had economists been treated by policy makers as more than an irksome necessity. But the President changed that. He proved to be an apt student, Heller discovered. "But seen from close by," he noted wryly, "the course of true economics was not always smooth and straight." Kennedy's education was periodically interrupted by political pressures. And during his first two years in the White House he was cautious. He resisted every CEA proposal to stimulate the economy. Kennedy had a businessman's abhorrence of inflation which did his father credit. During the Berlin crisis he wanted to raise taxes by $3 billion. Only strenuous protests from Heller and the CEA made him see the folly of increasing taxes while the economy was trying to recover from a recession.

The economy in 1961 was running at $50 billion a year below its full potential. The CEA, therefore, had few qualms about recommending large-scale expansionary measures to close the gap. It proposed a $10 billion tax cut plus big increases in government spending. The Treasury and the Federal Reserve encouraged the President's resistance to deficit spending. But, said Seymour Harris, "By 1963 he had clearly become a convert." He had come to accept the elementary Keynesian approach to the tax system. That is, during an economic downturn the tax system was a stabilizing influence: by sustaining government revenues, it sustained government spending, and sustained government spending played a central role in maintaining aggregate demand; thus, a recession was kept from turning into a depression. But when the economy was trying to recover from a recession, the tax system acted as a brake because taxes bit deeper and deeper as incomes rose; this slowed the growth of consumer spending and kept the recovery from running its full course. In late 1962 it was evident that Kennedy had learned this lesson. But he was hesitant to propose a tax cut while the budget was heavily in deficit; it looked too much like an act of political suicide.

Important Senators were against a tax cut. The Cabinet was against it. The Treasury was against it. Economists in government and out were almost all for it, however. In early 1963 the President overcame his own hesitation and went on television to propose a tax cut. Then he discovered that there was hardly any public support for such a step. He had made his proposal, but he chose not to fight for it. He did not exercise leadership. He did exactly what Eisenhower had done at such moments—he waited for a change in public opinion and in the meantime turned his attention to other business. For the rest of 1963 the proposed $10 billion tax cut lay dormant in Congress. And at the end of the year the economy had almost pulled out of the slump, more slowly by two or three years than was necessary, but with every passing week the tax cut became less and less important.

Under Kennedy less grandiose stimuli had been applied over the past two years. Federal agencies were directed to speed up purchases for which Congress had already appropriated the money. Home building and home buying were encouraged. Unemployment benefits were extended over a longer period of time. The Federal Reserve was persuaded to hold down interest rates, in hopes of stimulating long-term investment. Increased government spending on defense and the space program helped reflate the economy in a fashion which even economic conservatives found acceptable. An Investment Credit Act was sent to Congress in 1961 and was passed in 1962. It allowed a 7 percent tax deduction on new investment; in effect, a new machine priced at $100,000 now cost only $93,000. The taxpayers would make up the difference. The Administration pursued a "Buy American" policy more assiduously than the previous Republican administration had ever attempted. Under Kennedy 80 percent of foreign aid money had to be spent on American-made goods.

The President was solicitous of the goodwill of Wall Street and big business. The Commerce Department was allowed to shed itself of the Business Advisory Council—and then did a volte-face. The President decided that he needed the support of the large corporations whether or not he liked the people who ran them. From the ashes of the BAC sprang a new (well, not really) entity, the Business Council. In most respects it was a far more important body than the much better known National Association of Manufacturers or the U.S. Chamber of Commerce.

Under Robert Kennedy the Justice Department's Antitrust Division passed the time in tranquillity. Under the Kennedy Administration net corporate profits rose by 43 percent. Even so, the Administration was viewed in business circles with profound suspicion.

For one thing, there were very few businessmen in top posts under Kennedy. Under Eisenhower businessmen had filled one-third of the top jobs. For another thing, there were Kennedy's ties with labor. "Their gripe was not really that Kennedy was anti-business, but rather that he was *not* anti-labor." (Original italics.) Ironically, Kennedy's economic policies were bitterly criticized by labor leaders. They were too much like Eisenhower's. Yet labor remained publicly loyal to the Democratic President.

Businessmen were adamantly convinced that Kennedy was hostile to them. And when he attempted as part of a series of proposals for tax reform to cut down deductions for business expense accounts, a cry of anguish was raised in most of the best restaurants, bars, clubhouses, and resorts from Bangor to Bel-Air. Rumors proliferated. One story had it that a host of cherished institutions such as the Kentucky Derby were certain to be forced out of business once expense-account lunches and travel were curbed. The Administration's response to this chorus of impending calamity on the cocktail circuit was meekly to back down.

In January 1962 businessmen were outraged when the President spoke harshly about strategic stockpiles, a subject normally discussed in hushed and reverential tones. The United States held stockpiles of raw materials worth $8 billion. President Kennedy suggested that these stockpiles were less important to a future emergency than they were as a subsidy to business. He ordered them to be reduced.

What antagonized businessmen most, however, was the showdown with the steel companies in the spring of 1962. The confrontation arose, as a perverse fate would have it, from the Administration's ardent adoption of wage controls—which business had been urging for years. Stable prices were as much an article of faith along the New Frontier as they had been among the Eisenhower Crusaders.

By exploiting its traditional links with the trade unions, plus some adroit arm twisting from Secretary of Labor Arthur Goldberg (until recently the CIO's legal counsel), the Kennedy Administration was able to win the (reluctant) acceptance of wage controls. Of course, they were not called that. They were called guidelines. Eisenhower had tried, with some very modest success, to tie wage increases to increases in productivity. Kennedy did the same thing with more success. Increases could be calculated in various ways. This produced a variety of results. Somehow they nearly always came out close to 3 percent. The seeming precision of the Kennedy guidelines appears to have made them far more acceptable than the vague exhortations of the Eisenhower Administration.

The CEA considered wage and price guidelines an educational device, a way of teaching people to think of the economy as a whole. It was almost certain, however, that there would be a showdown at some point, and the odds were very high that it would involve steel. Truman had twice been dragged into a fight over steel prices. Eisenhower had twice been involved in clashes over steel and each time tried to buy the country out of trouble. There was little reason to expect that Kennedy would be spared. Every few years, when steel contracts ran out, there was a clash no Administration was able to ignore. And the Republicans had found that buying the industry off did not mean it stayed bought; the 1959 steel strike, coming only three years after the costly 1956 settlement, was one of the longest strikes in American history. "Steel," wrote one observer, "had become the supreme test of government."

The steelworkers disliked the guidelines but accepted a wage settlement of less than 3 percent. Ten days after the steelworkers accepted this modest raise Roger Blough, the president of U.S. Steel, called at the White House. He handed Kennedy a press release which announced that U.S. Steel was raising its price on most steels by an average of $6 a ton—which worked out to nearly 4 percent.

The President felt betrayed. Although there had been no explicit agreement that the steel companies would hold steel prices in line with steel wage increases, there had been, he believed, a tacit understanding to that effect. By making dramatic appeals to the nation and to the steel companies, Kennedy succeeded in persuading several of the middle-range steel companies to hold their prices in step with the wage guidelines. U.S. Steel was forced to back down.

Kennedy's swift and effective response to Blough's obstinacy was, of course, taken in business circles as the unanswerable proof that the Kennedy Administration was hostile to business. Yet the President was not emotionally lashing back because he felt that he had been double-crossed. His anger was unfeigned. But what he was defending was not his ego. He was protecting a carefully nurtured system of voluntary wage and price controls. Had it collapsed, either all the recent gains in real economic growth would have been destroyed by inflation or the Administration would have been forced to impose controls by law. There was an adage among economists: "As steel goes, so goes inflation." By and large that was true.

Blough's actions deserved a severe public rebuke anyway. They showed a wanton disregard for the dignity of the Presidency. He and other steel executives had been involved in the Administration's efforts to keep the increase in steelworkers' wages below 3 percent. Evidently Blough felt that the President of the United States could be treated in a cavalier way. Kennedy could be self-mocking and irreverent regarding his own person. He was so self-assured that he never descended to pomposity. But he held his office in high regard, and he was prepared to defend its honor. Blough was plainly astonished at the reaction he had provoked.

Kennedy's father had been associated briefly with the steel industry during his business career. Following the steel showdown the President remarked to his staff, "My father always told me steel men were sons-of-bitches. But I never realized till now how right he was."* To his friend Ben Bradlee he said more pungently, "They kicked us right in the balls. Is this the way the private enterprise system is supposed to work?"

He was magnanimous in victory. After the backdown of the steel companies he made numerous attempts to reassure business that he was eager to see it prosper. Businessmen remained sullen. When the Business Council met in Hot Springs in mid-May for its annual convention, there were lapel buttons reading S.O.B. CLUB on expensive, well-tailored suits. The stock market, in the doldrums for several months, turned skittish. Then, on May 28, 1962 ("Black Monday"), it went into its sharpest one-day decline since 1929. Buying orders flooded in. The tape ran nearly three hours late. When the New York Stock Exchange closed at the end of an amazingly hectic day, nearly $21 billion had been written off.† The next day the bargain hunters moved in. By Tuesday nightfall nearly all that $21 billion had been regained. These emotional gyrations—or rather, the downward parts of the gyrations—were blamed on the President. When the market came to its senses later in the summer of 1962, it set off on one of the longest unbroken bull markets in American history.

There was a curious aftermath to the steel affair. In 1963 the steel industry raised the basic price of steel almost to the levels U.S. Steel had sought in 1962. The middle-range producers put up their prices by $6 a ton. U.S. Steel, learning a trick in its old age, shrewdly settled for $4.85.

---

*Businessmen preferred the version which appeared in the *New York Times* on April 23, 1962: "My father always told me that all business men were sons-of-bitches but I never believed it till now!"

†One inevitable result of wild fluctuations on the stock market is that a lot of overcommitted companies go to the wall. The most spectacular crash on Black Monday was the financial empire of Edward M. Gilbert, head of a Tennessee lumber corporation. Before the accountants could get to the books, Gilbert was on a plane to Brazil, so heavily weighed down with money that he had to leave his wife and children behind.

This was an astute ploy. With the price leader in the industry keeping its prices competitive, this time the White House did nothing and said nothing.

In the field of foreign trade the Kennedy Administration worked for some long-overdue changes. The Trade Expansion Act of 1962 gave the President authority to reduce tariffs down to zero on a wide range of products in return for tariff concessions made by other countries on American goods. Under the rubric of pursuing better relations with the Russians, government officials in 1963 encouraged grain dealers to negotiate a large wheat sale with the Soviet Union. An agreement was reached in October to sell the Russians and their East European satellites 150 million bushels of wheat. The Great Wheat Deal signaled an important change in the Cold War. It repudiated at a stroke the Truman-Eisenhower policy of appeasing the right wing by discouraging trade with the Soviet Union. In 1962 the total volume of U.S.-Soviet trade was $30 million. The wheat deal alone was ten times that size.

It was also an attempt to help American farmers and cut sharply into the government wheat stockpile, which stood at close to 1 billion bushels. And just as steel was part of every President's education, so was agriculture. It was remarkable that when Benson had been the Secretary of Agriculture and a vacancy had appeared on the House Agriculture Committee, forty Democrats had applied to fill it; but when Kennedy took office and Orville Freeman became Secretary of Agriculture, it was hard to find any Democrat who was eager to fill a vacancy on the House or Senate committees on agriculture. It was a wonderful opportunity for cutting other people down, but no place to expose oneself.

Benson's solution to the problem of surpluses was to reduce price supports. This pressured marginal farmers into leaving the land. Freeman's answer to the surpluses was production controls. The 1962 farm bill provided fines and prison sentences for farmers who falsified their production records. Congressmen from farming areas had a diverting time conjuring up visions of red-faced farmers being hauled away in handcuffs to the Federal penitentiary because they were terrible bookkeepers. From Gettysburg the nation's most famous gentleman farmer since Thomas Jefferson announced that he would be honored to go to prison rather than submit to the tyrannical Democrat farm bill.

The penalties were made less Draconian; the controls were relaxed. But even farming interests normally friendly to Kennedy and Freeman disliked the principle of production controls. There was a jest in Congress that Benson had been the wrong man with the right program, while Freeman was the right man with the wrong program. There was more than a grain of truth in it.

The 1962 farm bill got through Congress by a very slender margin, and only after controls on feed grain production had been dropped. Instead of production controls, there was the policy of the reviled Benson—flexible price supports. The 1962 legislation set a goal of price supports as low as 50 percent of parity starting in 1964. That legislation setting such an objective could be passed marked the shift in Congress from being under rural to being under urban domination.

The Administration did not abandon its hopes of fixing production controls. Ever since the 1940s the government had each year held a series of referenda among farmers. Most of them offered price support at a certain level in exchange for production controls over certain crops. The alternative was no controls, no support. No such referendum had ever lost. That is, when actually faced with the alternative of a free market, the farmers had never voted in favor of it. In 1963 the wheat referendum was directed at one group of wheat farmers, those who grew fewer than fifteen acres of wheat each year. Until now small wheat farmers had been free of all production controls.

The Farm Bureau was still smarting over its defeat in 1962, when it had opposed the Administration's farm bill. It devoted its energies in 1963 to revenge and concentrated on defeating the wheat referendum. Naturally the issue involved was cast as freedom v. slavery, bureaucracy v. farming, and purity v. evil. The Birchite right threw itself into the wheat referendum struggle. Nearly 1.5 million small wheat farmers voted in the referendum, and 52 percent voted it down.

This defeat was not, however, a heroic stand for high principles and low prices. The Farm Bureau and the farmers who voted no on the referendum believed (rightly) that if wheat prices began to fall steeply, Congress would be forced to intervene. Their no vote was an attempt to put pressure on Congress, not a heady bid for independence.

Kennedy's notable lack of success at economic management led to taunts that his was "the Third Eisenhower Administration." But the economy did turn up, even if largely for reasons outside anything the Administration did. Real growth reached 5 percent in 1963. But unemployment remained close to 6 percent. Kennedy and his advisers were inordinately proud of rapid growth combined with stable prices. But this price stability was mainly due to the large amount of slack still in the economy, not to the guidelines on wages and prices, useful as they were.

Most Americans in 1963 had few serious financial worries in 1963, however. For 70 to 80 percent of the nation life was comfortable and secure. Real per capita income was 50 percent higher than it had been in 1945. For the nation as a whole real income had doubled. And this was with an economy which had spent most of the past eighteen years working well below capacity. Americans were so prosperous that the average family gave away more than $300 a year to friends, charity, or some nonprofit venture, was so prosperous that it saved ten percent of its income—three times what it had saved in 1950.

Nearly every major welfare measure broached during the New Deal had by now come to fruition. The only important failure was the lack of an equitable system of health and medical care.

Kennedy never shrank from the long-standing effort to put more Federal money into the public schools. He confronted the religious issue squarely and proposed to make several billion dollars available for school construction and larger teachers' salaries. But he flatly opposed aid to paochial schools as being unconstitutional. Catholics just as flatly fought his proposed school aid program and defeated it in the House.

Although religious issues appeared to be as sensitive as ever when viewed at this level, the savage passions that religious antagonisms had long aroused were rapidly abating. John Kennedy had shown that a Catholic President would not by any stretch of the imagination be in thrall to the Vatican. And at the Vatican the 1958 election of John XXIII had shown that there were Popes whose love for humanity transcended the boundaries of religious difference.

Pope John's liberalism horrified the hidebound, Irish-dominated Catholic clergy of the United States, however. The appearance in 1961 of the encyclical *Mater et Magistra*, with its favorable references to the welfare state, evoked muted protests from American priests of "*Mater si, magistra no.*" In 1963 he issued *Pacem in Terris*, which suggested an "opening to the left." This encyclical was not much concerned with theology; rather, it was a sincere and moving expression of concern with the perils of a thermonuclear war and the current state of human rights. This was the first Papal encyclical, moreover, to be addressed to all people, Catholics and non-Catholics alike. Conservative Catholics howled as though it were a peace treaty with the Kremlin.

Pope John offered them no further comfort when he called for major reforms within the Catholic Church. To the joy of young theologians and liberal church politicians he set in train the Second Vatican Council. When John XXIII died in June 1963 at the age of eighty-one, the entire Western world mourned his passing.

For Kennedy, however, the religious issue destroyed his attempt to double the level of Federal aid to education. Ironically, Eisenhower, who felt no deep commitment to aiding the schools and colleges, did more for them through the National Defense Education Act than Kennedy, who had a liberal's faith in education, ever achieved.

The President had little to show, in fact, on the domestic scene for his major initiatives as 1963 drew to a close. On November 8, 1963, *Congressional Quarterly* ran a Presidential box score. Of twenty-five major legislative proposals from the White House since January 1961 only eight had been passed into law. It was not an impressive showing, and the less so in light of the President's commitment to effect change, to generate movement, and to provide leadership.

Yet without one's being churlish, it is fair to say that this was what might have been expected. For all his bravura style, his wit, his grace, his intelligence, and his eloquence John Kennedy had never possessed more than the basic political gift—the ability to get himself elected. During his six years in the House he had not distinguished himself in any way, devoting his energies chiefly to private pleasures. In the Senate he was dogged by serious and painful illness. But even when fit, he had not, except for his stand on the St. Lawrence Seaway, shown himself unusually conscientious about his duties. Indeed, most of the period when he was in comparatively good health was spent on running for the White House.

His Presidency was of a piece with the rest of his political career: dazzling appearance; ordinary performance. It was a performance which no one would have troubled to criticize in a clearly run-of-the-mill politician. But Kennedy promised so much, he worked hard at appearing to be different, and he raised high expectations. Domestic politics clearly did not excite him as much as foreign policy, however, and the nuts-and-bolts political skills which he praised in others he never bothered to cultivate for himself.

Throughout the Kennedy Administration the President and the country were tormented by the knowledge that a Communist regime had taken power in Cuba. Castro's regime had transformed Miami, filling it with thousands of middle-class Cuban refugees—lawyers working as bus boys, doctors driving cabs, aristocratic matrons scrubbing floors. And from this seething community of exiles sporadic efforts were launched to harry Castro and to lure the United States into another effort to topple him.

Miami spawned dozens of Free Cuba movements. It ground out rumours that the Soviet Union was building the island into a military base which threatened the security of the United States. But for more than a year after the Bay of Pigs fiasco the Coast Guard thwarted the Free Cuba freedom fighters, and the CIA discounted the rumors. Then, in the summer of 1962, Soviet shipments to Cuba suddenly picked up. There were many more ships each month, and the cargoes were evidently heavier because the ships rode much lower in the water. By mid-September there were Soviet ships arriving every day at Havana. U-2 reconnaissance flights were doubled to keep pace with this activity.

The Soviet buildup revived popular demands that the Administration "do something" about Castro. The Russians in turn warned that if doing something meant another attack on Cuba, the result would be a major war. They maintained that the arms currently being supplied to the Cubans were of a defensive character only.

But at the debriefing station the CIA operated at Opa-locka, Florida, the stories being told by incoming refugees offered a different picture. Large missiles were being transported along Cuban roads at night, they said, and were hidden out of sight before dawn. Castro's personal pilot was said to have made drunken boasts in a bar that Cuba could now stand up to the Americans because it had its own missiles and nuclear warheads. Without any tangible proof these stories were properly discounted. But on October 14 a U-2 photographed the unmistakable signs of a missile launching area under construction at the western end of the island. It also picked out a medium range ballistic missile ready to be hoisted into firing position.

The President and his advisers argued over the proper response to make to this Soviet-Cuban demarche. Hardly any of those involved had the least doubt that the missiles had to be removed. The opinion of Dean Acheson, who was called in because of the President's great respect for his experience and skill in dealing with the Soviets, was that an immediate attack should be made to destroy the missiles and the launching sites. The view advanced by Stevenson, whom Kennedy had appointed ambassador to the UN, was that the missiles should be removed by persuasion and negotiation. Opinion was generally broken into those for and those against these opposite approaches.

The missile crisis was discussed as if it had altered the strategic balance between the United States and the Soviet Union. But it had no effect on the bulk of American retaliatory power—on the several score ICBMS in hardened sites, the fifty to sixty B-52s which were aloft at at any given moment, the several hundred Polaris missiles aboard nuclear submarines at present on station in the depths of the sea. And for several years the United States had lived with the knowledge that Soviet ICBMs could strike any target within the United States.

But the President was convinced that if he meekly accepted this daring initiative, the Soviets would be tempted to try something similar elsewhere. During one of the missile crisis meetings his note pad was later seen to be covered with "Berlin . . . Berlin . . . Berlin . . . Berlin . . . Berlin . . . Berlin."

The swiftest method for destroying the missiles was an air strike. But the Tactical Air Command advised that no matter how thorough the strike, at least 10 percent of the missiles would survive. In the carnage and confusion following an attack there would be hundreds of dead and badly wounded Russian airmen and soldiers. But some of them would survive along with some of the missiles. It was possible that the senior Soviet officer on the spot might be moved to avenge his dead comrades by obliterating Washington or some other American city with the missiles still intact. It was not likely. But was the risk worth taking? Robert Kennedy raised another consideration. Should the country which had suffered a sneak attack at Pearl Harbor and vilified the Japanese for it now descend to the same tactics?

McNamara suggested a middle way—a naval blockade, leading by stages to an air strike and an invasion as the last resort. This approach appealed to the President for its combination of toughness with flexibility. It had the further, and priceless, merit of offering the Russians a chance to retreat.

On the evening of October 22 the President went on television to tell the nation that there was a missile crisis. He showed the photographs, which indicated that work on the launching sites was being carried on at a furious pace. The President's tone was grim and unyielding. As he spoke, six Army divisions were ready to move, in Germany and the United States, to defend Berlin and invade Cuba. A landing force of 7,500 Marines was practicing on the beaches of Puerto Rico the invasion of "the Republic of Vieques," to overthrow the hated Communist dictator "Ortsac" (try reading it backward). More than 300 strategic bombers had been dispersed to civilian airfields. All 156 operational ICBMs were targeted to strike the Soviet Union and were ready to be launched within minutes of a Presidential command. More than 100 B-52s were airborne and heading for their fail-safe points on the perimeter of Soviet airspace. At sea, American attack carriers moved closer to Soviet waters. Nearly 200 Navy ships were deployed in the Caribbean to enforce the blockade.

The nation rallied to the President without a moment's doubt. They had grown tired of Khrushchev's blustering. They had chafed for more than three years at their powerlessness against Castro. By taking a firm stand over the Soviet missiles, Kennedy struck at Khrushchev and Castro alike. To many people, however, the blockade (euphemistically called a "quarantine" because a blockade has been a traditional and irrefutable *casus belli*) was not enough. For them nothing short of Castro's death or imprisonment would do. But the majority were satisfied to see Khrushchev and Castro humbled in public. This was, moreover, a showdown taken from the scenario of *High Noon*. It bristled with drama and tension. It was an exhilarating break from the usually remote forces of power politics and advanced technology.

The first vessel to be boarded was an old Liberty ship, the *Maruda*, Liberian-registered and under Soviet charter. Not so coincidentally the boarding parties came from the destroyers *John R. Pierce* and *Joseph P. Kennedy*. Yet even when Soviet ships bound for Cuba slowed down to a few knots, the work at the missile launching sites was being hurried forward. The preparations for an air strike were accordingly stepped up. Five million leaflets were printed in Spanish to inform the Cubans that they were being invaded because it was good for them.

On October 26 a reporter for ABC, John Scali, was settling down to a bologna sandwich in his cubicle at the State Department when a counselor at the Soviet Embassy asked him to come for lunch. Scali tried to decline this sudden invitation; not because he was addicted to bologna but because the Cuban missile crisis was a fast-breaking story and he was a reporter. The Russian insisted, hinting that the invitation involved the missile crisis. Scali thereafter found himself in the middle of a Soviet attempt to settle the crisis by involving a third party—that is, John Scali. The Soviets used him as a transmission belt along which Khrushchev could send reassuring signals to the President, without having to work through the Soviet and American diplomatic bureaucracies.

Once the Soviet Premier had decided to make a conciliatory and constructive offer—to remove the missiles in exchange for a pledge that the United States would not invade Cuba—the crisis was speedily resolved. And following what might easily have been the prelude to a nuclear catastrophe, the two governments decided to introduce a hot line (a pair of linked teletype machines) to improve communications between the leaders of the two nations. This might in future obviate the need to drag mere journalists into the great issues of state. Yet misunderstandings arose even so. Moscow's first hot line message, in reply to Washington's first communication, was; "Please explain what is meant by a quick brown fox jumping over a lazy dog?"

The missiles were removed from Cuba under UN supervision. There had been no good reason for installing them in the first place. But the American response had also been excessive. There was no need to raise matters to a flash point in order to deal with them. But the Kennedy Administration knew no other style. Most sobering of all, however, was that two modern governments were seriously prepared to risk a thermonuclear war over what was little more than a puerile act of folly.

The removal of the missiles led in turn to the clearing up of some old business—freeing the surviving prisoners of the Bay of Pigs operation. Castro had asked for and been denied a ransom of 400 tractors. But in early December 1962 there arrived in Florida trainloads and truck loads of medical supplies, bound for Cuba. There was everything from several tons of tranquilizers to a dozen large X-ray machines. The White House attempted to claim that the government had no hand in this; that this was a spontaneous, humanitarian gesture, which would provide the Cubans with $53 million in medical supplies in exchange for 1,113 prisoners. The drug companies had given their products free, as had the manufacturers of medical equipment. Railroads and trucking companies had transported the supplies to Florida without charge.

The tab, however, was being picked up by the taxpayer. This spontaneous gesture was run from the Justice Department, under the energetic supervision of Robert Kennedy. The humanitarianism was wrung from the donors only after tough negotiations in which the goods were to be provided in return for generous tax concessions.

At Christmas 1962 the survivors of Brigade 2506 were flown into Miami aboard commerical airliners. A delirious crowd of weeping, cheering relatives and well-wishers gave them an emotional welcome. Two days later the President reviewed the brigade at the Orange Bowl. Emotions were still at a very high pitch. Physical courage and sacrifice counted highly with John Kennedy. He was moved by the sight of these brave, unlucky men, his reserve cracked, and in a shrill, choked voice he impulsively vowed that one day "This flag"—he brandished it vigorously—"will be returned to this brigade in a free Havana."

In coming months the freebooting Miami Cubans, their ranks and their spirit revived by the returned prisoners, harassed Soviet ships tied up at Cuban ports. This embarrassed the American authorities, who could not control them, and the Cuban authorities, who could not intercept them. These pinpricks were no threat to Castro's power. But they were a threat to peace—as the exiles knew only too well. A war involving the United States was the best prospect they could see of destroying the Castro regime. There were scores of exile guerrilla groups, with cryptic names, such as Alpha 69 ("Alpha is just the beginning, and 69 is a swinging number"). Often they were jealous of and hostile toward one another. They were under the control of no one; their efforts were uncoordinated. Throughout the spring and summer of 1963 a second Cuban blockade was put into effect, this time looking to the Florida shore.

Americans gradually learned to tolerate the intolerable, a Communist regime only ninety miles away. And the Administration turned its attention to other matters. It took a fresh interest in reaching a test ban treaty in the wake of the Cuban missile crisis. So too did the Soviets.

Khrushchev spoke repeatedly after this episode of the responsibility of the great powers not to blunder into a thermonuclear war. By the spring of 1963 it was evident that the Russians were prepared to make an agreement which would ban further testing aboveground. After years of wrangling the two superpowers moved rapidly toward a formal and explicit agreement.

It should be noted, however, that the agreement came only after both sides had perfected the technology of fitting large warheads into their ICBMs. And the Test Ban Treaty did not put a stop to testing as such. Underground explosions continued. Both sides concentrated on perfecting smaller warheads, for battlefield use. But the treaty was hailed as a major step forward, and in an area where there had been no progress for nearly twenty years any movement was to be welcomed.

To champagne toasts and lighthearted music the draft of the treaty was initialed in Moscow. The clock on the *Bulletin of the Atomic Scientists* was moved back five minutes to stand at twelve minutes to midnight. The Senate promptly ratified the agreement, by 80 votes to 19.

In the afterglow of the Test Ban Treaty the President addressed the opening session of the UN General Assembly in September 1963. He used the occasion to propose joint U.S.-Soviet ventures in space and to endorse a Russian proposal that nuclear weapons be banned from outer space. American-Soviet relations had in the year after the Cuban missile crisis taken a remarkable turn for the better. The new spirit was known as detente.

Yet such is the perversity of human affairs that in these same twelve months the United States had slid ever deeper into war. On taking office the new Administration had reviewed the nation's military forces. It had thrown up its hands in gestures of shock and horror at what it found. The United States was not, it was discovered, prepared to fight several wars at once in various parts of the globe. It was prepared almost entirely for a war with the only country in the world capable of fighting it on roughly equal terms, the Soviet Union. This was considered appalling. The principal weak spot was the Army. It numbered slightly fewer than 1 million men.

Army generals certainly felt slighted. In a three-pronged military establishment they had the bluntest prong. The Army had no thrilling strategic mission to fulfill, unlike the Air Force and the Navy, which in a total war with the Soviet Union would carry the fight to the enemy. Army officers had spent a decade faulting the air-atomic strategy of the Eisenhower years. And the idea that the United States might beat Communist guerrillas at their own game fell on the receptive ears of the young President. Throughout his time in the White House he showed his favor to the Special Forces units. Under his direction the United States prepared to fight a limited war in rice paddies and jungles. The American foot was planted

firmly on the slippery slope of armed intervention. In effect the administration had repudiated the "Never Again" school of thought which had
governed policies regarding Asia since the Korean War.

Eisenhower had countenanced various measures to aid Asian countries
to resist the spreading of Communist power. But he had drawn the line
unmistakably at two points: no combat troops and no unilateral American
action. The Kennedy Administration, true to its nature, refused to draw
lines ("We shall bear any burden"). There was another difference between the two Presidents. Eisenhower consulted Congress over the
American role in Indochina. Kennedy never did.

The White House view in the first days of the new Administration was
summed up by Arthur Schlesinger: "There was in 1961 no alternative but
to continue" aid to the government of Ngo Dinh Diem. The next year
McNamara and Maxwell Taylor, who had been brought back from retirement to serve as Chairman of the Joint Chiefs of Staff, went to Vietnam to
make a report for the President. They concluded that the war was being
lost not through the corruption, the incompetence, or the remoteness of
the Diem regime—about which the United States could have done almost
nothing—but because of military weakness. (At this time the Army of the
Republic of Vietnam numbered 250,000; American estimates of the Viet
Cong placed their numbers at 15,000, and there were no North Vietnamese Army units in South Vietnam.) Throughout 1962 the U.S. military
presence in South Vietnam was raised from 500 advisers to 15,000 uni-
formed men. By the spring of 1963 the White House and the Defense Department seriously believed that this infusion of military support had
turned the tide. The war was, they said, being won.

A thin pretense was still maintained that the American soldiers in South
Vietnam were merely giving advice to their South Vietnamese counterparts. Their role was limited. Their numbers did not as yet permit them to
mount military operations of their own. But they did fire weapons, they
did fly combat helicopter missions, and they did take casualties. The President tacitly admitted the truth about the changed nature of the American
presence when he ordered that the Purple Heart be awarded to servicemen wounded in South Vietnam. There were scores of awards each week
throughout the summer and fall of 1963.

Yet there was surprisingly little public disquiet over these developments. Public opinion trusted the President's judgment. And the reputable press rallied en masse to his side. *Life* had devoted almost its entire
issue of October 27, 1961, to "The Lovely Land That May Blow Up."
The tone suggested that the gentlemen at *Life* rather hoped it would. *Time*
put Diem on the cover and reported that although he was not infallible, he
was a great patriot and a fervent anti-Communist; exactly the kind of person Americans could trust. In March 1962 *Life* returned to South Vietnam
with the cheering news: "Far-Off War We Have Decided to Win." American casualties were mounting rapidly, it reported. The faint of heart were
sternly warned, "Inevitably more will die."

In April 1962 *Newsweek* carried the same message: there was no alternative to fighting, and the United States had committed itself to seeing it through. "The U.S., in short, has passed the point of no return—short of victory—in the battle for South Vietnam." Two weeks later *Newsweek* carried a banner headline for Americans to ponder: VIETNAM—WHAT PRICE VICTORY? The attitude in the American press in these years was less what one might expect from reporters than from cheerleaders. Yet there is no doubt that it was an accurate reflection of the mainstream of public opinion.

The President's responses to Communist depredations in Vietnam were predictable. The Soviet Union had not begun to issue demands that the Western powers withdraw from Berlin only when Kennedy took office. They had been making such demands for years. The most dire threats had been made since 1958. Eisenhower saw them for the bluffing that they were and treated them accordingly. But Kennedy treated every such demand as a crisis and thereby created one. In South Vietnam there was the same pattern of overreaction, the same exaggeration of the importance of events which were unwelcome and destabilizing, but not fatal to American security interests. Eisenhower had a gift for making the right pointless gestures. Kennedy's gift was for making the wrong hair-raising kind.

What criticism there was of the unfolding war and the changed nature of the American commitment came from a handful of longtime pacifists and radicals and several young reporters, notably David Halberstam of *The New York Times* and Malcolm Brown of the Associated Press. Infuriated by Halberstam's reporting, the President tried to have him removed from South Vietnam. This suggested a certain resistance to bad news about the war.

A few liberal publications of limited circulation also offered outright condemnation of the war. Richard Lee Strout, writing in *The New Republic* as TRB, observed prophetically on March 5, 1962: "The South Vietnam affair is an ugly, little undeclared peripheral war to which we now seem irrevocably committed. It carries nothing but grief, no matter what happens." In October 1963 another *New Republic* reporter sent back from Southeast Asia a story which began bluntly: "The war in South Vietnam cannot be won." Taylor and McNamara had recently returned to the United States from their second tour of the battlefields. They assured the President that the war was being lost from military weakness and the rottenness of the Diem regime. To correct the former, there would be more American soldiers. To correct the latter, the United States would connive at Diem's overthrow.

But at present Madame Nhu was touring the United States to confront the skeptics and to plead for more American aid. "Lovely to look at," *Newsweek* conceded, "but delightful to Ngo?" She was in Los Angeles preparing to fly home when news arrived that her husband and her brother-in-law, President Diem, had been murdered in a coup d'etat.

By its complicity in Diem's demise the United States had turned the last corner on the road to root-and-branch commitment. Henceforth it would be responsible for the outcome of the war because it had become responsible for the character of whatever government, or governments, followed Diem's. It would be morally obliged to defend the new regime to arm it, to pay its bills, and to advise it. According to Kenneth P. O'Donnell, the President by now had the gravest misgivings about what he had done. "He told me privately . . . that after his re-election [in 1964] he would take the risk of unpopularity and make a complete withdrawal of American military forces from Vietnam." But whether he had the courage and determination to follow this desire through, to accept calumny and slander and be branded "the President who lost South Vietnam," will never be known.

On November 22, 1963, President John F. Kennedy flew to Dallas. It was a journey he was eager to make. He would court Texas's twenty-five Electoral College votes, with an eye to 1964. He would help effect a reconciliation between the conservative and liberal wings of the Texas Democratic Party. And he would savor the delights of being toasted and cheered. During the afternoon he was assassinated by a sniper, Lee Harvey Oswald. With his death an era ended.

What was dead besides John Kennedy was America's secular faith—its optimism. With their faith in themselves badly shaken, Americans reeled toward the future, instead of reaching out to seize it. There could be no escape from the price that History exacts from every people burning to be great. "Lightning," said the Romans, "always strikes the highest peaks."

41
Envoi

"GREAT MEN ARE NOT ALWAYS WISE." *Job.*

From 1945 through 1963 the American people were in hot pursuit of their destiny. That was the meaning of American life in those years. The fulfillment of their historic ambitions appeared within their grasp. Their view of themselves as a chosen people, of their country as a city on a hill, could now be made manifest. They reached out with both hands to take hold of History. To some extent the emotional life of wartime had been a preparation.

No one seriously doubted from 1945 to 1963 that their country was living through a historic hour. Awareness of this uniqueness heightened every emotion, made nearly every division bitter, made every question about the nature of American society appear heretical and every doubt about the nation's destiny appear a form of disloyalty.

Although their history had given them a priceless opportunity, it had not prepared them completely for the burdens they must now bear. Until the war Americans had been remarkably provincial. For all their riches, the availability of education, their advanced economy, their vibrant cities, they remained to a large degree isolated from many of the major intellectual and artistic currents of the twentieth century, in touch with them at second hand or not at all. The United States was a net importer of basic science. Its role in international affairs was rarely constructive, consisting chiefly of attitudinizing and pleasant self-delusion. The best American architecture was innovative, but unpopular at home. American art was feeble and derivative. There were a dozen to a score of American writers of international stature, but with very few exceptions they took European writers for their models or tried to immerse themselves in European culture.

Those nations which are moved by dreams of greatness do not shake off their past and start anew on the golden age. They carry into it the defects as well as the strengths which have made them what they are. Postwar America, with its high historic mission and its global responsibilities, bore the earmarks of its recent provincial, largely agricultural past. The small-town boosterism, the easy acceptance of the second-rate, the credulousness, the crass and bombastic commercialism, the tiresome moralizing, the most repellent vulgarities of popular culture—all continued to flourish after 1945. They provoked both astonishment and resentment among educated people elsewhere. The great nations of the past, went one gibe popular among European café intellectuals of the 1950s, had gone from barbarism to civilization to decadence, but the get-ahead Americans had skipped the middle stage.

In their awareness of their historic importance Americans sometimes saw themselves as modern Athenians—defending civilization against the militaristic, power-mad Spartans (the Russians, that is). Or else they were the new Romans, enjoying imperial sway over the civilized world and building roads that everyone envied. And just as the Romans had been dogged by a cultural inferiority complex vis-a-vis the subtle and artistic Greeks, so Americans seemed on occasion to stand in regard to Western Europe. And Europeans, naturally, encouraged it. Harold Macmillan once complacently informed the postwar British that it was their duty to be the new Greeks to the American Romans. America, however, was neither a reborn Athens or a new Rome. It was itself and nothing else.

The American people in these years carried three historic responsibilities: first, to develop their own highest attributes as a nation; second, to defend the integrity of Western civilization; third, to help bring a world community into existence. The first is the moral duty of every nation. The second is the moral duty which has devolved for 2,500 years, since the Battle of Marathon, on the most powerful nation in the West at any given time. The third is a moral duty imposed on the world's leading power by the twentieth century—that is, by the advent of thermonuclear weapons, the dissolution of empires, the sophistication of international trade, and the pressures of population growth. Pericles had been proud to call Athens "the school of Greece." In living up to its moral obiligations

America, as the world's richest and freest country, was called on after 1945 to be the school of the West and the world.

It was in some respects a generation ahead of other Western or Westernized nations (in, e.g., applied technology, educational democracy), but in others (e.g., social welfare, the production of high culture) it was a generation behind. In its longer resistance to the all-embracing paternalistic state and in its greater entrepreneurial drive it had remained longer in the nineteenth century than any Western European country, including Great Britain. Yet such is the irony of history that this seeming backwardness helped provide postwar America with the brashness, the ambition, and the energy which made it possible for Americans to see in clear and simple terms their historic role and impel them to seize it so firmly. Had they been a more sophisticated and reflective people, it is doubtful that they would have enjoyed the self-confidence to match themselves with the imperatives of the historic moment.

The life of great nations at the height of their powers is not characterized by sobriety and dignity. On the contrary, it is turbulent. In the febrile atmosphere generated by an outpouring of nervous energy, in the tensions produced by the fear that they may be found wanting, such people yield to excess. Their motto was written by the Romans: *Nunquam desistere scivimus*—We never knew when to stop. The French Revolution saw the French people try to come to grips with their history and in the process produce a score of bloody crimes such as the prison massacres of September 1792. Great Britain in the days of its Empire was not the orderly, declining Britain we know. It was enlivened, for example, by seven attempts to assassinate Queen Victoria; child prostitution flourished in the streets of London; and the militia were called out to suppress political agitation, in one instance leaving a score of innocents, including women and children, dead from saber wounds. Even as late as the 1920s the British openly countenanced terror, exercised by the Black and Tans. The sensible, hardheaded, and intelligent Dutch at their national zenith, in the 17th century, threw themselves into a speculative craze in tulip bulbs which led to suicides and murders, turned millionaires overnight into beggars, and wrecked the Dutch economy for a decade. The Germans in their ascendant phases have shown how readily the craving for historic fulfillment turns into murderous behavior. There is no example of a great nation which has not, while the fit has been on it, committed horrifying crimes and yielded to mind-boggling stupidity. By comparison with the great nations of the past, the postwar American people were certainly no worse and by and large far better. Their greatest disgrace was McCathyism and all that it entailed—the suicides, the wrecked careers, the calumnies, the low-grade terror, the stultification of the spirit which always attends cowardice and lies.

Great nations in their ascendant phases produce not only excess but high drama. The Hiss-Chambers confrontation was an episode of nearly unbelievable theatricality. So at times were the antics of HUAC. The year 1948 produced the most extraordinary election result of American history, and 1960 produced the most exciting election, and the man who took office may well have been the man who had lost. The development of thermonuclear weapons was probably the most momentous misapplications of knowledge in the history of man. The Oppenheimer hearing, the execution of the Rosenbergs, the turmoil over school desegregation, the career of Joe McCarthy—all were the stuff of epic drama. It was an era of individuals who were larger than life, of astonishing twists and turns in the plot, and of portentous denouements. It was an era which closed with high tragedy, the assassination of John F. Kennedy. Behind every great nation there stands a host of upheavals. No wonder that Carlyle once remarked that happy was the nation which had no history.

But great nations have no monopoly on excess. Appalling crimes are committed in places such as Paraguay and Uganda; and these are hardly great nations. The excesses of great nations, however, are public events. They are not kept out of sight. The source of the one kind of injustice or idiocy is the pursuit of power or wealth by a handful of people at the expense of others. But the excesses of great nations spring from an excited popular temper. In the one case the few are trying to control the many. In the other the many are trying to control History. The one is rooted in private viciousness. The other is the result of a collective will that has missed the target.

Nations in the throes of greatness live on their nerves. They are difficult to manage but easy to move. It is not hard for them to blind themselves to their own failings. Fifth-century Athens, for example, produced both Socrates and slave labor; Phidias and the massacre at Melos. Elizabethan England was entertained by William Shakespeare and the death by torture of Catholic recusants. In a later ascendant phase the British people of 1848 had among them both John Stuart Mill and the mills which inspired the *Communist Manifesto*.

But between the self-doubts and the self-confidence which reside side by side in everyone, the postwar balance lay clearly with the latter. It pressed Americans forward to make the future of the world the future of their country, and the future of their country the future of the world.

Although the past had not completely prepared it for the present, there was within the United States the best instrument of salvation. The principle of monarchy, said Montesquieu, is honor; of a tyranny, fear; but of a republic, education. Americans had a more profound faith in education than any other democratic people. They worked on Deweyan principles. They learned about the demands of greatness while trying to be great.

"If there is one test of national genius universally accepted," wrote Emerson in 1847, "it is success." By that test, he conceded, the English were in 1847 the greatest nation on earth. Yet in what did this greatness consist? There was a vulgar inclination to cast it in terms of industrial production or to count the many millions of people under British rule. All this drew the scorn of Matthew Arnold. Greatness, he maintained, consisted of those attributes of a people which win the approbation of mankind.

Following Arnold, I would argue that the test of greatness is the extent to which a nation has engaged itself in the important enterprises of its time. Size is no more a test of greatness in a people than a man's height or wealth is a test of individual greatness. And Emerson was right about the English not because they were the most advanced industrial power or boasted a vast empire, but because there was hardly an important human undertaking of the 19th century in which the British were not deeply involved—in the struggle to abolish slavery, in the development of modern science, in the advancement of literature, in the spreading of literacy and democracy, in the development of economics, in the application of technology to improve the conditions of ordinary life, in the development of law, in parliamentary reform, in the creation of new public institutions, in generating new ideas about urban development. Twentieth-century science, literature, liberalism, and economic thought all have deep roots in nineteenth-century Britain. It is this ardent, energetic, confident closing with the moral challenges of an age which develops the spiritual and emotional powers of the human race and therefore wins the approbation of mankind. After 1945 there was no important human enterprise in which there was not an active American presence.

Since the ancient Greeks it has been the democracies which have been most likely to be attracted to greatness so understood. A nondemocratic or antidemocratic people is far more likely to be misled into mere self-aggrandizement. Not that democracies are necessarily immune to this danger. But greatness, because its true objective (however dimly seen or sometimes lost to sight) is the advancement of the human spirit, is most naturally pursued by individuals acting freely together and remaining free to change their course. The pursuit of power, on the other hand, is a perversion of any moral or spiritual quest. It inevitably leads to the regimentation of effort and forecloses the option to alter course. Greatness aims to set the spirit free. Power aims to control behavior. Greatness and power may touch at various points. They are often confused. However fine the line between them, it can be drawn, even though people remain likely to hunger for both:

> The good want power, but to weep barren tears.
> The powerful goodness want: worse need for them.
> The wise want love; and those who love want wisdom;
> And all best things are thus confused to ill.
> Shelley, *Prometheus Unbound*

The drive for greatness as a force in the lives of nations is a little studied, less understood social and historical phenomenon. As a rule it must be safely in the past before it seems possible for twentieth-century writers and thinkers to consider it at all. This reflects the present shriveled view we take of ourselves and of the world that men have made. Yet the appetite for greatness lives on. We have lived through epic times but have no gift for epic song.

A great age, or a great people in their prime, will not necessarily produce great art, great literature, or great ideas. These are not the only avenues down which the human spirit advances. But the commitment to important enterprises leaves monuments for those with eyes to see. This is true whether, like the great nations of the West, they go out into the world or whether, like China, they expect the world to come to them.

The great human ventures of the postwar were social, economic, and educational; scientific, organizational, and technological; instead of being artistic, musical, and literary. This was the result of the rapid twentieth-century increase in democratic practices, in the fund of useful knowledge, and in universal secondary education, in an unprecedented growth of material production, and in the development of truly international institutions. These were combined with the decline of traditional cultural and political elites and the eradication, at least in the West, of extreme mass poverty. The past has not been without similar eras. France between 1789 and 1815 was deeply (and bloodily) engaged in political, social, and ethical issues of historic importance but produced almost no first-rate art, literature, or music.

The drive for greatness is both a historical event for an entire people and an expression of the deepest impulses of the individual psyche. In the individual it springs not simply from a love of glory but from a desire to serve the human race and at the same time give meaning to everyday life. It is the inevitable pursuit of a few individuals in every age; the calling of great artists, geniuses, religious visionaries, creative thinkers. But the ordinary man is not a genius or a visionary. And "Human life," wrote Ortega y Gasset, "by its very nature, has to be dedicated to something, an enterprise glorious or humble, a destiny illustrious or trivial. . . . If that life of mine, which concerns only myself, is not directed towards something, it will be disjointed, lacking in tension and form."

Caught up in the throes of greatness, people do not awake each morning and consciously begin to shape their actions of that day to serve great ends. Each individual has his or her personal life to live. But each of us also lives he life and times of our society. The American of the first eighteen postwar years would, because of his era and its moral imperatives, have been more likely to think about voting, wonder if blacks did not deserve a break, be uneasy about the death penalty, demand higher standards in the schools, be more conscientious about teaching his children to be good citizens, be more actively involved in the life of his community and country. Nothing seemed more natural than a concern with "national goals," the "quality of life," and "human rights." As people become consciously engaged with concerns such as these, moreover, their nature becomes more expansive, the range of their moral concerns is broadened, their sensitivity to the needs of the spirit is advanced.

The pursuit of national destiny coexists with those concerns which people would have to deal with anyway: employment, the family, sickness, old age, education, money. Remove the collective drive for greatness, life would still go on. But there would be an empty space. In the nations whose greatness lies firmly in the past it forms an echo chamber and gives forth hollow sounds, as it does in modern Britain, France, Italy, and

Spain. Modern man needs greatness and the dreams of greatness as much as his ancestors ever did. An obsession with greatness is part of our hunger for experience in the brief time that each of us enjoys.

In the case of great men and women, the drive to realize their destiny ends only with death. Societies have less staying power. Twenty to thirty years appear to be as long as they can live at the summit of commitment. Then may follow a century or only a few decades, in which they bask in their former glory and reap the rewards, and the sometimes bitter fruits, of what they have sown. By the early 1960s the drive for greatness which had really begun during the war was beginning to ebb.

Social morale, like national character or natural justice, is elusive. It makes itself felt in our emotional and spiritual life but expresses itself indirectly elsewhere. To me, the postwar religious revival was part of the drive for greatness. By the early 1960s that revival had clearly passed its peak. The percentage of eligible voters participating in Presidential elections rose steadily after 1944 and peaked in 1960. It has dropped just as steadily ever since. Suicide and homicide rates kept pace with the growth of population until the early 1960s: since then they have virtually doubled. The high postwar birthrate leveled off in the late 1950s and turned down in the early 1960s. And as we have seen, silent youth turned rebellious in the early 1960s and black protest turned violent. At the same time drug abuse began to spread from the poorest, most brutalized parts of society into the white middle class. Even had John F. Kennedy lived, the United States was about to pass through a crisis of nerve and authority.

But there was no mistaking the character of the age just past. The Fifties received a bad press even at the time, being derided as "the vacuum age," when there were "the bland leading the bland." Yet this was the very decade when American popular culture swept the world because it was the most vibrant and accessible. America represented, to the ordinary people at home and overseas, vigor and daring—thinking big, talking big, acting big. It was the craving for even greater excitement that Kennedy exploited so astutely.

No great nation in its prime is modest. The brazen boasting of Americans in the postwar could be matched sentiment for sentiment, if not word for word, by other great nations of the past. Even the Chinese, usually a private and modest people, in their great ages were far from reticent. They simply placed themselves at the center of the universe. When a nation is in its ascendancy, it likes to talk about it—usually at the top of its lungs.

"She has tamed the savage continent," wrote the greatest of American historians, Francis Parkman, "peopled the solitude, gathered wealth untold, waxed potent, imposing, redoubtable. And now it remains for her to prove, if she can, that the rule of the masses is consistent with the highest growth of the individual; that democracy can give the world a civilization as mature and pregnant, ideas as energetic and vitalizing, and types of manhood as lofty and strong as any of the systems which it boasts to supplant." The nature of the challenge was never put more concisely or elegantly.

Yet 100 years later another great gentleman-scholar, George Kennan, would say, "We have nothing to teach the world. We have to confess that we have not got the answers to the problems of human society in the modern age."

There is ample reason for a critical mind to despair of the United States if it emphasizes the excesses and the enduring provincial traits. It is also true that of their three moral obligations—to themselves, to the West, and to the world at large—American policy makers in the postwar tended too often to see only the second and to lose sight of the first and third. In pursuit of the defense of the democratic West they found a moral cause which could be used to justify the betrayal of their country's own highest attributes and to impede the development of a world community.

Yet I maintain that the American people, however narrowly or confusedly, advanced—at different rates—toward all three objectives. The American presence in the important ventures of mankind may at times have been a mixed blessing, but for the most part it was a force for good. The world became a kinder, more just place because of the role of the United States. At home, America became a kinder, more just place as well.

The American ascendancy of 1945 to 1963 was a positive development. It could be misled, miunderstood, put to the service of chauvinism and greed, power mania, or self-delusion. And it was. But out of the restless energy, the revival of optimism and self-confidence, arose countless opportunities for expansive, generous, brave spirits to express themselves freely. And even the policy makers were not always wrong. The enlightened self-interest of the Marshall Plan, the organization of idealism by means of the Peace Corps, the 55,000 dead in Korea who paid the price of mutual security, the outpouring of money for scientific and medical research serve as timeless examples of greatness in action. A nation in decline, by comparison, will turn grudging and envious, become self-occupied and mean-spirited. None of which describes the postwar United States.

The postwar also produced great men in the public arena. Here, in alphabetical order, are a handful: Acheson, Eisenhower, Kennan, Kennedy, Lilienthal, MacArthur, Marshall, Oppenheimer, and Truman. All were active in the life of their country from the early 1940s to the early 1960s. Could any comparable list be compiled for the years since 1963?

Americans did remain true to themselves despite the disgraces of the Cold War. Theirs remained an open society. No government had a more difficult time keeping its secrets; no government was so susceptible to aroused public opinion; no press was as free to print what it liked or a people as free to read or see or say what they liked. Despite the crudities of its visa policies, America shared with ancient Rome a remarkable capacity for "the absorption of outlying genius." Rich Americans scoured the world for artistic treasures. Rich American institutions scoured it for talented scientists, scholars, artists, writers, and thinkers and brought them to the United States. This was the rule except in a handful of cases—and thinking Americans considered the exceptions outrageous. They also pressed, successfully, for an end to such nonsense.

Although Americans were pursuing greatness, it was not an insular pursuit, reserved only for the native-born. Anyone who had something to offer was welcome to participate, whether in a laboratory or writing at a desk, painting pictures, or teaching in a university. There has never been anything like it except for a very brief period during the French Revolution.

Not only were they for the most part true to the openness and generosity which are their highest attributes as a people, but they also tried to advance the world community. No one believed more strongly in the United Nations. No one created more international bodies, or supported them more generously. In the Test Ban Treaty, the Atoms for Peace program, and the proposed joint ventures in space with the Soviet Union the Americans took the initiative. Had they met with a more forthcoming response, they would doubtless have gone still further. The worldwide spreading of American popular culture was another force which helped bind ordinary people in many lands in a shared experience.

Historic enterprises are the work of decades or centuries. No one should despair because there were setbacks and disappointments. The facts are that America remained free and used its free institutions to help create a better society. The West remained free and bound up its terrible self-inflicted wounds. The world was brought more tightly together than ever. American communications satellites, the ubiquitous Coca-Cola, American jet airliners, the Peace Corps, American films and music, American businesses and machinery, American books, and a thousand other American products spread around the world American ideas and values. And around the world it was young people especially who responded. They played American records, spoke American slang, wore American clothing, followed American idols. Behind their dress, their speech, their actions was a yearning for the vibrancy and life-affirming energy of American life. However vicariously, they needed to feel in touch with American achievements in order to make contact with their own time.

All history, however, ends in tragedy. We are too frail, too fallible for it to be otherwise. It is inevitable that any nation dreaming of greatness will have a reach that exceeds its grasp. But tragedy, as Nietzsche said, transcends pessimism. Our sense of tragedy comes from a spirit that loves life and responds to it, no matter how painful or desperate. What the American people had yet to learn when they launched themselves on the postwar drive for the greatness that would fulfill their destiny was that in reaching out for History they had embraced tragedy.

Tragedy is the highest form of drama. The theme is of greatness overreaching itself. But it can do no other. Here is the lesson every great nation has eventually learned: to be great is to struggle, to suffer, and to fail. John F. Kennedy in his brief life symbolized the postwar drive for greatness. In his sudden, cruel death he symbolized the falling short of a nation—the tragedy of his time, his country, of humanity itself.

Yet men must reach as high as they can see. Carl Schurz in a speech at Faneuil Hall in 1859 compared our ideals with the stars. By keeping our eyes on the stars, which are far beyond our reach, we may navigate safely through the darkness and over the water, until we reach our destination. So too with our ideals: so long as we have the courage to navigate by them, however unattainable they may be, we will journey with purpose until that day when we arrive at the destiny of man.

On November 22, 1963, Kennedy became immortal, not for anything he had done in life but for what he stood for in death. To the human heart there is nothing more romantic than loss. That romantic aura will cling to his name through generations yet unborn.

But something besides a President was buried. What was dead was a kind of innocence which I have called optimism. Americans had no sense of tragedy, of human limitations, until that day. Despite the Civil War, the assassination of Lincoln, the Depression, they had no true sense of the price that History exacts for greatness. After November 22, 1963, they saw themselves and the world realistically, or more realistically than they had ever done. And now when they looked on the future they were seized with foreboding. Ahead of them, they sensed, there stretched a bad and bitter time.

SOURCES

Sources

I: THE ROAD TO 1948

Chapter 1
The fanatical Japanese: Louis Halle, *The Cold War as History* (London: 1967), pp. 93–94. Peace looked "a little nondescript" to Jonathan Daniels, *Frontier on the Potomac* (New York: 1945), p. 222. Telephoning to Washington: *Time* (August 20, 1945). The "returning war correspondent" was Daniels, p. 235. Radio hams: *Time* (September 3, 1945). Price of bicycles: ibid. (December 17, 1945). Personal optimism: Hadley Cantril, *Public Opinion 1935–1946* (Princeton, New Jersey: 1951), p. 831.

Behavior of American servicemen overseas: R. Alton Lee, "The Army Mutiny of 1946," *Journal of American History* (October 1966); *Time* (January 21, 1946); *Life*, (February 11, 1946). Louis Falstein: "You're On Your Own," *New Republic* (October 8, 1945). Paraphrase of Belloc: *Life* (December 2, 1946). Thomas Eugene Atkins: *Time* (November 12, 1945). James Kutcher, *The Case of the Legless Veteran* (New York: 1973). John Keats, *The New Romans* (Philadelphia: 1973), pp. 136–38. Claude Eatherly: William Bradford Huie, *The Hiroshima Pilot* (New York: 1964). The Bridgeport story: Stuart Chase, *For This We Fought* (New York: 1946). The Peoria story: Ralph Martin, *The Best Is None Too Good* (New York: 1948). Communists and the veterans organizations: William Price, "The Veterans' House Divided," *The Nation* (May 25, 1946); Sam Stavitsky, "The Veterans Make Their Choice," *Harper's* (September 1946). Frank Smith: *Congressman from Mississippi* (New York: 1964), p. 64.

Value of the nation's housing stock: Harold C. Vatter, *The U.S. Economy in the 1950s* (New York: 1963), p. 49. Inflation in house prices: *The*

743

Nation (February 8, 1946). Jay Ramsey: *Time* (December 24, 1945). Leo Zale: Martin, p. 72. Marine in Pershing Square: *Time* (November 17, 1945). School superintendent: ibid. Glen Taylor: John Gunther, *Inside, USA*, 2nd ed.(New York: 1951), p. 114. For views of the Dymaxion house, inside and out, see *Life* (April 1, 1946). Housing policies under Truman: Nathan Strauss, *Two Thirds of a Nation* (New York: 1952), and Richard Davies, *Housing Reform and the Truman Administration* (Columbia, Mo.: 1966). Housing policies and public opinion: Cantril, p. 300. Richard L. Neuberger: "This Is a World I Never Fought For," *New York Times Magazine* (July 28, 1946).

Lilienthal: *Journals of David E. Lilienthal* (New York: 1964), Vol. 2, p. 56. The 52-20 Club: *Time* (January 6, 1947). Veterans' readjustment allowance: Bureau of Labor Statistics, "Readjustment of Veterans to Civilian Life" (Washington, D.C.: 1946), p. 4. Glamor jobs, glamor plants: *Time* (September 10, 1945).

"Happiest day of my life": ibid. (November 5, 1945). "As a result of this ordeal": Julian Cornwell, *The Trial of Ezra Pound* (London: 1964), p. 14; for a very detailed account of Pound's experiences in captivity, see David Heyman, *Ezra Pound: The Last Rower* (London: 1975). Opinion on the atomic bomb: George H. Gallup, *The Gallup Poll* (New York: 1972), p. 521. Opinion on aid to Russia: ibid., p. 535. Hitler: ibid., p. 544. Postwar military establishment: ibid., p. 647. John Bartlow Martin, "Middletown Revisited," *Harper's* (August 1946).

Chapter 2
"Over the ceiling": *Life* (April 1, 1946). Black market in lumber and nails: *Time*, (June 24 and August 26, 1946). Veterans without shirts: ibid. (February 14 and April 29, 1946). House in Portland: *The Nation* (July 13, 1946). "Used" Cadillacs: *New Republic* (July 7, 1947). Used-car black market in the South: Tristram Coffin, "So You Want a New Car," ibid. (September 7, 1946). Journey with nylons: *Life* (April 1, 1946). Oklahoma hound dog: *Time* (April 29, 1946). Evading OPA regulations: Stanley Goodman, "Make It Pay," *Harper's* (September 1946). Anti-OPA mail: *The Nation* (April 27, 1946). Public opinion on the OPA: Hadley Cantril, *Public Opinion 1935-1946* (Princeton, N.J.: 1951), p. 662. OPA agent in Los Angeles: the photograph appeared in *Time* (September 23, 1946). Stampede to the slaughterhouse: *New York Times* (July 21, 1946). Public outcry and mail to Taft: *Time* (May 6, 1946). Wartime rent controls: Chester Bowles, *Promises to Keep* (New York: 1971), p. 36. Effects of the "meat famine": *Time* (September 30, 1946). End of public support for price controls: Cantril, pp. 218, 437; cf. Jerry Voorhis, *Confessions of a Congressman* (Garden City, N.Y.: 1947), p. 327. Coconut experiment: Alfred Friendly, "What Will Your Dollar Buy in 1946?," *The Nation* (January 5, 1946). Miami landlord: Robert S. Allen, *Our Fair City* (New York: 1947), p. 94. The Treasury's "dominant position": Lester Chandler, *Inflation in the United States 1940-1948* (New York: 1951), p. 302. Defla-

tionary expectations: Milton Friedman, with Anna M. Schwartz, *A Monetary History of the United States 1867–1960* (Princeton, N.J.: 1963), pp. 584–85; cf. "Inflation Over," *Fortune* (December 1946) in which *Fortune*'s editors confidently predict deflation and falling prices in 1947.

"End of the Gravy Train": Sumner H. Slichter, *The Impact of Collective Bargaining on Management* (Washington, D.C.: 1960), p. 494. Forecast of 8 million unemployed: *Bureau of Labor Statistics Fact Book on Manpower* (Washington, D.C.: 1951), Table 6. Forecast of 20 million unemployed: W. S. Woytinsky, "What Was Wrong with Forecasts of Postwar Depression," *Journal of Political Economy* (April 1947); cf. Chandler, op. cit., pp. 225–28. Earnings figures: *Monthly Labor Review*, No. 64 (Washington, D.C.: 1947). "You're crazy as hell": Jonathan Daniels, *The Man from Independence* (Philadelphia: 1950), p. 325. Lewis versus Truman: Saul Alinsky, *John L. Lewis* (New York: 1949), pp. 291–93. Effects of the coal strike: *Time* (May 20, 1946). "Hercules wearing size 12 shoes": Alinsky, op. cit., p. 335. Health in Appalachia and the UMW hospitals: Ira Wolfert, *An Epidemic of Genius* (New York: 1960), pp. 158–59; Harry M. Caudill, *Night Comes to the Cumberlands* (Boston: 1962). CIO FORCES SHOWDOWN: *Life* (January 21, 1946). Man-days lost to strikes: *Monthly Labor Review*, op. cit. "Proud to be the lowest paid head": Frank Cormier and William J. Eaton, *Reuther*, (Englewood Cliffs, N.J.: 1970), p. 251. "A roly-poly extrovert": ibid., p. 230. Thomas and the GM strike: Irving Howe and B. J. Widick, *The UAW and Walter Reuther* (New York: 1949), p. 157.

"Cancellation of any large number": Herbert Somers, *Presidential Agency* (Cambridge, Mass.: 1950), p. 179. Surplus homing pigeons, etc.: *Time* (August 20 and September 24, 1945). "One Company": Blair Bolles, *How to Get Rich in Washington* (New York: 1952), p. 84. Blimps: *Life* (February 17, 1947). Veterans' cabs: *New Republic* (January 27, 1947). Preston Tucker: Bolles, pp. 85–87. Artificial limb indictment: John Gunther, *Inside USA*, rev. ed. (New York: 1951), p. xviii. Wage rises tied to productivity: advertising in *Business Week* (August 28, 1948). Boulwareism: Herbert R. Northrup, "The Case for Boulwareism," *Harvard Business Review* (September–October 1963). "Between 1930 and 1946": Martin Mayer, *Wall Street*, rev. ed. (New York: 1959), p. 18.

"The New Deal was not ahead of its time": Alvin Hansen, *Economic Issues of the 1960s* (New York: 1960), p. 3. The 1946 Employment Act: Stephen K. Bailey, *Congress Makes a Law* (Wesleyan, Conn.: 1950). "The hardest, meanest son of a bitch": Daniels, p. 305. Wallace in 1932: Richard Dalfiume, *American Politics Since 1945* (New York: 1969), p. 47. "New Frontiers": Dwight Macdonald, *Henry Wallace: The Man and the Myth* (New York: 1948), p. 25. Wallace at Madison Square Garden: David Shannon, *The Decline of American Communism* (New York: 1959). What Wallace told Truman: Alonzo Hamby, *Beyond the New Deal* (New York: 1974), p. 128. Truman was called a liar by *Time* (September 30, 1946). "A man of mediocre mind": Robert S. Allen and William V. Shannon, *The Truman Merry-Go-Round* (New York: 1950), p. 4. Truman and the KKK:

A DREAM OF GREATNESS

Daniels, p. 126. "Held open court": Cabell Phillips, *The Truman Presidency* (New York: 1966), p. 141. "A man that knew the Masonic handshake": James West, *Plainville USA* (New York: 1945), p. 82. "Kennedy campaign buttons": *The Nation* (October 18, 1946). WANTED: Ralph De Toledano, *Nixon* (New York: 1956), pp. 39–40. "Joe McCarthy was a tail gunner": Jack Anderson and Ronald W. May, *McCarthy: The Man, The Senator, The Ism* (Boston: 1952), p. 85. Events in Athens: Theodore H. White, "The Battle of Athens, Tennessee," *Harper's* (January 1947); *Time* (August 12, 1946). "Shadow of a meatball": *The Nation* (November 2, 1946). "He was his own boss": Phillips, p. 125. "Bluff, genial": *Time* (August 26, 1946). "Warmhearted, ingratiating and charming": Jack Anderson, "The Senate's Remarkable Upstart," *Saturday Evening Post* (August 9, 1947).

Chapter 3
New York snowfall: *Newsweek* (January 5, 1948). Texas City: *Time* (April 27, 1948). "For heaven's sake": ibid. (November 11, 1946). Rabbits' feet and "Graveyard Dust": Howard Whitman, "Merchants of Luck," *Collier's* (November 1948). Science fiction: Richard A. Gehman, "Imagination Runs Wild," *New Republic* (January 17, 1949). UFOs in 1897 and 1947: David Michael Jacobs, *The UFO Controversy in America* (Bloomington, Ind.: 1975), Chapter 1.

Divorce figures: Bureau of the Census, *Historical Statistics of the United States* (Washington, D.C.: 1957). Divorced couples in same house: *San Francisco Chronicle* (September 7, 1947). Marriage, divorce, and birth rates: Clyde V. Kiser et al., *Trends and Variations in Fertility in the United States* (Cambridge, Mass.: 1968), Table 4.1, p. 58; J. F. Dewhurst et al., *America's Needs and Resources: A New Survey* (New York: 1955), p. 55. Illegitimate births: Joseph Schacter and Mary McCarthy, *Illegitimate Births, United States 1938–1957* (Washington, D.C.: 1960). Changes in child-rearing practices: Martha Wolfenstein, "The Emergence of Fun Morality," in Eric Larrabee and Rolf Meyersohn, *Mass Leisure* (New York: 1958). Sales of Dr. Spock: Alice Payne Hackett, *70 Years of Best Sellers* (Boston: 1968), p. 12. "Place a premium": Gesell, p. 455. Standards of teachers: Benjamin Fine, *Our Children Are Cheated* (New York: 1947). Public support for aid to education: Hadley Cantril, *Public Opinion 1935–1946* (Princeton, N.J.: 1951), p. 188. High school principal: *Harper's* (January 1946). Curricula changes: John F. Latimer, *What's Happened to Our High Schools* (Washington, D.C.: 1958), Tables 1–3, pp. 23–29; Table 6, p. 36; Tables 10–11, pp. 44, 47. The Prosser Resolution passed in Chicago in 1945: the text is reproduced in U.S. Office of Education, Bulletin 22, "Life Adjustment for Every Youth" (Washington, D.C.: 1951). Superiority of "Health education": Harl R. Douglass, *Secondary Education for Life Adjustment of Every American Youth* (New York: 1952), p. 406. List of "real-life problems": Arthur Bestor, *Educational Wastelands* (Urbana, Ill.: 1953), pp. 84–86. "It is through the poetry": Harvard University, *General Education in a Free Society* (Cambridge, Mass.: 1944), p. 108. $1 billion a year from the GI Bill: Congressional Quarterly, *Congress and the Nation 1945–1964* (Washington, D.C.: 1965), p. 1118. Cake decorating etc.: *Time* (December 22, 1947). "My experience": Jacques Barzun, *The House of Intellect* (New York: 1959), p. 122. "It is what they don't want": *Fortune* (June 1949).

Combat pilots, Brahms "Lullaby": E. A. Strecker, *Their Mothers' Sons* (Philadelphia: 1951). "From all the stuff": *Time* (November 19, 1945). Hostile writing about women: Ferdinand Lundberg and Marynia Farnham, *Modern Woman: The Lost Sex* (New York: 1947); Agnes Rogers, "Is It Anyone We Know?," *Harper's* (June 1946); "Woman's Dilemma," *Life* (June 16, 1947). "We spoke of life as a rat race": John Keats, *The New Romans* (Philadelphia: 1973), p. 157. "The well-to-do residential community": Carl Von Rhode, "The Suburban Mind," *Harper's* (April 1946). "Nearly six feet": *Time* (July 3, 1950). "The slum of the future": ibid. $500 million windfall from overestimates of costs: *Newsweek* (July 26, 1954). Three million families: *Time* (May 17, 1948). Family living in Pennsylvania Station: *New York Times* (April 4, 1948). "It's too true": Alistair Cooke in *New Republic* (January 27, 1947). Rookeries racket: George A. Bernstein, "The Rookeries Racket," *The Nation* (November 13, 1948).

Demand for appliances: J. F. Dewhurst et al., *America's Needs and Resources* (New York: 1947), pp. 347–48. Percentage of homes with servants: Cantril, p. 791. "In the year 1948": James B. Conant, *Education in a Divided World*, (Cambridge, Mass. 1948) p. 80. San Francisco bank queues: *San Francisco Chronicle* (September 3, 1947). Price of sex in Seattle: *Time* (February 10, 1947). Newburyport: ibid. (December 15, 1947). Carpet widths in demand: Pauline Paro, "Effects of World War II on the Production and Distribution of House Furnishings," *BLS* (Washington, D.C.: 1951). Early disillusionment with suburban life: Keats, op. cit., pp. 148–49.

"These days of falsies": *San Francisco Chronicle* (September 1, 1947).

"Only the possible candidacy": Selden Menefee, "America: There Is No Peace," *The Nation* (March 27, 1948). "It is Not": Norris Schneider and Sanford M. Dornbusch, *Popular Religion: Inspirational Books in America* (Chicago: 1958), p. 13. "The American way of life": Cyril Connolly, "Blueprint for a Silver Age," *Harper's* (December 1947). "I rediscovered": Luigi Barzini, *Americans Are Alone in the World* (New York: 1953), p. 80. "I liked": Simone de Beauvoir, *America Day by Day* (New York: 1953), p. 128.

Chapter 4

Stetson Kennedy: *I Rode with the Ku Klux Klan* (London: 1954), p. 25. "I knelt in front of the altar": ibid., pp. 99–100. Woodward blinding: George McMillan, "Race Justice in Aiken," *The Nation* (November 23, 1946). Trial and cheering: Richard Kluger, *Simple Justice* (New York:

1976), pp. 297–98. Marcus Snipes: Langston Hughes, *Fight for Freedom* (New York: 1962). Roger Malcolm and Leon McAtee: *Time* (August 5, 1946). Willie Earle: Don Whitehead, *The FBI Story* (New York: 1956), pp. 253–54. Anguilla Prison: The only coherent published account is the long telegram in *New Republic* (July 28, 1947) from the county commissioner for Glynn County, Georgia; also, *New Republic* (August 25, 1947). "Big Duck" Mallard: *Time* (December 6, 1948/January 24, 1949). "Many of my friends": James Baldwin, *The Fire Next Time* (New York: 1963), p. 26. "It destroyed their fear": ibid. Spencer Logan, *A Negro's Faith in America* (New York: 1946) p. 62. Student opinion: *The Nation* (March 6, 1948). Truman's horror at racial atrocities: Richard M. Dalfiume, *Desegregation of the U.S. Armed Forces* (Columbia, Mo.: 1969), pp. 134, 144–45. "This is the situation": U.S. President's Committee on Civil Rights, *To Secure These Rights* (Washington, D.C.: 1947), p. 95. "Stirring in the womb of time": Lerone Bennett, *What Manner of Man* (Chicago: 1964), pp. 33–34. Truman's personal views on race: Jonathan Daniels, *The Man of Independence* (Philadelphia: 1950), p. 338. "If you do this": Arthur Mann, *The Jackie Robinson Story* (New York: 1951), pp. 183–84.

"Control of the mosquito": Thomas D. Clark, *The Emerging South*, 2nd ed. (New York: 1968), p. 31. Freight rates 37 percent higher: *Time* (May 19, 1947). "I always make sure": Harry Golden, *For 2¢ Plain* (Cleveland: 1959), p. 214. Ernie Starnes: Lawrence Lader, "It's Still Done the Hard Way," *New Republic* (September 1, 1947). The Klan and the unions: Carey McWilliams, "The Klan: Postwar Model," *The Nation* (December 14, 1947). Russell Manufacturing Company: Jack Barbash, *The Practice of Unionism* (New York: 1956), pp. 42–43. Lucy Randolph Mason: Lawrence Lader, "The Lady and the Sheriff," *New Republic* (January 5, 1948); Ralph McGill, *The South and the Southerner* (Boston: 1963), pp. 191–92. Despairing thoughtful Southerners: e.g., V. O. Key, Jr., *Southern Politics in State and Nation* (New York: 1949), p. 4. Proportion of blacks in Southern population: ibid., p. 131.

"They do not": James Baldwin, *Nobody Knows My Name* (New York: 1961), p. 65. The slums of prosperity: Daniel Seligman, "The Enduring Slums," *Fortune* (December 1957). Sleeping conditions on the South Side: William H. Whyte, *Industry and Society* (Westburyport, Conn.: 1946), p. 95. Health of blacks in big city ghettos: *New Republic* (March 8, 1948). Henry Laws: Carey McWilliams, "The House on 92nd Street," *The Nation* (June 8, 1946). Bethesda woman et al.: *The Nation* (January 10, 1948). "The evil that the FHA did": Charles Abrams, *Forbidden Neighbors* (New York: 1955), p. 236. "Credit-blacklist maps": Jane Jacobs, *The Death and Life of Great American Cities* (New York: 1961), pp. 299–300. "Mostly crude farmers": Lee Mortimer's column, quoted by C. Wright Mills, *Puerto Rican Journey* (New York: 1950), pp. 131–32. Color discrimination among Puerto Ricans: Dan Wakefield, *Island in the City* (Boston: 1959), p. 41.

Chapter 5

Public opinion on location of United Nations: Hadley Cantril, *Public Opinion 1935–1946* (Princeton: 1951), p. 913. "Misplaced generosity": Dean Acheson, *Present at the Creation* (New York: 1969), p. 112. "New York *is* the world's capital": *The Nation* (December 21, 1946). Opinion on the UN's prospects: Leonard S. Cottrell and Silvia Everhard, *American Opinion on World Affairs* (Princeton: 1948), p. 126. Steven Supina: *The Nation* (July 21, 1948). "Philanthropy": F. Emerson Andrews, *Attitudes Toward Giving* (New York: 1953), p. 6. Gerard and Kathleen Hale: *Life* (October 14, 1946). Claude Canaday: ibid. (May 6, 1946). CARE: F. Emerson Andrews, *Philanthropic Giving* (New York: 1956), pp. 85–87. $2 billion for relief: Robert H. Bremner, *American Philanthropy* (Chicago: 1960), p. 162. "To come as close as possible": Alan J. Matusow, *Farm Policies and Politics in the Truman Years* (Cambridge, Mass.: 1967), p. 5. Photographs of starving children: e.g., *Life* (May 6, 1946). La Guardia's call for British sacrifice: *The Nation* (April 20, 1946). "Pillsbury" on girls' panties: *Time* (March 11, 1946). McCormick's proposal: John Gunther, *Inside USA*, 2nd ed. (New York: 1951), p. 390. Photograph of burning potatoes: *Time* (May 26, 1947). Opposition to British loan: Cottrell and Everhard, p. 130. Opinion on Russian loan: Cantril, pp. 214, 740. "We were willing": Jerry Voorhis, *Confessions of a Congressman* (New York: 1947), p. 244.

"There at Potsdam": Jonathan Daniels, *The Man of Independence* (Philadelphia: 1950). Discussions on dropping the bomb: the only firsthand accounts by participants are Harry S. Truman, *Year of Decisions* (Garden City, N.Y.: 1955), and Henry Stimson, "The Decision to Use the Bomb," *Harper's* (February 1947). Order to 509th Composite Group: Cabell Phillips, *The Truman Presidency* (New York: 1966), pp. 57–60. People felt secure: Cottrell and Everhard, op. cit., p. 18. The worriers and the nonworriers: ibid., p. 109. The Bikini test as radio entertainment: John Crosby, *Out of the Blue* (New York: 1952), pp. 3–9. Pretest rumor and posttest opinion: William L. Lawrence, "The Bikini Tests and Public Opinion," *Bulletin of the Atomic Scientists* (September 1, 1946). "The deuterium bomb": Leonard Engel in *The Nation* (August 28, 1948). The opposition of scientists to the May-Johnson bill: Donald A. Strickland, *Scientists in Politics: The Atomic Scientists' Movement 1945–1946* (Purdue, Ind.: 1968). Press releases from FATS: Alice Kimball Smith, *A Peril and a Hope* (Chicago: 1965), 208. Congressional mail: James R. Newman and Byron S. Miller, *The Control of Atomic Energy* (New York: 1948), p. 12. "No fairy story": David E. Lilienthal, *Journals of David E. Lilienthal* (New York: 1964), Vol. 2, pp. 16–17. "My fellow citizens" and "immediate, swift and sure punishment": Bernard Baruch, *The Public Years* (New York: 1960), 339–40. Churchill warning: *New York Times* (August 17, 1945). Vannevar Bush and James B. Conant warnings: Joseph I. Lieberman, *The Scorpion and the Tarantula* (Boston: 1970), p. 50. "If she threw": U.S. Congress Joint Committee on Atomic Energy, 79th Congress, 2nd Session, *Hearings* (Washington, D.C.: 1946), Part 1, p. 175. The two leading atomic scientists were Hans Bethe and Frederick Seitz, Jr., in *One World or None* (New York: 1946), p. 46. Irving Langmuir's estimate: ibid. p. 48. Public opinion on U.S. A-bomb monopoly: Cantril, pp. 22–23; Cottrell and Everhard, pp. 113–14.

"For the first time": U.S. President's Scientific Research Board, *Science and Public Policy* (Washington, D.C.: 1947), Vol. 1, p. 5. "No adequate course": *New York Herald Tribune* (October 24, 1948). "If it is true": Louis Wellborn, "The Ordeal of Dr. Condon," *Harper's* (January 1950). Oppenheimer under surveillance: Philip M. Stern, *The Oppenheimer Case* (New York: 1969), p. 112.

"Today": Baruch, pp. 355–56. Public opinion on Soviet leaders: George H. Gallup, *The Gallup Poll 1935–1972* (New York: 1972), pp. 565, 582. Hostility toward American Communists: ibid., p. 587. Five to one opposition to sale of oil etc.: ibid, p. 707. Opinion favoring CIA: Cantril, p. 772. "In many Eastern European countries": Michael Straight, "Fixing the Blame for the Cold War," *New Republic* (September 15, 1947). "From now on": *The Nation* (August 28, 1948). "I can testify": Louis Halle, *The Cold War as History* (London: 1967), p. 38. "Chose Berlin": Herbert Feis, *From Trust to Terror* (New York: 1968), p. 28. "The Americans would probably be frustrated": *The Cold War* (New York: 1948), p. 20. Public support for the Truman doctrine: *Newsweek* (March 22, 1948). "President Monroe's hands-off doctrine": Freda Kirchwey, in *The Nation* (March 22, 1947). Kennan's role in the Marshall Plan: George Kennan, *Memoirs 1925–1950* (Boston: 1967), pp. 325–28. Public opinion on future war with Soviet Union: *Newsweek*, op. cit. "Not since the fateful days": ibid. (March 29, 1948). Draft card burning: Lawrence S. Wittner, *Rebels Against War* (New York: 1969), p. 163. The draftless draft: *Time* (May. 17, 1947). "The dreadful word": TRB, in *New Republic* (April 5, 1948).

Popularity of Administration's DP policy: Robert A. Divine, *American Immigration Policy 1925–1952* (New Haven, Conn.: 1957), p. 113. One person in 100 in favor of unrestricted Jewish immigration: Cantril, p. 387. Jewish quotas in professional schools in the 1940s: U.S. President's Commission on Higher Education, *Higher Education for American Democracy* (Washington, D.C.: 1948), Vol. 2, pp. 38–39. The cartoon was by David Low: reproduced in *The Nation* (January 5, 1946). "Fitting and just": ibid. (December 8, 1948). Opposition to majority rule: e.g., *New Republic* (November 26, 1945). "We do not always like": Joseph Lash, *Eleanor: The Years Alone* (New York: 1973), p. 124. "You can bank on us": Daniels, p. 318. "God put you in your mother's womb": Merle Miller, *Plain Speaking* (New York: 1974), p. 218.

Asheville convention: "UWF's Birthday Marks Half a Decade of Progress," *The Federalist* (February 1952). Twenty-three state legislatures: Wittner, op. cit., p. 209. "What, or who": *Time* (September 20, 1948). James Burnham expressed his doubts in *The Struggle for the World* (New

York: 1947), p. 15. Toynbee appeared on the cover of *Time* (March 17 1947).

Chapter 6
"Was to court social ostracism": Ralph De Toledano and Victor Lasky, *Seeds of Treason* (New York: 1950), p. 42. George H. Gallup, *The Gallup Poll 1935–1972* (New York: 1972), p. 639, contains the data on the two-thirds of the nation that believed Communists were disloyal and the Party should be banned. "Leninist discipline": Granville Hicks, *Where We Came Out* (New York: 1954), pp. 46–47. "Browder is our leader": Irving Howe and Louis Coser, *The American Communist Party* (Boston: 1957), pp. 443–44. Post-Duclos CP recruitment: David Shannon, *The Decline of American Communism* (New York: 1959), pp. 92–93. 700,000 ex-CP members: Morris Ernst and David Loth, *Report on the American Communist* (New York: 1952). Plaid shirts, guitar playing, etc.: Robert W. Iverson, *The Communists and the Schools* (New York: 1959), p. 235. "Since the imperfect tyranny": Dwight Macdonald, *Memoirs of a Revolutionist* (New York: 1957), p. 5. Liberal orthodoxy on foreign policy: Arthur M. Schlesinger, Jr., *The Vital Center* (Boston: 1949), pp. 221–26. "And the cryptic designation": ibid., pp. 167–68. "The long, slow ebb tide": Shannon, p. 97. CP policy forced on union members: ibid., pp. 73–75; see also the detailed account of the purge in Max Kempelman, *The Communists vs. the CIO* (New York: 1957). Union of Electrical, Radio and Machine Workers: Howe and Coser, p. 468.

Red cushion and telephone book: Gordon Kahn, *Hollywood on Trial* (New York: 1948), p. 4. "Mistaken to write off": Eric Bentley, *Thirty Years of Treason* (New York: 1971), p. 669. "Then gambled for his garments": Walter Goodman, *The Committee* (New York: 1968), pp. 173–74. "You have to take": Kahn, p. 16. "It's ours": Alvah Bessie, *Inquisition in Eden* (Berlin: 1967), p. 173. "By golly": Goodman, p. 308. HUAC's decision to abandon the Hollywood hearings: Robert K. Carr, *The House Committee on Un-American Activities 1945–1959* (Ithaca, N.Y.: 1952), pp. 74–75. "I was able": Elizabeth Bentley, *Out of Bondage* (New York: 1951). Confrontation between Bentley and William Taylor: Herbert Packer, *Ex-Communist Witnesses* (Palo Alto, Calif.: 1964), p. 62. Chambers and Mandel: Whittaker Chambers, *Witness* (New York: 1952), pp. 207, 536. "We will give them out": *Time* (January 3, 1949). Levine's accusations against Duggan: *New York Times* (January 6, 1949). "The man jumped": *New York Herald Tribune* (December 23, 1948). Twenty suicides: the most complete list is in Bessie, pp. 293–94. "You are here": Vern Countryman, *Un-American Activities in the State of Washington* (Ithaca, N.Y.: 1951), p. 24.

1,000 lost their jobs: Eleanor Bontecou, *The Federal Loyalty-Security Program* (Ithaca, N.Y.: 1952), p. 15. "Definitely needed": *New York Times* (March 23, 1947). Subscribing to the wrong magazines, etc.: Bontecou, pp. 101–48, cites scores of such instances. Kutcher's summary dismissal: James Kutcher, *The Case of the Legless Veteran* (New York: 1973). 2,000 dismissed: ACLU, "Our Uncertain Liberties" (New York: 1948).

Chapter 7

Legionnaires' attacks on the PCA: Joseph P. Lyford, "Brass Knuckle Patriots" *New Republic* (December 29, 1947). Communist ambitions for a third party: David Shannon, *The Decline of American Communism* (New York: 1959), pp. 114–15; James Wechsler, *The Age of Suspicion* (New York: 1954), p. 208. PCA fund-raising methods: *New Republic* (January 26, 1948). "We were convinced": John Gates, *The Story of an American Communist* (New York: 1958), p. 116. Defection of Kingdon and others: E. L. and F. H. Schapsmeier, *Prophet in Politics* (Ames, Iowa: 1970), p. 186; see also Curtis D. McDougall, *Gideon's Army*, three volumes (New York: 1965). Norman Thomas: Schapsmeier and Schapsmeier, p. 183. "Embryo Babbits": K. M. Schmidt, *Henry A. Wallace* (Syracuse, N.Y.: 1960), pp. 182–83. Glen Taylor's candidacy: Schapsmeier and Schapsmeier, p. 184; Schmidt, pp. 62–63.

The famous Clifford memorandum has never been published, but it was shown to Irwin Ross for his *The Loneliest Campaign* (New York: 1968), which quotes from it at length.

Kennedy v. Nixon debates over Taft-Hartley: Earl Mazo, *Richard Nixon* (New York: 1959), p. 49. Newspaper and Mail Deliverers Union: Sumner H. Slichter, *The Impact of Collective Bargaining on Management* (Washington, D.C.: 1960), p. 41. Balloting on the union shop: ibid., p. 56. "Green. We disaffiliate": Saul Alinsky, *John L. Lewis* (New York: 1949), p. 338. "The strike photographs": Samuel Lubell, *The Future of American Politics*, rev. ed. (New York: 1955), pp. 179–80. Superseniority: Slichter, p. 130.

Shifting party loyalties among farmers: Angus Campbell et al., *The American Voter* (New York: 1964), Chapter 13. Opposition of farmers to rigid price supports: Reo M. Christenson, *The Brannan Plan* (Ann Arbor, Mich.: 1959), p. 49. The shotgun wedding: ibid., p. 16. Productivity increase: Allen J. Matusow, *Farm Policies and Politics of the Truman Years* (Cambridge, Mass.: 1967), p. 111. Political loyalties in rural areas: Lubell, pp. 160, 168–69.

Popularity of Douglas and Truman: Jules Abels, *Out of the Jaws of Victory* (New York: 1959), p. 79. "The chances are less than even": ibid., p. 2. NBC's role in the walkout: Gilbert Seldes, *The Great Audience* (New York: 1950), p. 207. Conditions in southern Missouri: the transformation is described in detail in James West, *Plainsville USA* (New York: 1945). Federal government's tax bite in 1948: Randolph Paul, *Taxation in the United States* (Indianapolis: 1954), pp. 437–38. "On the wrong side of the birth rate": Lubell, p. 31. "Give 'em hell, Harry!": Robert G. Spivack,

"Harry Don't Fight Orthodox," *The Nation* (October 9, 1948). "The greatest pruning": Richard H. Rovere, *The American Establishment* (New York: 1962), p. 25. Difference in crowds discounted: *Time* (October 25, 1948). "The seat of the rebellion": V. O. Key, Jr., *Southern Politics in State and Nation* (New York: 1949), pp. 9–10. "I believe in God": Schmidt, p. 45. "By October": Shannon, p. 177. "Wallace barnstormed the country": Cabel Phillips, *The Truman Presidency* (New York: 1966), p. 203. Anita McCormick Blaine: Abels, p. 111. "Beyond dispute": Wechsler, p. 218. Gift offered to Williams: Max Lerner, *Actions and Passions* (New York 1949). "Labor did it": *New York Times* (November 4, 1948).

II: THE COLD WAR AS A WAY OF LIFE

Chapter 8

Brink's robbery: *Time* (January 30, 1950). "Odd-looking, snub-nosed": ibid. (August 7, 1950). "A victory for free enterprise": ibid. January 30, 1950). Sales of records: *Newsweek* (January 5, 1951). Louis Tirini: *Time* (November 12, 1951). "His book": ibid. (March 13, 1950). "Was enough to cost a man his job": Eric Larrabee, "Scientists in Collision: Was Velikovsky Right?," *Harper's* (August 1963). "In short": Jacques Barzun, *The House of Intellect* (New York: 1959), pp. 57–58.

Union with Britain: *New Republic* (August 29, 1949). Forty Senators: Joseph B. Gorman, *Kefauver* (New York: 1971), p. 72. BELIEF IN AMERICA: *Life* (February 28, 1949). "The War We May Fight": *Life* (May 7, 1951). "My own impression": *New Republic* (October 18, 1948). "They came close": Emmet John Hughes, *America the Vincible* (Garden City, N.Y.: 1959), p. 45. Riesman's "The Nylon War," originally published in 1951, is reproduced in his *Abundance for What?* (Garden City, N.Y.: 1964). "Peace is not and cannot": James Burnham, *The Struggle for the World* (New York: 1947), p. 134. 70 percent chose war: George M. Gallup, The Gallup Poll 1935–1972 (New York: 1972), p. 929.

"In some sense": *Fortune* (October 1948). Oppenheimer's reservations concerning the H-bomb are treated at length in Thomas H. Wilson, *The Great Weapons Heresy* (Boston: 1970). "Here's the one thing": Ralph Lapp, *Atoms and People* (New York: 1956), p. 106. "All AEC and contractor employees'': James R. Shepley and Clay Blair, Jr., *The Hydrogen Bomb* (New York: 1954), p. 110. The incident of the Bethe article: Gerard Piel, *Science in the Cause of Man* (New York: 1961).

Exemption of French conscripts: *New Republic* (January 21, 1952). "Our line of defense": Arthur M. Schlesinger, Jr., and Richard H. Rovere, *The General and the President* (New York: 1952), p. 90. THE TRUMAN DOCTRINE IS DEAD: *New Republic* (January 23, 1950). "The missing component": *New York Times* (January 13, 1950). Acheson's Berkeley speech: ibid. (March 17, 1950). Truman swore not to set foot in Russia: *Time* (March 6, 1950). "The rising frequency": ibid. (May 1, 1950). "At 12:07 Tuesday noon": TRB, in *New Republic* (July 10, 1950). "Never before": TRB (as Richard Lee Strout he was the Washington bureau chief of the CSM), in *New Republic* (July 10, 1950). Army surplus: *Time* (March 26, 1951). "Operation Common Knowledge": Dean Acheson, *Present at the Creation* (New York: 1969), pp. 447–48. Montana draft board: Schlesinger and Rovere, p. 141. "MacArthur has found time": ibid., pp. 137–38. MacArthur's attempted resignation: Douglas MacArthur, *Reminiscences* (New York: 1964), p. 370. "Whereas": Schlesinger and Rovere, pp. 10–11. Two-thirds considered dismissal a mistake: Gallup, p. 981. "On the day": Cabell Philips, *The Truman Presidency* (New York: 1966), p. 267. MacArthur's public tirades: *Time* (November 26, 1951). "It looks": *Newsweek* (June 18, 1951). Oppenheimer and tactical nuclear weapons: Robert Gilpin, *American Scientists and Nuclear Weapons Policy* (Princeton, N.J.: 1962), pp. 117–18.

"Military socialism": Blair Bolles, *How to Get Rich in Washington* (New York: 1952), p. 26. Economic effects of the Korean War on inflation and unemployment: J. F. Dewhurst et al., eds., *America's Needs and Resources: A New Survey* (New York: 1955), Figure 1, p. 4. Liquor stores: *Time* (November 12, 1951).

Chapter 9

The Housing Act of 1949: Richard Davies, *Housing Reform and the Truman Administration* (Columbia, Mo.: 1966). "The tumult and the shouting": *Newsweek* (May 9, 1949). Liberal reaction to Truman's Inaugural Address: *The Nation* (January 22, 1949). Fistfight in the House: *New York Times* (June 23, 1949). "Mom, this is something": Lee Nichols, *Breakthrough on the Color Front* (New York: 1954), p. 98.

"If allowance is made": J. F. Dewhurst et al., eds., *America's Needs and Resources* (New York: 1947), p. 248. On health, race, class, and illness: E. Gartly Jaco, ed., *Patients, Physicians and Illness* (Glencoe, Ill.: 1958), esp. Chapters 1–6, 12, 15, which are based on studies conducted between 1935 and 1955. Tests for hospital patients increased: Seymour Harris, *The Economics of American Medicine* (New York: 1964), p. 185. Cost of a hospital bed compared with daily wage: W. S. Woytinski et al., *Employment and Wages in the U.S.* (New York: 1953), p. 212. Spending on health and medicine compared with spending on alcohol and tobacco: Dewhurst et al., Appendix Six. "Are hospitalized for some infirmity": Frederick W. Taylor, "You're In—You're a Vet," *Harper's* (February 1948). HEALTH BY COMPULSION: *Life* (May 2, 1949). Number of people covered by Blue Cross, Blue Shield: Woytinski et al., pp. 209–10. Demand for refresher courses at government expense: James G. Burrow, *AMA: The Voice of American Medicine* (Baltimore: 1963), p. 309. Demand for surplus medical equipment: *Journal of the AMA* (July 4, 1947). "Slaves" and "clock watchers": ibid. (March 30, 1946). Cost of the AMA's publicity campaign: Irwin Ross, "Whitaker and Baxter," *Harper's* (July 1959); cf. the account of Whitaker and Baxter in Stanley J. Kelley, Jr., *Public Relations and Political Power* (Baltimore: 1956). Morris Fishbein: Milton Mayer, "The Rise and Fall of Dr. Fishbein," *Harper's* (November 1949); *Time* (December 5, 1949). AMA publicity campaign materials: Milton Mayer, "The Dogged Retreat of the Doctors" *Harper's* (December 1949). Untruths about the British National Health Service: see especially *Journal of the AMA* (March 16, 1946) p. 724; (March 30, 1946) p. 856; (August 3, 1946), p. 1150; (November 9, 1946), p. 1600.

"The U.S. farmer": *Time* October 31, 1949). Rural electrification: Marquis Childs, *The Farmer Takes a Hand* (New York: 1952). Art Wardner: *Time* (February 20, 1950). Couple in Buffalo: *Life* (January 9, 1952). Farm incomes in 1952: Herman P. Miller, *Income of the American People* (New York: 1955), pp. 22–24. The catechism of agriculture: Lauren Soth, *Farm Trouble* (Princeton, N.J.: 1957), p. 21. Three-to-one Democratic vote among farmers: Reo V. Christenson, *The Brannan Plan* (Ann Arbor, Mich.: 1959), p. 164. Opinion among farmers over the Brannan Plan: George H. Gallup, *The Gallup Poll 1935–1972* (New York: 1972), p. 822.

Supreme Court decision on President's seizure of the steel mills: *Youngstown Steel and Tube* v. *Sawyer*, 343 U.S. 579 (1952). Costs of the steel strike: Mary K. Hammond, "The Steel Strike of 1952," *Current History* (November 1952).

Chapter 10

CP members threatened with expulsion for vacationing at Miami Beach: *New York Times* (April 20, 1951). Purge of working-class CP members: Nathan Glazer, *The Social Basis of American Communism* (New York: 1961), pp. 127–129. "Their advance statements": *New Republic* (September 12, 1949); cf. K. M. Schmidt, *Henry Wallace* (Syracuse, New York: 1960), p. 99. "Conviction was almost": Irving Howe and Lewis Coser, *The American Communist Party* (Boston: 1957), p. 481. "A giant new edition": Don Whitehead, *The FBI Story* (New York: 1956), p. 287. "When I went out": Harold R. Medina, *The Anatomy of Freedom* (New York: 1959), Chapter 1. Medina on the cover: *Time* (Oct. 17, 1949). "Wait until the *putsch*": *Dennis* v. *United States*, 341 U.S. 494 (1951). Justification because of onerous defense burden: *New York Times*

(June 5, 1951). "May be thought of": ibid. (June 10, 1951). "The score was now": *Newsweek* (August 6, 1951). Tightening up bail requirements: *New Republic* (August 27, 1951).

Counterfeit currency plot: David J. Dallin, *Soviet Espionage* (New Haven, Conn.: 1955), pp. 393–96. Orlov wrote the book: Alexander Orlov, *Handbook of Intelligence and Guerrilla Warfare* (Ann Arbor, Mich.: 1963), p. 96. Soviet distinction between intelligence and research: ibid., pp. 5–7. "I was in the Fourth Section": Whittaker Chambers, *Witness* (New York: 1952), p. 210. Chambers was infatuated with the *narodniki*: ibid., pp. 76–78. "It is hard to believe": ibid., p. 27. "He told me": Meyer A. Zeligs, *Friendship and Fratricide* (New York: 1967), pp. 238–39. "Abel Gross": Chambers, p. 29. Put his name in the telephone book: Alistair Cooke, *A Generation on Trial* (New York: 1951), p. 250. "His autobiography": *Newsweek* (May 26, 1952). Plagiarizing Dostoevsky: John Chabot Smith, *Alger Hiss* (New York: 1976), p. 414. "I never got used to it": Chambers, p. 154. "No martyrdom was ever": I. F. Stone, *The Truman Era* (New York: 1953), p. 185. "In a kind of physical hush": Chambers, p. 561. "The weight of God's purpose": ibid., p. 571. "His theory of innocence by association": Ralph De Toledano and Victor Lasky, *Seeds of Treason* (New York: 1950), p. 214. "I dare say": Cooke, p. 257. "If he was innocent": ibid., p. 196. Article on the first Hiss jury: *Life* (July 18, 1949). "To determine his fitness": *Time* (ibid). Hiss Defense Fund: Smith, p. 251. RED HERRING CANNED: John Gunther, *Inside USA*, rev. ed. (New York: 1951), p. 614. "Hiss is one man": De Toledano and Lasky, pp. 279–80.

Civil Service Commission identification of Silvermaster as "probably a secret agent": Walter Goodman, *The Committee* (New York: 1968), p. 247. "We haven't shown our teeth": Herbert L. Packer, *Ex-Communist Witnesses* (Palo Alto, Calif.: 1962), pp. 87–88. Browder's reaction to Elizabeth Bentley's claims that she gave him orders: Walter and Miriam Schneir, *Invitation to an Inquest* (Baltimore: 1973), p. 311.

"I'm innocent," "a panic," "a riot": *Time* (July 4 and 11, 1949); cf. *Newsweek* (May 9, 1949). "A grueling job": *Life* (July 11, 1949).

"That agents of a foreign power": Whitehead, pp. 298–99. "The secret of the atomic bomb": U.S. Congress Joint Committee on Atomic Energy, *Soviet Atomic Espionage* (Washington, D.C.: 1951), p. 170. "Had a hell of a time": George Racey Jordan, *From Major Jordan's Diaries* (New York: 1952), p. 236. Sobell's behavior is described without being fully explained in Morton Sobell, *On Doing Time* (New York: 1973). The eminent trial lawyer was Louis Nizer, *The Implosion Conspiracy* (New York: 1974), pp. 194–95. Gold's perjured testimony and fantasy life: John Wexley, *The Judgement of Julius and Ethel Rosenberg* (New York: 1955), p. 49. Orlov identified Gold: Orlov, p. 38. Gold's testimony before Senate subcommittee: Schneir and Schneir, p. 367. "If a trial": Nizer, p. 249. Soviet atomic energy research in the 1930s and 1940s: Arnold Kramish, *Atomic Energy in the Soviet Union* (Palo Alto, Calif.: 1959); cf. Joseph I. Lieberman, *The Scorpion and the Tarantula* (Boston: 1970), p. 193.

Greenglass's poor memory and limited mathematical competence: Joint Committee on Atomic Energy, pp. 5–7. "The Russians have the skills": *New York Times* (March 17, 1954).

"Where Communism is concerned": Herbert A. Philbrick, *I Led Three Lives* (New York: 1952), p. 235.

Chapter 11

McCarthy's lowest grade was in "Legal Ethics": Jack Anderson and Ronald W. May, *McCarthyism* (Boston: 1951), p. 26. "McCarthy left no brick unturned": ibid., pp. 144–45. Financial favors shown to McCarthy by real estate men: Richard H. Rovere, *Senator Joe McCarthy* (New York: 1959), p. 89. McCarthy's role in investigation of the "Five Percenters": *Time* (September 5, 1949, et seq.). "A shameful farce" and "a deliberate and clever attempt": Rovere, pp. 158, 161. "The government is full of Communists": Anderson and May, p. 172. "Keep talking": James T. Patterson, *Mr. Republican* (Boston: 1972), p. 446. McCarthy and the China Lobby: Anderson and May, p. 195. Max Lerner: *New York Post* (April 5, 1950). "McCarthyism is Americanism": Rovere, p. 12. Most people thought the United States was losing the Cold War: George H. Gallup, *The Gallup Poll 1935–1972* (New York: 1972), p. 897. "For as long as the war": William F. Buckley, Jr., and L. Brent Bozell, *McCarthy and His Enemies* (Chicago: 1954), p. 246. "At frequent intervals": *Time* (April 10, 1950). "I believe you can ask": Rovere, p. 123. Budenz's appearance before Tydings subcommittee: Herbert L. Packer, *Ex-Communist Witnesses* (Palo Alto, Calif.: 1962), pp. 126–43. Freda Utley's appearance before Tydings subcommittee: Owen Lattimore, *Ordeal by Slander* (Boston: 1950), pp. 141–45. Jon M. Jonkel's management of Butler's campaign: Stanley J. Kelley, Jr., *Professional Public Relations and Political Power* (Baltimore: 1956), Chapter 4. Career of Thomas Hennings: Donald J. Kemper, *Decade of Fear: Senator Hennings and Civil Liberties* (Columbia, Mo.: 1965). "Certainly few had seemed": Anderson and May, p. 308. "A front man for traitors": *Time* (September 25, 1950). McCarthy's 60,000-word review of Marshall's career was published as *America's Retreat from Victory* (New York: 1951). Would sell his grandmother": Rovere, p. 143. "Yeah, yeah. I can listen": *Saturday Evening Post* (July 9, 1950). On McCarthy's self-conscious playacting: cf. James Wechsler, *The Age of Suspicion* (New York: 1954), p. 282; Anderson and May, and Rovere, were also under the same impression that he wanted to be noticed without necessarily intending to be taken seriously. "Joe was noticeably braver": Anderson and May, p. 207. "There was no doubt": Rovere, p. 60. McCarthy's shyness and restlessness: Anderson and May, p. 10. Observer who reflected on McCarthy's accessibility was Martin Merson, *The Private Diary of a Public Servant* (New York: 1955), p. 98. "Moonstruck souls wearing badges": Rovere, pp. 22–23. "Lincoln got the homage": *Time* (February 19, 1951). Truman's remarks at American Legion ceremony: *Newsweek* (August 27, 1951). Truman called McCarthy a liar:

Time (February 11, 1952). McCarthy was on the cover: ibid. (October 22, 1951).

Figures on loyalty screening: Civil Service Commission, *1953 Annual Report* (Washington, D.C.: 1954), p. 32; no complete figures are available for dismissals on security grounds. Seth Richardson on throwing dice: Arnold J. Heidenheimer, "Five Long Years of Loyalty," *New Republic* (January 28, 1951). Jew accused of wanting to burn the Bible: Adam Yarmolinsky, *Case Studies in Personnel Security* (Washington, D.C.: 1955), pp. 1–8. "What do you think": ibid., p. 12. The proofreader at the GPO: ibid., pp. 14–19. "Second-class citizens": ibid., p. 30. Kutcher was supported by the American Legion: James Kutcher, *The Case of the Legless Veteran* (New York: 1973), p. 109. "I felt that the government": O. Edmund Clubb, *The Witness and I* (New York: 1975), p. 251.

Budenz's break with the Party and return to Catholicism: Louis Budenz, *This Is My Story* (New York: 1947). Budenz made $10,000 a year as a witness: Richard H. Rovere, *The American Establishment* (New York: 1962), pp. 61–67. "I think you'll make": Harvey Matusow, *False Witness* (New York: 1955), p. 62. Paul Crouch: Richard H. Rovere, "The Kept Witnesses," *Harper's* (May 1955). Attempt by Immigration and Naturalization Service to protect Hewitt: Melvin Rader, *False Witness* (Seattle: 1969), p. 93. "I never saw the *Daily Worker*": Vern Countryman, *Un-American Activities in the State of Washington* (Ithaca, N.Y.: 1951), p. 310. "To eventual slaughter": *New York Times* (May 13, 1949). Paul H. Hughes: Roy Cohn, *McCarthy* (New York: 1966), pp. 178–80.

Oregon State University biology teachers: ACLU, "In the Shadow of Fear" (New York: 1949). Professor dismissed for "intellectual arrogance": Paul F. Lazarsfeld and Wagner F. Thickens, Jr. *The Academic Mind* (Glencoe, Ill.: 1959), pp. 52–53. University of Michigan's canceled debate: ACLU, "Security and Freedom" (New York: 1951). Barrows Dunham: I. F. Stone, *The Haunted Fifties* (New York: 1963), p. 35. The career of the Illinois Broyles Committee: Walter Gellhorn, *The States and Subversion* (Ithaca, N.Y.: 1952), pp. 54–139. The Supreme Court upheld the Feinberg Law: *Adler* v. *Board of Education*, 342 U.S. 485 (1952). Security-risk legislation in New York: Ralph S. Brown, Jr., *Loyalty and Security* (New Haven, Conn.: 1956), pp. 106–07. Detroit campaign against subversion: Gellhorn, pp. 206–07, 229–30. Allen Zoll: David Hulburd, *This Happened in Pasadena* (New York: 1951), pp. 87–89. "To collaborate with the Committee": Robert W. Iverson, *The Communists and the Schools* (New York: 1959), pp. 270–71. Faculty resistance based on principle: George R. Stewart, *The Year of the Oath* (Garden City, N.Y.: 1950). Faculty resistance based on threat to tenure: David P. Gardner, *The California Oath Controversy* (Berkeley and Los Angeles: 1967). The Gosling affair is the subject of Hulburd.

"A greater threat": Alfred Steinberg, "McCarran: Lone Wolf of the Senate," *Harper's* (November 1950). Overriding the Truman veto: *Time* (October 2, 1050). Little McCarran Acts: ACLU, *Security and Freedom* (New York: 1951). Pledge of Allegiance episode: John Gates, *The Story of an American Communist* (New York: 1958), pp. 145–46. The FBI had sifted through IPR's files: Anderson and May, pp. 343–46. "Did President Roosevelt promote Communist interests": Alan Barth, *Government by Investigation* (New York: 1955), p. 110. Truman's role in the Ellen Knauff case: Alonzo Hamby, *Beyond the New Deal* (New York: 1974), pp. 395–96. Mrs. Knauff recounts her side of events in *The Ellen Knauff Story* (New York: 1952). Other war brides were detained: *New Republic* (August 28, 1950). "It is nothing of the kind": *New York Times* (April 4, 1948). "Is this defending civil liberties": I. F. Stone, *The Truman Era* (New York: 1953), pp. 104–05. Scientific bodies shunned the United States: U.S. President's Commission on Immigration and Naturalization, *Whom Shall We Welcome?* (Washington, D.C.: 1953), p. 67.

Chapter 12
Sale of television sets: J. F. Dewhurst et al., eds., *America's Needs and Resources: A New Survey* (New York: 1955), p. 19. People trusted radio more than TV: Leo Bogart, *The Age of Television*, rev. ed. (New York: 1958), pp. 156–57. "Women proposed to him": Eric Barnouw, *The Golden Web* (New York: 1966), p. 298. Mrs. Horwich got *Ding Dong School* by mistake: *Newsweek* (February 2, 1953). "An odd, narcotic pull": *Time* (January 2, 1950). "I sure can remember": Ira O. Glick and Sidney J. Levy, *Living with Television* (Chicago: 1962), p. 31. "People forget what is the prime purpose": *Time* (December 15, 1947). On television creating the time it consumed: Bogart, pp. 65–66; Raymond F. Stewart, *The Social Impact of Television on Atlanta Households* (Atlanta: 1952), p. 61. Radio as a bad influence on the young: *Newsweek* (May 9, 1949).

Porter's decision to shift FM: Lawrence Lessing, *Man of High Fidelity: Edwin H. Armstrong* (Philadelphia: 1962), p. 258.

"In the large cities": Paul Lazarsfeld and Patricia M. Kendall, *Radio Listening in America* (Englewood Cliffs, N.J.: 1948), p. 13. Foreign screen time reserved for American films: Eric Rhode, *A History of the Cinema* (London: 1976), p. 437. 300 people blacklisted in Hollywood: David Robinson, *World Cinema* (London: 1973), p. 247.

"The firm had little difficulty": Harvey Matusow, *False Witness* (New York: 1955), p. 110. IN AN EMERGENCY: John Cogley, *Robert on Blacklisting* (New York: 1956). There is no mention of the Legion blacklist in the standard accounts, but see Phil Kerby, "The Legion Blacklist," *New Republic* (June 16, 1952). "My husband, a veteran of World War Two": Cogley, pp. 104–06. Letter to Leonard A. Block: ibid., pp. 54–55. "When the vice president asked me": Fred Friendly, *Due to Circumstances Beyond Our Control* (New York: 1967), p. 24. "The Vice President in charge of treason": Barnouw, p. 278. The seven charges made by Aware, Inc., are reproduced in full in Louis Nizer, *The Jury Returns* (Garden City, N.Y.: 1966), pp. 297–99. "As an investment in America": John Henry Faulk, *Fear on Trial* (New York: 1965), p. 49.

Dashiell Hammett knew no names: Lillian Hellman, *An Unfinished Woman* (Boston: 1969), p. 261.

Chapter 13
One-fourth approved of Truman's leadership: George H. Gallup, *The Gallup Poll 1935–1972* (New York: 1972), p. 995. "An utterly useless war": ibid., p. 1019. The best coverage of the tax scandals and the attempts to cover them up is to be found in "The Tax Thieves of 1951," *New Republic* (November 12, 1951 et seq.). Scott Lucas sought revenge: Joseph B. Gorman, *Kefauver* (New York: 1971), p. 83. Results of strengthening the tax laws to prosecute criminals: ibid., p. 99. Two-thirds had never heard of Stevenson: Gallup, p. 1056. Delegate votes at opening of Democratic convention: Paul T. David et al., *Presidential Nominating Politics in 1952* (Baltimore: 1954), Vol. 1, p. 65. Stevenson's vacillating path to the nomination: John Bartlow Martin and Eric Larrabee, "The Drafting of Adlai Stevenson," *Harper's* (October 1952). Democratic doubts about Stevenson's electability: e.g., *New Republic* September 15, 1952).

"Mr. Eisenhower has never voted": Sherman Adams, *First-Hand Report* (New York: 1961), p. 25. The Eisenhower presence: Emmet J. Hughes, *Ordeal of Power* (New York: 1964), pp. 10, 19–20. Order to restore Eisenhower's pay, privileges, and pension: Marquis Childs, *Eisenhower: Captive Hero* (New York: 1958), p. 127. Taft's ideas on foreign policy as a graphic display of sense cheek by jowl with nonsense: Robert A. Taft, *A Foreign Policy for Americans* (Garden City, N.Y.: 1951). "You must enforce the quota": James T. Patterson, *Mr. Republican* (Boston: 1972), p. 281. Taft told three reporters what he had told McCarthy: Richard H. Rovere, "What's Happened to Taft?" *Harper's* (April 1952). Candidate preferences by voter registration: Gallup, p. 1044. "All over Texas that day": Dwight D. Eisenhower, *Mandate for Change* (Garden City, N.Y.: 1963), p. 39; there is a photograph of one such fistfight, involving neatly dressed middle-aged men brawling on a suburban lawn, in *Newsweek* (June 9, 1952).

"The most courageous fighter": *New Republic* (September 20, 1948). Eisenhower's reasons for choosing Nixon; Eisenhower, p. 46, "To make me relent": *Newsweek* (September 15, 1952). Melee at Eugene: Earl Mazo, *Richard M. Nixon* (New York: 1959), p. 117. "There is one thing I believe": Adams, pp. 45–45. "We could hear": ibid., p. 47. Nixon burst into tears: Hughes, p. 37. Mail to the Republican National Committee, dog food to Nixon: Richard M. Nixon, *Six Crises* (Garden City, N.Y.: 1962), p. 126. "To think that an old soldier": Martin Mayer, *Madison Avenue USA* (New York: 1962), p. 283. Eisenhower's dullness was more moving than Stevenson's brilliance: *New Republic* (October 6, 1952). "Anyone who says": *New York Times* (October 21, 1952). "The full power of municipal government": ibid. (October 26, 1952). "Making off in broad daylight": Louis Harris, *Is There a Republican Majority?* (New York: 1954), p. 174. Domestic Communism was not an important issue: this is supported by a variety of polls reproduced in Angus Campbell et al., *The American Voter* (New York: 1964), Alfred De Grazia, *The Western Public* (Palo Alto, Calif.: 1954), and Arthur Kornhauser et al., *When Labor Votes* (New York: 1956). "Towards Senator McCarthy": Arthur

Larson, *Eisenhower: The President Nobody Knew* (New York: 1969), p. 21. "One party press": Edwin Emery, *The Press and America* (Englewood Cliffs, N.J.: 1972), p. 698.

III: ROCKING!

Chapter 14

Contactee who won 171,000 votes: David Michael Jacobs, *The UFO Controversy in America* (Bloomington, Ind.: 1975), p. 120. Thousands wrote to Congress and the White House opposing intervention in Indochina: *Newsweek* (June 14, 1954). "What would the U.S. gain?" George H. Gallup, *The Gallup Poll 1935–1972* (New York: 1972), p. 1243. "We believe in romance": *Newsweek* (April 1, 1957). Toll of Asian flu: ibid. (October 21, 1957). MacArthur's plan for ending Korean War: Douglas A. MacArthur, *Reminiscences* (New York: 1964), p. 384. Eisenhower's threat to use atomic weapons: Dwight D. Eisenhower, *Mandate for Change* (Garden City, N.Y.: 1963), pp. 179–81. "Shift from 'cold war' to 'cold peace'": David Shannon, *The Decline of American Communism* (New York: 1959). "In which I shall live without living," "No power on earth": Julius and Ethel Rosenberg, *The Rosenberg Letters* (New York: 1953), letter of February 9, 1953. "Would simply recruit their spies": Eisenhower, p. 225.

Oppenheimer argued for air defense: J. Robert Oppenheimer, "Atomic Weapons and American Policy," *Foreign Affairs* (July 1953). On relations between Strauss and Oppenheimer: Joseph and Stewart Alsop, "We Accuse!," *Harper's* (October 1954). "Based upon years of study": Philip M. Stern, *The Oppenheimer Case* (New York: 1969), p. 1. "It was as if": ibid., p. 353. "Any scientists": Gerard Peil, *Science in the Cause of Man* (New York: 1961), p. 130.

"Rooting out the egg-heads": *New Republic* (March 30, 1953). Attempt to put pressure on Judge Youngdahl: ibid. (November 1, 1954). Loyalty oath to fish in reservoirs: *New York Times* (May 7, 1957). "The suffering in terms of broken families": I. F. Stone, *The Haunted Fifties* (New York: 1963), p. 35. Revoking Communists' pension rights: Murray Kempton, *America Comes of Middle Age* (Boston: 1963), pp. 7–9.

"I will make the rules": James Kutcher, *The Case of the Legless Veteran* (New York: 1973), p. 202. Half those dismissed as "security risks" were hired under Eisenhower Administration: Earl Latham, *The Communist Controversy in Washington* (Cambridge, Mass.: 1966), pp. 314–15.

"Any controversial persons": Martin Merson, *The Private Diary of a*

Public Servant (New York: 1955), p. 15. "Once the dogs are set upon you": *New Republic* (February 23, 1953). Kaghan ordered to resign or be fired: Theodore Kaghan, "The McCarthyization of Theodore Kaghan," *The Reporter* (July 21, 1953). The race to denounce Matthews: Emmet J. Hughes, *Ordeal of Power* (New York: 1964), pp. 83–85. "I just will not": ibid., p. 81. Mamie snubbed Mrs. McCarthy: *Newsweek* (May 31, 1954). "If Eisenhower could have had his way": Sherman Adams, *First-Hand Report* (New York: 1961), p. 115. "We are going to be judged": Fred Friendly, *Due to Circumstances Beyond Our Control* (New York: 1967), p. 34. Eisenhower embraced Murrow: ibid., p. 51. Drop in support for McCarthy: Gallup, pp. 1201, 1247. McCarthyite candidates defeated: *Newsweek* (June 28/September 27, 1954). Role of Lyndon Johnson: Rowland Evans and Robert Novak, *Lyndon B. Johnson* (New York: 1966), pp. 81–82; William S. White *The Professional*, (Boston: 1964), pp. 195–98. "Admit One Anti-Communist": *Time* (November 22, 1954). Johnson's condemnation of McCarthy: Evans and Novak, p. 85.

CIA supported *Daily Worker*: Victor Marchetti and John D. Marks, *The CIA and the Cult of Intelligence* (New York: 1974), p. 165. *Yates* v. *United States*, 354 U.S. 298 (1957); *Watkins* v. *United States*, 354 U.S. 178 (1957); *Sweezy* v. *New Hampshire*, 354 U.S. 234 (1957). CP membership losses: Shannon, p. 360. The Fosterite rump: John Gates, *The Story of an American Communist* (New York: 1958), p. 193. "For all intents and purposes": Irving Howe and Louis Coser, *The American Communist Party* (Boston: 1957), p. 498.

Chapter 15
The impact of security hearings on American science: Vannevar Bush, "If We Alienate Our Scientists," *New York Times Magazine* (June 13, 1954). ARE YOU A RED DUPE?: Frank Jacobs, *The MAD World of William Gaines* (New York: 1972), p. 103. Town in Massachusetts: James MacGregor Burns, "The Crazy Politics of Fluoridation," *New Republic* (July 13, 1953). Only 7 percent opposed fluoridation: George Gallup, *The Gallup Poll 1935–1972* (New York: 1972), p. 103. 10,000 people lost their jobs: Ralph S. Brown, Jr., *Loyalty and Security* (New Haven, Conn.: 1956), pp. 181–82. "Enough copies managed to get into the hands": Robert W. Iverson, *The Communists and the Schools* (New York: 1959), p. 243. *American Review of Soviet Medicine*: Laurence S. Wittner, *Rebels Against War* (New York: 1969), pp. 161–62. Article by A. G. Lunts: Gerard Piel, *Science in the Cause of Man* (New York: 1961), p. 163. "I have taken this room": *Time* (April 10, 1950).

Fewer than 1 percent listed Communism: Samuel Stouffer, *Communism, Conformism and Civil Liberties* (Garden City, N.Y.: 1955), Chapter 3. Fewer than 8 percent rated McCarthy above Hoover and Eisenhower: ibid., p. 230. "We found in most areas": Barbara Ward, "Report to Europe on America," *New York Times Magazine* (June 20, 1954). Boston Public Library: Lawrence J. Kipp, "Boston—the Library Did Not

Burn," *New Republic* (June 29, 1953). Pasadena survey: Joseph A. Brandt, "This Too Happened in Pasadena," *Harper's* (November 1952). Turmoil in Scarsdale: Robert Shaplen, "Scarsdale's Battle of the Books," *Commentary* (December 1950). Dr. Alexander Solosko: *New Republic* (September 14, 1953). "Felt that the climate": Robert J. Donovan, *Eisenhower: The Inside Story* (New York: 1956), p. 175. One academic in three was intimidated: Paul F. Lazarsfeld and Wagner Thickens, Jr., *The Academic Mind: Social Scientists in a Time of Crisis* (Glencoe, Ill.: 1958).

Chapter 16

"Found evidence of suburban developments": Lewis Mumford, *The City in History* (New York: 1961), p. 483. Average house in 1950 and 1956: Burnham Kelly et al., *The Design and Production of Housing* (New York: 1959), p. 47. Gruen's concept of shopping centers: Victor Gruen and Larry Smith, *Shopping Towns U.S.A.* (New York: 1960). "At first they advertised Park Forest": William H. Whyte, Jr., *The Organization Man* (Garden City, N.Y.: 1957), p. 314.

Self-identification by class: Hadley Cantril, *Public Opinion 1935–1946* (Princeton, N.J.: 1951), p. 116; cf. Richard Centers, *The Psychology of Social Classes* (Princeton, N.J.: 1949), who put the working class in 1948 at 50 to 55 percent of the population, and Leonard Reissman, *Class in American Society* (Glencoe, Ill.: 1960), who put it at 55.8 percent in 1954. The Chicago study is broken down into percentages in Pierre Martineau, *Motivation in Advertising* (New York: 1957), p. 164. Rise in blue-collar work force: Richard M. Scammon and Benjamin Wattenberg, *This U.S.A.* (Garden City, N.Y.: 1965), pp. 166, 170. "If the worker earns like the middle class": Harvey Swados, *A Radical's America* (Boston: 1959), p. 112. Children learning class roles: Celia B. Stendler, *Children of Brasstown* (Urbana, Ill.: 1949); August B. Hollingshead, *Elmtown's Youth* (New York: 1949). "Like Molière's M. Jourdain": Reissman, p. 229. "It is most apparent in the upper class": C. Wright Mills, *The Power Elite* (New York: 1956), p. 30. One-third went down the social scale: Seymour M. Lipset and Reinhard Bendix, *Social Mobility in Industrial Society* (Berkeley and Los Angeles: 1959), p. 90. "Many white-collared office workers": Vance Packard, *The Status Seekers* (New York: 1959), p. 37. Working-class defeatism: Bennett M. Berger, *Working Class Suburb* (Berkeley and Los Angeles: 1959), pp. 20–21, 24–25. Undesirable consequences: Melvin Tumin, "Some Unapplauded Consequences of Social Mobility," *Social Forces* (October 1957–May 1958). "In Odessa, Texas": William Attwood, *Still the Most Exciting Country* (New York: 1956), p. 28. Changes of residence: Scammon and Wattenberg, p. 117. Cadillac sales: William H. Whyte, Jr., "The Cadillac Phenomenon," *Fortune* (February 1955). "The classic situation": Robert H. Boyle, "Country Clubs," *Sports Illustrated* (February 26/March 5, 1962). Life in a working suburb: cf. Berger, who studied Milpitas, California. "The socially retarded wife has become the great sorrow": William H. Whyte, Jr., "The

Wives of Management," *Fortune* (October/November 1957). One-third of psychiatric patients: Richard E. Gordon et al., *The Split-Level Trap* (New York: 1960). Portrait of a working-class housewife: Lee Rainwater et al., *Workingman's Wife* (New York: 1959), p. 32. "They are both symptoms": Max Lerner, *Unfinished Country* (New York: 1959), *New York Post* column of April 22, 1956. Changes in men's hairstyles: Herbert Mitgang, "About—Men's Haircuts," *New York Times Magazine* (June 2, 1957). The new servant class was an idea advanced by Russell Lynes, *A Surfeit of Honey* (New York: 1957). The British anthropologist was Geoffrey Gorer, who wrote *The Americans* (London: 1948). Women in films: Martha Wolfenstein and Nathan Leites, *The Movies* (New York: 1950).

Lectures on American literature and kitchens: *Virginia Quarterly Review* (Autumn 1952). "You might also say": Eric Larrabee, "What's Happening to Hobbies?," *New York Times Magazine* (December 27, 1953). "The motive of curiosity about ideas": Jacques Barzun, *The House of Intellect* (New York: 1959), p. 63. Bearded strangers asked for identification: John Keats, *The New Romans* (Philadelphia: 1967), p. 171. Article critical of conformity: "The Danger of Being Too Well Adjusted," *Reader's Digest* (December 1958).

Popularity of cards: Irving Crespi, "Card Playing in Mass Culture," in Bernard Rosenberg and David M. White, eds., *Mass Culture* (Glencoe, Ill.: 1957). Nation of nonjoiners: Charles R. Wright and Herbert H. Hyman, "Voluntary Association Memberships of American Adults," *American Sociological Review* (June 1958). D-I-Y sales: U.S. Department of Commerce Staff, "The D-I-Y Market," in Eric Larrabee and Rolf Meyersohn, eds., *Mass Leisure* (Glencoe, Ill.: 1958). Sales of paint and wallpaper: Christopher Tunnard and Henry Hope Reed, *American Skyline* (New York: 1956), p. 184. "All kinds of linkages," "A sloppy and inept garden": William M. Dobriner, *Class in Suburbia* (Englewood Cliffs, N.J.: 1963), p. 9. Pets in Beverly Hills outnumbered people: *Newsweek* (March 11, 1957). "The standard package": David Riesman, *Abundance for What?* (Garden City, N.Y.: 1964). "He had a 1955 car": Attwood, p. 37. Park Forest, Illinois: William H. Whyte, Jr., p. 353. Anaheim, California: Bruce Bliven, "The Golden Age of Live Now, Pay Later," *The Reporter* (May 3, 1956). "The tie that binds" etc.: Hugh R. King, "E Pluribus Togetherness," *Harper's* (August 1957). "He read books": Henry Steele Commager, *The American Mind* (New Haven, Conn.: 1950), p. 416. "But was this, at last, the real life": Keats, p. 158.

"A community rich in all the means": John Seeley, *Crestwood Heights* (Toronto: 1956), p. 410. "From such unpleasant realities": Herbert J. Gans, *The Levittowners* (New York: 1967), p. 26. "A chosen people": Harlan Douglas, *The Suburban Trend* (New York: 1925), p. 34. "The peer-group becomes the measure": David Riesman et al., *The Lonely Crowd* (New Haven, Conn.: 1952), p. 83. "The assumption [is]": ibid., p. 112. College students preparing for careers in business: Whyte, p. 80.

Chapter 17

"As the week nears its end": Frederick Morton, "The Art of Courtship," *Holiday* (March 1957). Going steady was small-town behavior in a big-city nation: Charles W. Cole, "American Youth Goes Monogamous," *Harper's* (March 1957). Parental opposition to going steady: George H. Gallup, *The Gallup Poll 1935–1972* (New York: 1972), p. 1325. Psychologists' criticisms of dating patterns: Albert Ellis, *The American Sexual Tragedy* (New York: 1954), pp. 56–61. "We want sex! We want sex!": Max Lerner, *Unfinished Country* (New York: 1959), *New York Post* column of May 20, 1952. "Sometimes a boy and girl": Harrison Salisbury, *The Shook-Up Generation* (New York: 1958), p. 34. "Don't get involved": David Riesman et al., *The Lonely Crowd* (New Haven, Conn.: 1952), p. 279. Organized crime and pornography: "Joey," with Dave Fisher, *Killer* (Chicago: 1973), pp. 120–121. "People's peculiarities were intensified": Polly Adler, *A House Is Not a Home* (New York: 1953), p. 253. Homosexual communities: William J. Helmer, "New York's 'Middle Class Homosexuals," *Harper's* (March 1963); cf. Donald Webster Cory (pseud.), *The Homosexual in America: A Subjective Approach* (New York: 1951). Sale of beds: Editors of *Look, The Decline of the American Male* (New York: 1958), p. 11.

"He always answered": Wardell B. Pomeroy, *Dr. Kinsey and the Institute for Sex Relations* (New York: 1972), p. 18. "Not to publish anything": ibid., p. 262. Only twenty statisticians could resolve the problems: William G. Cochran et al., *Statistical Problems in the Kinsey Report on Sexual Behavior in the Human Male* (Washington, D.C.: 1951), p. 4. The man who proved his claim in ten seconds: Pomeroy, p. 122. "Scholarly and skilled lawyer": Alfred C. Kinsey, *Sexual Behavior in the Human Male* (Philadelphia: 1948), p. 195. "The underworld requires": ibid., p.36. "They have faith": ibid., p. 41. "As well ask a horse-trader": ibid., p. 43. "Not remembering accurately": Pomeroy, pp. 120–21. "Statistical sense": Kinsey, pp. 20–21. "Because of possible inaccuracies": Cochran et al., p. 3. "Many of the most interesting": ibid., p. 152.

Discussing income was "too personal": Ronald Freedman et al., *Family Planning, Sterility and Population Growth* (New York: 1959), p. 14. Birthrates and the economy: Clyde V. Kiser et al., *Trends and Variations in Fertility in the United States* (Cambridge, Mass.: 1968), Chapter 12. Ideal family size: Freedman, pp. 222–23. Number of abortions annually: Mary Steichen Calderone, *Abortion in the United States* (New York: 1958), p. 180. Contraceptive methods used by members of different religions: Freedman, pp. 176, 185. Class and sex: Lee Rainwater, *And the Poor Get Children* (Chicago: 1960).

"Repeatedly they see sexual relations": W. Lloyd Warner and James C. Abegglen, *Big Business Leaders in America* (New York: 1955), p. 99. Figures on divorce: Richard C. Scammon and Benjamin Wattenberg, *This U.S.A.* (Garden City, N.Y.: 1965), p. 36.

Chapter 18

Most authorities credit Haley with the first rock 'n' roll hit, either for "Crazy Man Crazy" or "Rock Around the Clock," but see Carl Belz, *The Story of Rock* (New York: 1969), pp. 25–26, for several other contenders. "Not many people in the pop music audience": Charlie Gillette, *Making Tracks* (London: 1975), p. 102. "The sound of the city": Charlie Gillette, *The Sound of the City: The Rise of Rock and Roll* (New York: 1970). "If I could find a white man": Jerry Hopkins, *Elvis* (New York: 1971), p. 47. "Some Elvis Presley bobbysocks": ibid., p. 127. "The pop music business": *Time* (April 4, 1955). "Up to a point": *Life* (August 27, 1956). Washington rock 'n' roll fracas: *Newsweek* (June 18, 1956). "Inciting the unlawful destruction of property": ibid. (May 12, 1958). "This hooby-dooby": quoted by *Time* (July 23, 1956).

Estimated sale of comic books: Fredric Wertham, *Seduction of the Innocent* (New York: 1954), pp. 11, 307. William Gaines's private life: Frank Jacobs, *The MAD World of William Gaines* (New York: 1972), pp. 78, 94.

Adolescent slang: Harold Wentworth and Stuart Berg Flexner, *Dictionary of American Slang* (New York: 1967), and Elliott Horne, "For Cool Cats and Far Out Chicks," *New York Times Magazine* (August 18, 1957). James Dean cult: Ezra Goodman, "Delirium over a Dead Star," *Life* (September 24, 1956); *Time* (September 3, 1956. "It was their almost universal inability": Eugene Kinkead, *In Every War but One* (New York: 1959), p. 186. "Alienation, once seen as imposed": Kenneth Keniston, *The Uncommitted* (New York: 1965), p. 3. "An explicit rejection": ibid., p. 8. "A term like filiarchy": William H. Whyte, Jr. *The Organization Man* (Garden City, N.Y.: 1957), p. 378. Changes in parent-child relationships: Melvin L. Kohn, "Social Class and Parent-Child Relationships: An Interpretation," *American Journal of Sociology* (January 1963). Beliefs of adolescents: H. H. Remmer and D. H. Radler, *The American Teenager* (Indianapolis: 1957), pp. 169–79, 194, 218.

Allen Ginsberg, "Little Jack" Melody, et al.: Jane Kramer, *Allen Ginsberg in America* (New York: 1969), pp. 123–29. Kerouac developed thrombophlebitis: Ann Charters, *Kerouac* (San Francisco: 1972), p. 59. "This new prophet of the open fly": Lawrence Lipton, *The Holy Barbarians* (New York: 1959), p. 193. "All right. You want to do something big": ibid., pp. 196–98. "Permanent War Economy": Ned Polsky, *Hustlers, Beats and Others* (Chicago: 1967), p. 159. Description of Beat life-style: see Lipton and Polsky and Thomas F. Parkinson, ed. *A Casebook on the Beat* (New York: 1961). Francis Rigney and L. Douglas Smith, *The Real Bohemia* (New York: 1961). "Beats suffer": Polsky, p. 159. Kerouac voted Republican: Bruce Cook, *The Beat Generation* (New York: 1971), p. 85. Two of the most venomous attacks on the Beats were Norman Podhoretz's "The Know-Nothing Bohemians" and Paul O'Neill's "The Only Rebellion Around"; both are included in Parkinson's *Casebook*." They wanted it to be successful": Norman Mailer, *Advertisements for Myself* (New York: 1959), p. 244.

Chapter 19

Reported crimes, reported convictions: Federal Bureau of Investigation, *Crime in the U.S.: Uniform Crime Reports* (Washington, D.C.: 1961), p. 15. "A new kind of thief": Norman Jaspan and Hillel Black, *The Thief in the White Collar* (Philadelphia: 1960), p. 11. The mentality of the white-collar criminal: Donald R. Cressey, *Other People's Money* (Glencoe, Ill.: 1953). Gambling was the sixth biggest business: Daniel Bell, *The End of Ideology* (Glencoe, Ill.: 1960), p. 133. Numbers were an apprenticeship for aspiring crooks: "Joey," with Dave Fisher, *Killer* (Chicago: 1973), p. 81. Harry Gross: Charles Hamilton, ed., *Men of the Underworld* (New York: 1952), p. 114. "On the evening of December 26, 1946": Ed Reid and Ovid Demaris, *The Green Felt Jungle* (New York: 1963), p. 22. Dead man put under a crap table: ibid., p. 217. Crime and suicide rates in Las Vegas: ibid., p. 10.

Estimated turnover of gambling: Estes Kefauver, *Crime in America* (Garden City, N.Y.: 1951), p. 59. "With the gambling fines cut off": Bell, p. 138. The travails of Joseph Bonnano: Gay Talese, *Honor Thy Father* (Cleveland: 1972), p. 46. "A nationwide crime syndicate," "Behind the local mobs": Kefauver, p. 24. "There is no one massive organization": Ramsey Clark, *Crime in America* (New York: 1971), p. 74. Carmine Lombardozzi: Donald R. Cressey, *Theft of a Nation* (New York: 1969), p. 99. Profaci sold adulterated olive oil: Kefauver, p. 31. "There is big money": Clark, pp. 74–75. "You don't kill a man": "Joey," p. 81. The conspiracy to kill Anastasia was between Costello's main rival, Vito Genovese, and Joe Profaci. Profaci's henchmen Tony Strollo and the Gallo brothers (Joey and Lawrence) set up the killing. The Gallos brought Nazarian from New England, with the approval of the Providence boss, Raymond Patriarca, on the sensible assumption that Anastasia would instantly recognize any hit man hired in New York. The Gallos were present during the killing, but Nazarian pulled the trigger; see Vincent Teresa, *My Life in the Mafia* (New York: 1973). The Cosa Nostra and drugs: Peter Maas, *The Valachi Papers* (New York: 1969), Chapter 11. The marijuana legacy of the Beats: Ned Polsky, *Hustlers, Beats and Others* (Chicago: 1967), p. 172. Girl who found "community" in marijuana smoking: John Clellon Holmes, "This Is the Beat Generation," *New York Times Magazine* (November 16, 1954). The Harrison Act and the Prohibition Bureau: Alden Stevens, "Make Dope Legal," *Harper's* (November 1952). Fumbling Bunch of Idiots: "Joey," p. 257. William F. Harrah: Keith Monroe, "The New Gambling King," *Harper's* (January 1962). 254 percent crime increase: Herbert A. Bloch and Gilbert Geis, *Man, Crime and Society* (New York: 1962), pp. 148–149.

The reformed gang leader was Ira Henry Freeman, author of *Out of the Burning* (New York: 1960). "A $20,000,000 slum," "They are fiendishly contrived": Harrison Salisbury, *The Shook-Up Generation* (New York: 1958), p. 75. The Chaplains and the Mau Maus: David Wilkerson, *The Cross and the Switchblade* (New York: 1963), pp. 56–57. Los Angeles gangs: Salisbury, p. 198. "By 1957 the fight thing": Claude Brown, *Man-*

child in the Promised Land (New York: 1965), p. 621. Blaming rock 'n' roll, comics, and television for juvenile delinquency: George H. Gallup, *The Gallup Poll 1935–1972* (New York: 1972), p. 1284; *Time* (November 1, 1954). The seven-year-old juvenile delinquent: Benjamin Fine *1,000,000 Delinquents* (Cleveland: 1955), p. 285. 400,000 convictions each year: ibid., p. 268. The eminent journalist was Albert Deutsch, *Our Rejected Children* (Boston: 1950). Typical training school euphemisms and punishments: ibid., pp. 15–16. Juvenile delinquents not created merely by poverty or rebelliousness: Richard A. Cloward and Lloyd E. Ohlin, *Delinquency and Oportunity* (Glencoe, Ill.: 1960); cf. Alfred K. Cohen, *Delinquent Boys* (Glencoe, Ill.: 1955) and Henry Williamson, *Hustler!* (Garden City, N.Y.: 1965). Delinquency varied according to neighborhood: Irving Sperlberg, *Racketville, Slumtown and Haulberg* (Chicago: 1964). Differences between homes of delinquents and nondelinquents: Sheldon and Eleanor Glueck, *Unraveling Juvenile Delinquency* (Cambridge, Mass.: 1950). Teenage torturers: *Newsweek* (August 10, 1954). Growing interest in psychopathy: *Time* (December 6, 1954). "Psychopathy is more widespread": Robert M. Lindner, *Rebel Without a Cause* (New York: 1945), p. 12. "It can be suggested," "Not love as the search for a mate": Norman Mailer, "The White Negro," in *Advertisements for Myself* (New York: 1959), pp. 185, 291.

"The New Prison has abolished stripes": John Bartlow Martin, *Break Down the Walls* (New York: 1954), Chapter 10. Chino State Institution: Kenyon J. Scudder, *Prisoners Are People* (Garden City, N.Y.: 1952). The wave of prison riots: Gresham M. Sykes, *The Society of Captives* (Princeton: 1958), pp. 112–20; cf. Martin.

Chapter 20
The health of blacks: E. Gartley Jaco, ed., *Patients, Physicians and Illness*, rev. ed. (Glencoe, Ill.: 1958), p. 27. The travels of Ray Sprigle are recounted in his *In the Land of Jim Crow* (New York: 1949); of John Howard Griffin in his *Black Like Me* (Boston: 1961). "Some of the most energetic people": James Baldwin *Nobody Knows My Name* (New York: 1961), p. 74. "I was forced to recognize": James Baldwin, *Notes of a Native Son* (Boston: 1955), p. 14. On the changing role of Africa in the self-image of American blacks, see Harold Isaacs, *The New World of Negro Americans* (New York: 1963). Happy reminiscences about the chain gang: Claude Brown, *Manchild in the Promised Land* (New York: 1965) p. 275. Registration practices in Louisiana: A. J. Liebling, *The Earl of Louisiana* (New York: 1961), p. 67. Southerners found it hard to say "Knee-grow": William D. Workman, Jr., *The Case for the South* (New York: 1961), p. 47. "I think everybody said it real loud": Brown, pp. 166–67. "He knew he was black": James Baldwin, "Notes of a Native Son," *Harper's* (November 1955).

"Who are generally opposed": E. Franklin Frazier, *Black Bourgeoisie* (Glencoe, Ill.: 1957), p. 104. "Anybody with money": C. Eric Lincoln, in Harold L. Sheppard, ed., *Poverty and Wealth in America* (Chicago: 1970),

p. 193. Fear of genuine competition: Frazier, pp. 216–17. Number of blacks moving in was equal to number of whites moving out: Charles E. Silberman, *Crisis in Black and White* (New York: 1964), p. 31. Black immigrants felt safer in the city: Eli Ginzberg, *The Negro Potential* (New York: 1956), p. 21. Donald Howard: Charles Abrams, *Forbidden Neighbors* (New York: 1955), p. 119. "Liberty City": ibid., p. 130. The Braden prosecution: Anne Braden, *The Wall Between* (New York: 1957). Lower incidence of suicide in black ghettos: Kenneth B. Clark, *Dark Ghetto* (New York: 1965), p. 81. "Horse was the new thing": Brown, p. 99. "Harlem had changed": ibid., pp. 179–80. Changing pattern of illegitimacy: Jessie Bernard, *Marriage and Family Among Negroes* (Englewood Cliffs, N.J.: 1966), p. 9.

Black contact with white power structure in Atlanta: Floyd Hunter, *Community Power Structure* (Garden City, N.Y.: 1963), pp. 139–40. NAACP membership losses: Langston Hughes, *Fight for Freedom* (New York: 1962), p. 114. Conditions at Scott's Branch School: John Bartlow Martin, *The Deep South Says "Never"* (New York: 1957), pp. 46–47. "If the NAACP was cotton": Murray Kempton, *America Comes of Middle Age* (Boston: 1963), p. 155. How the NAACP found Oliver Brown: Richard Kluger, *Simple Justice* (New York: 1976), p. 395. "Came to the conclusion": Daniel Berman, *It Is So Ordered* (New York: 1966), p. 9; cf. John D. Weaver, *Warren: The Man, the Court, the Era* (New York: 1967), p. 211. "So that the whole question": Kluger, p. 540. Gap in expenditures and teachers' salaries would be closed by 1963: Harry Ashmore, *The Negro and the Schools* (Chapel Hill, N.C.: 1954), pp. 61–63, 102–21. Expenditures on education in Mississippi: Thomas D. Clark, *The Emerging South*, rev. ed. (New York: 1968), p. 193.

The contentious Vinson Court: C. Herman Pritchett, *Civil Liberties and the Vinson Court* (New York: 1954), Table 1, p. 21. "It has no fixed left": *Time* (September 21, 1953). Warren's appointment and Brownell's pleas: Weaver, pp. 183, 192–93. "Earl Warren is honest, likable and clean": John Gunther, *Inside USA*, rev. ed. (New York: 1951), pp. 39–40. Suspicion that Warren was a liberal at heart: TRB, in *New Republic* (October 5, 1953). Examples of the distorted history in the *Brown* v. *Board* briefs: Berman, pp. 81–83. The lachrymose reporter was I. F. Stone, *The Haunted Fifties* (New York: 1963), p. 61. Had Vinson lived, the decision would not have been unanimous: Anthony Lewis, *Portrait of a Decade* (New York: 1964), p. 28. "Dear Fellow American": Martin, pp. 1–2. "I'm living crammed right in the middle": ibid., p. 13. "That God chose members of the white race": Howard H. Quint, *Profile in Black and White: A Frank Portrait of South Carolina* (Washington, D.C.: 1958), p. 32. "In spite of his basic inferiority": Tom Brady, *Black Monday* (Winona, Miss.: 1955), p. 11. "The social, political and economic": ibid., p. 7. "Whenever and wherever": ibid., p. 13. Public opinion outside the South supported *Brown*: George H. Gallup, *The Gallup Poll 1935–1972* (New York: 1972), p. 1253. "I'll fill the jail": Martin, p. 5.

Martin Luther King, Jr.'s suicide attempts: Lerone Bennett, *What Manner of Man* (Chicago: 1964), pp. 18–19. Bus passenger arrangements in Montgomery: Martin Luther King, Jr., *Stride Toward Freedom* (New York: 1958), pp. 38–39. "If you will protest": ibid., p. 61. Attitude of middle-class whites toward boycott: Wilma Dykeman and James Stokely, *Neither Black nor White* (New York: 1957), p. 283. "We must love our white brothers": King, pp. 131–32. King asked to be struck down: William Robert Miller, *Martin Luther King* (New York: 1968), p. 59. King applied for a gun permit: King, p. 134. "For some 50 years": Bennett, pp. 85–86.

White Citizens' Councils were strong in the Black Belt, weak outside: Neil R. McMillen, *The Citizens' Councils* (Urbana, Ill.: 1971), pp. 43–46. "In practice they resemble": Numan V. Bartley, *The Rise of Massive Resistance* (Baton Rouge, La.: 1969), p. 193. Blacks expected *Brown* would be complied with: Louis Lomax, *The Negro Revolt* (New York: 1962), p. 74. Councils' power over politicians: Dan Wakefield, *Revolt in the South* (New York: 1960), pp. 50–51. Falstaff and other surrenders: Hodding Carter III, *The South Strikes Back* (Garden City, N.Y.: 1959), pp. 159–60. "This nigger woman's one": Martin, p. 30. "But what I really need": Dykeman and Stokely, p. 109. Klan floggings and bombings: Bartley, p. 208. Castration of Judge Aaron: James Graham Cook, *The Segregationists* (New York: 1962), pp. 140–43. "That river's full": Wakefield, p. 32. "The wild rumor had spread": Frank E. Smith, *Congressman from Mississippi* (New York: 1964), p. 263. Death ascribed to "causes unknown": Carter, p. 116. Rock Quarry camp: *Time* (August 13, 1956). "With far more real provocation": Harry Ashmore, *Epitaph for Dixie* (New York: 1958), p. 120. "A thin-lipped, hating man": Bartley, p. 118. "The Negro race, as a race": James J. Kilpatrick, *The Southern Case for School Segregation* (New York: 1962), p. 96. "Enthusiastically, Southerners": Martin, p. 35. The Committee of 52: Quint, p. 28.

"The greatest thing that has happened": Martin, p. 12. Dubious character of the poll test: Kluger, pp. 355–56. Julius Waties Waring: Bruce Bliven, "Judge Waring Moves North," *New Republic* (May 5, 1958); cf. Kluger. The Federal judges in the South and the pressures on them: J. W. Peltason, *58 Lonely Men* (New York: 1961). "It is our responsibility": Brooks Hayes, *A Southern Moderate Speaks* (Chapel Hill, N.C.: 1959), p. 130. Frederick John Kasper: James Rorty, "Hate Monger with Literary Trimmings," *Commentary* (December 1956). Pupil placement laws are considered in detail in Reed Sarratt, *The Ordeal of Desegregation* (New York: 1966). Only 2 percent of black children were at school with whites: Martin, p. 163. "Integration has always worked well": Baldwin, *Nobody*, p. 99. "Since no one in the South": Harry Golden, *Only in America* (Cleveland: 1958), p. 106. "You is getin to smart": Walter Lord, *The Past That Would Not Die* (New York: 1965), p. 76.

Chapter 21

56 percent of men, 69 percent of women: Samuel Stouffer, *Communism, Conformity and Civil Liberties* (Garden City, N.Y.: 1955), p. 141.

Half claimed to go to church weekly: George H. Gallup, *The Gallup Poll 1935–1972* (New York: 1972), p. 1253. Church membership: J. F. Dewhurst et al., *America's Needs and Resources: A New Survey* (New York: 1955), pp. 418–419. Church construction boom: Will Herberg, *Protestant, Catholic, Jew*, rev. ed. (Garden City, N.Y.: 1960), p. 50. "Surprising as it may seem": J. Paul Williams, *What Americans Believe and How They Worship* (New York: 1962), p. 473. Churches topped trust poll: Paul Lazarsfeld and Patricia Kendall, *Radio Listening in America* (Englewood Cliffs, N.J.: 1948), Table 20, p. 46. Belief in Christ and the Devil: Gallup, pp. 1481–83. Teenagers trusted clergymen, believed in God: H. H. Remmers and D. H. Radler, *The American Teenager* (Indianapolis: 1957), pp. 169–74. "Since Communists are anti-God": William Lee Miller, "Piety Along the Potomac," *The Reporter* (August 17, 1954). "Today there is a suspicion": A. Roy Eckhart, *The Surge of Piety in America* (New York: 1958) p. 25. Religious bodies screened refugees: Peter L. Berger, *The Noise of Solemn Assemblies* (Garden City, N.Y.: 1961), p. 64. "God's Float": Miller. "I am the most intensely religious man": *Chicago Daily News* (January 12, 1952). "The most widespread of all": Williams, p. 12. "Secularism is too widespread": Merrimon Cunninggim, *The College Seeks Religion* (New Haven, Conn.: 1947), p. 259. On church membership figures, see N. J. Demerath, "Trends and Anti-trends in Religious Change," in Eleanor B. Sheldon and Wilbert E. Moore, *Indicators of Social Change* (New York: 1968). Indianapolis department store: David Riesman, *Abundance for What?* (Garden City, N.Y.: 1964), p. 144. "The cult of reassurance": Martin E. Marty, *The New Shape of American Religion* (New York: 1959), p. 15. Pray *big*: Norman Vincent Peale, *The Power of Positive Thinking* (Englewood Cliffs, N.J.: 1952), pp. 7–8. God's judgment on Christ's ministry: A. Roy Eckhart, "The New Look in American Piety," *Christian Century* (November 17, 1954). "Societal religion": Williams. "Persons of cultivated taste": Herbert W. Schneider, *Religion in 20th Century America*, rev. ed. (Cambridge, Mass.: 1964), p. 150. "What is your religion?": *Current Population Reports*, Series P-20, No. 79 (Washington, D.C.: 1958). Southern Methodists, Southern Baptists: George Hansen, "How to Tell a Baptist from a Methodist in the South," *Harper's* (February 1963); cf. Kenneth K. Bailey, *Southern White Protestantism in the 20th Century* (New York: 1964). The solitary nickel: Dan Wakefield, *Revolt in the South* (New York: 1960), p. 70. "*This* hand has never": Wilma Dykeman and James Stokely, *Neither Black nor White* (New York: 1957), p. 261. The pentecostal revival: Daniel E. Harrell Jr. *All Things are Possible* (Bloomington, Ind.: 1975). Young reformers among Southern Baptists: Samuel S. Hill, Jr., "The Southern Baptists," *Christian Century* (January 9, 1963). Business did more for blacks than churches: Bailey, pp. 148–49. "The faith may be described as childlike": James Baldwin, "Harlem Ghetto: Winter 1948," *Commentary* (February 1948).

"The choice between humility and comfort": H.-J. Duteil, *The Great American Parade* (New York: 1953), p. 91. "The American Catholic clergy'': ibid., p. 155. Wife told to resist her husband: *American Ecclesiastical Review*, 1946 Vol. 112, p. 265. "Faced with the threat of decline": *National Catholic Almanac 1948*, p. 380. "Pushed Bible reading": Lawrence H. Fuchs, *John F. Kennedy and American Catholicism* (New York: 1967), pp. 132–33. "If it takes 40,000 priests": J. H. Fichter, *Parochial School* (South Bend, Ind.: 1959), p. 86. Segregated retreats: Bradford Daniel, ed., *Black, White and Gray* (New York: 1964), p. 151.

"The more a man gives away": Judith R. Kramer and Seymour Leventman, *Children of the Gilded Ghetto* (New Haven, Conn.: 1961), p. 100. "Jewishness" of suburban Jewish life: cf. Nathan Glazer *American Judaism*, rev. ed. (Chicago: 1972), Chapter 7. The Jews of Park Forest: Herbert J. Gans, "Park Forest: Birth of a Jewish Community," *Commentary* (April 1951); see also Harry Gersh, "The New Suburbanites of the 50's—Jewish Division," *Commentary* (March 1954). Decline in the observance of the sacraments: Marshall Sklare and Joseph Greenbaum, *Jewish Identity on the Suburban Frontier* (New York: 1967), pp. 49–56. "The synagogue in America": Will Herberg, "The Postwar Revival of the Synagogue," *Commentary* (April 1950). Intermarriage on the increase: Erich Rosenthal, "Studies of Jewish Intermarriage in the United States," *American Jewish Year Book 1963*. Jews at Harvard Business School: E. Digby Baltzell, *Protestant Establishment* (New York: 1964), p. 322. "Persons of Negro blood": Charles Abrams, *Forbidden Neighbors* (New York: 1955), p. 241. Preference was shown to black applicants: Vincent S. Carruthers, "The 'Narrow Door' to College Admissions," *New Republic* (September 13, 1954). "Just as society must have a scapegoat": Baldwin, "Harlem Ghetto." Half the teachers were Jewish: estimate of Nathan Glazer and Daniel P. Moynihan, *Beyond the Melting Pot* (Cambridge, Mass.: 1963), p. 146. "Them goddamned Jews": Claude Brown, *Manchild in the Promised Land* (New York: 1965), p. 336. Fire Island: Abrams, p. 202. $1.4 billion was raised: *American Jewish Year Book 1957*, Table i, p. 185. "Bonds for Israel": Harry Golden, *For 2¢ Plain* (Cleveland: 1959), p. 59.

Chapter 22

"When Joseph M. Dodge," "never more money": Sherman Adams, *First-Hand Report* (New York 1961), p. 134. Economic policies of the Eisenhower Administration: A. E. Holmans, *United States Fiscal Policy 1945–1959* (New York: 1961), pp. 235–71. "Seemed to believe in no function": Marquis Childs, *Eisenhower: Captive Hero* (New York: 1958), p. 160. "I cannot conceive of one": Robert J. Donovan, *Eisenhower: The Inside Story* (New York: 1956), p. 25. Tidelands oil: Edward R. Bartley, *The Tidelands Oil Controversy* (Austin, Texas: 1953). Admirals in the Texas Navy: John Bainbridge, *The Super Americans* (Garden City, New York: 1961), p. 87. $2 billion a year: Philip M. Stern, *The Great Treasury Raid* (New York: 1964) p. 21. "Those bastards": Aaron Wildavsky, *Dixon-Yates* (New Haven, Conn.: 1962) p. 6. "Throughout the Midwest":

William R. Willoughby, *The St. Lawrence Seaway* (Madison, Wis.: 1961), p. 258.
"A criminal raid": Donovan, p. 173. Eisenhower intended to use the Emergency Fund: ibid., p. 323. Eisenhower's attitude toward Republican right wing: Arthur Larson, *Eisenhower: The President Nobody Knew* (New York: 1969), pp. 49–58. Democratic leadership and Eisenhower: William J. White, *The Professional: Lyndon B. Johnson* (Boston: 1964), p. 175. "The United States is now": *Newsweek* (July 16, 1954). The Federal highway program: Helen Leavitt, *Superhighway-Superhoax* (Garden City, N.Y.: 1970). "When it comes down": Donovan, p. 223. Letter of disgust at "New Dealers": ibid., p. 62.

"Whether expanding at philosophic length": Emmet J. Hughes, *Ordeal of Power* (New York: 1962), pp. 46–47. Dulles was admired: Richard Goold-Adams, *The Time of Power* (London: 1962). Dulles's obsession with "rollback": Townsend Hoopes, *The Devil and John Foster Dulles* (Boston: 1973), p. 128. Eisenhower's denial of a policy change: *New York Times* (January 14, 1954). Dulles claimed that he had been misunderstood: John Foster Dulles, "A Policy for Security and Peace," *Foreign Affairs* (April 1954). Eisenhower's opinion of Dulles: Dwight D. Eisenhower, *Waging Peace* (New York: 1966), pp. 361–67. "He seems to be building": Adams, p. 84. "A 12-day civil war": *Life* (July 12, 1954).

Conservative ideas: William F. Buckley, Jr., *Up from Liberalism* (New York: 1959). "It is less individualistic": Clinton Rossiter, *Conservatism in America* (New York: 1955) pp. 200–02. Eisenhower's decision to run again: Adams, pp. 180–81. "When you are shaking hands": Herbert J. Muller, *Adlai Stevenson* (New York: 1967), pp. 175–76. "He can't be a virgin twice": Lord Kinross, *The Innocents at Home* (London: 1959), p. 67. Kennedy's "availability": Donald Malcolm, "The Man Who Wants Second Place," *New Republic* (July 30, 1956). Press coverage of test ban proposal: cf. *Newsweek* (October 29, 1956), which found the idea shocking.

Washington correspondents' disesteem of Eisenhower: Childs, p. 220. "Lose the vote of every liberal": Hughes, p. 133. For a fair-minded appraisal of the Eisenhower Presidency, cf. Clinton Rossiter, *The American Presidency* (New York: 1964), pp. 127–35.

Chapter 23
Conflicting recollections: Emmet J. Hughes, *Ordeal of Power* (New York: 1962), p. 176; Arthur Larson, *Eisenhower: The President Nobody Knew* (New York: 1969), pp. 137–38, 141; Dwight D. Eisenhower, *Waging Peace 1956–1961* (Garden City, N.Y.: 1966), p. 150; Sherman Adams, *First-Hand Report* (New York: 1961), pp. 253–54. Eisenhower's initiatives to end segregation: Robert J. Donovan, *Eisenhower: The Inside Story* (New York: 1956), pp. 155–59. Brownell's role in civil rights bill: J. W. Anderson, *Eisenhower, Brownell and the Congress* (Alabama: 1964). Johnson and the civil rights bill: Rowland Evans and Robert Novack,

Lyndon B. Johnson: The Exercise of Power (New York: 1966), Chapter 7.

Blossom's premonition of trouble: Virgil T. Blossom, *It has Happened Here* (New York: 1959), p. 8. The fatal flaw in the Blossom plan: Numan V. Bartley, *The Rise of Massive Resistance* (Baton Rouge, La.: 1969), p. 254. "Everybody knows": *New York Times* (July 18, 1957). Faubus agreed that peaceful desegregation was possible: Blossom, p. 66. *Birth of a Nation*: Benjamin Muse, *Ten Years of Prelude* (New York: 1964), p. 41. "To combat the legend": John Gunther, *Inside U.S.A.*, rev. ed. (New York, 1951), p. 843. "Throw a lit stick of dynamite": *Newsweek* (September 2, 1957). Faubus wanted Federal government to intervene: Blossom, p. 53. Elizabeth Eckford: Daisy Bates, *The Long Shadow of Little Rock* (New York: 1962), pp. 65–66; Anthony Lewis, *Portrait of a Decade* (New York: 1964), pp. 47–48. Eisenhower's attempts to settle the Little Rock crisis: Eisenhower, pp. 163–170. Role of Brooks Hays and its consequences: Brooks Hays, *A Southern Moderate Speaks* (Chapel Hill, N.C.: 1959). "We went through every room": *New York Times* (September 24, 1957). Faubus betrayed the moderates and cultivated the Citizens' Councils: Harry Ashmore, *Epitaph for Dixie* (New York: 1958), p. 41. Effects of crisis on Little Rock and Arkansas: *New Republic* (November 2, 1959); Benjamin Wattenberg and Richard Scammon, *This USA* (Garden City, N.Y.: 1965), p. 95. Effects on the Citizens Councils: Hodding Carter III, *The South Strikes Back* (Garden City, N.Y.: 1959), pp. 84, 189. Assassination attempt: Blossom, p. 150. Public support for the President: George H. Gallup, *The Gallup Poll 1935–1972* (New York: 1972), p. 1517.

IV: FALLING SHORT

Chapter 24

Mike Todd's party: *Newsweek* (October 28, 1957). "How can an old man": *Time* (July 13, 1958). Hail Marys, skywriting: I. F. Stone, *The Haunted Fifties* (New York: 1963), p. 284. QUIZ CHAMP VAN DOREN: *Time* (February 11, 1957). Van Doren's confession: *New York Times* (November 3, 1959). "Probably the climate of the Fifties": Eric Goldman, "Goodbye to the Fifties—and Good Riddance," *Harper's* (January 1960). Chessman was on the cover of *Time* (March 21, 1960). Trend in executions from the 1920s to 1960s: Benjamin Wattenberg and Richard Scammon, *This U.S.A.* (Garden City, N.Y.: 1965), p. 26. The Chessman version: Caryl Chessman, *Cell 2455 Death Row* (Englewood Cliffs, N.J.: 1954); *Trial by Ordeal* (Englewood Cliffs, N.J.: 1955). "Only one betrayed the trust": Vernon J. Scudder, *Prisoners Are People* (Garden City, N.Y.: 1952), p. 208. The pro-Chessman lobby: e.g., Elizabeth Hardwick, "The Chessman Case," *Partisan Review* (Summer 1960). "A very arrogant, mean, hating man": Louis Nizer, *The Jury Returns* (Garden City, N.Y.: 1966), p. 93. Barbie: *Life* (August 23, 1963). Ione Marshall: ibid. August 5, 1957).

Russians got the idea for Sputnik from the American press: Leonid Vladimirov, *The Russian Space Bluff* (New York: 1971), pp. 52–58. "My pet project": Arthur Larson, *Eisenhower: The President Nobody Knew* (New York: 1969), pp. 26–27. Missile stories: *Time* (January 30, 1956); *Life* (February 27, 1956). Organization of high-level science: Bernard Barber, *Science and the Social Order* (New York: 1952). "Seven men cut out of the same stone": *Time* (April 20, 1959). "A Russian astronaut is very likely": *Newsweek* (December 29, 1958). NASA was lobbying for the moon project: ibid. Poll on scientific leadership: George H. Gallup, *The Gallup Poll 1935–1972* (New York: 1972), p. 1653. "Informed people agree": James M. Gavin, *War and Peace in the Space Age* (New York: 1958), p. 17. "The Missile Gap": Maxwell Taylor, *The Uncertain Trumpet* (New York: 1960), p. 13. "The words 'missile gap' ": *Newsweek* op. cit. Thomas S. Gates, Jr.: *Time* (February 1, 1960). On think tanks: Bruce L. R. Smith, *The RAND Corporation* (Cambridge, Mass.: 1966); Paul Dickson, *Think Tanks* (New York: 1972); Joseph Kraft, "RAND: Arsenal of Ideas," *Harper's* (July 1960); and Edward L. Katzenbach, Jr., "Ideas: A New Defense Industry" *The Reporter* (March 2, 1961). Spending on research and development: because of changing definitions and changes in accounting methods, there simply are no reliable figures on total R&D spending before 1964; my figures are an averaging of half a dozen estimates. Summer study: Theodore H. White, "U.S. Science—the Troubled Quest," *The Reporter* (September 14, 1954). Federal support for humanities and social sciences: Charles V. Kidd, *American Universities and Federal Research* (Cambridge, Mass.: 1959), Appendix Table A7, p. 69. "The plain fact is": Don K. Price, "The Scientific Establishment," *Science* (June 19, 1962). Unraveling nucleic acids: James D. Watson, *The Double Helix* (New York: 1968); Bernard Bailyn and Donald Fleming, *The Intellectual Migration* (Cambridge, Mass.: 1969); Ruth Moore, *The Coil of Life* (New York: 1961). Comparative incidence and costs of TB and polio: Seymour Harris, *The Economics of American Medicine* (New York: 1964), Table 3, p. 36. "An ominous precursor": Fred Davis, *Passage Through Crisis* (Indianapolis: 1963), p. 39.

The changing character of invention: Jacob Schmookler, "Technological Progress and the Modern Corporation," in E. S. Mason, ed., *The Corporation and Modern Society* (Cambridge, Mass.: 1959); cf. Aaron Warner et al., *The Impact of Science on Technology* (New York: 1965). Transistorized hearing aids: *Time* (March 12, 1956). Growth of the electronics industry: Harold G. Vatter, *The U.S. Economy in the 1950's* (New York: 1963), p. 152; Charles Silberman, "The Coming Shake-Out in Electronics," *Fortune* (August 1960). "New industrial complex": Vatter, p. 184.

I. I. Rabi: Ralph E. Freeman, ed., *Postwar Economic Trends* (New York: 1961), p. 42. Doubling employment of instrument makers: Bureau of Labor Statistics, *Employment and Earnings Statistics for the United States 1909–1960* (Washington, D.C.: 1961). "Will find in the monuments": Alvin Weinberg, "Impact of Large-Scale Science on the United States," *Science* (July 21, 1961). Where research scientists came from: R. H. Knapp and H. B. Goodrich, *Origins of American Scientists* (Chicago: 1952). Motivation of scientists: Anne Roe, *The Making of a Scientist* (New York: 1953). Wastage of scientific talent: H. H. Remmers and D. H. Radler, *The American Teenager* (Indianapolis: 1957), p. 165. Ambivalent attitudes: Margaret Meade and Rhoda Metraux, "The Image of the Scientist Among High School Students," *Science* (August 20, 1957). "The great edifice of modern physics": C. P. Snow, *The Two Cultures and the Scientific Revolution* (Cambridge: 1959), pp. 14–15.

"Why do they permit themselves": Robert Jungk, *Tomorrow Is Already Here* (New York: 1954), pp. 62–63.

Chapter 25

"Here was tangible proof": William Attwood, *Still the Most Exciting Country* (New York: 1956), p. 89. Columbus, Ohio: Alexander Werth, *America in Doubt* (London: 1959). "Warning-Yellow": Donald Robinson, "If H-Bombs Fall," *Saturday Evening Post* (May 25, 1957). "The Chairman of the Atomic Energy Good News Commission": Herbert Block, *Herblock's Special for Today* (New York: 1958), p. 12. Perfecting the "clean" bomb: Lewis Strauss, *Men and Decisions* (Garden City, N.Y.: 1962), pp. 419–20; Willard Libby, *Time* (May 6, 1957). Gaither Committee: Morton Halperin, "The Gaither Committee and the Policy Process," *World Politics* (April 1961). "Will fortify people against mass hysteria": Federal Civil Defense Administration, "The Church and Civil Defense" (Washington, D.C.: 1956). Town in New Hampshire, tornado belt in Texas: Attwood, p. 94. Alterations to homes, stocking emergency supplies: George H. Gallup, *The Gallup Poll 1935–1972* (New York: 1972), p. 1732.

"It was an accident": James Shepley and Clay Blair, Jr., *The Hydrogen Bomb* (New York: 1954), p. 228. "Inevitable. It has achieved the realization": William L. Laurence, *Men and Atoms* (New York: 1959), p. 268. Albert Wohlstetter and the bases study: Paul Dickson, *Think Tanks* (New York: 1972), pp. 59–61; cf. Joseph Kraft, "RAND: Arsenal of Ideas," *Harper's* (July 1960). Winning a thermonuclear war: Edward Teller, "Alternative to Security," *Foreign Affairs* (December 1957). "Master of the challenges": Henry Kissinger, *Nuclear Weapons and Foreign Policy* (New York: 1957), p. 61. "Moreover if we utilize": ibid., p. 152. "A defeatist": ibid., p. 188. "Despite widespread belief": Herman Kahn, *On Thermonuclear War* (Princeton, N.J.: 1960), p. 21. "We must be willing": ibid., p. 529. "These men struck me": Attwood, pp. 106–07. "Murderers": Dorothy Day, "Conscience and Civil Defense," *New Republic* (August 22, 1957). SANE and Senator Dodd: Lawrence S. Wittner, *Rebels Against War* (New York: 1969), p. 246. Bigelow: Albert Bigelow, *The Voyage of the Golden Rule* (Garden City, N.Y.: 1959). Reynolds: Earle Reynolds, *The Forbidden Voyage* (New York: 1961). The fictitious Eatherley: Gunther Anders, *Burning Conscience* (New York: 1962). The real Eatherley: William Bradford Huie, *The Hiroshima Pilot* (New York: 1964). AEC's monitors detected test at 2,300 miles: *New York Times* (March 12, 1958). Problems of a test ban: Robert S. Gilpin, *American Scientists and Nuclear Weapons Policy* (Princeton, N.J.: 1962), pp. 225–38, 244–45.

Chapter 26

"To impede, thwart, delay or frustrate": *Newsweek* (August 3, 1959). "In Arkansas": ibid. (August 24, 1959). Encyclopedia salesmen: Ernest Q. Campbell et al., *When a City Closes Its Schools* (Chapel Hill, N.C.: 1960), pp. 21–22. "Now Russian is the rage": Jacques Barzun, *The House of Intellect* (New York: 1959), p. 121. For a picture of Russian engineers at work in the early 1950s, see Alexander Solzhenitzyn, *The First Circle* (New York: 1970). Low pay of science graduates: Charles C. Cole, Jr., *Encouraging Scientific Talent* (New York: 1956), p. 103. Right-wing criticism of textbooks: E. Merrill Root, *Brainwashing in the High Schools* (New York: 1958). Middle-class teachers and lower-class students: Edgar Z. Friedenberg, *The Vanishing Adolescent* (Boston: 1960), pp. 67–68. "There is no hope": David Stevenson "Who Will Teach the Teachers?" *New Republic* (January 13, 1958). "Nearly 150 had a long-standing hatred": H. S. Dyer et al., *Problems in Mathematical Education* (Princeton, N.J.: 1956), p. 11. Education majors: Henry Chauncey, "The Use of the Selective Service Qualification Test in the Deferment of College Students," *Science* (July 25, 1952). "We don't teach subject matter": Arthur Bestor, *Educational Wastelands* (Urbana, Ill.: 1953), pp. 118–19. Number of states rose from eighteen to forty-three: James B. Conant, *The Education of American Teachers* (New York: 1963), p. 17. Cost of education was $35 billion: Theodore W. Schultz, *The Economic Value of Education* (New York: 1963), pp. 34, 62. Half of top students did not go to college: Cole, pp. 71–72, 145. Economic return on diplomas and degrees: Schultz pp. 63–65. Federal spending on education: Congressional Quarterly, *Congress and the Nation 1945–1964* (Washington, D.C.: 1965), p. 1199. Television and adult education: *Newsweek* (October 7, 1957). Conant and Rickover: *Life* (January 13, 1958).

"Almost everywhere we went": William Attwood, *Still the Most Exciting Country* (New York: 1956), p. 56. Growth of kindergartens: Benjamin Wattenberg and Richard Scammon, *This USA* (Garden City, N.Y.: 1965), pp. 204–05. Shortage of classrooms and teachers: I. L. Kandel, *American Education in the 20th Century* (Cambridge, Mass.: 1957), p. 217. Expenditures on education: Seymour E. Harris, *More Resources for Education* (New York: 1960), Table 2, p. 6. Boom in school construction: Fritz

Machlup, *The Production and Distribution of Knowledge in the United States* (Princeton, N.J.: 1962), Table IV-3, p. 71. Differences in per pupil expenditures: James B. Conant, *Slums and Suburbs* (New York: 1961), p. 80. Vocational and nonvocational education: ibid., pp. 5–6. George Goldfarb: *Newsweek* (February 10, 1958); cf. Harrison Salisbury, *The Shook-Up Generation* (New York: 1958). "At a station labelled 'high school' ": W. Lloyd Warner et al., *Who Shall Be Educated* (New York: 1944), p. 48. Hostility toward vocational high school graduates: Martin Mayer, *The Schools* (New York: 1961), p. 205. Impact of postwar educational psychology: R. Freeman Butts and Lawrence Cremin, *A History of Education in American Culture* (New York: 1953); Ronald Gross and Judith Murphy, *The Revolution in the Schools* (New York: 1964). "Of an intelligence virtually unparalleled": Mayer, p. 86. "The simple fact is": B. F. Skinner, "The Science of Learning and the Art of Teaching," *Harvard Educational Review* (Spring 1954). The "teacher-engineer": Simon Ramo, "A New Technique of Education," *Engineering and Science* (October 1957). "As one nears the question": Mayer, p. 225. Correlation of IQ score and social class: August B. Hollingshead, *Elmtown's Youth* (New York: 1949), pp. 194–200. Postwar rise in aptitude testing: Lawrence Bloomgarden, "Our Changing Elite Colleges," *Commentary* (February 1960). SAT math scores at Harvard: *Time* (March 7, 1960). "Geniuses used to be rare": John W. Gardner, *Excellence* (New York: 1961) p. 46. Marilyn Monroe: W. J. Weatherby, *Conversations with Marilyn* (London: 1976).

College students per 1,000 people: Charles Lewis Taylor and Michael C. Hudson, *World Handbook of Political and Social Indicators* (New Haven, Conn.: 1972), Table 4.4, p. 229. University of California: Peter F. Drucker, *America's Next 20 Years* (New York: 1957), p. 53. Eighteen- to twenty-one-year-olds at college: Martin Trow, "The Second Transformation of American Secondary Education," *Educational Journal of Comparative Sociology* (September 1961). PhD production: Mary Irwin, ed., *American Colleges and Universities* (Washington, D.C.: 1956), pp. 66–67. Too few PhDs: Dale Wolfle, *America's Resources of Specialized Talent* (New York: 1954), p. 126. "The mere holding of a bachelor's degree": Conant, pp. 93–94. "No knowledge that is precise": Barzun, pp. 98–99. "A knowledge of comic strips": David Riesman, *Constraint and Variety in American Education* (Lincoln, Neb.: 1956), p. 37. "There is no valid reason": Hyman Rickover, *Education and Freedom* (New York: 1959), pp. 126–27. Remarkable high school transcript: A. Whitney Griswold, *Liberal Education and the Democratic Ideal* (New Haven, Conn.: 1959), p. 29. "*In*-credible subjects": Jacques Barzun, *Teacher in America* (Boston: 1945), p. 91. Educational value of the PhD: Paul Samuelson, in Ralph E. Freeman, ed., *Postwar Economic Trends in the United States* (New York: 1960), pp. 43–44. "One of the most remarkable features": Robert M. Hutchins, *Great Books* (New York: 1954), p. 80. Standards in engineering education: Norbert Wiener, *The Human Use of Human Beings* (Boston: 1950), p. 155. "Liberal culture, receptive to ideas": Daniel Bell,

The End of Ideology (Glencoe, Ill.: 1960), p. 314. Department of Social Relations: Riesman, p. 66. Bright students were attracted to psychology: Wolfle, pp. 199–200.

"Almost any program of study and research": Robert M. Hutchins, *Some Observations on American Education* (Cambridge, England: 1956), p. 15. "The Federal grant university": Clark Kerr, *The Uses of the University* (Cambridge, Mass.: 1963), p. 45. $1.5 billion in Federal money: J. Kenneth Little, *A Survey of Federal Programs in Higher Education* (Washington, D.C.: 1962), p. 6. Riverside and Irvine: Kerr, p. 89. From thirty-two percent to sixty-one percent: Harold Orlans, *The Effects of Federal Programs on Higher Education* (Washington, D.C.: 1962), p. 140. UC and University of Iowa's respective shares: Little, p. 3. Numbers of students in various Federally-financed programs: ibid., pp. 14–19. Effect of NDEA on social sciences: ibid., p. 25. CIA and *The Dynamics of Soviet Society*: Victor Marchetti and John D. Marks, *The CIA and the Cult of Intelligence* (New York: 1974), p. 175. "At some of our major universities": Riesman, p. 69. Screening and loyalty oaths: Charles V. Kidd, *American Universities and Federal Research* (Cambridge, Mass.: 1959) p. XL.

Chapter 27

Number and characteristics of "culture consumers": Alvin Toffler, *The Culture Consumers* (New York: 1964), pp. 28–29. Spending on tickets: Editors of *Fortune, America in the Sixties* (New York: 1960), pp. 195–196. Sales of musical instruments: Jacques Barzun, *Music in American Life* (Bloomington, Ind.: 1962), pp. 33–34. Number of children learning to play instruments: Toffler, p. 43. Lincoln Center: Robert A. Caro *The Power Broker* (New York: 1974) pp. 1009–1012, 1014–1115. Herbert Kupferberg "The Cultural Monopoly at Lincoln Center," *Harper's* (October 1961). Doubts about the culture boom: Jacques Barzun, "America's Passion for Culture," *Harper's* (March 1954); *Time* (December 23, 1957). The Great Books and Webster's Third: Dwight Macdonald, *Against the American Grain* (New York: 1962). "A spectre haunts our culture": Lionel Trilling, "The Liberal Imagination," *American Quarterly* (Fall 1949).

"Where no museums existed": Rudi Blesh, *Modern Art USA* (New York: 1956), p. 230. "To control art in the United States": *Congressional Record* (March 11, 1949), pp. 2364–65. "It's become a kind of super WPA": *New Republic* (June 2, 1958). "The students requested permission": *New York Times* (October 28, 1950). "I wish they did": Russell Lynes, *The Tastemakers* (New York: 1954), pp. 282–83. "Since resemblance to nature": *Times Literary Supplement, The American Imagination* (London: 1960), p. 130. "Abstract Expressionism": Robert M. Coates, "The Art Galleries," *New Yorker* (March 30, 1946). "Every time he stretches canvas": Barbara Rose, *American Art Since 1900* (New York: 1967), p. 150. "The first American to paint pictures": Irving Sandler, *Abstract Expressionism* (London: 1970), p. 44. Jackson Pollock: Peggy Guggenheim, *Confessions of an Art Addict* (London: 1960) pp. 132, 140. Frank O'Hara, *Jackson Pollock* (New York: 1959). De Kooning: Harriet Janis and Rudi Blesh, *De Kooning* (New York: 1960). Art critics and Pop Art: see the collection of head-scratching essays in Gregory Battcock, ed., *The New Art* (New York: 1966). Parke-Bernet auction: *Time* (December 1, 1958). Renoir canvas cut up: *Newsweek* (March 16, 1959). "Prices are unheard of": Guggenheim, p. 172. "I watched them": Louis Kronenberger, *The Cart and the Horse* (New York: 1964), p. 201.

The American architectural Grand Tour: Ian MacCallum, *Architecture USA* (London: 1959), p. 9. Aluminum in postwar construction: Editors of *Architectural Forum*, *Building USA* (New York: 1958), p. 68. "I would not be surprised": William Attwood, *Still the Most Exciting Country* (New York: 1956), p. 97. Taxes and the Seagram Building: Richard J. Whalen, *A City Destroying Itself* (New York 1965), p. 44. "Form follows sales": John Burchard and Albert Bush-Brown, *The Architecture of America*, rev. ed. (London: 1967), pp. 347–48. Guggenheim Museum would bounce: Henry-Russell Hitchcock and Arthur Drexler, *Built in USA* (New York: 1952), p. 27. "Designed into the structural members": Harrison Gill, "What Makes Architecture Modern?," *Harper's* (July 1953).

Employment in "printing, publishing, and allied industries": Bureau of Labor Statistics, *Employment and Earnings Statistics in the United States 1909–1960* (Washington, D.C.: 1961), p. 165. Sales of Peyton Place: Alice Payne Hackett, *70 Years of Bestsellers 1895–1965* (New York: 1968), p. 41. Erle Stanley Gardner: ibid., p. 61. Forty percent read mysteries: George H. Gallup, *The Gallup Poll 1935–1972* (New York: 1972), p. 943. Faulkner was out of print in 1945: Willard Thorp, *American Writing in the 20th Century* (Cambridge, Mass.: 1960), p. 260. Growth of book sales: Roger H. Smith, ed., *The American Reading Public* (New York: 1964), p. 53. Nonfiction outsold fiction best-sellers: Hackett, pp. 200, 213. Export of American books: Smith, p. 118. "A writer isn't a writer": William Barrett, "Writers and Their Work," in George B. De Huszar, ed., *The Intellectuals* (Glencoe, Ill.: 1960); cf. Malcolm Cowley, *The Literary Situation* (New York: 1954). The visiting Frenchman was H.-J. Duteil, *The Great American Parade* (New York: 1953), p. 122. Seymour Krim, *Views of a Near-Sighted Cannoneer* (New York: 1961), describes a literary scene in which his mental breakdown appears as the most logical outcome of events. "Probably the best fiction": *New Republic* (June 23, 1958). "This story of the two-year rape": ibid. (October 27, 1958).

Chapter 28

"The organization is more important": John K. Jessup, "A Political Role for the Corporation," *Fortune* August 1952. For a profile of postwar corporation presidents, see Mabel Newcomer, *The Big Business Executive* (New York: 1955). "Corporation executives are not capitalists": A. A. Berle, *Power Without Property* (New York: 1959), p. 68. "Recruited from the grab-bag": Daniel Bell, *The End of Ideology* (Glencoe, Ill.: 1960), pp. 89–90. "What do the Socialists have to gain": John R. Bunting, *The Hidden Face of Free Enterprise* (New York: 1964), p. 39. Fathers of executives: W. Lloyd Warner and James C. Abegglen, *Big Business Leaders in America* (New York: 1955), p. 14. Religion and education of executives: Newcomer, pp. 48, 70. Top 5 percent of income earners: Herman P. Miller, *Rich Man, Poor Man* (New York: 1971), Table IX-2, p. 153. Man who could spend $10: Vance Packard, *The Pyramid Climbers* (New York: 1962), p. 30. Self-image of business executives: Francis X. Sutton et al., *The American Business Creed* (Cambridge, Mass.: 1956) pp. 30, 93, 105, 148. "We'll be able to arrange the walls": *Wall Street Journal* (October 19, 1957). 250,000 business VPs: Editors of *Fortune, The Executive Life* (Garden City, N. Y.: 1956), p. 150. "Nevertheless, Chrysler was not one": Harry M. Trebing, ed., *The Corporation in the American Economy.* (Chicago: 1971), p. 37. "The social strains": Bell, p. 98. Business failure rates: Harold G. Vatter, *The U.S. Economy in the 1950s* (New York: 1963), pp. 150–151, 206.

Efforts of pro-business lobbies: U.S. House of Representatives Select Committee on Lobbying Activities, *General Interim Report*, 81st Congress, 2nd Session (Washington, D.C.: 1950) pp. 8–12. "The Gospel of Social Responsibility": Earl Cheit, ed., *The Business Establishment* (New York: 1964), p. 152. "The public be cultivated": Wilbert E. Moore, *The Conduct of the Corporation* (New York: 1962), p. 282. Response to Levitt: Vance Packard, *The Waste Makers* (New York: 1960), pp. 226–227. Courses in public relations: Alfred McClung Lee, "Trends in Public Relations Training," *Public Opinion Quarterly* (Spring 1947); "Management's Self-Conscious Spokesmen," *Fortune* (November 1955). "The rise of the public relations industry": John Kenneth Galbraith, *The Affluent Society* (Boston: 1958), p. 155. Praise of bigness: David Lilienthal, *Big Business* (New York: 1952). Three in four, one in ten: Cheit, p. 132. Sources of investment capital: Berle, pp. 39–45. Charles Lynch: Martin Mayer, *Wall Street*, rev. ed. (New York: 1959), pp. 109–114. People's Capitalism and the New York Stock Exchange: J. A. Livingston, *The American Stockholder* (Philadelphia: 1958), pp. 23–24. "Executives' Capitalism": Michael D. Reagan, "What 17 Million Shareholders Share," *New York Times Magazine* (February 23, 1964). Growth of foundations: Warren Weaver, *U.S. Philanthropic Foundations* (New York: 1967), pp. 60–61. "To my arguments": Jacques Barzun, *The House of Intellect* (New York: 1959), p. 199. "A tendency for the [professors]": David Riesman, *Constraint and Variety in American Education* (Lincoln, Neb.: 1956), p. 36. "A distinctively American combination": Dwight Macdonald, *The Ford Foundation* (New York: 1956), p. 57. One third of Fund was spent on administration: Thomas C. Reeves, *Freedom and the Foundations* (New York: 1969), p. 282. Proposals made to Ford: Macdonald, pp. 112–113.

Importance of advertising as a source of values: Packard, p. 295. Growth of advertising expenditure: A. H. Hansen, *Economic Issues of the 1960s* (New York: 1960), p. 75; Vatter, p. 176. Increase in personal indebtedness: Hansen, p. 65. "Was taking on about $750": Packard, p. 142. Prewar ratio of production and distribution costs: Twentieth Century Fund, *Does Distribution Cost Too Much?* (New York: 1939) pp. 21, 47. Money spent on packaging: Packard, p. 51. "Glamorous, financially rewarding": Martin Mayer, *Madison Avenue* (New York: 1958), p. 37. Early deaths of advertising executives: ibid., p. 22. Advertising men thought they were helping consumers: Sutton, p. 148. "The function of advertising": Otto Kleppner, "Is There Too Much Advertising?," *Harper's* (February 1951). Advertising as "folk art": Pierre Martineau, *Motivation in Advertising* (New York: 1957), pp. 189–190. "There is no work called for": ibid., p. 5. Increased sales of Coke and popcorn: Mayer, pp. 233–234. "It came to be regarded": Vance Packard, *The Hidden Persuaders* (New York: 1957), p. 99. Furniture advertising caused confusion: Editors of *Fortune, America in the Sixties* (New York: 1960), p. 124. Monsignor Sheen switched: Mayer, p. 211. Shortcomings of Motivation Research: Alfred Politz, " 'Motivation Research' from a Research Viewpoint," *Public Opinion Quarterly* (Winter 1956–1957). "The Cellini of Chrome": *Time* (November 4, 1957). "More car per car": Gilbert Burck and Sanford S. Parker, "Detroit's Next Decade," *Fortune* (October 1959). The Edsel's genesis is reconstructed in John Brooks, *The Fate of the Edsel and Other Business Adventures* (New York: 1959). "No materal shall give offense": Alexander McKendrick, *Prime Time* (New York: 1969), p. 449. The billboard subsidy and the penalty on trees: Peter Blake, *God's Own Junkyard* (New York; 1964), p. 11. Curtis Publishing Company, *Reader's Digest: Wall Street Journal* (March 17, 1949). *Time-Life's* $20 million subsidy: this was a fact John F. Kennedy was delighted to bring to the attention of Henry Luce; Theodore Sorensen, *Kennedy* (1965), p. 353. *Time-Life* production costs and sales income: David Cort, *Is There an American in the House?* (New York: 1960) p. 93. Advertising Council: J. A. R. Pimlott, "Public Service Advertising," *Public Opinion Quarterly* (Spring 1948).

"A taciturn thoughtful financial man": Osborn Elliott, *Men at the Top* (New York: 1959), p. 7. Kaiser's fortune: "The Arrival of Henry Kaiser," *Fortune* (July 1951). "The ablest, brainiest and most ruthless": John Gunther and Bernard Quint, *Days to Remember* (New York: 1956), p. 206. Young's Texas friends: Philip M. Stern, *The Great Treasury Raid* (New York: 1964), p. 22; John Brooks, *The Seven Fat Years* (New York: 1958). "Some shareholders, overwhelmed by attention": Livingston, p. 139. Edwin H. Land: Francisco Bello, "The Magic That Made Polaroid," *Fortune* (April 1959). Ford shares: Brooks, "This Way to the Ford Stock, Boys." General Motors: Peter F. Drucker, *The Conduct of the Corporation* (New York: 1946). Warren, Michigan: Benjamin Wattenberg and Richard Scammon, *This USA* (Garden City, N. Y.: 1965), p. 201.

Number and size of small businesses: John H. Bunzell, *The American Small Businessman* (New York: 1962), pp. 31–33. RFC promoted competition: John Kenneth Galbraith, *American Capitalism* (Boston: 1956), p.

35. Cost of monopoly and oligopoly: Leonard W. Weiss, *Economics and American Industry* (New York: 1961), p. 507. Attitudes toward competition: Bunting, p. 41. Return on capital in 1920s and 1950s: Chase Manhattan Bank, "Business in Brief" (November/December 1959). "Many officials privately confide": *New York Times* (February 4, 1961). Concentration produced 50 percent higher profits: Weiss, pp. 500–503. Steel was responsible for half of inflation: Otto Eckstein, *Steel and the Postwar Inflation* (A report for the Joint Economic Committee, 86th Congress, 1st Session) (Washington, D.C.: 1959), p. 34. GE and Du Pont aimed at 20 percent: Gardiner C. Means, *Pricing Power and the Public Interest* (New York: 1962), p. 240. Corruption at Sears, Continental Foods, Whirlpool, *New York Times*, Hearst press: Robert F. Kennedy, *The Enemy Within* (New York: 1960), pp. 219–226, 232–234. Nella Bogart: Murray Kempton, *America Comes of Middle Age* (Boston: 1963). "Is the Stock Exchange honest?": Mayer, *Wall Street*, pp. 74–75. Mrs. Emily Rogers: Mayer, *Madison Avenue*, p. 90. The eight-year price-fixing conspiracy: John Herling, *The Great Price Conspiracy* (Washington, D.C.: 1962); Richard Austin Smith, "The Incredible Electrical Conspiracy," *Fortune* (April and May 1961). W. F. Oswalt: John G. Fuller, *The Gentlemen Conspirators* (New York: 1962), pp. 13–14. Press coverage: *New Republic* (February 20, 1961). "Many of the defendants": Smith (May 1961). Survey of 1,700 executives and managers: Raymond C. Baumhart, "How Ethical Are Businessmen?" *Harvard Business Review* (July–August 1961).

Chapter 29

Real family income rose by $1,000: Herman P. Miller, *Rich Man, Poor Man* (New York: 1971), p. 37. Public debt as percentage of GNP: Council of Economic Advisers, *Economic Report to the President* (Washington, D.C.: 1960), p. 210. Government spending was less stable than private investment: Bert G. Hickman, *Growth and Stability in the Postwar Economy* (Washington, D.C.: 1960), pp. 30–33. Eisenhower defended do-nothing economic policy: *New York Times* (October 21, 1958). "Buy": Vance Packard, *The Waste Makers* (New York: 1960), p. 27. "Customers suddenly started robbing": ibid., p. 221. "A rise which rarely faltered": Harold G. Vatter, *The U.S. Economy in the 1950's* (New York: 1963), p. 48. Unions made an issue of economic growth rates: Frank C. Pierson, *Unions in Postwar America* (New York: 1967), p. 47.

Hard-core unemployed: Stanley Lebergott, ed., *Men Without Work* (Englewood Cliffs, New Jersey: 1964), Table 8, p. 35. Employment in aircraft and shipbuilding: Bureau of Labor Statistics, *Employment and Earnings Statistics for the U.S. 1909–1960* (Washington, D.C.: 1961), pp. 215–216, 222–223. Employment in construction, government, agriculture, and mining: H. S. Perloff et al., *Regions, Resources and Economic Growth* (Baltimore: 1960), Table 130, p. 303. Workers' fantasies of independence: Eli Chinoy, *Automobile Workers and the American Dream*

(Garden City, N. Y.: 1955). Public opinion: George H. Gallup, *The Gallup Poll 1935–1972* (New York: 1972), pp. 1484, 1505. Changes in the workweek: Joseph S. Zeisel, "The Workweek in American Industry," U.S. Department of Labor, *Monthly Labor Review* (Washington,D.C.: January 1959). Changes in lifetime pattern of work: Seymour L. Wolfbein, "The Changing Length of Working Life," in Eric Larrabee and R. Meyersohn, eds., *Mass Leisure* (Glencoe, Ill.: 1958). Public opinion toward labor: Gallup, pp. 1484, 1505. "A national sentiment of being pro-labor": B.J. Widick, *Labor Today* (Boston: 1964), p. 166. "The worst setback": Michael D. Reagan, *The Managed Economy* (New York: 1963), pp. 126–128, quoting A. H. Raskin. Surveys to raise morale: Loren Baritz, *The Servants of Power* (Middletown, Conn.: 1960), p. 154. Aptitude testing to weed out liberals and radicals: ibid., p. 159. Rubber Workers at University of Alabama, Teamsters at Central High: Harry Ashmore, *Epitaph for Dixie* (New York: 1958), p. 130. "This is what happens": Bradford Daniel, ed., *Black, White and Gray* (New York: 1964), p. 11. Liberals' disappointment with labor: Widick, p. 202. "It may interest you": *New York Post* (September 9, 1955). "The labor business": Paul Jacobs, *The State of the Unions* (New York: 1963), p. 17. The ILGWU: ibid., pp. 126–127; Kenneth B. Clark, *Dark Ghetto* (New York: 1965), p. 44.

Attempts to get members to union meetings: Jack Barbash, *The Practice of Unionism* (New York: 1956), p. 65. Unions' private welfare programs: ibid., pp. 302–303. UMW's casualties: Ira Wolfert, *An Epidemic of Genius* (New York: 1960), p. 157. Number of welfare and pension plans: John Hutchinson, *The Imperfect Union* (New York: 1970), p. 358. The Select Committee: John L. McClellan, *Crime Without Punishment* (New York: 1962); Robert F. Kennedy, *The Enemy Within* (New York: 1960); Clark R. Mollenhoff, *Tentacles of Power* (Cleveland: 1965). *My Fair Lady* twenty-four times: McClellan, pp. 98–99. Beck's crimes: ibid., pp. 39, 42. Hoffa's wink: Kennedy, p. 75. "One night Bob and I": Pierre Salinger, *With Kennedy* (Garden City, N. Y.: 1966), p. 19. Landrum-Griffin's passage through Congress: Alan K. McAdams, *Power and Politics in Labor Legislation* (New York: 1964).

Chapter 30

The young graduate student was James West (pseudonym of Carl Withers), *Plainville USA* (New York: 1945). Fifteen years of change are recorded in Art Gallagher, Jr., *Plainville Fifteen Years Later* (New York: 1961). Farm sizes: Edward C. Higbee, *Farms and Farmers in the Urban Age* (New York: 1963), p. 99; Lowry Nelson, *American Farm Life* (Cambridge, Mass.: 1954), p. 20. Assets and liabilities: U.S. Department of Agriculture, "The Balance Sheet of Agriculture," *Agriculture Information Bulletin*, No. 90 (Washington, D.C.: 1952). Capital investment per farm worker: J. F. Dewhurst, *America's Needs and Resources: A New Survey* (New York: 1955), p. 911. Cost of corn production: Higbee, p. 22.

Top one-fourth grew three-fourths: U.S. Department of Agriculture, *A Place to Live* (Washington, D.C.: 1963), p. 15. Big business's response to competition from co-ops: *Time* (February 15, 1960). Harvested cropland declined: *A Place to Live*, p. 172. Lamar and Linden Ratliff: Higbee, p. 25. Productivity gains: John D. Kendrick, *Postwar Productivity Trends in the U.S. 1948–1969* (New York : 1973), Table 5–1, pp. 78—79. "To find a diet": Rachel Carson, *Silent Spring* (Boston: 1962), p. 148. 90 percent were still family farms: *A Place to Live*, p. 167. "One could see," "Cleveland business executive": ibid., p. 11. Health on farms: Helen L. Johnston, "Health Trends in Rural America," in ibid. Rural population was mainly nonfarm: Bureau of the Census, *Census of Population 1960: Summary of General Social and Economic Characteristics* (Washington, D.C.: 1962), p. 216. Life-style of rural nonfarm population: Lee Taylor and Arthur R. Jones, Jr., *Rural Life and Urbanized Society* (New York: 1964). "People who live on farms": Dale E. Hathaway, *Government and Agriculture* (New York: 1963), p. 32. "With whitewall tires": Vance Packard, *The Hidden Persuaders* (New York: 1957), p. 143. "He gets up in the morning": John Bunzel, *The American Small Businessman* (New York: 1962), p. 250.

Plainville and the GI farmer: Gallagher, pp. 18–19. "Where the population was once thought": John Kenneth Galbraith, *The Affluent Society* (Boston: 1958), p. 103. Net farm income in 1947 and 1957: Congressional Quarterly, *Congress and the Nation 1945–1964* (Washington, D.C.: 1965), p. 669. Nonfarm income almost equal to farm income: Higbee, pp. 11–12. Farmers paid more income tax: Hathaway, Table 2, p. 348. Rising value of farms: Higbee, pp. 16–17. Minimum capital requirements of farming: ibid., pp. 81–82. "I told him," "by asking in return": Sherman Adams, *First-Hand Report* (New York: 1962), pp. 171–172. "Benson has a talent": *Time* (November 4, 1957). Attack on Benson at Sioux Falls: *Life* (October 21, 1957). "Enveloped in a kind of celestial optimism": Adams, p. 172. Rise in farm program costs: *Congress and the Nation*, p. 671. "When we asked": William Attwood, *Still the Most Exciting Country* (New York: 1956), p. 39. Differences in parity payments: Rockefeller Panel Report, *Prospect for America* (Garden City, N. Y.: 1961), p. 294. Programs under PL 480: *Congress and the Nation*, p. 177. Reduction in crop acreage: *A Place to Live*, pp. 172–73. Crops in Liberty ships: Edward L. Dale, Jr., *Conservatives in Power* (Garden City, N. Y.: 1960), p. 186. Stanley Yankus: *New York Times* (April 25, 1960). Jack A. Harris: Higbee, pp. 23–24. Billie Sol Estes: Fred J. Cook, *The Corrupted Land* (New York: 1966), pp. 161–66. First asset seized was cotton allotments: Higbee, p. 108. Agriculture emphasis in state vocational training programs: Stanley Lebergott, ed., *Men Without Work* (Englewood Cliffs, N. J.: 1964), p. 40. Food prices dropped in real terms: *New York Times* (December 19, 1961); Harold G. Vatter, *The U.S. Economy in the 1950's* (New York: 1963), p. 1. Food's share of the family budget: Bureau of Labor Statistics, *Contrasts in Spending by Urban Families* (Washington, D.C.: 1965), p. 1252.

Chapter 31

1,000 people a day: J. F. Dewhurst, *America's Needs and Resources* (New York: 1947), Table 16, p. 45. "Better that they go home": C. Hartley Grattan. "The Future of the Pacific Coast," *Harper's* (March 1945). ("Loaded with furniture": Carey McWilliams, "Look What's Happened to California," *Harper's* (October 1949). "A unique way of life": "The California Way of Life," *Life* (October 22, 1945). California was the ideal vacation spot: George H. Gallup, *The Gallup Poll 1935–1972* (New York: 1972), pp. 925–26. A tenth wanted to move to California: Hadley Cantril, ed., *Public Opinion 1935–1946* (Princeton, N. J.: 1951) p. 449; cf. Gallup, p. 1461. "California is for the United States": Luigi Barzini, *Americans Are Alone in the World* (New York: 1953), p. 36. Shift in manufacturing: Victor R. Fuchs, *Changes in the Location of Manufacturing in the U.S. Since 1929* (New Haven, Conn.: 1962), p. 9. "Which city do you think": Gallup, p. 1406. More employment in aircraft than automobile industry: Harold G. Vatter, *The U.S. Economy in the 1950's* (New York: 1963), p. 187. California's housing bonanza: Emmet J. Hughes and Todd May, "Housing: The Stalled Revolution," *Fortune* (April 1957). California accounted for half of increase in service employment: H. S. Perloff et al., *Regions, Resources and Economic Growth* (Baltimore: 1960), pp. 256–262. "California is no longer a place": R. L. Duffus, "The Two States of California," *New York Times Magazine* (December 18, 1955). Most highly educated adult population: Bureau of the Census, *Census of the Population: 1960* (Washington, D.C.: 1964) Vol. 1, Part 1, Fig. 77, S–48. Newcomers were better educated than residents: McWilliams. California teachers were more stable: David G. Ryans, *Characteristics of Teachers* (Washington, D.C.: 1960), pp. 396–97. "Everyone is taking a course": C. Page Smith, "The Pacific Coast: A Study of Southern California," *Current History* (May 1961). "In California universal higher education": *Harper's* (October 1961). "Surfurbia": a term coined by Reyner Banham, *Los Angeles: The Architecture of Four Ecologies* (New York: 1971), p. 41. "Slurbs": a term coined by *Newsweek* (September 23, 1963). "We took Dick Nixon": Theodore H. White, *The Making of the President 1960* (New York: 1961), p. 28. Suicide rates: Margaret S. Clark, *Medicine Today* (New York: 1960), pp. 142–43. "One vast Pittsburgh": Bruce Bliven, "The California Culture," *Harper's* (January 1955).

Florida became the top vacation spot: Gallup, p. 1304. Most newcomers were retired: *Newsweek* (January 5, 1959). Brevard County: Benjamin Wattenberg and Richard Scammon, *This USA* (Garden City, N. Y.: 1965), p. 201. Florida's prosperity: William F. Rivers, "Florida: The State with the Two–Way Stretch," *Harper's* (February 1955). One–fourth of Texas's income: Vatter, p. 187. "California compares to Texas": John Gunther, *Inside USA*, rev. ed. (New York: 1951), p. 9. New Mexico: Albert Rosenfeld, "New Mexico Cashes In," *Harper's* (January 1954).

80 percent favored statehood: Gallup, p. 927. "A major objective": Fred Friendly, *Due to Circumstances Beyond Our Control* (New York: 1967), p. 91. GONE OUT OF BUSINESS: *Newsweek* (March 23, 1959).

Chapter 32

"Ben Hogan for President": Marquis Childs, *Eisenhower: Captive Hero* (New York: 1958), p. 229. Students in Columbus: Alexander Werth, *America in Doubt* (London: 1959), pp. 60–61. "That will curl your hair": *Time* (February 18, 1957). "Negativism was triumphant": Arthur Larson, *Eisenhower: The President Nobody Knew* (New York: 1969), p. 155. "The USA has become more bureaucratic": Robert Jungk, *Tomorrow Is Already Here* (New York: 1954), p. 176. Employment in Federal, state, and local government: Bureau of Labor Statistics, *Employment and Earnings Statistics for the U.S. 1909–1960* (Washington, D.C.: 1961), pp. 466–67, 470–71. Adams's instructions to the staff: Emmet J. Hughes, *Ordeal of Power* (New York: 1964), p. 54. Adams and Ezra Pound: Julien Cornell, *The Trial of Ezra Pound* (London: 1966), pp. 123–25.

"Growth is fast-becoming": Vance Packard, *The Waste Makers* (New York: 1960), p. 29. Productivity since the Civil War: Solomon Fabricant, "Productivity and Economic Growth," in Eli Ginzberg, ed., *Technology and Social Change* (New York: 1964). Productivity since V-J Day: John D. Kendrick, *Postwar Productivity Trends in the U.S. 1948–1969* (New York: 1973), Table 3–1, p. 37. One of the sober men was A. A. Berle, *Power Without Property* (New York: 1954), p. 121. Soviet growth rates: Bruce M. Russett et al., eds., *World Handbook of Political and Social Indicators* (New Haven, Connecticut: 1964), Table 45, p. 160. Khrushchev's boasts: Walter Lippmann, *The Communist World and Ours* (Boston: 1959), pp. 22–24. Eisenhower and the polls: Larson, p. 108. Most people believed the United States was losing: George H. Gallup, *The Gallup Poll 1935–1972* (New York: 1972), p. 1534. 1.5 million Americans lived abroad: Bureau of the Census, *Census of Population: 1960* , (Washington D.C.: 1964) Vol. 1, Part 1, p. xvii. "It is difficult to describe": Gary F. Powers and Curt Gentry, *Operation Overflight* (New York: 1971), p. 7. U-2 stories: *Time* (January 20 and July 21, 1958). "I am an American": Powers, p. 45.

Eisenhower would have run for a third term: Sherman Adams, *First-Hand Report* (New York: 1962), p. 327. "The new Nixon": Earl Mazo, *Richard Nixon* (New York: 1959), p. 136. "Nixonland": ibid., p. 8. Nixon's ruthlessness would make him a strong President: Margaret Halsey, *The Pseudo-Ethic* (New York: 1963), p. 13. Nixon's changing fortunes in the polls: *Newsweek* (May 26, 1958/November 30, 1959); *Time* (December 15, 1958/September 29, 1959). "God never permits": the entire letter is in Joan Myers, ed., *John Fitzgerald Kennedy as We Remember Him* (Chicago: 1963), p. 75. Religious habits: Kenneth P. O'Donnell and David Powers, *Johnny, We Hardly Knew Ye* (New York: 1973), p. 366. "A man who wore": Laurence H. Fuchs, *John F. Kennedy and American Catholicism* (New York: 1967), p. 163. "Wild-eyed ADA people": O'Donnell and Powers, p. 370. Kennedy took McCarthy for a ride: Roy Cohn, *McCarthy* (New York: 1966), p. 16. Joe Kennedy contributed $3,000: Richard J. Whalen, *The Founding Father* (Boston: 1964) p. 427. He was charming and evasive: Eleanor Roosevelt, *On My Own* (New York: 1958), pp.

163–164. Kennedy and the Seaway: Theodore Sorensen, *Kennedy* (New York: 1966), pp. 65–66. Use of the Catholic issue to exert pressure: *Time* (May 2, 1960); *New Republic* (June 25, 1960). "The Kennedys were not only," estimated $1.5 million: Whalen, p. 453. "He climbed back into the car": Sorensen, p. 28. Going price of a county sheriff: Merle Miller, *Plain Speaking* (New York: 1974), pp. 187–188. *Private Property*: Ben Bradlee, *Conversations with Kennedy* (New York: 1975), p. 27. Stevenson demonstration: Theodore H. White, *The Making of the President 1960* (New York: 1961), p. 198. "He dressed like a riverboat gambler": Rowland Evans and Robert Novak, *Lyndon B. Johnson: The Exercise of Power* (New York: 1966), p. 90. Johnson's defense of the Court: ibid., pp. 166–67. "He'll never accept it": Chester Bowles, *Promises to Keep* (N. Y.: 1971), pp. 293–94; Bradlee, pp. 30–31. Kennedy was surprised: Pierre Salinger, *With Kennedy* (Garden City, N. Y.: 1966), p. 44; Evelyn Lincoln, *Kennedy and Johnson* (New York: 1968), pp. 96–98. Kennedy's explanation to O'Donnell: O'Donnell, pp. 221–22. Johnson was seeking VP nomination at least a year in advance: Evans and Novak, pp. 275–76. "The whole story": Salinger, p. 56. "I note the tremendous growth": White, p. 263. The debates helped both Kennedy and Nixon: Stanley Kraus, ed., *The Great Debates* (New York: 1962), p. 151. Newspaper endorsements: Edwin Emergy, *The Press and America* (Englewood Cliff, N. J.: 1973), Table 1, p. 697. "Count the nuns": Bradlee, p. 20. George V. Allen laments: *Time* (February 1, 1960). "If you give me a week": Earl Mazo and Stephen Hess, *Nixon* (New York: 1968), pp. 238–39. Nixon asked not to risk Eisenhower's health: ibid., pp. 139–46. Religion cost Kennedy 1.5 million votes: Philip E. Converse et al., "Stability and Change in 1960: A Reinstating Election," *American Political Science Review* (June 1961). Religious and ethnic identification in the 1960 election: Lucy Dawidowicz and Leon J. Goldstein, *Politics in a Pluralist Democracy: The 1960 Election* (New York: 1963). Kennedy's lack of appeal to young voters: V. O. Key, Jr., *The Responsible Electorate* (Cambridge, Mass.: 1966), p. 117. "Nixon is a shifty-eyed, goddamn liar": Miller, p. 178. "Mr. President, with a little bit of luck": Bradlee, p. 33. 100,000 nonexistent voters: Mazo and Hess, pp. 247–48. "Our country cannot afford": ibid., p. 249. "The conjuction of an immense military establishment": *New York Times* (January 18, 1961).

V: LIGHTNING ALWAYS STRIKES THE HIGHEST PEAKS

Chapter 33
"I wish I'd let that money sit": Fred J. Cook, *The Corrupted Land* (New York: 1966), pp. 9—12. TO THE HONEST COLORED MAN: *Life* (May 19, 1961). Wilfredo Roman Oquendo: *Time* (August 4, 1961). "The richest refugees": *Newsweek* (November 20, 1961). Astronauts' welcome: ibid. (March 12, 1962). "Twice a week—forever": *Time* (November 2, 1962). "He's surely got the country": *Newsweek* (February 25, 1962). Jewelry heist: *Time* (November 22, 1963). "The development of stretch pants": ibid. (January 12, 1962). Yo-yos in Nashville: *Newsweek* (May 22, 1961). "In other words": *Time* (December 7, 1962). "Give me Liberty": ibid. (July 22, 1962).

"Would probably be a no-nonsense type": James MacGregor Burns, *John Kennedy* (New York: 1960), p. 269. "Kennedy has picked": TRB, in *New Republic* (December 26, 1960). Kennedy's view of politics: Theodore H. White, *The Making of the President 1960* (New York: 1961), p. 269. Kennedy's thermal underwear: David Halberstam, *The Best and the Brightest* (New York: 1973), p. 241. Kennedy's physical ills: Theodore Sorensen, *Kennedy* (New York: 1966), p. 45; Benjamin Bradlee, *Conversations with Kennedy* (New York: 1975), p. 68; Pierre Salinger, *With Kennedy* (Garden City, N. Y.: 1966), p. 75. Taste in films: Kenneth P. O'Donnell and David F. Powers, *Johnny, We Hardly Knew Ye* (New York: 1973), p. 395. The Hoffa Unit: Victor Navasky, *Kennedy Justice* (New York: 1971); Clark R. Mollenhoff, *Tentacles of Power* (Cleveland: 1965), pp. 338–40. On the Marilyn Monroe-Robert Kennedy affair, see W. R. Weatherby, *Conversations with Marilyn* (London: 1976) pp. 216–21. "If other nations falter": White, p. 452. "If we make our country": Sorensen, p. 436. "I love everything": E. Digby Baltzell, *Protestant Establishment* (New York: 1964), p. 301.

Khrushchev told Lippmann about the invasion: Walter Lippmann, *The Coming Tests with Russia* (Boston: 1961), p. 17. Webb's tantalizing prospect: Sorensen, pp. 592–93. Lack of enthusiasm among scientists: Alvin M. Weinberg, "The Impact of Large-Scale Science on the United States," *Science* (July 21, 1961). Khrushchev at Vienna disclaims interest in the Moon: Sorensen, pp. 592–93. "It should be made clear": Maxwell Taylor, *The Uncertain Trumpet* (New York: 1960), p. 146. Shelters and crowbars: *Time* (October 20, 1961). Kennedy's shelter: *Newsweek* (March 25, 1963). Charles Davis episode: L. C. McHugh, "Ethics at the Shelter Doorway," *America* (September 30, 1961). Pamphlets were mailed back: *Time* (February 23, 1962). Herman Kahn and SUC: J. J. Sullivan, ed., *Protective Construction in a Nuclear Age* (New York: 1959–1961), Vol. 1, pp. 36–37. Portland abandoned civil defense: *Newsweek* (June 10,

1963). President declared milk safe: *Time* (February 2, 1962). "It was as if": *Life* (July 20, 1962).

"Wealthy businessmen, retired military officers": *Newsweek* (March 11, 1963). "I am a good friend": Robert Welch, *The Blue Book of the John Birch Society* (Belmont, Mass.: 1961), p. 148. "What is not only needed": ibid., p. 107. Birch Society membership and income: Alan F. Westin, "The John Birch Society," *Commentary* (April 1961). "The sad truth," "the most completely opportunistic": Robert Welch, *The Politician* (Belmont, Mass.: 1963), pp. 5–6. "An anti-Communist phone service": John D. Weaver, "Santa Barbara: Dilemma in Paradise," *Holiday* (June 1961). Half Birch members were Catholics: Westin. Size and wealth of radical right: Westin, "The Deadly Parallels: Radical Right and Radical Left," *Harper's* (April 1962). Boeing's lecturer: ibid. "Anti-Communism and the Corporations," *Commentary* (December 1963). For an excellent account of a CACC "school," see Raymond E. Holfinger et al., "America's Radical Right," in David Apter, ed., *Ideology and Discontent* (New York: 1964). Mental health movement was a Communist plot: Fred Schwartz, *You Can Trust the Communists* (Englewood Cliffs, N. J.: 1960), p. 116. "I have four lovely daughters": Murray Kempton, *America Comes of Middle Age* (Boston: 1963), pp. 341–42. "If you left me naked": Donald Janson and Bernard Eismann, *The Far Right* (New York: 1963), p. 112. Russian peat moss: *Newsweek* (December 4, 1961). Radical right in Houston and Dallas: Willie Morris, "Houston's Superpatriots," *Harper's* (October 1961). "A mixture of blackmail and bribery": Barry Goldwater, *The Conscience of a Conservative* (Shepherdsville, Ky.: 1960), p. 27.

"Name that boy": Evelyn Lincoln, *Kennedy and Johnson* (New York: 1968), p. 26. " 'Ordered' me not to return": Walter Heller, *New Dimensions of Political Economy* (Cambridge, Mass.: 1966), p. 11. "And where is the pressure": B. J. Widick, *Labor Today* (Boston: 1964), p. vii. "We stand on the brink": *Newsweek* (September 4, 1961). "I want to be around": *Time* (October 20, 1961). "Running for Governor of the United States": Earl Mazo and Stephen Hess, *Nixon* (New York: 1968), p. 281. "Just think what you're going to be missing": *Time* (November 16, 1961).

Chapter 34

Fewer than 1 million poor: Editors of *Fortune, America in the Sixties* (New York: 1960), pp. xiii, 102. "More people die": J. K. Galbraith, *The Affluent Society* (Boston: 1958), p. 103. "Nobody starves in America": Edmund G. Love, "Subways Are for Sleeping," *Harper's* (March 1956). Among the few who looked to see how many poor people there were and found there were many millions were Helen Hill Miller, "Today's 'One-Third of a Nation,'" *New Republic* (November 17, 1958), and Alvin Hansen, *Economic Issues of the 1960s* (New York: 1960). "The failure of the great society," "war on poverty": Michael Harrington, *The Other America* (New York: 1963), pp. 88, 167. "The poor get less": ibid., p. 158. Forty percent were ill-housed, etc.: David R. Hunter, *The Slums: Challenge and Response* (New York: 1964). 32 million poor: Robert J.

Lampman, *The Low Income Population and Economic Growth* (A Study for the Joint Economic Committee, 86th Congress, 1st Session) (Washington, D.C.: 1959). 34.5 million poor: Mollie Orshansky, :"Counting the Poor," *Social Security Bulletin* (Washington, D.C.: January 1965). Postwar changes in distribution of income and wealth: Robert J. Lampman, *Changes in the Share of Wealth Held by Top Wealth Holders* (New York: 1960). Income distribution in the United States and elsewhere: Charles Lee Taylor and Michael C. Hudson, *World Handbook of Political and Social Indicators* (New Haven, Conn.: 1972), Table 4.13, pp. 263–64. Unattached individuals living in poverty: Leon H. Keyserling, *Progress and Poverty* (New York: 1965), p. 17. Percentage of youth unemployment: Edgar May, *The Wasted Americans* (New York: 1964), Table 6, p. 68. Education among the poor: Lampman, *The Low Income Population and Economic Growth* (Washington, D.C.: 1959), p. 4. Growth of ADC: M. Elaine Burgess and Donald O. Price, *An American Dependency Challenge* (Chicago: 1963), p. xii; Department of HEW, *Health, Education and Welfare Trends* (Washington, D.C.: 1964), p. vi. Scope of OASDI: Herman P. Miller, *Rich Man, Poor Man* (New York: 1971), Table VIII-1, p. 133. Effects of transfers and government spending: ibid., Table II-5, p. 19. $21 billion from friends, etc.: James N. Morgan et al., *Income and Welfare in the United States* (New York: 1962), p. 7. Spending patterns on health, education, and welfare: Congressional Quarterly, *Congress and the Nation 1945–1964* (Washington, D.C.: 1965), p. 1279. "The United States has arrived": Morgan, pp. 3–4; cf. Harold G. Vatter, *The U.S. Economy in the 1950's* (New York: 1963), p. 1.

Newburgh, New York: May, Chapter 2; *Newsweek* (July 22, 1963). "Welfare! Welfare! Welfare!": *Time* (July 14, 1961). Private pension plans: *Congress and the Nation*, p. 1211. "Anyone who has struggled": James Baldwin, *Nobody Knows My Name* (New York: 1961), p. 60. "It is of some interest": David Caplowitz, in P. B. Shostak and W. Gomberg, eds., *Blue Collar World* (Englewood Cliffs, N. J.: 1964), p. 113. "Portable consumer durable goods": Elliot Liebow, *Tally's Corner* (Boston: 1967), p. 66. The psychological isolation of the poor: Genevieve Knupfer, "Portrait of the Underdog," *Public Opinion Quarterly* (Spring 1947). Working wives by income groups: Eleanor B. Sheldon and Wilbert E. Moore, *Indicators of Social Change* (New York: 1968), Table 10, p. 749.

"We used to own the slaves": U.S. Senate Subcommittee on Migratory Labor, *The Migrant Farm Worker in America*, 86th Congress, 2nd Session (Washington, D.C.: 1960), p. 13; cf. U.S. President's Commission on Migratory Labor, *Migratory Labor in American Agriculture* (Washington, D.C.: 1951). Mexicans "paroled" to farmers: Louisa R. Shotwell, *The Harvesters* (Garden City, N. Y.: 1961), p. 77. "The plight of the agricultural migrant": *The Migrant Farm Worker in America*, p. 52. Low productivity of migrant farm workers: Dale E. Hathaway, *Government and Agriculture* (New York: 1963), pp. 178, 181.

Urbanization of Mexican-Americans: Leo Grebler et al., *The Mexican-American People* (New York: 1970), pp. 112–17. "The Mexican-American thinks of himself": William E. Madsen, *The Mexican-Americans of South*

Texas (New York: 1964), p. 15. Operation Wetback: Stan Steiner, *La Raza* (New York: 1970), p. 128; Joan W. Moore and Alfredo Cuellar, *Mexican-Americans* (Englewood Cliffs, N. J.: 1970), p. 91. Living standards of Mexican-Americans: Miller, p. 98. "The only thing most people in Mexico get": Edward Banfield, *Big City Politics* (New York: 1965), p. 76. Plane flight from San Juan: Dan Wakefield, *Island in the City* (Boston: 1959), p. 28. Luis Ferre: Nathan Glazer and Daniel P. Moynihan, *Beyond the Melting Pot*, 2nd ed. (Cambridge, Mass.: 1970), p. 100. East 100th Street: Wakefield, p. 232. Advertising Puerto Rico: Martin Mayer, *Madison Avenue, USA* (New York: 1958), p. 62; cf. David Ogilvy, *Confessions of an Advertising Man* (New York: 1963). Neoyorquismos: Fredric Wertham, *Circle of Guilt* (New York: 1956), p. 127. *Aspira*: Glazer and Moynihan, p. 128. Spiritualism: Wakefield, pp. 59–65.

Number of Indians in 1960: William A. Brophie and Sophie D. Aberle, *The Indian: America's Unfinished Business* (Oklahoma City: 1966), p. 11; Stan Steiner, *The New Indians* (New York: 1967), pp. 176–77. Unemployment rates: Steiner, pp. 199–200. The Unarillas: Brophie and Aberle, pp. 183–84. Sale of 3 million acres: Dorothy Van Der Mark, "The Raid on the Reservations," *Harper's* (March 1956); Brophie and Aberle, p. 219. The Tuscaroras: Edmund Wilson, *Apologies to the Iroquois* (New York: 1960), pp. 139–49. Settling Indian claims: Brophie and Aberle, p. 29; "Not that they starve": Vachel Lindsay, *Collected Poems* (New York: 1925) p. 70.

Chapter 35
Population concentration in the 1950s: Conrad and Irene Taeuber, *The Changing Population of the U.S.* (New York: 1958), p. 23. Concentration in the SMAs: ibid., p. 133. Dade County: Edward Sofen, *The Miami Metropolitan Experiment* (Bloomington, Ind.: 1963). Honesty in local government: Edward C. Banfield and James Q. Wilson, *City Politics* (New York: 1965), pp. 329–30.

Slum population: David R. Hunter, *The Slums* (New York: 1964), p. 3. "Slums of despair": Charles Stokes, "A Theory of Slums," *Land Economics* (August 1962). Life on skid row: Donald J. Bogue, *Skid Row in American Cities* (Chicago: 1963); Edmund G. Love, *Subways Are for Sleeping* (1958); Samuel E. Wallace, *Skid Row as a Way of Life* (New York: 1968). Boston's West End: Herbert J. Gans, *The Urban Villagers* (New York: 1962). "The first instance in which": Charles E. Silberman, *Crisis in Black and White* (New York: 1964), p. 318. Number of housing units razed and number built: Congressional Quarterly, *Congress and the Nation 1945–1964* (Washington, D.C.: 1965), p. 465; Jeanne R. Low, *Cities in a Race with Time* (New York: 1967), p. 232. "The building in which you live": taken from a notice issued by Boston Redevelopment Agency, in Martin Anderson, *Federal Bulldozer: A Critical Analysis of Urban Renewal 1949–1962* (Cambridge, Mass.: 1964). Housing standards: U.S. Housing and Home Finance Agency, *Housing Statistics* (Washington,

D.C.: 1961). Dilapidated rural housing: Anderson, Table 13.2, p. 203. "A public purpose": *Berman* v. *Parker*, 348 U.S. 26 (1954). "One of the most successful": Harold Kaplan, *Urban Renewal Politics: Slum Clearance in Newark* (New York: 1963), p. 15. "We took an awful chance": ibid., p. 24. White families moving into black areas: Blake McKelvey, *The Emergence of Metropolitan America* (New Brunswick, N.J.: 1968), p. 172. Thirty to fifty cents: Anderson, pp. 138–144. Federal spending on urban renewal: *Congress and the Nation*, p. 496. Taft's expectations: Lowe, p. 253. Housing reform was a cause: Richard Davies, *Housing Reform During the Truman Administration* (Columbia, Mo.:1966), p. 4. Racism less important than other factors: Nathan Glazer and Davis McEntire, eds., *Studies in Housing* (Berkeley and Los Angeles: 1960). pp. 27-29. "Once upon a time": Daniel Seligman, "The Enduring Slums," *Fortune* (December 1957). Evictions because of an "undesirable": Dan Wakefield, *Island in the City* (Boston: 1959), p. 244. "The projects in Harlem are hated": James Baldwin, "Fifth Avenue, Uptown," *Esquire* (July 1960). Cost of public housing: Seligman.

Teamsters applied BLS standard to New Yorkers: Hunter, p. 28. La Guardia had resignation pads printed: Robert A. Caro, *The Power Broker* (New York: 1974), p. 448. Kennedys' building: Richard J. Whalen, *The Patriarch* (Boston: 1964), p. 379. Urban renewal under Moses: Caro, pp. 963–966, 969–976, 1005–1009. Organized crime moved into public housing: ibid., p. 1044. Ethnicity endured in New York: Nathan Glazer and Daniel P. Moynihan, *Beyond the Melting Pot*, 2nd ed. (Cambridge, Mass.: 1970). Community newspapers in Chicago: Daniel Bell, *The End of Ideology* (Glencoe, Ill.: 1960), p. 33. Number of heroin victims: White House Conference on Narcotics and Drug Abuse, *Proceedings* (Washington, D.C.: 1963), p. 16. Drugs created more employment than construction: ibid. p. 19. Drugs and the crime rate: Isidor Chein et al., *Narcotics, Delinquency and Social Policy* (New York: 1964), pp. 57–65. Successful criminals avoided dope: Claude Brown, *Manchild in the Promised Land* (New York: 1965), p. 331. "This . . . offense is to me": Frederic J. Sondern, *Brotherhood of Evil* (New York: 1959), p. 97.

"Walking down Levittown streets": William J. Dobriner, *Class in Suburbia* (Englewood Cliffs, N.J.: 1963), pp. 105–06. Wave of fear: *Time* (November 23, 1962). Lure of desert living: *Life* (March 23, 1962). FHA insured 5 million units: *Congress and the Nation*, p. 459. Mortgage money in city and suburb: Jane Jacobs, *The Death and Life of Great American Cities* (New York: 1961), p. 310. Majority were in middle-income range: Anderson, Fig. 13.3, p. 207. "For better or worse": *Time* (June 20, 1960).

Chapter 36

Infant mortality rates: Sam Shapiro et al., *Infant, Perinatal, Maternal and Childhood Mortality in the United States* (Cambridge, Mass.: 1968), Table 5.1, p. 116. Death rates on skid row: Donald J. Bogue, *Skid Row in American Cities* (Chicago: 1963), p. 230. "The immediate cure": *Time*

(May 24, 1963). Spending on health: U. S. Department of Health, Education, and Welfare, *Health, Education and Welfare Trends* (Washington, D.C.: 1964) p. 25. Doctors' incomes: Seymour E. Harris, *The Economics of American Medicine* (New York: 1964), p. 143. Number of doctors, number of hospital beds: Bruce M. Russett et al., eds, *World Handbook of Political and Social Indicators* (New Haven, Conn.: 1964), Table 8, p. 47; Table 61, p. 211. Doctors' incomes by region: Seymour Harris, Chapter 6. Sickness rates among the poor: U.S. Public Health Service, *National Health Survey* (Washington, D.C.: 1945). 50 million drank fluoridated water: *Health, Education and Welfare Trends,* p. 38. Rich and poor neglected teeth: F.J. Dewhurst et al., *America's Needs and Resources* (New York: 1947), p. 250. In the 641 communities which held referenda on the issue, fluoridation by the spring of 1962 had been rejected in 393: *Newsweek* (April 16, 1962). Women were lighter, men heavier: Marguerite S. Clark, *Medicine Today* (New York: 1960), pp. 295–96. Spending on quack medicine: *Newsweek* (January 28, 1963). "Even the false doctors": Ira O. Glick and Sidney J. Levy, *Living with Television* (Chicago: 1962), p. 190. Profitability of drug companies: Richard Harris, *The Real Voice* (New York: 1964), p. 63. "I had not the faintest idea": Seymour Harris, p. 7. Ten to twenty times cost: Richard Harris, pp. 33, 60, 62. "We can't put two people in bed": ibid, p. 64. Dr. Welch's "honorariums": ibid., p. 112. The fight to market thalidomide in the United States: Henning Sjostrom and Robert Nilsson, *Thalidomide and the Power of the Drug Companies* (Baltimore: 1972), pp. 112–130. Confrontation on the Senate floor: Richard Harris, pp. 169–178. Medical insurance of the over-sixty-fives: Seymour Harris, p. 365. "The President never got over": Theodore Sorensen, *Kennedy* (New York: 1965), p. 385. PHS appropriations: Congressional Quarterly, *Congress and the Nation 1945–1964* (Washington, D.C.: 1965), p. 1148, "A Godsend": Julian Samora, ed., *La Raza: Forgotten Americans* (South Bend, Ind.: 1966), p. 78. "Late every night": *Time* (March 10, 1961).

Estimated incidence of mental illness: Albert Deutsch, *The Shame of the States* (New York: 1948) p. 31. Admission and release rates: *Health, Education, and Welfare Trends,* p. 30. Number of mental patients in various hospitals:' Marvin K. Opler, ed., *Culture and Mental Health* (New York: 1959), p. 395. Forty-three cents a day: Deutsch, p. 175. American Freudianism: cf. Karen Horney, *Are You Considering Psychoanalysis?* (New York: 1946). "After the war": Betty Friedan, *The Feminine Mystique* (New York: 1963) p. 110. "Psychoanalysts are all the rage": Simone de Beauvoir, *America Day by Day* (New York: 1953), p. 66. "And I cannot forget": William Attwood, *Still the Most Exciting Country* (New York: 1956), p. 97. Suicides and estimated suicides: Clark, p. 137. "Has been replaced": Daniel Bell, *The End of Ideology* (Glencoe, Ill.: 1960), p. 13. Twenty million on tranquilizers: Editors of *Fortune, America in the Sixties* (New York: 1960), pp. 27–28. "Is an affront": Francis Bello, "The Tranquilizer Question," *Fortune* (May 1957). Tranquilizers and research into mental illness: Ian Stevenson, "Tranquilizers and the Mind," *Harp-*

er's (July 1957). Pyschiatry in Manhattan: Leo Srole et al., *Mental Health in the Metropolis: The Midtown Study* (New York: 1962), p. 153. Psychiatry in New Haven: August B. Hollingshead and F. C. Redlich, *Social Class and Mental Illness* (New Haven, Conn.: 1958), p. 375. 23.4 percent were impaired: Srole, p. 138. Class differences in diagnosis and treatment: Hollingshead and Redlich, pp. 266–275.

Chapter 37

"The ultra-rapid computing machine": Norbert Wiener, *Cybernetics, or Control in the Animal and the Machine*, 2nd ed. (Cambridge, Mass.: 1961), p. 14. Development of the transistor: Richard G. Nelson, "The Link Between Science and Invention," in National Bureau of Economic Research, *The Rate and Direction of Inventive Activity* (Princeton, N.J.: 1962). "As if one were addressing": George A. W. Boehm, "The Next Generation of Computers," *Fortune* (March 1959). "Businessmen bringing their records": Ira Wolfert, *An Epidemic of Genius* (New York: 1960), p. 226.

Time spent machine tending: Peter F. Drucker, *America's Next 20 Years* (New York: 1957), p. 19. Rising wages of unskilled: Victor Fuchs, *The Growing Importance of the Service Industries* (New York: 1965), p. 13. 13 percent were wasting their time: Gunnar Myrdal, *Challenge to Affluence* (New York: 1963). pp. 17–20. "To equip factories": William Peterson, "The New American Family," *Commentary* (January 1956). Capital investment and productivity gains: John W. Kendrick, *Postwar Productivity Trends in the U.S. 1948–1969* (Princeton, N.J.: 1973), Chart 5-3, p. 84. Chrysler and GM: Frank Marquart, "The Auto Worker," in *Voices of Dissent* (New York: 1958). "The fact that the UMW threw": Frank C. Pierson, *Unions in Postwar America* (New York: 1967), p. 47. Lewis and Eaton: Nat Caldwell and Gene S. Graham, "The Strange Romance Between John L. Lewis and Cyrus Eaton," *Harper's* (December 1961). Criticism of Lewis: B. J. Widick, *Labor Today* (Boston: 1964), p. 180. The ILGWU: Harvey Swados, *A Radical's America* (Boston: 1959), pp. 45–64. Varying estimates of unemployment owing to automation: *New York Times* (October 2, 1963). Westinghouse strike: Daniel Bell, *Work and Its Discontents* (Boston: 1956), pp. 53–54. Gulf Oil strike: *Wall Street Journal* (January 17, 1962.) "If conspicuous consumption": Bell, pp. 18–19. Hearings: U.S. House of Representatives Subcommittee on Unemployment and the Impact of Automation, 87th Congress, 1st Session, *Impact of Automation on Employment* (Washington, D.C.: 1961). West coast longshoremen: William Gomberg, "The Job as Property," *The Nation* (October 21, 1960).

Advent of the service economy: Eleanor B. Sheldon and Wilbert E. Moore, *Indicators of Social Change* (New York: 1968), Table 1, p. 154. Services accounted for entire increase in employment: Bureau of Labor Statistics, *Employment and Earnings Statistics for the U.S. 1909–1960*

(Washington, D.C. 1961), pp. 439, 448, 463; Bert G. Hickman, *Growth and Stability of the Postwar Economy* (Washington, D.C.: 1960), pp. 71–73. Spending on television: Vance Packard, *The Waste Makers* (New York: 1960), p. 124. Coopers and barbers: U.S. Department of Labor, *Occupational Outlook Handbook* (Washington, D.C. : 1951), Chart 1, p. 13. Percentage of work force engaged in manufacturing: Bruce M. Russett et al., eds., *World Handbook of Political and Social Indicators* (New Haven, Conn.: 1964), Table 53, p. 185. Number of workers in manufacturing rose: *Employment and Earnings Statistics*, p. 30. New jobs were on service side, not production side: Editors of *Fortune, America in the Sixties* (New York: 1960), pp. 54–55. One-third wore white collars: Bureau of the Census, *Census of Population 1960* (Washington, D.C.: 1961), Vol. I, Part 1, p. lxxiii. Employment in service sector of women, over sixty-fives, part-timers: Fuchs, Table 8, p. 15. Elevator operators: *Impact of Automation on Employment*, p 103. Union membership in service sector: Fuchs, p. 13. Growth of Retail Clerks International: Michael Harrington, *The Retail Clerks* (New York: 1962), p. 7. Self-employment in 1948 and 1962: John E. Bregger, "Self-Employment in the United States 1948–1962," *Monthly Labor Review* (January 1963). "The post-industrial society": Daniel Bell, "The Post-Industrial Society," in Eli Ginzberg, ed., *Technology and Social Change* (New York: 1964). Division of R&D expenditures: National Academy of Sciences, *Federal Support of Basic Research in Institutions of Higher Learning* (Washington, D.C.: 1964), Chart 2, p. 61. Clerical workers' growth since Civil War: *Employment and Earnings Statistics*, p. 131. Increase in chemists, engineers, etc.,: Editors of *Fortune*, p. 55. The new breed: "The Egghead Millionaires," *Fortune* (September 1960). "When the Census Bureau purchased": Herman P. Miller, *Rich Man, Poor Man* (New York: 1971), p. 155 . Unions and the "men of knowledge": Harold R. Wilensky, *Intellectuals in Labor Unions* (New York: 1956). Number of scientists and engineers in various industries: U.S. Congress Select Committee on Small Business, 89th Congress, 1st Session, *The Role and Effects of Technology on the Nation's Economy* (Washington, D.C.: 1963), Part 2, p. 172. Polaroid shares: Hobart Rowen, *The Free Enterprisers* (New York: 1964), p. 140. IBM shares: Thomas B. Watson, *A Business and Its Beliefs* (New York: 1963), p. 9. IBM trained 100,000 a year: Stanley Lebergott, ed., *Men Without Work* (Englewood Cliffs, N.J.: 1964), p. 40. Mercury capsule: Editors of *Fortune, The Space Industry* (Englewood Cliffs, N.J.: 1962), p. 88. Educational achievements of workers: Lebergott p. 29. Education and paychecks: Miller, Table X-5, p. 175. Income rose three times faster than investment: Theodore W. Schultz, "Investment in Man: An Economist's View," *Social Science Review* (January 1959). Education and knowledge added to productivity: Edward F. Denison, *The Sources of Economic Growth in the U.S.* (New York: 1962), pp. 267–78. Pursuit of knowledge accounted for one-third of the GNP: Fritz Machlup, *The Production and Distribution of Knowledge in the United States* (Princeton, N.J.: 1962), Table IX-1, pp. 354–57. Cost of educational deficiencies: Harold L. Wilensky and Charles N. Lebeaux,

Industrial Society and Social Welfare (New York: 1958), p. xxv. 10 percent increase a year: Machlup, p. 374. New products, old businesses: Dexter M. Keezer, *New Forces in American Business* (New York: 1959), pp. 61–63.

"Exactly like our brains": Mortimer Taube, *Computers and Common Sense* (New York: 1961) dissects this and other such fallacies; see also Charles Silberman, *The Myths of Automation* (New York: 1963). The machines might transcend human performance: Norbert Wiener, "Some Moral and Technological Consequences of Automation," *Science* (May 6, 1960). "We can only hand it over": Wiener, *Cybernetics*, p. 28.

Chapter 38

ADC cases continued to rise: U.S. Department of Labor, *The Negro Family* (Washington, D.C.: 1965), p. 13. "One high government official": Herman P. Miller, *Rich Man, Poor Man*, (New York: 1971), p. 55. Black growth rate: Reynolds Farley, *Growth of the Black Population* (New York: 1970), p. 23. Black and white birth rates: Miller, Table V-2, p. 57. Percentage of white children in New York public schools: Nathan Glazer and Daniel P. Moynihan, *Beyond the Melting Pot*, 2nd ed. (Cambridge, Mass.: 1970), p. 48. Powell called for equal rights in organized crime: *New York Times* (January 7, 1960). Powell's 1962 reelection campaign: *U.S. News and World Report* (April 23, 1963). Washington race riot: *Time* (December 7, 1962). "Northerners, provincials that they are" : V. O. Key, Jr., and Alexander Heard, *Southern Politics in State and Nation* (New York: 1949), p. 229. Voting in Atlanta: Edward C. Banfield and James Q. Wilson, *City Politics* (Cambridge, Mass.: 1963), p. 29. "The largest number": John Williams, *This Is My Country Too* (New York: 1966), p. 54. Cleaning up the South: Thomas B. Clark, *The Emerging South*, 2nd ed. (New York: 1968), pp. 98–102. Declining proportion of blacks: Miller, Table V-6, p. 63. Albany, Georgia: Charles E. Silberman, *Crisis in Black and White* (New York: 1964), p. 11. Last lynching: Benjamin Wattenberg and Richard Scammon, *This USA* (Garden City, N.Y.: 1965) p. 25.

Black Elks: E. Franklin Frazier, *Black Bourgeoisie* (Glencoe, Ill.: 1957), pp. 92–93. "The Supreme Ruler": C. Eric Lincoln, *The Black Muslims in America* (Boston: 1961), p. 12. "I was in the presence": Monroe Berger, "The Black Muslims," *Horizon* (January 1964). "The natural religion for the black man": Malcolm X, with Alex Haley, *The Autobiography of Malcolm X* (New York: 1966), p. 155. Muslim membership and wealth: from Berger, Lincoln, Malcolm X, and E. Essien-Udom, *Black Nationalism* (Chicago: 1962), pp. 8–11. "Members of the brotherhood": *Time* (March 31, 1961). "A very beautiful thing has happened": Silberman, pp. 55–56. "Most of the things white people say" : Berger. "They are on the whole": Peter Goldman, *The Death and Life of Malcolm X* (New York: 1973) p. 96. Malcolm X's sermons: ibid., pp. 42–44. "The Trial": Lincoln, pp. 3–4. "Negroes who do not join": Berger.

Number of black college students: Bureau of the Census, *Census of*

Population: 1960, Vol. I, Part 1 (Washington, D.C.: 1961), Table 102, pp. 1–242. "Sit-down strike": *New York Times* (Febuary 3, 1960). For an excellent first hand account of personal encounters at sit-ins, see Merrill Proudfoot, *Diary of a Sit-In* (Chapel Hill, N.C.: 1962). "There is nothing more humiliating": Louis E. Lomax, *The Negro Revolt* (New York: 1962), p. 76. "My basic strength": *Time* (August 30, 1963). "Southerners now dream": Harry Golden, *Mr. Kennedy and the Negroes* (Cleveland: 1964), p. 117. Jail experiences of SNCC volunteers: Howard Zinn, *SNCC: The New Abolitionists* (Boston: 1964), pp. 23–24. Connor blamed Mother's Day: James Peck, *Freedom Ride* (New York: 1962), p. 124. Violence in Montgomery: *Newsweek* (May 29, 1961). Convoy on the road to Jackson: Lerone Bennett, *What Manner of Man* (Chicago: 1964), p. 126. "Kill 'em!": Anthony Lewis, *Portrait of a Decade* (New York: 1964), pp. 91–92. "Personally I feel only affection": Carleton Putnam, *Race and Reason: A Yankee View* (Washington, D.C. : 1961), p. 7. "Race and Reason Day": Neil R. McMillen, *The Citizens' Councils* (Urbana, Ill.: 1971), pp. 166–67. Interracial intercourse: Putnam, pp. 39–40.

"A group of children": Lewis, p. 157. "Many of these pioneer children": Robert Coles, *Children in Crisis* (Boston: 1967), p. 120. "In my experience": ibid., p. 67. Charlotte's schools: Harry Golden, *For 2¢ Plain* (Cleveland: 1959), p. 252. Desegregation by A.D. 9256: James Cook, *The Segregationists* (New York: 1962). Central High in Kansas City: Martin Mayer, *The Schools* (New York: 1961), p. 127. "Having a white child": Silberman, p. 301. School transfers: Glazer and Moynihan, pp. 48–49. Busing accounted for one-third of budgets: National Education Association, *Yearbook 1953* (Washington, D.C.: 1953), pp. 15–16. "One, two, three, four": Calvin Trillin, *An Education in Georgia* (New York: 1964), pp. 60–61. Clennon King: Walter Lord, *The Past That Would Not Die* (New York: 1965), p. 76. Clyde Kennan: James Silver, *Mississippi: The Closed Society* (New York: 1964), pp. 93–94. "I returned to my home state": James Meredith, *Three Years in Mississippi* (Bloomington, Ind.: 1966), p. 20. "A wiry young man": Lord, p. 96. Medgar Evers: Langston Hughes, *Fight for Freedom* (New York: 1962), p. 181. "It is time to move": Lord, p. 182. Barnett's proposed scenario: Theodore Sorensen, *Kennedy* (New York: 1965), p. 543. "Never, never, never": Silver, pp. 118–119. Meredith's tears: Meredith, p. 214. "They came rollin' down from Memphis": Silver, pp. 130–31. "John Patterson out-nigguhed me" : Marshall Frady, *Wallace* (New York: 1969), p. 127. "As your governor": *Newsweek* (May 14, 1962). "In the name of the greatest people": Frady, p. 142. "I'm gonna make race": ibid., p. 140.

"An air of incipient martyrdom" : Bennett, p. 193. "I got on my marching shoes": Louis E. Lomax, "When Nonviolence Meets Black Power," in C. Eric Lincoln, ed., *Martin Luther King Jr.* (New York: 1970). Colored Broadcasting System: *New York Times* (August 15, 1962). "Whites and blacks": ibid. (April 12, 1960). "Nigras and whites": Robert S. Allen, *Our Fair City* (New York: 1947), p. 105. King's strategy for Birmingham: Martin Luther King, Jr., *Why We Can't Wait* (New York: 1964), pp.

54–55. "Who'll go to jail": W. R. Miller, *Martin Luther King, Jr.* (New York: 1968), pp. 135–36. Treatment of girls in Birmingham jail: ibid., p. 143. William L. Moore: Murray Kempton, "Pilgrimage to Jackson," *New Republic* (May 11, 1963). "The Negro most feared": Cook, p. 93. Assassination of Medgar Evers: Lewis, p. 226. Byron de La Beckwith: Frank Smith, *Congressman from Mississippi* (New York: 1964), p. 105. Anxiety over the March on Washington: Warren R. Young and William Lambert, "Marchers' Master Plan," *Life* (June 28, 1963). White speakers were embarrassed: Miller, p. 163. "Deep fervor and quiet dignity": *New York Times* (September 1, 1963). Racial bombings 1956–1963: David M. Chalmers, *Hooded Americanism* (New York: 1965), pp. 356–365. Racial killings and bombings in 1963: Golden, *Mr. Kennedy*, p. 225; Miller, p. 176. Whites not allowed to pass collection buckets: Nat Hentoff, *The New Equality* (New York: 1964), p. 28. White attitudes toward blacks: William Brink and Louis Harris, *The Negro Revolution in America* (New York: 1964), pp. 140–43. "See the Japs": *New Republic* (September 21, 1963). "He has done more": Brink and Harris, p. 91.

Chapter 39

Loss of reformist zeal: e.g., *Barenblatt* v. *United States*, 360 US 109 (1959); *Uphaus* v. *United States*, 360 US 72 (1959). Reapportionment case: *Baker* v. *Carr*, 369 US 186 (1962). Board of Regents' prayer: *Engel* v. *Vitale*, 370 US 421 (1962). Court banned Bible reading: *Abingdon School District* v. *Schemp/Murray* v. *Curlett*, 374 US 203 (1963). 146 attempts to amend Constitution: Theodore Becker and Malcolm M. Freeley, eds., *The Impact of Supreme Court Decisions* (New York: 1969), p. 28. Confessions and illegal evidence: *Mapp* v. *Ohio*, 367 US 643 (1961). "If the petitioner would of had attorney": *Gideon* v. *Wainwright*, 372 US 335 (1963); cf. Anthony Lewis, *Gideon's Trumpet* (New York: 1964). "How did you get out": *Time* (December 28, 1959). "The Communists have gone respectable": Mark Sherwin, *The Extremists* (New York: 1963), p. 11. Strange death of Whittaker Chambers: Meyer A. Zeligs, *Friendship and Fratricide* (New York: 1967). pp. 21–30. Censorship: *Roth* v. *United States* 354 US 476 (1957). Leo F. Koch: *Time* (May 10, 1963). "If an education": Betty Friedan, *The Feminine Mystique* (New York: 1963), p. 150. Growing self-awareness: cf. *Harper's* (October 1962) supplement "The American Female." "They don't sell out": Louis Kronenberger, *Company Manners* (Indianapolis: 1962), p. 117. Class of '55. David Riesman, "The Found Generation," in his *Abundance for What?* (Garden City, N.Y.: 1964). Class of '61: James A. Davies, *Undergraduate Career Decisions* (Chicago: 1965) p. 222–26. Americans had not adjusted successfully: Kenneth Keniston, *The Uncommitted* (New York: 1965), p. 211. "Had an extraordinary moment": Murray Kempton, "Oh Dad, Poor Dad," *New Republic* (September 28, 1963). SDS: the Port Huron statement is reproduced in Mitchell Cohen and Daniel Hale, eds., *The New Student Left* (Boston: 1967). Protests and rioting doubled: Charles Lewis Taylor and

Michael C. Hudson, *World Handbook of Political and Social Indicators*, 2nd ed. (New Haven, Conn.: 1972), Tables 3.2, 3.3, pp. 88–101. "We can easily say": Benjamin Wattenberg and Richard Scammon, *This USA* (Garden City, N.Y.: 1965), p. 203. Spending on education in the postwar: U.S. Department of Health, Education and Welfare, *Health, Education and Welfare Trends* (Washington, D.C.: 1964) pp. 63–69. Hours worked: Herman P. Miller, *Rich Man, Poor Man* (New York: 1971), p. 183. Sales of *Europe: Time* (July 26, 1963). They would give up their cars and refrigerators: Gary A. Steiner, *The People Look at Television* (New York: 1963), pp. 22–24; cf. Ira O. Glick and Sidney J. Levy, *Living with Television* (Chicago: 1962). "I was subtly influenced": Fred Friendly, *Due to Circumstances Beyond Our Control* (New York: 1969), p. 135. "Compared to Elvis": Jerry Hopkins, *Elvis* (New York: 1971), p. 267. "Their songs": *Time* (November 15, 1963). "Funny being equivalent": Lawrence Goldman, *Ladies and Gentlemen, Lenny Bruce!!* (New York: 1974), p. 152. Kennedy's obscenities: Ben Bradlee, *Conversations with Kennedy* (New York: 1975). Although he was artistically honest, Lenny Bruce was evasive about his drug addiction in the autobiographical *How to Talk Dirty and Influence People* (Chicago: 1972); some of the best routines are available on several records and are printed in John Cohen, ed., *The Essential Lenny Bruce* (New York: 1973). Fred Whipple's $1,000 bet: Editors of *Fortune, The Space Industry* (New York: 1962), p. 2.

Chapter 40
Kennedy's interest in macroeconomics: Walter M. Heler, *New Dimensions in Political Economy* (Cambridge, Mass.: 1966), p. 49. Kennedy's views on deficits: Seymour E. Harris, *Economics of the Kennedy Years* (New York: 1964), pp. 59–60. "The course of true economics": Heller, p. 30. "By 1963": Harris, p. 5. The BAC and the BC: Hobart Rowen, *The Free Enterprisers* (New York: 1964), pp. 69–77. 43 percent rise in net profits: Harris, p. 51. "Their gripe": Rowen, p. 118. Kennedy's policies were much the same as Eisenhower's: Bernard Nossiter, *The Mythmakers* (Boston: 1964), pp. 7–9. "Steel had become": Grant McConnell, *Steel and the Presidency, 1962* (New York: 1963), p. 63. "My father always told me": Theodore Sorensen, *Kennedy* (New York: 1965), p. 504. "They kicked us": Ben Bradlee, *Conversations with Kennedy* (New York: 1975), p. 76. S.O.B. CLUB: *Newsweek* (May 21, 1962). Forty sought the vacancy: Don F. Hadwiger and Ross B. Talbot, *Pressures and Protests* (San Francisco: 1965), p. 51. The Gettysburg martyr: ibid., p. 117. Per capita income rose 50 percent: U.S. Department of Health, Education and Welfare, *Health, Education and Welfare Trends* (Washington, D.C.: 1964), pp. 55–59. National income rose 100 percent: Edward F. Denison, *Accounting for U.S. Economic Growth 1929–1969* (Washington, D.C.: 1975), Table 2-1, p. 11. Gifts and savings: Harold G. Vatter, *The U.S. Economy in the 1950s* (New York: 1963), p. 3. "Berlin . . . Berlin . . . ": Kenneth P. O'Donnell and David F.

Powers, *Johnny, We Hardly Knew Ye* (Boston: 1972), p. 354. Readiness of the armed forces: Elie Abel, *The Missiles of October* (Philadelphia: 1966), pp. 97, 107–08. "Please explain": Jim Bishop, *A Day in the Life of President Kennedy* (New York: 1964) p. 49. "Alpha is just the beginning": *Newsweek* (April 15, 1963). Spirit of detente: ibid. (September 30, 1963). "There was in 1961": Arthur M. Schlesinger, Jr., *A Thousand Days* (Boston: 1965), p. 497. Diem was on the cover of *Time,* August 4, 1961. "Inevitably more will die": *Life* (March 16, 1962). "The U.S. in short": *Newsweek* (April 23, 1962). VIETNAM: ibid. (May 7, 1962). "Lovely to look at": ibid. (October 21, 1963). "He told me privately": O'Donnell and Powers, pp. 12–13.

ESSAY IN
BIBLIOGRAPHY

Essay in
Bibliography

We are able to think clearly about the past only because most people and public events are rapidly forgotten. But what is also lost is the sense of ebb and flow that is a part of everday life, of change, renewal, endings, and beginnings. Yet it is possible to recapture that sense of unfolding. What yesterday considered important, was moved by, or thrilled at, still lives in yesterday's journalism. Newspaper and magazine accounts are necessarily incomplete; occasionally they are biased; they can garble the truth as well as preserve it. Nevertheless, they are accessible, they are direct, but most of all, they carry within them the power to awaken a sense of how life appeared to unfold to people at that time. Journalism is the last word to take as final, and the best with which to begin.

Every historian of American society is entitled to lament that there is no truly national newspaper. The *Wall Street Journal* and the *Christian Science Monitor* are national newspapers in the sense of being printed in different parts of the country. But they are really newspapers of the Northeastern and mid-Atlantic states. This is even more the case with the *New York Times*, which probably has more to say about life in Paris and London than Houston and San Francisco.

But I have turned repeatedly to the *New York Times* and relied on its splendid *Index*. I have also read every issue of the two leading newsmagazines, *Time* and *Newsweek*, from V-J Day through 1963. Until about 1960 they took much of their coverage of international and national politics from the *New York Times* and the *New York Herald Tribune* and rewrote it to suit their own styles and editorial policies. But in the "back of the book" their reporting was their own, and they took the entire country for their province.

In my first book, *Days of Sadness, Years of Triumph*, I made clear that

I had scoured newsmagazines and other periodicals. Naturally, I was criticized for this.* Yet, unrepentant, I have read every issue of *The New Republic, Harper's* and *Life.* I have searched *Commentary* and *Fortune* because these two very different publications offered some of the most useful reporting on social change to be written in the postwar. *The New Yorker* was read with care not only because it is probably the most elegantly written magazine in the United States but because a clever social history could be put together using nothing but *New Yorker* cartoons and advertisements. Much of its best reporting on American society also found its way between hard covers and may be found in its rightful place elsewhere in this bibliography. In its comparatively brief existence *The Reporter* attracted some of the most perceptive journalists then practicing. The *Saturday Review* also repaid study, being involved directly in issues of social concern such as the investigation of the drug companies' prices and practices.

Besides relying heavily on journalism, I have sought to widen the avenues to social history by turning to the contemporary literature in the social sciences. During the 1930s the social sciences for the first time attracted large numbers of graduate students. These students often were moved by a hope that if they learned something about the workings of society, they might be able to help tackle the Depression. The Depression was ended by the outbreak of war in Europe in 1939. The harvest of youthful enthusiasm was reaped, however, in the 1940s and 1950s. Tens of thousands of young economists, political scientists, sociologists, anthropologists, criminologists, and psychologists took their PhDs and set out to succeed in their chosen careers. Comparatively young, filled with zeal, and remarkably free to explore new approaches in theory and methodology, they seized on the largest possible social issues with a sense that everything needed to be done.

The results of this outburst of energy are uneven. First-rate ideas are often choked by second-rate writing, an excellent method of investigation is wasted on a theory that is little more than a tautology, and so on. Yet methodology and jargon had not yet been sufficiently advanced to obliterate the people being studied. Some of the social scientists of the postwar—David Riesman, Herbert J. Gans, Elliot Liebow—were extraordinarily good reporters by any reckoning.

As with all periods of intellectual innovation, this one did not last very long, from about 1948 to about 1959. Yet the works it produced have set standards against which subsequent social science research has measured itself (nearly always, of course, to its own advantage, or so it has claimed). Even now breathes there an ambitious social scientist with soul so dead that he would not want his own work to supplant some giant such

---

*The first large-scale American social history was McMaster's *History of the People of the United States.* When the first volume appeared approximately 100 years ago, several important reviewers noticed that McMasters had been reading a lot of old newspapers. He was severely berated for having stooped so low. Newspapers are no longer scorned as being unworthy of a serious man's time. But periodicals, I discovered, are.

as the Kinsey reports, *The Authoritarian Personality*, *The Lonely Crowd*, or *The Voter Decides*?

The social science monographs I have drawn upon are to be found listed at appropriate places in the bibliography. The scholarly journals I have searched are the *American Economic Review*, the *American Historical Review*, the *American Journal of Sociology*, the *American Political Science Review*, the *American Sociological Review*, and *Public Opinion Quarterly*.

I have cast this bibliography in essay form instead of providing a long list of books for several reasons. First, I am happy to acknowledge my debts, but debts vary. Secondly, lists of books are unreadable; the eye soon glazes over. Thirdly, the comments I offer on the books listed further illuminate my approach to writing social history.

Some selections are likely to strike the reader as being odd to the point of quixoticism. But I have not adhered to the common practice of listing only reputable or widely accepted works as being those alone which are worth remembering or reading long after their original publication. To take an extreme example, *The Blue Book of the John Birch Society* is as witless a work as any published between 1945 and 1963. Yet this book was taken as gospel by tens of thousands of ostensibly sane and responsible people. To know what was in their minds, it is necessary to read this book. I have also included scores of works which are of a poor standard. But they happen to be the best or the only works available on a topic which is important.

The careful reader will notice that some books have been listed twice. This is because some works are so important to different categories of social history that to restrict them to one would be entirely arbitrary and needless. Double-listing fewer than twenty works has added very little to this bibliography's length.

General

William Manchester, *The Glory and the Dream* (Boston: 1974) is a massive work which completely overlaps the period, but offers no perspective; the trivial and the important receive equal treatment. Eric Goldman, *The Crucial Decade—and After* (New York: 1960)concentrates primarily on the first postwar decade, and its emphasis is national politics. Godfrey Hodgson, *In Our Times* (Garden City, N.Y.: 1976) is similarly concerned with domestic politics since 1945. Alonzo Hamby, *The Imperial Years* (New York: 1976) and Lawrence S. Wittner, *Cold War America* (New York: 1974) are chiefly interested in Cold War issues but take a passing glance at the domestic scene. Joseph Goulden, *The Best Years* (New York: 1975) is a nostalgic, entertaining account of everday life 1945–1950.

Population: Growth and Change

The basic material is to be found in Bureau of the Census, *Census of Population: 1950* (Washington, D.C.: 1952) and *Census of Population:1960* (Washington, D.C. 1961). Especially useful are the volumes entitled *Characteristics of the Population*. Between decennial censuses the bureau compiles and publishes serial reports on population change, and much of the most interesting material on social trends appears in these reports. The well-known bureau publication *Historical Statistics of the United States from Colonial Times to 1957* (Washington, D.C.: 1958) contains important material on the first postwar decade in summary form. The assiduous student can turn to the annual *Statistical Abstract of the United States* and make his or her own comparative statistical studies from any given year to any other year.

Donald J. Bogue, *The Population of the United States* (Glencoe, Ill.: 1959) is an ambitious combination of sociology and population data up to 1957. Ansley J. Coale and Melvin Zelnick, *New Estimates of Fertility and Population in the United States* (Princeton, N.J.: 1963) is an important work clarifying and correcting the 1950 and 1960 censuses. Reynolds Farley, *Growth of the Black Population: A Study of Demographic Trends* (Chicago: 1970) corrects census data undercounting in black neighborhoods. Ronald Freedman et al., *Family Planning, Sterility and Population Growth* (New York: 1960) is based on a 1955 survey of 3,000 women of childbearing age. The same study, but this time including black women, was conducted in 1960, and the results were published in Pascal K. Whelpton et al., *Fertility and Family Planning in the United States* (Princeton, N.J.: 1966). Conrad and Irene B. Taeuber, *The Changing Population of the United States* (New York: 1958) is a useful study of population trends by an eminent authority on population statistics. Clyde V. Kiser et al., *Trends and Variations in Fertility in the United States* (Cambridge, Mass.: 1966) breaks new ground. There is another groundbreaking work, combining data drawn from the United States and other countries, which offers some intriguing comparisons between countries: Bruce M. Russett et al., eds., *World Handbook of Political and Social Indicators* (New Haven, Conn.: 1964). The sources involved, however, vary widely in reliability and compatibility, so conclusions need to be drawn with care. Another important attempt to use social statistics in an imaginative way is the collection of essays in Eleanor B. Sheldon and Wilbert E. Moore, eds., *Indicators of Social Change* (New York: 1968). Charles E. Westoff et al., *Family Growth in Metropolitan America* (Princeton, N. J.: 1961) on the other hand, is a useful family planning survey of 1,165 urban couples which uses an elaborate mathematical apparatus to no great effect. Ben J. Wattenberg and Richard C. Scammon, *This USA* (Garden City, N.Y.: 1965) is a lively, iconoclastic look at American society relying onCensus Bureau figures;it is coauthored by a former director of the bureau.

Social Structure

General

Richard Centers, *The Psychology of Social Classes* (Princeton, N.J.: 1949) is based on a survey made at the end of the war; it finds four major social classes. William M. Dobriner, *Class in Suburbia* (Englewood Cliffs, N.J.: 1963) refutes the idea that suburbs work a class transformation on those who move there. As the twig is bent: August B. Hollingshead, *Elmtown's Youth* (New York:1949) and Celia Burns Stendler, *Children of Brasstown* (Urbana, Ill.: 1949) show how early—and decisively—the young learn their class roles. August B. Hollingshead and Frederick C. Redlich, *Social Class and Mental Illness* (New York: 1958) is a seminal work indicating that psychoses are more common among the lower classes, neuroses among the upper. Leonard Reissman, *Class in American Society* (Glencoe, Ill.: 1960) is a thorough survey of the literature. William H. Whyte, Jr., *The Organization Man* (Garden City, N.Y.: 1957) is a stimulating study. Class differences among public high schools constitute the great divide in James B. Conant, *Slums and Suburbs* (New York.: 1961). Class differences in taste and behavior are the subject of Louis Kronenberger, *Company Manners* (Indianapolis: 1962) and appear in all the books by Vance Packard.

E. Digby Baltzell, *The Protestant Establishment* (New York: 1964) traces the declining fortunes of upper-class WASPs, owing, in his view, to their moral blindness. The Editors of *Fortune* profiled twenty-one successful (i.e., rich) businessmen prominent in the 1950s in *The Art of Success* (Philadelphia: 1956) and offered a sympathetic account of life at the top in *The Executive Life* (Garden City, New York: 1956). Vance Packard, *The Pyramid Climbers* (New York: 1962) takes a less enthusiastic view of the executive life. The ordinary middle classes at midcentury are studied, brilliantly, in C. Wright Mills, *White Collar* (New York: 1951).

Bennett M. Berger, *Working Class Suburb* (Berkeley and Los Angeles: 1959) is a valuable study which corrects the idea that suburbs are uniquely middle-class. Eli Chinoy, *Automobile Workers and the American Dream* (Garden City, New York: 1955) demonstrates that the dream is chiefly—as workers themselves come to realize—a daydream. Ira Wolfert, *An Epidemic of Genius* (New York: 1960) is self-consciously literary but contains some observant portraits of workers. Harvey Swados, *A Radical's America* (Boston: 1959) is worthwhile. Lee Rainwater et al.,*Workingman's Wife* (New York: 1959) is part social study and part marketing manual. Arthur B. Shostak and William Gomberg, eds., *Blue Collar World* (Englewood Cliffs, N.J.: 1964) contains a dozen of the best studies of the working class in the 1950s and early 1960s.

C. Wright Mills's most famous book, *The Power Elite* (New York: 1956), is angry and overstates its case at almost every point. Yet it cannot be ignored. For as a commentary on postwar American social structure there is nothing else so trenchant or so determined to deal with the most important questions of social class. Other illuminating studies of class as power are Arthur J. Vidich and Joseph Bensman, *Small Town in Mass Society* (Princeton, N.J.: 1958), concerning a small town in upper New York State, and Floyd Hunter, *Community Power Structure* (Chapel Hill, N.C.: 1953), on Atlanta's upper class. James West (pseudonym of Carl Withers), *Plainville USA* (New York: 1945) and Art Gallagher, Jr., *Plainville 15 Years Later* (New York: 1961) form a unique and valuable account of social change in a rural community in Missouri.

Social and Occupational Mobility
The best broad study is Seymour Martin Lipset and Reinhard Bendix, *Social Mobility in Industrial Society* (Berkeley and Los Angeles: 1959), which considers the subject historically and internationally. Whether upward mobility was getting easier is covered by Mabel Newcomer, *The Big Business Executive* (New York: 1955) and W. Lloyd Warner and James C. Abegglen, *Occupational Mobility in American Business and Industry* (Minneapolis: 1955). They arrive at opposite conclusions. An entertaining, and often astute, account of upward mobility is Vance Packard, *The Status Seekers* (New York: 1959).

Incomes and Wealth
The best introduction is a splendid book on incomes and wealth by a Census Bureau statistician, Herman P. Miller, *Rich Man, Poor Man* (New York: 1964; rev. ed., 1971). It is a sensible, dispassionate work on an emotive subject. Gabriel Kolko, *Wealth and Power in America* (New York: 1962) fails to recognize the limitations of the economic data it relies on. John Bainbridge, *The Super-Americans* (Garden City, N.Y.: 1961) offeres an amused, yet sympathetic account of life among Texas millionaires. Robert J. Lampman, *Changes in the Share of Wealth by Top Wealth-holders 1922–1956* (New York: 1960) needs to be used with caution becuse it is based on estate tax data. Many fortunes, accounting for a great deal of private wealth, are never subjected to estate tax, for various reasons. Osborn Elliott, *Men at the Top* (New York: 1959) profiles rich businessmen of the 1950s.

Social Welfare

General
A useful introduction is U.S. Department of Health, Education and Welfare, *Health, Education and Welfare Trends* (Washington, D.C.: 1964), Parts 1 and 2, which contains a wealth of material from the end of

the war to the 1960s. Federal attempts to deal with welfare problems are clearly covered year by year in Congressional Quarterly, *Congress and the Nation 1945–1964* (Washington, D.C.: 1965), a monumental work of reference. Michael Harrington, *The Other America* (Baltimore: 1963) is a lucid, angry work by someone who had lived in poverty; his claim that there were 50 million poor within the affluent society was credited with launching the Johnsonian "war on poverty." Harrington relied for much of his data on Robert J. Lampman, *The Low Income Population and Economic Growth* (Washington, D.C.: 1959), a basic source. Also useful is Leon H. Keyserling, *Progress or Poverty* (Washington, D.C.: 1964). Edgar May, *The Wasted Americans* (New York: 1964) is an investigative reporter's account of how welfare programs worked or, more often, failed to work. M. Elaine Burgess and Daniel O. Price, *An American Dependency Challenge* (Chicago: 1963) is a major study of the Aid to Dependent Children program. Edmund G. Love, *Subways Are for Sleeping* (New York: 1957) contains vivid portraits of people who lived by their wits, without money or regular employment, in New York in the 1950s. Samuel E. Wallace, *Skid Row as a Way of Life* (Totowa, N.J.: 1965) is an excellent short sociological study. Sara Harris, *Skid Row, USA* (Garden City, New York: 1963) describes life along the Bowery in 1961. Donald J. Bogue, *Skid Row in American Cities* (Chicago: 1963) offers an in-depth study, focusing mainly on Chicago's skid row in 1957 and 1958. Harry M. Caudill, *Night Comes to the Cumberlands* (Boston: 1962) is a brilliant work on an impoverished region. Thomas R. Ford, ed., *The Southern Appalachia Region* (Lexington, Ky.: 1962) is also useful. Herman P. Miller, *Rich Man, Poor Man* (New York: 1964; rev. ed., 1971) is a lively and imaginative work by a former Census Bureau expert. Three Bureau of Labor Statistics reports repay study: *Statistics Related to the Standards of Living of U.S. Families* (Washington, D.C.: 1959); *Contrasts in Spending by Urban Families: Trends Since 1950 and Variations in 1960–1961* (Washington, D.C.: 1965); and *Surveys of Consumer Expenditure: 1961–1962* (Washington, D.C.:1963).

The terrible hardship of migratory workers is covered in President's Commission on Migratory Labor, *Migratory Labor in American Agriculture* (Washington, D.C.: 1951). That conditions did not change markedly for the better in the next ten years is made clear by U.S. Congress, Senate Committee on Labor and Public Welfare, Subcommittee on Migratory Labor, *The Migrant Farm Worker in America* (a report prepared by Daniel H. Pollitt and Selma M. Levine), 86th Congress, 2nd Session. (Washington, D.C.: 1960). Louisa R. Shotwell, *The Harvesters* (Garden City, N.Y.: 1961) is a journalistic attempt to awaken concern.

Private charity is covered in F. Emerson Andrews, *Philanthropic Giving* (New York: 1950); *Attitudes Toward Giving* (New York: 1953); and *Philanthropic Foundations* (New York: 1956); Robert H. Bremner, *American Philanthropy* (Chicago: 1960); and Warren Weaver, *U.S. Philanthropic Foundations* (New York: 1967).

Other works of interest are: Eli Ginzberg, *Human Resources* (New

York: 1958); K. W. Kapp, *The Social Cost of Private Enterprise* (Cambridge, Mass.: 1950); Earl Raab and Hugh Folk, *The Pattern of Dependent Poverty in California* (Berkeley: 1963); and Harold L. Wilensky and Charles N. Lebeaux, *Industrial Society and Social Welfare* (New York: 1965).

The reentry of the war veterans into American society was a success story, of a major social problem avoided. Stuart Chase, *For This We Fought* (New York: 1946); Ralph G. Martin, *The Best Is None Too Good* (New York: 1948); and Charles G. Bolte, *The New Veteran* (New York: 1945) are firsthand reports. John Keats, *The New Romans* (Philadelphia: 1967) contains a caustic and funny account of one man's return to civilian life. David R. B. Ross, *Preparing for Ulysses* (New York: 1969) is an excellent scholarly work on the efforts made by Washington, the states, and veterans organizations. The Bureau of Labor Statistics, *Readjustment of Veterans to Civilian Life* (Washington, D.C.: 1946) is based on interviews with returning veterans about their experiences.

Health

There is no comprehensive history of medicine available for the postwar. Health, like education, does not interest historians much, even though it is among the first of human concerns. Almost without exception, people are more interested in their own bodies than in the body politic. But the proverbial man from Mars would never grasp that if he relied entirely on historians for descriptions of human society.

Geoffrey Marks and William K. Beatty, *The Story of Medicine in America* (New York: 1973) covers postwar developments in its later chapters.

There is a good study of the American Medical Association; James G. Burrow, *AMA: Voice of American Medicine* (Baltimore: 1963). Marguerite S. Clark, *Medicine Today* (New York: 1960) is a survey of the important developments in postwar medical research, by a noted science writer. Fred Davis, *Passage Through Crisis* (Indianapolis: 1963) is a study of families in which someone had been stricken with one of the most dreaded diseases of the period, polio. Donald Hunter, *The Diseases of Occupations* (2nd ed., Boston: 1957; and later eds.) is a famous work. It depicts the costs to health of work in an industrialized society in a brilliant and understated manner; part history, part medical book, part occupational sociology, it is almost beyond praise. E. Gartly Jaco, ed., *Patients, Physicians and Illness* (Glencoe, Ill,: 1958) offers a sociological perspective. Robert E. Rothenburg et al., *Group Medicine and Health Insurance in Action* (New York: 1949) is by a group of New York doctors who attempted to apply their experiences in wartime military medicine to peacetime civilian patients. Seymour E. Harris, *The Economics of American Medicine* (New York: 1964) considers one of the most emotive aspects of medicine in an unemotional way.

An important public health study is Sam Shapiro et al., *Infant, Perinatal, Maternal and Childhood Care in the United States* (Cambridge,

Mass.: 1968), which concentrates on the 1950s and early 1960s. There is also Rachel Carson, *Silent Spring* (Boston: 1962), which portrays the widespread use of pesticides as a menace to public health.

Sylvia A. Law, *Blue Cross: What Went Wrong?* (New Haven, Conn.: 1974) is valuable both as history and as an analysis of a unique institution.

Albert Deutsch, *The Shame of the States* (New York: 1948) provides a good, horrifying account of state mental hospitals shortly before the discovery of tranquilizers. There has been no comparable work since. Leo Srole et al., *Mental Health in the Metropolis: The Midtown Manhattan Study* (New York: 1962) is an important, controversial study. August B. Hollingshead and Frederick C. Redlich, *Social Class and Mental Illness* (New Haven, Conn.: 1958) is another important work, concerned with the social origins of mental patients. Arthur Kornhauser, *Mental Health of the Industrial Worker,* (New York: 1965) is an important study of automobile workers in the 1950s. It establishes the close correspondence between job satisfaction and positive mental health. There is a seminal study of the mental health of an entire suburb, John R. Seeley et al., *Crestwood Heights* (Toronto: 1956). Also useful are Marvin K. Opler, ed., *Culture and Mental Health* (New York: 1959) and Frank Riessman et al., *Mental Health of the Poor* (New York: 1964). For the Americanization of Freudianism, see Karen Horney, ed., *Are You Considering Psychoanalysis?* (New York: 1946).

Housing

Housing was one of the most urgent social problems of the immediate postwar years. Richard O. Davies, *Housing Reform During the Truman Administration* (Columbia, Mo.: 1966) is a good account of Truman's initiatives. Burnham Kelly et al., *Design and Production of Houses* (New York: 1959) is critical of postwar housing, but in a constructive way. Robert Moore Fisher, *Twenty Years of Public Housing* (New York: 1959) is somewhat disappointing. Most of the period from 1945 to 1963 is covered in Martin Meyerson et al., *Housing, People and Cities* (New York: 1962). U.S. Housing and Home Finance Agency, *Housing Statistics* (Washington, D.C.: 1961) contains most of the relevant figures.

The Urban Crisis

Urbs and Suburbs

The best introduction to what went wrong with cities in general is Lewis Mumford, *The City in History* (New York: 1961). The twentieth-century deterioration of the American city is surveyed by Blake McKelvey, *The Emergence of Metropolitan America 1915–1966* (New Brunswick, N.J.: 1968). The Editors of *Fortune, The Exploding Metropolis* (Garden

City, N. Y.: 1958) is useful. Victor Gruen, *The Heart of Our Cities* (New York: 1964) examines the damage done by the automobile. Peter Blake, *God's Own Junkyard* (New York: 1964) and Gordon Mitchell, *Sick Cities* (Baltimore: 1961) contain many striking pictures of urban ugliness between 1945 and 1961. There is also Percival and Paul Goodman, *Communitas* (Chicago: 1947). It is hard to decide where to place this work. It is stimulating. Its criticisms of urban failure are telling. Yet its prescriptions are impossible to take seriously. Edward Sofen, *The Miami Metropolitan Experiment* (Bloomington, Ind.: 1963) is a careful, academic account of the appearance of reform and the absence of its contents.

New York deserves, and receives, special attention. Jane Jacobs, *The Death and Life of Great American Cities* (New York: 1961) is mostly about New York. It is a lively, argumentative, and brilliant study. Robert A. Caro, *The Power Broker: Robert Moses and the Fall of New York* (New York: 1974) is overlong and overwritten; even so, it is a marvelous account of a great city's despoliation. Richard J. Whalen, *A City Destroying Itself* (New York: 1965) is a short, able work on the same theme.

David R. Hunter, *The Slums* (New York: 1964) surveyed the urban crisis as of 1963. The solution had presumably been set in motion in 1949. According to Hunter and Martin Anderson, *The Federal Bulldozer: A Critical Analysis of Urban Renewal 1949–1961* (Cambridge, Mass.: 1964), it wasn't. Jeanne R. Lowe, *Cities in a Race with Time* (New York: 1967) offers a knowledgeable survey of urban renewal in five East Coast cities. A detailed account of urban renewal in Newark, New Jersey, is Harold Kaplan, *Urban Renewal Politics* (New York: 1963). Herbert J. Gans, *The Urban Villagers* (New York: 1962) provides a graphic description of a cohesive neighborhood condemned by urban planners blind to the realities of working-class life. The racial element in the urban crisis is the subject of two works: Charles Abrams, *Forbidden Neighbors* (New York: 1955) and Morton Grodzins, *The Metropolitan Areas as a Racial Problem* (Pittsburgh: 1958). There is a shrewd and original account of ethnic elements in the life of New York: Nathan Glazer and Daniel P. Moynihan, *Beyond the Melting Pot*, second ed., (Cambridge, Mass.: 1970). Edward C. Banfield, *Big City Politics* (New York: 1965) provides a lively short account of how nine of the biggest cities were actually run in the postwar.

The most incisive study available of life in a postwar suburb is Herbert J. Gans *The Levittowners* (New York: 1967), based on his experiences as a resident of the third Levittown from 1959 to 1961. The first Levittown is studied in depth by William H. Dobriner, *Class in Suburbia* (Englewood Cliffs, N.J.: 1963). William H. Whyte, Jr., *The Organization Man* (Garden City, N. Y.: 1957) is illuminating on the character of the people who moved to the suburbs. But as Bennett M. Berger, *Working Class Suburb* (Berkeley and Los Angeles: 1959) demonstrates, not all suburbanites were middle-class. John R. Seeley et al., *Crestwood Heights* (Toronto: 1956) offers an excellent account of life in a Toronto suburb that was probably much like its American counterparts. Richard E. Gordon et al.,

The Split-Level Trap (New York: 1960) is a disappointing study of Bergen County, New Jersey, based on a study of psychiatric patients.

Suburban shopping centers are explained with skill and force in Victor Gruen and Larry Smith, *Shopping Towns USA* (New York: 1960), a work written for architects and planners, but very readable. Like all the best architectural writing, it is infused with a missionary zeal. There are a score of superficial attacks on suburban life as it developed in the postwar. Almost all can be ignored. But John Keats, *The Crack in the Picture Window* (Boston: 1957) is mordantly funny, and A. C. Spectorsky, *The Exurbanites* (Philadelphia: 1957) considers the upper middle class who moved beyond the suburbs to create what he terms "Exurbs." There is also Robert C. Wood, *Suburbia: Its People and Their Politics* (Boston: 1958), concerning a suburb in Massachusetts.

The Crisis in Architecture

John Burchard and Albert Bush-Brown, *The Architecture of America*, rev. ed. (London: 1967) is the best survey of American architecture in this century. It is a distinguished work with an unabashed belief in modernism. Henry-Russell Hitchcock and Arthur Drexler, *Built in U.S.A.: Postwar Architecture* (New York: 1952) is useful for the 1940s. Wayne Andrews, *Architecture, Ambition and Americans* (New York: 1955) provides a historical perspective. Hitchcock and Philip Johnson, *The International Style*, rev. ed. (New York: 1966) dates in its original version from 1932 and coined the term "International Style." The 1966 edition is useful because it contains Hitchcock's 1951 and 1965 reappraisals of modern architectural styles. In order to grasp the ideas which lie behind modern architecture, the most valuable work is Segfried Giedion, *Space, Time And Architecture*, rev. ed. (Cambridge, Mass.: 1967). John Jacobus, *Twentieth Century Architecture 1940–1965* (New York and Washington, D.C.: 1966) concentrates on American architecture but places it in its proper historical and international setting. Ian McCallum, *Architecture USA* (London: 1959) is an enjoyable Grand Tour by a young English architect. The details of domestic architecture are superbly illustrated and clearly explained in Kate E. Rogers, *Modern House U.S.A.* (New York: 1962). Christopher Tunnard and Henry Hope Reed, *American Skyline* (New York: 1956) is useful. The best way to understand important buildings and cities is, naturally, to go and see them. Editors of *Architectural Forum*, *Building, USA* (New York: 1965) provides an excellent short introduction to most of the important buildings of the postwar. Reyner Banham, *Los Angeles: The Architecture of Four Ecologies* (New York: 1971) offers an imaginative view of one of the leading cities in American architecture. For a contrasting view see William Bronson, *How to Kill a Golden State* (Garden City, N. Y.: 1968).

The Economy

General
There is a first-rate, important account of reconversion policy making: Herman Somers, *Presidential Agency* (Cambridge, Mass.: 1950). There is also J. F. Dewhurst et al., *America's Needs and Resources* (New York: 1947), which surveyed the economy and much of American society at the end of the war. It is a lucid work which was bold enough to set targets for economic and social growth for the first postwar decade. The later edition, published in 1955, brings the earlier work up to date through the end of the Truman Administration. The Editors of *Fortune* wrote *America in the Sixties* (New York: 1960) ostensibly to prefigure the coming decade. But nearly all its material is drawn from the 1950s and usefully charts some of the noteworthy economic and social developments of the decade. The same is true of Alvin Hansen, *Economic Issues of the 1960s* (New York: 1960). George Katona, *The Mass Consumption Society* (New York: 1964) is a good study of changes in consumer spending and consumer expectations between 1945 and 1963. Victor Fuchs, *Changes in the Location of Manufacturing in the United States Since 1929* (New Haven, Conn.: 1962) is important; so is his *The Growing Importance of the Service Industries* (New York: 1965). Robert Lekachman, *The Age of Keynes* (New York: 1966) examines the growing public and political acceptance of Keynesian economics after the war and is mildly Keynesian. Bernard D. Nossiter, *The Mythmakers* (Boston: 1964) examines government's approach to the economy under Eisenhower and Kennedy and finds little to choose between them. Michael D. Reagan, *The Managed Economy* (New York: 1963) finds it managed in favor of big business. Harold G. Vatter, *The U.S. Economy in the 1950s* (New York: 1963) is stimulating. There is also the Report of the Rockefeller Panel, *Prospect for America* (Garden City, N.Y.: 1961). U.S. Senate Subcommittee of the Select Committee on Small Business, 88th Congress, 1st Session, *The Role and Effects of of Technology in the Nation's Economy* (Washington, D.C.; 1963) examines the growing importance of automation as a force in the economy.

Fiscal and Monetary Policies
The last three chapters of Lester V. Chandler, *Inflation in the United States 1940-1948* (New York: 1951) provide a good short account of the inflationary boom which accompanied the ending of wartime price controls. Edward S. Flash, Jr., *Economic Advice and Presidential Leadership* (New York: 1965) is a scholarly history of that postwar innovation the Council of Economic Advisers and its periodic attempts to dabble in Keynesian demand management without encouraging inflation. The CEA, as Flash says, is a creation both illogical and important. It is hard to imagine any President attempting to influence the economy now without hav-

ing the CEA, or some body like it, to influence him. Stephen K. Bailey, *Congress Makes a Law* (New York: 1950) is the classic account of the enactment of the Employment Act of 1946, and Edwin G. Nourse, *Economics in the Public Service* (New York: 1953) is the account by the first chairman of the CEA of the efforts to make certain that the 1946 act worked. Walter W. Heller, *New Dimensions of Political Economy* (Cambridge, Mass.: 1966) is an examination of the principal issues confronting economic policy makers after 1950 by the most successful chairman of the CEA; it is a work written with verve and wit. For a good critical account of economic policy making during Heller's tenure, however, see Hobart Rowen, *The Free Enterprisers* (New York: 1964), economic journalism of a high order. Randolph E. Paul, *Taxation in the United States* (Indianapolis: 1954) is a valuable account of fiscal policies through the Korean War by a former Treasury tax expert. Philip M. Stern, *The Great Treasury Raid* (New York: 1964) offers a highly readable, well-informed account of the anomalies and iniquities of taxation in the postwar. The monetarist view of the postwar is fairly put in Milton Friedman and Anna J. Schwartz, *A Monetary History of the United States 1867–1960* (Princeton, N. J.: 1963). Ralph E. Freeman, ed., *Postwar Economic Trends in the United States* (New York: 1960) offers a choice of analyses. Edwin L. Dale, Jr., *Conservatives in Power: A Study in Frustration* (Garden City, N. Y.: 1960) draws from the Eisenhower years the moral that the budget is beyond the control of any new Administration, no matter what its economic policies. Seymour Harris, *Economics of the Kennedy Years* (New York: 1964) has no doubts that Kennedy became a good Keynesian, albeit reluctantly. Burt G. Hickman, *Growth and Stability of the Postwar Economy* (Washington, D.C.: 1960) is pedestrian but sound. The best account, however, is A. E. Holmans, *United States Fiscal Policy 1945–1959* (New York: 1961); well-written, by an English Keynesian, but no dogmatist, it is a model work of economic history and analysis. The annual report of the Council of Economic Advisers is a primary source of material on a wide range of government activities but chiefly concerns economic policy.

Economic Growth

The pioneering efforts of Edward F. Denison, *The Sources of Economic Growth in the United States and the Alternatives Before Us* (New York: 1962) and *Accounting for United States Economic Growth 1929–1969* (Washington, D.C.: 1965) are, as great works should be, controversial. In the second work Denison corrects some of the mistakes in method which were criticized in the first. He also has better figures to work from. Some of his estimates are admittedly guesses, but they are very intelligent guesses. John W. Kendrick and Maude R. Peche, *Postwar Productivity Trends in the United States 1948–1969* (Princeton, N. J.: 1973) is important and, like Denison, readable. There is also Harvey S. Perloff et al., *Regions, Resources and Economic Growth* (Baltimore: 1960), which sensibly rose above the late 1950s' view that economic growth was the key to success in the Cold War and that the Soviets were running away with it, which was the implicit thesis of Walt Whitman Rostow, *The Stages of Economic Growth* (New York: 1960).

Business

Walter Adams, ed., *The Structure of American Industry*, third ed., (New York: 1961) and the latter chapters of Thomas C. Cochran, *The American Business System* (Cambridge, Mass.: 1957) offer a good useful introduction based on recent history. John Brooks, *The Seven Fat Years* (New York: 1958) is an entertaining, informative account of Wall Street from 1950 through 1957. The only extended work on the small entrepreneurs is John H. Bunzel, *The American Small Businessman* (New York: 1962), which strikes a persuasive balance of views. Vance Packard, *The Pyramid Climbers* (New York: 1962) is a slightly disappointing examination of the lives of big businessmen. There is a collection of slightly mocking essays on the same theme: Earl F. Cheit, ed., *The Business Establishment* (New York: 1964). It was often claimed that the best-run business in the country was GM or IBM. On the former, see Peter F. Drucker, *The Concept of the Corporation* (New York: 1946); on the latter, see Thomas B. Watson, *A Business and Its Beliefs* (New York: 1967). Both works occasionally verge on the mystical. The central pillar in manufacturing industry is the subject of Otto Eckstein and Gary Fromm, *Steel and the Postwar Inflation* (Washington, D.C.: 1959). Gardiner C. Means, *Pricing Power and the Public Interest* (New York: 1962) takes the postwar steel industry as a crucial example of "administered prices." The Editors of *Fortune, The Space Industry* (Englewood Cliffs, N. J.: 1962) surveys the growth of an entirely new industry between 1945 and the 1960s. John Kenneth Galbraith, *American Capitalism* (Boston: 1956) surveys the rise of "countervailing power" among buyers in the postwar. By contrast A. A. Berle, *Power without Property* (New York: 1959) is concerned with the growth of oligopoly. J. S. Livingstone, *The American Stockholder* (Philadelphia: 1958) takes a skeptical look at the "People's Capitalism" drive of the 1950s. Martin Mayer, *Wall Street*, rev. ed. (New York: 1959) offers an excellent journalistic account of the Street and those who worked there. John Brooks, *The Fate of the Edsel and Other Business Adventures* (New York: 1963) is alive to the human and at times dramatic side of business, while John R. Bunting, *The Hidden Face of Free Enterprise* (New York: 1964) is concerned with the "split personality" of businessmen. Francis X. Sutton et al., *The American Business Creed* (Cambridge, Mass.: 1956) is a somewhat disappointing study of the ideology of businessmen in the early 1950s. Blair Bolles, *How to Get Rich in Washington* (New York: 1952) is a critical study of lobbying by business interests. Robert K. Lane, *The Regulation of Businessmen* (New Haven: 1954) is a sociological study of business attitudes toward government regulation. For contrasting views of American capitalism at midcentury see Seymour Harris, ed., *Saving American Capitalism* (New York: 1948); Alvin Hansen, *The American Economy* (New York: 1957); Dexter M. Keezer, *New Forces in American Business* (New York: 1959); David E. Lilienthal, *Big Business* (New York: 1952); Edward S. and Leonard Weiss, *Economics and American Industry* (New York: 1961). Richard Eells, *The Corporation and the Arts* (New York: 1967) examines an important new development in business history. The Department of Commerce publication *Survey of Current Business* covers such aspects of business as investment, employment, and consumer spending each month.

Labor

Government agencies collect and publish a variety of statistics, for a variety of purposes. The definitions and arrangements of the raw data vary from time to time; occasionally, where politically sensitive areas are involved, from administration to administration. At the same time it is worth remembering that some of the best statisticians in the country are employed in Federal agencies, especially in the Bureau of the Census and in the Bureau of Labor Statistics. For a good historical survey of employment and earnings see Bureau of Labor Statistics, *Employment and Earnings Statistics for the United States 1909–1960* (Washington, D.C.: 1961). The BLS *Factbook on Manpower*, rev. ed. (Washington, D.C.: 1954) covers employment in industries and services in the first postwar decade. Another BLS publication, *How the Government Measures Unemployment* (Washington, D.C.: 1962) is a useful guide to a complex subject often misunderstood. Stanley Lebergott, ed., *Men Without Work* (Englewood Cliffs, N. J.: 1964) stresses the shortcomings in postwar vocational training programs. W. S. Woytinsky et al., *Employment and Wages in the United States* (New York: 1953) studies various aspects of the transition of labor from World War II to the Korean War. Gunnar Myrdal, *Challenge to Affluence* (New York: 1963) is an astute short work which traces the economic slowdown in the 1950s to structural unemployment. U.S. House of Representatives, Subcommittee on Unemployment of the Committee on Education and Labor, 87th Congress, 1st Session, *Impact of Automation on Unemployment* (Washington, D.C.: 1961) is valuable.

Arthur F. McClure, *The Truman Adminstration and the Problems of Postwar Labor 1945–1948* (Rutherford, N. J.: 1969) is a useful scholarly account. Jack Barbash, *The Practice of Unionism* (New York: 1956) is an incisive study of what labor unions were really like and how they operated in the first decade after the war. Frank C. Pierson, (New York: 1967) covers the entire period, but in a pedestrian way. B.J. Widick, *Labor Today* (Boston: 1964) laments the failure of postwar labor to live up to its prewar promise. Michael Harrington, *The Retail Clerks* (New York: 1962) reports on one of the few unions which had a boom in membership in the postwar. It was a union for a new kind of worker, one whose collar was neither white nor blue. Sumner H. Slichter et al., *The Impact of Collective*

Bargaining on Management (Washington, D.C.: 1960) covers far more ground than the title suggests. Paul Jacobs, *The State of the Unions* (New York: 1973) is by one of the most thoughtful labor journalists of the postwar. Max M. Kampelman, *The Communist Party and the CIO* (New York: 1957) is a careful account of a historic struggle. Thomas R. Brooks, *Toil and Trouble*, 2nd. rev. ed. (New York: 1971) is probably the best short account of American unions, especially since the war.

Postwar labor legislation was inextricably linked with labor racketeering. The most useful work on labor corruption, placed in its historic setting, is John Hutchinson, *The Imperfect Union* (New York: 1970). Harry A. Millis and Emily Clark Brown, *From the Wagner Act to Taft-Hartley* (Chicago: 1950) is a dispassionate account of the Taft-Hartley Act. Alan K. McAdams, *Power and Politics in Labor Legislation* (New York: 1964) does the same with the Landrum-Griffin Act. McAdams needs to be read in conjunction, however, with John L. McClellan, *Crime Without Punishment* (New York: 1962); Robert Kennedy, *The Enemy Within* (New York: 1960); and Clark R. Mollenhoff, *The Tentacles of Power* (Cleveland: 1965).

There are three useful biographies of postwar labor leaders: Saul Alinsky, *John L. Lewis* (New York: 1949); Frank Cormier and William J. Eaton, *Reuther* (Englewood Cliffs, N. J.: 1970); and Joseph Goulden, *Meany* (New York: 1972). Melvyn Dubofsky and Warren Van Tine, *John L. Lewis* (New York: 1974) is by far the best biography of Lewis, however. Yet its authors do not like their subject very much.

The increasing importance of the "men of knowledge" within labor unions is described in Harold L. Wilensky, *Intellectuals in Labor Unions* (Glencoe, Ill.: 1956). Also see Loren Baritz, *The Servants of Power* (Middletown, Conn.: 1960).

Agriculture

The Department of Agriculture's Yearbook for 1963, *A Place to Live* (Washington, D.C.: 1963) and Bureau of the Census, *1959 Census of Agriculture—A Summary of the 48 States* (Washington, D.C.: 1961) provide overall views of agriculture in the 1950s. Edward Higbee, *Farms and Farmers in an Urban Age* (New York: 1963) is a brilliant work on the social, economic, and political realities of postwar agriculture. Wallace Wilcox, *Social Responsibility in Farm Leadership* (New York: 1956) examines the permanent crisis in agriculture as an ethical as well as an economic dilemma.

Lauren Soth, *Farm Trouble* (Princeton, N. J.: 1957) takes a robustly unsentimental view of the farmer's distress. Other useful works are: Grant McConnell, *The Decline of Agrarian Democracy* (Berkeley and Los Angeles: 1953); Lowry Nelson, *American Farm Life* (Cambridge, Mass.: 1954); Wayne C. Rohrer and Louis H. Douglas, *The Agrarian Transition in America* (Indianapolis: 1968); and Lee Taylor and Arthur R. Jones, Jr., *Rural Life and Urbanized Society* (New York: 1964).

Government agricultural policy (or the attempts to create one) in the period is covered by a leading agricultural economist, Dale E. Hathaway, *Government and Agriculture* (New York: 1963). Hathaway's work assumes an elementary knowledge of macroeconomic theory, but it is an essential account of postwar agriculture as a complex social and political challenge. Reo D. Christenson, *The Brannan Plan* (Ann Arbor, Mich.: 1959) and Allen J. Matusow, *Farm Policies and Politics in the Truman Years* (Cambridge, Mass.: 1967) are careful and conventional. To date there is no objective account of farm policy during the Eisenhower years, but there is Ezra Taft Benson, *Crossfire* (Garden City, N.Y.: 1962). Kennedy's farm program—especially the wheat referendum of 1963—is well served by a lively and learned study, Don F. Hadwiger and Ross B. Talbot, *Pressures and Protests* (San Francisco: 1965).

Politics

Presidential

There are some good biographies of the Presidents of the period, but none which is outstanding. Truman and Eisenhower were diligent memorialists. But memoirs are usually intended to preserve reputations. Theirs are not exceptions.

That splendidly edited series, *Public Papers of the U.S. Presidents*, cannot be overlooked. The relevant volumes are *Harry S. Truman* (Washington, D.C.: 1961–1966); *Dwight D. Eisenhower* (Washington, D.C.: 1960–1961); and *John F. Kennedy* (Washington, D.C.: 1962–1964).

Jonathan Daniels, *The Man of Independence* (Philadelphia: 1950) is an important source of material of Truman's life until he became Vice President. Truman didn't like the book, although it was written with his cooperation. *Frontier on the Potomac* (New York: 1945) by the same author is a good journalistic account of life in Washington at the time Truman became President. Robert S. Allen and William V. Shannon, *The Truman Merry-Go-Round* (New York: 1950) is full of Washington gossip, almost all of it hostile to Truman and his Administration. It is good for conveying the depth of the contempt which the capital city felt for the President. Cabell Phillips, *The Truman Presidency* (New York: 1966) is the best and most balanced biography to date. A less successful attempt is Alfred Steinberg, *The Man from Missouri* (New York: 1962). While still in office, Truman allowed use to be made of his papers for *Mr. President* (New York: 1952) by William Hillman. But the end result was a strangely stilted and curious exercise in Presidential veneration. The more intriguing, therefore, is Merle Miller, *Plain Speaking* (New York: 1974), compiled from interviews. Truman expressing himself directly and at length is engrossing. He gives himself the benefit of every doubt. Yet these conversations are more open and forceful and persuasive than his formal memoirs,

Year of Decision (Garden City, N.Y.: 1955) and *Years of Trial and Hope* (Garden City, N.Y.: 1956). Margaret Truman, *Harry S. Truman* (New York: 1973) is loyal, and predictable.

Richard S. Kirkendall, ed., *The Truman Period as a Research Field* (Columbia, Mo: 1967) is a useful introduction to the major topics. There is also Barton J. Bernstein and Allen J. Matusow, eds., *The Truman Administration* (New York: 1966). But it is neither a history nor an authoritative collection of complete documents. Richard J. Neustadt, *Presidential Power* (New York: 1960), which is based on the Truman Administration, might more aptly be called "The Limits of Presidential Power." Robert J. Donovan, *Conflict and Crisis* (New York: 1977) is a careful account of Truman's first three years in the White House.

The Korean War as such is outside the scope of this work. One aspect of it, however, became an important issue in domestic politics: Truman's clash with MacArthur. Arthur M. Schlesinger and Richard H. Rovere, *The General and the President* (New York: 1952) finds MacArthur to be a menace to peace and the Constitution. John W. Spanier, *The Truman-MacArthur Controversy and the Korean War* (Cambridge, Mass.: 1959) is less entertaining and more persuasive. The general's account is to be found in his *Reminiscences* (New York: 1964), which is gracefully written. The famous address is available as *Address at the Joint Meeting of the Two Houses of Congress* (Senate Document No. 36) 82nd Congress, 1st Session (Washington, D.C.: 1951).

The most convincing portrait of Eisenhower is to be found in Emmet John Hughes *The Ordeal of Power* (New York: 1964). Arthur Larson, *Eisenhower: The President Nobody Knew* (New York: 1969) contradicts the stereotypical views and draws effectively on his experience as one of Eisenhower's special assistants. Herbert S. Parmet, *Eisenhower and the American Crusades* (New York: 1963) and Peter Lyon, *Eisenhower: Portrait of the Hero* (Boston: 1974) are both thorough, and thoroughly pedestrian. Merlo J. Pusey, *Eisenhower the President* (New York: 1956) is a dull account of Eisenhower's first term. A good, sometimes critical account by a knowledgeable Washington journalist is Marquis Childs, *Eisenhower: Captive Hero* (New York: 1958). Robert J. Donovan, *Eisenhower, the Inside Story* (New York: 1956) is valuable because it is based on Cabinet minutes; unfortunately it is badly written. Sherman Adams, *First-Hand Report* (New York: 1961) is self-effacing. Eisenhower's memoirs are *Mandate for Change* (Garden City, N. Y.: 1963) and *Waging Peace* (Garden City, N. Y.: 1966).

James Tracy Crown, *The Kennedy Literature* (New York: 1968) is a valuable guide to sources. There is a convincing portrait of Kennedy the man in James MacGregor Burns, *John Kennedy: A Political Profile* (New York: 1960), a work Kennedy did not like. The most complete account of Kennedy as man and President is Theodore Sorensen, *Kennedy* (New York: 1965); it is a work which has many of Kennedy's own characteristic strengths and weaknesses, e.g., the use of candor to mislead. Arthur M. Schlesinger, Jr., *A Thousand Days* (Boston: 1965) offers a slightly broader view of the Kennedy Administration. Kenneth P. O'Donnell and David F. Powers, *Johnny, We Hardly Knew Ye* (Boston: 1972) is an excellent account until Kennedy becomes President, after which he becomes ten feet tall and never used any expression stronger than "Gosh!" Benjamin C. Bradlee, *Conversations with Kennedy* (New York: 1975) is an honest and moving account. Pierre Salinger, *With Kennedy* (Garden City, N. Y.: 1966) is banal; so is Hugh Sidey, *John F. Kennedy* (New York: 1964). William Manchester, *Portrait of a President* (Boston: 1962) is useful chiefly to show the almost complete identification with Kennedy that prevailed among men of a certain age and class. Jim Bishop, *A Day in the Life of President Kennedy* (New York: 1964) is reverential. There is a less enchanted glimpse of the President to be descried in Richard J. Whalen, *The Founding Father* (New York: 1964), a biography of Joseph Kennedy. The best-known work to attack Kennedy directly as both man and President is Victor Lasky, *JFK: The Man and the Myth* (New York: 1963), a work which chokes on its own indignation and has no sense of proportion. Joan Myers, ed., *John Fitzgerald Kennedy as We Remember Him* (Chicago:1964) is the best of the many picture books and contains some excellent photographs of the Kennedy entourage. The President's first year in the White House is covered in two pedestrian accounts: Helen Fuller, *Year of Trial* (New York: 1962) and Stan Opotowsky, *The Kennedy Government* (New York: 1961). Kennedy's effectiveness in handling domestic political problems has been examined in two works: Jim F. Heath, *John F. Kennedy and the Business Community* (Chicago: 1969), which is unilluminating about either, and Grant McConnell, *Steel and the Presidency 1962* (New York: 1963), which depicts the Presidency under Kennedy as an office characterized by great responsibilities and little real power. Lawrence H. Fuchs, *John F. Kennedy and American Catholicism* (New York: 1967) is a useful study of a sensitive subject. On his relations with Lyndon B. Johnson, Evelyn Lincoln, *Kennedy and Johnson* (New York: 1968) consists mainly of gossip hostile to Johnson, and Tom Wicker, *JFK and LBJ* (New York: 1968) is at its best describing Kennedy's dealings not with his Vice President but with Congress.

Congressional

Congressional Quarterly, *Congress and the Nation 1945–1964* (Washington, D.C.: 1965) is an outstanding survey of Federal legislation in the postwar. It brings to bear an unmatched knowledge of the interests involved in the major issues and explains clearly the course of every important bill, including those which failed to be enacted. For the pressures on Congress in the Forties see V. O. Key, Jr., *Politics, Parties and Pressure Groups* (New York: 1952). There is a masterly account of Congressional politics in the Fifties contained in Rowland Evans and Robert Novak, *Lyndon B. Johnson: The Exercise of Power* (New York: 1968).

Some of the legislative struggles of the period have been studied at length: the Employment Act of 1946, Stephen K, Bailey, *Congress Makes a Law* (New York: 1950); the Selective Service Act of 1948, Clyde E. Jacobs and John F. Gallagher, *The Selective Service Act* (New York: 1968); the Dangerous Drugs Act of 1963, Richard Harris, *The Real Voice* (New York: 1964); the Landrum-Griffin Act, Alan K. McAdams, *Power and Politics in Labor Legislation* (New York: 1964); the St. Lawrence Seaway, William R. Willoughby, *The St. Lawrence Seaway* (Madison, Wis.: 1961); the Dixon-Yates contract, Aaron Wildavsky, *Dixon-Yates: A Study in Power Politics* (New Haven, Conn.: 1962).

Party

The authorized biography of Robert A. Taft, James T. Patterson, *Mr. Republican* (Boston: 1972) is thorough and not uncritical. It tentatively breasts the murky waters of "psychohistory." William S. White, *The Taft Sory* (New York: 1954) is less ambitious. The dilemma the Korean War posed the Republicans—how to support a war against the Communists without actually supporting Truman—is analyzed by Robert J. Caridi, *The Korean War and American Politics* (Philadelphia: 1969). There is a disenchanted view of Republicanism by one of Eisenhower's speech writers: Arthur Larson, *A Republican Looks at His Party* (New York: 1956). The True Faith, however, appears to have been in the possession of Republicans such as Barry Goldwater, *The Conscience of a Conservative* (Shepherdsville, Ky.: 1960). This was an enormous best-seller, although it reads like a piece of campaign literature. The postwar conservative revival is lucidly discussed in Clinton Rossiter, *Conservatism in America* (New York: 1955).

On what it was like to be a Congressman and have Richard Nixon for an opponent, see Jerry Voorhis, *Confessions of a Congressman* (Garden City, N. Y.: 1947). The role of the Democratic Party's strongest interest group is ably analyzed in Fay Calkins, *The CIO and the Democratic Party* (Chicago: 1952). Postwar liberals are fashionably derided as Cold Warriors. What is forgotten is the reluctance with which the Cold War was swallowed. It was a bitter pill, as Arthur M. Schlesinger, Jr., *The Vital Center* (Boston: 1949) evidences. The general concerns of the liberal wing of the party were, by definition, the concerns of Eleanor Roosevelt. Joseph Lash, *Eleanor: The Years Alone* (New York: 1973) is sound but reverential. A useful memoir by another keeper of the liberal flame in the years of Republicanism is Chester Bowles, *Promises to Keep* (New York: 1971). There is a dull but well-researched biography of Estes Kefauver: Joseph Bruce Gorman, *Kefauver* (New York: 1971).

Electoral

There are two good accounts of the 1948 election: Jules Abels, *Out of the Jaws of Victory* (New York: 1959) and Irwin Ross, *The Loneliest Campaign* (New York: 1968). Samuel Lubell, *The Future of American Politics* (New York: 1952) offers an intriguing analysis of underlying

trends based mainly on the 1948 election and the decline of machine politics in the big cities. Alexander Heard, *A Two-Party South* (Chapel Hill,
N.C.: 1952) is a study of the Dixiecrats. Unfortunately there is no full-
length biography of Thomas Dewey. Henry Wallace, however, is a subject of enduring interest. Karl M. Schnidt, *Henry A. Wallace: Quixotic
Crusade 1948* (Syracuse, N. Y.: 1960) and Norman D. Markowitz, *The
Rise and Fall of the People's Century* (New York: 1973) are perceptive
and often critical. The best defense of Wallace is E.L. and F. H. Schapsmeier, *Prophet in Politics* (Ames, Iowa: 1970). Dwight Macdonald,
Henry Wallace: The Man and the Myth (New York: 1948) is witty and
hostile. Curtis D. MacDougall, *Gideon's Army*, 3 vols. (New York: 1965)
offers the most thorough account of the Progressive Party and a highly
personal one. I. F. Stone, *The Truman Era* (New York: 1953) offers some
of the most astute writing available on the Progressives.

For Eisenhower's opponent in the 1952 and 1956 elections, see Herbert
J. Muller, *Adlai E. Stevenson* (New York: 1962), a work full of longing
and regret, and Stuart Gary Brown, *Conscience in Politics* (Syracuse, N.
Y.: 1961), a dull academic study. For the definitive, and masterly, biography, however, see John Bartlow Martin, *Triumph of Failure: Adlai Stevenson and the World* (Garden City, N. Y.: 1977).

Louis Harris, *Is There a Republican Majority?* (New York: 1954) takes
a close look at the 1952 election returns. Angus Campbell et al., *The Voter
Decides* (Evanston, Ill.: 1954) was a seminal approach to election analysis
when it appeared. Taking the 1952 result, it concentrated not so much on
votes as on voters. A decade later Campbell et al. produced *The American Voter* (New York: 1964), which extended these techniques to the
elections of 1948 and 1956 and restudied the 1952 election. The results are
impressive. Paul T. David et al., *Presidential Nominating Politics in 1952*,
5 vols. (Baltimore: 1952) is exhaustive but undistinguished. The postwar
style of political campaigns—dominated by television and by advertising
methods—emerged for the first time in 1952. At first blush it was a style
which appalled and intrigued, as two works make clear: Stanley Kelley,
Jr., *Public Relations and Political Power* (Baltimore: 1956) and Charles A.
H. Thomson, *Television and Presidential Politics* (Washington, D.C.:
1960). Charles A. H. Thomson and Frances M. Shattuck, *The 1956 Presidential Campaign* (Washington, D.C.: 1960) is useful, as is Lucy S. Dawi-
dowitz and Leon J. Goldstein, *Politics in a Pluralist Demcracy* (New
York: 1963), which examines the role played by religion and ethnic identification in the 1960 election. But the essential account is Theodore H.
White, *The Making of the President 1960* (New York: 1961), which is one
of the best disquisitions ever written on American politics. Less brilliant
but as painstaking is Paul T. David et al., *The Presidential Election and
Transition* (Washington, D.C.: 1961). Kennedy's opponent in 1960 never
failed to stir deep passions. For the worshiper's view, Ralph De Toledano, *Nixon* (New York: 1956) is required reading. Less entranced but still
sympathetic—and important for its account of Nixon's years in Congress
and as Vice President—is Earl Mazo, *Nixon* (New York: 1959). Mazo lat-

er became a Nixon speech writer and still later, in company with Stephen Hess, updated the earlier work to produce *Nixon* (New York: 1968). For his view of the 1952 and 1960 elections, see Richard M. Nixon, *Six Crises* (Garden City, N. Y.: 1962). For a thoroughly hostile portrait, there is William Costello, *The Facts About Nixon* (New York: 1960). The central event of the 1960 campaign is covered at length in Sidney Kraus, ed., *The Great Debates* (Bloomington, Ind.: 1967), which contains transcripts of all four debates.

The Presidential elections from 1948 to 1960 are seen as being decided soberly in V. O. Key Jr., *The Responsible Electorate* (Cambridge, Mass.: 1966). Arthur M. Schlesinger, Jr., and Fred L. Israel, eds., *A History of American Elections 1789–1968* (New York: 1968) offers, in Volume 4, reliable but lackluster accounts of each of the postwar contests. This work is valuable for its extensive reproduction of materials used in the campaigns.

Two worthwile collections of political journalism from the 1950s, by very different reporters, are Richard H. Rovere, *The Eisenhower Years* (New York: 1956) and I. F. Stone, *The Haunted Fifties* (New York: 1963).

The Cold War as a Way of Life

Foreign Policy

Foreign policy as such is outside the scope of this book. But it would be false and arbitrary to exclude it entirely. Foreign policy is an important expression of a nation's conception of itself, besides being an expression of its interests. Much of the writing by and about the Presidents of the period contains useful material on America's relations with the rest of the world. Two Secretaries of State who were instrumental in the formulation of the American side of the Cold War have left memoirs: James F. Byrnes, *Speaking Frankly* (New York: 1947) is written close to events; Dean G. Acheson, *Present at the Creation* (New York: 1969) is leisurely and urbane. George Kennan, *Memoirs* (Boston: 1967) reflects one of the finest minds of the age at work on serious problems of policy.

D. F. Fleming, *The Cold War and Its Origins*, 2 vols. (Garden City, N. Y.: 1961) has the merit of tracing the Cold War back to 1917. Gabriel Kolko, *The Politics of War* (New York: 1968) in contrast traces it to the conflicts in U.S.-Soviet relations during the Second World War, especially those involving liberation movements. Walter LeFeber, *America, Russia and the Cold War* (New York: 1967) refers Cold War conflicts back to domestic tensions. Herbert Feis, *From Trust to Terror* (New York: 1970) is an orthodox view by a former State Department official. Robert G. Kaiser, *Cold Winter, Cold War* (New York: 1974) pins responsibility squarely on the Truman Doctrine. The most trenchant criticism of containment, however, remains the prophetic Walter Lippmann, *The Cold War* (New York: 1948); it might have been written yesterday. The most satisfactory account is Louis Halle, *The Cold War as History* (London: 1967). Almost as lucid is John Spanier, *American Foreign Policy Since World War II*, 2nd ed. (New York: 1965). Joseph Marion Jones, *The Fifteen Weeks* (New York: 1955) is an exciting firsthand account of the creation of the Marshall Plan. Harry Bayard Price, *The Marshall Plan and Its Meaning* (Ithaca, N. Y.: 1955) examines what followed. Ross Y. Koen, *The China Lobby in American Politics* (New York: 1974) is a splendid account of a sordid business. Foreign policy under Eisenhower is tellingly dissected by Emmet John Hughes, *America the Vincible* (Garden City, N. Y.: 1959). John Robinson Beal, *John Foster Dulles* (New York: 1957) remains an important source of ideas and material on Eisenhower's Secretary of State. Richard Goold-Adams, *The Time of Power* (London: 1962) is by an admirer of Dulles. There is an excellent, critical biography: Townsend Hoopes, *The Devil and John Foster Dulles* (Boston: 1973). A useful, if somewhat black-and-white, dissection of foreign policy under Kennedy is Louise Fitzsimmons, *The Kennedy Doctrine* (New York: 1972). Haynes Johnson, *The Bay of Pigs* (New York: 1964) is the authorized account of Brigade 2506. There is a firsthand version of the Cuban missile crisis: Robert F. Kennedy, *Thirteen Days* (New York: 1969). More complete however is Elie Abel, *The Missile Crisis* (Philadelphia: 1966). For the people who made foreign policy in the Kennedy years, David Halberstam, *The Best and the Brightest* (New York: 1973) is a graveyard of reputations. Victor Marchetti and John D. Marks, *The CIA and the Cult of Intelligence* (New York: 1973) contains some interesting material on how the CIA served foreign policy ends at home.

There is an extensive Cold War literature which is more in the nature of theological disputation than historical inquiry. From an embarrassment of riches I choose one example as being representative: Richard J. Walton, *Henry Wallace, Harry Truman and the Cold War* (New York: 1976).

Programs and Investigations

There is an excellent general account: Eleanor Bontecou, *The Federal Loyalty-Security Program* (Ithaca, N. Y.: 1953). Ralph S. Brown, Jr., *Loyalty and Security* (New Haven, Conn.: 1956) is equally valuable. He dissects the oath mania with great skill. There are two works which hold Truman's Loyalty-Security program responsible for McCarthyism. The earlier, and more charitable, version is Carey McWilliams, *Witch Hunt* (Boston: 1950). The later version is Athan Theoharis, *Seeds of Repression* (Chicago: 1971). Less persuasive is Ralph M. Freeland, *The Truman Doctrine and the Origins of McCarthyism* (New York: 1972). He blames it on the Marshall Plan. Truman comes off badly also in Alan D. Harper, *The Politics of Loyalty* (New York: 1969). Edward A. Shils, *The Torment of Secrecy* (Glencoe, Ill.: 1956) combines political sociology with high-minded indignation. There are several good reports from the front lines: O. Edmund Clubb, *The Witness and I* (New York: 1975) is an understated telling of his ludicrous "trial" by the State Department's Loyalty-Security Board; the situation at USIA is described in Martin Merson, *The Private Diary of a Public Servant* (New York: 1955). There are several extraordinary case studies in an early journalistic account, Bert Andrews, *Washington Witch Hunt* (New York: 1948). Cedric Belfrage, *The American Inquisition 1945–1960* (Indianapolis: 1973) is part history, part polemic, part personal account from an avowedly left-wing angle. The VA's use of the Loyalty-Security machinery to deprive a soldier who had lost both legs in combat of his disability pension is told by the veteran concerned, James Kutcher, in *The Case of the Legless Veteran*, rev. ed. (London: 1973). Sober, legalistic accounts of what happened to some civil servants and servicemen are collected in Adam Yarmolinsky, *Case Studies in Personnel Security* (Washington, D.C.: 1955). Most involved cruelty exaggerated by farce. Earl Latham, *The Communist Controversy in Washington* (Cambridge, Mass.: 1968) offers a lucid guide to these complex events. David Caute, *The Great Fear* (New York: 1978) is the most thorough study of McCarthyism and filled with illuminating detail. It is, nonetheless, very long on indignation and very short on analysis.

Walter Gellhorn, *Security, Loyalty and Science* (New York: 1950) is a valuable early study and helps set the scene for much of what happened; notably the ordeal of Robert Oppenheimer. The best work on this episode is Robert M. Stern, *The Oppenheimer Case: Security on Trial* (New York: 1969). John Major, *The Oppenheimer Hearing* (New York: 1971) is a fine dispassionate account. Charles P. Curtis, *The Oppenheimer Case* (New York: 1955) contains long extracts from the hearing transcript. Peter Michelmore, *The Swift Years* (Philadelphia: 1969) is a useful, if less than definitive, biography of Oppenheimer. Thomas W. Wilson, Jr., *The Great Weapons Heresy* (Boston: 1970) claims that Oppenheimer was driven out of government service for arguing that nuclear weapons create insecurity, rather than security. James R. Shepley and Clay Blair, Jr., *The Hydrogen Bomb* (New York: 1954) is one of the classics of Cold War literature.

The role of the FBI was important but has not yet been the subject of the separate and authoritative study it deserves. Fred J. Cook, *The FBI Nobody Knows* (New York: 1964) is critical, yet woefully short of inside information. The best account of the bureau is Sanford J. Ungar, *FBI* (Boston: 1976); scattered throughout it is material from 1945 to 1963.

The role Congress played in investigating loyalty and security questions is thoughtfully examined in Alan Barth, *Government by Investigation* (New York: 1955). His earlier work, *The Loyalty of Free Men* (New York: 1951) is valuable and more far-reaching. A comprehensive account of the House Un-American Activities Committee throughout the period is Walter Goodman, *The Committee* (New York: 1968), a lively and somewhat eccentric work. Robert K. Carr, *The House Committee on Un-American Activities 1945–1950* (Ithaca, N. Y.: 1952) offers a lawyer's view. The Hollywood Ten's version of their encounter with the committee is in Gordon Kahn, *Hollywood on Trial* (New York: 1948). A very useful work, containing much fascinating testimony from various of HUAC's hearings, is Eric Bentley, *Thirty Years of Treason* (New York: 1971). William F. Buckley, Jr., et al., *The Committee and Its Critics* (New York: 1962) puts the case for the defense.

The activities of the "little HUACs," which sprang to life in the various states are ably covered in Walter Gellhorn, *The States and Subversion* (Ithaca, N. Y.: 1952). Edward L. Barrett, Jr., *The Tenney* Committee (Ithaca, N. Y.: 1951) and Vern Countryman, *Un-American Activities in the States of Washington* (Ithaca, N. Y.: 1951) are important studies. Melvin Rader, *False Witness* (Seattle: 1969) tells an extraordinary story. David P. Gardner, *The California Oath: Its Controversy* (Berkeley and Los Angeles: 1967) is thorough but wooden. There is also George R. Stewart, *The Year of the Oath* (Garden City, N. Y.: 1950).

Trials

David A. Shannon, *The Decline of American Communism: A History of the Communist Party of the United States Since 1945* (New York: 1959) is excellent as both history and analysis. Also useful are Nathan Glazer, *The Social Basis of American Communism* (New York: 1961) and Irving Howe and Lewis Coser, *The American Communist Party* (Boston: 1957). The postwar was a terrible time for former CP members. Whatever mistakes they had made, many of them paid for them very heavily. Their vulnerability and prosaic humanity are evident in Murray Kempton, *Part of Our Time* (New York: 1955). Morris Ernst and David Loth, *Report on the American Communist* (New York: 1952) attempts to build a profile based on interviews and questionnaires. A more useful sociological study is Gabriel Almond, *The Appeals of Communism* (Princeton, N.J.: 1954). Also see Harold W. Chase, *Security and Liberty: The Problem of Native Communists 1947–1955* (Garden City, N.Y.: 1955). Nathan Glazer, *The Social Basis of American Communism* (New York: 1961) is useful, and Joseph R. Starobin, *American Communism in Crisis* (Cambridge, Mass.: 1972) is an insider's account by a long-time CP staff member.

There is an important and persuasive account of his life in the Party by a onetime editor of the *Daily Worker*, John Gates, *The Story of an American Communist* (New York: 1958). Gates was one of the eleven CP leaders tried before Harold Medina, whose account of the trial is in his *The Anatomy of Freedom* (New York: 1959). Elizabeth Bentley, *Out of Bondage* (New York: 1951) is written like a romance thriller. Herbert A. Philbrick, *I Led Three Lives* (New York: 1952) is interesting, while Louis Budenz, *This Is My Story* (New York: 1947) is tedious, pompous, and pathetic. Harvey Matusow, *False Witness* (New York: 1955) is the confession of a former paid witness and perjurer. There is an excellent study of the problems posed by the testimony of former Party members: Herbert L. Packer, *Ex-Communist Witnesses* (Palo Alto, Calif.: 1962).

The most famous such witness was Whittaker Chambers. His biography, *Witness* (New York: 1952), is a fascinating combination of fact and fiction. William F. Buckley, Jr., *Odyssey of a Friend* (New York: 1970), based on Buckley's correspondence with Chambers, reveals Chambers as an extremely attractive man—witty, compassionate, lively, thoughtful in his relations with others. On the other hand, John Chabot Smith, *Alger Hiss: The True Story* (New York: 1976) is an important and disturbing book. If Chambers really did frame Hiss, then this is almost certainly how it was done, and why. Meyer A. Zeligs, *Friendship and Fratricide* (New York: 1967) is a psychiatrist's interpretation; it also contains much important information on the lives and personalities of the two men. The two Hiss trials are reconstructed with extraordinary skill by Alastair Cooke, *A Generation on Trial* (New York: 1951). Earl Jowitt, *The Strange Case of Alger Hiss* (London: 1953) applies a very strict standard to the evidence in Chambers's case against Hiss and finds it wanting. Alger Hiss, *In the Court of Public Opinion* (New York: 1957) is evasive and unconvincing. Ralph De Toledano and Victor Lasky, *The Seeds of Treason* (New York: 1950) offers no new information for analysis; it is simply mean-spirited and vindictive.

Walter and Miriam Schneir, *Invitation to an Inquest* (Baltimore: 1973) is a brilliant investigation of the Rosenberg case. Louis Nizer, *The Implosion Conspiracy* (Garden City, N.Y.: 1973), offers both a masterly reconstruction of the trial and a first-rate commentary on the legal and moral issues involved. John Wexley, *The Judgment of Julius and Ethel Rosenberg* (New York: 1955) reproduces much of the court record and concludes that the Rosenbergs were framed. Morton Sobell, *On Doing Time* (New York: 1974) casts serious doubt on the trial. Of interest is Jonathan Root, *The Betrayers* (New York: 1963). Julius and Ethel Rosenberg, *The Rosenberg Letters* (London: 1953) protest their innocence in this poignant correspondence with each other and with their children.

McCarthy

The Senator was *sui generis;* he was also the product of his time. To understand his appeal to large numbers of Americans in the postwar, the works of several right-wing authors provide as good an introduction as any. For example, John T. Flynn, *The Road Ahead* (New York: 1949), *While You Slept* (New York: 1951), and *The Decline of the American Republic* (New York: 1955); James Burnham, *The Struggle for the World* (New York: 1947) and *The Web of Subversion* (New York: 1949); and William F. Buckley, Jr., *Up from Liberalism* (New York: 1959). And for the True Faith see, for example, Joseph R. McCarthy, *America's Retreat from Victory* (New York: 1951), which offers invective and pseudoscholarship cast in a prose style derived from hack literature, right down to the erratic spelling and garbled syntax.

The essential works of the radical right of the late 1950s, early 1960s are Robert Welch, *The Blue Book of the John Birch Society* (Belmont, Mass.:

1960), an inimitable work, and *The Politician* (Belmont, Mass.: 1963), which, in a field crowded with competition, is a masterpiece of its kind. Also see Fred Schwartz, *You Can Trust the Communists (. . . to Do Exactly as They Say!)* (Englewood Cliffs, N.J.: 1961), an evangelical anti-Communist manifesto.

Daniel Bell, ed., *The New American Right* (Garden City, N.J.: 1955) and *The Radical Right* (Garden City, N.Y.: 1963) offer several explanations for the right-wing extremism of the 1950s, early 1960s. Other works in the same vein are Richard Hofstadter, *The Paranoid Style in American Politics* (New York: 1965); Donald Janson and Bernard Eismann, *The Far Right* (New York: 1963); and Harry and Bonaro Overstreet, *The Strange Tactics of Extremism* (New York: 1964). Mark Sherwin, *The Extremists* (New York: 1963) looks under a variety of rocks. A valuable account of what could happen to a community once anti-Communist hysteria was rampant is David Hulburd, *This Happened in Pasadena* (New York: 1951).

There are two good books about McCarthy but no authoritative, even-handed biography. Jack Anderson and Ronald May, *McCarthy—the Man, the Senator, the Ism* (Boston: 1952) is the principal account of McCarthy's life until he became famous, or infamous. Richard H. Rovere, *Senator Joe McCarthy* (New York: 1959) charts the decline and fall. Both works are grimly funny. Fred J. Cook, *The Nightmare Decade: The Life and Times of Joe McCarthy* (New York: 1971) is a polemic. Roy Cohn, *McCarthy* (Cleveland: 1968) is disingenuous. There is a useful biography of one of the few Senators, Thomas C. Hennings, who fought McCarthy from first to last: Donald J. Kemper, *Decade of Fear* (Columbia, Mo.: 1965). The defense of McCarthy is William F. Buckley, Jr., and L. Brent Bozell, *McCarthy and His Enemies* (Chicago: 1954; rev. ed., Chicago: 1961), but its pretensions to objectivity cannot be taken seriously. Bozell was one of McCarthy's assistants. Two of the Senator's victims have given their own versions of events: Owen Lattimore, *Ordeal by Slander* (Boston: 1950) and James Wechsler, *The Age of Suspicion* (New York: 1954). Wechsler is important, moreover, for his account of life on the left circa 1941–1951. Also see Michael Paul Rogin, *The Intellectuals and McCarthy* (Cambridge, Mass.: 1969).

Blacklisting

Stefan Kanfer, *A Journal of the Plague Years* (New York: 1973) is an essential account of blacklisting; often incisive, it is, unhappily, sometimes pretentious. In most respects the best general account remains John Cogley, *Report on Blacklisting* (New York: 1956), a study financed by the Fund for the Republic. Thomas C. Reeves, *Freedom and the Foundation* (New York: 1969) examines the operations of the fund and its Cold War vicissitudes. Merle Miller, *The Judges and the Judged* (Garden City, N.Y.: 1952) is an early and tentative study of blacklisting. But it offers valuable portraits of the principal figures involved in compiling and publishing the blacklists. There is a memorable description of John Henry Faulk's struggle to clear his name in Louis Nizer, *The Jury Returns* (Garden City, N.Y.: 1966). John Henry Faulk, *Fear on Trial* (New York: 1964) is a poignant account of his travails, but without self-pity. Lillian Hellman, *Scoundrel Time* (Boston: 1976) is amusing and moving, while Alvah Bessie, *Inquisition in Eden* (New York: 1965) is bitter and funny. One of the Hollywood Ten, Dalton Trumbo, *Additional Dialogue* (New York: 1970) clearly bore his misfortunes—including imprisonment—with courage, resilience, and wry humor. Robert Vaughn, *Only Victims* (New York: 1972) is a wretchedly ill-written account of blacklisting in the theater.

The Supreme Court

Almost all the works concerning the postwar Supreme Court have been principally interested in race. And perhaps the social consequences of its role in the race problem have been more far-reaching than any of its other activities. Yet the balance is undoubtedly wrong.

Anthony Lewis, *Gideon's Trumpet* (New York: 1964) must surely be the best introduction to the Supreme Court—what it does, how it does it—ever written. And the story of Clarence Gideon's demand for justice is undeniably moving. There is only one lengthy account of the Vinson Court: C. Herman Pritchett, *Civil Liberties and the Vinson Court* (Chicago: 1954). Theodore L. Becker and Malcolm M. Feeley, eds., *The Impact of Supreme Court Decisions*, 2nd ed. (New York: 1969) contains half a dozen useful studies based on decisions of the Court under Vinson and Warren. Ernest R. Bartley, *The Tidelands Oil Controversy* (Austin, Texas: 1953) is a valuable study of one of the most important Constitutional questions between the states and the Federal government in the postwar. There is an adequate biography of Warren: John D. Weaver, *Warren: The Man, the Court, the Era* (New York: 1967). There are several noteworthy views of the Court in Richard H. Sayler et al., *The Warren Court: A Critical Analysis* (New York: 1968). Contrasting views are taken by two distinguished lawyers: Archibald Cox, *The Warren Court* (Cambridge, Mass.: 1968) and Philip B. Kurland, *Politics, the Constitution and the Warren Court* (Chicago: 1970). Kurland is highly critical. The Court's active attempts to advance racial equality provoked the anger of many Congressmen. Two useful accounts are Walter F. Murphy, *Congress and the Court* (Chicago: 1952) and C. Herman Pritchett, *Congress vs. the Supreme Court, 1957–1960* (Minneapolis: 1961).

Other works concerning the Supreme Court will be found under the entry Blacks—The Courts.

Blacks

General

The most reliable biography of Martin Luther King, Jr., is Lerone Bennett *What Manner of Man?* (Chicago: 1964). William Robert Miller, *Martin Luther King Jr.* (New York: 1968) is valuable for its account of the pressures on King and his relations with the SCLC, but is otherwise disappointing. There are some useful contributions in C. Eric Lincoln, ed., *Martin Luther King, Jr.* (New York: 1970). L. D. Reddick, *Crusader Without Violence* (New York: 1959) is valuable for its many illuminating references to the black middle-class milieu which produced King. Martin Luther King, Jr., *Stride Toward Freedom* (New York: 1958) is an impressive account of the Montgomery bus boycott by the man it made famous. His later *Why We Can't Wait* (New York: 1964), on the other hand, is a potboiler.

Other biographical and autobiographical accounts of greater or lesser importance include Claude Brown, *Manchild in the Promised Land* (New York: 1965), a brilliant and powerful description of growing up in, and away from, postwar Harlem. The autobiographical writings of James Baldwin, *Notes of a Native Son* (Boston: 1955), *Nobody Knows My Name* (New York: 1961), and *The Fire Next Time* (New York, 1963) are written with elegance. John A. Williams *This is My Country Too* (New York: 1966) is of interest. Henry Williamson, *Hustler!* (Garden City, N.Y.: 1965) is a remarkable autobiography by a black criminal living on Chicago's South Side. Robert F. Williams, *Negroes with Guns* (New York: 1958) blazes with anger.

There is, unfortunately, no good history of the NAACP in the postwar. Langston Hughes, *Fight for Freedom* (New York: 1962) does not really try to fill the need. A good general account of the open struggle by blacks for racial justice—and the often covert counterresistance of the white majority, is Charles E. Silberman, *Crisis in Black and White* (New York: 1964). Nat Hentoff, *The New Equality* (New York: 1964) takes an ultraliberal view of the civil rights movement. Harold Isaacs, *The New World of Negro Americans* (New York: 1963) attempts to describe it as being largely a response to events in the Third World. Louis E. Lomax, *The Negro Revolt* (New York: 1962) is a gifted black journalist's view of the civil rights movement as a struggle for identity. August Meier and Elliott Rudwick, eds., *Black Protest in the Sixties* is a collection of articles from the *New York Times*, concerning marches, sit-ins, and Freedom Rides. One of the most trenchant works on social structure among Negroes is E. Franklin Frazier, *Black Bourgeoisie: The Rise of a New Middle Class* (Glencoe, Ill.: 1957). Public opinion—among blacks and whites—at the time of the March on Washington is surveyed in depth by William Brink and Louis Harris, *The Negro Revolution in America* (New York: 1964).

Other useful accounts of opinion on race are in Bruno Bettelheim and Morris Janowitz, *Social Change and Prejudice* (New York: 1964) and Bradford Daniel, ed., *Black, White and Gray* (New York: 1964). The work by Daniel is particularly noteworthy for Norman Podhoretz's "My Negro Problem—and Ours" and Ronnie Dugger's "Confessions of a White Liberal." August Meier and Elliott Rudnick, *CORE* (New York: 1968) is a comprehensive history of a leading black pressure group.

E. U. Essien-Udom, *Black Nationalism* (Chicago: 1962) is an excellent account, by a Nigerian, of the Black Muslims. C. Eric Lincoln, *The Black Muslims in America* (Boston: 1961) is less perceptive. Malcolm X and Alex Haley, *The Autobiography of Malcolm X* (New York: 1965) is a work of painful honesty. Peter Goldman, *The Death and Life of Malcolm X* (New York: 1973) is an uncritical account, concerned chiefly with the short period between Malcolm's break with Elijah Muhammad and his murder.

A good introduction to the social setting in which most, if not all, of the black population lived is U.S. Department of Labor, *The Negro Family* (Washington, D.C.: 1965). It should be read in conjunction with Jessie Bernard, *Marriage and Family Among Negroes* (Englewood Cliffs, N.J.: 1966), a creative combination of history and sociology. Reynolds Farley, *Growth of the Black Population* (New York: 1970) provides needed corrections to the Census data. Eli Ginzberg, *The Negro Potential* (New York: 1956) considers the problem of wasted human resources from the point of view of an expert on manpower. The delayed but rapid urbanization of the Negro population began to attract the attention of serious writers. The early work by Horace R. Cayton and St. Clair Drake, *Black Metropolis* (New York: 1945), about Chicago's South Side, is still important. There is also Robert C. Weaver, *Negro Ghetto* (New York: 1948). Morton Grodzins, *The Metropolitan Area as a Racial Problem* (Pittsburgh: 1958) proved to be a prophetic essay. Karl and Alma Taeuber, *Negroes in Cities* (Chicago: 1965) is an imaginative study of residential segregation patterns between 1940 and 1960. Charles Abrams, *Forbidden Neighbors* (New York: 1955) is a good account of prejudice in housing. And the extraordinary events which followed when a white couple sold a house in a Louisville suburb to a young Negro couple are related in Anne Braden, *The Wall Between* (New York: 1957). Kenneth B. Clark, *Dark Ghetto* (New York: 1965) is a psychologist's depiction of Harlem as a machine for mangling personalities. Elliot Liebow, *Tally's Corner* (Boston: 1967), a study of Negro street-corner men in Washington in 1962 and 1963, is a minor classic of social anthropology.

By the end of the war it was clear that the question of racial equality would be the most critical domestic issue of the postwar, if one assumed another Depression would be avoided. Truman wasted little time in coming to grips with the issue. And the report of the President's Committee on Civil Rights, *To Secure These Rights* (Washington, D.C.: 1947), was remakably ambitious in the aims it set. The attempt to create a permanent FEPC failed; see Louis Coleridge Kesselman, *The Social Politics of the*

FEPC (Chapel Hill, N.C.: 1948) and the standard work, Louis Ruchames, *Race, Jobs and Politics* (New York: 1953). But the Executive branch was able to assure success elsewhere—in the armed forces. Richard M. Dalfiume, *Desegregation of the U.S. Armed Forces* (Columbia, Mo.: 1969) is the best account. There is also Lee Nichols, *Breakthrough on the Color Front* (New York: 1954). The civil rights bill of 1957 is the subject of an a splendid scholarly monograph: J. W. Anderson, *Eisenhower, Brownell and the Congress* (University, Ala.: 1964). The efforts of blacks to organize for conventional political activities in one city (Chicago) are described in detail in James Q. Wilson, *Negro Politics* (Glencoe, Ill.: 1960). James W. Prothro, *Negroes and the New Southern Politics* (New York: 1966) examines black voting—and prevention of blacks from voting—from every conceivable angle. Samuel Lubell, *White and Black: Test of a Nation* (New York: 1964) cautioned, however, that desegregation was not integration.

The Courts

Richard Kluger, *Simple Justice* (New York: 1976) is an exhaustive and important account of *Brown*, written largely in women's fiction prose. Clement E. Vose, *Caucasians Only* (Berkeley and Los Angeles: 1967) offers is a careful account of the 1948 racial covenant cases which vindicated the NAACP's main strategy. These cases showed beyond a doubt which way the winds of legal change were blowing, leading in time to the school desegregation cases. Albert P. Blaustein and Clarence Clyde Ferguson, Jr., *Desegregation and the Law* (New Brunswick, N.J.: 1959) considers *Brown* v. *Board of Education* from three perspectives: in terms of constitutional history, in terms of the backgrounds of the nine judges, and in terms of law as an expression of social forces. Other works concerned chiefly with the Brown decision are: Daniel M. Berman, *It Is So Ordered* (New York: 1966); Loren E. Miller, *The Petitioners* (New York: 1966); and Idus A. Newby, *Challenge to the Court*, rev. ed. (Baton Rouge, La.: 1970). Jack Greenberg, *Race Relations and American Law* (New York: 1959) is an essential survey of such matters as miscegenation statutes and racial covenants.

The Federal judges in the South who had to bear much of the burden of putting the Supreme Court's decision into effect—often against their personal beliefs—are viewed with sympathy in a valuable work: J. W. Peltason, *58 Lonely Men* (New York: 1961).

The Schools

Two of the main figures in the events at Little Rock Central High School have written interesting, if self-justifying, accounts: Daisy Bates, *The Long Shadow of Little Rock* (New York: 1962) is bitter, with reason; Virgil T. Blossom, *It Has Happened Here* (New York: 1959) is a thoughtful reappraisal by the superintendent of schools. Robert Coles, *Children in Crisis* (Boston: 1967) is a psychiatrist's sensitive exploration of the impact of the school desegregation struggles on the children involved, black and white. To anyone who cares about children or moral courage it is a deeply moving work.

The integration of the University of Georgia by Charlayne Hunter and Hamilton Holmes is described vividly by Calvin Trillin in *An Education in Georgia* (New York: 1964). James Meredith provides his own version of the integration of the University of Mississippi in *Three Years in Mississippi* (Bloomington, Ind.: 1966); a studiously unrevealing work. Meredith stood in awe of himself as someone with "Divine Responsibility." He allows nothing which might cast doubt on his divinity to intrude. Walter Lord, *The Past That Would Not Die* (New York: 1965) is a meticulous reconstruction of James Meredith and the United States v. Ole Miss.

Two useful attempts to survey the effectiveness of the Brown decision on the schools over the decade 1954–1964 are: Benjamin Muse, *Ten Years of Prelude* (New York: 1964) and Reed Sarratt, *The Ordeal of Desgregation* (New York: 1966).

Contrasting views by two prominent Southern newspaper editors are offered by Harry Ashmore, *The Negro and the Schools* (Chapel Hill, N.C.: 1954) and James J. Kilpatrick, *The Southern Case for School Segregation* (New York: 1962).

The South

There is more to the South than race. Yet in the period covered by this work the dominant issue in Southern life was the struggle concerning segregation. Thomas D. Clark, *The Emerging South*, 2nd ed., (New York: 1968) is the most satisfactory general account of the postwar South. A work which captures Southern sentiments in the mid-1950s with remarkable skill is Wilma Dykeman and James Stokely, *Neither Black Nor White* (New York: 1957). Two disenchanted professors who described affairs in the states they knew best are Howard H. Quint, *Profile in Black and White: A Frank Portrait of South Carolina* (Washington, D. C.: 1958) and James Silver, *Mississippi: The Closed Society* (New York: 1964). Events in Virginia are described in Ernest Q. Campbell et al., *When a City Closes Its Schools* (Chapel Hill, N.C.: 1960) and Benjamin Muse, *Virginia's Massive Resistance* (Bloomington, Ind.: 1961). Two noted liberal newspaper editors, Southern-born both, who viewed the region with sadness and affection and insight are Harry S. Ashmore, *An Epitaph for Dixie* (New York: 1958) and Ralph McGill, *The South and the Southerner* (Boston: 1963). Robert Penn Warren, *Segregation: The Inner Conflict of the South* (New York: 1956) surveys the guilty conscience. There are memorable portraits of the ordinary people, black and white, who found themselves caught up in the struggle in Murray Kempton, *America Comes of Middle Age* (Boston: 1963) and Harry Golden, *Mr. Kennedy and the Negroes* (Cleveland: 1964). Notable firsthand accounts by white participants are

James Peck, *Freedom Ride* (New York: 1962) and Merrill Proudfoot, *Diary of a Sit-In* (Chapel Hill, N.C.: 1962). Two white men who passed for black were Ray Sprigle, *In the Land of Jim Crow* (Garden City, N.Y.: 1949) and John Howard Griffin, *Black Like Me* (Boston: 1961), a vivid and moving account. Frank Smith, *Congressman from Mississippi* (New York: 1964) describes an elected white politician's painful struggles with his conscience. No such anxieties beset Carleton Putnam, *Race and Reason* (Washington, D.C.: 1961), who defended the South on the grounds that blacks were by nature inferior. William D. Workman, *The Case for the South* (New York: 1960) assumes that everyone already agrees with that. The masterpiece of this genre, however, is Tom P. Brady, *Black Monday* (Winona, Miss.: 1955).

The *New York Times*'s reporting on the civil rights struggles from 1954 to 1964 provides the basis for a very useful guide to these turbulent events: Anthony Lewis, *Portrait of a Decade* (New York: 1964).

Politics in the South manages to be both simpler and more Byzantine than politics anywhere else. V. O. Key, Jr., *Southern Politics in State and Nation* (New York: 1949) remains the standard introduction. How the race issue could destroy a good man's career is the unstated theme of Brooks Hays, *A Southern Moderate Speaks* (Chapel Hill, N.C.: 1959). A. J. Liebling, *The Ear of Louisiana* (New York: 1961) is witty and telling. Marshall Frady, *Wallace* (New York: 1969) is an absorbing account of politics in Alabama since the war. Robert Sherrill, *Gothic Politics in the Deep South* (New York: 1968) is filled with telling anecdotes and sharply etched portraits.

There is an excellent survey of the South's embittered response to the Supreme Court's desegregation decision: Numan V. Bartley, *The Rise of Massive Resistance* (Baton Rouge, La.: 1969). For the early days of the Citizens' Councils and especially its leaders and organizers, John Bartlow Martin, *The Deep South Says "Never"* (New York: 1957) is essential. Other important accounts are: Hodding Carter III, *The South Strikes Back* (Garden City, N.Y.: 1959); James Grahm Cook, *The Segregationists* (New York: 1962); Neil R. McMillen, *The Citizens' Council: Organized Resistance to the Second Reconstruction 1954–1964* (Urbana, Ill.: 1971); and Dan Wakefield, *Revolt in the South* (New York: 1960).

The Citizens' Councils represented "respectable" protest. The Klan represented the dregs. David M. Chalmers, *Hooded Americanism* (Princeton, N.J.: 1965) is a history of the Klan. But its knowledge of the postwar KKK is severely limited. Stetson Kennedy, *I Rode With the KKK* (London: 1954) is the account of a brave and resourceful man who investigated the postwar Klan revival. Allowance must be made for the pulp-fiction prose.

Howard Zinn, *SNCC: The New Abolitionists* (Boston: 1964) is starry-eyed, yet provides good firsthand descriptions of youthful protest in the face of violence.

Other Minorities

Leo Grebler et al., *The Mexican-American People* (New York: 1970) is the most comprehensive and most systematic study of Mexican-Americans in the postwar era. Its merits are obscured, however, by the lumpy sociologese of its prose. Matt S. Meier and Feliciano Rivera, *The Chicanos* (New York: 1972) is disorganized and badly written. Stan Steiner, *La Raza* (New York: 1970) is sentimental. Carey McWilliams, *North from Mexico* (New York: 1949) sets a very high standard. Julian Samora, ed., *La Raza: Forgotten Americans* (South Bend, Ind.: 1966) is a useful collection of short studies. Celia Heller, *Mexican-American Youth* (New York: 1966) makes melancholy reading. Ernesto Galarzo, *Merchants of Labor* (Santa Barbara, Calif.: 1964) is the most impressive study made of the bracero program, concentrating on its implementation in California. William Madsen, *The Mexican-Americans of South Texas* (New York: 1964) is a scholarly and sympathetic study. Joan W. Moore and Alfredo Cuellar, *Mexican-Americans* (Englewood Cliffs, N.J.: 1970) is useful. (For other entries concerning Mexican-American migrant farmworkers, see Social Welfare.)

C. Wright Mills et al., *The Puerto Rican Journey* (New York: 1950) is based on interviews with 1,100 Puerto Rican families in New York in 1948. There are three remarkably good studies from a decade later: Elena Padilla, *Up From Puerto Rico* (New York: 1958); Christopher Rand, *Puerto Ricans* (New York: 1958); and Dan Wakefield, *Island in the City* (Boston: 1959). Frederic Wertham, *Circle of Guilt* (New York: 1956) concerns Puerto Rican street gangs, the police, and the press.

The most authoritative general survey of the postwar condition of the Indians is William A. Brophie and Sophie D. Aberle, *The Indian: America's Unfinished Business* (Oklahoma City: 1966). Stan Steiner, *The New Indians* (New York: 1968)) wisely allows his subjects to explain themselves at length. Edmund Wilson, *Apologies to the Iroquois*—and *The Mohawks in High Steel* by Joseph Mitchell [New York: 1960]—is a splendid book concerning the resurgence of nationalism among the Iroquois in the 1950s.

Subcultures

The only full-length study of the Beats, Bruce Cook, *The Beat Generation* (New York: 1971) is superficial. Ann Charters, *Kerouac* (San Francisco: 1973) is an uncritical but important work. Jane Kramer, *Allen Ginsberg in America* (New York: 1969) offers a winning portrait of the most endearing of the Beats. John Clellon Holmes, *Go* (New York: 1953) is a novel which offers a labored autobiographical account of Beat life in New York around 1951. The best account of daily life among the Beat and near Beat, however, is Lawrence Lipton, *The Holy Barbarians* (New York: 1959), describing the community in Venice West. Ned Polsky, *Hustlers, Beats and Others* (Chicago: 1967) offers a short, striking account of Greenwich Village in 1960. There are some delightful vignettes in Jane Kramer, *Off Washington Square* (New York: 1969). Martin Duberman, *Black Mountain* (New York: 1972) is a strange, experimental book about a strange, experimental community. Francis J. Rigney and L. Douglas Smith, *The Real Bohemia* (New York: 1961) is a study of North Beach Beats. There is a very useful collection of Beat writings: Thomas Parkinson, ed., *A Casebook on the Beat* (New York: 1961). Elias Wilentz, *Beat Scene* (New York: 1960) contains some striking photographs.

For Greenwich Village literary hipsterism, see Seymour Krim, *Views of a Near-Sighted Cannoneer* (New York: 1961) and Norman Mailer, *Advertisements for Myself* (New York: 1959). For show business hipsterism, see Lenny Bruce, *How to Talk Dirty and Influence People* (Chicago: 1972) and Albert Goldman with Lawrence Schiller, *Ladies and Gentlemen, Lenny Bruce!!* (New York: 1974). William Lee (pseudonym of William Burroughs), *Junkie* (New York: 1953) is a fictionalized autobiographical account of dope and hipsterism.

Crime

U.S. Senate Special Committee to Investigate Organized Crime in Interstate Commerce, 81st Congress, 2nd Session and 82nd Congress, 1st Session *Hearings* and *Report* (Washington, D.C.: 1950–1951) is important. Its history is set out in Estes Kefauver, *Crime in America* (Garden City, N.Y.: 1951). Kefauver exaggerated the Mafia. Ramsey Clark, *Crime in America* (New York: 1970), on the other hand, is skeptical of the larger claims made about criminals' organizations and criminals' wealth. There is a valuable essay on crime and the myth of crime "waves" in Daniel Bell, *The End of Ideology* (Glencoe, Ill.: 1960). Bell also has some telling comments to make concerning labor racketeering. Donald R. Cressey, *Theft of the Nation* (New York: 1969) insists that there is an organization and describes its historical, social, and political setting. Frederick Sondern, Jr., *Brotherhood of Evil* (New York: 1959) is the most thorough account available of the 1957 meeting in Apalachin, N.Y. His principal sources were narcotics agents, and Sondern blames the Mafia squarely for the postwar Harlem heroin "plague." There is a remarkable account of life in a Mafia family in the postwar: Gay Talese, *Honor Thy Father* (Cleveland: 1972). Talese romanticizes the gangsters by accepting them entirely on their own terms, which was presumably the tacitly understood price of cooperation. John Bartlow Martin, *My Life in Crime* (New York:

1952) appears absolutely genuine. "Joey," with Dave Fisher, *Killer: The Autobiography of "Joey," a Professional Killer* (Chicago: 1973) contains nothing concerning criminals' methods or identifiable events that is not likely to be known to crime reporters or the NYPD. For that reason much of it can be accepted as true, and the nonmoral tone is convincing. Peter Maas, *The Valachi Papers* (New York 1969) is undeniably authentic. So is Vincent Teresa with Thomas C. Renner, *My Life in the Mafia* (New York: 1973), which is much more informative. Ed Reid and Ovid Demaris, *The Green Felt Jungle* (New York: 1963) is a knowledgeable account of the town the crooks built, Las Vegas.

John Bartlow Martin, *Break Down the Walls* (New York: 1954) is a study of the rioting which swept through the prisons in the early 1950s and especially at Jackson Prison in Michigan. Gresham M. Sykes, *The Society of Captives* (Princeton, N.J.: 1958) concerns the maximum security prison at Trenton, New Jersey. Kenyon J. Scudder, *Prisoners Are People* (Garden City, N.Y.: 1952) is an account of the pioneering California Institute for Men at Chino by its first superintendent. The most controversial prisoner of the period wrote two books: Caryl Chessman, *Cell 2455: Death Row* (Englewood Cliffs, N.J.; 1954) and *Trial by Ordeal* (Englewood Cliffs, N.J.: 1955).

White-collar crime is committed by people who don't consider themselves *real* criminals. But the money they take from other people is real enough. I enjoyed Donald R. Cressey, *Other People's Money* (Glencoe, Ill.: 1953), a study of embezzlers. Norman Jaspan with Hillel Black, *The Thief in the White Collar* (Philadelphia: 1960) is by an authority on the subject, but written in a gee-whiz style. John Herling, *The Great Price Conspiracy* (Washington, D.C.: 1962) is a thorough account of the electrical industry's conspiracy to bilk its customers. John G. Fuller, *The Gentlemen Conspirators* (New York: 1962) is less substantial but contains sympathetic portraits of the "Unlucky Seven" who went to jail. Robert F. Kennedy, *The Enemy Within* (New York: 1960) is a firsthand account of the investigation of labor racketeering. It is a valuable book, and one written with wit and charm. Clark Mollenhoff, *Tentacles of Power* (Cleveland: 1965), on the other hand, gracelessly (and often) intrudes on his narrative to cast himself as the unsung hero of "the Great Investigation" of the Teamsters.

The White House Conference on Narcotics and Drug Abuse, *Proceedings and Appendix to Proceedings* (Washington, D.C.: 1963) confronts the unsatisfactory state of knowledge about the most repugnant criminal enterprise of the postwar. Nevertheless it contains much fascinating and authentic detail about the narcotics trade. Like polio, its principal source of victims was among the young. Isidor Chein et al., *Narcotics, Delinquents and Social Policy* (New York: 1964) is an important study of addiction among male adolescents in Manhattan, Brooklyn, and the Bronx. It casts doubt on the notion that addiction is a major cause of crime. There is a compelling view of the heroin plague as it came to Harlem in the late 1940s in Claude Brown, *Manchild in the Promised Land* (New York:

1965), a work which also offers a firsthand account of life in a fighting gang.

Albert K. Cohen, *Delinquent Boys: The Culture of the Gang* (Glencoe, Ill.: 1955) is a study which provokes thought, based on close observation of gangs in Chicago. Frederic Wertham, *Seduction of the Innocent* (New York: 1954) blamed the relentless increase in juvenile delinquency after the late 1930s on comic books. Another work by Wertham, *Circle of Guilt* (New York: 1956), describes how a harmless Puerto Rican stickball team became a fighting gang. Ira Henry Freeman, *Out of the Burning* (New York: 1960) is the story of a Harlem gang leader. Bernard Fine, *1,000,000 Delinquents* (Cleveland: 1955) is useful. Albert Deutsch, *Our Rejected Children* (Boston: 1950) examines the state training schools for delinquents; the usual result was to train them for criminal careers. The most ambitious study of juvenile delinquency during the period was Sheldon and Eleanor Glueck, *Unraveling Juvenile Delinquency* (Cambridge, Mass.: 1950), which matched 500 juvenile delinquents with a control group of 500 nondelinquents. It offers many blinding glimpses of the obvious. David Wilkerson, *The Cross and the Switchblade* (New York: 1963) is an interesting account of one man's attempts to work with delinquents. Harrison Salisbury, *The Shook-Up Generation* (New York: 1958) is an investigation of delinquency by one of the country's best reporters. Irving Sperlberg, *Racketville, Slumtown, Haulburg* (New York: 1964) attempts to describe different delinquent subcultures. Richard A. Cloward and Lloyd E. Ohlin, *Delinquency and Opportunity* (Glencoe, Ill.: 1960) relates delinquency to social class.

Youth

Benjamin Spock, *The Pocket Book of Baby and Child Care* (New York: 1946) and Arnold Gesell and Francis L. Ilg, *The Child from Five to Ten* (New York: 1946) helped mold the middle-class young of an entire generation. Erik Erickson, *Childhood and Society* (New York: 1952) contains some trenchant comments on American childhood at midcentury. Eli Ginzberg, ed., *The Nation's Children*, 3 vols. (New York: 1960) contains much important material, but not always used to its best advantage. Of interest is Margaret Mead and Martha Wolfenstein, eds., *Childhood and Contemporary Cultures* (Chicago: 1955), a work which compares American ways of child rearing with those practiced in other cultures.

H. H. Remmers and D. H. Radler, *The American Teenager* (Indianapolis: 1957) is a comprehensive study of adolescent opinion based on thousands of interviews and 15,000 attitude tests. Adolescents had the sympathy of Edgar Z. Friedenberg, *The Vanishing Adolescent*, 2nd ed. (Boston: 1964) and Paul Goodman, *Growing Up Absurd* (New York: 1960). Remarkably, both works were popular with the young, at least, with college students. Kenneth Keniston, *The Uncommitted* (New York: 1965) is, even after allowing for the slipperiness of "alienation," a brilliant work.

Education

Grade Schools and High Schools

Two helpful surveys, concerned chiefly with secondary education, are R. Freeman Butts and Laurence A. Kromin, *A History of Education in American Culture* (New York: 1953) and I. L. Kandel, *American Education in the 20th Century* (Cambridge, Mass.: 1957). The Kandel work is particularly good.

Benjamin Fine, *Our Children Are Cheated* (New York: 1947) is a hand-wringing report on secondary and elementary schools shortly after the end of the war. The best work on all aspects of secondary education in the postwar is Martin Mayer, *The Schools* (New York: 1961), which makes some telling comparisons with education in Europe. Roman Catholic schools are the subject of a sociological account, Joseph H. Fichter, *Parochial School* (South Bend, Ind.: 1959). But Professor Fichter's faith in Catholic education proves too strong for him to take a detached view. The impact of postwar experimental psychology on secondary education is covered in Ronald Gross and Judith Murphy, eds. *The Revolution in the Schools* (New York: 1964). Other works of value are James B. Conant, *Education in a Divided World* (Cambridge, Mass.: 1948); Paul Woodring, *A Fourth of a Nation* (New York: 1957), and James B. Conant, *The American High School Today* (New York: 1959).

The economic constraints on the schools are examined in Seymour E. Harris, *More Resources for Education* (New York: 1960), and the economic return on high school diplomas and college degrees is covered in a lucid, imaginative short book by Theodore W. Schultz, *The Economic Value of Education* (New York: 1963).

But the principal general concern with education in the period was not economic. It was, as it deserved to be, a concern with quality. Inevitably—and unhappily—this concern became entangled with, and occasionally indistinguishable from, the Cold War. The shortcomings of the high schools came in for serious and perceptive criticism from the former president of Harvard, James B. Conant, *The American High School Today* (New York: 1959) and *Slums and Suburbs* (New York: 1961). Reading methods were attacked in an unlikely best-seller, Rudolf C. Flesch, *Why Johnny Can't Read* (New York: 1955). Flesch in turn was attacked by two "teachers of teachers," Sam Duker and Thomas P. Nally, *The Truth About Your Child's Reading* (New York: 1956). Before Sputnik much of the criticism of education focused on life adjustment courses and the anti-intellectual attitudes of life adjustment theorists. Harl R. Douglass, *Secondary Education for Life Adjustment of American Youth* (New York: 1952), for example, has to be read to be believed. Some of the more ludicrous practical consequences of this approach are examined in Arthur E. Bestor, *Educational Wastelands* (Urbana, Ill.: 1953), a work which stirred deep passions. Less effective was Mortimer Smith, *The Diminished Mind* (Chicago: 1954). Sputnik added a new dimension: the schools were held responsible for national setbacks in the Cold War. Representative works on this unedifying theme were John Francis Latimer, *What's Happened to Our High Schools* (Washington, D.C.: 1958) and E. Merrill Root, *Brainwashing in the High Schools* (New York, 1958). A more considered, yet nonetheless alarmed, treatment is Hyman Rickover, *Education and Freedom* (New York: 1959). Robert W. Iverson, *The Communists and the Schools* (New York: 1959) examined the question of subversion directly. He found very little, and that little inept.

There were were serious deficiencies in teacher education, a problem which had less to do with methods than with the fact that teaching failed to attract a proper share of the brightest and most enthusiastic college graduates. H. S. Dyer et al., *Problems in Mathematical Education* (Princeton, N.J.: 1956) makes clear the innumeracy of many teachers. David G. Ryans, *Characteristics of Teachers* (Washington, D.C.: 1960) draws together the results of nearly 100 separate studies, almost all disquieting.

Colleges and Universities.

Even before the war ended, a committee of Harvard professors had considered the shape of postwar education and issued an influential report (more influential in colleges than in high schools), *General Education in a Free Society* (Cambridge, Mass.: 1945). Shortly after the war came the report of the President's Commission on Higher Education, *Higher Education for American Democracy*, 6 vols. (Washington, D.C.: 1947), which provides a good view of the state of the colleges and universities at that time. It set a variety of ambitious goals to make good the wartime losses. The arguments it provoked can be found in Gail Kennedy, ed., *Education for Democracy* (New York: 1952). Seymour E. Harris, *The Market for College Graduates* (Cambridge, Mass.: 1949) doubted that there would be enough jobs for the number of college graduates the President's commission called for. Ernest Havemann and Patricia Salter West, *They Went to College* (New York: 1952) offers a useful profile of the Class of '47. In similar vein is James A. Davis, *Undergraduate Career Decisions* (Chicago: 1965), which provides a portrait of the Class of '61 based on a survey of 57,000 students.

There are some valuable articles on higher education in the first decade after the war in Mary Irwin, ed., *American Universities and Colleges* (Washington, D.C.: 1956). And the astringent, often unfashionable, sensible views of one of the higher education's most serious critics appear in Robert M. Hutchins, *The University of Utopia* (Chicago: 1953), *The Conflict of Education in a Democratic Society* (New York: 1953), and *Some Observations on American Education* (Cambridge, England: 1956). Two other university presidents to express their concern were A. Whitney Griswold, *Liberal Education and the Democratic Ideal* (New Haven,

Conn.: 1959) and Clark Kerr, *The Uses of the University* (Cambridge, Mass.: 1963). Teachers' colleges were found wanting in James B. Conant, *The Education of American Teachers* (New York: 1963). The teachers' side is put forward in Myron Lieberman, *Education as a Profession* (Englewood Cliffs, N.J.: 1956). Two bitterly funny books about academic life are Jacques Barzun, *Teacher in America* (Boston: 1945) and *The House of Intellect* (New York: 1959). David Riesman, *Constraint and Variety in American Education* (Lincoln, Neb.: 1956) saw higher learning becoming bureaucratic and institutionalized.

The problem of assuring that the brightest, rather than the privileged, went on to college is the subject of two important studies: W. Lloyd Warner et al., *Who Shall Be Educated?* and, especially, Dael Wolfle, *America's Resources of Specialized Talent* (New York: 1954). Also of value are Byron S. Hollinshead, *Who Should Go to College?* (New York: 1952) and Charles C. Cole, Jr., *Encouraging Scientific Talent* (New York: 1956).

The strongest single outside influence on higher education after the war was the Federal government. Its role is examined in four useful studies: Charles V. Kidd, *American Universities and Federal Research* (Cambridge, Mass.: 1959); J. Kenneth Little, *A Survey of Federal Programs in Higher Education* (Washington, D.C.: 1962); National Academy of Science, Committee on Science and Public Policy, *Federal Support of Basic Research in Institutions of Higher Learning* (Washington, D.C.: 1964); and Harold Orlans, *The Effect of Federal Programs on Higher Education* (Washington, D.C. 1962).

The impact of the Cold War on the colleges and universities is covered in two very different works: Paul Lazarsfeld and Wagner Thielens, Jr., *The Academic Mind: Social Scientists in a Time of Crisis* (Glencoe, Ill.: 1958) and Albert Parry, *America Learns Russian* (Syracuse, N.Y.: 1967). A young Roman Catholic who inherited a multimillion-dollar fortune, William F. Buckley, Jr., argued that Yale was in the grip of left-wing teachers in *God and Man at Yale* (Chicago: 1951). It is a curious work, combining anguish over the declining value of money with an impassioned plea for an end to academic freedom. Throughout the 1950s it remained a popular book among young American conservatives. The hiring and (rarely) the firing of academics are explored by Theodore Caplow and Reece J. McGee, *The Academic Marketplace* (New York: 1958), a work which casts light on a number of intellectual byways.

Science and Technology

General

Vannevar Bush, *Science: The Endless Frontier* (Washington D.C.: 1945) is a famous report describing the state of science in America at the end of the war and setting forth recommendations on what should be done in the postwar era. Truman commissioned a report of his own. The President's Scientific Research Board, *Science and Public Policy*, 5 vols. (Washington D.C.: 1947) called for a doubling of American scientific activity within a decade. Such a goal assumed a major role for the government in the growth of science, a role virtually as pervasive as that achieved in wartime. Don K. Price, *Government and Science* (New York: 1954) and *The Scientific Estate* (Cambridge, Mass.: 1965) dispassionately examine the results. Bernard Barber, *Science and the Social Order* (Glencoe, Ill.: 1952) describes the formal and informal organization of science. Richard J. Barber, *The Politics of Research* (Washington D.C.: 1966) deals with an important subject but is disappointing. Paul Dickson, *Think Tanks* (New York: 1972) is a lively short account of a remarkable postwar phenomenon. Also of interest is the somewhat superficial Leonard Silk, *The Research Revolution* (New York: 1960). Gerard Piel, *Science in the Cause of Man* (New York: 1961) is a collection of essays on postwar science, most of them pessimistic, by the publisher of *Scientific American*.

There is a tendency to regard scientists as exotics. R. H. Knapp and H. B. Goodrich, *Origins of Americans Scientists* (Chicago: 1952) and Anne Roe, *The Making of a Scientist* (New York: 1953) attempt to explain where they usually come from and the kind of people they are likely to be. Regarding those who came from abroad, Donald Fleming and Bernard Bailyn, eds., *The Intellectual Migration: Europe and America 1930–1960* (Cambridge, Mass.: 1969) is an important work. The problems involved in making sure that precious scientific talent was not frittered away are examined by Charles C. Cole, Jr., *Encouraging Scientific Talent* (New York: 1956).

The most portentous scientific breakthrough of the period occurred in the least glamorous field: biology. There is a good general survey, Ruth Moore, *The Science of Life* (New York: 1961). There is also James D. Watson *The Double Helix* (New York: 1968), an incomparable work describing what some scientific research is really like, by one of the discoverers of DNA.

Much of the research in biology was supported by the large foundations; Rockefeller money, for example, financed the laboratory at Cambridge, England, where DNA was first unraveled and the laboratory in New York where it was first synthesized. There is a lively and hostile work, Dwight Macdonald, *The Ford Foundation* (New York: 1956), which goes far beyond Ford to attack foundations in general. Warren Weaver, *U.S. Philanthropic Foundations* (New York: 1967) is a valuable history, description, and, in a sense, defense of the foundations. Thomas Reeve, *Freedom and the Foundation* (New York: 1969) is an excellent scholarly account of the turbulent history of the Ford Foundation in the 1950s.

David Michael Joseph, *The UFO Controversy in America* (Bloomington, Ind.: 1975) is an enthralling account of pseudoscience and popular fantasy.

Learning to Live with the Bomb

Norman Cousins, *Modern Man Is Obsolete* (New York: 1946) is a famous *Saturday Review* editorial expanded to book length. But the work which really pricked the nation's conscience and marked the beginning of serious doubts about the future by people other than intellectuals was John Hersey, *Hiroshima* (New York: 1946), a work of great force.

The best account of the scientists' attempts to assure civilian control over atomic energy projects is Alice Kimball Smith, *A Peril and a Hope* (Chicago: 1965). There is also Donald A. Strickland, *Scientists in Politics* (Purdue, Ind.: 1968), and the background to the scientists' fears is traced in Robert Jungk, *Brighter Than a Thousand Suns* (New York: 1958), a unique and valuable work. James R. Newman and Byron S. Miller, *The Control of Atomic Energy* (New York: 1948) is an insider's account of the Atomic Energy Act.

The early attempts to secure international control over atomic energy in retrospect seem doomed to failure. Bernard Baruch, *The Public Years* (New York: 1960) is a complacent memoir. Margaret Coit, *Mr. Baruch* (Boston: 1958) is not much better. David E. Lilienthal, *The Journals of David E. Lilienthal*, Vol. 2, *The Atomic Energy Years* (New York: 1964) is exceptionally good. Lewis L. Strauss, *Men and Decisions* (Garden City, N.Y.: 1962) is self-congratulatory and guarded. Joseph I. Lieberman, *The Scorpion and the Tarantula* (Boston: 1970) is a reliable general account of the various attempts to reach an international agreement before the first Russian A-bomb explosion.

Robert Gilpin, *American Scientists and Nuclear Weapons Policy* (Princeton, N.J.: 1962) is a skillful and dispassionate study of the efforts made by scientists to help ensure that the search for an agreement was not abandoned. On the other hand, Henry Kissinger, *Nuclear Weapons and Foreign Policy* (New York: 1957) is an extraordinary attempt to create a rationale for the use of tactical nuclear weapons without triggering a global disaster. But the masterwork of "crackpot realism" is undoubtedly Herman Kahn, *On Thermonuclear War* (Princeton, N.J.: 1960). The fault, however, is less Kahn's than the inherent black humor of nuclear deterrence.

There are straightforward, modest accounts by the two men who attempted to protest atomic weapons testing on the high seas: Arnold Bigelow, *The Voyage of the Golden Rule* (Garden City, N.Y.: 1959) and Earle Reynolds, *The Forbidden Voyage* (New York: 1961). There is an important general history of pacifism between Pearl Harbor and the Test Ban Treaty: Lawrence S. Wittner, *Rebels Against War* (New York: 1969).

Virtually everything involving the Bomb had an element of the bizarre. Claude Eatherly and Gunther Anders, *Burning Conscience* (New York: 1962) needs to be read in conjunction with William Bradford Huie, *The Hiroshima Pilot* (New York: 1964). William Laurence, *Men and Atoms* (New York: 1959) is by the *New York Times* science editor. Its thesis is that the hydrogen bomb is a boon to humanity, and continued testing the necessary perfection of that boon. Thomas E. Dufwa, *How to Survive in an Atomic Attack* (New York: 1963) is a compendium of helpful hints. U.S. Office of Civil and Defense Mobilization, *The Family Fallout Shelter* (Washington, D.C.: 1959) and *Fallout Protection* (Washington, D.C.: 1961) are also full of advice.

Toward the Knowledge Society

A useful place to begin is with the essays in Eleanor B. Sheldon and Wilbert E. Moore, eds., *Indicators of Social Change* (New York: 1968). Fritz Machlup, *The Production and Distribution of Knowledge in the United States* (Princeton, N.J.: 1962) is imaginative but too ambitious for the material available. The same limitation holds for another bold effort, David A. McLelland, *The Achieving Society* (Princeton, N.J.: 1961). National Bureau of Economic Research, *The Rate and Direction of Inventive Activity* (Princeton, N.J.: 1962) is important. There are several useful essays in Eli Ginzberg, ed., *Technology and Social Change* (New York: 1964).

Norbert Wiener, *Cybernetics: or Control and Communication in the Animal and the Machine*, 2nd ed. (Cambridge, Mass.: 1961) is one of the most important books of the postwar. His *Human Use of Human Beings: Cybernetics and Society* (Boston: 1959) is, however, more accessible. There is a clear, well-written, sensible introduction to automation: Editors of *Scientific American, Automatic Control* (New York: 1955). It draws on automation in its early days for its examples. There are two works which stood against the most common responses to automation (alarm or euphoria): Charles Silberman, *The Myths of Automation* (New York: 1966), a work of robust common sense, and Mortimer Taube, *Computers and Common Sense: The Myth of Thinking Machines* (New York: 1961). Ben B. Seligman, *Most Notorious Victory* (New York: 1966) and G. G. Somers et al., *Adjusting to Technological Change* (New York: 1963) are useful symposia based on the first generation of automation. U.S. Senate Subcommittee of the Select Committee on Small Business, 88th Congress, 1st Session, *Hearings on the Role and Effect of Technology in the Nation's Economy* (Washington, D.C.: 1963) offers a general view at the end of the period.

Religion

Herbert Wallace Schneider, *Religion in 20th Century America*, rev. ed. (Cambridge, Mass.: 1964) and J. Paul Williams, *What Americans Believe and How They Worship*, rev. ed. (New York: 1962) are reliable and thorough. A. Roy Eckhardt, *The Surge of Piety in America* (New York: 1958) takes an ironic look at the postwar revival not so much of religion as interest in religion. Will Herberg, *Protestant, Catholic, Jew*, rev. ed. (Garden

City, N.Y.: 1960) considered this revival a part of the struggle by ethnic groups to retain a sense of their identity. Martin E. Marty, *The New Shape of American Religion* (New York: 1959) and Leo Pfeffer, *Creeds in Competition* (New York: 1958) are of some interest. The commercialization of religion is examined in James H. Barnett, *The American Christmas* (New York: 1954), a work which never lives up to its promise. David E. Harrell, Jr., *All Things Are Possible* (Bloomington, Ind: 1975) is a reliable account of the postwar Pentecostal revival.

Paul Blanshard, *American Freedom and Catholic Power* (Boston: 1949) overstates its case. Not even the Catholic Church is run strictly by the book. The replies to Blanshard were angry and confused; see James M. O'Neill, *Catholicism and American Freedom* (New York: 1952) for a notable example. There is a valuable account of conversion to Catholicism: Thomas Merton, *The Seven Storey Mountain* (New York: 1948). Kenneth K. Bailey, *Southern White Protestantism in the 20th Century* (New York: 1964) is a useful guide to a bewildering assortment of creeds. Nathan Glazer, *American Judaism*, rev. ed. (Chicago: 1972) is a short and perceptive history whose later chapters cover the postwar. Judith R. Kramer and Seymour Leventman, *Children of the Gilded Ghetto* (New Haven, Conn.: 1961) is an important study of a Jewish community in the Midwest. Marshall Sklare and Joseph Greenblum, *Jewish Identity on the Suburban Frontier* (New York: 1967) is an astute study of a subject which inspired dozens of self-indulgent postwar novels.

Religion was no more impervious to the currents of Cold War tension than any other important aspect of American life. There is a fine account: Ralph Lord Roy, *Communism and the Churches* (New York: 1960). William E. Miller et al., *Religion and the Free Society* (Santa Barbara, Calif.: 1958) has some interesting suggestions to offer. Peter L. Berger, *The Noise of Solemn Assemblies* (Garden City, N.Y.: 1961) offers a sociological critique of postwar religious bodies.

Joshua L. Liebman, *Peace of Mind* (New York: 1946) and Norman Vincent Peale, *The Power of Positive Thinking* (Englewood Cliffs, N.J.: 1952) need to be read, or at least sampled, to recapture the religious tone and outlook of the period. Liebman offered nondenominational religion braced with Freudian psychology. Peale probed accurately the anxieties of those millions described in *The Lonely Crowd* and *The Organization Man* and fashioned a set of quasi-religious beliefs to match.

Public Opinion

The massive collection of polls made by Hadley Cantril, *Public Opinion 1935–1946* (Princeton, N.J.: 1951) is useful for the state of public opinion at the end of the war and during the first postwar year. Laurence S. Cottrell, Jr., and Sylvia Eberhard, *American Opinion on World Affairs* (Princeton, N.J.: 1948) charts rising Cold War tempers. Samuel A. Stouffer,, *Communism, Conformity and Civil Liberties* (Garden City, N.Y.: 1955) is important. George H. Gallup, *The Gallup Polls 1935–1971*, 3 vols. (New York: 1972) is invaluable and splendidly organized. William Brink and Louis Harris, *The Negro Revolution in America* (New York: 1964) is an exhaustive survey of opinion on race among Negroes and whites in 1963. *Public Opinion Quarterly* contains a variety of polls on topics great and small. *POQ* is valuable also for its explanations of how polls are designed, what they do, how reliable they are, and what they are used for.

Two excellent biographies of two very different men are: Alexander Kendrick, *Prime Time: The Life of Edward R. Murrow* (New York: 1969) and W. A. Swanberg, *Luce and His Empire* (New York: 1972).

The latter chapters of Edwin Emery, *The Press and America*, 3rd ed. (Englewood Cliffs, N.J.: 1972) provide a thoughtful interpretative account of the press in the postwar.

Popular Culture

By the end of the period the principal popular diversion was television. There is an excellent three-volume history of broadcasting: Erik Barnouw, *The Tower of Babel*. Volume 2, *The Golden Web 1933–1953* (New York: 1966) and Volume 3, *The Image Empire, from 1953* (New York: 1970) are well written and comprehensive. There is a gossipy, yet serious account of the rise of television as seen from within: Fred W. Friendly, *Due to Circumstances Beyond Our Control* (New York: 1967). It is a story of conscience versus commerce. Lawrence Lessing, *Man of High Fidelity* (Philadelphia: 1956) is a biography of Edwin Armstrong, a man of great gifts utterly destroyed in the scramble by others to profit from his inventions. Gilbert Seldes, *The Great Audience* (New York: 1950) is a thoughtful examination of television, showing that it was failing to live up to its promise almost from the first moment of its commercial and popular success. In a later work, *The Public Arts* (New York: 1956), Seldes took another look at television and compared it with radio and the movies. Gary B. Steiner, *The People Look at Television* (New York: 1963) is the best survey undertaken of audience attitudes toward television during the period. An early, limited study is Raymond F. Stewart, *The Social Impact of Television on Atlanta Households* (Atlanta, Ga.: 1952). Wilbur Schramm et al., *The People Look at Educational Television* (Palo Alto, Calif.: 1963) is important. Ira O. Glick and Sidney J. Levy, *Living with Television* (Chicago: 1962) surveys most of the best studies and includes a major study of their own. Leo Bogart, *The Age of Television*, 2nd ed., rev. (New York: 1958) describes the growth of television in the first postwar decade. William Schramm et al., *Television in the Lives of Our Children* (Palo Alto, Calif.: 1961) is an impressive study of one of the most important aspects of television as a force in popular culture. Michael Straight, *Trial by Television* (Boston: 1954) is an important early work on television's impact on politics, concentrating on the Army-McCarthy Hearings. Vincent Terrace, *The Complete Encyclopedia of Television Programs 1947–1976* (Cranbury, N.J.: 1976) is reliable and well illustrated. Of the many popular works concerning television in the 1940s and 1950s I choose one as being representative: Stan Opotowsky, *TV: The Big Picture* (New York: 1961).

On radio during its painful transition the witty and perceptive criticism of John Crosby, *Out of the Blue* (New York: 1952) can hardly be faulted. The surveys of televison audiences—especially their likes and dislikes—grew out of the earlier surveys of radio audiences. Paul Lazarsfeld, *The People Look at Radio* (Chapel Hill, N.C.: 1946); Lazarsfeld and Patricia Kendall, *Radio Listening in America* (Englewood Cliffs, N.J.: 1949); and Lazarsfeld and Frank N. Stanton, eds., *Communications Research 1948–1949* (New York: 1949) are the essential works. An amusing inside account of radio at the end of its golden age is Fred Allen, *Treadmill to Oblivion* (Boston: 1952).

There are hundreds of books on Hollywood and the movies. Any attempt at selection soon becomes arbitrary. The work which has had the widest influence, however, is Arthur Knight, *The Liveliest Art* (New York: 1957). For a broader historical effort see Benjamin Hampton, *History of the American Film Industry* (New York: 1970). Charles Higham and Joel Greenberg, *Hollywood in the Forties* (New York: 1968) is an excellent short history of Hollywood in its heyday which misses nothing of importance. There are two excellent works on the biggest star of the 1950s, from two very different perspectives: Fred L. Guiles, *Norma Jean* (New York: 1969) and W. J. Weatherby, *Conversations with Marilyn* (London: 1975). There is a long, detailed account of the making of a single film—*The Red Badge of Courage*—in Lillian Ross, *Reporting* (New York: 1964), a work which offers some brilliant short accounts of other aspects of popular culture, from a Junior League Ball to the Miss America pageant. Martha Wolfenstein and Nathan Leites, *Movies: A Psychological Study* (Glencoe, Ill.: 1950) attempts to dissect several common Hollywood movie plots of the 1940s and explain their audience appeal.

Douglas Miller and Marion Nowack, *The Fifties* (Garden City, New York: 1976) is an impressionistic work on the popular culture of that decade and is concerned mainly with ridiculing its subject.

Charlie Gillett, *The Sound of the City* (New York: 1970) is a lively and enthusiastic history of the rise of rock 'n' roll. There are dozens of books on Elvis Presley, but the best by far is Jerry Hopkins, *Elvis* (New York: 1971).Carl Belz, *The Story of Rock* (New York: 1972) argues that rock music is a modern form of folk art. Charlie Gillett, *Making Tracks* (New York: 1975) follows the fortunes of Atlantic Recores. Ely J. Kahn, *The Voice* (New York: 1947) is an amused and amusing account of the meteoric rise of the first of the postwar pop idols, Frank Sinatra. There is an absorbing book on the lives of jazz musicians in the late 1940s and early 1950s: Stephen Longstreet, *The Real Jazz—Old and New* (Baton Rouge, La.: 1956).

Advertising sank billions of dollars each year into attempts to fashion popular tastes. It was so pervasive a force in American life that it became an integral part of popular culture, affecting tastes, fashions, diversions, attitudes, but in a hit-or-miss way. Martin Mayer, *Madison Avenue U.S.A.* (New York: 1958) is an excellent study. Vance Packard, *The Hidden Persuaders* (New York: 1957) is worthwhile, even though he too often takes the researchers' claims at face value. David Ogilvy, *Confessions of an Advertising Man* (New York: 1963) is conceited but stylishly written. Ogilvy, however, provides an instructive example of a highly intelligent man making himself believe what he wants to believe for the sake of comfort and convenience. Pierre Martineau, *Motivation in Advertising* (New York: 1957), in contrast, believes that advertising is both the chief American art form and the secret of the country's economic success. More prosaically, Martineau attempts to explain how to exploit irrationality in a rational way. Shepherd Mead, *How to Succeed in Business Without Really Trying* (New York: 1952) is a satire based on his experiences as an advertising executive; it is funny only because it has the ring of truth.

Much of the best reporting on popular culture in the immediate postwar period has been collected in two works: Eric Larrabee and Rolf Meyerson, eds., *Mass Leisure* (Glencoe, Ill.: 1958) and Bernard Rosenberg and David M. White, *Mass Culture: The Popular Arts in America* (Glencoe, Ill.: 1957). On comic books, see Frank Jacobs, *The Mad World of William M. Gaines* (New York: 1972) and Les Daniels, *COMIX: A History of Comic Books in America* (New York: 1971).

The Higher Culture

Peggy Guggenheim, *Confessions of an Art Addict* (New York: 1960) is a spirited autobiography by a woman who served American art nobly and well, even if more or less by accident at first. Rudi Blesh, *Modern Art USA* (New York: 1956) is important. John I. H. Bauer, *Between the Fairs: 25 Years of American Art 1939–1964* (New York: 1964) is useful, as is Sam Hunter, *American Painting and Sculpture* (New York: 1959). There are some good illustrations in Museum of Modern Art, *The New American Painting* (New York: 1959). Barbara Rose, *American Art Since 1900* (New York: 1967) is a serious work—that is, it invites disagreement. Irving Sadler, *Abstract Expressionism: The Triumph of American Painting* (London: 1970). On the early years of Pop Art, see Gregory Battcock, *The New Art* (New York: 1966). There are two worthwhile biographies of the best of the abstract expressionists: Harold Rosenberg, *Willem De Kooning* (New York: 1972) and Harriet Janis and Rudi Blesh, *De Kooning* (New York: 1960). Frank O'Hara, *Jackson Pollock* (New York: 1959) is useful. On the interaction between modern art and modern society see the often trenchant essays in Harold Rosenberg, *Discovering the Present* (Chicago: 1973).

Jacques Barzun, *Music in American Life* (Bloomington, Ind.: 1962) is an "essay" which is as good as a survey, and more provocative.

On the writer's life during the period, Malcolm Cowley, *The Literary Situation* (New York: 1954) has a good description. His account of the various aspects of publishing is also noteworthy. Julian Cornell, *The Trial of Ezra Pound* (London: 1966) tells an extraordinary tale and a true one. Walter Miller, *The Book Industry* (New York: 1949) and Roger H. Smith, ed., *The American Reading Public* (New York: 1964) are of value. Edmund Wilson, *The Bit Between My Teeth: A Literary Chronicle of 1950–1965* (New York: 1965) contains some notable gems.

Russell Lynes, *The Tastemakers* (New York: 1954) is a very funny survey of postwar changes in artistic and literary taste. There is also Harold Rosenberg, *The Tradition of the New* (New York: 1959). The *Times Literary Supplement, The American Imagination* (New York: 1960) is a survey which offers praise without condescension. Alvin Toffler, *The Culture Consumers* (New York: 1964) tries too hard to be clever. Nevertheless, it is a useful report on money and the arts. Alice Payne Hackett, *70 Years of Best Sellers* (New York: 1967) is a useful work which charts changing tastes and moods in culture high and low.

Social Criticism

Even in its most complacent periods America has never lacked for home-grown critics. Nor has it ever been viewed with indifference by foreigners. And so it will be for as long as America matters. Harold J. Laski, *The American Democracy* (New York: 1948) and Max Lerner, *America as a Civilization* (New York: 1957) are the two most exhaustive attempts at description and analysis of American life made during the period. The temperaments of the two men were different: Laski, a British Socialist, was less infatuated with American ways, and less optimistic about the country's future, than was Lerner. But ultimately each produced a Ganges of a book—a mile wide but ankle deep. In its way David Riesman et al., *The Lonely Crowd* (New Haven, Conn.: 1950) is more daring than either of these works. *The Lonely Crowd* is full of ideas. Its central argument, that Americans were developing a new kind of character, is intriguing. But the work as a whole never quite reaches up to the interestingness of the ideas in it. Riesman and Nathan Glazer, later produced *Faces in the Crowd* (New Haven, Conn.: 1952) which discusses at length twenty of the individuals interviewed in the course of researching the earlier book. Riesman simply gave off ideas as generators produce electricity. His *Individualism Reconsidered* (Garden City, N.Y.: 1955) and *Abundance for What?* (Garden City, N.Y.: 1964) are well worth reading.

David M. Potter, *People of Plenty* (New York: 1954) sees the American character being shaped ineluctably by prosperity. John Kenneth Galbraith, *The Affluent Society* (Boston: 1958) acknowledges the prosperity but argues that the country's priorities are all wrong and most of its economic thinking confused. It is a work of respectable radicalism. Vance Packard, *The Waste Makers* (New York: 1960) is simply appalled at the profligacy of American consumption. Packard turns his attention to the loss of privacy in *The Naked Society* (New York: 1964).

The country's moral fiber was tested and found rotting. See Fred J. Cook, *The Corrupted Land* (New York: 1966); Margaret Halsey, *The Pseudo-Ethic* (New York: 1963); William Lederer, *A Nation of Sheep* (New York: 1961); and a collection of articles from *Dissent* magazine, *Voices of DISSENT* (New York: 1958). Jacques Barzun, *The House of Intellect* (New York: 1959) decides that when character declines, brains swiftly follow.

Betty Friedan, *The Feminine Mystique* (New York: 1963) is another fascinating critique which has many telling points to make without ever being able to organize them into a coherent and persuasive argument. But its major claim is doubtless sound: there was much despair among middle-class housewives. Jessica Mitford, *The American Way of Death* (New York: 1963) is both very serious and very funny. Russell Lynes, *A Surfeit of Honey* (New York: 1957) is less serious but is nevertheless a shrewd examination of postwar American mores, as is Dwight Macdonald, *Against the American Grain* (New York: 1962).

H.-J. Duteil, *The Great American Parade*, trans. by Fletcher Pratt (New York: 1953) was a best-seller in Europe. It is a mine of misinformation, some of it hilarious, with translation to match. Geoffrey Gorer, *The Americans: A Study in National Character* (London: 1948) is pretentious but occasionally strikes the target squarely.

Graham Hutton, *Midwest at Noon* (Chicago: 1946) is an Englishman's view of the Midwest, based on long acquaintance and an open mind. Robert Jungk, *Tomorrow Is Already Here*, trans. by Marguerite Waldman (New York: 1954) sees the drive for mastery over nature threatening all that is best in American life. There is a wry, astute, and very readable work by a noted English travel writer, Lord Kinross, *The Innocents at Home* (London: 1959) which is far better than the patronizing title suggests. Jacques Maritain, *Reflections on America* (New York: 1958) is so busy loving America that there's little time left to see it. Jan Olof Olsson, *Welcome to Tombstone*, trans. by Maurice Michael (London: 1956) concerns life in the once-legendary Arizona small town during the early 1950s. Olsson, a Swede, stayed there long enough to be invited to impersonate Ike Clanton for Tombstone's annual "Helldorado." Alexander Werth, *America in Doubt* (London: 1959) traces the development of a noted French correspondent's understanding of America and describes life as he saw it in Columbus, Ohio.

Simone de Beauvoir, *America Day by Day* (New York: 1953) is particularly valuable for its descriptions of life among American intellectuals.

Luigi Barzini, Jr., *Americans Are Alone in the World* (New York: 1953) appears to be all anecdotes but is instead a serious book. Andre Siegfried, *America at Mid-Century* (New York: 1955) is an uneven, stimulating analysis by a noted French intellectual. Wyndham Lewis, *America and Cosmic Man* (Garden City, N.Y.: 1949) is a work which is half daft and half shrewd.

There were two American foreign correspondents who "rediscovered" their own country. John Gunther, *Inside U.S.A.* (New York: 1947; rev. ed., New York: 1951) is a triumph of reporting. Gunther's reputation was such that he could go anywhere, meet anyone. William Attwood came back after nine years, roamed across America, and then wrote *Still the Most Exciting Country* (New York: 1956). It has a fidelity to life and thought among ordinary people in the mid-1950s that is remarkable.

A. J. Liebling, *The Press* (New York: 1964) is a witty, brilliant, biting account of American journalism from 1947 to 1963.

The novels of the postwar era at times described and often criticized American life or at least some aspect of it of which the author had special knowledge. Allen Drury, *Advise and Consent* (Garden City, N.Y.: 1959) grew out of more than a decade's reporting on Congress. In places its descriptions carry conviction. Cameron Hawley, *Executive Suite* (Boston: 1952) conveys faithfully the heroic view of themselves which business executives privately cultivate. The most stunning novel of the postwar was Joseph Heller, *Catch-22* (New York: 1961), for reasons which are discussed in the text. Philip Roth, *Goodbye, Columbus* (New York: 1959) contains some inspired evocations of the identity crisis of American Jews. Nelson Algren, *The Man with the Golden Arm* (Garden City, N.Y.: 1949) is a moving novel of life among the drifters and grifters, the petty hoods, and the hapless junkies around Division Street, Chicago. Evan Hunter, *The Blackboard Jungle* (New York: 1954) is a telling account of the illiterate, the violent and the despairing in New York's manual arts high schools. Jack Kerouac, *On the Road* (New York: 1957) portrays a way of life and a state of mind with unmistakable fidelity. Warren Miller, *The Cool World* (Boston: 1959) is a graphic short novel about a teenage black gang leader. Sloan Wilson, *The Man in the Gray Flannel Suit* (New York: 1955) is a lament for a generation, the young men who came back from the war only to exchange one uniform for another. Vladimir Nabokov, *Lolita* (New York: 1958) not only is very funny and an oddly nonerotic, yet convincing description of sexual passion, but also contains a memorable depiction of philistine vulgarity in American life. J. F. Powers, *Morte D'Urban* (Garden City, N.Y.: 1962) is a brilliant novel which, in its portrait of the priest-as-hustler, stands as a masterful commentary on the interactions of postwar society and religion.

Sex

Helen Gurley Brown, *Sex and the Single Girl* (New York: 1962) is amusing when it isn't ghastly. But it was probably taken seriously, at least in part, by many thousands of single women. It characterizes the increasing aggressiveness about sexual freedom which was an important feature of postwar life. Albert Ellis, *The Folklore of Sex* (New York: 1951) and *The American Sexual Tragedy* (New York: 1954) sort through books, plays, films, magazines, and radio shows to arrive at popular attitudes toward sex. Gail Greene, *Sex and the College Girl* (New York: 1964) is an impressionistic survey culled from interviews with 600 coeds. Alfred C. Kinsey et al., *Sexual Behavior in the Human Male* (Philadelphia: 1948) and *Sexual Behavior in the Human Female* (Philadelphia: 1953) have an importance separate from the intrincic value of the material they contain. For an evaluation of these works, please consult the text. There is a very good biography of Kinsey by one of his principal assistants: Wardell B. Pomeroy, *Dr. Kinsey and the Institute of Sex Research* (New York: 1972). Pomeroy offers an able defense of the reports. Cornelia V. Christenson, *Kinsey* (Bloomington, Ind.: 1970) puts her emphasis on the man, rather than the work. William G. Cochran et al., *Statistical Problems of the Kinsey Report* (Washington, D.C.: 1951) remains the most important of the many analyses of Kinsey's methods.

Lee Rainwater, *And the Poor Get Children* (Chicago: 1960) examines the effects of class on sexual behavior. Ira L. Reiss, *Pre-Marital Sexual Standards in America* (Glencoe, Ill.: 1960) compares belief with practice. Joseph Schacter and Mary McCarthy, *Illegitimate Births: United States 1938–1957* (Washington, D.C.: 1960) describes and interprets the dramatic rise in illegitimacy which began during the war and continued through the 1950s.

Russell Lynes, *A Surfeit of Honey* (New York: 1957) offers a witty look at changing sex roles. A similar enterprise is the Editors of *Look, The Decline of the American Male* (New York: 1958). Margaret Mead, *Male and Female* (New York: 1955) compares American sexual practices and standards at midcentury with those of other societies. John Rechy, *City of Night* (New York: 1963) portrays the world of the male hustler—the lavatory liaisons, the drag queens, the gay bars—in convincing detail. Donald Webster Coty (pseud.), *The Homosexual in America* (New York: 1951) is an honest account based on a lifetime of homosexuality by a man who had a family and a stable marriage.

INDEX

Matthew Effect, 478, 538

sit down strike, 673-4